RON SHANDLER'S **2024**

BASEBALL FORECASTER

AND ENCYCLOPEDIA OF FANALYTICS

Copyright © 2023, USA TODAY Sports Media Group LLC.
No part of this publication may be reproduced, stored in a retrieval system, or transmitted in any form by any means, electronic, mechanical, photocopying, or otherwise, without the prior written permission of the publisher, Triumph Books LLC, 814 North Franklin Street, Chicago, Illinois 60610.

Triumph Books and colophon are registered trademarks of Random House, Inc.

This book is available in quantity at special discounts for your group or organization. For further information, contact:

Triumph Books LLC
814 North Franklin Street
Chicago, Illinois 60610
(312) 337-0747
www.triumphbooks.com

Printed in U.S.A.
ISBN: 978-1-63727-319-7

Rotisserie League Baseball is a registered trademark of the
Rotisserie League Baseball Association, Inc.

Statistics provided by Baseball Info Solutions

Cover design by Brent Hershey
Front cover photograph by Charles LeClaire-USATODAY Sports
Author photograph by Kevin Hurley

Ron Shandler's

BASEBALL FORECASTER

Editors

Ray Murphy
Brent Hershey

Associate Editors

Brandon Kruse
Ryan Bloomfield

• • • • • •

Tech/Data/Charts

Matt Cederholm
Mike Krebs

Graphic Design

Brent Hershey

Player Commentaries

Chris Blessing
Ryan Bloomfield
Alain de Leonardis
Brent Hershey
Brandon Kruse
Dan Marcus
Ray Murphy
Stephen Nickrand
Kristopher Olson
Greg Pyron
Brian Rudd
Paul Sporer
Jock Thompson
Rod Truesdell
Corbin Young

Research and Articles

Andy Andres
Ryan Bloomfield
Ed DeCaria
Jon Enriquez
Zach Larson
Doug Otto
Michael Weddell

Prospects

Chris Blessing
Jeremy Deloney
Rob Gordon
Tom Mulhall

Injury Chart

Rick Wilton

Acknowledgments

Producing the *Baseball Forecaster* is a team effort; the list of credits to the left are the heavy lifters. On behalf of Ron, Brent, and Ray, our most sincere thanks to each of you.

We are just as grateful to the rest of the BaseballHQ.com staff, who do the yeoman's work in populating the website with 12 months of incredible content: Dave Adler, Sarah Allan, Matt Beagle, Alex Beckey, Bob Berger, Derrick Boyd, Brian Brickley, Tim Cavanaugh, Brant Chesser, Jake Crumpler, Patrick Davitt, Alan Davison, Doug Dennis, Brian Entrekin, Jim Ferretti, Greg Fishwick, Neil FitzGerald, Arik Florimonte, Rick Green, Phil Hertz, Ed Hubbard, Cary James, Greg Jewett, Brad Johnson, Tom Kephart, Chris Lee, David Martin, Bill McKnight, Landon Moblad, Matthew Mougalian, Josh Paley, Nick Richards, Sara Sanchez, Peter Sheridan, Adam Sloate, Skip Snow, Matthew St-Germain, Jeffrey Tomich, Shelly Verougstraete, Steve Weimer, Ryan Williams and Michael Yachera.

Thank you to all our industry colleagues—you are technically competitors, but also comrades working to grow this industry. That is never more evident than at our First Pitch Forum live events. Hope to see many of you again in person in either Florida or Arizona in 2024.

Thank you to Ryan Bonini and the team at USA Today Sports Media Group, as well as all the support from the folks at Triumph Books and Action Printing.

And of course, thank *you*, readers, for your interest in what we all have to say. Your kind words, support and (respectful) criticism move us forward on the fanalytic continuum more than you know. We are grateful for your readership.

•

From Brent Hershey In theory, the first "regular" offseason in several years should make this project less complicated. But the fact is the names you see to your left and above continue to push themselves as analysts, writers and editors, and the quality of what you're about to read and digest keeps improving. Kinda like a certain coverboy in his prime. Thanks to Brandon and Ryan for the assist in keeping us on message and maintaining the lofty standards that readers have come to expect. Thanks to Ron for blazing this trail (in its fourth decade!) that Ray and I now help maintain. And thanks to Ray for the friendship, honesty and trust that goes into any successful partnership. For Lorie, Dillon and Eden, it's so exciting to see us grow together also. I'm confident our best days as a family are still ahead of us.

From Ray Murphy A close friend passed away this summer. Baseball was a throughline in our relationship. We watched Sid Bream beat Barry Bonds' throw on a tiny tv with rabbit ears. We attended Game 5 of the 2000 World Series; the pinnacle of fandom for a couple of born-and-raised New Yorkers. And I vividly remember a morning spent on a golf course, bantering about our fantasy league. By the time we reached the 18th hole, we had agreed to a 16-player trade. Those in-person interactions are the best part of this hobby. Rest in peace, Greg.

Partnering with Ron, Brent, Brandon, Ryan, and our entire team each fall is practically muscle memory; it is remarkable how much gets accomplished after the last pitch of the regular season. I'm deeply appreciative of every contribution, particularly Brandon catching when I mistakenly pasted Giovanny Gallegos' commentary onto Carlos Carrasco's player box! Finally, a quick shout-out to my wife Jennifer and my now-12-year-old daughters Bridget and Grace, who are old enough to be offended if I don't mention them here. Love you, girls!

From Ron Shandler The first edition of this book came out a month after the Mets won the 1986 World Series. After a few years, a friend asked me how long I was going to continue it. I laughed and said, "Probably until the next time the Mets win the World Series." So here we are.

While I wait out another year, I wrote a historical memoir that you might find of interest (RonShandler.com/FantasyExpert). You need longevity to write about history firsthand, and longevity only comes with help from others.

So, none of this would have been possible without the dozens of writers and analysts who fueled this book, ably led now by Ray, Brent, Brandon and Ryan; the hundreds of thousands of dedicated readers like yourself; a trio of loving and patient women who keep me alive; and all the MLB contributors, particularly Orel Hershiser, Derek Jeter, Salvador Perez and a single Carlos-Beltran-freezing curveball from rookie Adam Wainwright that kept up their end of the bargain, dammit.

Table of Contents

One-Off

by Ron Shandler

Ronald Acuña, Jr.

Any conversation or analysis of 2023 begins with Ronald Acuña, Jr. and one incredible, historic season. We can talk about the fine seasons of Freddie Freeman, Mookie Betts, and Matt Olson, all MVP-caliber in any other year. We can recognize the accomplishments of Gerrit Cole and Félix Bautista and the big profits realized by Kyle Bradish and Justin Steele owners. And, of course, we can continue to revere Shohei Ohtani, whose combined earnings as batter and pitcher would be more notable if most leagues were allowed to use him in both roles simultaneously. However, those combined earnings still fell $11 short of what Acuña posted at the plate in 2023.

Ronald Acuña, Jr. earned $63 in 2023, based on a 15-team mixed league and 66/33 batter/pitcher split, according to the valuation engine at BaseballHQ.com. That is unheard of in the modern-day game. Since the beginning of the Rotisserie Era (1980-), there have been a handful of $50 seasons, but nobody has come within $8 of what Acuña accomplished this year.

Batter	Year	R$	AB	R	HR	RBI	SB	BA
Ronald Acuña, Jr.	**2023**	**$63**	**643**	**149**	**41**	**106**	**73**	**.337**
Larry Walker	1997	$55	568	143	49	130	33	.366
Mike Schmidt	1981*	$55	354	78	31	91	12	.316
Aaron Judge	2022	$54	570	133	62	131	16	.311
Jose Canseco	1988	$52	610	120	42	124	40	.307
Jeff Bagwell	1994*	$52	400	104	39	116	15	.368
Vladimir Guerrero	2002	$52	614	106	39	111	40	.338
Matt Kemp	2011	$50	602	115	39	126	40	.324
Andre Dawson	1981*	$50	394	71	24	64	26	.302

Pitcher	Year	R$	IP	W	Sv	K	ERA	WHIP
Pedro Martinez	2000	$51	217	18	0	284	1.74	0.74

**Strike-shortened season*

There is no Barry Bonds on this list. He topped out at $48 in 1993 and 2001. No Rickey Henderson either—he peaked at $49 in 1982. Albert Pujols? His best was $43 in both 2005 and 2009. Mike Trout's high-water mark was the $47 he earned in his 2012 rookie year. On the pitching side, Greg Maddux's best was the $44 he earned in 1995. Randy Johnson? $47 in 1999 and 2001. Clayton Kershaw's best was $44 in 2015. Surprisingly, Roger Clemens never cracked $40 in his 24-year career, topping out at $39 in 1997.

You'll notice that some of those $50-plus stat lines seem miles behind what we might expect from a performance even marginally close to Acuña's. Roto values are normalized to the caliber of league productivity each year, which explains the disconnect. For instance, Jose Canseco's stat line in the low-offense 1988 season generated a higher dollar value than Alex Rodriguez's arguably better line in the high-offense 1998 season (124-42-123-46-.310), which earned only $46. That's also why Rickey Henderson's 130-SB performance only earned $49 during a season in which over two dozen players stole 30 or more bases. And why Barry Bonds' 72-homer performance only earned $48 during the presumably juiced 2001 campaign.

Admittedly, there is some variability in these earnings calculations depending upon which Rotisserie valuation system you use and the league parameters. Peter Kreutzer of AskRotoman.com calculated Acuña's 2023 value at $69. RotoWire.com also had him at $69. FanGraphs.com had $66. Razzball.com has a Historical Fantasy Baseball Player Rater that includes everyone who has donned a uniform since 1903. It is based on a 12-team mixed league and values Acuña's season at $71, ranking him No. 1 in the database—essentially *the best season ever*. Better than Honus Wagner in 1908 ($67), Ty Cobb in 1909 ($66) or Babe Ruth in 1921 ($65). It's incredible.

Acuña's performance is also notable because 2023 was not a low-offense year. Run scoring was up 7.8% from 2022, home runs were up 12.5%, and stolen bases were up a ridiculous 40.9%. Overall, 2023 production was about average compared to the last seven years, but still a high caliber of competition. He didn't ride the 2023 wave—he surfed straight past it onto a beach in the next county.

I encourage you to look at Acuña's player box later in the book and just admire it. It's quite impressive:

- He increased his contact rate by 14%, from 73% in 2022 to 87%. Who does that?
- His career-high .337 BA was not inflated by BABIP (h%); that level barely budged from last year. His .324 xBA reinforced that he was legit.
- He tied his career high of 41 HR, but xHR said his skills merited 48! And this was despite a 49 percent ground ball rate.
- He came within one stolen base of *doubling* his previous career high. The bases were only 4.5 inches closer, not 4.5 feet.

From a fantasy perspective, Acuña also achieved something that no other player has done since we began keeping records in 2004 (when the National Fantasy Baseball Championship started providing industry Average Draft Position rankings). Not only did Acuña finish with the No. 1 earnings, but he was also ranked No. 1 coming into the season.

For 20 years, not even back when A-Rod, Albert Pujols, and Mike Trout dominated the game, did anyone ever earn the most roto dollars after entering the season as No. 1 in the ADP rankings.

Year	ADP #1	Finish	Earned #1 from ADP	
2004	A.Rodriguez	15	I.Suzuki	71
2005	A.Rodriguez	2	D.Lee	35
2006	A.Rodriguez	3	J.Reyes	15
2007	A.Pujols	24	A.Rodriguez	4
2008	A.Rodriguez	11	A.Pujols	10
2009	H.Ramirez	2	A.Pujols	2
2010	A.Pujols	2	C.Gonzalez	119
2011	A.Pujols	14	M.Kemp	23
2012	M.Kemp	96	M.Trout	228
2013	R.Braun	314	M.Cabrera	2
2014	M.Trout	4	J.Altuve	92
2015	M.Trout	10	J.Arrieta	97
2016	M.Trout	3	M.Betts	16
2017	M.Trout	18	C.Blackmon	17
2018	M.Trout	10	M.Betts	7
2019	M.Trout	18	J.Verlander	21
2020	R.Acuña, Jr.	28	S.Bieber	22
2021	R.Acuña, Jr.	54	T.Turner	8
2022	T.Turner	5	A.Judge	32
2023	R.Acuña, Jr.	1	R.Acuña, Jr.	1

I know, I know—this is not that meaningful, kinda random, and not at all projectible. There is only a 33 percent chance of a first-round pick earning back first-round value at all, so nailing No. 1 is a dart throw at best. Still, Acuña was the first player to pull it off in two decades. Also interesting:

- Mike Trout went 1.01 six times but earned it back only once, two years before he started the 6-year run.
- The only players who were the top earners more than once were Albert Pujols and Mookie Betts.
- How much roto value have our No. 1 picks returned?
  - Top 5 (40%).
  - Top 15 (65%).
  - Top 30 (90%).
- From what ADP did the actual No. 1 earners come from?
  - Top 5 (20%).
  - Top 15 (40%).
  - Top 30 (65%).

If nothing else, our No. 1 picks have had high floors.

Gut predictions, my report card

In 2023, we played a different game under a new set of rules that had the potential to upend some of the statistical benchmarks we've come to rely on. You can find complete analyses of the impacts in the Research Abstracts section.

Last year, in these pages, I speculated on what the fallout might look like and offered up the possibility of chaos (because nothing engages readers more than fear-induced hysteria). In those speculations, I made some "gut predictions." Since I am not one to hide from things like wrong predictions (usually), here is a full report of my gut's assertions back in November 2022. (My gut writes *in italics.*)

The schedule (Every team plays every other team, fewer intra-division games): *One of the Central Division winners will have a sub-.500 record. One of the other division winners will make a run at 120 victories.*

I went out on a limb here but with a solid supporting branch. At mid-season, this looked much more likely; the Twins were leading the AL Central at only 41-42, and the Rays were on pace for 111 wins. Unfortunately for my gut, they kept playing the game for another three months.

The clock (15/20 second pitch clock): *Starting pitchers will be mostly unaffected. Bullpen management will become even tougher than it already is, with more underperformances, more injuries, and more closer turnover.*

This was mainly business as usual—pitchers just adjusted—though the closer pool was more stable than we've seen in a while. More on that later and in the Encyclopedia.

The bases (Larger 18" bases, 4.5" shorter distance between them, and limit of three pickoff attempts): *League-wide stolen base attempts will rise 20 percent, and at least five players will exceed 50 bags.*

I nearly nailed this. One more Bobby Witt swipe and three more from C.J. Abrams would have yielded four 50-SB runners. Attempts were up 32.5 percent, blowing past my gut.

The defense (Limited shifting—2B/SS must be on opposite sides of 2B): *Hitters who had been shifted against the most will see an average 15-point increase in batting average, but some could see a 30-40 point boost. Some pitchers will see a 0.10 increase in ERA. However, these bumps are just averages and will not affect every player equally.*

With that prediction, I included a list of the highest contact hitters (75%+ ct%) who were shifted against the most (75% or more). I thought they would likely be most affected. How did I do?

Hitters	2022	2023	Var
Yordan Alvarez	.306	.293	-.013
Kyle Tucker	.257	.284	+.027
Josh Naylor	.256	.308	+.052
Adley Rutschman	.254	.277	+.023
Salvador Perez	.254	.255	+.001
Keibert Ruiz	.251	.260	+.009
Marcus Semien	.248	.276	+.028
Corey Seager	.245	.327	+.082
Anthony Santander	.240	.257	+.017
Max Kepler	.227	.260	+.033
Jonah Heim	.227	.258	+.031
Anthony Rizzo	.224	.244	+.020
Jesse Winker	.219	.199	-.020
Rowdy Tellez	.219	.215	-.004
Carlos Santana	.202	.240	+.038
MEAN			**+.023**

Not too bad, though some of this probably would have happened anyway due to normal regression. Gut projecting is fun!

But it's making me a little hungry.

View from 38,000 feet

Each year in these pages, I've been including a 10-year scan of league-wide data. The purpose is to objectively examine the trends without getting bogged down in "now." With the 2023 rule changes, there has been a surge toward planting a stake in "now," so this year's exercise potentially becomes more important. Maybe.

		|—Players with—|		
Year	**Tot HR**	**20+ HR**	**30+ HR**	**HR/FB%**
2014	4186	57	11	9.5%
2015	4909	64	20	11.4%
2016	5610	111	35	12.8%
2017	6105	118	41	13.7%
2018	5585	100	27	12.7%
2019	6776	130	58	15.3%
*2020	6221	119	53	14.8%
2021	5944	102	43	13.6%
2022	5215	71	23	11.4%
2023	5868	102	29	12.7%

** Pro-rated to full season*

There was little in the new rules that would have affected power (pitchers rushing pitches to beat the clock, maybe?), so 2023 looks like a typical season, with 2022 being an outlier compared to recent years. In fact, 2023 looks very much like 2018.

		Three True	
Year	**Singles%**	**Outcomes%**	**K%**
2013	67.6%	30.3%	18.9%
2014	68.3%	30.3%	19.4%
2015	66.5%	30.7%	19.5%
2016	65.1%	32.3%	20.2%
2017	63.8%	33.5%	20.6%
2018	64.2%	33.7%	21.6%
2019	61.7%	35.1%	22.3%
2020	62.8%	36.1%	22.9%
2021	63.3%	35.1%	23.2%
2022	65.2%	33.4%	22.4%
2023	63.7%	34.5%	22.7%

We might have expected the defensive shift limitations to boost singles, but that was not the case. The league-level batting average only rose from .243 to .248, a four-year high… which is mostly noise. That fact makes the SB spike even more notable.

		|—Players with—|	
Year	**Tot SB**	**20+**	**30+**
2013	2693	40	16
2014	2764	39	15
2015	2505	30	7
2016	2537	28	14
2017	2527	29	6
2018	2474	28	11
2019	2280	21	8
*2020	2387	29	9
2021	2213	19	6
2022	2487	24	6
2023	3503	51	18

** Pro-rated to full season*

We shortened the distance between the bases. We limited the number of times a pitcher could hold a runner on. We gave runners a pitch clock so they could time their attempts better. The result was a 40.9 percent increase in steals from 2022 and the most since 1987. This total was the ninth highest of *all time* (the other seven seasons in the rankings were all from 1887-1915). This past year wasn't just a mere jump—it was a spike to one of the all-time speediest seasons ever.

There were 0.90 steal attempts per game, up from 0.68 in 2022 and the highest since 2012. There were 0.72 successful steals per game, up from 0.51 in 2022 and the highest since 1997.

The stolen base success rate was 80.2%, up from 75.4% in 2022 and possibly the highest ever. Caught stealing data is spotty from the first half of the last century, so we don't know for sure. In 2021, the success rate was 75.7%, and that's the highest level I can find behind 2023. Compare that to the lowest confirmed success rate—55.1% in 1952.

These past years were all interesting in their own ways. Look:

	2023	**2012**	**1997**	**1987**	**1952**
Total stolen bases	3503	3229	3308	3585	771
Attempts/game	0.90	0.90	1.08	1.21	0.56
Successful SB/gm	0.72	0.66	0.73	0.85	0.31
Success rate	80%	74%	68%	70%	55%
No. of teams	30	30	28	26	16
Total base-stealers	437	412	414	367	190
No. 20+ SB players	51	48	42	58	5
No. 40+ SB players	6	6	11	14	0

There are many ways to cut and dice the 2023 data and get into the weeds, but Ryan Bloomfield has written a more in-depth look at the stolen base situation in the Research Abstracts section. I'll let him take the baton on this.

	|——Number of Pitchers with——|			
Year	**200 IP**	**200 K**	**15 W**	****10 W**
2014	34	13	25	83
2015	28	18	13	70
2016	15	12	23	70
2017	15	16	17	74
2018	13	18	19	59
2019	15	24	16	74
*2020	6	20	19	70
2021	4	17	5	54
2022	8	11	14	63
2023	5	17	8	59

**Prorated to full season* ***Includes relief pitchers*

There are conflicting reports about whether the pitch clock increased the frequency or severity of pitcher injuries. Still, as far as stat accumulation, we seem to have plateaued in this space. Particularly notable is the fact that there has been no post-pandemic recovery; the innings restrictions from 2020 and 2021 should have washed out by now, yet here we are. We did have one 20-game winner this year (Spencer Strider), making for a three-year trend of one per year. There have been fifteen 20-game winners over the past ten years. There were fifteen 20-game winners in 1969 alone.

	INNINGS		**WINS**	
Year	**Starters**	**Relievers**	**Starters**	**Relievers**
2016	63.3%	36.7%	67.1%	32.9%
2017	61.9	38.1	67.5	32.5
2018	59.9	40.1	62.3	37.7
2019	57.9	42.1	59.7	40.3
2020	55.5	44.5	52.2	47.8
2021	57.3	42.7	55.4	44.6
2022	58.7	41.3	59.4	40.6
2023	58.0	42.0	57.7	42.3

The math is straightforward. Regardless of how deep into games starters go these days, every team still has a nearly fixed number of innings to allocate (approximately 1440). If you don't have an adequate number of starting pitchers willing or able to shoulder a greater percentage of that workload, the innings will flow out to the bullpen, draining away some of the Wins with them. It's a closed system. Here is the other part of that equation:

Year	IP/GS	CG%
2016	5.65	1.7%
2017	5.51	1.2%
2018	5.36	0.9%
2019	5.18	0.9%
2020	4.78	1.6%
2021	5.02	1.0%
2022	5.20	0.7%
2023	5.14	0.7%

Tampa first introduced us to the Opener in 2018, and we're now living in a world where some teams employ the tactic, some teams don't, and a bullpen game is often viewed as a sign of weakness. In 2020 and 2021, I was excited to see pitching roles start to blur, but the game's caretakers said, "No!" Commissioner Rob Manfred was entirely upfront about his goal of restoring the dominance of starting pitchers. We have dug in on the roles of "starter" and "reliever" rather than entertain having a single role of "pitcher," which would open up miles and miles of new strategic roadways and off-ramps. One can dream.

Manfred's solution? Let's reduce the number of pitchers per team from 13 to 12 while at the same time continuing to push the human limits of fastball velocity; injuries be damned.

Apparently, he longs for the days when baseball was great:

	INNINGS		WINS	
Year	Starters	Relievers	Starters	Relievers
1969	73.6%	26.4%	74.3%	25.7%

Year	IP/GS	CG%
1969	7.01	25.9%

Admittedly, for fantasy leaguers, this would allow us to project wins more accurately, but we're not returning to the 1969 game any time soon. So, the starter/reliever roles will remain intact at some level, but not enough to make wins any easier to project. They have really become a crapshoot.

This past fall in the XFL, we proposed to replace the Wins category with Innings Pitched. This league is a 15-team mixed keeper/dynasty hybrid composed of owners who are old enough to remember doing stats by hand but progressive enough to realize that the game has changed. The vote was 46.7 percent for, 46.7 percent against, and 6.7 percent willing to go along with the majority. Thank you very much.

Tout Wars does run one league (out of eight) that uses Innings Pitched and Saves-plus-Holds, and the participants love it. So there.

Anyway, I am in favor of optimizing the controllable elements of any game format. Enough luck is already baked into the stats that we don't need to be pulling levers on categories that are nearly random. So, boot Wins. (And replace them with Innings Pitched, which has become a popular replacement category. Pitch well; accumulate innings. It's more simple math.)

		Number of Pitchers with				
Year	Saves	30+	20+	5+	1+	%20+
2014	1264	17	25	46	135	18.5
2015	1292	19	28	44	146	19.2
2016	1276	15	22	52	135	16.3
2017	1179	10	23	51	163	14.1
2018	1244	8	20	50	166	12.0
2019	1180	11	22	53	200	11.0
2021	1191	9	19	62	198	9.6
2022	1232	10	18	65	223	8.1
2023	1241	12	23	54	215	10.7

The past three years have seen some stabilization in the closer market. The number of 20-save closers jumped from 18 in 2022 to 23 in 2023, meaning that over three-quarters of MLB teams deployed a go-to guy long enough to reach 20, the highest level since 2017.

This is particularly notable because we were speculating that the pitch clock might most negatively impact closers. They are the ones throwing harder and needing more time to recover between pitches. This particular pool of closers did not seem to be affected on a league-wide basis. At least not in 2023.

That diminished risk might justify an increase in closer pricing and negate the need to reach for frontliners in the second and third rounds. But it's also possible that we might not see the injury fallout until 2024. And so, we must consider...

Could 2023 be just a...?

The new rules affected many aspects of the 2023 game—some obvious, some that might not yet be apparent. People are already trying to dig in their heels on these results and tell us what we must do in 2024. The mindset has become infective: "What have we learned from 2023 that we need to take into next year?"

And why not learn from 2023? American League pitchers posted a lower aggregate ERA (4.28) than National League arms (4.38) for the first time since 1972, the year before the adoption of the DH. So, it must be time to start chasing AL pitchers.

Nope. The designated hitter is in both leagues; the edge could swing either way.

Ten players amassed over 700 plate appearances, up from five in 2022 and two in 2021. So, it must be okay to start projecting more playing time.

Nope. IL days are as prevalent as ever. All you'll be doing is overvaluing players.

That 80 percent stolen base success rate? That must be the new standard, so let's start projecting SB for everyone! Here are some more SB for fast guys. Here are some more SB for players on teams that like to run. Here are some more SB for teams that didn't like to run but may now realize they probably should. Let's even project a few more bags for slower players because everyone else is doing it and, you know, pizza box bases. Everyone should be thinking, "I wanna get me some of dem steals!"

Nope. (Pizza box bases, haha. Steal second, open base, grab a slice of pepperoni.)

Okay, maybe some of this is possible. But what if 2023 was a little bit of an anomaly, a year when the league was just dipping its toes into the new rule pool? What if 2023 was just a test year? What if it all was just a one-off?

After all, teams may review baserunning data and find ways to optimize the running game even more or find ways to combat it. The scouting reports on players who succeeded or failed spectacularly will be pored over by opposing teams to mine intelligence. Teams may reassess their pitcher usage in response to the clock. They might conduct research on defensive shifting to optimize fielder positioning even more. It seems to me that these are all fluid situations. Anyone who commits to a course of action based on 2023 data alone sets themselves up for surprises in 2024.

How should we handle this? Since 2023 data may or may not be meaningful, I think we have to go back to some basic concepts and start at the beginning.

The beginning

My entire perspective about the stats and the projections process starts with a fundamental forecasting concept and a passage from the 2011 edition of the *Forecaster*:

> *When Albert Pujols hit 42 HR this past season, that was interpreted as a finite and accurate measure. When he hits 41, 49, 32, 37, and 47 HR over five years, those data points are seen as a valid range of values. But they're not.*
>
> *Pujols' 42 HR described a unique confluence of events shaped by his health, ballpark dimensions, wind currents, and the particular assortment of pitchers he faced last season. Of the thousands of pitches he saw, a handful of changes in velocity or location could have shifted that 42 HR to 41, or 48, or 36. This book defines "errant gust of wind" as a standard unit of measure describing the same phenomenon.*
>
> *The truth is, that 42 was an almost arbitrary stopping point along a continuum of possibilities this year. Yet we use that 42 as absolute input in our projection models.*

Assigning a number to a specific level of performance gives us a false sense of precision. This is especially important this year because of the rush to find meaning in the 2023 data. Any shifts in expectation could still be more noise than signal.

In a book that you use to help you evaluate and project player performance, the last thing you want to hear is that all the data is fuzzy. The truth is, while Ronald Acuña, Jr. went 41-73 this year, he could just as well have gone 35-75 or 42-50 or 48-57 (his "x" stats!) or any number of different variations and still have exhibited the same set of skills. But we're all going into next year projecting off 41-73, using those specific numbers as precise data input to his 2024 projection. As long as Acuña is more human than robot, that input is not fuzzy enough.

There was a tweet (I will always call it a tweet; let Musk come after me) after the season ended that went something like this:

> - *Stolen bases increased 40%*
> - *Nearly all high-priced closers returned positive value.*
> - *There were more impact rookies than any year in recent memory.*
>
> *Will these trends continue?*

No. Those are not trends. They are single data points and quite possibly just one-offs.

In fact, the whole idea of creating trends from these single data points is also flawed. You can't look at Acuña's 26-41-24-15-41 home run scan and say, "This is a 35-HR hitter." Nor can you look at Sean Murphy's 17-18-21 home run trend and say, "Next up, 23." Or Kyle Schwarber's 32-46-47 trend and think, "Possibly 50." These hitters didn't spend the past few years hopping around some well-defined output range. No, these hitters started every year at zero. They had to use their skills foundation and claw their way up through a *"unique confluence of events shaped by health, ballpark dimensions, wind currents, and the particular assortment of pitchers faced last season"* to get to some unknown statistical stopping point. And now, with new benchmarks and moving goalposts (sorry, football, ugh), we can trust the numbers even less.

Just because Ronald Acuña, Jr. hit 41 HRs and stole 73 bases does not mean he can be inked in for a floor of 35/60. Research has shown that the next data point in Sean Murphy's HR trend is far more likely to be 17 than 25. And at Schwarber's current cruising altitude, 38 is well within the range of 2024 home run expectations.

Add in the fact that all the new variables often interacted. The increase in SB was driven by the larger bases *and* the restriction on pickoff attempts *and* the pitch clock *and* the defensive shift limitations, all to varying degrees. Rising ERAs were likely affected by the increase in SB *and* defensive shift limitations *and* the pitch clock and on and on.

And all of it—*all of it*—could just be a one-off. The 2023 season was a sample size of one. Not only that, with the annual inflows and outflows of players old and new, every season is also a completely new marketplace. That's why you can't read very much into the stabilization of the closer market. You can't draw conclusions about the depth of any one position based on how talent shook out last year. And you can't plant any sort of stake in the first year of fallout from the new rules. In 2024, it may all be different again.

Where does this leave us for March drafts?

With about 99.999999% certainty, we know that Acuña will open 2024 as the top pick in the ADP rankings. (It would have been 100%, but some guy in Glendale, Arizona, is going to pick Corbin Carroll first. There's always one.)

But wait a minute—that D-backs fan might actually be playing better odds. I posted the following poll last September:

> *Ronald Acuña, Jr. is currently earning over $60 in roto dollars and leads the #2 earner, Freddie Freeman, by nearly $20. If you had to choose which player will be the top earner in 2024, who would you pick—Acuña or the field?*

The poll was online for barely five minutes, with Acuña zooming in front of the field, 55% to 45%, when this occurred:

Chris got it immediately. And, had he not offered his reality check, these final poll results might have been even more skewed:

Ronald Acuna, Jr. is currently earning over $60 in roto dollars and leads the #2 earner, Freddie Freeman, by nearly $20. If you had to choose which player will be the top fantasy earner in 2024, who would you pick?

Ronald Acuna, Jr.	50.2%
The field	49.8%

No! No, no, no, no, no! "The field" should have won in a landslide. Just look at the chart of No. 1s shown earlier. Only once in the past 20 years has a player repeated at No. 1. Analyst Ariel Cohen also commented: "Repeating as the No. 1 overall is a low-chance outcome. Ronald Acuña as a first-rounder versus not a first-rounder is more even money."

That's correct. But when granted the top pick, the field could be anybody; the path of least resistance is to go with the guy who did it last and was off the charts. But it almost guarantees that you will be wrong.

In creating projections, it is natural to rely on the most recent data as a reference point, and that has always been dangerous. We see Acuña's $63 earnings and think, "Even if he regresses 33 percent, that's still a $40-plus season, which is likely better than we could project for almost anyone else." (Hence, these poll results.) In 2024, many fantasy leaguers will consider Ronald Acuña's floor as higher than the ceilings of 90 percent of the rest of the league. (That might seem reasonable, but it's hyperbole.) Even in this book, with projections driven by five years of history, it was tough to regress Acuña's projection much lower than 35 HR, 48 steals, and a .304 BA. (Believe me, we tried.) This is still a $51 line!

And I'll be taking the under on that. Regression and gravity are a bitch.

All of this is the same line of flawed thinking that boosted Aaron Judge and his $54 season in 2022 to rank as the second overall pick in 2023; he earned just $21, ranked 41st. It's also the same line of thinking that boosted Shane Bieber into the 2021 first round after his elite 77-inning 2020 season and Jonathan Villar into the second round. It also boosted one-off wonders Charlie Blackmon and Corey Kluber into the 2018 first round and Jean Segura as high as ADP 17 in 2017. All were coming off notable single-season performances; all fell far short of their ADP.

But 2024 will not be an extension of 2023—it begins as a blank slate. This is a fundamental principle of the entire process. Embracing that fact will help keep projections in perspective.

Does that mean Acuña shouldn't be the No. 1 overall pick in 2024? It doesn't matter—just try to pry him away from that spot. But will he earn the most roto dollars? I'm still taking the field.

Granted, the field is vast. But history has shown that you could pick any player in the first few rounds and have a pretty good shot at getting a decent return. The marketplace has historically been so bad at projecting earnings that it almost doesn't matter the order in which you rank the top players; the talent distribution is flatter than you think.

Admittedly, 2023 was a little different. The market did a good job with the first round; after that, the usual brand of hit-or-miss mediocrity.

ADP	Player	Earnings
1	Acuña Jr., Ronald	$63
2	Judge, Aaron	$21
3	Turner, Trea	$25
4	Ramírez, José	$25
5	Rodríguez, Julio	$33
6	Tucker, Kyle	$31
7	Ohtani, Shohei	$34 + $18
8	Witt Jr., Bobby	$35
9	Betts, Mookie	$36
10	Guerrero Jr., Vlad	$16
11	Soto, Juan	$26
12	Alvarez, Yordan	$19
13	Freeman, Freddie	$42
14	Machado, Manny	$15
15	Bichette, Bo	$19
	ROUND 1 mean	**$29**
	Range	**$15-$63**
16	Tatis Jr., Fernando	$21
17	Burnes, Corbin	$21
18	Trout, Mike	$4
19	Cole, Gerrit	$37
20	Alonso, Pete	$17
21	Riley, Austin	$27
22	Devers, Rafael	$21
23	Goldschmidt, Paul	$18
24	Realmuto, J.T.	$11
25	Alcantara, Sandy	$3
26	Strider, Spencer	$26
27	Harris II, Michael	$18
28	Semien, Marcus	$28
29	deGrom, Jacob	($2)
30	Arenado, Nolan	$15
	ROUND 2 mean	**$18**
	Range	**($2)-$37**

ADP	Player	Earnings
31	Lindor, Francisco	$27
32	Nola, Aaron	$9
33	Arozarena, Randy	$19
34	Chisholm Jr., Jazz	$10
35	Varsho, Daulton	$6
36	Woodruff, Brandon	$10
37	Clase, Emmanuel	$13
38	Olson, Matt	$36
39	Verlander, Justin	$17
40	McClanahan, Shane	$9
41	Scherzer, Max	$14
42	Robert Jr., Luis	$23
43	Schwarber, Kyle	$13
44	Seager, Corey	$27
45	Mullins, Cedric	$7
	ROUND 3 mean	**$16**
	Range	**$6-$36**
46	Cease, Dylan	($6)
47	Albies, Ozzie	$27
48	Smith, Will	$11
49	Hader, Josh	$16
50	Bieber, Shane	$1
51	Garcia, Adolis	$22
52	Javier, Cristian	$0
53	Wheeler, Zack	$21
54	Carroll, Corbin	$36
55	Urias, Julio	$2
56	Castillo, Luis	$24
57	Gausman, Kevin	$21
58	Romano, Jordan	$12
59	Perez, Salvador	$9
60	Cruz, Oneil	($11)
	ROUND 4 mean	**$12**
	Range	**($11)-$36**

Good job in Round 1; Acuña helped, obviously. The earnings of picks in Rounds 2 and 3 were pretty much indistinguishable, and Round 4 was not that far behind. Still, 2023 was a better year than most. We're usually a lot crappier at this:

	MEAN EARNINGS ($)					
ADP	2023	2022	2021	2019	2018	5YR
Round 1	29	26	19	26	27	24
Round 2	18	15	16	18	19	17
Round 3	16	24	15	18	17	18
Round 4	12	11	16	14	10	13

It looks like the market struggled to accurately assess talent after the short 2020 season. I wouldn't argue if you decided to toss out those 2021 results. And yes, Judge was a third-rounder in 2022.

Still, while it is accepted that the first round is where all the $30 players should live, our recent track record shows that we can't always count on that. Nor can we rely on our second-round picks returning more value than third-rounders. As it turns out, $35 earners and ($10) losers can be found in almost any early round.

The first round yielded higher-value picks overall, but it hardly mattered who you picked at any seed. Acuña blew up the bank from 1.01, but you could dig deeper and find Gerrit Cole (2.04), Matt Olson (3.08), and Corey Seager (3.14) as high earners as well. Freddie Freeman (2.01), Aaron Judge (3.02), and Paul Goldschmidt (2.15) were all megadollar earners outside the first round in 2022. Bo Bichette (2.08), Vlad Guerrero, Jr. (3.03), and Starling Marte (3.04) returned first-round money in 2021. Justin Verlander (2.06), Gerrit Cole (2.09) and Cody Bellinger (3.12) did it in 2019. And José Ramírez (2.05), Francisco Lindor (2.06), J.D. Martinez (2.08), Jacob deGrom (3.03), Verlander (3.07), and Christian Yelich (3.11) were all $35-plus earners in 2018.

All these great players being drafted from everywhere is making me think about ice cream. (I told you I was getting hungry.)

Average Deliciousness Position

We all have our personal preferences when it comes to the frosty goodness of our favorite ice cream. Lately, I've been going to this one shop that has a flavor called Stellar Coffee. It's rich coffee ice cream with fudge and dark chocolate-covered espresso drops... and it's wonderful. But you know what? If you offered me a pint of Haagen Dazs vanilla on a hot afternoon, I wouldn't send you away. Either one would be refreshing. Both would be delicious.

Now that I'm thinking about it... here is the current first-round ADP ranking for the favorite ice cream flavors in the United States *(from a YouGov.com survey of 1,000 Americans)*:

1	Vanilla
2	Chocolate
3	Cookies and Cream
4	Strawberry
5	Chocolate Chip
6	Butter Pecan
7	Chocolate Chip Cookie Dough
8	Mint Chocolate Chip
9	Caramel
10	Neopolitan
11	Rocky Road
12	Chocolate Peanut Butter
13	Coffee
14	Pistachio
15	Cherry

This is the national ADP. However, Chocolate is the No. 1 pick in 15 states. If you are in a league in Pennsylvania, Washington, or Oregon, pick 1.01 would be Mint Chocolate Chip. Rocky Road gets the top nod in California, Montana, and Nevada. Strawberry is tops in Washington, DC. Coffee is first off the board in Massachusetts, New Mexico, Rhode Island, and Hawaii. Apparently, that was not enough to raise my personal fave higher than the 13th-ranked pick. Heck, Moose Tracks is the favorite in Iowa, Michigan, and Wisconsin but doesn't even crack the first-round rankings at all. Spencer Strider was the Moose Tracks of 2023.

I look at this list and think, "I hate strawberry—how could it go so high? Peanut butter is much better on bread with jelly, but not in ice cream. And who still eats Neopolitan? That was my grandparents' flavor." But it doesn't matter; there are enough other flavors in the first round that I can find something that satisfies my sweet tooth. Nearly any of them will be delicious.

Similarly, I could look at the earlier ADP list and think, "I hate Aaron Judge—how could he go so high? Juan Soto was much better in Washington, not in San Diego. And who is still drafting Vlad Guerrero? He was my grandparents' flavor."

Something like that.

But it doesn't matter; there are enough other players in the first round that can provide a solid foundation to my roster, and really, *any flavor of superstar can be delicious.* So, if you're the 8th seed and you're sitting at the beginning of the draft praying, "Please, Kyle Tucker, drop to me, drop to me, drop to me..." well, that's a lot of wasted anxiety.

Of course, if your roster construction plan has you gravitating to certain positions or statistical profiles in subsequent rounds, that can shape your choices. But your plan will change a half dozen times over the rest of the draft. So, if you're agonizing over whether Jose Altuve will still be there at 2.11 or whether Framber Valdez will make it to the third round... I can assure you that nearly anyone still waiting for you in those early rounds can be delicious. The mean earnings chart above bears that out.

Tasty young morsels

On another level of deliciousness are tasty young morsels that we often elevate in perceived value and cost because of FOMO. Word gets out about the incredible, new, mega-flavorful experience of Dark Chocolate Almond Truffle Maple Chip Fudge, and we have to be first in line to try it. $20 for a single scoop? YES, PLEASE.

Similarly, major league teams have started promoting young players faster than ever, partly due to the Prospect Promotion Incentive in the new collective bargaining agreement (where teams can earn an additional amateur or international draft pick if their player places in the Rookie of the Year voting). Those new, delicious flavors have been causing massive waves of fantasy draft day FOMO, too. In 2023, many delivered both unexpected productivity and mouthwatering yumminess. Researchers are still looking into what was in the water supply in Cincinnati.

I got to enjoy the experience of watching one of those rising stars suddenly POP in real-time back on March 4, 2023.

It was a spring training game between the St. Louis Cardinals and the home Washington Nationals at the Ballpark of the Palm Beaches. This was also First Pitch Florida weekend, and the conference attendees had our block of seats on the first base line.

In the third inning, with the Cards down 2-0, well-hyped prospect Jordan Walker stepped to the plate and launched a massive shot that cleared the left center field fence, the left center field berm, and landed with a thud about 20 feet further onto the concrete concourse just left of the concession stand selling pizza. It scattered the innocent bystanders, unaware that their personal pan was about to add a topping other than pepperoni.

The shot was Herculean, and we could only stare in awe at this massive feat of strength. I was sitting with the NFBC's Greg Ambrosius and Shawn Childs, who I had shared space with at the previous evening's LABR-NL draft. Upon Walker's shot, Greg sprang to his feet and yelled, "Walker! Yes! Sixteen bucks, baby!" in celebration of their acquisition the night before. Then, in the 7th inning, with his team down a run, Walker did it again, another massive shot. This time, it was with a runner on, and it put the Cards up for good.

Walker's ADP was 171 coming into the day but immediately spiked. From March 16 through Opening Day, his ADP was all the way up to 112, with the earliest pick inside the Top 50. He was going ahead of Max Muncy (118), Nick Castellanos (120), and Christian Walker (121), players with far more experience and highly productive track records.

It didn't matter that Walker's two-homer feat was accomplished against what was expected to be the worst pitching staff in the majors, specifically—Cade Cavalli (who might have already been nursing a bum elbow when he was pulled from a game ten days later en route to Tommy John surgery) and Chad Kuhl (who hadn't posted a draft-worthy ERA for eight years, and that was in Triple-A). But there he was, going as high as the fourth round in the NFBC. Even though March 4, 2023, might just have been a one-off.

For every Julio Rodriguez who explodes out of the gate, there are many more Jered Kelenics who take years even to begin to find footing or Jo Adells who never do. Remember that Mike Trout hit .220 in his first exposure to the majors. A-Rod hit .204 and .232 in his first two short stints in the majors. Greg Maddux went 8-18 with a 5.59 ERA in his first two seasons. Jacob deGrom never cracked a Top 100 prospect list, and Aaron Judge was ranked behind Bradley Zimmer, Nomar Mazara, and Victor Robles on 2016's Top 100 prospect list.

So, Jordan Walker finished March with a final slash line of .277/.299/.492, which included just one more HR in his 67 plate appearances. His .791 OPS didn't exactly herald superstardom, but it was enough to land him a roster spot on Opening Day. That's all you can hope for from a spring training performance.

He then opened the season with a 12-game hitting streak, and everyone's avarice felt validated. But after 73 AB, a .718 OPS, some defensive miscues, and the Cardinals' need to right their sinking ship, Walker was sent down to AAA-Memphis. Five weeks and a .928 OPS later, he was back in St. Louis, where he stayed the rest of the season. Walker would go on to hit .276 with 16 HR, 51 RBI, and 7 SB, earning $13.

While that represented a $3 loss for Greg and Shawn, it was a representative line for a 21-year-old rookie. Here are the lines of all the other 21 and younger rookies in their first 400 PA season in the majors (since 2010). They are ranked by their rookie year roto earnings:

	ROOKIE YEAR									YEAR 2	
Player	**Age**	**Yr**	**MLBA**	**ADP**	**HR**	**SB**	**BA**	**OPS**	**R$**	**ADP2**	**R$**
Trout,M	20	2012	9A	228	30	49	.326	.963	$47	3	$40
Rodriguez,J	21	2022	9B	199	28	25	.284	.853	$34	5	$33
Harris,M	21	2022	9D	**	19	20	.297	.853	$30	30	$22
Acuña,R	20	2018	10D	96	26	16	.293	.917	$24	8	$43
Bellinger,C	21	2017	9D	445	39	10	.267	.933	$23	26	$21
Soto,J	19	2018	9C	**	22	5	.292	.923	$19	33	$29
Harper,B	19	2012	10D	257	22	18	.270	.817	$17	15	$14
Hosmer,E	21	2011	9B	**	19	11	.293	.799	$16	51	$5
Torres,G	21	2018	9B	319	24	6	.271	.820	$16	64	$24
DeLaCruz,E	**21**	**2023**	**9C**	**548**	**13**	**35**	**.235**	**.710**	**$16**		
Correa,C	20	2015	9B	**	22	14	.279	.857	$15	6	$18
Tovar,E	**21**	**2023**	**9D**	**211**	**15**	**11**	**.253**	**.695**	**$15**		
Heyward,J	20	2010	9B	203	18	11	.277	.849	$14	56	-$1
Freeman,F	21	2011	9C	256	21	4	.282	.795	$14	120	$14
Lindor,F	21	2015	9B	397	12	12	.313	.835	$14	63	$25
Walker,J	**21**	**2023**	**9B**	**143**	**16**	**7**	**.276**	**.787**	**$13**		
Guerrero,V	20	2019	10C	49	15	0	.272	.772	$9	56	$20
Mazara,N	21	2016	8C	427	20	0	.266	.739	$8	202	$10
Castro,S	20	2010	9C	**	3	10	.300	.755	$6	146	$23
Greene,R	21	2022	9C	311	5	1	.253	.682	$6	194	$13
Álvarez,F	**21**	**2023**	**9C**	**463**	**25**	**2**	**.209**	**.721**	**$6**		
Russell,A	21	2015	9C	472	13	4	.242	.696	$3	123	$8
Bogaerts,X	21	2014	9C	166	12	2	.240	.660	$2	164	$24
Odor,R	20	2014	8C	**	9	4	.259	.698	$2	235	$7

*MLBA represents their prospect rating from the Minor League Baseball Analyst (number represents potential 1-10; letter represents odds of reaching potential A-F). ADP was their draft ranking coming into that first season. ** means they were not drafted in the Top 500 players. ADP2 was their ranking the following pre-season and R$ was the eventual earnings that year.*

Only the very best get to see 400 plate appearances at age 21 or younger, so this starts as a potentially elite group—note all the 9 and 10 ratings from the *Minor League Baseball Analyst*. In Year 2, you can see how their rookie performances drove their ADPs. You can also see what the resulting sophomore years earned back.

While this is an admittedly tiny sample—elite players rarely constitute a critical mass—those who earned at least $20 in their rookie year had a solid $20 floor in their sophomore campaign, with a high upside. Those who earned less than $20 were only a 40 percent bet to rise into the $20s in their second year, though their odds of improving at all was 73%. So, we can probably expect *some* growth from Walker (and the other trio of 2023 specimens), but I would be reluctant to draft him as if he will be a $20 earner next year. In snake draft terms, $20 is a fourth rounder.

That's the problem with these young morsels. You might end up with Xander Bogaerts, who starts slow and improves, or Nomar Mazara, who starts slow and stagnates. Or even a Jason Heyward who is expected to do something big then doesn't. That makes a high draft pick or $20 investment for any of them somewhat risky.

But that hasn't stopped early drafters from pushing 2024's new flavors up the board even more than they used to. If the CBA is incentivizing MLB teams to accelerate young players, shouldn't we be replacing our boring 15th and 20th-rounders with well-hyped minor leaguers as well? *To a point.* First of all, last season's large influx may have just been the 2020 minor league non-season washing itself out. It's also possible that the more prospects organizations push up, the lower the odds *their* guy will place in the Rookie of the Year voting. That could effectively result in a pullback in 2024.

Once again, 2023 was a sample size of one.

So, if you feel compelled to grab a player like Elly De La Cruz a few rounds early based on his electric debut (.307 in his first 95 plate appearances) and season's worth of counting stats (13 HR, 35 SB), don't forget that his last two months (.199 over 220 plate appearances) might inform his short-term playing time opportunities. If you're already in on post-season wunderkind Evan Carter (.300/.417/.500 in 70 PA), remember that opposing teams will be spending the winter looking for weaknesses to exploit. And if you've already decided that Jacksons Chourio and Holliday are going to be on your team no matter what, remember that they're both still at least a year away from being able to legally drink.

Sadly, it also doesn't take much research to discover that Dark Chocolate Almond Truffle Maple Chip Fudge is not all that it's cracked up to be. In fact, "almond truffle maple" is not even an ice cream flavor—it's a plank flooring color from Home Depot. Call it the Addison Russell of ice cream flavors. (So much for my appetite.)

Fantasy Expert

So, I've written a book. No, not this book—you already know about the *Baseball Forecaster*. I wrote another book. It is a historical memoir that chronicles the first 25 years of the fantasy baseball industry, as reported by someone who lived it (me). After nearly 40 years in this industry, it is the first book I have ever written with more words than numbers.

It is called *Fantasy Expert*, a moniker of pure irony that seemed to be fitting for the journey I have been on. I have hated the term FANTASY forever. I don't like being called an EXPERT. But it's the story of the many writers and analysts who were saddled with that tag in the 1980s, 1990s, and early 2000s. The official promo calls it "part memoir, part madcap history," and I'll add "part romance novel," but you'll have to make it to page 99 to know what that means.

Bottom line: *Fantasy Expert* is the Stellar Coffee of baseball memoirs.

Check out page 286 for more information. You can also view chapter summaries, excerpts, outtakes, and share your own stories at RonShandler.com/FantasyExpert.

The official release date is February 20, 2024. If you're reading this before February 20, you can pre-order it at amazon.com. Or, if you'd prefer that Jeff Bezos's cut goes into my pocket instead, order it directly from the publisher at TriumphBooks.com.

CONSUMER ADVISORY

AN IMPORTANT MESSAGE FOR FANTASY LEAGUERS REGARDING PROPER USAGE OF THE *BASEBALL FORECASTER*

This document is provided in compliance with authorities to outline the prospective risks and hazards possible in the event that the Baseball Forecaster is used incorrectly. Please be aware of these potentially dangerous situations and avoid them. The publisher assumes no risk related to any financial loss or stress-induced illnesses caused by ignoring the items as described below.

1. The statistical projections in this book are intended as general guidelines, not as gospel. It is highly dangerous to use the projected statistics alone, and then live and die by them. That's like going to a ballgame, being given a choice of any seat in the park, and deliberately choosing the last row in the right field corner with an obstructed view. The projections are there, you can look at them, but there are so many better places to sit.

We have to publish those numbers, but they are stagnant, inert pieces of data. This book focuses on a live forecasting process that provides the tools so that you can understand the leading indicators and draw your own conclusions. If you at least attempt your own analyses of the data, and enhance them with the player commentaries, you can paint more robust, colorful pictures of the future.

In other words...

If you bought this book purely for the projected statistics and do not intend to spend at least some time learning about the process, then you might as well just buy an $8 magazine.

2. The player commentaries in this book are written by humans, just like you. These commentaries provide an overall evaluation of performance and likely future direction, but 70-word capsules cannot capture everything. Your greatest value will be to use these as a springboard to your own analysis of the data. Odds are, if you take the time, you'll find hidden indicators that we might have missed. Forecaster veterans say that this self-guided excursion is the best part of owning the book.

3. This book does not attempt to tackle playing time. Rather than making arbitrary decisions about how roles will shake out, the focus is on performance. The playing time projections presented here are merely to help you better evaluate each player's talent. Our online preseason projections update provides more current AB and IP expectations based on how roles are being assigned.

4. The dollar values in this book are intended solely for player-to-player comparisons. They are not driven by a finite pool of playing time—which is required for valuation systems to work properly—so they cannot be used for bid values to be used in your own draft.

There are two reasons for this:

a. The finite pool of players that will generate the finite pool of playing time will not be determined until much closer to Opening Day. And, if we are to be brutally honest, there is really no such thing as a finite pool of players.

b. Your particular league's construction will drive the values; a $10 player in a 10-team mixed league will not be the same as a $10 player in a 12-team NL-only league.

Note that book dollar values also cannot be compared to those published at BaseballHQ.com as the online values are generated by a more finite player pool.

5. Do not pass judgment on the effectiveness of this book based on the performance of a few individual players. The test, rather, is on the collective predictive value of the book's methods. Are players with better base skills more likely to produce good results than bad ones? Years of research suggest that the answer is "yes." Does that mean that every high skilled player will do well? No. But many more of them will perform well than will the average low-skilled player. You should always side with the better percentage plays, but recognize that there are factors we cannot predict. Good decisions that beget bad outcomes do not invalidate the methods.

6. If your copy of this book is not marked up and dog-eared by Draft Day, you probably did not get as much value out of it as you might have.

7. This edition of the Forecaster is not intended to provide absorbency for spills of more than 7.5 ounces.

8. This edition is not intended to provide stabilizing weight for more than 18 sheets of 20 lb. paper in winds of more than 45 mph.

9. The pages of this book are not recommended for avian waste collection. In independent laboratory studies, 87% of migratory water fowl refused to excrete on interior pages, even when coaxed.

10. This book, when rolled into a cylindrical shape, is not intended to be used as a weapon for any purpose, including but not limited to insect extermination, canine training or to influence bidding behavior at a fantasy draft.

Welcome to the 38th Edition

If you are new to the *Baseball Forecaster*, the sheer volume of information in this book may seem a bit daunting. We don't recommend you assess its contents over a single commute to work, particularly if you drive. But do set aside some time this winter; instead of staring out the window, waiting for baseball to begin again, try immersing yourself in all the wisdom contained in this tome. There's a ton of it, and the payoff—Yoo-Hoo or otherwise—is worth it.

But where to begin?

The best place to start is with the Encyclopedia of Fanalytics, which provides the foundation concepts for everything else that appears in these pages. It's our research archive and collective memory, just as valuable for veterans as it is for rookies. Take a cursory read-through, lingering at any section that looks interesting. You'll keep coming back here frequently.

Then just jump in. Close your eyes, flip to a random page, and put your finger down anywhere. Oh, look—the "other" De La Cruz—Bryan, not Elly. Despite a "down" second half (thanks, h%), a lot of his relevant skills—contact, FB%, Brl% among them—were on the rise. Still just 27 with a bunch of MLB PA under his belt... maybe there's another level lurking. See, you've learned something already!

What's New in 2024?

2023's rules change were a primary focus of our research efforts this year, including:

- The explosion of stolen bases was massively impactful in 2023, and we have full coverage: Ryan Bloomfield has an essay on the overview of the surge (pg. 68). Ed DeCaria revised our expected Stolen Base (xSB) metric to reflect the new environment (pg. 69). The new xSB data appears in all of the batter boxes.
- Also in the new "new rules" umbrella, Andy Andres has an essay on the pitch clock, and whether clock-driven changes to pitch tempo impacted batters (pg. 67).
- Following up on last year's "Future of Playing Time" essay, Ed DeCaria is back with a Year Two revision. See "High-precision playing time analytics" on pg 70.

Also, answers to questions, such as: How should we adjust 2024 category targets based on those 2023 environment changes? Is the Santana Plan still relevant after 15 years? How much does age matter when assessing minor leaguers? And more....

Updates

The Baseball Forecaster page at BaseballHQ.com is at www.baseballhq.com/bf2024. This is your headquarters for all information and updates regarding this book. Here you will find links to the following:

Content Updates: In a project of this magnitude, there are occasionally items that need clarification or correction. You can find them here.

Free Projections Update: As a buyer of this book, you get one free 2024 projections update. This is a set of Excel spreadsheet files that will be posted on or about March 1, 2024. Remember to keep the book handy when you visit as the access codes are hidden within these pages.

Electronic book: The complete PDF version of the *Forecaster*—plus Excel versions of most key charts—is available free to those who bought the book directly through the BaseballHQ.com website. These files will be available in January 2024 for most of you; those who have an annual standing order should have received the PDF just before Thanksgiving. Contact us if you do not receive information via e-mail about access. Information about the e-book version can be found through the website.

If you purchased the book online or at a bookstore, or would like these files earlier, you can purchase them from us for $9.95. Reach us at support@baseballhq.com for more information.

Beyond the Forecaster

The *Baseball Forecaster* is just the beginning. The following companion products and services are described in more detail in the back of the book.

BaseballHQ.com is our home website. It provides regular updates to everything in this book, including daily updated statistics and projections. A subscription to BHQ gets you more than 1,000 articles over the course of a year updated daily from spring training through the end of the regular season, customized tools, access to data going back over a decade, plus much more. For a free peek, sign up for our BaseballHQFriday newsletter at www.baseballhq.com/friday.

We take this show on the road twice a year via our *First Pitch Forums* weekend conferences. We just completed our 28th year of our Arizona Fall League symposium, *First Pitch Arizona*. It's the ultimate fantasy baseball getaway, where you can meet top industry analysts and network with fellow fantasy leaguers. We are also planning *First Pitch Florida* in 2024, with three days of baseball talk, spring training games and the legendary LABR expert league drafts. Find out more about these events on page 287 and at BaseballHQ.com.

The 19th edition of the *Minor League Baseball Analyst* is the *Forecaster's* prospect companion, with stat boxes for 900-plus prospects, essays on prospects, lists upon lists, and more. In an era where rookies matter, it's an essential resource and available in January.

RotoLab is the best draft software on the market and comes pre-loaded with our projections. Learn more at www.rotolab.com.

Even further beyond the Forecaster

Visit us on *Facebook* at www.facebook.com/baseballhq. "Like" the BaseballHQ page for updates, photos from events and links to other important stuff.

Follow us on *Twitter/X*. Site updates are tweeted from @BaseballHQ and many of our writers share their insights from their own personal accounts. We even have a list to follow: www.twitter.com/BaseballHQ/lists/hq-staff.

But back to baseball. Your winter comfort awaits.

—Brent Hershey and Ray Murphy

For new readers...

Everything begins here. The information in the following pages represents the foundation that powers everything we do.

You'll learn about the underlying concepts for our unique mode of analysis. You'll find answers to long-asked questions, interesting insights into what makes players tick, and innovative applications for all this newfound knowledge.

This Encyclopedia is organized into several logical sections:

1. Fundamentals
2. Batters
3. Pitchers
4. Prospects
5. Gaming

Enough talking. Jump in.

Remember to breathe.

For veteran readers...

As we do in each edition, this year's ever-expanding Encyclopedia includes relevant research results we've published over the past year. We've added some of the essays from the Research Abstracts section in the 2023 *Forecaster* as well as some other essays from BaseballHQ.com.

And we continue to mold the content to best fit how fantasy leaguers use their information. Many readers consider this their fantasy information bible.

Okay, time to jump-start the analytical process for 2024. Remember to breathe—it's always good advice.

Abbreviations

Fundamentals

What is Fanalytics?

Fanalytics is the scientific approach to fantasy baseball analysis. A contraction of "fantasy" and "analytics," fanalytic gaming might be considered a mode of play that requires a more strategic and quantitative approach to player analysis and game decisions.

The three key elements of fanalytics are:

1. **Performance analysis**
2. **Performance forecasting**
3. **Gaming analysis**

For performance analysis, we tap into the vast knowledge of the sabermetric community. Founded by Bill James, this area of study provides objective and progressive new ways to assess skill. What we do in this book is called "component skills analysis." We break down performance into its component parts, then reverse-engineer it back into the traditional measures with which we are more familiar.

Our forecasting methodology is one part science and one part art. We start with a computer-generated baseline for each player, driven by the performance analysis and a contextual assessment of the player's role and expected playing time. We then make subjective adjustments based on a variety of factors, such as discrepancies in skills indicators and historical guidelines gleaned from more than 35 years of research. We don't rely on a rigid model; our method forces us to get our hands dirty.

You might say that our brand of forecasting is more about finding logical journeys than blind destinations.

Gaming analysis is an integrated approach designed to help us win our fantasy leagues. It takes the knowledge gained from the first two elements and adds the strategic and tactical aspect of each specific fantasy game format.

Component Skills Analysis

Familiar gauges like HR and ERA have long been used to measure skill. In fact, these gauges only measure the outcome of an individual event, or series of events. They represent statistical output. They are "surface stats."

Raw skill is the talent beneath the stats. Players use these skills to create the individual events, or components, that are the building blocks of measures like HR and ERA. Our approach:

1. It's not about batting average; it's about seeing the ball and making contact. We target hitters based on elements such as their batting eye (walks to strikeouts ratio), how often they make contact and the type of contact they make. We then combine these components into an "expected batting average." By comparing each hitter's actual BA to how he should be performing, we can draw conclusions about the future.

2. It's not about home runs; it's about power. From the perspective of a round bat meeting a round ball, it may be only a fraction of an inch at the point of contact that makes the difference between a HR and a long foul ball. When a ball is hit safely, often it is only a few inches that separate a HR from a double or long fly out. We can now measure elements like swing speed, exit velocity and launch angle to provide a more granular perspective. We must incorporate all these components to paint a complete picture of power.

3. It's not about ERA; it's about getting the ball over the plate and minimizing the damage of contact. Forget ERA. You want to draft pitchers who walk few batters (Control), strike out many (Dominance) and succeed at both in tandem (Command). You generally want pitchers who keep the ball on the ground (because home runs are bad), though some fly ball pitchers can succeed under the right conditions. All of this translates into an "expected ERA" that you can use to validate a pitcher's actual performance.

4. It's never about wins. For pitchers, winning ballgames is less about skill than it is about offensive support. As such, projecting wins is a high-risk exercise and valuing hurlers based on their win history is dangerous. Current trends in pitching usage—which fragment roles and spread innings to more pitchers—dilute our ability to project wins even more. Target skill; wins may or may not come, but it's your best hope. Many leagues are switching to tracking innings instead.

5. It's not about saves; it's about opportunity first and skills second. While the highest-skilled pitchers have the best potential to succeed as closers, they still must be given the ball with the game on the line in the 9th inning, and that is a decision left to others. Over the past 10 years, over 55% of relievers drafted for saves failed to hold the role for the entire season (that percentage is over 63% since 2018). The lesson: Don't take chances on draft day. There will always be saves in the free agent pool. Or toss out a wider net over the bullpen pool and switch to Saves-plus-Holds.

Accounting for "luck"

Luck has been used as a catch-all term to describe random chance. When we use the term here, we're talking about unexplained variances that shape the statistics. While these variances may be random, they are also often measurable and projectable. To get a better read on "luck," we use formulas that capture the external variability of the data.

Through our research and the work of others, we have learned that when raw skill is separated from statistical output, what's remaining is often unexplained variance. The aggregate totals of many of these variances, for all players, is often a constant. For instance, while a pitcher's ERA might fluctuate, the rate at which his opposition's batted balls fall for hits will tend towards roughly 30%. Large variances can be expected to regress towards 30%.

Why is all this important? Analysts complain about the lack of predictability of many traditional statistical metrics. The reason they find it difficult is that they are trying to project performance using metrics that are loaded with external noise. Raw skills metrics follow better-defined trends during a player's career. Then, as we get a better handle on the variances—explained and unexplained—we can construct a more complete picture of what a player's statistics really mean.

Baseball Forecasting

Forecasting in perspective

The crystal ball aura of "predicting the future" conceals the fact that forecasting is a process. We might define it as "the systematic process of determining likely end results." At its core, it's scientific.

However, the *outcomes* of forecasted events are what are most closely scrutinized and are used to judge the success or failure of the forecast. That said, as long as the process is sound, the forecast has done the best job it can do. *In the end, forecasting is about analysis, not prophecy.*

Baseball performance forecasting is inherently a high-risk exercise with a very modest accuracy rate. This is because the process involves not only statistics, but also unscientific elements, from random chance to human volatility. And even from within the statistical aspect, multiple elements need to be evaluated, from skill to playing time to a host of external variables.

Every system is comprised of the same core elements:

- Players will tend to perform within the framework of history and trends.
- Skills will develop and erode as a player ages.
- Statistics will be shaped by a player's health, role and environment.

While all systems are built from these same elements, they also are constrained by the same limitations. We are all still trying to project a bunch of human beings, each one...

- with his own individual skill set
- with his own rate of growth and decline
- with his own ability to resist and recover from injury
- limited to opportunities determined by other people
- generating a group of statistics largely affected by external noise.

Research has shown that the best accuracy rate that can be attained by any system is about 70%. In fact, a simple system that uses three-year averages adjusted for age ("Marcel") can attain a success rate of 65%. This means all the advanced systems are fighting for occupation of the remaining 5%.

But there is a bigger question… *what exactly are we measuring?* When we search for accuracy, what does that mean? In fact, any quest for accuracy is going to run into a brick wall of paradoxes:

- If a slugging average projection is dead on, but the player hits 10 fewer HR than expected (and likely, 20 more doubles), is that a success or a failure?
- If a projection of hits and walks allowed by a pitcher is on the mark, but the bullpen and defense implode and inflate his ERA by a run, is that a success or a failure?
- If the projection of a speedster's rate of stolen base success is perfect, but his team replaces the manager with one that doesn't run, and the player ends up with half as many SB as expected, is that a success or a failure?
- If a batter is traded to a hitters' ballpark and all the touts project an increase in production, but he posts a statistical line exactly what would have been projected had he not been traded to that park, is that a success or a failure?
- If the projection for a bullpen closer's ERA, WHIP and peripheral numbers is perfect, but he saves 20 games instead of 40 because the GM decided to bring in a high-priced free agent at the trading deadline, is that a success or a failure?
- If a player is projected to hit .272 in 550 AB and only hits .249, is that a success or failure? Most will say "failure." But wait a minute! The real difference is only two hits per month. That shortfall of 23 points in batting average is because a fielder might have made a spectacular play, or a screaming liner might have been hit right at someone, or a long shot to the outfield might have been held up by the wind... once every 14 games. Does that constitute "failure"?

Even if we were to isolate a single statistic that measures "overall performance" and run our accuracy tests on it, the results will still be inconclusive.

According to OPS, these players were virtually identical in 2023:

BATTER	HR	RBI	SB	BA	OBA	SLG	OPS
Crawford,JP	19	65	2	.266	.380	.438	.818
Rodríguez,J	32	103	37	.275	.333	.485	.818
Schwarber,K	47	104	0	.197	.343	.474	.817

If I projected Julio Rodríguez-caliber stats and ended up with J.P. Crawford's numbers, I'd hardly call that an accurate projection. According to Rotisserie dollars, these players were also dead-on in 2023:

BATTER	HR	RBI	Runs	SB	BA	R$
Soto,J	35	109	97	12	.275	$26
Hoerner,N	9	68	98	43	.283	$26

It's not so simple for someone to claim they have accurate projections. And so, it is best to focus on the bigger picture, especially when it comes to winning at fantasy baseball.

More on this: "The Great Myths of Projective Accuracy"

http://www.baseballhq.com/great-myths-projective-accuracy

Baseball Forecaster's forecasting process

Our approach is to assemble component skills in such a way that they can be used to validate our observations, analyze their relevance and project a likely future direction.

In a perfect world, if a player's raw skills improve, then so should his surface stats. If his skills decline, then his stats should follow. But sometimes a player's skill indicators increase while his surface stats decline. These variances may be due to a variety of factors.

Our forecasting process is based on the expectation that events tend to move towards universal order. Surface stats will eventually approach their skill levels. Unexplained variances will regress to a mean. And from this, we can identify players whose performance may potentially change.

For most of us, this process begins with the previous year's numbers. Last season provides us with a point of reference, so it's a natural way to begin the process of looking into the future. Component skills analysis allows us to validate those numbers. A batter with few HR but elevated power metrics has a good probability of improving his future HR output. A pitcher whose ERA was poor while his pitching support metrics were solid might be a good bet for ERA improvement.

Of course, these leading indicators do not always follow the rules. There are more shades of grey than blacks and whites. When indicators are in conflict—for instance, a pitcher who is displaying both a rising strikeout rate and a rising walk rate—then we must find ways to sort out what these indicators might be saying.

It is often helpful to look at leading indicators in a hierarchy. A rank of the most important pitching indicators might be: K-BB%, K%, BB% and GB/FB rate. For batters, contact rate tops the list, followed by power, walk rate and speed.

Assimilating additional research

Once we've painted the statistical picture of a player's potential, we then use additional criteria and research results to help us add some color to the analysis. These other criteria include the player's health, age, changes in role, ballpark and a variety of other factors. We also use the research results described in the following pages.

The final element of the process is assimilating the news into the forecast. This is the element that many fantasy leaguers tend to rely on most since it is the most accessible. However, it is also the element that provides the most noise. Players, management and the media have absolute control over what we are allowed to know. Factors such as hidden injuries, messy divorces and clubhouse unrest are routinely kept from us, while we are fed red herrings and media spam. *We will never know the entire truth.*

Quite often, all you are reading is just other people's opinions... a manager who believes that a player has what it takes to be a regular or a team physician whose diagnosis is that a player is healthy enough to play. These words from experts have some element of truth but cannot be wholly relied upon to provide an accurate expectation of future events. As such, it is often helpful to develop an appropriate cynicism for what you read.

For instance, if a player is struggling for no apparent reason and there are denials about health issues, don't dismiss the possibility that an injury does exist. There are often motives for such news to be withheld from the public.

And so, as long as we do not know all the facts, we cannot dismiss the possibility that any one fact is true, no matter how often the media assures it, deplores it, or ignores it. Don't believe everything you read; use your own judgment. If your observations conflict with what is being reported, that's powerful insight that should not be ignored.

Also remember that nothing lasts forever in major league baseball. *Reality is fluid.* One decision begets a series of events that lead to other decisions. Any reported action can easily be reversed based on subsequent events. My favorite examples are announcements of a team's new bullpen closer. Those are about the shortest realities known to man.

We need the media to provide us with context for our analyses, and the real news they provide is valuable intelligence. But separating the news from the noise is difficult. In most cases, the only thing you can trust is how that player actually performs.

Embracing imprecision

Precision in baseball prognosticating is a fool's quest. There are far too many unexpected variables and noise that can render our projections useless. The truth is, the best we can ever hope for is to accurately forecast general tendencies and percentage plays.

However, even when you follow an 80 percent play, for instance, you will still lose 20 percent of the time. That 20 percent is what skeptics use as justification to dismiss prognosticators; they conveniently ignore the more prevalent 80 percent. The paradox, of course, is that fantasy league titles are often won or lost by those exceptions. Still, long-term success dictates that you always chase the 80 percent and accept the fact that you will be wrong 20 percent of the time. Or, whatever that percentage play happens to be.

For fantasy purposes, playing the percentages can take on an even less precise spin. The best projections are often the ones that are just far enough away from the field of expectation to alter decision-making. In other words, it doesn't matter if I project Player X to bat .320 and he only bats .295; it matters that I project .320 and everyone else projects .280. Those who follow my less-accurate projection will go the extra dollar to acquire him in their draft.

Or, perhaps we should evaluate the projections based on their intrinsic value. For instance, coming into 2023 would it have been more important for me to tell you that Pete Alonso was going to hit 40 home runs or that Matt Olson would hit 40? By season's end, the Alonso projection would have been more accurate, but the Olson projection—even though it was off by more than twice as much—would have been far more valuable. The Olson projection might have persuaded you to go an extra buck on Draft Day, yielding more profit.

And that has to be enough. Any tout who projects a player's statistics dead-on will have just been lucky with his dart throws that day.

Perpetuity

Forecasting is not an exercise that produces a single set of numbers. It is dynamic, cyclical and ongoing. Conditions are constantly changing, and we must react to those changes by adjusting our expectations. A pre-season projection is just a snapshot in time. Once the first batter steps to the plate on Opening Day, that projection has become obsolete. Its value is merely to provide a starting point, a baseline for what is about to occur.

During the season, if a projection appears to have been invalidated by current performance, the process continues. It is then that we need to ask... What went wrong? What conditions have changed? In fact, has *anything* changed? We need to analyze the situation and revise our expectations, if necessary. This process must be ongoing.

When good projections go bad

All we can control is the process. We simply can't control outcomes. However, one thing we *can* do is analyze the misses to see *why* they occurred. This is always a valuable exercise each year. It puts a proper focus on the variables that were out of our control as well as providing perspective on those players with whom we might have done a better job.

In general, we can organize these forecasting misses into several categories. To demonstrate, here are players whose 2023 Rotisserie earnings varied significantly from our projections.

Performances that exceeded expectation

Development beyond the growth trend: These are young players for whom we knew there was skill. Some of them were prized prospects in the past who have taken their time ascending the growth curve. Others were a surprise only because their performance spike arrived sooner than anyone anticipated... Corbin Carroll, Nico Hoerner, Bryson Stott, CJ Abrams, James Outman, Matt McLain, Spencer Torkelson, Kyle Bradish, George Kirby, Justin Steele, Tanner Bibee, Bailey Ober, Bobby Miller, Cole Ragans

Skilled players who just had big years: We knew these guys were good too; we just didn't anticipate they'd be this good... Ronald Acuña, Matt Olson, Yandy Díaz, Ha-Seong Kim, Eduardo

Rodriguez, Josh Lowe, Kodai Senga, David Bednar, Zach Eflin, Jordan Montgomery

Unexpected health: We knew these players had the goods; we just didn't know whether they'd be healthy or would stay healthy all year... Cody Bellinger, Christian Yelich, Michael Wacha, Sonny Gray

Unexpected playing time: These players had the skills—and may have even displayed them at some time in the past—but had questionable playing time potential coming into this season. Some benefited from another player's injury, a rookie who didn't pan out or leveraged a short streak into a regular gig... TJ Friedl, Chas McCormick, Jarren Duran, Isaac Paredes, Brent Rooker, Lane Thomas, Nolan Jones, Jake Burger, Yainer Diaz, Orlando Arcia, Braxton Garrett

Unexpected role: This category is reserved for players who played their way into, or backed into, a larger role than anticipated. For most, there was already some previously demonstrated skill: Alexis Díaz, Paul Sewald, Jhoan Duran, Carlos Estévez, Evan Phillips, Will Smith, Adbert Alzolay, Tanner Scott, Nick Pivetta, Michael King, Seth Lugo

Unexpected discovery of the Fountain of Youth: These players should have been done, or nearly done, or at least headed down the far side of the bell curve. That's what the trends were pointing to. The trends were wrong... Marcell Ozuna, Justin Turner, Clayton Kershaw, Yusei Kikuchi, Craig Kimbrel

Surprise, yes, but not as good as it looked: These are players whose numbers were pretty, but unsupported by their skills metrics. Enjoy them now, but be wary of next year... Blake Snell, José Berríos, Bryce Elder

Who the heck knows? Maybe there are reasonable explanations, but this year was so far off the charts for... JP Crawford, Mitch Keller, Dane Dunning

Performances that fell short of expectation

Hobbled masses yearning to breathe free: These are players who got hurt, may not have returned fully healthy, or may have never been fully healthy (whether they'd admit it or not)... Oneil Cruz, Michael Brantley, Logan O'Hoppe, Tyler O'Neill, Mitch Haniger, Mike Trout, Jorge Polanco, CJ Cron, Kris Bryant, Starling Marte, Jazz Chisholm, Riley Greene, Cedric Mullins, Aaron Judge, Anthony Rizzo, Rowdy Tellez, Thairo Estrada, Vinnie Pasquantino, Byron Buxton, Manny Machado, Jeffrey Springs, Triston McKenzie, Trevor Rogers, Jacob deGrom, Tyler Mahle, Drew Rasmussen, Kyle Wright, Nick Lodolo, Dustin May, Brandon Woodruff, Carlos Rodón, Nestor Cortes, José Urquidy, Joe Musgrove, Shane McClanahan, Hunter Greene, Shane Bieber, Justin Verlander, Luis Garcia (HOU), Max Fried

Accelerated skills erosion: These are players who we knew were on the downside of their careers or had soft peripherals but who we did not think would plummet so quickly. In some cases, there were injuries involved, but all in all, 2023 might have been the beginning of the end for... Giancarlo Stanton, Tim Anderson, Javier Báez, José Abreu, Sal Perez, JT Realmuto, Lance Lynn, Yu Darvish

Inflated expectations: Here are players who we really should not have expected much more than what they produced. Some had short or spotty track records, others had soft peripherals coming into 2023, and still others were inflated by media hype. Player performance trends simply don't progress or regress in a straight line; still, the skills trends were intriguing enough to take a leap of faith. We were wrong... Alejandro Kirk, MJ Melendez, Daulton Varsho, Brady Singer, Reid Detmers, Dylan Cease

Unexpected loss of role: This category is reserved for would-be closers who lost the job before they could return profit... Scott Barlow, Daniel Bard, Ryan Helsley, Jorge López, Jose Leclerc

Surprise, yes, but not as bad as it looked: These are players whose numbers were disappointing but supported by better skills metrics. Diss them now, but keep an open mind for next year... Nolan Arenado, Vlad Guerrero Jr, Pete Alonso, José Ramírez, Joe Ryan, Aaron Nola

Who the heck knows? Maybe any one of these players could have been slotted into another category, but they still remain head-scratchers... Bo Bichette, Alek Manoah, Cristian Javier

About fantasy baseball touts

As a group, there is a strong tendency for all pundits to provide numbers that are publicly palatable, often at the expense of potential accuracy. That's because committing to either end of the range of expectation poses a high risk. Few touts will put their credibility on the line like that, even though we all know that those outliers are inevitable. Among our projections, you will find no .350 hitters or 70-steal speedsters. *Someone* is going to post a sub-2.50 ERA next year, but damned if any of us will commit to that. So, we take an easier road. We'll hedge our numbers or split the difference between two equally possible outcomes.

In the world of prognosticating, this is called the *comfort zone*. This represents the outer tolerances for the public acceptability of a set of numbers. In most circumstances, even if the evidence is outstanding, prognosticators will not stray from within the comfort zone.

As for this book, occasionally we do commit to outlying numbers when we feel the data support it. But overall, most of the numbers here can be nearly as cowardly as everyone else's. We get around this by providing "color" to the projections in the capsule commentaries, often listing UPside or DOWNside projections. That is where you will find the players whose projection has the best potential to stray beyond the limits of the comfort zone.

As analyst John Burnson once wrote: "The issue is not the success rate for one player, but the success rate for all players. No system is 100% reliable, and in trying to capture the outliers, you weaken the middle and thereby lose more predictive pull than you gain. At some level, everyone is an exception!"

Validating Performance

Performance validation criteria

The following is a set of support variables that helps determine whether a player's statistical output is an accurate reflection of his skills. From this we can validate or refute stats that vary from expectation, essentially asking, is this performance "fact or fluke?"

1. Age: Is the player at the stage of development when we might expect a change in performance?

2. Health: Is he coming off an injury, reconditioned and healthy for the first time in years, or a habitual resident of the IL?

3. Minor league performance: Has he shown the potential for greater things at some level of the minors? Or does his minor league history show a poor skill set that might indicate a lower ceiling?

4. Historical trends: Have his skill levels over time been on an upswing or downswing?

5. Component skills indicators: Looking beyond batting averages and ERAs, what do his support metrics look like?

6. Ballpark, team, league: Pitchers going to Colorado will see their ERA spike. Pitchers going to Oakland will see their ERA improve.

7. Team performance: Has a player's performance been affected by overall team chemistry, or the environment fostered by a winning or losing club?

8. Batting stance, pitching style/mastery: Has a change in performance been due to a mechanical adjustment?

9. Usage pattern, lineup position, role: Has a change in RBI opportunities been a result of moving further up or down in the batting order? Has pitching effectiveness been impacted by moving from the bullpen to the rotation?

10. Coaching effects: Has the coaching staff changed the way a player approaches his conditioning, or how he approaches the game itself?

11. Off-season activity: Has the player spent the winter frequenting workout rooms or banquet tables?

12. Personal factors: Has the player undergone a family crisis? Experienced spiritual rebirth? Given up red meat? Taken up testosterone?

13. MLB rule changes: How have the balanced schedule, defensive shift limitations, larger bases and pitch clock impacted a player's performance numbers?

Skills ownership

Once a player displays a skill, he owns it. That display could occur at any time—earlier in his career, back in the minors, or even in winter ball play. And while that skill may lie dormant after its initial display, the potential is always there for him to tap back into that skill at some point, barring injury or age. That dormant skill can reappear at any time given the right set of circumstances.

Caveats:

1. The initial display of skill must have occurred over an extended period. An isolated 1-hit shutout in Single-A ball amidst a 5.00 ERA season is not enough. The shorter the display of skill in the past, the more likely it can be attributed to random chance. The longer the display, the more likely that any reemergence could be for real.

2. If a player has been suspected of using performance enhancing drugs at any time, all bets are off.

Corollaries:

1. Once a player displays a vulnerability or skills deficiency, he owns that as well. That vulnerability could be an old injury problem, an inability to hit breaking pitches, or just a tendency to go into prolonged slumps.

2. The probability of a player correcting a skills deficiency declines with each year that deficiency continues to exist.

Risk Analysis

Risk management and reliability grades

Forecasts are constructed with the best data available, but there are factors that can impact the variability. One way we manage this risk is to assign each player Reliability Grades. The more certainty we see in a data set, the higher the reliability grades assigned to that player. The following variables are evaluated:

Health: Players with a history of staying healthy and off the IL are valuable to own. Unfortunately, while the ability to stay healthy can be considered skill, it is not very projectable. We can track the number of days spent on the injured list and draw rough conclusions using letter grades.

"A" level players accumulated fewer than 30 days on the major league IL over the past five years. "F" grades go to those who've spent more than 120 days on the IL. Recent IL stays are given a heavier weight in the calculation. There is also an adjustment for older players, who have a higher likelihood of getting hurt. That is the only forward-looking element of the grade.

Playing Time and Experience (PT/Exp): The greater the pool of MLB history to draw from, the greater our ability to construct a viable forecast. Length of service—and consistent service—is important. So, players who bounce up and down from the majors to the minors are higher risk players. And rookies are all high risk.

For batters, we simply track plate appearances. Major league PA have greater weight than minor league PA. "A" level players would have averaged at least 550 major league PA per year over the past three years. "F" graded players averaged fewer than 250 major league PA per year.

For pitchers, workload can be a double-edged sword. On one hand, small IP samples are deceptive in providing a read on a pitcher's true potential. Even a consistent 65-inning reliever can be considered higher risk since it would take just one bad outing to skew an entire season's work.

On the flipside, high workload levels also need to be monitored, especially in the formative years of a pitcher's career. Exceeding those levels elevates the risk of injury, burnout, or breakdown. So, tracking workload must be done within a range of innings. The grades capture this.

Consistency: Consistent performers are easier to project and garner higher reliability grades. Players that mix mediocrity with occasional flashes of brilliance or badness generate higher risk projections. Even those who exhibit a consistent upward or downward trend cannot be considered truly consistent as we do not know whether those trends will continue. Typically, they don't. *(See next: Using 3-year trends as leading indicators)*

"A" level players are those whose runs created per game level (xERA for pitchers) has fluctuated by less than half a run during each of the past three years. "F" grades go to those whose RC/G or xERA has fluctuated by two runs or more.

Remember that these grades have nothing to do with the quality of performance; they strictly refer to confidence in our expectations. So, a grade of AAA for a bad player only means that there is a high probability he will perform as poorly as we've projected.

Using 3-year trends as leading indicators *(Ed DeCaria)*

It is almost irresistibly tempting to look at three numbers moving in one direction and expect that the fourth will continue that progression. However, for both hitters and pitchers riding positive trends over any consecutive three-year period, not only do most players not continue their positive trend into a fourth year, their Year 4 performance usually regresses significantly. This is true for every metric tested (whether related to playing time, batting skills, pitching skills, running skills, luck indicators, or valuation). Negative trends show similar reversals, but tend to be more "sticky," meaning that rebounds are neither as frequent nor as strong as positive trend regressions.

Reliability and age

Peak batting reliability occurs at ages 29 and 30, followed by a minor decline for four years. So, to draft the most reliable batters, and maximize the odds of returning at least par value on your investments, you should target the age range of 28-34.

The most reliable age range for pitchers is 29-34. While we are forever looking for "sleepers" and hot prospects, it is very risky to draft any pitcher under 27 or over 35.

Evaluating reliability *(Bill Macey)*

When you head into an upcoming auction or draft, consider the following regarding risk and reliability:

- Reliability grades do help identify more stable investments: players with "B" grades in both Health and PT/Experience are more likely to return a higher percentage of their projected value.
- While top-end starting pitching may be more reliable than ever, the overall pool of pitchers is fraught with uncertainty and they represent a less reliable investment than batters.
- There does not appear to be a significant market premium for reliability, at least according to the criteria measured by BaseballHQ.com.
- There are only two types of players: risky and riskier. So, while it may be worth going the extra buck for a more reliable player, be warned that even the most reliable player can falter—don't go overboard bidding up a AAA-rated player simply due to his Reliability grades.

Normal production variance *(Patrick Davitt)*

Even if we have a perfectly accurate understanding of a player's "normal" performance level, his actual performance can vary widely over any 150-game span—including the 150-game span we call "a season." A .300 career hitter can perform in a range of .250-.350, a 40-HR hitter from 30-50, and a 3.70/1.15 pitcher from 2.60/0.95 to 6.00/1.55. And all these results must be considered "normal."

Health Analysis

Injury primer *(James C. Ferretti, DO)*

Every player injury and recovery process is unique. Still, you can gain a sizable advantage with a better understanding of both injuries and the corresponding medical terms. An overview of the human musculoskeletal system:

- *Bones:* The rigid support framework which is also a foundation for the other moving parts.
- *Cartilage:* Soft tissue that acts as a cushion and prevents wear—usually in areas where bones are close to each other.
- *Muscles:* Bundles of fibers that bend and stretch to perform work.
- *Tendons:* Bundles of (less bendy/stretchy) fibers that attach muscles to bones.
- *Ligaments:* Bundles of (even less bendy/stretchy) fibers that attach bones to other bones.

Some common ailments:

A **fracture** is simply a break in a bone, which means it isn't able to act as a stabilizer or absorb/distribute forces. Time to heal and/or long-term effects? Usually 4-6 weeks, though sometimes longer, though once the new bone has matured, it's as good as new.

Strains/sprains are tears of the fibers of muscles/tendons (strains) and ligaments (sprains). Most doctors categorize them on a Grade 1, 2, 3, scale, from less severe to most.

Time to heal and/or long-term effects? A rough estimate is 2-4 weeks for a Grade 1, 4-8 weeks for a Grade 2, and at least 8 weeks for a Grade 3. There can be long-term effects, notably that the repaired areas contain fibrous ("scar") tissue, which is neither as strong nor as flexible as the original tissue and is more prone to re-injury.

Inflammation is an irritation of soft tissues, often from overuse or repetitive motion and the structures affected get "angry." Even if they occur for different reasons, inflammation and a Grade 1 strain can behave similarly—and both can keep a player out for weeks. Long-term effects? Injury/pain can recur, or even worsen without adequate time to heal. (So, maybe your player coming back early isn't such good news after all.)

Some widely-used injury terms:

"No structural damage" sounds reassuring, but it's often misleading. When medical imagers unaffiliated with MLB clubs make an injury diagnosis, they might term it a fracture, dislocation, soft tissue tear, or inflammation; all of which are bad news. Or they may call it "normal," or "negative," which is good news. But rarely would they describe an injury in terms of "no structural damage," because it's not an actual diagnosis. Rather, it's a way of saying that whatever body part being imaged is intact, with no broken bone or soft tissue tear. This is not the same as a "normal" or "negative" diagnosis. When you hear "no structural damage", continue to keep a close eye on the situation.

Similarly, **"day-to-day"** sounds reassuring—but really doesn't tell you anything other than "We aren't sure," which can be far more worrisome.

"X-Rays are negative": Imaging a player is usually prompted by sudden or increasing onset of pain. Most baseball injuries, though, are to soft tissue, which is never diagnosed with an X-ray alone. Unless there's suspicion of a broken bone or joint injury, an X-ray probably isn't going to tell you much. We often see writers and analysts use a "negative" X-ray report to justify that the injury is "not believed to be serious." Don't make that mistake—await the results of more definitive imaging/tests, like a CAT scan or MRI.

Injured list statistics

Year	#Players	3yr Avg	IL Days	3yr Avg
2013	442	419	29,551	28,523
2014	422	424	25,839	28,599
2015	454	439	28,982	28,124
2016	478	451	31,329	28,717
2017	533	488	30,913	30,408
2018	574	528	34,284	32,175
2019	563	557	36,394	33,864
2020*	456	-	13,518	-
2021**	835	657	47,693	39,457
2022	726	708	44,389	42,825
2023	677	746	44,551	45,544

*Due to the 60-game season, 2020 data is not included in 3-year averages.
** The 2021 data includes 103 players/1,467 days whose only "injury" loss was due to a COVID-19 quarantine, and another 78 players who had other injuries in addition to a COVID quarantine.

IL days as a leading indicator *(Bill Macey)*

Players who are injured in one year are likely to be injured in a subsequent year:

% IL batters in Year 1 who are also DL in year 2	38%
Under age 30	36%
Age 30 and older	41%
% IL batters in Year 1 and 2 who are also DL in year 3	54%
% IL pitchers in Year 1 who are also DL in year 2	43%
Under age 30	45%
Age 30 and older	41%
% IL pitchers in Yr 1 and 2 who are also DL in year 3	41%

Previously injured players also tend to spend a longer time on the IL. The average number of days on the IL was 51 days for batters and 73 days for pitchers. For the subset of these players who get hurt again the following year, the average number of days on the IL was 58 days for batters and 88 days for pitchers.

How a batter's age affects IL stays *(Jeff Zimmerman)*

Some players seem to get more than their fair share of injuries, but for those hitters with the "injury-prone" tag, it only takes one healthy season to make a difference. After breaking up hitters into three age groups (25 and younger; 26-29; 30 and older), a study examined length and frequency of IL stints. Among the findings:

1. If someone in the youngest group goes on the IL once, they aren't as likely to again the next season. The probability increases after two IL seasons, however, from 33% to 43%.
2. The best health is exhibited by the middle group. It seems this age is the sweet spot for avoiding injuries. The hitters have shown they can hold up to a full season, but their bodies have not started to break down.
3. Not surprisingly, the oldest group takes longer to heal. The IL-related stats hover above the league average, but the IL rate doesn't increase as a player racks up previous injuries.

Do overworked hitters wear down? *(Jeff Zimmerman)*

A study compared the first- and second-half statistics for batters who played the most games over the entire season from 2002-16. These players were continually run out on the field, and one figures that fatigue would show up in their statistics. In actuality, their output improves the more they play. Though this concept goes against conventional wisdom, it is true: If a hitter plays more, the more likely he is healthy and not wearing down.

In-Season Analysis

The weight of early season numbers

Early season strugglers who surge later in the year often get little respect because they have to live with the weight of their early numbers all season long. Conversely, quick starters who fade late get far more accolades than they deserve.

For instance, take Mitch Keller's month-by-month ERA in 2023. The perception is that his 4.21 mark reflected another mediocre year but doesn't nearly show how much he struggled in the second half. Keller had a 3.34 ERA at mid-season—but crashed at a 5.24 level after the break:

Month	ERA	Cum ERA
Mar-Apr	3.53	3.53
May	3.00	3.25
June	3.56	3.34
July	6.28	3.97
August	4.20	4.01
Sept-Oct	5.28	4.21

Courtship period

Any time a player is put into a new situation, he enters a courtship period. This period might occur when a player switches leagues, or switches teams. It could be the first few games when a minor leaguer is called up. It could occur when a reliever moves into the rotation, or when a lead-off hitter is moved to another spot in the lineup. There is a team-wide courtship period when a manager is replaced. Any external situation that could affect a player's performance sets off a new decision point in evaluating that performance.

During this period, it is difficult to get a true read on how a player is going to ultimately perform. He is adjusting to the new situation. Things could be volatile during this time. For instance, a role change that doesn't work could spur other moves. A rookie hurler might buy himself a few extra starts with a solid debut, even if he has questionable skills.

It is best not to make a roster decision on a player who is going through a courtship period. Wait until his stats stabilize. Don't cut a struggling pitcher in his first few starts after a managerial change. Don't pick up a hitter who smacks a pair of HR in his first game after having been traded. Unless, of course, talent and track record say otherwise.

Half-season fallacies

A popular exercise is to analyze players who are consistent first half to second half surgers or faders. There are several fallacies with this analytical approach.

1. There are very few players who show consistent changes in performance from one half of the season to the other.

2. Multi-year scans may not show any consistency at all. A player whose 5-year batting average shows a 15-point rise in the 2nd half, for instance, may actually have experienced a BA decline in several of those years, a fact that might have been offset by a huge BA rise in one of the years.

3. The season's midpoint is an arbitrary delineator of performance swings. Some players are slow starters and might be more appropriately evaluated as pre-May and post-May. Others bring up their game in a pennant chase and might see a performance swing with an August 15 cut-off. Each player may have his own individual tendency, if, in fact, one exists at all.

Half-season tendencies

Despite the above, it stands to reason logically that there might be some underlying tendencies on a more global scale, first half to second half. In fact, one would think that the player population as a whole might decline in performance as the season drones on. There are many variables that might contribute to a player wearing down—workload, weather, boredom—and the longer a player is on the field, the higher the likelihood that he is going to get hurt. A recent 5-year study uncovered the following tendencies:

Batting

Overall, batting skills held up pretty well, half to half. There was a 5% erosion of playing time, likely due, in part, to September roster expansion.

Power: First half power studs (20 HR in 1H) saw a 10% drop-off in the second half. 34% of first half 20+ HR hitters hit 15 or fewer in the second half and only 27% were able to improve on their first half output.

Speed: Second half speed waned as well. About 26% of the 20+ SB speedsters stole *at least 10 fewer bases* in the second half. Only 26% increased their second half SB output at all.

Batting average: 60% of first half .300 hitters failed to hit .300 in the second half. Only 20% showed any second half improvement at all. As for 1H strugglers, managers tended to stick with their full-timers despite poor starts. Nearly one in five of the sub-.250 1H hitters managed to hit *more than* .300 in the second half.

Pitching

Overall, there was some slight erosion in innings and ERA despite marginal improvement in skills metrics.

ERA: For those who pitched at least 100 innings in the first half, ERAs rose an average of 0.40 runs in the 2H. Of those with first half ERAs less than 4.00, only 49% were able to maintain a sub-4.00 ERA in the second half.

Wins: Pitchers who won 18 or more games in a season tended to pitch *more* innings in the 2H and had slightly better skills metrics.

Saves: Of those closers who saved 20 or more games in the first half, only 39% were able to post 20 or more saves in the 2H, and 26% posted fewer than 15 saves. Aggregate ERAs of these pitchers rose from 2.45 to 3.17, half to half.

In-season trends in hitting and pitching *(Zach Larson)*

League-wide baselines not only change each season, but monthly within a season as well, due to a variety of factors (such as weather). A study of the 2021 and 2022 seasons found some general trends, including the fact that hitters do tend to perform better in warmer weather. Some of the variances between the two years can be attributed to post-pandemic and post-lockout factors.

2022 MLB stats by month (per game):

Month	GP	R	HR	RBI	SB	AVG	K	SV	ERA	WHIP
Apr	634	4.03	0.91	3.82	0.48	0.231	8.50	0.27	3.72	1.24
May	839	4.43	1.08	4.22	0.52	0.246	8.21	0.25	4.10	1.28
Jun	808	4.49	1.19	4.30	0.52	0.246	8.32	0.24	4.14	1.29
Jul	780	4.32	1.10	4.12	0.51	0.245	8.46	0.26	3.97	1.27
Aug	840	4.22	1.04	4.07	0.50	0.245	8.33	0.24	3.93	1.27
Sep/Oct	958	4.17	1.09	3.99	0.54	0.240	8.58	0.25	3.91	1.25

2021 MLB stats by month (per game):

Month	GP	R	HR	RBI	SB	AVG	K	SV	ERA	WHIP
Apr	766	4.26	1.14	4.01	0.46	0.232	9.07	0.24	3.98	1.25
May	834	4.41	1.12	4.19	0.46	0.239	8.92	0.25	4.06	1.29
Jun	796	4.66	1.28	4.46	0.45	0.246	8.69	0.24	4.43	1.32
Jul	742	4.62	1.29	4.41	0.44	0.248	8.51	0.23	4.39	1.32
Aug	828	4.54	1.24	4.35	0.45	0.246	8.51	0.25	4.26	1.29
Sep/Oct	892	4.67	1.27	4.49	0.47	0.250	8.38	0.25	4.42	1.32

Can in-season deficiencies in ratio categories be overcome?

(Patrick Davitt)

Many fantasy players think that we can't move the decimals (BA, ERA, WHIP) later in the season because the majority of AB/IP are in the books and the ratio's large denominators make it too hard. While it's true we can't move as much late as early, we can still gain points. We tested this idea at the two-thirds mark in the season. Using teams and stats in a 15-team mixed expert's league, we built tables to see how much an owner could gain—first just by dropping a poor performer, and then by replacing a poor performer with a good performer.

Both methods found that it's still possible to gain points. (Obviously, stratification of league standings will vary.)

Batting Average

The BA test projected a team to finish with a .257 BA. With 190 remaining projected AB per batter, we found that by dropping a player and not replacing him:

- Drop a .235 hitter: Team BA .25756
- .225 hitter: .25783
- .215 hitter: .25810

The gains are amplified when the poor hitter is replaced with a high projected BA hitter. Dropping a .215 pBA hitter and adding a .305 guy jumps team pBA to .25927. Dropping a .245 and adding a .265 still gains 57 baseline points. Again, depending on how close your league standings are, this matters.

ERA

Gains in pitching decimals can be greater because the denominator is smaller than BA. This study used a team with a 4.00 final pERA in 1,325 IP. Let's drop a poor performer with 55 pIP:

- Dropping a 4.50 pERA pitcher, finished at 3.976
- 5.00 pitcher: 3.954
- 5.50 pitcher: 3.933

And now, by adding a low-pERA replacement: Dropping a 5.50 disaster for a 2.75 stud means a final pERA of 3.885, an improvement of .115.

Again, much depends on how each category is stratified.

Surprisingly productive years *(Ed DeCaria)*
Here's a skills-based method of finding productive in-season roster additions:

1. Consider all batters projected for 50% or less playing time, all starting pitchers projected for 10% or less of his team's innings pitched (about 140 IP), and all relief pitchers projected for less than 4% of his team's innings pitched (about 50 IP)
2. Using each player's projected skills—not stats—in the form of his Mayberry scores, include only batters whose sum of three Mayberry skills (power, speed, and hitting) was 7 or higher (8 or higher for mixed leagues). For pitchers, only consider players whose sum of two Mayberry skills (xERA and strikeout rate) was 4 or higher (5 or higher for mixed leagues). For relievers, we also counted Mayberry's saves potential score, so we included only relievers whose sum of three scores was 7 or higher (8 or higher for mixed leagues).
3. Examine the specific situation of each player that met our first two criteria and assign a realistic playing time upside given his skills and injury, consistency, and forecast risk, and that of the player(s) ahead of him on his team's depth chart.
4. Calculate a single number that measured their "projected skill" over their "potential playing time" to arrive at their "potential value."
    a. For hitters, take his Mayberry sum and multiply it by his potential playing time (pPT). Then rank batters by this metric and subtract the minimum value of the group from all players, so that the least valuable batter had a marginal score (mSCORE) of zero. Then use mSCORE to calculate each player's "share" of the total and multiply that by the league's total wasted dollars (using a 65/35 batter/pitcher split) to determine each batter's potential value (pR$).
    b. Similarly for pitchers, take the Mayberry sum multiplied by potential innings percentage (pPT) and rank pitchers by this metric. Subtract the minimum value of the group from all pitchers, then use mSCORE to calculate each pitcher's "share" of the total and multiply that by the league's total wasted dollars (using a 65/35 batter/pitcher split) to determine each pitcher's potential value (pR$).

Use these rankings to produce lists of players who are projected for far less than full playing time despite good or even great skills. A well-timed pick-up of any one of these players could be a boon to most teams' chances of winning their league.

Teams

Johnson Effect *(Bryan Johnson)*: Teams whose actual won/loss record exceeds or falls short of their statistically projected record in one season will tend to revert to the level of their projection in the following season.

Law of Competitive Balance *(Bill James)*: The level at which a team (or player) will address its problems is inversely related to its current level of success. Low performers will tend to make changes to improve; high performers will not. This law explains the existence of the Plexiglass and Whirlpool Principles.

Plexiglass Principle *(Bill James)*: If a player or team improves markedly in one season, it will likely decline in the next. The opposite is true but not as often (because a poor performer gets fewer opportunities to rebound).

Whirlpool Principle *(Bill James)*: All team and player performances are forcefully drawn to the center. For teams, that center is a .500 record. For players, it represents their career average level of performance.

Other Diamonds

The Fanalytic Fundamentals

1. This is not a game of accuracy or precision. It is a game of human beings and tendencies.
2. Draft skills, not stats. Draft skills, not roles.
3. A player's ability to post acceptable stats despite lousy support metrics will eventually run out.
4. Once you display a skill, you own it.
5. Virtually every player is vulnerable to a month of aberrant performance. Or a year.
7. Exercise excruciating patience.

Forecasting Fundamental

We interpret a player's stat line as a fixed measure of performance. But each data point represents a unique confluence of events that were shaped by variables such as health, ballpark dimensions, wind currents, and the particular assortment of pitchers or hitters he faced during the season. Each piece of data is really just an almost arbitrary stopping point along a continuum of possibilities. That's why we cannot use those stats as absolute input to a projections model and expect precise output.

Aging Axioms

1. Age is the only variable for which we can project a rising trend with 100% accuracy. (Or, age never regresses.)
2. The aging process slows down for those who maintain a firm grasp on the strike zone. Plate patience and pitching command can preserve any waning skill they have left.
3. Negatives tend to snowball as you age.

Steve Avery List

Players who hang onto MLB rosters for six years searching for a skill level they only had for three.

Bylaws of Badness

1. Some players are better than an open roster spot, but not by much.
2. Some players have bad years because they are unlucky. Others have *many* bad years because they are bad... and lucky.

Christie Brinkley Law of Statistical Analysis

Never get married to the model.

Employment Standards

1. If you are right-brain dominant, own a catcher's mitt and are under 40, you will always be gainfully employed.
2. Some teams believe that it is better to employ a player with any experience because it has to be better than the devil they don't know.
3. It's not so good to go *pffft* in a contract year.

Brad Fullmer List

Players whose leading indicators indicate upside potential, year after year, but consistently fail to reach that full potential. Players like Byron Buxton, Andrew Heaney and Chris Paddack head the list once again.

Good Luck Truisms

1. Good luck is rare, and everyone has more of it than you do. That's the law.
2. An Unreasonably Good Luck Year can be considered "winning UGLY."

The Gravity Principles

1. It is easier to be crappy than it is to be good.
2. All performance starts at zero, ends at zero and can drop to zero at any time.
3. The odds of a good performer slumping are far greater than the odds of a poor performer surging.
4. Once a player is in a slump, it takes several 3-for-5 days to get out of it. Once he is on a streak, it takes a single 0-for-4 day to begin the downward spiral. *Corollary:* Once a player is in a slump, not only does it take several 3-for-5 days to get out of it, but he also has to get his name back on the lineup card.
5. Eventually, all performance comes down to earth. It may take a week, or a month, or may not happen until he's 45, but eventually it's going to happen.

Health Homilies

1. Staying healthy is a skill.
2. A $40 player can get hurt just as easily as a $5 player but is eight times tougher to replace.
3. Chronically injured players never suddenly get healthy.
4. There are two kinds of pitchers: those that are hurt and those that are not hurt... yet.
5. Players with back problems are always worth $10 less.
6. "Opting out of surgery" usually means it's coming anyway, just later.

The Health Hush

Players get hurt and potentially have a lot to lose, so there is an incentive for them to hide injuries. HIPAA laws restrict the disclosure of health information. Team doctors and trainers have been instructed not to talk with the media. So, when it comes to information on a player's health status, we're all pretty much in the dark.

The Livan Level

The point when a player's career Runs Above Replacement level has dropped so far below zero that he has effectively canceled out any possible remaining future value. (Similarly, the Dontrelle Demarcation.)

The Momentum Maxims

1. A player will post a pattern of positive results until the day you add him to your roster.
2. Patterns of negative results are more likely to snowball than correct.
3. When an unstoppable force meets an immovable object, the wall always wins.

Noise

Irrelevant or meaningless pieces of information that can distort the results of an analysis. In news, this is opinion or rumor. In forecasting, this is random variance or irrelevant data. In ballparks, this is a screaming crowd cheering for a team down 12-3 with two outs and bases empty in the bottom of the ninth.

Paradoxes and Conundrums

1. Is a player's improvement in performance from one year to the next a point in a growth trend, an isolated outlier or a complete anomaly?
2. A player can play through an injury, post rotten numbers and put his job at risk… or… he can admit that he can't play through an injury, allow himself to be taken out of the lineup/rotation, and put his job at risk.
3. Did irregular playing time take its toll on the player's performance or did poor performance force a reduction in his playing time?
4. Is a player only in the game versus right-handers because he has a true skills deficiency versus left-handers? Or is his poor performance versus left-handers because he's never given a chance to face them?
5. The problem with stockpiling bench players in the hope that one pans out is that you end up evaluating performance using data sets that are too small to be reliable.
6. There are players who could give you 20 stolen bases if they got 400 AB. But if they got 400 AB, they would likely be on a bad team that wouldn't let them steal.

Paths to Retirement

1. **The George Brett Path:** Get out while you're still putting up good numbers and the public perception of you is favorable. Like Chipper Jones, Mariano Rivera and David Ortiz.
2. **The Steve Carlton Path:** Hang around the majors long enough for your numbers to become so wretched that people begin to forget your past successes. New retirees who, sadly, took this path are Miguel Cabrera and Adam Wainwright. Two others within sight of those final plate appearances are Josh Donaldson and Joey Votto.
3. **The Johan Santana Path:** Stay on the injured list for so long that nobody realizes you've officially retired until your name shows up on a Hall of Fame ballot. Others who took this path include Carl Crawford and Jacoby Ellsbury. A player like Anthony Rendon could be next.

Process-Outcome Matrix *(Russo and Schoemaker)*

	Good Outcome	**Bad Outcome**
Good Process	Deserved Success	Bad Break
Bad Process	Dumb Luck	Poetic Justice

Quack!

An exclamation in response to the educated speculation that a player has used performance enhancing drugs. While it is rare to have absolute proof, there is often enough information to suggest that, "if it looks like a duck and quacks like a duck, then odds are it's a duck."

Rules of Regression

1. The two strongest forces on Earth are regression and gravity.
2. The most accurate forecast is often just a regression to a player's career average.
3. Regression doesn't punch a time clock. *(Todd Zola)*

Surface Stats

All those wonderful statistics we grew up with that those mean bean counters are telling us don't matter anymore. Home runs, RBI, batting average, won-loss record. Let's go back to the 1960s and make baseball great again! [EDITOR: No.]

Tenets of Optimal Timing

1. If a second half fader had put up his second half stats in the first half and his first half stats in the second half, then he probably wouldn't even have had a second half.
2. Fast starters can often buy six months of playing time out of one month of productivity.
3. Poor 2nd halves don't get recognized until it's too late.
4. "Baseball is like this. Have one good year and you can fool them for five more, because for five more years they expect you to have another good one." — Frankie Frisch

The Three True Outcomes

1. Strikeouts
2. Walks
3. Home runs

The Three True Handicaps

1. Has power but can't make contact.
2. Has speed but can't hit safely.
3. Has potential but is too old.

Zombie

A player who is indestructible, continuing to get work, year after year, no matter how dead his skills metrics have become. Thankfully, it appears that zombies Jhoulys Chacin and Mike Minor were finally reburied after 2022. But Dallas Keuchel, Chase Anderson, and Tommy Milone are still among the walking dead now.

Batters

Batting Eye, Contact and Batting Average

Batting average (BA, or Avg)

This is where it starts. BA is a grand old nugget that has long outgrown its usefulness. We revere .300 hitters as superstars and think of .250 hitters as middingly acceptable, yet the difference between the two is one hit every five games. BA is a poor evaluator of performance in that it neglects the offensive value of the base on balls and assumes that all hits are created equal.

Walk rate (bb%)

(BB / (AB + BB))

A measure of a batter's plate patience. **BENCHMARKS:** The best batters will have levels more than 10%. Those with poor plate patience will have levels of 5% or less.

On base average (OB)

(H + BB + HBP) / (AB + BB + HBP + Sac Flies)

Addressing a key deficiency with BA, OB gives value to events that get batters on base but are not hits. An OB of .350 can be read as "this batter gets on base 35% of the time." When a run is scored, there is no distinction made as to how that runner reached base. So, two-thirds of the time—about how often a batter comes to the plate with the bases empty—a walk really is as good as a hit. **BENCHMARKS:** We know what a .300 hitter is, but what represents "good" for OB? That comparable level would likely be .340, with .290 representing the comparable level of futility.

Ground ball, line drive, fly ball percentages (G/L/F)

The percentage of balls in play that are hit on the ground, as line drives, and in the air. For batters, increased fly ball tendency may foretell a rise in power skills; increased line drive tendency may foretell an improvement in batting average. A study of 2017-2021 batted ball data shows league averages for each:

BIP Type	Total%	Out%
Ground ball	43%	72%
Line drive	21%	28%
Fly ball	37%	85%

Line drives and luck *(Patrick Davitt)*

Given that each individual batter's hit rate sets its own baseline, and that line drives (LD) are the most productive type of batted ball, a study looked at the relationship between the two. Among the findings were that hit rates on LDs are much higher than on FBs or GBs, with individual batters consistently falling into the 72-73% range. Ninety-five percent of all batters fall between the range of 60%-86%; batters outside this range regress very quickly, often within the season.

Note that batters' BAs did not always follow their LD% up or down, because some of them enjoyed higher hit rates on other batted balls, improved their contact rates, or both. Still, it's justifiable to bet that players hitting the ball with authority but getting fewer hits than they should will correct over time.

Batting eye (Eye)

(Walks / Strikeouts)

A measure of a player's strike zone judgment. **BENCHMARKS:** The best hitters have Eye ratios more than 1.00 (indicating more walks than strikeouts) and are the most likely to be among a league's .300 hitters. Ratios less than 0.30 represent batters who likely also have lower BAs.

Batting eye as a leading indicator

There is a correlation between strike zone judgment and batting average but research shows that this is more descriptive than predictive.

However, we can create percentage plays for the different levels:

For Eye	Pct who bat	
Levels of	.300+	.250-
0.00 - 0.25	7%	39%
0.26 - 0.50	14%	26%
0.51 - 0.75	18%	17%
0.76 - 1.00	32%	14%
1.01 - 1.50	51%	9%
1.51 +	59%	4%

Any batter with an eye ratio more than 1.50 has about a 4% chance of hitting less than .250 over 500 at bats.

Of all .300 hitters, those with ratios of at least 1.00 have a 65% chance of repeating as .300 hitters. Those with ratios less than 1.00 have less than a 50% chance of repeating.

Only 4% of sub-.250 hitters with ratios less than 0.50 will mature into .300 hitters the following year.

In this study, only 37 batters hit .300-plus with a sub-0.50 eye ratio over at least 300 AB in a season. Of this group, 30% were able to accomplish this feat on a consistent basis. For the other 70%, this was a short-term aberration.

Chase rate (Chase%)

A Statcast plate discipline metric defined as the percentage of pitches thrown outside the zone that a batter swings at. **BENCHMARKS:** The league-wide chase rate in 2023 was 29%. The lower (better) chase rates are typically below 25%, while the free-swingers are above 33%.

Contact rate (ct%)

((AB - K) / AB)

Measures a batter's ability to get wood on the ball and hit it into the field of play. **BENCHMARKS:** Those batters with the best contact skill will have levels of 80% or better. The hackers will have levels of 70% or less.

Contact rate as a leading indicator

The more often a batter makes contact with the ball, the higher the likelihood that he will hit safely.

	Batting Average					
Contact Rate	2019	2020	2021	2022	2023	+/-
0% - 60%	.179	.184	.188	.185	.192	+.007
61% - 65%	.223	.212	.222	.216	.227	+.011
66% - 70%	.241	.224	.225	.225	.234	+.009
71% - 75%	.252	.248	.245	.239	.246	+.007
76% - 80%	.264	.261	.261	.249	.254	+.005
81% - 85%	.277	.269	.268	.263	.271	+.008
Over 85%	.282	.284	.273	.271	.272	+.001

The limitations to defensive shifting are noticeable within this data, but the impact appears more pronounced at the lower contact levels.

Contact rate and walk rate as leading indicators

We looked at seasons from 2000-2021 to see how well both walk rate (BB%) and strikeout rate (K%; loosely inverse to contact rate, ct%) correlate with batting average:

Year	BB%	K%
All	0.01	-0.47
2000	0.14	-0.39
2007	0.00	-0.41
2014	-0.07	-0.53
2021	-0.06	-0.55

A correlation of zero literally means zero correlation, and that's what we see right down the line with walk rate: it doesn't matter to batting average. Strikeouts, however, have quite solid negative correlations: as strikeouts go up, BA goes down, and vice versa.

HCt and HctX *(Patrick Davitt)*

HCt= hard hit ball rate x contact rate

HctX= Player HCt divided by league average Hct, normalized to 100

The combination of making contact and hitting the ball hard might be the most important skills for a batter. HctX correlates very strongly with BA, and at higher BA levels often does so with high accuracy. Its success with HR was somewhat limited, probably due to GB/FB differences. **BENCHMARKS:** The average major-leaguer has a HctX of 100. Elite batters have an HctX of 135 or above; weakest batters have HctX of 55 or below.

Balls in play (BIP)

(AB – K)

The total number of batted balls that are hit fair, both hits and outs. An analysis of how these balls are hit—on the ground, in the air, hits, outs, etc.—can provide analytical insight, from player skill levels to the impact of luck on statistical output.

Batting average on balls in play *(Voros McCracken)*

(H – HR) / (AB – HR – K)

Or, BABIP. Also called hit rate (h%). The percent of balls hit into the field of play that fall for hits. **BENCHMARK:** Every hitter establishes his own individual hit rate that stabilizes over time. A batter whose seasonal hit rate varies significantly from the h% he has established over the preceding three seasons (variance of at least +/- 3%) is likely to improve or regress to his individual h% mean (with over-performer declines more likely and sharper than under-performer recoveries). Three-year h% levels strongly predict a player's h% the following year.

Pitches/plate appearance as a leading indicator for BA *(Paul Petera)*

The deeper a batter works a count (via pitches per plate appearance, or P/PA), the more likely his batting average will fall (e.g., more strikeouts) but his OBA will rise (e.g., more walks):

P/PA	OBA	BA
4.00+	.360	.264
3.75-3.99	.347	.271
3.50-3.74	.334	.274
Under 3.50	.321	.276

Players with an unusually high or low BA for their P/PA in one year tend to regress heavily the next:

	YEAR TWO	
YEAR ONE	BA Improved	BA Declined
Low P/PA and Low BA	77%	23%
High P/PA and High BA	21%	79%

Expected batting average *(John Burnson)*

*xCT% * [xH1% + xH2%]*

where

xH1% = GB% x [0.0004 PX + 0.062 ln(SX)]
+ LD% x [0.93 - 0.086 ln(SX)]
+ FB% x 0.12

and

xH2% = FB% x [0.0013 PX - 0.0002 SX - 0.057]
+ GB% x [0.0006 PX]

A hitter's expected batting average is calculated by multiplying the percentage of balls put in play (contact rate) by the chance that a ball in play falls for a hit. The likelihood that a ball in play falls for a hit is a product of the speed of the ball and distance it is hit (PX), the speed of the batter (SX), and the distribution of ground balls, fly balls, and line drives. We further split it out by non-homerun hit rate (xH1%) and homerun hit rate (xH2%). **BENCHMARKS:** In general, xBA should approximate batting average closely. Those hitters who have large variances between the two gauges are candidates for further analysis. **LIMITATION:** xBA tends to understate a batter's true value if he is an extreme ground ball hitter (G/F ratio over 3.0) with a low PX. These players are not inherently weak but choose to take safe singles rather than swing for the fences.

Expected batting average variance

xBA – BA

The variance between a batter's BA and his xBA is a measure of over- or under-achievement. A positive variance indicates the potential for a batter's BA to rise. A negative variance indicates the potential for BA to decline. **BENCHMARK:** Discount variances that are less than 20 points. Any variance of more than 30 points is regarded as a strong indicator of future change.

Power

Slugging average (Slg)

(Singles + (2 x Doubles) + (3 x Triples) + (4 x HR)) / AB

A measure of the total number of bases accumulated (or the minimum number of runners' bases advanced) per at bat. It is a misnomer; it is not a true measure of a batter's slugging ability because it includes singles. Slg also assumes that each type of hit has proportionately increasing value (i.e. a double is twice as valuable as a single, etc.) which is not true. For instance, with the bases loaded, a HR always scores four runs, a triple always scores three, but a double could score two or three and a single could score one, or two, or even three. **BENCHMARKS:** Top batters will have levels over .450. The bottom batters will have levels less than .350.

Home runs to fly ball rate (HR/F)

The percent of fly balls that are hit for HR.

HR/F rate as a leading indicator *(Joshua Randall)*

Each batter establishes an individual home run to fly ball rate that stabilizes over rolling three-year periods; those levels strongly predict the HR/F in the subsequent year. A batter who varies significantly from his HR/F is likely to regress toward his individual HR/F mean, with over-performance decline more likely and more severe than under-performance recovery.

Estimating HR rate for young hitters *(Matt Cederholm)*

Over time, hitters establish a baseline HR/F, but how do we measure the HR output of young hitters with little track record? Since power is a key indicator of HR output, we can look at typical HR/F for various levels of power, as measured by xPX:

	HR/F percentiles				
xPX	10	25	50	75	90
<=70	0.9%	2.0%	3.8%	5.5%	7.4%
71-80	3.3%	5.1%	6.4%	8.1%	10.0%
81-90	3.8%	5.4%	7.4%	9.0%	11.0%
91-100	4.7%	6.6%	8.9%	11.3%	13.0%
101-110	6.6%	8.3%	10.9%	13.0%	16.2%
111-120	7.4%	9.8%	11.9%	14.7%	17.1%
121-130	8.5%	10.9%	12.8%	15.5%	17.4%
131-140	9.7%	11.9%	14.6%	17.1%	20.4%
141-160	11.3%	13.1%	16.5%	19.2%	21.5%
161+	14.4%	16.5%	19.4%	22.0%	25.8%

To predict changes in HR output, look at a player and project his HR as if his HR/F was at the median for his xPX level. For example, if a player with a 125 xPX exceeds a 12.8% HR/F, we would expect a decline in the following season. The greater the deviation from the mean, the greater the probability of an increase or decline.

Expected home run total (xHR) *(Arik Florimonte)*

A study assessing all baseball conditions from 2015-2019 created a model for expected home run rate (xHR) given exit velocity (EV) and launch angle (LA) found in MLB's Statcast system. The model was applied to the entire database of batted balls to calculate the likelihood of each batted ball becoming a home run.

The xHR metric is not a measure of whether a specific batted ball should have been a home run. Rather, it is a measure of how often a ball struck in the way it was turns out to be a home run. By comparing a hitter's actual home run total to xHR over a given year, we can estimate how much of that performance was earned or unearned and adjust home run expectations for the following season.

Expected home runs to fly ball rate (xHR/F) *(Arik Florimonte)*

A player's xHR divided by his fly balls in a given season. While previous years' HR/F results do have some useful correlation to current year's result, xHR/F does even better in that it has added benefit for shorter periods of time. In predicting the next month's results, xHR/F from one month does as well as two months of HR/F. And for equal samples, a batter's xHR/F is about 15-25% better correlated to the upcoming result over a similar period. This additional predictive value persists for up to about two years, at which time xHR/F and HR/F are roughly equally valuable.

Is fly ball carry a skill? *(Arik Florimonte)*

Using Statcast data from 2015-17, we determined that "Carry"—how much a fly ball travels compared to its projected distance based on Launch Angle and Exit Velocity—is a repeatable skill for batters. Specific findings from this study include:

- Carry is well-correlated from year to year, with Prior Year Carry explaining 47% of Current Year Carry.
- On average, a batter will retain two-thirds of his fly ball Carry from year to year.
- Batters with unlucky HR totals in Year 0 tend to see an improvement in Year 1. Of those with high Carry in Year 0, 88% saw improvement in the difference between HR/F and xHR/F (expected HR/F), and the average gain is +0.059 (including non-gainers).

Hard-hit fly balls as a skill *(Arik Florimonte)*

A study of batted ball data from 2002-2020 found we should seek batters that produce hard-hit fly balls. Among the key findings:

- The ability to hit the ball hard is good, the ability to hit fly balls and line drives is also good, and the ability to do both at once is even better.
- All three of these metrics have good correlation year to year, meaning each can reliably be called a "skill."
- When evaluating batters whose xPX, which uses hard-hit fly balls and line drives as inputs, seems out of line with hard-hit rate and FB% or LD%, we should expect some regression, and the real talent level probably lies somewhere in the middle.

Launch angle (LA)

A Statcast metric defined by MLB.com as the vertical angle at which the ball leaves a player's bat after being struck. In other words, it's a precise measure for how high (or low) a ball is hit. **BENCHMARKS:** The league-wide average launch angle in 2023 was 12.8 degrees. We can convert launch angle ranges into traditional batted ball trajectories as follows:

Batted ball type	Launch angle
Groundball	Less than 10 degrees
Line drive	10-25 degrees
Flyball	25-50 degrees
Pop-up	Greater than 50 degrees

Exit velocity (EV)

A Statcast metric defined by MLB.com as the speed of the baseball as it comes off the bat, immediately after a batter makes contact. In other words, it's a precise measure of how hard a ball is hit. Batters with higher average exit velocities make harder contact and are more likely to see favorable outcomes than those with lower exit velocities. **BENCHMARKS:** The league-wide average exit velocity in 2023 was 89.0 miles per hour. Top batters will average above 90 mph with bottom batters struggling to reach 87 mph.

Barrel rate (Brl%)

A "barrel" is a Statcast metric defined by MLB.com as a well-struck ball where the combination of exit velocity and launch angle generally leads to a minimum .500 batting average and 1.500 slugging percentage. Barrel rate (Brl% in hitter boxes) is simply the number of barrels divided by the number of batted balls for a given hitter. **BENCHMARKS:** The league-wide barrel rate in 2023 was 8.1%. A rate of >12% is generally considered top tier.

Quality of batted ball score (QBaB) *(Arik Florimonte)*

For batters, greater exit velocity and greater mean launch angle are better. In addition, reduced launch angle variability is correlated with better batted ball results. The Quality of Batted Ball score (QBaB) assigns A-F grades for exit velocity, launch angle, and launch angle variability based on percentile groups with the thresholds below:

Percentile	Grade	Exit Velocity (mph)	Launch Angle	Launch Angle Variability
90+	A	> 90.8	> 17.6°	< 23.95°
70-90	B	89.2 – 90.8	14.1° – 17.6°	23.95° – 25.64°
30-70	C	88.6 – 89.2	9.2° – 14.1°	25.64° – 27.91°
10-30	D	84.1 – 88.6	5.7° – 9.2°	27.91° – 29.45°
10-	F	< 84.1	< 5.7°	> 29.45°

These scores can be useful in several ways:

- QBaB is very well correlated with batter output.
- Higher EV grades are always desirable.
- Higher LA grades are good for power, but do not help batting average.
- Smaller Launch Angle Variation is good for batting average, but impact on power is murky.
- QBaB scores are very sticky. It is extremely rare for a great hitter to become terrible and vice versa.
- Batters who have great QBaB scores but underperform tend to recover; the converse is true for those with poor scores.

QBaB over short samples—exit velocity *(Arik Florimonte)*

Using Statcast data from 2015-2020, we determined that QBaB scores for exit velocity can be meaningful over short sample sizes. Specifically:

- Over any sample size, a QBaB "A" for exit velocity is correlated with improved QBaB scores over the next 25 batted balls (1-2 weeks), and "F" scores portended worse results.
- The magnitude of the differences in outcomes changes steadily and dramatically as sample size increases.
- A single batted ball in the top 10% of all batted balls is a surprisingly good indicator of upcoming exit velocity goodness.

As you make roster decisions throughout the year, be sure to check in on the rolling 100- and 25- batted ball exit velocity trends.

Linear weighted power (LWPwr)

((Doubles x .8) + (Triples x .8) + (HR x 1.4)) / (At bats- K) x 100

A variation of Pete Palmer's linear weights formula that considers only events that are measures of a batter's pure power. **BENCHMARKS:** Top sluggers typically top the 17 mark. Weak hitters will have a LWPwr level of less than 10.

Linear weighted power index (PX)

(Batter's LWPwr / League LWPwr) x 100

LWPwr is presented in this book in its normalized form to get a better read on a batter's accomplishment in each year. For instance, a 30-HR season today is much less of an accomplishment than 30 HR hit in a lower offense year like 2014. **BENCHMARKS:** A level of 100 equals league-average power skills. Any player with a value of more than 100 has above-average power skills, and those more than 150 are the Slugging Elite.

Expected LW power index (xPX) *(Bill Macey)*

*2.6 + 269*HHLD% + 724*HHFB%*

Previous research has shown that hard-hit balls are more likely to result in hits and hard-hit fly balls are more likely to end up as HR. As such, we can use hard-hit ball data to calculate an expected skills-based power index. This metric starts with hard-hit ball data, which measures a player's fundamental skill of making solid contact, and then places it on the same scale as PX (xPX). In the above formula, HHLD% is calculated as the number of hard-hit line drives divided by the total number of balls put in play. HHFB% is similarly calculated for fly balls. The variance between PX and xPX can be viewed as a leading indicator for other power metrics.

Pitches/plate appearance as a leading indicator for PX *(Paul Petera)*

Batters who work deeper into the count (via pitches per plate appearance, or P/PA) tend to display more power (as measured by PX) than batters who don't:

P/PA	PX
4.00+	123
3.75-3.99	108
3.50-3.74	96
Under 3.50	84

Players with an unusually high or low PX for their P/PA in one year tend to regress heavily the next:

	YEAR TWO	
YEAR ONE	PX Improved	PX Declined
Low P/PA and High PX	11%	89%
High P/PA and Low PX	70%	30%

Doubles as a leading indicator for home runs *(Bill Macey)*

There is little support for the theory that hitting many doubles in year x leads to an increase in HR in year x+1. However, it was shown that batters with high doubles rates (2B/AB) also tend to hit more HR/AB than the league average; oddly, they are unable to sustain the high 2B/AB rate but do sustain their higher HR/AB rates. Batters with high 2B/AB rates and low HR/AB rates are more likely to see HR gains in the following year, but those rates will still typically trail the league average. And, batters who experience a surge in 2B/AB typically give back most of those gains in the following year without any corresponding gain in HR.

Opposite field home runs *(Ed DeCaria)*

Opposite field HR serve as a strong indicator of overall home run power (AB/HR). Power hitters (lower AB/HR rates) hit a far higher percentage of their HR to the opposite field or straight away (over 30%). Conversely, non-power hitters hit almost 90% of their home runs to their pull field.

	Performance in Y2-Y4 (% of Group)		
Y1 Trigger	<=30 AB/HR	5.5+ RC/G	$16+ R$
2+ OppHR	69%	46%	33%
<2 OppHR	29%	13%	12%

Players who hit just two or more OppHR in one season were 2-3 times as likely as those who hit zero or one OppHR to sustain strong AB/HR rates, RC/G levels, or R$ values over the following three seasons.

	Y2-Y4 Breakout Performance (% Breakout by Group, Age <=26 Only)		
	AB/HR	RC/G	R$
Y1 Trigger	>35 to <=30	<4.5 to 5.5+	<$8 to $16+
2+ OppHR	32%	21%	30%
<2 OppHR	23%	12%	10%

Roughly one of every 3-4 batters aged 26 or younger experiences a *sustained three-year breakout* in AB/HR, RC/G or R$ after a season in which they hit 2+ OppHR, far better odds than the one in 8-10 batters who experience a breakout without the 2+ OppHR trigger.

A 2015 Brad Kullman study that examined hard hit balls of all types (flies, liners, and grounders) by hitters with 100 or more plate appearances offered a broader conclusion. His research found that hitters who can effectively use the whole field are more productive in virtually every facet of hitting than those with an exclusively pull-oriented approach.

Home runs in bunches or droughts *(Patrick Davitt)*

A study from 2010-2012 on HR data showed that batters hit HR in a random manner, with game-gaps between HR that correspond roughly to their average days per HR. Hitters do sometimes hit HR with greater or lesser frequency in short periods, but these periods are not predictive. It appears pointless to try to "time the market" by predicting the beginning or end of a drought or a bunch, or by assuming the end of one presages the beginning of the other, despite what the ex-player in the broadcast booth tells you.

Power breakout profile

It is not easy to predict which batters will experience a power spike. We can categorize power breakouts to determine the likelihood of a player taking a step up or a surprise performer repeating his feat. Possibilities:

- Increase in playing time
- History of power skills at some time in the past
- Redistribution of already demonstrated extra base hit power
- Normal skills growth
- Situational breakouts, particularly in hitter-friendly venues
- Increased fly ball tendency
- Use of illegal performance-enhancing substances
- Miscellaneous unexplained variables

Speed

Wasted talent on the base paths

We refer to some players as having "wasted talent," a high level skill that is negated by a deficiency in another skill. Among these types are players with blazing speed negated by a sub-.300 on base average.

These players can have short-term value. However, their stolen base totals are tied so tightly to their "green light" that any change in managerial strategy could completely erase that value. A higher

OB mitigates that downside; the good news is that plate patience can be taught.

There have always been a handful of players who had at least 20 SB with an OBP less than .300, putting their future SB at risk. The rise in 2023 steals did yield a slightly higher number of "wasted talent" speedsters, led by perennial rule-defier Jorge Mateo (32 SB, .267 OBP). Joining him were Brice Turang (26, .285), Anthony Volpe (24, .283), Ji-Hwan Bae (24, .296), Brenton Doyle (22, .250) and Harrison Bader (20, .274).

Stolen base attempt rate (SBA%)

(SB + CS) / (BB + Singles + HBP)

A rough approximation of how often a baserunner attempts a stolen base. Provides a comparative measure for players on a given team and, as a team measure, the propensity of a manager to give a "green light" to his runners.

Stolen base success rate (SB%)

SB / (SB + CS)

The rate at which baserunners are successful in their stolen base attempts. **BENCHMARK:** It is generally accepted that an 80% rate is the minimum required for a runner to provide value.

Speed score *(Bill James)*

A measure of the various elements that comprise a runner's speed skills. Although this formula (a variation of James' original version) may be used as a leading indicator for stolen base output, SB attempts are controlled by managerial strategy which makes speed score somewhat less valuable.

Speed score is calculated as the mean value of the following four elements:

1. Stolen base efficiency = *(((SB + 3)/(SB + CS + 7)) - .4) x 20*
2. Stolen base freq. = *Square root of ((SB + CS)/(Singles + BB)) / .07*
3. Triples rating = *(3B / (AB - HR - K))* and the result assigned a value based on the following chart:

< 0.001	0	0.0105	6
0.001	1	0.013	7
0.0023	2	0.0158	8
0.0039	3	0.0189	9
0.0058	4	0.0223+	10
0.008	5		

4. Runs scored as a percentage of times on base = *(((R - HR) / (H + BB - HR)) - .1) / .04*

Speed score index (SX)

(Batter's speed score / League speed score) x 100

Normalized speed scores get a better read on a runner's accomplishment in context. A level of 100 equals league average speed skill. Values more than 100 indicate above average skill, more than 200 represent the Fleet of Feet Elite.

Statistically scouted speed (Spd) *(Ed DeCaria)*

*(104 + {[(Runs–HR+10*age_wt)/(RBI-HR+10)]/lg_av*100} / 5*
*+ {[(3B+5*age_wt)/(2B+3B+5)]/lg_av*100} / 5*
*+ {[(SoftMedGBhits+25*age_wt)/(SoftMedGB+25)]/lg_av*100} / 2*
*- {[Weight (Lbs)/Height (In)^2 * 703]/lg_av*100}*

A skills-based gauge that measures speed without relying on stolen bases. Its components are:

- *(Runs – HR) / (RBI – HR)*: This metric aims to minimize the influence of extra base hit power and team run-scoring rates on perceived speed.
- *3B / (2B + 3B)*: No one can deny that triples are a fast runner's stat; dividing them by 2B+3B instead of all balls in play dampens the power aspect of extra base hits.
- *(Soft + Medium Ground Ball Hits) / (Soft + Medium Ground Balls)*: Faster runners are more likely than slower runners to beat out routine grounders. Hard hit balls are excluded from numerator and denominator.
- *Body Mass Index (BMI)*: Calculated as *Weight (lbs) / Height (in)2 * 703*. All other factors considered, leaner players run faster than heavier ones.

In this book, the formula is scaled with a midpoint of 100.

Expected stolen bases (xSB) *(Ed DeCaria)*

See updated research on this topic on page 69.

Roto Speed (RSpd)

(Spd x (SBO + SB%))

An adjustment to the measure for raw speed that considers a runner's opportunities to steal and his success rate. This stat is intended to provide a more accurate predictive measure of stolen bases for the Mayberry Method.

Overall Performance Analysis

On base plus slugging average (OPS)

A simple sum of the two gauges, it is considered one of the better evaluators of overall performance. OPS combines the two basic elements of offensive production—the ability to get on base (OB) and the ability to advance baserunners (Slg). **BENCHMARKS:** The game's top batters will have OPS levels more than .850. The worst batters will have levels less than .660.

Adjusted on base plus slugging average (OPS+)

OPS scaled to league average to account for year-to-year fluctuations in league-wide statistical performance. It's a snapshot of a player's overall skills compared to an average player; also used in platoon situations (vL+; vR+). **BENCHMARK:** A level of 100 means a player had a league-average OPS in that given season.

Base Performance Value (BPV)

(Walk rate - 5) x 2) + ((Contact rate - 75) x 4)
+ ((Power Index - 80) x 0.8) + ((Spd - 80) x 0.3)

A single value that describes a player's overall raw skill level. This formula combines the individual raw skills of batting eye, contact rate, power and speed.

Base Performance Index (BPX)

BPV scaled to league average to account for year-to-year fluctuations in league-wide statistical performance. It's a snapshot of a player's overall skills compared to an average player. **BENCHMARK:** A level of 100 means a player had a league-average BPV in that given season.

Linear weights *(Pete Palmer)*

((Singles x .46) + (Doubles x .8) + (Triples x 1.02)
+ (Home runs x 1.4) + (Walks x .33) + (Stolen Bases x .3)
- (Caught Stealing x .6) - ((At bats - Hits) x Normalizing Factor)

(Also referred to as Batting Runs.) Formula whose premise is that all events in baseball are linear; that is, the output (runs) is directly proportional to the input (offensive events). Each event is then weighted according to its relative value in producing runs. Positive events—hits, walks, stolen bases—have positive values. Negative events—outs, caught stealing—have negative values.

The normalizing factor, representing the value of an out, is an offset to the level of offense in a given year. It changes every season, growing larger in high offense years and smaller in low offense years. The value is about .26 and varies by league.

LW is not included in the player boxes, but the LW concept is used with the linear weighted power gauge.

Runs Above Replacement (RAR)

An estimate of the number of runs a player contributes above a "replacement level" player. "Replacement" is defined as the level of performance at which another player can easily be found at little or no cost to a team. What constitutes replacement level is a topic that is hotly debated. There are a variety of formulas and rules of thumb used to determine this level for each position (replacement level for a catcher will be very different from replacement level for an outfielder). Our estimates appear below.

One of the major values of RAR for fantasy applications is that it can be used to assemble an integrated ranking of batters and pitchers for drafting purposes.

To calculate RAR for batters:

- Start with a batter's runs created per game (RC/G).
- Subtract his position's replacement level RC/G.
- Multiply by number of games played: (AB - H + CS) / 25.5.

Replacement levels used in this book:

POS	AL	NL
CA	3.32	3.38
1B	3.80	4.23
2B	3.51	3.81
3B	3.70	3.91
SS	3.69	3.87
LF	3.79	3.91
CF	3.77	3.84
RF	3.86	4.03
DH	4.18	4.00

RAR can also be used to calculate rough projected team won-loss records. *(Roger Miller)* Total the RAR levels for all the players on a team, divide by 10 and add to 53 wins.

Runs created *(Bill James)*

(H + BB – CS) x (Total bases + (.55 x SB)) / (AB + BB)

A formula that converts all offensive events into a total of runs scored. As calculated for individual teams, the result approximates a club's actual run total with great accuracy. The above is the "stolen base" version of the formula. There is also a more complex "technical version" and a multi-tiered 2002 version that helps to normalize extreme on-base and slugging performers.

Runs created per game (RC/G)

Runs Created / ((AB - H + CS) / 25.5)

RC expressed on a per-game basis might be considered the hypothetical ERA compiled against a particular batter. Another way to look at it: A batter with a RC/G of 7.00 would be expected to score 7 runs per game if he were cloned nine times and faced an average pitcher in every at bat. Cloning batters is not a practice we recommend. **BENCHMARKS:** Few players surpass the level of a 10.00 RC/G, but any level more than 7.50 can still be considered very good. At the bottom are levels less than 3.00.

Skill-specific aging patterns for batters *(Ed DeCaria)*

Recognized peak age for *overall* batting value is a player's late 20s. But individual skills do not peak uniformly at the same time:

Contact rate (ct%): Ascends modestly by about a half point of contact per year from age 22 to 26, then holds steady within a half point of peak until age 35, after which players lose a half point of contact per year.

Walk rate (bb%): Trends the opposite way with age compared to contact rate, as batters tend to peak at age 30 and largely remain there until they turn 38.

Stolen Base Opportunity (SBO): Typically, players maintain their SBO through age 27, but then reduce their attempts steadily in each remaining year of their careers.

Stolen base success rate (SB%): Aggressive runners (>14% SBO) tend to lose about 2 points per year as they age. However, less aggressive runners (<=14% SBO) actually improve their SB% by about 2 points per year until age 28, after which they reverse course and give back 1-2 pts every year as they age.

GB%/LD%/FB%: Both GB% and LD% peak at the start of a player's career and then decline as many hitters seemingly learn to elevate the ball more. But at about age 30, hitter GB% ascends toward a second late-career peak while LD% continues to plummet and FB% continues to rise through age 38.

Hit rate (h%): Declines linearly with age. This is a natural result of a loss of speed and change in batted ball trajectory.

Isolated Power (ISO): Typically peaks from age 24-26. Similarly, home runs per fly ball, opposite field HR %, and Hard Hit % all peak by age 25 and decline somewhat linearly from that point on.

Catchers and late-career performance spikes *(Ed Spaulding)*

Many catchers—particularly second line catchers—have their best seasons late in their careers. Some possible reasons why:

1. Catchers often get to the big leagues for defensive reasons and not their offensive skills. These skills take longer to develop.
2. The heavy emphasis on learning the catching/ defense/ pitching side of the game detracts from their time to learn about, and practice, hitting.
3. Injuries often curtail their ability to show offensive skills, though these injuries (typically jammed fingers, bruises on the arms, rib injuries from collisions) often don't lead to time on the injured list.
4. The time spent behind the plate has to impact the ability to recognize, and eventually hit, all kinds of pitches.

Playing Time

Playing time building blocks *(Ed DeCaria)*

The following six metrics work together to explain how batters have accumulated past playing time, and can help fantasy managers to forecast future playing time. (See page 70 for additional new research on this topic.) At a high level, Total PA can be broken down into these components:

- *Active Weeks (AW)*: Number of weeks during which the player was active on an MLB roster at the start of the week.
- *Plate Appearances per Active Week (PAAW):* Average number of PA by the player per week, during weeks that he was available.
- *Ghost Plate Appearances as % of Total PA (GPA%):* Playing time earned during weeks when the player wasn't active at the start of the week, but was subsequently activated later in the week.

Where Total PA is mostly just *AW * PAAW*, but for completeness we divide by *(1 – GPA%)* to get Total PA. From here, PAAW can be further broken down into these components:

- *Starts per Active Week (SAW):* Average number of games started by the player per week, during weeks he was available.
- *Plate Appearances per Start (PAS):* Average number of times the player came to bat in games that they started.
- *Extra Plate Appearances per Active Week (EAW):* Average number of times per week that the player came off the bench to hit.

Where P*AAW = SAW * PAS + EAW*. At the most granular level, *Total PA = AW * (SAW * PAS + EAW) / (1 – GPA%)*, but as a shortcut for most fantasy-relevant players, simply *AW * SAW * PAS* captures 95%+ of their Total PA. Players with very similar Total PA can take very different paths, and just knowing how often they were available (AW), how often they started when available (SAW), and how often they came to the plate when they started (PAS) tells a very clear story in just three numbers.

Plate appearances as a leading indicator *(Patrick Davitt)*

Cumulative plate appearances, especially during the first two years of a young player's career, can also have predictive value in assessing a coming spike in production. Three main conclusions:

- When projecting players, MLB experience is more important than age.
- Players who amass 800+ PA in their first two seasons are highly likely to have double-digit Rotisserie dollar value in Year 3.
- Also target young players in the season where they attain 400 PA, as they are twice as likely as other players to grow significantly in value.

When do hitters get platooned? *(Jeff Zimmerman)*

We created a talent baseline to determine when a hitter might get platooned by examining 24 actual platoon pairs from the 2017 season. We compared the more extreme hitter's projected OPS splits entering the year. Among the main findings:

- Normally, a spread of ~200 points of OPS is needed to start a platoon. In only two instances did a platoon happen with a projected split under 130 points.
- For most teams to implement a platoon, they need at least one player to have a projected platoon OPS around .830.
- The minimum projected OPS in which teams begin using platoons is around .590. A player could have a 200-point spread, but if the low projected OPS is over .700, teams aren't likely to add another player to make up the difference.

The simple rule of an ".800-.600 OPS spread" works great for an average platoon benchmark. Owners may want to relax the values to snare a few more players with a .775-.625 OPS spread, or an ".800-.600 OPS spread with shrinkage".

In-Season Analysis

Sample size reliability *(Russell Carleton)*

At what sample size do skill and luck each represent 50 percent contributors to a specific metric?

*Measured in plate appearances	
60:	Contact rate
120:	Walk rate
160:	ISO (Isolated power)
170:	HR rate
320:	Slg
460:	OBP

*Measured via balls in play:	
50:	HR/F
80:	GB%; FB%
600:	LD%
820:	Hit rate (BABIP)

**Unlisted metrics did not stabilize over a full season of play.*

How to read: "After 60 plate appearances, the luck-to-skill ratio for contact rate has evened out. If a player with a career 70 percent contact rate has an 85 percent contact rate after 60 PA, we can attribute 50% of that new rate to a new skill and the other 50% to random chance." These levels represent the point at which these metrics become useful, though not as direct predictors. Their value is as another data point in the forecasting process.

Can we trust in-season sample size? *(Arik Florimonte)*

When a batter's performance deviates from their established history, when can you trust the change? And are there any metrics that are better in short periods than long? Using data from 2010-2017 and filtering for full-time players (≥ 350 PA in a season, or ≥ 75 PA in a month), we were able to answer these questions.

Not surprisingly, there is no magic date for believing the current season's results more than the previous season's; rather, it's more of a continuum. We were able to estimate the point in the season current year-to-date results are more predictive than the prior year's results, noted in the table below by the change from white blocks to black. We also note at which point the previous month alone offers better predictive value than the entire previous year ("PM>PY").

	Months of the Season						PM>PY starting...
Hard%	A	M	J	J	A	S	June
Soft%	A	M	J	J	A	S	May
HR/FB	A	M	J	J	A	S	Never
GB%	A	M	J	J	A	S	Never
LD%	A	M	J	J	A	S	Never
FB%	A	M	J	J	A	S	Never
IFFB%	A	M	J	J	A	S	Never
K%	A	M	J	J	A	S	Never
BB%	A	M	J	J	A	S	Never

Prior Year is Better
Year-to-date is Better

Note that due to the data filters used, a month in the chart above can be equated to roughly 90 plate appearances.

Key takeaways:

- Don't buy hard into early changes in batter plate skills until at least June
- Changes in ground ball and fly ball rates take a while to become firm; true "swing changers" can't really be discerned until mid-summer.
- In both of the above, it might pay to speculate earlier if you can stash a player on reserve.
- Don't expect the prior year's Soft% to continue but pay attention to the current year's Soft contact rates.
- Generally, projections based on prior years' skills should remain your fallback position but keep moving the needle toward the current year's results as the year goes on.

Batting order facts *(Ed DeCaria)*

Eighty-eight percent of today's leadoff hitters bat leadoff again in their next game, 78% still bat leadoff 10 games later, and 68% still bat leadoff 50 games later. Despite this level of turnover after 50 games, leadoff hitters have the best chance of retaining their role over time. After leadoff, #3 and #4 hitters are the next most likely to retain their lineup slots.

On a season-to-season basis, leadoff hitters are again the most stable, with 69% of last year's primary leadoff hitters retaining the #1 slot next year.

Plate appearances decline linearly by lineup slot. Leadoff batters receive 10-12% more PA than when batting lower in the lineup. #9 batters get 9-10% fewer PA. These results mirror play-by-play data showing a 15-20 PA drop by lineup slot over a full season.

Walk rate is largely unaffected by lineup slot.

Batting order has no discernable effect on contact rate.

Hit rate slopes gently upward as hitters are slotted deeper in the lineup.

As expected, the #3-4-5 slots are ideal for non-HR RBI, at the expense of #6 hitters. RBI are worst for those in the #1-2 slots. Batting atop the order sharply increases the probability of scoring runs.

The leadoff slot easily has the highest stolen base attempt rate. #4-5-6 hitters attempt steals more often when batting out of those slots than they do batting elsewhere.

DOMination and DISaster rates

Week-to-week consistency is measured using a batter's BPV compiled in each week. A player earns a DOMinant week if his BPV was greater or equal to 50 for that week. A player registers a DISaster if his BPV was less than 0 for that week. The percentage of Dominant weeks, DOM%, is calculated as the number of DOM weeks divided by the total number of weeks played.

Is week-to-week consistency a repeatable skill? *(Bill Macey)*

To test whether consistent performance is a repeatable skill for batters, we examined how closely related a player's DOM% was from year to year.

YR1 DOM%	AVG YR2 DOM%
< 35%	37%
35%–45%	40%
46%–55%	45%
56%+	56%

Quality/consistency score (QC)

(DOM% – (2 x DIS%)) x 2)

Using the DOM/DIS percentages, this score measures both the quality of performance as well as week–to-week consistency.

	Sample configurations		
DOM%	Neutral	DIS%	QC
100	0	0	200
70	20	10	100
60	30	10	80
50	30	20	20
50	25	25	0
40	30	30	-40
30	20	50	-140
20	20	60	-200
0	100	0	-400

Projecting RBI *(Patrick Davitt)*

Evaluating players in-season for RBI potential is a function of the interplay among four factors:

- Teammates' ability to reach base ahead of him and to run the bases efficiently
- His own ability to drive them in by hitting, especially XBH
- Number of Games Played
- Place in the batting order

3-4-5 Hitters:
(0.69 x GP x TOB) + (0.30 x ITB) + (0.275 x HR) – (.191 x GP)

6-7-8 Hitters:
(0.63 x GP x TOB) + (0.27 x ITB) + (0.250 x HR) – (.191 x GP)

9-1-2 Hitters:
(0.57 x GP x TOB) + (0.24 x ITB) + (0.225 x HR) – (.191 x GP)

...where *GP = games played, TOB = team on-base pct.* and *ITB = individual total bases (ITB).*

Apply this pRBI formula after 70 games played or so (to reduce the variation from small sample size) to find players more than 9 RBI over or under their projected RBI. There could be a correction coming.

You should also consider other factors, like injury or trade (involving the player or a top-of-the-order speedster) or team SB philosophy and success rate.

Remember: the player himself has an impact on his TOB. When we first did this study, we excluded the player from his TOB and got better results. The formula overestimates projected RBI for players with high OBP who skew his teams' OBP but can't benefit in RBI from that effect.

What can foul balls tell us? *(Nick Trojanowski)*

Foul balls, because of their relatively meager influence on in-game outcomes, have been examined far less often than balls in play. Using 2008-17 data for every 500+ pitch season, we found that hitting foul balls is a skill, in that it's repeatable from year to year. Other findings:

1. Hitters who swing at more pitches, regardless of location, hit more foul balls, regardless of contact rate.
2. Routinely fouling off pitches doesn't regularly lead to better outcomes, and in fact tends to make walks less likely.

Other Diamonds

It's a Busy World Shortcut

For marginal utility-type players, scan their PX and Spd history to see if there's anything to mine for. If you see triple digits anywhere, stop and look further. If not, move on.

Errant Gust of Wind

A unit of measure used to describe the difference between your home run projection and mine.

Mendoza Line

Named for Mario Mendoza, it represents the benchmark for batting futility. Usually refers to a .200 batting average, but can also be used for low levels of other statistical categories. Note that Mendoza's lifetime batting average was actually a much more robust .215.

Old Player Skills

Power, low batting average, no speed and usually good plate patience. Young players, often those with a larger frame, who possess these "old player skills" tend to decline faster than normal, often in their early 30s.

Power Peak Postulate

A player's career power trend is not a climb up to a single peak and then descent. It is more of a mountain range, with many peaks of varying elevations.

Esix Snead List

Players with excellent speed and sub-.300 on base averages who get a lot of practice running down the line to first base, and then back to the dugout.

Pitchers

Strikeouts and Walks

Fundamental skills

The contention that pitching performance is unreliable is a fallacy driven by the practice of attempting to project pitching stats using gauges that are poor evaluators of skill.

How can we better evaluate pitching skill? We can start with the statistical categories generally unaffected by external factors. These stats capture the outcome of an individual pitcher versus batter match-up without regard to supporting offense, defense or bullpen:

Walks Allowed, Strikeouts and Ground/Fly Balls

Even with only these stats to observe, there is a wealth of insight that these measures can provide.

Control rate (Ctl, bb/9), or opposition walks per game

BB allowed x 9 / IP

Measures how many walks a pitcher allows per game equivalent. **BENCHMARK:** The best pitchers will have bb/9 of 2.5 or less.

Walk rate (BB%)

(BB / TBF)

Measures how many walks a pitcher allows as a percentage of total batters faced.

Approximate Conversions

Ctl	Ball%	BB%
1.5	<31	4.1
1.7	31	4.8
1.8	32	5.0
2.2	33	5.9
2.3	34	6.1
2.7	35	7.2
2.9	36	7.6
3.2	37	8.3
3.4	38	8.7
3.8	39	9.6
4.1	40	10.5
4.7	41	11.6
5.4	>41	12.8

BENCHMARK: For those who used a Ctl rate of 2.5 or less as a benchmark for potential skills upside, the comparable level on the BB% scale would be about 6.6%. Better (and easier to remember): target pitchers with a rate of 6% or lower. The league-wide BB% in 2023 was 8.6%.

Dominance rate (Dom, k/9), or opposition strikeouts/game

Strikeouts recorded x 9 / IP

Measures how many strikeouts a pitcher allows per game equivalent. **BENCHMARK:** The best pitchers will have k/9 levels of 9.0 or higher.

Swinging strike rate as leading indicator *(Stephen Nickrand)*

Swinging strike rate (SwK%) measures the percentage of total pitches against which a batter swings and misses. SwK% can help us validate and forecast a SP's Dominance (K/9) rate, which in turn allows us to identify surgers and faders with greater accuracy. An expected Dominance rate can be estimated from SwK%; and a pitcher's individual SwK% does not regress to league norms.

BENCHMARKS: The few starters per year who have a 12.0% or higher SwK% are near-locks to have a 9.0 Dom or 25% K%. In contrast, starters with a 7.0% or lower SwK% have nearly no chance at posting even an average Dom. Finally, use an 9.5% SwK% as an acceptable threshold when searching for SP based on this metric; raise it to 10.5% to begin to find SwK% difference-makers.

Strikeout rate (K%)

(K / TBF)

Measures how many strikeouts a pitcher produces as a percentage of total batters faced.

Approximate Conversions

K/9	SwK%	K%
5.4	<6.0	13.2
5.6	6.0	14.1
6.1	7.0	15.2
6.6	8.0	17.5
7.3	9.0	19.1
7.8	10.0	20.5
8.5	11.0	22.2
9.3	12.0	24.8
9.9	13.0	27.1
10.7	14.0	29.2
11.3	15.0	31.6
12.0	16.0	33.5
12.9	>16.0	36.0

BENCHMARK: For those who used a Dominance rate of 9.5 as a benchmark for potential skills upside, the comparable level on the K% scale would be about 25%. The league-wide K% in 2022 was 22.7%.

Command ratio (Cmd)

(Strikeouts / Walks)

A measure of a pitcher's ability to get the ball over the plate. There is no more fundamental a skill than this, and so it is used as a leading indicator to project future rises and falls in other gauges, such as ERA. **BENCHMARKS:** Baseball's best pitchers will have ratios in excess of 3.0. Pitchers with ratios less than 1.0—indicating that they walk more batters than they strike out—have virtually no potential for long-term success. If you make no other changes in your approach to drafting pitchers, limiting your focus to only pitchers with a command ratio of 3.0 or better will substantially improve your odds of success.

Strikeout rate minus walk rate (K-BB%)

(K% – BB%)

Measures a pitchers' strikeout rate (K%) minus walk rate (BB%) and is a leading indicator for future performance.

Approx Conversions		Correlated
K/BB	K-BB%	ERA
<1.0	-4%	8.43
1.0-2.0	7%	5.44
2.1-3.0	15%	4.26
3.1-4.0	19%	4.00
4.1-5.0	23%	3.73
>5.0	26%	3.13

BENCHMARK: For those who used a Command ratio of 3.0 as a benchmark for potential skills upside, the comparable level on the K-BB% scale would be about 18%. Better (and easier to remember): target pitchers with a rate of 20% or higher. The league-wide K-BB% in 2023 was 14.1%.

Fastball velocity and Dominance rate *(Stephen Nickrand)*

It is intuitive that an increase in fastball velocity for starting pitchers leads to more strikeouts. But how much?

Research shows that the vast majority of SP with significant fastball velocity gains follow this three-step process:

1. They experience a significant Dom gain during the same season.
2. Most often, they give back those Dom gains during the following season.
3. They are likely to increase their Dom the following season, but the magnitude of the Dom increase usually is small.

By contrast, the vast majority of SP with significant fastball velocity losses are likely to experience a significant Dom decrease during the same season.

Those SP with significant fastball velocity losses from one season to the next are just as likely to experience a fastball velocity or Dom increase as they are to experience a fastball or Dom decrease, and the amounts of the increase/decrease are nearly identical.

How aging affects fastball velocity, swinging strikes and strikeout rate *(Ed DeCaria)*

On average, pitchers lose about 0.2 mph per season off their fastballs. Over time, this coincides with decreases in swinging strike rate (SwK%) and overall strikeout rate (K/PA)—the inevitable effects of aging. But one thing that pitchers can do to delay these effects is to throw more first pitch strikes.

Power/contact rating

(BB + K) / IP

Measures the level by which a pitcher allows balls to be put into play. In general, extreme power pitchers can be successful even with poor defensive teams. Power pitchers tend to have greater longevity in the game. Contact pitchers with poor defenses behind them are high risks to have poor W-L records and ERA. **BENCHMARKS:** A level of 1.13+ describes pure throwers. A level of .93 or less describes high contact pitchers.

Balls in Play

Balls after contact (BAC)

(Batters faced – (BB + HBP + SAC)) + H – K

The total number of batted balls that are hit fair, both hits and outs. An analysis of how these balls are hit—on the ground, in the air, hits, outs, etc.—can provide analytical insight, from player skill levels to the impact of luck on statistical output.

Balls in play (BIP)

(Batters faced – (BB + HBP + SAC)) + H – K - HR

The total number of batted balls that are hit into the field of play. Essentially, BAC minus home runs.

Batting average on balls in play *(Voros McCracken)*

(H – HR) / (Batters faced – (BB + HBP + SAC)) + H – K – HR

Abbreviated as BABIP; also called hit rate (H%), this is the percent of balls hit into the field of play that fall for hits. In 2000, Voros McCracken published a study that concluded "there is little if any difference among major league pitchers in their ability to prevent hits on balls hit in the field of play." His assertion was that, while a Johan Santana would have a better ability to prevent a batter from getting wood on a ball, or perhaps keeping the ball in the park, once that ball was hit in the field of play, the probability of it falling for a hit was virtually no different than for any other pitcher.

Among the findings in his study were:

- There is little correlation between what a pitcher does one year in the stat and what he will do the next. This is not true with other significant stats (BB, K, HR).
- You can better predict a pitcher's hits per balls in play from the rate of the rest of the pitcher's team than from the pitcher's own rate.

This last point brings a team's defense into the picture. It begs the question, when a batter gets a hit, is it because the pitcher made a bad pitch, the batter took a good swing, or the defense was not positioned correctly?

BABIP as a leading indicator *(Voros McCracken)*

The league average is 30%, which is also the level that individual performances will regress to on a year-to-year basis. Any +/- variance of 3% or more can affect a pitcher's ERA.

Pitchers will often post hit rates per balls-in-play that are far off from the league average, but then revert to the mean the following year. As such, we can use that mean to project the direction of a pitcher's ERA.

Subsequent research has shown that ground ball or fly ball propensity has some impact on this rate.

Hit rate *(See Batting average on balls in play)*

Opposition batting average (OBA)

Hits allowed / (Batters faced – (BB + HBP + SAC))

The batting average achieved by opposing batters against a pitcher. **BENCHMARKS:** The best pitchers will have levels less than .235; the worst pitchers will have levels more than .280.

Opposition on base average (OOB)

(Hits allowed + BB) / ((Batters faced – (BB + HBP + SAC)) + Hits allowed + BB)

The on base average achieved by opposing batters against a pitcher. **BENCHMARK:** The best pitchers will have levels less than .290; the worst pitchers will have levels more than .350.

Walks plus hits divided by innings pitched (WHIP)

Essentially the same measure as opposition on base average but used for Rotisserie purposes. **BENCHMARKS:** A WHIP of less than 1.15 is considered top level; more than 1.50 indicative of poor performance. Levels less than 1.00—allowing fewer runners than IP—represent extraordinary performance and are rarely maintained over time.

Expected walks plus hits divided by innings pitched (xWHIP) *(Arik Florimonte)*

Hit rate luck makes an amplified contribution to WHIP, due to its impact on both the numerator (hits) and denominator (outs). To neutralize the effect, Expected WHIP (xWHIP) assumes that a pitcher's walk rate, strikeout rate, rate of hit batters, and ground-ball-to-flyball ratio reflect their true skill, but assigns league average rates of line drives, hits per batted ball type (xH%), and double plays per ground ball (xDP%). xWHIP better captures a pitcher's true skill and is therefore more useful for predicting future results.

Ground ball, line drive, fly ball percentages (G/L/F)

The percentage of balls in play that are hit on the ground, as line drives, and in the air. For pitchers, the ability to keep the ball on the ground can contribute to his statistical output exceeding his demonstrated skill level. A study of 2017-2021 batted ball data shows league averages for each:

BIP Type	Total%	Out%
Ground ball	43%	72%
Line drive	21%	28%
Fly ball	37%	85%

Ground ball tendencies *(John Burnson)*

Ground ball pitchers tend to give up fewer HR than do fly ball pitchers. There is also evidence that GB pitchers have higher hit rates. In other words, a ground ball has a higher chance of being a hit than does a fly ball that is not out of the park.

GB pitchers have lower strikeout rates. We should be more forgiving of a low strikeout rate if it belongs to an extreme ground ball pitcher.

GB pitchers have a lower ERA but a higher WHIP than do fly ball pitchers. On balance, GB pitchers come out ahead, even when considering strikeouts, because a lower ERA also leads to more wins.

Extreme GB/FB pitchers *(Patrick Davitt)*

Among pitchers with normal strikeout levels, extreme GB pitchers (>37% of all batters faced) have ERAs about 0.4 runs lower than normal-GB% pitchers but only slight WHIP advantages. Extreme FB% pitchers (>32% FB) show no ERA benefits.

Among High-K (>=24% of BF), however, extreme GBers have ERAs about 0.5 runs lower than normal-GB pitchers, and WHIPs about five points lower. Extreme FB% pitchers have ERAs about 0.2 runs lower than normal-FB pitchers, and WHIPs about 10 points lower.

Revisiting fly balls *(Jason Collette)*

The increased emphasis on defensive positioning is often associated with infield shifting, but the same data also influences how outfielders are positioned. Some managers are positioning OFs more aggressively than just the customary few steps per a right- or left-handed swinging batter.

Before dismissing flyball pitchers as toxic assets, pay more attention to park factors and OF defensive talent. In particular, be a little more willing to roster fly ball pitchers who pitch both in front of good defensive OFs and in good pitchers' parks.

Line drive percentage as a leading indicator *(Seth Samuels)*

The percentage of balls-in-play that are line drives is beyond a pitcher's control. Line drives do the most damage; from 2017-2022, here were the expected hit rates and number of total bases per type of BIP.

Trajectory	% of BIP	BABIP	BAC	TB/BIP
Ground balls	42.6%	.236	.236	.258
Line drives	20.5%	.680	.687	.901
Fly balls	35.5%	.119	.239	.721
Bunts	1.3%	.422	.422	.423

Despite the damage done by LDs, pitchers do not have any innate skill to avoid them. There is little relationship between a pitcher's LD% one year and his rate the next year. All rates tend to regress towards the mean of 20.5%.

Home run to fly ball rate (HR/F)

The percent of fly balls that are hit for home runs.

HR/F as a leading indicator *(John Burnson)*

McCracken's work focused on "balls in play," omitting home runs from the study. However, pitchers also do not have much control over the percentage of fly balls that turn into HR. Research shows that there is an underlying rate of HR as a percentage of fly balls which in 2023 was 12.7%. A pitcher's HR/F rate will vary each year but always tends to regress to that mean. The element that pitchers do have control over is the number of fly balls they allow. That is the underlying skill or deficiency that controls their HR rate.

Exit velocity, barrel rate and launch angle for pitchers *(Stephen Nickrand)*

Though primarily used to evaluate batter performance and skill, Statcast metrics such as exit velocity, barrel rate, and launch angle have moderate-to-strong correlations to several pitching indicators:

- There is a modest correlation between the average exit velocity and barrel rate allowed by starting pitchers to both their ERA and HR/9.
- As a pitchers' exit velocity and barrel rate go up, so does their ERA and HR/9; and vice-versa.
- A significant deviation from a pitcher's average exit velocity baseline usually results in a regression towards that prior baseline during the following season.
- Starting pitchers experience a lot of volatility in their Barrel%. There is no pattern of them regressing to their prior barrel rate baseline, partly because launch angle has been steadily increasing in the game over the past four seasons.

Expected home run total (xHR) *(Arik Florimonte)*

A study assessing all baseball conditions from 2015-2019 created a model for expected home run rate (xHR) given exit velocity (EV) and launch angle (LA) found in MLB's Statcast system. The model was applied to the entire database of batted balls to calculate the likelihood of each batted ball becoming a home run.

The xHR metric is not a measure of whether a specific batted ball should have been a home run. Rather, it is a measure of how often a ball struck in the way it was turns out to be a home run. By comparing a pitcher's actual home runs allowed total to xHR over a given year, we can estimate how much of that performance was earned or unearned and adjust home runs allowed expectations for the following season.

Expected home runs per fly ball rate (xHR/F) *(Arik Florimonte)*

A pitcher's xHR allowed divided by his fly balls given up in a season. It is well-established that a pitcher's HR/F in one season is not a valid predictor for the pitcher's following year's HR/F. Despite this, biases may linger against pitchers who have "proven" to have acute gopheritis, or in favor of pitchers who managed to avoid surrendering HR. Unfortunately, knowing a pitcher's xHR/F history provides negligible improvement to predictive models. If a pitcher's xHR/F is high, it means that he was hit hard, but it does not mean he will be hit hard again. Once park factors are considered, regression to league average HR/F is still the best predictor.

What can foul balls tell us? *(Nick Trojanowski)*

Foul balls, because of their relatively meager influence on in-game outcomes, have been examined far less often than balls in play. Using 2008-17 data for every 500+ pitch season, we found that inducing foul balls is a skill, in that it's repeatable from year to year. Other findings:

1. Pitchers who induce more swings at strikes allow more fouls, but pitchers who induce more chases do not.
2. Groundball pitchers tend to give up fewer foul balls than flyball pitchers.

Runs

Expected earned run average (xERA)

Gill and Reeve version: *(.575 x H [per 9 IP]) + (.94 x HR [per 9 IP]) + (.28 x BB [per 9 IP]) – (.01 x K [per 9 IP]) – Normalizing Factor*

John Burnson version (used in this book):
(xER x 9)/IP, where xER is defined as
xER% x (FB/10) + (1-xS%) x [0.3 x (BIP – FB/10) + BB]
where xER% = 0.96 – (0.0284 x (GB/FB))
and
xS% = (64.5 + (K/9 x 1.2) – (BB/9 x (BB/9 + 1)) / 20)
+ ((0.0012 x (GB%^2)) – (0.001 x GB%) - 2.4)

xERA represents an equivalent of what a pitcher's real ERA might be, calculated solely with skills-based measures. It is not influenced by situation-dependent factors.

Expected ERA variance

xERA – ERA

The variance between a pitcher's ERA and his xERA is a measure of over or underachievement. A positive variance indicates the potential for a pitcher's ERA to rise. A negative variance indicates the potential for ERA improvement. **BENCHMARK:** Discount variances that are less than 0.50. Any variance more than 1.00 (one run per game) is regarded as a strong indicator of future change.

Projected xERA or projected ERA?

Which should we be using to forecast a pitcher's ERA? Projected xERA is more accurate for looking ahead on a purely skills basis. Projected ERA includes *situation-dependent* events—bullpen support, park factors, etc.—which are reflected better by ERA. The optimal approach is to use both gauges as *a range of expectation* for forecasting purposes.

Strand rate (S%)

(H + BB – ER) / (H + BB – HR)

Measures the percentage of allowed runners a pitcher strands (earned runs only), which incorporates both individual pitcher skill and bullpen effectiveness. **BENCHMARKS:** The most adept at stranding runners will have S% levels over 75%. Those with rates over 80% will have artificially low ERAs which will be prone to relapse. Levels below 65% will inflate ERA but have a high probability of regression.

Expected strand rate *(Michael Weddell)*

*73.935 + K/9 - 0.116 * (BB/9*(BB/9+1))*
*+ (0.0047 * GB%^2 - 0.3385 * GB%)*
+ (MAX(2,MIN(4,IP/G))/2-1)
+ (0.82 if left-handed)

This formula is based on three core skills: strikeouts per nine innings, walks per nine innings, and ground balls per balls in play, with adjustments for whether the pitcher is a starter or reliever (measured by IP/G), and his handedness.

Strand rate as a leading indicator *(Ed DeCaria)*

Strand rate often regresses/rebounds toward past rates (usually 69-74%), resulting in Year 2 ERA changes:

% of Pitchers with Year 2 Regression/Rebound

Y1 S%	RP	SP	LR
<60%	100%	94%	94%
65	81%	74%	88%
70	53%	48%	65%
75	55%	85%	100%
80	80%	100%	100%
85	100%	100%	100%

Typical ERA Regression/Rebound in Year 2

Y1 S%	RP	SP	LR
<60%	-2.54	-2.03	-2.79
65	-1.00	-0.64	-0.93
70	-0.10	-0.05	-0.44
75	0.24	0.54	0.75
80	1.15	1.36	2.29
85	1.71	2.21	n/a

Starting pitchers (SP) have a narrower range of strand rate outcomes than do relievers (RP) or swingmen/long relievers (LR). **Relief pitchers** with Y1 strand rates of <=67% or >=78% are likely to experience a +/- ERA regression in Y2. **Starters and swingmen/long relievers** with Y1 strand rates of <=65% or >=75% are likely to experience a +/- ERA regression in Y2. Pitchers with strand rates that deviate more than a few points off their individual expected strand rates are likely to experience some degree of ERA regression in Y2. Over-performing (or "lucky") pitchers are more likely than underperforming (or "unlucky") pitchers to see such a correction.

Wins

Expected Wins (xW) *(Matt Cederholm)*

[(Team runs per game)^1.8]/[(Pitcher ERA)^1.8 + (Team runs per game)^1.8] x 0.72 x GS

Starting pitchers' win totals are often at odds with their ERA. Attempts to find a strictly skill-based analysis of this phenomenon haven't worked, but there is a powerful tool in the toolbox: Bill James' Pythagorean Theorem. While usually applied to team outcomes, recent research has shown that its validity holds up when applied to individual starting pitchers.

One key to applying the Pythagorean Theorem is factoring in no-decisions. Research shows that the average no-decision rate is 28% of starts, regardless of the type or quality of the pitcher or his team, with no correlation in ND% from one season to the next.

Overall, 70% of pitchers whose expected wins varied from actual wins showed regression in wins per start in the following year, making variation from Expected Wins a good leading indicator.

Projecting/chasing wins

Five events need to occur for a pitcher to post a single win...

1. He must pitch well, allowing few runs.
2. The offense must score enough runs.
3. The defense must successfully field all batted balls.
4. The bullpen must hold the lead.
5. The manager must leave the pitcher in for 5 innings, and not remove him if the team is still behind.

Of these five events, only one is within the control of the pitcher. As such, projecting or chasing wins based on skills alone can be an exercise in futility.

Home field advantage and wins *(Ed DeCaria)*

Pitchers starting at home are 7% more likely to earn a Win than when they start on the road. This extra Win potential comes from two sources: 1) home starting pitchers tend to go deeper into games than away starters, and 2) even when home starters only last 5-6 IP, they are more likely to get the Win.

Usage

Batters faced per game *(Craig Wright)*

((Batters faced – (BB + HBP + SAC)) + H + BB) / G

A measure of pitcher usage and one of the leading indicators for potential pitcher burnout.

Workload

Research suggests that there is a finite number of innings in a pitcher's arm. This number varies by pitcher, development cycle, and pitching style and repertoire. We can measure a pitcher's potential for future arm problems and/or reduced effectiveness (burnout):

Sharp increases in usage from one year to the next. Common wisdom has suggested that pitchers who significantly increase their workload from one year to the next are candidates for burnout symptoms. This has often been called the Verducci Effect, after writer Tom Verducci. Michael Weddell tested pitchers with sharp workload increases during the period 1988-2008 and found that no such effect exists.

Starters' overuse. Consistent "batters faced per game" (BF/G) levels of 28.0 or higher, combined with consistent seasonal IP totals of 200 or more may indicate burnout potential, especially with pitchers younger than 25. Within a season, a BF/G of more than 30.0 with a projected IP total of 200 may indicate a late season fade.

Relievers' overuse. Warning flags should be up for relievers who post more than 100 IP in a season, while averaging fewer than 2 IP per outing.

When focusing solely on minor league pitchers, research results are striking:

Stamina: Virtually every minor league pitcher who had a BF/G of 28.5 or more in one season experienced a drop-off in BF/G the following year. Many were unable to ever duplicate that previous level of durability.

Performance: Most pitchers experienced an associated drop-off in their BPVs in the years following the 28.5 BF/G season. Some were able to salvage their effectiveness later on by moving to the bullpen.

Effects of short-term workloads on relief pitcher value

(Arik Florimonte)

Using game logs from 2002-17, we studied the effects of recent workload on relief pitcher performance. After accounting for factors such as selection and usage bias—good pitchers get used on short rest more often—we discovered there is almost no measurable performance impact. Pitchers used heavily for several days, including the day before, show perhaps a 5-10% reduction in BPV.

Pitchers who have thrown often in the recent past are less likely to be used, which can significantly reduce their value, with a 36% reduction in saves and a 64% reduction in games pitched when "worn out".

In leagues with daily lineup changes, monitoring RP workloads can help owners decide to start rested closers of lesser quality, and therefore lower cost, over more expensive closers who may be worn out.

Protecting young pitchers *(Craig Wright)*

There is a link between some degree of eventual arm trouble and a history of heavy workloads in a pitcher's formative years. Some recommendations from this research:

Teenagers (A-ball): No 200 IP seasons and no BF/G over 28.5 in any 150 IP span. No starts on three days rest.

Ages 20-22: Average no more than 105 pitches per start with a single game ceiling of 130 pitches.

Ages 23-24: Average no more than 110 pitches per start with a single game ceiling of 140 pitches.

When possible, a young starter should be introduced to the majors in long relief before he goes into the rotation.

Overall Performance Analysis

Base Performance Value (BPV)

((K/9 - 5.0) x 18)
+ ((4.0 - bb/9) x 27))
+ (Ground ball rate as a whole number - 40%)

A single value that describes a player's overall raw skill level. The formula combines the individual raw skills of dominance, control and the ability to keep the ball down in the zone, all characteristics that are unaffected by most external factors. In tandem with a pitcher's strand rate, it provides a more complete picture of the elements that contribute to ERA, and therefore serves as an accurate tool to project likely changes in ERA. Note that the league-normalized version (BPX) is what appears in this book.

Base Performance Index (BPX)

BPV scaled to league average to account for year-to-year fluctuations in league-wide statistical performance. It's a snapshot of a player's overall skills compared to an average player. BENCHMARK: A level of 100 means a player had a league-average BPV in that given season.

Runs Above Replacement (RAR)

An estimate of the number of runs a player contributes above a "replacement level" player.

Batters create runs; pitchers save runs. But are batters and pitchers who have comparable RAR levels truly equal in value? Pitchers might be considered to have higher value. Saving an additional run is more important than producing an additional run. A pitcher who throws a shutout is guaranteed to win that game, whereas no matter how many runs a batter produces, his team can still lose given poor pitching support.

To calculate RAR for pitchers:

1. Start with the replacement level league ERA.
2. Subtract the pitcher's ERA. (To calculate projected RAR, use the pitcher's xERA.)
3. Multiply by number of games played, calculated as plate appearances (IP x 4.34) divided by 38.
4. Multiply the resulting RAR level by 1.08 to account for the variance between earned runs and total runs.

Skill-specific aging patterns for pitchers *(Ed DeCaria)*

For pitchers, prior research has shown that pitcher value peaks somewhere in their late 20s to early 30s. But how does aging affect each demonstrable pitching skill?

Strikeout rate (k/9): Declines fairly linearly beginning at age 25.

Walk rate (bb/9): Improves until age 25 and holds somewhat steady until age 29, at which point it begins to steadily worsen. Deteriorating k/9 and bb/9 rates result in inefficiency, as it requires far more pitches to get an out. For starting pitchers, this affects the ability to pitch deep into games.

Innings Pitched per game (IP/G): Among starters, it improves slightly until age 27, then tails off considerably with age, costing pitchers nearly one full IP/G by age 33 and one more by age 39.

Hit rate (H%): Among pitchers, H% appears to increase slowly but steadily as pitchers age, to the tune of .002-.003 points per year.

Strand rate (S%): Very similar to hit rate, except strand rate decreases with age rather than increasing. GB%/LD%/FB%: Line drives increase steadily from age 24 onward, and outfield flies increase beginning at age 31. Because 70%+ of line drives fall for hits, and 10%+ of fly balls become home runs, this spells trouble for aging pitchers.

Home runs per fly ball (HR/F): As each year passes, a higher percentage of a pitcher's fly balls become home runs allowed increases with age.

Catchers' effect on pitching *(Thomas Hanrahan)*

A typical catcher handles a pitching staff better after being with a club for a few years. Research has shown an improvement in team ERA from a catcher's rookie season to his prime years with a club. Expect a pitcher's ERA to be higher than expected if he is throwing to a rookie backstop.

First productive season *(Michael Weddell)*

To find those starting pitchers who are about to post their first productive season in the majors (10 wins, 150 IP, ERA of 4.00 or less), look for:

- Pitchers entering their age 23-26 seasons, especially those about to pitch their age 25 season.
- Pitchers who already have good skills, shown by an xERA in the prior year of 4.25 or less.
- Pitchers coming off at least a partial season in the majors without a major health problem.
- To the extent that one speculates on pitchers who are one skill away, look for pitchers who only need to improve their control (bb/9).

Bounceback fallacy *(Patrick Davitt)*

It is conventional wisdom that a pitcher often follows a bad year (value decline of more than 50%) with a significant "bounceback" that offers profit opportunity for the canny owner. But research showed the owner is extremely unlikely to get a full bounceback, and in fact, is more likely to suffer a further decline or uselessly small recovery than even a partial bounceback. The safest bet is a $30+ pitcher who has a collapse—but even then, bid to only about half of the previous premium value.

Closers

Saves

Six events need to occur for a relief pitcher to post a single save:

1. The starting pitcher and middle relievers must pitch well.
2. The offense must score enough runs.
3. It must be a reasonably close game.
4. The manager must put the pitcher in for a save opportunity.
5. The pitcher must pitch well and hold the lead.
6. The manager must let him finish the game.

Of these six events, only one is within the control of the relief pitcher. As such, projecting saves for a reliever has less to do with skills than opportunity. However, pitchers with excellent skills may create opportunities for themselves.

Saves conversion rate (Sv%)

Saves / Save Opportunities

The percentage of save opportunities that are successfully converted. **BENCHMARK:** We look for a minimum 80% for long-term success.

Leverage index (LI) *(Tom Tango)*

Leverage index measures the amount of swing in win probability indexed against an average value of 1.00. Thus, relievers who come into games in various situations create a composite score and if that average score is higher than 1.00, then their manager is showing enough confidence in them to try to win games with them. If the average score is below 1.00, then the manager is using them, but not showing nearly as much confidence that they can win games.

Origin of closers

History has long maintained that ace closers are not easily recognizable early on in their careers, so that every season does see its share of the unexpected. Adbert Alzolay, Tanner Scott, Jason Adam, Hunter Harvey ...who would have thought it a year ago?

Accepted facts, all of which have some element of truth:

- You cannot find major league closers from pitchers who were closers in the minors.
- Closers begin their careers as starters.
- Closers are converted set-up men.
- Closers are pitchers who were unable to develop a third effective pitch.

More simply, closers are a product of circumstance.

Are the minor leagues a place to look at all? In the 41 years from 1990 to 2021, there were nearly 500 twenty-save seasons recorded in Double-A and Triple-A ball. Only 16 of those pitchers ever saved 20 games in the majors, and only eight had multiple 20-save seasons: John Wetteland, Mark Wohlers, Ricky Bottalico, Braden Looper, Francisco Cordero, Craig Kimbrel, A.J. Ramos and Kirby Yates.

One of the reasons that minor league closers rarely become major league closers is because, in general, they do not get enough innings in the minors to sufficiently develop their arms into big-league caliber. In fact, organizations do not look at minor league closing performance seriously, assigning that role to pitchers who they do not see as legitimate prospects. The average age of minor league closers over the past decade has been 27.5.

Elements of saves success

The task of finding future closing potential comes down to looking at two elements:

Talent: The raw skills to mow down hitters for short periods.

Opportunity: The more important element, yet the one that pitchers have no control over.

Some pitchers have Talent, but not Opportunity. These pitchers are not given a chance to close for a variety of reasons (e.g. being blocked by a solid front-liner in the pen, being left-handed, etc.), but are good to own because they will not likely hurt your pitching staff. You just can't count on them for saves, at least not in the near term.

Some pitchers have Opportunity, but not Talent. MLB managers decide who to give the ball to in the 9th inning based on their own perceptions about what skills are required to succeed, even if those perceived "skills" don't translate into acceptable metrics.

Those pitchers without the metrics may have some initial short-term success, but their long-term prognosis is poor and they are high risks to your roster. Recent examples include Lou Trivino, Ian Kennedy and Gregory Soto.

Closers' job retention *(Michael Weddell)*

Of pitchers with 20 or more saves in one year, only 67.5% earned 20 or more saves the following year. The variables that best predicted whether a closer would avoid this attrition:

- *Saves history:* Career saves was the most important factor.
- *Age:* Closers are most likely to keep their jobs at age 27. For long-time closers, their growing career saves totals more than offset the negative impact of their advanced ages. Older closers without a long history of racking up saves tend to be bad candidates for retaining their roles.
- *Performance:* Actual performance, measured by ERA+, was of only minor importance.
- *Being right-handed:* Increased the odds of retaining the closer's role by 9% over left-handers.

Closer volatility history

Year	Closers Drafted	Avg R$	Closers Failed	Failure %	New Sources
2014	28	$15.54	11	39%	15
2015	29	$14.79	13	45%	16
2016	33	$13.30	19	58%	17
2017	32	$13.63	17	53%	15
2018	27	$13.22	17	63%	20
2019	31	$13.29	18	58%	14
2020*	27	$14.30	19	70%	26
2021	33	$11.79	21	64%	22
2022	35	$12.66	25	71%	14
2023	32	$14.13	16	50%	12

**The 2020 data should be mostly ignored due to the vagaries of the short season.*

Drafted refers to the number of saves sources purchased in both LABR and Tout Wars experts leagues each year. These only include relievers drafted specifically for saves speculation. *Avg R$* refers to the average purchase price of these pitchers in the AL-only and NL-only leagues. *Failed* is the number (and percentage) of saves sources drafted that did not return at least 50% of their value that year. The failures include those that lost their value due to ineffectiveness, injury or managerial decision. *New Sources* are arms drafted for less than $5 (if drafted at all) but finished with at least 10 saves.

Except for the anomalous 2020 data, the $14.13 average closer investment in 2023 was the highest since 2015, a surprising level given the record-setting failure rate last year; we would have expected a softer market. As it turned out, this year's drafters' hit rate was the best since 2015, but the losses were deeper for closers who failed. That led to some oddities; drafters spent $75 on Kenley Jansen, Raisel Iglesias, and Ryan Pressly, but the trio earned back only $24 despite notching over 90 saves.

The $452 spent on closers returned $199 overall, much better than last year's $443-$65, but still a losing investment. As a result, drafters may feel empowered to bid deeper again in 2024 given the perceived lower risk, but we don't know if 2023 was a one-off. Historically, saves investments are risky by nature; don't let one year with "only" a 50% failure rate dictate your risk assessment.

Closers and multi-year performance *(Patrick Davitt)*
A team having an "established closer"—even a successful one—in a given year does not affect how many of that team's wins are saved in the next year. However, a top closer (40-plus saves) in a given year has a significantly greater chance to retain his role in the subsequent season.

Research of saves and wins data over several seasons found that the percentage of wins that are saved is consistently 50%-54%, irrespective of whether the saves were concentrated in the hands of a "top closer" or passed around to the dreaded "committee" of lesser closers. But it also found that about two-thirds of high-save closers reprised their roles the next season, while three-quarters of low-save closers did not. Moreover, closers who held the role for two or three straight seasons averaged 34 saves per season while closers new to the role averaged 27.

Saves chances and wins *(Patrick Davitt)*
Do good teams get more saves because they generate more wins, or do poor teams get more saves because more of their wins are by narrow margins. The "good-team" side is probably on firmer ground, though there are enough exceptions that we should be cautious about drawing broad inferences.

The 2014 study confirmed what Craig Neuman found years earlier: The argument "more wins leads to more saves" is generally correct. Over five studied seasons, the percentage of wins that were saved (Sv%W) was about 50%, and half of all team-seasons fell in the Sv%W range of 48%-56%. As a result, high-saves seasons were more common for high-win teams.

That wins-saves connection for individual team-seasons was much less solid, however, and we observed many outliers. Data for individual team-seasons showed wide ranges of both Sv%W and actual saves.

Finally, higher-win teams do indeed get more blowout wins, but while poorer teams had a higher percentage (73%) of close wins (three runs or fewer) than better teams (56%), good teams' higher number of wins meant they still had more close wins, more save opportunities and more saves, again with many outliers among individual team-seasons.

Other Relievers

Reliever Efficiency Percent (REff%)
(Wins + Saves + Holds) / (Wins + Losses + SaveOpps + Holds)
This is a measure of how often a reliever contributes positively to the outcome of a game. A record of consistent, positive impact on game outcomes breeds managerial confidence, and that confidence could pave the way to save opportunities. For those pitchers suddenly thrust into a closer's role, this formula helps gauge their potential to succeed based on past successes in similar roles.
BENCHMARK: Minimum of 80%.

Vulture
A pitcher, typically a middle reliever, who accumulates an unusually high number of wins by preying on other pitchers' misfortunes. More accurately, this is a pitcher typically brought into a game after a starting pitcher has put his team behind, and then pitches well enough and long enough to allow his offense to take the lead, thereby "vulturing" a win from the starter. This concept has been losing its relevance with the rising use of Openers. Today's "vulture" is the bulk inning relief pitcher who follows the one-inning Opener and does not have to pitch five innings to qualify for a Win.

In-Season Analysis

Sample size reliability *(Russell Carleton)*
At what sample size do skill and luck each represent 50 percent contributors to a specific metric?

*Measured in batters faced	
60:	K/PA
120:	BB/PA

Note that 120 batters faced is roughly equivalent to just shy of five outings for a starting pitcher.

*Measured via balls in play:	
50:	HR/F
80:	GB%; FB%
600:	LD%
820:	Hit rate (BABIP)

**Unlisted metrics did not stabilize over a full season of play.*

How to read: "After 50 balls in play, the luck-to-skill ratio for home run to fly ball rate has evened out. If a player with a career HR/F rate of 12 percent has an 8 percent rate after 50 balls in play, we can attribute 50% of that new rate to a new skill and the other 50% to random chance." These levels represent the point at which these metrics become useful, though not as direct predictors. Their value is as another data point in the forecasting process.

Can we trust in-season sample size? *(Arik Florimonte)*
When a pitcher's performance deviates significantly from their established history, when can you trust the change? And are there any metrics that are better in short periods than long? Using data from 2010-2017 and filtering for full-time players (≥ 120 IP in a season, or ≥ 25 IP in a month), there is no magic date for believing the current season's results more than the previous season's; rather, it's more of a continuum. We were able to estimate the point in the season current year-to-date results are more predictive than the prior year's results, noted in the table below by the change from white blocks to black. We also note at which point the previous month alone offers better predictive value than the entire previous year ("PM>PY").

	Months of the Season						PM>PY starting...
K%	A	M	J	J	A	S	July
BB%	A	M	J	J	A	S	Never
GB%	A	M	J	J	A	S	Never
FB%	A	M	J	J	A	S	Never
Soft%	A	M	J	J	A	S	Always
Hard%	A	M	J	J	A	S	May

Prior Year is Better
Year-to-date is Better

Note that due to the date filters used, a month here is roughly equivalent to 25-35 IP, or around 125 batters faced.

Key takeaways:

- Don't fully buy into a change in GB/FB mix or K/BB until June (although you may still want to speculate earlier if you can stash a player on reserve)
- Don't expect last year's hard and soft contact tendencies to continue into the current year.
- Pay some attention to the current year's Soft% and Hard%— there is useful information there—but remember that at best, future outcomes are still 80% noise and regression.
- There is essentially no month-to-month or year-to-year correlation for HR/FB for pitchers. There may be pitchers with a "homer problem," but it is not possible to identify them by looking at home run rates.
- Generally, projections based on prior years' skills should remain your fallback position but keep moving the needle toward the current year's results as the year goes on.

Pure Quality Starts

Pure Quality Starts (PQS) says that the smallest unit of measure should not be the "event" but instead be the "game." Within that game, we can accumulate all the strikeouts, hits and walks, and evaluate that outing as a whole. After all, when a pitcher takes the mound, he is either "on" or "off" his game; he is either dominant or struggling, or somewhere in between.

In PQS, we give a starting pitcher credit for exhibiting certain skills in each of his starts. Then by tracking his "PQS Score" over time, we can follow his progress. A starter earns one point for each of the following criteria:

1. *The pitcher must go more than 6 innings (record at least one out in the 7th).* This measures stamina.
2. *He must allow fewer hits than innings pitched.* This measures hit prevention.
3. *His number of strikeouts must equal to or more than 5.* This measures dominance.
4. *He must strike out at least three times as many batters as he walks (or have a minimum of three strikeouts if he hasn't walked a batter).* This measures command.
5. *He must not allow a home run.* This measures his ability to keep the ball in the park.

A perfect PQS score is 5. Any pitcher who averages 3 or more over the course of the season is probably performing admirably. The nice thing about PQS is it allows you to approach each start as more than an all-or-nothing event.

Note the absence of earned runs. No matter how many runs a pitcher allows, if he scores high on the PQS scale, he has hurled a good game in terms of his base skills. The number of runs allowed—a function of not only the pitcher's ability but that of his bullpen and defense—will tend to even out over time.

It doesn't matter if a few extra balls got through the infield, or the pitcher was given the hook in the fourth or sixth inning, or the bullpen was able to strand their inherited baserunners. When we look at performance in the aggregate, those events do matter, and will affect a pitcher's skills metrics and ERA. But with PQS, the minutia is less relevant than the overall performance.

In the end, a dominating performance is a dominating performance, whether Spencer Strider hurls 7 IP of scoreless baseball or gives up 2 runs while striking out 9 in 6 IP. And a disaster is still a disaster, whether Alek Manoah gets pulled in the first inning after allowing 6 runs or is hooked after 4 IP after 7 runs scored.

(A proposed change to this formula is discussed in the research section on page 75.)

Skill versus consistency

Two pitchers have identical 4.50 ERAs and identical 3.0 PQS averages. Their PQS logs look like this:

PITCHER A:	3	3	3	3	3
PITCHER B:	5	0	5	0	5

Which pitcher would you rather have on your team? The risk-averse manager would choose Pitcher A as he represents the perfectly known commodity. Many fantasy leaguers might opt for Pitcher B because his occasional dominating starts show that there is an upside. His Achilles Heel is inconsistency—he is unable to sustain that high level. Is there any hope for Pitcher B?

- If a pitcher's inconsistency is characterized by more poor starts than good starts, his upside is limited.
- Pitchers with extreme inconsistency rarely get a full season of starts.
- However, inconsistency is neither chronic nor fatal.

The outlook for Pitcher A is actually worse. Disaster avoidance might buy these pitchers more starts, but history shows that the lack of dominating outings is more telling of future potential. In short, consistent mediocrity is bad.

PQS DOMination and DISaster rates *(Gene McCaffrey)*

DOM% is the percentage of a starting pitcher's outings that rate as a PQS-4 or PQS-5. DIS% is the percentage that rate as a PQS-0 or PQS-1.

DOM/DIS percentages open up a new perspective, providing us with two separate scales of performance. In tandem, they measure consistency.

Quality/consistency score (QC)

(DOM% – (2 x DIS%)) x 2)

Using PQS and DOM/DIS percentages, this score measures both the quality of performance as well as start-to-start consistency.

DOM%	Neutral	DIS%	QC
	Sample configurations		
100	0	0	200
70	20	10	100
60	30	10	80
50	30	20	20
50	25	25	0
40	30	30	-40
30	20	50	-140
20	20	60	-200
0	100	0	-400

Predictive value of PQS *(Arik Florimonte)*

Using data from 2010-2015, research showed that PQS values can be used to project future starts. A pitcher who even threw only one PQS-DOM start had a slightly better chance of throwing another DOM in his subsequent start. For a pitcher who posts two, three, or even four PQS-DOMs in a row, the streak portends better results. The longer the streak, the better the results.

Fantasy owners best positioned to take advantage are those who can frequently choose from multiple similar SP options, such as in a DFS league, or streaming in traditional leagues. In either case, make your evaluations as you normally would (e.g. talent first, then matchups, ballpark or by using BaseballHQ.com's Pitcher Matchups Tool)—and then give a value bump to the pitcher with the hot streak.

PQS correlation with Wins

PQS		Wins	Losses	No Decision
4-5	DOM	60%	14%	26%
2-3		34%	27%	39%
0-1	DIS	10%	57%	33%

PQS correlation with Quality Starts *(Ed DeCaria)*

PQS	QS%	% of all starts	% of all QS	QS Index
0	4%	14%	1%	11
1	9%	22%	4%	17
2	23%	25%	9%	37
3	46%	20%	18%	91
4	71%	14%	28%	204
5	99%	7%	39%	601

High pitch counts and PQS *(Paul Petera)*

A 2017 study found that high-scoring PQS starters who also ran up high pitch counts continued to thrive in their next start (and beyond). Taking three seasons of PQS and pitch-count data, starts were grouped by pitch count into five cohorts and averaged by PQS. The study then calculated the average PQS scores in the subsequent starts and found that pitchers with higher pitch counts are safer bets to throw well in their next start (and beyond) than those who throw fewer pitches. Near-term fatigue or other negative symptoms do not appear to be worthy of concern; so, do not shy away from these pitchers solely for that reason.

In-season ERA/xERA variance as a leading indicator

(Matt Cederholm)

Pitchers with large first-half ERA/xERA variances will see regression towards their xERA in the second half, if they are allowed (and are able) to finish out the season. Starters have a stronger regression tendency than relievers, which we would expect to see given the larger sample size. In addition, there is substantial attrition among all types of pitchers, but those who are "unlucky" have a much higher rate.

An important corollary: While a pitcher underperforming his xERA is very likely to rebound in the second half, such regression hinges on his ability to hold onto his job long enough to see that regression come to fruition. Healthy veteran pitchers with an established role are more likely to experience the second half boost than a rookie starter trying to make his mark.

Pure Quality Relief *(Patrick Davitt)*

A system for evaluating reliever outings. The scoring:

1. Two points for the first out, and one point for each subsequent out, to a maximum of four points.
2. One point for having at least one strikeout for every four full outs (one K for 1-4 outs, two Ks for 5-8 outs, etc.).
3. One point for zero baserunners, minus one point for each baserunner, though allowing the pitcher one unpenalized runner for each three full outs (one baserunner for 3-5 outs, two for 6-8 outs, three for nine outs)
4. Minus one point for each earned run, though allowing one ER for 8– or 9-out appearances.
5. An automatic PQR-0 for allowing a home run.

Using first half reliever stats as a leading indicator

(Steve Weimer)

A study of reliever data from 2019, 2021, and 2022 was conducted to determine which first-half statistics best predicted second-half results. The findings:

- K-BB% is the first-half statistic most strongly correlated with second-half reliever value. Ball% and SwK% had a similarly strong relation to second-half ratios. Focus on all three to identify ratio-protecting relievers.
- Of the 122 relievers who posted over a 20% K-BB% in the first half, just over two-thirds contributed positively to the ratio categories in the second half. When we factor in their contribution to strikeouts as well as ERA and WHIP, they were worth more than two standings points in the second half.

Contextual factors must also be considered (park factors, strength of opposing offenses), and by bypassing relievers who meet the relevant first-half thresholds but whose skills have clearly declined in the second half (i.e. drop in velocity or strikeout rate), fantasy players should be able to do even better than the hit rates described above.

Avoiding relief disasters *(Ed DeCaria)*

Relief disasters (defined as ER>=3 and IP<=3), occur in 5%+ of all appearances. The chance of a disaster exceeds 13% in any 7-day period. To minimize the odds of a disaster, we created a model that produced the following list of factors, in order of influence:

1. Strength of opposing offense
2. Park factor of home stadium
3. BB/9 over latest 31 days (more walks is bad)
4. Pitch count over previous 7 days (more pitches is bad)
5. Latest 31 Days ERA>xERA (recent bad luck continues)

Daily league owners who can slot relievers by individual game should also pay attention to days of rest: pitching on less rest than one is accustomed to increases disaster risk.

April ERA as a leading indicator *(Stephen Nickrand)*

A starting pitcher's April ERA can act as a leading indicator for how his ERA is likely to fare during the balance of the season. A study looked at extreme April ERA results to see what kind of in-season forecasting power they may have. From 2010-2012, 42 SP posted an ERA in April that was at least 2.00 ER better than their career ERA. The findings:

- Pitchers who come out of the gates quickly have an excellent chance at finishing the season with an ERA much better than their career ERA.
- While April ERA gems see their in-season ERA regresses towards their career ERA, their May-Sept ERA is still significantly better than their career ERA.
- Those who stumble out of the gates have a strong chance at posting an ERA worse than their career average, but their in-season ERA improves towards their career ERA.
- April ERA disasters tend to have a May-Sept ERA that closely resembles their career ERA.

Using K–BB% to find SP buying opportunities *(Arik Florimonte)*

Research showed that finding pitchers who have seen an uptick in K–BB% over the past 30 days is one way to search for mid-season replacements from the waiver wire. Using 2014-2016 player-seasons and filtering for starting pitchers with ≥ 100 IP, the K–BB% mean is about 13%. The overall MLB mean is approximately 12%, and the top 50 SP tend to be 14% or higher.

The findings:

- Last 30 days K–BB% is useful as a gauge of next 30 days performance.
- Pitchers on the upswing are more likely to climb into the elite ranks than other pitchers of similar YTD numbers; pitchers with a larger uptick show a greater likelihood.
- Last-30 K–BB% surgers could be good mid-season pickups if they are being overlooked by other owners in your league.

Second-half ERA reduction drivers *(Stephen Nickrand)*

It's easy to dismiss first-half-to-second-half improvement among starting pitchers as an unpredictable event. After all, the midpoint of the season is an arbitrary cutoff. Performance swings occur throughout the season.

A study of SP who experienced significant 1H-2H ERA improvement from 2010-2012 examined what indicators drove second-half ERA improvement. Among the findings for those 79 SP with a > 1.00 ERA 1H-2H reduction:

- 97% saw their WHIP decrease, with an average decrease of 0.26
- 97% saw their strand (S%) rate improve, with an average increase of 9%
- 87% saw their BABIP (H%) improve, with an average reduction of 5%
- 75% saw their control (bb/9) rate improve, with an average reduction of 0.8
- 70% saw their HR/9 rate improve, with an average decrease of 0.5
- 68% saw their swinging strike (SwK%) rate improve, with an average increase of 1.4%
- 68% saw their BPV improve, with an average increase of 37
- 67% saw their HR per fly ball rate (HR/F) improve, with an average decrease of 4%
- 53% saw their ground ball (GB%) rate improve, with an average increase of 5%
- 52% saw their dominance (k/9) rate improve, with an average increase of 1.3

These findings highlight the power of H% and S% regression as it relates to ERA and WHIP improvement. In fact, H% and S% are more often correlated with ERA improvement than are improved skills. They also suggest that improved control has a bigger impact on ERA reduction than does increased strikeouts.

Pitcher home/road splits *(Stephen Nickrand)*

One overlooked strategy in leagues that allow frequent transactions is to bench pitchers when they are on the road. Research reveals that several pitching stats and indicators are significantly and consistently worse on the road than at home.

Some home/road rules of thumb for SP:

- If you want to gain significant ground in ERA and WHIP, bench all your average or worse SP on the road.
- A pitcher's win percentage drops by 15% on the road, so don't bank on road starts to catch up in wins.
- Control erodes by 10% on the road, so be especially careful with keeping wild SP in your active lineups when they are away from home.
- HR/9, groundball rate, hit rate, strand rate, and HR/F do not show significant home vs. road variances.

Other Diamonds

The Pitching Postulates

1. Never sign a soft-tosser to a long-term contract.
2. Right-brain dominance has a very long shelf life.
3. A fly ball pitcher who gives up many HR is expected. A GB pitcher who gives up many HR is making mistakes.
4. Never draft a contact fly ball pitcher who plays in a hitter's park.
5. Only bad teams ever need an innings-eater.
6. Never chase wins.

Dontrelle Willis List

Pitchers with skills metrics so horrible that you have to wonder how they can possibly draw a major league paycheck year after year.

Chaconian

Having the ability to post many saves despite sub-Mendoza metrics and an ERA in the stratosphere. (See: Shawn Chacón, 2004.)

Coors Chum
Soft-tossing fly ball/line drive contact pitchers in the Colorado system. By rights, they should not be allowed anywhere near Coors Field, not even to buy a hot dog. Like Chase Anderson, Ty Blach, Chris Flexen and Connor Seabold.

ERA Benchmark
A half run of ERA over 200 innings comes out to just one earned run every four starts.

The Knuckleballers Rule
Knuckleballers don't follow no stinkin' rules.

Brad Lidge Lament
When a closer posts a 62% strand rate, he has nobody to blame but himself.

Vin Mazzaro Vindication
Occasional nightmares (2.1 innings, 14 ER) are just a part of the game.

PQS Benchmark
Generally, a single DISaster outing requires two DOMinant outings just to get back to par.

The Five Saves Certainties

1. On every team, there will be save opportunities and someone will get them. At a bare minimum, there will be at least 30 saves to go around, and not unlikely more than 45.
2. Any pitcher could end up being the chief beneficiary. Bullpen management is a fickle endeavor.
3. Relief pitchers are often the ones that require the most time at the start of the season to find a groove. The weather is cold, the schedule is sparse and their usage is erratic.
4. Despite the talk about "bullpens by committee," managers prefer a go-to guy. It makes their job easier.
5. As many as 50% of the saves in any year will come from pitchers who are undrafted.

Soft-tosser land
The place where feebler arms leave their fortunes in the hands of the defense, variable hit and strand rates, and park dimensions. It's a place where many live, but few survive.

Vintage Eck Territory
A BPX of over 300. From 1989-1992, Dennis Eckersely posted sub-2.00 ERAs and 300-plus BPXs three times. He had an ERA of 0.61 in 1990. In 1989 and 1990, he posted K/BB ratios over 18.0.

Prospects

General

Minor league prospecting in perspective

In our perpetual quest to be the genius who uncovers the next Mike Trout when he's still in high school, there is an obsessive fascination with minor league prospects. That's not to say that prospecting is not important. The issue is perspective:

1. From 2006 to 2015, 14% of players selected in the first round of the Major League Baseball First Year Player Draft went on to have at least one $20 season in the Majors. From those in the top 10, 32% posted at least one $20 MLB season.
2. Some prospects are going to hit the ground running (Corbin Carroll) and some are going to immediately struggle (Brett Baty), no matter what level of hype follows them.
3. Some prospects are going to start fast (since the league is unfamiliar with them) and then fade (as the league figures them out). Others will start slow (since they are unfamiliar with the opposition) and then improve (as they adjust to the competition). So, if you make your free agent and roster decisions based on small early samples sizes, you are just as likely to be an idiot as a genius.
4. How any individual player will perform relative to his talent is largely unknown because there is a psychological element that is vastly unexplored. Some transition to the majors seamlessly and some not, regardless of how talented they are.
5. Still, talent is the best predictor of future success, so major league equivalent base performance indicators still have a valuable role in the process. As do scouting reports, carefully filtered.
6. Follow the player's path to the majors. Did he have to repeat certain levels? Was he allowed to stay at a level long enough to learn how to adjust to the level of competition? A player with only two great months at Double-A is a good bet to struggle if promoted directly to the majors because he was never fully tested at Double-A, let alone Triple-A.
7. Younger players holding their own against older competition is a good thing. Older players reaching their physical peak, regardless of their current address, can be a good thing too. The J.P. Frances, Brent Rookers and Jake Burgers can have some very profitable years.
8. Remember team context. A prospect with superior potential often will not unseat a steady but unspectacular incumbent, especially one with a large contract.
9. Don't try to anticipate how a team is going to manage their talent, both at the major and minor league level. You might think it's time to promote Jackson Holliday and give him an everyday role. You are not running the Orioles.
10. Those who play in shallow, one-year leagues should have little cause to be looking at the minors at all. The risk versus reward is so skewed against you, and there is

so much talent available with a track record, that taking a chance on an unproven commodity makes little sense.

11. Decide where your priorities really are. If your goal is to win, prospect analysis is just a *part* of the process, not the entire process.

Factors affecting minor league stats *(Terry Linhart)*

1. Often, there is an exaggerated emphasis on short-term performance in an environment that is supposed to focus on the long-term. Two poor outings don't mean a 21-year-old pitcher is washed up.
2. Ballpark dimensions and altitude create hitters parks and pitchers parks. Also, some parks have inconsistent field quality which can artificially depress defensive statistics while inflating stats like batting average. However, these are now isolated issues affecting only some parks (e.g. Chattanooga, Daytona, Durham). When MLB took over managing the minor leagues, they gave MiLB organizations five years (starting in 2021) to correct issues or risk losing their affiliation agreement.
3. Some players' skills are so superior to the competition at their level that you can't get a true picture of what they're going to do from their stats alone.
4. Many pitchers are told to work on secondary pitches in unorthodox situations just to gain confidence in the pitch. The result is an artificially increased number of walks.
5. The #3, #4, and #5 pitchers in the lower minors are truly longshots to make the majors. They often possess only two pitches and are unable to disguise the off-speed offerings. Hitters can see inflated statistics in these leagues.
6. MLB has experimented with a variety of rule changes in the minor leagues since 2021. This includes the use of automated strike zones with a full challenge system at all levels of Triple-A in 2023. The Double-A Southern and Texas Leagues have also experimented with using a pre-tacked baseball during portions of the last two seasons, with mostly negative feedback. These moves specifically have affected strike out rates and walk rates in the environments in which they were tested.

Minor league level versus age

See updated research on this topic on page 74.

Triple-A experience as a leading indicator

The probability that a minor leaguer will immediately succeed in the majors can vary depending upon the level of Triple-A experience he has amassed at the time of call-up.

	BATTERS		PITCHERS	
	< 1 Yr	Full	<1 Yr	Full
Performed well	57%	56%	16%	56%
Performed poorly	21%	38%	77%	33%
2nd half drop-off	21%	7%	6%	10%

The odds of a batter achieving immediate MLB success was slightly more than 50/50. More than 80% of all pitchers promoted with less than a full year at Triple-A struggled in their first year in the majors. Those pitchers with a year in Triple-A succeeded at a level equal to that of batters.

When do Top 100 prospects get promoted? *(Jeff Zimmerman)*

We created a simple procedure to determine if—and when—a player will make it to the majors in the season after being ranked in BaseballHQ.com's HQ100 prospect list (2010-17). We examined only the prospects who had not yet played in the majors, and found that the chances of a major league call-up for a healthy hitter or pitcher who last played in each level to be as follows:

- As a veteran in a foreign league: 100%
- In Triple-A: 90%
- In Double-A: 50%
- In A-ball: 20%
- Other: 0%

Additionally, to increase the odds of a call-up, take the (1) higher-ranked player; (2) the older player; and (3) the player on a contending team.

Major League Equivalency (MLE) *(Bill James)*

A formula that converts a player's minor or foreign league statistics into a comparable performance in the major leagues. These are not projections, but conversions of current performance. MLEs contain adjustments for the level of play in individual leagues and teams. They work best with Triple-A stats, not quite as well with Double-A stats, and hardly at all with the lower levels. Foreign conversions are still a work in process. James' original formula only addressed batting. Our research has devised conversion formulas for pitchers, however, their best use comes when looking at skills metrics, not traditional stats.

Adjusting to the competition

All players must "adjust to the competition" at every level of professional play. Players often get off to fast or slow starts. During their second tour at that level is when we get to see whether the slow starters have caught up or whether the league has figured out the fast starters. That second half "adjustment" period is a good baseline for projecting the subsequent season, in the majors or minors.

Premature major league call-ups often negate the ability for us to accurately evaluate a player due to the lack of this adjustment period. For instance, a hotshot Double-A player might open the season in Triple-A. After putting up solid numbers for a month, he gets a call to the bigs, and struggles. The fact is, we do not have enough evidence that the player has mastered the Triple-A level. We don't know whether the rest of the league would have caught up to him during his second tour of the league. But now he's labeled as an underperformer in the bigs when in fact he has never truly proven his skills at the lower levels.

Bull Durham prospects

There is some potential talent in older players—age 26, 27 or higher—who, for many reasons (untimely injury, circumstance, bad luck, etc.), don't reach the majors until they have already been downgraded from prospect to suspect. Equating potential with age is an economic reality for major league clubs, but not necessarily a skills reality.

Skills growth and decline are universal, whether at the major league level or in the minors. So a high-skills journeyman in Triple-A is just as likely to peak at age 27 as a major leaguer of the same age. The question becomes one of opportunity—will the parent club see fit to reap the benefits of that peak performance?

Prospecting these players for your fantasy team is, admittedly, a high-risk endeavor, though there are some criteria you can use. Look for a player who is/has:

- Optimally, age 27-28 for overall peak skills, age 30-31 for power skills, or age 28-31 for pitchers.
- At least two seasons of experience at Triple-A. Career Double-A players are generally not good picks.
- Solid base skills levels.
- Shallow organizational depth at their position.
- Notable winter league or spring training performance.

Players who meet these conditions are not typically draftable, but worthwhile reserve or FAB picks.

Deep-league prospecting primer *(Jock Thompson)*

There's no substitute for having a philosophy, objective, and plan for your fantasy farm system. Here's a prospecting process checklist:

Commit to some prospecting time. Sounds intuitive, but some owners either don't have the time or won't take the time to learn about their league's available prospects.

Have a prospecting framework/philosophy. Such as TINSTAPP—there is no such thing as a pitching prospect. The non-linear rise and development of prospects can be frustrating in general, but much more so with pitchers. Unlike with hitters, you're usually safe in forgoing low-minors pitching, and are better off speculating on near-ready pitching names.

Have objectives. Upside vs. MLB proximity is an ongoing dilemma, but rebuilders will always need to take on some far-away high-ceiling flyers.

Devise a strategy and stick with it. You'll need an idea as to how you'll 1) acquire available talent; and 2) upgrade your roster deficiencies. Above all, play out the year. Your team will improve by making good free agent assessments all season—not by taking off in August and September.

Always account for defense. A plus glove is a real advantage in finding MLB opportunity. Versatility and athleticism are even better, and often feed multi-position eligibility.

Consider all the variables. Things like age, opportunity, organization, venue, and club positional needs should all be factors.

Exercise excruciating patience - with legit hitting prospects. Even the most highly regarded prospects do not grow to the moon in linear fashion.

Speculate readily and be nimble with your in-season pitching moves. If you see something that looks more promising than what you have, grab it fast. If you don't, someone else will.

Pay attention and dig into in-season minor league developments. All of these lights can flicker on and turn into big edges if you can identify them. For example: a plus hit tool guy suddenly begins tapping into power, a pitcher makes in-season mechanical changes, a hitter makes across-the-board improvement following a position change.

Don't dismiss late bloomers with extended MLB opportunity. Like the more publicized names, plenty of lesser prospects have playable talent, and are just late figuring out how to unlock it.

Batters

Identifying batting average-led breakouts *(Chris Blessing)*

Much of the chatter around prospect "breakouts" centers around power, but there is a subset of minor leaguers who can provide batting-average-led value. While minor league swing data is much less accessible than for MLB players, key phrases in scouting reports can hold clues to what type of player could emerge. Players who post elite contact rates and low chase rates, possess a solid spray (or all-fields) approach, and have exemplary bat control can often find success early in their MLB careers. Often, these players exhibit topspin-heavy, line-drive and ground-ball contact characteristics. While profiles such as these have tended to decline in recent years, players with many plate appearances and batting-average-forward results like Jeff McNeil and Luis Arraez can become fantasy assets in the right team construction.

MLE PX as a leading indicator *(Bill Macey)*

Looking at minor league performance (as MLE) in one year and the corresponding MLB performance the subsequent year:

	Year 1 MLE	Year 2 MLB
Observations	496	496
Median PX	95	96
Percent PX > 100	43%	46%

In addition, 53% of the players had a MLB PX in year 2 that exceeded their MLE PX in year 1. A slight bias towards improved performance in year 2 is consistent with general career trajectories.

Year 1 MLE PX	Year 2 MLB PX	Pct. Incr	Pct. MLB PX > 100
<= 50	61	70.3%	5.4%
51-75	85	69.6%	29.4%
76-100	93	55.2%	39.9%
101-125	111	47.4%	62.0%
126-150	119	32.1%	66.1%
> 150	142	28.6%	76.2%

Slicing the numbers by performance level, there is a good amount of regression to the mean.

Players rarely suddenly develop power at the MLB level if they didn't previously display that skill in the minors. However, the relatively large gap between the median MLE PX and MLB PX for these players, 125 to 110, confirms the notion that the best players continue to improve once they reach the major leagues.

MLE contact rate as a leading indicator *(Bill Macey)*

There is a strong positive correlation (0.63) between a player's MLE ct% in Year 1 and his actual ct% at the MLB level in Year 2.

MLE ct%	Year 1 MLE ct%	Year 2 MLB ct%
< 70%	69%	68%
70% - 74%	73%	72%
75% - 79%	77%	75%
80% - 84%	82%	77%
85% - 89%	87%	82%
90% +	91%	86%
TOTAL	**84%**	**79%**

There is very little difference between the median MLE BA in Year 1 and the median MLB BA in Year 2:

MLE ct%	Year 1 MLE BA	Year 2 MLB BA
< 70%	.230	.270
70% - 74%	.257	.248
75% - 79%	.248	.255
80% - 84%	.257	.255
85% - 89%	.266	.270
90% +	.282	.273
TOTAL	.261	.262

Excluding the <70% cohort (which was a tiny sample size), there is a positive relationship between MLE ct% and MLB BA.

Pitchers

Skills metrics as a leading indicator for pitching success

The percentage of hurlers that were good investments in the year that they were called up varied by the level of their historical minor league skills metrics prior to that year.

Pitchers who had:	Fared well	Fared poorly
Good indicators	79%	21%
Marginal or poor indicators	18%	82%

The data used here were MLE levels from the previous two years, not the season in which they were called up. The significance? Solid current performance is what merits a call-up, but this is not a good indicator of short-term MLB success, because a) the performance data set is too small, typically just a few month's worth of statistics, and b) for those putting up good numbers at a new minor league level, there has typically not been enough time for the scouting reports to make their rounds.

East Asia Baseball *(Tom Mulhall)*

There has been a slow but steady influx of MLB-ready players from East Asian professional leagues to Major League Baseball, which is especially important in dynasty leagues with larger reserve or farm clubs. The Japanese major leagues (Nippon Professional Baseball) are generally considered to be equivalent to Triple-A ball with the pitching possibly better. The Korean league (Korean Baseball Organization) is considered slightly less competitive with less depth, and is roughly comparable to Double-A ball.

When evaluating the potential of Asian League prospects, the key is not to just identify the best players—the key is to identify impact players who have the desire and opportunity to sign with a MLB team. Opportunity is crucial, since players must have a certain number years of professional experience in order to qualify for international free agency, or hope that their team "posts" them early for full free agency. With the success of players like Ichiro, Darvish and Ohtani, it is easy to overestimate the value of drafting these players. Most don't have that impact. Still, for owners who are allowed to carry a large reserve or farm team at reduced salaries, rostering these players before they sign with a MLB club could be a real windfall, especially if your competitors do not do their homework. This is especially true in deeper dynasty leagues.

When doing your own research, note that in both Japan and Korea, the family name may be listed first, followed by the given name. The Forecaster will "westernize" those names for familiarity and ease of use. Names are sometimes difficult to translate into English so the official NPB or KBO designation will be used.

Japan

Baseball was first introduced in 1872 with professional leagues founded in the 1920s. It reached widespread popularity in the 1930s, partially due to exhibition games against American barnstorming teams that included Babe Ruth, Lou Gehrig, and Jimmie Foxx. Baseball is now considered the most popular spectator and participatory sport in Japan. The Nippon Professional Baseball (NPB) has two leagues, the Central League and Pacific League, each consisting of six teams. The Pacific League is currently considered superior to the more conservative Central League. There is also a strong amateur Industrial League, where players like Hideo Nomo and Kosuke Fukudome were discovered.

Statistics are difficult to compare due to differences in the way the game is played in Japan:

1. While strong on fundamentals, Japanese baseball's guiding philosophy remains risk avoidance. Runners rarely take extra bases, batters focus on making contact rather than driving the ball, and managers play for one run at a time. Bunts are more common. As a result, offenses score fewer runs per number of hits, and pitching stats tend to look better.
2. Stadiums in Japan usually have smaller dimensions and shorter fences. This should mean more HR, but given the style of play, it is the foreign born players who make up much of Japan's power elite. While a few Japanese power hitters such as Shohei Ohtani and Hideki Matsui made a full equivalent transition to MLB, it is still rare for the power to be entirely duplicated. (Note that the more conservative Central League still does not use the designated hitter.)
3. There are more artificial turf fields, which increases the number of ground ball singles. A few stadiums still use all dirt infields.
4. Teams are limited to having four foreign players on an active roster, and they cannot all be hitters or pitchers.
5. Teams have smaller pitching staffs and use a six-man rotation. Starters usually pitch once a week, typically on the same day since Monday is an off-day for the entire league. Some starters will also occasionally pitch in relief between starts. Managers push for complete games, no matter what the score or situation. Because of the style of offense, higher pitch counts are common. Despite superior conditioning, Japanese pitchers tend to burn out early due to overuse.
6. The ball is smaller and lighter, and the strike zone is slightly closer to the batter. Their ball also has more tack than the current MLB ball, which allows for a better spin rate.
7. There is an automatic ejection for hitting a batter in the area of the head and for arguing a call for more than three minutes.
8. Travel is less exhausting, with much shorter distances between teams.

9. If the score remains even after 12 innings, the game goes into the books as a tie.
10. There are 143 games in a season, as opposed to 162 in MLB. (There are no double-headers, as a rule.)

Players may sign with a MLB team out of high school, but this is a rare occurrence and most players sign with a NPB team. Player movement between players signed to a Japanese team and MLB teams is severely restricted by their "posting" system. Japanese teams have far greater control over player contracts than MLB teams. While domestic free agency usually comes a year sooner, players must have nine years of experience before they obtain international free agency. If a player wishes to play in the ML sooner than that, his team must agree to "post" him for free agency. Posting usually occurs in the penultimate year of the player's contract but can come sooner if the club agrees. Some teams are more willing to do that than others, usually those with financial problems. Unfortunately, since not all time spent on Injured Reserve counts towards free agency, some teams manipulate the system to delay the required service time. (For example, the SoftBank Hawks are notorious for manipulated the IR to delay the required service time towards free agency.)

The good news is that under the new posting system, a player now has 45 days from his posting to negotiate with all interested MLB teams, rather than be restricted to a single team with the highest posting bid. The Japanese team then receives a "release fee" from the MLB club based on a percentage of the total guaranteed value of the contract, usually around 15-20%. This release fee is received if and only if the player signs with a MLB team.

Korea

Baseball was probably introduced in Korean around 1900. Professional leagues developed long after they did in Japan, with the Korean Baseball Organization (KBO) being founded in 1981. The KBO currently has ten teams in one league with no divisions. While many solid players have come from Korea, their professional league is considered a rung lower than Japan, mostly because of less depth in players.

When comparing statistics, consider:

1. Stadiums were very hitter friendly. For example, Jung-ho Park had 40 HR the year before joining the Pirates, and just 15 in his first ML season. To address this issue, a "dejuiced" ball was introduced in 2019 which has decreased the number of home runs.
2. Starting with the 2024 season, KBO will use ABS (automated ball-strike system), aka "robot umps", along with a pitch clock.
3. Since there is just one League, the designated hitter rule is universal.
4. Again, there are much shorter travel times in a smaller country.
5. Like Japan, tie games are allowed.
6. The KBO also uses a "pre-tacked" baseball, like Japan.
7. Ejections are rare, as players and managers seldom argue with calls.
8. Korea also plays fewer games, currently 144 in a season.

The KBO has a very similar posting system to Japan, although a Korean team is allowed to post only one player per off-season while a Japanese team has no limits. However, the requisite experience time is "just" seven years.

China/Taiwan

As with other Asian countries, baseball was introduced long ago to China, possibly in the mid-nineteenth century. Professional baseball is in its infancy, although MLB signed an agreement with the Chinese Baseball Association (CBA) in 2019 to help with development. Baseball in Taiwan is more advanced, with the Chinese Professional Baseball League (CPBL) beginning play in 1990. The best players usually sign with a Japanese team but some players have played MLB ball. Coverage on the Chinese leagues will expand as their impact grows.

A list of Asian League players who could move to the majors appears in the Prospects section of the Forecaster beginning on page 237.

Other Diamonds

Age 26 Paradox

Age 26 is when a player begins to reach his peak skill, no matter what his address is. If circumstances have him celebrating that birthday in the majors, he is a breakout candidate. If circumstances have him celebrating that birthday in the minors, he is washed up.

A-Rod 10-Step Path to Stardom

Not all well-hyped prospects hit the ground running. More often they follow an alternative path:

1. Prospect puts up phenomenal minor league numbers.
2. The media machine gets oiled up.
3. Prospect gets called up, but struggles, Year 1.
4. Prospect gets demoted.
5. Prospect tears it up in the minors, Year 2.
6. Prospect gets called up, but struggles, Year 2.
7. Prospect gets demoted.
8. The media turns their backs. Fantasy leaguers reduce their expectations.
9. Prospect tears it up in the minors, Year 3. The public shrugs its collective shoulders.
10. Prospect is promoted in Year 3 and explodes. Some lucky fantasy leaguer lands a franchise player for under $5.

Jesús Luzardo is one current player who seems to have successfully ascended all 10 steps. Others currently stuck at one of the interim steps and may or may not ever reach Step 10 include Vidal Bruján, Jo Adell, and Carter Kieboom. Lewis Brinson was stuck in a step 6-7-8-9 loop for three years and exiled to a parallel universe – in Japan.

Bull Durham Gardening Tip

Late bloomers have fewer flowering seasons.

Developmental Dogmata

1. Defense is what gets a minor league prospect to the majors; offense is what keeps him there. *(Deric McKamey)*

2. Rapidly promoted minor leaguers often fail because they are never allowed to master the skill of "adjusting to the competition."
3. Rookies promoted in-season often perform better than those who make the club out of spring training. Inferior March competition can inflate the latter group's perceived talent level.
4. Young players rarely lose their inherent skills. Pitchers may uncover weaknesses and the players may have difficulty adjusting. These are bumps along the growth curve, but they do not reflect a loss of skill.
5. Late bloomers have smaller windows of opportunity and much less chance for forgiveness.
6. The greatest risk in this game is to pay for performance that a player has never achieved.

Quad-A Player

Some outwardly talented prospects simply have a ceiling that's spelled "A-A-A." They may be highly rated prospects—even minor league stars—but are never able to succeed in the majors. They have names like Scott Kingery, Franklin Barreto, Danny Hultzen, Andy Marte and Brandon Wood.

Rule 5 Reminder

Don't ignore the Rule 5 draft lest you ignore the possibility of players like Jose Bautista, Johan Santana, and Jayson Werth. All were Rule 5 draftees.

The following players were acquired in the first round of the Rule 5 Draft who became at least serviceable Major Leaguers:

Year	Players who eventually stuck
2014	Mark Canha, Delino Deshields, Odúbel Herrera
2015	Joey Rickard, Jake Cave, Ji-Man Choi
2016	Caleb Smith, Anthony Santander
2017	Nestor Cortes, Victor Reyes, Brad Keller, Elieser Hernandez
2018	Jordan Romano, Connor Joe
2020	Akil Baddoo, Garrett Whitlock, Tyler Wells
2022	Ryan Noda, Blake Sabol

Trout Inflation

The tendency for rookies to go for exorbitant draft prices following a year when there was a very good rookie crop.

Gaming

Standard Rules and Variations

Rotisserie Baseball was invented as an elegant confluence of baseball and economics. Whether by design or accident, the result has lasted for more than four decades. But what would Rotisserie and fantasy have been like if the Founding Fathers knew then what we know now about statistical analysis and game design? You can be sure things would be different.

The world has changed since the original game was introduced yet some leagues use the same rules today. New technologies have opened up opportunities to improve elements of the game that might have been limited by the capabilities of the 1980s. New analytical approaches have revealed areas where the original game falls short.

As such, there are good reasons to tinker and experiment; to find ways to enhance the experience.

Following are the basic elements of fantasy competition, those that provide opportunities for alternative rules and experimentation. This is by no means an exhaustive list, but at minimum provides some interesting food-for-thought.

Player pool

Standard: American League-only, National League-only or Mixed League.

AL/NL-only typically drafts 8-12 teams (pool penetration of 49% to 74%). Mixed leagues draft 10-18 teams (31% to 55% penetration), though 15 teams (46%) is a common number.

Drafting of reserve players will increase the penetration percentages. A 12-team AL/NL-only league adding six reserves onto 23-man rosters would draft 93% of the available pool of players on all teams' 25-man rosters.

The draft penetration level determines which fantasy management skills are most important to your league. The higher the penetration, the more important it is to draft a good team. The lower the penetration, the greater the availability of free agents and the more important in-season roster management becomes.

There is no generally-accepted optimal penetration level, but we have often suggested that 75% (including reserves) provides a good balance between the skills required for both draft prep and in-season management.

Alternative pools: There are many options here. Certain leagues draft from within a small group of major league divisions or teams. Some competitions, like home run leagues, only draft batters.

Positional structure

Standard: 23 players. One at each defensive position (though three outfielders may be from any of LF, CF or RF), plus one additional catcher, one middle infielder (2B or SS), one corner infielder (1B or 3B), two additional outfielders and a utility player/designated hitter (which often can be a batter who qualifies anywhere). Nine pitchers, typically holding any starting or relief role.

Open: 25 players. One at each defensive position (plus DH), 5-man starting rotation and two relief pitchers. Nine additional players at any position, which may be a part of the active roster or constitute a reserve list.

40-man: Standard 23 plus 17 reserves. Used in many keeper and dynasty leagues.

50-man: Standard 23 plus 27 reserves. Used in many draft-and-hold leagues.

Reapportioned: In recent years, new obstacles are being faced by 12-team AL/NL-only leagues thanks to changes in the real game. The 14/9 split between batters and pitchers no longer reflects how MLB teams structure their rosters. Of the 30 teams, each with 26-man rosters, not one contained 14 batters for any length of time.

For fantasy purposes in AL/NL-only leagues, that left a disproportionate draft penetration into the batter and pitcher pools. Assuming MLB teams rostering 13 batters and 13 pitchers:

	BATTERS	PITCHERS
On all MLB rosters	195	195
Players drafted	168	108
Pct.	86%	55%

These drafts are depleting 31% more batters out of the pool than pitchers. Add in those leagues with reserve lists—perhaps an additional six players per team removing another 72 players —and post-draft free agent pools are very thin, especially on the batting side.

The impact is less in 15-team mixed leagues, though the FA pitching pool is still disproportionately deep.

	BATTERS	PITCHERS
On all rosters	390	390
Drafted	210	135
Pct.	54%	35%

One solution is to reapportion the number of batters and pitchers that are rostered. Adding one pitcher slot and eliminating one batter slot may be enough to provide better balance. The batting slot most often removed is the second catcher, since it is the position with the least depth. However, that only serves to populate the free agent pool with a dozen or more worthless catchers.

Beginning in the 2012 season, the Tout Wars AL/NL-only experts leagues opted to eliminate one of the outfield slots and replace it with a "swingman" position. This position could be any batter or pitcher, depending upon the owner's needs at any given time during the season.

Selecting players

Standard: The three most prevalent methods for stocking fantasy rosters are:

Snake/Straight/Serpentine draft: Players are selected in order with seeds reversed in alternating rounds. This method has become the most popular due to its speed, ease of implementation and ease of automation.

In these drafts, the underlying assumption is that value can be ranked relative to a linear baseline. Pick #1 is better than pick #2, which is better than pick #3, and the difference between each pick is assumed to be somewhat equivalent. While a faulty assumption, we must believe in it to assume a level playing field.

Auction: Players are sold to the highest bidder from a fixed budget, typically $260. Auctions provide the team owner with more control over which players will be on his team but can take twice as long as snake drafts.

The baseline is $0 at the beginning of each player put up for bid. The final purchase price for each player is shaped by many wildly variable factors, from roster need to geographic location of the draft. A $30 player can mean different things to different drafters.

One option that can help reduce the time commitment of auctions is to force minimum bids at each hour mark. You could mandate $15 openers in hour #1; $10 openers in hour #2, etc. This removes some nominating strategy, however.

Pick-a-player / Salary cap: Players are assigned fixed dollar values and owners assemble their roster within a fixed cap. This type of roster-stocking is an individual exercise which results in teams typically having some of the same players.

In these leagues, "value assessment" is taken out of the hands of the owners. Each player has a fixed cost, pre-assigned based on past season performance and/or future expectation.

Stat categories

Standard: The standard statistical categories for Rotisserie leagues are:

4x4: HR, RBI, SB, BA, W, Sv, ERA, WHIP

5x5: HR, R, RBI, SB, BA, W, Sv, K, ERA, WHIP

6x6: Categories typically added are Holds and OPS.

7x7, etc.: Any number of categories may be added.

In general, the more categories you add, the more complicated it is to isolate individual performance and manage the categorical impact on your roster. There is also the danger of redundancy; with multiple categories measuring like stats, certain skills can get over-valued. For instance, home runs are double-counted when using the categories of both HR and slugging average. (Though note that HR are actually already triple-counted in standard 5x5—HR, runs, and RBI)

If the goal is to have categories that create a more encompassing picture of player performance, it is actually possible to accomplish more with less:

Modified 4x4: HR, (R+RBI-HR), SB, OBA, (W+QS), (Sv+Hld), K, ERA

This provides a better balance between batting and pitching in that each has three counting categories and one ratio category. In fact, the balance is shown to be even more notable here:

	BATTING	PITCHING
Pure skill counting stat	HR	K
Ratio category	OBA	ERA
Dependent upon managerial decision	SB	(Sv+Hold)
Dependent upon team support	(R+RBI-HR)	(W+QS)
Alternative or addition to team support:		
Usage/stamina/health	Plate app	Innings

Replacing saves: The problem with the Saves statistic is that we have a scarce commodity that is centered on a small group of players, thereby creating inflated demand for those players. With the high failure rate for closers, the incentive to pay full value for the commodity decreases. The higher the risk, the lower the prices.

We can increase the value of the commodity by reducing the risk. We might do this by increasing the number of players that contribute to that category, thereby spreading the risk around. One way we can accomplish this is by changing the category to Saves + Holds.

Holds are not perfect, but the typical argument about them being random and arbitrary can apply to saves as well. In fact, many of the pitchers who record holds are far more skilled and valuable than closers; they are often called to the mound in much higher leverage situations (a fact backed up by a scan of each pitcher's Leverage Index).

Neither stat is perfect, but together they form a reasonable proxy for overall bullpen performance.

In tandem, they effectively double the player pool of draftable relievers while also flattening the values allotted to those pitchers. The more players around which we spread the risk, the more control we have in managing our pitching staffs.

Replacing wins: Some have argued for replacing the Wins statistic with W + QS (quality starts). This method of scoring gives value to a starting pitcher who pitches well but fails to receive the win due to his team's poor offense or poor luck. However, with the decline in the average length of starts, the number of QS outings has dropped sharply. W+QS was a good idea a few years ago; less so now. A replacement stat gaining in popularity is Innings Pitched. Pitchers left on the mound for more innings are more likely to be helping your team, regardless of whether they are in line for a win or quality start.

Keeping score

Standard: These are the most common scoring methods:

Rotisserie: Players are evaluated in several statistical categories. Totals of these statistics are ranked by team. The winner is the team with the highest cumulative ranking.

Points: Players receive points for events that they contribute to in each game. Points are totaled for each team and teams are then ranked.

Head-to-Head (H2H): Using Rotisserie or points scoring, teams are scheduled in daily or weekly matchups. The winner of each matchup is the team that finishes higher in more categories (Rotisserie) or scores the most points.

Free agent acquisition

Standard: Three methods are the most common for acquiring free agent players during the season.

First come first served: Free agents are awarded to the first owner who claims them.

Reverse order of standings: Access to the free agent pool is typically in a snake draft fashion with the last place team getting the first pick, and each successive team higher in the standings picking afterwards.

Free agent budget (FAB): Teams are given a set budget at the beginning of the season (typically, $100 or $1000) from which they bid on free agents in a closed auction process.

Vickrey FAB: Research has shown that more than 50% of FAB dollars are lost via overbid on an annual basis. Given that this is a scarce commodity, a system to better manage these dollars might be desirable. The Vickrey system conducts a closed auction in the same way as standard FAB, but the price of the winning bid is set at the amount of the second highest bid, plus $1. In some cases, gross overbids (at least $10 over) are reduced to the second highest bid plus $5.

This method was designed by William Vickrey, a Professor of Economics at Columbia University. His theory was that this process reveals the true value of the commodity. For his work, Vickrey was awarded the Nobel Prize for Economics (and $1.2 million) in 1996.

The season

Standard: Leagues are played out during the course of the entire Major League Baseball season.

Split-season: Leagues are conducted from Opening Day through the All-Star break, then re-drafted to play from the All-Star break through the end of the season.

50-game split-season: Leagues are divided into three 50-game seasons with one-week break in between.

Monthly: Leagues are divided into six seasons or rolling four-week seasons.

The advantages of these shorter time frames:

- They can help to maintain interest. There would be fewer abandoned teams.
- There would be more shots at a title each year.
- Given that drafting is considered the most fun aspect of the game, these splits multiply the opportunities to participate in some type of draft. Leagues may choose to do complete re-drafts and treat the year as distinct mini-seasons. Or, leagues might allow teams to drop their five worst players and conduct a restocking draft at each break.

Daily games: Participants select a roster of players from one day's MLB schedule. Scoring is based on an aggregate points-based system rather than categories, with cash prizes awarded based on the day's results. The structure and distribution of that prize pool varies across different types of events, and those differences can affect roster construction strategies. Although scoring and prizes are based on one day's play, the season-long element of bankroll management provides a proxy for overall standings.

In terms of projecting outcomes, daily games are drastically different than full-season leagues. Playing time is one key element of any projection, and daily games offer near-100% accuracy in projecting playing time: you can check pre-game lineups to see exactly which players are in the lineup that night. The other key component of any projection is performance, but that is plagued by variance in daily competitions. Even if you roster a team full of the most advantageous matchups, the best hitters can still go 0-for-4 on a given night.

Draft Process

Draft-day cheat sheet *(Patrick Davitt)*

1. Know what players are available, right to the bottom of the pool.
2. Know what every player is worth in your league format.

3. Know why you think each player is worth what you think he's worth.
4. Identify players you believe you value differently from the other owners.
5. Know each player's risks.
6. Know your opponents' patterns.
7. For sure, know the league rules and its history, and what it takes to win.

Draft preparation with a full-season mindset *(Matt Dodge)*

Each of the dimensions of your league setup—player pool, reserve list depth; type and frequency of transactions, scoring categories, etc.—should impact your draft day plan. But it may also be helpful to look at them in combination.

Sources of additional stats after draft day

League Player Pool

Reserve List	Mixed 15 team	AL- or NL-only 12 team
Short	free agents	trades, free agents
Long	free agents, trades	trades

Review the prior season's transactions for your league and analyze the successful teams' category contributions from trade acquisitions and free agent pickups. Trades are often necessary to add specific stats in AL/NL-only leagues as the player pool penetration is generally much deeper, and the size of a reserve roster further reduces the help possible from the free agent pool.

Draft strategies related to in-season player acquisition

Trade Activity

FA Pool	Low	High
Shallow	solid foundation (STR)	tradable commodoties surplus counting stats
Deep	gamble on upside (S&S)	ultimate flexibility

Trading activity is a function of multiple factors. Keeper leagues provide opportunities for owners to contend this year or play for next year. However, those increased opportunities are often controlled by rules to prevent "dump trading." Stratification of the standings in redraft leagues can cause lower ranked owners to lose interest, reducing the number of effective trading partners as the season goes on.

When deep rosters create a shallow free agent pool in a league with little trading, draft day success becomes paramount. In this case, a Spread the Risk strategy designed to accumulate at bats, innings, and saves is recommended. If the free agent pool is deep, the drafter can take more risks with a Stars and Scrubs approach, acquiring "lottery ticket" players with upside, knowing that replacements are readily available if the upside plays don't hit.

In leagues where trading is prevalent, a shallow free agent pool means you should acquire players on draft day with the intent of trading them. This could mean acquiring a category surplus (frequently saves and/or steals), and then trading it in-season to shore up other categories. In a keeper league, this includes grabbing a few bargains (to interest rebuilding teams) or grabbing top performers to flip in trade (if you are on "the two year plan").

Draft Day Considerations for In-season Roster Management

Reserve List Txn Freq	4 x 4 League Format	5 x 5 League Format
Daily	careful SP management batting platoons positional flexibility	RP (K, ERA, WHIP) batting platoons positional flexibility
Weekly	SP (2 start weeks) cover risky starters	SP (2 start weeks) cover risky starters

Owners must be careful with pitching, due to the negative impact potential of ERA and WHIP. Blindly streaming pitchers on a daily basis can be counter-productive, particularly in 4x4 leagues. In 5x5, the Strikeouts category can make a foundation of high Dom relievers a useful source of mitigation for the invariable starting pitching disappointments.

The degree to which these recommendations can be implemented is also dependent on the depth of the reserve list. Those with more reserves can do more than those with fewer, obviously, but the key is deciding up front how you plan to use your reserves, and then tailoring your draft strategy toward that usage.

The value of mock drafts *(Todd Zola)*

Most assume the purpose of a mock draft is to get to know the market value of the player pool. But even more important, mock drafting is general preparation for the environment and process, thereby allowing the drafter to completely focus on the draft when it counts. Mock drafting is more about fine-tuning your strategy than player value. Here are some tips to maximize your mock drafting experience.

1. Make sure you can seamlessly use an on-line drafting room, draft software or your own lists to track your draft or auction. The less time you spend looking, adding and adjusting names, the more time you can spend on thinking about what player is best for your team. This also gives you the opportunity to make sure your draft lists are complete and assures all the players are listed at the correct position(s).

2. Alter the draft slots of your mocks. The flow of each mock will be different, but if you do a few mocks with an early initial pick, a few in the middle and a few with a late first pick, you may learn you prefer one of the spots more than the others. If you're in a league where you can choose your draft spot, this helps you decide where to select. Once you know your spot, a few mocks from that spot will help you decide how to deal with positional runs.

3. Use non-typical strategies and consider players you rarely target. We all have our favorite players. Intentionally passing on those players not only gives you an idea when others may draft them but it also forces you to research players you normally don't consider. The more players you have researched, the more prepared you'll be for the events that occur during your real draft.

Snake Drafting

Snake draft first round history

The following tables compare pre-season projected player rankings (using Average Draft Position data from Mock Draft Central and National Fantasy Baseball Championship) and actual end-of-season results. The 18-year success rate of identifying each season's top talent is only 33.7%. Even if we extend the study to the top two rounds, the hit rate is only around 50%.

2016	ADP	ACTUAL = 7	
1	Mike Trout	1	Mookie Betts
2	Paul Goldschmidt	2	Jose Altuve (11)
3	Bryce Harper	3	Mike Trout (1)
4	Clayton Kershaw	4	Jonathan Villar
5	Josh Donaldson	5	Jean Segura
6	Carlos Correa	6	Max Scherzer (15)
7	Nolan Arenado	7	Paul Goldschmidt (2)
8	Manny Machado	8	Charlie Blackmon
9	Anthony Rizzo	9	Clayton Kershaw (4)
10	Giancarlo Stanton	10	Nolan Arenado (7)
11	Jose Altuve	11	Daniel Murphy
12	Kris Bryant	12	Kris Bryant (12)
13	Miguel Cabrera	13	Joey Votto
14	Andrew McCutchen	14	Jon Lester
15	Max Scherzer	15	Madison Bumgarner

2017	ADP	ACTUAL = 5	
1	Mike Trout	1	Charlie Blackmon
2	Mookie Betts	2	Jose Altuve (4)
3	Clayton Kershaw	3	Corey Kluber
4	Jose Altuve	4	Max Scherzer (12)
5	Kris Bryant	5	Paul Goldschmidt (7)
6	Nolan Arenado	6	Giancarlo Stanton
7	Paul Goldschmidt	7	Chris Sale
8	Manny Machado	8	Aaron Judge
9	Bryce Harper	9	Dee Gordon
10	Trea Turner	10	Clayton Kershaw (3)
11	Josh Donaldson	11	Nolan Arenado (6)
12	Max Scherzer	12	Jose Ramirez
13	Anthony Rizzo	13	Joey Votto
14	Madison Bumgarner	14	Marcell Ozuna
15	Carlos Correa	15	Elvis Andrus

2018	ADP	ACTUAL = 3*	
1	Mike Trout	1	Mookie Betts (7)
2	Jose Altuve	2	Christian Yelich
3	Nolan Arenado	3	J.D. Martinez
4	Trea Turner	4	Max Scherzer (11)
5	Clayton Kershaw	5	Jacob deGrom
6	Paul Goldschmidt	6	Jose Ramirez
7	Mookie Betts	7	Francisco Lindor
8	Giancarlo Stanton	8	Trevor Story
9	Charlie Blackmon	9	Justin Verlander
10	Bryce Harper	10	Mike Trout (1)
11	Max Scherzer	11	Blake Snell
12	Chris Sale	12	Javier Baez
13	Corey Kluber	13	Whit Merrifield
14	Carlos Correa	14	Aaron Nola
15	Kris Bryant	15	Manny Machado

**2018 represents the lowest first round hit rate in 15 years. However, the next four players on the list would be: 16) Trea Turner (4); 17) Chris Sale (12); 18) Nolan Arenado (3); 19) Corey Kluber (13)*

2019	ADP	ACTUAL = 4	
1	Mike Trout	1	Justin Verlander
2	Mookie Betts	2	Gerrit Cole
3	Jose Ramirez	3	Christian Yelich (6)
4	Max Scherzer	4	Ronald Acuna (8)
5	J.D. Martinez	5	Cody Bellinger
6	Christian Yelich	6	Rafael Devers
7	Nolan Arenado	7	Anthony Rendon
8	Ronald Acuna	8	Jacob deGrom (10)
9	Trea Turner	9	Jonathan Villar
10	Jacob deGrom	10	Trevor Story
11	Alex Bregman	11	Nolan Arenado (7)
12	Chris Sale	12	Ketel Marte
13	Francisco Lindor	13	D.J. LeMahieu
14	Aaron Judge	14	Zack Greinke
15	Jose Altuve	15	Xander Bogaerts

Similar to 2018, the next players on the 2019 list would be: 16) Alex Bregman (11); 17) Mookie Betts (2); 18) Mike Trout (1); 19) Trea Turner (9)

2020	ADP	ACTUAL = 5	
1	Ronald Acuna	1	Shane Bieber
2	Christian Yelich	2	Trea Turner (8)
3	Cody Bellinger	3	Fernando Tatis, Jr.
4	Gerrit Cole	4	Jose Ramirez (11)
5	Mookie Betts	5	Trevor Bauer
6	Mike Trout	6	Mookie Betts (5)
7	Francisco Lindor	7	Freddie Freeman
8	Trea Turner	8	Jose Abreu
9	Jacob deGrom	9	Manny Machado
10	Trevor Story	10	Marcell Ozuna
11	Jose Ramirez	11	Yu Darvish
12	Juan Soto	12	Trevor Story (10)
13	Justin Verlander	13	Adalberto Mondesi
14	Nolan Arenado	14	Juan Soto (12)
15	Max Scherzer	15	Kenta Maeda

2021	ADP	ACTUAL = 3	
1	Ronald Acuna	1	Trea Turner (8)
2	Fernando Tatis, Jr.	2	Shohei Ohtani*
3	Juan Soto	3	Bo Bichette
4	Mookie Betts	4	Vladimir Guerrero, Jr.
5	Jacob deGrom	5	Starling Marte
6	Mike Trout	6	Max Scherzer
7	Gerrit Cole	7	Fernando Tatis, Jr. (2)
8	Trea Turner	8	Jose Ramirez (10)
9	Shane Bieber	9	Walker Buehler
10	Jose Ramirez	10	Cedric Mullins III
11	Christian Yelich	11	Marcus Semien
12	Trevor Story	12	Whit Merrifield
13	Freddie Freeman	13	Teoscar Hernandez
14	Trevor Bauer	14	Bryce Harper
15	Cody Bellinger	15	Zack Wheeler

** Includes earnings as both hitter and pitcher. Ohtani ranked 9th overall on his hitting stats alone.*

2022	ADP	ACTUAL = 3	
1	Trea Turner	1	Aaron Judge
2	Jose Ramirez	2	Shohei Ohtani (7)*
3	Juan Soto	3	Freddie Freeman
4	Vladimir Guerrero, Jr.	4	Paul Goldschmidt
5	Bo Bichette	5	Trea Turner (1)
6	Gerrit Cole	6	Jose Ramirez (2)
7	Shohei Ohtani	7	Justin Verlander
8	Bryce Harper	8	Manny Machado
9	Corbin Burnes	9	Pete Alonso
10	Kyle Tucker	10	Dansby Swanson
11	Mike Trout	11	Francisco Lindor
12	Rafael Devers	12	Julio Rodriguez
13	Ronald Acuna	13	Jose Altuve
14	Mookie Betts	14	Sandy Alcantara
15	Luis Robert	15	Yordan Alvarez

** Includes earnings as both hitter and pitcher. Ohtani ranked outside the top 15 on his hitting or pitching stats alone. So if you are in a league where you can only use Ohtani as batter or pitcher in any given week, he drops out of the ranking here. In that case, move up the players ranked 3-15 and add Mookie Betts (14) at No. 15.*

2023	ADP	ACTUAL = 6	
1	Ronald Acuna	1	Ronald Acuna (1)
2	Aaron Judge	2	Shohei Ohtani (7)*
3	Trea Turner	3	Freddie Freeman (13)
4	Jose Ramirez	4	Gerrit Cole
5	Julio Rodriguez	5	Mookie Betts (9)
6	Kyle Tucker	6	Matt Olson
7	Shohei Ohtani	7	Corbin Carroll
8	Bobby Witt	8	Bobby Witt, Jr.
9	Mookie Betts	9	Julio Rodriguez (5)
10	Vlad Guerrero, Jr.	10	Kyle Tucker (6)
11	Juan Soto	11	Blake Snell
12	Yordan Alvarez	12	Cody Bellinger
13	Freddie Freeman	13	Marcus Semien
14	Manny Machado	14	Corey Seager
15	Bo Bichette	15	Francisco Lindor

** Includes earnings as both hitter and pitcher. Ohtani ranked 8th overall on his hitting stats alone.*

ADP attrition

Why is our success rate so low in identifying what should be the most easy-to-project players each year? We rank and draft players based on the expectation that those ranked higher will return greater value in terms of productivity and playing time, as well as being the safest investments. However, there are many variables affecting where players finish.

Earlier, it was shown that players spend an inordinate number of days on the injured list. In fact, of the players projected to finish in the top 300, the number who were placed on the injury list, demoted or designated for assignment has been extreme:

Year	Pct. of top-ranked 300 players who lost PT
2013	51%
2014	53%
2015	47%
2016	47%
2017	58%
2018	60%
2019	59%
2020*	43%
2021	71%
2022	59%
2023	54%

**In 60 games.*

Considering that well over half of each season's very best players had fewer at-bats or innings pitched than we projected, it shows how tough it is to rank players each year.

The Ineptitude of ADPs

What is our true aptitude in accurately ranking players each year? It's very, very bad. Using the ADPs from a 15-team mixed league (2018 and 2019), we looked at each player, round by round and tagged each one:

- PROFIT: Turned a profit on the round he was drafted in
- PAR: Earned back the exact value of the round he was drafted in
- LOSS: Took a 1-3 round loss on his draft round
- BUST: Took a 4-plus round loss on his draft round
- DISASTER: Returned earnings outside the top 750 players, essentially undraftable in a league with 50-man rosters. Disasters are subsets of Busts.

2018

Rds	Profit	Par	Loss	Bust	Dis
1-5	21%	8%	27%	44%	4%
6-10	24%	7%	24%	45%	4%
11-15	27%	3%	9%	61%	27%
16-20	37%	1%	8%	53%	25%
21-25	41%	1%	4%	53%	21%
26-30	40%	0%	0%	60%	35%
31-35	15%	0%	0%	85%	76%
36-40	15%	1%	0%	84%	79%
41-45	19%	3%	1%	77%	76%
46-50	28%	0%	3%	69%	68%

2019

Rds	Profit	Par	Loss	Bust	Dis
1-5	20%	13%	21%	45%	4%
6-10	28%	8%	12%	52%	5%
11-15	35%	0%	5%	60%	15%
16-20	31%	3%	7%	60%	27%
21-25	37%	3%	4%	56%	39%
26-30	39%	4%	7%	51%	33%
31-35	35%	0%	1%	64%	49%
36-40	32%	0%	3%	65%	55%
41-45	37%	0%	3%	60%	57%
46-50	33%	0%	3%	64%	64%

For starters, there is no such thing as "Player-X is a Y-rounder." We had virtually no ability to identify exactly where a player should be drafted. Over the first five rounds, we got about 90 percent of them wrong and nearly half our picks were full-out busts. Over the rest of the draft, the right answers were blind dart throws.

Our percentage of profitable picks increased as we progressed through the active draft rounds. However, much of that is just probability; the deeper into a draft, the more room for picks to finish higher. In most cases the draft round was random. Rounds 21-30 were the sweet spot for profitable picks. We fared best after the active part of the draft was mostly over.

2018

Rds	Profit	Par	Loss	Bust	Dis
1-23	30%	4%	16%	50%	15%
24-50	24%	1%	1%	75%	64%

2019

Rds	Profit	Par	Loss	Bust	Dis
1-23	30%	5%	10%	55%	16%
24-50	35%	1%	3%	60%	51%

In the active roster draft, a third of our picks performed at par or better; two thirds performed worse than where we drafted them. Fully half of them could have been considered busts. In other words, *every player we drafted had, at best, only a one-in-three chance of being a good pick.*

Ignore ADP (mostly) *(Matt Cederholm)*

Using ADP as a draft tool will usually lead to suboptimal outcomes. Why is ADP bad? Anchoring. Anchoring is a cognitive bias where our estimate of a quantity is tied to previous or known estimates.

It begins right after the season ends, as early drafts begin for the next season. Those early drafts, done with highly imperfect information, inform the drafts that follow, and it eventually rolls up into the spring drafts. Early ADPs anchor future drafts, despite the ever-shifting landscape of information and analysis. Aside from catastrophic news, ADPs tend to change slowly.

In general, you should ignore ADPs and pick the best players, based on your research and rankings. Make sure that your rankings are rational—don't take someone early because you think "this is the year." But if you're sure the value is there, the ADP shouldn't matter.

Here's a good rule of thumb, though it's a very loose heuristic. In general, only be concerned with ADP if you're torn between two or more players or if the ADP is more than double the draft slot you're picking from. That widens your band as the draft progresses.

Importance of the early rounds *(Bill Macey)*

It's long been said that you can't win your league in the first round, but you can lose it there. An analysis of data from actual drafts reveals that this holds true—those who spend an early round pick on a player that severely under-performs expectations rarely win their league and seldom even finish in the top 3.

At the same time, drafting a player in the first round that returns first-round value is no guarantee of success. In fact, those that draft some of the best values still only win their league about a quarter of the time and finish in the top 3 less than half the time. Research also shows that drafting pitchers in the first round is a risky proposition. Even if the pitchers deliver first-round value, the opportunity cost of passing up on an elite batter makes you less likely to win your league.

Benefits of structured snake drafting *(Dan Marcus)*

We analyzed NFBC data from 2018-2022, excluding 2020, to determine whether there's an advantage to any one particular draft strategy in the first five rounds. Some highlights:

- The most common league-winning build was two starting pitchers in the first five rounds. Such an approach has accounted for 41% and 45% of league winners in 12-team and 15-team leagues, respectively.
- In 15-team leagues, 41% of league winners have drafted a starting pitcher in the first round. This number dropped to 28% in 12-team leagues.
- Selecting an early closer appears to be effective—50% of 15-team winners took one in the first five rounds in 2022—while two early closers is unpopular and perhaps ineffective.

The Impact of the draft on final statistics *(Todd Zola)*

Which has more impact on your team's final standings—your draft or in-season roster management? The standings correlation based on draft-to-final results ranges from 0.42 to 0.94, with the mean around 0.73. The top hitting counting stat drafted is home runs; the fewest is stolen bases. The top pitching counting stat drafted is saves; the fewest is wins. More hitting is acquired at the draft or auction than pitching. The in-season influx of stats is greatest in mixed leagues, suggesting that owners should practice patience with in-season free agents in AL/NL formats while being cautiously aggressive in mixed formats.

Top teams almost always improve ratio categories from their drafted rosters, despite available free agents sporting poorer aggregate ratios. This is most applicable to improving your pitching staff as the year progresses, but it's easier said than done.

Being top-three in saves is far more important in mixed leagues than in AL/NL. Most mixed champions draft the majority of saves while AL/NL winners often acquire saves in season.

What is the best seed to draft from?

Most drafters like mid-round so they never have to wait too long for their next player. Some like the swing pick, suggesting that getting two players at 15 and 16 is better than a 1 and a 30. Many drafters assume that the swing pick means you'd be getting something like two $30 players instead of a $40 and $20.

Equivalent auction dollar values reveal the following facts about the first two snake draft rounds:

In an AL/NL-only league, the top seed would get a $44 player (at #1) and a $24 player (at #24) for a total of $68; the 12th seed would get two $29s (at #12 and #13) for $58.

In a mixed league, the top seed would get a $47 and a $24 ($71); the 15th seed would get two $28s ($56).

Since the talent level flattens out after the 2nd round, low seeds never get a chance to catch up:

$ difference between first player/last player selected

Round	12-team	15-team
1	$15	$19
2	$7	$8
3	$5	$4
4	$3	$3
5	$2	$2
6	$2	$1
7-17	$1	$1
18-23	$0	$0

The total value each seed accumulates at the end of the draft is hardly equitable:

Seed	Mixed	AL/NL-only
1	$266	$273
2	$264	$269
3	$263	$261
4	$262	$262
5	$259	$260
6	$261	$260
7	$260	$260
8	$261	$260
9	$261	$258
10	$257	$260
11	$257	$257
12	$258	$257
13	$254	
14	$255	
15	$256	

The counter-argument to this focuses on whether we can reasonably expect "accurate projections" at the top of the draft. Given the snake draft first round history, a case could be made that any seed might potentially do well. In fact, an argument can be made that the last seed is the best spot because it essentially provides two picks from the top 13 players (in a 12-team league) during the part of the draft with the steepest talent decline.

Using ADPs to determine when to select players *(Bill Macey)*

Although average draft position (ADP) data provides a good idea of where in the draft each player is selected, it can be misleading when trying to determine how early to target a player. This chart summarizes the percentage of players drafted within 15 picks of his ADP as well as the average standard deviation by grouping of players.

ADP Rank	% within 15 picks	Standard Deviation
1-25	100%	2.5
26-50	97%	6.1
51-100	87%	9.6
100-150	72%	14.0
150-200	61%	17.4
200-250	53%	20.9

As the draft progresses, the picks for each player become more widely dispersed and less clustered around the average. Most top 100 players will go within one round of their ADP-converted round. However, as you reach the mid-to-late rounds, there is much more uncertainty as to when a player will be selected. Pitchers have slightly smaller standard deviations than do batters (i.e. they tend to be drafted in a narrower range). This suggests that drafters may be more likely to reach for a batter than for a pitcher.

Using the ADP and corresponding standard deviation, we can estimate the likelihood that a given player will be available at a certain draft pick. We estimate the predicted standard deviation for each player as follows:

Stdev = -0.42 + 0.42*(ADP - Earliest Pick)

(That the figure 0.42 appears twice is pure coincidence; the numbers are not equal past two decimal points.)

If we assume that the picks are normally distributed, we can use a player's ADP and estimated standard deviation to estimate the likelihood that the player is available with a certain pick (MS Excel formula):

=1-normdist(x,ADP,Standard Deviation,True)

where «x» represents the pick number to be evaluated.

We can use this information to prepare for a snake draft by determining how early we may need to reach to roster a player. Suppose you had the 8th pick in a 15-team league draft and your target was a player with an ADP of 128.9 and an earliest selection at pick 94. This would yield an estimated standard deviation of 14.2. You could have then entered these values into the formula above to estimate the likelihood that this player was still available at each of the following picks:

Pick	Likelihood Available
83	100%
98	99%
113	87%
128	53%
143	16%
158	2%

ADPs and scarcity *(Bill Macey)*

Most players are selected within a round or two of their ADP with tight clustering around the average. But every draft is unique and every pick in the draft seemingly affects the ordering of subsequent picks. In fact, deviations from "expected" sequences can sometimes start a chain reaction at that position. This is most often seen in runs at scarce positions such as the closer; once the first one goes, the next seems sure to closely follow.

Research also suggests that within each position, there is a correlation within tiers of players. The sooner players within a generally accepted tier are selected, the sooner other players within the same tier will be taken. However, once that tier is exhausted, draft order reverts to normal.

How can we use this information? If you notice a reach pick, you can expect that other drafters may follow suit. If your draft plan is to get a similar player within that tier, you'll need to adjust your picks accordingly.

Mapping ADPs to auction value *(Bill Macey)*

Reliable average auction values (AAV) are often tougher to come by than ADP data for snake drafts. However, we can estimate predicted auction prices as a function of ADP, arriving at the following equation:

$$y = -9.8\ln(x) + 57.8$$

where ln(x) is the natural log function, x represents the actual ADP, and y represents the predicted AAV.

This equation does an excellent job estimating auction prices (r2=0.93), though deviations are unavoidable. The asymptotic nature of the logarithmic function, however, causes the model to predict overly high prices for the top players. So be aware of that and adjust.

Auction Value Analysis

Auction values (R$) in perspective

R$ is the dollar value placed on a player's statistical performance in a Rotisserie league, and designed to measure the impact that player has on the standings.

There are two primary methods to calculate a player's value from his projected (or actual) statistics.

Standings Gain Points: First described in the book, *How to Value Players for Rotisserie Baseball*, by Art McGee. SGP converts a player's statistics in each Rotisserie category into the number of points those stats will allow you to gain in the standings. These are then converted back into dollars.

Percentage Valuation Method: In PVM, a least valuable, or replacement performance level is set for each category (in a given league size) and then values are calculated representing the incremental improvement from that base. A player is then awarded value in direct proportion to the level he contributes to each category. This process is often accomplished with the use of z-scores.

As much as these methods serve to attach a firm number to projected performance, the winning bid for any player is still highly variable depending upon many factors:

- the salary cap limit
- the number of teams in the league
- each team's roster size
- the impact of any protected players
- each team's positional demands at the time of bidding

- the statistical category demands at the time of bidding
- external factors, e.g. media inflation or deflation of value

In other words, a $30 player is only a $30 player if someone in your draft pays $30 for him.

Roster slot valuation *(John Burnson)*

When you draft a player, what have you bought?

"You have bought the stats generated by this player."

No. You have bought the stats generated by his slot. Initially, the drafted player fills the slot, but he need not fill the slot for the season, and he need not contribute from Day One. If you trade the player during the season, then your bid on Draft Day paid for the stats of the original player plus the stats of the new player. If the player misses time due to injury or demotion, then you bought the stats of whoever fills the time while the drafted player is missing. At season's end, there will be more players providing positive value than there are roster slots.

Before the season, the number of players projected for positive value must equal the total number of roster slots. However, the projected productivity should be adjusted by the potential to capture extra value in the slot. This is especially important for injury-rehab cases and late-season call-ups. For example, if we think that a player will miss half the season, then we would augment his projected stats with a half-year of stats from a replacement-level player at his position. Only then would we calculate prices. Essentially, we want to apportion $260 per team among the slots, not the players.

Average player value by draft round

Rd	AL/NL	Mxd
1	$34	$34
2	$26	$26
3	$23	$23
4	$20	$20
5	$18	$18
6	$17	$16
7	$16	$15
8	$15	$13
9	$13	$12
10	$12	$11
11	$11	$10
12	$10	$9
13	$9	$8
14	$8	$8
15	$7	$7
16	$6	$6
17	$5	$5
18	$4	$4
19	$3	$3
20	$2	$2
21	$1	$2
22	$1	$1
23	$1	$1

Benchmarks for auction players:

- All $30 players will go in the first round.
- All $20-plus players will go in the first four rounds.
- Double-digit value ends pretty much after Round 11.
- The $1 end game starts at about Round 21.

How likely is it that a $30 player will repeat? *(Matt Cederholm)*

From 2003-2008, 205 players earned $30 or more (using single-league 5x5 values). Only 70 of them (34%) earned $30 or more in the next season.

In fact, the odds of repeating a $30 season aren't good. As seen below, the best odds during that period were 42%. And as we would expect, pitchers fare far worse than hitters.

	Total>$30	# Repeat	% Repeat
Hitters	167	64	38%
Pitchers	38	6	16%
Total	205	70	34%
*High-Reliability**			
Hitters	42	16	38%
Pitchers	7	0	0%
Total	49	16	33%
100+ BPV			
Hitters	60	25	42%
Pitchers	31	6	19%
Total	91	31	19%
*High-Reliability and 100+ BPV**			
Hitters	12	5	42%
Pitchers	6	0	0%
Total	18	5	28%

**Reliability figures are from 2006-2008*

For players with multiple seasons of $30 or more, the numbers get better. Players with consecutive $30 seasons, 2003-2008:

	Total>$30	# Repeat	% Repeat
Two Years	62	29	55%
Three+ Years	29	19	66%

Still, a player with two consecutive seasons at $30 in value is barely a 50/50 proposition. And three consecutive seasons is only a 2/3 shot. Small sample sizes aside, this does illustrate the nature of the beast. Even the most consistent, reliable players fail 1/3 of the time. Of course, this is true whether they are kept or drafted anew, so this alone shouldn't prevent you from keeping a player.

Dollar values: expected projective accuracy

There is a 65% chance that a player projected for a certain dollar value will finish the season with a value within plus-or-minus $5 of that projection. Therefore, if you value a player at $25, you only have about a 2-in-3 shot of him finishing between $20 and $30.

If you want to raise your odds to 80%, the range becomes +/- $9, so your $25 player can finish anywhere between $16 and $34.

How well do elite pitchers retain their value? *(Michael Weddell)*

An elite pitcher (one who earns at least $24 in a season) on average keeps 80% of his R$ value from year 1 to year 2. This compares to the baseline case of only 52%.

Historically, 36% of elite pitchers improve, returning a greater R$ in the second year than they did the first year. That is an impressive performance considering they already were at an elite level. 17% collapse, returning less than a third of their R$ in the second year. The remaining 47% experience a middling outcome, keeping more than a third but less than all of their R$ from one year to the next.

Valuing closers

Given the high risk associated with the closer's role, it is difficult to determine a fair draft value. Typically, those who have successfully held the role for several seasons will earn the highest draft price, but valuing less stable commodities is troublesome.

A rough rule of thumb is to start by paying $10 for the role alone. Any pitcher tagged the closer on draft day should merit at least $10. Those without a firm appointment may start at less than $10. Then add anywhere from $0 to $15 for support skills.

In this way, the top level talents will draw upwards of $20-$25. Those with moderate skill will draw $15-$20, and those with more questionable skill in the $10-$15 range.

Realistic expectations of $1 end-gamers *(Patrick Davitt)*

Many fantasy articles insist AL- or NL-only (mono) leagues are won or lost with $1 batters, because "that's where the profits are." But are they?

A 2011 analysis showed that when considering $1 players in deep mono leagues, managing $1 end-gamers should be more about minimizing losses than fishing for profit. In the cohort of batters projected $0 to -$5, 82% returned losses, based on a $1 bid. Two-thirds of the projected $1 cohort returned losses. In addition, when considering $1 players, speculate on speed.

Advanced Drafting Concepts

Stars & Scrubs v. Spread the Risk

Stars & Scrubs (S&S): A Rotisserie auction strategy in which a roster is anchored by a core of high priced stars and the remaining positions filled with low-cost players.

Spread the Risk (STR): An auction strategy in which available dollars are spread evenly among all roster slots.

Both approaches have benefits and risks. An experiment was conducted in 2004 whereby a league was stocked with four teams assembled as S&S, four as STR and four as a control group. Rosters were then frozen for the season.

The Stars & Scrubs teams won all three ratio categories. Those deep investments ensured stability in the categories that are typically most difficult to manage. On the batting side, however, S&S teams amassed the least amount of playing time, which in turn led to bottom-rung finishes in HR, RBI and Runs.

One of the arguments for the S&S approach is that it is easier to replace end-game losers (which, in turn, may help resolve the playing time issues). Not only is this true, but the results of this experiment show that replacing those bottom players is critical to success.

The Spread the Risk teams stockpiled playing time, which led to strong finishes in many counting stats, including clear victories in RBI, wins and strikeouts. This is a key tenet in drafting philosophy; we often say that the team that compiles the most AB will be among the top teams in RBI and Runs.

The danger is on the pitching side. More innings did yield more wins and Ks, but also destroyed ERA/WHIP.

So, what approach makes the most sense? **The optimal strategy might be to STR on offense and go S&S with your pitching staff.** STR buys more AB, so you immediately position yourself well in four of the five batting categories. On pitching, it might be more advisable to roster a few core arms, though that immediately elevates your risk exposure. Admittedly, it's a balancing act, which is why we need to pay more attention to risk analysis.

The LIMA Plan

The LIMA Plan is a strategy for Rotisserie leagues (though the underlying concept can be used in other formats) that allows you to target high skills pitchers at very low cost, thereby freeing up dollars for offense. LIMA is an acronym for Low Investment Mound Aces, and also pays tribute to Jose Lima, a $1 pitcher whose $24 breakout in 1998 breakout exemplified the power of the strategy. In a $260 league:

1. Budget a maximum of $60 for your pitching staff.
2. Allot no more than $30 of that budget for acquiring saves.
3. Ignore ERA. Draft only pitchers with:
   - Strikeout rate of 25% or greater.
   - Walk rate of less than 10%.
   - Home run rate of less than 3.5% (which correlates roughly to a HR/9 rate of 1.3).
4. Draft as few innings as your league rules will allow. This is intended to manage risk. For some game formats, this should be a secondary consideration.
5. Maximize your batting slots. Spend $200 on batters who have:
   - Contact rate of at least 80%
   - Walk rate of at least 10%
   - PX or Spd level of at least 100

Spend no more than $29 for any player and try to keep the $1 picks to a minimum.

The goal is to ace the batting categories and carefully pick your pitching staff so that it will finish in the upper third in ERA, WHIP and saves (and Ks in 5x5), and an upside of perhaps 9th in wins. In a competitive league, that should be enough to win, and definitely enough to finish in the money. Worst case, you should have an excess of offense available that you can deal for pitching.

The strategy works because it better allocates resources. Fantasy leaguers who spend a lot for pitching are not only paying for expected performance, they are also paying for better defined roles—#1 and #2 rotation starters, ace closers, etc.—which are expected to translate into more IP, wins and saves. But roles are highly variable. A pitcher's role will usually come down to his skill and performance; if he doesn't perform, he'll lose the role.

The LIMA Plan says, let's invest in skill and let the roles fall where they may. In the long run, better skills should translate into more innings, wins and saves. And as it turns out, pitching skill costs less than pitching roles do.

In *snake draft leagues,* you may be able to delay drafting starting pitchers until Round 6, 7 or 8. In *shallow mixed leagues,* the LIMA Plan may not be necessary; just focus on the support metrics. In *simulation leagues,* build your staff around those metrics.

Variations on the LIMA Plan

LIMA Extrema: Limit your total pitching budget to only $30, or less. This can be particularly effective in shallow leagues where

LIMA-caliber starting pitcher free agents are plentiful during the season.

SANTANA Plan: Instead of spending $30 on saves, you spend it on a starting pitcher anchor. In 5x5 leagues, allocating those dollars to a high-end LIMA-caliber starting pitcher can work well as long as you pick the right anchor and can acquire saves during the season.

Total Control Drafting (TCD)

On Draft Day, we make every effort to control as many elements as possible. In reality, the players that end up on our teams are largely controlled by the other owners. Their bidding affects your ability to roster the players you want. In a snake draft, the other owners control your roster even more. We are only able to get the players we want within the limitations set by others.

However, an optimal roster can be constructed from a fanalytic assessment of skill and risk combined with more assertive draft day demeanor.

Why this makes sense

1. Our obsession with projected player values is holding us back. If a player on your draft list is valued at $20 and you agonize when the bidding hits $23, odds are about two chances in three that he could really earn anywhere from $15 to $25. What this means is, in some cases, and within reason, you should just pay what it takes to get the players you want.

2. There is no such thing as a bargain. Most of us *don't* just pay what it takes because we are always on the lookout for players who go under value. But we really don't know which players will cost less than they will earn because prices are still driven by the draft table. The concept of "bargain" assumes that we even know what a player's true value is.

3. "Control" is there for the taking. Most owners are so focused on their own team that they really don't pay much attention to what you're doing. There are some exceptions, and bidding wars do happen, but in general, other owners will not provide that much resistance.

How it's done

1. Create your optimal draft pool.

2. Get those players.

Start by identifying which players will be draftable based on the LIMA or Mayberry criteria. Then, at the draft, focus solely on your roster. When it's your bid opener, toss a player you need at about 50%-75% of your projected value. Bid aggressively and just pay what you need to pay. Of course, don't spend $40 for a player with $25 market value, but it's okay to exceed your projected value within reason.

From a tactical perspective, mix up the caliber of openers. Drop out early on some bids to prevent other owners from catching on to you.

In the end, it's okay to pay a slight premium to make sure you get the players with the highest potential to provide a good return on your investment. It's no different than the premium you might pay for a player with position flexibility or to get the last valuable shortstop. With TCD, you're just spending those extra dollars up front to ensure you are rostering your targets. As a side benefit, TCD almost assures that you don't leave money on the table.

Mayberry Method

The Mayberry Method (MM) asserts that we really can't project player performance with the level of precision that advanced metrics and modeling systems would like us to believe.

MM is named after the fictional TV village where life was simpler. MM evaluates skill by embracing the imprecision of the forecasting process and projecting performance in broad strokes rather than with hard statistics.

MM reduces every player to a 7-character code. The format of the code is 5555 AAA, where the first four characters describe elements of a player's skill on a scale of 0 to 5. These skills are indexed to the league average so that players are evaluated within the context of the level of offense or pitching in a given year.

The three alpha characters are our reliability grades (Health, Experience and Consistency) on the standard A-to-F scale. The skills numerics are forward-looking; the alpha characters grade reliability based on past history.

Batting

The first character in the MM code measures a batter's power skills. It is assigned using the following table:

Power Index	MM
0 - 49	0
50 - 79	1
80 - 99	2
100 - 119	3
120 - 159	4
160+	5

The second character measures a batter's speed skills. RSpd takes our Statistically Scouted Speed metric (Spd) and adds the elements of opportunity and success rate, to construct the formula of RSpd = Spd x (SBO + SB%).

RSpd	MM
0 - 39	0
40 - 59	1
60 - 79	2
80 - 99	3
100 - 119	4
120+	5

The third character measures expected batting average.

xBA Index	MM
0-87	0
88-92	1
93-97	2
98-102	3
103-107	4
108+	5

The fourth character measures playing time.

Role	PA	MM
Potential full-timers	450+	5
Mid-timers	250-449	3
Fringe/bench	100-249	1
Non-factors	0-99	0

Pitching

The first character in the pitching MM code measures xERA, which captures a pitcher's overall ability and is a proxy for ERA, and even WHIP.

xERA Index	MM
0-80	0
81-90	1
91-100	2
101-110	3
111-120	4
121+	5

The second character measures strikeout ability.

K/9 Index	MM
0-76	0
77-88	1
89-100	2
101-112	3
113-124	4
125+	5

The third character measures saves potential.

Description	Saves est.	MM
No hope for saves; starting pitchers	0	0
Speculative closer	1-9	1
Closer in a pen with alternatives	10-24	2
Frontline closer with firm bullpen role	25+	3

The fourth character measures **playing time.**

Role	IP	MM
Potential #1-2 starters	180+	5
Potential #3-4 starters	130-179	3
#5 starters/swingmen	70-129	1
Relievers	0-69	0

Overall Mayberry Scores

The real value of Mayberry is to provide a skills profile on a player-by-player basis. It allows us to look at players like this...

Player A	4455 AAB
Player B	5245 BBD
Player C	5255 BAB
Player D	5155 BAF

...and make an objective, unbiased evaluation without being swayed by preconceived notions and baggage. The following calculation can provide a single, overall value for each player.

Batting MM Score =
(PX score + Spd score + xBA score + PA score)
x PA score

Pitching MM Score =
((xERA score x 2) + K/9 score + Saves score + IP score)
x (IP score + Saves score)

The highest score you can get for either is 100. That makes the result of the formula easy to assess.

Adding Reliability Grades to Mayberry *(Patrick Davitt)*

Research shows that players with higher reliability grades met their Mayberry targets more often than their lower-reliability counterparts. Players with all "D" or "F" reliability scores under-perform Mayberry projections far more often. Those results can be reflected by multiplying a player's MM Score by each of three reliability bonuses or penalties:"

	Health	Experience	Consistency
A	x 1.10	x 1.10	x 1.10
B	x 1.05	x 1.05	x 1.05
C	x 1.00	x 1.00	x 1.00
D	x 0.90	x 0.95	x 0.95
F	x 0.80	x 0.90	x 0.90

Let's perform the overall calculations for Player A (4455 AAB), using these Reliability adjustments.

Player A: 4455 AAB
= (4+4+5+5) x 5
= 90 x 1.10 x 1.10 x 1.05
= 114.3

Portfolio3 Plan concepts

When it comes to profitability, all players are not created equal. Every player has a different role on your team by virtue of his skill set, dollar value/draft round, position and risk profile. When it comes to a strategy for how to approach a specific player, one size does not fit all.

We need some players to return fair value more than others. A $40/first round player going belly-up is going to hurt you far more than a $1/23rd round bust. End-gamers are easily replaceable.

We rely on some players for profit more than others. First-rounders do not provide the most profit potential; that comes from players further down the value rankings.

We can afford to weather more risk with some players than with others. Since high-priced early-rounders need to return at least fair value, we cannot afford to take on excessive risk. Our risk tolerance opens up with later-round/lower cost picks.

Players have different risk profiles based solely on what roster spot they are going to fill. Catchers are more injury prone. A closer's value is highly dependent on managerial decision. These types of players are high risk even if they have great skills. That needs to affect their draft price or draft round.

For some players, the promise of providing a scarce skill, or productivity at a scarce position, may trump risk. Not always, but sometimes. The determining factor is usually price.

Previously, we created a model that integrated these types of players into a roster planning tool, called the Portfolio3 Plan. However, over time, variables like baseball's changing statistical environment and the shifting MLB roster construction affected the utility of the model. The rigid player allocation framework of the tiers began to erode, and no fudging could retain the integrity of the model. So we have retired it. The Mayberry Method includes the relevant player evaluators that Portfolio3 used; you can rely on those to create your own roster plan that balances skill and risk.

Head-to-Head Leagues

Consistency in Head-to-Head leagues *(Dylan Hedges)*

Few things are as valuable to H2H league success as filling your roster with players who can produce a solid baseline of stats, week in and week out. In traditional leagues, while consistency is not as important—all we care about are aggregate numbers—filling your H2H team with consistent players can make roster management easier.

Consistent batters have good plate discipline, walk rates and on base percentages. These are foundation skills. Those who add power to the mix are obviously more valuable, however, the ability to hit home runs consistently is rare.

Consistent pitchers demonstrate similar skills in each outing; if they also produce similar results, they are even more valuable.

We can track consistency but predicting it is difficult. Many fantasy leaguers try to predict a batter's hot or cold streaks, or individual pitcher starts, but that is typically a fool's errand. The best we can do is find players who demonstrate seasonal consistency; in-season, we must manage players and consistency tactically.

Building a consistent Head-to-Head team *(David Martin)*

Focusing on certain metrics helps build consistency, which is the roster holy grail for H2H players. Our filters for such success are:

- Contact rate = minimum 80%
- xBA = minimum .280
- PX (or Spd) = minimum 120
- RC/G = minimum 5.00

Ratio insulation in Head-to-Head leagues *(David Martin)*

On a week-to-week basis, inequities are inherent in the head-to-head game. One way to eliminate your competitor's advantage in the pure numbers game is to build your team's pitching foundation around the ratio categories.

One should normally insulate at the end of a draft, once your hitters are in place. To obtain several ratio insulators, target pitchers that have:

- K-BB% greater than 19%
- K% greater than 20%
- xERA less than 3.30

While adopting this strategy may compromise wins, research has shown that wins come at a cost to ERA and WHIP. Roster space permitting, adding two to four insulators to your team will improve your team's weekly ERA and WHIP.

A Head-to-Head approach to the Mayberry Method *(David Martin)*

Though the Mayberry Method was designed for use in Rotisserie leagues, a skill set analysis about whether a player is head-to-head league material is built into each seven-digit Mayberry code. By "decoding" Mayberry and incorporating quality-consistency (QC) scores, one can assemble a team that has the characteristics of a successful H2H squad.

In reviewing the MM skills scores, we can correlate the power and contact skills as follows:

- PX > 4 or 5 = PX of 120 or higher
- xBA > 4 or 5 = xBA index of 103 or higher

Only full-time players will have an opportunity to produce the counting statistics required, so to create a top tier of players, we need to limit our search to those who earn a 5 for playing time. This top tier should be sorted by QC scores so that the more consistent players are ranked higher.

To create the second tier of players, lower the power index to 3, but keep all other skill requirements intact:

PWR	SPD	BA	PT	HLTH
3	N/A	4/5	5	A/B

The interplay between tiers is important; use Tier 2 in conjunction with Tier 1 and not simply after the top tier options are exhausted. For example, it might make sense to dip into Tier 2 if there is a player available with a higher QC score.

Additionally, while the H2H MM codes do not target players based on their speed skills, the second column of the MM codes contains this information. Though you are de-prioritizing the speed skill, you do not need to punt the steals category. You will typically find that the tiers nonetheless contain multiple players with a MM speed score of 3 or higher, so you can still be competitive in the steal category most weeks applying this approach.

Consistency in points leagues *(Bill Macey)*

Week-to-week consistency is also important in points-based games. A study showed that not only do players with better skills post more overall points in this format, but that the format caters to consistent performances on a week-to-week basis, even after accounting for differences in total points scored and playing-time.

Therefore, when drafting your batters in points-based head-to-head leagues, ct% and bb% make excellent tiebreakers if you are having trouble deciding between two players with similarly projected point totals. Likewise, when rostering pitchers, favor those who tend not to give up home runs.

In-Season Roster Management

Rotisserie category management tips *(Todd Zola)*

1. Disregard whether you are near the top or the bottom of a category; focus instead on the gaps directly above and below your squad.
2. Prorate the difference in stats between teams.
3. ERA tends to move towards WHIP.
4. As the season progresses, the number of AB/IP do not preclude a gain/loss in the ratio categories.
5. An opponent's point lost is your point gained.
6. *Most important!* Come crunch time, forget value, forget names, and forget reputation. It's all about stats and where you are situated within each category.

Which is more important—quality or quantity? *(Steve Weimer)*

We examined the importance of AB and IP in three of the largest 2022 competitions hosted by the NFBC. The findings:

- The correlation between AB and total hitting points is quite strong.
- Teams that maximize AB tend to do well in runs and RBI, and teams that do well in runs and RBI tend to do well in total hitting points. Taking advantage of this by maximizing AB should be a core part of one's hitting strategy.
- The strongest predictors of total pitching points are easily the pure "quality" ratio categories: ERA and WHIP.

- Teams with more innings tend to do better in strikeouts and wins, but worse in the other three pitching categories. Exercise caution in streaming starting pitchers.

As a general plan of attack: quantity over quality for hitting, quality over quantity for pitching. Teams that successfully pile up AB and protect pitching ratios tend to find themselves toward the top of the standings, and in a strong position from which to pursue specific categories as necessary down the stretch.

Sitting stars and starting scrubs *(Ed DeCaria)*

In setting your pitching rotation, conventional wisdom suggests sticking with trusted stars despite difficult matchups. But does this hold up? And can you carefully start inferior pitchers against weaker opponents? Here are the ERAs posted by varying skilled pitchers facing a range of different strength offenses:

	OPPOSING OFFENSE (RC/G)				
Pitcher (ERA)	5.25+	5.00	4.25	4.00	<4.00
3.00-	3.46	3.04	3.04	2.50	2.20
3.50	3.98	3.94	3.44	3.17	2.87
4.00	4.72	4.57	3.96	3.66	3.24
4.50	5.37	4.92	4.47	4.07	3.66
5.00+	6.02	5.41	5.15	4.94	4.42

Recommendations:

1. Never start below replacement-level pitchers.
2. Always start elite pitchers.
3. Other than that, never say never or always.

Playing matchups can pay off when the difference in opposing offense is severe.

Two-start pitcher weeks *(Ed DeCaria)*

A two-start pitcher is a prized possession. But those starts can mean two DOMinant outings, two DISasters, or anything else in between, as shown by these results:

PQS Pair	% Weeks	ERA	WHIP	Win/Wk	K/Wk
DOM-DOM	20%	2.53	1.02	1.1	12.0
DOM-AVG	28%	3.60	1.25	0.8	9.2
AVG-AVG	14%	4.44	1.45	0.7	6.8
DOM-DIS	15%	5.24	1.48	0.6	7.9
AVG-DIS	17%	6.58	1.74	0.5	5.7
DIS-DIS	6%	8.85	2.07	0.3	5.0

Weeks that include even one DISaster start produce terrible results. Unfortunately, avoiding such disasters is much easier in hindsight. But what is the actual impact of this decision on the stat categories?

ERA and WHIP: When the difference between opponents is extreme, inferior pitchers can be a better percentage play. This is true both for 1-start pitchers and 2-start pitchers, and for choosing inferior one-start pitchers over superior two-start pitchers.

Strikeouts per Week: Unlike the two rate stats, there is a massive shift in the balance of power between one-start and two-start pitchers in the strikeout category. Even stars with easy one-start matchups can only barely keep pace with two-start replacement-level arms in strikeouts per week.

Wins per week are also dominated by the two-start pitchers. Even the very worst two-start pitchers will earn a half of a win on average, which is the same rate as the very best one-start pitchers.

The bottom line: If strikeouts and wins are the strategic priority, use as many two-start weeks as the rules allow, even if it means using a replacement-level pitcher with two tough starts instead of a mid-level arm with a single easy start. But if ERA and/or WHIP management are the priority, two-start pitchers can be very powerful, as a single week might impact the standings by over 1.5 points in ERA/WHIP, positively or negatively.

Tactics to improve free agent pickups *(Cary James)*

When you peruse the contents of your league's waiver wire, you have a few in-house methods to narrow down possible candidates:

Previous Production: For hitters, past production helps you form a decision, but it does not guarantee an outcome. This is a better hack for pitchers, especially when determining the legitimacy of a breakout start.

Rostership Percentage: For both hitters and pitchers, rostership percentage serves to weaken your decision-making process. Ignore this filter.

Transaction Trends: Most sites have a tool that allows you to see the Top 50-100 popular pickups over the last 24 hours. Once we exclude daily streamers, this tool delivers. We can use this in tandem with a watch list to see if your window for cheap acquisition is closing.

Rest-of-Season Projections: To ignore these is folly. Combine them with season-to-date production and weigh them against category totals to analyze weaknesses as the season goes on.

Rest-of-season projections and transaction trends are your best in-house tools when attempting to resist both recency and outcome bias.

Top 12 trading tips *(Fred Zinkie)*

We all need to make trades to win our leagues. And while every negotiation is unique, here are some quick tips that should make anyone more effective on the trade market.

1. Learn how the other owner wishes to communicate. Some owners prefer email, others like the league website, some prefer a Twitter DM, and texting is often a desirable option. And there are even some who still want a phone call. The easy way to figure this out is to send your initial contact in multiple ways. Generally, the other owner's preferred method is the one they use to send their initial reply.

2. All negotiations start with an offer. Don't beat around the bush—give the other owner something concrete to work with. You can start with your best deal or merely a respectable proposal, but you should get the ball rolling with a firm offer.

3. Check your ego at the door. You should enter trade talks with low expectations and a willingness to accept a different point of view. The other owner is not necessarily wrong when they disagree with your opinions on player values or what makes sense for their roster.

4. Be willing to unbalance your roster. Owners who draft a balanced team and then only seek out deals that maintain that balance are going to miss out on buying opportunities. To improve your roster—especially during the first half—you should be willing to have stretches with weak hitting, poor starting pitching, or a lack of saves. The goal is to acquire value.

5. Proofread. Always take the extra minute to proofread your communication and ensure your thoughts are clear. Beyond looking for typos, be sure that all players mentioned are the ones you intend to mention. Keep your initial communication to a couple sentences.

6. Be prompt. Trading can be inconvenient, but an active trader makes time when the opportunity arises. Don't get yourself fired or abandon your children in search of the perfect trade, but in general, you should be willing to work around your competitor's schedule.

7. Send multiple offers. Submitting multiple offers lets the other owner pick the proposal they like best. If you don't want to take the time to send multiple offers, you can at least mention that you would be willing to trade Player X, Y, or Z to get your desired return.

8. Be clear about all the players who interest you on the other team. An easy way to start negotiations is to mention all players who interest you on the other team. Again, this gives some control to the other owner, who can now tell you which players are most available.

9. The message board is your last resort. Trade messages can make you appear desperate. This is especially true when trying to unload a certain player. Like a house that sits on the market, the asking price on your player tends to drop once a couple days have passed.

10. Look for owners who may be desperate. Because most owners seek to achieve roster balance, you can find value by helping those who have an immediate need. And you can always help since you are the rare owner willing to unbalance their roster to obtain value. Look at the standings, as owners who are low in a roto category are likely to trade away value in order to address their weakness.

11. Look for owners who have a surplus. On the opposite end of the spectrum, owners can be willing to make deals when they have a surplus of a position or skill. Targeting the owner who is running away with the steals category could get you SB at a reasonable price.

12. Have the guts to trade away overachievers. This is one of the hardest tips to put into practice, but experience tells us that most players who have surprising stretches return to normal at some point. If it sometimes seems too good to be true, it probably is.

Other Diamonds

The Universal Tenets of Fantasy Economics

- This is not a game of projections. It is a game of market value versus real value.
- We don't need precisely accurate projections. All we need are projections accurate enough to tell us when the marketplace is wrong.
- Every player you draft has only a one-in-three chance of returning even par value.
- The marketplace is generally wrong, so we don't have to buy into anything it tells us.
- The variance between market cost and real value (in dollars or draft rounds) is far more important than the accuracy of any player projection.
- The market cost of a veteran player is driven more by the certainty of past performance than the uncertainty of future potential.
- The market cost of a young player is driven more by the promise of future potential than the questionable validity of past performance.
- Your greatest competitive advantage is to leverage the variance between market cost and real value.
- In summary, if you are convinced that a player is worth $25 and land him for $21, you will have overpaid if the rest of the league sees him as just a $17 player… even if he is really worth $30.

Cellar value
The dollar value at which a player cannot help but earn more than he costs. Always profit here.

Crickets
The sound heard when someone's opening draft bid on a player is also the only bid.

End-game wasteland
Home for players undraftable in the deepest of leagues, who stay in the free agent pool all year. It's the place where even crickets keep quiet when a name is called at the draft.

FAB Forewarnings

1. Spend early and often.
2. Emptying your budget for one prime league-crosser is a tactic that should be reserved for the desperate.
3. If you chase two rabbits, you will lose them both.

Free Agent Aphorism
Every time we acquire a player in-season—especially early on—we're likely replacing a player who was rostered through more careful in-depth analysis.

The Hope Hypothesis

- Hope can keep you interested but will have no effect on how a player performs.
- Hope is sometimes referred to as "wishcasting" and may sound more scientific but really it's just plain old hope with a random number attached.
- In the end, hope has virtually no intrinsic value and you can't win with it alone.
- Yet, hope will cost you about $5 over market value at the draft table.

The Ice Cream-ADP Metaphor
Ice cream is delicious. On any given day, cookies-and-cream can provide just as much cooling enjoyment as rocky road. So don't obsess over your first-round pick. Any flavor of superstar will be delicious.

The Loser's Lament
"I hate everybody." (Typically uttered at some point in the season by just about everyone who plays this game.)

Daily Fantasy Baseball

Daily Fantasy Sports (DFS) is an offshoot of traditional fantasy sports. Many of the same analytic methods that are integral to seasonal fantasy baseball are just as relevant for DFS.

General Format

1. The overwhelming majority of DFS contests are pay-for-play where the winners are compensated a percentage of their entry fee, in accordance with the rules of that game.

2. DFS baseball contests are generally based on a single day's slate of games, or a subset of the day's games (i.e., all afternoon games or all evening games)

3. Most DFS formats are points-based salary cap games.

Most Popular Contests

1. Cash Games: Three variants (50/50, Multipliers, and Head-to-Head) all pay out a flat prize to a portion of the entries.

2. GPP (Guaranteed prize pool) Tournaments: The overall winner earns the largest prize and prizes scale downward.

3. Survivor: A survivor contest is a multiple-slate format where a portion of the entries survives to play the following day.

4. Qualifiers/Satellites: Tournaments where the prize(s) consist of entry tickets to a larger tournament.

DFS Analysis

1. Predicting single-day performance entails adjusting a baseline projection based on that day's match-up. This adjusted expectation is considered in context with a player's salary to determine his potential contributions relative to the other players.

2. Weighted on base average (wOBA) is a souped-up version of OBP, and is a favorite metric to help evaluate both hitters and pitchers. (For more useful DFS metrics, see next section)

3. Pitching: In DFS, innings and strikeouts are the two chief means of accruing points, so they need to be weighed heavily in pitching evaluation.

Tips for Players New to DFS

1. Start slow and be prepared to lose: While cogent analysis can increase your chances of winning, the variance associated with a single day's worth of outcomes doesn't assure success. Short-term losing streaks are inevitable, so start with low cost cash games before embarking on tournament play.

2. Minimize the number of sites you play: The DFS space is dominated by two sites but there are other options. At the beginning, stick to one or two. Once you're comfortable, consider expanding to others.

3. Bankroll management: The recommended means to manage your bankroll is to risk no more than 10% on a given day in cash games, or 2% in tournaments.

4. General Strategies

A. Cash Games: Conventional wisdom preaches to be conservative in cash games. Upper level starting pitchers make excellent cash game options. For hitters, it's best to spread your choices among several teams. In general, you're looking for players with a high floor rather than a high ceiling.

B: GPP Tournaments: In tournaments (with a larger number of entrants), a common ploy is to select a lesser priced, though risky, pitcher with a favorable match-up. It's also very common to overload—or stack—several batters from the same team, hoping that squad scores a bunch of runs.

5. Miscellaneous Tips

A. Pay extra attention to games threatened by weather, as well as players who are not a lock to be in the lineup.

B. Avoid playing head-to-head against strangers until you're comfortable and have enjoyed some success.

C. Stay disciplined. The worst thing you can do is eat up your bankroll quickly by entering into tournaments.

D. Most importantly, have fun. Obviously, you want to win, but hopefully you're also in it for the challenge of mastering the unique skills intrinsic to DFS.

Using BaseballHQ Tools in DFS

Here are some of the additional skill metrics to consider:

Cash Game Metrics

bb%: This simple indicator may receive only a quick glance when building lineups, but it is imperative in providing insight on a batter's underlying approach and plate discipline. Walks also equal points in all DFS scoring structures.

ct%: Another byproduct of good plate discipline, reflecting the percentage of balls put in play. Players with strong contact rates tend to provide a higher floor, and less chance of a negative score from a free swinger with a high strikeout rate.

xBA: Measures a hitter's BA by multiplying his contact rate by the chance that a ball in play falls for a hit. Hitters whose BA is far below their xBA may be "due" for some hits.

Tournament / GPP Metrics

PX / xPX: Home runs are the single greatest multi-point event. Using PX (power index) and xPX (expected power index) together can help identify underperformers who are due in the power category.

Choosing Pitchers in DFS

The criteria for choosing a pitcher(s) may be more narrow than for full-season league, but the skills focus should remain.

Major Considerations

• Overall skills. Look for the following minimums: BB% under 7%, K% over 23%, K-BB% over 16%, and max 1.0 hr/9.

• Home/Away. In 2023, MLB pitchers logged a 4.23 ERA, 8.5% BB%, 23.2% K% (14.7% K-BB%) at home; 4.44 ERA, 8.7% BB%, 22.3% K% (13.6% K-BB%) on the road.

• Is he pitching at Coors Field? (Even the best pitchers are a risky start there.)

Moderate Considerations

• Recent performance. Examine Ks and BBs over last 4-5 starts.

• Strength of opponent. Refer to opposing team's OPS for the season, as well as more recent performance.

Minor Considerations

• L/R issues. Does the pitcher/opponent have wide platoon splits?

• Park. Is the game at a hitter's/pitcher's/neutral park?

• Previous outings. Has he faced this team already this season? If so, how did he fare? (Skills; not just his ERA.)

You should be left with a tiered list of pitching options, ripe for comparing individual risk/reward level against their price point.

The Okrent Rule
There is nothing more interesting than my fantasy team and nothing less interesting than your fantasy team.

Pastanalysis
A performance evaluation methodology or draft plan that involves tossing a bunch of players against the wall to see who sticks.

Professional Free Agent (PFA)
Player whose name will never come up on draft day but will always end up on a roster at some point during the season as an injury replacement.

Seasonal Assessment Standard
If you still have reason to be reading the boxscores during the last weekend of the season, then your year has to be considered a success.

The Three Cardinal Rules for Winners
If you cherish this hobby, you will live by them or die by them...

1. Revel in your success; fame is fleeting.
2. Exercise excruciating humility.
3. 100% of winnings must be spent on significant others.

Did the pitch clock change batting performance?

by Andy Andres

Watching games this past season, we observed certain batters changing their approach within a plate appearance. Rafael Devers, for example, needed to give up his routine between pitches, which led us to wonder if the pitch clock had any effect on a hitter's performance.

Some understanding of pitch tempo might help first. The figure below shows trends in annual MLB average pitch tempo, defined as the time between pitches following a called ball or a called strike. The three lines represent pitch tempo with bases empty (the bottom line, naturally the fastest tempo), with "Men on Base" (the top line, the slowest)—both datasets are from MLB's Statcast—and the middle line from FanGraphs.com's "Pace," which uses both base states together in its calculation.

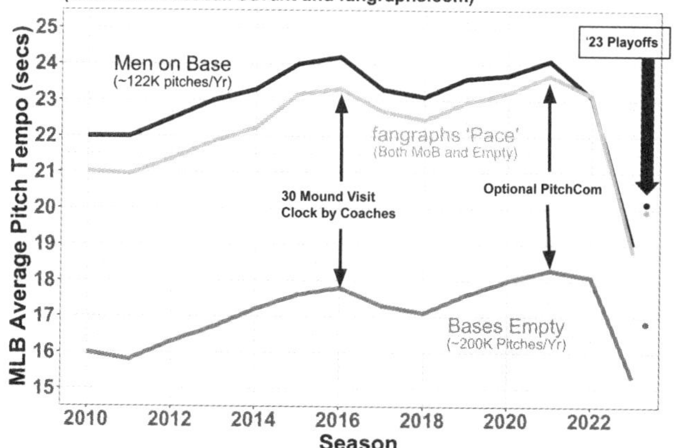

It is nice that the two different ways of measuring pitch tempo (from Statcast and from FanGraphs) are aligned and that they both show the same trends:

- An increasing average pitch tempo until the 2016 season.
- Then a decrease after the 30-second mound visit rule.
- And then increasing tempo until we see a small effect of the usage of PitchCom. The PitchCom decrease in 2022 is likely due to the reduced need for varied pitch signaling when a runner is on second base.

The dramatic drop in pitch tempo in 2023 has led to reduced average Time of Game, likely one of the biggest stories of the 2023 MLB season. Both reductions are a result of the new pitch clock rules. 2023 playoff data for both Pace and Statcast pitch tempos is also shown, which demonstrates an increase of at least one second compared to the regular season, which is very interesting, and something to be researched in the future.

To see if batters' performance was impacted by the pitch clock, the differences between wRC+ and xwOBA for the 2022 and 2023 seasons were measured. These were chosen because they are more generalized measures of batting outcomes (wRC+) and batted ball quality (xwOBA), two things that would likely change if the batter performance changed between the seasons.

Among the changes in pitch tempo between 2022 and 2023, it was thought that pitch tempo with the bases empty was the most likely to impact batting performance because it was the shortest time relative to the other measures of pitch tempo available. In total, 197 batters saw at least 500 pitches that counted towards pitch tempo data in both seasons.

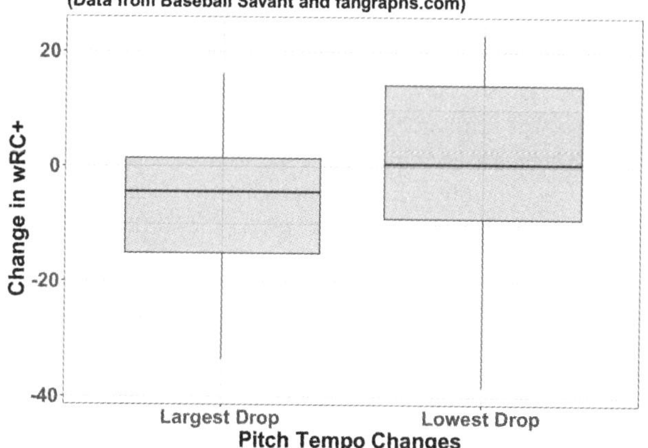

This boxplot compares batters with the lowest drop in pitch tempo changes (representing batters that did not have to adjust much to the new pitch clock) vs. the batters with the largest difference (batters that had to make the biggest adjustments). There was a slight decrease in 2023 wRC+ in the batters that had the larger adjustment, but it was not statistically significant. Who were the batters with the biggest pitch tempo challenges?

Batter	Tempo Difference (Bases Empty)	Change in wRC	Change in xwOBA
Christian Vázquez	-7.691	-33.54	-0.036
Mark Canha	-6.399	-15.27	-0.001
J.D. Martinez	-5.987	16.19	0.021
Josh Naylor	-5.858	9.15	0.018
Pete Alonso	-5.648	-20.02	0.017
J.D. Davis	-5.266	-14.82	-0.027
Bryce Harper	-4.977	3.33	0.017
Brandon Nimmo	-4.914	-2.37	0.013
Miguel Rojas	-4.781	-0.49	-0.002
Willson Contreras	-4.661	-4.38	0.011

There are many things that will impact a change in wRC+ or xwOBA from year to year (injury, changes in approach, aging, etc.), but there may be something to consider and watch for in the players on this list. In particular, J.D. Davis and Christian Vázquez had real decreases in both measures of batted ball quality and batting performance outcomes.

Further work will look to measure how well batters that had to make the largest tempo adjustments in 2023 may have improved over the whole of the 2023 season. It is thought that the biggest impact of the pitch clock happened early in 2023, and potentially they learned to adapt to the new rules.

Deep-diving 2023's stolen base surge

by Ryan Bloomfield

Bigger bases. A pitch clock. Limited pickoff throws. We knew change was coming to the stolen base landscape in 2023, but how drastic would it be? Which players would it affect the most? How many bags would we have to draft at the table? We now have the answers.

Our dive into 2023's stolen base changes starts with some league-wide basics:

Season	SB	SB%	SBA%
2018	2474	72.1	8.0%
2019	2280	73.3	7.5%
2021	2213	75.7	7.0%
2022	2486	75.4	7.7%
2023	3503	80.2	10.0%

We saw the most stolen bases in a season since 1987 (3,585) with a 41% increase compared to 2022, an all-time high in stolen base success rate (SB%), and a major spike in stolen base attempt rate (SBA%). Breaking down these league-wide numbers into smaller buckets gives us a better idea of where these increases came from:

Number of Players

SB	2022	2023	Change
1-10	357	323	-10%
11-20	54	72	+33%
21-30	14	28	+100%
31-40	4	8	+100%
40+	1	6	+500%

Number of Players (min. 200 PA, 5 attempts)

SB%	2022	2023	Change
<= 60%	43	25	-42%
61-70%	30	22	-27%
71-80%	56	63	+13%
81-90%	46	77	+67%
90%+	23	36	+57%

Several takeaways:

- We saw 10% fewer single-digit SBers in 2023, though this group still encompassed the majority of players.
- The next few groups saw major increases: 18 more hitters stole between 11 and 20 bases, and twice as many stole between 21 and 40 bases compared to 2022.
- The elite tier grew, too. Six players stole more than 40 in 2023, while Jon Berti was the sole member of that club in 2022, leading the league with 41 SB.
- The groups with over 70%, 80%, and 90% success rates saw the largest growth. Given that the "break-even" point for SB% settles in the low-to-mid 70s, teams had plenty of reason to keep those lights green.

Another way to slice this is to see where players' stolen base attempt rates (SBA%) moved in 2023 based on their 2022 bucket (min. 200 PA in both seasons):

2023 SBA%	Players with 2022 SBA% 0-5%	5-10%	10-15%	15-20%	20-25%	>25%
0-5%	98 (80%)	15 (27%)	0 (0%)	0 (0%)	0 (0%)	0 (0%)
5-10%	23 (18%)	19 (35%)	13 (34%)	4 (17%)	2 (22%)	1 (8%)
10-15%	0 (0%)	12 (22%)	13 (34%)	4 (17%)	1 (11%)	1 (8%)
15-20%	1 (1%)	3 (5%)	7 (18%)	7 (29%)	2 (22%)	3 (25%)
20-25%	1 (1%)	3 (5%)	4 (11%)	5 (21%)	0 (0%)	1 (8%)
>25%	0 (0%)	3 (5%)	1 (3%)	4 (17%)	4 (44%)	6 (50%)
TOTAL	123	55	38	24	9	12

For example, 80% of hitters with a sub-5% SBA% in 2022 finished with a <5% SBA% again in 2023, and 98% of them ran less than 10% of the time. Translation: if you didn't run before the rule changes, you probably didn't run after them either.

Nearly three-fourths of those with a 5-10% SBA% in 2022 ran more often or as frequently in 2023, and the same can be said for two-thirds of the 10-15% group. The middle class of the SB pool sure did its part in driving the league-wide surge.

Stolen Base Attempt Rates by Team

The league-wide increase didn't just come from a few teams, either. Here's the percent increase in SBA% by team from 2022 to 2023:

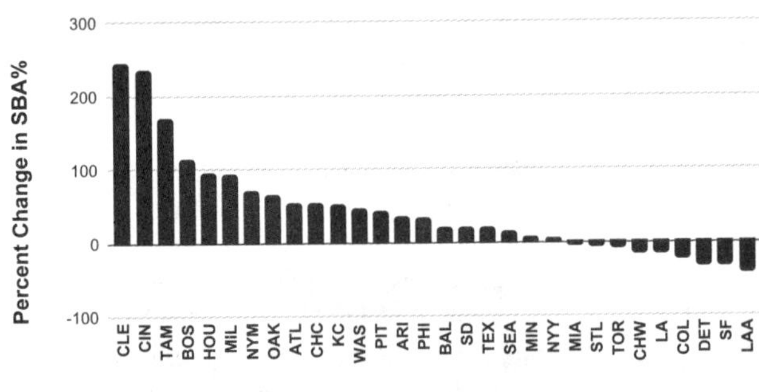

- Twenty-one of 30 teams ran more often. Four of them (CLE, CIN, TAM, BOS) saw their attempt rates double.
- Eleven teams had a 50% or higher increase. By contrast, nearly every team that ran less often did so by a thin margin.

Category Targets

The surge had a major impact on our fantasy teams and standings as well. Using the NFBC's 12-team Online Championship format (2,388 total teams in 2022; 2,460 teams in 2023), we can compare the spread of SB totals by fantasy team:

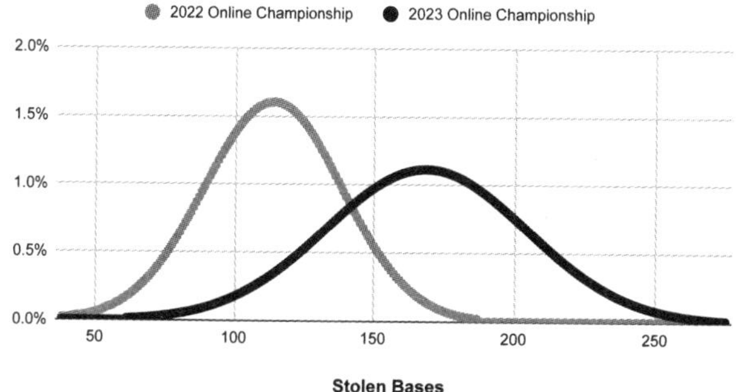

Not only did you need more steals to compete in the category—the 50th percentile SB total jumped from 113 to 166 this year—but the flatter curve in 2023 meant you also needed more bags to move up in the standings. To go from the 50th to 80th percentile in 2022, you needed just 21 SB (from 113 to 134); that number jumped to 32 in 2023 (from 166 to 198).

Conclusion

The stolen base landscape has drastically changed: runners were far more successful, and thus more aggressive, as a result of the new rules; the number of 10+, 20+, and 30+ base stealers jumped dramatically; and you needed more SB than ever to compete and move up in the category. Given 2023's all-time high in SB success rate, there's little incentive for teams to slow down in 2024. The bags will keep coming.

Revisiting Expected Stolen Bases (xSB)

by Ed DeCaria

In 2023, we witnessed the biggest single-season change to league-wide stolen base per game totals in the last 100 years, driven by both stolen base attempt rate (SBA%) increasing by 2.3% (as we define it, from 7.7% in 2022 to 10.0% in 2023) and stolen base success rate (SBS%) increasing by 5.0% (from 75.0% in 2022 to 80.0% in 2023).

In light of this massive shift, we felt compelled to re-evaluate our Expected Stolen Bases (xSB) metric to make sure it still reflects the way the game is now being played.

A bit of history: The original research piece that introduced xSB was focused primarily on separating the "will to steal" from the "skill to steal." To achieve this objective, we constructed two models for expected stolen base attempt rate (xSBA%), one that made use of players' past stolen base attempt rates as an independent variable, and one that used only other measures of stolen base skill like speed and past success rate, but *not* their past attempt rates. We then used the delta between the two models' regression equations to represent the "will to steal," because the only difference between the resulting modeled attempt rates was the player's own choice to run more or less than otherwise expected.

The final output of this exercise was to take a player's actual (or projected) stolen base totals and split them into 1) SB-Skill, which were those SB attributed to the player's general opportunity, speed, technique, etc., and 2) SB-Will, which were however many SB were left over (+ or -). Ironically, these skill vs. will splits have been mostly lost to research history, while their byproduct—the unified xSB metric—has been enshrined in the player boxes of this book for several years now.

Back to the present, one characteristic of xSB as defined is that it is a lagging indicator, because it uses the prior year's attempt rate as part of the model to calculate the next year's xSBA%. This suited our research goal at the time, but especially in a year where the macro stolen base environment has seen such major change, the gap between xSB informed by prior year's SBA% and actual SB driven by this year's SBA% renders the metric almost meaningless.

So, our goal in refreshing the xSB metric now is to ensure that it represents what was expected to have happened on the basepaths given a player's expected level of aggressiveness/passiveness (xSBA%), as informed by their general speed profile and "established level" of aggressiveness/passiveness.

For this, we have to get creative, because we're essentially trying to use SBA% itself as one of several inputs to a modeled xSBA%. What we settled on is a dual definition of "established SBA%" (eSBA%) depending on the usage:

- When projecting xSBA% for a new year (y2), eSBA% is the player's *prior* year (y1) SBA%, i.e., his "previously established SBA%"
- When estimating xSBA% for a past year (y1), eSBA% is the player's SBA% for *that* year (y1), i.e., his "newly established SBA%") as opposed to that season's prior season (y0)

This eliminates the lag effect, while still leaving xSB free to deviate from actual SB, because we are still using a modeled xSBA% based in part on the player's actual SBA%, but taking into consideration other skill factors as well. The new modeled xSBA% formula (which was derived using the first of the two definitions above) is:

$$xSBA\% = -0.09 + 0.856 * LgSBA + 0.00000484 * Spd^{\wedge}2 + 0.687 * eSBA\% - 0.313 * eSBA\%^{\wedge}2$$

In lay terms, this is saying "Given the league environment, the player's speed, and the player's aggressiveness, the expectation is that he would have attempted to steal x% of the time."

To calculate total xSB, we still use three main components: Times on First (TOF), Expected SB Attempt Rate (xSBA%), and Expected SB Success Rate (xSBS%), where:

$$xSB = TOF * xSBA\% * xSBS\%$$

and where:

$$TOF = H - 2B - 3B - HR + BB + HBP$$

$$xSBS\% = 0.894 * LgSBS\% + 0.395 * eSBA\%$$

All player boxes and other tables in this book now use the new version of xSB.

High-precision playing time analytics

by Ed DeCaria

Last year, we introduced a formula to break down batters' Total Plate Appearances (PA) into six new metrics that combine to tell their playing time "story" without any words. The Total PA formula is:

*Total PA = Active Weeks (AW) * Plate Appearances per Active Week (PAAW) / (1 - Ghost Plate Appearance % (GPA%)), where:*

*PAAW = Starts per Active Week (SAW) * Plate Appearances per Start (PAS) + Extra PA per Active Week (EAW)*

As a mental shortcut, AW * PAAW accounts for 99% of Total PA for most players, and alone reveals distinct accumulation patterns for players with otherwise similar PA totals. Almost as simple, AW * SAW * PAS accounts for about 94% of Total PA and further highlights each player's main playing time strengths and weaknesses.

To illustrate these metrics' narrative power, here are the 2023 playing time stories of Amed Rosario and Jake Burger, as told in numbers:

Player	PA	AW	PAAW	SAW	PAS	EAW	GPA%
Rosario, Amed	545	27	20.2	4.3	4.34	1.2	0.0%
Burger, Jake	540	25	21.4	5.2	3.98	0.5	0.7%

Both ended up with nearly 550 Total PA, but their paths could not have been more different. Rosario was on the active roster for more weeks than Burger (27 vs. 25 AW, with Burger losing another 0.7% Ghost PA). However, Burger earned more total playing time when active (21.4 vs. 20.2 PAAW). This was due mainly to Burger starting far more games per week than Rosario (5.2 vs. 4.3 SAW), which was offset by Rosario coming up to the plate far more times per start (4.34 vs. 3.98 PAS) and coming off the bench to bat more often (1.2 vs. 0.5 EAW). We'll revisit this pair a bit later.

Definitions of these six metrics can be found in the Encyclopedia entry "Playing time building blocks" on page 31. We've since reworked the calculations to stop using imputed full-season data and transaction logs, and start using daily box/lineup data, which not only improves data accuracy and scalability, but also opens up far more analytic capabilities. Let's walk through a few:

Multi-year progression

We can now easily analyze playing time trends over multiple years. Kyle Schwarber presents an interesting case:

Year	Age	PA	AW	PAAW	SAW	PAS
2019	26	610	27	22.6	5.1	4.25
2020	27	224	10	22.4	↑ 5.6	↓ 3.89
2021	28	471	↓ 19	24.4	5.6	↑ 4.28
2022	29	669	↑ 27	24.8	5.7	4.36
2023	30	720	27	26.7	↑ 5.9	↑ 4.50

In 2019, Schwarber was active all year, with great-but-not-elite PAS and good-not-great SAW, which earned him 610 Total PA (~70th percentile among 15-team mixed 5x5 >=$1 players, which is the player pool filter used throughout this essay).

In 2020, he was active all 10 weeks and increased his SAW, but saw his PAS drop concurrently (see next section for more on this).

In 2021, he maintained his higher SAW, and his higher PAS returned, which resulted in near-elite PAAW, but he missed 8 weeks.

In 2022, he was active all year, maintained a high SAW (85th percentile), and upped his PAS further (75th percentile), leading to a then-career high 669 PA.

In 2023, he pushed his SAW and PAS even further into super-elite territory (90th + percentile), netting him 720 PA (t-6th in MLB).

Expect to see some of these playing time building blocks inside the Forecaster multi-year player boxes starting next year.

Opposing SP (OppSP) handedness

Typically when we think about platoon splits, we think only of players in "strict" platoons like LHBs Joc Pederson or Eddie Rosario, or less fantasy-relevant RHBs like Austin Slater or Rob Refsnyder. But while very few players are in such strict platoons, almost *every* player tends to start more/less often depending on OppSP hand.

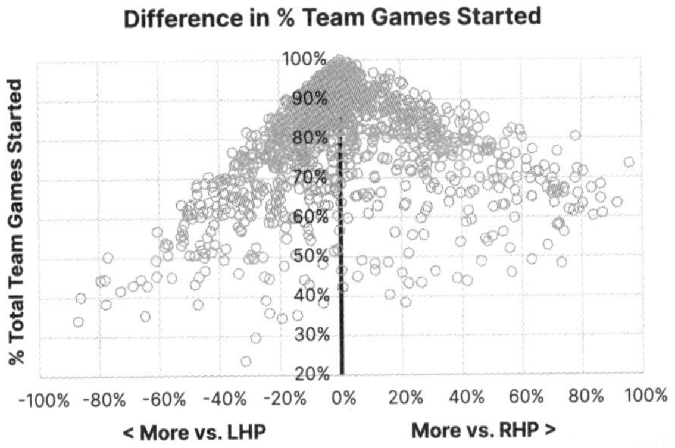

Difference in % Team Games Started

% Total Team Games Started
100%
90%
80%
70%
60%
50%
40%
30%
20%
-100% -80% -60% -40% -20% 0% 20% 40% 60% 80% 100%
< More vs. LHP
More vs. RHP >

Each circle represents a player season. The y-axis is the % of all team games started (%GS) by a player (during AW only), so the higher up the axis, the higher the player's SAW. The x-axis is the player's %GS vs. RHP (%vR) minus %GS vs. LHP (%vL). The further from center the mark is, the more playing time tilts toward one OppSP hand or the other. Even players who we think of as full-time (90%+ GS) exhibit OppSP hand splits; in 2023 for example, Corbin Carroll started 96%vR but only 78%vL, while Alec Bohm only started 86%vR but 98%vL. Such mini- and micro-platoons are prevalent across all MLB teams and defensive positions.

OppSP hand also impacts PAS, specifically when:

- Players are assigned different lineup slots
- Players are substituted out when an RP enters
- Lineups turn over more/less often as teams hit better/worse

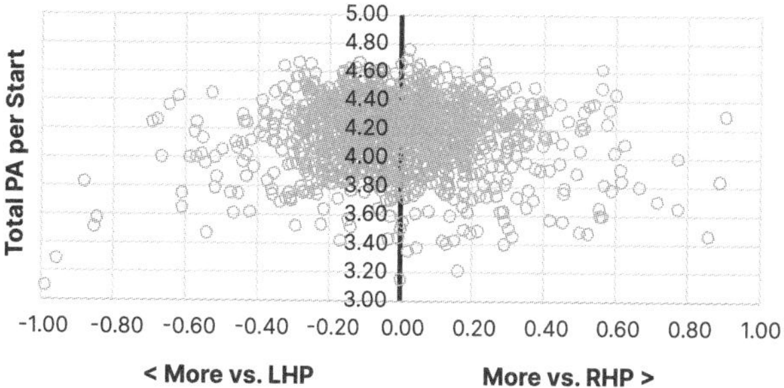

Here the y-axis is the player's overall PAS, while the x-axis is the player's PAS vs. RHP (PAS-R) minus PAS vs. LHP (PAS-L). The further left or right of center the mark, the more PA that player gets when facing an OppSP of one hand or the other. In 2023 for example, Tommy Edman not only started 85%vR vs. 100%vL, he garnered only 3.86 PAS-R vs. 4.41 PAS-L. Players with only mild %GS splits can also have material PAS splits (and these can often be reverse splits), such as Kyle Tucker who started 96%vR and %vL, but earned only 4.17 PAS-R compared to 4.49 PAS-L.

In addition to %vR/%vL and PAS-R/PAS-L, two other metrics that help unravel the mysteries of SAW and PAS are:

- *#R/#L:* Most frequent (i.e., mode) lineup slot by OppSP hand
- *wTmX:* wOBA of player's team, excluding player's own wOBA, which impacts how frequently the lineup turns over

Let's take a closer look at Kyle Schwarber's path to elite Total PA:

Year	Age	PA	AW	PAAW	SAW	PAS	%vR	%vL	PAS-R	PAS-L	#R	#L	wTmX
2019	26	610	27	22.6	5.1	4.25	95%	47%	4.25	4.20	1	1	336
2020	27	224	10	22.4	↑ 5.6	↓ 3.89	96%	↑ 82%	3.89	3.89	↓ 4	↓ 5	↓ 305
2021	28	471	↓ 19	24.4	5.6	↑ 4.28	100%	↓ 72%	4.33	4.14	4	6	↑ 331
2022	29	669	↑ 27	24.8	5.7	4.36	96%	↑ 91%	4.40	4.26	1	1	320
2023	30	720	27	26.7	↑ 5.9	↑ 4.50	97%	↑ 98%	4.50	4.50	1	1	↑ 328

In 2019, Schwarber was heavily platooned (only 47% GS vs. LHP), which explains his middling SAW. But he typically batted leadoff that year, which kept his PAS above average.

In 2020, he started far more often vs. LHP, but he was dropped to 4th or 5th in the order and the rest of his teammates were horrid (.305 wTmX), which cratered his PAS (10th percentile). (The Cubs also played eight 7-inning games that year, which didn't help.)

In 2021, Schwarber started every game vs. RHP, but gave back 10%vL. Meanwhile his teammates performed much better, which boosted his PAS despite still only batting mid-lineup.

In 2022, he once again boosted his %vL to 91%, and was put back into the leadoff spot, lifting both his SAW and PAS.

In 2023, *everything* clicked, as he started nearly every game and batted leadoff vs. both RHP and LHP, and his team was one of the top offenses in MLB. This is how you max out Total PA (and these metrics are how you explain it)!

Sub-season insights

Beyond the season-long metrics, we can now use daily box/lineup data to spot even more deeply hidden playing time trends, highs, and lows. Returning to our comparison of Amed Rosario vs. Jake Burger, as useful as the building block metrics are in explaining their respective paths to playing time in 2023, even they still don't convey the full shape of those paths. These other new metrics do:

- Trend: Absolute monthly change in SAW (TrS) and PAS (TrP); players with higher SAW or PAS toward end of season have + values, and vice versa
- Max of Rolling 5 Weeks SAW (MxS) and PAS (MxP)
- Min of Rolling 5 Weeks SAW (MnS) and PAS (MnP)

Player	PA	AW	PAAW	SAW	PAS	MxS	MnS	TrS	MxP	MnP	TrP
Rosario, Amed	545	27	20.2	4.3	4.34	6.0	2.1	-0.5	4.68	3.71	-0.18
Burger, Jake	540	25	21.4	5.2	3.98	6.0	4.0	0.3	4.29	3.52	0.13

Both Rosario and Burger went through at least one 5-week stretch of playing every day (6.0 MxS), but that's where the similarities stopped. Rosario bottomed out at 2.1 SAW (MnS), and his SAW fell by nearly 0.5 per month (the single worst trend among 425+ PA players). Conversely, Burger never dipped below 4.0 SAW in any active 5-week stretch, and his SAW increased by 0.3 monthly.

On the other hand, even at his best, Burger's PAS fell short of Rosario's season-long average. But while Rosario's PAS was at times elite (4.68 MxP), it tanked as the season went on, dropping -0.18 per month (3rd worst trend among 425+ PA players), whereas Burger's rose steadily by 0.13 per month.

These were huge in-season trends that would be totally hidden to fantasy managers without these additional playing time analytics (or without exceptionally good memories, and even then the insights would not be so neatly quantified!).

Summary

For too long, fantasy managers have been living in a world where the only batter playing time metric they ever see is Total PA. This is akin to only understanding batter performance through the lens of Total Hits per year. That is now unimaginable, yet this has been the reality on the playing time front for literally *decades*.

Our new playing time metrics have turned this world ~~upside down~~ right-side up. We can now paint a much more vivid picture of batter playing time through a combination of our original building block metrics, OppSP split metrics, team performance metrics, and other sub-season insights, with even more on the way. In the coming months and years, we will continue to make these data and related insights more accessible to readers of this book and subscribers to BaseballHQ.com. *See tables on starting on page 281 for 2023 playing time data by defensive position.*

Playing time projection, and endless possibilities

by Ed DeCaria

Now that we've established a core set of playing time metrics (see previous essay), it's time to get more serious about projecting playing time: both how projections are created and how they're used.

While projecting playing time is extremely challenging and still highly exploratory, we hope to demonstrate that there is merit in systematically calculating playing time *baselines*, which can then serve as the foundation for modeling other possible *scenarios*.

Year-over-year stability

The core building blocks of playing time are stable. All correlate positively year-over-year, with moderate-to-high strength:

- AW: y1 explains 29% of y2 (R=0.54) (yes, we adjusted for 2020)
- PAAW: y1 explains 50% of y2 (R=0.71)
- SAW: y1 explains 44% of y2 (R=0.67)
- PAS: y1 explains 27% of y2 (R=0.52)
- EAW: y1 explains 15% of y2 EAW (R=0.39)

PAAW is the most stable, itself driven by SAW more than PAS, while AW is more variable year-over-year. We include EAW only to show that even the weakest building block metric maintains some stability. Drilling one level deeper:

- y1 %GS vs. same-hand SP explains 50% of y2 (R=0.71), while y1 %GS vs. opposite-hand SP only explains 27% of y2 (R=0.52)
- Such divergence was *not* true of PAS; y1 PAS by both OppSP hands are stable, but one no more than the other

One major caveat is that the above values are for the entire player pool. When we limit the player pool to only those who earned >=$1 in 15-team mixed 5x5 leagues, most of the R values come down slightly (though EAW jumps up a bit) with the critical exception that Active Weeks nosedives to R=0.08, meaning *y1 AW has almost no statistical bearing on y2 AW.* There is a slight 2020 penalty in that R-value, but the truth is that injury, health, demotion, free agency, suspension, retirement, or performance factors can all impact a player's active status at any time.

So when it comes to creating baseline playing time projections, especially for established players, it's critical to weigh all building blocks appropriately, which means de-emphasizing past AW. To that end, here is a group of low-AW, high-PAAW batters from 2023:

Name	PA	AW	PAAW	AW27	Name	PA	AW	PAAW	AW27
McLain, Matt	403	15	26.9	725	Blackmon, Charlie	413	18	22.9	620
Gelof, Zack	300	11	26.2	707	Jones, Nolan	424	18	22.9	618
De La Cruz, Elly	427	17	25.1	678	Ward, Taylor	409	18	22.7	614
Judge, Aaron	458	18	24.9	674	Chisholm Jr., Jazz	385	17	22.6	611
Mauricio, Ronny	108	4	24.3	655	Trout, Mike	362	16	22.6	611
Meadows, Parker	145	6	24.2	653	Greene, Riley	416	18	22.6	611
Pasquantino, Vinnie	259	11	23.5	636	Davis, Henry	255	11	22.5	609
Young, Jacob	121	5	23.4	632	Carter, Evan	75	3	22.3	603
Altuve, Jose	410	17	23.4	631					

Project 27 AW for any of these players and they reach 600+ PA (in fact, we foresee "AW27" as a common shortcut for playing time pseudo-projection in the future). Even 23 AW gets them to 500+!

Aging

Not accounted for in the above stability metrics, each of our core playing time building blocks has a distinct aging pattern that can be used to inform baseline projections:

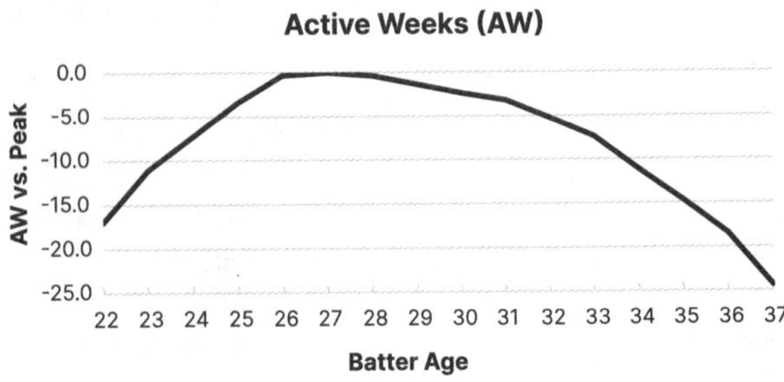

AW peaks at age 27. This is driven primarily by more players coming into the league than exiting the league until age 28, and then vice versa thereafter. But even among players active in back-to-back seasons, there is still generally a multi-year (at least two) progression toward a brief AW peak before disruption and attrition set in.

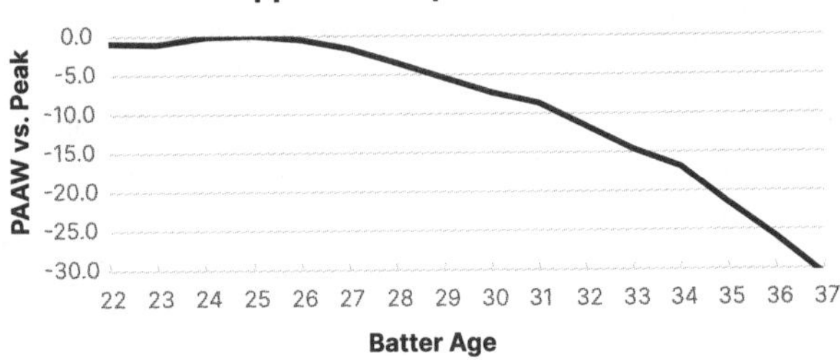

PAAW peaks earlier than AW, at age 25, but there's only a very slight buildup to that peak followed by a slow decline through age 31, then a cliff as most players hang on for 1-2 more years before exiting the league.

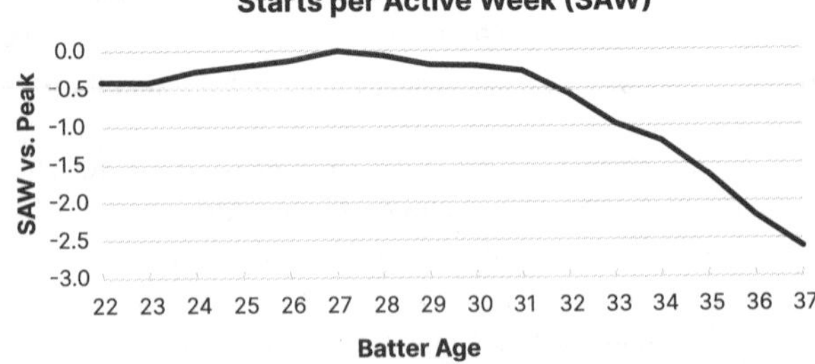

SAW peaks at age 27, but is generally quite flat, as players begin their careers only 0.4-0.5 SAW from peak, and hold within 0.3-0.4 of peak until age 31, after which SAW starts to fall rapidly. We can see a more precise cause here:

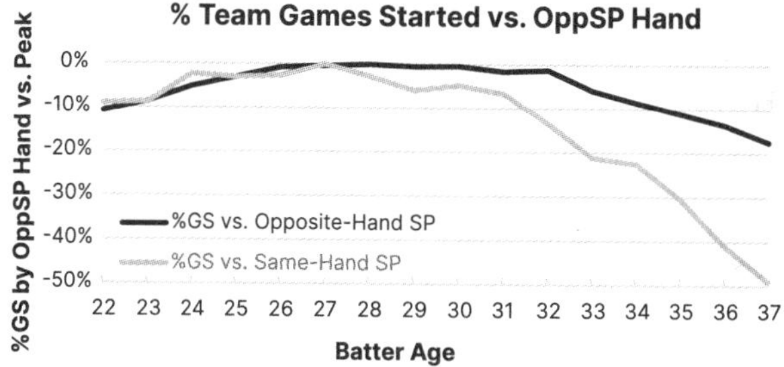

Batters actually continue to start vs. opposite-handed SPs near their peak rate from age 26 through 32, and even then only decline modestly through the end of their careers. What drops more rapidly is starts vs. same-handed SPs, with an average absolute decline of 8% GS per season after age 32. For RHBs, that is a fast track to fantasy irrelevance. Lookin' at you, 32-year-old Hunter Renfroe.

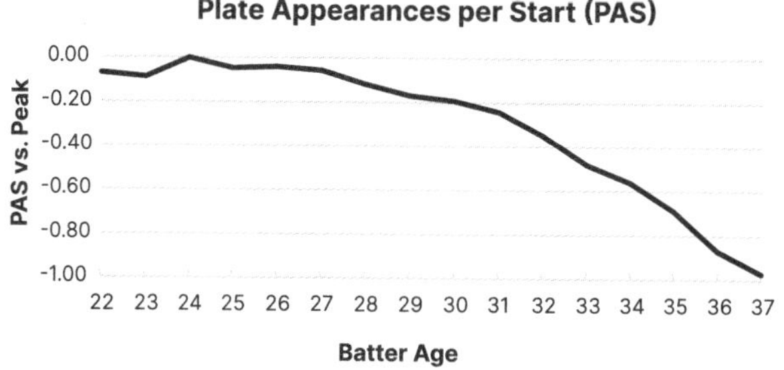

PAS peaks much earlier than SAW at age 24. A typical batter starts their career at close to peak PAS and holds it through age 27, then starts to decline by -0.05 per year through age 31, then by -0.12 per year through retirement.

Projection vs. possibility

With so many factors in play (we've only scratched the surface here), trying to project Total PA directly via a regression model produces watered-down results. A better approach is to project individual building blocks and their sub-components (e.g., AW, SAW, % GS by OppSP hand, PAS, EAW, wOBA) using hard data and player age, and then use our overall playing time formula to recombine them into a Total PA baseline.

The benefit of such baseline projections is not only that they are grounded in logic, but that they are self-explanatory in the form of their narrative building blocks and, most importantly, they are theoretically editable by fantasy managers who disagree with them.

It is this last point that we want to dwell on, because many batters experience marked changes in playing time from year to year, and there are many indicators (both opportunities and threats) that won't be reflected in their baseline projections, but which individual fantasy managers may feel strongly will influence one aspect of playing time or another. These include but are not limited to:

- Player wOBA vs. teammates by OppSP hand
- Team wOBA by OppSP hand
- Defensive prowess at one position
- Defensive flexibility at multiple positions
- wOBA vs. others at defensive position(s)
- Team's prospects nearing majors
- Team's free agent signings
- Player's or teammates' health
- Player's or teammates' MiLB options
- Contract size relative to total team payroll
- Reputation (prospect status/grade, awards)
- Team W-L record

Based on such factors, fantasy managers can override the calculation variables like AW, SAW, or PAS, and the player's Total PA projection will update automatically in kind.

Take a player like Ha-Seong Kim. He had a great 2023, but there are myriad ways his playing time could shake out in 2024:

Year	Age	PA	AW	PAAW	SAW	PAS	%vR	%vL	PAS-R	PAS-L	#R	#L	wTmX+
2021	26	298	26	11.2	2.4	3.74	35%	49%	3.93	3.38	7	7	83
2022	27	582	27	21.6	5.3	4.05	83%	96%	3.99	4.15	7	1	95
2023	28	626	27	23.2	5.3	4.29	86%	96%	4.26	4.37	1	1	103
Base	**29**	**572**	**26**	**21.9**	**5.2**	**4.16**	**84%**	**95%**	**4.02**	**4.50**	**6**	**1**	**100**
Rosy	**29**	**671**	**27**	**24.8**	**5.5**	**4.53**	**88%**	**98%**	**4.54**	**4.50**	**1**	**1**	**105**
Sour	**29**	**516**	**25**	**20.6**	**5.0**	**4.08**	**78%**	**95%**	**3.94**	**4.44**	**7**	**2**	**97**
Tank	**29**	**433**	**25**	**17.3**	**4.4**	**3.84**	**65%**	**93%**	**3.73**	**4.12**	**9**	**5**	**94**

Kim's calculated baseline (illustrative only) SAW and PAS assume that he will continue to primarily lead off for the Padres vs. LHP, but due to aging and his poor track record vs. RHP (not shown), he will sink back down the lineup and lose a few starts, and miss a week of play at some point. His baseline Total PA is therefore 572.

However, suppose a fantasy manager is optimistic that with another year of growth, he'll be able to improve vs. RHP, enabling him to regain the leadoff slot despite heavy competition, and even gain a few extra starts. They can create a rosy scenario where SAW and PAS reflect this, and Kim's Total PA increases to 671.

Alternatively, say a fantasy manager starts to sour on Kim, and assumes performance regression and further lineup displacement, and assumes a two-week IL stint. Compared to his baseline, Kim loses 1 AW, his SAW drops another 0.2, and his PAS drops another 0.08. Combined, these lead to only 516 Total PA.

Finally, say a fantasy manager looks at Kim's splits and fears his playing time vs. RHP (%vR and PAS-R) could really tank, and that other Padres stars will occupy the top lineup slots even vs. LHPs. Mild tweaks to these building blocks further drop Kim's Total PA all the way down to 433.

Retaking control

With these insights and capabilities, the era of black box playing time projections will soon come to an end, giving fantasy managers both a sense of confidence in those projections and the direct ability to create their own logical or whimsical scenarios in preparation for their drafts, trades, free agent bids, and other decisions.

MiLB age as a leading indicator of MLB outcomes

by Doug Otto

It's common knowledge that advanced performance at a young age is a significant indicator of future success. As with just about any other "skill," this certainly applies to baseball. It doesn't take much scouting expertise to understand the importance of making an MLB debut before most college players get drafted, or of playing in Double-A before most high schoolers graduate.

But what about the less obvious cases? Is there reason to be suspicious of a 23-year-old slashing .300/.400/.500 at High-A? How much slack should we give a 20-year-old struggling at Double-A? Answering these questions requires evaluating multiple facets of a player's game; however, understanding the extent to which age factors into a player's development may be helpful for projecting future performance.

Debut Age

Before looking at minor league age, let's see how MLB debut age correlates with MLB performance. Using publicly available data from FanGraphs, we included all batters and pitchers who made their debut between 1990 and 2022 and logged at least 300 career PA or 150 career IP, respectively. Batter performance is measured using FanGraphs' Offensive Runs Above Average (OFF, the higher the better), and pitcher value is measured using FanGraphs' Runs Above Replacement (RAR, the higher the better). A player's season age is defined as their age as of June 30:

Debut Age	Batter Value	Pitcher Value
≤20	7.7	24.3
21-22	0.7	20.5
23-24	-1.8	18.1
25-26	-5.5	15.4
27≥	-7.1	14.1

There appears to be a linear trend for both batters and pitchers such that production value declines as debut age increases. This is consistent with an intuitive understanding of the value of reaching the majors at a young age.

Minor League Age Scores

While this is a helpful start, we still want to know if age can be used as a barometer for future performance while a player is still developing in the minor leagues. We can use the following historical data to try to answer this question:

- We included all players' full-season minor league data (Short Season A, Single-A, High-A, Double-A, and Triple-A) from 2006 to 2019.
- We included all players' MLB data from 2010 to 2023 to capture major leaguers with more complete minor league track records. In addition, including only minor league data up through 2019 helps exclude those who might currently be in the minors at lower levels.
- To avoid rehab assignments, minor league seasons for players who already exceeded rookie limits in the majors were excluded.
- Finally, only batters with at least 300 total minor league PA and pitchers with at least 150 IP were included.
- This leaves us with 5,805 minor league batters and 4,326 pitchers.

For each level, batter and pitcher age was converted to an age score (standardized z-score relative to the distribution of ages). This allows us to compare age across all levels of non-rookie minor league ball. Once the age scores were calculated, each player was given a weighted average score by taking the average of a player's score at each level weighted by PA for batters and IP for pitchers. Players were then grouped by "Age Group" ranges from -2 (younger) to +2 (older), which encompasses roughly 95% of players. The table below shows the age range for each age score group by level for batters (B) and pitchers (P):

	Single-A		High-A		Double-A		Triple-A	
Age Group	B	P	B	P	B	P	B	P
-2 or Less	16-18	16-18	17-19	17-18	17-20	18-19	17-20	18-19
-1.99 to -1	19-20	19-20	20-21	19-21	21-22	20-22	21-22	20-23
-0.99 to 0	21	21-22	22	22-23	23-24	23-24	23-25	24-26
0 to 0.99	22-23	23-24	23-24	24-25	25-26	25-27	26-27	27-30
1 to 1.99	24-25	25	25-26	26-28	27-28	28-29	28-30	31-33
2 or More	26+	26+	27+	29+	29+	30+	31+	34+

The table below shows MLB value (again using FanGraphs' OFF metric) by Age Group for batters per 600 PA:

Age Group	Number	% in MLB	Value/600 PA
-2 or Less	73	79.5	9.3
-1.99 to -1	632	57	0.5
-0.99 to 0	1,885	29.1	-1.9
0 to 0.99	2,170	11.2	-5.2
1 to 1.99	448	4.9	-6.8
2 or More	53	3.8	-7.4

For batters, there appears to be a linear relationship between minor league age and reaching the majors, as well as offensive production. In fact, only batters with an age score of -2 or less had appreciably positive offensive production, while even players with age scores between -1 and -2 had only middling MLB outcomes.

The table below shows MLB outcomes for pitchers using RAR (set to a rate per 180 IP as a starter and 60 IP as a reliever):

Age Group	Number	% in MLB	SP Val/180 IP	RP Val/60 IP
-2 or Less	19	68.4	17.7	-0.1
-1.99 to -1	414	57.2	17.3	0.9
-0.99 to 0	1,759	41.6	12.2	1.1
0 to 0.99	1,502	28.5	9.1	1.6
1 to 1.99	210	31.9	6.3	2.3
2 or More	24	29.2	5.5	0.6

While a similar trend can be seen by age for pitchers, it is less pronounced than that of the trend observed for batters. In contrast to batters, where only those with an age score of less than -2 had significantly positive SP value outcomes, pitchers with an age score of less than -1 appeared to have similarly positive outcomes. There appears to be no correlation between minor league age score and RP value per 60 IP.

Regression

These results are indicative of a significant statistical relationship between minor league age and future production, but there are other factors at play that could be influencing these trends. Valuable skill sets such as power and plate discipline for batters, and stuff and control for pitchers have always played a large role in future production and should not be ignored. We can use regression analyses to control for these potentially confounding variables and isolate the effect of age.

For the batter regression models, we'll operationalize age as whether the batter had a weighted age score -2 or less while controlling for ISO, BB% and K%.

- For the first model, the dependent variable was whether the batter reached the majors. Results of the regression showed that batters with a minor league age score below -2 were over 17 times more likely than older batters to make the majors when controlling for the other variables.
- The second regression analysis included MLB offensive value as the dependent variable. Results showed that being in the -2 or less age score group results in an average value boost of 19.6 per 600 PA for batters.

Because the pitcher age score findings revealed a smaller difference between pitchers with a minor league age score of -2 or less and pitchers with an age score between -1 and -2, age will be categorized as those with an age score of -1 or less vs. those higher than -1. The control variables for the pitcher regression were ERA, IP per start, and the interaction between BB/9 and K/9.

- Results of the first regression analysis for pitchers showed that having a minor league age score of -1 or less increased the likelihood of making the major leagues by a factor of 1.3.
- Because the initial findings showed no real correlation between age and relief pitcher value, only starting pitcher value was used as the dependent variable for the second regression analysis. Results showed that having a minor league age score resulted in an average increase of 5.9 per 180 IP.

Conclusion

The results of these analyses show that the youngest minor leaguers tend to have better MLB outcomes than their older counterparts. The effect was more distinct among batters than starting pitchers, and there appeared to be no correlation for relievers. While being relatively old as a minor leaguer does not mean that a player cannot have success as a major leaguer, their minor league production should be taken with healthy skepticism. Overall, minor league age should be heavily considered when evaluating minor league players, especially batters.

As a guide, the table below shows the cutoffs for low-risk ages among batters and pitchers at each level of full-season ball.

Level	Batters	Starting Pitchers
Single-A	18 or younger	20 or younger
High-A	19 or younger	21 or younger
Double-A	20 or younger	22 or younger
Triple-A	20 or younger	23 or younger

Checking in on Pure Quality Starts

by Jon Enriquez

The Pure Quality Starts (PQS) system has long been a reliable way to summarize a starting pitcher's performance at a glance with a stat you can calculate in your head. When a pitcher achieves each one of five different outcomes in a start, they earn a PQS point, and they receive an overall score between 0 and 5. The outcomes, along with the current standard, are:

- Stamina – pitching deep into games, specifically more than 6 IP per start (IP>6)
- Hit prevention – allowing fewer hits than innings pitched (H<IP)
- Dominance – posting 5 or more strikeouts (K>=5)
- Command – more than 3 strikeouts for each walk (K/BB>=3, or K>=3 if BB=0)
- Home run prevention – keeping the ball in the park (HR=0)

These standards were set deliberately so that each would be met in 50% of all starts (or as close to it as possible). But these were last set to reflect the game as it was in 2012-2014, so here's a look at how well these benchmarks have withstood the changes of the last decade:

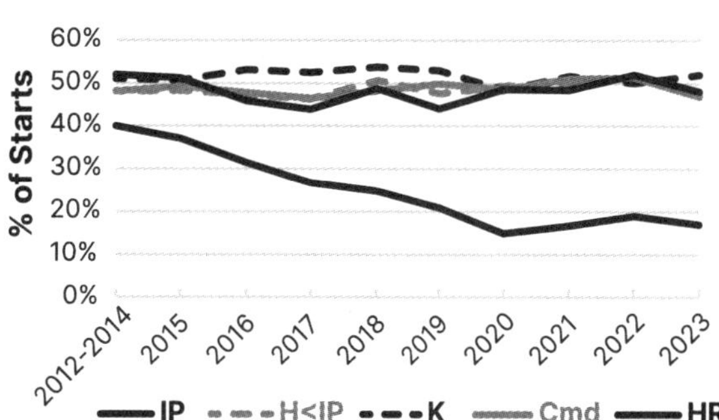

Four of the five criteria have held up very well, with achievement continuing to hover around 50% of starts. But the IP component stands out. Even at the time the current standard was set, the pivotal decision was to either set it to >6 IP such that ~40% of starts would qualify, or to >=6 IP such that ~60% of starts would qualify. We selected the latter. But in the ensuing years, the percentage of starters who pitched into the seventh inning declined steadily for years before leveling out in recent seasons, to the point that in 2023, just 17.3% of starts qualified for that point.

As a result, the distribution of PQS scores is no longer normally distributed. In 2014:

- 29% of starts had a PQS-4 or 5 – DOMinant (DOM) starts
- 40% of starts had a PQS-2 or 3 – DECent (DEC) starts
- 31% of starts had a PQS-0 or 1 – DISaster (DIS) starts

That's a normal, balanced distribution. But in 2023, just 20% were DOMinant, 45% were DECent, and 35% were DISasters, which is no longer a normal distribution. When the standards were last set, the problem we needed to solve was that it was too easy to earn a DOM score. In 2023, the problem is that it's now too hard.

To bring balance back to PQS, we are again tweaking the IP standard. We are now adopting the standard of *6 or more IP.* With this revision, we have restored a more normal distribution. Here is a similar chart showing the starts for 2023 (which is very similar to that of 2022, not shown):

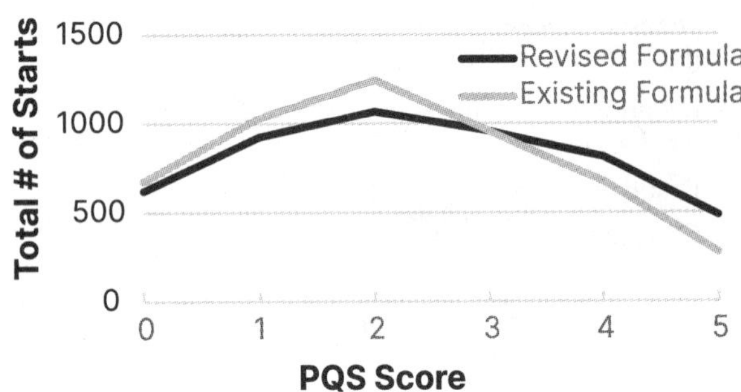

The distribution under the revised formula is now 26% DOMinant to 32% DISaster, which isn't quite balanced, but it's a lot closer. One mitigating effect is that even though the IP threshold is now easier to achieve, starters who pitch exactly 6 IP must still allow no more than 5 hits to get both their IP>=6 point and their H<IP point.

Of course, just because the data are more normally distributed doesn't automatically mean the change is worthwhile. The obvious question is whether this change cheapens PQS by awarding points for outcomes that aren't really that good. Put another way, is a 6 IP start really "DOMinant"?

Let's look at some examples. Under both the current formula and the new formula, all of the performances on the left side of this table would qualify as PQS-4 DOMinant starts:

Examples: DOMinant Starts						Tweaked: Still DOMinant?						
IP	H	BB	K	HR	PQS	IP	H	BB	K	HR	PQS	NewPQS
6.1	6	1	4	0	4	6.0	5	1	4	0	3	4
6.1	7	2	6	0	4	6.0	7	2	6	0	3	4
6.1	6	3	9	1	4	6.0	5	3	9	1	3	4
6.1	5	4	10	0	4	6.0	4	4	10	0	3	4

On the right are slightly modified versions of those starts. Under the existing IP>6 standard, these tweaked versions would have resulted in a PQS-3 rating, but under the revised IP>=6 standard, they will now be considered PQS-4 DOMinant as well.

In our view, these starts aren't that different, and in fact starts like those on the right side often produce better rate stats than the ones on the left side (i.e., there's a reason those SPs were removed after one out in the 7th inning). There will always be exceptions, but a newly earned PQS-4 or PQS-5 under the revised formula when a pitcher goes exactly 6 IP will most often feel like a dominant performance.

Under the revised standard, starts can earn no more than one additional point compared to the previous standard, and can never lose a point. Thus, there are no starts classified as DISasters under the existing formula that have been reclassified as DOMinant. About 7% of starts were reclassified from DECent to DOMinant, and 3% more were reclassified from DISaster to DECent, but most stayed the same:

2023	New PQS					
Current	Count			%		
PQS	DIS	DEC	DOM	DIS	DEC	DOM
DOM	0	0	955	0%	0%	20%
DEC	0	1862	341	0%	38%	7%
DIS	1541	161	0	32%	3%	0%

All things considered, this is a common sense change that keeps the overall PQS system aligned with how the game is played on the field. The new formula will be implemented at the BaseballHQ.com website and in future editions of the *Forecaster*.

Looking ahead to 2024 category targets

by Zach Larson

There are many tasks on fantasy managers' to-do lists as we prepare for draft season. As we calculate and tweak our interpretations of players' situations and skill sets, it behooves us to know how many of these statistics we need to fill our respective buckets. Granted, it's not an exact science—MLB presents us with several ever-changing variables each season to keep us on our toes. This year, we saw new changes like pitch clocks, base size changes, and defensive restrictions added to the usual mystery of baseball design specs and teams changing their ballpark dimensions—and perhaps even more things we don't know about now but may find out later.

Despite this uncertainty, we still have a valuable resource: league scoring history. While we're striving to do as well as possible in each category, we do have some restrictions—limited resources (i.e. draft capital) being Number One. There's a concept called value engineering: understanding the relationship between cost and functionality, striving to fulfill the product's requirements while minimizing each dollar we spend. With this idea in mind, we don't need to top each category to win our league; we simply can do well in each one. In fact, finishing in first place in a category by more than one is technically a waste of resources.

In 5x5 roto leagues, we generally need about 100 points (12-team leagues) or 120 points (15-teamers) for a first-place finish. These winning scores amount to a third-place finish in each category in 12-team leagues and a fourth-place finish in 15-team leagues. You can look at your home league's history to see the numbers required to win. Due to the accessibility and representative quality of the data, we'll use the National Fantasy Baseball Championship (NFBC) platform to look at targets for 15-team and 12-team mixed leagues:

12-team Mixed Leagues, 3rd place

Year	R	HR	RBI	SB	AVG	K	W	SV	ERA	WHIP
2021	1093.0	322.4	1050.9	124.9	.2624	1406.9	90.0	72.2	3.606	1.157
2022	1004.7	278.2	980.1	131.5	.2568	1362.0	92.4	69.4	3.343	1.135
2023	1131.3	321.8	1098.7	196.5	.2629	1448.6	93.4	78.5	3.747	1.199

15-team Mixed Leagues, 4th place

Year	R	HR	RBI	SB	AVG	K	W	SV	ERA	WHIP
2021	1075.2	314.9	1033.8	118.5	.2606	1380.9	87.6	69.3	3.690	1.171
2022	986.8	268.9	962.9	127.5	.2549	1337.6	90.1	64.9	3.417	1.147
2023	1074.7	302.6	1042.5	182.0	.2597	1368.7	88.9	69.4	3.860	1.218

As outlined in the tables above, we see a big jump in stolen bases, which surprises no one (even Rip Van Winkle had dreams about stolen bases.) We saw modest increases in offense and subsequent declines in pitching ratios, which also correlate to many of the rule changes seemingly designed to promote run scoring.

The following table looks at the 2023 percent change compared to the three-year (2021-23) average:

2023 Percent Change vs Three-Year Average

Lg Siz	R	HR	RBI	SB	AVG	K	W	SV	ERA	WHIP
12-team	5.1%	4.7%	5.3%	30.2%	0.8%	3.0%	1.6%	7.0%	-5.1%	-3.0%
15-team	2.8%	2.4%	2.9%	27.5%	0.5%	0.5%	0.1%	2.2%	-5.6%	-3.3%

When compared to 2021, we see three-year highs in R, RBI, and SB, but fewer HR. Could this mean that because stolen bases are more prevalent, they will be easier to acquire, and draft capital should prioritize power? Will some hidden pendulum swing back to give pitchers more advantages, or will the elite ratio arms be worth their premium draft prices?

Establish Your Approach

Instead of hyper-focusing on specific numbers, a better approach would be to do what you're likely already doing when drafting a team: absorb as much upside as possible while mitigating risk. Extract value in each phase of the fantasy season. Establish core strengths early and leverage upside plays when presented at a discount during the draft. In-season, recognize the opportunity cost of hoping for prospect hype or an injured player's impactful return. Maximize your FAB dollars so they have the most time to impact your team before losing the ability to acquire stats as the season ticks away. Targets are just another reference point for building your team in a historically successful way.

Targets aren't just valuable for preseason draft planning; they can also be helpful during the season. Keep an eye on them as you investigate the month-over-month trends and see if any rule changes have had the expected impact. If things appear to be trending higher or lower than you expected, make the necessary moves while you still have time to impact your bottom line. Targets can help us all season long by identifying ways to attack our leagues by continuing to out-maneuver our opposition.

In any competition, it's up to you to leverage every piece of information you have to your advantage. Nothing is certain—this year's rule changes might mitigate the past seasons' relevance. We could see 2023 as a weird year that bucks all the statistical trends. On the other hand, we may uncover something that ultimately gave us a decided advantage. Only time will tell, but rarely does putting in extra work lead you astray.

Exploring FAB usage rates

by Zach Larson

Few things cause as much hand-wringing as creating Free Agent Budget (FAB) bids. If you are unaccustomed to FAB bid construction, on its best days, it can feel like something between a hunch and a coin flip—and on its most peculiar, requiring some archaic form of spellcasting from a lost world. We have spent time exploring ways to help fantasy managers create bids relative to their specific leagues, but zooming out and looking at the FAB environment from a distance can also be helpful.

For this exercise, we looked at two popular contests in the NFBC: the Online Championship (composed of 205 separate 12-team mixed leagues) and the Main Event (53 separate 15-team mixed leagues). By breaking down how teams spend money by week, we hope to learn how to budget most efficiently so that we are competitive early in the season—when the bids offer the most potential return—while still having enough left in the tank for the home stretch.

FAB Spend Chart

Wk	12-team Remaining	12-team Spent	15-team Remaining	15-team Spent	Main Event Lg Winners
0	95.4%	4.6%	99.2%	0.8%	0.7%
1	88.9%	6.5%	92.8%	6.4%	5.0%
2	81.8%	7.1%	85.8%	7.0%	5.5%
3	74.0%	7.8%	77.1%	8.7%	5.4%
4	67.3%	6.7%	70.4%	6.8%	6.1%
5	59.9%	7.4%	62.6%	7.8%	6.2%
6	52.5%	7.4%	53.3%	9.3%	6.8%
7	46.0%	6.4%	45.8%	7.5%	6.8%
8	41.6%	4.4%	40.6%	5.2%	5.4%
9	37.8%	3.8%	35.9%	4.7%	6.5%
10	34.2%	3.7%	31.6%	4.3%	5.9%
11	28.2%	6.0%	25.0%	6.5%	8.9%
12	25.7%	2.4%	22.2%	2.8%	3.0%
13	23.4%	2.3%	19.4%	2.8%	4.0%
14	22.0%	1.4%	17.7%	1.7%	2.3%
15	20.3%	1.7%	15.7%	2.0%	3.6%
16	19.4%	0.9%	14.5%	1.2%	1.3%
17	17.6%	1.8%	12.3%	2.2%	5.0%
18	16.6%	1.0%	11.1%	1.2%	1.3%
19	15.4%	1.2%	9.7%	1.4%	1.8%
20	14.0%	1.4%	8.3%	1.4%	2.6%
21	13.1%	0.9%	7.3%	1.0%	1.6%
22	12.1%	0.9%	6.4%	0.9%	1.3%
23	11.4%	0.8%	5.6%	0.8%	1.0%
24	10.8%	0.6%	5.2%	0.5%	0.9%
25	10.3%	0.5%	4.7%	0.4%	0.9%
26	9.9%	0.4%	4.4%	0.3%	0.5%

We can gain insight into the macro-environment by looking at the above chart. If we break the season into thirds, teams spend 60-65% by Memorial Day (Week 9). Most of the remaining FAB

(30-35%) is spent over the next two months, bringing us to early August (Week 19) and the season's home stretch. When unspent FAB is considered (10% for 12-team leagues and 5% for 15-team leagues), the data shows that managers are earmarking around 5% for the final weeks.

These spending habits could stem from a variety of reasons. As MLB teams appear more comfortable bringing young players up earlier, especially when paired with league incentives to do so, high-value targets appear sooner. Early spending also supports the idea that fantasy managers are aware of the inflationary nature of FAB dollars and are keen on spending them earlier in the season when they can deliver the most value, as 20 weeks of stats are better than 15, which are better than 10, and so on.

Notes on 2023 Main Event league winners

- Main Event League winners were slightly less aggressive early in the season, spending 54.3% of their budget through Week 9, as opposed to 64.1% in 15-team leagues and 62.2% in 12-team leagues.
- They spent more of their budget in the final stretch (10.5%, compared to 6.7% in 15-team and 12-team leagues). This is likely due to competing in an overall competition where every stat is critical, even though their individual league standings could be unimpacted.
- They spent 99.98% of their FAB budget.
- They made 56.2 transactions, on average (2,981 total moves).

Beware of Hammer-Chasing

When we think about FAB, we want to understand what it truly is at its core: another resource to acquire stats. We can sometimes overvalue our FAB dollars, treating them like they have some inherent value when they solely represent our ability to make roster moves (and in a $0 bid environment, not even that) to buy futures on statistics.

Some will want to maintain the "hammer," or the most FAB at any given time, to acquire a mid-to-late season impact player. This isn't a bad strategy, but don't overvalue its worth. There is an inherent opportunity cost risk when you bypass players that could help you now for a theoretical advantage in the future. Compounding this late-season inflation with the dead money from abandoned teams (around 4-10%) at the end of the season leads to an environment where players may cost less when you have fewer opponents to bid against.

Act With Purpose

Make sure you have a specific plan for each player you bid on. After doing some roster assessment, you can identify some essential items: your short-term and long-term needs, and how many roster spots you have available to address them. A short-term add to ensure a legal roster will likely have a different impact than a potential long-term add to replace an anchor starter.

Looking at FAB from a top-level approach gives us season-long parameters to work within. It helps guide us when drilling down bids on specific targets while ensuring that our micro-level decisions align with our overall plan. This process will help you define your feelings about each potential addition and not fall victim to hype or lack of due diligence. If you are willing to go above what you perceive as fair market value, ask yourself why. Is it because you have confidence in the player being a long-term solution to a need, or is it a luxury item that the industry is high on, but less valuable to your specific situation? Ensure that every available resource best impacts your bottom line.

Assessing the Santana Plan

by Michael Weddell

The Santana Plan is a roster construction strategy—a modification of the LIMA Plan that advocates spending no more than $60 out of $260 on your pitching staff—that revolves around one elite starting pitcher (a "Santana Plan anchor"). The rest of your pitching staff needs to be low-priced as you acquire a saves source and try to stay as close to the $60 budget for your pitching staff as possible.

We've been pushing this version of the Santana Plan for 15 years, starting back when Johan Santana (the namesake) still was the premier example of a reliable, elite starter. Most of our annual articles on BaseballHQ.com focus on each spring's crop of Santana Plan anchors, so let's use this opportunity to take a step back and re-assess how well the strategy works.

Santana Plan performance

A Santana Plan anchor is a starting pitcher who has performed at elite (or near-elite) performance levels over the two most recent seasons. More specifically, they must have earned at least $24 during each of the prior two years based on strikeouts, innings, xERA, and xWHIP. We make the calculations for you and announce each year's Santana Plan anchors each preseason on BaseballHQ.com.

From 2009-22, Santana Plan anchors retained 79% of their prior-year value compared to only 52% for the pitching pool as a whole. ("Value" means R$ using the categories mentioned above). This is a huge, actionable difference, which is why we urge you to draft one elite starter from the subset of the pool that retains 79% of its value. Other results:

- Historically, 28% of Santana Plan anchors improved, returning a greater R$ in the year they were named anchors than the prior year. This is quite impressive considering that they were already performing at an elite level.
- Just 13% of them collapsed, returning less than one-third of their R$.
- The remaining 55% experienced a middling outcome, keeping more than one-third but less than all of their prior R$.

Comparing other expensive starting pitchers

Let's shake up our kaleidoscope and consider a different method of measuring Santana Plan anchors. Maybe fantasy players should just buy expensive starters without regard for which ones appear on the Santana list. Perhaps the market already accurately reflects the best wisdom about which top starters to purchase. Perhaps our annual list of who to buy is superfluous.

This new method of evaluating Santana Plan anchors also will use historical average auction values, which should be a more robust test:

- We used NFBC ADP data from 2014-23.
- We listed the Santana Plan anchors for each of those ten years, looked up their ADPs, and converted their ADPs to average auction values using Bill Macey's formula found on page 57 in this book.
- We then computed the end-of-year R$ using BaseballHQ's Custom Draft Guide to see how much of the original investment was returned.
- To create a matched set, we then did the same thing for the same number of pitchers each year who had the earliest ADPs, but were not Santana Plan anchors. We then compared the results.

The Santana Plan anchors returned 75% of their value from 2014-23. The control group of other expensive starting pitchers returned just 61%. We conclude that BaseballHQ's annual list of Santana Plan anchors provides substantial additional value beyond the "just buy the starters with early ADPs" control method.

The control group might have had a hidden disadvantage, however. We let the Santana Plan first pick who it wanted (peak Clayton Kershaw from 2014-18, for example) and then the control group selected among the leftovers, often resulting in less expensive pitchers. However, even when we look at the subset of Santana Plan anchors with ADPs later than 60, we find that those pitchers returned 91% of their value, better than the overall 75% average for the Santana Plan anchors.

A few last technical notes:

- We set a floor of $0 for the R$ earned by pitchers so that our calculations weren't excessively affected by disasters. If a pitcher's R$ was far below $0, in practice, the fantasy owner is replacing that pitcher on their roster, typically because the pitcher was injured early in the season.
- We excluded pitchers who did not play, or who we know began the season on the IL, even if they were Santana Plan anchors.
- We excluded Shohei Ohtani because his ADP was affected by eligibility as a hitter.

Frequently Asked Questions

If buying one Santana Plan anchor is good, shouldn't we also consider purchasing two elite starters, doubling down on the strategy?

No, don't buy two Santana Plan starters. Possible exceptions are if you are in a keeper league and have a great set of underpriced batters entering draft day, or you are intentionally competing by writing off saves. A key feature of the LIMA and the Santana Plan is spending less on pitching than most of your opponents, and you can't do that by acquiring two elite starters on draft day.

Isn't the Santana Plan outdated given the more granular pitching data available to today's fantasy players? Why look at the preceding two years' worth of data when a sharp fantasy player can tell when a pitcher's velocity increases, when a new pitch is added, or when a pitchers' K-BB% suddenly increases?

Good questions, but no, the Santana Plan isn't outdated as demonstrated by this article. Recency bias–exaggerating recent performance changes instead of considering a full two-year track record–remains a real phenomenon.

How do I apply the Santana Plan to a draft, not an auction, format?

It's the same principle. Pick a Santana Plan anchor early on, then load up on batters and one reliable saves source. You still want to invest more early-round picks on batters than your competitors.

Conclusion

The Santana Plan continues to be a valuable, effective roster construction strategy. We'll continue to publish preseason articles on BaseballHQ.com naming each year's Santana Plan anchors.

The following section contains player boxes for every batter who had significant playing time in 2023 and/or is expected to get fantasy roster-worthy plate appearances in 2024. You will find some prospects here, but only those who logged MLB plate appearances in 2023 and who we project to play a significant role in 2024. For more complete prospect coverage, see our Prospects section.

Snapshot Section

The top band of each player box contains the following information:

Age as of July 1, 2024.

Bats shows which side of the plate he bats from—(L)eft, (R)ight or (B)oth.

Positions: Up to three defensive positions are listed and represent those for which he appeared a minimum of 20 games in 2023. Note that an additional multiposition chart (with 20-, 10- and 5-game eligibility minimums) can be found on page 280.

Ht/Wt: Each batter's height and weight.

Reliability Grades analyze each batter's forecast risk, on an A-F scale. High grades go to those who have accumulated few disabled list days (Health), have a history of substantial and regular major league playing time (PT/Exp) and have displayed consistent performance over the past three years, using RC/G (Consist).

LIMA Plan Grade evaluates how well a batter would fit into a team using the LIMA Plan draft strategy. Best grades go to batters who have excellent base skills, are expected to see regular playing time, and are in the $10-$30 Rotisserie dollar range. Lowest grades will go to poor skills, few AB and values less than $5 or more than $30.

Random Variance Score (Rand Var) measures the impact random variance had on the batter's 2023 stats and the probability that his 2024 performance will exceed or fall short of 2023. The variables tracked are those prone to regression—h%, HR/F and xBA to BA variance. Players are rated on a scale of −5 to +5 with positive scores indicating rebounds and negative scores indicating corrections. Note that this score is computer-generated and the projections will override it on occasion.

Mayberry Method (MM) acknowledges the imprecision of the forecasting process by projecting player performance in broad strokes. The four digits of MM each represent a fantasy-relevant skill—power, speed, batting average and playing time (PA)—and are all on a scale of 0 to 5. For additional information and specifics of MM, see page 60.

Commentaries provide a brief analysis of his skills and the potential impact on 2024 performance. MLB statistics are listed first for those who played only a portion of 2023 at the major league level. Note that these commentaries generally look at performance related issues only. Role and playing time expectations may impact these analyses, so you will have to adjust accordingly. Upside (UP) and downside (DN) statistical potential appears for some players; these are less grounded in hard data and more speculative of skills potential.

Commentaries that end with "(CB)" were written by BaseballHQ.com Director of Prospect Analysis Chris Blessing. As those players still have rookie eligibility and minimal MLB experience, we've decided it is more beneficial to describe the player's scouting attributes than to focus on his statistical or performance history. The author for the balance of any page's commentaries is noted after the final box on each page.

Player Stat Section

The past five years' statistics represent the total accumulated in the majors as well as in Triple-A, Double-A ball and various foreign leagues during each year. All non-major league stats have been converted to a major league equivalent (MLE) performance level. Minor league levels below Double-A are not included.

Nearly all baseball publications separate a player's statistical experiences in the major leagues from the minor leagues and outside leagues. While this may be appropriate for official record-keeping purposes, it is not an easy-to-analyze snapshot of a player's complete performance for a given year.

Bill James has proven that minor league statistics (converted to MLEs), at Double-A level or above, provide as accurate a record of a player's performance as major league statistics. Other researchers have also devised conversion factors for foreign leagues. Since these are adequate barometers, we include them in the pool of historical data for each year.

Team designations: An asterisk (*) appearing with a team name means that Triple-A and/or Double-A numbers are included in that year's stat line. Any stints of less than 20 AB are not included (to screen out most rehab appearances). A designation of "a/a" means the stats were accumulated at both AA and AAA levels that year. "for" represents a foreign or independent league. The designation "2TM" appears whenever a player was on more than one major league team, crossing leagues, in a season. "2AL" and "2NL" represent more than one team in the same league. Players who were cut during the season and finished 2023 as a free agent are designated as FAA (Free agent, AL) and FAN (Free agent, NL).

Stats: Descriptions of all the categories appear in the Encyclopedia.

- The leading decimal point has been suppressed on some categories to conserve space.

- Data for platoons (vL+, vR+), xHR and xHR/F, balls-in-play (G/L/F) and batted ball characteristics (HctX, QBaB, Brl%) are for major league performance only.
- Formulas that use BIP data, like xBA and xPX, only appear for years in which G/L/F data is available.

After the traditional five rotisserie stat categories, expected HR, expected SB, and expected BA are presented for comparison. On-base average and slugging average appear next, and then OPS+, which is adjusted to league average, for both OPS itself, and OPS splits vs. left-handed and right-handed pitchers.

Batting eye and contact skill are measured with walk rate (bb%), contact rate (ct%). Eye is the ratio of walks to strikeouts.

Once the ball leaves the bat, it will either be a (G)round ball, (L)ine drive or (F)ly ball. Hit rate (h%), also referred to as batting average on balls-in-play (BABIP), measures how often a ball put into play results in a base hit. Hard contact index (HctX) measures the frequency of hard contact, compared to overall league levels. QBaB is a quality-of-contact metric that encapsulates average exit velocity, average launch angle, and launch angle variability, and Brl% is a percentage of batted balls hit with the optimal exit velocity and launch angle combination.

Linear weighted power index (PX) measures a batter's skill at hitting extra base hits as compared to overall league levels. xPX measures power by assessing how hard the ball is being hit (rather than the outcomes of those hits). And the ratio of home runs to fly balls shows the results of those hits. Expected home runs to fly balls give a sense of whether the player over or underperformed in the power department.

To assess speed, first look at on-base average (does he get on base?), then Spd (is he fast enough to steal bases?), then SBA (how often is he attempting to steal bases?) and finally, SB% (when he attempts, what is his rate of success?).

The final section includes two overall performance measures: runs above replacement (RAR) and base performance index (BPX, which is BPV indexed to each year's league average) and the Rotisserie value (R$).

2024 Projections

Forecasts are computed from a player's trends over the past five years. Adjustments were made for leading indicators and variances between skill and statistical output. After reviewing the leading indicators, you might opt to make further adjustments.

Although each year's numbers include all playing time at the Double-A level or above, the 2024 forecast only represents potential playing time at the major league level, and again is highly preliminary.

Note that the projected Rotisserie values in this book will not necessarily align with each player's historical actuals. Since we currently have no idea who is going to play shortstop for the Marlins, or whether Junior Caminero is going to break camp with the Rays, it is impossible to create a finite pool of playing time, something which is required for valuation. So the projections are roughly based on a 12-team AL/NL league, and include an inflated number of plate appearances, league-wide. This serves to flatten the spread of values and depress individual player dollar projections. In truth, a $25 player in this book might actually be worth $21, or $28. This level of precision is irrelevant in a process that is driven by market forces anyway. So, don't obsess over it.

Be aware of other sources that publish perfectly calibrated Rotisserie values over the winter. They are likely making arbitrary decisions as to where free agents are going to sign and who is going to land jobs in the spring. We do not make those leaps of faith here.

Bottom line... It is far too early to be making definitive projections for 2024, especially on playing time. Focus on the skill levels and trends, then consult BaseballHQ.com for playing time revisions as players change teams and roles become more defined. A free projections update will be available online in March.

Do-it-yourself analysis

Here are some data points you can look at in doing your own player analysis:

- Variance between vL+ and vR+ OPS+
- Growth or decline in walk rate (bb%)
- Growth or decline in contact rate (ct%)
- Growth or decline in G/L/F individually, or concurrent shifts
- Variance in 2023 hit rate (h%) to 2020-2022 three-year average
- Variance between BA and xBA each year
- Variance between 2023 HR and 2023 xHR
- Growth or decline in HctX level
- Growth or decline in QBaB scores
- Growth or decline in Brl%
- Growth or decline in power index (PX) rate
- Variance between PX and xPX each year
- Variance in 2023 HR/F rate to 2020-2022 three-year average
- Variance in 2023 HR/F rate to 2023 xHR/F rate
- Growth or decline in statistically scouted speed (Spd) score
- Concurrent growth/decline of gauges like ct%, FB, PX, xPX, HR/F
- Concurrent growth/decline of gauges like OB, Spd, SBA, SB%

Abrams,CJ

Age: 23 Pos: SS | Bats: L Ht: 6' 2" Wt: 185
Health A | PT/Exp A | Consist B
LIMA Plan D+ | Rand Var +2 | MM 2535

Despite doing little in first half to earn the role, was promoted to leadoff spot on July 7 and blossomed there. Exciting 2nd-half trifecta of more walks, more contact, more hard contact says these gains are sustainable. Elite Spd and SB% say there's no reason for green light to flicker. xBA points to headroom for BA as h% creeps up, with... UP: 70 SB

Yr	Tm	PA	R	HR	RBI	SB	BA	xHR	xSB	xBA	OBP	SLG	OPS+	vL+	vR+	bb%	ct%	Eye	G	L	F	h%	HctX	QBaB	Brl%	PX	xPX	HR/F	xHR/F	Spd	SBA%	SB%	RAR	BPX	R$
19																																			
20																																			
21	aa	174	20	1	18	10	259		6		311	364	93			7	76	0.31				34				78				87	30%	82%		27	$6
22	2 NL *	480	63	7	42	17	255	3	17	243	274	351	89	54	100	2	81	0.14	51	18	31	30	88	DDf	2%	61	65	3%	4%	134	23%	67%	-16.1	69	$16
23	WAS	614	83	18	64	47	245	17	35	257	300	412	97	69	107	5	79	0.27	44	18	38	28	94	CCf	7%	94	96	11%	10%	138	39%	92%	6.9	161	$24
1st Half		273	31	7	34	9	234	7	9	250	279	395	92	74	100	3	75	0.14	47	17	36	28	82	DCf	6%	97	83	10%	10%	132	21%	82%	-5.9	96	$11
2nd Half		341	52	11	30	38	254	10	26	262	316	427	100	64	112	7	82	0.42	41	19	40	28	103	CBd	8%	92	106	11%	10%	143	51%	95%	7.4	218	$37
24	Proj	630	97	15	68	52	251	13	31	251	305	390	95	64	108	5	80	0.27	44	19	36	29	92		5%	81	84	8%	8%	132	41%	85%	4.5	113	$33

Abreu,José

Age: 37 Pos: 1B | Bats: R Ht: 6' 3" Wt: 235
Health A | PT/Exp A | Consist C
LIMA Plan B+ | Rand Var +3 | MM 3035

Missed 10 days in August with a bad back, but spent entire season hitting like a 36-year old with a bad back. Tepid second-half recovery provides only mild optimism: hard contact (HctX, QBaB, Brl%) was his standout skill at peak. If that's gone, odds are against a late-30s rebound. His ceiling is 2nd half x 2, but hope to pay for less.

Yr	Tm	PA	R	HR	RBI	SB	BA	xHR	xSB	xBA	OBP	SLG	OPS+	vL+	vR+	bb%	ct%	Eye	G	L	F	h%	HctX	QBaB	Brl%	PX	xPX	HR/F	xHR/F	Spd	SBA%	SB%	RAR	BPX	R$
19	CHW	693	85	33	123	2	284	37	2	272	330	503	115	140	106	5	76	0.24	46	22	32	33	107	ACb	13%	117	104	21%	24%	82	3%	50%	14.3	130	$24
20	CHW	262	43	19	60	0	317	18	0	295	370	617	131	114	136	7	75	0.31	45	24	32	35	122	ACb	14%	163	127	33%	31%	74	0%	0%	19.3	280	$38
21	CHW	659	86	30	117	1	261	27	0	261	351	481	114	132	109	9	75	0.43	46	19	35	30	114	ACc	10%	126	99	20%	18%	73	1%	100%	15.9	162	$22
22	CHW	679	85	15	75	0	304	25	2	261	378	446	117	120	116	9	82	0.56	48	20	32	35	133	ADc	9%	93	105	10%	16%	87	0%	0%	31.8	162	$26
23	HOU	594	62	18	90	0	237	19	3	238	296	383	93	100	89	7	76	0.32	45	19	36	28	88	CCd	9%	86	87	12%	13%	86	1%	0%	-1.3	50	$12
1st Half		337	26	6	41	0	240	6	2	222	291	344	87	85	88	6	75	0.27	46	19	35	30	84	BCd	6%	68	80	7%	7%	80	1%	0%	-10.0	-25	$7
2nd Half		257	36	12	49	0	233	13	1	258	304	435	100	117	91	8	77	0.40	44	18	38	25	94	CCd	12%	111	97	17%	19%	93	0%	0%	-0.6	157	$14
24	Proj	560	69	20	88	0	254	23	2	254	321	428	103	111	100	8	77	0.38	46	19	35	29	107		10%	102	98	15%	17%	78	0%	34%	8.1	127	$19

Abreu,Wilyer

Age: 25 Pos: OF | Bats: L Ht: 6' 0" Wt: 180
Health A | PT/Exp B | Consist B
LIMA Plan C | Rand Var 0 | MM 2413

2-14-.216 in 85 PA at BOS. Swing change in minors last year unlocked some power and put him on a late-blooming prospect track. Flashed above-average patience, pop, and speed in late-season callup. That broad skill base, strong-side platoon fit, and ability to handle all three OF spots give him a lot of paths to end-game profit.

Yr	Tm	PA	R	HR	RBI	SB	BA	xHR	xSB	xBA	OBP	SLG	OPS+	vL+	vR+	bb%	ct%	Eye	G	L	F	h%	HctX	QBaB	Brl%	PX	xPX	HR/F	xHR/F	Spd	SBA%	SB%	RAR	BPX	R$
19																																			
20																																			
21																																			
22	aa	534	72	12	49	21	213		13		327	356	97			14	63	0.46				31				119				91	18%	86%		24	$15
23	BOS *	422	55	17	57	8	249	4	11	247	333	436	105	54	127	11	72	0.44	42	21	38	30	116	ACc	9%	112	88	10%	20%	124	9%	79%	12.8	136	$12
1st Half		195	23	6	21	2	219		4	226	302	376	93	0	0	11	68	0.37	44	20	36	29	0		0%	98	-21	0%		124	7%	64%	-2.0	36	$1
2nd Half		228	32	11	37	6	275	4	6	265	359	488	114	53	126	12	75	0.53	42	21	38	32	121	ACc	10%	122	88	10%	20%	114	11%	86%	12.8	204	$18
24	Proj	315	42	9	40	9	243	15	8	228	335	393	100	43	108	12	70	0.46	41	21	39	32	109		9%	98	79	12%	20%	121	13%	85%	5.4	90	$12

Acuña Jr.,Ronald

Age: 26 Pos: RF | Bats: R Ht: 6' 0" Wt: 205
Health C | PT/Exp A | Consist B
LIMA Plan C | Rand Var -2 | MM 4455

Restored to full health, he surged right past his 2019 explosion. Staggering ct% gains rendered this masterpiece. xPX and Spd are actually "good not great," but sheer volume of hard-hit balls extracts amazing production from those skills. Repeat? Gravity is undefeated, but he could lose one-third of his value and still be in mix for #1 producer next year.

Yr	Tm	PA	R	HR	RBI	SB	BA	xHR	xSB	xBA	OBP	SLG	OPS+	vL+	vR+	bb%	ct%	Eye	G	L	F	h%	HctX	QBaB	Brl%	PX	xPX	HR/F	xHR/F	Spd	SBA%	SB%	RAR	BPX	R$
19	ATL	712	127	41	101	37	280	49	28	254	365	518	122	125	120	11	70	0.40	38	24	38	34	111	BBb	15%	128	139	25%	30%	128	24%	80%	21.5	163	$42
20	ATL	202	46	14	29	8	250	16	5	263	406	581	131	111	136	19	63	0.63	35	22	43	30	129	AAc	16%	217	186	33%	37%	89	16%	89%	13.3	360	$29
21	ATL	360	72	24	52	17	283	25	12	277	394	596	136	145	134	14	71	0.58	31	23	46	32	113	AAc	20%	185	139	24%	25%	102	23%	74%	27.6	358	$23
22	ATL	533	71	15	50	29	266	26	21	241	351	413	108	100	111	10	73	0.42	48	18	34	33	110	ACf	13%	102	109	13%	22%	97	27%	73%	8.7	86	$27
23	ATL	735	149	41	106	73	337	48	57	324	416	596	138	130	140	11	87	0.95	49	20	30	34	163	ADc	15%	126	132	24%	28%	127	38%	84%	96.1	393	$63
1st Half		381	76	21	54	39	336	25	28	326	415	604	139	137	140	11	86	0.88	50	19	31	34	153	ADc	16%	138	121	24%	28%	115	41%	85%	49.9	400	$64
2nd Half		354	73	20	52	34	339	23	30	322	418	587	136	121	139	11	88	1.06	49	21	30	33	174	ADb	15%	114	143	24%	28%	143	36%	83%	43.8	396	$62
24	Proj	630	110	35	85	48	304	39	36	296	392	551	129	122	131	12	80	0.65	47	21	33	33	139		16%	133	131	24%	27%	104	32%	80%	60.2	300	$51

Adames,Willy

Age: 28 Pos: SS | Bats: R Ht: 6' 0" Wt: 210
Health B | PT/Exp A | Consist B
LIMA Plan B | Rand Var +5 | MM 4225

Concussion cost him a couple of weeks in May/June; effects likely lingered as June was his worst month. Mediocre full-season line tamped down by 1st-half h% and HctX dips, but bounced back to career norms in 2nd half. Overall picture is one of stability: 30+ HRs might stay just out of reach, but xBA says he should rebound off this BA floor.

Yr	Tm	PA	R	HR	RBI	SB	BA	xHR	xSB	xBA	OBP	SLG	OPS+	vL+	vR+	bb%	ct%	Eye	G	L	F	h%	HctX	QBaB	Brl%	PX	xPX	HR/F	xHR/F	Spd	SBA%	SB%	RAR	BPX	R$
19	TAM	584	69	20	52	4	254	22	5	246	317	418	102	80	112	8	71	0.30	47	23	30	32	104	CCb	8%	94	91	18%	19%	105	4%	67%	-4.6	33	$11
20	TAM	205	29	8	23	2	259	7	3	240	332	481	108	129	100	10	60	0.27	43	25	32	39	90	CCf	10%	165	111	23%	20%	122	7%	67%	5.0	120	$16
21	2 TM	555	77	25	73	5	262	24	6	248	337	481	112	105	116	10	69	0.37	37	23	41	33	106	BBc	11%	142	131	18%	17%	105	7%	56%	13.8	162	$18
22	MIL	617	83	31	98	8	238	32	6	248	298	458	107	98	110	8	71	0.30	34	20	46	28	108	CAc	13%	149	170	17%	17%	89	9%	73%	3.3	159	$22
23	MIL	636	73	24	80	5	217	27	7	236	310	407	98	103	96	11	70	0.43	36	19	45	26	101	CAd	12%	120	133	14%	15%	82	6%	63%	2.5	93	$11
1st Half		315	35	12	35	4	203	13	3	227	289	373	91	83	93	10	70	0.39	37	19	44	24	91	DBd	13%	106	133	14%	15%	65	9%	67%	-7.3	25	$9
2nd Half		321	38	12	45	1	231	14	4	245	330	440	104	125	98	12	70	0.48	35	19	46	28	111	CAc	12%	134	133	13%	16%	104	3%	50%	4.2	168	$14
24	Proj	630	80	27	85	6	245	28	7	242	322	449	106	106	106	10	70	0.37	36	20	43	30	104		12%	132	139	16%	17%	96	6%	64%	17.5	127	$22

Adams,Jordyn

Age: 24 Pos: OF | Bats: R Ht: 6' 2" Wt: 180
Health A | PT/Exp C | Consist A
LIMA Plan F | Rand Var 0 | MM 2501

0-1-.128 in 40 PA at LAA. Tools-laden prospect has struggled to hit professional pitching at each stop up the minors ladder; finally took a step forward this year (albeit at PCL Salt Lake), earning Sept callup. His speed is undeniable, as is the raw plate approach. Will need another big step forward in plate skills to move BA to "tolerable" levels.

Yr	Tm	PA	R	HR	RBI	SB	BA	xHR	xSB	xBA	OBP	SLG	OPS+	vL+	vR+	bb%	ct%	Eye	G	L	F	h%	HctX	QBaB	Brl%	PX	xPX	HR/F	xHR/F	Spd	SBA%	SB%	RAR	BPX	R$
19																																			
20																																			
21																																			
22	aa	223	21	3	13	9	199		6		248	275	74			6	61	0.17				31				62				119	20%	100%		-186	$1
23	LAA *	488	47	10	43	28	209	0	27	207	262	340	82	0	47	7	62	0.19	50	17	33	31	73	ADc	0%	96	73	0%	0%	158	38%	78%	-12.8	-43	$8
1st Half		282	31	8	32	16	208		15	212	263	363	86	0	0	7	62	0.20	44	20	36	30	0		0%	105	-21	0%		163	36%	82%	-7.4	-7	$11
2nd Half		206	16	2	11	12	210	0	11	198	260	309	77	0	47	6	61	0.18	50	17	33	33	73	ADc	0%	85	73	0%	0%	135	41%	74%	-8.9	-114	$2
24	Proj	175	16	3	12	9	205	3	7	196	249	315	77	44	90	6	62	0.17	50	17	33	31	66		3%	84	66	9%	8%	141	31%	84%	-6.1	-116	$4

Adams,Riley

Age: 28 Pos: CA | Bats: R Ht: 6' 4" Wt: 249
Health A | PT/Exp D | Consist F
LIMA Plan D | Rand Var -4 | MM 4011

Broken hamate bone ended his season in Sept. We called his numbers "cringe-worthy" a year ago; it's got to be tough to improve when you're playing only 1-2x a week. He thumped LHPs (small sample warning), and also improved his CS% behind the plate. That may be enough to keep him employed, but not to make him relevant to us.

Yr	Tm	PA	R	HR	RBI	SB	BA	xHR	xSB	xBA	OBP	SLG	OPS+	vL+	vR+	bb%	ct%	Eye	G	L	F	h%	HctX	QBaB	Brl%	PX	xPX	HR/F	xHR/F	Spd	SBA%	SB%	RAR	BPX	R$
19	aa	317	44	11	37	3	252		3		323	431	104			10	61	0.27				38				122				109	5%	73%		-19	$6
20																																			
21	2 TM *	253	28	7	22	0	211	4	1	212	301	390	95	96	106	11	58	0.31	46	20	34	33	80	CCb	14%	140	105	10%	20%	103	0%	0%	-0.3	0	$0
22	WAS *	269	21	8	21	0	176	5	0	187	234	310	77	56	97	7	62	0.20	45	15	41	25	88	BCd	10%	107	105	13%	13%	71	2%	0%	-11.4	-97	-$4
23	WAS	158	8	4	21	0	273	3	1	258	331	476	110	131	89	7	69	0.24	34	25	40	37	98	BAc	5%	143	98	10%	8%	83	0%	0%	8.3	104	$1
1st Half		71	4	3	9	0	266	2	1	260	329	516	116	155	66	9	66	0.27	38	26	36	36	87	CBf	8%	156	110	20%	13%	125	0%	0%	4.2	157	-$7
2nd Half		87	4	1	12	0	278	1	0	262	333	443	105	108	104	6	71	0.22	32	25	44	38	106	BAb	3%	134	89	4%	4%	64	0%	0%	3.2	86	-$4
24	Proj	210	16	6	24	0	237	6	1	227	309	412	99	101	97	8	65	0.25	40	21	40	34	92		8%	130	101	11%	11%	79	1%	44%	4.3	31	$4

RAY MURPHY

Adell,Jo

Age: 25	Pos: OF		Health	C	LIMA Plan	D+
Bats: R	Ht: 6' 3"	Wt: 215	PT/Exp	B	Rand Var	0
			Consist	B	MM	3403

3-6-.207 in 62 PA at LAA. Spent his summer pounding Triple-A pitching (again), but made contact in barely half of PA during big-league cup-o-coffee (again). Halfway through his 20s, the story remains the same: tantalizing power still shackled by awful plate skills, which show little sign of growth. Hopes for meaningful payoff are flickering at best.

Yr	Tm	PA	R	HR	RBI	SB	BA	xHR	xSB	xBA	OBP	SLG	OPS+	vL+	vR+	bb%	ct%	Eye	G	L	F	h%	HctX	QBaB	Brl%	PX	xPX	HR/F	xHR/F	Spd	SBA%	SB%	RAR	BPX	R$
19	a/a	303	40	7	25	6	257		3		315	415	101			8	67	0.25				36				110				97	9%	100%		11	$5
20	LAA	132	9	3	7	0	161	3	1	167	212	266	63	74	58	5	56	0.13	43	19	38	26	72	BCf	4%	82	60	12%	12%	114	5%	0%	-15.8	-256	-$4
21	LAA *	465	53	18	70	7	234	4	8	235	271	419	95	104	92	5	67	0.15	47	20	33	31	88	DCd	9%	118	83	13%	13%	127	12%	68%	-7.9	38	$11
22	LAA *	451	42	16	46	6	208	7	7	213	249	385	90	79	97	5	59	0.13	39	21	41	31	64	CBd	10%	146	85	12%	11%	112	14%	57%	-14.6	0	$6
23	LAA *	365	46	20	41	7	219	3	7	228	280	445	99	92	98	8	62	0.22	48	12	39	29	76	CCf	9%	154	108	23%	23%	106	12%	85%	3.2	71	$7
1st Half		293	36	16	35	6	218	1	5	202	285	442	99	226	137	9	62	0.24	50	0	50	28	126	AFf	50%	153	353	100%	100%	88	13%	83%	0.8	50	$14
2nd Half		72	9	3	7	1	223	2	1	239	262	459	98	67	95	5	63	0.14	48	13	39	30	74	DCf	6%	161	92	17%	17%	133	9%	100%	0.0	118	-$4
24	Proj	**350**	**40**	**10**	**38**	**5**	**217**	**24**	**6**	**213**	**268**	**376**	**88**	**82**	**91**	**6**	**62**	**0.17**	**45**	**18**	**37**	**32**	**77**		**8%**	**117**	**83**	**14%**	**32%**	**114**	**10%**	**78%**	**-6.4**	**39**	**$4**

Albies,Ozzie

Age: 27	Pos: 2B		Health	F	LIMA Plan	D+
Bats: B	Ht: 5' 8"	Wt: 165	PT/Exp	A	Rand Var	0
			Consist	D	MM	3345

Erased memories of 2022's injury-plagued campaign by reclaiming 2021 peak, with a touch more contact and a little less FB tilt. Those adjustments boosted BA while not dragging down HR (or xHR), a nice enhancement. The three odd-year full seasons in this box are remarkably consistent, setting an easy (and plenty attractive) baseline.

Yr	Tm	PA	R	HR	RBI	SB	BA	xHR	xSB	xBA	OBP	SLG	OPS+	vL+	vR+	bb%	ct%	Eye	G	L	F	h%	HctX	QBaB	Brl%	PX	xPX	HR/F	xHR/F	Spd	SBA%	SB%	RAR	BPX	R$
19	ATL	702	102	24	86	15	295	26	16	284	352	500	118	153	107	8	83	0.48	38	25	37	33	121	CBb	7%	103	114	12%	13%	133	11%	79%	32.0	259	$28
20	ATL	124	21	6	19	3	271	5	3	231	306	466	103	64	114	4	75	0.17	41	14	45	32	82	DBd	9%	108	82	15%	13%	131	15%	75%	-0.4	136	$14
21	ATL	686	103	30	106	20	259	28	15	259	310	488	110	128	103	7	80	0.37	31	20	49	28	113	BAc	9%	126	129	12%	11%	116	18%	83%	14.9	269	$31
22	ATL *	296	39	9	40	3	251	8	5	247	292	411	100	100	99	5	80	0.30	38	18	44	28	114	CBd	5%	101	125	9%	9%	97	13%	38%	-2.6	152	$8
23	ATL	658	96	33	109	13	280	28	13	280	336	513	116	138	110	7	82	0.43	38	20	42	29	122	CBc	8%	121	138	16%	13%	106	9%	93%	39.1	261	$30
1st Half		351	44	20	59	6	259	16	5	286	311	506	112	151	99	7	83	0.43	39	18	43	26	122	CBc	9%	124	139	17%	14%	100	8%	100%	14.7	279	$28
2nd Half		307	52	13	50	7	304	12	8	274	365	522	120	116	121	8	80	0.43	36	21	42	34	122	CAb	7%	117	138	14%	13%	114	10%	88%	22.8	239	$31
24	Proj	**630**	**95**	**27**	**99**	**13**	**277**	**24**	**13**	**265**	**329**	**485**	**112**	**119**	**109**	**7**	**81**	**0.38**	**37**	**20**	**44**	**30**	**117**		**8%**	**114**	**130**	**13%**	**12%**	**111**	**11%**	**74%**	**31.3**	**226**	**$32**

Allen,Nick

Age: 25	Pos: SS		Health	A	LIMA Plan	D+
Bats: R	Ht: 5' 8"	Wt: 166	PT/Exp	A	Rand Var	+1
			Consist	B	MM	1413

4-20-.221 with 5 SB in 329 PA at OAK. If you were going to try and conjure a fantasy skill set out of a profile that started with bottom-shelf QBaB and Brl%, you would probably focus on ct%, Spd, GBs, and defense. But then you'd look at what you had made, throw it back in the kettle, and start over with at least some ability to hit a ball hard.

Yr	Tm	PA	R	HR	RBI	SB	BA	xHR	xSB	xBA	OBP	SLG	OPS+	vL+	vR+	bb%	ct%	Eye	G	L	F	h%	HctX	QBaB	Brl%	PX	xPX	HR/F	xHR/F	Spd	SBA%	SB%	RAR	BPX	R$
19																																			
20																																			
21	a/a	359	34	4	29	8	241		8		284	331	85			6	74	0.23				31				60				100	18%	55%		-38	$6
22	OAK *	513	48	5	28	8	202	2	8	224	255	277	75	107	65	7	78	0.32	52	17	32	25	67	FFf	1%	55	56	5%	3%	111	12%	66%	-27.4	14	$1
23	OAK *	476	48	5	30	12	230	2	14	236	277	314	81	92	67	6	84	0.40	53	14	33	26	80	FFf	1%	47	62	5%	2%	140	13%	85%	-9.8	104	$5
1st Half		258	28	2	13	7	227	1	7	239	280	314	81	99	47	7	84	0.47	51	14	35	26	75	FFf	1%	54	57	4%	4%	124	14%	86%	-8.9	118	$
2nd Half		218	20	3	17	5	234	1	8	228	274	313	79	88	76	5	83	0.32	53	14	33	27	83	FFf	1%	39	64	6%	2%	165	12%	83%	-7.9	89	$2
24	Proj	**385**	**38**	**5**	**25**	**8**	**222**	**2**	**10**	**227**	**270**	**308**	**79**	**103**	**69**	**6**	**80**	**0.32**	**52**	**15**	**33**	**27**	**75**		**1%**	**52**	**59**	**5%**	**3%**	**122**	**13%**	**73%**	**-11.9**	**50**	**$6**

Alonso,Pete

Age: 29	Pos: 1B		Health	A	LIMA Plan	D+
Bats: R	Ht: 6' 3"	Wt: 245	PT/Exp	A	Rand Var	+5
			Consist	B	MM	4145

Missed a chunk of June with HBP-induced wrist injury, which seems a likely cause for 2nd-half ct% dip. That ct% combined with appalling season-long h% to tank the BA, but xBA is unconcerned and points to strong recovery. Uptick in FB% might prevent BA from coming all the way back, but obviously is good for HRs. Still.... UP: 50 HR

Yr	Tm	PA	R	HR	RBI	SB	BA	xHR	xSB	xBA	OBP	SLG	OPS+	vL+	vR+	bb%	ct%	Eye	G	L	F	h%	HctX	QBaB	Brl%	PX	xPX	HR/F	xHR/F	Spd	SBA%	SB%	RAR	BPX	R$
19	NYM	693	103	53	120	1	260	49	2	271	358	583	130	131	129	10	69	0.39	41	18	41	28	101	BBc	16%	176	153	31%	28%	91	1%	100%	24.5	252	$2
20	NYM	239	31	16	35	1	231	15	0	243	326	490	108	93	115	10	71	0.39	39	17	44	24	91	BBd	13%	142	100	25%	23%	71	2%	100%	-5.2	160	$1
21	NYM	637	81	37	94	3	262	38	2	269	344	519	118	123	117	9	77	0.47	39	18	43	28	120	ABd	15%	138	129	20%	20%	87	2%	100%	18.0	258	$2
22	NYM	685	95	40	131	5	271	36	2	274	352	518	123	117	125	10	79	0.52	36	20	44	28	116	BAc	12%	143	112	19%	17%	63	3%	83%	27.7	238	$3
23	NYM	658	92	46	118	4	217	46	4	265	318	504	112	116	110	10	73	0.43	37	16	48	21	104	BAc	15%	158	135	23%	23%	71	4%	80%	11.2	225	$2
1st Half		320	48	25	58	3	221	23	3	276	316	520	114	118	112	10	78	0.49	37	16	47	19	115	CBc	15%	151	151	24%	22%	76	4%	100%	6.5	271	$2
2nd Half		338	44	21	60	1	213	22	2	255	320	488	109	113	107	11	69	0.39	36	16	48	22	93	BAc	15%	166	117	21%	22%	74	3%	50%	2.3	196	$2
24	Proj	**665**	**94**	**44**	**121**	**4**	**256**	**43**	**4**	**265**	**347**	**526**	**120**	**120**	**120**	**10**	**75**	**0.45**	**37**	**17**	**46**	**27**	**108**		**14%**	**151**	**125**	**22%**	**21%**	**70**	**3%**	**81%**	**34.5**	**232**	**$3**

Altuve,Jose

Age: 34	Pos: 2B		Health	D	LIMA Plan	A
Bats: R	Ht: 5' 6"	Wt: 166	PT/Exp	A	Rand Var	-3
			Consist	C	MM	3455

Fractured thumb kept him out til June; oblique strain shelved him for much of July. When active, the production was vintage, but underlying skills are showing wear: once-elite ct% is now merely good, hard-hit metrics (never his strength) are sagging further, return of GB tilt lowers HR ceiling. And big-PA seasons get tougher in mid-30s.

Yr	Tm	PA	R	HR	RBI	SB	BA	xHR	xSB	xBA	OBP	SLG	OPS+	vL+	vR+	bb%	ct%	Eye	G	L	F	h%	HctX	QBaB	Brl%	PX	xPX	HR/F	xHR/F	Spd	SBA%	SB%	RAR	BPX	R$
19	HOU *	570	91	31	74	6	291	25	9	291	345	535	122	147	116	7	83	0.46	50	18	33	30	116	CCd	8%	115	85	23%	19%	125	8%	55%	24.8	281	$2
20	HOU	210	32	5	18	2	219	5	3	252	286	344	84	66	89	8	80	0.44	49	21	30	25	99	DDf	5%	71	68	11%	11%	103	11%	40%	-9.7	100	$
21	HOU	678	117	31	83	5	278	19	5	284	350	489	115	107	119	10	85	0.73	39	22	39	28	107	CBf	6%	108	90	16%	10%	97	5%	63%	29.3	292	$2
22	HOU	604	103	28	57	18	300	21	13	297	387	533	130	152	122	11	83	0.76	41	20	39	32	110	DBc	8%	139	99	17%	13%	111	11%	95%	56.0	352	$3
23	HOU *	432	76	17	51	14	297	15	16	281	369	496	118	114	129	10	80	0.58	48	19	33	33	87	DCf	8%	110	82	18%	16%	131	14%	81%	33.9	250	$1
1st Half		160	24	6	18	5	239	4	5	281	325	424	103	78	131	11	79	0.62	48	22	30	26	75	CCd	8%	107	57	21%	14%	92	18%	69%	2.6	193	$
2nd Half		272	52	11	33	9	331	11	11	281	404	537	127	128	126	10	81	0.55	48	18	34	38	93	DCf	8%	112	94	17%	17%	147	12%	90%	27.9	275	$2
24	Proj	**560**	**94**	**22**	**59**	**15**	**284**	**20**	**14**	**281**	**363**	**483**	**116**	**114**	**117**	**10**	**82**	**0.62**	**45**	**20**	**35**	**31**	**97**		**8%**	**110**	**86**	**16%**	**14%**	**117**	**12%**	**82%**	**36.1**	**272**	**$2**

Alu,Jake

Age: 27	Pos: LF 2B		Health	A	LIMA Plan	D
Bats: L	Ht: 5' 10"	Wt: 175	PT/Exp	A	Rand Var	+2
			Consist	C	MM	1333

2-16-.226 with 5 SB in 175 PA at WAS. High-minors skills suggested a potentially-useful power/speed blend, but he only brought the speed part to his MLB debut. Sketchy plate skills (6% BB%, 74% ct% with WAS), ground-ball tilt, and lack of barrels say there's a lot to fix, and he's not that young. Cheap speed is easy to find; look elsewhere.

Yr	Tm	PA	R	HR	RBI	SB	BA	xHR	xSB	xBA	OBP	SLG	OPS+	vL+	vR+	bb%	ct%	Eye	G	L	F	h%	HctX	QBaB	Brl%	PX	xPX	HR/F	xHR/F	Spd	SBA%	SB%	RAR	BPX	R$
19																																			
20																																			
21	aa	207	19	4	17	4	233		4		269	356	86			5	76	0.20				29				79				95	18%	52%		19	$
22	a/a	537	57	15	57	11	249		8		298	409	100			7	76	0.29				30				110				87	14%	75%		117	$1
23	WAS *	486	45	6	45	16	231	3	14	254	279	319	81	85	77	6	78	0.30	55	21	24	29	87	CFb	3%	56	52	7%	11%	99	19%	77%	-12.8	4	$
1st Half		246	22	4	25	9	248	0	7	291	292	361	89	0	71	6	80	0.31	70	20	10	30	33	FFc	0%	73	-21	0%	0%	96	21%	79%	-3.9	75	$
2nd Half		240	23	2	20	7	214	2	7	234	265	275	73	84	77	6	76	0.29	53	21	25	27	90	CDb	3%	38	59	7%	7%	114	16%	75%	-12.2	-61	$
24	Proj	**280**	**28**	**3**	**27**	**7**	**236**	**2**	**7**	**249**	**290**	**333**	**85**	**87**	**85**	**6**	**77**	**0.27**	**53**	**21**	**25**	**30**	**81**		**2%**	**65**	**53**	**7%**	**4%**	**98**	**15%**	**75%**	**-5.8**	**41**	**$**

Álvarez,Francisco

Age: 22	Pos: CA		Health	A	LIMA Plan	C+
Bats: R	Ht: 5' 10"	Wt: 233	PT/Exp	B	Rand Var	+2
			Consist	A	MM	4115

Prodigious power was as advertised right out of the gate in first full MLB season, but rest of the skill set is still-developing. Underneath the flat second-half stats are some encouraging gains in bb%, HctX, and LD%. He'll need more of all of those to become better than a low-BA power source behind the plate, but he's got time yet. Stash.

Yr	Tm	PA	R	HR	RBI	SB	BA	xHR	xSB	xBA	OBP	SLG	OPS+	vL+	vR+	bb%	ct%	Eye	G	L	F	h%	HctX	QBaB	Brl%	PX	xPX	HR/F	xHR/F	Spd	SBA%	SB%	RAR	BPX	R$
19																																			
20																																			
21																																			
22	NYM *	469	53	20	54	0	210	1	0	211	293	395	97	0	163	10	65	0.33	50	13	38	27	142	CBa	20%	135	204	33%	33%	57	0%	0%	1.5	28	$
23	NYM	423	51	25	63	2	209	20	1	238	284	437	98	82	106	8	71	0.31	44	13	43	22	103	BCf	13%	131	126	21%	17%	48	2%	100%	6.0	79	$
1st Half		202	25	13	27	0	214	9	0	241	272	460	100	48	121	7	73	0.26	47	11	42	22	96	CCf	11%	139	114	22%	16%	62	0%	0%	2.2	136	$
2nd Half		221	26	12	36	2	205	11	1	230	294	415	96	105	89	10	69	0.35	41	15	43	23	110	ACf	14%	123	139	20%	19%	51	4%	100%	1.4	43	$
24	Proj	**490**	**58**	**28**	**70**	**2**	**231**	**31**	**1**	**229**	**309**	**455**	**105**	**93**	**111**	**9**	**69**	**0.31**	**43**	**14**	**43**	**27**	**104**		**13%**	**137**	**129**	**21%**	**24%**	**42**	**1%**	**100%**	**16.0**	**60**	**$1**

RAY MURPHY

Alvarez,Yordan

Age: 27 Pos: DH LF — Bats: L Ht: 6'5" Wt: 225
Health D — PT/Exp A — Consist D
LIMA Plan B+ — Rand Var 0 — MM 5155

Spring bout of hand soreness threatened to cloud his season; that was a non-factor but then oblique injury cost him nearly all of June/July. Last year in this space, we said "he's just a launch-angle tweak (and a full season of health) away from... UP: 50+ HR". He's delivered the first part, now it's just a question of health. UP: 50+ HR, still.

Yr	Tm	PA	R	HR	RBI	SB	BA	xHR	xSB	xBA	OBP	SLG	OPS+	vL+	vR+	bb%	ct%	Eye	G	L	F	h%	HctX	QBaB	Brl%	PX	xPX	HR/F	xHR/F	Spd	SBA%	SB%	RAR	BPX	R$
19	HOU *	610	95	44	130	1	305	27	0	295	396	632	142	144	148	13	71	0.53	38	25	37	35	126	ACa	17%	183	155	33%	33%	71	1%	56%	57.8	300	$30
20	HOU	9	2	1	4	0	250	0	0	338	333	625	127	183	33	0	88	0.00	57	14	29	17	202	ADf		153	116	50%	0%	105	0%	0%	0.0	424	-$1
21	HOU	598	92	33	104	1	277	40	1	272	346	531	120	120	121	8	73	0.34	38	23	39	32	118	ACc	16%	151	153	21%	26%	88	1%	100%	31.1	223	$25
22	HOU	561	95	37	97	1	306	45	2	304	406	613	144	140	146	14	77	0.74	39	22	39	33	150	ACb	21%	182	170	25%	31%	79	1%	50%	63.9	376	$33
23	HOU	496	77	31	97	0	293	36	4	288	407	583	135	120	143	14	78	0.75	35	19	45	31	142	ABc	18%	159	155	21%	25%	92	0%	0%	51.2	339	$23
1st Half		242	41	17	55	0	277	18	1	281	388	589	134	134	133	14	73	0.58	39	17	44	30	135	ABc	19%	181	157	26%	27%	84	0%	0%	21.6	321	$23
2nd Half		254	36	14	42	0	308	18	3	294	425	577	135	107	152	15	82	1.00	32	22	47	32	149	ABc	17%	140	153	18%	23%	104	0%	0%	26.7	371	$21
24	**Proj**	**560**	**91**	**40**	**107**	**0**	**296**	**45**	**3**	**295**	**398**	**610**	**138**	**127**	**145**	**13**	**77**	**0.66**	**36**	**20**	**44**	**31**	**140**		**18%**	**175**	**158**	**24%**	**27%**	**84**	**1%**	**58%**	**60.7**	**333**	**$30**

Amaya,Jacob

Age: 25 Pos: SS — Bats: R Ht: 6'0" Wt: 180
Health A — PT/Exp A — Consist A
LIMA Plan D — Rand Var +2 — MM 1301

0-2-.222 in 9 PA at MIA. Light-hitting defensive standout who spent summer at AAA before Sept promotion. BA-dependent profile without the BA. On surface, .252/.345/.407 AAA line is encouraging. However, outclassed by 93 MPH+ velocity (.204/.344/.324) due to below-avg strength and slow bat speed. Minimal SB impact expected too. (CB)

Yr	Tm	PA	R	HR	RBI	SB	BA	xHR	xSB	xBA	OBP	SLG	OPS+	vL+	vR+	bb%	ct%	Eye	G	L	F	h%	HctX	QBaB	Brl%	PX	xPX	HR/F	xHR/F	Spd	SBA%	SB%	RAR	BPX	R$
19																																			
20																																			
21	aa	451	42	9	33	3	177		2		239	272	70			8	72	0.29				22				59				96	3%	100%		-69	-$4
22	a/a	523	51	12	43	4	203		5		274	316	84			9	72	0.35				26				75				104	5%	61%		0	$3
23	MIA *	541	60	11	47	5	211	0	8	256	281	328	83	54	68	9	75	0.39	75	13	13	26	153	DFa	0%	74	73	0%	0%	109	6%	69%	-13.8	46	$4
1st Half		254	26	6	26	2	227	0	4	253	275	361	87	54	69	6	73	0.25	75	13	13	28	149	DFa	0%	82	73	0%	0%	122	6%	59%	-7.1	32	$3
2nd Half		287	34	4	21	3	196		4	235	285	297	79	0	0	11	77	0.55	44	20	36	24	0		0%	66	-21	0%		106	6%	75%	-12.3	64	$1
24	**Proj**	**245**	**26**	**3**	**20**	**2**	**216**	**3**	**3**	**216**	**284**	**302**	**80**	**79**	**81**	**9**	**74**	**0.37**	**44**	**20**	**36**	**28**	**87**		**3%**	**57**	**62**	**5%**	**5%**	**114**	**5%**	**73%**	**-6.8**	**15**	**$3**

Amaya,Miguel

Age: 25 Pos: CA — Bats: R Ht: 6'1" Wt: 185
Health A — PT/Exp F — Consist A
LIMA Plan D+ — Rand Var -1 — MM 3303

5-18-.214 in 156 PA at CHC. Multiple injuries had removed the still-developing-prospect sheen, but he finally reached the majors and even flashed some plate patience and above-average pop. It's unsurprisingly raw, given the low PA totals in this box, but there's reason to be intrigued by the emerging patience+power here. Dynasty stash.

Yr	Tm	PA	R	HR	RBI	SB	BA	xHR	xSB	xBA	OBP	SLG	OPS+	vL+	vR+	bb%	ct%	Eye	G	L	F	h%	HctX	QBaB	Brl%	PX	xPX	HR/F	xHR/F	Spd	SBA%	SB%	RAR	BPX	R$
19																																			
20																																			
21	aa	95	8	1	10	1	189		1		327	262	81			17	70	0.68				26				56				93	4%	100%		-38	-$2
22	aa	106	9	2	12	0	220		0		284	360	91			8	66	0.27				30				105				105	0%	0%		0	-$2
23	CHC *	261	27	8	30	1	224	5	2	214	302	388	94	94	93	10	66	0.33	34	19	47	30	72	DAd	10%	115	114	12%	12%	80	2%	100%	3.3	4	$2
1st Half		165	17	5	19	1	249	3	2	243	327	433	104	131	97	10	63	0.32	29	29	41	36	74	CAc	11%	138	111	14%	21%	92	2%	100%	5.2	50	$0
2nd Half		96	10	3	11	0	181	1	1	185	292	313	82	70	89	10	70	0.36	37	12	51	22	74	DBd	9%	80	115	10%	3%	95	0%	0%	-2.8	-21	-$5
24	**Proj**	**350**	**35**	**12**	**41**	**1**	**225**	**11**	**3**	**214**	**346**	**392**	**101**	**105**	**98**	**9**	**67**	**0.31**	**34**	**19**	**47**	**30**	**74**		**10%**	**112**	**113**	**12%**	**11%**	**85**	**1%**	**100%**	**4.7**	**5**	**$7**

Anderson,Brian

Age: 31 Pos: 3B RF — Bats: R Ht: 6'3" Wt: 208
Health F — PT/Exp B — Consist B
LIMA Plan D — Rand Var 0 — MM 1201

Back injury landed him on the IL in mid-July and he couldn't crack the lineup upon his return. Comparing current skills to 2019-20 peak shows that, while he still generates walks and barrels at a decent clip, the losses of contact and power have crippled his productivity. Plus speed has never translated into bags either, leaving little path to value.

Yr	Tm	PA	R	HR	RBI	SB	BA	xHR	xSB	xBA	OBP	SLG	OPS+	vL+	vR+	bb%	ct%	Eye	G	L	F	h%	HctX	QBaB	Brl%	PX	xPX	HR/F	xHR/F	Spd	SBA%	SB%	RAR	BPX	R$
19	MIA	520	57	20	66	5	261	20	3	263	342	468	112	103	114	8	75	0.39	45	19	35	31	115	BCc	9%	117	108	16%	16%	87	5%	83%	-1.7	144	$13
20	MIA	229	27	11	38	0	255	11	2	239	345	465	108	103	109	10	67	0.33	49	21	30	33	96	CCc	10%	125	120	27%	27%	116	0%	0%	-0.3	96	$17
21	MIA	264	24	7	28	5	249	8	3	214	337	378	98	58	111	10	72	0.40	49	15	36	32	86	CCc	8%	80	93	11%	13%	97	7%	100%	-0.5	12	$5
22	MIA *	410	45	9	29	1	218	12	2	223	292	347	90	104	90	9	69	0.34	50	18	31	29	92	CDd	10%	95	82	11%	16%	103	1%	100%	-11.7	7	$2
23	MIL	361	38	9	40	1	226	12	7	219	310	368	92	81	96	10	66	0.33	47	19	33	31	87	CCd	10%	93	105	13%	17%	135	5%	25%	-3.2	4	$3
1st Half		314	34	9	37	0	227	11	4	216	318	374	95	74	101	11	66	0.37	48	18	34	31	88	CCd	11%	98	109	15%	18%	108	4%	0%	-4.1	-4	$8
2nd Half		47	4	0	3	1	222	1	1	220	255	333	80	107	66	4	67	0.13	43	27	30	33	81	ACa	6%	64	79	0%	11%	172	11%	100%	-1.8	-71	-$7
24	**Proj**	**210**	**23**	**4**	**25**	**1**	**238**	**7**	**2**	**219**	**321**	**350**	**92**	**91**	**92**	**10**	**69**	**0.36**	**47**	**20**	**32**	**32**	**88**		**9%**	**77**	**91**	**9%**	**17%**	**95**	**4%**	**67%**	**-0.8**	**32**	**$5**

Anderson,Tim

Age: 31 Pos: SS — Bats: R Ht: 6'1" Wt: 185
Health F — PT/Exp A — Consist C
LIMA Plan B — Rand Var +4 — MM 1545

In some years, the OF fence seems 5000 feet away. Maybe it was injuries, as his first two weeks were hot (.298 BA, 5 SB) before spraining a knee. Off-field issues may have been a factor too. RandVar offers hope, but double-digit HR were always a stretch for his power profile, and speed is a skill of the young. Keep bounceback hopes modest.

Yr	Tm	PA	R	HR	RBI	SB	BA	xHR	xSB	xBA	OBP	SLG	OPS+	vL+	vR+	bb%	ct%	Eye	G	L	F	h%	HctX	QBaB	Brl%	PX	xPX	HR/F	xHR/F	Spd	SBA%	SB%	RAR	BPX	R$
19	CHW *	541	83	19	59	17	333	16	14	279	352	505	119	117	120	3	79	0.13	49	24	28	40	88	CDa	5%	94	84	17%	15%	115	16%	77%	22.2	119	$28
20	CHW	221	45	10	21	5	322	12	7	274	357	529	118	197	92	5	76	0.20	55	19	26	39	101	CDa	10%	114	101	24%	29%	155	12%	71%	12.8	212	$31
21	CHW	551	94	17	61	18	309	16	18	278	338	469	111	113	110	4	77	0.18	55	23	22	37	107	BFa	8%	94	85	19%	18%	136	18%	72%	20.9	138	$31
22	CHW	351	50	6	25	13	301	8	9	276	339	395	104	135	97	4	83	0.25	55	24	21	35	104	CFa	6%	59	73	10%	14%	121	13%	100%	8.5	93	$17
23	CHW	524	52	1	25	13	245	4	15	246	286	296	79	96	73	5	75	0.21	61	22	17	32	86	CFa	3%	37	38	2%	6%	131	12%	87%	-11.2	-61	$6
1st Half		263	26	0	12	9	231	2	7	244	270	267	74	101	65	5	78	0.25	64	20	16	30	93	CFa	4%	30	37	0%	6%	102	16%	90%	-12.5	-79	$0
2nd Half		261	26	1	13	4	260	2	8	245	303	325	85	92	82	5	73	0.18	58	25	17	35	79	CFa	2%	45	38	3%	6%	150	7%	80%	-6.4	-61	$4
24	**Proj**	**525**	**68**	**7**	**36**	**15**	**273**	**9**	**15**	**261**	**310**	**365**	**93**	**110**	**87**	**4**	**78**	**0.21**	**57**	**23**	**20**	**34**	**94**		**5%**	**59**	**59**	**9%**	**11%**	**130**	**13%**	**86%**	**3.0**	**26**	**$19**

Andrus,Elvis

Age: 35 Pos: 2B SS — Bats: R Ht: 6'0" Wt: 210
Health B — PT/Exp A — Consist B
LIMA Plan C — Rand Var -1 — MM 1233

Missed three weeks in May with an oblique injury. Also missed: any sign of 2022's unlikely power outburst. Made a late attempt to hold value with a 2nd-half BA spike, but that was mostly h% noise between the halves. Age, below-average Spd suggest SB in jeopardy, which means double-digit R$ has likely left the building for good.

Yr	Tm	PA	R	HR	RBI	SB	BA	xHR	xSB	xBA	OBP	SLG	OPS+	vL+	vR+	bb%	ct%	Eye	G	L	F	h%	HctX	QBaB	Brl%	PX	xPX	HR/F	xHR/F	Spd	SBA%	SB%	RAR	BPX	R$
19	TEX	648	81	12	72	31	275	14	22	271	313	393	98	102	95	5	84	0.35	51	21	28	31	112	CDc	4%	60	72	8%	10%	115	24%	79%	-6.5	115	$26
20	TEX	111	11	3	7	3	194	4	2	249	252	330	77	76	77	7	85	0.53	49	15	36	20	118	CDf	6%	71	120	10%	13%	83	20%	75%	-6.5	160	$3
21	OAK	541	60	3	37	12	243	6	8	257	294	320	84	65	94	6	84	0.38	46	24	30	29	93	CDf	2%	49	71	2%	5%	102	11%	86%	-16.0	69	$10
22	2 AL	577	66	17	58	18	249	12	10	264	303	404	100	116	94	7	83	0.42	46	17	36	27	107	CCd	4%	97	71	11%	8%	69	17%	82%	7.5	155	$20
23	CHW	406	39	6	44	12	251	4	10	255	304	358	90	91	90	6	81	0.35	55	17	28	30	92	CFd	3%	66	51	7%	5%	81	17%	75%	1.4	54	$8
1st Half		222	17	2	17	6	202	1	5	239	281	263	74	62	79	8	80	0.46	52	21	27	24	69	DFd	2%	38	38	5%	2%	73	17%	67%	-10.6	-29	-$3
2nd Half		184	22	4	27	6	307	3	5	274	332	466	108	135	100	4	82	0.22	59	12	29	36	117	CFd	3%	97	65	10%	7%	90	17%	86%	9.1	150	$12
24	**Proj**	**315**	**34**	**6**	**33**	**10**	**255**	**5**	**7**	**258**	**303**	**376**	**93**	**95**	**92**	**6**	**82**	**0.36**	**52**	**18**	**31**	**29**	**101**		**3%**	**74**	**65**	**8%**	**6%**	**81**	**17%**	**79%**	**1.9**	**102**	**$11**

Aranda,Jonathan

Age: 26 Pos: DH — Bats: L Ht: 6'0" Wt: 210
Health A — PT/Exp A — Consist C
LIMA Plan D+ — Rand Var -2 — MM 2213

2-13-.230 in 103 PA at TAM. As a below-average defender (DH-only now), it takes a plus bat to stick on a big-league roster. Minors profile suggested he could meet that standard, but it hasn't translated yet in two big-league stints: too many Ks, too many GB. Even 2022's smattering of hard contact didn't repeat. Work to be done, clock now ticking.

Yr	Tm	PA	R	HR	RBI	SB	BA	xHR	xSB	xBA	OBP	SLG	OPS+	vL+	vR+	bb%	ct%	Eye	G	L	F	h%	HctX	QBaB	Brl%	PX	xPX	HR/F	xHR/F	Spd	SBA%	SB%	RAR	BPX	R$
19																																			
20																																			
21	aa	299	41	8	44	3	280		4		341	452	109			8	73	0.34				36				106				114	7%	57%		112	$10
22	TAM *	522	60	14	66	4	247	3	2	223	305	389	98	40	89	8	70	0.28	55	13	33	33	116	ADd	8%	105	113	11%	17%	80	3%	100%	-0.5	14	$13
23	TAM *	503	69	20	68	1	263	2	4	236	346	452	109	45	100	11	69	0.41	54	14	32	34	88	CDf	5%	122	54	11%	11%	75	2%	36%	19.7	68	$15
1st Half		280	37	11	38	1	277		3	243	358	469	113	0	0	11	69	0.41	44	20	36	36	0		0%	125	-21	0%		80	4%	22%	9.6	86	$16
2nd Half		223	32	8	30	1	246	2	2	236	332	430	103	45	100	11	68	0.41	54	14	32	32	88	CDf	5%	117	54	11%	11%	88	2%	100%	2.8	64	$9
24	**Proj**	**315**	**41**	**8**	**42**	**2**	**258**	**9**	**3**	**223**	**338**	**401**	**101**	**44**	**106**	**9**	**70**	**0.34**	**54**	**14**	**32**	**35**	**99**		**6%**	**97**	**78**	**12%**	**14%**	**83**	**3%**	**72%**	**3.5**	**58**	**$10**

AY MURPHY

Arcia,Orlando

Age: 29	Pos: SS		Health	B	LIMA Plan	B+
Bats: R	Ht: 6'0"	Wt: 187	PT/Exp	A	Rand Var	-2
			Consist	B	MM	2235

Missed four weeks in April/May after getting plunked on wrist. Surprise winner of everyday SS job fared just about as well as his track record suggested. Slapped tons of first-half GB (wrist still sore?) and they found holes regularly enough to prop up BA. 2nd half saw a few more FB, more hard contact, so next step could be... UP: 25 HR.

Yr	Tm	PA	R	HR	RBI	SB	BA	xHR	xSB	xBA	OBP	SLG	OPS+	vL+	vR+	bb%	ct%	Eye	G	L	F	h%	HctX	QBaB	Brl%	PX	xPX	HR/F	xHR/F	Spd	SBA%	SB%	RAR	BPX
19	MIL	546	51	15	59	8	223	13	8	242	283	350	88	95	85	8	78	0.39	51	18	31	26	89	CDd	5%	66	86	13%	11%	106	11%	62%	-23.6	52
20	MIL	189	22	5	20	2	260	6	1	269	317	416	97	83	103	7	82	0.44	46	23	31	29	121	CCb	5%	86	110	11%	14%	87	5%	100%	0.4	152
21	2 NL *	399	50	14	42	5	225	2	4	258	284	389	92	107	67	8	82	0.47	51	16	33	24	70	CDf	3%	88	50	10%	10%	84	11%	57%	-11.3	165
22	ATL	234	25	9	30	0	244	8	1	234	316	416	104	84	112	9	76	0.41	46	16	38	28	118	BCd	8%	108	116	15%	13%	101	0%	0%	0.2	134
23	ATL	533	66	17	65	1	264	16	4	256	321	420	101	136	92	7	79	0.38	54	17	30	30	102	CFf	7%	91	84	15%	14%	93	1%	100%	11.1	121
1st Half		241	33	7	28	1	296	6	3	261	349	439	108	157	96	7	78	0.35	58	18	24	35	93	CFd	7%	85	78	17%	14%	102	2%	100%	8.1	104
2nd Half		292	33	10	37	0	238	10	1	247	298	404	95	119	88	8	80	0.41	50	15	34	26	109	CDf	7%	95	89	14%	14%	89	0%	0%	-1.7	139
24	**Proj**	**560**	**66**	**20**	**73**	**2**	**253**	**17**	**4**	**251**	**314**	**416**	**100**	**113**	**96**	**8**	**79**	**0.41**	**51**	**17**	**33**	**29**	**102**		**6%**	**94**	**89**	**15%**	**13%**	**89**	**2%**	**67%**	**9.9**	**131**

Arenado,Nolan

Age: 33	Pos: 3B		Health	A	LIMA Plan	A
Bats: R	Ht: 6'2"	Wt: 215	PT/Exp	A	Rand Var	0
			Consist	D	MM	3155

Disappointing season really consisted of a completely reasonable 1st half followed by a substantial 2nd half fade. Bac issues in 2nd half look like a plausible culprit for that fade, manifesting in loss of launch angle and thus power. Consistent track record points to rebound, but back problems in mid-30s tend to not suddenly abate.

Yr	Tm	PA	R	HR	RBI	SB	BA	xHR	xSB	xBA	OBP	SLG	OPS+	vL+	vR+	bb%	ct%	Eye	G	L	F	h%	HctX	QBaB	Brl%	PX	xPX	HR/F	xHR/F	Spd	SBA%	SB%	RAR	BPX
19	COL	662	102	41	118	3	315	27	6	287	379	583	133	143	129	9	84	0.67	36	19	45	32	123	BAd	8%	124	139	18%	12%	110	3%	60%	43.7	333
20	COL	201	23	8	26	0	253	6	0	251	303	434	98	89	101	7	89	0.75	37	16	47	25	126	CAf	5%	87	103	10%	8%	77	0%	0%	-3.8	264
21	STL	653	81	34	105	2	255	21	1	271	312	494	111	127	107	8	84	0.52	31	19	50	25	116	CAf	7%	123	127	14%	8%	88	2%	100%	16.2	296
22	STL	620	73	30	103	5	293	22	4	292	358	533	126	131	125	8	87	0.72	30	20	50	29	121	CAd	8%	136	116	12%	9%	71	5%	63%	36.3	334
23	STL	612	71	26	93	3	266	20	7	270	315	459	105	89	111	7	82	0.41	39	21	40	28	113	CBd	7%	102	93	14%	11%	91	4%	50%	17.0	186
1st Half		334	37	16	54	2	278	13	5	264	326	490	112	122	109	7	80	0.38	37	19	44	30	114	CAd	8%	112	110	15%	12%	96	6%	40%	11.5	196
2nd Half		278	34	10	39	1	252	7	2	278	302	421	98	64	112	7	84	0.45	41	22	36	26	112	CBd	6%	91	73	13%	9%	83	2%	100%	1.3	179
24	**Proj**	**595**	**73**	**27**	**94**	**3**	**271**	**20**	**4**	**275**	**327**	**481**	**111**	**101**	**114**	**8**	**84**	**0.52**	**35**	**20**	**44**	**28**	**117**		**7%**	**111**	**104**	**13%**	**10%**	**81**	**4%**	**61%**	**25.8**	**251**

Arias,Gabriel

Age: 24	Pos: SS 1B		Health	A	LIMA Plan	D+
Bats: R	Ht: 6'1"	Wt: 217	PT/Exp	A	Rand Var	0
			Consist	C	MM	2113

Got near-full-time role post-trade deadline, and formerly-ignorable skill set showed some life. He clearly got more aggressive per bb%, but it worked for him (see HctX, Brl%, PX/xPX). Lest we get carried away: still too little ct% and too many GB%. But he forged one plus skill from thin air, if he invents another we'll get interested.

Yr	Tm	PA	R	HR	RBI	SB	BA	xHR	xSB	xBA	OBP	SLG	OPS+	vL+	vR+	bb%	ct%	Eye	G	L	F	h%	HctX	QBaB	Brl%	PX	xPX	HR/F	xHR/F	Spd	SBA%	SB%	RAR	BPX
19																																		
20																																		
21	aaa	465	48	10	41	4	250		3		297	387	94			6	72	0.24				33				92				96	5%	77%		15
22	CLE *	360	36	9	26	4	189	1	5	239	240	299	76	76	102	6	69	0.22	67	20	13	25	56	DFa	4%	75	52	25%	25%	129	7%	78%	-19.1	-38
23	CLE	345	36	10	26	3	210	14	5	218	275	352	86	43	108	8	64	0.25	52	18	30	29	93	BFf	10%	103	111	17%	24%	85	10%	43%	-7.0	-57
1st Half		152	13	4	6	0	189	5	3	190	296	318	84	47	110	13	62	0.40	53	15	33	27	77	CFf	6%	93	98	15%	19%	103	8%	0%	-6.6	-64
2nd Half		193	23	6	20	3	224	9	3	235	259	377	86	38	106	4	66	0.13	52	20	28	31	104	BFf	12%	109	120	18%	27%	80	12%	75%	-5.9	-57
24	**Proj**	**420**	**46**	**13**	**34**	**4**	**229**	**19**	**6**	**224**	**284**	**375**	**90**	**44**	**114**	**7**	**67**	**0.23**	**52**	**18**	**30**	**31**	**93**		**10%**	**98**	**111**	**17%**	**24%**	**86**	**8%**	**58%**	**-4.1**	**-41**

Arozarena,Randy

Age: 29	Pos: LF		Health	A	LIMA Plan	D+
Bats: R	Ht: 5'11"	Wt: 185	PT/Exp	A	Rand Var	+1
			Consist	A	MM	4435

R$ deemed year disappointing but a lot of nice elements: more walks, more hard contact (all of HctX, QBaB, Brl%), more FBs. All of those pop the lid on a higher HR tier. Meanwhile, SB lag amid league-wide boom was frustrating, but corrected in (otherwise cruddy) 2nd half. Sew that together and you get... UP: 30 HR, 30 SB.

Yr	Tm	PA	R	HR	RBI	SB	BA	xHR	xSB	xBA	OBP	SLG	OPS+	vL+	vR+	bb%	ct%	Eye	G	L	F	h%	HctX	QBaB	Brl%	PX	xPX	HR/F	xHR/F	Spd	SBA%	SB%	RAR	BPX
19	STL *	395	56	13	45	16	299	1	18	259	354	481	116	162	115	8	77	0.37	56	13	31	36	100	BFf	6%	100	42	20%	20%	129	30%	51%	3.2	163
20	TAM	76	15	7	11	4	281	4	2	280	382	641	136	193	109	8	66	0.27	47	19	35	31	99	BDf	14%	208	113	47%	27%	111	20%	100%	5.0	320
21	TAM	604	94	20	69	20	274	17	23	240	356	459	112	125	103	9	68	0.33	49	18	33	37	89	BDf	8%	123	89	17%	14%	145	19%	67%	16.2	131
22	TAM	645	72	20	89	32	263	20	25	259	327	445	109	129	104	7	73	0.29	51	16	33	33	101	BDf	8%	127	88	14%	14%	110	30%	73%	11.7	152
23	TAM	654	95	23	83	22	254	24	31	235	364	425	107	112	106	12	72	0.51	43	18	39	31	112	ACf	12%	101	118	15%	15%	147	17%	69%	19.3	136
1st Half		352	53	16	58	9	287	16	15	240	398	488	121	115	123	13	72	0.54	41	18	42	35	126	ACf	15%	115	151	18%	18%	136	14%	56%	19.2	171
2nd Half		302	42	7	25	13	217	8	15	229	325	353	91	107	87	12	72	0.48	46	18	36	28	97	BCf	9%	84	80	10%	12%	151	20%	81%	-3.0	89
24	**Proj**	**630**	**89**	**25**	**78**	**25**	**259**	**22**	**28**	**251**	**351**	**457**	**111**	**130**	**104**	**10**	**72**	**0.40**	**46**	**18**	**36**	**32**	**103**		**10%**	**121**	**101**	**17%**	**15%**	**123**	**22%**	**69%**	**21.1**	**135**

Arraez,Luis

Age: 27	Pos: 2B		Health	B	LIMA Plan	D+
Bats: L	Ht: 5'10"	Wt: 175	PT/Exp	A	Rand Var	-4
			Consist	C	MM	1255

First-half run at .400 was fun to see. BPX column shows that his skills didn't fade in 2nd half; he just couldn't keep the h% in the 40s. How does he hit .354 with such a small Brl%? His secret super power is the 3rd letter of QBaB: launch angle variability. He keeps his contact in the narrow range of angles that yield LDs, and he has that skill perfected.

Yr	Tm	PA	R	HR	RBI	SB	BA	xHR	xSB	xBA	OBP	SLG	OPS+	vL+	vR+	bb%	ct%	Eye	G	L	F	h%	HctX	QBaB	Brl%	PX	xPX	HR/F	xHR/F	Spd	SBA%	SB%	RAR	BPX
19	MIN *	600	77	4	48	6	333	5	9	297	398	418	113	97	122	10	92	1.29	41	29	29	36	110	CCa	3%	46	73	5%	6%	110	5%	52%	23.9	215
20	MIN	121	16	0	13	0	321	3	1	293	364	402	102	74	110	7	90	0.73	41	29	29	36	104	CCa	3%	55	88	0%	10%	100	0%	0%	1.5	200
21	MIN	479	58	2	42	2	294	6	8	275	357	376	101	89	104	9	89	0.90	46	26	28	33	102	CCa	2%	44	63	2%	6%	136	3%	50%	4.4	196
22	MIN	603	88	8	49	4	316	10	8	287	375	420	113	96	117	8	92	1.16	41	26	33	33	112	CCb	4%	63	75	5%	6%	106	4%	50%	23.8	238
23	MIA	617	71	10	69	3	354	10	10	314	393	469	117	102	122	6	94	1.03	43	28	29	36	114	CCa	3%	60	73	6%	6%	107	3%	60%	49.1	250
1st Half		334	36	3	41	1	389	3	6	319	440	482	126	115	129	8	94	1.47	45	30	25	41	109	CCa	2%	52	57	4%	4%	105	2%	33%	34.3	243
2nd Half		283	35	7	28	2	314	7	4	308	337	454	107	89	113	4	94	0.59	40	27	33	32	119	CCa	5%	68	92	8%	8%	112	3%	100%	13.4	257
24	**Proj**	**665**	**85**	**9**	**65**	**4**	**328**	**11**	**10**	**297**	**376**	**434**	**111**	**95**	**116**	**7**	**92**	**1.00**	**42**	**27**	**30**	**34**	**112**		**3%**	**58**	**75**	**5%**	**6%**	**107**	**3%**	**58%**	**40.3**	**235**

Baddoo,Akil

Age: 25	Pos: LF		Health	B	LIMA Plan	C
Bats: L	Ht: 6'1"	Wt: 214	PT/Exp	B	Rand Var	+2
			Consist	C	MM	2403

11-34-.218 with 14 SB in 357 PA at DET. Missed most of June with a quad injury; strict platoon otherwise (only 10 PA vL). Recovered 2021's power/speed blend, but not BA (thanks, h%). Got more aggressive in 2nd half, yielding more Brl%/PX at the cost of BA/OBP. HR/SB seem top of range for underlying skills. Hard to see a path forward.

Yr	Tm	PA	R	HR	RBI	SB	BA	xHR	xSB	xBA	OBP	SLG	OPS+	vL+	vR+	bb%	ct%	Eye	G	L	F	h%	HctX	QBaB	Brl%	PX	xPX	HR/F	xHR/F	Spd	SBA%	SB%	RAR	BPX
19																																		
20																																		
21	DET	461	60	13	55	18	259	16	15	233	330	436	105	71	116	10	70	0.37	40	21	39	34	90	DCd	9%	108	118	11%	14%	134	20%	82%	8.8	115
22	DET *	348	39	4	19	14	221	3	19	200	303	319	88	76	80	11	70	0.40	42	18	40	30	69	DCf	2%	68	63	4%	6%	165	28%	56%	-11.4	24
23	DET *	402	44	12	39	15	219	12	12	229	312	372	93	60	94	12	71	0.47	46	16	38	27	85	CCf	6%	95	90	13%	14%	96	20%	79%	0.5	57
1st Half		203	20	4	20	7	234	4	6	225	343	356	96	45	96	14	77	0.72	45	14	41	28	80	CDf	4%	76	76	7%	9%	103	16%	77%	0.5	107
2nd Half		200	24	8	19	8	204	8	6	231	280	388	90	89	92	9	66	0.31	47	17	36	26	88	CCf	9%	118	103	20%	20%	93	25%	80%	-3.0	29
24	**Proj**	**420**	**48**	**10**	**36**	**16**	**233**	**12**	**17**	**221**	**314**	**376**	**95**	**76**	**97**	**11**	**70**	**0.40**	**44**	**17**	**39**	**30**	**80**		**6%**	**91**	**86**	**10%**	**12%**	**122**	**23%**	**69%**	**0.1**	**56**

Bader,Harrison

Age: 30	Pos: CF		Health	F	LIMA Plan	C
Bats: R	Ht: 6'0"	Wt: 210	PT/Exp	B	Rand Var	+3
			Consist	C	MM	1513

7-40-.232 with 20 SB in 344 PA at NYY/CIN. Oblique injury in April, hamstring in June, groin in September. Hard to pa any judgments amid litany of injuries, but they sure didn't slow him on the bases. Former power/speed profile is now speed-forward. Health grade, low PA totals are the story. If he ever conquers those... UP: 30 SB.

Yr	Tm	PA	R	HR	RBI	SB	BA	xHR	xSB	xBA	OBP	SLG	OPS+	vL+	vR+	bb%	ct%	Eye	G	L	F	h%	HctX	QBaB	Brl%	PX	xPX	HR/F	xHR/F	Spd	SBA%	SB%	RAR	BPX
19	STL *	475	72	17	50	13	214	15	12	214	302	394	96	89	95	11	67	0.38	38	17	44	27	88	CBd	10%	105	141	12%	15%	132	14%	82%	-4.5	56
20	STL	125	21	4	11	3	226	7	4	219	336	443	103	160	86	10	62	0.33	41	15	44	32	90	DBf	12%	148	147	14%	24%	153	14%	75%	-1.7	144
21	STL	401	45	16	50	9	267	13	8	248	324	460	108	104	109	7	77	0.32	43	16	41	31	96	DCf	7%	112	106	14%	11%	105	14%	69%	5.6	169
22	2 TM *	339	41	6	33	18	245	4	15	218	284	354	90	79	95	5	79	0.26	40	16	44	29	88	FBf	4%	67	77	5%	4%	149	27%	85%	-4.9	93
23	2 TM *	382	45	7	41	21	218	9	16	217	256	324	79	126	69	5	80	0.26	37	17	47	25	97	DBf	5%	60	96	6%	7%	115	31%	87%	-10.8	57
1st Half		175	20	6	24	8	219	5	7	227	243	380	85	170	79	3	84	0.19	35	13	52	23	101	DAf	9%	79	104	10%	8%	135	33%	79%	-4.9	164
2nd Half		207	25	1	17	13	217	3	8	208	272	275	74	104	60	6	78	0.31	38	19	43	27	93	DBf	3%	42	90	2%	5%	90	30%	93%	-7.6	-50
24	**Proj**	**315**	**40**	**7**	**34**	**17**	**232**	**8**	**12**	**222**	**283**	**361**	**88**	**110**	**81**	**6**	**78**	**0.27**	**39**	**17**	**45**	**28**	**93**		**6%**	**75**	**97**	**7%**	**8%**	**113**	**28%**	**87%**	**-3.2**	**76**

RAY MURPHY

Bae,Ji Hwan

Age: 24	Pos: 2B CF	Health	B	LIMA Plan	C
Bats: L	Ht: 6' 1" Wt: 185	PT/Exp	B	Rand Var	0
		Consist	A	MM	1423

2-32-.231 with 24 SB in 371 PA at PIT. Put himself on radar with 2 HR / 9 SB April, but that was his best month. Ankle injury cost him several weeks in 2nd half. PRO: Elite wheels, keeps ball on the ground to play to that strength. CON: Poor contact quality, low BA/xBA, and non-existent power. Marginal OBP keeps us marginally interested.

Yr Tm	PA	R	HR	RBI	SB	BA	xHR	xSB	xBA	OBP	SLG	OPS+	vL+	vR+	bb%	ct%	Eye	G	L	F	h%	HctX	QBaB	Brl%	PX	xPX	HR/F	xHR/F	Spd	SBA%	SB%	RAR	BPX	R$
19																																		
20																																		
21 aa	349	47	5	23	15	244		15		307	346	90			8	72	0.33				32				64				134	27%	63%		0	$10
22 PIT *	489	59	5	41	23	247	0	22	272	301	351	92	18	145	7	79	0.37	56	24	20	30	51	FFf		71	-4	0%	0%	145	28%	72%	-8.3	110	$17
23 PIT *	408	60	3	33	25	236	3	23	241	303	322	85	81	83	9	72	0.34	60	18	22	32	64	DFd	2%	64	38	4%	6%	128	34%	74%	-6.1	-11	$10
1st Half	239	37	2	19	20	238	2	16	233	301	308	83	82	84	8	73	0.31	56	19	24	32	57	DFd	3%	51	33	6%	6%	124	43%	77%	-5.0	-46	$12
2nd Half	169	23	1	14	5	232	0	6	251	310	341	88	80	82	10	70	0.38	65	17	18	33	77	CFf	1%	82	48	0%	0%	124	21%	64%	-2.3	21	$1
24 Proj	420	57	1	34	21	240	1	20	243	305	319	86	86	85	8	74	0.35	62	18	20	32	69		2%	57	42	2%	1%	122	28%	70%	-5.3	36	$11

Báez,Javier

Age: 31	Pos: SS	Health	A	LIMA Plan	B
Bats: R	Ht: 6' 0" Wt: 190	PT/Exp	A	Rand Var	+4
		Consist	C	MM	1415

Production took another dive and he lost PT in Sept. Scan of BA/xBA shows that 2021 BA is a clear outlier. Power skills that waned in 2022 outright crashed in 2023, so 20 HR looks out of reach now. Spd/SB% is the only bright spot. At this stage, anything more than a recovery to 2022 levels is wishcasting, barring some kind of QBaB reboot.

Yr Tm	PA	R	HR	RBI	SB	BA	xHR	xSB	xBA	OBP	SLG	OPS+	vL+	vR+	bb%	ct%	Eye	G	L	F	h%	HctX	QBaB	Brl%	PX	xPX	HR/F	xHR/F	Spd	SBA%	SB%	RAR	BPX	R$
19 CHC	561	89	29	85	11	281	31	12	272	316	531	117	134	112	5	71	0.18	50	18	32	35	91	ADa	13%	145	108	24%	26%	125	17%	61%	9.2	178	$24
20 CHC	235	27	8	24	3	203	9	2	222	238	360	79	85	77	3	66	0.09	50	18	32	27	97	CCf	8%	100	87	17%	19%	111	8%	100%	-13.5	-52	$9
21 2 NL	542	79	30	86	18	265	27	16	237	319	490	111	127	106	5	64	0.15	47	19	34	36	95	BCd	13%	145	117	28%	25%	131	19%	78%	12.4	85	$27
22 DET	590	64	17	67	9	238	19	10	242	278	393	95	117	88	4	74	0.18	50	17	34	29	86	CCc	8%	103	94	12%	14%	132	9%	82%	-7.9	93	$15
23 DET	546	58	9	59	12	222	12	13	234	267	325	81	88	78	4	75	0.19	50	18	32	28	87	CCd	5%	63	59	7%	10%	131	10%	100%	-13.1	7	$8
1st Half	333	32	6	42	6	223	6	7	234	258	331	81	83	80	4	76	0.16	50	18	32	27	82	CDd	3%	63	57	8%	8%	130	9%	100%	-13.3	11	$9
2nd Half	213	26	3	17	6	219	6	6	230	282	316	81	94	75	6	74	0.24	50	18	32	28	96	CCc	8%	62	64	7%	13%	126	13%	100%	-8.0	-4	$3
24 Proj	560	62	12	59	12	234	15	13	229	282	358	88	100	83	5	72	0.19	50	18	33	30	90		8%	79	81	10%	12%	121	11%	88%	-7.8	43	$15

Bailey,Patrick

Age: 25	Pos: CA	Health	A	LIMA Plan	D
Bats: B	Ht: 6' 2" Wt: 207	PT/Exp	D	Rand Var	0
		Consist	F	MM	2313

7-48-.233 in 353 PA at SF. Made MLB debut on May 19 with a nice splash (5-26-.309 in 132 1st half MLB PA). But that wave broke as pitchers adjusted and regression took hold in 2nd half. Expected HR points to 15-20 HR upside at peak, but the ct%/BA issues were present in minors and foretell more growing pains ahead.

Yr Tm	PA	R	HR	RBI	SB	BA	xHR	xSB	xBA	OBP	SLG	OPS+	vL+	vR+	bb%	ct%	Eye	G	L	F	h%	HctX	QBaB	Brl%	PX	xPX	HR/F	xHR/F	Spd	SBA%	SB%	RAR	BPX	R$
19																																		
20																																		
21																																		
22																																		
23 SF *	468	39	10	60	3	233	12	3	226	284	352	87	112	76	7	69	0.23	43	22	34	31	91	CCd	10%	82	100	9%	15%	81	3%	100%	-8.2	-61	$6
1st Half	247	23	8	38	2	273	6	2	260	318	437	103	167	102	6	70	0.21	38	31	31	36	111	BCa	14%	108	126	19%	22%	90	4%	100%	2.1	21	$11
2nd Half	221	16	2	22	1	187	6	1	191	253	256	69	88	58	7	69	0.25	46	17	36	26	77	CCf	8%	52	84	4%	12%	82	2%	100%	-16.9	-146	-$4
24 Proj	420	34	9	52	1	221	15	3	223	278	341	85	110	73	7	69	0.23	43	23	34	30	91		10%	82	101	10%	16%	80	1%	100%	-3.7	-79	$6

Baker,Luken

Age: 27	Pos: DH	Health	A	LIMA Plan	D
Bats: R	Ht: 6' 4" Wt: 265	PT/Exp	A	Rand Var	-2
		Consist	F	MM	2211

2-10-.209 in 99 PA at STL. Flashed improved power and ct% in second year at AAA. The ct% gains didn't carry over to tiny MLB sample, but he did show patience and enticing QBaB/xPX. Defensive limitations are an obstacle to PT and put added pressure on bat. Worth a flyer, but this skillset isn't hard to find, so don't get attached.

Yr Tm	PA	R	HR	RBI	SB	BA	xHR	xSB	xBA	OBP	SLG	OPS+	vL+	vR+	bb%	ct%	Eye	G	L	F	h%	HctX	QBaB	Brl%	PX	xPX	HR/F	xHR/F	Spd	SBA%	SB%	RAR	BPX	R$
19																																		
20																																		
21 a/a	377	34	16	45	0	193		0		244	374	85			6	66	0.20				24				120				77	0%	0%		-4	$0
22 aaa	486	32	12	41	0	170		0		207	268	67			5	68	0.15				22				68				82	0%	0%		-124	-$6
23 STL *	450	55	23	74	0	248	3	1	256	332	468	109	68	99	11	69	0.41	36	24	40	30	128	ABb	7%	138	134	9%	14%	65	0%	0%	14.5	111	$12
1st Half	276	34	14	39	0	248	0	1	241	329	459	108	54	137	11	68	0.37	33	22	44	31	122	ABa	0%	134	173	0%	0%	62	0%	0%	6.9	68	$13
2nd Half	175	21	9	35	0	248	2	1	271	337	483	111	71	95	12	72	0.48	37	24	39	29	134	ABb	9%	144	126	11%	11%	70	0%	0%	6.1	179	$8
24 Proj	175	17	5	24	0	231	4	0	222	295	361	90	74	100	8	69	0.29	37	24	39	30	121		8%	87	113	11%	9%	74	0%	100%	-2.7	23	$4

Barrero,Jose

Age: 26	Pos: SS	Health	B	LIMA Plan	F
Bats: R	Ht: 6' 2" Wt: 175	PT/Exp	B	Rand Var	0
		Consist	F	MM	1401

2-17-.218 with 3 SB in 149 PA at CIN. Suddenly appeared on radar with a .900+ OPS in upper levels of minors in 2021. However, he hasn't produced anything close to that since. PRO: Spd/SB% indicate SB are best path to value. CON: Dreadful ct%/HctX caps BA; subpar xPX/Brl% stymies power potential. Low ceiling; watch your head.

Yr Tm	PA	R	HR	RBI	SB	BA	xHR	xSB	xBA	OBP	SLG	OPS+	vL+	vR+	bb%	ct%	Eye	G	L	F	h%	HctX	QBaB	Brl%	PX	xPX	HR/F	xHR/F	Spd	SBA%	SB%	RAR	BPX	R$
19																																		
20 CIN	68	4	0	2	1	194	1	2	185	206	194	53	78	42	1	61	0.04	39	34	27	32	36	CDd	2%	0	10	0%	9%	132	14%	50%	-7.1	-440	-$3
21 CIN *	416	54	17	57	14	264	1	13	217	324	462	108	79	86	8	69	0.29	36	12	52	34	69	BAb	9%	126	61	0%	6%	142	19%	76%	6.7	150	$18
22 CIN *	402	32	10	27	8	169	2	7	160	204	271	67	70	53	4	53	0.10	40	17	43	28	60	CAc	2%	91	85	5%	5%	117	18%	70%	-33.9	-231	-$2
23 CIN *	453	43	16	51	15	210	3	13	216	259	381	87	74	91	6	60	0.17	40	22	38	31	68	CBf	3%	128	43	6%	9%	125	23%	82%	-8.4	-18	$7
1st Half	196	17	3	20	3	189	3	4	204	259	297	76	74	91	9	62	0.25	40	22	38	29	70	CBf	3%	91	43	6%	9%	109	14%	60%	-10.7	-96	-$4
2nd Half	258	26	13	31	12	226		9	226	260	443	95	0	0	4	58	0.11	44	20	36	33	0		0%	156	-21	0%		135	30%	91%	-2.1	36	$15
24 Proj	210	20	2	21	6	205	3	7	174	264	291	76	81	73	6	59	0.15	39	19	42	33	63		5%	73	53	5%	6%	121	17%	80%	-8.7	-67	$4

Bart,Joey

Age: 27	Pos: CA	Health	B	LIMA Plan	F
Bats: R	Ht: 6' 2" Wt: 238	PT/Exp	C	Rand Var	+2
		Consist	B	MM	1201

0-5-.207 in 95 PA at SF. Injuries (back, groin) shelved him for over a month in 1st half. Provided glimmer of 20 HR upside in 2022, but power metrics took a tumble in 2023. Given history of poor ct%/xBA, he'll need that power in order to be viable offensively. At this stage, not even a 2nd CA candidate until he gives us a reason to reconsider.

Yr Tm	PA	R	HR	RBI	SB	BA	xHR	xSB	xBA	OBP	SLG	OPS+	vL+	vR+	bb%	ct%	Eye	G	L	F	h%	HctX	QBaB	Brl%	PX	xPX	HR/F	xHR/F	Spd	SBA%	SB%	RAR	BPX	R$
19 aa	86	9	3	11	0	302		2		358	505	119			8	72	0.31				39				112				117	9%	0%		111	$0
20 SF	111	15	0	7	0	233	2	1	183	288	320	81	67	85	3	60	0.07	52	16	32	39	98	CCb	5%	69	78	0%	10%	141	0%	0%	-4.1	-212	$1
21 SF *	272	26	6	32	0	233	0	0	263	273	349	85	181	0	5	61	0.14	25	50	25	36	0	CAf	0%	91	-22	0%	0%	78	0%	0%	-5.3	-173	$2
22 SF *	320	37	12	27	2	214	11	2	195	282	355	90	91	94	8	59	0.23	43	21	36	32	86	CBc	10%	107	99	21%	21%	81	4%	67%	-3.4	-124	$3
23 SF *	320	30	3	23	1	193	1	1	183	250	277	72	62	83	7	63	0.20	43	17	40	30	63	DBf	6%	70	59	0%	4%	65	2%	100%	-10.9	-200	-$3
1st Half	161	13	1	11	1	203	1	1	178	226	268	68	68	92	3	67	0.09	45	15	40	30	62	FBf	5%	54	47	0%	5%	70	3%	100%	-7.7	-221	-$7
2nd Half	160	17	2	12	0	184	0	1	222	275	287	76	0	23	11	59	0.31	25	38	38	29	90	ACf	13%	91	135	0%	0%	78	0%	0%	-5.0	-157	-$5
24 Proj	175	19	2	14	0	208	3	1	178	291	289	80	70	85	7	61	0.19	47	17	36	33	82		6%	69	72	5%	7%	85	1%	78%	-4.5	-169	$1

Basabe,Osleivis

Age: 23	Pos: SS	Health	A	LIMA Plan	D
Bats: R	Ht: 6' 1" Wt: 165	PT/Exp	C	Rand Var	0
		Consist	D	MM	2531

1-12-.218 in 94 PA at TAM. Struggled to put bat on ball in teeny MLB sample after Aug debut, but ct% was a strength in minors. Power is relegated to shooting gaps, so plus wheels and SB potential are the start of a value proposition. Possibly a future "good BA/20 SB" profile, but that's unlikely for 2024.

Yr Tm	PA	R	HR	RBI	SB	BA	xHR	xSB	xBA	OBP	SLG	OPS+	vL+	vR+	bb%	ct%	Eye	G	L	F	h%	HctX	QBaB	Brl%	PX	xPX	HR/F	xHR/F	Spd	SBA%	SB%	RAR	BPX	R$
19																																		
20																																		
21																																		
22 aa	245	28	0	18	10	281		6		332	388	102			7	87	0.59				32				77				106	17%	100%		197	$7
23 TAM *	501	47	4	53	11	240	1	19	241	282	339	85	101	70	6	78	0.27	60	13	27	30	77	CFf	3%	64	72	6%	6%	153	18%	59%	-8.8	82	$7
1st Half	278	21	3	25	6	240		11	240	286	340	86	0	0	6	80	0.32	44	20	36	29	0		0%	60	-21	0%		144	21%	45%	-9.9	93	$4
2nd Half	223	26	1	27	6	239	1	7	240	277	337	83	100	69	5	76	0.21	60	13	27	31	75	CFf	3%	69	72	6%	6%	147	15%	85%	-6.5	50	$6
24 Proj	210	22	2	20	7	257	3	7	252	309	384	95	121	82	6	78	0.30	54	16	30	32	68		3%	84	65	5%	6%	139	17%	80%	1.4	120	$7

GREG PYRON

Batten,Matthew

Age: 29 Pos: 2B | Bats: R Ht: 5' 11" Wt: 180

Health A | PT/Exp A | Consist A | LIMA Plan F | Rand Var +3 | MM 1301

2-11-.258 with 2 SB in 139 PA at SD. Versatile defender saw lots of playing time in Sept, but hit only .218 BA with 0 HR in 101 PA. Poor ct% and no power are his M.O. Showed slightly better ct% in MLB, but puny Brl%, QBaB, HctX, and xPX confirm lack of pop. Spd is his best asset if he can ever fix the plate approach, but time is running out.

Yr	Tm	PA	R	HR	RBI	SB	BA	xHR	xSB	xBA	OBP	SLG	OPS+	vL+	vR+	bb%	ct%	Eye	G	L	F	h%	HctX	QBaB	Brl%	PX	xPX	HR/F	xHR/F	Spd	SBA%	SB%	RAR	BPX	R$
19	a/a	382	45	4	36	6	252		9		297	351	90			6	72	0.23				34				62				113	17%	39%		-44	$5
20																																			
21	a/a	476	46	4	26	18	224		15		282	283	78			7	65	0.23				34				44				115	22%	71%		-204	$8
22	SD *	372	32	6	24	9	190	0	7	220	249	281	75	89	14	7	70	0.26	62	15	23	25	47	DFd		67	-14	0%	0%	96	16%	78%	-23.6	-69	$0
23	SD *	521	57	9	38	16	181	0	17	198	253	276	72	129	81	9	66	0.28	40	20	39	25	41	DCf	1%	69	24	6%	0%	124	22%	70%	-27.0	-86	$1
1st Half		326	34	6	25	14	158		11	195	227	254	66	0	0	8	63	0.24	44	20	36	23	0		0%	72	-21	0%		106	30%	85%	-23.2	-150	$2
2nd Half		195	23	3	13	2	220	0	6	212	297	314	83	128	80	10	71	0.38	40	20	39	29	45	DCf	1%	65	24	6%	0%	124	15%	31%	-7.7	-11	$0
24	**Proj**	**175**	**18**	**2**	**12**	**4**	**203**	**0**	**5**	**197**	**273**	**285**	**76**	**102**	**63**	**8**	**68**	**0.28**	**40**	**20**	**39**	**28**	**41**		**1%**	**60**	**22**	**5%**	**0%**	**123**	**18%**	**61%**	**-6.7**	**-86**	**-$1**

Baty,Brett

Age: 24 Pos: 3B | Bats: L Ht: 6' 3" Wt: 210

Health B | PT/Exp B | Consist B | LIMA Plan D+ | Rand Var +3 | MM 1003

9-34-.212 in 386 PA at NYM. Sent to AAA in Aug. after brutal 2nd half start, hit well at AAA, but struggled again in Sept recall. Too much swing-and-miss the main problem. When he does make contact, shows above-average exit velocity, but GB% stifles power. Launch angle tweak needed, so improvement (43% GB%) in Sept is notable. Stay patient.

Yr	Tm	PA	R	HR	RBI	SB	BA	xHR	xSB	xBA	OBP	SLG	OPS+	vL+	vR+	bb%	ct%	Eye	G	L	F	h%	HctX	QBaB	Brl%	PX	xPX	HR/F	xHR/F	Spd	SBA%	SB%	RAR	BPX	R$
19																																			
20																																			
21	aa	169	12	4	16	1	219		1		293	331	86			9	65	0.30				32				81				86	3%	100%		-112	-$1
22	NYM *	437	55	15	45	1	247	1	3	221	309	403	101	31	99	8	66	0.26	53	17	30	34	87	ACa	7%	114	77	22%	11%	77	6%	22%	-4.0	-3	$10
23	NYM *	501	54	15	55	3	217	11	5	232	280	348	86	64	87	8	68	0.28	50	22	27	28	79	BDc	8%	85	61	13%	16%	86	5%	58%	-10.8	-50	$6
1st Half		258	31	8	31	3	255	6	5	252	325	401	99	89	93	9	70	0.35	50	25	25	33	86	ADc	7%	93	52	14%	17%	101	8%	58%	1.2	29	$10
2nd Half		243	23	7	24	0	178	5	1	205	233	295	71	47	79	7	66	0.21	50	19	31	23	72	DFd	10%	76	73	13%	16%	81	0%	0%	-14.8	-125	-$1
24	**Proj**	**420**	**45**	**10**	**44**	**2**	**232**	**11**	**3**	**216**	**298**	**347**	**88**	**67**	**97**	**8**	**67**	**0.27**	**49**	**21**	**29**	**32**	**78**		**8%**	**79**	**65**	**13%**	**14%**	**74**	**4%**	**42%**	**-5.6**	**-50**	**$9**

Bauers,Jake

Age: 28 Pos: RF LF 1B | Bats: L Ht: 6' 1" Wt: 195

Health A | PT/Exp C | Consist F | LIMA Plan D | Rand Var -1 | MM 4213

12-30-.202 with 3 SB in 272 PA at NYY. Altered swing at AAA in 2022 seeking more power, but injuries kept him from showing it until 2023. Flashed career-best xPX/Brl% and hope for more palatable BA (xBA) in strong-side platoon. 2nd half crash may have been caused by bout of left shoulder inflammation. If so, that opens door to... UP: 25 HR

Yr	Tm	PA	R	HR	RBI	SB	BA	xHR	xSB	xBA	OBP	SLG	OPS+	vL+	vR+	bb%	ct%	Eye	G	L	F	h%	HctX	QBaB	Brl%	PX	xPX	HR/F	xHR/F	Spd	SBA%	SB%	RAR	BPX	R$
19	CLE *	524	57	15	55	10	226	10	9	227	310	373	95	95	94	11	69	0.39	39	24	38	30	74	CBc	5%	90	65	12%	10%	100	12%	64%	-10.5	4	$9
20																																			
21	2 AL	314	27	4	19	6	209	7	5	203	290	277	78	73	79	10	72	0.38	33	25	42	28	75	CAf	5%	43	73	5%	8%	105	9%	86%	-15.5	-88	$1
22	aaa	228	14	5	18	5	137		5		236	245	68			11	53	0.28				22				93				98	20%	59%		-200	-$5
23	NYY *	362	40	19	45	7	221	17	6	247	306	470	106	64	98	11	64	0.34	38	19	43	28	93	CCf	19%	172	161	19%	27%	76	13%	78%	9.2	139	$7
1st Half		228	27	13	32	5	229	9	3	268	327	508	114	79	112	13	67	0.45	37	20	44	27	107	BBc	20%	183	171	18%	24%	78	11%	100%	10.1	239	$10
2nd Half		135	14	6	13	2	210	8	3	214	274	414	93	45	83	8	58	0.21	40	19	41	30	75	CCf	18%	153	146	19%	31%	91	16%	46%	-2.0	-7	-$1
24	**Proj**	**315**	**29**	**13**	**30**	**5**	**241**	**17**	**7**	**227**	**327**	**430**	**104**	**87**	**108**	**11**	**65**	**0.37**	**36**	**22**	**42**	**32**	**81**		**12%**	**126**	**113**	**17%**	**22%**	**96**	**11%**	**61%**	**5.6**	**-17**	**$9**

Bell,Josh

Age: 31 Pos: DH 1B | Bats: B Ht: 6' 4" Wt: 261

Health A | PT/Exp A | Consist B | LIMA Plan B+ | Rand Var 0 | MM 3035

Poor 1st half prompted trade to MIA, where change in latitude brought a change in attitude. Traded some ct% for gains in exit velocity and Brl%. If you squint, 2nd half isn't that far removed from 2019 peak. However, he has never been able to hold that FB% level; it predictably faded in Sept (32%). Split 2022-2023 for your new baseline.

Yr	Tm	PA	R	HR	RBI	SB	BA	xHR	xSB	xBA	OBP	SLG	OPS+	vL+	vR+	bb%	ct%	Eye	G	L	F	h%	HctX	QBaB	Brl%	PX	xPX	HR/F	xHR/F	Spd	SBA%	SB%	RAR	BPX	R$
19	PIT	613	94	37	116	0	277	38	-	291	367	569	130	106	137	12	78	0.63	44	19	37	29	122	ACc	13%	150	135	24%	25%	62	1%	0%	30.5	278	$23
20	PIT	223	22	8	22	0	226	8	0	212	305	364	89	77	93	10	70	0.37	56	19	26	28	117	ADd	9%	77	57	22%	22%	79	0%	0%	-7.1	-52	$8
21	WAS	568	75	27	88	0	261	24	0	278	347	476	113	114	112	11	80	0.64	54	20	27	28	122	AFc	9%	115	101	25%	23%	65	0%	0%	8.6	212	$17
22	2 NL	644	78	17	71	0	266	18	2	263	362	422	111	114	109	13	82	0.79	50	19	31	30	105	CDd	7%	95	74	12%	13%	86	1%	0%	10.6	190	$18
23	2 TM	615	52	22	74	0	247	25	1	236	325	419	101	115	95	10	76	0.47	48	18	34	29	101	BCd	10%	103	95	15%	18%	50	1%	0%	9.2	79	$12
1st Half		307	17	8	38	0	228	9	1	228	319	377	95	94	96	12	74	0.54	50	19	31	28	95	BDc	9%	96	84	13%	15%	51	1%	0%	-5.5	54	$4
2nd Half		308	35	14	36	0	265	16	1	243	331	459	107	136	95	9	77	0.40	47	16	37	30	106	BCd	12%	109	106	18%	20%	59	0%	0%	4.9	111	$16
24	**Proj**	**595**	**65**	**22**	**75**	**0**	**256**	**24**	**1**	**253**	**339**	**436**	**106**	**114**	**103**	**11**	**78**	**0.55**	**50**	**18**	**32**	**29**	**107**		**9%**	**104**	**92**	**17%**	**18%**	**64**	**0%**	**0%**	**14.7**	**135**	**$18**

Bellinger,Cody

Age: 28 Pos: CF 1B | Bats: L Ht: 6' 4" Wt: 203

Health C | PT/Exp A | Consist F | LIMA Plan D+ | Rand Var -5 | MM 3435

Delivered resurgent season, as shoulder woes appear to finally be behind him. Stellar 2nd half followed month-long IL stint (left knee). PRO: Dramatic ct% gains; Spd/SBA%/SB% back 15+ SB. CON: xHR questions HR rebound; xBA doesn't fully support BA surge. Next step likely back a bit, rather than toward 2019, but his ceiling has risen.

Yr	Tm	PA	R	HR	RBI	SB	BA	xHR	xSB	xBA	OBP	SLG	OPS+	vL+	vR+	bb%	ct%	Eye	G	L	F	h%	HctX	QBaB	Brl%	PX	xPX	HR/F	xHR/F	Spd	SBA%	SB%	RAR	BPX	R$
19	LA	660	121	47	115	15	305	45	14	306	406	629	143	137	145	14	81	0.88	31	26	42	31	137	AAb	13%	155	165	25%	24%	120	11%	75%	77.1	419	$37
20	LA	243	33	12	30	6	239	11	4	267	333	455	105	87	114	12	80	0.71	38	22	41	25	124	CBd	9%	111	120	17%	16%	93	12%	86%	0.7	256	$22
21	LA	350	39	10	36	3	165	10	3	205	240	302	74	52	83	9	70	0.33	31	22	48	20	88	CAd	7%	82	110	9%	9%	109	6%	75%	-23.3	0	-$2
22	LA	550	70	19	68	14	210	17	11	225	265	389	93	82	97	7	70	0.25	36	17	47	26	107	BAd	8%	124	128	11%	10%	118	18%	82%	-10.6	107	$14
23	CHC	556	95	26	97	20	307	18	20	279	356	525	120	133	113	7	83	0.46	36	21	43	33	98	CBc	6%	117	108	14%	10%	120	18%	77%	41.7	271	$32
1st Half		216	35	7	23	10	276	5	9	253	333	458	108	137	94	8	79	0.41	37	19	45	32	80	DAf	5%	107	72	10%	7%	127	23%	83%	8.6	204	$13
2nd Half		340	60	19	74	10	326	12	11	295	371	567	127	129	125	7	85	0.50	35	22	43	33	110	CBb	6%	123	129	17%	11%	115	16%	71%	32.0	318	$46
24	**Proj**	**560**	**88**	**24**	**87**	**16**	**277**	**19**	**16**	**253**	**334**	**475**	**111**	**113**	**110**	**8**	**77**	**0.39**	**35**	**20**	**45**	**32**	**102**		**7%**	**114**	**116**	**13%**	**10%**	**114**	**15%**	**78%**	**26.7**	**197**	**$31**

Belt,Brandon

Age: 36 Pos: DH 1B | Bats: L Ht: 6' 3" Wt: 231

Health F | PT/Exp A | Consist F | LIMA Plan C | Rand Var -4 | MM 4123

Health was again an issue at times (hamstring, illness, back spasms). Displayed typically elite xPX, still rakes vR. Don't be alarmed by ct% crash, as it was mostly 1st half and may have been influenced by injuries, limited spring training. Stable skills back a repeat on per-PA basis, but another 400 PA isn't a lock given health, age, and platoon split.

Yr	Tm	PA	R	HR	RBI	SB	BA	xHR	xSB	xBA	OBP	SLG	OPS+	vL+	vR+	bb%	ct%	Eye	G	L	F	h%	HctX	QBaB	Brl%	PX	xPX	HR/F	xHR/F	Spd	SBA%	SB%	RAR	BPX	R$
19	SF	616	76	17	57	4	234	27	4	238	339	403	103	92	105	13	76	0.65	28	23	49	28	107	CAa	9%	95	139	9%	14%	89	4%	57%	-12.2	130	$
20	SF	179	25	9	30	0	309	12	0	292	425	591	135	72	148	17	76	0.83	31	27	42	36	125	BBc	17%	161	160	19%	26%	77	0%	0%	17.7	364	$1
21	SF	381	65	29	59	3	274	24	3	265	378	597	134	113	139	13	68	0.47	27	23	50	31	108	CAc	17%	190	165	27%	22%	96	5%	60%	23.3	312	$1
22	SF	298	25	8	23	1	213	13	1	207	326	350	96	84	100	12	68	0.46	27	23	50	28	86	CAc	13%	96	140	10%	15%	86	1%	100%	-8.3	7	$
23	TOR	404	53	19	43	0	254	20	3	231	369	490	117	77	122	15	58	0.43	30	22	48	37	88	CAc	15%	181	153	20%	21%	94	0%	0%	19.5	139	$
1st Half		215	23	6	20	0	257	6	2	215	363	443	110	56	116	14	55	0.36	29	24	46	44	86	BAa	11%	169	148	13%	13%	95	0%	0%	4.7	43	$
2nd Half		189	30	13	23	0	250	14	1	250	376	545	124	99	127	17	63	0.53	31	19	50	31	90	DAf	19%	194	159	27%	29%	87	0%	0%	10.7	243	$1
24	**Proj**	**350**	**46**	**18**	**39**	**1**	**248**	**19**	**2**	**237**	**361**	**482**	**116**	**88**	**121**	**14**	**65**	**0.48**	**29**	**22**	**49**	**32**	**94**		**15%**	**158**	**152**	**19%**	**21%**	**84**	**1%**	**69%**	**15.2**	**155**	**$1**

Benintendi,Andrew

Age: 29 Pos: LF | Bats: L Ht: 5' 9" Wt: 180

Health C | PT/Exp A | Consist C | LIMA Plan B+ | Rand Var 0 | MM 1335

Traded power for contact in 2022 and is now another year further from 2017-18 pop. As expected, bloated 2022 h% regressed and BA tumbled. Improved SB% and PA uptick contributed to SB spike, but track record says to expect pullback. Late-2022 right wrist injury lingered for much of 2023. If wrist is healthy, 2019 redux is still in play.

Yr	Tm	PA	R	HR	RBI	SB	BA	xHR	xSB	xBA	OBP	SLG	OPS+	vL+	vR+	bb%	ct%	Eye	G	L	F	h%	HctX	QBaB	Brl%	PX	xPX	HR/F	xHR/F	Spd	SBA%	SB%	RAR	BPX	R$
19	BOS	615	72	13	68	10	266	22	9	243	343	431	107	111	105	10	74	0.42	38	21	41	34	98	CBa	8%	99	107	8%	13%	113	9%	77%	9.1	115	$1
20	BOS	52	4	0	1	1	103	1	2	120	314	128	59	47	61	21	56	0.65	57	5	38	18	60	FFf	4%	28	57	0%	13%	111	20%	33%	-5.3	-292	-$
21	KC	538	63	17	73	8	276	20	10	254	324	442	105	108	104	7	80	0.37	39	21	41	31	115	CBc	9%	94	133	10%	12%	102	13%	47%	5.5	165	$1
22	2 AL	521	54	5	51	8	304	12	10	250	373	399	109	95	115	10	83	0.68	43	22	35	36	114	CCb	5%	63	96	4%	9%	121	7%	73%	20.4	145	$2
23	CHW	621	72	5	45	13	262	8	12	265	326	356	93	97	92	8	84	0.58	39	26	35	30	84	DBb	3%	60	58	3%	5%	93	9%	87%	4.8	111	$1
1st Half		332	39	1	23	9	282	3	8	268	347	372	99	92	100	9	84	0.60	44	24	32	33	84	CCb	3%	63	39	1%	4%	102	11%	90%	6.1	132	$1
2nd Half		289	33	4	22	4	239	5	4	264	301	337	86	103	82	8	84	0.57	33	29	38	27	84	DBc	3%	57	80	5%	6%	86	7%	80%	-4.1	93	$
24	**Proj**	**560**	**64**	**9**	**53**	**10**	**272**	**12**	**10**	**259**	**336**	**392**	**100**	**101**	**99**	**9**	**82**	**0.54**	**39**	**24**	**36**	**32**	**98**		**5%**	**73**	**86**	**6%**	**8%**	**102**	**9%**	**74%**	**11.0**	**127**	**$1**

GREG PYRON

Benson,Will

Age: 26 Pos: RF LF | Bats: L Ht: 6' 5" Wt: 230

Health A | PT/Exp B | Consist C | LIMA Plan C+ | Rand Var -4 | MM 4505

11-31-.275 with 19 SB in 329 PA at CIN. Thrived in platoon role following late-May promotion. PRO: Bat crackles per QBaB, Brl%, xPX along with FB%; elite Spd and improved SB%, strong bb%. CON: Awful ct% threatens to ruin everything else, with xBA pointing out some of the risk. But this is a power/speed profile worthy of consideration.

Yr	Tm	PA	R	HR	RBI	SB	BA	xHR	xSB	xBA	OBP	SLG	OPS+	vL+	vR+	bb%	ct%	Eye	G	L	F	h%	HctX	QBaB	Brl%	PX	xPX	HR/F	xHR/F	Spd	SBA%	SB%	RAR	BPX	R$
19																																			
20																																			
21	a/a	410	52	13	38	10	177		10		288	352	88			14	54	0.34				28				141				122	19%	65%		-27	$3
22	CLE *	420	51	10	29	9	208	1	10	217	295	343	90	23	68	11	65	0.35	47	19	33	29	46	FDf	0%	102	48	0%	8%	120	15%	66%	-11.3	10	$5
23	CIN *	445	66	13	36	25	246	11	25	227	347	447	108	54	128	13	62	0.41	37	23	39	36	93	BBc	10%	138	140	15%	15%	159	26%	86%	16.3	129	$14
1st Half		231	33	5	12	12	228	4	14	206	345	381	100	81	121	15	64	0.50	39	18	42	33	78	BBc	12%	99	102	10%	13%	170	22%	85%	2.3	71	$6
2nd Half		214	33	8	24	13	266	7	11	245	350	516	117	47	132	11	60	0.32	36	26	38	40	101	BCb	9%	181	163	19%	16%	137	31%	87%	12.5	182	$16
24	Proj	455	63	12	38	18	237	12	19	214	339	406	102	48	110	12	62	0.36	39	22	39	35	73		9%	122	102	12%	12%	140	20%	79%	7.1	68	$13

Berti,Jon

Age: 34 Pos: SS 3B | Bats: R Ht: 5' 10" Wt: 190

Health D | PT/Exp A | Consist B | LIMA Plan C+ | Rand Var -4 | MM 1533

A lot went right here: career-high PA, boosted ct%, h% cooperated, and BPX spiked to new heights. But in a "How was the play, Mrs. Lincoln?" sort of way, the only thing that matters is that 2022's SBA% vanished and, at his age, likely isn't coming back. Even if he logs another 400 PA, can't count on more than 20-25 SB... and that's no longer rare.

Yr	Tm	PA	R	HR	RBI	SB	BA	xHR	xSB	xBA	OBP	SLG	OPS+	vL+	vR+	bb%	ct%	Eye	G	L	F	h%	HctX	QBaB	Brl%	PX	xPX	HR/F	xHR/F	Spd	SBA%	SB%	RAR	BPX	R$
19	MIA *	361	63	9	30	21	264	6	15	264	339	400	102	123	99	10	73	0.41	53	26	21	34	91	CFc	4%	79	59	16%	16%	133	24%	87%	1.6	56	$15
20	MIA	149	21	2	14	9	258	2	6	219	388	350	98	88	102	15	69	0.62	53	20	27	36	62	DFd	3%	63	40	9%	9%	98	22%	82%	0.9	-40	$16
21	MIA	271	35	4	19	8	210	3	7	245	311	313	86	75	92	12	74	0.52	59	20	21	27	76	CFc	2%	66	49	11%	8%	107	17%	67%	-10.9	23	$3
22	MIA	404	47	4	28	41	240	9	28	233	324	338	94	97	93	10	75	0.47	53	17	30	31	86	CFd	6%	70	85	5%	11%	144	43%	89%	-3.1	79	$22
23	MIA	424	53	7	33	16	294	9	20	261	344	405	102	108	99	7	80	0.38	54	20	26	35	92	DFf	5%	64	67	9%	11%	145	18%	73%	12.0	111	$14
1st Half		244	29	2	15	8	276	4	10	239	318	347	91	107	85	6	78	0.28	49	22	29	35	88	DFf	4%	46	63	4%	8%	126	18%	67%	-2.8	0	$7
2nd Half		180	24	5	18	8	319	5	9	293	378	485	116	109	121	8	83	0.56	60	18	23	36	97	DFd	6%	88	72	16%	16%	145	19%	80%	11.8	236	$12
24	Proj	385	50	7	31	22	260	8	18	255	332	377	97	97	97	9	78	0.45	55	19	26	32	87		5%	71	68	10%	12%	126	26%	81%	6.3	95	$17

Bethancourt,Christian

Age: 32 Pos: CA | Bats: R Ht: 6' 3" Wt: 205

Health A | PT/Exp B | Consist B | LIMA Plan D | Rand Var 0 | MM 2311

Unable to fully replicate 2022 breakthrough, as ct%/Brl% dipped and HR/F slipped. The GB% didn't help matters either (despite decent wheels for a backstop). Given his age, BA risk and average-at-best skills across the board, he's just barely hanging on the edge of the "viable second catcher in an -only league" line.

Yr	Tm	PA	R	HR	RBI	SB	BA	xHR	xSB	xBA	OBP	SLG	OPS+	vL+	vR+	bb%	ct%	Eye	G	L	F	h%	HctX	QBaB	Brl%	PX	xPX	HR/F	xHR/F	Spd	SBA%	SB%	RAR	BPX	R$
19																																			
20																																			
21	aaa	349	29	8	38	3	209		2		250	331	80			5	72	0.20				26				78				82	6%	66%		-42	$1
22	2 AL	333	39	11	34	5	252	15	4	247	283	409	98	96	99	4	75	0.15	45	19	35	30	107	BCd	12%	105	111	13%	18%	101	9%	83%	3.4	79	$9
23	TAM	332	49	11	33	1	225	11	2	227	254	381	86	88	86	4	71	0.14	49	14	38	28	99	CCf	8%	100	110	13%	13%	97	2%	100%	-0.8	11	$4
1st Half		191	28	7	21	0	236	8	1	236	258	418	92	111	89	3	71	0.12	47	14	39	29	107	BCf	10%	119	109	14%	16%	91	0%	0%	0.3	61	$3
2nd Half		141	21	4	12	1	211	3	1	212	248	331	78	67	82	5	71	0.18	51	14	35	27	88	DDf	5%	75	111	12%	9%	107	4%	100%	-3.6	-46	-$1
24	Proj	245	32	7	25	2	230	9	2	227	262	372	87	86	87	4	73	0.16	48	16	36	29	100		9%	91	111	12%	14%	101	5%	85%	-0.8	20	$6

Betts,Mookie

Age: 31 Pos: RF 2B | Bats: R Ht: 5' 9" Wt: 180

Health B | PT/Exp A | Consist C | LIMA Plan C | Rand Var -2 | MM 4355

Consistent above-average ct%/elite HctX combo sets the foundation. Improvements in QBaB and Brl% suggest the power is sustainable, even xHR has conceded agreement. Slight BA pullback is possible and double-digit SB are at risk with Spd/SB% slippage, but those are quibbles. Added 2B eligibility is a significant plus. BPX string says it all.

Yr	Tm	PA	R	HR	RBI	SB	BA	xHR	xSB	xBA	OBP	SLG	OPS+	vL+	vR+	bb%	ct%	Eye	G	L	F	h%	HctX	QBaB	Brl%	PX	xPX	HR/F	xHR/F	Spd	SBA%	SB%	RAR	BPX	R$
19	BOS	706	135	29	80	16	295	37	17	279	391	524	127	117	130	14	83	0.96	31	25	44	31	124	AAb	10%	113	134	13%	17%	133	9%	84%	35.6	341	$31
20	LA	246	47	16	39	10	292	10	9	277	366	562	123	69	141	10	83	0.63	32	21	46	29	149	BAb	8%	129	179	19%	12%	145	19%	83%	13.5	396	$40
21	LA	550	93	23	58	10	264	18	13	272	367	487	117	117	118	12	82	0.79	35	22	43	28	137	BAc	8%	120	140	14%	11%	137	10%	67%	16.2	346	$21
22	LA	639	117	35	82	12	269	29	10	285	340	533	124	138	118	9	82	0.53	34	19	48	27	137	BAc	10%	154	159	16%	13%	111	10%	86%	34.0	355	$33
23	LA	693	126	39	107	14	307	36	14	293	408	579	134	148	130	14	82	0.90	28	24	49	32	137	AAb	12%	146	173	17%	15%	95	8%	82%	73.8	364	$38
1st Half		368	64	22	56	7	271	20	7	289	372	555	127	141	123	14	80	0.79	30	21	49	27	139	AAb	12%	153	186	18%	16%	94	10%	78%	26.9	357	$35
2nd Half		325	62	17	51	7	347	16	7	300	449	606	143	154	138	15	84	1.04	26	26	48	37	134	AAa	13%	139	158	15%	15%	98	7%	88%	45.2	379	$40
24	Proj	665	124	35	94	12	294	31	15	285	388	551	129	135	126	12	82	0.79	31	22	47	31	136		11%	139	161	16%	14%	107	8%	84%	60.3	363	$39

Bichette,Bo

Age: 26 Pos: SS | Bats: R Ht: 6' 0" Wt: 190

Health B | PT/Exp A | Consist B | LIMA Plan D+ | Rand Var -1 | MM 3355

Two separate IL stints limited him in 2nd half (right patellar tendinitis, right quad strain). Prior to that, he delivered 1st round value in first half with career best BA/xBA, ct%, and HctX helping to offset diminished SB. Leg injuries could continue to cap SB totals, and GB% lean is a drag on HR upside. But there's plenty of value in the bat-to-ball skill.

Yr	Tm	PA	R	HR	RBI	SB	BA	xHR	xSB	xBA	OBP	SLG	OPS+	vL+	vR+	bb%	ct%	Eye	G	L	F	h%	HctX	QBaB	Brl%	PX	xPX	HR/F	xHR/F	Spd	SBA%	SB%	RAR	BPX	R$
19	TOR *	451	62	18	49	17	287	10	15	279	335	508	117	150	119	7	76	0.30	44	23	34	34	86	BCc	9%	125	97	22%	20%	119	27%	65%	7.8	204	$19
20	TOR	128	18	5	23	4	301	7	3	281	328	512	112	112	111	4	78	0.19	41	26	33	35	102	BCc	13%	120	111	16%	22%	116	19%	80%	5.1	212	$16
21	TOR	690	121	29	102	25	298	29	15	272	343	484	114	129	109	6	79	0.29	49	21	30	34	117	ADd	10%	103	91	19%	19%	102	15%	96%	33.8	158	$42
22	TOR	697	91	24	93	13	290	22	12	269	333	469	114	111	114	6	76	0.26	49	20	31	35	116	ADb	10%	120	106	16%	14%	94	13%	62%	25.1	148	$34
23	TOR	601	69	20	73	5	306	22	11	290	339	475	111	120	109	4	80	0.23	46	27	27	36	117	BDc	10%	95	86	17%	18%	116	5%	63%	33.4	146	$23
1st Half		373	43	15	51	3	317	14	6	309	346	507	117	136	113	4	82	0.23	47	29	24	36	131	AFb	10%	106	96	21%	20%	96	7%	50%	20.5	179	$31
2nd Half		228	26	5	22	2	290	8	5	257	329	421	101	95	103	5	77	0.24	44	25	31	36	93	CDd	9%	76	69	10%	16%	149	3%	100%	4.7	93	$9
24	Proj	630	83	24	80	11	297	25	13	277	335	483	112	118	111	5	78	0.25	45	24	31	35	110		10%	108	90	17%	17%	111	10%	75%	33.6	145	$32

Biggio,Cavan

Age: 29 Pos: 2B RF 1B | Bats: L Ht: 6' 2" Wt: 200

Health C | PT/Exp B | Consist A | LIMA Plan D | Rand Var -2 | MM 2301

Struggled in reserve role before becoming more of a lineup regular over final several weeks. 2nd half BA leap wasn't supported by xBA and it came with a substantial drop in Brl% and xHR/F. Appears to still be tinkering with approach, but that's been the case for basically all of his 20s, and eventually we all have to grow up and move on.

Yr	Tm	PA	R	HR	RBI	SB	BA	xHR	xSB	xBA	OBP	SLG	OPS+	vL+	vR+	bb%	ct%	Eye	G	L	F	h%	HctX	QBaB	Brl%	PX	xPX	HR/F	xHR/F	Spd	SBA%	SB%	RAR	BPX	R$
19	TOR *	595	85	21	71	18	249	14	12	228	375	439	113	103	112	17	69	0.64	25	28	47	32	94	CAa	9%	112	151	15%	13%	105	11%	94%	15.0	115	$19
20	TOR	264	41	8	28	6	250	6	4	242	375	432	107	118	101	16	72	0.67	38	21	41	31	88	CBd	5%	116	110	13%	9%	107	8%	100%	6.2	188	$23
21	TOR *	379	40	10	36	3	209	6	3	210	307	340	89	73	99	12	67	0.43	38	22	40	28	83	CBc	6%	86	111	10%	9%	95	4%	75%	-9.0	-27	$2
22	TOR *	339	49	6	26	3	204	7	4	220	312	345	93	76	98	13	68	0.48	35	21	44	28	80	CAc	7%	114	97	8%	9%	115	4%	100%	-1.4	86	$2
23	TOR	338	54	9	40	5	235	9	6	219	340	370	97	97	97	12	70	0.45	38	21	42	31	91	CBc	7%	88	109	11%	11%	96	7%	71%	4.7	11	$6
1st Half		141	20	7	16	2	194	7	3	212	262	388	89	46	94	7	66	0.23	39	13	48	23	98	CAc	16%	122	142	18%	18%	98	15%	50%	-4.1	25	-$1
2nd Half		197	34	2	24	3	269	2	4	227	396	356	102	117	96	16	73	0.68	38	26	37	36	85	CBc	2%	63	86	5%	5%	100	4%	100%	4.6	14	$8
24	Proj	245	37	6	26	3	226	6	4	219	336	364	96	91	97	13	69	0.48	37	21	42	30	87		7%	95	108	10%	10%	103	6%	81%	1.9	42	$6

Blackmon,Charlie

Age: 38 Pos: DH RF | Bats: L Ht: 6' 3" Wt: 221

Health C | PT/Exp A | Consist B | LIMA Plan B | Rand Var 0 | MM 2353

Fractured right hand sidelined him from mid-June to mid-August. Best asset (last asset?) is ct%, which hasn't been this high since 2012. That still sets a sturdy BA floor, but there's not much above ground level: power has been subpar in this decade; SB tally can be counted on one hand. Now just a deep-league streamer during Coors homestands.

Yr	Tm	PA	R	HR	RBI	SB	BA	xHR	xSB	xBA	OBP	SLG	OPS+	vL+	vR+	bb%	ct%	Eye	G	L	F	h%	HctX	QBaB	Brl%	PX	xPX	HR/F	xHR/F	Spd	SBA%	SB%	RAR	BPX	R$
19	COL	634	112	32	86	2	314	30	7	298	364	576	130	131	129	6	82	0.38	39	23	38	34	114	CBb	8%	129	132	18%	17%	121	5%	29%	34.2	304	$27
20	COL	247	31	6	42	2	303	7	2	265	356	448	107	121	98	8	80	0.43	36	28	35	36	100	DCf	5%	81	92	10%	11%	90	4%	67%	5.9	116	$25
21	COL	582	76	13	78	3	270	15	3	266	351	411	105	105	105	9	82	0.59	47	22	31	31	112	CCd	7%	77	91	10%	11%	100	2%	100%	-2.5	158	$17
22	COL	577	60	16	78	4	264	12	6	260	314	419	104	106	103	6	79	0.29	43	23	34	31	100	DCd	4%	92	100	11%	8%	116	4%	80%	-1.9	134	$18
23	COL	413	57	8	40	4	279	8	6	274	363	440	109	113	108	9	85	0.71	36	23	40	31	109	DAc	5%	90	102	6%	6%	104	4%	80%	14.8	225	$10
1st Half		242	34	5	26	0	265	6	2	265	347	422	105	84	112	9	84	0.64	33	23	45	29	106	DAc	6%	89	103	6%	7%	95	2%	0%	1.0	204	$7
2nd Half		171	23	3	14	4	297	3	4	290	386	466	115	157	102	11	85	0.82	42	24	34	33	112	CBc	3%	92	99	7%	7%	112	8%	100%	7.8	254	$6
24	Proj	420	56	10	50	4	280	10	6	273	352	443	109	118	106	9	83	0.54	41	23	36	32	107		5%	91	100	9%	9%	109	5%	85%	14.1	195	$17

GREG PYRON

Bleday,JJ

Age: 26	Pos: LF CF		Health	B	LIMA Plan	D+
Bats: L	Ht: 6' 3"	Wt: 205	PT/Exp	A	Rand Var	+1
			Consist	B	MM	2205

10-27-.195 in 303 PA at OAK. 4th overall pick of 2019 MLB draft suffered mid-August ACL sprain in left knee, essentially ending his season. PRO: Patience, launch angle, ct% gains. CON: Horrid BA/xBA, merely pedestrian pop, ct% dropped each month. Pedigree and lost 2020 season buys him some more time.

Yr	Tm	PA	R	HR	RBI	SB	BA	xHR	xSB	xBA	OBP	SLG	OPS+	vL+	vR+	bb%	ct%	Eye	G	L	F	h%	HctX	QBaB	Brl%	PX	xPX	HR/F	xHR/F	Spd	SBA%	SB%	RAR	BPX	R$
19																																			
20																																			
21	aa	450	43	9	45	4	180		4		277	309	80			12	71	0.46				23				83				101	7%	55%		23	-$
22	MIA *	580	58	17	51	5	173	5	5	199	274	325	85	62	88	12	64	0.38	24	24	53	23	74	DAd	8%	114	108	7%	7%	93	6%	68%	-21.5	0	$
23	OAK *	424	52	14	40	6	209	9	7	230	313	377	94	65	99	13	74	0.59	43	14	43	24	97	CBd	6%	101	91	13%	11%	94	8%	71%	0.3	121	$
1st Half		268	33	8	26	5	219	2	6	245	321	396	98	70	103	13	79	0.70	41	15	45	24	105	DBf	3%	103	63	11%	4%	104	11%	67%	1.0	200	$
2nd Half		156	19	6	13	1	193	6	2	199	301	345	87	62	94	13	66	0.46	47	12	41	24	85	BBc	10%	96	124	15%	18%	94	3%	100%	-2.7	0	-$
24	**Proj**	**490**	**55**	**15**	**45**	**5**	**220**	**14**	**6**	**215**	**320**	**374**	**95**	**72**	**103**	**13**	**71**	**0.49**	**36**	**17**	**47**	**27**	**86**		**8%**	**97**	**102**	**11%**	**10%**	**91**	**5%**	**73%**	**0.3**	**43**	**$**

Bogaerts,Xander

Age: 31	Pos: SS		Health	A	LIMA Plan	B+
Bats: R	Ht: 6' 2"	Wt: 218	PT/Exp	A	Rand Var	0
			Consist	B	MM	2445

Left wrist soreness began in March and lingered all season, requiring a cortisone injection in March and another in July. Slugged 4 HR prior to Apr 18 HBP on that wrist, subsequently scuffled until post-ASB. Overall, the underlying skills support a similar BA (see 2nd half xBA) and near 20 HR, but expect some SB pullback at his age.

Yr	Tm	PA	R	HR	RBI	SB	BA	xHR	xSB	xBA	OBP	SLG	OPS+	vL+	vR+	bb%	ct%	Eye	G	L	F	h%	HctX	QBaB	Brl%	PX	xPX	HR/F	xHR/F	Spd	SBA%	SB%	RAR	BPX	R$
19	BOS	698	110	33	117	4	309	28	4	283	384	555	130	127	130	11	80	0.62	41	19	40	34	107	BCc	8%	130	116	17%	14%	88	3%	67%	51.8	278	$3
20	BOS	225	36	11	28	8	300	11	4	261	364	502	115	132	106	9	80	0.51	46	18	36	33	117	CDf	9%	103	116	19%	19%	94	13%	100%	13.8	200	$3
21	BOS	603	90	23	79	5	295	21	4	270	370	493	119	111	122	10	79	0.55	40	23	37	34	113	BCd	10%	114	103	15%	13%	96	4%	83%	30.3	219	$2
22	BOS	631	84	15	73	8	307	14	8	265	377	456	118	145	110	9	79	0.48	46	22	32	37	105	CCd	6%	101	71	11%	10%	101	5%	80%	28.8	162	$2
23	SD	665	83	19	58	19	285	18	19	265	350	440	108	107	108	8	82	0.51	50	17	33	32	100	CDf	6%	87	80	12%	11%	119	12%	90%	28.7	179	$2
1st Half		334	40	8	28	9	252	9	8	244	335	378	98	90	101	11	79	0.56	52	16	32	30	95	CFf	7%	75	81	11%	12%	96	11%	90%	1.5	93	$1
2nd Half		331	43	11	30	10	318	9	11	283	366	500	117	131	113	7	84	0.45	49	17	34	35	105	CCd	5%	98	80	13%	10%	133	12%	91%	22.0	254	$2
24	**Proj**	**630**	**83**	**20**	**64**	**12**	**288**	**18**	**12**	**267**	**357**	**455**	**111**	**117**	**109**	**9**	**81**	**0.52**	**47**	**19**	**34**	**33**	**105**		**7%**	**97**	**85**	**13%**	**12%**	**108**	**8%**	**88%**	**33.1**	**192**	**$2**

Bohm,Alec

Age: 27	Pos: 3B 1B		Health	A	LIMA Plan	B
Bats: R	Ht: 6' 5"	Wt: 218	PT/Exp	A	Rand Var	+2
			Consist	B	MM	2245

Looks like a breakout, but underlying metrics look more like just a skills consolidation. Career-high HR was driven by positive HR/F regression and slight FB% uptick. xBA, ct% and LD% all say BA has staying power, which becomes his best skill as compared to not-quite-average power and speed. Squint to see small growth; be careful bidding on it.

Yr	Tm	PA	R	HR	RBI	SB	BA	xHR	xSB	xBA	OBP	SLG	OPS+	vL+	vR+	bb%	ct%	Eye	G	L	F	h%	HctX	QBaB	Brl%	PX	xPX	HR/F	xHR/F	Spd	SBA%	SB%	RAR	BPX	R$
19	aa	263	34	14	38	2	252		3		323	478	111			10	82	0.57				25				107				100	7%	45%		233	$
20	PHI	180	24	4	23	1	338	7	2	259	400	481	117	113	118	9	78	0.44	53	21	25	42	87	BFb	10%	89	73	13%	22%	104	4%	50%	8.1	128	$
21	PHI *	481	52	8	51	6	245	9	4	235	302	342	88	108	79	7	71	0.28	53	25	23	33	110	AFb	7%	66	78	11%	15%	87	6%	84%	-10.9	-81	$
22	PHI	631	79	13	72	2	280	16	8	258	315	398	101	131	89	5	81	0.28	46	23	30	33	112	BCc	7%	72	86	9%	11%	126	3%	40%	0.0	110	$
23	PHI	611	74	20	97	4	274	18	5	281	327	437	104	125	96	7	83	0.45	42	24	34	30	107	BCc	6%	91	81	13%	11%	76	3%	80%	17.3	157	$
1st Half		289	33	9	54	2	277	8	3	262	322	427	103	127	93	6	82	0.35	43	21	36	31	104	BCc	7%	84	77	11%	10%	82	4%	67%	4.7	121	$
2nd Half		322	41	11	43	2	271	9	2	298	332	447	105	123	98	8	84	0.54	42	27	32	29	109	CCc	5%	97	85	14%	11%	80	3%	100%	8.4	200	$
24	**Proj**	**595**	**74**	**16**	**82**	**4**	**273**	**16**	**6**	**267**	**325**	**411**	**101**	**120**	**93**	**7**	**81**	**0.38**	**46**	**24**	**30**	**32**	**107**		**7%**	**81**	**81**	**12%**	**12%**	**90**	**4%**	**70%**	**13.3**	**118**	**$**

Brantley,Michael

Age: 37	Pos: LF		Health	F	LIMA Plan	B
Bats: L	Ht: 6' 2"	Wt: 209	PT/Exp	D	Rand Var	+5
			Consist	B	MM	1253

2-7-.278 in 57 PA at HOU. Activated from IL in late-August (recovery from Aug 2022 surgery to repair labrum in right shoulder). Soreness in that shoulder restricted his availability in Sept. Elite plate skills and BA track record, but these days he is just a one-category producer. Health grade and age warn of potential ... DN: 200 PA.

Yr	Tm	PA	R	HR	RBI	SB	BA	xHR	xSB	xBA	OBP	SLG	OPS+	vL+	vR+	bb%	ct%	Eye	G	L	F	h%	HctX	QBaB	Brl%	PX	xPX	HR/F	xHR/F	Spd	SBA%	SB%	RAR	BPX	R$
19	HOU	637	88	22	90	3	311	19	2	306	372	503	121	103	127	8	89	0.77	45	24	31	32	128	CCa	6%	92	89	14%	12%	75	3%	60%	23.8	252	$
20	HOU	187	24	5	22	2	300	5	1	284	364	476	112	83	123	9	84	0.61	47	22	31	34	126	CCc	5%	102	104	11%	11%	85	4%	100%	7.1	248	$
21	HOU	508	68	8	47	1	311	11	4	293	362	437	110	78	127	6	89	0.62	46	26	28	34	125	BCb	6%	70	80	7%	9%	114	1%	100%	8.8	231	$
22	HOU	277	28	5	26	1	288	7	1	282	370	416	111	103	115	11	88	1.03	44	24	31	31	123	BCa	6%	77	100	7%	10%	79	2%	50%	5.4	207	
23	HOU *	113	11	3	14	0	247	0	1	299	319	373	94	82	103	9	97	3.16	38	25	38	24	134	BCb	0%	62	74	10%	0%	81	0%	0%	-0.3	289	
1st Half		30	3	0	3	0	176		0	259	347	235	80	0	0	21	94	4.61	44	20	36	19	0		0%	40	-21	0%		90	0%	0%	-1.6	286	-$
2nd Half		82	8	3	11	0	270	0	0	306	309	417	98	81	102	5	97	2.17	38	25	38	25	135	BCb	0%	68	74	10%	0%	81	0%	0%	-0.2	289	
24	**Proj**	**385**	**45**	**8**	**44**	**1**	**279**	**8**	**2**	**290**	**334**	**408**	**102**	**83**	**109**	**8**	**90**	**0.84**	**43**	**24**	**32**	**29**	**128**		**4%**	**71**	**87**	**7%**	**7%**	**85**	**2%**	**76%**	**9.7**	**248**	**$**

Bregman,Alex

Age: 30	Pos: 3B		Health	B	LIMA Plan	A
Bats: R	Ht: 6' 0"	Wt: 192	PT/Exp	A	Rand Var	0
			Consist	A	MM	2145

Another year past 2019—and it's time to move on. The consistent seasons since paint a clear picture: Strong ct% sets the BA floor, which xBA confirms. xPX holds out hope for more power, but Brl% and xHR say there's not enough hard contact to take advantage. But there's bankable safety in that pile of PA, 20ish HR and 180+ runs and RBI.

Yr	Tm	PA	R	HR	RBI	SB	BA	xHR	xSB	xBA	OBP	SLG	OPS+	vL+	vR+	bb%	ct%	Eye	G	L	F	h%	HctX	QBaB	Brl%	PX	xPX	HR/F	xHR/F	Spd	SBA%	SB%	RAR	BPX	R$
19	HOU	690	122	41	112	5	296	20	5	303	423	592	141	165	130	17	85	1.43	32	23	46	29	131	BAc	5%	138	135	19%	9%	95	3%	83%	61.5	430	$
20	HOU	180	19	6	22	0	242	4	0	284	350	451	106	129	96	13	83	0.92	34	25	41	26	123	CBc	4%	113	92	11%	8%	85	0%	0%	1.7	308	
21	HOU *	440	58	13	58	1	262	10	1	253	345	411	104	114	103	11	86	0.87	41	18	41	28	110	CBd	6%	80	93	10%	8%	86	1%	100%	8.5	215	$
22	HOU	656	93	23	93	1	259	18	1	271	366	454	116	99	125	13	86	1.13	33	19	48	27	116	CAd	7%	115	126	10%	8%	69	2%	33%	25.5	293	$
23	HOU	724	103	25	98	3	262	18	12	262	363	441	110	94	116	13	86	1.06	35	19	46	27	117	CAc	5%	90	128	10%	7%	122	2%	75%	31.2	286	$
1st Half		371	48	12	53	3	246	9	6	246	345	405	103	83	110	13	85	1.00	33	19	49	26	105	CAc	4%	79	134	9%	7%	117	3%	100%	5.5	239	$
2nd Half		353	55	13	45	0	279	10	6	278	382	478	116	102	123	13	87	1.13	38	19	43	29	131	CBc	6%	102	123	12%	9%	125	1%	0%	17.6	336	$
24	**Proj**	**665**	**97**	**24**	**93**	**2**	**264**	**18**	**6**	**267**	**365**	**452**	**112**	**103**	**116**	**13**	**86**	**1.05**	**36**	**19**	**45**	**27**	**119**		**6%**	**99**	**121**	**11%**	**8%**	**94**	**2%**	**61%**	**30.2**	**291**	**$**

Brennan,Will

Age: 26	Pos: RF		Health	A	LIMA Plan	B
Bats: L	Ht: 6' 0"	Wt: 200	PT/Exp	A	Rand Var	0
			Consist	B	MM	1245

Not a bad rookie season. Bat-to-ball skills and wheels are his best assets as a strong-side platoon guy. However, non-existent Brl% and near-failing QBaB tell us there isn't more power lurking. Speed skills aren't great either, but aggression on bases gives him a chance to add value, as long as he keeps SB% up. Worth a flyer for SB.

Yr	Tm	PA	R	HR	RBI	SB	BA	xHR	xSB	xBA	OBP	SLG	OPS+	vL+	vR+	bb%	ct%	Eye	G	L	F	h%	HctX	QBaB	Brl%	PX	xPX	HR/F	xHR/F	Spd	SBA%	SB%	RAR	BPX
19																																		
20																																		
21	aa	164	22	2	16	2	249		2		314	317	87			9	78	0.44				31				45				96	9%	42%		-12
22	CLE *	605	50	10	77	15	261	1	11	270	302	383	97	47	141	6	85	0.39	53	18	29	29	127	BFa	7%	78	104	9%	9%	91	15%	77%	-2.6	145
23	CLE	455	41	5	41	13	266	4	12	278	299	356	89	67	95	4	87	0.28	46	25	29	30	73	DCc	2%	56	42	5%	4%	87	17%	72%	-3.3	96
1st Half		227	21	5	26	6	273	3	6	294	304	407	97	57	107	3	85	0.22	45	26	28	30	75	DDc	3%	79	51	10%	6%	87	18%	67%	-0.4	136
2nd Half		228	20	0	15	7	259	1	6	260	294	306	81	75	82	4	88	0.36	47	23	30	29	71	DCd	2%	33	34	0%	2%	95	16%	78%	-6.9	68
24	**Proj**	**455**	**43**	**4**	**47**	**12**	**272**	**6**	**11**	**266**	**315**	**359**	**92**	**73**	**97**	**5**	**85**	**0.35**	**46**	**24**	**29**	**31**	**73**		**2%**	**55**	**41**	**4%**	**6%**	**90**	**15%**	**73%**	**-0.9**	**97**

Brown,Seth

Age: 31	Pos: RF LF		Health	B	LIMA Plan	B
Bats: L	Ht: 6' 1"	Wt: 223	PT/Exp	A	Rand Var	-3
			Consist	A	MM	4115

Missed most of Apr/May (left oblique strain). Power skills remain in fine shape, highlighted by career-best xPX, improved exit velocity, xHR, and a few more FBs. xBA says BA is locked in this range, and Spd/SBA%/age cast serio doubt on return of double-digit SB. Cheap power can be useful, but loss of 1B eligibility dings his utility.

Yr	Tm	PA	R	HR	RBI	SB	BA	xHR	xSB	xBA	OBP	SLG	OPS+	vL+	vR+	bb%	ct%	Eye	G	L	F	h%	HctX	QBaB	Brl%	PX	xPX	HR/F	xHR/F	Spd	SBA%	SB%	RAR	BPX
19	OAK *	561	84	25	88	7	245	2	5	246	291	473	106	60	123	6	66	0.19	33	29	38	32	92	CBd	12%	139	93	0%	10%	98	8%	85%	-6.9	70
20	OAK	5	0	0	0	0	0	1		0	0	0	0	0	0	0	60	0.00	33	0	67	0	81	CAf	33%	0	223	0%	50%	94	#DIV/0!	0%	-1.0	-516
21	OAK	307	43	20	48	4	214	16	2	243	274	480	104	69	107	7	68	0.26	31	19	50	23	95	CAf	14%	161	144	21%	16%	74	10%	80%	-0.5	158
22	OAK	555	55	25	73	11	230	25	6	246	305	444	106	77	113	9	71	0.35	36	20	44	27	108	CBf	13%	142	117	16%	16%	66	11%	85%	5.8	128
23	OAK	378	33	14	52	3	222	18	3	227	286	405	94	62	101	8	71	0.30	36	16	48	27	110	BBf	12%	117	153	12%	16%	68	5%	75%	-0.2	50
1st Half		161	14	7	22	2	203	8	2	197	267	378	88	29	103	8	64	0.25	35	14	52	26	107	ABf	13%	116	179	14%	16%	78	10%	67%	-3.9	-32
2nd Half		217	19	7	30	1	236	10	1	248	301	426	98	94	99	8	75	0.35	38	17	45	28	113	BBf	12%	118	137	10%	15%	68	2%	100%	1.3	121
24	**Proj**	**455**	**48**	**18**	**65**	**4**	**225**	**21**	**3**	**231**	**291**	**417**	**97**	**65**	**103**	**8**	**70**	**0.29**	**35**	**19**	**46**	**28**	**106**		**13%**	**123**	**137**	**13%**	**15%**	**67**	**5%**	**73%**	**-0.1**	**93**

GREG PYRON

Bryant,Kris

Age: 32 Pos: RF DH
Bats: R Ht: 6'5" Wt: 230

Health	F	LIMA Plan	B
PT/Exp	A	Rand Var	+2
Consist	D	MM	3235

Another injury-marred season, as a heel bruise cost him a month in 1st half and fractured finger shelved him for 45 games in 2nd half. Has now appeared in just 122 total games since signing a seven-year contract in Mar 2022. Stable xPX, xHR/F says power is still intact, if healthy, but as we've seen recently, that's a huge "if".

Yr	Tm	PA	R	HR	RBI	SB	BA	xHR	xSB	xBA	OBP	SLG	OPS+	vL+	vR+	bb%	ct%	Eye	G	L	F	h%	HctX	QBaB	Brl%	PX	xPX	HR/F	xHR/F	Spd	SBA%	SB%	RAR	BPX	R$
19	CHC	634	108	31	77	4	282	28	6	259	382	521	125	147	119	12	73	0.51	36	21	43	33	91	CAb	9%	133	105	18%	16%	116	2%	100%	25.6	222	$22
20	CHC	147	20	4	11	0	206	5	2	205	293	351	85	107	78	8	69	0.30	37	18	45	26	87	DAb	5%	87	111	10%	12%	141	0%	0%	-8.8	32	$3
21	2 NL	586	86	25	73	10	265	20	8	261	353	481	115	124	111	11	74	0.46	37	23	39	31	109	CBc	10%	130	133	17%	13%	102	8%	83%	18.0	200	$22
22	COL	181	28	5	14	0	306	5	1	273	376	475	120	137	108	9	83	0.63	40	21	39	34	124	DCd	7%	108	137	10%	10%	106	0%	0%	11.0	245	$5
23	COL	335	36	10	31	0	233	11	2	242	313	367	93	95	92	9	77	0.43	38	23	39	27	103	DBd	6%	76	125	11%	12%	80	0%	0%	-2.1	46	$3
1st Half		228	22	5	18	0	260	6	2	253	338	363	96	98	94	9	80	0.53	36	27	37	30	96	CBc	5%	57	103	8%	10%	88	0%	0%	0.4	50	$2
2nd Half		107	14	5	13	0	177	5	0	229	262	375	86	84	86	8	71	0.29	44	13	43	19	119	FCd	8%	120	177	17%	17%	77	0%	0%	-3.8	71	-$3
24	**Proj**	**490**	**68**	**18**	**50**	**1**	**262**	**18**	**3**	**249**	**340**	**436**	**106**	**120**	**101**	**9**	**76**	**0.42**	**40**	**20**	**40**	**31**	**111**		**7%**	**104**	**139**	**13%**	**13%**	**89**	**1%**	**85%**	**13.1**	**135**	**$13**

Burger,Jake

Age: 28 Pos: 3B DH
Bats: R Ht: 6'2" Wt: 230

Health	B	LIMA Plan	B
PT/Exp	A	Rand Var	0
Consist	C	MM	4025

Late-bloomer's breakout came replete with skills support. Power had been displayed previously in small MLB samples; is largely backed by xHR/F and elite Brl%. 2nd half ct% spike and xBA points to some BA upside, and strength vR bolsters staying power. If those second-half skill gains stick around for a full year... UP: 40 HR, .265 BA

Yr	Tm	PA	R	HR	RBI	SB	BA	xHR	xSB	xBA	OBP	SLG	OPS+	vL+	vR+	bb%	ct%	Eye	G	L	F	h%	HctX	QBaB	Brl%	PX	xPX	HR/F	xHR/F	Spd	SBA%	SB%	RAR	BPX	R$
19																																			
20																																			
21	CHW *	369	37	13	41	0	223	2	2	232	267	395	91	44	139	6	64	0.17	43	26	30	31	102	ACc	13%	117	108	14%	29%	124	0%	0%	-9.5	0	$3
22	CHW *	340	33	11	35	0	221	11	3	207	270	371	91	146	94	6	69	0.21	42	15	42	28	98	BCd	15%	99	125	17%	23%	121	1%	0%	-11.1	17	$2
23	2 TM	540	71	34	80	1	250	29	3	268	309	518	113	122	109	6	70	0.21	43	18	39	29	116	ACf	17%	165	129	25%	22%	79	2%	50%	18.4	171	$17
1st Half		242	32	18	38	1	220	14	2	264	273	520	109	116	105	6	64	0.16	40	20	40	25	112	ACc	19%	195	153	32%	25%	81	6%	50%	1.5	171	$13
2nd Half		298	39	16	42	0	275	14	1	266	339	517	116	128	112	7	75	0.28	45	17	38	31	120	ACf	15%	143	112	21%	18%	81	0%	0%	13.0	189	$21
24	**Proj**	**560**	**66**	**32**	**72**	**0**	**256**	**33**	**4**	**244**	**315**	**490**	**110**	**130**	**103**	**6**	**69**	**0.22**	**43**	**17**	**40**	**31**	**109**		**16%**	**145**	**127**	**22%**	**23%**	**91**	**1%**	**31%**	**19.1**	**97**	**$21**

Burleson,Alec

Age: 25 Pos: LF DH
Bats: L Ht: 6'2" Wt: 212

Health	A	LIMA Plan	D+
PT/Exp	A	Rand Var	+2
Consist	B	MM	1233

Rookie season was a little better than it seemed. Elite ct% sets high BA floor and xBA says he was victimized by low h%. Power metrics were a tick below average overall and 2nd half FB% dip reinforces that weakness. Defensive issues could continue to curtail PT. Late-Sept left thumb surgery (fracture), but expected ready for spring training.

Yr	Tm	PA	R	HR	RBI	SB	BA	xHR	xSB	xBA	OBP	SLG	OPS+	vL+	vR+	bb%	ct%	Eye	G	L	F	h%	HctX	QBaB	Brl%	PX	xPX	HR/F	xHR/F	Spd	SBA%	SB%	RAR	BPX	R$
19																																			
20																																			
21	a/a	437	35	11	44	1	214		1		255	328	80			5	77	0.24				25				66				81	2%	53%		-12	$1
22	STL *	503	48	13	59	4	252	2	3	261	286	377	94	93	75	5	82	0.27	50	21	29	28	110	BFd	9%	76	117	9%	18%	91	4%	100%	-3.7	97	$12
23	STL	344	34	8	36	3	244	10	3	276	300	390	94	82	95	7	86	0.51	41	22	37	26	109	CCd	6%	83	96	8%	10%	78	5%	75%	0.0	171	$4
1st Half		182	20	5	17	0	223	5	2	275	282	380	91	46	95	7	88	0.60	40	21	40	23	99	CCf	4%	82	89	9%	9%	97	3%	0%	-3.6	221	-$2
2nd Half		162	14	3	19	3	268	5	2	277	321	403	98	119	96	7	83	0.44	43	24	33	31	119	CCc	7%	84	105	7%	12%	71	8%	100%	2.4	132	$3
24	**Proj**	**280**	**26**	**6**	**31**	**2**	**257**	**11**	**2**	**259**	**305**	**384**	**95**	**92**	**95**	**6**	**83**	**0.36**	**42**	**22**	**36**	**29**	**111**		**6%**	**75**	**99**	**8%**	**14%**	**75**	**4%**	**86%**	**1.1**	**116**	**$8**

Busch,Michael

Age: 26 Pos: 3B
Bats: L Ht: 6'0" Wt: 207

Health	A	LIMA Plan	D
PT/Exp	A	Rand Var	0
Consist	B	MM	4213

2-12-.167 in 81 PA at LA. Older prospect who slugged 27 HR in Triple-A. Below-average athlete, his bat carries the profile but he lacks a true defensive home. A patient hitter who improved aggressiveness within zone. Improved ct% and BA and increased hard hit rates. Power plays to the gaps and pull side. (CB)

Yr	Tm	PA	R	HR	RBI	SB	BA	xHR	xSB	xBA	OBP	SLG	OPS+	vL+	vR+	bb%	ct%	Eye	G	L	F	h%	HctX	QBaB	Brl%	PX	xPX	HR/F	xHR/F	Spd	SBA%	SB%	RAR	BPX	R$
19																																			
20																																			
21	aa	454	57	14	46	1	217		2		295	379	93			10	63	0.30				31				117				90	4%	28%		-15	$4
22	a/a	594	70	21	64	2	211		2		266	379	91			7	63	0.21				29				131				83	3%	66%		0	$8
23	LA *	512	64	21	65	4	245	3	5	243	318	445	104	63	76	10	70	0.36	59	9	33	30	81	CFf	7%	124	82	13%	20%	90	4%	100%	13.9	104	$13
1st Half		264	33	6	32	2	244	1	3	247	329	401	100	105	70	11	68	0.40	66	14	21	33	67	CFf	7%	111	65	0%	17%	93	3%	100%	4.0	46	$8
2nd Half		249	31	15	34	2	247	2	2	219	307	491	108	0	86	8	73	0.32	47	0	53	27	105	AAb	6%	137	111	22%	22%	94	4%	100%	8.3	168	$14
24	**Proj**	**315**	**39**	**12**	**37**	**2**	**229**	**15**	**2**	**232**	**289**	**408**	**96**	**66**	**103**	**9**	**67**	**0.28**	**38**	**22**	**40**	**30**	**90**		**6%**	**120**	**93**	**15%**	**20%**	**93**	**3%**	**78%**	**1.5**	**57**	**$8**

Butler,Lawrence

Age: 23 Pos: CF
Bats: L Ht: 6'4" Wt: 185

Health	A	LIMA Plan	C
PT/Exp	C	Rand Var	0
Consist	F	MM	2513

4-10-.211 in 129 PA at OAK. Improved ct% while not losing offensive upside in the upper minors. Tall and muscular, athleticism and power potential carries his profile. But aggressive approach, coupled with whiff issues and poor angles, hasn't allowed power to play up in games. Plus runner with chance for 20 SB someday. (CB)

Yr	Tm	PA	R	HR	RBI	SB	BA	xHR	xSB	xBA	OBP	SLG	OPS+	vL+	vR+	bb%	ct%	Eye	G	L	F	h%	HctX	QBaB	Brl%	PX	xPX	HR/F	xHR/F	Spd	SBA%	SB%	RAR	BPX	R$
19																																			
20																																			
21																																			
22																																			
23	OAK *	520	52	12	54	13	221	6	13	215	265	346	83	56	84	6	75	0.23	41	15	44	27	96	CBf	9%	76	118	10%	15%	124	14%	85%	-12.0	39	$8
1st Half		292	35	6	30	8	240		8	244	292	369	91	0	0	7	77	0.32	44	20	36	29	0		0%	80	-21	0%		120	16%	79%	-4.4	82	$10
2nd Half		229	21	7	27	6	210	6	5	209	246	339	79	56	83	5	73	0.18	41	15	44	26	94	CBf	9%	76	118	10%	15%	124	14%	100%	-9.1	4	$5
24	**Proj**	**420**	**43**	**15**	**47**	**8**	**228**	**20**	**11**	**225**	**276**	**388**	**91**	**68**	**96**	**6**	**75**	**0.24**	**41**	**15**	**44**	**27**	**85**		**8%**	**94**	**106**	**11%**	**15%**	**126**	**11%**	**88%**	**-3.2**	**35**	**$12**

Buxton,Byron

Age: 30 Pos: DH
Bats: R Ht: 6'2" Wt: 190

Health	F	LIMA Plan	B
PT/Exp	B	Rand Var	+3
Consist	F	MM	5523

Sept 2022 knee surgery limited him early and new injuries (hip, hamstring, knee) plagued him all year, ultimately ending his season in Aug. Underwent Oct 2023 arthroscopic knee surgery to alleviate patellar tendinitis. Drop in ct% creates a BA ceiling (see xBA plunge), and he hasn't logged 400 PA since 2017. Project more at your own risk.

Yr	Tm	PA	R	HR	RBI	SB	BA	xHR	xSB	xBA	OBP	SLG	OPS+	vL+	vR+	bb%	ct%	Eye	G	L	F	h%	HctX	QBaB	Brl%	PX	xPX	HR/F	xHR/F	Spd	SBA%	SB%	RAR	BPX	R$
19	MIN	295	48	10	46	14	262	11	9	263	314	513	114	128	109	6	75	0.28	29	22	49	32	92	BAf	8%	148	92	10%	11%	120	35%	82%	2.1	256	$12
20	MIN	135	19	13	27	2	254	12	2	255	267	577	112	100	115	1	72	0.06	36	13	51	25	104	AAf	14%	168	116	27%	24%	119	15%	67%	0.9	256	$16
21	MIN *	277	54	21	38	9	309	19	6	313	346	658	138	136	139	5	74	0.22	40	22	38	34	130	ACd	18%	207	141	29%	29%	121	19%	90%	23.9	431	$18
22	MIN	382	61	28	51	6	224	25	7	254	306	526	118	128	113	9	66	0.29	31	18	51	24	120	AAf	16%	201	165	24%	22%	145	8%	100%	5.6	303	$14
23	MIN	347	49	17	42	9	207	16	7	222	294	438	100	85	105	10	64	0.32	32	14	54	26	88	AAf	15%	156	137	16%	15%	114	13%	100%	0.4	136	$7
1st Half		272	38	14	31	7	210	12	6	226	305	445	103	89	108	11	66	0.37	34	13	53	25	83	BAf	13%	153	122	17%	14%	119	13%	100%	-1.2	161	$12
2nd Half		75	11	3	11	2	197	5	1	207	253	409	89	69	97	7	59	0.19	24	17	60	28	103	AAf	20%	168	193	12%	20%	101	18%	100%	-2.5	61	-$3
24	**Proj**	**385**	**62**	**23**	**55**	**9**	**229**	**25**	**8**	**244**	**295**	**499**	**109**	**104**	**111**	**8**	**66**	**0.24**	**31**	**17**	**52**	**28**	**107**		**17%**	**179**	**155**	**19%**	**20%**	**113**	**14%**	**94%**	**8.2**	**217**	**$16**

Caballero,Jose

Age: 27 Pos: 2B SS
Bats: R Ht: 5'10" Wt: 185

Health	A	LIMA Plan	D+
PT/Exp	D	Rand Var	-1
Consist	C	MM	1501

4-26-.221 with 26 SB in 280 PA at SEA. Non-prospect made an impact on bases thanks to blazing speed, SBA%, and top-tier SB%. Though bb% boosts OBP, BA/xBA and lack of pop are significant concerns. Defensive versatility creates avenues to PT, but absent improved bat, chances could dry up.

Yr	Tm	PA	R	HR	RBI	SB	BA	xHR	xSB	xBA	OBP	SLG	OPS+	vL+	vR+	bb%	ct%	Eye	G	L	F	h%	HctX	QBaB	Brl%	PX	xPX	HR/F	xHR/F	Spd	SBA%	SB%	RAR	BPX	R$
19																																			
20																																			
21	aa																																		
22	aa	119	13	1	8	9	166		6		318	233	78			18	71	0.78				22				50				100	32%	79%		-17	$0
23	SEA *	314	42	5	31	29	223	4	22	202	315	329	88	102	80	11	72	0.49	32	20	48	29	61	FAf	4%	68	62	5%	5%	129	35%	87%	0.7	25	$9
1st Half		202	24	4	24	14	240	3	12	217	355	366	99	116	90	15	77	0.77	30	21	50	29	72	FAd	4%	73	72	6%	6%	126	26%	81%	1.7	129	$9
2nd Half		112	18	1	7	15	196	1	10	177	295	268	76	89	60	6	65	0.18	37	18	45	29	45	FAf	3%	58	44	4%	4%	123	57%	94%	-5.1	-154	$3
24	**Proj**	**245**	**34**	**3**	**21**	**25**	**209**	**3**	**18**	**189**	**337**	**292**	**86**	**98**	**75**	**11**	**70**	**0.42**	**34**	**19**	**47**	**28**	**56**		**3%**	**58**	**55**	**4%**	**4%**	**122**	**36%**	**87%**	**-3.5**	**-28**	**$11**

GREG PYRON

Cabrera,Miguel

Age: 41 Pos: DH | Bats: R Ht: 6' 4" Wt: 267 | Health B | PT/Exp A | Consist B | LIMA Plan | Rand Var | MM

Probably should've hung up the spikes after topping 3,000 hits and appearing in the All-Star Game in 2022, but we can only imagine it's tough to walk away from $32 million. Finished with a lifetime .306 BA, 511 HR, .901 OPS, 2 MVP awards, and 12 All-Star appearances. Next stop: Cooperstown.

Yr Tm	PA	R	HR	RBI	SB	BA	xHR	xSB	xBA	OBP	SLG	OPS+	vL+	vR+	bb%	ct%	Eye	G	L	F	h%	HctX	QBaB	Brl%	PX	xPX	HR/F	xHR/F	Spd	SBA%	SB%	RAR	BPX	R$
19 DET	549	41	12	59	0	282	15	-	245	346	398	103	135	94	9	78	0.44	44	24	32	34	119	BCa	6%	64	93	10%	12%	54	0%	0%	-5.2	0	$1
20 DET	231	28	10	35	1	250	12	0	253	329	417	99	146	89	10	75	0.47	42	26	32	29	92	ACb	10%	86	81	20%	24%	51	2%	100%	-1.0	28	$1
21 DET	526	48	15	75	0	256	20	0	224	316	386	96	95	97	8	75	0.34	48	20	32	31	114	ACc	8%	76	107	13%	17%	57	0%	0%	-12.7	-15	$1
22 DET	433	25	5	43	1	254	7	0	217	305	317	88	97	85	6	75	0.28	53	22	25	33	76	BFb	5%	44	56	7%	9%	55	1%	100%	-15.3	-117	$
23 DET	370	21	4	34	0	257	6	1	232	322	353	92	93	91	8	78	0.42	50	21	29	32	101	CDc	4%	66	60	5%	8%	58	0%	0%	-2.7	0	$
1st Half	172	10	1	12	0	238	3	0	221	320	318	87	105	81	11	77	0.56	55	19	26	30	95	CDc	5%	59	49	3%	10%	63	0%	0%	-5.3	0	-$
2nd Half	198	11	3	22	0	273	3	0	243	323	383	95	83	100	6	78	0.30	47	23	31	34	106	CDd	3%	73	69	7%	7%	59	0%	0%	-1.8	11	$
24 Proj																																		

Cabrera,Oswaldo

Age: 25 Pos: LF RF | Bats: B Ht: 6' 0" Wt: 200 | Health A | PT/Exp B | Consist B | LIMA Plan D+ | Rand Var +1 | MM 1303

5-29-.211 with 8 SB in 330 PA at NYY. 2021 MLE indicated presence of power, but MLB contact quality has been merely average. Made ct% gains in 2023, though it was mostly in 1st half and BA/xBA still hovered near the Mendoza Line. Spd/SBA%/SB% all back double-digit SB if he can hit enough to justify 400 PA. Skills don't merit it yet.

Yr Tm	PA	R	HR	RBI	SB	BA	xHR	xSB	xBA	OBP	SLG	OPS+	vL+	vR+	bb%	ct%	Eye	G	L	F	h%	HctX	QBaB	Brl%	PX	xPX	HR/F	xHR/F	Spd	SBA%	SB%	RAR	BPX	R$
19																																		
20																																		
21 a/a	501	59	25	73	17	243		11		295	466	104			7	70	0.24				29				139				85	23%	76%		119	$1
22 NYY *	368	42	12	40	10	230	5	9	218	291	406	99	103	105	8	68	0.27	28	22	50	30	87	DAc	7%	125	122	11%	9%	110	20%	66%	-3.0	76	$
23 NYY *	373	40	6	33	9	208	4	7	212	269	300	78	80	78	8	76	0.34	45	15	40	26	83	DCf	3%	58	90	6%	5%	82	12%	89%	-11.5	-32	$
1st Half	200	23	4	19	5	202	3	4	220	254	301	76	94	73	7	79	0.33	48	13	39	23	75	DCf	4%	58	74	8%	6%	81	14%	81%	-8.9	7	$
2nd Half	174	17	2	14	4	215	1	3	202	287	298	79	61	84	9	71	0.35	40	19	41	29	94	DCf	2%	58	117	3%	3%	99	10%	100%	-5.3	-64	-$
24 Proj	385	43	8	40	10	220	7	9	210	282	340	85	83	86	8	71	0.30	37	19	44	29	86		5%	79	108	7%	6%	102	15%	79%	-7.5	27	$

Call,Alex

Age: 29 Pos: CF LF | Bats: R Ht: 5' 11" Wt: 188 | Health A | PT/Exp A | Consist C | LIMA Plan D+ | Rand Var +2 | MM 2211

8-38-.200 with 9 SB in 439 PA at WAS. Saw more MLB action than expected, but didn't do much with the opportunity. PRO: Plate skills are serviceable; good sprint speed. CON: Not much happens after contact; raw wheels haven't yet translated into SB%. We might pull for the PRO if he was 23; at 29, CON makes him undraftable.

Yr Tm	PA	R	HR	RBI	SB	BA	xHR	xSB	xBA	OBP	SLG	OPS+	vL+	vR+	bb%	ct%	Eye	G	L	F	h%	HctX	QBaB	Brl%	PX	xPX	HR/F	xHR/F	Spd	SBA%	SB%	RAR	BPX	R$
19 aa	313	26	5	27	4	190		6		241	294	74			6	64	0.19				28				71				111	18%	44%		-137	-
20																																		
21 a/a	424	47	10	35	10	209		8		279	338	85			9	79	0.47				24				75				93	18%	63%		96	
22 2 TM *	419	56	13	45	9	227	1	8	236	312	389	99	85	123	11	73	0.47	36	22	42	27	88	DBc	1%	107	109	14%	3%	107	13%	67%	-0.4	121	$
23 WAS *	483	46	9	40	11	200	8	14	214	297	307	82	100	74	12	80	0.69	38	15	47	23	88	DBf	5%	63	99	6%	6%	107	16%	58%	-14.6	100	
1st Half	289	27	4	22	7	207	3	6	221	290	295	80	101	70	10	80	0.57	42	17	41	25	74	DBf	4%	56	79	4%	4%	91	13%	78%	-9.8	46	
2nd Half	195	19	5	18	4	189	5	8	206	308	326	86	100	79	15	81	0.88	33	12	55	20	108	DAf	7%	73	127	7%	7%	133	20%	38%	-6.6	186	
24 Proj	245	26	7	23	5	204	4	7	225	304	354	90	90	90	11	77	0.54	36	17	46	23	92		4%	87	108	9%	5%	111	16%	55%	-4.4	96	

Caminero,Junior

Age: 20 Pos: 3B | Bats: R Ht: 5' 11" Wt: 157 | Health A | PT/Exp D | Consist F | LIMA Plan B | Rand Var -2 | MM 2123

1-7-.235 in 36 PA at TAM. Went from High-A to MLB in whirlwind 2023, slugging 31 MiLB HR. Average athlete who is near projection. Offensive explosiveness is driven by lower half strength and plus-plus bat speed. Unusual batted ball profile: Hits topspin-heavy liners to pull side, but natural swing plane produces loft to RCF gap. (CB)

Yr Tm	PA	R	HR	RBI	SB	BA	xHR	xSB	xBA	OBP	SLG	OPS+	vL+	vR+	bb%	ct%	Eye	G	L	F	h%	HctX	QBaB	Brl%	PX	xPX	HR/F	xHR/F	Spd	SBA%	SB%	RAR	BPX	R$
19																																		
20																																		
21																																		
22																																		
23 TAM *	375	48	17	56	2	274	1	10	246	327	464	108	118	70	7	79	0.37	62	8	31	30	111	DFf	12%	98	56	13%	13%	143	6%	36%	14.1	186	$
1st Half	112	14	4	15	0	279		3	251	336	450	108	0	0	8	76	0.36	44	20	36	33	0		0%	95	-21	0%		137	10%	0%	1.5	143	-
2nd Half	264	34	13	41	2	272	1	6	254	323	470	107	117	69	7	79	0.37	62	8	31	29	112	DFf	12%	100	56	13%	13%	143	5%	69%	7.8	204	$
24 Proj	385	49	14	57	2	277	13	10	239	330	442	106	150	84	7	78	0.37	48	15	38	32	101		10%	88	50	13%	13%	136	7%	26%	11.1	180	$

Campusano,Luis

Age: 25 Pos: CA | Bats: R Ht: 5' 11" Wt: 232 | Health D | PT/Exp D | Consist F | LIMA Plan B | Rand Var -5 | MM 1235

Underwent April 2023 left thumb surgery (torn ligament), sidelining him for three months. Impressive 2nd half, albeit a small sample, led by elite ct% with BA/xBA that's extremely rare for a CA. There's a 20-HR peak here, though mayb not yet. Assume 2024 growing pains but exciting long-term potential.

Yr Tm	PA	R	HR	RBI	SB	BA	xHR	xSB	xBA	OBP	SLG	OPS+	vL+	vR+	bb%	ct%	Eye	G	L	F	h%	HctX	QBaB	Brl%	PX	xPX	HR/F	xHR/F	Spd	SBA%	SB%	RAR	BPX	R$
19																																		
20 SD	4	2	1	1	0	333	0	0	471	500	1333	243	348	0	0	33	0.00	0	0	100	0	135	AA		1071	722	100%	0%	95	0%	0%	1.0	2484	
21 SD *	348	29	9	29	1	215	0	1	244	263	357	85	0	41	6	73	0.25	39	26	35	27	104	ABf	0%	90	54	0%	0%	88	2%	100%	-7.9	19	
22 SD *	388	38	8	38	0	219	1	0	199	259	323	82	83	84	5	76	0.22	45	13	42	27	113	CBf	6%	68	77	6%	6%	70	0%	0%	-9.9	-28	
23 SD	174	27	7	30	0	319	5	1	284	356	491	115	150	103	4	87	0.33	41	22	36	33	109	CCc	8%	87	91	13%	10%	68	0%	0%	13.0	171	
1st Half	22	3	1	2	0	238	1	0	207	227	429	90	194	46	0	71	0.00	25	13	63	29	127	AAa	19%	117	276	10%	10%	88	0%	0%	-0.1	29	-
2nd Half	152	24	6	28	0	331	4	1	296	375	500	118	142	110	5	89	0.47	43	24	33	34	106	CCc	6%	83	68	14%	10%	67	0%	0%	12.4	200	
24 Proj	455	52	12	56	1	256	11	1	257	310	391	96	116	89	6	80	0.28	43	24	33	30	95		6%	78	61	11%	10%	69	0%	100%	8.0	71	

Candelario,Jeimer

Age: 30 Pos: 3B 1B | Bats: B Ht: 6' 1" Wt: 216 | Health B | PT/Exp A | Consist F | LIMA Plan B | Rand Var +2 | MM 3335

Rebounded from a dreadful 2022 campaign to set new career-high in HR, but xHR is a tad skeptical. Meanwhile ct% column has been stable year-to-year and xBA points to further BA recovery toward 2021 BA peak. Even at his age anc with a lack of a standout skill upside, he can hang in this value range.

Yr Tm	PA	R	HR	RBI	SB	BA	xHR	xSB	xBA	OBP	SLG	OPS+	vL+	vR+	bb%	ct%	Eye	G	L	F	h%	HctX	QBaB	Brl%	PX	xPX	HR/F	xHR/F	Spd	SBA%	SB%	RAR	BPX
19 DET *	556	57	15	59	3	227	9	2	236	313	392	97	80	91	11	72	0.44	37	23	40	29	93	CBc	6%	95	86	9%	10%	84	3%	75%	-20.5	44
20 DET	206	30	7	29	1	297	8	2	262	369	503	116	144	107	10	74	0.41	40	26	34	37	107	BCc	10%	118	118	15%	17%	118	4%	50%	6.5	180
21 DET	626	75	16	67	0	271	22	2	267	351	443	109	102	112	10	76	0.48	39	26	34	33	103	CCc	9%	109	108	11%	15%	97	0%	0%	16.2	162
22 DET	467	49	13	50	0	217	15	2	232	272	361	90	95	88	6	75	0.26	42	19	40	26	91	CCd	9%	95	100	10%	12%	101	1%	0%	-17.0	66
23 2 NL	575	77	22	70	8	251	18	7	269	336	471	110	107	111	9	75	0.42	40	19	41	29	96	CBc	8%	136	107	14%	12%	82	7%	89%	19.6	189
1st Half	336	42	11	39	4	264	10	4	275	339	475	112	91	121	9	77	0.41	36	22	42	31	108	CBc	7%	131	110	11%	10%	80	7%	80%	10.6	204
2nd Half	239	35	11	31	4	233	8	3	260	331	466	108	137	98	11	71	0.42	46	15	39	27	78	CCd	10%	144	102	19%	14%	88	7%	100%	5.2	182
24 Proj	525	68	18	63	4	252	17	5	255	331	444	106	110	105	9	74	0.39	41	20	39	30	93		9%	119	104	13%	13%	93	4%	85%	15.0	147

Canha,Mark

Age: 35 Pos: LF DH RF | Bats: R Ht: 6' 2" Wt: 209 | Health B | PT/Exp A | Consist A | LIMA Plan B | Rand Var 0 | MM 2335

Often gets overlooked because he doesn't post eye-catching numbers in any category, but he has now produced five consecutive seasons of mid-teens value, with typically strong bb% boosting his appeal in OBP leagues. Plate skills sti look solid and stable, but long-term slippage in PX/xPX and Spd look like Father Time taking hold.

Yr Tm	PA	R	HR	RBI	SB	BA	xHR	xSB	xBA	OBP	SLG	OPS+	vL+	vR+	bb%	ct%	Eye	G	L	F	h%	HctX	QBaB	Brl%	PX	xPX	HR/F	xHR/F	Spd	SBA%	SB%	RAR	BPX
19 OAK	497	80	26	58	3	273	22	9	256	396	517	126	111	132	13	74	0.63	41	18	41	31	101	CBd	10%	124	100	21%	18%	140	3%	60%	18.2	244
20 OAK	243	32	5	33	4	246	8	5	225	387	408	106	128	99	15	72	0.69	35	20	44	32	108	BAb	8%	102	126	8%	13%	131	5%	100%	-0.1	160
21 OAK	625	93	17	61	12	231	14	16	245	358	387	102	99	104	12	75	0.60	41	23	36	28	97	CCd	7%	90	96	12%	10%	147	8%	86%	-4.0	169
22 NYM	542	71	13	61	3	266	10	4	250	367	403	109	103	112	9	79	0.49	45	20	35	31	98	CCd	5%	89	82	10%	8%	92	2%	75%	9.5	117
23 2 NL	507	51	11	62	11	262	11	9	247	355	400	103	111	98	10	82	0.62	44	16	40	30	102	CCf	5%	81	79	8%	8%	81	8%	92%	10.9	136
1st Half	243	27	6	25	6	245	6	4	255	337	394	100	100	100	11	81	0.63	46	17	37	28	98	CCd	5%	89	92	9%	9%	71	10%	100%	3.0	139
2nd Half	264	24	5	37	5	278	4	6	238	371	405	105	122	97	10	83	0.62	43	15	42	32	107	CBf	4%	74	67	6%	5%	99	8%	83%	6.4	146
24 Proj	455	57	12	57	8	255	10	8	247	358	401	104	107	103	11	79	0.58	43	18	38	30	101		5%	87	85	10%	8%	100	6%	88%	9.6	146

GREG PYRON

Canzone,Dominic

Age: 26 Pos: LF	Health A	LIMA Plan D+
Bats: L Ht: 6'1" Wt: 190	PT/Exp B	Rand Var +2
	Consist D	MM 2123

6-21-.220 in 182 PA at ARI/SEA. Lightly-skilled bat couldn't maintain PCL-infused numbers in MLB as Eye evaporated from 0.98 to just 0.25 upon call-up. Stopped running after a pair of double-digit SB seasons in 2021-22, going just 2-for-5 in MLB. Interesting 2nd half xPX was all done in the majors, but upside is limited without better plate skills.

Yr	Tm	PA	R	HR	RBI	SB	BA	xHR	xSB	xBA	OBP	SLG	OPS+	vL+	vR+	bb%	ct%	Eye	G	L	F	h%	HctX	QBaB	Brl%	PX	xPX	HR/F	xHR/F	Spd	SBA%	SB%	RAR	BPX	R$
19																																			
20																																			
21	aa	140	17	5	19	1	296		1		349	470	112			7	75	0.32				37				103				102	6%	37%		112	$4
22	a/a	406	44	11	49	8	224		5		261	367	89			5	75	0.20				27				96				86	14%	77%		48	$8
23	2 TM *	462	58	14	62	2	248	9	5	260	298	417	97	85	90	7	81	0.37	43	18	40	28	131	BBd	12%	98	139	11%	16%	84	6%	36%	2.0	154	$10
1st Half		267	34	8	39	1	258		5	266	321	425	102	0	0	8	81	0.48	44	20	36	29	0		0%	95	-21	0%		107	8%	24%	2.7	179	$12
2nd Half		195	24	6	23	1	234	9	1	264	266	406	91	84	90	4	81	0.23	43	18	40	26	132	BBd	12%	103	139	11%	16%	80	3%	100%	-2.3	150	$4
24	Proj	350	42	10	45	4	246	16	4	246	291	403	95	95	95	6	78	0.27	43	18	40	29	119		11%	96	125	10%	16%	83	8%	63%	0.1	114	$7

Carlson,Dylan

Age: 25 Pos: CF RF	Health D	LIMA Plan D+
Bats: B Ht: 6'2" Wt: 205	PT/Exp A	Rand Var +2
	Consist B	MM 2323

Nothing went his way as a pair of injuries (oblique, ankle that required surgery) stunted his output and his season was over by Aug 10. Solid 1st half skills despite worsening platoon split that could start to eat up PA vR. Age and prospect pedigree keep him on the radar but upside is limited if he can't recapture his 2020-21 power levels.

Yr	Tm	PA	R	HR	RBI	SB	BA	xHR	xSB	xBA	OBP	SLG	OPS+	vL+	vR+	bb%	ct%	Eye	G	L	F	h%	HctX	QBaB	Brl%	PX	xPX	HR/F	xHR/F	Spd	SBA%	SB%	RAR	BPX	R$
19	a/a	536	80	21	57	17	265		17		330	470	111			9	75	0.38				32				109				128	21%	66%		163	$20
20	STL	119	11	3	16	1	200	5	1	239	252	364	82	73	83	7	68	0.23	45	24	32	26	98	CCd	9%	108	131	13%	21%	99	11%	50%	-8.3	16	$2
21	STL	619	79	18	65	2	266	17	4	245	343	437	107	126	102	9	72	0.38	38	25	38	34	84	CBc	7%	108	102	12%	11%	110	2%	67%	7.8	108	$16
22	STL	488	56	8	42	5	236	11	5	253	316	380	98	118	90	9	78	0.48	42	21	37	28	95	DCd	5%	98	98	6%	9%	103	6%	71%	-1.0	148	$8
23	STL	255	27	5	27	3	219	6	4	230	318	333	89	104	81	10	78	0.53	44	18	38	26	97	CBc	6%	67	95	8%	9%	101	4%	100%	-3.6	61	$1
1st Half		169	18	5	19	2	245	6	3	247	320	391	97	110	90	7	77	0.34	47	20	34	29	96	BCc	9%	81	98	13%	15%	109	5%	100%	0.0	79	$1
2nd Half		86	9	0	8	1	162	1	1	187	314	206	70	89	61	17	79	1.00	38	14	48	20	98	CBf	0%	35	91	0%	4%	95	4%	100%	-4.6	36	-$7
24	Proj	350	41	7	36	4	236	9	5	234	328	364	95	112	88	11	77	0.53	41	19	39	29	95		5%	80	100	7%	10%	99	5%	82%	1.0	89	$8

Carpenter,Kerry

Age: 26 Pos: RF DH	Health B	LIMA Plan B
Bats: L Ht: 6'2" Wt: 220	PT/Exp A	Rand Var -3
	Consist C	MM 4135

20-64-.278 in 459 PA at DET. Prototypical platoon power bat smashed vR after an early shoulder injury. Success vL dried up in the 2nd half despite expanded PT (started 15 of last 18 vL) and remains a risk. If real, the 2nd half Spd could deliver 10+ SBs. With a sharper Eye and improvement vL, power metrics say there's... UP: 30 HR.

Yr	Tm	PA	R	HR	RBI	SB	BA	xHR	xSB	xBA	OBP	SLG	OPS+	vL+	vR+	bb%	ct%	Eye	G	L	F	h%	HctX	QBaB	Brl%	PX	xPX	HR/F	xHR/F	Spd	SBA%	SB%	RAR	BPX	R$
19																																			
20																																			
21	aa	437	43	11	57	4	227		5		265	363	86			5	76	0.21				27				84				84	13%	36%		27	$6
22	DET *	493	56	25	61	2	250	5	7	246	293	476	109	84	121	6	71	0.21	40	15	44	30	103	CBc	11%	152	159	19%	16%	82	15%	14%	1.9	145	$15
23	DET *	497	60	21	66	6	266	19	6	247	319	450	105	89	115	7	72	0.27	45	20	36	33	104	BCc	10%	110	115	19%	18%	92	5%	100%	16.7	64	$16
1st Half		188	21	9	21	0	240	7	1	247	291	439	100	137	109	7	70	0.24	40	22	39	29	96	ABd	13%	125	130	21%	18%	76	0%	0%	1.3	64	$3
2nd Half		309	39	12	45	6	282	12	6	246	350	457	109	78	117	8	73	0.30	47	19	34	35	108	BCb	9%	101	107	17%	17%	110	7%	100%	12.4	75	$23
24	Proj	525	61	26	68	5	254	23	7	249	316	469	108	85	113	7	72	0.25	43	18	39	30	103		11%	129	134	19%	17%	90	9%	45%	10.5	90	$20

Carroll,Corbin

Age: 23 Pos: LF RF CF	Health A	LIMA Plan D+
Bats: L Ht: 5'10" Wt: 165	PT/Exp A	Rand Var 0
	Consist D	MM 4545

Met or exceeded a lofty set of expectations, returning 1st round caliber earnings. Concerns over severe PX split by half are mitigated by xPX improvement, and the late-Jun shoulder scare may have played a role (Brl%, HR/F dips). Fully healthy, he's Acuña-lite, and could someday contend for #1 overall. Next step for the eager... UP: 30 HR/60 SB

Yr	Tm	PA	R	HR	RBI	SB	BA	xHR	xSB	xBA	OBP	SLG	OPS+	vL+	vR+	bb%	ct%	Eye	G	L	F	h%	HctX	QBaB	Brl%	PX	xPX	HR/F	xHR/F	Spd	SBA%	SB%	RAR	BPX	R$
19																																			
20																																			
21																																			
22	ARI *	508	64	17	50	20	247	3	21	260	315	448	108	83	130	9	68	0.31	48	25	27	33	77	DDf	5%	142	71	20%	15%	156	25%	75%	9.4	176	$20
23	ARI	645	116	25	76	54	285	20	48	274	362	506	118	97	126	9	78	0.46	44	19	37	33	106	CCf	8%	121	117	15%	12%	168	36%	92%	46.5	279	$38
1st Half		324	60	17	44	24	289	12	19	293	365	557	126	100	135	9	78	0.45	46	16	38	32	104	BCf	9%	151	112	20%	14%	145	33%	92%	28.3	339	$39
2nd Half		321	56	8	32	30	281	8	29	257	358	453	110	94	116	9	78	0.46	42	22	36	33	107	CCf	6%	91	122	10%	10%	186	38%	91%	16.5	218	$35
24	Proj	630	108	24	74	44	273	20	40	269	352	489	115	90	125	9	76	0.41	44	21	35	32	101		7%	123	99	16%	13%	164	31%	87%	35.7	231	$41

Carter,Evan

Age: 21 Pos: OF	Health A	LIMA Plan C+
Bats: L Ht: 6'4" Wt: 190	PT/Exp C	Rand Var -2
	Consist F	MM 3515

5-12-.307 with 3 SB in 75 PA at TEX. Late-season darling possesses above-average toolshed. Patient with discerning eye, has improved aggressiveness early in counts. All-fields approach morphed into pull-side power in MLB, but HR gains not feasible. Platoon concerns throughout career, only 1 XBH vLHP in 2023. Above average on bases. (CB)

Yr	Tm	PA	R	HR	RBI	SB	BA	xHR	xSB	xBA	OBP	SLG	OPS+	vL+	vR+	bb%	ct%	Eye	G	L	F	h%	HctX	QBaB	Brl%	PX	xPX	HR/F	xHR/F	Spd	SBA%	SB%	RAR	BPX	R$
19																																			
20																																			
21																																			
22	aa	25	6	1	5	1	376		1		467	558	145			15	68	0.53				53				144				102	22%	56%		166	-$1
23	TEX *	543	69	14	58	21	259	2	29	232	354	412	104	12	169	13	70	0.48	44	21	36	34	116	CDc	10%	95	165	36%	14%	150	21%	63%	14.4	96	$17
1st Half		230	25	5	26	7	270		11	232	359	388	102	0	0	12	76	0.57	44	20	36	34	0		0%	67	-21	0%		130	20%	52%	2.8	82	$9
2nd Half		314	44	10	32	14	253	2	17	230	353	433	106	12	168	13	65	0.44	44	21	36	36	108	CDc	10%	119	165	36%	14%	155	22%	71%	9.1	107	$22
24	Proj	455	58	14	49	16	262	12	23	234	350	432	107	80	112	13	69	0.47	44	21	36	34	97		9%	105	149	14%	12%	155	19%	64%	14.5	97	$20

Casas,Triston

Age: 24 Pos: 1B	Health A	LIMA Plan C+
Bats: L Ht: 6'4" Wt: 252	PT/Exp A	Rand Var -1
	Consist C	MM 4145

Fantastic example of how the metrics can help you stick with a struggling bat in-season as xPX, xHR, xHR/F, and Brl% all advocated a hold for brighter days. Contact profile improved and the power unlocked at a level that looks sustainable, as long as the shoulder injury that ended his season in mid-September doesn't linger.

Yr	Tm	PA	R	HR	RBI	SB	BA	xHR	xSB	xBA	OBP	SLG	OPS+	vL+	vR+	bb%	ct%	Eye	G	L	F	h%	HctX	QBaB	Brl%	PX	xPX	HR/F	xHR/F	Spd	SBA%	SB%	RAR	BPX	R$
19																																			
20																																			
21	a/a	355	50	10	47	6	257		6		351	424	106			13	75	0.58				31				99				106	9%	63%		146	$10
22	BOS *	390	42	12	38	1	231	3	1	225	329	403	104	86	116	13	72	0.52	57	8	36	29	100	DFf	6%	122	113	26%	16%	72	1%	100%	3.2	114	$5
23	BOS	502	66	24	65	0	263	28	2	253	367	490	117	110	118	14	71	0.56	37	21	42	32	107	ABd	13%	137	135	19%	22%	78	0%	0%	29.9	164	$15
1st Half		274	30	9	27	0	226	14	1	232	328	400	100	93	101	14	69	0.51	39	20	41	29	103	ACf	14%	113	124	13%	21%	82	0%	0%	-0.1	71	$5
2nd Half		228	36	15	38	0	309	14	1	279	412	598	136	126	139	15	73	0.62	34	22	44	36	111	BBc	13%	164	147	24%	23%	81	0%	0%	24.6	275	$20
24	Proj	525	67	29	65	2	268	25	3	260	368	523	122	106	127	14	72	0.57	44	16	40	31	105		13%	152	128	22%	19%	76	2%	73%	35.0	159	$21

Castellanos,Nick

Age: 32 Pos: RF	Health B	LIMA Plan B
Bats: R Ht: 6'4" Wt: 203	PT/Exp A	Rand Var -2
	Consist F	MM 4335

Classic "doing too much" in Year 1 of a big deal in 2022; nagging injuries made things worse. Much better in 2023, though still short of CIN highs, particularly in xPX and HR/F. Huge h% drove 1st half success. Modest xBA underscores continued drop in ct% while tenuous plate skills trend is a yellow flag. HR repeat more likely than a BA one.

Yr	Tm	PA	R	HR	RBI	SB	BA	xHR	xSB	xBA	OBP	SLG	OPS+	vL+	vR+	bb%	ct%	Eye	G	L	F	h%	HctX	QBaB	Brl%	PX	xPX	HR/F	xHR/F	Spd	SBA%	SB%	RAR	BPX	R$
19	2 TM	664	100	27	73	2	289	39	6	280	337	525	119	158	110	6	77	0.29	38	23	40	34	113	CCa	11%	134	131	14%	21%	124	3%	50%	14.4	244	$21
20	CIN	242	37	14	34	0	225	15	2	258	298	486	104	100	105	8	68	0.28	35	26	39	26	101	ABa	16%	154	161	24%	25%	125	4%	0%	-5.2	208	$16
21	CIN	585	95	34	100	3	309	28	3	297	362	576	129	129	129	7	77	0.34	38	27	36	35	127	BCb	11%	152	146	23%	19%	90	3%	75%	41.2	285	$31
22	PHI	558	56	13	62	7	263	17	5	233	305	389	98	99	98	5	75	0.22	42	20	38	33	91	CBc	6%	87	100	9%	11%	93	6%	88%	-0.9	38	$16
23	PHI	671	79	29	106	11	272	27	11	256	311	476	107	125	100	5	70	0.19	41	22	37	34	104	CBb	10%	130	110	18%	16%	99	9%	85%	21.3	100	$26
1st Half		346	50	12	54	6	316	12	7	272	358	516	120	133	114	7	73	0.27	43	23	34	40	109	CCc	11%	130	114	15%	15%	107	9%	75%	23.7	161	$31
2nd Half		325	29	17	52	5	225	14	4	239	262	435	94	118	85	4	67	0.13	39	21	40	28	98	CBa	10%	129	106	20%	17%	94	9%	100%	-3.9	39	$18
24	Proj	665	81	28	98	8	261	27	8	252	305	457	105	116	100	6	71	0.21	40	22	38	32	104		10%	125	116	17%	16%	91	7%	83%	15.3	119	$27

PAUL SPORER

Castro,Harold

Age: 30	Pos: 2B	Health A	LIMA Plan D
Bats: L	Ht: 5' 10" Wt: 195	PT/Exp B	Rand Var 0
		Consist B	MM 1123

2022's skills gains, specifically in ct% and Brl%, might have been enough to make him a useful BA-forward asset in Coors. Except he neglected to bring those skills with him. Terrible plate patience, virtually no hard contact, bunches of GBs without the speed to exploit them... thin air can't solve these problems. Also no longer a multi-position piece.

Yr Tm	PA	R	HR	RBI	SB	BA	xHR	xSB	xBA	OBP	SLG	OPS+	vL+	vR+	bb%	ct%	Eye	G	L	F	h%	HctX	QBaB	Brl%	PX	xPX	HR/F	xHR/F	Spd	SBA%	SB%	RAR	BPX	R$
19 DET *	498	46	8	58	5	290	7	9	254	313	394	98	62	102	3	76	0.14	52	25	22	37	104	CDa	4%	55	67	8%	12%	123	9%	47%	-15.7	-22	$12
20 DET	54	6	0	3	0	347	1	0	262	407	429	111	109	111	9	78	0.45	47	29	24	45	66	CCa	3%	64	59	0%	11%	103	0%	0%	1.9	52	$2
21 DET	339	35	3	37	1	283	6	1	262	310	359	92	62	97	4	77	0.19	41	34	26	36	90	CCa	3%	50	77	5%	10%	88	2%	50%	-3.6	-54	$7
22 DET	443	37	7	47	0	271	12	2	262	300	381	96	102	96	4	81	0.22	44	26	30	32	84	DCb	6%	72	80	7%	12%	91	1%	0%	-4.9	66	$9
23 COL	270	24	1	31	1	252	4	2	236	275	314	80	33	86	3	74	0.14	46	26	28	34	82	DCb	3%	49	69	2%	7%	84	2%	100%	-6.9	-100	$2
1st Half	179	19	1	22	0	281	2	1	247	298	345	88	25	95	3	78	0.14	44	27	29	35	79	DCc	3%	46	70	3%	5%	92	0%	0%	-2.4	-50	$1
2nd Half	91	5	0	9	1	195	1	1	212	231	253	65	45	69	4	67	0.14	48	24	28	29	89	DDa	3%	55	65	0%	6%	79	6%	100%	-6.3	-196	-$7
24 Proj	315	27	2	35	2	254	5	2	242	280	331	84	62	87	4	75	0.15	46	27	28	33	87		4%	55	72	4%	8%	82	3%	68%	-4.3	-63	$3

Castro,Rodolfo

Age: 25	Pos: 2B SS	Health A	LIMA Plan F
Bats: B	Ht: 6' 0" Wt: 205	PT/Exp B	Rand Var 0
		Consist B	MM 1101

6-24-.211 in 256 PA at PIT/PHI. We warned a year ago that his 2nd half power surge (.231 ISO) wasn't a harbinger for future success, with lagging metrics and platoon issues that could cap his PT. Worse yet, GB lean became a GB tilt, sapping his power altogether. vR+ column says he should never see light of day vs. 70% of pitchers in league.

Yr Tm	PA	R	HR	RBI	SB	BA	xHR	xSB	xBA	OBP	SLG	OPS+	vL+	vR+	bb%	ct%	Eye	G	L	F	h%	HctX	QBaB	Brl%	PX	xPX	HR/F	xHR/F	Spd	SBA%	SB%	RAR	BPX	R$
19																																		
20																																		
21 PIT *	430	46	15	49	5	211	3	4	235	253	375	86	117	75	5	72	0.20	53	15	32	26	94	CDf	10%	102	84	26%	16%	83	12%	54%	-18.9	19	$5
22 PIT *	572	49	18	53	9	217	9	11	230	277	379	93	127	91	8	68	0.26	48	19	33	28	72	DCf	7%	111	90	19%	15%	123	13%	58%	-13.5	48	$9
23 2 NL *	310	26	7	31	1	189	7	4	189	267	312	79	111	59	8	65	0.26	56	13	31	28	71	CDd	8%	75	59	13%	15%	83	7%	20%	-11.5	-121	-$1
1st Half	213	19	6	22	1	234	7	4	211	319	367	94	127	62	9	71	0.35	53	14	33	30	84	CCd	8%	84	65	14%	16%	85	9%	20%	-2.9	-14	$1
2nd Half	97	7	1	9	0	134	0	0	139	189	198	52	29	47	6	54	0.15	80	5	15	23	22	FFf	5%	52	17	0%	0%	96	0%	0%	-8.7	-350	-$9
24 Proj	175	15	4	17	1	206	3	2	200	269	319	81	92	73	7	65	0.22	59	13	28	29	63		7%	79	62	13%	11%	101	8%	48%	-5.4	-88	$2

Castro,Willi

Age: 27	Pos: LF CF 3B	Health A	LIMA Plan C+
Bats: B	Ht: 6' 1" Wt: 206	PT/Exp A	Rand Var -1
		Consist B	MM 2523

SB breakout wasn't solely a function of new rules, though he did double his SBA%. Just as important is the OBP spike that got him to 1B much more often. Got more patient (bb%) and more aggressive (ct%) at the same time, and for the better (HctX, Brl%). Position versatility, viability vR, SB% all say this is repeatable. xSB says, "Almost."

Yr Tm	PA	R	HR	RBI	SB	BA	xHR	xSB	xBA	OBP	SLG	OPS+	vL+	vR+	bb%	ct%	Eye	G	L	F	h%	HctX	QBaB	Brl%	PX	xPX	HR/F	xHR/F	Spd	SBA%	SB%	RAR	BPX	R$
19 DET *	607	76	11	63	15	279	2	15	238	324	431	105	107	81	6	74	0.26	36	24	39	36	64	DAb	2%	87	43	4%	8%	137	14%	74%	-3.3	78	$19
20 DET	140	21	6	24	0	349	7	3	253	381	550	124	131	122	5	71	0.18	42	27	31	46	82	DCc	10%	111	78	21%	24%	156	2%	0%	8.5	120	$17
21 DET *	473	62	10	40	11	227	10	11	238	266	361	86	94	82	5	75	0.21	46	21	33	28	67	DCd	5%	78	55	9%	10%	133	15%	73%	-15.6	46	$9
22 DET *	427	48	8	32	11	238	4	10	241	268	358	89	92	92	4	77	0.17	42	23	36	29	73	DCd	3%	81	49	8%	4%	113	18%	68%	-11.4	52	$9
23 MIN	409	60	9	34	33	257	9	26	230	339	411	102	86	110	8	72	0.34	39	19	42	33	92	DCf	7%	95	98	9%	9%	132	36%	87%	10.7	86	$15
1st Half	203	32	5	16	15	250	6	11	224	312	380	95	93	95	6	71	0.20	36	23	41	33	89	FCf	9%	87	112	10%	12%	114	35%	88%	-0.1	0	$10
2nd Half	206	28	4	18	18	264	3	15	239	366	443	109	73	121	12	74	0.51	43	16	42	34	94	DBf	5%	104	83	8%	6%	135	37%	86%	8.4	164	$14
24 Proj	385	53	9	35	24	254	8	16	237	321	404	99	90	103	7	74	0.29	41	21	38	32	82		5%	91	74	9%	8%	127	30%	84%	5.6	79	$19

Cave,Jake

Age: 31	Pos: LF	Health B	LIMA Plan D
Bats: L	Ht: 6' 0" Wt: 200	PT/Exp B	Rand Var +1
		Consist B	MM 3211

5-21-.212 in 203 PA at PHI. According to BPX column, this was actually a big leap forward in skills. Did extend some recent growth trends: even more ct%, held most of FB gains, decent Brl%. But it still just doesn't add up to much. If he was five years younger, we'd be curious if there's another step forward to come. But he's not.

Yr Tm	PA	R	HR	RBI	SB	BA	xHR	xSB	xBA	OBP	SLG	OPS+	vL+	vR+	bb%	ct%	Eye	G	L	F	h%	HctX	QBaB	Brl%	PX	xPX	HR/F	xHR/F	Spd	SBA%	SB%	RAR	BPX	R$
19 MIN *	436	57	14	55	4	280	10	4	264	335	478	112	120	108	7	67	0.25	53	25	22	39	121	BDa	13%	123	110	29%	36%	112	4%	100%	16.1	63	$1
20 MIN	123	17	4	15	0	221	3	2	223	285	389	89	71	96	4	61	0.11	50	25	25	32	86	CDa	4%	106	95	24%	18%	126	8%	0%	-7.3	-88	$
21 MIN *	212	18	4	17	1	205	3	2	220	257	308	78	33	88	6	61	0.18	50	30	20	31	59	DDb	6%	76	60	15%	15%	101	7%	31%	-12.5	-181	-$
22 MIN *	523	52	12	52	8	199	7	8	205	253	348	85	93	91	7	65	0.21	36	20	44	28	109	BBc	10%	111	152	10%	13%	136	9%	100%	-17.9	14	$
23 PHI *	459	55	15	51	4	236	7	6	244	293	426	98	53	91	7	69	0.26	39	20	41	30	90	CBc	8%	129	113	9%	13%	89	9%	51%	2.5	86	$
1st Half	278	36	9	36	4	260	2	5	253	315	468	107	71	88	7	70	0.27	38	19	44	34	77	CBc	8%	148	146	5%	10%	85	15%	51%	6.7	143	$1
2nd Half	181	19	6	15	0	200	4	1	224	259	360	84	42	91	7	69	0.25	40	20	40	25	96	BBc	7%	98	94	12%	12%	113	0%	0%	-5.0	11	-$
24 Proj	175	19	5	18	1	217	6	2	224	274	374	89	67	94	7	66	0.21	41	22	37	30	91		8%	108	115	12%	14%	105	7%	61%	-3.0	7	$

Chapman,Matt

Age: 31	Pos: 3B	Health B	LIMA Plan B+
Bats: R	Ht: 6' 0" Wt: 215	PT/Exp A	Rand Var -1
		Consist A	MM 4215

PRO: Steady FB%, xHR, xPX all say the power outage was undeserved; lingering finger injury likely a key factor in 2nd-half collapse. CON: Even ignoring 2nd half, xBA says h%-fueled 1st half BA recovery was a mirage. A rebound to 2022 level is a nice baseline expectation, possibly available at a recency-bias-driven discount.

Yr Tm	PA	R	HR	RBI	SB	BA	xHR	xSB	xBA	OBP	SLG	OPS+	vL+	vR+	bb%	ct%	Eye	G	L	F	h%	HctX	QBaB	Brl%	PX	xPX	HR/F	xHR/F	Spd	SBA%	SB%	RAR	BPX	R$
19 OAK	670	102	36	91	1	249	36	3	261	342	506	117	118	116	11	75	0.50	41	15	43	27	117	ABf	12%	137	107	19%	19%	101	1%	50%	11.2	233	$1
20 OAK	152	22	10	25	0	232	12	0	244	276	535	108	84	112	5	62	0.15	26	24	51	29	104	AAf	18%	198	150	22%	27%	109	0%	0%	0.0	208	$1
21 OAK	622	75	27	72	3	210	29	8	195	314	403	98	110	92	13	62	0.40	34	15	52	28	76	BAf	14%	126	130	16%	17%	131	3%	60%	-1.6	58	$
22 TOR	621	83	27	76	2	229	30	4	230	324	433	107	105	108	11	68	0.40	34	17	49	28	120	AAf	13%	142	154	15%	17%	95	3%	50%	7.9	134	$1
23 TOR	581	66	17	54	4	240	28	9	224	330	424	103	120	99	11	68	0.38	35	16	49	32	111	AAf	17%	131	140	10%	16%	116	4%	67%	13.0	118	$1
1st Half	344	42	11	38	3	262	19	5	237	340	459	109	141	102	10	69	0.35	36	17	47	35	124	ABd	18%	141	153	11%	19%	99	6%	60%	9.6	139	$1
2nd Half	237	24	6	16	1	206	10	4	204	316	373	93	91	94	12	66	0.41	33	14	53	28	90	AAf	16%	116	120	8%	14%	131	2%	100%	-3.4	82	$
24 Proj	595	74	26	70	3	227	30	6	228	320	444	105	111	103	11	67	0.37	34	16	50	29	104		15%	145	137	15%	17%	102	3%	65%	12.0	117	$1

Chisholm Jr.,Jazz

Age: 26	Pos: CF	Health F	LIMA Plan C
Bats: L	Ht: 5' 11" Wt: 184	PT/Exp A	Rand Var -3
		Consist B	MM 4523

First, the good: a HR shy of 20/20 despite fewer than 100 gms. Now, the bad: more injuries, continued extreme platoon, meager ct% fell further, flyball growth regressed, and all his power indicators dipped. SB% spike offset Spd loss, aided by rule changes. Still a ton of upside, but now that he's an OF, the Buxton parallels ring truer.

Yr Tm	PA	R	HR	RBI	SB	BA	xHR	xSB	xBA	OBP	SLG	OPS+	vL+	vR+	bb%	ct%	Eye	G	L	F	h%	HctX	QBaB	Brl%	PX	xPX	HR/F	xHR/F	Spd	SBA%	SB%	RAR	BPX	R$
19 aa	455	63	21	61	18	220		17		320	442	106			13	61	0.38				30				133				152	21%	81%		85	$1
20 MIA	62	8	2	6	2	161	3	2	183	242	321	75	121	59	8	66	0.26	37	11	51	20	72	DBf	11%	91	145	11%	17%	141	36%	50%	-5.9	-4	$
21 MIA	507	70	18	53	23	248	17	21	241	303	425	100	91	104	7	69	0.23	49	20	31	32	87	BDf	9%	110	88	18%	17%	144	28%	74%	-3.1	85	$2
22 MIA	240	39	14	45	12	254	13	10	267	325	535	122	73	132	9	69	0.32	37	22	41	30	111	BCf	17%	181	159	23%	22%	131	34%	71%	10.0	276	$1
23 MIA	383	50	19	51	22	250	19	16	240	304	457	104	65	117	7	66	0.22	48	17	36	32	93	CDf	12%	129	125	23%	23%	108	30%	88%	10.6	61	$1
1st Half	183	20	9	21	14	246	9	10	234	302	443	102	54	115	7	66	0.21	48	18	34	32	101	BDf	12%	120	141	24%	24%	114	39%	88%	3.4	32	$1
2nd Half	200	30	10	30	8	254	9	6	244	305	470	105	71	118	7	67	0.23	48	16	37	32	85	CCf	13%	136	110	23%	20%	107	21%	89%	6.0	89	$1
24 Proj	420	61	21	62	22	248	21	17	242	311	470	107	80	116	8	67	0.26	44	18	38	32	94		13%	138	129	21%	21%	126	29%	81%	13.0	123	$2

Clemens,Kody

Age: 28	Pos: 1B	Health A	LIMA Plan D
Bats: L	Ht: 6' 1" Wt: 200	PT/Exp B	Rand Var +3
		Consist B	MM 2211

4-13-.230 in 148 PA at PHI. Up and down from AAA/MLB for the second straight season for Roger's boy, and while there's some interesting quality of contact here, there's just not nearly enough bat-meeting-ball. Strikeouts and h% level have kept BA low—just as poor SB% has undermined ample Spd. Lots of ways to improve; not much time.

Yr Tm	PA	R	HR	RBI	SB	BA	xHR	xSB	xBA	OBP	SLG	OPS+	vL+	vR+	bb%	ct%	Eye	G	L	F	h%	HctX	QBaB	Brl%	PX	xPX	HR/F	xHR/F	Spd	SBA%	SB%	RAR	BPX	R$
19 aa	53	5	1	4	0	163		0		252	267	72			11	60	0.30				24				75				105	0%	0%		-159	
20																																		
21 aaa	397	53	14	48	3	220		5		275	406	94			7	72	0.28				26				105				135	5%	74%		115	
22 DET *	381	39	13	45	4	196	4	5	212	240	375	87	127	59	5	68	0.18	38	14	48	25	59	BBc	5%	120	70	12%	10%	116	10%	64%	-20.8	52	
23 PHI *	409	47	16	46	4	210	3	7	245	278	394	92	43	95	9	70	0.32	41	22	36	25	81	BBc	6%	111	78	11%	8%	111	10%	55%	-9.1	79	
1st Half	162	16	4	14	1	220	3	1	232	262	345	83	43	95	5	72	0.20	41	22	36	28	83	BBc	6%	82	78	11%	8%	93	3%	100%	-6.5	-18	
2nd Half	248	32	12	32	4	204	0	7	252	289	427	97	0	0	11	69	0.39	44	20	36	23	0	AF	0%	132	-21	0%		125	16%	51%	-4.3	150	$
24 Proj	210	24	6	24	2	226	3	4	223	284	388	92	99	91	7	70	0.26	40	19	41	29	73		6%	100	75	12%	6%	114	9%	60%	-2.8	77	

PAUL SPORER

Colás,Oscar

Age: 25 Pos: RF | Bats: L Ht: 6' 1" Wt: 209

Health A | PT/Exp C | Consist C | LIMA Plan D+ | Rand Var 0 | MM 1103

5-19-.216 with 4 SB in 263 PA at CHW. Cuban-born slugger tore through three MiLB levels in 2022, then met his match in the majors. Poor batting eye, low contact rate highlight trouble with swing decisions. Pounded the ball into the dirt way too often, wide launch angle variability speaks to lack of swing optimization. Needs more seasoning.

Yr Tm	PA	R	HR	RBI	SB	BA	xHR	xSB	xBA	OBP	SLG	OPS+	vL+	vR+	bb%	ct%	Eye	G	L	F	h%	HctX	QBaB	Brl%	PX	xPX	HR/F	xHR/F	Spd	SBA%	SB%	RAR	BPX	R$
19																																		
20																																		
21																																		
22 a/a	248	28	12	24	1	253		3		285	445	103			4	67	0.14				33				131				99	10%	27%		41	$5
23 CHW *	491	56	12	38	5	217	5	7	223	261	338	82	72	80	6	71	0.20	51	16	32	28	93	CDf	8%	80	80	9%	9%	96	8%	64%	-14.3	-32	$4
1st Half	287	31	8	26	3	229	1	4	232	276	366	88	36	83	6	73	0.24	60	12	28	28	82	DFf	9%	88	58	6%	6%	98	7%	77%	-6.7	21	$6
2nd Half	204	25	4	12	2	202	4	3	209	240	301	73	82	78	5	69	0.16	47	18	34	27	95	CDf	8%	68	91	10%	10%	101	10%	50%	-11.8	-104	-$1
24 Proj	385	45	7	32	3	230	7	6	206	272	328	82	72	85	5	69	0.17	48	18	34	31	90		8%	68	78	9%	8%	90	8%	42%	-12.9	-15	$4

Conforto,Michael

Age: 31 Pos: RF | Bats: L Ht: 6' 1" Wt: 215

Health B | PT/Exp A | Consist A | LIMA Plan B | Rand Var +2 | MM 2225

First year back from major shoulder surgery almost a carbon copy of 2021. Recurring left hamstring issues cost him about a month and may have contributed to second half swoon; also dealt with nagging calf, heel issues earlier. First half shows the upside, but if health, vL trends continue, cracking $20 again will be tough.

Yr Tm	PA	R	HR	RBI	SB	BA	xHR	xSB	xBA	OBP	SLG	OPS+	vL+	vR+	bb%	ct%	Eye	G	L	F	h%	HctX	QBaB	Brl%	PX	xPX	HR/F	xHR/F	Spd	SBA%	SB%	RAR	BPX	R$
19 NYM	648	90	33	92	7	257	33	5	262	363	494	119	98	127	13	73	0.56	36	24	40	29	92	BBc	12%	128	120	20%	20%	86	5%	78%	10.2	178	$20
20 NYM	233	40	9	31	3	322	10	3	270	412	515	123	114	128	10	72	0.42	41	30	28	41	106	CCc	11%	117	108	22%	24%	84	8%	50%	11.7	116	$29
21 NYM	479	52	14	55	1	232	16	0	241	344	384	100	79	109	12	74	0.57	45	21	34	28	112	CCc	9%	93	110	13%	15%	73	1%	100%	-6.5	77	$6
22																																		
23 SF	470	58	15	58	4	239	15	4	228	334	384	98	81	103	11	74	0.50	45	16	38	29	98	CCf	8%	86	101	13%	13%	78	3%	100%	2.8	43	$9
1st Half	276	39	12	42	2	236	10	2	237	333	422	103	93	106	12	70	0.47	49	16	35	28	95	BCf	10%	111	103	20%	17%	77	3%	100%	3.7	71	$14
2nd Half	194	19	3	16	2	243	6	2	214	335	331	90	62	98	11	79	0.56	40	17	43	29	104	CBf	6%	54	99	5%	11%	87	4%	100%	-2.5	25	$1
24 Proj	455	58	16	55	4	244	18	3	243	344	406	103	86	109	12	74	0.51	43	21	37	29	103		9%	97	106	14%	16%	78	4%	78%	7.3	76	$14

ontreras,William

Age: 26 Pos: CA DH | Bats: R Ht: 6' 0" Wt: 180

Health A | PT/Exp A | Consist B | LIMA Plan B | Rand Var +2 | MM 3435

Only took one full season to eclipse more famous older brother and achieve fantasy breakout. A lot to like here: above-average walk rate shows selectivity; solid contact rate provides good BA floor; snags a few bags with decent speed. But, oh, that elite exit velocity [drool]. Improving dreadful launch angle even a bit could yield... UP: 30 HR

Yr Tm	PA	R	HR	RBI	SB	BA	xHR	xSB	xBA	OBP	SLG	OPS+	vL+	vR+	bb%	ct%	Eye	G	L	F	h%	HctX	QBaB	Brl%	PX	xPX	HR/F	xHR/F	Spd	SBA%	SB%	RAR	BPX	R$
19 aa	207	26	3	19	0	253		1		311	351	92			8	79	0.39				31				58				98	0%	0%		30	$0
20 ATL	10	0	0	1	0	400	0	0	391	400	500	119	0	150	0	60	0.00	17	67	17	67	81	DAa	17%	102	140	0%	0%	112	0%	0%	1.0	-168	-$2
21 ATL *	350	40	15	46	0	235	8	1	237	299	419	99	91	98	8	70	0.31	49	19	32	29	94	ADd	11%	110	90	23%	23%	106	0%	0%	3.1	77	$6
22 ATL *	426	53	20	51	2	275	22	5	247	346	481	117	145	111	10	70	0.36	53	15	32	35	113	BDd	14%	137	126	27%	30%	126	2%	100%	24.6	166	$15
23 MIL	611	86	17	78	6	289	22	10	265	367	457	112	146	98	10	77	0.50	55	16	29	35	112	AFf	9%	106	97	14%	18%	108	4%	86%	39.4	164	$22
1st Half	267	34	9	29	1	247	10	3	260	337	421	104	129	92	11	77	0.52	56	15	29	28	95	BFf	10%	101	98	17%	19%	116	1%	100%	7.7	168	$9
2nd Half	344	52	8	49	5	321	12	7	266	391	485	118	162	102	10	76	0.49	54	17	29	40	124	AFd	9%	110	96	12%	18%	108	6%	83%	29.3	171	$30
24 Proj	560	74	23	70	4	275	25	6	258	348	470	112	139	102	10	74	0.41	53	16	30	33	110		11%	119	106	20%	22%	113	3%	88%	34.3	141	$23

ontreras,Willson

Age: 32 Pos: CA DH | Bats: R Ht: 6' 1" Wt: 225

Health B | PT/Exp A | Consist A | LIMA Plan B+ | Rand Var 0 | MM 4145

Can't argue with the consistency of these results. Two-year surge in contact rate, HctX bode well for sustaining above-average BA; no problems vL or vR; hits the ball really hard. It may be tempting to extrapolate a career year from bonkers 2nd half but a 41% h% is unsustainable. One of the most reliable options at a difficult position.

Yr Tm	PA	R	HR	RBI	SB	BA	xHR	xSB	xBA	OBP	SLG	OPS+	vL+	vR+	bb%	ct%	Eye	G	L	F	h%	HctX	QBaB	Brl%	PX	xPX	HR/F	xHR/F	Spd	SBA%	SB%	RAR	BPX	R$
19 CHC	409	57	24	64	1	272	20	3	263	355	533	123	143	117	9	72	0.37	50	16	34	32	92	CDc	12%	141	128	27%	23%	99	3%	33%	19.8	185	$13
20 CHC	225	37	7	26	1	243	10	2	234	356	407	101	71	110	9	70	0.35	47	20	33	31	99	BDd	10%	103	125	16%	23%	79	5%	33%	0.7	20	$15
21 CHC	483	61	21	57	5	237	22	4	233	340	438	107	121	101	11	67	0.38	50	16	34	30	106	ACc	11%	131	127	22%	23%	79	7%	56%	9.4	69	$11
22 CHC	487	65	22	55	4	243	22	4	272	349	466	115	120	114	9	75	0.44	51	16	33	27	137	BDd	10%	141	129	21%	21%	94	5%	67%	16.3	214	$14
23 STL	495	55	20	67	6	264	22	6	268	358	467	112	122	109	10	74	0.46	46	21	33	31	127	ACd	12%	125	108	19%	21%	63	7%	67%	26.1	136	$15
1st Half	298	30	8	31	5	214	12	4	248	305	366	92	90	92	10	74	0.41	46	19	34	26	125	ACc	10%	99	103	12%	18%	63	9%	83%	-0.8	57	$6
2nd Half	197	25	12	36	1	343	10	2	298	439	627	144	158	138	12	74	0.53	46	23	31	41	130	ADf	15%	166	114	32%	26%	72	5%	33%	27.6	275	$18
24 Proj	455	60	22	64	4	268	22	5	265	365	491	118	127	114	10	73	0.43	48	19	33	32	124		12%	136	119	23%	23%	75	6%	57%	28.6	168	$20

ooper,Garrett

Age: 33 Pos: 1B DH | Bats: R Ht: 6' 5" Wt: 235

Health F | PT/Exp A | Consist B | LIMA Plan C | Rand Var 0 | MM 3033

Health has long been an issue but finished season with only a minimum-stay IL stint for an ear infection. Despite surge in homers, tumbling Eye and exit velocity are disquieting trends. Still, if he continues to stroke line drives at a high rate, we could see a couple more seasons of moderate results. Dependable later-round pick, budget accordingly.

Yr Tm	PA	R	HR	RBI	SB	BA	xHR	xSB	xBA	OBP	SLG	OPS+	vL+	vR+	bb%	ct%	Eye	G	L	F	h%	HctX	QBaB	Brl%	PX	xPX	HR/F	xHR/F	Spd	SBA%	SB%	RAR	BPX	R$
MIA	421	52	15	50	0	281	18	1	255	344	446	109	89	116	8	71	0.30	52	25	23	36	100	CFb	10%	93	93	24%	29%	96	0%	0%	-0.5	19	$10
MIA	133	20	6	20	0	283	6	0	276	353	500	113	153	93	8	74	0.35	46	26	28	34	94	BCa	10%	127	72	24%	24%	71	0%	0%	0.7	152	$11
MIA	250	30	9	33	1	284	9	2	244	380	465	116	132	109	12	68	0.44	51	22	27	38	94	ADa	11%	115	101	23%	23%	97	3%	50%	7.2	81	$7
MIA	469	37	9	50	0	261	16	0	258	337	415	107	87	112	9	71	0.34	44	26	29	35	106	BDb	11%	119	121	10%	18%	77	0%	0%	0.4	76	$9
2 NL	457	42	17	61	0	251	17	2	241	304	419	99	122	91	7	69	0.23	43	24	33	33	97	CCa	10%	107	119	18%	18%	75	0%	0%	1.1	-4	$9
Half	251	20	10	36	0	250	10	1	238	291	424	98	111	94	5	68	0.17	42	23	35	32	99	ABa	10%	109	130	18%	18%	89	0%	0%	-1.4	-4	$8
Half	206	22	7	25	0	253	7	0	245	320	414	99	132	86	9	69	0.32	45	25	30	33	93	CCb	10%	105	106	18%	18%	64	0%	0%	0.7	0	$6
Proj	385	39	13	49	0	262	14	1	249	330	430	104	118	99	8	70	0.30	46	24	30	34	98		10%	111	111	17%	20%	72	1%	50%	8.1	39	$12

rrea,Carlos

Age: 29 Pos: SS | Bats: R Ht: 6' 4" Wt: 220

Health B | PT/Exp A | Consist C | LIMA Plan B+ | Rand Var +4 | MM 3035

Missed last two weeks with plantar fasciitis but admitted he battled the injury for several months. Could that have led to big dropoff in roto value? Quality of contact, swing decisions were still solid. Big dip in hit rate took a bite out of offense. Total absence of stolen bases puts pressure on other categories; foot injury specter looms. Caution.

Yr Tm	PA	R	HR	RBI	SB	BA	xHR	xSB	xBA	OBP	SLG	OPS+	vL+	vR+	bb%	ct%	Eye	G	L	F	h%	HctX	QBaB	Brl%	PX	xPX	HR/F	xHR/F	Spd	SBA%	SB%	RAR	BPX	R$
HOU *	344	43	21	60	1	277	18	1	274	357	554	126	134	125	11	73	0.46	39	21	40	31	114	CCd	13%	149	132	26%	22%	95	1%	100%	15.9	233	$11
HOU	221	22	5	25	0	264	6	0	231	326	383	94	101	91	7	76	0.33	50	21	29	33	110	CCf	6%	71	86	11%	13%	85	0%	0%	-2.3	4	$11
HOU	640	104	26	92	0	279	21	1	277	366	485	117	115	118	12	79	0.65	42	24	35	31	118	BCd	9%	116	102	17%	14%	92	0%	0%	30.9	238	$23
MIN	590	70	22	64	0	291	27	3	250	366	467	118	132	113	10	77	0.50	43	20	38	34	121	BCd	12%	110	111	14%	18%	94	1%	0%	29.5	159	$22
MIN	580	60	18	65	0	230	18	3	251	312	399	97	105	94	10	75	0.45	46	20	34	27	111	BCf	10%	104	89	14%	14%	89	0%	0%	6.0	107	$8
Half	316	27	11	37	0	218	11	2	248	291	404	95	88	97	9	74	0.39	45	18	37	26	98	CCf	12%	113	81	14%	14%	95	0%	0%	-3.5	121	$6
Half	264	33	7	28	0	245	6	1	255	337	393	99	125	90	12	76	0.54	47	22	30	30	127	ACd	7%	93	98	13%	11%	85	0%	0%	1.3	96	$8
Proj	560	68	20	67	0	259	20	3	255	340	437	107	117	103	11	76	0.49	43	21	36	30	117		10%	107	100	15%	14%	87	0%	26%	18.7	140	$18

wser,Colton

Age: 24 Pos: OF | Bats: L Ht: 6' 3" Wt: 195

Health A | PT/Exp C | Consist B | LIMA Plan D | Rand Var 0 | MM 2203

0-4-.115 in 77 PA at BAL. Big start in AAA but left aggressiveness there and struggled mightily in MLB debut. Strong, athletic prospect with knack for hard contact. Natural up-the-middle approach with HR power to both gaps, though present swing trajectory doesn't allow for power to truly play. Above-average runner who times jumps well. (CB)

Yr Tm	PA	R	HR	RBI	SB	BA	xHR	xSB	xBA	OBP	SLG	OPS+	vL+	vR+	bb%	ct%	Eye	G	L	F	h%	HctX	QBaB	Brl%	PX	xPX	HR/F	xHR/F	Spd	SBA%	SB%	RAR	BPX	R$
a/a	313	48	12	29	1	251		3		328	425	107			10	63	0.31				36				135				98	4%	37%		41	$7
BAL *	446	66	11	48	7	227	0	9	224	330	357	94	64	57	13	63	0.41	48	25	28	33	64	CFc	3%	94	79	0%	0%	106	8%	68%	1.1	-43	$8
Half	238	39	6	29	5	276		6	219	382	416	109	0	0	15	67	0.51	44	20	36	39	0		0%	93	-21	0%		115	8%	81%	9.8	25	$12
Half	208	28	4	20	2	173	0	4	210	271	292	76	64	56	12	59	0.33	48	25	28	26	60	CFc	3%	96	79	0%	0%	105	9%	51%	-9.5	-107	-$1
Proj	280	42	5	28	3	230	5	5	215	336	340	93	134	87	12	63	0.37	48	25	28	35	54		2%	85	71	12%	12%	107	6%	59%	-2.2	-15	$7

N DE LEONARDIS

Crawford,Brandon

Age: 37	Pos: SS		Health	D	LIMA Plan	D
Bats: L	Ht: 6' 1"	Wt: 223	PT/Exp	A	Rand Var	+5
			Consist	F	MM	2211

When analyzing a 37-year-old SS, the first thing that comes to mind is, "This guy can still play short?!" Glove remained slick, and bumps in barrel rate and exit velocity prevented complete offensive collapse, but steep two-year drop in contact rate, dwindling PA due to nagging old man injuries may be enough to consider hanging them up.

Yr	Tm	PA	R	HR	RBI	SB	BA	xHR	xSB	xBA	OBP	SLG	OPS+	vL+	vR+	bb%	ct%	Eye	G	L	F	h%	HctX	QBaB	Brl%	PX	xPX	HR/F	xHR/F	Spd	SBA%	SB%	RAR	BPX
19	SF	560	58	11	59	3	228	15	2	252	304	350	90	83	92	9	77	0.45	48	23	28	28	104	CDb	5%	69	106	10%	14%	79	4%	60%	-19.6	22
20	SF	193	26	8	28	1	256	7	1	259	326	465	105	84	110	8	73	0.32	42	23	35	31	102	CCd	9%	127	123	18%	16%	72	7%	33%	1.5	124
21	SF	549	79	24	90	11	298	27	9	266	373	522	123	98	133	10	78	0.53	40	19	41	34	101	CBd	11%	126	137	15%	17%	104	9%	79%	33.4	258
22	SF	458	50	9	52	1	231	11	2	225	308	344	92	93	92	9	76	0.40	47	18	36	28	86	CCd	7%	73	95	8%	10%	95	2%	50%	-12.0	34
23	SF	320	31	7	38	3	194	10	2	216	273	314	80	81	80	9	71	0.35	42	18	40	25	83	BCd	10%	77	91	9%	12%	72	4%	100%	-10.3	-39
1st Half		194	19	4	23	3	221	5	2	227	301	343	88	80	91	10	70	0.37	43	21	36	29	72	CCf	8%	84	75	9%	11%	63	7%	100%	-4.0	-36
2nd Half		126	12	3	15	0	153	5	1	195	230	270	68	83	64	8	73	0.30	41	13	46	18	99	BBc	13%	65	115	8%	13%	93	0%	0%	-9.0	-39
24	Proj	**175**	**20**	**5**	**23**	**1**	**217**	**6**	**1**	**226**	**294**	**354**	**89**	**87**	**89**	**9**	**74**	**0.38**	**43**	**18**	**39**	**26**	**91**		**10%**	**83**	**105**	**10%**	**13%**	**86**	**4%**	**78%**	**-2.3**	**36**

Crawford,J.P.

Age: 29	Pos: SS		Health	A	LIMA Plan	B+
Bats: L	Ht: 6' 2"	Wt: 202	PT/Exp	A	Rand Var	-2
			Consist	C	MM	2235

Exciting new level or just a career year? PRO: More exit velocity goosed power, but improved launch angle made the bigger difference; change in approach reflected in career-high bb% as well as drop in ct%. CON: Gulf between HR vs xHR, PX vs xPX casts doubt on power repeat; Brl%, xHR/F still well below average. Better—but only modestly so.

Yr	Tm	PA	R	HR	RBI	SB	BA	xHR	xSB	xBA	OBP	SLG	OPS+	vL+	vR+	bb%	ct%	Eye	G	L	F	h%	HctX	QBaB	Brl%	PX	xPX	HR/F	xHR/F	Spd	SBA%	SB%	RAR	BPX
19	SEA *	527	58	9	57	7	236	5	7	242	321	371	96	62	108	11	75	0.51	45	20	35	29	74	DCc	3%	79	69	8%	5%	109	8%	71%	-16.3	78
20	SEA	232	33	2	24	6	255	3	7	240	336	338	90	86	91	10	81	0.59	44	23	33	31	96	DCd	2%	46	83	4%	6%	138	13%	67%	-5.1	96
21	SEA	687	89	9	54	3	273	6	6	256	338	376	98	95	100	8	82	0.51	46	24	31	32	75	DCd	2%	66	42	6%	4%	98	5%	33%	0.0	104
22	SEA	603	57	6	42	3	243	6	7	258	339	336	96	93	97	11	85	0.85	45	23	31	28	82	DDf	2%	59	58	4%	4%	112	3%	60%	-5.2	152
23	SEA	638	94	19	65	2	266	11	5	263	380	438	111	102	116	15	77	0.75	39	23	38	32	97	CBc	5%	106	73	12%	7%	88	1%	100%	31.6	175
1st Half		317	44	7	30	1	246	4	3	258	361	384	102	79	112	15	78	0.81	41	23	36	29	101	CCd	3%	86	63	9%	5%	94	1%	100%	3.8	150
2nd Half		321	50	12	35	1	286	7	3	269	398	492	120	124	119	15	75	0.70	37	23	40	34	93	DBc	6%	128	82	15%	9%	86	1%	100%	20.3	214
24	Proj	**595**	**85**	**12**	**56**	**3**	**265**	**9**	**7**	**255**	**363**	**396**	**104**	**98**	**107**	**13**	**79**	**0.70**	**41**	**23**	**36**	**31**	**88**		**4%**	**81**	**66**	**8%**	**6%**	**100**	**3%**	**64%**	**16.8**	**157**

Cron,C.J.

Age: 34	Pos: 1B		Health	F	LIMA Plan	C+
Bats: R	Ht: 6' 4"	Wt: 235	PT/Exp	A	Rand Var	0
			Consist	C	MM	4233

Plagued with recurring back issues from May all the way through end of season, requiring three IL stints. 2021 walk rate looks like a mirage now, so we're left with a one-and-a-half tool slugger, if you include league-average contact rate. Burly, plodding middle-aged dudes with wonky backs are an archetype. Don't cast him as your hero.

Yr	Tm	PA	R	HR	RBI	SB	BA	xHR	xSB	xBA	OBP	SLG	OPS+	vL+	vR+	bb%	ct%	Eye	G	L	F	h%	HctX	QBaB	Brl%	PX	xPX	HR/F	xHR/F	Spd	SBA%	SB%	RAR	BPX
19	MIN	499	51	25	78	0	253	33	-	262	311	469	108	142	94	6	77	0.27	42	22	36	28	109	ACc	15%	113	114	20%	26%	59	0%	0%	-1.9	104
20	DET	52	9	4	8	0	190	4	0	264	346	548	119	80	133	17	62	0.56	38	15	46	18	106	DAf	19%	235	194	33%	33%	88	0%	0%	0.5	396
21	COL	547	70	28	92	1	281	26	0	267	375	530	124	133	121	11	75	0.51	39	19	42	32	111	CBd	11%	145	115	19%	17%	71	1%	100%	29.8	238
22	COL	631	79	29	102	0	257	28	2	251	315	468	111	97	117	7	71	0.26	39	20	40	31	98	CCf	11%	138	104	17%	17%	94	0%	0%	14.5	138
23	2 TM	278	38	12	37	0	248	13	1	245	295	434	99	101	99	6	75	0.26	42	18	40	29	105	CCf	14%	109	135	15%	17%	66	0%	0%	4.1	71
1st Half		167	23	6	21	0	240	8	0	252	287	422	97	104	94	7	76	0.30	39	19	42	28	109	CBf	16%	112	143	12%	16%	65	0%	0%	-1.1	100
2nd Half		111	15	6	16	0	260	6	0	233	306	452	102	92	105	5	73	0.21	47	16	37	30	98	DCd	11%	105	124	21%	21%	79	0%	0%	0.9	46
24	Proj	**350**	**46**	**17**	**54**	**0**	**258**	**18**	**1**	**250**	**315**	**464**	**107**	**107**	**106**	**7**	**74**	**0.28**	**42**	**19**	**39**	**30**	**103**		**12%**	**121**	**120**	**18%**	**19%**	**73**	**0%**	**100%**	**8.6**	**114**

Cronenworth,Jake

Age: 30	Pos: 1B 2B		Health	B	LIMA Plan	A
Bats: L	Ht: 6' 0"	Wt: 187	PT/Exp	A	Rand Var	+3
			Consist	B	MM	2435

A fractured wrist ended his season in late August, capping off a disappointing first year on his new long-term contract. You can see how essential those high PA totals were to accumulating roto value in 2021-22. Three-year slide in barrel rate is concerning, doesn't make much use of good speed. Buy the MI/CI eligibility, hope for plenty of PT.

Yr	Tm	PA	R	HR	RBI	SB	BA	xHR	xSB	xBA	OBP	SLG	OPS+	vL+	vR+	bb%	ct%	Eye	G	L	F	h%	HctX	QBaB	Brl%	PX	xPX	HR/F	xHR/F	Spd	SBA%	SB%	RAR	BPX
19	aaa	384	60	8	36	10	283		10		358	433	109			10	78	0.53				35				84				121	15%	62%		137
20	SD	192	26	4	20	3	285	9	3	295	354	477	110	72	128	9	83	0.60	45	25	29	33	122	BCb	10%	108	104	10%	21%	107	9%	75%	0.3	276
21	SD	638	94	21	71	4	266	18	8	281	340	460	110	105	112	9	84	0.61	42	22	36	29	102	CCd	7%	102	95	12%	10%	125	5%	57%	5.4	288
22	SD	681	88	17	88	3	239	18	6	229	332	390	102	100	103	10	78	0.53	35	17	48	28	87	CAd	6%	97	97	8%	8%	111	2%	100%	-7.5	152
23	SD	521	54	10	48	6	229	10	10	250	312	378	94	90	96	9	79	0.47	37	22	41	27	82	DBc	4%	86	91	7%	7%	131	6%	86%	-6.2	154
1st Half		342	35	7	27	3	208	6	6	235	311	345	90	93	88	11	75	0.53	36	23	41	25	81	DBc	4%	79	97	8%	7%	131	4%	100%	-9.1	104
2nd Half		179	19	3	21	3	267	5	4	277	313	436	101	83	107	5	85	0.32	39	21	40	30	85	DBd	6%	97	81	5%	9%	128	11%	75%	0.8	239
24	Proj	**616**	**77**	**14**	**70**	**7**	**250**	**17**	**11**	**257**	**324**	**413**	**101**	**91**	**105**	**9**	**81**	**0.48**	**39**	**21**	**40**	**29**	**91**		**6%**	**94**	**93**	**8%**	**9%**	**124**	**6%**	**76%**	**6.5**	**194**

Crow-Armstrong,Pete

Age: 22	Pos: CF		Health	A	LIMA Plan	D+
Bats: L	Ht: 6' 1"	Wt: 180	PT/Exp	D	Rand Var	-5
			Consist	F	MM	3503

0-1-.000 in 19 PA at CHC. Summoned for a little big league action in Sept. Plus athlete, glove carries bat to playing time. Aggressive approach with ct% concerns. Hit career high in HR, sacrificing contact for a steeper launch angle, increasing loft. Struggles with velocity up. Plus runner; should develop into a SB threat. (CB)

Yr	Tm	PA	R	HR	RBI	SB	BA	xHR	xSB	xBA	OBP	SLG	OPS+	vL+	vR+	bb%	ct%	Eye	G	L	F	h%	HctX	QBaB	Brl%	PX	xPX	HR/F	xHR/F	Spd	SBA%	SB%	RAR	BPX
19																																		
20																																		
21																																		
22																																		
23	CHC *	490	74	13	60	29	238	1	28	170	295	401	95	34	21	7	67	0.24	33	0	67	33	61	FFf	11%	108	104	0%	25%	135	41%	69%	-1.0	43
1st Half		251	38	7	37	18	251		17	239	301	416	98	0	0	7	71	0.24	44	20	36	33	0		0%	101	-21	0%		138	47%	70%	0.6	71
2nd Half		240	38	7	25	12	230	0	12	170	296	399	94	33	21	9	63	0.26	33	0	67	33	57	FFf	11%	120	104	0%	0%	133	35%	70%	-1.2	32
24	Proj	**315**	**49**	**7**	**38**	**14**	**245**	**7**	**19**	**214**	**307**	**401**	**97**	**96**	**97**	**8**	**66**	**0.26**	**38**	**20**	**42**	**35**	**92**		**6%**	**106**		**9%**	**9%**	**141**	**32%**	**65%**	**1.2**	**48**

Cruz,Oneil

Age: 25	Pos: SS		Health	F	LIMA Plan	C+
Bats: L	Ht: 6' 7"	Wt: 220	PT/Exp	D	Rand Var	+4
			Consist	F	MM	4425

Fractured fibula during home plate collision ended his season on April 9. This walking toolshed in the body of an NBA small forward showed hints of progress to contact, walk, flyball, vL, SB% rates over an admittedly minuscule sample. If he can marry towering power and speed to modest gains in those areas... UP: 25 HR/25 SB

Yr	Tm	PA	R	HR	RBI	SB	BA	xHR	xSB	xBA	OBP	SLG	OPS+	vL+	vR+	bb%	ct%	Eye	G	L	F	h%	HctX	QBaB	Brl%	PX	xPX	HR/F	xHR/F	Spd	SBA%	SB%	RAR	BPX
19	aa	134	14	1	17	3	269		3		349	409	105			11	70	0.42				38				89				125	11%	74%		48
20																																		
21	PIT *	301	48	13	38	14	269	1	10	280	320	482	110	0	248	7	71	0.27	60	20	20	33	234	AFa	40%	128	178	100%	100%	125	26%	80%	7.0	162
22	PIT *	592	71	22	77	17	214	17	19	227	278	395	95	75	119	8	65	0.25	49	17	34	28	109	ADf	16%	126	119	24%	24%	136	24%	61%	-16.5	69
23	PIT	40	7	1	4	3	250	1	2	197	375	375	102	177	87	18	75	0.88	44	8	48	30	24	BCf	4%	73	39	8%	8%	129	23%	100%	1.6	121
1st Half		40	7	1	4	3	250	1	2	197	375	375	103	178	87	18	75	0.88	44	8	48	30	24	BCf	4%	73	39	8%	8%	129	23%	100%	1.3	125
2nd Half																									0%									
24	Proj	**525**	**65**	**22**	**67**	**14**	**249**	**23**	**14**	**244**	**312**	**471**	**107**	**128**	**101**	**9**	**69**	**0.32**	**44**	**16**	**40**	**32**	**58**		**9%**	**139**	**71**	**17%**	**18%**	**137**	**18%**	**69%**	**16.9**	**84**

d'Arnaud,Travis

Age: 35	Pos: CA		Health	D	LIMA Plan	D+
Bats: R	Ht: 6' 2"	Wt: 210	PT/Exp	B	Rand Var	+5
			Consist	C	MM	3133

Concussion cost him a month early in the season. Despite his age, exit velocity, xPX confirm he can still sting the ball. Sharp dropoff in contact rate during 2nd half could indicate proximity to the edge of age-related cliff, although at least some of his overall offensive slide was due to plunging hit rate, which should normalize. Still a solid CA2 pick.

Yr	Tm	PA	R	HR	RBI	SB	BA	xHR	xSB	xBA	OBP	SLG	OPS+	vL+	vR+	bb%	ct%	Eye	G	L	F	h%	HctX	QBaB	Brl%	PX	xPX	HR/F	xHR/F	Spd	SBA%	SB%	RAR	BPX
19	3 TM	391	52	16	69	0	251	15	0	248	312	433	103	123	90	8	76	0.38	41	21	39	29	109	BBf	8%	97	100	15%	14%	70	1%	0%	2.2	74
20	ATL	184	19	9	34	1	321	10	1	259	386	533	122	66	136	9	70	0.32	43	27	30	42	129	ADb	11%	126	122	26%	29%	84	2%	100%	15.9	96
21	ATL	229	21	7	26	0	220	7	0	252	284	388	92	113	87	7	75	0.32	46	22	31	26	95	BDd	8%	106	80	14%	14%	66	0%	0%	-2.0	77
22	ATL	426	61	18	60	0	268	15	1	267	319	472	112	133	106	4	77	0.21	45	19	36	31	106	CCf	8%	130	103	16%	14%	89	0%	0%	15.2	176
23	ATL	292	31	11	39	0	225	11	1	247	288	397	93	106	90	7	75	0.31	42	20	37	26	108	BCf	9%	103	122	15%	15%	67	0%	0%	2.3	64
1st Half		137	18	7	21	0	279	7	1	258	358	492	116	136	110	10	80	0.56	46	16	37	30	124	BDd	11%	113	139	19%	19%	84	0%	0%	8.8	200
2nd Half		155	13	4	18	0	179	4	0	237	226	317	73	77	72	5	71	0.17	38	24	38	22	95	ACf	8%	93	107	10%	10%	63	0%	0%	-6.7	-39
24	Proj	**315**	**36**	**12**	**44**	**0**	**238**	**12**	**1**	**252**	**297**	**417**	**98**	**111**	**94**	**7**	**75**	**0.28**	**43**	**21**	**36**	**28**	**106**		**8%**	**109**	**109**	**15%**	**15%**	**67**	**0%**	**68%**	**5.9**	**92**

ALAIN DE LEONARDIS

Davis,Henry

Age: 24 Pos: RF | Bats: R Ht: 6'2" Wt: 210

Health	F	LIMA Plan	D+
PT/Exp	C	Rand Var	0
Consist	F	MM	3125

7-27-.213 with 3 SB in 255 PA at PIT. Catching prospect called up mid-June, strained hand cost him about a month. While sturdy walk rate, xPX hint at a potentially useful slugger, barrel rate, QBaB suggest he's still a few degrees from fully tapping into raw power. Lost CA eligibility hurts fantasy value—now a late-round OF dart throw.

Yr	Tm	PA	R	HR	RBI	SB	BA	xHR	xSB	xBA	OBP	SLG	OPS+	vL+	vR+	bb%	ct%	Eye	G	L	F	h%	HctX	QBaB	Brl%	PX	xPX	HR/F	xHR/F	Spd	SBA%	SB%	RAR	BPX	R$
19																																			
20																																			
21																																			
22	aa	124	12	2	12	2	169		2		224	293	73			7	72	0.25				21				95				91	16%	64%		17	-$3
23	PIT *	486	51	16	48	11	237	5	14	236	332	403	100	87	90	12	71	0.49	45	18	37	30	111	CCf	7%	102	106	12%	9%	94	16%	53%	10.9	75	$10
1st Half		265	28	9	29	9	257	1	11	286	353	438	108	146	90	13	73	0.54	58	27	15	32	134	CDb	7%	108	70	20%	20%	109	20%	61%	10.1	132	$12
2nd Half		221	23	7	20	2	215	4	4	213	309	363	91	73	89	12	70	0.45	41	16	43	27	103	CCf	7%	95	116	11%	8%	86	11%	31%	-1.2	21	$3
24	**Proj**	**490**	**50**	**17**	**48**	**7**	**231**	**15**	**12**	**238**	**322**	**401**	**99**	**109**	**94**	**10**	**71**	**0.39**	**44**	**20**	**37**	**29**	**115**		**7%**	**108**	**98**	**15%**	**13%**	**83**	**12%**	**48%**	**-0.8**	**47**	**$9**

Davis,J.D.

Age: 31 Pos: 3B | Bats: R Ht: 6'3" Wt: 218

Health	C	LIMA Plan	C+
PT/Exp	A	Rand Var	0
Consist	B	MM	3215

Finally played a full season as a lineup regular, posting decent-yet-unspectacular results. First half looked like he was on track to equal promise of 2019; big dips in line drive rate, h%, sagging exit velocity tanked 2nd half. Improved defense should help sustain PT, but groundball lean, ct% cap value. Buy the worm burners, hope for more loft.

Yr	Tm	PA	R	HR	RBI	SB	BA	xHR	xSB	xBA	OBP	SLG	OPS+	vL+	vR+	bb%	ct%	Eye	G	L	F	h%	HctX	QBaB	Brl%	PX	xPX	HR/F	xHR/F	Spd	SBA%	SB%	RAR	BPX	R$
19	NYM	453	65	22	57	3	307	23	4	278	369	527	124	127	122	8	76	0.39	47	23	30	36	110	ACa	11%	115	111	23%	24%	107	2%	100%	19.4	178	$17
20	NYM	229	26	6	19	0	247	8	1	229	371	389	101	101	100	14	71	0.55	56	20	24	32	102	BFc	9%	89	73	19%	25%	106	0%	0%	-6.9	56	$10
21	NYM *	255	23	7	27	1	274	6	1	234	363	445	111	93	121	12	60	0.35	39	31	30	43	76	BCb	12%	135	95	15%	18%	100	1%	100%	5.0	12	$5
22	2 NL	365	46	12	35	1	248	19	4	221	340	418	107	106	107	11	62	0.32	45	21	34	36	98	ACc	17%	134	117	18%	28%	125	2%	50%	0.1	52	$7
23	SF	544	61	18	69	1	248	18	3	240	325	413	101	98	101	10	68	0.34	53	20	28	33	98	ADb	10%	108	86	20%	20%	80	1%	100%	3.9	18	$12
1st Half		299	35	10	45	1	284	11	2	255	361	456	112	109	113	10	69	0.37	50	25	25	38	107	ADb	11%	112	93	22%	24%	85	1%	100%	10.7	43	$17
2nd Half		245	26	8	24	0	205	7	1	215	282	361	87	89	86	9	68	0.31	56	14	30	26	86	BDc	8%	103	78	17%	15%	81	0%	0%	-7.9	-4	$3
24	**Proj**	**455**	**50**	**15**	**48**	**1**	**247**	**17**	**3**	**231**	**332**	**410**	**102**	**99**	**103**	**10**	**66**	**0.33**	**49**	**21**	**30**	**34**	**94**		**12%**	**114**	**95**	**18%**	**22%**	**96**	**1%**	**77%**	**8.5**	**34**	**$12**

De La Cruz,Bryan

Age: 27 Pos: LF | Bats: R Ht: 6'2" Wt: 175

Health	A	LIMA Plan	B+
PT/Exp	A	Rand Var	0
Consist	A	MM	2235

Not the breakout some were hoping for after eye-popping expected power stats in 2022, but still posted good ROI. Looking past hit rate vagaries, substantial ct%, launch angle improvements in 2nd half reveal path for growth. Pairing those with established exit velocity pushes us to call last year's ... UP: 30 HR, and raise you a .270 BA

Yr	Tm	PA	R	HR	RBI	SB	BA	xHR	xSB	xBA	OBP	SLG	OPS+	vL+	vR+	bb%	ct%	Eye	G	L	F	h%	HctX	QBaB	Brl%	PX	xPX	HR/F	xHR/F	Spd	SBA%	SB%	RAR	BPX	R$
19	aa	290	40	4	21	6	256		8		311	366	94			7	75	0.32				33				64				133	17%	53%		26	$4
20																																			
21	MIA *	502	49	14	52	2	274	4	9	240	316	411	100	129	101	6	73	0.23	48	22	30	35	98	CCc	5%	84	75	11%	9%	141	7%	29%	-3.1	65	$13
22	MIA *	407	45	15	50	5	252	17	3	266	292	434	103	71	114	5	72	0.20	42	28	31	31	123	BCa	12%	126	146	17%	23%	88	6%	100%	4.5	97	$11
23	MIA	625	60	19	78	4	257	20	6	254	304	411	97	95	98	6	75	0.28	41	23	36	31	109	BCc	9%	95	111	12%	13%	90	4%	80%	6.8	71	$15
1st Half		331	35	9	43	3	276	8	5	257	323	421	102	104	101	7	72	0.27	45	26	28	36	108	ADa	7%	95	105	14%	13%	102	5%	75%	7.1	39	$17
2nd Half		294	25	10	35	1	236	11	2	250	282	400	92	88	94	6	79	0.30	37	20	43	26	109	CBc	11%	95	117	11%	12%	85	2%	100%	-2.2	114	$9
24	**Proj**	**595**	**62**	**20**	**69**	**5**	**256**	**21**	**7**	**256**	**301**	**417**	**99**	**89**	**102**	**6**	**75**	**0.26**	**42**	**24**	**34**	**31**	**112**		**10%**	**100**	**118**	**14%**	**14%**	**94**	**6%**	**66%**	**6.7**	**79**	**$19**

De La Cruz,Elly

Age: 22 Pos: SS 3B | Bats: B Ht: 6'2" Wt: 150

Health	A	LIMA Plan	B
PT/Exp	B	Rand Var	+1
Consist	C	MM	4535

13-44-.235 with 35 SB in 427 PA at CIN. Greatest thing since sliced bread? PRO: Flash-caliber speed, SBA% a recipe for monster SBs; exit velocity—especially ridiculous 119.2 max EV—provides spark for fireworks. CON: Abysmal ct% dampens BA outlook; extreme GB caps HR; needs work vL. Young, raw, and beats the hell out of pumpernickel loaf.

Yr	Tm	PA	R	HR	RBI	SB	BA	xHR	xSB	xBA	OBP	SLG	OPS+	vL+	vR+	bb%	ct%	Eye	G	L	F	h%	HctX	QBaB	Brl%	PX	xPX	HR/F	xHR/F	Spd	SBA%	SB%	RAR	BPX	R$
19																																			
20																																			
21																																			
22	aa	202	24	7	24	14	274		8		316	476	112			6	63	0.16				40				167				99	40%	86%		93	$10
23	CIN *	602	91	22	67	42	241	14	44	255	307	440	102	67	109	9	63	0.26	54	24	22	34	84	BFc	9%	133	79	25%	26%	170	44%	74%	9.5	107	$24
1st Half		278	45	12	35	16	267	2	19	280	330	502	114	30	142	9	65	0.27	61	22	17	36	79	BFb	5%	156	89	27%	18%	170	39%	68%	9.2	200	$24
2nd Half		324	46	10	32	26	219	12	25	235	291	387	92	77	98	9	62	0.25	51	25	23	32	84	AFd	10%	112	76	24%	29%	171	47%	79%	-5.0	25	$25
24	**Proj**	**560**	**77**	**20**	**64**	**39**	**243**	**20**	**32**	**249**	**304**	**443**	**102**	**62**	**119**	**8**	**63**	**0.23**	**51**	**24**	**25**	**35**	**82**		**8%**	**141**	**81**	**24%**	**24%**	**144**	**44%**	**79%**	**11.4**	**96**	**$30**

DeJong,Paul

Age: 30 Pos: SS | Bats: R Ht: 6'0" Wt: 205

Health	B	LIMA Plan	F
PT/Exp	B	Rand Var	-1
Consist	B	MM	2101

14-38-.207 in 400 PA at STL/TOR/SF. Missed the first three weeks of the season due to back issues, and one might reasonably wonder if those lingered throughout the season, especially given awful 2nd half. Then we put on our readers and see he's made a career of optimizing launch angle with little else to recommend. Hard pass.

Yr	Tm	PA	R	HR	RBI	SB	BA	xHR	xSB	xBA	OBP	SLG	OPS+	vL+	vR+	bb%	ct%	Eye	G	L	F	h%	HctX	QBaB	Brl%	PX	xPX	HR/F	xHR/F	Spd	SBA%	SB%	RAR	BPX	R$
19	STL	664	97	30	78	9	233	30	8	245	318	444	105	94	107	9	74	0.42	38	18	44	26	107	CAc	9%	114	123	15%	15%	99	9%	64%	-8.7	144	$17
20	STL	174	17	3	25	1	250	6	1	208	322	349	89	52	96	10	67	0.34	27	28	44	35	105	CAc	8%	68	152	6%	13%	86	2%	100%	-2.9	-116	$9
21	STL	402	44	19	45	4	197	18	3	221	284	390	93	82	96	9	71	0.34	38	16	47	22	100	DBf	11%	111	151	16%	15%	95	6%	80%	-12.0	81	$4
22	STL *	449	39	15	56	4	163	8	3	195	223	309	75	71	76	7	65	0.22	33	17	50	21	85	CAf	10%	108	102	9%	12%	52	10%	52%	-31.5	-72	-$1
23	3 TM *	437	46	15	46	4	211	12	5	214	255	360	84	86	82	5	66	0.18	40	19	41	28	82	DBf	7%	99	90	13%	12%	71	9%	50%	-12.6	-71	$4
1st Half		253	35	13	34	3	234	10	4	224	296	447	102	118	98	8	64	0.24	35	18	47	30	97	CAd	11%	140	133	20%	16%	84	9%	60%	0.6	43	$12
2nd Half		184	11	2	12	1	181	2	2	201	207	249	61	61	61	2	69	0.07	44	21	35	25	66	FCf	2%	50	44	5%	5%	69	10%	33%	-15.9	-204	-$7
24	**Proj**	**210**	**21**	**6**	**23**	**2**	**196**	**7**	**2**	**205**	**256**	**332**	**81**	**76**	**82**	**6**	**67**	**0.20**	**37**	**19**	**44**	**25**	**86**		**8%**	**90**	**102**	**11%**	**11%**	**74**	**8%**	**55%**	**-7.9**	**-57**	**$3**

Delay,Jason

Age: 29 Pos: CA | Bats: R Ht: 5'11" Wt: 200

Health	A	LIMA Plan	D
PT/Exp	F	Rand Var	-5
Consist	C	MM	1211

1-18-.251 in 187 PA at PIT. Unless you're desperate—and we mean, like, drinking your own urine after a plane crash in the Andes and contemplating cannibalism desperate—to play an actual live human as your 2nd CA who might hit his only HR or steal his only base all year when you happen to play him, don't delay here. We repeat: Do not Delay.

Yr	Tm	PA	R	HR	RBI	SB	BA	xHR	xSB	xBA	OBP	SLG	OPS+	vL+	vR+	bb%	ct%	Eye	G	L	F	h%	HctX	QBaB	Brl%	PX	xPX	HR/F	xHR/F	Spd	SBA%	SB%	RAR	BPX	R$
19	aa	243	20	7	34	1	219		1		258	369	87			5	71	0.18				28				89				92	2%	100%		-19	$0
20																																			
21	a/a	97	5	1	5	0	135		0		160	212	51			3	60	0.07				21				63				93	0%	0%		-281	-$5
22	PIT *	261	23	1	16	1	195	1	2	197	238	257	70	87	67	5	71	0.20	42	20	38	27	87	DBd	2%	53	57	3%	3%	99	6%	23%	-13.6	-107	-$4
23	PIT *	217	23	1	21	1	255	2	2	243	312	353	91	92	90	7	74	0.31	43	25	32	34	60	FCc	3%	75	65	3%	5%	100	2%	100%	2.3	7	$1
1st Half		109	10	1	10	0	268	2	1	239	327	381	97	117	86	7	71	0.25	41	26	33	37	60	FCb	4%	81	76	4%	9%	116	0%	0%	1.8	0	-$6
2nd Half		108	13	0	11	1	242	0	1	246	306	324	85	64	96	8	76	0.39	46	23	31	32	58	FCf	2%	69	51	0%	0%	85	4%	100%	-0.6	18	-$3
24	**Proj**	**175**	**17**	**1**	**16**	**1**	**228**	**1**	**2**	**224**	**287**	**312**	**82**	**83**	**81**	**6**	**73**	**0.25**	**43**	**23**	**34**	**31**	**70**		**2%**	**65**	**60**	**2%**	**3%**	**91**	**3%**	**64%**	**-2.5**	**-35**	**$2**

Devers,Rafael

Age: 27 Pos: 3B | Bats: L Ht: 6'0" Wt: 240

Health	A	LIMA Plan	D+
PT/Exp	A	Rand Var	+1
Consist	A	MM	4155

Another very solid year from the perennial early-round 3B stalwart. If we're going to pick nits, didn't dominate vR quite as much and got even slower, which when coupled with already poor defense might hasten his move to DH at a relatively early age. Has consistently under-slammed xHR which might one day mean... UP: 40 HR

Yr	Tm	PA	R	HR	RBI	SB	BA	xHR	xSB	xBA	OBP	SLG	OPS+	vL+	vR+	bb%	ct%	Eye	G	L	F	h%	HctX	QBaB	Brl%	PX	xPX	HR/F	xHR/F	Spd	SBA%	SB%	RAR	BPX	R$
19	BOS	702	129	32	115	8	311	32	8	298	361	555	127	103	137	7	82	0.40	44	21	34	34	107	ACc	9%	126	93	18%	18%	84	10%	50%	36.5	252	$34
20	BOS	248	32	11	43	0	263	13	0	255	310	483	105	80	118	5	71	0.19	45	20	35	32	120	ACc	12%	135	78	19%	23%	75	0%	0%	1.2	108	$20
21	BOS	664	101	38	113	5	279	41	3	278	352	538	122	102	135	9	76	0.43	41	20	38	31	124	ACd	15%	148	124	22%	24%	63	6%	50%	38.9	235	$30
22	BOS	614	84	27	88	3	295	29	2	285	358	521	125	103	132	8	79	0.44	42	20	37	33	124	ACf	12%	142	115	16%	17%	68	3%	75%	41.1	241	$29
23	BOS	656	90	33	100	5	271	37	4	274	351	500	116	111	118	9	78	0.49	43	18	39	29	132	ACf	13%	129	121	18%	21%	59	4%	83%	37.8	196	$25
1st Half		350	46	20	66	1	256	21	2	272	326	505	114	119	111	9	77	0.42	40	18	42	27	126	ACf	13%	140	134	20%	21%	53	3%	50%	12.1	196	$27
2nd Half		306	44	13	34	4	288	16	3	275	379	494	118	101	125	11	80	0.59	46	18	36	32	139	ACf	12%	116	106	17%	21%	76	5%	100%	17.8	207	$22
24	**Proj**	**630**	**91**	**31**	**96**	**4**	**282**	**34**	**4**	**277**	**356**	**512**	**119**	**104**	**125**	**9**	**78**	**0.46**	**43**	**19**	**38**	**31**	**128**		**13%**	**132**	**115**	**18%**	**20%**	**67**	**3%**	**69%**	**40.1**	**215**	**$30**

AIN DE LEONARDIS

Díaz,Aledmys

Age: 33	Pos: 3B SS		Health	D	LIMA Plan	D+
Bats: R	Ht: 6' 1"	Wt: 195	PT/Exp	B	Rand Var	+2
			Consist	B	MM	1233

You might have expected a PT bump in moving to talent-starved OAK, but it didn't happen. Maybe they realized what we see—there's just no life in this bat. Makes enough ct%, but doesn't hit balls hard or square them up, and HOU-to-OAK move predictably tanked his HR/F. Position eligibility used to be part of his appeal, but no longer.

Yr	Tm	PA	R	HR	RBI	SB	BA	xHR	xSB	xBA	OBP	SLG	OPS+	vL+	vR+	bb%	ct%	Eye	G	L	F	h%	HctX	QBaB	Brl%	PX	xPX	HR/F	xHR/F	Spd	SBA%	SB%	RAR	BPX
19	HOU *	270	37	9	40	2	253	7	2	265	334	431	106	105	117	10	84	0.76	46	17	37	27	94	CCf	6%	87	70	13%	10%	109	3%	100%	-1.9	226
20	HOU	59	8	3	6	0	241	1	0	287	254	483	98	59	118	2	79	0.08	43	22	35	26	91	CCd	2%	136	77	19%	6%	89	0%	0%	-1.2	232
21	HOU	319	28	8	45	0	259	7	0	258	317	405	99	107	95	5	79	0.26	42	24	34	30	111	CCd	6%	90	89	10%	9%	76	1%	0%	-8.7	88
22	HOU	327	35	12	38	1	243	8	1	265	287	403	98	107	94	6	83	0.34	40	23	37	26	104	DCf	7%	93	78	13%	9%	84	3%	50%	-7.3	148
23	OAK	344	25	4	24	1	229	4	3	242	280	337	84	86	82	5	79	0.26	47	19	34	28	90	CCf	3%	72	70	5%	5%	96	1%	100%	-11.2	54
1st Half		208	15	2	13	1	204	2	1	218	260	283	74	74	74	5	79	0.24	52	15	33	25	90	CDd	3%	53	70	4%	4%	86	2%	100%	-14.2	-21
2nd Half		136	10	2	11	0	266	2	1	273	311	419	99	99	98	5	80	0.28	41	24	36	32	89	CCf	2%	100	71	6%	6%	107	0%	0%	-0.6	157
24	Proj	350	33	5	37	1	245	7	2	250	297	362	90	92	89	6	81	0.31	43	21	35	29	97		4%	74	76	6%	7%	92	2%	67%	-2.9	116

Díaz,Elias

Age: 33	Pos: CA		Health	A	LIMA Plan	D+
Bats: R	Ht: 6' 1"	Wt: 223	PT/Exp	A	Rand Var	-5
			Consist	C	MM	2113

By R$, this looks like your classic mid-30s catcher breakout. But it was really just a PA surge coupled with a h% spike. BPX trend highlights the state of the underlying skills, and the direction they're trending. Throw in second-half collapse, of both R$ and BPX, and we see what RandVar is telling us: bidding on a repeat is a trap to be avoided.

Yr	Tm	PA	R	HR	RBI	SB	BA	xHR	xSB	xBA	OBP	SLG	OPS+	vL+	vR+	bb%	ct%	Eye	G	L	F	h%	HctX	QBaB	Brl%	PX	xPX	HR/F	xHR/F	Spd	SBA%	SB%	RAR	BPX
19	PIT *	362	35	2	31	0	249	4	-	235	299	317	85	90	80	7	81	0.38	47	21	31	30	88	CDf	2%	43	46	3%	5%	73	0%	0%	-10.9	-11
20	COL	73	4	2	9	0	235	2	0	235	288	353	85	87	83	7	78	0.33	40	25	36	27	125	CCf	11%	64	119	11%	11%	71	0%	0%	-1.3	0
21	COL	371	52	18	44	0	246	12	0	272	310	464	106	104	107	8	82	0.50	41	19	40	25	118	CBf	8%	115	104	16%	11%	73	0%	0%	9.6	235
22	COL	381	29	9	51	0	228	7	1	233	281	368	92	105	83	7	77	0.30	48	16	36	27	105	CCf	6%	92	99	9%	7%	91	1%	0%	-2.8	79
23	COL	526	48	14	72	1	267	13	4	236	316	409	99	79	106	6	76	0.29	47	17	36	33	117	CCc	6%	88	90	10%	10%	89	1%	100%	15.7	54
1st Half		288	27	9	45	0	284	9	2	247	337	452	108	97	111	8	77	0.37	46	17	36	34	124	CCd	8%	100	105	12%	12%	90	0%	0%	13.8	121
2nd Half		238	21	5	27	1	249	4	2	218	290	360	88	61	99	5	74	0.20	48	17	36	32	109	CCc	4%	72	71	8%	7%	84	2%	100%	-0.3	-36
24	Proj	420	37	10	50	1	243	9	2	234	294	377	92	86	95	7	77	0.31	46	18	36	29	112		6%	83	91	9%	8%	78	1%	65%	4.1	67

Diaz,Jordan

Age: 23	Pos: 3B 2B		Health	A	LIMA Plan	D+
Bats: R	Ht: 5' 10"	Wt: 175	PT/Exp	C	Rand Var	0
			Consist	B	MM	3023

10-37-.221 in 293 PA at OAK. PRO: There's a little life in his bat (xHR/F, Brl%, exit velocity). CON: Marginal ct% with hefty GB% shrinks the denominator for "hard-hit balls in the air"; xBA says the BA peril is real. Multi-position eligibility makes it easy to fit him into your lineup, but that's like saying "At least I have a short drive to my dentist."

Yr	Tm	PA	R	HR	RBI	SB	BA	xHR	xSB	xBA	OBP	SLG	OPS+	vL+	vR+	bb%	ct%	Eye	G	L	F	h%	HctX	QBaB	Brl%	PX	xPX	HR/F	xHR/F	Spd	SBA%	SB%	RAR	BPX
19																																		
20																																		
21																																		
22	OAK *	559	45	11	53	0	260	0	2	227	285	379	94	85	89	3	82	0.20	67	10	24	30	51	CFd		79	57	0%	0%	102	0%	0%	-5.8	110
23	OAK *	455	31	13	45	0	226	8	3	225	266	364	86	81	91	5	76	0.22	53	17	30	27	92	BFd	6%	84	77	16%	13%	86	2%	0%	-8.9	32
1st Half		241	17	7	26	0	233	2	2	229	262	376	87	64	117	4	77	0.17	42	18	40	27	88	CCd	6%	86	71	17%	9%	99	4%	0%	-8.8	64
2nd Half		214	14	6	19	0	218	6	1	216	276	350	85	88	82	7	74	0.27	57	17	26	26	92	BFf	7%	81	80	16%	16%	90	0%	0%	-7.8	14
24	Proj	420	31	16	40	0	239	7	2	240	282	410	95	86	101	5	77	0.22	51	17	32	27	90		6%	101	76	16%	8%	85	1%	10%	-0.8	65

Diaz,Yainer

Age: 25	Pos: CA DH		Health	A	LIMA Plan	B+
Bats: R	Ht: 6' 0"	Wt: 195	PT/Exp	B	Rand Var	0
			Consist	D	MM	4353

Bat-first catcher hit his way out of the backup spot and into a semi-regular DH/1B by summer. And with good reason: behold that 2nd half. "Swing at everything" isn't a liability when you're spraying LDs everywhere. 2nd half xHR caution: he's not a pure power play, but full-season line is well-supported and sets him as a real asset in the CA pool.

Yr	Tm	PA	R	HR	RBI	SB	BA	xHR	xSB	xBA	OBP	SLG	OPS+	vL+	vR+	bb%	ct%	Eye	G	L	F	h%	HctX	QBaB	Brl%	PX	xPX	HR/F	xHR/F	Spd	SBA%	SB%	RAR	BPX
19																																		
20																																		
21																																		
22	HOU *	476	48	16	62	1	240	1	3	199	276	400	96	0	88	5	78	0.23	50	0	50	27	114	AAf	17%	96	110	0%	33%	113	1%	100%	2.4	124
23	HOU	377	51	23	60	0	282	23	1	289	308	538	115	84	127	3	79	0.15	43	20	37	30	124	BCc	12%	141	134	22%	22%	80	0%	0%	24.7	218
1st Half		161	17	7	17	0	268	11	1	260	280	477	104	53	119	2	80	0.10	42	16	42	30	113	ACc	14%	122	120	13%	21%	93	0%	0%	4.9	179
2nd Half		216	34	16	43	0	292	11	1	310	329	584	123	100	134	4	79	0.19	44	24	32	30	131	BCc	11%	157	145	31%	21%	80	0%	0%	17.6	264
24	Proj	420	52	25	63	0	265	25	2	282	299	510	111	82	122	4	79	0.19	43	20	36	28	124		12%	134	135	22%	22%	85	0%	100%	21.5	187

Díaz,Yandy

Age: 32	Pos: 1B		Health	B	LIMA Plan	B+
Bats: R	Ht: 6' 2"	Wt: 215	PT/Exp	A	Rand Var	-5
			Consist	D	MM	2145

Owner of one of the game's best Eye ratios cashed it in in favor of a more aggressive approach, to great effect. Seein HctX climb while ct% shrunk tells us he was finding more pitches to drive: Brl%, "little c" in QBaB provide receipts. xHR and xBA both say he overachieved a bit in 2023, but a 2022-23 mashup is very attainable.

Yr	Tm	PA	R	HR	RBI	SB	BA	xHR	xSB	xBA	OBP	SLG	OPS+	vL+	vR+	bb%	ct%	Eye	G	L	F	h%	HctX	QBaB	Brl%	PX	xPX	HR/F	xHR/F	Spd	SBA%	SB%	RAR	BPX
19	TAM	347	53	14	38	2	267	13	3	276	340	476	113	137	101	10	80	0.57	51	17	32	29	118	AFc	10%	108	115	18%	16%	102	5%	50%	5.7	222
20	TAM	138	16	2	11	0	307	1	1	261	428	386	108	100	111	17	85	1.35	66	23	11	35	96	CFf	2%	41	22	18%	9%	104	0%	0%	2.0	160
21	TAM	541	62	13	64	1	256	13	4	242	353	387	102	110	95	13	82	0.81	52	16	32	29	116	BDf	7%	73	79	11%	11%	113	1%	50%	1.0	181
22	TAM	558	71	9	57	3	296	11	5	270	401	423	117	125	114	14	87	1.30	50	19	32	32	135	ADd	5%	82	86	7%	8%	94	3%	50%	24.7	252
23	TAM	600	95	22	78	0	330	20	6	282	410	522	127	148	120	11	82	0.69	52	19	29	37	140	ADc	9%	109	92	18%	16%	97	1%	0%	57.5	243
1st Half		315	55	12	39	0	318	10	3	286	403	511	125	129	124	12	82	0.72	51	21	28	35	135	ADc	9%	108	88	19%	16%	93	0%	0%	23.5	236
2nd Half		285	40	10	39	0	343	9	3	277	418	534	129	166	116	10	82	0.66	53	18	29	39	145	AFd	10%	109	96	17%	15%	102	1%	0%	26.1	250
24	Proj	595	84	18	72	1	302	16	6	271	392	466	118	131	112	12	83	0.83	52	19	29	33	132		8%	94	87	14%	13%	100	2%	39%	36.0	231

Domínguez,Jasson

Age: 21	Pos: CF		Health	A	LIMA Plan	D+
Bats: B	Ht: 5' 10"	Wt: 190	PT/Exp	C	Rand Var	0
			Consist	F	MM	3421

4-7-.258 with 1 SB in 33 PA at NYY. Suffered right elbow tear, requiring Tommy John surgery in Sept and will not be recovered to start season. Better from LH side, he works counts and gets on base at high rate. Sells out for a power-over-hit profile and is an above average runner. SB plays up due to elite reactions. (CB)

Yr	Tm	PA	R	HR	RBI	SB	BA	xHR	xSB	xBA	OBP	SLG	OPS+	vL+	vR+	bb%	ct%	Eye	G	L	F	h%	HctX	QBaB	Brl%	PX	xPX	HR/F	xHR/F	Spd	SBA%	SB%	RAR	BPX
19																																		
20																																		
21																																		
22	aa																																	
23	NYY *	555	76	16	67	33	239	2	25	229	332	393	99	39	161	12	68	0.43	48	17	35	32	120	BFf	17%	101	207	50%	25%	94	29%	79%	10.3	25
1st Half		300	44	8	31	16	186		13	204	311	318	86	0	0	15	62	0.48	44	20	36	26	0		0%	89	-21	0%		114	25%	84%	-5.5	-43
2nd Half		257	35	8	38	17	304	2	13	260	368	488	116	38	160	9	74	0.39	48	17	35	38	132	BFf	17%	115	207	50%	25%	89	31%	76%	16.7	129
24	Proj	245	35	7	32	14	257	8	11	235	342	422	105	79	112	11	70	0.42	48	17	35	34	119		11%	107	186	14%	15%	96	28%	79%	7.7	60

Donaldson,Josh

Age: 38	Pos: 3B		Health	F	LIMA Plan	D+
Bats: R	Ht: 6' 1"	Wt: 210	PT/Exp	B	Rand Var	+5
			Consist	C	MM	4011

Hamstring injury cost him most of April/May, then long-troublesome calf another month across July/August. Landed in MIL via waivers in Sept and showed some signs of life... well, as much as you can while posting what might be the lowest h% we've ever seen in these pages. Best to consider that late power a dead cat bounce.

Yr	Tm	PA	R	HR	RBI	SB	BA	xHR	xSB	xBA	OBP	SLG	OPS+	vL+	vR+	bb%	ct%	Eye	G	L	F	h%	HctX	QBaB	Brl%	PX	xPX	HR/F	xHR/F	Spd	SBA%	SB%	RAR	BPX
19	ATL	659	96	37	94	4	259	36	3	270	379	521	125	117	126	15	72	0.65	42	21	36	29	118	ACd	16%	145	124	26%	25%	79	3%	67%	19.5	219
20	MIN	102	14	6	11	0	222	5	0	226	373	469	112	82	118	18	70	0.75	55	10	34	24	98	ADf	7%	134	98	30%	25%	85	0%	0%	0.7	208
21	MIN	543	73	26	72	0	247	31	0	253	352	475	114	128	107	14	75	0.65	43	17	40	27	123	ABd	17%	132	120	19%	22%	78	0%	0%	17.5	223
22	NYY	546	59	15	62	2	222	17	2	225	308	374	97	99	96	10	69	0.36	43	18	39	29	101	BCf	10%	114	109	12%	13%	78	3%	50%	-10.5	45
23	2 TM *	228	24	15	29	0	156	12	0	223	260	414	92	128	76	12	71	0.48	48	9	44	13	113	ACf	16%	146	141	25%	24%	56	0%	0%	-4.2	154
1st Half		108	14	9	14	0	152	8	0	233	221	439	90	116	77	8	69	0.29	50	5	45	10	121	ACf	25%	161	162	32%	32%	65	0%	0%	-4.1	157
2nd Half		120	10	6	15	0	161	4	0	215	295	389	92	135	75	16	72	0.68	46	11	43	15	106	ACf	9%	133	123	19%	15%	67	0%	0%	-2.3	171
24	Proj	245	28	13	31	0	209	13	1	233	310	433	102	124	93	13	71	0.50	46	13	41	23	111		14%	134	126	21%	20%	72	1%	53%	3.2	149

RAY MURPHY

Donovan,Brendan

Age: 27	Pos: 2B LF		Health	C	LIMA Plan	C+
Bats: L	Ht: 6' 1"	Wt: 195	PT/Exp	A	Rand Var	0
			Consist	B	MM	1243

Spring training focus on getting to hard contact yielded gains in Brl%, HctX and xPX. June elbow injury scuttled those plans and resulted in season-ending surgery. Positional versatility, plate skills are additional positives, but struggles vLHP, lots of GB and minimal SB appeal lessen the "next step" potential. Assuming health, could be a useful piece.

Yr	Tm	PA	R	HR	RBI	SB	BA	xHR	xSB	xBA	OBP	SLG	OPS+	vL+	vR+	bb%	ct%	Eye	G	L	F	h%	HctX	QBaB	Brl%	PX	xPX	HR/F	xHR/F	Spd	SBA%	SB%	RAR	BPX	R$
19	aaa																																		
20																																			
21	a/a	321	38	6	35	8	243		8		303	350	90			8	76	0.35				30				66				93	21%	49%		4	$7
22	STL *	530	71	6	49	2	274	6	5	266	366	368	104	105	110	12	82	0.82	53	24	24	32	95	CFb	3%	64	72	7%	8%	102	3%	40%	8.6	128	$14
23	STL	371	48	11	34	5	284	9	8	273	365	422	107	77	114	9	84	0.62	46	23	30	31	120	CCc	6%	70	110	13%	11%	111	5%	83%	12.8	157	$10
1st Half		293	37	9	26	4	280	7	5	270	372	413	108	81	113	11	83	0.71	46	23	31	31	117	CCb	7%	68	109	14%	11%	100	5%	80%	8.6	146	$14
2nd Half		78	11	2	8	1	301	2	2	284	338	452	107	62	116	4	85	0.27	48	23	29	33	132	BDc	3%	77	112	11%	11%	126	5%	100%	3.0	175	-$2
24	Proj	420	57	11	42	5	279	9	8	271	358	419	106	80	112	9	82	0.55	48	23	29	31	113		4%	77	95	12%	10%	114	6%	64%	14.8	127	$13

Doyle,Brenton

Age: 26	Pos: CF		Health	A	LIMA Plan	C+
Bats: R	Ht: 6' 3"	Wt: 200	PT/Exp	B	Rand Var	0
			Consist	A	MM	2505

10-48-.203 with 22 SB in 431 PA at COL. A study in contrasts: Power and speed metrics justify the HR/SB appeal ... but that ct% and xBA point to a BA black hole. Solid Brl% for a debut, but neither exit velocity nor launch angle excites on their own. The kicker? Defensive prowess could lead to a PA total that hurts more than helps.

Yr	Tm	PA	R	HR	RBI	SB	BA	xHR	xSB	xBA	OBP	SLG	OPS+	vL+	vR+	bb%	ct%	Eye	G	L	F	h%	HctX	QBaB	Brl%	PX	xPX	HR/F	xHR/F	Spd	SBA%	SB%	RAR	BPX	R$
19																																			
20																																			
21																																			
22	a/a	522	47	16	44	13	211		10		234	360	84			3	64	0.08				30				109				116	19%	79%		-45	$8
23	COL *	484	55	13	52	23	208	13	22	211	252	357	83	79	82	5	62	0.15	47	18	35	30	92	DCd	9%	104	119	12%	16%	156	32%	82%	-12.5	-32	$9
1st Half		236	32	9	26	13	221	6	13	209	276	383	90	68	96	7	61	0.20	47	17	36	31	98	DDd	11%	107	114	16%	16%	157	32%	81%	-3.0	-18	$11
2nd Half		248	23	4	26	10	197	7	9	212	236	333	77	88	72	4	62	0.11	47	19	34	30	88	DCd	7%	101	124	9%	15%	139	32%	83%	-11.0	-68	$4
24	Proj	490	51	12	49	19	219	16	18	206	258	354	84	82	85	4	63	0.12	47	18	35	32	92		9%	95	120	12%	16%	120	25%	82%	-12.3	-46	$14

Drury,Brandon

Age: 31	Pos: 2B 1B		Health	B	LIMA Plan	B
Bats: R	Ht: 6' 2"	Wt: 230	PT/Exp	A	Rand Var	-3
			Consist	C	MM	4035

Sneaky good. Given full-time AB over the past two seasons (spread over three orgs, no less!), he's responded with remarkable consistency: above-average power, passable BA, mid-500s PA at multiple positions. His repeated trick of out-pacing xHR is curious to say the least, but no reason to think he can't play it back.

Yr	Tm	PA	R	HR	RBI	SB	BA	xHR	xSB	xBA	OBP	SLG	OPS+	vL+	vR+	bb%	ct%	Eye	G	L	F	h%	HctX	QBaB	Brl%	PX	xPX	HR/F	xHR/F	Spd	SBA%	SB%	RAR	BPX	R$
19	TOR	447	43	15	41	0	218	18	0	248	262	380	89	86	90	6	73	0.22	42	24	34	26	97	CCd	9%	93	99	14%	17%	73	1%	0%	-20.0	4	$2
20	TOR	49	3	0	1	0	152	1	0	216	184	174	47	74	21	4	80	0.22	34	26	39	19	69	FAd	5%	17	72	0%	7%	92	0%	0%	-5.5	-104	-$5
21	NYM *	313	24	9	33	0	204	2	0	210	240	345	80	120	98	5	70	0.16	52	16	32	26	97	BCf	6%	93	95	20%	10%	66	0%	0%	-16.5	-54	-$1
22	2 NL	568	87	28	87	2	263	20	3	271	320	492	115	134	107	7	76	0.30	41	20	39	30	116	CCd	11%	145	120	18%	13%	85	4%	40%	23.2	207	$23
23	LAA	523	61	26	83	0	262	20	4	264	306	497	109	108	110	5	72	0.18	42	19	38	31	104	BCd	11%	144	113	19%	15%	97	2%	0%	21.3	157	$16
1st Half		307	36	14	45	0	277	12	4	258	322	500	113	92	119	5	72	0.20	42	19	39	34	96	BCc	12%	137	103	18%	15%	115	3%	0%	11.9	154	$19
2nd Half		216	25	12	38	0	241	8	1	272	282	493	105	128	96	4	72	0.16	43	20	38	27	116	BCf	10%	152	126	21%	14%	74	0%	0%	3.7	157	$11
24	Proj	560	69	27	85	1	261	20	2	259	306	481	108	117	104	5	73	0.20	43	19	37	31	107		10%	134	113	19%	14%	70	2%	24%	19.0	122	$22

Dubón,Mauricio

Age: 29	Pos: 2B CF		Health	A	LIMA Plan	C+
Bats: R	Ht: 6' 0"	Wt: 173	PT/Exp	A	Rand Var	-1
			Consist	D	MM	1333

Rode a Dusty Fascination to career-best PA and MLB R$. Elite contact has its appeal (see BA column), but in this case it's mostly empty. Best employed against LHP, the power is well below average, and despite plus Spd, pre-2023 efficiency has been a problem. Remember that accumulators depend entirely on who is filling out the lineup card.

Yr	Tm	PA	R	HR	RBI	SB	BA	xHR	xSB	xBA	OBP	SLG	OPS+	vL+	vR+	bb%	ct%	Eye	G	L	F	h%	HctX	QBaB	Brl%	PX	xPX	HR/F	xHR/F	Spd	SBA%	SB%	RAR	BPX	R$
19	2 NL *	636	76	17	53	11	260	2	13	287	291	393	95	115	97	4	84	0.28	48	27	26	29	91	DCb	2%	68	74	18%	9%	118	15%	51%	-9.9	133	$15
20	SF	176	21	4	19	2	274	5	6	231	337	389	96	116	88	9	77	0.42	34	26	40	33	96	DBd	4%	61	108	8%	10%	165	10%	40%	-1.8	104	$12
21	SF *	453	47	10	42	8	248	5	8	240	294	368	91	99	84	6	79	0.31	40	22	38	29	90	DCd	4%	71	97	10%	10%	111	13%	62%	-11.1	77	$10
22	2 TM	265	31	5	24	2	214	3	4	231	252	313	80	107	64	5	88	0.43	39	17	45	23	95	FBf	2%	58	78	5%	3%	112	10%	40%	-10.6	145	$1
23	HOU	492	76	10	46	7	278	7	12	272	309	411	98	116	93	4	85	0.27	45	21	34	31	88	CCd	5%	75	72	7%	5%	139	8%	78%	9.1	182	$14
1st Half		270	44	4	19	5	288	3	6	287	315	412	100	120	94	4	87	0.30	47	22	30	32	85	DDd	5%	74	63	6%	4%	129	8%	100%	5.8	200	$12
2nd Half		222	32	6	27	2	267	4	6	253	302	410	96	112	90	4	82	0.24	43	19	39	30	93	CCd	4%	76	83	9%	6%	151	8%	50%	0.9	164	$10
24	Proj	350	47	6	34	4	255	6	8	248	292	366	90	106	83	5	84	0.31	42	20	38	29	92		4%	63	81	6%	6%	126	9%	58%	-1.1	149	$11

Duran,Ezequiel

Age: 25	Pos: SS LF 3B DH		Health	A	LIMA Plan	C
Bats: R	Ht: 5' 11"	Wt: 185	PT/Exp	B	Rand Var	-2
			Consist	C	MM	2313

First full season looks good on surface, but warning signs abound. Was clearly over his head early on, as h%, xHR/F exceeded his MiLB track record. The 2nd half? Well, let's just say the league adjusted. Positional utility should give him plenty of real-life chances to respond, but poor Eye is among the challenges to overcome. Your move, Zeke.

Yr	Tm	PA	R	HR	RBI	SB	BA	xHR	xSB	xBA	OBP	SLG	OPS+	vL+	vR+	bb%	ct%	Eye	G	L	F	h%	HctX	QBaB	Brl%	PX	xPX	HR/F	xHR/F	Spd	SBA%	SB%	RAR	BPX	R$
19																																			
20																																			
21																																			
22	TEX *	561	58	15	61	13	238	4	13	246	273	395	95	101	88	5	73	0.18	51	16	33	30	77	DCf	5%	113	63	10%	8%	106	22%	59%	-10.3	86	$15
23	TEX	439	55	14	46	8	276	17	12	241	324	443	105	113	101	5	70	0.19	40	22	38	36	96	BCd	9%	108	103	13%	15%	125	12%	67%	13.2	64	$13
1st Half		241	35	12	34	4	308	14	6	268	349	537	121	156	107	4	72	0.16	39	23	38	38	118	ACc	13%	141	131	19%	23%	124	12%	57%	13.9	171	$19
2nd Half		198	20	2	12	4	235	3	5	205	294	324	84	61	93	7	69	0.23	41	20	39	33	69	CCf	3%	65	67	4%	6%	125	11%	80%	-5.9	-71	$0
24	Proj	420	48	11	42	9	255	11	11	234	300	402	96	100	95	5	71	0.19	44	19	36	33	84		6%	99	81	10%	11%	108	15%	65%	1.9	52	$14

Duran,Jarren

Age: 27	Pos: CF LF		Health	B	LIMA Plan	B
Bats: L	Ht: 6' 2"	Wt: 212	PT/Exp	B	Rand Var	-4
			Consist	C	MM	3535

8-40-.295 with 24 SB in 361 PA at BOS. It wasn't ONLY the new SB rules. Made both more and better contact, especially in the 2nd half, though Aug toe injury and surgery wiped out final six weeks. His skill set, experience and opportunity seem to have consolidated. Assuming health, the next step could look like ... UP: 15 HR, 40 SB

Yr	Tm	PA	R	HR	RBI	SB	BA	xHR	xSB	xBA	OBP	SLG	OPS+	vL+	vR+	bb%	ct%	Eye	G	L	F	h%	HctX	QBaB	Brl%	PX	xPX	HR/F	xHR/F	Spd	SBA%	SB%	RAR	BPX	R$
19	aa	340	37	1	17	25	247		21		291	323	85			6	73	0.23				34				46				149	42%	75%		-48	$10
20																																			
21	BOS *	379	52	13	37	14	221	1	11	234	276	395	92	60	86	7	67	0.23	49	19	31	29	109	CDf	4%	110	105	10%	5%	125	25%	76%	-9.1	35	$10
22	BOS *	518	54	9	41	18	226	6	14	230	271	369	91	63	98	6	69	0.20	51	15	34	31	83	CDd	8%	106	92	7%	13%	119	23%	79%	-8.0	38	$12
23	BOS *	408	51	9	44	25	281	9	17	272	334	468	109	101	115	7	72	0.29	41	26	33	37	103	BCc	5%	130	89	10%	11%	103	30%	93%	22.0	146	$16
1st Half		280	30	5	33	16	282	6	10	265	339	458	109	84	120	8	69	0.28	42	27	31	39	92	BDc	6%	135	83	9%	13%	93	27%	94%	13.6	107	$18
2nd Half		128	21	4	11	9	277	2	7	287	328	487	110	144	106	6	80	0.33	40	24	36	32	123	BCd	4%	121	98	12%	6%	125	37%	90%	6.3	243	$7
24	Proj	560	72	12	50	32	267	12	24	254	321	428	103	85	106	7	74	0.27	46	21	34	34	101		6%	105	94	9%	9%	117	29%	85%	15.6	104	$27

Duvall,Adam

Age: 35	Pos: CF RF		Health	F	LIMA Plan	C+
Bats: R	Ht: 6' 1"	Wt: 215	PT/Exp	B	Rand Var	0
			Consist	C	MM	5223

21-58-.247 with 4 SB in 353 PA at BOS. Mashed 4 HR/13 RBI in first eight games; missed two months with a broken wrist; picked up right where he left off in June. An amazing per-PA power threat, his absurd FB% assures both below-average BA (ct%) and lofty HR totals (Brl%; HR/F). Welcome to Home Runs and Health Grade Roulette. Good luck.

Yr	Tm	PA	R	HR	RBI	SB	BA	xHR	xSB	xBA	OBP	SLG	OPS+	vL+	vR+	bb%	ct%	Eye	G	L	F	h%	HctX	QBaB	Brl%	PX	xPX	HR/F	xHR/F	Spd	SBA%	SB%	RAR	BPX	R$
19	ATL *	534	72	33	89	1	223	12	2	221	284	479	106	157	104	8	70	0.29	27	12	60	25	109	AAf	16%	138	182	20%	24%	104	1%	100%	2.9	148	$12
20	ATL	209	34	16	33	0	237	16	0	251	301	532	111	117	108	7	72	0.28	29	17	54	24	89	CAf	14%	162	136	22%	22%	94	0%	0%	2.6	244	$18
21	2 NL	555	67	38	113	5	228	37	3	231	281	491	106	83	114	6	66	0.20	30	17	53	26	97	BAd	16%	160	148	21%	20%	85	5%	100%	2.5	123	$18
22	ATL	315	39	12	36	0	213	14	1	215	276	401	96	118	88	7	65	0.21	29	19	52	28	95	CAc	13%	141	132	12%	14%	84	3%	0%	-4.5	45	$3
23	BOS *	380	48	22	60	4	240	21	4	248	291	518	110	102	118	7	65	0.21	20	23	57	30	92	CAc	13%	187	135	17%	17%	93	6%	100%	13.9	189	$11
1st Half		137	18	6	20	2	235	7	2	244	303	485	108	126	114	9	66	0.29	16	27	57	30	73	CAd	15%	171	128	13%	18%	94	7%	100%	3.7	179	$1
2nd Half		243	30	16	40	2	243	14	2	252	288	536	111	92	119	6	64	0.16	22	21	57	30	101	BAc	12%	196	138	19%	17%	91	5%	100%	8.2	196	$16
24	Proj	420	57	25	70	3	231	25	3	240	293	492	108	107	108	7	66	0.22	25	20	55	28	93		14%	173	138	18%	18%	82	5%	81%	9.9	144	$16

RENT HERSHEY

Edman,Tommy

Age: 29 Pos: 2B SS CF | Bats: B Ht: 5' 10" Wt: 180
Health A | PT/Exp A | Consist B | LIMA Plan B | Rand Var +2 | MM 2545

Skills-wise, a near-carbon-copy from previous two years. Three differences: July wrist injury cost him four weeks; fewer runs, as he hit ninth more often than leadoff; SB not quite as impactful amid league-wide surge. Still quite the useful cog, as well-rounded production from three positions doesn't grow on trees.

Yr	Tm	PA	R	HR	RBI	SB	BA	xHR	xSB	xBA	OBP	SLG	OPS+	vL+	vR+	bb%	ct%	Eye	G	L	F	h%	HctX	QBaB	Brl%	PX	xPX	HR/F	xHR/F	Spd	SBA%	SB%	RAR	BPX
19	STL *	557	89	16	59	22	288	10	17	273	323	470	110	134	111	5	81	0.28	41	25	35	33	116	CBb	5%	90	108	12%	11%	139	18%	96%	13.1	189
20	STL	227	29	5	26	2	250	4	4	248	317	368	91	111	85	7	76	0.33	51	23	26	30	92	DDd	4%	66	67	12%	10%	114	10%	33%	-5.9	36
21	STL	691	91	11	56	30	262	15	21	270	308	387	95	108	92	5	85	0.40	46	22	32	29	102	CDd	4%	73	79	6%	9%	116	22%	86%	-6.7	181
22	STL	630	95	13	57	32	265	13	22	263	324	400	103	109	100	7	81	0.41	49	20	31	31	104	CDd	6%	86	90	9%	9%	122	22%	91%	5.2	155
23	STL	528	69	13	47	27	248	11	21	270	307	399	96	98	95	7	82	0.42	51	17	32	28	114	CDf	5%	84	83	10%	9%	118	26%	87%	4.9	171
1st Half		297	44	7	28	14	242	5	11	270	310	396	97	112	90	8	83	0.52	51	16	33	27	131	CDf	5%	85	101	10%	7%	124	22%	93%	0.5	193
2nd Half		231	25	6	19	13	257	5	10	268	303	402	95	84	101	5	82	0.29	51	17	31	29	92	CDf	5%	82	62	11%	9%	106	31%	81%	-0.7	136
24	**Proj**	**595**	**82**	**14**	**54**	**29**	**258**	**12**	**22**	**266**	**312**	**400**	**98**	**101**	**96**	**6**	**82**	**0.38**	**49**	**19**	**32**	**29**	**106**		**5%**	**82**	**82**	**10%**	**9%**	**119**	**24%**	**86%**	**10.9**	**157**

Edwards,Xavier

Age: 24 Pos: 2B | Bats: B Ht: 5' 10" Wt: 175
Health A | PT/Exp A | Consist D | LIMA Plan C | Rand Var -5 | MM 0403

0-3-.295 in 84 PA at MIA. Enjoyed big season at AAA (.351/.429/.457) prior to callup. Short-statured switch-hitter with plus ct% skills. Slasher profile from LH side with plus bat control. More of a threat for XBH from RH side. Not much drop off of production from either side of the plate. Plus runner with great reactions and jumps on SB attempts. (CB)

Yr	Tm	PA	R	HR	RBI	SB	BA	xHR	xSB	xBA	OBP	SLG	OPS+	vL+	vR+	bb%	ct%	Eye	G	L	F	h%	HctX	QBaB	Brl%	PX	xPX	HR/F	xHR/F	Spd	SBA%	SB%	RAR	BPX
19																																		
20																																		
21	aa	319	31	0	21	15	264		15		329	320	89			9	83	0.58				32				36				118	30%	55%		65
22	aaa	380	34	3	23	5	201		6		267	279	77			8	74	0.35				26				60				98	12%	52%		-21
23	MIA *	491	69	5	37	28	302	0	25	253	359	379	101	79	93	8	89	0.83	47	18	35	33	66	FDf	2%	42	46	0%	0%	127	22%	86%	17.3	168
1st Half		229	32	1	14	10	288	0	10	313	343	352	95	116	108	8	92	1.00	65	24	12	31	83	FFd	0%	35	-21	0%	0%	131	16%	90%	3.8	182
2nd Half		262	37	4	23	18	315	0	15	230	373	403	105	51	89	9	87	0.73	40	16	44	35	59	FCf	2%	48	72	0%	0%	120	25%	84%	12.5	150
24	**Proj**	**280**	**33**	**2**	**20**	**12**	**263**	**2**	**11**	**212**	**335**	**333**	**92**	**71**	**96**	**8**	**83**	**0.55**	**40**	**16**	**44**	**31**	**53**		**2%**	**43**	**65**	**2%**	**2%**	**120**	**19%**	**74%**	**0.7**	**84**

Encarnacion-Strand,Christian

Age: 24 Pos: 1B DH | Bats: R Ht: 6' 0" Wt: 224
Health A | PT/Exp C | Consist B | LIMA Plan B | Rand Var 0 | MM 4135

13-37-.270 in 241 PA at CIN. Back injury pushed AAA debut to late April, where he hit 20 HR and was called up by July. Power carried over to majors (Brl%, xHR/F), but so did strikeouts, which hints at BA pullback if elevated h% falls. Strong Sept (.304 BA, 8 HR) a sign things started to click. If so... UP: 30 HR.

Yr	Tm	PA	R	HR	RBI	SB	BA	xHR	xSB	xBA	OBP	SLG	OPS+	vL+	vR+	bb%	ct%	Eye	G	L	F	h%	HctX	QBaB	Brl%	PX	xPX	HR/F	xHR/F	Spd	SBA%	SB%	RAR	BPX
19																																		
20																																		
21																																		
22	aa	197	16	9	31	1	272		2		297	468	108			4	68	0.11				35				131				96	5%	37%		52
23	CIN *	540	69	28	75	3	272	11	3	261	319	492	111	92	115	6	70	0.23	35	27	39	34	96	BAb	10%	136	115	22%	19%	75	2%	100%	18.8	89
1st Half		257	32	13	33	1	265		2	256	313	493	110	0	0	7	69	0.23	44	20	36	33	0		0%	141	-21	0%		92	2%	100%	6.9	114
2nd Half		283	37	15	42	3	279	11	2	261	325	492	110	92	114	6	70	0.23	35	27	39	34	97	BAb	10%	131	115	22%	19%	69	4%	100%	9.9	75
24	**Proj**	**490**	**54**	**25**	**72**	**3**	**252**	**23**	**4**	**255**	**304**	**462**	**105**	**90**	**110**	**5**	**70**	**0.19**	**35**	**27**	**39**	**31**	**87**		**9%**	**129**	**104**	**20%**	**19%**	**72**	**4%**	**77%**	**7.6**	**76**

Escobar,Eduardo

Age: 35 Pos: 3B 2B | Bats: B Ht: 5' 10" Wt: 193
Health A | PT/Exp A | Consist C | LIMA Plan D+ | Rand Var 0 | MM 2211

Acquired by LAA for cash considerations in June; they should've asked for a refund. Hard contact vanished with lowest HctX of any non-speedster (<5 SB, min. 300 PA), while ct% sunk to new lows in 2nd half. A chance power rebounds to 2021-22 levels, but at this age, your only cash consideration is the dollar bin.

Yr	Tm	PA	R	HR	RBI	SB	BA	xHR	xSB	xBA	OBP	SLG	OPS+	vL+	vR+	bb%	ct%	Eye	G	L	F	h%	HctX	QBaB	Brl%	PX	xPX	HR/F	xHR/F	Spd	SBA%	SB%	RAR	BPX
19	ARI	699	94	35	118	5	269	30	6	268	320	511	115	123	111	7	80	0.38	33	23	45	29	114	CAa	7%	116	152	15%	13%	112	4%	83%	13.2	226
20	ARI	222	22	4	20	1	212	5	2	236	270	335	80	74	83	7	80	0.37	36	24	40	25	97	CAd	5%	64	80	6%	8%	115	2%	100%	-12.2	84
21	2 NL	599	77	28	90	1	253	25	3	254	314	472	108	119	104	8	77	0.39	32	21	47	28	110	CAd	9%	119	134	14%	13%	112	1%	100%	14.6	215
22	NYM	542	58	20	69	0	240	21	2	245	295	430	103	114	97	7	74	0.31	30	23	47	29	91	CAb	9%	123	122	11%	12%	94	2%	0%	3.5	134
23	2 TM	309	32	6	31	2	226	4	6	221	269	344	84	104	71	6	73	0.23	43	20	37	29	61	DCf	4%	65	54	8%	5%	146	5%	67%	-5.6	4
1st Half		145	21	4	17	2	246	2	3	262	292	403	95	113	78	6	78	0.30	43	26	31	29	78	CCd	5%	80	72	12%	6%	137	6%	100%	-0.4	107
2nd Half		164	11	2	14	0	208	2	2	181	250	292	73	90	65	6	69	0.19	44	14	42	29	47	DBf	3%	51	35	4%	4%	128	3%	0%	-9.1	-118
24	**Proj**	**245**	**26**	**7**	**29**	**1**	**234**	**6**	**3**	**230**	**284**	**386**	**92**	**106**	**85**	**7**	**74**	**0.28**	**37**	**21**	**42**	**29**	**80**		**6%**	**88**	**87**	**10%**	**8%**	**120**	**3%**	**56%**	**-1.2**	**67**

Espinal,Santiago

Age: 29 Pos: 2B 3B | Bats: R Ht: 5' 10" Wt: 187
Health B | PT/Exp B | Consist C | LIMA Plan D+ | Rand Var +2 | MM 1241

A few minor dings (April wrist, May hamstring), but another year in utility role with little category juice. Bat-to-ball ability is his one plus skill, but PX/xPX says all that contact is hollow, and speed skills aren't conducive to more SB. Useful in an -only league pinch given LD% stroke, position eligibility, but undraftable otherwise.

Yr	Tm	PA	R	HR	RBI	SB	BA	xHR	xSB	xBA	OBP	SLG	OPS+	vL+	vR+	bb%	ct%	Eye	G	L	F	h%	HctX	QBaB	Brl%	PX	xPX	HR/F	xHR/F	Spd	SBA%	SB%	RAR	BPX
19	a/a	507	49	6	62	10	262		12		314	361	93			7	82	0.44				31				57				87	20%	41%		67
20	TOR	66	10	0	6	1	267	1	1	253	308	333	85	96	69	6	73	0.25	30	40	30	36	77	FCc	2%	56	78	0%	8%	106	6%	100%	-1.5	-60
21	TOR	246	32	2	17	6	311	1	6	259	376	405	107	108	106	9	86	0.73	43	22	35	35	86	DCd	2%	58	55	3%	2%	131	9%	86%	8.7	196
22	TOR	491	51	7	51	6	267	5	7	260	322	370	98	116	92	7	85	0.53	43	23	34	30	92	DCc	3%	68	69	5%	4%	88	10%	50%	4.0	128
23	TOR	254	30	2	25	2	248	2	3	257	310	335	88	89	87	7	84	0.50	44	22	34	29	87	DCc	1%	58	58	3%	3%	87	5%	67%	-0.5	93
1st Half		128	17	1	11	2	221	1	2	255	307	301	83	71	90	10	86	0.75	50	19	31	25	82	DDf	0%	51	47	3%	3%	87	9%	67%	-3.5	111
2nd Half		126	13	1	14	0	274	1	1	262	312	368	92	100	81	5	83	0.30	37	26	37	32	92	DCb	2%	64	69	3%	3%	97	0%	0%	0.3	86
24	**Proj**	**245**	**28**	**2**	**25**	**3**	**266**	**2**	**4**	**260**	**323**	**356**	**93**	**98**	**89**	**7**	**84**	**0.51**	**41**	**24**	**34**	**31**	**88**		**2%**	**59**	**63**	**3%**	**3%**	**100**	**8%**	**59%**	**1.5**	**116**

Estrada,Thairo

Age: 28 Pos: 2B SS | Bats: R Ht: 5' 10" Wt: 185
Health B | PT/Exp A | Consist A | LIMA Plan B | Rand Var -2 | MM 2335

A full-blown breakout through June, then hand fracture cost him all of July and never recovered. Pre-injury power skills, FB% took steps forward, as did SB aggressiveness and success; all of which tanked in 2nd half. Can't quite use 1st half pace as baseline, but healthy off-season could yield... UP: 20 HR, 30 SB.

Yr	Tm	PA	R	HR	RBI	SB	BA	xHR	xSB	xBA	OBP	SLG	OPS+	vL+	vR+	bb%	ct%	Eye	G	L	F	h%	HctX	QBaB	Brl%	PX	xPX	HR/F	xHR/F	Spd	SBA%	SB%	RAR	BPX
19	NYY *	322	43	10	38	6	239	2	4	269	274	408	94	58	111	5	77	0.21	53	20	27	28	74	CDb	4%	92	60	23%	15%	108	11%	85%	-6.8	89
20	NYY	52	8	1	3	1	167	1	1	189	231	229	61	93	36	2	60	0.05	59	21	21	25	67	FFf	3%	37	60	17%	17%	110	9%	100%	-5.7	-356
21	SF *	356	44	12	49	5	268	5	6	256	315	431	102	93	127	6	80	0.35	51	17	32	30	84	DDf	7%	90	108	23%	16%	109	12%	51%	0.6	158
22	SF	541	71	14	62	21	260	9	17	269	322	402	103	117	96	6	82	0.37	51	20	30	29	85	DDf	5%	86	74	12%	8%	121	20%	78%	1.8	159
23	SF	530	63	14	49	23	271	11	20	250	315	416	100	87	105	4	76	0.18	44	21	35	33	94	DCf	5%	89	85	11%	9%	106	24%	77%	8.0	57
1st Half		315	46	9	31	18	272	8	14	247	327	434	104	101	105	5	73	0.19	41	21	38	34	89	DCd	6%	104	111	11%	10%	111	29%	82%	7.1	79
2nd Half		215	17	5	18	5	268	3	6	254	298	390	93	66	104	3	79	0.16	48	21	30	32	100	DCf	4%	70	52	10%	6%	102	16%	63%	-0.4	39
24	**Proj**	**560**	**68**	**16**	**61**	**22**	**264**	**13**	**16**	**259**	**312**	**413**	**99**	**89**	**104**	**5**	**79**	**0.24**	**46**	**21**	**33**	**31**	**89**		**5%**	**87**	**79**	**12%**	**10%**	**102**	**21%**	**76%**	**9.5**	**100**

Fairchild,Stuart

Age: 28 Pos: LF RF CF | Bats: R Ht: 6' 0" Wt: 205
Health A | PT/Exp C | Consist A | LIMA Plan D | Rand Var 0 | MM 3321

5-28-.228 with 10 SB in 255 PA at CIN. Bounced between AAA and majors with few spurts of fantasy utility. Ran more often with mild success, but couldn't hold 2022's power gains and paltry xBA hardly budged. A modest HR/SB threat with regular playing time, but recent OBP history says that's a stretch.

Yr	Tm	PA	R	HR	RBI	SB	BA	xHR	xSB	xBA	OBP	SLG	OPS+	vL+	vR+	bb%	ct%	Eye	G	L	F	h%	HctX	QBaB	Brl%	PX	xPX	HR/F	xHR/F	Spd	SBA%	SB%	RAR	BPX
19	aa	171	22	4	15	3	257		3		334	421	104			10	83	0.67				29				89				108	12%	55%		211
20																																		
21	ARI *	185	18	5	17	4	214	0	4	236	269	367	87	86	0	7	71	0.26	42	25	33	28	72	FCf	0%	91	61	0%	0%	148	14%	76%	-6.7	58
22	3 TM *	314	36	14	22	5	227	4	7	223	282	423	100	116	111	7	63	0.21	43	18	39	31	96	CCd	8%	144	157	21%	17%	138	14%	53%	-2.6	83
23	CIN *	355	45	8	35	12	223	7	12	225	294	370	90	94	98	9	67	0.30	39	22	39	31	69	FCd	8%	102	81	9%	12%	116	20%	73%	-2.8	14
1st Half		211	29	6	25	9	230	6	8	223	309	413	99	105	98	10	64	0.31	38	19	43	33	74	DBc	8%	133	111	9%	13%	120	23%	81%	1.9	71
2nd Half		145	16	2	10	3	213	1	4	241	273	309	79	70	98	8	72	0.29	43	28	28	28	51	FCf	7%	64	12	8%	8%	107	16%	58%	-5.5	-46
24	**Proj**	**245**	**29**	**7**	**21**	**6**	**225**	**6**	**7**	**235**	**312**	**389**	**96**	**92**	**99**	**8**	**69**	**0.29**	**42**	**22**	**36**	**29**	**75**		**8%**	**108**	**95**	**13%**	**10%**	**105**	**15%**	**68%**	**-1.6**	**51**

RYAN BLOOMFIELD

Farmer,Kyle

Age: 33	Pos: 2B 3B SS	Health	B	LIMA Plan	D+
Bats: R	Ht: 6' 0" Wt: 205	PT/Exp	A	Rand Var	-1
		Consist	A	MM	2121

Fractured jaw, surgery from April 12 HBP likely had at least some impact on 1st half underperformance. 2nd half saw him reboot as slightly different hitter, with career-high FB% and better launch angle, though net gain in power wasn't all that sizable. Even if return to full-time role is unlikely, has enough pop to provide deep league value as reserve.

Yr	Tm	PA	R	HR	RBI	SB	BA	xHR	xSB	xBA	OBP	SLG	OPS+	vL+	vR+	bb%	ct%	Eye	G	L	F	h%	HctX	QBaB	Brl%	PX	xPX	HR/F	xHR/F	Spd	SBA%	SB%	RAR	BPX	R$
19	CIN	197	22	9	27	4	230	7	2	235	279	410	95	114	84	5	68	0.17	40	24	35	29	94	DAb	6%	103	80	20%	16%	70	13%	80%	-7.5	-44	$3
20	CIN	70	4	0	4	1	266	2	1	235	329	313	85	118	64	7	80	0.38	37	27	35	33	114	BAb	6%	36	101	0%	11%	83	5%	100%	-2.3	-40	$1
21	CIN	529	60	16	63	2	263	11	4	259	316	416	101	107	99	4	80	0.23	41	24	35	30	118	CBc	4%	85	109	12%	8%	107	4%	40%	0.0	115	$13
22	CIN	583	58	14	78	4	255	12	4	263	315	386	99	133	87	6	81	0.33	45	24	32	29	108	DCb	4%	82	91	10%	9%	84	5%	57%	-1.3	100	$15
23	MIN	369	49	11	46	2	256	10	6	243	317	408	99	105	95	6	74	0.27	42	21	37	31	103	DCd	7%	90	115	12%	11%	107	7%	33%	3.5	57	$8
1st Half		180	25	4	16	1	248	4	2	244	306	358	91	95	89	6	72	0.22	42	28	30	32	110	CCc	8%	70	115	11%	11%	102	2%	100%	-2.9	-43	$1
2nd Half		189	24	7	30	1	263	6	4	246	328	456	106	114	101	7	77	0.33	43	14	42	31	97	DBd	6%	108	115	13%	11%	104	11%	20%	1.8	143	$8
24	Proj	245	30	7	33	2	255	7	3	247	313	399	98	112	91	6	76	0.26	43	22	35	31	106		6%	85	106	11%	10%	88	7%	44%	1.9	72	$5

Fermin,Freddy

Age: 29	Pos: CA	Health	A	LIMA Plan	D
Bats: R	Ht: 5' 10" Wt: 200	PT/Exp	C	Rand Var	-2
		Consist	D	MM	2033

9-32-.281 in 235 PA at KC. Mid-Sept fractured finger cut short out-of-nowhere success story, which included incredible six-week run where he hit .360 with 1.017 OPS. Overall MLB numbers came with skill support, so we can't really call him a fluke; still, previous outlook was that of career backup CA. Worth a speculative flyer, but have a solid Plan B.

Yr	Tm	PA	R	HR	RBI	SB	BA	xHR	xSB	xBA	OBP	SLG	OPS+	vL+	vR+	bb%	ct%	Eye	G	L	F	h%	HctX	QBaB	Brl%	PX	xPX	HR/F	xHR/F	Spd	SBA%	SB%	RAR	BPX	R$
19	aa	110	10	2	10	0	232		1		251	328	80			2	77	0.11				28				51				99	9%	0%		-52	-$2
20																																			
21	a/a	304	35	6	34	1	228		1		285	347	87			7	78	0.35				27				71				94	3%	38%		46	$2
22	KC *	327	25	7	31	1	198	0	1	166	257	318	81	0	0	7	75	0.32	50	0	50	24	0	BBf		83	-14	0%	0%	72	3%	36%	-9.2	17	-$1
23	KC *	288	34	12	41	0	272	8	2	266	323	459	107	105	107	7	77	0.33	45	22	33	31	114	CCc	10%	105	114	16%	15%	91	0%	0%	14.0	125	$7
1st Half		147	16	7	26	0	254	4	1	267	324	460	108	98	112	9	78	0.46	48	20	32	28	98	CDf	11%	110	115	19%	19%	110	0%	0%	5.9	186	$3
2nd Half		141	18	5	15	0	290	4	1	263	319	458	105	109	103	4	76	0.19	43	24	33	35	124	BCa	9%	101	114	15%	12%	78	0%	0%	6.2	71	$3
24	Proj	315	34	11	37	0	245	10	2	256	291	411	96	96	96	6	76	0.28	45	22	33	28	114		10%	97	114	15%	14%	75	2%	30%	5.7	64	$9

Fletcher,Dominic

Age: 26	Pos: OF	Health	A	LIMA Plan	D
Bats: L	Ht: 5' 9" Wt: 185	PT/Exp	A	Rand Var	0
		Consist	A	MM	2211

2-14-.301 in 102 PA at ARI. Finger fracture in Sept froze MLB BA at very misleading level, as xBA was .237. 2nd half HctX, QBaB, xPX can be dismissed, as they're based on 5 PA. So what isn't misleading? Subpar ct% and PX, struggles vL (54% ct%), and despite Spd, might be worst basestealer you'll ever see. Let others chase that .300 mirage.

Yr	Tm	PA	R	HR	RBI	SB	BA	xHR	xSB	xBA	OBP	SLG	OPS+	vL+	vR+	bb%	ct%	Eye	G	L	F	h%	HctX	QBaB	Brl%	PX	xPX	HR/F	xHR/F	Spd	SBA%	SB%	RAR	BPX	R$
19																																			
20																																			
21	aa	419	41	10	38	2	219		5		251	353	83			4	69	0.14				29				84				123	7%	37%		-35	$2
22	a/a	553	54	6	40	5	237		11		278	350	89			5	74	0.22				31				80				122	13%	34%		31	$7
23	ARI *	404	50	7	40	3	238	2	8	232	297	366	90	57	129	8	74	0.32	51	15	34	31	95	CDd	4%	82	95	8%	8%	127	8%	39%	-4.0	57	$5
1st Half		258	31	3	25	1	267	1	7	234	313	385	96	57	133	6	76	0.29	52	15	33	34	95	CDd	5%	71	91	9%	5%	141	8%	20%	-0.4	71	$6
2nd Half		146	20	3	14	2	186	0	2	221	267	329	81	0	88	10	69	0.35	25	25	50	24	140	ABa	0%	103	166	0%	0%	94	7%	100%	-4.7	25	-$2
24	Proj	245	28	4	21	2	224	1	4	229	276	355	87	46	105	7	72	0.26	52	15	33	29	86		4%	87	82	8%	2%	114	10%	46%	-5.4	27	$4

Flores,Wilmer

Age: 32	Pos: 1B DH 3B	Health	B	LIMA Plan	B+
Bats: R	Ht: 6' 2" Wt: 213	PT/Exp	A	Rand Var	-1
		Consist	D	MM	3345

Maintained 2022's career-high FB%, paired it with ct% rebound, and voila! New high in HR. (And in fewer PA, too.) But before getting any 30-HR upside stars in your eyes, note that xPX was only league average, and xHR didn't back the output. Skills did support best BA since 2019, and with more PA likely, has good shot at repeating HR total anyway.

Yr	Tm	PA	R	HR	RBI	SB	BA	xHR	xSB	xBA	OBP	SLG	OPS+	vL+	vR+	bb%	ct%	Eye	G	L	F	h%	HctX	QBaB	Brl%	PX	xPX	HR/F	xHR/F	Spd	SBA%	SB%	RAR	BPX	R$
19	ARI	285	31	9	37	0	317	7	-	290	361	487	117	137	104	5	88	0.48	37	25	38	33	114	CBc	5%	84	93	10%	8%	75	0%	0%	7.1	204	$7
20	SF	213	30	12	32	1	268	9	1	280	315	515	110	127	102	6	82	0.36	33	23	44	27	118	CAc	6%	125	130	17%	13%	92	2%	100%	1.9	276	$20
21	SF	436	57	18	53	1	262	12	2	270	335	447	107	109	106	9	86	0.73	38	21	41	27	108	CAc	6%	92	107	13%	9%	99	1%	100%	8.9	258	$12
22	SF	602	72	19	71	0	229	16	2	246	316	394	101	99	101	10	80	0.57	34	19	47	25	105	CAc	6%	102	102	10%	8%	97	0%	0%	-5.9	186	$11
23	SF	454	51	23	60	0	284	16	2	284	355	509	118	120	116	9	84	0.65	32	21	47	29	103	DAd	8%	116	100	14%	10%	71	0%	0%	27.6	257	$15
1st Half		188	21	8	24	0	250	6	1	255	319	446	105	109	101	9	80	0.50	28	20	52	27	93	CAd	7%	110	93	11%	8%	77	0%	0%	3.3	182	$4
2nd Half		266	30	15	36	0	308	10	1	304	380	553	126	128	124	9	88	0.83	34	22	43	30	109	DAd	8%	120	105	17%	11%	74	0%	0%	21.8	321	$20
24	Proj	525	63	21	65	0	268	17	2	267	339	456	109	112	107	9	84	0.60	35	21	44	28	105		7%	101	103	12%	9%	82	0%	100%	17.7	242	$19

lorial,Estevan

Age: 26	Pos: CF	Health	A	LIMA Plan	D
Bats: L	Ht: 6' 1" Wt: 195	PT/Exp	A	Rand Var	+5
		Consist	A	MM	3401

0-8-.230 with 3 SB in 71 PA at NYY. Cups of coffee keep getting tiny bit bigger each year, but lack of traction reflects how far prospect standing has fallen. Raw power, speed remain enticing, but lousy ct%, mediocre SB% make him risky bet if he gets real shot in 2024. 20/20 dreams could quickly turn into nightmare if BA lands him on bench.

Yr	Tm	PA	R	HR	RBI	SB	BA	xHR	xSB	xBA	OBP	SLG	OPS+	vL+	vR+	bb%	ct%	Eye	G	L	F	h%	HctX	QBaB	Brl%	PX	xPX	HR/F	xHR/F	Spd	SBA%	SB%	RAR	BPX	R$
19																																			
20	NYY	3	0	0	0	0	333	0	0	301	333	333	88	0	89	0	33	0.00	0	100	0	100	0	FA		0	-26	0%		118	0%	0%	0.0	-912	-$3
21	NYY *	409	58	15	39	11	193	0	12	195	275	366	88	39	170	10	60	0.29	50	7	43	27	88	BFd	7%	126	192	17%	0%	120	25%	55%	-17.0	0	$6
22	NYY *	477	51	11	33	29	215	1	22	198	284	350	90	91	34	9	57	0.23	47	18	35	34	42	FCf	6%	121	59	0%	17%	109	41%	71%	-9.9	-69	$15
23	NYY *	524	61	19	61	20	225	1	22	219	302	411	97	114	82	10	57	0.26	43	24	33	35	56	DBf	2%	140	57	0%	7%	116	28%	62%	1.1	-4	$13
1st Half		280	35	14	31	11	233		14	222	307	454	104	0	0	10	57	0.25	44	20	36	35	0		0%	160	-21	0%		133	35%	53%	1.3	57	$16
2nd Half		244	26	5	30	9	216	1	7	210	296	360	89	113	81	10	58	0.27	43	24	33	35	56	DBf	2%	119	57	0%	7%	100	20%	79%	-3.0	-75	$8
24	Proj	175	20	4	17	8	216	4	8	202	305	345	89	141	80	10	58	0.25	43	24	33	35	50		2%	107	51	12%	12%	109	27%	67%	-3.2	-35	$5

ord,Mike

Age: 31	Pos: DH	Health	A	LIMA Plan	D
Bats: L	Ht: 6' 0" Wt: 225	PT/Exp	B	Rand Var	-3
		Consist	B	MM	4111

16-34-.228 in 251 PA at SEA. Finally rekindled power stroke that created so many false hopes back in 2019. And given poor ct%, mediocre HctX and QBaB, and HR/F - xHR/F gap, there's even less to get excited about this time around. A player in his 30s who still routinely sports asterisks next to his Tm designation is a pretty dependable red flag.

Yr	Tm	PA	R	HR	RBI	SB	BA	xHR	xSB	xBA	OBP	SLG	OPS+	vL+	vR+	bb%	ct%	Eye	G	L	F	h%	HctX	QBaB	Brl%	PX	xPX	HR/F	xHR/F	Spd	SBA%	SB%	RAR	BPX	R$
19	NYY *	492	74	32	69	0	255	6	-	270	334	523	119	193	105	11	78	0.55	37	18	44	26	111	ABc	10%	133	135	24%	12%	58	1%	0%	12.6	222	$14
20	NYY	84	5	2	11	0	135	3	0	233	226	270	66	14	72	8	78	0.44	51	19	31	14	129	BDc	7%	79	96	11%	17%	69	0%	0%	-9.2	64	-$3
21	NYY *	363	29	13	34	1	162	3	0	172	241	310	76	48	83	9	62	0.28	38	11	51	21	103	ABf	19%	98	154	16%	16%	73	2%	100%	-28.1	-108	-$4
22	4 TM *	274	16	4	14	0	186	2	0	216	271	278	78	109	81	10	74	0.46	33	23	44	23	103	CAd	3%	66	84	8%	5%	76	0%	0%	-13.4	-14	-$5
23	SEA *	441	52	23	66	1	219	12	2	231	294	434	99	124	107	10	69	0.34	32	19	50	25	94	CAf	17%	130	134	23%	17%	67	1%	100%	4.6	68	$8
1st Half		255	30	13	44	1	209	4	1	237	274	417	95	0	110	8	73	0.34	29	20	51	22	80	CAf	19%	117	119	29%	19%	74	2%	100%	-4.7	96	$10
2nd Half		186	22	10	22	0	233	8	1	220	344	459	109	136	105	12	62	0.34	33	18	49	31	92	BAf	17%	153	140	21%	17%	73	0%	0%	2.6	57	$5
24	Proj	245	25	12	28	0	207	10	1	227	301	408	97	104	96	10	69	0.37	35	19	46	24	97		13%	124	121	17%	14%	69	1%	85%	-2.1	39	$5

ortes,Nick

Age: 27	Pos: CA	Health	A	LIMA Plan	D+
Bats: R	Ht: 5' 11" Wt: 198	PT/Exp	B	Rand Var	+3
		Consist	B	MM	1203

2021's MLB power skills were small-sample fluke (34 PA), but now it seems even 2022's larger sample wasn't sustainable. Trends in QBaB, Brl%, xPX, and xHR/F are very discouraging, and all that's left is empty ct%, ability to hit LHP (career .768 OPS). If roster flexibility allows you to platoon him, great; if not, 2023 R$ says everything.

Yr	Tm	PA	R	HR	RBI	SB	BA	xHR	xSB	xBA	OBP	SLG	OPS+	vL+	vR+	bb%	ct%	Eye	G	L	F	h%	HctX	QBaB	Brl%	PX	xPX	HR/F	xHR/F	Spd	SBA%	SB%	RAR	BPX	R$
19																																			
20																																			
21	MIA *	390	36	9	42	6	212	2	5	196	270	331	83	110	161	7	80	0.41	30	13	57	24	171	AAd	22%	67	217	31%	15%	98	10%	71%	-10.8	81	$4
22	MIA *	352	50	11	33	6	220	7	7	231	277	356	90	92	101	7	80	0.38	40	17	42	24	111	BBf	7%	79	122	12%	10%	127	11%	65%	-4.4	124	$6
23	MIA	323	33	6	26	4	204	6	5	214	263	299	77	115	63	5	80	0.29	46	13	41	24	106	CCf	4%	56	86	6%	6%	90	9%	67%	-9.5	14	$0
1st Half		185	18	4	15	3	216	4	3	213	266	304	78	146	60	7	78	0.32	44	17	39	26	108	CCf	5%	48	94	8%	8%	95	10%	75%	-4.9	-25	-$2
2nd Half		138	15	2	11	1	187	3	2	216	257	293	74	89	67	4	83	0.24	49	8	44	21	103	CCf	3%	66	76	4%	7%	94	8%	50%	-6.5	79	-$5
24	Proj	315	34	7	25	4	209	7	5	220	276	323	82	97	76	6	80	0.34	44	14	42	24	107		5%	65	99	7%	7%	102	9%	66%	-6.5	74	$5

RANDON KRUSE

Fraley,Jake

Age: 29 Pos: RF LF DH | Bats: L Ht: 6' 0" Wt: 195

Health	F	LIMA Plan	C+
PT/Exp	B	Rand Var	+1
Consist	A	MM	3333

Was electric from May through early Aug, when he fractured his toe and missed four weeks. Struggled in Sept return; Oct toe surgery tells us why. Plate skills look healthy, but exit velocity remains sub-par. HR/SB combo is belied by xHR/xSB red flags which cap his ceiling below 1st half electricity. Strong-side platoon makes him more valuable.

Yr	Tm	PA	R	HR	RBI	SB	BA	xHR	xSB	xBA	OBP	SLG	OPS+	vL+	vR+	bb%	ct%	Eye	G	L	F	h%	HctX	QBaB	Brl%	PX	xPX	HR/F	xHR/F	Spd	SBA%	SB%	RAR	BPX
19	SEA *	452	60	16	68	18	251	0	14	207	299	444	103	31	57	6	72	0.24	31	12	58	31	38	FAf	4%	111	2	0%	0%	107	29%	70%	-11.2	81
20	SEA	29	3	0	0	2	154	0	2	182	241	269	68	19	83	7	58	0.18	27	33	40	27	47	FAc	7%	82	40	0%	0%	141	60%	67%	-2.8	-176
21	SEA *	311	33	11	41	12	218	7	7	224	352	379	100	72	112	17	64	0.58	39	26	34	29	79	DCc	6%	105	111	18%	14%	85	17%	79%	-5.1	12
22	CIN *	293	38	13	31	5	253	9	4	244	333	437	109	67	122	11	72	0.43	43	20	37	30	85	DCc	8%	117	106	20%	15%	93	8%	82%	3.2	114
23	CIN	380	41	15	65	21	256	8	14	268	339	443	107	68	111	10	79	0.52	38	23	39	28	92	DBc	6%	107	80	14%	8%	64	27%	81%	10.8	150
1st Half		240	29	11	50	13	274	6	9	272	354	476	114	27	127	11	82	0.64	38	21	41	29	99	DBc	8%	108	91	15%	8%	65	27%	76%	7.5	196
2nd Half		140	12	4	15	8	226	2	5	261	314	387	95	238	87	9	74	0.38	39	26	35	27	79	FBb	2%	104	58	13%	6%	81	28%	89%	-2.5	86
24	**Proj**	**350**	**40**	**13**	**48**	**15**	**250**	**8**	**11**	**251**	**339**	**425**	**105**	**82**	**109**	**11**	**74**	**0.45**	**40**	**23**	**37**	**30**	**85**		**6%**	**107**	**89**	**16%**	**9%**	**82**	**20%**	**82%**	**8.4**	**103**

France,Ty

Age: 29 Pos: 1B | Bats: R Ht: 5' 11" Wt: 215

Health	A	LIMA Plan	B+
PT/Exp	A	Rand Var	+3
Consist	B	MM	2235

Contact skills still look healthy, but power metrics and BA have trended poorly in lockstep for a while now. Mediocre exit velocity, fluky 2nd-half struggles vL and HR/F collapse created a perfect 2023 storm. BA skills remain playable; xHR says HR drop-off shouldn't have been this bad. At the bottom of his R$ range; a rebound seems likely.

Yr	Tm	PA	R	HR	RBI	SB	BA	xHR	xSB	xBA	OBP	SLG	OPS+	vL+	vR+	bb%	ct%	Eye	G	L	F	h%	HctX	QBaB	Brl%	PX	xPX	HR/F	xHR/F	Spd	SBA%	SB%	RAR	BPX
19	SD *	518	77	24	85	1	288	7	3	270	330	510	116	107	91	6	77	0.27	43	21	37	33	112	CBc	6%	118	96	14%	14%	99	3%	25%	6.9	167
20	2 TM	155	19	4	23	0	305	6	0	265	368	468	111	82	130	7	74	0.30	38	31	32	39	95	DBc	9%	100	108	12%	18%	92	0%	0%	2.8	76
21	SEA	650	85	18	73	0	291	20	1	268	368	445	112	119	108	7	81	0.43	46	23	31	33	112	CCc	7%	88	84	12%	14%	94	0%	0%	14.7	158
22	SEA	612	65	20	84	0	276	15	1	270	340	437	110	103	113	6	83	0.37	48	21	31	30	110	CCc	6%	95	80	14%	11%	80	0%	0%	12.8	155
23	SEA	665	79	12	58	1	250	17	3	255	337	366	96	97	95	6	80	0.37	42	23	35	29	89	CCc	7%	72	65	7%	10%	68	1%	100%	-0.4	46
1st Half		355	51	7	36	1	267	8	2	271	332	401	100	121	94	6	81	0.31	43	24	33	31	82	DCc	6%	84	53	8%	9%	65	1%	100%	-0.6	86
2nd Half		310	28	5	22	0	230	8	2	234	342	325	90	70	97	8	79	0.43	40	22	37	27	97	CBc	7%	57	80	6%	10%	79	0%	0%	-9.7	14
24	**Proj**	**595**	**72**	**15**	**67**	**0**	**265**	**17**	**2**	**259**	**344**	**402**	**102**	**99**	**104**	**7**	**80**	**0.37**	**44**	**23**	**34**	**31**	**100**		**7%**	**81**	**77**	**10%**	**11%**	**80**	**0%**	**78%**	**5.8**	**96**

Franco,Wander

Age: 23 Pos: SS | Bats: B Ht: 5' 10" Wt: 189

Health	C	LIMA Plan	C
PT/Exp	A	Rand Var	0
Consist	B	MM	3555

Prodigious talent's HR/SB breakout interrupted by off-field issues; didn't play again after Aug 12. Running game blossomed with SBA% spike. Power arrived with exit velocity bump, soaring Brl%, HR/F supported by xHR—and 2nd half surge says it was gaining steam. Future now up to MLB; no player will have a more consequential off-season.

Yr	Tm	PA	R	HR	RBI	SB	BA	xHR	xSB	xBA	OBP	SLG	OPS+	vL+	vR+	bb%	ct%	Eye	G	L	F	h%	HctX	QBaB	Brl%	PX	xPX	HR/F	xHR/F	Spd	SBA%	SB%	RAR	BPX
19																																		
20																																		
21	TAM *	484	81	13	71	7	293	6	11	291	347	496	116	139	96	8	86	0.61	45	20	34	32	102	CCf	5%	103	80	8%	7%	140	10%	56%	21.7	338
22	TAM *	368	48	6	35	8	283	7	6	292	341	420	108	110	104	8	89	0.80	44	25	31	30	111	CDf	4%	82	81	7%	8%	105	10%	87%	10.5	245
23	TAM	491	65	17	58	30	281	17	27	301	344	475	112	125	108	9	84	0.61	47	23	29	30	125	BDc	8%	101	104	15%	15%	120	33%	75%	25.5	261
1st Half		353	46	9	42	26	283	10	21	306	343	459	110	115	108	8	86	0.64	48	25	28	31	120	CDc	6%	95	93	12%	13%	108	39%	76%	12.3	254
2nd Half		138	19	8	16	4	274	7	6	285	348	516	117	158	109	9	81	0.54	46	20	34	28	138	ACc	11%	115	134	24%	21%	149	17%	67%	6.5	286
24	**Proj**	**595**	**83**	**24**	**69**	**31**	**282**	**20**	**19**	**299**	**341**	**492**	**114**	**133**	**109**	**8**	**85**	**0.62**	**46**	**23**	**32**	**29**	**120**		**7%**	**106**	**99**	**16%**	**14%**	**127**	**27%**	**78%**	**33.7**	**273**

Frazier,Adam

Age: 32 Pos: 2B | Bats: L Ht: 5' 10" Wt: 181

Health	A	LIMA Plan	C+
PT/Exp	A	Rand Var	+3
Consist	D	MM	1343

Strange season. 1st-half surface stats say he traded BA for power, but elite plate skills, LD% and poor h% luck say otherwise. xHR discredits early HR surge; he didn't leave the yard again after July 30. Running game still modestly helpful and xBA says he deserved better. Will continue to evolve into a platoon option with a humble ceiling.

Yr	Tm	PA	R	HR	RBI	SB	BA	xHR	xSB	xBA	OBP	SLG	OPS+	vL+	vR+	bb%	ct%	Eye	G	L	F	h%	HctX	QBaB	Brl%	PX	xPX	HR/F	xHR/F	Spd	SBA%	SB%	RAR	BPX
19	PIT	608	80	10	50	5	278	10	10	283	336	417	104	93	107	7	86	0.53	41	26	33	31	89	CCb	2%	70	69	6%	6%	129	7%	50%	-1.3	207
20	PIT	230	22	7	23	1	230	6	2	250	297	364	88	70	92	7	83	0.49	44	21	35	25	85	DCd	4%	68	67	11%	10%	87	7%	25%	-8.7	120
21	2 NL	639	83	5	43	10	305	4	14	288	368	411	107	102	109	8	88	0.70	41	29	30	34	86	DCb	1%	62	53	3%	3%	129	8%	67%	17.1	223
22	SEA	602	61	3	42	11	238	4	12	250	301	311	87	81	89	8	87	0.63	41	24	35	27	79	DCc	2%	46	55	2%	2%	110	11%	65%	-10.1	114
23	BAL	454	59	13	60	11	240	6	10	277	300	396	95	83	97	7	83	0.47	37	27	37	26	83	DBc	3%	85	69	10%	5%	91	15%	73%	4.7	161
1st Half		277	36	9	35	7	226	3	6	295	298	387	94	85	96	9	87	0.75	38	28	34	23	84	DCb	3%	82	67	12%	4%	85	16%	70%	-1.6	211
2nd Half		177	23	4	25	4	262	3	4	252	303	409	96	67	97	5	78	0.22	35	24	41	31	80	DBd	3%	90	72	8%	6%	104	13%	80%	1.4	96
24	**Proj**	**350**	**43**	**5**	**37**	**7**	**255**	**4**	**8**	**264**	**313**	**369**	**93**	**84**	**96**	**7**	**84**	**0.48**	**39**	**26**	**36**	**29**	**82**		**2%**	**66**	**64**	**6%**	**4%**	**106**	**12%**	**69%**	**1.7**	**149**

Freeman,Freddie

Age: 34 Pos: 1B | Bats: L Ht: 6' 5" Wt: 220

Health	A	LIMA Plan	C
PT/Exp	A	Rand Var	-2
Consist	B	MM	4355

Exit velocity downtick didn't matter. Talk up his post-season struggles if you think it'll help, because that and age are all you've got. Rock-solid plate skills, LD% inflicted elite damage vL and vR alike. Launch angle gains brought power back, and xHR says it could have been better. Running game exploded with rules change. Still a PA monster.

Yr	Tm	PA	R	HR	RBI	SB	BA	xHR	xSB	xBA	OBP	SLG	OPS+	vL+	vR+	bb%	ct%	Eye	G	L	F	h%	HctX	QBaB	Brl%	PX	xPX	HR/F	xHR/F	Spd	SBA%	SB%	RAR	BPX
19	ATL	692	113	38	121	6	295	41	5	296	389	549	130	104	138	13	79	0.69	38	28	34	32	128	BBa	13%	128	133	24%	25%	90	5%	67%	36.0	263
20	ATL	262	51	13	53	2	341	17	2	326	462	640	146	93	163	17	83	1.22	32	31	37	37	146	ABa	15%	162	143	20%	26%	92	2%	100%	30.2	496
21	ATL	695	120	31	83	8	300	38	8	285	393	503	123	103	131	12	82	0.79	43	24	33	32	129	ACb	12%	104	114	19%	24%	103	5%	73%	35.9	265
22	LA	708	117	21	100	13	325	33	11	295	407	511	130	115	136	12	83	0.82	39	27	34	36	135	ACa	10%	116	140	12%	19%	101	7%	81%	53.1	283
23	LA	730	131	29	102	23	331	35	19	305	410	567	133	136	131	10	81	0.60	35	28	37	37	122	BBa	11%	138	123	15%	18%	100	11%	96%	77.8	307
1st Half		381	65	14	54	11	315	19	9	295	396	533	127	135	123	11	80	0.62	33	28	38	36	124	BBa	12%	129	121	14%	18%	93	11%	92%	31.5	271
2nd Half		349	66	15	48	12	349	16	10	316	424	603	139	136	139	9	82	0.57	37	27	36	39	119	BBa	10%	148	125	17%	18%	106	12%	100%	44.3	350
24	**Proj**	**665**	**120**	**27**	**100**	**17**	**326**	**34**	**13**	**301**	**408**	**550**	**131**	**122**	**135**	**11**	**82**	**0.69**	**38**	**27**	**35**	**36**	**127**		**11%**	**129**	**128**	**16%**	**20%**	**99**	**9%**	**91%**	**70.2**	**308**

Freeman,Tyler

Age: 25 Pos: 3B | Bats: R Ht: 6' 0" Wt: 190

Health	A	LIMA Plan	D
PT/Exp	D	Rand Var	+1
Consist	D	MM	0431

4-18-.242 with 5 SB in 168 PA at CLE. Career .311 minor league hitter with elite ct% found a tad more MLB playing time; even advanced his bb% and running game. But as an infield utility type with sub-par power and exit velocity, finding consistent PA will be a challenge. LD%, xBA hint at BA upside, but all depends on opportunity.

Yr	Tm	PA	R	HR	RBI	SB	BA	xHR	xSB	xBA	OBP	SLG	OPS+	vL+	vR+	bb%	ct%	Eye	G	L	F	h%	HctX	QBaB	Brl%	PX	xPX	HR/F	xHR/F	Spd	SBA%	SB%	RAR	BPX
19																																		
20																																		
21	aa	171	21	2	16	3	295		3		322	423	102			4	86	0.28				34				79				103	13%	60%		181
22	CLE *	398	39	4	29	5	224	0	5	236	260	276	76	88	83	5	87	0.38	52	18	30	25	68	DCf	2%	32	34	0%	0%	105	7%	66%	-15.3	55
23	CLE *	270	36	5	30	12	248	3	9	268	307	364	91	90	90	8	80	0.43	48	25	28	29	70	DFf	3%	69	65	12%	9%	108	18%	100%	4.0	89
1st Half		159	24	1	16	8	271	0	6	285	333	378	97	50	112	8	81	0.48	54	25	21	33	85	DFf	0%	72	57	0%	0%	108	20%	100%	3.4	114
2nd Half		111	13	4	14	4	216	3	3	253	271	344	83	99	64	7	79	0.36	43	24	32	23	59	DDd	5%	64	70	17%	13%	111	15%	100%	-2.1	61
24	**Proj**	**175**	**21**	**2**	**17**	**5**	**242**	**2**	**4**	**255**	**303**	**326**	**86**	**87**	**85**	**6**	**83**	**0.37**	**50**	**22**	**28**	**28**	**69**		**2%**	**49**	**52**	**6%**	**4%**	**110**	**12%**	**89%**	**-2.7**	**88**

Frelick,Sal

Age: 24 Pos: RF CF | Bats: L Ht: 5'9" Wt: 175

Health	A	LIMA Plan	B
PT/Exp	C	Rand Var	+1
Consist	C	MM	1435

3-24-.246, 7 SB in 223 PA at MIL. UCL surgery to left thumb kept 2021 1st-round pick out until June; made MLB debut July. Rust, inexperience showed throughout, and he's yet to develop double-digit HR power. But he wasn't overmatched—and elite plate skills, running game, glove point to bright future. Could be undervalued on draft day.

Yr	Tm	PA	R	HR	RBI	SB	BA	xHR	xSB	xBA	OBP	SLG	OPS+	vL+	vR+	bb%	ct%	Eye	G	L	F	h%	HctX	QBaB	Brl%	PX	xPX	HR/F	xHR/F	Spd	SBA%	SB%	RAR	BPX
19																																		
20																																		
21																																		
22	a/a	442	55	7	35	13	286		13		332	396	103			6	86	0.49				32				66				119	16%	69%		162
23	MIL *	395	48	5	37	13	229	2	13	248	313	322	86	77	99	11	83	0.73	53	16	31	26	69	FDf	3%	55	51	6%	4%	109	17%	74%	-5.2	121
1st Half		112	12	1	6	4	203		5	233	262	273	73	0	0	7	82	0.44	44	20	36	24	0		0%	42	-21	0%		124	30%	57%	-6.2	54
2nd Half		283	36	4	31	8	240	2	7	253	333	343	91	76	98	12	84	0.87	53	16	31	27	70	FDf	3%	60	51	6%	4%	104	12%	88%	0.1	146
24	**Proj**	**455**	**56**	**6**	**39**	**17**	**256**	**4**	**15**	**252**	**319**	**359**	**93**	**74**	**98**	**9**	**84**	**0.59**	**53**	**16**	**31**	**29**	**63**		**2%**	**59**	**46**	**6%**	**4%**	**117**	**19%**	**74%**	**-0.2**	**129**

JOCK THOMPSON

Friedl,T.J.

Age: 28 Pos: CF LF | Bats: L Ht: 5' 10" Wt: 180 | Health A | PT/Exp A | Consist C | LIMA Plan B+ | Rand Var -3 | MM 2525

Seized CF job early, never looked back despite May/June IL stints, 2nd half h% regression. Stable ct%, bb%, plus base-running and some luck drove value; friendly home venue (13 HR, .926 OPS) didn't hurt. But poor exit velocity, xHR/F say this is a ceiling. Plus glove, speed, reverse splits help keep him in the lineup, but don't pay for a full repeat.

Yr Tm	PA	R	HR	RBI	SB	BA	xHR	xSB	xBA	OBP	SLG	OPS+	vL+	vR+	bb%	ct%	Eye	G	L	F	h%	HctX	QBaB	Brl%	PX	xPX	HR/F	xHR/F	Spd	SBA%	SB%	RAR	BPX	R$
19 aa	252	33	5	25	11	216		9		298	356	91			10	74	0.45				27				78				133	27%	72%		78	$4
20																																		
21 CIN *	457	55	11	30	10	229	0	13	219	296	360	90	113	106	9	80	0.48	30	20	50	26	87	CAd	7%	70	70	7%	0%	135	17%	55%	-15.8	138	$8
22 CIN *	483	56	14	51	14	233	5	13	227	298	404	99	157	102	8	77	0.40	32	18	50	27	98	FAf	5%	103	116	9%	6%	124	16%	76%	0.2	155	$14
23 CIN	556	73	18	66	27	279	5	26	262	352	467	112	130	107	8	82	0.52	38	20	42	31	83	FCf	3%	99	69	11%	3%	137	23%	82%	25.4	236	$23
1st Half	246	31	6	31	14	309	1	11	265	373	479	117	140	113	9	80	0.48	38	23	39	37	65	FCf	2%	98	37	9%	2%	118	22%	93%	16.9	186	$19
2nd Half	310	42	12	35	13	255	4	16	260	336	458	107	124	102	9	83	0.57	39	17	44	27	97	FCf	4%	99	95	13%	4%	151	23%	72%	7.0	271	$22
24 Proj	455	59	12	49	19	255	6	19	243	332	413	102	127	98	9	80	0.49	37	20	43	29	92		4%	86	89	8%	4%	133	20%	78%	9.2	186	$16

Gallo,Joey

Age: 30 Pos: 1B LF | Bats: L Ht: 6' 5" Wt: 250 | Health C | PT/Exp A | Consist C | LIMA Plan D | Rand Var 0 | MM 5203

21-40-.177 in 332 PA at MIN. Fast start was quickly derailed by multiple IL stints and 2nd half slump that torpedoed his playing time by year-end. Power, exit velocity rejoined bb% at elite levels, but plunging ct% neutralized it all and began to obliterate fantasy usefulness in late May. R$ says these HRs are not worth the BA drag.

Yr Tm	PA	R	HR	RBI	SB	BA	xHR	xSB	xBA	OBP	SLG	OPS+	vL+	vR+	bb%	ct%	Eye	G	L	F	h%	HctX	QBaB	Brl%	PX	xPX	HR/F	xHR/F	Spd	SBA%	SB%	RAR	BPX	R$
19 TEX	297	54	22	49	4	253	28	3	240	389	598	136	163	124	18	53	0.46	27	26	47	37	95	AAc	26%	251	199	37%	47%	89	8%	67%	18.8	278	$11
20 TEX	226	23	10	26	2	181	12	1	194	301	378	90	82	94	13	59	0.37	27	18	55	24	99	CAf	14%	137	173	17%	20%	88	4%	100%	-12.3	0	$7
21 2 AL	616	90	38	77	6	199	38	3	212	351	458	111	104	115	18	57	0.52	33	17	51	25	88	BAf	19%	179	160	27%	27%	79	4%	100%	12.2	131	$13
22 2 TM	410	48	19	47	3	160	21	3	186	280	357	90	61	98	14	53	0.34	28	19	53	22	77	CAf	17%	160	141	19%	21%	101	3%	100%	-12.1	3	$1
23 MIN *	363	40	22	44	1	172	22	2	192	288	423	97	95	102	14	50	0.32	29	12	58	24	74	AAf	19%	204	186	26%	27%	83	3%	50%	-0.7	61	$2
1st Half	240	28	16	31	0	188	16	1	212	294	474	105	91	114	13	52	0.32	28	12	60	25	81	AAf	21%	225	194	25%	27%	85	0%	0%	2.2	154	$6
2nd Half	123	12	6	13	1	141	5	2	154	275	324	81	103	82	16	45	0.33	33	13	54	22	59	BAf	14%	158	165	29%	24%	87	7%	50%	-5.1	-129	-$4
24 Proj	350	42	21	42	2	189	21	3	194	315	431	102	99	103	15	51	0.36	30	16	54	27	76		18%	190	166	25%	25%	87	4%	71%	1.8	26	$7

Garcia,Adolis

Age: 31 Pos: RF | Bats: R Ht: 6' 1" Wt: 205 | Health A | PT/Exp A | Consist B | LIMA Plan B | Rand Var -4 | MM 4325

LD% retreat, ct% keep BA shaky. But reprised all of his 2022 hard contact as notable launch angle improvement, patience and pitch selection helped bump FB% and power to another level. Disappearance of running game fueled R$ decline; Spd, SBA% and age suggest it may not return, though SB% offers hope. But production looks like a lock.

Yr Tm	PA	R	HR	RBI	SB	BA	xHR	xSB	xBA	OBP	SLG	OPS+	vL+	vR+	bb%	ct%	Eye	G	L	F	h%	HctX	QBaB	Brl%	PX	xPX	HR/F	xHR/F	Spd	SBA%	SB%	RAR	BPX	R$
19 aaa	507	71	23	71	10	205		12		230	396	87			3	62	0.09				28				118				116	31%	47%		-48	$10
20 TEX	7	0	0	0	0	0	0	0	0	143	0	19	0	67	14	33	0.25	50	0	50	0	0	FDf		0	-26	0%	0%	101	0%	0%	-1.1	-820	-$4
21 TEX	622	77	31	90	16	243	30	12	231	286	454	102	95	105	5	67	0.16	43	16	41	31	106	BBd	12%	134	127	20%	19%	112	18%	76%	-1.7	73	$23
22 TEX	657	88	27	101	25	250	30	22	247	300	456	107	104	108	6	70	0.22	41	19	40	31	120	ACf	13%	142	139	16%	18%	140	24%	81%	8.1	169	$32
23 TEX	632	108	39	107	9	245	41	9	253	328	508	114	117	113	10	68	0.37	37	16	47	28	119	ABd	16%	163	174	22%	23%	94	7%	90%	29.0	196	$25
1st Half	361	61	20	67	6	259	21	5	255	327	503	114	119	112	9	71	0.34	35	18	46	30	130	ABd	15%	149	183	19%	19%	95	8%	100%	14.9	186	$34
2nd Half	271	47	19	40	3	226	20	4	250	328	515	114	113	114	12	65	0.40	39	13	48	25	103	ABd	17%	185	160	26%	27%	94	7%	75%	9.0	225	$20
24 Proj	630	98	34	100	10	241	37	14	241	306	473	107	104	108	8	67	0.27	40	17	44	30	115		14%	149	152	20%	22%	107	11%	70%	13.7	153	$27

Garcia,Avisail

Age: 33 Pos: RF | Bats: R Ht: 6' 4" Wt: 250 | Health F | PT/Exp C | Consist C | LIMA Plan D | Rand Var +4 | MM 2303

3-12-.185 in 116 PA at MIA. 2023 never lifted off. Back woes shelved him from May through July, strained hamstring finished him in late August. Injuries the obvious story here, but so is age—and that combination rarely ends well. MLB contract still fuels playing time hope. But volatile skills history, poor ct%, GB% trends make 2021 seem far away.

Yr Tm	PA	R	HR	RBI	SB	BA	xHR	xSB	xBA	OBP	SLG	OPS+	vL+	vR+	bb%	ct%	Eye	G	L	F	h%	HctX	QBaB	Brl%	PX	xPX	HR/F	xHR/F	Spd	SBA%	SB%	RAR	BPX	R$
19 TAM	530	61	20	72	10	282	26	8	260	332	464	110	108	110	6	74	0.25	46	22	32	34	103	BCc	12%	100	90	17%	22%	97	11%	71%	-1.2	78	$18
20 MIL	207	20	2	15	1	238	5	2	232	333	326	88	114	75	10	73	0.41	48	24	27	32	81	CDc	4%	63	68	6%	14%	80	7%	25%	-10.8	-48	$6
21 MIL	515	68	29	86	8	262	27	5	265	330	490	113	127	108	7	74	0.31	47	21	32	30	113	BCc	12%	128	117	26%	24%	69	10%	67%	7.5	135	$21
22 MIA *	411	33	8	36	5	221	11	3	208	259	310	81	81	83	5	68	0.16	56	18	26	30	88	CFd	7%	65	93	12%	17%	81	5%	100%	-17.3	-134	$4
23 MIA *	165	13	6	18	2	181	5	2	206	237	340	79	71	79	7	61	0.19	54	13	33	25	108	BCc	12%	111	110	13%	22%	93	7%	100%	-7.1	-79	-$2
1st Half	90	7	4	9	1	172	3	1	189	206	314	71	45	88	4	61	0.11	50	15	35	23	92	BCf	13%	92	110	19%	19%	74	7%	100%	-5.8	-182	-$8
2nd Half	75	6	2	9	1	193	1	1	223	272	373	87	83	46	10	62	0.28	61	9	30	28	142	ADa	9%	134	109	0%	14%	98	8%	100%	-1.9	18	-$6
24 Proj	315	31	8	38	4	235	12	4	220	297	368	91	92	91	7	69	0.24	50	18	32	31	109		11%	86	103	13%	18%	90	7%	85%	-3.3	-43	$8

Garcia,Luis

Age: 24 Pos: 2B | Bats: L Ht: 6' 2" Wt: 212 | Health A | PT/Exp A | Consist A | LIMA Plan B | Rand Var +2 | MM 1245

9-50-.266 in 482 PA at WAS. Aug demotion to AAA sent a message; Sept finish (.850 OPS, 3 HR in 73 PA) hints at message received—but questions remain. Elite ct% is wasted by too many GBs; average speed and exit velocity don't help; more patience, less chase might. Ceiling seems apparent, but still has time to improve. Track his off-season.

Yr Tm	PA	R	HR	RBI	SB	BA	xHR	xSB	xBA	OBP	SLG	OPS+	vL+	vR+	bb%	ct%	Eye	G	L	F	h%	HctX	QBaB	Brl%	PX	xPX	HR/F	xHR/F	Spd	SBA%	SB%	RAR	BPX	R$
19 aa	542	68	4	31	11	268		12		292	350	89			3	84	0.20				31				46				128	13%	69%		67	$11
20 WAS	139	18	2	16	1	276	3	1	259	302	366	89	37	106	4	78	0.17	61	23	16	34	82	FFf	5%	55	41	12%	18%	87	6%	50%	-4.6	-24	$9
21 WAS *	401	50	17	42	1	257	5	2	288	300	458	104	105	90	6	81	0.32	56	20	24	28	105	CFd	5%	109	68	13%	11%	92	5%	21%	1.2	208	$9
22 WAS *	574	57	13	68	5	272	12	6	264	302	413	101	81	107	4	77	0.19	51	22	27	33	103	CFc	8%	93	112	9%	16%	99	7%	56%	2.3	83	$18
23 WAS *	585	72	10	59	10	259	12	12	273	301	373	92	90	95	6	86	0.44	53	19	28	29	107	CFd	6%	63	85	8%	11%	104	10%	72%	0.4	143	$14
1st Half	318	36	5	37	4	276	10	7	274	309	388	95	86	99	5	87	0.45	56	18	26	30	117	CFc	7%	59	94	7%	15%	109	10%	50%	1.8	146	$14
2nd Half	267	36	5	22	6	239	3	5	267	284	356	86	102	88	6	85	0.42	48	20	33	26	87	CDf	4%	67	68	9%	7%	103	11%	100%	-2.9	139	$9
24 Proj	490	59	10	50	7	274	13	8	270	308	402	97	89	100	5	83	0.30	53	20	27	31	99		6%	74	82	10%	12%	100	8%	68%	8.9	125	$18

Garcia,Maikel

Age: 24 Pos: 3B | Bats: R Ht: 6' 0" Wt: 145 | Health A | PT/Exp A | Consist A | LIMA Plan B | Rand Var -1 | MM 1535

4-50-.272 with 23 SB in 515 PA at KC. Athletic rookie not at all overmatched in his first extended MLB opportunity, with the possibility of more. Running game, speed, solid plate skills offer a floor. Elite Hard hit% hints at some HR gains with a launch angle tweak. Plus glove at SS/3B and age completes this growth-stock profile.

Yr Tm	PA	R	HR	RBI	SB	BA	xHR	xSB	xBA	OBP	SLG	OPS+	vL+	vR+	bb%	ct%	Eye	G	L	F	h%	HctX	QBaB	Brl%	PX	xPX	HR/F	xHR/F	Spd	SBA%	SB%	RAR	BPX	R$
19																																		
20																																		
21																																		
22 KC *	544	66	6	40	24	246	0	23	248	295	351	91	158	68	6	78	0.32	53	18	29	31	40	DFd		78	30	0%	0%	144	28%	73%	-9.1	114	$18
23 KC *	621	67	5	62	26	260	8	31	246	320	347	91	106	88	8	75	0.35	48	25	27	34	114	ADd	4%	58	105	4%	8%	147	22%	71%	1.6	32	$17
1st Half	310	31	3	32	16	263	4	14	251	323	357	93	118	90	8	76	0.36	49	24	27	34	118	ADc	6%	66	121	5%	10%	125	25%	78%	-1.4	43	$15
2nd Half	311	36	2	30	10	258	4	17	240	312	337	88	91	87	8	75	0.34	47	25	27	34	112	AFd	3%	50	94	3%	7%	170	20%	63%	-5.7	32	$13
24 Proj	560	70	8	56	24	266	8	28	254	317	375	95	112	90	7	76	0.34	48	25	27	34	114		4%	72	105	7%	7%	134	23%	72%	4.8	68	$24

Garrett,Stone

Age: 28 Pos: LF | Bats: R Ht: 6' 2" Wt: 195 | Health A | PT/Exp B | Consist C | LIMA Plan D+ | Rand Var -5 | MM 4313

Older rookie held his own as short-side platoon, then mashed as a full-timer in Aug before fractured fibia ended his season. Power metrics, exit velocity and 53 HR in previous two minor league seasons attest to legitimate power; doesn't look overmatched vR. But entrenched ct%, age hint that everyday play could be elusive.

Yr Tm	PA	R	HR	RBI	SB	BA	xHR	xSB	xBA	OBP	SLG	OPS+	vL+	vR+	bb%	ct%	Eye	G	L	F	h%	HctX	QBaB	Brl%	PX	xPX	HR/F	xHR/F	Spd	SBA%	SB%	RAR	BPX	R$
19 aa	431	58	13	67	16	228		13		263	390	90			4	66	0.14				31				99				112	31%	67%		-44	$12
20																																		
21 a/a	424	38	14	47	10	206		8		229	347	79			3	65	0.08				28				94				87	24%	62%		-123	$6
22 ARI *	486	50	17	58	11	206	4	10	205	237	379	87	123	114	4	66	0.12	34	14	52	27	92	AAc	10%	128	135	15%	15%	128	21%	75%	-19.2	48	$9
23 WAS	268	40	9	40	3	269	9	4	245	343	457	109	113	104	10	65	0.32	32	29	39	38	110	ABd	10%	137	124	15%	15%	104	6%	75%	9.6	79	$7
1st Half	159	22	5	23	3	275	5	3	237	340	437	106	124	84	8	67	0.28	34	27	39	38	121	ABf	8%	113	126	13%	13%	106	7%	100%	4.5	32	$5
2nd Half	109	18	4	17	0	261	5	1	260	349	489	113	95	130	12	62	0.37	28	32	40	38	93	AAc	12%	179	121	17%	21%	102	4%	0%	4.1	171	$1
24 Proj	280	38	11	40	5	254	13	6	232	309	454	105	104	104	7	65	0.22	32	23	45	35	100		10%	142	128	15%	17%	105	12%	65%	6.2	47	$11

OCK THOMPSON

Garver,Mitch

Age: 33 Pos: DH CA | Bats: R Ht: 6' 1" Wt: 220

Health F | PT/Exp C | Consist F | LIMA Plan D+ | Rand Var -2 | MM 4023

Logged significant IL time again but rebounded late and crushed down the stretch. Plus power-and-patience combo, big FB% remain intact; elevated ct%, LD% stretched BA in the second half. Still qualifies at CA, will again find most of his PA at DH in the real game. Still risky, yet fantasy worthy in 2-catcher leagues; age/health should inform your bid.

Yr	Tm	PA	R	HR	RBI	SB	BA	xHR	xSB	xBA	OBP	SLG	OPS+	vL+	vR+	bb%	ct%	Eye	G	L	F	h%	HctX	QBaB	Brl%	PX	xPX	HR/F	xHR/F	Spd	SBA%	SB%	RAR	BPX	R$
19	MIN	359	70	31	67	0	273	26	1	278	365	630	138	163	124	11	72	0.47	39	14	47	28	118	ABd	16%	186	159	29%	24%	89	0%	0%	23.5	330	$1
20	MIN	81	8	2	5	0	167	2	0	150	247	264	68	107	49	9	49	0.19	39	22	39	30	82	AAf	8%	79	77	14%	14%	96	0%	0%	-6.8	-372	-$
21	MIN *	271	32	13	35	1	247	15	0	242	341	479	113	100	136	12	65	0.41	31	23	46	32	122	AAc	17%	157	183	21%	24%	59	3%	50%	2.6	115	$
22	TEX	215	23	10	24	1	207	9	1	229	298	404	99	144	82	11	72	0.43	34	17	49	23	105	CAd	9%	126	133	15%	13%	86	4%	50%	-5.1	128	$
23	TEX	343	45	19	50	0	270	17	2	253	370	500	119	126	115	13	72	0.54	30	21	48	31	105	BAd	13%	132	119	18%	17%	77	0%	0%	18.6	164	$1
1st Half		89	11	3	13	0	238	4	1	206	315	400	98	133	86	10	64	0.31	43	16	41	33	92	BCf	14%	116	77	14%	19%	91	0%	0%	-1.0	-11	-$
2nd Half		254	34	16	37	0	282	13	1	271	390	537	125	123	125	14	75	0.66	26	23	50	31	109	BAc	12%	137	132	20%	16%	70	0%	0%	16.3	221	$1
24	**Proj**	**315**	**41**	**16**	**44**	**1**	**249**	**16**	**1**	**240**	**342**	**468**	**111**	**127**	**104**	**12**	**70**	**0.45**	**34**	**20**	**47**	**30**	**106**		**12%**	**134**	**128**	**18%**	**18%**	**75**	**1%**	**50%**	**10.2**	**146**	**$**

Gelof,Zack

Age: 24 Pos: 2B | Bats: R Ht: 6' 3" Wt: 205

Health A | PT/Exp B | Consist D | LIMA Plan C+ | Rand Var 0 | MM 4425

14-32-.267 with 14 SB in 300 PA at OAK. Called up in July, quickly entrenched himself as a top-of-the-lineup regular. Small MLB sample, but running game looks sustainable; HR may need launch angle tweak and a few more FB to keep up. Struggles vL, ct%, h% make MLB BA repeat dubious. Glove and age point to an early 2B draft darling.

Yr	Tm	PA	R	HR	RBI	SB	BA	xHR	xSB	xBA	OBP	SLG	OPS+	vL+	vR+	bb%	ct%	Eye	G	L	F	h%	HctX	QBaB	Brl%	PX	xPX	HR/F	xHR/F	Spd	SBA%	SB%	RAR	BPX	R$
19																																			
20																																			
21	aaa																																		
22	a/a	419	37	10	40	6	206		5		262	322	83			7	64	0.21				29				89				95	9%	72%		-97	$
23	OAK *	587	74	20	57	25	248	11	22	249	313	436	102	66	132	9	66	0.28	41	26	34	34	98	BCc	11%	134	111	22%	17%	115	26%	76%	17.3	86	$
1st Half		253	31	5	19	11	223		11	210	297	353	89	0	0	10	62	0.28	44	20	36	34	0		0%	103	-21	0%		111	31%	64%	-4.5	-54	$
2nd Half		334	43	15	38	15	267	11	12	272	325	498	111	65	131	8	69	0.27	41	26	34	34	102	BCc	11%	154	111	22%	17%	112	24%	88%	16.4	179	$2
24	**Proj**	**525**	**61**	**18**	**51**	**17**	**242**	**18**	**15**	**236**	**309**	**415**	**99**	**59**	**114**	**8**	**65**	**0.25**	**42**	**25**	**34**	**33**	**92**		**10%**	**123**	**100**	**17%**	**17%**	**113**	**19%**	**76%**	**8.3**	**10**	**$1**

Gimenez,Andres

Age: 25 Pos: 2B | Bats: L Ht: 5' 11" Wt: 161

Health A | PT/Exp A | Consist F | LIMA Plan B | Rand Var +1 | MM 2535

2022 h% always looked unsustainable, even with upward-trending ct% and speed. Abysmal chase% and stagnant exit velocity now suggest that BA won't retrace fully any time soon. Launch angle uptick and few more FBs helped keep a floor under the power, but SB is the R$ fuel here. Buy the running game, youth and health, hope for more growth.

Yr	Tm	PA	R	HR	RBI	SB	BA	xHR	xSB	xBA	OBP	SLG	OPS+	vL+	vR+	bb%	ct%	Eye	G	L	F	h%	HctX	QBaB	Brl%	PX	xPX	HR/F	xHR/F	Spd	SBA%	SB%	RAR	BPX	R$
19	aa	456	54	9	37	28	235		24		276	363	88			5	74	0.21				30				74				124	47%	64%		11	$
20	NYM	132	22	3	12	8	263	3	8	237	333	398	97	96	98	5	76	0.25	45	21	34	32	64	DCf	3%	70	35	10%	10%	177	25%	89%	-0.7	108	$
21	CLE *	428	45	12	38	17	232	4	12	222	269	382	89	78	89	5	70	0.17	50	13	38	30	83	DDf	4%	99	85	10%	8%	111	26%	79%	-10.0	23	$
22	CLE	557	66	17	69	20	297	15	19	263	371	466	119	124	117	6	77	0.30	46	21	33	36	87	DCd	6%	107	79	14%	12%	141	14%	87%	30.7	176	$
23	CLE	616	76	15	62	30	251	13	27	252	314	399	97	96	97	5	80	0.29	45	17	37	29	87	FCf	6%	84	79	9%	8%	132	25%	83%	9.0	139	$
1st Half		313	37	6	31	10	246	5	12	248	315	382	95	108	90	5	81	0.31	47	16	37	28	83	FCd	4%	74	80	7%	6%	141	17%	77%	-1.6	143	$
2nd Half		303	39	9	31	20	256	8	15	255	312	415	98	86	105	5	78	0.27	44	19	37	30	91	FCf	8%	93	77	11%	10%	122	33%	87%	4.1	132	$
24	**Proj**	**595**	**76**	**17**	**65**	**29**	**260**	**15**	**26**	**252**	**323**	**416**	**101**	**99**	**102**	**5**	**79**	**0.26**	**46**	**18**	**36**	**30**	**87**		**5%**	**90**	**75**	**11%**	**9%**	**140**	**23%**	**82%**	**11.5**	**122**	**$**

Goldschmidt,Paul

Age: 36 Pos: 1B DH | Bats: R Ht: 6' 3" Wt: 220

Health A | PT/Exp A | Consist F | LIMA Plan B+ | Rand Var 0 | MM 3335

Began 2023 as advertised, but faded in the second half. GB% spike, absence of authoritative contact confirmed by exit velocity and launch angle struggles. Perhaps he was pressing; the sum here is still pretty good and history, skills point to a rebound. But is age hinting at a new normal? Heed the Consistency grade. DN: 20 HR, .260 BA.

Yr	Tm	PA	R	HR	RBI	SB	BA	xHR	xSB	xBA	OBP	SLG	OPS+	vL+	vR+	bb%	ct%	Eye	G	L	F	h%	HctX	QBaB	Brl%	PX	xPX	HR/F	xHR/F	Spd	SBA%	SB%	RAR	BPX	R$
19	STL	680	97	34	97	3	260	39	4	251	346	476	114	134	108	11	72	0.47	38	22	39	30	119	BBb	11%	116	140	20%	23%	101	2%	75%	4.2	137	$
20	STL	230	31	6	21	1	304	11	2	264	417	466	117	134	114	16	77	0.86	35	28	38	37	88	CCc	11%	97	114	11%	20%	99	1%	100%	6.5	204	$
21	STL	679	102	31	99	12	294	42	8	269	365	514	121	145	115	10	77	0.49	36	24	40	33	131	ABc	14%	125	141	16%	22%	101	7%	100%	33.4	238	$
22	STL	649	106	35	115	7	317	33	6	282	404	578	139	186	127	12	75	0.56	40	19	41	37	110	BBc	12%	169	131	20%	19%	97	4%	100%	62.0	310	$
23	STL	686	89	25	80	11	268	30	10	251	363	447	110	111	110	13	73	0.54	41	22	37	33	113	ACc	12%	110	127	15%	19%	78	7%	85%	24.9	107	$
1st Half		363	51	15	46	8	286	18	7	266	375	492	119	99	125	12	75	0.56	39	21	39	34	133	ABc	13%	125	148	16%	19%	81	9%	89%	20.3	182	$
2nd Half		323	38	10	34	3	248	12	4	234	350	396	101	123	92	13	71	0.52	43	22	35	32	90	CCf	10%	93	102	14%	17%	78	4%	75%	2.6	32	$
24	**Proj**	**630**	**85**	**25**	**81**	**7**	**278**	**30**	**7**	**255**	**367**	**469**	**115**	**132**	**110**	**12**	**74**	**0.53**	**40**	**22**	**38**	**34**	**111**		**12%**	**118**	**127**	**16%**	**19%**	**88**	**5%**	**88%**	**32.9**	**176**	**$**

Gomes,Yan

Age: 36 Pos: CA | Bats: R Ht: 6' 2" Wt: 212

Health B | PT/Exp A | Consist C | LIMA Plan D+ | Rand Var -1 | MM 2333

Inherited primary catcher job on what was ostensibly a rebuilding club and held on throughout, posting highest PA total in five years. Power has begun to wane even as BA skills hold steady. R$ history and surprisingly good health illustrate sneaky value in two-catcher formats. But age now suggests he'll be hard-pressed to repeat.

Yr	Tm	PA	R	HR	RBI	SB	BA	xHR	xSB	xBA	OBP	SLG	OPS+	vL+	vR+	bb%	ct%	Eye	G	L	F	h%	HctX	QBaB	Brl%	PX	xPX	HR/F	xHR/F	Spd	SBA%	SB%	RAR	BPX
19	WAS	358	36	12	43	2	223	13	1	230	316	389	97	122	89	11	73	0.45	39	19	42	27	83	CAc	7%	94	91	12%	13%	84	2%	100%	-3.8	63
20	WAS	119	14	4	13	1	284	4	1	262	319	468	105	126	97	5	80	0.27	36	24	40	33	101	BAc	6%	99	93	11%	11%	120	4%	100%	4.2	184
21	2 TM	375	49	14	52	0	252	13	0	260	301	421	99	121	88	5	78	0.24	39	25	36	29	111	BCc	9%	95	118	14%	13%	90	0%	0%	3.2	100
22	CHC	293	23	8	31	2	235	7	1	260	260	365	89	94	86	3	83	0.17	45	22	33	26	91	DDf	3%	78	91	10%	9%	60	4%	100%	-3.8	69
23	CHC	419	44	10	63	1	267	12	4	250	315	408	99	111	92	5	79	0.26	37	22	40	32	95	CBd	8%	84	90	8%	10%	107	1%	100%	10.6	96
1st Half		181	25	7	24	1	265	6	2	224	309	410	98	114	89	5	78	0.24	33	19	48	30	91	CAf	10%	75	98	11%	10%	107	2%	100%	3.6	54
2nd Half		238	19	3	39	0	269	5	2	270	319	407	98	108	94	5	80	0.27	40	25	35	33	98	CCc	6%	90	84	5%	8%	98	0%	0%	4.8	114
24	**Proj**	**315**	**33**	**9**	**44**	**1**	**255**	**9**	**2**	**253**	**299**	**399**	**96**	**109**	**89**	**5**	**79**	**0.24**	**40**	**23**	**38**	**30**	**96**		**7%**	**84**	**94**	**10%**	**10%**	**81**	**2%**	**100%**	**5.6**	**90**

Gonzales,Nick

Age: 25 Pos: 2B | Bats: R Ht: 5' 10" Wt: 190

Health A | PT/Exp B | Consist A | LIMA Plan D | Rand Var 0 | MM 3201

2-13-.209 in 128 PA at PIT. Rebounded from injury-filled 2022 to post solid numbers at AAA, but too many whiffs for short-limbed hitter; eroding ct% has stymied BA upside. Sprays ball across diamond, but struggles to get to hard contact. Below-average HR and SB potential puts added pressure on BA-dependent profile. (CB)

Yr	Tm	PA	R	HR	RBI	SB	BA	xHR	xSB	xBA	OBP	SLG	OPS+	vL+	vR+	bb%	ct%	Eye	G	L	F	h%	HctX	QBaB	Brl%	PX	xPX	HR/F	xHR/F	Spd	SBA%	SB%	RAR	BPX
19																																		
20																																		
21																																		
22	aa	289	31	4	22	3	218		4		298	342	91			10	61	0.30				34				114				96	10%	49%		-38
23	PIT *	543	65	12	48	3	230	2	10	235	294	392	93	77	87	8	66	0.27	58	14	28	32	79	DDb	4%	113	53	9%	9%	134	6%	39%	-1.7	54
1st Half		273	32	6	26	1	216	1	6	202	292	382	92	79	132	10	63	0.29	55	5	40	31	129	DBc	7%	115	104	25%	13%	143	7%	17%	-3.7	36
2nd Half		270	33	6	22	2	244	1	4	252	295	403	94	76	74	7	70	0.24	59	16	25	33	64	DDb	3%	111	37	0%	7%	120	5%	68%	0.5	68
24	**Proj**	**245**	**28**	**4**	**20**	**2**	**226**	**4**	**4**	**217**	**312**	**370**	**94**	**82**	**99**	**9**	**65**	**0.28**	**57**	**12**	**31**	**33**	**85**		**4%**	**109**	**64**	**10%**	**9%**	**111**	**7%**	**48%**	**-1.1**	**18**

Gonzalez,Oscar

Age: 26 Pos: RF | Bats: R Ht: 6' 4" Wt: 240

Health A | PT/Exp A | Consist B | LIMA Plan D | Rand Var +2 | MM 1121

2-12-.214 in 180 PA at CLE. Poor start led to quick demotion and year-long AAA-to-MLB shuttle, wiping away any 2022 playing time edge. Collapse of ct% was the primary culprit, though exit velocity was nothing special even in better days. Entrenched GB%, poor patience complete dismal outlook. Even with an uptick, still fantasy FA list fodder.

Yr	Tm	PA	R	HR	RBI	SB	BA	xHR	xSB	xBA	OBP	SLG	OPS+	vL+	vR+	bb%	ct%	Eye	G	L	F	h%	HctX	QBaB	Brl%	PX	xPX	HR/F	xHR/F	Spd	SBA%	SB%	RAR	BPX
19	aa	99	7	1	9	0	187		0		211	272	67			3	81	0.16				22				52				95	0%	0%		15
20																																		
21	a/a	495	53	24	63	1	255		1		280	452	101			3	73	0.13				30				115				83	2%	40%		69
22	CLE *	576	54	17	65	1	268	10	3	268	294	426	102	104	115	3	80	0.18	51	21	28	31	117	CFd	7%	102	89	13%	12%	91	3%	33%	2.2	128
23	CLE *	529	48	11	55	1	221	4	4	239	249	350	82	68	79	4	71	0.13	49	21	30	29	89	CDd	8%	84	81	5%	11%	106	1%	100%	-15.3	-18
1st Half		273	23	6	31	1	216	2	2	236	240	345	80	90	47	3	73	0.12	45	21	34	27	67	CDf	5%	82	57	5%	10%	103	2%	100%	-11.9	-11
2nd Half		255	25	5	24	0	227	2	2	238	258	356	83	47	98	4	70	0.14	53	21	26	31	105	BDa	10%	86	101	6%	11%	109	0%	0%	-8.4	-36
24	**Proj**	**175**	**17**	**3**	**19**	**0**	**243**	**4**	**1**	**241**	**273**	**362**	**87**	**78**	**92**	**4**	**74**	**0.14**	**50**	**21**	**29**	**31**	**100**		**8%**	**78**	**85**	**9%**	**11%**	**94**	**2%**	**52%**	**-3.4**	**42**

JOCK THOMPSON

Goodman,Hunter

Age: 24	Pos: RF	Health	A	LIMA Plan	D+
Bats: R	Ht: 6' 1" Wt: 210	PT/Exp	C	Rand Var	+3
		Consist	F	MM	2101

1-17-.200 in 77 PA at COL. Rookie struggled in small sample after late-season callup. Power metrics look formidable and backed up by 70 HR in MiLB over the last two seasons. Struggles vR, ct% are less optimistic; poor mobility puts his defensive home into question. Has a chance; now a 2024 dart throw at best.

Yr	Tm	PA	R	HR	RBI	SB	BA	xHR	xSB	xBA	OBP	SLG	OPS+	vL+	vR+	bb%	ct%	Eye	G	L	F	h%	HctX	QBaB	Brl%	PX	xPX	HR/F	xHR/F	Spd	SBA%	SB%	RAR	BPX	R$
19																																			
20																																			
21																																			
22	aa	46	3	1	2	1	192		1		223	283	72			4	72	0.14				24				51				110	11%	100%		-100	-$4
23	COL *	514	49	26	86	1	220	2	3	257	270	460	99	114	80	6	70	0.23	44	17	40	26	107	CCf	10%	150	140	5%	11%	86	3%	47%	-3.0	146	$10
1st Half		291	30	15	44	0	216		1	264	276	451	100	0	0	8	72	0.29	44	20	36	24	0		0%	148	-21	0%		76	0%	0%	-2.7	161	$11
2nd Half		225	22	13	47	1	240	2	2	267	282	513	107	113	79	6	69	0.19	44	17	40	28	105	CCf	10%	169	140	5%	11%	109	6%	47%	2.4	204	$13
24	**Proj**	**245**	**24**	**3**	**45**	**1**	**231**	**7**	**2**	**215**	**277**	**353**	**86**	**105**	**82**	**7**	**70**	**0.24**	**44**	**17**	**40**	**32**	**95**		**9%**	**89**	**126**	**5%**	**11%**	**87**	**3%**	**50%**	**-4.5**	**187**	**$2**

Gordon,Nick

Age: 28	Pos: CF	Health	C	LIMA Plan	C+
Bats: L	Ht: 6' 0" Wt: 160	PT/Exp	D	Rand Var	+5
		Consist	D	MM	2533

Struggled early before fractured shin ended his season in late May. Abysmal bb% still looks glaring, GB% suspect and baserunning may be stagnating. But the contact skills are intriguing and xPX, HR/F still hint at more, perhaps with a launch angle tweak. Age, handedness, versatility will keep giving him opportunity. UP: 15 HR/15 SB

Yr	Tm	PA	R	HR	RBI	SB	BA	xHR	xSB	xBA	OBP	SLG	OPS+	vL+	vR+	bb%	ct%	Eye	G	L	F	h%	HctX	QBaB	Brl%	PX	xPX	HR/F	xHR/F	Spd	SBA%	SB%	RAR	BPX	R$
19	aaa	307	41	3	33	12	271		8		307	417	100			5	76	0.21				35				94				104	26%	72%		74	$9
20																																			
21	MIN *	292	27	6	30	15	240	6	11	244	284	355	88	71	94	6	74	0.24	52	22	26	30	133	ACa	7%	68	88	11%	16%	132	26%	82%	-6.7	19	$9
22	MIN	443	45	9	50	6	272	20	9	253	316	427	105	76	113	4	74	0.18	41	24	35	35	122	BCb	9%	110	135	8%	19%	130	10%	60%	4.3	117	$13
23	MIN	93	13	2	7	0	176	3	0	274	185	319	69	94	65	1	88	0.09	47	18	35	18	119	CCd	5%	76	109	7%	11%	121	0%	0%	-5.4	189	-$3
1st Half		93	13	2	7	0	176	3	0	274	185	319	69	95	66	1	88	0.09	47	18	35	18	119	CCd	5%	76	109	7%	11%	121	0%	0%	-7.0	189	-$9
2nd Half																									0%										
24	**Proj**	**315**	**40**	**7**	**34**	**9**	**251**	**11**	**7**	**252**	**287**	**394**	**93**	**84**	**95**	**4**	**77**	**0.17**	**45**	**21**	**34**	**31**	**123**		**7%**	**88**	**107**	**9%**	**15%**	**135**	**17%**	**78%**	**-0.3**	**98**	**$11**

Gorman,Nolan

Age: 24	Pos: 2B DH	Health	A	LIMA Plan	C+
Bats: L	Ht: 6' 1" Wt: 210	PT/Exp	A	Rand Var	0
		Consist	B	MM	4215

Poor ct% keeps ceiling intact, but progress is otherwise visible—and there's plenty to like. Power metrics, FB% look firm; improving pitch selection, patience, exit velocity hint at more. Success vL gave him more opportunities, may have shed platoon outlook. Even his running game ticked up. Age, health offer 30+ HR upside at a scarce position.

Yr	Tm	PA	R	HR	RBI	SB	BA	xHR	xSB	xBA	OBP	SLG	OPS+	vL+	vR+	bb%	ct%	Eye	G	L	F	h%	HctX	QBaB	Brl%	PX	xPX	HR/F	xHR/F	Spd	SBA%	SB%	RAR	BPX	R$
19																																			
20																																			
21	a/a	505	48	16	51	5	230		3		269	368	87			5	74	0.20				28				81				88	6%	81%		-4	$8
22	STL *	493	67	24	52	3	223	18	3	215	282	417	99	93	103	8	61	0.21	27	25	48	31	93	BAb	14%	147	170	16%	21%	92	3%	100%	-3.3	17	$11
23	STL	464	59	27	76	7	236	28	6	238	328	478	110	113	109	11	64	0.36	29	23	48	30	93	AAc	17%	159	137	22%	22%	65	8%	78%	16.7	93	$14
1st Half		289	31	16	49	4	232	15	4	241	318	461	107	103	107	11	65	0.36	29	24	46	29	86	AAd	13%	146	112	21%	19%	67	9%	67%	6.9	82	$17
2nd Half		175	28	11	27	3	243	13	2	234	343	507	115	119	113	12	61	0.35	28	21	51	32	105	AAc	23%	182	183	23%	28%	83	7%	100%	8.7	139	$10
24	**Proj**	**525**	**70**	**29**	**71**	**6**	**232**	**34**	**5**	**228**	**307**	**457**	**105**	**110**	**104**	**9**	**64**	**0.28**	**28**	**23**	**49**	**30**	**95**		**17%**	**150**	**160**	**20%**	**23%**	**79**	**6%**	**87%**	**13.8**	**63**	**$19**

Grandal,Yasmani

Age: 35	Pos: CA	Health	C	LIMA Plan	D
Bats: B	Ht: 6' 2" Wt: 225	PT/Exp	A	Rand Var	0
		Consist	F	MM	1201

Fortunate BA and contact kept him in early playing time, but regression, nagging injuries and woeful production gradually put an end to it. Once-formidable power remained MIA. And decent plate skills aren't enough to save a health-challenged, slow-footed 35-year-old catcher. He's edging closer to fantasy irrelevance.

Yr	Tm	PA	R	HR	RBI	SB	BA	xHR	xSB	xBA	OBP	SLG	OPS+	vL+	vR+	bb%	ct%	Eye	G	L	F	h%	HctX	QBaB	Brl%	PX	xPX	HR/F	xHR/F	Spd	SBA%	SB%	RAR	BPX	R$
19	MIL	632	79	28	77	5	246	28	3	259	380	468	117	129	112	17	73	0.78	39	23	38	28	114	BBc	11%	120	133	20%	20%	80	3%	83%	36.4	178	$15
20	CHW	194	27	8	27	0	230	8	0	222	351	422	103	118	99	15	64	0.52	36	23	41	31	109	BBc	8%	125	161	19%	19%	67	0%	0%	3.7	36	$11
21	CHW *	410	64	24	64	0	239	18	0	247	408	498	124	142	125	22	69	0.92	41	19	40	27	119	ACd	13%	150	153	28%	22%	61	0%	0%	26.7	231	$11
22	CHW *	421	19	7	32	1	210	5	1	212	312	289	85	108	72	13	77	0.64	43	21	36	25	83	BCf	5%	50	59	6%	6%	74	1%	100%	-6.8	-7	-$1
23	CHW	405	33	8	33	0	234	7	2	217	309	339	88	92	87	9	76	0.42	45	18	37	29	89	CCd	5%	65	74	8%	7%	73	0%	0%	1.1	0	$2
1st Half		248	18	6	21	0	260	5	1	227	319	388	97	101	95	7	78	0.35	46	19	36	31	95	CCd	6%	78	78	10%	8%	75	0%	0%	4.1	43	$2
2nd Half		157	15	2	12	0	191	2	1	195	293	257	74	75	74	12	74	0.51	44	18	38	24	80	CCd	3%	41	67	5%	5%	76	0%	0%	-5.4	-79	-$5
24	**Proj**	**245**	**23**	**7**	**24**	**0**	**222**	**6**	**1**	**219**	**327**	**345**	**92**	**105**	**88**	**13**	**74**	**0.58**	**43**	**19**	**38**	**27**	**93**		**6%**	**74**	**88**	**11%**	**10%**	**72**	**0%**	**92%**	**2.0**	**29**	**$4**

Greene,Riley

Age: 23	Pos: CF	Health	C	LIMA Plan	C+
Bats: L	Ht: 6' 3" Wt: 200	PT/Exp	A	Rand Var	-3
		Consist	F	MM	3435

Shin stress fracture shelved him for 38 days in May; Tommy John surgery to non-throwing elbow ended him in Sept. But despite challenged ct%, gains were evident. Whittled away at lofty GB%, as LD% soared; exit velocity now top shelf as power metrics grow. Spd, SB%, age still promising. With health, more growth... UP: .290, 20 HR/20 SB.

Yr	Tm	PA	R	HR	RBI	SB	BA	xHR	xSB	xBA	OBP	SLG	OPS+	vL+	vR+	bb%	ct%	Eye	G	L	F	h%	HctX	QBaB	Brl%	PX	xPX	HR/F	xHR/F	Spd	SBA%	SB%	RAR	BPX	R$
19																																			
20																																			
21	a/a	536	79	20	70	13	284		11		352	489	116			10	68	0.33				38				128				129	10%	93%		131	$24
22	DET *	484	53	6	46	3	250	13	9	230	313	356	95	105	93	8	69	0.30	56	20	24	35	98	BFd	10%	81	89	8%	21%	134	6%	44%	-2.3	0	$8
23	DET	416	51	11	37	7	288	19	10	259	349	447	108	94	113	8	70	0.31	49	26	25	39	111	ADa	11%	102	114	17%	29%	133	6%	100%	20.5	71	$12
1st Half		224	29	5	18	6	296	10	8	255	362	443	110	96	115	9	68	0.33	53	26	22	41	100	AFa	10%	95	112	17%	33%	150	9%	100%	11.6	57	$9
2nd Half		192	22	6	19	1	280	9	2	265	333	451	106	90	110	7	71	0.28	45	27	28	36	124	ADa	13%	110	117	17%	25%	108	2%	100%	7.0	82	$6
24	**Proj**	**595**	**83**	**18**	**69**	**8**	**282**	**24**	**12**	**254**	**342**	**451**	**109**	**100**	**112**	**8**	**70**	**0.29**	**50**	**24**	**26**	**38**	**108**		**11%**	**109**	**105**	**18%**	**24%**	**131**	**6%**	**80%**	**25.9**	**56**	**$25**

Grichuk,Randal

Age: 32	Pos: LF RF CF	Health	B	LIMA Plan	D+
Bats: R	Ht: 6' 2" Wt: 216	PT/Exp	A	Rand Var	+1
		Consist	A	MM	3233

16-44-.267 in 471 PA at COL/LAA. Pre-season hernia surgery delayed season, slowed him early before power returned. BA, contact skills have held up surprisingly well with age, though historically atrocious chase tendency keeps lid intact. Poor OBP won't improve; all of his real damage is now vL. Short-side platoon role looks inevitable.

Yr	Tm	PA	R	HR	RBI	SB	BA	xHR	xSB	xBA	OBP	SLG	OPS+	vL+	vR+	bb%	ct%	Eye	G	L	F	h%	HctX	QBaB	Brl%	PX	xPX	HR/F	xHR/F	Spd	SBA%	SB%	RAR	BPX	R$
19	TOR	628	75	31	80	2	232	27	4	247	280	457	102	109	98	6	72	0.21	39	19	42	27	93	BBf	9%	122	93	17%	15%	119	3%	67%	-15.2	130	$12
20	TOR	231	38	12	35	1	273	11	1	262	312	481	105	124	97	6	77	0.27	41	22	37	30	109	CCf	11%	110	95	19%	18%	94	4%	50%	1.9	156	$23
21	TOR	545	59	22	81	0	241	19	2	239	281	423	97	100	96	5	78	0.24	40	17	43	27	107	BBf	8%	103	98	13%	11%	87	3%	0%	-8.2	119	$11
22	COL	538	60	19	73	4	259	16	6	239	299	425	103	130	88	4	75	0.19	51	13	36	31	119	BDf	7%	105	114	14%	12%	126	3%	100%	2.3	110	$17
23	2 TM *	505	68	16	45	2	253	12	5	264	299	432	100	134	95	6	78	0.30	41	21	39	29	122	BCf	7%	108	107	12%	9%	100	4%	50%	4.3	150	$10
1st Half		242	32	3	20	1	258	3	4	257	310	384	95	119	103	7	77	0.32	40	25	35	33	108	BBc	6%	87	83	6%	6%	109	5%	33%	-1.4	86	$4
2nd Half		263	36	13	25	1	248	9	2	273	293	476	104	148	88	5	79	0.27	41	17	41	26	133	CCf	8%	127	124	16%	11%	92	2%	100%	3.7	211	$12
24	**Proj**	**280**	**36**	**10**	**33**	**1**	**252**	**8**	**2**	**253**	**298**	**435**	**100**	**123**	**91**	**5**	**77**	**0.24**	**43**	**18**	**39**	**29**	**117**		**7%**	**108**	**106**	**13%**	**11%**	**96**	**3%**	**60%**	**3.4**	**140**	**$9**

Grisham,Trent

Age: 27	Pos: CF	Health	A	LIMA Plan	C
Bats: L	Ht: 5' 11" Wt: 224	PT/Exp	A	Rand Var	+3
		Consist	C	MM	3215

Rebounded some, but not to relevance. Depressed ct% again the primary culprit, along with depressed h% despite LD bounce. Average exit velocity, speed, mysterious issues vR don't help his efforts. But xBA says he deserved better; so does excellent chase%. Ditto xHR/F and power metrics. Can't bet on it, but with a fix ... UP: 20 HR, .260

Yr	Tm	PA	R	HR	RBI	SB	BA	xHR	xSB	xBA	OBP	SLG	OPS+	vL+	vR+	bb%	ct%	Eye	G	L	F	h%	HctX	QBaB	Brl%	PX	xPX	HR/F	xHR/F	Spd	SBA%	SB%	RAR	BPX	R$
19	MIL *	613	87	31	87	12	267	4	9	262	364	520	122	99	101	13	75	0.62	38	19	43	30	94	CBc	5%	129	90	13%	8%	86	11%	68%	33.8	219	$23
20	SD	251	42	10	26	10	251	13	7	247	352	456	107	98	110	12	70	0.48	41	25	34	31	95	DCf	11%	116	111	20%	26%	111	16%	91%	3.2	136	$28
21	SD	527	61	15	62	13	242	10	8	249	327	413	102	112	98	10	74	0.45	41	22	37	30	90	CCf	5%	106	95	12%	8%	73	14%	72%	-0.3	100	$15
22	SD	524	58	17	53	7	184	17	4	208	284	341	89	89	88	11	67	0.38	43	13	43	23	88	DCf	8%	110	110	14%	14%	80	7%	88%	-15.3	10	$4
23	SD	554	67	13	50	15	198	19	11	225	315	352	91	107	85	14	67	0.49	35	22	43	26	82	CBf	12%	111	110	10%	15%	78	14%	83%	-4.5	36	$6
1st Half		300	35	8	23	8	209	14	7	233	318	384	96	117	88	13	68	0.46	34	22	44	28	93	BAd	16%	124	123	11%	19%	92	16%	73%	-1.0	93	$7
2nd Half		254	32	5	27	7	185	5	4	216	311	313	84	92	82	15	66	0.52	37	22	41	25	69	DCf	8%	95	94	9%	9%	67	11%	100%	-5.3	-25	$5
24	**Proj**	**455**	**57**	**13**	**48**	**11**	**206**	**14**	**7**	**225**	**312**	**367**	**93**	**101**	**90**	**13**	**69**	**0.46**	**39**	**20**	**41**	**26**	**84**		**9%**	**109**	**105**	**12%**	**13%**	**74**	**12%**	**84%**	**-1.6**	**46**	**$11**

OCK THOMPSON

Grissom,Vaughn

Age: 23 Pos: SS	Health A	LIMA Plan D	
Bats: R Ht: 6'3" Wt: 210	PT/Exp C	Rand Var -1	
	Consist A	MM 1431	

0-9-.280 with 5 SB in 80 PA at ATL. Defensive limitations blocked path to everyday SS, so spent most of the season at AAA (.330/.419/.501). Plate skills, running game look like immediate value drivers, even if he hasn't unlocked either piece of QBaB in big-league trials. Still growth-age, may need scenery change to unlock opportunity.

Yr	Tm	PA	R	HR	RBI	SB	BA	xHR	xSB	xBA	OBP	SLG	OPS+	vL+	vR+	bb%	ct%	Eye	G	L	F	h%	HctX	QBaB	Brl%	PX	xPX	HR/F	xHR/F	Spd	SBA%	SB%	RAR	BPX
19																																		
20																																		
21																																		
22	ATL *	250	32	7	27	11	307	5	9	262	347	447	112	132	103	6	79	0.29	44	25	31	36	89	DDc	8%	86	113	15%	15%	125	20%	77%	8.6	117
23	ATL *	521	63	6	56	10	289	1	13	268	352	415	104	70	105	9	80	0.49	57	17	27	35	70	DFc	7%	82	54	0%	6%	114	9%	76%	18.3	146
1st Half		318	36	1	31	8	277	1	10	260	328	377	97	74	94	7	82	0.43	58	15	27	33	76	DFc	6%	65	51	0%	7%	124	13%	71%	1.0	125
2nd Half		202	27	5	25	2	308	0	3	288	388	479	117	53	190	12	77	0.57	50	25	25	38	39	FFa	13%	110	73	0%	0%	97	4%	100%	13.3	182
24	**Proj**	**175**	**22**	**2**	**20**	**5**	**280**	**3**	**5**	**255**	**352**	**395**	**102**	**96**	**106**	**8**	**79**	**0.42**	**52**	**19**	**28**	**34**	**81**		**6%**	**74**	**76**	**6%**	**8%**	**112**	**12%**	**79%**	**4.6**	**142**

Grossman,Robbie

Age: 34 Pos: LF DH RF	Health A	LIMA Plan D+	
Bats: B Ht: 6'0" Wt: 209	PT/Exp A	Rand Var 0	
	Consist D	MM 3213	

Forgettable 1st half was followed by h%-fueled, OBP-forward 2nd half in part-time role. HR, xHR at odds with power metrics despite sturdy FB%; 2021 looks increasingly like an anomaly. Plate discipline is his only rock-steady skill. And after two years of struggles vR, his playing time is in question. Best employed in OBP leagues only.

Yr	Tm	PA	R	HR	RBI	SB	BA	xHR	xSB	xBA	OBP	SLG	OPS+	vL+	vR+	bb%	ct%	Eye	G	L	F	h%	HctX	QBaB	Brl%	PX	xPX	HR/F	xHR/F	Spd	SBA%	SB%	RAR	BPX
19	OAK	482	57	6	38	9	240	8	8	250	334	348	94	76	96	12	80	0.69	41	25	34	29	95	CCc	2%	60	81	5%	7%	107	10%	69%	-14.5	93
20	OAK	192	23	8	23	8	241	6	5	275	344	482	110	59	117	11	77	0.55	39	23	38	27	88	CBc	5%	134	98	16%	12%	98	20%	89%	2.5	276
21	DET	671	88	23	67	20	239	19	16	229	357	415	106	117	101	15	72	0.63	29	24	46	29	81	CAb	8%	104	105	12%	10%	114	13%	80%	9.6	142
22	2 TM	477	40	7	45	6	209	7	4	206	310	311	88	123	72	12	69	0.43	31	24	45	29	84	DAb	4%	79	105	6%	6%	81	7%	75%	-13.9	-41
23	TEX	420	56	10	49	1	238	8	3	233	340	394	100	128	86	14	72	0.58	32	21	47	30	104	CAc	7%	104	123	8%	7%	94	1%	100%	7.3	104
1st Half		246	36	7	33	0	219	5	1	218	297	358	90	105	83	10	72	0.39	34	19	47	27	94	CAd	6%	88	117	9%	7%	92	0%	0%	-4.6	25
2nd Half		174	20	3	16	1	268	3	2	256	402	449	115	157	92	19	73	0.89	29	24	47	35	120	CAb	8%	128	131	6%	6%	88	2%	100%	9.1	221
24	**Proj**	**315**	**38**	**7**	**33**	**4**	**236**	**6**	**4**	**231**	**344**	**386**	**100**	**128**	**88**	**14**	**72**	**0.58**	**32**	**23**	**45**	**30**	**97**		**6%**	**101**	**114**	**8%**	**7%**	**89**	**6%**	**81%**	**5.0**	**101**

Guerrero Jr.,Vladimir

Age: 25 Pos: 1B DH	Health A	LIMA Plan B+	
Bats: R Ht: 6'2" Wt: 240	PT/Exp A	Rand Var +2	
	Consist D	MM 3155	

Power was off despite FB% rebound, even with exit velocity, bb%, ct% still in terrific shape. Maybe it was playing through a mid-May knee injury that lingered throughout. Or new Rogers Centre dimensions that capped him at 10 HR and a .391 Slg. And/or something else. Age and talent give him a mulligan, but don't pay for 2021. Yet.

Yr	Tm	PA	R	HR	RBI	SB	BA	xHR	xSB	xBA	OBP	SLG	OPS+	vL+	vR+	bb%	ct%	Eye	G	L	F	h%	HctX	QBaB	Brl%	PX	xPX	HR/F	xHR/F	Spd	SBA%	SB%	RAR	BPX
19	TOR *	548	58	18	76	1	277	18	1	259	343	448	109	89	113	9	81	0.53	50	17	33	31	98	BDd	8%	88	89	12%	15%	84	1%	48%	6.4	148
20	TOR	243	34	9	33	1	262	9	1	283	329	462	105	116	101	8	83	0.53	55	17	28	28	130	AFc	9%	103	72	18%	18%	100	2%	100%	-1.1	248
21	TOR	698	123	48	111	4	311	42	3	299	401	601	138	129	141	12	82	0.78	45	19	36	31	139	ACd	15%	146	128	27%	23%	88	2%	80%	69.8	373
22	TOR	706	90	32	97	8	274	27	5	284	339	480	116	100	119	8	82	0.50	52	17	31	29	137	AFf	11%	121	107	20%	17%	71	6%	73%	27.6	221
23	TOR	682	78	26	94	5	264	28	6	271	345	444	107	103	108	10	83	0.67	46	18	35	28	124	ACd	11%	96	95	15%	16%	59	4%	63%	23.5	179
1st Half		357	37	12	52	4	274	18	4	274	347	445	108	106	109	9	83	0.55	47	20	33	30	127	ADc	14%	95	104	14%	20%	67	6%	67%	7.7	164
2nd Half		325	41	14	42	1	253	9	2	266	342	442	106	101	107	11	84	0.82	45	17	38	26	120	BCf	9%	97	86	15%	10%	60	2%	50%	5.8	207
24	**Proj**	**665**	**87**	**30**	**95**	**5**	**273**	**28**	**5**	**277**	**349**	**476**	**113**	**106**	**115**	**10**	**83**	**0.63**	**48**	**18**	**34**	**29**	**128**		**11%**	**108**	**101**	**18%**	**16%**	**67**	**4%**	**68%**	**29.3**	**226**

Gurriel Jr.,Lourdes

Age: 30 Pos: LF DH	Health B	LIMA Plan B+	
Bats: R Ht: 6'4" Wt: 215	PT/Exp A	Rand Var +4	
	Consist A	MM 3255	

Put 2022, Oct wrist surgery behind him with rebound to 2021 production levels, despite depressed h%. PX, xHR sugges power isn't all this. But fine bat-to-ball skills again made a difference, negating chronic bb%; ct%, HctX combo has never looked better. Still a sneaky-good fantasy asset; where this free agent lands should inform your bidding.

Yr	Tm	PA	R	HR	RBI	SB	BA	xHR	xSB	xBA	OBP	SLG	OPS+	vL+	vR+	bb%	ct%	Eye	G	L	F	h%	HctX	QBaB	Brl%	PX	xPX	HR/F	xHR/F	Spd	SBA%	SB%	RAR	BPX
19	TOR *	468	66	23	71	6	268	20	8	260	303	508	112	138	110	5	74	0.20	39	18	43	31	112	BBf	11%	133	145	20%	20%	116	14%	49%	-1.1	185
20	TOR	224	28	11	33	3	308	10	3	282	348	534	117	108	120	6	77	0.29	41	26	33	36	94	ACd	12%	127	91	20%	19%	100	8%	75%	9.2	216
21	TOR	541	62	21	84	1	276	20	4	267	319	466	108	101	111	6	80	0.31	45	21	34	31	106	BCc	10%	106	93	15%	15%	107	3%	25%	7.8	188
22	TOR	492	52	5	52	3	291	9	6	262	343	400	105	95	108	6	82	0.37	45	24	32	35	118	BCc	4%	78	79	4%	8%	108	5%	43%	9.3	124
23	ARI	592	65	24	82	5	261	19	5	284	309	463	105	110	103	6	81	0.32	43	21	36	28	130	BCc	8%	113	127	15%	12%	83	4%	100%	15.7	193
1st Half		305	35	13	49	1	270	10	2	289	321	489	111	106	113	6	82	0.37	46	19	35	29	121	CCd	8%	121	125	16%	12%	93	2%	100%	11.1	239
2nd Half		287	30	11	33	4	253	10	3	279	296	435	99	114	93	5	81	0.27	40	24	36	28	140	ACc	9%	104	130	14%	13%	76	7%	100%	2.7	146
24	**Proj**	**560**	**63**	**22**	**75**	**5**	**277**	**18**	**6**	**279**	**323**	**470**	**109**	**110**	**108**	**6**	**80**	**0.31**	**43**	**22**	**35**	**31**	**122**		**8%**	**111**	**110**	**15%**	**12%**	**94**	**5%**	**68%**	**20.7**	**171**

Gurriel,Yulieski

Age: 40 Pos: 1B	Health A	LIMA Plan D	
Bats: R Ht: 6'0" Wt: 215	PT/Exp A	Rand Var 0	
	Consist D	MM 1331	

It's been said that sometimes things are their most beautiful when coming to an end—but rarely with respect to a 40-year-old's stat line. Long-time full-timer now a shadow of his former self in bench role. Eeked out a few more walks, but empty contact is his only real remaining skill. Age, exit velocity, dismal 2nd half say MLB career may be over.

Yr	Tm	PA	R	HR	RBI	SB	BA	xHR	xSB	xBA	OBP	SLG	OPS+	vL+	vR+	bb%	ct%	Eye	G	L	F	h%	HctX	QBaB	Brl%	PX	xPX	HR/F	xHR/F	Spd	SBA%	SB%	RAR	BPX
19	HOU	612	85	31	104	5	298	12	4	306	343	541	122	112	126	6	88	0.57	38	22	39	29	118	BBf	4%	113	79	16%	6%	80	6%	63%	18.8	304
20	HOU	230	27	6	22	0	232	6	1	258	274	384	87	115	75	5	87	0.44	38	20	42	24	127	BCd	3%	78	123	8%	8%	96	2%	0%	-15.9	208
21	HOU	605	83	15	81	1	319	10	0	263	383	462	116	126	111	10	87	0.87	41	20	39	34	120	BCf	3%	78	83	8%	5%	75	1%	50%	25.1	212
22	HOU	584	53	8	53	8	242	5	4	255	288	360	92	104	86	5	87	0.41	41	19	41	27	103	CBf	2%	79	80	4%	3%	78	7%	100%	-18.6	155
23	MIA	329	32	4	27	4	245	3	7	242	304	359	90	85	93	8	85	0.59	41	17	43	28	100	CBf	2%	65	71	4%	3%	140	5%	100%	-3.9	189
1st Half		206	18	3	16	4	267	2	6	247	320	396	98	85	103	7	87	0.63	37	18	45	29	96	CAd	2%	68	83	4%	3%	150	8%	100%	1.0	232
2nd Half		123	14	1	11	0	207	1	1	224	276	297	78	84	73	9	82	0.55	48	14	38	24	105	CCf	2%	61	50	3%	3%	99	0%	0%	-5.9	93
24	**Proj**	**105**	**12**	**2**	**11**	**1**	**251**	**1**	**1**	**249**	**306**	**373**	**93**	**97**	**91**	**7**	**86**	**0.55**	**42**	**18**	**41**	**28**	**107**		**2%**	**73**	**74**	**5%**	**4%**	**91**	**4%**	**92%**	**-0.3**	**170**

Hampson,Garrett

Age: 29 Pos: SS CF RF	Health A	LIMA Plan D	
Bats: R Ht: 5'11" Wt: 196	PT/Exp B	Rand Var -5	
	Consist C	MM 2511	

3-23-.275 with 5 SB in 253 PA at MIA. Versatile as ever, and 2nd half h% luck fueled his small sample BA shine. But the good news ends there, as bottom rung exit velocity is as entrenched as ever; HctX, Brl%, PX all singing along. Ev lost the green light for his running game, which has long been the only speculative reason for rostering him. Pass.

Yr	Tm	PA	R	HR	RBI	SB	BA	xHR	xSB	xBA	OBP	SLG	OPS+	vL+	vR+	bb%	ct%	Eye	G	L	F	h%	HctX	QBaB	Brl%	PX	xPX	HR/F	xHR/F	Spd	SBA%	SB%	RAR	BPX
19	COL *	439	50	9	33	19	243	6	17	224	290	378	92	100	92	6	72	0.24	43	19	37	32	75	DCd	4%	77	73	11%	8%	152	25%	79%	-20.5	30
20	COL	184	25	5	11	6	234	7	7	204	287	383	89	71	100	7	64	0.22	36	25	39	33	68	FCd	8%	90	141	13%	18%	178	18%	86%	-7.1	-4
21	COL	494	69	11	33	17	234	12	21	234	289	380	92	111	83	7	74	0.28	39	23	38	29	107	FCd	5%	87	139	9%	10%	174	23%	71%	-16.6	127
22	COL	226	29	2	15	12	211	3	11	203	287	307	84	117	65	9	68	0.33	48	16	35	30	70	FDf	4%	69	89	4%	7%	164	27%	86%	-7.2	-3
23	MIA *	350	41	3	26	9	274	3	11	232	335	368	96	95	101	8	73	0.33	43	24	33	37	80	FCd	3%	67	74	6%	6%	140	9%	100%	4.4	14
1st Half		176	22	1	11	5	228	2	4	212	297	316	84	94	88	9	71	0.34	40	19	41	31	66	FCd	3%	72	76	3%	6%	112	12%	100%	-4.3	-18
2nd Half		174	19	2	16	4	320	1	7	258	374	420	107	97	118	8	74	0.33	46	30	24	42	98	DDc	1%	63	72	13%	6%	156	7%	100%	8.1	39
24	**Proj**	**210**	**26**	**4**	**16**	**7**	**254**	**3**	**8**	**231**	**316**	**378**	**95**	**101**	**92**	**8**	**71**	**0.31**	**44**	**22**	**34**	**34**	**83**		**4%**	**80**	**91**	**8%**	**7%**	**132**	**16%**	**87%**	**2.3**	**28**

Haniger,Mitch

Age: 33 Pos: LF	Health F	LIMA Plan C	
Bats: R Ht: 6'2" Wt: 214	PT/Exp B	Rand Var +5	
	Consist C	MM 4323	

6-28-.209 in 229 PA at SF. Another 100+ IL days for injury magnet. Strained oblique delayed season until late April, fractured forearm shelved him in mid-June, more back woes ended him in late Sept. That he never got untracked is unsurprising, despite stable exit velocity and xPX that still projects well. Now a low-risk dart throw; hope for health.

Yr	Tm	PA	R	HR	RBI	SB	BA	xHR	xSB	xBA	OBP	SLG	OPS+	vL+	vR+	bb%	ct%	Eye	G	L	F	h%	HctX	QBaB	Brl%	PX	xPX	HR/F	xHR/F	Spd	SBA%	SB%	RAR	BPX
19	SEA	283	46	15	32	4	220	14	3	240	314	463	108	128	101	11	67	0.37	35	20	45	26	82	CAc	11%	143	116	20%	19%	99	7%	100%	-3.6	130
20																																		
21	SEA	691	110	39	100	1	253	36	4	248	318	485	110	125	103	8	73	0.32	43	16	41	29	111	BBd	13%	131	133	21%	19%	112	1%	100%	11.2	181
22	SEA *	273	34	12	37	0	238	12	1	233	309	418	103	107	103	9	72	0.37	37	20	43	28	113	AAc	11%	115	113	16%	17%	86	0%	0%	2.6	90
23	SF *	260	29	7	30	1	197	9	1	228	247	346	81	95	82	6	71	0.23	35	21	44	25	104	ABc	11%	98	132	9%	14%	80	2%	100%	-8.8	0
1st Half		173	21	5	24	1	228	7	1	234	269	379	89	101	85	5	72	0.20	34	22	44	29	110	ABb	11%	98	131	9%	15%	70	3%	100%	-3.1	4
2nd Half		87	8	2	6	0	134	2	0	217	205	284	66	87	72	8	68	0.28	40	18	43	17	90	ACd	10%	100	135	12%	12%	104	0%	0%	-6.3	7
24	**Proj**	**385**	**51**	**18**	**45**	**1**	**240**	**17**	**2**	**241**	**304**	**444**	**103**	**110**	**99**	**8**	**71**	**0.30**	**38**	**19**	**43**	**29**	**102**		**11%**	**124**	**127**	**16%**	**16%**	**93**	**1%**	**100%**	**6.8**	**66**

JOCK THOMPSON

Happ,Ian

Age: 29 Pos: LF | Bats: B Ht: 6' 0" Wt: 205
Health A | PT/Exp A | Consist A
LIMA Plan B | Rand Var +2 | MM 4335

Career-best BA from 2022 retreated to norms with h% regression, even as ct%, xBA consolidated. But plenty to like in this profile. Exit velocity looks entrenched; improved pitch selection fueled bb% rebound, boding well for power. Even running game took a step forward. Health adds to optimistic outlook; now multiple value paths to a repeat.

Yr	Tm	PA	R	HR	RBI	SB	BA	xHR	xSB	xBA	OBP	SLG	OPS+	vL+	vR+	bb%	ct%	Eye	G	L	F	h%	HctX	QBaB	Brl%	PX	xPX	HR/F	xHR/F	Spd	SBA%	SB%	RAR	BPX	R$
19	CHC *	569	77	23	72	9	225	10	7	222	319	420	102	107	128	12	66	0.41	43	16	42	29	79	BBd	14%	117	102	26%	24%	103	8%	80%	-11.7	56	$13
20	CHC	231	27	12	28	1	258	11	3	259	361	505	115	93	122	13	68	0.48	45	22	33	32	99	BDc	10%	150	121	27%	25%	94	7%	25%	3.5	196	$17
21	CHC	535	63	25	66	9	226	20	6	242	323	434	104	89	109	12	66	0.40	46	21	33	28	93	CCf	11%	133	115	24%	19%	89	9%	82%	-0.1	92	$13
22	CHC	641	72	17	72	9	271	17	9	257	342	440	111	110	111	9	74	0.39	46	20	33	34	100	BCd	7%	120	105	12%	12%	98	8%	69%	19.2	141	$22
23	CHC	691	86	21	84	14	248	22	15	256	360	431	108	93	113	14	74	0.65	42	21	37	30	93	BCd	9%	113	93	13%	14%	102	9%	82%	23.8	164	$19
1st Half		345	31	7	38	6	254	9	7	244	380	406	108	88	114	17	70	0.65	44	24	33	34	79	BCc	8%	104	74	11%	14%	102	8%	75%	10.3	96	$13
2nd Half		346	55	14	46	8	242	13	7	267	341	455	108	96	113	13	77	0.64	40	19	41	27	107	BCf	10%	121	108	15%	14%	102	11%	89%	11.0	232	$24
24	Proj	**630**	**79**	**23**	**77**	**12**	**255**	**22**	**11**	**254**	**352**	**448**	**110**	**98**	**114**	**13**	**72**	**0.52**	**44**	**21**	**36**	**31**	**96**		**9%**	**122**	**102**	**16%**	**15%**	**98**	**9%**	**79%**	**24.5**	**150**	**$20**

Harper,Bryce

Age: 31 Pos: DH 1B | Bats: L Ht: 6' 3" Wt: 210
Health D | PT/Exp A | Consist D
LIMA Plan C | Rand Var -2 | MM 4255

Season delayed by rehab from offseason elbow surgery, but returned faster than anticipated. Power, vintage exit velocity took awhile to rebound, but both returned with a vengeance in the 2nd half. Contact skills, bb% finished plus as ever; ditto consistent baserunning skills. OF eligibility is a question, but still a premium 1B pick off the draft board.

Yr	Tm	PA	R	HR	RBI	SB	BA	xHR	xSB	xBA	OBP	SLG	OPS+	vL+	vR+	bb%	ct%	Eye	G	L	F	h%	HctX	QBaB	Brl%	PX	xPX	HR/F	xHR/F	Spd	SBA%	SB%	RAR	BPX	R$
19	PHI	682	98	35	114	15	260	40	9	261	372	510	122	132	116	15	69	0.56	38	24	38	32	115	ACc	15%	145	152	23%	27%	87	10%	83%	18.9	181	$27
20	PHI	244	41	13	33	8	268	20	7	266	420	542	128	126	128	20	77	1.14	36	18	46	28	125	BCc	17%	141	148	20%	30%	121	13%	80%	11.4	404	$31
21	PHI	599	101	35	84	13	309	39	11	293	429	615	143	109	159	17	73	0.75	41	22	37	36	128	ACc	18%	186	152	27%	30%	107	9%	81%	64.2	408	$35
22	PHI	426	63	18	65	11	286	23	8	287	364	514	124	109	131	11	76	0.53	41	24	34	33	118	ACc	13%	148	124	18%	23%	84	14%	73%	21.0	252	$22
23	PHI	546	84	21	72	11	293	26	12	279	401	499	123	119	124	15	74	0.67	45	25	30	36	122	ADc	15%	126	117	20%	25%	94	8%	79%	37.9	200	$23
1st Half		226	31	3	22	5	293	8	5	246	394	398	108	72	128	15	74	0.67	47	24	29	38	103	BDc	12%	73	100	7%	19%	98	8%	83%	7.6	61	$9
2nd Half		320	53	18	50	6	293	18	6	301	406	571	132	158	121	15	74	0.67	43	26	31	34	136	ACc	17%	164	129	30%	30%	92	9%	75%	28.5	307	$32
24	Proj	**630**	**100**	**32**	**90**	**12**	**291**	**36**	**13**	**286**	**395**	**543**	**129**	**119**	**133**	**14**	**74**	**0.66**	**42**	**24**	**35**	**34**	**122**		**15%**	**152**	**128**	**23%**	**26%**	**92**	**9%**	**75%**	**54.0**	**258**	**$35**

Harris II,Michael

Age: 23 Pos: CF | Bats: L Ht: 6' 0" Wt: 195
Health A | PT/Exp A | Consist A
LIMA Plan D+ | Rand Var 0 | MM 4455

Early back issues shelved him for 3 weeks; May knee injury didn't help. And though QBaB gains were evident from the get-go, 1st-half GB% remained elevated. But he was a house afire from June on; power reappeared, h% spiked and LD% began to soar in July. Running game still plus, even with SB% dip. With 600+ PA ... UP: 1st round value.

Yr	Tm	PA	R	HR	RBI	SB	BA	xHR	xSB	xBA	OBP	SLG	OPS+	vL+	vR+	bb%	ct%	Eye	G	L	F	h%	HctX	QBaB	Brl%	PX	xPX	HR/F	xHR/F	Spd	SBA%	SB%	RAR	BPX	R$
19																																			
20																																			
21																																			
22	ATL *	628	101	23	90	29	291	19	21	281	330	495	117	91	134	5	75	0.23	56	17	27	36	111	CFd	10%	137	109	23%	23%	118	24%	84%	31.8	193	$41
23	ATL	539	76	18	57	20	293	19	18	286	331	477	110	107	111	5	80	0.25	47	22	31	34	122	BDd	10%	107	96	15%	15%	113	19%	83%	25.9	182	$23
1st Half		227	30	7	22	10	263	7	8	261	313	421	101	101	100	6	79	0.30	52	16	32	30	116	BDf	9%	90	86	13%	13%	119	21%	91%	4.2	132	$11
2nd Half		312	46	11	35	10	314	11	9	302	344	517	116	112	118	4	81	0.21	44	27	30	36	127	BDd	11%	118	103	15%	15%	107	18%	77%	20.5	211	$29
24	Proj	**560**	**89**	**22**	**84**	**22**	**288**	**22**	**18**	**284**	**330**	**492**	**113**	**99**	**118**	**5**	**78**	**0.24**	**51**	**20**	**29**	**34**	**118**		**10%**	**121**	**101**	**18%**	**18%**	**111**	**21%**	**84%**	**29.6**	**184**	**$34**

Hayes,Ke'Bryan

Age: 27 Pos: 3B | Bats: R Ht: 5' 10" Wt: 205
Health C | PT/Exp A | Consist B
LIMA Plan B | Rand Var +1 | MM 3345

Power remained dormant through lackluster 1st half, but it reappeared again in early August following five weeks on the IL with lower back issues. 2nd-half launch angle improvement, Brl%, HctX gains support the small sample PX/xPX. Were injuries the primary obstacle here? May not cost much to find out. With health ... UP: .280, 20+ HR.

Yr	Tm	PA	R	HR	RBI	SB	BA	xHR	xSB	xBA	OBP	SLG	OPS+	vL+	vR+	bb%	ct%	Eye	G	L	F	h%	HctX	QBaB	Brl%	PX	xPX	HR/F	xHR/F	Spd	SBA%	SB%	RAR	BPX	R$
19	aaa	464	54	8	45	10	245		6		304	376	94			8	78	0.39				30				78				99	11%	90%		78	$9
20	PIT	95	17	5	11	1	376	4	2	305	442	682	149	175	140	9	76	0.45	48	22	31	45	138	ADd	9%	167	112	25%	20%	142	4%	100%	14.5	412	$13
21	PIT *	421	53	7	40	9	254	8	6	251	312	378	95	101	92	8	75	0.34	57	18	25	32	110	BFd	5%	80	76	9%	11%	103	10%	90%	-2.8	54	$10
22	PIT	560	55	7	41	20	244	9	16	242	314	345	93	106	88	9	76	0.39	49	22	29	31	102	AFf	4%	71	74	6%	8%	119	18%	80%	-10.7	52	$15
23	PIT	525	65	15	61	10	271	15	14	263	309	453	104	114	99	5	79	0.27	42	19	39	32	119	ACc	7%	105	116	10%	10%	128	15%	63%	12.5	182	$16
1st Half		303	34	5	32	8	254	7	11	251	290	397	94	102	91	5	79	0.25	44	19	37	31	109	ACc	7%	84	101	6%	8%	144	21%	62%	-3.3	139	$12
2nd Half		222	31	10	29	2	295	8	3	281	333	531	117	127	110	6	79	0.30	39	19	41	33	132	ABd	9%	135	135	15%	12%	101	6%	67%	12.8	239	$15
24	Proj	**560**	**67**	**17**	**58**	**13**	**263**	**14**	**12**	**261**	**315**	**441**	**104**	**115**	**98**	**7**	**78**	**0.33**	**44**	**20**	**36**	**31**	**117**		**7%**	**106**	**102**	**12%**	**10%**	**104**	**14%**	**75%**	**14.5**	**128**	**$21**

Hays,Austin

Age: 28 Pos: LF | Bats: R Ht: 6' 0" Wt: 205
Health B | PT/Exp A | Consist B
LIMA Plan B+ | Rand Var -4 | MM 3235

More decent production, 2nd half fade with launch angle volatility. 1st half R$ was driven by BA and unsustainable h%. Lost exit velocity and average afterward, as ct% dipped and GB% spiked in 2022 repeat. Relative HR stability, lineup context help an unexciting skill set. Ongoing QBaB woes stamp this as the top of a narrow performance range.

Yr	Tm	PA	R	HR	RBI	SB	BA	xHR	xSB	xBA	OBP	SLG	OPS+	vL+	vR+	bb%	ct%	Eye	G	L	F	h%	HctX	QBaB	Brl%	PX	xPX	HR/F	xHR/F	Spd	SBA%	SB%	RAR	BPX	R$
19	BAL *	384	55	15	45	10	242	2	9	260	282	438	100	48	177	5	75	0.22	41	22	37	28	80	ACa	6%	111	107	20%	10%	112	24%	63%	-12.4	126	$10
20	BAL	134	20	4	9	2	279	3	4	236	328	393	96	95	96	6	80	0.32	49	19	32	32	62	DCf	4%	57	42	13%	10%	141	13%	40%	-4.6	80	$10
21	BAL	529	73	22	71	4	256	21	6	261	308	461	106	122	94	5	78	0.26	43	18	38	29	98	CCf	9%	114	92	15%	14%	119	6%	57%	4.0	200	$16
22	BAL	582	66	16	60	2	250	15	6	256	306	413	102	98	103	6	79	0.30	43	19	38	29	105	CCf	5%	107	103	10%	9%	117	5%	33%	-0.8	169	$13
23	BAL	566	76	16	67	5	275	21	7	245	325	444	105	106	104	7	73	0.27	45	17	38	35	106	BCf	9%	111	103	11%	14%	99	5%	83%	19.2	89	$17
1st Half		301	42	8	34	2	312	13	5	252	352	491	115	112	117	6	75	0.26	41	18	41	39	115	BCd	11%	116	109	9%	15%	118	4%	67%	17.8	150	$19
2nd Half		265	34	8	33	3	232	7	2	235	294	390	92	99	90	8	71	0.28	50	16	34	30	95	CDf	7%	105	95	14%	12%	77	5%	100%	-1.4	25	$10
24	Proj	**560**	**74**	**18**	**66**	**5**	**259**	**18**	**7**	**249**	**312**	**431**	**102**	**101**	**102**	**6**	**75**	**0.28**	**45**	**18**	**37**	**31**	**100**		**7%**	**107**	**97**	**12%**	**12%**	**98**	**6%**	**63%**	**9.9**	**120**	**$20**

Heim,Jonah

Age: 29 Pos: CA | Bats: B Ht: 6' 4" Wt: 220
Health A | PT/Exp A | Consist C
LIMA Plan B | Rand Var -2 | MM 2135

First half QBaB gains fueled early BA, power jumps until another 2nd half collapse intervened. Strained wrist in late July was a factor; finished hitting .189 with 4 HR over final 185 PA after return from IL. Intriguing 1st half hints at more than previous iterations. Even with fade history ... UP: .275, 20+ HR.

Yr	Tm	PA	R	HR	RBI	SB	BA	xHR	xSB	xBA	OBP	SLG	OPS+	vL+	vR+	bb%	ct%	Eye	G	L	F	h%	HctX	QBaB	Brl%	PX	xPX	HR/F	xHR/F	Spd	SBA%	SB%	RAR	BPX	R$
19	a/a	315	34	7	43	0	270		1		335	408	103			9	82	0.55				31				78				83	1%	0%		130	$5
20	OAK	41	5	0	5	0	211	1	0	202	268	211	64	87	56	7	92	1.00	43	17	40	23	117	DBf	6%	0	66	0%	7%	113	0%	0%	-2.6	76	-$2
21	TEX	285	22	10	32	3	196	8	1	239	239	358	82	99	75	7	76	0.26	40	18	42	21	116	CBf	6%	93	117	11%	9%	56	9%	75%	-10.2	62	$0
22	TEX	450	51	16	48	2	227	11	2	245	298	399	99	117	91	9	79	0.47	39	18	43	25	111	CBf	6%	106	106	12%	8%	83	2%	100%	4.9	152	$8
23	TEX	501	61	18	95	2	258	18	2	261	317	438	103	117	100	8	79	0.42	36	21	43	29	119	CBc	8%	105	123	12%	12%	63	2%	100%	19.8	132	$16
1st Half		296	41	12	56	2	282	12	2	277	334	484	112	115	111	7	81	0.40	32	24	44	31	123	BAb	9%	116	136	12%	12%	75	3%	100%	16.8	193	$23
2nd Half		205	20	6	39	0	223	6	0	228	293	370	89	123	86	9	77	0.44	43	17	41	26	114	CBd	7%	88	102	10%	10%	63	0%	0%	0.0	61	$5
24	Proj	**490**	**55**	**17**	**77**	**2**	**250**	**15**	**2**	**247**	**310**	**419**	**100**	**118**	**95**	**8**	**79**	**0.41**	**39**	**19**	**42**	**28**	**115**		**7%**	**99**	**112**	**11%**	**10%**	**62**	**2%**	**83%**	**14.3**	**117**	**$16**

Henderson,Gunnar

Age: 23 Pos: 3B SS | Bats: L Ht: 6' 2" Wt: 210
Health A | PT/Exp A | Consist A
LIMA Plan B+ | Rand Var 0 | MM 4445

Full season debut from pedigreed prospect sprouted 2nd half wings with more aggressive approach. Sacrificed patience, OBP in the process, but contact skills and HR, BA spikes more than compensated. Launch angle can still use some work, but exit velocity, HR/F are already top-shelf; even running game hints at upside. He's just getting started.

Yr	Tm	PA	R	HR	RBI	SB	BA	xHR	xSB	xBA	OBP	SLG	OPS+	vL+	vR+	bb%	ct%	Eye	G	L	F	h%	HctX	QBaB	Brl%	PX	xPX	HR/F	xHR/F	Spd	SBA%	SB%	RAR	BPX	R$
19																																			
20																																			
21	aa																																		
22	BAL *	591	79	19	69	16	256	5	15	256	342	437	110	63	124	12	69	0.43	60	16	24	33	104	AFd	10%	125	92	20%	25%	128	13%	78%	17.9	141	$23
23	BAL	622	100	28	82	10	255	28	15	265	325	489	111	83	121	9	72	0.35	45	19	36	31	115	ACc	11%	138	120	19%	19%	137	10%	77%	27.9	207	$22
1st Half		270	38	11	30	5	239	11	8	240	341	453	109	71	119	13	64	0.40	44	21	35	33	110	ACb	13%	142	135	21%	21%	134	10%	71%	6.2	129	$12
2nd Half		352	62	17	52	5	267	17	7	283	313	515	112	89	121	6	77	0.30	48	18	36	30	119	ACc	11%	136	111	18%	18%	134	9%	83%	13.7	261	$31
24	Proj	**630**	**95**	**28**	**80**	**13**	**263**	**30**	**16**	**261**	**337**	**492**	**114**	**77**	**125**	**10**	**71**	**0.38**	**48**	**18**	**34**	**32**	**111**		**11%**	**139**	**109**	**21%**	**22%**	**131**	**11%**	**79%**	**31.6**	**180**	**$29**

JOCK THOMPSON

Hernández,Kiké

Age: 32	Pos: SS 2B CF	Health C	LIMA Plan D+
Bats: R	Ht: 5' 11" Wt: 190	PT/Exp A	Rand Var 0
		Consist C	MM 2223

Perked up after trade deadline move to LA (.731 OPS over 185 AB). But BA and power skills have been stagnant over the past two seasons; exit velocity history is constructive. Still versatile as ever, but his only consistent offensive skill has been contact. That makes him more valuable in the real game than in ours.

Yr	Tm	PA	R	HR	RBI	SB	BA	xHR	xSB	xBA	OBP	SLG	OPS+	vL+	vR+	bb%	ct%	Eye	G	L	F	h%	HctX	QBaB	Brl%	PX	xPX	HR/F	xHR/F	Spd	SBA%	SB%	RAR	BPX	R$
19	LA	460	57	17	64	4	237	15	2	242	304	411	99	105	94	8	77	0.37	36	21	43	27	107	CAc	6%	92	107	12%	11%	88	4%	100%	-7.6	89	$9
20	LA	148	20	5	20	0	230	5	1	251	270	410	90	88	91	4	78	0.19	40	20	39	26	107	CBf	6%	101	104	12%	12%	121	4%	0%	-4.5	152	$7
21	BOS	585	84	20	60	1	250	23	4	256	337	449	108	116	103	10	78	0.55	33	21	46	28	114	BAd	8%	116	123	11%	12%	122	1%	100%	7.7	254	$1
22	BOS	402	48	6	45	0	222	7	2	233	291	338	89	109	83	8	80	0.48	39	18	43	26	103	CBf	5%	82	78	5%	6%	97	2%	0%	-13.7	121	$3
23	2 TM	508	57	11	61	4	237	9	5	232	289	357	88	86	88	7	79	0.35	37	19	44	28	85	CBf	5%	73	73	7%	6%	86	4%	80%	-5.7	57	$8
1st Half		291	34	6	29	3	225	5	4	220	282	333	84	89	82	7	77	0.33	38	18	44	27	77	CBf	4%	67	60	7%	5%	90	6%	75%	-9.4	18	$6
2nd Half		217	23	5	32	1	253	4	2	250	300	389	93	83	98	7	82	0.39	36	20	43	29	96	CAd	5%	82	89	7%	6%	87	2%	100%	-1.1	121	$7
24	**Proj**	**385**	**47**	**9**	**48**	**2**	**237**	**9**	**3**	**240**	**299**	**375**	**92**	**96**	**90**	**8**	**80**	**0.41**	**37**	**19**	**43**	**27**	**98**		**6%**	**85**	**87**	**7%**	**7%**	**95**	**3%**	**65%**	**-0.9**	**120**	**$6**

Hernández,Teoscar

Age: 31	Pos: RF DH	Health B	LIMA Plan B
Bats: R	Ht: 6' 2" Wt: 215	PT/Exp A	Rand Var 0
		Consist B	MM 4225

QBaB shows another season of launch angle struggles. LD%, ct% dipped again. xBA suggests he may never retrace lofty BA levels but it's still a plus by today's standards, making this a minor quibble. Exit velocity, barrel rate remain in fine shape, buoying power even at new GB% levels—and xHR say he was unlucky (again). So 30+ HR is still out there.

Yr	Tm	PA	R	HR	RBI	SB	BA	xHR	xSB	xBA	OBP	SLG	OPS+	vL+	vR+	bb%	ct%	Eye	G	L	F	h%	HctX	QBaB	Brl%	PX	xPX	HR/F	xHR/F	Spd	SBA%	SB%	RAR	BPX	R$
19	TOR *	544	67	30	74	8	228	25	8	226	299	461	105	116	103	9	64	0.28	39	18	43	29	97	ABf	12%	138	144	23%	22%	114	10%	74%	-11.1	74	$1
20	TOR	206	33	16	34	6	289	18	4	262	340	579	122	122	121	7	67	0.22	36	26	38	35	133	ABb	18%	169	165	33%	37%	98	15%	86%	11.8	188	$3
21	TOR	595	92	32	116	12	296	32	9	268	346	524	119	157	108	6	73	0.24	38	25	36	35	109	ACc	14%	134	109	22%	22%	96	11%	75%	20.0	162	$3
22	TOR	535	71	25	77	6	267	31	5	265	316	491	114	137	109	6	70	0.22	44	22	34	34	133	ACc	15%	159	143	21%	26%	92	8%	67%	9.3	166	$2
23	SEA	678	70	26	93	7	258	33	10	230	305	435	101	110	98	6	66	0.18	43	19	37	35	108	ACd	14%	118	123	17%	21%	103	6%	78%	5.6	11	$2
1st Half		342	39	15	48	4	254	18	7	232	304	451	103	122	97	6	65	0.18	39	22	39	34	103	ACc	14%	129	134	19%	22%	121	8%	67%	-0.7	46	$2
2nd Half		336	31	11	45	3	261	15	3	225	307	419	98	96	99	5	68	0.18	47	17	36	35	112	ACd	14%	107	112	14%	20%	84	4%	100%	-1.7	-18	$1
24	**Proj**	**630**	**78**	**29**	**95**	**8**	**261**	**34**	**8**	**245**	**310**	**463**	**106**	**120**	**102**	**6**	**68**	**0.20**	**43**	**21**	**37**	**34**	**115**		**14%**	**132**	**128**	**19%**	**23%**	**92**	**8%**	**76%**	**15.8**	**83**	**$2**

Heyward,Jason

Age: 34	Pos: RF CF	Health F	LIMA Plan D+
Bats: L	Ht: 6' 5" Wt: 240	PT/Exp B	Rand Var -1
		Consist D	MM 2123

Scenery change made fantasy afterthought rosterable again. Plate skills firmed up: Ct% improved, Brl% edged up, FB% climbed and launch angle tweak put HR back in play. But just 28 PA vL points to playing time cap, and age waits for no one. Strong-side platoon could deliver more of the same, but he offers more downside than up from here.

Yr	Tm	PA	R	HR	RBI	SB	BA	xHR	xSB	xBA	OBP	SLG	OPS+	vL+	vR+	bb%	ct%	Eye	G	L	F	h%	HctX	QBaB	Brl%	PX	xPX	HR/F	xHR/F	Spd	SBA%	SB%	RAR	BPX	R$
19	CHC	589	78	21	62	8	251	12	8	258	343	429	107	77	114	12	79	0.62	46	20	34	28	96	CCc	6%	88	82	15%	9%	110	7%	73%	-6.8	159	$1
20	CHC	181	20	6	22	2	265	5	2	271	392	456	113	74	125	17	75	0.81	46	28	27	32	119	CCa	4%	103	114	20%	17%	110	4%	100%	4.6	200	$1
21	CHC	353	35	8	30	5	214	8	4	245	280	347	86	84	87	8	79	0.40	51	17	33	25	99	CDf	5%	77	77	10%	10%	99	8%	83%	-16.3	92	$
22	CHC	151	15	1	10	1	204	3	1	207	278	277	79	61	82	7	77	0.34	46	16	38	26	99	CCf	5%	51	92	3%	8%	93	3%	100%	-7.6	-24	-$
23	LA	374	56	15	40	2	269	10	4	262	340	473	111	101	112	9	81	0.53	41	15	44	29	109	CBf	8%	116	105	13%	8%	79	4%	50%	13.8	214	$1
1st Half		190	32	8	20	2	258	6	3	264	353	479	114	27	119	12	78	0.61	41	15	44	29	108	CAd	9%	131	122	14%	11%	93	6%	67%	7.0	250	$
2nd Half		184	24	7	20	0	281	4	1	259	326	468	107	134	104	7	84	0.43	42	15	43	30	109	CCf	7%	104	90	11%	6%	67	2%	0%	5.5	189	$
24	**Proj**	**350**	**44**	**10**	**34**	**3**	**245**	**9**	**3**	**245**	**318**	**400**	**98**	**83**	**101**	**9**	**79**	**0.47**	**44**	**16**	**39**	**28**	**105**		**6%**	**91**	**96**	**10%**	**9%**	**81**	**4%**	**68%**	**2.3**	**132**	**$**

Hicks,Aaron

Age: 34	Pos: CF LF RF	Health F	LIMA Plan C
Bats: B	Ht: 6' 1" Wt: 205	PT/Exp B	Rand Var -4
		Consist B	MM 1403

Cut in late May after struggling in part-time role; fared better with more playing time in BAL (.806 OPS). But inability to stay whole again exposed by hamstring, back injuries that shelved him for 40 days in the 2nd half. Exit velocity is in full retreat; patience, pitch selection, SBs are the only reasons for rostering. Maybe an OBP flyer; otherwise avoid.

Yr	Tm	PA	R	HR	RBI	SB	BA	xHR	xSB	xBA	OBP	SLG	OPS+	vL+	vR+	bb%	ct%	Eye	G	L	F	h%	HctX	QBaB	Brl%	PX	xPX	HR/F	xHR/F	Spd	SBA%	SB%	RAR	BPX	R$
19	NYY	255	41	12	36	1	235	9	2	227	325	443	106	94	112	12	67	0.43	43	16	41	29	89	BCf	9%	122	98	19%	15%	92	5%	33%	-2.6	78	$
20	NYY	211	28	6	21	4	225	7	4	261	379	414	105	103	106	19	78	1.08	45	20	35	26	93	CCf	7%	105	75	13%	16%	115	8%	80%	-1.3	276	$1
21	NYY	126	13	4	14	0	194	4	0	213	294	333	86	112	74	11	72	0.47	35	20	45	23	89	BAd	10%	81	109	11%	11%	86	0%	0%	-4.3	15	-$
22	NYY	453	54	8	40	10	216	10	12	201	330	313	91	89	91	14	72	0.57	44	16	39	28	90	CCf	6%	63	70	7%	9%	135	10%	77%	-8.7	24	$
23	2 AL	312	44	8	36	6	253	5	6	221	353	383	100	131	91	13	74	0.61	46	15	39	31	71	DCf	4%	77	57	10%	6%	102	7%	100%	7.7	68	$
1st Half		171	25	5	17	3	228	3	3	212	327	376	96	105	94	13	73	0.55	43	12	45	28	68	DBf	6%	86	74	10%	6%	96	7%	100%	0.7	64	$
2nd Half		141	19	3	19	3	283	1	3	230	383	392	105	154	86	14	76	0.69	51	18	32	35	74	DDf	2%	65	37	10%	3%	106	6%	100%	5.2	64	$
24	**Proj**	**350**	**46**	**9**	**39**	**6**	**237**	**7**	**6**	**218**	**341**	**364**	**97**	**116**	**89**	**13**	**73**	**0.58**	**44**	**17**	**39**	**29**	**81**		**5%**	**76**	**68**	**10%**	**8%**	**112**	**7%**	**88%**	**3.6**	**58**	**$1**

Hiura,Keston

Age: 27	Pos: DH	Health A	LIMA Plan D
Bats: R	Ht: 6' 0" Wt: 202	PT/Exp B	Rand Var
		Consist B	MM 4101

Dropped from 40-man roster in late March, then pulverized AAA pitching between knee, elbow injuries that eventually kept him from another MLB audition; a free agent this winter. Still owns intriguing power and exit velocity, both still negated by abysmal ct%. Defensive challenges also work against him; dart-throw only.

Yr	Tm	PA	R	HR	RBI	SB	BA	xHR	xSB	xBA	OBP	SLG	OPS+	vL+	vR+	bb%	ct%	Eye	G	L	F	h%	HctX	QBaB	Brl%	PX	xPX	HR/F	xHR/F	Spd	SBA%	SB%	RAR	BPX	R$
19	MIL *	579	85	35	85	14	298	20	11	262	351	577	128	94	140	7	66	0.24	38	24	38	39	100	ABb	14%	170	140	24%	25%	108	14%	73%	29.3	178	$2
20	MIL	246	30	13	32	3	212	14	3	211	297	410	94	89	95	7	61	0.19	43	20	37	28	72	CBc	13%	124	111	26%	28%	96	9%	60%	-9.6	-52	$1
21	MIL *	388	30	9	35	4	185	7	3	183	256	327	80	55	86	9	53	0.20	37	22	41	31	81	BBf	15%	125	133	10%	18%	88	7%	78%	-27.2	-158	-$
22	MIL *	319	39	18	43	5	230	14	7	217	302	460	108	87	123	9	54	0.22	37	25	38	35	91	ABb	16%	189	155	30%	30%	102	15%	47%	-2.3	59	$
23	aaa	337	38	17	53	0	244		2		292	437	99			6	63	0.19				33				127				80	3%	0%		-21	$
1st Half		164	19	10	26	0	249		2		300	470	105			7	64	0.20				32				143				86	6%	0%		36	$
2nd Half		172	18	7	27	0	239		1	211	285	406	93			6	62	0.17	44	20	36	33	0			113	-21	0%		86	0%	0%	-3.5	-71	$
24	**Proj**	**175**	**20**	**9**	**25**	**1**	**233**	**9**	**2**	**218**	**314**	**434**	**103**	**84**	**111**	**7**	**59**	**0.20**	**39**	**22**	**38**	**33**	**84**		**14%**	**144**	**133**	**24%**	**25%**	**89**	**7%**	**47%**	**-0.2**	**-17**	**$**

Hoerner,Nico

Age: 27	Pos: 2B SS	Health C	LIMA Plan D+
Bats: R	Ht: 6' 1" Wt: 200	PT/Exp A	Rand Var -2
		Consist A	MM 1545

Speed, running game, ct% were already driving his value; new rules made him a fantasy star. Out-hit xBA for a third consecutive season despite mediocre exit velocity, even repeated unlikely HR total. Hamstring injury slowed him in May / June, but he didn't miss a beat in the 2nd half. With health, no reason why young legs can't do this again.

Yr	Tm	PA	R	HR	RBI	SB	BA	xHR	xSB	xBA	OBP	SLG	OPS+	vL+	vR+	bb%	ct%	Eye	G	L	F	h%	HctX	QBaB	Brl%	PX	xPX	HR/F	xHR/F	Spd	SBA%	SB%	RAR	BPX	R$
19	CHC *	370	48	6	38	7	277	1	9	298	322	399	100	111	100	6	87	0.53	53	25	22	30	80	DFa	2%	60	48	20%	7%	135	12%	64%	-1.0	193	$
20	CHC	125	19	0	13	3	222	1	3	230	312	259	76	81	73	10	78	0.50	55	21	24	29	92	CFf	1%	29	59	0%	5%	113	14%	60%	-8.4	-40	$
21	CHC *	196	15	0	17	5	290	1	5	246	353	352	97	87	110	9	82	0.53	48	23	29	35	80	CDc	2%	48	41	0%	3%	110	13%	63%	-0.3	69	$
22	CHC	517	60	10	55	20	281	6	18	274	327	410	104	106	104	5	88	0.49	46	21	33	30	92	CCc	2%	73	66	7%	4%	146	17%	91%	9.3	234	$2
23	CHC	688	98	9	68	43	283	5	38	260	346	383	99	102	98	7	87	0.59	47	19	34	31	83	DCc	2%	56	67	5%	3%	135	25%	86%	17.3	171	$2
1st Half		337	46	5	42	19	283	2	16	270	332	395	100	103	98	6	88	0.56	47	19	34	31	72	DCc	2%	60	51	5%	2%	132	23%	90%	8.2	196	$2
2nd Half		351	52	4	26	24	282	3	22	249	360	370	99	100	98	9	85	0.62	46	19	35	32	94	DCc	2%	51	83	4%	3%	134	27%	83%	7.2	139	$2
24	**Proj**	**630**	**82**	**8**	**62**	**39**	**280**	**6**	**27**	**261**	**343**	**382**	**99**	**98**	**100**	**7**	**86**	**0.55**	**48**	**20**	**32**	**32**	**86**		**2%**	**58**	**63**	**5%**	**3%**	**126**	**25%**	**84%**	**17.0**	**157**	**$3**

Hoskins,Rhys

Age: 31	Pos: 1B	Health F	LIMA Plan B
Bats: R	Ht: 6' 4" Wt: 245	PT/Exp C	Rand Var 0
		Consist B	MM 4135

2023 aborted by torn ACL in March. But at last look, plus power was still intact despite FB% swoon and exit velocity dip; HR, HR/F, xHR/F add confirmation. Stable ct%, plus patience say he won't be a BA or OBP liability. There's no reason why he can't produce at these levels again, no matter where this free agent lands.

Yr	Tm	PA	R	HR	RBI	SB	BA	xHR	xSB	xBA	OBP	SLG	OPS+	vL+	vR+	bb%	ct%	Eye	G	L	F	h%	HctX	QBaB	Brl%	PX	xPX	HR/F	xHR/F	Spd	SBA%	SB%	RAR	BPX	R$
19	PHI	703	86	29	85	2	226	29	5	236	364	454	113	136	105	17	70	0.67	29	21	50	27	111	BAc	10%	131	143	14%	14%	106	2%	50%	-1.8	185	$1
20	PHI	185	35	10	26	1	245	12	1	247	384	503	118	162	100	16	72	0.67	29	19	52	28	94	BAc	15%	150	161	18%	21%	93	2%	100%	1.6	268	$1
21	PHI	443	64	27	71	3	247	31	2	267	334	530	119	127	115	11	72	0.44	29	20	51	27	101	AAc	17%	172	152	19%	22%	73	5%	60%	10.5	277	$1
22	PHI	671	81	30	79	2	246	31	2	255	332	462	112	132	106	11	71	0.43	36	23	42	29	101	BAc	11%	144	124	17%	18%	81	2%	67%	8.3	166	$1
23																																			
1st Half																																			
2nd Half																																			
24	**Proj**	**560**	**86**	**27**	**77**	**2**	**247**	**30**	**3**	**254**	**357**	**480**	**115**	**141**	**104**	**13**	**71**	**0.53**	**34**	**21**	**45**	**29**	**100**		**13%**	**145**	**145**	**17%**	**19%**	**83**	**2%**	**62%**	**23.2**	**227**	**$2**

JOCK THOMPSON

Ibanez,Andy

Age: 31	Pos: 2B OF		Health	A	LIMA Plan	D+
Bats: R	Ht: 5' 11"	Wt: 205	PT/Exp	B	Rand Var	-2
			Consist	F	MM	2221

11-41-.264 in 383 PA at DET. Most HR he's ever hit in majors, but... couldn't sustain 1st half gains in HctX and QBaB, output remained primarily platoon-based (152 PX vL, 76 vR), and 2nd half BA surge wasn't backed by skills. Still, career .796 OPS vL means you can carve out some value in deep leagues and DFS, so don't overlook him.

Yr	Tm	PA	R	HR	RBI	SB	BA	xHR	xSB	xBA	OBP	SLG	OPS+	vL+	vR+	bb%	ct%	Eye	G	L	F	h%	HctX	QBaB	Brl%	PX	xPX	HR/F	xHR/F	Spd	SBA%	SB%	RAR	BPX	R$
19	aaa	506	64	15	46	5	255		7		312	411	100			8	78	0.37				30				85				100	10%	41%		100	$10
20																																			
21	TEX *	394	45	12	43	1	274	7	2	262	317	448	105	122	93	6	84	0.40	37	20	43	30	106	CBd	7%	96	102	7%	7%	110	1%	100%	8.8	231	$10
22	TEX *	425	33	4	26	6	188	3	6	196	234	261	70	72	81	6	79	0.29	43	12	45	23	88	CBf	6%	52	108	2%	7%	102	11%	68%	-26.6	10	-$3
23	DET *	455	51	14	51	2	256	13	4	253	309	427	100	110	97	7	79	0.37	44	16	40	29	113	CCd	9%	101	101	9%	11%	95	3%	63%	9.7	154	$10
1st Half		253	32	9	27	1	230	8	2	247	276	415	95	115	87	6	78	0.29	44	13	43	26	137	ACc	13%	110	137	10%	13%	74	4%	48%	-3.2	132	$6
2nd Half		202	19	5	24	1	290	5	3	256	348	443	107	107	107	9	81	0.49	44	19	38	34	90	CCf	6%	89	68	9%	9%	113	2%	100%	7.3	171	$7
24	Proj	**245**	**28**	**7**	**29**	**2**	**260**	**7**	**3**	**246**	**312**	**417**	**100**	**105**	**97**	**7**	**80**	**0.38**	**43**	**16**	**40**	**30**	**101**		**8%**	**92**	**101**	**10%**	**9%**	**100**	**5%**	**65%**	**5.1**	**125**	**$4**

India,Jonathan

Age: 27	Pos: 2B		Health	C	LIMA Plan	B
Bats: R	Ht: 6' 0"	Wt: 200	PT/Exp	A	Rand Var	+1
			Consist	C	MM	3335

Plantar fasciitis ruined 2nd half, just like leg injuries doomed 2022. R$ in 2021, 1st half of 2023 show he's a $20+ player when healthy, but healthy is not a reliable state for him, especially with penchant for being HBP (53 in three years). Before you chase 20 HR/20 SB upside, make sure you can build his injury risk into your budget.

Yr	Tm	PA	R	HR	RBI	SB	BA	xHR	xSB	xBA	OBP	SLG	OPS+	vL+	vR+	bb%	ct%	Eye	G	L	F	h%	HctX	QBaB	Brl%	PX	xPX	HR/F	xHR/F	Spd	SBA%	SB%	RAR	BPX	R$
19	aa	132	22	3	13	4	252		3		369	358	101			16	73	0.68				32				58				110	9%	100%		15	$1
20																																			
21	CIN	631	98	21	69	12	269	21	9	260	376	459	115	112	116	11	73	0.50	44	23	33	33	102	CCc	10%	118	96	16%	16%	102	8%	80%	19.3	165	$23
22	CIN	431	48	10	41	3	249	9	7	239	327	378	100	99	100	7	76	0.33	41	23	36	30	85	DBd	5%	84	81	10%	9%	124	6%	43%	-4.1	79	$9
23	CIN	529	78	17	61	14	244	16	11	251	338	407	102	87	107	10	76	0.48	39	22	39	29	104	BBc	8%	98	103	12%	12%	89	12%	88%	9.7	111	$15
1st Half		371	61	11	45	12	254	11	10	255	345	411	104	89	109	9	78	0.48	40	21	39	29	103	BBc	7%	93	94	11%	11%	90	14%	86%	7.0	129	$26
2nd Half		158	17	6	16	2	222	5	2	242	323	400	98	82	103	12	70	0.48	35	24	41	27	106	BBb	9%	111	129	15%	13%	96	5%	100%	1.4	93	$1
24	Proj	**511**	**71**	**18**	**56**	**11**	**256**	**16**	**9**	**248**	**350**	**428**	**107**	**97**	**110**	**10**	**74**	**0.45**	**40**	**23**	**38**	**31**	**97**		**7%**	**104**	**100**	**14%**	**13%**	**100**	**9%**	**83%**	**17.3**	**100**	**$20**

Isbel,Kyle

Age: 27	Pos: CF		Health	B	LIMA Plan	B
Bats: L	Ht: 5' 11"	Wt: 190	PT/Exp	B	Rand Var	0
			Consist	C	MM	2425

5-34-.240 with 7 SB in 313 PA at KC. Behind this pedestrian output, there is growth: note ct% gain, SB% improvement, and xPX upside, while ignoring vL+ (inflated by 45% h%). 2nd half suggests he can deliver double-digit value even in platoon role, with more power potential lying in wait. A speculative bid could net you... UP: 15 HR, 15 SB

Yr	Tm	PA	R	HR	RBI	SB	BA	xHR	xSB	xBA	OBP	SLG	OPS+	vL+	vR+	bb%	ct%	Eye	G	L	F	h%	HctX	QBaB	Brl%	PX	xPX	HR/F	xHR/F	Spd	SBA%	SB%	RAR	BPX	R$
19																																			
20																																			
21	KC *	509	60	11	46	18	233	1	16	211	292	366	90	120	104	8	74	0.32	35	18	47	29	80	DAf	4%	81	52	4%	4%	132	21%	75%	-11.9	69	$14
22	KC	278	32	5	28	9	211	4	10	220	264	340	85	70	89	6	71	0.21	43	19	38	28	101	CCf	5%	87	96	7%	6%	132	28%	60%	-9.8	21	$4
23	KC *	348	50	6	38	7	239	6	7	245	285	382	91	108	86	6	80	0.32	40	17	43	28	111	CCf	6%	91	118	5%	6%	106	12%	88%	-0.5	132	$6
1st Half		146	16	2	13	2	207	3	2	240	255	341	82	97	73	6	80	0.32	48	12	40	24	108	BCf	8%	86	103	3%	9%	103	12%	67%	-5.1	114	-$5
2nd Half		202	34	4	25	5	262	3	4	247	303	412	97	113	93	6	80	0.32	36	19	45	31	113	CBd	4%	94	127	6%	5%	109	12%	100%	3.0	146	$10
24	Proj	**455**	**60**	**9**	**48**	**13**	**236**	**8**	**12**	**235**	**285**	**379**	**91**	**80**	**94**	**6**	**78**	**0.29**	**40**	**18**	**43**	**28**	**103**		**6%**	**88**	**100**	**7%**	**6%**	**117**	**19%**	**77%**	**-3.0**	**84**	**$14**

Jankowski,Travis

Age: 33	Pos: LF		Health	D	LIMA Plan	D
Bats: L	Ht: 6' 2"	Wt: 190	PT/Exp	C	Rand Var	-4
			Consist	F	MM	0511

Healthy season, new SB rules helped him tap speed to degree not seen since Padres heyday. At 33, he is who he is: he's not gonna hit for power, and he's not gonna hit for average, despite what that luck-fueled 1st half BA might have you believe. Above-average OBP should keep modest PA, SB coming; but that F Consistency grade is well-earned.

Yr	Tm	PA	R	HR	RBI	SB	BA	xHR	xSB	xBA	OBP	SLG	OPS+	vL+	vR+	bb%	ct%	Eye	G	L	F	h%	HctX	QBaB	Brl%	PX	xPX	HR/F	xHR/F	Spd	SBA%	SB%	RAR	BPX	R$
19	SD *	197	21	0	7	6	227	0	6	155	287	256	75	0	62	8	76	0.35	47	6	47	30	29	FCf	0%	23	8	0%	0%	113	22%	58%	-11.1	-100	$0
20	CIN	17	3	0	0	2	67	0	1	169	176	67	32	0	40	12	53	0.29	63	25	13	13	0	FFf	0%	0	-26	0%	0%	107	100%	67%	-2.4	-512	-$2
21	PHI *	221	34	1	14	8	248	1	10	246	356	333	95	100	98	14	78	0.77	49	23	27	31	58	FFf	2%	55	52	4%	4%	157	18%	66%	-2.8	131	$5
22	2 TM *	213	26	1	5	11	161	0	8	189	263	186	64	70	60	12	68	0.43	71	10	19	23	40	FFf	0%	19	3	0%	0%	139	22%	90%	-14.4	-152	-$1
23	TEX	287	34	1	30	19	263	1	14	253	357	332	94	82	95	12	83	0.83	50	21	29	31	86	DDd	0%	46	32	2%	2%	117	23%	95%	5.4	107	$8
1st Half		138	21	0	13	10	310	0	8	280	416	397	111	145	106	15	82	0.95	57	23	20	38	80	FFd	0%	60	17	0%	0%	132	23%	91%	8.3	168	$4
2nd Half		149	13	1	17	9	221	1	6	229	302	275	78	10	86	10	84	0.71	45	19	36	26	92	DCd	0%	33	45	3%	3%	96	23%	100%	-3.5	50	$2
24	Proj	**175**	**22**	**0**	**13**	**10**	**241**	**0**	**8**	**234**	**337**	**292**	**86**	**78**	**88**	**12**	**79**	**0.65**	**53**	**20**	**27**	**30**	**66**		**0%**	**36**	**26**	**1%**	**1%**	**117**	**21%**	**87%**	**-1.6**	**20**	**$6**

Jansen,Danny

Age: 29	Pos: CA		Health	F	LIMA Plan	C+
Bats: R	Ht: 6' 2"	Wt: 215	PT/Exp	C	Rand Var	+2
			Consist	D	MM	4233

Fractured right middle finger flipped his season the bird on Sept 1, cutting short resurgent 2nd half (.895 OPS, career-best ct%). Third straight year injuries have given one-finger salute to PA and R$, and second straight with Health grade warning not to F around. Elite power may seem right up your(s) alley, but bid too high, and you might sit and spin.

Yr	Tm	PA	R	HR	RBI	SB	BA	xHR	xSB	xBA	OBP	SLG	OPS+	vL+	vR+	bb%	ct%	Eye	G	L	F	h%	HctX	QBaB	Brl%	PX	xPX	HR/F	xHR/F	Spd	SBA%	SB%	RAR	BPX	R$
19	TOR	384	41	13	43	0	207	13	1	237	279	360	89	101	82	8	77	0.39	39	20	41	23	114	CBd	6%	78	97	12%	12%	91	1%	0%	-5.2	63	$1
20	TOR	147	18	6	20	0	183	6	0	243	313	358	89	55	105	14	74	0.68	36	25	39	19	65	FBf	9%	93	74	17%	17%	95	0%	0%	-2.7	120	$4
21	TOR *	229	36	12	31	0	221	9	0	272	292	459	103	79	119	9	77	0.43	31	24	45	23	105	BAf	9%	136	117	17%	14%	81	0%	0%	2.8	231	$3
22	TOR	248	34	15	44	1	260	15	1	267	339	516	121	116	123	10	80	0.57	34	16	51	26	144	BAf	13%	147	160	17%	17%	81	2%	100%	15.6	283	$9
23	TOR	301	38	17	53	0	228	12	1	251	312	474	107	107	107	8	77	0.37	34	14	52	23	109	CAf	11%	139	130	16%	11%	75	0%	0%	9.7	207	$6
1st Half		181	22	10	33	0	214	7	0	246	271	446	98	93	100	7	74	0.30	32	16	52	23	116	CAf	11%	135	141	15%	11%	69	0%	0%	1.8	154	$5
2nd Half		120	16	7	20	0	250	6	1	260	375	520	121	125	119	9	81	0.53	37	10	53	24	98	CAf	11%	144	112	16%	14%	92	0%	0%	6.0	311	$3
24	Proj	**315**	**44**	**18**	**54**	**0**	**235**	**16**	**1**	**258**	**326**	**478**	**110**	**104**	**113**	**9**	**78**	**0.46**	**34**	**16**	**50**	**24**	**113**		**11%**	**135**	**128**	**16%**	**14%**	**82**	**1%**	**89%**	**13.0**	**239**	**$12**

Jeffers,Ryan

Age: 27	Pos: CA		Health	B	LIMA Plan	C+
Bats: R	Ht: 6' 4"	Wt: 235	PT/Exp	B	Rand Var	-5
			Consist	C	MM	4223

Outhit his competition enough over final two months to move from time share to primary catcher, and while 2nd half BA was inflated, ct% rebound was encouraging, and power skills evoked promise of 2020-21. Also owned career-best bb% while continuing to rip barrels and mash lefties. At his age, could finally be ready for... UP: 20 HR

Yr	Tm	PA	R	HR	RBI	SB	BA	xHR	xSB	xBA	OBP	SLG	OPS+	vL+	vR+	bb%	ct%	Eye	G	L	F	h%	HctX	QBaB	Brl%	PX	xPX	HR/F	xHR/F	Spd	SBA%	SB%	RAR	BPX	R$
19	aa	95	12	4	8	0	279		0		343	467	112			9	77	0.42				32				101				102	0%	0%		148	-$1
20	MIN	62	5	3	7	0	273	4	0	182	355	436	105	93	110	8	65	0.26	53	17	31	36	110	ACf	14%	89	112	27%	36%	109	0%	0%	1.5	-60	$2
21	MIN *	389	38	18	47	0	196	14	1	217	269	394	91	99	88	9	61	0.25	42	21	37	26	98	BCc	14%	136	157	24%	24%	96	1%	0%	-6.8	4	$2
22	MIN *	273	28	9	31	1	203	11	1	225	277	360	90	127	77	9	73	0.38	35	19	46	24	99	CBd	14%	104	115	10%	16%	75	2%	100%	-2.5	62	$1
23	MIN	335	46	14	43	3	276	15	9	239	369	490	117	127	113	10	67	0.35	39	18	42	36	90	CBd	12%	137	102	17%	18%	142	5%	60%	21.6	157	$10
1st Half		150	17	3	10	0	254	4	4	222	361	405	105	84	116	11	64	0.33	39	23	39	37	78	CBc	7%	112	67	10%	13%	135	2%	0%	3.3	36	-$3
2nd Half		185	29	11	33	3	294	10	5	254	375	556	126	183	111	10	70	0.38	40	15	45	36	99	CBf	14%	155	127	22%	20%	133	8%	75%	16.6	236	$15
24	Proj	**385**	**51**	**17**	**52**	**2**	**254**	**17**	**5**	**236**	**339**	**459**	**109**	**123**	**103**	**10**	**68**	**0.35**	**40**	**19**	**41**	**32**	**96**		**13%**	**130**	**115**	**17%**	**18%**	**105**	**4%**	**64%**	**17.7**	**100**	**$14**

Jimenez,Eloy

Age: 27	Pos: DH		Health	F	LIMA Plan	B
Bats: R	Ht: 6' 4"	Wt: 240	PT/Exp	A	Rand Var	0
			Consist	B	MM	3035

Logged another 32 IL days in 2023, plus another 9 day-to-day games (calf, groin, heel), and even when healthy, wasn't all that healthy (see 2nd half). When he's right, 30-HR upside remains intact: 8 HR, 142 PX, 24% HR/F in 131 PA in May/June. But we haven't seen that guy over a full season since 2019; odds of him showing up now aren't great.

Yr	Tm	PA	R	HR	RBI	SB	BA	xHR	xSB	xBA	OBP	SLG	OPS+	vL+	vR+	bb%	ct%	Eye	G	L	F	h%	HctX	QBaB	Brl%	PX	xPX	HR/F	xHR/F	Spd	SBA%	SB%	RAR	BPX	R$
19	CHW *	526	71	32	80	0	268	30	2	255	310	509	113	109	116	6	71	0.21	48	18	34	31	94	ACc	13%	128	102	27%	26%	107	0%	0%	3.3	126	$16
20	CHW	226	26	14	41	0	296	15	0	268	332	559	118	112	120	5	74	0.21	52	20	28	34	132	AFd	16%	150	125	31%	33%	84	0%	0%	11.0	212	$24
21	CHW *	270	25	11	38	0	243	10	0	239	292	416	97	78	110	6	70	0.24	48	22	29	30	114	BDc	11%	108	104	22%	22%	65	0%	0%	-7.3	12	$4
22	CHW *	388	45	17	58	0	276	19	1	239	336	460	113	118	123	8	75	0.36	50	17	33	32	144	ADc	15%	112	143	22%	26%	85	0%	0%	8.0	117	$13
23	CHW	489	50	18	64	0	272	16	2	246	317	441	103	100	104	6	80	0.32	53	16	31	31	123	ADf	9%	96	88	16%	14%	81	0%	0%	9.3	121	$13
1st Half		227	26	11	38	0	275	10	1	245	322	483	110	108	111	7	74	0.27	52	15	32	32	125	ADd	13%	124	106	22%	20%	76	0%	0%	5.3	118	$12
2nd Half		262	24	7	26	0	269	6	2	247	313	404	97	90	98	6	84	0.39	54	16	30	30	121	BFf	7%	75	74	11%	10%	90	0%	0%	-1.5	136	$8
24	Proj	**490**	**52**	**23**	**68**	**0**	**269**	**24**	**1**	**251**	**320**	**469**	**108**	**101**	**110**	**7**	**77**	**0.31**	**51**	**17**	**31**	**30**	**126**		**11%**	**114**	**106**	**21%**	**21%**	**79**	**0%**	**0%**	**14.7**	**112**	**$19**

BRANDON KRUSE

Joe,Connor

Age: 31	Pos: RF 1B LF	Health	B	LIMA Plan	D+
Bats: R	Ht: 6' 0" Wt: 205	PT/Exp	A	Rand Var	0
		Consist	C	MM	2233

Leaving Coors didn't affect power, mainly because his power has never lived up to the potential of his plus skills. Which makes it hard to get too excited about 2nd half gains in ct%, HctX, and QBaB, even though they were career-best marks. Worth a flyer in deep leagues, but most likely outcome is another year of near-replacement-level results.

Yr	Tm	PA	R	HR	RBI	SB	BA	xHR	xSB	xBA	OBP	SLG	OPS+	vL+	vR+	bb%	ct%	Eye	G	L	F	h%	HctX	QBaB	Brl%	PX	xPX	HR/F	xHR/F	Spd	SBA%	SB%	RAR	BPX	R$
19	SF *	422	57	10	46	1	228	0	2	229	315	370	95	31	0	11	71	0.44	70	10	20	29	25	FFc	0%	87	-36	0%	0%	83	3%	22%	-16.4	19	$4
20																																			
21	COL *	311	34	14	49	1	273	7	0	272	355	477	114	128	112	11	75	0.51	33	28	38	32	119	CBc	10%	119	138	15%	13%	80	1%	100%	10.7	165	$9
22	COL	467	56	7	28	6	238	7	11	242	338	359	99	104	95	12	76	0.57	46	21	33	30	86	DCd	5%	82	78	7%	7%	148	6%	75%	-0.1	138	$7
23	PIT	472	63	11	42	3	247	12	9	252	339	421	104	110	98	11	73	0.45	36	23	41	31	106	CBd	8%	114	120	9%	10%	116	7%	38%	7.3	154	$8
1st Half		260	34	6	24	3	236	8	6	244	327	415	102	122	88	11	68	0.37	38	23	38	32	92	CBf	10%	125	122	10%	14%	111	14%	38%	0.2	104	$6
2nd Half		212	29	5	18	0	261	4	2	263	354	429	106	97	111	11	80	0.62	34	22	44	30	123	BAc	6%	103	118	8%	6%	117	0%	0%	5.6	218	$5
24	**Proj**	**350**	**45**	**8**	**33**	**2**	**248**	**7**	**5**	**249**	**342**	**403**	**102**	**106**	**100**	**11**	**75**	**0.51**	**39**	**23**	**38**	**31**	**103**		**7%**	**99**	**108**	**9%**	**8%**	**109**	**4%**	**54%**	**5.0**	**147**	**$**

Jones,Nolan

Age: 26	Pos: LF RF	Health	A	LIMA Plan	C+
Bats: L	Ht: 6' 4" Wt: 195	PT/Exp	A	Rand Var	-5
		Consist	F	MM	4435

20-62-.297 with 20 SB in 424 PA at COL. Breakout season showcased elite power with surprisingly adept running game, and wasn't just Coors (.928 OPS home, .934 away). Got help from h%, leaving nearly 40-point gap between BA, xBA, but even there, had encouraging growth in Sept (76% ct%, .290 xBA). Next step could be... UP: 30 HR, 30 SB

Yr	Tm	PA	R	HR	RBI	SB	BA	xHR	xSB	xBA	OBP	SLG	OPS+	vL+	vR+	bb%	ct%	Eye	G	L	F	h%	HctX	QBaB	Brl%	PX	xPX	HR/F	xHR/F	Spd	SBA%	SB%	RAR	BPX	R$
19	aa	208	31	8	21	2	252		2		360	460	113			14	63	0.46				35				134				118	4%	100%		93	$
20																																			
21	aaa	383	43	9	34	7	201		5		290	352	88			11	59	0.30				31				122				91	11%	76%		-50	$
22	CLE *	326	35	7	38	2	220	3	2	219	282	342	88	0	102	8	64	0.24	35	30	35	32	102	CBc	15%	97	147	11%	16%	98	4%	66%	-9.6	-62	$
23	COL *	591	81	28	86	23	296	24	23	259	381	544	126	121	129	12	67	0.41	43	20	38	40	110	BCd	16%	162	151	22%	27%	132	17%	85%	51.7	218	$3
1st Half		290	37	13	38	8	303	7	8	271	380	539	126	93	143	11	67	0.38	47	23	30	41	113	ACa	12%	160	126	24%	33%	126	10%	100%	24.9	207	$2
2nd Half		301	44	15	48	15	290	18	15	254	385	548	126	132	123	13	66	0.44	41	19	41	38	108	CCf	18%	165	161	22%	26%	138	23%	79%	24.7	236	$3
24	**Proj**	**560**	**77**	**26**	**76**	**19**	**264**	**30**	**13**	**252**	**349**	**492**	**115**	**106**	**118**	**11**	**67**	**0.39**	**43**	**20**	**37**	**34**	**107**		**15%**	**149**	**147**	**21%**	**25%**	**119**	**17%**	**82%**	**30.6**	**99**	**$2**

Judge,Aaron

Age: 32	Pos: RF DH	Health	D	LIMA Plan	D+
Bats: R	Ht: 6' 7" Wt: 282	PT/Exp	A	Rand Var	+1
		Consist	F	MM	5055

Torn ligament in big toe cost him almost two months and prevented another run at big HR numbers. Higher FB%, slightly lower PX combined to take bite out of BA, but given half-season xBA split, fair to assume injury played a role. Age, health history suggest you shouldn't go all-in on rebound, though 1st half skills confirm 2022 beast still lurks.

Yr	Tm	PA	R	HR	RBI	SB	BA	xHR	xSB	xBA	OBP	SLG	OPS+	vL+	vR+	bb%	ct%	Eye	G	L	F	h%	HctX	QBaB	Brl%	PX	xPX	HR/F	xHR/F	Spd	SBA%	SB%	RAR	BPX	R$
19	NYY	446	75	27	55	3	272	29	3	256	381	540	127	156	116	14	63	0.45	40	27	32	36	117	ACa	20%	163	150	35%	38%	88	4%	60%	22.1	141	$1
20	NYY	113	23	9	22	0	257	8	0	259	336	554	118	120	117	9	68	0.31	39	20	41	28	116	ABa	12%	166	111	32%	29%	72	4%	0%	3.0	188	$1
21	NYY	633	89	39	98	6	287	39	1	268	373	544	126	135	122	12	71	0.47	41	23	36	34	136	ACa	18%	149	141	28%	28%	53	4%	86%	44.6	177	$3
22	NYY	692	133	62	131	16	311	69	8	302	425	686	157	141	162	16	69	0.63	37	19	44	35	145	ABa	27%	239	200	36%	40%	61	9%	84%	102.7	417	$5
23	NYY	458	79	37	75	3	267	47	3	272	406	613	139	142	138	19	65	0.68	30	20	50	31	141	AAa	28%	217	223	31%	39%	52	3%	75%	51.3	314	$2
1st Half		213	42	19	40	3	291	24	3	290	404	674	148	79	163	17	64	0.56	30	23	48	34	150	AAa	31%	246	229	35%	44%	60	7%	75%	28.0	379	$2
2nd Half		245	37	18	35	0	245	23	1	252	408	557	130	205	116	22	65	0.79	31	17	52	27	134	AAb	25%	191	217	28%	35%	58	0%	0%	20.0	271	$1
24	**Proj**	**560**	**98**	**44**	**104**	**4**	**279**	**51**	**4**	**273**	**401**	**608**	**138**	**143**	**137**	**17**	**67**	**0.62**	**35**	**20**	**45**	**32**	**139**		**25%**	**202**	**195**	**32%**	**37%**	**54**	**3%**	**70%**	**61.4**	**304**	**$3**

Julien,Edouard

Age: 25	Pos: 2B DH	Health	A	LIMA Plan	C+
Bats: L	Ht: 6' 2" Wt: 195	PT/Exp	B	Rand Var	0
		Consist	C	MM	4325

16-37-.263 in 408 PA at MIN. Elite bb% has always been skill that drives his profile, and in 2nd half it led to elite power, though xHR, xHR/F caution against a repeat. There are still flaws in his game—too many Ks, too many grounders, and struggles vL—but his patience is enough reason to invest yours as he tries to work through it.

Yr	Tm	PA	R	HR	RBI	SB	BA	xHR	xSB	xBA	OBP	SLG	OPS+	vL+	vR+	bb%	ct%	Eye	G	L	F	h%	HctX	QBaB	Brl%	PX	xPX	HR/F	xHR/F	Spd	SBA%	SB%	RAR	BPX	R$
19																																			
20																																			
21																																			
22	aa	465	50	11	44	12	244		12		350	373	102			14	64	0.45				35				100				104	15%	61%		-7	$1
23	MIN *	564	80	19	52	5	257	16	7	245	372	439	111	60	123	15	62	0.49	50	26	24	37	83	CDa	13%	133	109	31%	31%	96	3%	100%	29.9	61	$1
1st Half		295	35	7	24	3	245	4	3	233	343	403	102	36	112	13	61	0.39	51	23	26	37	53	CDb	11%	128	70	21%	21%	81	4%	100%	6.2	-4	$
2nd Half		269	45	12	28	2	271	12	5	256	405	482	120	71	128	18	63	0.61	50	27	23	37	100	BDa	14%	139	130	38%	38%	120	2%	100%	18.5	139	$1
24	**Proj**	**490**	**65**	**20**	**47**	**8**	**253**	**19**	**9**	**247**	**367**	**448**	**112**	**57**	**120**	**15**	**63**	**0.48**	**50**	**26**	**24**	**35**	**81**		**13%**	**135**	**106**	**31%**	**31%**	**109**	**8%**	**69%**	**23.4**	**45**	**$1**

Julks,Corey

Age: 28	Pos: LF	Health	A	LIMA Plan	D
Bats: R	Ht: 6' 1" Wt: 185	PT/Exp	A	Rand Var	0
		Consist	B	MM	1401

6-33-.245 with 15 SB in 323 PA at HOU. Got the full luck/regression experience in one roller coaster season, going from spring afterthought (729 ADP) to 1st half fantasy darling to Triple-A demotion in August. And while 2nd half bumps in bb%, HctX, and xPX might merit optimism, double-digit R$ ain't likely to return. But it was one hell of a ride.

Yr	Tm	PA	R	HR	RBI	SB	BA	xHR	xSB	xBA	OBP	SLG	OPS+	vL+	vR+	bb%	ct%	Eye	G	L	F	h%	HctX	QBaB	Brl%	PX	xPX	HR/F	xHR/F	Spd	SBA%	SB%	RAR	BPX	R$
19	aa	41	3	0	4	0	145		0		220	145	51			9	52	0.20				28				0				111	0%	0%		-515	-$
20																																			
21	aa	362	51	11	27	11	239		10		289	401	95			7	70	0.24				31				105				110	23%	66%		54	$1
22	aaa	557	60	19	53	13	202		11		251	351	85			6	69	0.21				25				98				109	18%	68%		7	$
23	HOU *	441	51	8	40	19	228	7	17	239	292	348	87	84	90	8	74	0.35	36	25	39	29	84	CBb	5%	81	77	7%	8%	128	24%	81%	-4.2	64	$
1st Half		232	31	6	27	12	259	5	11	236	306	389	95	98	94	6	72	0.25	38	25	38	33	77	CBc	5%	84	65	10%	8%	128	27%	80%	0.9	32	$1
2nd Half		209	20	2	13	7	192	1	6	241	276	301	78	62	76	10	76	0.48	32	26	41	24	100	CBa	6%	77	104	0%	4%	112	19%	84%	-7.9	79	-$
24	**Proj**	**175**	**20**	**2**	**15**	**6**	**217**	**3**	**5**	**219**	**277**	**308**	**80**	**72**	**83**	**7**	**72**	**0.28**	**34**	**26**	**40**	**29**	**91**		**5%**	**65**	**88**	**4%**	**6%**	**111**	**20%**	**76%**	**-5.4**	**41**	**$**

Jung,Josh

Age: 26	Pos: 3B	Health	B	LIMA Plan	C
Bats: R	Ht: 6' 2" Wt: 214	PT/Exp	A	Rand Var	-2
		Consist	F	MM	4135

Fractured thumb and subsequent surgery stole six weeks from breakout sophomore season, and he wasn't the same upon return (.515 OPS over final 54 PA). Prior to that, improvements in vR+, ct%, and QBaB from shaky rookie debut were positive signs. BA may regress a bit, but power should be here to stay. UP: 30 HR, .275 BA

Yr	Tm	PA	R	HR	RBI	SB	BA	xHR	xSB	xBA	OBP	SLG	OPS+	vL+	vR+	bb%	ct%	Eye	G	L	F	h%	HctX	QBaB	Brl%	PX	xPX	HR/F	xHR/F	Spd	SBA%	SB%	RAR	BPX	R$
19																																			
20																																			
21	a/a	329	43	15	48	2	288		2		341	506	116			7	72	0.29				36				136				85	5%	41%		150	$
22	TEX *	203	18	8	28	3	206	5	2	233	231	393	88	120	75	3	62	0.09	41	25	34	28	102	DBc	10%	142	155	25%	25%	88	10%	100%	-6.1	-3	$
23	TEX	515	75	23	70	1	266	25	6	249	315	467	106	134	98	6	68	0.20	36	24	39	34	114	ABb	12%	129	139	18%	19%	103	4%	25%	16.3	75	$
1st Half		344	56	17	50	1	270	18	4	256	323	487	111	142	101	6	69	0.22	36	25	39	34	122	ABb	12%	136	151	20%	21%	108	4%	33%	10.2	118	$2
2nd Half		171	19	6	20	0	256	7	1	233	298	425	98	116	93	5	67	0.15	37	23	40	35	98	ABb	11%	116	116	14%	16%	94	3%	0%	-0.2	0	$
24	**Proj**	**525**	**66**	**28**	**75**	**3**	**257**	**29**	**5**	**254**	**305**	**485**	**108**	**136**	**97**	**6**	**68**	**0.19**	**37**	**24**	**38**	**32**	**110**		**11%**	**147**	**140**	**22%**	**23%**	**84**	**5%**	**63%**	**16.7**	**45**	**$2**

Kelenic,Jarred

Age: 24	Pos: LF RF	Health	B	LIMA Plan	C+
Bats: L	Ht: 6' 1" Wt: 206	PT/Exp	A	Rand Var	-5
		Consist	C	MM	3215

11-49-.253 with 13 SB in 416 PA at SEA. 'Twas a season even more Kelenic-y than ever before, with dizzying highs (.846 OPS in April/May) and soul-crushing lows (.637 OPS after 6/1, fractured foot after kicking water cooler in July). Could he repeat 1st half over full season? Possibly! Will he? Have your inanimate objects handy for attack.

Yr	Tm	PA	R	HR	RBI	SB	BA	xHR	xSB	xBA	OBP	SLG	OPS+	vL+	vR+	bb%	ct%	Eye	G	L	F	h%	HctX	QBaB	Brl%	PX	xPX	HR/F	xHR/F	Spd	SBA%	SB%	RAR	BPX	R$
19	aa	91	12	6	18	3	255		2		324	556	122			9	78	0.46				25				145				111	17%	100%		300	$
20																																			
21	SEA *	514	63	21	64	11	206	15	7	230	280	393	92	67	96	9	71	0.36	43	16	42	24	85	CBd	10%	112	111	15%	16%	71	16%	67%	-13.3	65	$
22	SEA *	555	57	18	58	11	199	8	9	208	254	372	89	60	83	7	69	0.24	37	11	52	25	93	DAf	14%	124	138	13%	15%	78	19%	62%	-20.4	45	$
23	SEA *	456	49	12	52	14	251	13	12	246	325	413	101	104	101	10	64	0.31	43	29	28	36	86	ACb	10%	121	80	16%	19%	83	18%	73%	8.3	4	$
1st Half		312	37	11	37	11	252	12	9	251	327	453	107	121	102	10	63	0.30	42	28	30	36	88	ACb	11%	147	101	21%	23%	93	20%	79%	7.4	68	$
2nd Half		144	12	1	15	3	250	1	3	243	321	328	88	36	98	9	67	0.32	45	32	23	37	76	BCa	7%	69	25	0%	7%	78	14%	57%	-2.7	-114	-
24	**Proj**	**490**	**54**	**16**	**58**	**15**	**248**	**16**	**11**	**234**	**319**	**418**	**101**	**78**	**110**	**9**	**67**	**0.32**	**41**	**21**	**38**	**33**	**86**		**11%**	**118**	**93**	**14%**	**14%**	**74**	**18%**	**71%**	**7.9**	**5**	**$**

BRANDON KRUSE

Kemp,Tony

Age: 32 Pos: LF 2B
Bats: L Ht: 5' 6" Wt: 160

Health	A	LIMA Plan	D+
PT/Exp	A	Rand Var	+5
Consist	C	MM	1431

Unlucky hit rate led to reduced PA in Aug/Sept, even though skills were pretty much the same. That's the thing about this type of empty-contact, speed-and-defense profile though: teams are always looking for someone better, especially if BA/OBP starts to slip. Might still be worth a SB flyer in deep leagues, but double-digit R$ looks unlikely to return.

Yr	Tm	PA	R	HR	RBI	SB	BA	xHR	xSB	xBA	OBP	SLG	OPS+	vL+	vR+	bb%	ct%	Eye	G	L	F	h%	HctX	QBaB	Brl%	PX	xPX	HR/F	xHR/F	Spd	SBA%	SB%	RAR	BPX	R$
19	2 TM	279	31	8	29	4	212	3	5	241	291	380	93	103	90	8	81	0.49	41	16	43	23	99	DBc	2%	80	110	10%	4%	122	13%	50%	-11.5	156	$2
20	OAK	114	15	0	4	3	247	1	2	253	363	301	88	16	94	13	85	1.07	35	29	35	29	92	FAb	1%	39	97	0%	4%	97	11%	75%	-2.6	112	$4
21	OAK	397	54	8	37	8	279	3	8	254	382	418	110	100	113	13	85	1.02	35	23	42	31	90	DBc	1%	75	98	7%	3%	123	8%	80%	12.8	242	$13
22	OAK	558	61	7	46	11	235	4	8	247	307	334	91	84	92	8	86	0.65	41	20	39	26	73	FCf	2%	62	79	4%	2%	98	9%	92%	-3.8	141	$11
23	OAK	419	42	5	27	15	209	3	14	259	303	304	83	126	76	11	89	1.10	48	18	34	22	84	DCd	1%	50	67	5%	3%	117	18%	79%	-6.1	193	$3
1st Half		236	25	3	16	7	196	2	6	254	289	289	79	135	71	11	88	1.00	48	18	34	21	89	FCd	2%	47	75	5%	3%	109	14%	88%	-7.9	164	-$1
2nd Half		183	17	2	11	8	226	1	8	265	322	323	87	117	81	11	90	1.25	47	19	34	24	76	DDd	1%	53	57	4%	2%	120	23%	73%	-2.7	221	$1
24	**Proj**	**245**	**28**	**3**	**19**	**7**	**231**	**2**	**7**	**254**	**320**	**335**	**90**	**105**	**87**	**11**	**87**	**0.91**	**43**	**20**	**37**	**25**	**82**		**1%**	**58**	**77**	**5%**	**3%**	**116**	**14%**	**78%**	**-2.3**	**184**	**$3**

Kepler,Max

Age: 31 Pos: RF
Bats: L Ht: 6' 4" Wt: 225

Health	C	LIMA Plan	B+
PT/Exp	A	Rand Var	-2
Consist	C	MM	3235

First extended injury-free period since 2nd half of 2021 (15 xHR, 161 xPX), but just as important may have been the new shift limitations - he had been shifted against 90% of the time in 2022. Thrived vL for first time since 2019. Health grade might not fully reflect risk, as over/under on .250 BA, 20 HR hinges on avoiding even non-IL dings and dents.

Yr	Tm	PA	R	HR	RBI	SB	BA	xHR	xSB	xBA	OBP	SLG	OPS+	vL+	vR+	bb%	ct%	Eye	G	L	F	h%	HctX	QBaB	Brl%	PX	xPX	HR/F	xHR/F	Spd	SBA%	SB%	RAR	BPX	R$
19	MIN	596	98	36	90	1	252	22	2	275	336	519	118	122	116	10	81	0.61	36	17	47	25	119	BAd	9%	131	113	18%	11%	68	5%	17%	9.0	267	$18
20	MIN	196	27	9	23	3	228	7	1	257	321	439	101	49	120	11	79	0.61	32	22	46	24	103	CAd	5%	112	95	15%	11%	79	7%	100%	-1.2	216	$14
21	MIN	490	61	19	54	10	211	19	7	249	306	413	99	69	110	11	77	0.56	37	19	44	23	113	BBd	11%	112	134	13%	13%	109	9%	100%	-3.3	215	$9
22	MIN	446	54	9	43	3	227	12	4	254	318	348	94	95	94	11	83	0.74	46	20	34	25	108	CCf	7%	75	77	8%	11%	93	4%	60%	-7.0	152	$6
23	MIN	491	72	24	66	1	260	24	4	258	332	484	111	101	114	9	76	0.42	38	18	44	29	117	ABc	12%	127	142	16%	16%	96	2%	50%	20.4	193	$15
1st Half		202	24	11	25	0	209	9	1	237	277	418	95	79	98	8	75	0.33	39	15	46	21	95	BCf	11%	113	118	17%	14%	77	3%	0%	-3.7	114	$3
2nd Half		289	48	13	41	1	297	14	3	271	370	531	122	112	125	10	76	0.49	37	20	43	35	132	ABb	13%	137	159	15%	16%	110	1%	100%	21.2	250	$23
24	**Proj**	**490**	**69**	**20**	**61**	**3**	**255**	**20**	**5**	**255**	**334**	**447**	**107**	**94**	**111**	**10**	**78**	**0.52**	**39**	**19**	**42**	**28**	**114**		**10%**	**109**	**121**	**14%**	**13%**	**97**	**4%**	**73%**	**14.1**	**192**	**$18**

Kieboom,Carter

Age: 26 Pos: 3B
Bats: R Ht: 6' 2" Wt: 200

Health	F	LIMA Plan	D+
PT/Exp	D	Rand Var	-1
Consist	A	MM	1103

4-11-.207 in 94 PA at WAS. Former boom prospect has slowly gone bust, this time due to shoulder and oblique injuries that kept him on IL or in minors most of the season. When he did play, skills remained disappointingly lackluster. Still young enough to turn things around, but there's not much reason to put your faith in that outcome at this point.

Yr	Tm	PA	R	HR	RBI	SB	BA	xHR	xSB	xBA	OBP	SLG	OPS+	vL+	vR+	bb%	ct%	Eye	G	L	F	h%	HctX	QBaB	Brl%	PX	xPX	HR/F	xHR/F	Spd	SBA%	SB%	RAR	BPX	R$
19	WAS *	507	65	15	63	4	262	2	5	221	344	418	105	55	70	11	72	0.45	48	13	39	33	109	ACc	9%	90	137	22%	22%	101	4%	64%	-6.6	56	$12
20	WAS	122	15	0	9	0	202	0	1	196	344	212	74	103	58	14	67	0.52	41	30	29	30	56	DCc	0%	9	27	0%	0%	113	2%	0%	-10.0	-244	$0
21	WAS *	416	45	10	37	1	208	5	2	229	294	324	85	84	85	11	74	0.46	49	21	30	25	90	DDd	4%	71	69	13%	11%	101	2%	40%	-15.0	19	$1
22																																			
23	WAS *	263	30	8	29	1	212	2	3	219	281	346	85	108	73	9	68	0.30	47	19	34	27	74	DCf	5%	85	64	20%	10%	99	3%	55%	-5.9	-29	$1
1st Half		133	13	2	14	1	214		2	213	301	329	86	0	0	11	67	0.38	44	20	36	30	0		0%	81	-21	0%		114	6%	55%	-3.8	-32	-$5
2nd Half		130	18	6	15	0	209	2	1	223	259	363	84	107	72	6	70	0.22	47	19	34	25	76	DCf	5%	89	64	20%	10%	95	0%	0%	-4.3	-25	-$1
24	**Proj**	**385**	**38**	**8**	**31**	**1**	**213**	**7**	**4**	**220**	**308**	**311**	**85**	**106**	**73**	**10**	**70**	**0.36**	**45**	**24**	**31**	**28**	**72**		**3%**	**63**	**50**	**10%**	**10%**	**100**	**3%**	**43%**	**-9.9**	**-40**	**$4**

Kiermaier,Kevin

Age: 34 Pos: CF
Bats: L Ht: 6' 1" Wt: 210

Health	D	LIMA Plan	C+
PT/Exp	A	Rand Var	0
Consist	B	MM	2433

Three factors—staying healthy (only 10 IL days!), ct% rebound, and new SB rules—combined to help restore fantasy relevance, though career-low xPX is a new red flag, and xHR suggests power will regress. Improvement vL was mostly due to 37% h%, so probably best to continue viewing him as strong-side platoon guy with high injury risk.

Yr	Tm	PA	R	HR	RBI	SB	BA	xHR	xSB	xBA	OBP	SLG	OPS+	vL+	vR+	bb%	ct%	Eye	G	L	F	h%	HctX	QBaB	Brl%	PX	xPX	HR/F	xHR/F	Spd	SBA%	SB%	RAR	BPX	R$
19	TAM	480	60	14	55	19	228	14	15	261	278	398	94	109	87	5	77	0.25	54	17	29	27	88	CDd	6%	88	59	14%	14%	136	26%	79%	-12.5	115	$13
20	TAM	159	16	3	22	8	217	4	6	250	321	362	91	59	96	13	70	0.48	56	24	20	29	88	CFf	6%	85	75	16%	21%	130	23%	89%	-3.3	52	$13
21	TAM	390	54	4	37	9	259	4	12	243	328	388	98	92	101	8	72	0.33	57	18	25	35	82	DFf	4%	84	69	6%	6%	152	14%	64%	-1.8	69	$10
22	TAM	221	28	7	22	6	228	6	4	239	281	369	92	88	93	6	70	0.23	52	20	28	29	83	CFd	7%	97	97	18%	15%	92	15%	86%	-2.5	7	$4
23	TOR	408	58	8	36	14	265	5	13	272	322	419	101	95	103	7	77	0.34	56	19	25	33	81	DFc	3%	92	47	11%	7%	133	16%	93%	11.0	132	$11
1st Half		222	33	4	18	9	272	3	9	273	330	436	105	94	108	7	77	0.35	56	18	26	34	98	DFc	3%	94	55	10%	8%	149	17%	100%	7.5	161	$9
2nd Half		186	25	4	18	5	256	2	4	269	312	399	96	97	96	7	76	0.33	55	21	24	31	62	CFc	4%	90	37	13%	6%	100	14%	83%	1.7	82	$6
24	**Proj**	**385**	**53**	**7**	**38**	**10**	**255**	**7**	**11**	**253**	**313**	**389**	**96**	**94**	**97**	**7**	**74**	**0.30**	**55**	**20**	**26**	**33**	**80**		**5%**	**85**	**63**	**11%**	**10%**	**122**	**13%**	**82%**	**3.8**	**77**	**$14**

Kim,Ha-Seong

Age: 28 Pos: 2B 3B SS
Bats: R Ht: 5' 9" Wt: 168

Health	A	LIMA Plan	B
PT/Exp	A	Rand Var	-3
Consist	B	MM	1425

Last four half-season splits show SB breakout has been gradual process of getting on base more and earning manager's trust: OBP—.322, .328, .346, .356; SBA%—9%, 12%, 20%, 33%. However, given BA/xBA gap and fact that bb% was highest he's ever owned, some regression is likely. Add in HR/xHR gap, and betting on a full repeat looks risky.

Yr	Tm	PA	R	HR	RBI	SB	BA	xHR	xSB	xBA	OBP	SLG	OPS+	vL+	vR+	bb%	ct%	Eye	G	L	F	h%	HctX	QBaB	Brl%	PX	xPX	HR/F	xHR/F	Spd	SBA%	SB%	RAR	BPX	R$
19	for	596	109	11	101	30	287		18		354	431	109			9	86	0.74				32	0			76				100	21%	87%	15.1	207	$31
20	for	528	98	16	97	21	283		13		356	434	105			10	88	0.98				29	0			73				98	15%	91%	8.5	256	$79
21	SD	298	27	8	34	6	202	5	5	224	270	352	85	91	83	7	73	0.31	41	17	41	24	87	DCf	4%	90	74	10%	6%	117	12%	86%	-12.0	69	$2
22	SD	582	58	11	59	12	251	11	11	248	325	383	100	107	97	9	81	0.51	40	21	39	29	96	DBf	4%	85	97	7%	7%	115	10%	86%	1.3	155	$16
23	SD	626	84	17	60	38	260	11	31	242	351	398	102	121	93	12	77	0.60	41	21	39	31	84	DCf	4%	81	73	10%	7%	111	26%	81%	18.1	114	$24
1st Half		298	39	10	31	13	258	8	11	236	346	418	105	118	96	12	74	0.52	38	20	42	31	80	DBd	6%	96	99	13%	10%	103	20%	81%	8.8	104	$18
2nd Half		328	45	7	29	25	262	3	21	247	356	379	99	124	90	12	80	0.70	43	21	36	31	88	DCf	3%	69	52	9%	4%	119	32%	81%	7.7	132	$27
24	**Proj**	**609**	**76**	**13**	**62**	**31**	**252**	**11**	**21**	**239**	**332**	**378**	**97**	**111**	**91**	**10**	**79**	**0.54**	**40**	**20**	**39**	**30**	**89**		**4%**	**76**	**80**	**8%**	**6%**	**109**	**23%**	**82%**	**11.4**	**133**	**$26**

Kiner-Falefa,Isiah

Age: 29 Pos: CF LF 3B
Bats: R Ht: 5' 11" Wt: 190

Health	A	LIMA Plan	C
PT/Exp	A	Rand Var	+1
Consist	A	MM	1333

Arrival of Anthony Volpe shifted him to utility role, brought run of $20+ seasons to an end. Resulting lack of reps seems responsible for 2nd half ct% dropping to career-worst level, though it's concerning enough to hedge your bet on BA rebound. Glove, relative youth should get him another shot, just don't assume a R$ resurgence.

Yr	Tm	PA	R	HR	RBI	SB	BA	xHR	xSB	xBA	OBP	SLG	OPS+	vL+	vR+	bb%	ct%	Eye	G	L	F	h%	HctX	QBaB	Brl%	PX	xPX	HR/F	xHR/F	Spd	SBA%	SB%	RAR	BPX	R$
19	TEX *	324	31	3	31	5	230	2	3	235	283	327	84	75	91	7	78	0.33	50	17	33	29	98	CDc	1%	62	85	2%	4%	104	7%	100%	-17.5	30	$2
20	TEX	228	28	3	10	8	280	3	14	259	329	370	93	119	82	6	85	0.44	62	16	22	32	101	CFd	2%	42	33	8%	8%	198	20%	62%	-8.6	184	$20
21	TEX	677	74	8	53	20	271	5	18	263	312	357	92	79	98	4	86	0.31	54	20	26	31	95	DFc	2%	49	49	6%	3%	130	14%	80%	-9.2	123	$22
22	NYY	531	66	4	48	22	261	3	14	260	314	327	91	96	89	7	85	0.49	55	21	24	30	75	DFc	1%	45	34	4%	3%	96	18%	85%	-6.2	69	$20
23	NYY	361	39	6	37	14	242	4	13	259	306	340	88	85	89	8	79	0.40	49	25	26	29	87	CDc	3%	59	53	9%	6%	102	21%	74%	-3.2	32	$7
1st Half		191	27	5	22	9	256	4	9	269	305	381	94	74	101	6	82	0.39	46	24	30	29	87	CDd	5%	65	69	12%	9%	118	28%	69%	-1.1	114	$8
2nd Half		170	12	1	15	5	227	0	4	245	306	293	81	105	75	10	74	0.41	54	25	21	30	88	CFb	1%	50	31	4%	0%	87	14%	83%	-4.7	-57	-$1
24	**Proj**	**350**	**38**	**4**	**33**	**13**	**263**	**2**	**11**	**256**	**320**	**344**	**91**	**92**	**91**	**7**	**81**	**0.40**	**53**	**22**	**25**	**31**	**87**		**2%**	**51**	**45**	**6%**	**4%**	**103**	**17%**	**78%**	**0.0**	**52**	**$13**

Kirilloff,Alex

Age: 26 Pos: 1B OF
Bats: L Ht: 6' 2" Wt: 195

Health	F	LIMA Plan	C+
PT/Exp	C	Rand Var	-2
Consist	A	MM	3243

11-41-.270 in 319 PA at MIN. Injuries continue to define his career. Recovery from offseason wrist surgery delayed start of 2023, shoulder issue cost him all of Aug and required offseason surgery that may delay start of 2024. BA, power upside began to emerge in 2nd half, but any speculation should be tempered by glancing at that PA column.

Yr	Tm	PA	R	HR	RBI	SB	BA	xHR	xSB	xBA	OBP	SLG	OPS+	vL+	vR+	bb%	ct%	Eye	G	L	F	h%	HctX	QBaB	Brl%	PX	xPX	HR/F	xHR/F	Spd	SBA%	SB%	RAR	BPX	R$
19	aa	402	44	8	40	7	276		8		324	402	101			7	79	0.34				33				69				105	13%	51%		67	$9
20																																			
21	MIN	231	23	8	34	1	251	12	1	260	299	423	99	106	96	6	76	0.27	49	22	29	30	108	ADb	13%	101	136	17%	25%	95	4%	50%	-2.1	104	$4
22	MIN *	300	35	9	41	1	265	4	2	234	312	409	102	70	97	6	75	0.28	55	15	30	32	102	BDd	6%	95	97	9%	12%	101	1%	100%	2.8	79	$8
23	MIN *	388	44	14	53	2	275	9	4	273	336	454	108	65	117	8	72	0.33	40	31	29	34	101	CCb	7%	111	114	18%	15%	88	3%	65%	15.2	79	$11
1st Half		225	21	6	22	1	264	3	3	272	348	404	103	61	117	11	71	0.44	44	34	23	34	102	CCa	6%	93	104	16%	12%	94	3%	52%	2.4	36	$4
2nd Half		163	23	8	31	1	289	6	1	277	321	519	114	74	117	4	74	0.18	35	28	37	34	99	CBc	9%	133	125	20%	17%	93	3%	100%	6.9	146	$10
24	**Proj**	**385**	**47**	**14**	**59**	**2**	**271**	**13**	**4**	**263**	**331**	**444**	**106**	**82**	**112**	**7**	**75**	**0.29**	**45**	**24**	**31**	**33**	**102**		**8%**	**104**	**113**	**17%**	**16%**	**94**	**4%**	**66%**	**9.7**	**93**	**$16**

BRANDON KRUSE

Kirk,Alejandro

Age: 25	Pos: CA		Health	B	LIMA Plan	D+
Bats: R	Ht: 5' 8"	Wt: 245	PT/Exp	A	Rand Var	+4
			Consist	B	MM	1133

Breakout 1st half of 2022 (.314 BA, 10 HR, 11% Brl%, 14% HR/F) disappearing into rearview. In over 700 PA since, he's hit .253 with 12 HR, 5% Brl%, 8% HR/F. Exit velocity continues to decline, 50% GB remains stuck, and while elite ct% ensures BA floor, the ceiling is getting lower. Young enough to take a flyer, hope for resurgence.

Yr	Tm	PA	R	HR	RBI	SB	BA	xHR	xSB	xBA	OBP	SLG	OPS+	vL+	vR+	bb%	ct%	Eye	G	L	F	h%	HctX	QBaB	Brl%	PX	xPX	HR/F	xHR/F	Spd	SBA%	SB%	RAR	BPX	R$
19																																			
20	TOR	25	4	1	3	0	375	1	0	291	400	583	131	37	168	4	83	0.25	55	20	25	42	135	ADb	5%	115	61	20%	20%	67	0%	0%	3.2	220	$
21	TOR *	242	25	10	36	0	262	8	0	268	335	452	108	134	91	10	85	0.74	41	20	39	27	113	ABc	11%	98	97	14%	14%	33	0%	0%	8.0	192	$
22	TOR	541	59	14	63	0	285	15	0	259	372	415	111	105	113	12	88	1.09	50	19	31	30	144	BDc	7%	73	102	11%	12%	61	0%	0%	25.4	183	$1
23	TOR	422	34	8	43	0	250	8	0	255	334	358	94	99	92	10	88	0.93	50	20	30	27	110	CDd	5%	59	78	8%	8%	36	0%	0%	7.0	111	$
1st Half		211	14	3	21	0	253	3	0	249	336	328	91	78	95	10	88	0.87	51	22	27	28	83	CFf	5%	40	58	7%	7%	46	0%	0%	0.3	64	-$
2nd Half		211	20	5	22	0	247	5	0	261	332	387	97	112	89	11	88	1.00	49	18	33	26	137	CCc	5%	77	97	9%	9%	39	0%	0%	3.9	175	$
24	**Proj**	**385**	**37**	**10**	**45**	**0**	**264**	**10**	**0**	**258**	**349**	**393**	**102**	**108**	**99**	**11**	**87**	**0.96**	**49**	**19**	**32**	**28**	**125**		**7%**	**69**	**91**	**10%**	**10%**	**45**	**0%**	**100%**	**13.1**	**158**	**$**

Kjerstad,Heston

Age: 25	Pos: DH		Health	A	LIMA Plan	D+
Bats: L	Ht: 6' 3"	Wt: 205	PT/Exp	C	Rand Var	0
			Consist	F	MM	3233

2-3-.233 in 33 PA at BAL. Split 2023 between AA and AAA before callup. Loads of loud contact with great angles between the gaps. Unorthodox swing creates difficulties lofting the ball to the pull side and limits present HR totals. Lacks plate discipline—near 40% MiLB chase rate carried over to MLB. Still, wouldn't bet that BA craters. (CB)

Yr	Tm	PA	R	HR	RBI	SB	BA	xHR	xSB	xBA	OBP	SLG	OPS+	vL+	vR+	bb%	ct%	Eye	G	L	F	h%	HctX	QBaB	Brl%	PX	xPX	HR/F	xHR/F	Spd	SBA%	SB%	RAR	BPX	R$
19																																			
20																																			
21																																			
22																																			
23	BAL *	542	67	16	43	4	250	2	12	244	296	410	96	0	106	6	76	0.27	30	25	45	30	123	AAa	20%	94	154	22%	22%	140	8%	44%	2.0	121	$1
1st Half		283	35	10	24	3	251		6	264	294	431	99	0	0	6	78	0.28	44	20	36	29	0		0%	102	-21	0%		124	11%	46%	-0.5	161	$1
2nd Half		259	32	6	19	1	249	2	5	229	298	386	92	0	105	7	73	0.26	30	25	45	32	119	AAa	20%	84	154	22%	22%	141	3%	39%	-2.3	57	$
24	**Proj**	**280**	**34**	**12**	**25**	**2**	**249**	**15**	**5**	**257**	**299**	**452**	**103**	**69**	**104**	**7**	**75**	**0.28**	**36**	**23**	**41**	**29**	**107**		**10%**	**118**	**139**	**15%**	**18%**	**132**	**6%**	**50%**	**3.0**	**99**	**$**

Knizner,Andrew

Age: 29	Pos: CA		Health	A	LIMA Plan	D
Bats: R	Ht: 6' 1"	Wt: 225	PT/Exp	C	Rand Var	-2
			Consist	C	MM	2211

Waited out Yadi's retirement only to be blocked anew, but that didn't stop him from quietly turning in best power skills of career, with new highs in FB%, Brl%, xPX, and xHR/F. Traded some plate discipline to get there, but xBA says it was worth it. Could be a name to tuck away in deep leagues should opportunity knock and lead to more double-digit HR.

Yr	Tm	PA	R	HR	RBI	SB	BA	xHR	xSB	xBA	OBP	SLG	OPS+	vL+	vR+	bb%	ct%	Eye	G	L	F	h%	HctX	QBaB	Brl%	PX	xPX	HR/F	xHR/F	Spd	SBA%	SB%	RAR	BPX	R$
19	STL *	322	39	11	33	4	234	1	2	219	286	378	92	56	100	7	81	0.40	62	3	36	25	101	CDf	3%	71	85	14%	7%	82	6%	100%	-6.0	85	$
20	STL	17	1	0	4	0	250	0	0	228	235	313	73	78	70	0	69	0.00	67	25	8	36	116	AFc	0%	56	57	0%	0%	80	0%	0%	-0.6	-212	-$
21	STL	185	18	1	9	0	174	2	0	210	281	236	71	37	84	11	76	0.51	52	18	30	22	84	CDf	4%	45	58	3%	5%	74	0%	0%	-10.0	-54	-$
22	STL	293	28	4	25	0	215	4	0	207	301	300	85	71	89	9	76	0.42	45	17	38	27	89	DBf	4%	59	64	5%	5%	64	1%	0%	-6.9	-28	-$
23	STL	241	30	10	31	2	241	9	2	236	288	424	97	91	100	5	72	0.19	40	17	43	29	93	CBf	8%	112	97	14%	13%	94	4%	100%	4.3	68	$
1st Half		113	16	5	15	1	222	6	1	238	250	417	91	96	89	4	69	0.12	37	19	44	27	82	CBd	11%	125	116	16%	19%	97	6%	100%	-0.4	57	-$
2nd Half		128	14	5	16	1	259	4	1	232	320	431	101	86	110	6	75	0.28	43	15	42	30	104	BCf	5%	101	81	14%	11%	91	3%	100%	3.4	82	$
24	**Proj**	**210**	**24**	**7**	**22**	**1**	**236**	**6**	**1**	**226**	**302**	**384**	**94**	**81**	**99**	**7**	**75**	**0.31**	**43**	**16**	**41**	**28**	**93**		**6%**	**90**	**81**	**11%**	**10%**	**76**	**3%**	**86%**	**2.2**	**29**	**$**

Kwan,Steven

Age: 26	Pos: LF		Health	A	LIMA Plan	B+
Bats: L	Ht: 5' 9"	Wt: 170	PT/Exp	A	Rand Var	+2
			Consist	A	MM	1555

BA slid 30 points while xBA gained 20, taking him from overvalued to under. So which is it? 2023 xBA required elite ct%, LD% along with PX that xPX says he can't sustain. But really, skills were nearly identical in both years, which shows how easily his BA can fluctuate. Safe bet is to just call him a .280 hitter and rake in the R and SB.

Yr	Tm	PA	R	HR	RBI	SB	BA	xHR	xSB	xBA	OBP	SLG	OPS+	vL+	vR+	bb%	ct%	Eye	G	L	F	h%	HctX	QBaB	Brl%	PX	xPX	HR/F	xHR/F	Spd	SBA%	SB%	RAR	BPX	R$
19																																			
20																																			
21	a/a	323	49	9	33	4	281		5		341	435	107			8	88	0.74				30				77				117	7%	66%		254	$1
22	CLE	638	89	6	52	19	298	4	24	265	373	400	109	90	115	10	89	1.03	42	23	35	33	74	DCd	1%	59	40	3%	2%	154	12%	79%	20.6	248	$2
23	CLE	718	93	5	54	21	268	4	24	285	340	370	97	90	100	10	88	0.93	45	25	30	30	66	DCb	1%	59	29	3%	2%	131	12%	88%	13.3	218	$1
1st Half		370	55	2	25	13	261	1	13	273	339	350	94	105	90	10	86	0.84	44	25	31	30	53	DCc	1%	56	10	2%	1%	129	15%	87%	1.8	182	$
2nd Half		348	38	3	29	8	276	3	10	298	342	391	99	77	111	9	90	1.07	46	26	28	30	80	DDb	1%	62	49	4%	4%	130	10%	89%	7.1	254	$
24	**Proj**	**630**	**86**	**5**	**53**	**19**	**281**	**4**	**20**	**276**	**350**	**383**	**101**	**87**	**106**	**9**	**89**	**0.92**	**44**	**24**	**32**	**31**	**71**		**1%**	**57**	**36**	**3%**	**3%**	**139**	**12%**	**84%**	**15.9**	**238**	**$2**

Langeliers,Shea

Age: 26	Pos: CA		Health	A	LIMA Plan	B
Bats: R	Ht: 6' 0"	Wt: 205	PT/Exp	A	Rand Var	+2
			Consist	B	MM	4215

2nd half growth saw him tap into power skills while finding his stroke vL, and only bad luck on h% kept it from being more valuable. That .251 xBA in 2nd half suggests he can make this skill set work over the long-term as long as PX remains elite. Our scouting report classified his ceiling as "bomb power." Next step could be... UP: 30 HR

Yr	Tm	PA	R	HR	RBI	SB	BA	xHR	xSB	xBA	OBP	SLG	OPS+	vL+	vR+	bb%	ct%	Eye	G	L	F	h%	HctX	QBaB	Brl%	PX	xPX	HR/F	xHR/F	Spd	SBA%	SB%	RAR	BPX	R$
19																																			
20																																			
21	a/a	372	49	18	44	1	227		1		293	424	99			9	66	0.28				29				126				86	1%	100%		42	$
22	OAK *	529	47	15	52	3	206	5	3	223	254	355	86	112	94	6	67	0.20	38	22	40	27	91	CBf	11%	109	95	17%	14%	90	4%	68%	-10.2	-3	$
23	OAK	490	52	22	63	3	205	24	7	224	268	413	93	79	99	7	68	0.24	36	15	49	25	94	BAf	13%	129	119	15%	16%	120	6%	60%	1.4	96	$
1st Half		275	27	9	32	1	203	10	3	203	266	359	86	58	95	7	68	0.23	35	15	50	26	85	CAf	11%	100	95	10%	12%	114	4%	50%	-5.3	7	$
2nd Half		215	25	13	31	2	208	14	3	251	270	482	102	96	104	8	68	0.25	38	15	47	23	105	AAf	17%	165	149	20%	22%	119	9%	67%	3.2	204	$
24	**Proj**	**490**	**52**	**23**	**59**	**3**	**220**	**23**	**5**	**230**	**278**	**431**	**97**	**94**	**98**	**7**	**68**	**0.24**	**36**	**18**	**46**	**27**	**94**		**13%**	**134**	**114**	**16%**	**16%**	**87**	**5%**	**68%**	**7.2**	**68**	**$**

Larnach,Trevor

Age: 27	Pos: LF RF		Health	D	LIMA Plan	D
Bats: L	Ht: 6' 4"	Wt: 223	PT/Exp	B	Rand Var	-1
			Consist	A	MM	4103

8-40-.213 in 212 PA at MIN. While power upside continues to look scary good (note that 2nd half xPX is only based on 35 MLB PA), true horror is lousy ct% rates, which keep frightening away PA. High FB% haunts BA, and vL+ suggests he's unlikely to flee platoon boogeyman. Hope for a treat, but he'll probably put another apple in your bag instead.

Yr	Tm	PA	R	HR	RBI	SB	BA	xHR	xSB	xBA	OBP	SLG	OPS+	vL+	vR+	bb%	ct%	Eye	G	L	F	h%	HctX	QBaB	Brl%	PX	xPX	HR/F	xHR/F	Spd	SBA%	SB%	RAR	BPX	R$
19	aa	177	24	7	21	0	286		1		369	439	112			12	67	0.39				39				88				101	0%	0%		-26	
20																																			
21	MIN *	357	39	9	33	1	212	10	1	190	293	343	87	71	102	10	59	0.28	46	18	35	32	81	BCb	9%	101	84	13%	18%	83	1%	100%	-10.1	-135	
22	MIN *	227	23	6	21	0	215	9	0	212	288	360	92	100	101	9	64	0.29	42	19	39	31	104	BCb	11%	121	147	12%	22%	82	0%	0%	-4.4	-3	
23	MIN *	508	62	18	71	2	212	10	7	198	307	387	95	56	105	12	59	0.33	33	19	48	32	110	BBb	13%	128	185	15%	19%	105	4%	40%	-0.6	-18	
1st Half		257	35	9	41	1	222	9	4	202	322	405	100	65	100	13	57	0.34	33	22	45	34	98	CBb	14%	136	143	14%	21%	112	3%	50%	1.3	-4	
2nd Half		251	28	8	29	1	202	2	3	176	292	369	89	0	129	11	60	0.32	30	10	60	29	159	AAa	10%	121	378	17%	17%	98	6%	35%	-5.1	-32	
24	**Proj**	**280**	**33**	**10**	**33**	**1**	**219**	**14**	**2**	**201**	**305**	**391**	**95**	**70**	**102**	**11**	**61**	**0.31**	**37**	**17**	**46**	**32**	**116**		**11%**	**125**	**130**	**14%**	**19%**	**93**	**2%**	**43%**	**-0.1**	**-34**	

Laureano,Ramón

Age: 29	Pos: RF CF		Health	D	LIMA Plan	C
Bats: R	Ht: 5' 11"	Wt: 203	PT/Exp	A	Rand Var	0
			Consist	C	MM	3413

Another year, another step further away from 2019 peak. Although new rules helped him restore SB%, health and subpar OPS+ keep him from full-time role, and xSB says he's maxed out at a dozen SB at this PA level. 2nd half line came mostly with CLE, and career-best Eye might be something, but he's just an end game speculation at best.

Yr	Tm	PA	R	HR	RBI	SB	BA	xHR	xSB	xBA	OBP	SLG	OPS+	vL+	vR+	bb%	ct%	Eye	G	L	F	h%	HctX	QBaB	Brl%	PX	xPX	HR/F	xHR/F	Spd	SBA%	SB%	RAR	BPX	R$
19	OAK	481	79	24	67	13	288	22	8	263	340	521	119	117	119	6	72	0.22	36	25	39	35	99	BBc	10%	134	108	19%	18%	101	14%	87%	14.5	137	$
20	OAK	222	27	6	25	2	213	8	2	225	338	366	93	85	96	11	68	0.41	43	22	35	28	91	CCf	9%	96	100	13%	18%	85	5%	67%	-7.5	0	$
21	OAK	378	43	14	39	12	246	18	9	253	317	443	104	117	98	7	71	0.28	43	22	35	31	94	CCc	11%	124	108	16%	21%	96	20%	71%	0.3	112	$
22	OAK *	422	54	13	35	12	199	17	10	225	252	351	85	97	93	6	69	0.23	43	18	39	25	101	CBd	12%	110	101	14%	18%	98	22%	67%	-17.4	31	
23	2 AL	404	46	9	35	12	224	12	12	229	304	371	92	107	84	8	68	0.29	45	19	36	30	88	CCf	10%	98	84	10%	13%	136	14%	92%	-2.1	39	
1st Half		219	21	5	17	8	213	7	7	222	274	361	87	104	80	6	66	0.19	43	20	37	29	83	CCd	10%	99	90	10%	14%	129	19%	100%	-5.8	-11	
2nd Half		185	25	4	18	4	239	5	5	236	341	384	98	109	89	11	71	0.43	46	18	35	31	94	CCf	10%	96	78	10%	13%	129	10%	80%	0.2	86	
24	**Proj**	**385**	**44**	**10**	**32**	**11**	**226**	**14**	**10**	**232**	**306**	**377**	**94**	**104**	**89**	**8**	**70**	**0.29**	**45**	**20**	**36**	**30**	**94**		**10%**	**101**	**93**	**12%**	**16%**	**112**	**15%**	**78%**	**-3.8**	**55**	**$**

BRANDON KRUSE

Lawlar,Jordan

Age: 21	Pos: SS	Health	A	LIMA Plan	C+
Bats: R	Ht: 6'2" Wt: 190	PT/Exp	C	Rand Var	-1
		Consist	D	MM	1515

0-0-.129 in 34 PA at ARI. Disciplined hitter, struggled in bigs facing MLB sliders for first time. However, enjoyed first healthy season as pro, showing no ill effects from past shoulder injuries. Premium athlete with abundant tool shed. Hitability off the charts with avg power playing to all fields. Double-plus runner should contribute SB right away. (CB)

Yr	Tm	PA	R	HR	RBI	SB	BA	xHR	xSB	xBA	OBP	SLG	OPS+	vL+	vR+	bb%	ct%	Eye	G	L	F	h%	HctX	QBaB	Brl%	PX	xPX	HR/F	xHR/F	Spd	SBA%	SB%	RAR	BPX	R$
19																																			
20																																			
21																																			
22	aa	91	11	2	7	1	171		1		226	252	68			7	65	0.20				23				51				114	11%	53%		-172	-$3
23	ARI *	487	64	11	44	24	222	0	22	208	284	353	87	47	44	8	73	0.31	53	5	42	28	15	FCf	0%	83	19	0%	0%	130	30%	79%	-7.3	50	$11
1st Half		262	30	6	22	16	200		12	230	262	335	82	0	0	8	70	0.28	44	20	36	26	0		0%	89	-21	0%		135	38%	88%	-9.5	36	$7
2nd Half		226	35	6	23	9	254	0	9	212	318	386	95	47	44	9	76	0.38	53	5	42	31	15	FCf	0%	80	19	0%	0%	121	23%	67%	-1.0	79	$12
24	Proj	455	63	9	43	21	231	9	24	226	315	353	92	99	87	9	74	0.36	48	16	36	29	86		4%	78	17	8%	8%	123	22%	80%	-3.0	62	$13

Lee,Jung-hoo

Age: 25	Pos: LF	Health	A	LIMA Plan	B+
Bats: L	Ht: 0'0" Wt: 0	PT/Exp	A	Rand Var	0
		Consist	C	MM	2455

Pristine bat-to-ball skills in KBO (more BB than K in each of last five seasons) should help him bear immediate fruit in majors, putting eilte BA in play right away. Hit-over-power profile confirmed by just one >15 HR season overseas. Speed more modest than moderate, but good enough to put double-digit bags in play. UP: .300+ BA, 20 SB

Yr	Tm	PA	R	HR	RBI	SB	BA	xHR	xSB	xBA	OBP	SLG	OPS+	vL+	vR+	bb%	ct%	Eye	G	L	F	h%	HctX	QBaB	Brl%	PX	xPX	HR/F	xHR/F	Spd	SBA%	SB%	RAR	BPX	R$
19	for	610	89	4	66	12	313		19		354	440	110			6	93	0.96				33	0			57				153	12%	60%	7.2	293	$22
20	for	591	83	9	98	11	310		9		365	477	112			8	92	1.07				33	0			88				106	9%	83%	16.7	352	$71
21	for	514	76	4	82	9	335		9		400	492	123			10	92	1.43				36	0			86				112	8%	73%	37.4	362	$27
22	for	606	83	14	110	5	325		10		384	521	128			9	95	1.76				33	0			100				134	3%	100%	52.8	407	$34
23	for	368	49	4	44	5	297		8		373	418	108			11	93	1.81				31	0			67				107	7%	62%	15.7	296	$11
1st Half																																			
2nd Half																																			
24	Proj	525	68	8	60	10	283	8	8	287	343	450	109	108	109	8	88	0.78	44	20	36	31	101		7%	91		5%	5%	126	10%	82%	22.7	362	$21

Lee,Korey

Age: 25	Pos: CA	Health	A	LIMA Plan	D
Bats: R	Ht: 6'2" Wt: 210	PT/Exp	B	Rand Var	-2
		Consist	A	MM	1103

1-3-.077 in 70 PA at CHW. Among bats with 70+ PA, his OPS was the lowest in the majors. Crazy 9% hit rate was the driver, as was near-flunking QBaB. Those warts support perception of him as a defense-first backstop. No reason to roster him even as a caddy right now, but tuck away former 8C prospect pedigree and follow from a distance.

Yr	Tm	PA	R	HR	RBI	SB	BA	xHR	xSB	xBA	OBP	SLG	OPS+	vL+	vR+	bb%	ct%	Eye	G	L	F	h%	HctX	QBaB	Brl%	PX	xPX	HR/F	xHR/F	Spd	SBA%	SB%	RAR	BPX	R$
19																																			
20																																			
21	a/a	234	20	6	23	2	209		2		256	347	83			6	77	0.27				24				82				92	7%	66%		58	$0
22	HOU *	453	47	16	51	7	183	0	6	190	225	341	80	64	59	5	62	0.15	56	0	44	25	0	FCf		120	-14	0%	0%	118	12%	87%	-15.2	-17	$3
23	CHW *	418	30	5	27	9	198	1	8	189	234	277	70	6	55	4	67	0.14	51	13	36	28	30	DDf	4%	60	18	6%	6%	78	18%	64%	-16.6	-179	-$1
1st Half		291	24	4	21	8	226		8	214	257	321	79	0	0	4	70	0.14	44	20	36	31	0		0%	70	-21	0%		97	23%	63%	-8.4	-96	$3
2nd Half		127	5	1	6	1	134	1	1	145	182	174	48	6	54	6	60	0.15	51	13	36	21	27	DDf	4%	31	18	6%	6%	84	5%	100%	-10.7	-343	-$11
24	Proj	385	30	5	32	4	180	2	5	182	224	259	66	5	97	5	65	0.16	51	13	36	26	24		4%	60	16	6%	3%	68	8%	66%	-18.4	-119	$0

LeMahieu,DJ

Age: 35	Pos: 3B 1B	Health	B	LIMA Plan	B
Bats: R	Ht: 6'4" Wt: 220	PT/Exp	A	Rand Var	+1
		Consist	A	MM	1245

Name recognition kept ADP under 250 again, but that won't happen in 2024. Long gone is the value he used to provide in batting average; see concurrent ugly trends in both BA and xBA. Homers in teens should stick, but if he's your starting 1B or 3B, you'll need to cover for his marginal power elsewhere. This is a profile that isn't aging gracefully.

Yr	Tm	PA	R	HR	RBI	SB	BA	xHR	xSB	xBA	OBP	SLG	OPS+	vL+	vR+	bb%	ct%	Eye	G	L	F	h%	HctX	QBaB	Brl%	PX	xPX	HR/F	xHR/F	Spd	SBA%	SB%	RAR	BPX	R$
19	NYY	655	109	26	102	5	327	25	7	302	375	518	124	148	114	7	85	0.51	50	24	26	35	119	ADb	8%	92	90	19%	19%	109	4%	71%	38.5	230	$31
20	NYY	216	41	10	27	3	364	5	4	327	421	590	134	131	135	8	89	0.86	57	22	21	37	128	AFb	3%	104	76	27%	14%	135	4%	100%	22.6	396	$33
21	NYY	679	84	10	57	4	268	10	5	262	349	362	98	92	100	11	84	0.78	52	22	26	30	94	BFc	4%	53	62	8%	8%	101	3%	67%	-3.3	127	$15
22	NYY	541	74	12	46	4	261	10	6	259	357	377	104	112	101	12	85	0.94	53	18	28	29	85	CFd	5%	68	68	11%	9%	97	4%	57%	6.1	169	$14
23	NYY	562	55	15	44	2	243	13	7	252	327	390	98	103	96	11	75	0.48	55	19	26	30	103	BFd	6%	88	82	15%	13%	106	3%	50%	6.4	89	$8
1st Half		284	28	7	27	0	225	7	3	245	289	368	90	85	91	8	73	0.32	54	18	27	28	95	BFd	6%	89	79	13%	13%	103	3%	0%	-8.2	46	$3
2nd Half		278	27	8	17	2	264	6	4	259	367	414	106	123	101	14	77	0.68	56	20	25	31	111	CFc	6%	87	86	18%	13%	106	2%	100%	6.3	132	$8
24	Proj	490	59	12	42	3	253	11	6	261	339	386	99	104	98	11	80	0.64	54	20	26	29	100		5%	76	76	13%	12%	102	3%	64%	7.7	141	$13

Lewis,Kyle

Age: 28	Pos: DH	Health	F	LIMA Plan	D
Bats: R	Ht: 6'4" Wt: 222	PT/Exp	D	Rand Var	-4
		Consist	D	MM	2201

1-2-.157 in 54 PA at ARI. Former top prospect days are firmly in the rearview now. Still, a few reasons why he could resurface... 1) Elite 1.098 OPS and really good plate discipline in Triple-A; 2) Hasn't gotten an extended look in majors last two seasons; 3) Still in prime years. If he can find a team in need of DH ... there are worse flyers out there.

Yr	Tm	PA	R	HR	RBI	SB	BA	xHR	xSB	xBA	OBP	SLG	OPS+	vL+	vR+	bb%	ct%	Eye	G	L	F	h%	HctX	QBaB	Brl%	PX	xPX	HR/F	xHR/F	Spd	SBA%	SB%	RAR	BPX	R$
19	SEA *	587	70	17	74	3	248	6	5	202	323	404	101	72	140	10	61	0.28	51	14	35	37	69	BCa	23%	108	144	40%	40%	107	4%	57%	-13.6	-56	$11
20	SEA	242	37	11	28	5	262	10	5	215	364	437	106	105	106	14	66	0.48	43	20	36	35	87	CCd	11%	101	97	22%	20%	119	8%	83%	4.4	36	$24
21	SEA	147	15	5	11	2	246	6	2	224	333	392	100	88	103	11	72	0.43	33	24	43	31	101	BBd	14%	87	118	13%	15%	108	5%	100%	-2.3	46	$1
22	SEA *	224	23	10	24	0	164	3	0	194	238	322	79	56	82	9	62	0.25	46	16	38	20	73	BBf	11%	110	93	21%	21%	87	0%	0%	-14.9	-62	-$3
23	ARI *	324	33	9	47	0	248	1	1	200	306	388	95	81	40	8	68	0.26	33	17	50	34	110	CAd	7%	96	104	7%	7%	70	0%	0%	0.3	-50	$5
1st Half		140	13	4	17	0	207	0	1	177	268	344	84	70	85	8	63	0.23	27	13	60	29	103	CAf	11%	102	162	11%	0%	82	0%	0%	-6.6	-82	-$4
2nd Half		184	20	5	29	0	281	0	1	223	336	422	102	104	23	8	71	0.28	40	20	40	37	115	BAa	5%	92	46	0%	0%	79	0%	0%	2.0	-7	$7
24	Proj	210	22	7	26	1	230	6	1	203	303	374	93	100	88	9	66	0.30	39	18	43	31	96		10%	96	99	13%	11%	87	2%	90%	-2.2	-28	$5

Lewis,Royce

Age: 25	Pos: 3B	Health	F	LIMA Plan	B
Bats: R	Ht: 6'2" Wt: 200	PT/Exp	F	Rand Var	-3
		Consist	F	MM	4445

15-52-.309 with 6 SB in 239 PA at MIN. Former 1st overall pick showed flashes of elite upside after recovery from another knee injury. However, that was sandwiched between oblique and hamstring issues. BA and power likely to be his impact areas given surgeries. A huge "IF", but if he stays off IL... UP: .300 BA, 30 HR

Yr	Tm	PA	R	HR	RBI	SB	BA	xHR	xSB	xBA	OBP	SLG	OPS+	vL+	vR+	bb%	ct%	Eye	G	L	F	h%	HctX	QBaB	Brl%	PX	xPX	HR/F	xHR/F	Spd	SBA%	SB%	RAR	BPX	R$
19	aa	145	17	2	13	6	233		4		289	360	90			7	75	0.32				30				80				108	27%	74%		52	$1
20																																			
21																																			
22	MIN *	184	24	5	14	8	265	2	6	245	317	445	108	150	115	7	75	0.31	31	20	49	33	113	BAf	6%	128	142	12%	12%	107	26%	77%	4.0	179	$6
23	MIN *	294	46	19	62	9	306	12	8	259	364	552	125	106	131	8	72	0.33	35	21	44	36	91	BBf	12%	139	101	21%	17%	99	14%	81%	27.3	171	$16
1st Half		140	18	7	23	4	311	3	4	240	337	490	113	116	112	4	67	0.12	43	24	33	42	74	CCf	9%	109	76	18%	14%	105	14%	76%	6.8	-7	$7
2nd Half		154	28	12	39	6	300	9	5	282	388	615	135	96	144	13	77	0.63	29	19	52	31	106	AAd	14%	165	119	22%	18%	100	16%	85%	16.9	346	$18
24	Proj	455	66	28	69	13	279	20	14	272	344	545	122	103	128	8	74	0.35	35	21	44	31	93		12%	154	102	21%	15%	106	15%	80%	32.3	173	$27

Lindor,Francisco

Age: 30	Pos: SS	Health	A	LIMA Plan	D+
Bats: B	Ht: 5'11" Wt: 190	PT/Exp	A	Rand Var	0
		Consist	B	MM	3435

One of four players with both 30+ HR and SB, and did it on cusp of age 30 with a bone spur in his elbow. Can he repeat? PRO: Elite QBaB, sets up career-best exit velocity and barrel rate; swing plane is in HR sweetspot now. CON: Mediocre Spd and good-not-great Statcast sprint speed; prior SB% suggests regression. Even still, a $30 player.

Yr	Tm	PA	R	HR	RBI	SB	BA	xHR	xSB	xBA	OBP	SLG	OPS+	vL+	vR+	bb%	ct%	Eye	G	L	F	h%	HctX	QBaB	Brl%	PX	xPX	HR/F	xHR/F	Spd	SBA%	SB%	RAR	BPX	R$
19	CLE	654	101	32	74	22	284	25	15	292	335	518	118	108	122	7	84	0.47	44	20	37	29	122	ACd	8%	115	104	17%	14%	106	19%	81%	24.7	274	$30
20	CLE	266	30	8	27	6	258	8	5	270	335	415	100	97	100	9	83	0.59	38	26	36	28	102	BCc	6%	85	82	11%	11%	97	12%	75%	1.0	192	$21
21	NYM	524	73	20	63	10	230	19	9	245	322	412	101	97	102	11	79	0.60	39	19	42	25	104	BCf	8%	96	114	13%	13%	108	11%	71%	-3.2	185	$14
22	NYM	706	98	26	107	16	270	27	18	254	339	449	112	110	112	8	79	0.44	43	18	39	31	107	CCf	8%	105	110	13%	14%	128	12%	73%	14.8	197	$33
23	NYM	687	108	31	98	31	254	28	22	259	336	470	110	123	103	10	77	0.48	34	20	46	28	111	AAd	10%	122	121	14%	13%	94	21%	89%	27.9	200	$30
1st Half		359	49	17	55	9	223	17	6	257	306	446	103	119	96	10	75	0.44	32	20	48	24	118	AAc	12%	131	150	15%	15%	73	14%	90%	2.4	179	$24
2nd Half		328	59	14	43	22	288	10	17	263	369	497	117	127	111	10	79	0.53	36	20	43	32	104	BAd	9%	113	90	14%	10%	120	27%	88%	19.9	232	$38
24	Proj	665	103	28	93	25	260	25	20	257	338	457	109	114	107	10	79	0.50	38	20	42	29	108		9%	110	111	14%	13%	111	18%	83%	26.7	206	$34

STEPHEN NICKRAND

Loftin,Nick

Age: 25	Pos: 1B	Health A	LIMA Plan D+
Bats: R	Ht: 6' 1" Wt: 180	PT/Exp B	Rand Var +1
		Consist B	MM 1333

0-10-.323 in 68 PA at KC. Model of consistency in MiLB, traits carried over to MLB. Great bat-to-ball skills, limiting whiffs despite high chase rate. Very BA-dependent profile, especially difficult to maintain with pull heavy approach. Below average power, doesn't show up against average or better velocity. Fits nearly anywhere on the diamond. (CB)

Yr	Tm	PA	R	HR	RBI	SB	BA	xHR	xSB	xBA	OBP	SLG	OPS+	vL+	vR+	bb%	ct%	Eye	G	L	F	h%	HctX	QBaB	Brl%	PX	xPX	HR/F	xHR/F	Spd	SBA%	SB%	RAR	BPX	R$
19																																			
20																																			
21																																			
22	a/a	547	62	9	39	17	204		13		249	301	78			6	79	0.29				24				65				98	23%	71%		41	$8
23	KC *	405	37	8	47	6	235	1	10	258	285	352	87	145	91	6	83	0.41	49	20	31	26	86	DCc	8%	66	87	0%	6%	120	12%	56%	-5.4	129	$6
1st Half		186	15	5	25	2	228		3	268	263	369	87	0	0	5	86	0.35	44	20	36	24	0		0%	76	-21	0%		95	9%	63%	-5.6	164	$0
2nd Half		219	22	3	22	4	242	1	8	244	303	336	86	144	90	8	80	0.45	49	20	31	29	83	DCc	8%	56	87	0%	6%	138	15%	53%	-5.5	89	$4
24	**Proj**	**280**	**28**	**5**	**27**	**6**	**239**	**4**	**8**	**248**	**292**	**341**	**87**	**122**	**69**	**6**	**81**	**0.36**	**49**	**20**	**31**	**28**	**75**		**7%**	**61**	**78**	**7%**	**6%**	**124**	**14%**	**62%**	**-6.6**	**89**	**$4**

Longoria,Evan

Age: 38	Pos: 3B DH	Health F	LIMA Plan D
Bats: R	Ht: 6' 1" Wt: 213	PT/Exp C	Rand Var 0
		Consist B	MM 3001

Yes, he again missed a few games to injury (strained back), but this PT hit comes mainly from doing a lot of sitting on the bench. And while 1st-half power metrics were terrific, it all went deep into the tank from July on. He's got that first half to cling to, but at 38, it's highly possible we see... DN: Hangs 'em up on a fine career

Yr	Tm	PA	R	HR	RBI	SB	BA	xHR	xSB	xBA	OBP	SLG	OPS+	vL+	vR+	bb%	ct%	Eye	G	L	F	h%	HctX	QBaB	Brl%	PX	xPX	HR/F	xHR/F	Spd	SBA%	SB%	RAR	BPX	R$
19	SF	508	59	20	69	3	254	24	5	250	325	437	105	118	99	8	75	0.38	41	22	37	30	115	BCa	8%	96	123	16%	19%	119	3%	75%	-8.9	119	$1
20	SF	209	26	7	28	0	254	13	1	258	297	425	96	112	89	5	80	0.28	50	18	32	29	125	ACb	11%	92	115	14%	26%	97	2%	0%	-6.4	136	$1
21	SF	291	45	13	46	1	261	14	1	255	351	482	114	148	102	12	73	0.51	41	19	40	31	129	ABb	13%	136	150	17%	19%	79	3%	50%	10.3	196	$
22	SF *	323	33	14	42	0	244	14	1	238	309	439	106	114	104	9	68	0.29	37	22	41	31	95	AAd	12%	138	132	18%	18%	91	0%	0%	1.8	93	$
23	ARI	237	25	11	28	0	223	12	1	225	295	422	98	99	96	10	65	0.32	38	19	43	28	102	ABc	11%	131	130	18%	20%	64	0%	0%	1.5	25	$
1st Half		147	23	11	22	0	250	11	0	266	313	553	119	128	109	9	66	0.29	34	20	46	29	139	AAb	15%	193	190	27%	27%	66	0%	0%	6.9	207	$
2nd Half		90	2	0	6	0	177	1	0	133	267	203	63	54	73	11	65	0.36	46	17	37	27	40	BCd	4%	25	27	0%	5%	75	0%	0%	-6.3	-268	-$1
24	**Proj**	**175**	**18**	**6**	**21**	**0**	**229**	**7**	**1**	**221**	**303**	**390**	**95**	**97**	**93**	**10**	**68**	**0.34**	**40**	**20**	**40**	**30**	**95**		**10%**	**107**	**114**	**14%**	**17%**	**80**	**1%**	**49%**	**0.5**	**26**	**$**

Lopez,Nicky

Age: 29	Pos: 2B 3B	Health A	LIMA Plan D
Bats: L	Ht: 5' 11" Wt: 180	PT/Exp A	Rand Var +3
		Consist D	MM 0441

While 2021 appears to be an outlier, xBA says he's been pretty much the same hitter for five years. But with his playing time now drying up, the category that drove most of his value—steals—is being gutted. A return to 500 PA seems highly unlikely, so an empty .260-BA upside is the only reason to roster him.

Yr	Tm	PA	R	HR	RBI	SB	BA	xHR	xSB	xBA	OBP	SLG	OPS+	vL+	vR+	bb%	ct%	Eye	G	L	F	h%	HctX	QBaB	Brl%	PX	xPX	HR/F	xHR/F	Spd	SBA%	SB%	RAR	BPX	R$
19	KC *	533	65	4	40	8	257	2	9	277	304	349	90	90	80	6	89	0.59	62	16	22	28	78	DFb	1%	50	5	3%	3%	121	10%	64%	-13.9	167	$
20	KC	192	15	1	13	0	201	1	3	242	286	266	73	58	79	9	76	0.44	55	26	19	26	73	FFf	2%	47	51	4%	4%	85	11%	0%	-16.2	-48	-$
21	KC	565	78	2	43	22	300	3	21	269	365	378	102	96	104	9	85	0.66	55	21	23	35	87	DFf	1%	46	48	2%	3%	151	13%	96%	11.3	162	$2
22	KC	480	51	0	20	13	227	3	15	252	281	273	78	69	82	6	86	0.46	54	21	25	27	82	FFf	2%	30	46	0%	3%	149	14%	81%	-21.2	86	$
23	2 TM	262	32	1	25	6	231	1	8	269	326	307	86	77	88	10	82	0.65	57	23	20	28	81	DFc	1%	44	40	3%	3%	126	11%	75%	-4.2	86	$
1st Half		144	14	0	11	3	222	0	6	257	355	308	91	85	92	14	78	0.73	58	22	20	29	54	FFc	0%	49	18	0%	0%	147	12%	60%	-2.4	86	-$
2nd Half		118	18	1	14	3	241	1	2	279	291	306	81	67	84	6	87	0.50	56	23	21	27	111	CFc	2%	39	61	5%	5%	89	10%	100%	-2.6	71	$
24	**Proj**	**175**	**22**	**1**	**14**	**5**	**241**	**1**	**5**	**264**	**312**	**309**	**85**	**76**	**88**	**8**	**84**	**0.56**	**56**	**22**	**22**	**28**	**85**		**1%**	**41**	**43**	**2%**	**3%**	**122**	**12%**	**79%**	**-2.2**	**90**	**$**

Lowe,Brandon

Age: 29	Pos: 2B	Health F	LIMA Plan C+
Bats: L	Ht: 5' 10" Wt: 185	PT/Exp A	Rand Var 0
		Consist D	MM 4323

A partial rebound, tempered by more injury issues (herniated disc, fractured patella). When on the field, he continues to deliver plus power and a decent OBP. But that's two years of back issues in a row; big slippage vL is also a concern. There's clearly a lot of risk in this projection, but if healthy, he could again be among the top 2B producers.

Yr	Tm	PA	R	HR	RBI	SB	BA	xHR	xSB	xBA	OBP	SLG	OPS+	vL+	vR+	bb%	ct%	Eye	G	L	F	h%	HctX	QBaB	Brl%	PX	xPX	HR/F	xHR/F	Spd	SBA%	SB%	RAR	BPX	R$
19	TAM	327	42	17	51	5	270	20	4	235	336	514	118	94	123	8	62	0.22	30	27	43	38	92	AAb	16%	156	130	22%	26%	117	7%	100%	10.2	93	$1
20	TAM	224	36	14	37	3	269	15	3	261	362	554	122	148	112	11	70	0.43	33	24	43	31	122	BAc	18%	161	154	24%	25%	121	5%	100%	12.8	276	$2
21	TAM	615	97	39	99	7	247	34	4	261	340	523	119	90	132	11	69	0.41	34	22	44	28	99	CBd	14%	171	137	24%	21%	89	6%	88%	26.2	242	$2
22	TAM	266	31	8	25	1	221	9	2	236	308	383	98	111	95	10	74	0.44	38	21	41	27	92	CBf	10%	103	97	11%	13%	106	2%	100%	0.9	114	$
23	TAM	436	58	21	68	7	231	21	6	231	328	443	105	69	111	11	68	0.42	41	15	45	28	107	ABd	11%	130	129	18%	18%	92	7%	100%	14.9	107	$1
1st Half		201	26	9	29	3	205	9	3	204	299	398	95	60	99	12	64	0.38	39	11	49	26	99	ABc	12%	123	135	16%	16%	110	7%	100%	0.0	50	$
2nd Half		235	32	12	39	4	254	12	3	254	353	483	113	73	122	11	72	0.46	41	17	41	29	114	ABd	10%	136	125	20%	20%	82	7%	100%	10.6	168	$1
24	**Proj**	**420**	**58**	**20**	**61**	**5**	**236**	**20**	**5**	**240**	**327**	**452**	**107**	**91**	**111**	**11**	**70**	**0.40**	**38**	**18**	**44**	**28**	**103**		**12%**	**133**	**124**	**18%**	**18%**	**95**	**5%**	**98%**	**13.8**	**144**	**$1**

Lowe,Josh

Age: 26	Pos: RF DH	Health A	LIMA Plan C+
Bats: L	Ht: 6' 4" Wt: 205	PT/Exp A	Rand Var -3
		Consist D	MM 4525

Finally got a full helping of playing time, and delivered a solid year—but not one without warts. PRO: Superb SB% means bags are a given; contact and vL improvements give BA floor. CON: Exit velocity, xPX suggest some power pull-back; walk rate diving; xBA points to BA regression. A solid multi-category bat, just don't bid on a full repeat.

Yr	Tm	PA	R	HR	RBI	SB	BA	xHR	xSB	xBA	OBP	SLG	OPS+	vL+	vR+	bb%	ct%	Eye	G	L	F	h%	HctX	QBaB	Brl%	PX	xPX	HR/F	xHR/F	Spd	SBA%	SB%	RAR	BPX	R$
19	aa	507	68	17	61	29	241		22		329	419	104			12	67	0.40				32				107				117	31%	75%		52	$2
20																																			
21	TAM *	457	66	19	68	24	264	0	14	280	351	475	113	0	276	12	65	0.38	100	0	0	36	0	FF	0%	145	-22	0%		109	21%	100%	20.5	127	$2
22	TAM *	532	60	11	60	21	242	5	15	206	309	397	100	38	104	9	57	0.22	36	25	39	40	67	CCc	5%	145	111	4%	11%	125	20%	90%	1.8	3	$1
23	TAM	501	71	20	83	32	292	22	22	264	335	500	114	96	117	6	73	0.25	40	21	39	36	94	CCc	11%	131	94	15%	16%	105	31%	91%	32.3	157	$2
1st Half		263	36	12	48	19	285	13	12	264	327	504	114	88	117	6	72	0.23	38	21	40	35	81	CBd	12%	141	85	17%	18%	95	38%	90%	14.0	154	$2
2nd Half		238	35	8	35	13	300	9	10	264	345	495	114	101	116	6	75	0.27	41	21	38	37	108	CCc	10%	120	103	13%	14%	118	25%	93%	14.2	164	$2
24	**Proj**	**525**	**68**	**16**	**73**	**29**	**267**	**16**	**20**	**244**	**328**	**448**	**106**	**69**	**115**	**8**	**70**	**0.30**	**38**	**23**	**39**	**35**	**85**		**9%**	**122**	**102**	**12%**	**12%**	**115**	**26%**	**90%**	**19.2**	**105**	**$2**

Lowe,Nathaniel

Age: 28	Pos: 1B	Health A	LIMA Plan B
Bats: L	Ht: 6' 4" Wt: 220	PT/Exp A	Rand Var +1
		Consist C	MM 3335

Faded badly late (.553 OPS in Sept.), and it's hard to explain the 40% drop in barrels. Otherwise, this would have looked much like 2022, considering the expected HR and BA regression. Family health issues may have played a role in the late swoon, and he's not old by any means. So there's hope. But his 2022 looks like an anomaly now.

Yr	Tm	PA	R	HR	RBI	SB	BA	xHR	xSB	xBA	OBP	SLG	OPS+	vL+	vR+	bb%	ct%	Eye	G	L	F	h%	HctX	QBaB	Brl%	PX	xPX	HR/F	xHR/F	Spd	SBA%	SB%	RAR	BPX	R$
19	TAM *	558	76	20	71	1	252	7	1	244	350	432	108	136	101	13	69	0.49	40	24	36	32	99	ACc	11%	110	93	19%	19%	78	1%	100%	3.5	59	$
20	TAM	76	10	4	11	1	224	3	1	229	316	433	99	48	114	12	58	0.32	46	28	26	31	60	CDa	15%	141	82	40%	30%	94	6%	100%	-1.5	0	$
21	TEX	642	75	18	72	8	264	20	8	239	357	415	106	103	108	12	71	0.49	55	18	27	34	103	AFc	10%	94	87	17%	18%	114	4%	100%	10.4	77	$
22	TEX	645	74	27	76	2	302	25	6	263	358	492	120	129	116	7	75	0.33	48	21	31	36	116	BDc	10%	118	98	20%	18%	107	2%	50%	36.0	152	$2
23	TEX	724	89	17	82	1	262	17	6	256	360	414	106	87	114	13	74	0.56	48	22	30	33	108	BDd	7%	99	95	12%	12%	95	0%	100%	23.9	107	$
1st Half		379	53	9	45	0	276	9	3	246	369	433	110	94	117	13	75	0.59	47	23	30	34	109	BDd	7%	101	99	12%	12%	89	0%	0%	11.3	129	$2
2nd Half		345	36	8	37	1	246	8	4	245	351	394	101	77	110	13	71	0.54	48	22	30	32	107	BDc	6%	96	91	13%	13%	106	1%	100%	2.4	82	$
24	**Proj**	**665**	**80**	**21**	**77**	**2**	**269**	**20**	**6**	**255**	**356**	**439**	**109**	**99**	**113**	**12**	**73**	**0.48**	**48**	**22**	**30**	**34**	**106**		**8%**	**107**	**93**	**17%**	**15%**	**103**	**2%**	**83%**	**23.9**	**106**	**$2**

Luciano,Marco

Age: 22	Pos: SS	Health A	LIMA Plan D+
Bats: R	Ht: 6' 2" Wt: 178	PT/Exp F	Rand Var +2
		Consist F	MM 3205

0-0-.231 in 45 PA at SF. Backfields darling, hasn't quite lived up to billing. On surface, appears disciplined at the plate, though doesn't swing early in counts to avoid whiffs, which are abundant in the zone the deeper he gets. Massive power, but whiff issues dampen production. Powerful physique, foot speed slowing by the day. (CB)

Yr	Tm	PA	R	HR	RBI	SB	BA	xHR	xSB	xBA	OBP	SLG	OPS+	vL+	vR+	bb%	ct%	Eye	G	L	F	h%	HctX	QBaB	Brl%	PX	xPX	HR/F	xHR/F	Spd	SBA%	SB%	RAR	BPX	R$
19																																			
20																																			
21																																			
22																																			
23	SF *	350	36	10	30	6	197	0	5	221	292	344	87	154	54	12	59	0.33	55	23	23	30	98	AFd	0%	117	104	0%	0%	93	8%	100%	-5.5	-61	
1st Half		198	23	7	24	4	192		3	222	299	379	93	0	0	13	59	0.38	44	20	36	27	0		0%	145	-21	0%		104	10%	100%	-2.7	46	
2nd Half		154	15	3	8	2	212	0	2	206	302	327	85	153	53	11	58	0.31	55	23	23	34	97	AFd	0%	93	104	0%	0%	105	5%	100%	-4.0	-129	
24	**Proj**	**525**	**55**	**11**	**42**	**8**	**205**	**11**	**9**	**184**	**299**	**328**	**86**	**151**	**54**	**12**	**59**	**0.32**	**45**	**15**	**41**	**32**	**81**		**5%**	**103**	**94**	**10%**	**10%**	**81**	**9%**	**81%**	**-8.7**	**-59**	

ROD TRUESDELL

Lux,Gavin

Age: 26 Pos: DH | Bats: L Ht: 6' 2" Wt: 190

Health	F	LIMA Plan	B
PT/Exp	D	Rand Var	
Consist	C	MM	2335

Season wiped away after torn ACL in spring. PRO: Rising ct% and Spd give him more upside on basepaths; last xHR supports uptick in homers. CON: Regression from 2022 hit rate likely to offset steady xBA gains; QBaB still needs work. All need to be viewed through lens of a missed year, but metrics/age hint of a step up... UP: .280, 15 HR, 20 SB

Yr Tm	PA	R	HR	RBI	SB	BA	xHR	xSB	xBA	OBP	SLG	OPS+	vL+	vR+	bb%	ct%	Eye	G	L	F	h%	HctX	QBaB	Brl%	PX	xPX	HR/F	xHR/F	Spd	SBA%	SB%	RAR	BPX	R$
19 LA *	588	94	24	72	10	304	2	13	268	369	513	122	58	104	9	74	0.40	39	27	33	37	135	CCa	6%	112	164	12%	12%	132	10%	65%	30.0	170	$25
20 LA	69	8	3	8	1	175	2	1	216	246	349	79	37	87	9	70	0.32	48	14	39	20	109	CCa	7%	101	110	18%	12%	102	8%	100%	-3.6	40	$0
21 LA *	453	61	8	53	4	239	7	8	236	315	354	92	72	103	10	75	0.45	47	21	31	30	93	BCc	4%	69	79	9%	9%	143	4%	80%	-9.3	77	$8
22 LA	471	66	6	42	7	276	11	13	252	346	399	106	96	109	10	77	0.49	49	22	29	34	97	CDd	6%	80	86	6%	11%	156	7%	78%	6.6	145	$15
23																																		
1st Half																																		
2nd Half																																		
24 Proj	455	65	12	48	5	265	11	10	249	337	425	105	77	112	10	75	0.44	47	20	34	33	106		6%	94	105	12%	11%	134	7%	66%	9.9	138	$13

Machado,Manny

Age: 31 Pos: 3B DH | Bats: R Ht: 6' 3" Wt: 218

Health	A	LIMA Plan	B+
PT/Exp	A	Rand Var	+1
Consist	D	MM	3245

Elbow surgery at end of season could sideline him into spring. Before that, apparent down season was fueled by lowest hit rate of career. Underpinnings of 30-HR, 100-RBI profile remain really solid, including premium batted ball quality and an amazing eight straight 600+ PA seasons, save for COVID year. Another place to target injury profit.

Yr Tm	PA	R	HR	RBI	SB	BA	xHR	xSB	xBA	OBP	SLG	OPS+	vL+	vR+	bb%	ct%	Eye	G	L	F	h%	HctX	QBaB	Brl%	PX	xPX	HR/F	xHR/F	Spd	SBA%	SB%	RAR	BPX	R$
19 SD	661	81	32	85	5	256	26	6	251	334	462	110	151	98	10	78	0.51	42	17	41	28	118	ACf	8%	101	121	17%	14%	99	5%	63%	-4.6	167	$18
20 SD	254	44	16	47	6	304	14	5	294	370	580	126	123	127	10	83	0.70	37	22	41	30	131	BBd	11%	134	108	21%	18%	106	14%	67%	15.4	384	$38
21 SD	640	92	28	106	12	278	30	9	271	347	489	115	109	117	10	82	0.62	39	20	41	30	137	ACf	13%	112	123	15%	16%	97	9%	80%	27.5	262	$29
22 SD	644	100	32	102	9	298	23	7	274	366	531	127	120	130	10	77	0.47	38	21	42	34	128	ABc	10%	146	127	17%	12%	92	6%	90%	44.1	255	$37
23 SD	601	75	30	91	3	258	26	6	251	319	462	107	120	102	8	80	0.46	40	15	45	27	117	ABf	10%	108	117	15%	13%	86	4%	60%	18.0	182	$19
1st Half	292	33	11	36	3	243	8	4	237	284	408	95	123	84	6	79	0.28	44	13	42	27	99	BCd	7%	93	98	12%	9%	100	7%	75%	-2.2	121	$12
2nd Half	309	42	19	55	0	273	17	2	265	353	517	117	115	118	11	81	0.65	36	17	47	28	135	ABf	14%	123	134	18%	16%	73	1%	0%	16.7	243	$25
24 Proj	560	79	28	90	6	275	24	6	263	342	492	114	118	113	9	80	0.51	39	18	43	30	125		11%	118	121	16%	14%	82	5%	73%	30.5	228	$27

Madrigal,Nick

Age: 27 Pos: 3B | Bats: R Ht: 5' 8" Wt: 175

Health	F	LIMA Plan	C+
PT/Exp	C	Rand Var	+2
Consist	D	MM	0353

2-28-.263 with 10 SB in 294 PA at CHC. Few can connect bat and ball better, and it's a skill that makes return to .300 BA possible. However, batted ball quality is stuck in the mud; he has barreled four balls in the past *four* seasons. As a 3B, that lack of thump is hard to overlook. With MI eligibility, this becomes more appealing... UP: .300 BA, 15 SB

Yr Tm	PA	R	HR	RBI	SB	BA	xHR	xSB	xBA	OBP	SLG	OPS+	vL+	vR+	bb%	ct%	Eye	G	L	F	h%	HctX	QBaB	Brl%	PX	xPX	HR/F	xHR/F	Spd	SBA%	SB%	RAR	BPX	R$
19 a/a	306	51	2	25	16	314		15		369	408	108			8	96	2.17				32				46				125	28%	63%		281	$13
20 CHW	109	8	0	11	2	340	0	2	283	376	369	99	59	109	4	93	0.57	55	26	19	36	83	FFc	0%	19	10	0%	0%	117	8%	67%	-0.4	132	$9
21 CHW	215	30	2	21	1	305	1	5	302	349	425	106	135	94	5	92	0.65	60	20	20	33	81	DFc	1%	61	14	6%	3%	164	5%	33%	4.2	292	$6
22 CHC *	270	24	0	10	3	250	0	3	255	295	281	82	76	87	6	87	0.48	61	21	18	29	68	DFc	0%	25	30	0%	0%	102	5%	75%	-11.2	38	$1
23 CHC *	358	45	3	32	10	277	1	10	293	309	383	94	83	93	4	90	0.46	56	19	25	30	85	DFc	1%	61	29	3%	2%	116	14%	83%	3.1	193	$9
1st Half	211	31	2	20	7	302	1	8	300	344	423	105	95	93	6	88	0.55	61	17	21	34	77	FFc	1%	68	15	4%	4%	137	16%	78%	6.1	221	$9
2nd Half	147	14	1	13	3	244	0	2	286	260	330	80	61	92	2	93	0.29	50	21	29	26	95	DFc	0%	53	46	3%	0%	84	10%	100%	-4.9	157	-$1
24 Proj	350	41	2	28	7	283	1	8	285	331	363	95	89	98	5	90	0.51	57	21	22	31	81		0%	48	27	2%	1%	111	10%	76%	2.7	165	$12

Maldonado,Martín

Age: 37 Pos: CA | Bats: R Ht: 6' 0" Wt: 230

Health	A	LIMA Plan	D
PT/Exp	A	Rand Var	0
Consist	A	MM	3103

If he were 10 years younger, concurrent upward trends of xPX and xHR would put 20 homers on table. At 37, that's not happening. Worse, a .200 BA is his ceiling given subpar QBaB and ct%. It's a damaging batting average, too, since he keeps getting 400 PA. Not-so-fun fact: among hitters with 500+ PA since 2020, his .170 BA vR ranks dead last.

Yr Tm	PA	R	HR	RBI	SB	BA	xHR	xSB	xBA	OBP	SLG	OPS+	vL+	vR+	bb%	ct%	Eye	G	L	F	h%	HctX	QBaB	Brl%	PX	xPX	HR/F	xHR/F	Spd	SBA%	SB%	RAR	BPX	R$
19 3 TM	374	46	12	27	0	213	13	-	237	293	378	93	96	91	9	74	0.37	48	17	35	25	103	CCc	8%	95	95	14%	15%	69	0%	0%	-1.4	44	$1
20 HOU	165	19	6	24	1	215	5	0	217	350	378	97	113	88	16	62	0.53	35	28	37	29	64	DBd	8%	106	79	19%	16%	57	2%	100%	0.6	-56	$8
21 HOU	426	40	12	36	0	172	10	0	200	272	300	79	91	73	11	66	0.37	37	21	42	22	75	CBd	6%	82	101	12%	10%	73	0%	0%	-18.0	-92	-$4
22 HOU	379	40	15	45	0	186	13	0	212	248	352	85	107	76	6	66	0.19	42	17	41	23	84	CBc	8%	116	103	16%	14%	52	0%	0%	-10.3	-41	$1
23 HOU	407	33	15	36	0	191	16	0	205	258	348	83	110	74	7	62	0.22	35	21	43	26	82	DBf	9%	109	129	16%	17%	40	0%	0%	-6.2	-132	$0
1st Half	218	14	5	13	0	174	5	0	202	256	284	74	95	69	9	64	0.26	37	24	39	24	79	FBf	6%	77	97	11%	11%	47	0%	0%	-8.8	-171	-$8
2nd Half	189	19	10	23	0	209	10	0	209	261	419	92	119	79	7	59	0.17	33	19	48	29	86	DAf	11%	148	166	21%	21%	52	0%	0%	-0.3	-57	$3
24 Proj	315	31	12	33	0	195	12	0	208	268	358	86	108	77	8	64	0.25	38	20	42	26	82		8%	110	119	16%	15%	53	0%	100%	-3.6	-76	$4

Marcano,Tucupita

Age: 24 Pos: SS | Bats: L Ht: 6' 0" Wt: 180

Health	C	LIMA Plan	D+
PT/Exp	C	Rand Var	-1
Consist	B	MM	1321

3-18-.233 with 5 SB in 220 PA at PIT. Cursory glance offers little reason for intrigue, but here are a few... 1) +3.6 mph exit velocity from 2022; 2) GB dipped while Brl% jumped in 1st half; 3) ct% + Spd puts double-digit steals in play. Knee injury ended season early, which means a reserve round pick could give you a few bucks of profit.

Yr Tm	PA	R	HR	RBI	SB	BA	xHR	xSB	xBA	OBP	SLG	OPS+	vL+	vR+	bb%	ct%	Eye	G	L	F	h%	HctX	QBaB	Brl%	PX	xPX	HR/F	xHR/F	Spd	SBA%	SB%	RAR	BPX	R$
19																																		
20																																		
21 SD *	445	51	5	32	9	214	0	10	241	296	289	80	80	63	10	82	0.65	63	14	23	25	86	DFb	0%	42	42	0%	0%	114	13%	58%	-21.9	73	$4
22 PIT *	400	43	5	28	5	228	2	11	222	293	336	89	88	76	8	75	0.37	45	18	38	29	70	FCf	2%	75	82	5%	5%	142	15%	37%	-13.1	72	$4
23 PIT *	267	22	4	25	7	256	4	7	261	291	396	94	64	91	5	82	0.28	40	21	39	30	91	DCf	5%	85	85	5%	6%	119	17%	78%	1.1	157	$3
1st Half	229	21	4	23	6	262	4	6	272	299	426	99	70	96	5	82	0.30	37	23	41	30	99	DCf	7%	100	94	6%	7%	119	16%	86%	3.5	207	$5
2nd Half	38	1	0	2	1	222	0	1	180	237	222	62	38	68	3	81	0.14	54	14	32	28	55	FFf	0%	0	42	0%	0%	122	22%	50%	-2.6	-121	-$8
24 Proj	245	26	2	20	5	233	2	6	235	295	333	86	76	89	8	80	0.44	46	18	36	28	72		2%	63	71	3%	4%	130	14%	62%	-4.1	120	$5

Margot,Manuel

Age: 29 Pos: CF RF | Bats: R Ht: 5' 11" Wt: 180

Health	D	LIMA Plan	C+
PT/Exp	A	Rand Var	0
Consist	A	MM	1333

Even if we give him a mulligan due to midseason elbow surgery, this profile ain't aging well. Used to buy him for hope of SB given ct% + Spd combo, but shaky acumen on basepaths keeps inhibiting that upside, and subpar batted ball components limits hope of both BA and power. Only hanging on to steady MLB work due to good glove.

Yr Tm	PA	R	HR	RBI	SB	BA	xHR	xSB	xBA	OBP	SLG	OPS+	vL+	vR+	bb%	ct%	Eye	G	L	F	h%	HctX	QBaB	Brl%	PX	xPX	HR/F	xHR/F	Spd	SBA%	SB%	RAR	BPX	R$
19 SD	441	59	12	37	20	234	6	17	238	304	387	96	123	85	9	78	0.43	43	16	40	27	90	CBf	4%	81	82	10%	5%	153	24%	83%	-12.8	152	$12
20 TAM	159	19	1	11	12	269	3	9	251	327	352	90	83	92	8	83	0.52	45	23	32	32	97	DDf	4%	55	86	3%	8%	125	38%	75%	-3.7	124	$19
21 TAM	464	55	10	57	13	254	9	15	250	313	382	96	102	90	8	83	0.53	46	18	36	28	101	CCf	5%	69	80	8%	7%	136	18%	62%	-5.4	181	$15
22 TAM	363	36	4	47	7	274	4	8	250	325	375	99	123	92	7	80	0.35	45	23	32	33	91	CDf	3%	70	62	5%	5%	122	11%	70%	0.5	93	$11
23 TAM	336	39	4	38	9	264	5	9	257	310	376	93	90	95	5	82	0.33	46	20	35	31	107	CCf	4%	72	62	4%	6%	107	15%	75%	0.9	114	$7
1st Half	221	29	3	26	7	260	4	7	254	317	380	95	103	93	7	82	0.42	45	18	36	30	112	CCf	5%	75	66	5%	7%	115	17%	78%	-0.4	136	$8
2nd Half	115	10	1	12	2	270	1	2	263	296	369	90	70	100	3	83	0.16	46	22	32	32	99	CCd	1%	68	56	3%	3%	97	12%	67%	-1.6	79	-$2
24 Proj	350	38	5	40	10	265	5	10	253	312	374	94	96	93	6	82	0.35	46	21	34	31	99		3%	70	66	5%	5%	108	16%	71%	1.6	115	$13

Marsh,Brandon

Age: 26 Pos: CF LF | Bats: L Ht: 6' 4" Wt: 215

Health	A	LIMA Plan	C+
PT/Exp	A	Rand Var	-5
Consist	C	MM	3515

3 reasons a breakout could happen... 1) Exit velocity and barrel rate jumped; 2) doubled walk rate, late ct% gains; 3) making progress vL. Even if impact from likely h% regression sends BA south, another year of batted ball gains, a friendlier green light on basepaths, and escaping strict platoon would bring... UP: 20 HR, 20 SB

Yr Tm	PA	R	HR	RBI	SB	BA	xHR	xSB	xBA	OBP	SLG	OPS+	vL+	vR+	bb%	ct%	Eye	G	L	F	h%	HctX	QBaB	Brl%	PX	xPX	HR/F	xHR/F	Spd	SBA%	SB%	RAR	BPX	R$
19 aa	405	45	7	40	17	281		12		361	404	106			11	72	0.44				37				77				99	19%	76%		11	$14
20																																		
21 LAA *	364	43	4	24	7	237	6	7	220	300	346	89	76	100	8	62	0.24	44	31	25	37	100	ADa	11%	84	122	6%	17%	130	9%	88%	-9.1	-104	$5
22 2 TM	461	49	11	52	10	245	14	11	216	295	384	96	68	104	6	63	0.18	43	25	33	36	91	CCc	7%	107	130	13%	16%	134	14%	71%	-3.6	-28	$12
23 PHI	472	58	12	60	10	277	14	13	236	372	458	113	97	118	13	64	0.41	45	21	34	40	86	BCa	9%	128	93	13%	16%	127	9%	83%	25.2	89	$15
1st Half	275	32	7	32	4	279	8	7	231	358	463	112	85	121	11	63	0.34	44	21	35	42	89	ACa	9%	132	97	13%	15%	138	7%	80%	13.3	82	$12
2nd Half	197	26	5	28	6	274	5	6	242	391	451	114	115	113	15	66	0.53	46	21	32	38	81	CCa	9%	121	88	14%	14%	110	12%	86%	10.6	100	$11
24 Proj	525	63	14	61	14	257	16	13	228	339	421	104	86	110	11	65	0.33	44	22	34	37	89		9%	116	110	13%	15%	123	12%	86%	15.6	25	$20

STEPHEN NICKRAND

Marte,Ketel

Age: 30	Pos: 2B		Health	C	LIMA Plan	A
Bats: B	Ht: 6' 1"	Wt: 210	PT/Exp	A	Rand Var	0
			Consist	F	MM	3355

Sparkling rebound season keyed by... doing the same things just a little bit better? In truth, good health and better fortune likely the biggest reasons for this, as his base skills remain consistently solid. Looking ahead, xHR points to a small power regression; otherwise, there's no reason not to bid on a repeat.

Yr	Tm	PA	R	HR	RBI	SB	BA	xHR	xSB	xBA	OBP	SLG	OPS+	vL+	vR+	bb%	ct%	Eye	G	L	F	h%	HctX	QBaB	Brl%	PX	xPX	HR/F	xHR/F	Spd	SBA%	SB%	RAR	BPX	R$
19	ARI	628	97	32	92	10	329	28	10	307	389	592	136	139	133	8	85	0.62	43	22	35	34	123	BCc	9%	122	107	19%	17%	116	7%	83%	62.7	337	$32
20	ARI	195	19	2	17	1	287	4	1	274	323	409	97	143	78	4	88	0.33	46	21	33	32	114	CDd	4%	71	80	4%	8%	107	2%	100%	-1.9	208	$11
21	ARI	374	52	14	50	2	318	12	1	295	377	532	125	159	109	8	82	0.52	46	22	32	35	134	ACd	9%	123	116	16%	13%	91	2%	100%	27.7	285	$17
22	ARI	558	68	12	52	5	240	12	4	263	321	407	103	114	99	10	79	0.54	42	19	39	28	120	BCd	6%	115	108	8%	8%	92	5%	83%	2.9	203	$11
23	ARI	650	94	25	82	8	276	18	15	277	358	485	115	118	113	11	81	0.65	45	19	36	30	126	ACf	8%	109	99	15%	11%	133	6%	80%	37.1	264	$23
1st Half		348	61	15	44	6	285	12	9	274	365	502	119	118	119	10	81	0.61	44	18	39	31	123	BCd	10%	111	120	15%	12%	130	7%	86%	22.0	271	$29
2nd Half		302	33	10	38	2	265	6	6	280	351	466	110	118	106	12	80	0.69	46	21	33	30	130	ACf	6%	107	75	14%	8%	129	4%	67%	13.5	254	$15
24	**Proj**	**630**	**84**	**21**	**76**	**6**	**275**	**17**	**9**	**278**	**349**	**472**	**113**	**125**	**107**	**10**	**81**	**0.59**	**44**	**20**	**36**	**31**	**126**		**7%**	**111**	**100**	**13%**	**10%**	**111**	**5%**	**81%**	**34.2**	**251**	**$22**

Marte,Noelvi

Age: 22	Pos: 3B		Health	A	LIMA Plan	C+
Bats: R	Ht: 6' 1"	Wt: 181	PT/Exp	D	Rand Var	0
			Consist	F	MM	2533

3-15-.316 in 123 PA at CIN. Adjusted to upper minors pitching, earning late promotion. Improved ct% by shortening swing, reacting to spin better, but still prone to chase off-speed pitches fading away. High hard contact rate carried over to MLB. Needs to elevate ball to cash in on raw power; instinctive runner who maximizes average speed. (CB)

Yr	Tm	PA	R	HR	RBI	SB	BA	xHR	xSB	xBA	OBP	SLG	OPS+	vL+	vR+	bb%	ct%	Eye	G	L	F	h%	HctX	QBaB	Brl%	PX	xPX	HR/F	xHR/F	Spd	SBA%	SB%	RAR	BPX	R$
19																																			
20																																			
21																																			
22																																			
23	CIN *	491	61	12	46	18	262	3	20	273	318	406	99	92	120	8	77	0.36	53	22	25	32	120	AFc	8%	87	69	14%	14%	135	20%	74%	7.5	129	$14
1st Half		234	27	7	18	7	244		8	249	296	390	94	0	0	7	77	0.32	44	20	36	29	0		0%	85	-21	0%		131	17%	76%	-2.2	114	$6
2nd Half		257	35	6	28	11	279	3	11	275	338	422	103	91	119	8	77	0.40	53	22	25	34	120	AFc	8%	90	69	14%	14%	129	23%	73%	5.2	139	$17
24	**Proj**	**420**	**54**	**11**	**41**	**16**	**263**	**11**	**17**	**248**	**324**	**414**	**101**	**83**	**108**	**8**	**77**	**0.36**	**45**	**18**	**37**	**31**	**108**		**7%**	**92**	**62**	**10%**	**10%**	**128**	**21%**	**75%**	**8.4**	**129**	**$18**

Marte,Starling

Age: 35	Pos: RF		Health	F	LIMA Plan	C+
Bats: R	Ht: 6' 1"	Wt: 195	PT/Exp	A	Rand Var	+1
			Consist	D	MM	2445

Migraines, strained groin did in his 2nd half. If it weren't for a rebooted running game, the 1st half would've been an equal disaster, as power and BA went bye-bye. It's possible a nagging sore neck caused issues, but in truth, several troubling signs were already there in 2022 (see HctX, xPX). History points to better things, but at 35, it's no given.

Yr	Tm	PA	R	HR	RBI	SB	BA	xHR	xSB	xBA	OBP	SLG	OPS+	vL+	vR+	bb%	ct%	Eye	G	L	F	h%	HctX	QBaB	Brl%	PX	xPX	HR/F	xHR/F	Spd	SBA%	SB%	RAR	BPX	R$
19	PIT	586	97	23	82	25	295	25	20	297	342	503	117	108	119	4	83	0.27	50	21	28	32	108	CDc	8%	102	88	19%	20%	135	22%	81%	8.3	233	$3
20	2 NL	250	36	6	27	10	281	8	8	272	340	430	102	92	106	5	82	0.29	53	19	28	32	97	DFd	6%	83	74	12%	16%	124	19%	83%	-1.8	172	$2
21	2 TM	526	89	12	55	47	308	16	33	276	381	456	115	104	120	8	79	0.43	55	21	24	37	106	CFd	8%	88	69	14%	18%	141	33%	90%	24.1	177	$4
22	NYM	505	76	16	63	18	292	15	21	278	347	468	115	123	112	5	79	0.27	49	22	29	34	88	CDc	7%	107	75	15%	14%	147	21%	67%	15.3	203	$2
23	NYM	341	38	5	28	24	248	9	17	232	301	324	85	89	83	5	78	0.23	52	18	30	30	86	CFd	6%	43	80	7%	13%	105	31%	86%	-6.7	-32	$
1st Half		305	35	4	25	21	252	8	16	235	304	326	86	90	84	5	79	0.24	51	19	30	31	87	CFc	6%	43	76	6%	12%	105	31%	84%	-6.8	-21	$1
2nd Half		36	3	1	3	3	212	1	2	204	278	303	79	72	79	6	70	0.20	61	13	26	27	74	DFf	4%	49	120	17%	17%	98	33%	100%	-1.3	-139	-$
24	**Proj**	**455**	**62**	**13**	**48**	**22**	**264**	**14**	**20**	**268**	**324**	**413**	**101**	**102**	**101**	**6**	**80**	**0.30**	**54**	**18**	**27**	**30**	**88**		**6%**	**85**	**88**	**14%**	**15%**	**114**	**23%**	**79%**	**5.8**	**128**	**$2**

Martinez,J.D.

Age: 36	Pos: DH		Health	B	LIMA Plan	B
Bats: R	Ht: 6' 3"	Wt: 230	PT/Exp	A	Rand Var	-3
			Consist	C	MM	5345

Sold out for power with career-worst contact rate—but it worked! Exit velocity and barrels were elite, and PX was close to a career high. This approach puts BA at risk if the hard contact regresses at all, and a 2nd-half strained groin could be a sign of things to come as he moves into his upper-30s. Otherwise, pencil in 25+ HR and bid away.

Yr	Tm	PA	R	HR	RBI	SB	BA	xHR	xSB	xBA	OBP	SLG	OPS+	vL+	vR+	bb%	ct%	Eye	G	L	F	h%	HctX	QBaB	Brl%	PX	xPX	HR/F	xHR/F	Spd	SBA%	SB%	RAR	BPX	R$
19	BOS	656	98	36	105	2	304	37	2	280	383	557	130	192	109	11	76	0.52	43	22	35	35	121	ACa	12%	131	127	23%	24%	91	1%	100%	40.1	222	$2
20	BOS	237	22	7	27	1	213	11	0	238	291	389	90	89	91	9	72	0.37	35	21	44	26	104	BBc	11%	114	150	10%	16%	60	2%	100%	-7.9	72	$
21	BOS	633	92	28	99	0	286	32	1	267	349	518	119	112	122	9	74	0.37	34	24	42	34	117	ABb	12%	142	140	16%	18%	92	0%	0%	21.7	212	$2
22	BOS	595	76	16	62	0	274	27	1	253	341	448	112	140	104	9	73	0.36	38	22	40	35	110	CBb	12%	129	132	10%	17%	83	0%	0%	11.4	134	$1
23	LA	477	61	33	103	1	271	33	2	272	321	572	122	125	120	7	66	0.23	36	22	42	34	131	ABa	17%	196	181	27%	27%	81	1%	100%	30.8	211	$2
1st Half		288	39	19	56	1	259	21	1	276	302	563	118	107	122	6	67	0.19	34	23	44	31	129	AAa	18%	198	190	24%	27%	79	2%	100%	9.8	221	$2
2nd Half		189	22	14	47	0	290	12	1	261	349	586	126	149	117	9	64	0.28	40	22	39	37	134	ABb	17%	192	166	33%	28%	80	0%	0%	13.4	193	$1
24	**Proj**	**490**	**64**	**27**	**88**	**1**	**265**	**29**	**1**	**264**	**326**	**515**	**115**	**128**	**110**	**8**	**69**	**0.30**	**37**	**22**	**40**	**33**	**122**		**15%**	**161**	**156**	**21%**	**23%**	**80**	**1%**	**100%**	**22.7**	**182**	**$2**

Massey,Michael

Age: 26	Pos: 2B		Health	A	LIMA Plan	C+
Bats: L	Ht: 6' 0"	Wt: 190	PT/Exp	A	Rand Var	+1
			Consist	B	MM	2225

His first full MLB season was... okay? He owns a little pop, did alright against right-handers, and 2nd-half skills growth (led by ct%) was nice. The problem is, a just-okay long-side platoon bat is probably about his ceiling. That said, with a bit of experience now and at peak age—and if you squint really hard... UP: 20 HR

Yr	Tm	PA	R	HR	RBI	SB	BA	xHR	xSB	xBA	OBP	SLG	OPS+	vL+	vR+	bb%	ct%	Eye	G	L	F	h%	HctX	QBaB	Brl%	PX	xPX	HR/F	xHR/F	Spd	SBA%	SB%	RAR	BPX	R$
19																																			
20																																			
21																																			
22	KC *	559	50	13	63	11	251	9	6	228	290	395	97	91	98	5	72	0.20	35	20	44	32	109	CBc	14%	107	159	7%	16%	73	11%	82%	3.8	31	$1
23	KC	461	42	15	55	6	229	15	6	244	274	381	89	80	91	5	77	0.24	30	25	45	26	97	CAd	8%	88	108	10%	10%	78	9%	75%	-1.4	50	$
1st Half		204	15	4	20	3	217	7	3	202	279	315	82	92	77	7	67	0.23	30	24	46	30	93	CAc	10%	67	123	7%	13%	81	9%	75%	-6.3	-132	-$
2nd Half		257	27	11	35	3	238	8	3	276	270	430	95	65	100	4	84	0.26	31	25	45	24	99	CAd	6%	100	98	12%	9%	87	9%	75%	-0.5	186	$1
24	**Proj**	**490**	**45**	**14**	**59**	**8**	**238**	**20**	**7**	**235**	**291**	**384**	**93**	**83**	**95**	**5**	**75**	**0.22**	**32**	**23**	**45**	**29**	**102**		**10%**	**91**	**129**	**9%**	**13%**	**77**	**9%**	**80%**	**-1.2**	**45**	**$1**

Mateo,Jorge

Age: 29	Pos: SS		Health	A	LIMA Plan	D+
Bats: R	Ht: 6' 0"	Wt: 182	PT/Exp	A	Rand Var	+1
			Consist	A	MM	2513

One-trick pony's window as a full-time player has just about shut. That means another 30+ steals is an increasingly unlikely proposition—not to mention that he's approaching the age where speed skills often begin to diminish. Heed the warning of that 2nd half, when younger, better players replaced him in the lineup... DN: <200 PA, <15 SB

Yr	Tm	PA	R	HR	RBI	SB	BA	xHR	xSB	xBA	OBP	SLG	OPS+	vL+	vR+	bb%	ct%	Eye	G	L	F	h%	HctX	QBaB	Brl%	PX	xPX	HR/F	xHR/F	Spd	SBA%	SB%	RAR	BPX	R$
19	aaa	554	72	13	60	18	249		20		279	418	96			4	69	0.13				34				98				145	30%	59%		26	$1
20	SD	28	4	0	2	1	154	0	1	207	185	269	60	67	44	4	58	0.09	13	47	40	27	102	CAd		122	107	0%	0%	107	50%	100%	-2.5	-120	-$
21	2 TM	209	19	4	14	10	247	4	7	227	293	376	92	90	93	4	72	0.16	39	23	38	33	71	DCf	6%	86	61	8%	8%	119	29%	77%	-4.1	8	$
22	BAL	531	63	13	50	35	221	13	30	225	267	379	91	87	93	5	70	0.18	38	20	41	29	80	DBf	6%	109	95	9%	9%	167	46%	80%	-12.5	103	$2
23	BAL	349	58	7	34	32	217	8	24	229	267	340	83	101	70	6	74	0.27	44	18	38	27	92	CCf	5%	76	94	8%	9%	140	54%	86%	-4.9	50	$1
1st Half		239	37	6	27	22	217	6	14	230	267	346	84	103	74	6	75	0.27	43	18	40	26	91	CCf	7%	81	97	9%	9%	105	53%	88%	-6.4	36	$
2nd Half		110	21	1	7	10	218	2	9	230	269	327	80	97	62	6	73	0.26	48	19	33	29	94	CDd	3%	67	89	4%	8%	177	55%	83%	-3.8	54	$
24	**Proj**	**280**	**42**	**5**	**25**	**21**	**226**	**6**	**17**	**226**	**271**	**359**	**86**	**95**	**81**	**5**	**72**	**0.20**	**42**	**20**	**38**	**29**	**85**		**5%**	**85**	**89**	**7%**	**9%**	**144**	**46%**	**81%**	**-4.4**	**53**	**$**

Maton,Nick

Age: 27	Pos: 3B 2B		Health	D	LIMA Plan	D
Bats: L	Ht: 6' 2"	Wt: 178	PT/Exp	B	Rand Var	+3
			Consist	B	MM	3211

8-32-.173 in 293 PA at DET. Another disappointing season, though to be fair, it's tough to fall off the floor. Flyball profile still hints at power, but with that subpar exit velocity, it's not coming. There's nothing in these skills to suggest he's making progress, either, and he's no young pup anymore. Time to move on.

Yr	Tm	PA	R	HR	RBI	SB	BA	xHR	xSB	xBA	OBP	SLG	OPS+	vL+	vR+	bb%	ct%	Eye	G	L	F	h%	HctX	QBaB	Brl%	PX	xPX	HR/F	xHR/F	Spd	SBA%	SB%	RAR	BPX	R$
19	aa	70	5	2	5	1	197		1		291	341	88			12	74	0.52				23				80				102	13%	46%		67	-
20																																			
21	PHI *	365	36	6	33	4	203	2	5	219	285	321	83	120	85	10	66	0.33	33	30	37	29	71	CBd	6%	84	83	7%	7%	117	7%	65%	-17.1	-38	
22	PHI *	318	34	8	40	2	215	3	2	227	295	377	95	112	125	10	67	0.34	32	25	43	29	91	DBf	7%	124	144	26%	16%	99	4%	62%	-3.4	62	
23	DET *	451	50	10	50	3	194	8	6	204	295	321	84	66	81	12	70	0.48	36	16	48	25	81	DBd	8%	86	106	9%	9%	96	6%	48%	-10.6	18	
1st Half		255	25	6	24	0	172	7	3	192	290	296	80	12	82	14	69	0.54	35	15	50	22	80	DAc	9%	82	101	9%	10%	92	3%	0%	-10.5	4	-
2nd Half		196	25	4	26	3	220	1	4	226	302	353	89	334	77	11	71	0.40	36	22	42	29	86	FBf	6%	90	125	13%	7%	113	9%	71%	-3.0	43	
24	**Proj**	**175**	**19**	**5**	**21**	**1**	**206**	**5**	**2**	**230**	**296**	**373**	**92**	**113**	**88**	**11**	**68**	**0.40**	**35**	**23**	**42**	**26**	**84**		**7%**	**112**	**121**	**12%**	**11%**	**110**	**6%**	**62%**	**-1.5**	**30**	

ROD TRUESDELL

Matos,Luis

Age: 22 Pos: CF | Bats: R Ht: 5' 11" Wt: 160
Health A | PT/Exp C | Consist F | LIMA Plan B+ | Rand Var 0 | MM 1535

2-14-.250 with 3 SB in 253 PA at SF. While 8D prospect didn't do much in first MLB look (.661 OPS), seeds of a BA/SB contributor are there... 1) Upper-tier 86% ct% after call-up; 2) Elite Spd; 3) Showed both average and power in majors vL (.310 BA, .825 OPS). Marginal batted ball profile says he needs more time, but he's a keeper. UP: .280 BA, 40 SB

Yr Tm	PA	R	HR	RBI	SB	BA	xHR	xSB	xBA	OBP	SLG	OPS+	vL+	vR+	bb%	ct%	Eye	G	L	F	h%	HctX	QBaB	Brl%	PX	xPX	HR/F	xHR/F	Spd	SBA%	SB%	RAR	BPX	R$
19																																		
20																																		
21																																		
22																																		
23 SF *	529	56	10	44	15	275	3	19	265	333	404	100	111	77	8	88	0.72	45	17	37	30	94	DDd	2%	71	93	3%	4%	136	15%	73%	11.8	239	$14
1st Half	307	41	8	32	14	300	1	17	284	359	444	110	100	82	9	90	0.89	47	20	33	31	93	DFf	6%	73	107	6%	6%	152	23%	71%	13.8	289	$23
2nd Half	222	15	2	12	1	239	1	3	246	296	348	87	112	73	7	85	0.55	44	17	39	27	93	CDc	1%	67	88	2%	2%	121	2%	100%	-2.8	171	-$2
24 Proj	455	43	6	34	20	263	5	13	257	327	374	96	117	85	8	87	0.66	45	18	37	29	93		3%	65	96	4%	3%	119	20%	85%	5.7	218	$13

Mauricio,Ronny

Age: 23 Pos: 2B | Bats: B Ht: 6' 3" Wt: 166
Health A | PT/Exp A | Consist D | LIMA Plan C+ | Rand Var +4 | MM 2415

2-8-.248 with 7 SB in 108 PA at NYM. Super aggressive hitter with chase rate north of 40%. Struggles expanding the zone in most counts and from both sides of the plate. OBP will always be BA-driven. Power is calling card and plays to all fields, especially from LH side. Versatile defender; quick reactions and solid first step play up average run tool. (CB)

Yr Tm	PA	R	HR	RBI	SB	BA	xHR	xSB	xBA	OBP	SLG	OPS+	vL+	vR+	bb%	ct%	Eye	G	L	F	h%	HctX	QBaB	Brl%	PX	xPX	HR/F	xHR/F	Spd	SBA%	SB%	RAR	BPX	R$
19																																		
20																																		
21 aa	33	2	1	1	2	277		1		310	375	94			5	59	0.12				45				74				106	22%	100%		-235	-$1
22 aa	526	49	18	62	14	214		13		240	368	86			3	71	0.12				26				104				86	30%	53%		10	$12
23 NYM *	624	64	16	58	24	238	2	22	264	278	374	89	66	105	5	75	0.23	47	26	27	29	114	BDf	6%	84	86	11%	11%	117	25%	75%	-6.4	57	$14
1st Half	321	31	7	30	9	241		11	253	271	379	89	0	0	4	78	0.19	44	20	36	29	0		0%	85	-21	0%		119	25%	61%	-5.9	100	$11
2nd Half	303	32	10	28	15	233	2	12	251	285	370	88	66	104	7	72	0.26	47	26	27	29	109	BDf	6%	82	86	11%	11%	122	26%	87%	-2.4	18	$16
24 Proj	490	48	14	50	17	227	16	16	223	264	366	86	67	102	5	73	0.19	37	20	43	28	98		5%	86	77	9%	11%	114	27%	69%	-8.2	35	$15

McCarthy,Jake

Age: 26 Pos: RF | Bats: L Ht: 6' 2" Wt: 215
Health A | PT/Exp A | Consist C | LIMA Plan C+ | Rand Var +1 | MM 1525

2-16-.243 with 26 SB in 312 PA at ARI. Speedster looked the part before weak bat ate into PT late. 98th percentile sprint speed, elite Spd both confirm that legs are legit. That's his only skill though (see badly flunking QBaB), and as a one-trick-pony, those PA can dry up quickly when his MLB team needs more production. In the right spot... UP: 40 SB

Yr Tm	PA	R	HR	RBI	SB	BA	xHR	xSB	xBA	OBP	SLG	OPS+	vL+	vR+	bb%	ct%	Eye	G	L	F	h%	HctX	QBaB	Brl%	PX	xPX	HR/F	xHR/F	Spd	SBA%	SB%	RAR	BPX	R$
19																																		
20																																		
21 ARI *	420	49	11	36	20	207	1	19	205	264	374	88	92	100	7	66	0.23	58	3	39	29	44	FFf	3%	104	82	14%	7%	161	35%	76%	-19.6	42	$10
22 ARI *	505	71	11	58	29	282	6	24	264	330	425	107	107	109	7	78	0.32	49	22	29	34	90	DFf	5%	93	80	12%	9%	138	29%	78%	11.0	145	$29
23 ARI *	519	61	6	37	35	255	3	32	257	308	361	91	86	88	7	79	0.37	51	22	27	31	74	FFf	2%	60	53	4%	5%	144	34%	79%	-1.9	86	$16
1st Half	287	34	4	21	19	251	3	20	263	307	367	92	92	95	8	80	0.42	53	21	26	30	88	FFc	4%	60	65	6%	9%	161	35%	78%	-2.3	125	$13
2nd Half	232	28	2	16	15	261	0	12	250	308	355	90	77	77	6	78	0.31	47	23	30	32	51	FDf	0%	61	31	0%	0%	114	32%	81%	-1.7	32	$11
24 Proj	455	59	6	41	28	257	6	26	244	320	372	95	93	95	7	76	0.31	51	19	30	32	71		3%	70	63	6%	6%	143	30%	77%	0.1	92	$21

McCormick,Chas

Age: 29 Pos: LF CF RF | Bats: R Ht: 6' 0" Wt: 208
Health B | PT/Exp A | Consist B | LIMA Plan B | Rand Var -1 | MM 3325

Five-category production in 2nd half fueled title runs for those who got him at his 546 ADP. Can gains stick? PRO: xHR likes new power level; SB% jump shows he made good use of much stronger green light. CON: Still does most of his damage vL; 23rd percentile exit velocity. We may have already seen his peak, but descent should be gentle.

Yr Tm	PA	R	HR	RBI	SB	BA	xHR	xSB	xBA	OBP	SLG	OPS+	vL+	vR+	bb%	ct%	Eye	G	L	F	h%	HctX	QBaB	Brl%	PX	xPX	HR/F	xHR/F	Spd	SBA%	SB%	RAR	BPX	R$
19 a/a	420	50	11	51	12	228		14		323	354	94			12	80	0.72				26				56				150	15%	73%		141	$9
20																																		
21 HOU	320	47	14	50	4	257	14	3	219	319	447	105	112	102	8	63	0.24	36	22	42	36	93	BAc	10%	128	144	18%	18%	87	8%	67%	3.5	0	$10
22 HOU	407	47	14	44	4	245	16	7	236	332	407	105	136	92	11	70	0.43	43	22	35	31	92	CCc	10%	105	110	16%	18%	123	7%	57%	6.5	93	$10
23 HOU	457	59	22	70	19	273	21	17	255	353	489	115	136	105	9	71	0.34	41	21	38	33	98	CBb	11%	128	133	20%	19%	104	21%	76%	23.2	132	$20
1st Half	175	19	7	24	8	258	6	6	244	339	458	109	99	113	9	70	0.32	37	21	42	33	91	DBb	8%	126	127	16%	13%	105	21%	89%	6.0	111	$7
2nd Half	282	40	15	46	11	282	15	11	262	362	508	118	155	99	9	72	0.36	43	21	36	34	102	CCc	13%	130	137	24%	24%	101	21%	69%	15.2	150	$28
24 Proj	560	71	21	74	16	259	24	16	240	339	431	106	127	97	10	71	0.37	42	22	36	33	95		11%	105	127	17%	19%	102	15%	73%	15.2	105	$25

McCutchen,Andrew

Age: 37 Pos: DH | Bats: R Ht: 5' 11" Wt: 195
Health D | PT/Exp A | Consist C | LIMA Plan C+ | Rand Var -2 | MM 2223

On a 20/20 path in 1st half before elbow and Achilles injuries derailed him. Those are reminders that the $20 version is long gone. Neither underlying power nor speed are coming back as he pushes 40. Inflated hit rate propped up batting average, which means you want to follow steady xBA as your guide. Still a useful piece at his likely cost.

Yr Tm	PA	R	HR	RBI	SB	BA	xHR	xSB	xBA	OBP	SLG	OPS+	vL+	vR+	bb%	ct%	Eye	G	L	F	h%	HctX	QBaB	Brl%	PX	xPX	HR/F	xHR/F	Spd	SBA%	SB%	RAR	BPX	R$
19 PHI	262	45	10	29	2	256	9	2	255	378	457	115	117	114	16	75	0.78	45	18	37	30	95	BCb	7%	109	101	17%	15%	100	4%	67%	4.0	189	$5
20 PHI	241	32	10	34	4	253	11	2	245	324	433	100	123	91	9	78	0.46	35	22	44	28	126	BAc	8%	96	151	14%	15%	92	7%	100%	0.1	144	$21
21 PHI	574	78	27	80	6	222	22	3	252	334	444	107	140	90	14	73	0.61	40	19	40	25	108	CBd	9%	131	126	19%	15%	79	5%	86%	-2.8	188	$14
22 MIL	580	66	17	69	8	237	17	7	243	316	384	99	103	97	10	76	0.46	42	21	37	28	104	CCd	9%	97	104	11%	11%	77	10%	57%	-10.3	90	$15
23 PIT	473	55	12	43	11	256	11	11	244	378	397	106	107	105	16	74	0.75	43	22	36	32	94	BCd	7%	88	90	11%	10%	89	9%	79%	13.6	100	$11
1st Half	305	38	10	28	9	278	8	9	252	390	440	114	110	115	16	76	0.78	40	22	38	33	103	BCd	8%	95	99	14%	11%	97	12%	75%	10.8	154	$17
2nd Half	168	17	2	15	2	217	3	2	228	357	319	91	102	85	17	71	0.70	47	21	32	29	77	CCc	5%	75	71	6%	10%	80	4%	100%	-3.8	14	-$2
24 Proj	420	51	12	46	7	239	11	6	240	349	386	101	110	96	14	74	0.64	43	21	36	29	97		7%	93	99	12%	12%	79	7%	76%	4.5	102	$12

McGuire,Reese

Age: 29 Pos: CA | Bats: L Ht: 6' 0" Wt: 218
Health B | PT/Exp D | Consist A | LIMA Plan D | Rand Var -5 | MM 1223

Some will view him as a decent second catcher in deep leagues, since he hasn't been a BA drain the past two seasons. Problem is, chronically poor xBA continues to show his downside, and we can't expect his balls-in-play fortune to last another year. In absence of decent BA, he's utterly unrosterable given "FFF" batted ball quality.

Yr Tm	PA	R	HR	RBI	SB	BA	xHR	xSB	xBA	OBP	SLG	OPS+	vL+	vR+	bb%	ct%	Eye	G	L	F	h%	HctX	QBaB	Brl%	PX	xPX	HR/F	xHR/F	Spd	SBA%	SB%	RAR	BPX	R$
19 TOR *	368	39	9	35	3	246	2	2	273	303	387	96	95	127	8	80	0.41	40	28	32	28	88	DCc	4%	77	85	20%	8%	93	4%	100%	4.2	104	$4
20 TOR	45	2	1	1	0	73	0	0	191	73	146	29	0	50	0	73	0.00	66	10	24	7	35	FFf	3%	36	8	14%	0%	85	0%	0%	-5.6	-200	-$6
21 TOR	217	22	1	10	0	253	2	0	239	310	343	90	63	97	7	78	0.34	40	24	36	32	71	DCc	3%	69	59	2%	4%	88	0%	0%	-2.0	35	$0
22 2 AL	273	25	3	22	1	269	4	1	234	307	369	96	85	98	4	78	0.21	39	23	39	34	59	DCf	3%	73	55	4%	5%	91	2%	100%	2.7	24	$4
23 BOS	202	15	1	16	2	267	2	3	233	310	358	91	118	87	5	72	0.21	55	20	25	37	64	FFf	3%	70	57	3%	6%	94	6%	67%	2.7	-54	$1
1st Half	114	11	0	11	0	267	0	1	227	313	352	91	152	83	6	70	0.22	53	21	26	38	49	FFf	1%	79	38	0%	0%	90	4%	0%	0.3	-61	-$6
2nd Half	88	4	1	5	2	268	1	2	238	307	366	91	81	93	5	74	0.19	58	19	24	35	83	FFd	5%	60	81	7%	7%	103	9%	100%	1.0	-43	-$5
24 Proj	280	23	3	21	2	241	3	2	241	287	348	87	83	88	6	75	0.24	47	22	31	31	69		3%	74	63	5%	5%	89	5%	83%	-0.2	-3	$5

McKinstry,Zach

Age: 29 Pos: 3B 2B RF SS LF | Bats: L Ht: 6' 0" Wt: 180
Health B | PT/Exp A | Consist A | LIMA Plan C+ | Rand Var +2 | MM 2415

Swiss army knife added some steals to underwhelming profile, and voilà, the best season of his career. Before you dismiss, contact rate and speed have never been better, so there might be 20 SB here. Lack of quality batted balls limits hope for impactful results in other areas. Fits best as a deep-league middle infielder.

Yr Tm	PA	R	HR	RBI	SB	BA	xHR	xSB	xBA	OBP	SLG	OPS+	vL+	vR+	bb%	ct%	Eye	G	L	F	h%	HctX	QBaB	Brl%	PX	xPX	HR/F	xHR/F	Spd	SBA%	SB%	RAR	BPX	R$
19 a/a	462	55	15	62	6	259		9		311	432	103			7	75	0.30				31				94				107	15%	38%		85	$11
20 LA	7	1	0	0	0	286	0	0	275	286	429	95	0	95	0	57	0.00	50	50	0	50	173	DFf		153	99	0%		112	0%	0%	0.0	-52	-$2
21 LA *	331	42	12	43	4	213	5	4	239	267	388	90	88	93	7	73	0.27	43	18	39	25	110	CCa	8%	106	143	17%	12%	103	12%	51%	-12.4	92	$5
22 2 NL *	390	40	7	27	7	221	4	9	228	282	344	89	65	93	8	73	0.32	37	25	38	28	80	DCf	4%	79	100	12%	9%	134	13%	64%	-13.7	48	$4
23 DET	518	60	9	35	16	231	12	19	227	302	351	89	88	89	8	76	0.39	35	22	43	29	85	CBb	8%	74	92	6%	8%	135	18%	73%	-3.4	75	$8
1st Half	265	34	6	22	11	251	7	10	230	335	381	98	83	99	11	77	0.54	35	20	45	30	86	CBb	10%	77	94	7%	9%	120	17%	92%	2.1	111	$11
2nd Half	253	26	3	13	5	210	5	9	225	269	322	80	88	79	6	74	0.26	35	24	41	27	83	DAb	6%	71	91	4%	7%	141	20%	50%	-12.5	32	$1
24 Proj	490	56	11	41	15	233	12	14	232	296	371	91	85	92	8	74	0.32	37	23	40	29	87		6%	84	103	8%	9%	126	19%	70%	-3.7	66	$14

STEPHEN NICKRAND

McLain,Matt

Age: 24 Pos: SS 2B | Bats: R Ht: 5' 11" Wt: 180

Health	B	LIMA Plan	B
PT/Exp	B	Rand Var	-2
Consist	F	MM	4525

16-50-.290 with 14 SB in 403 PA at CIN. PRO: Excelled in first taste of MLB with multi-category success; plate skills improving; solid barrels. CON: Faded in 2nd half before oblique strain ended season; QBaB, xPX don't fully support HR outburst; BA also stands to regress. Exciting youngster, but let 2nd half numbers be your guide for 2023.

Yr	Tm	PA	R	HR	RBI	SB	BA	xHR	xSB	xBA	OBP	SLG	OPS+	vL+	vR+	bb%	ct%	Eye	G	L	F	h%	HctX	QBaB	Brl%	PX	xPX	HR/F	xHR/F	Spd	SBA%	SB%	RAR	BPX	R$
19																																			
20																																			
21																																			
22	aa	419	45	13	39	18	196		12		288	364	92			11	61	0.33				28				134				106	24%	84%		21	$9
23	CIN *	566	83	25	75	20	288	14	27	262	352	518	118	134	112	9	69	0.31	39	24	37	37	94	CCd	11%	148	110	17%	15%	146	22%	65%	34.6	204	$26
1st Half		356	52	16	53	10	303	7	16	270	367	556	126	139	122	9	70	0.34	38	22	40	39	101	CCd	14%	159	129	14%	14%	148	22%	53%	24.3	264	$34
2nd Half		210	31	9	22	10	263	6	9	246	326	454	105	128	102	9	66	0.27	40	26	34	35	86	CCf	8%	127	91	22%	15%	122	23%	83%	5.5	75	$14
24	**Proj**	**560**	**74**	**19**	**63**	**23**	**259**	**18**	**23**	**241**	**344**	**441**	**108**	**124**	**102**	**10**	**68**	**0.34**	**39**	**25**	**36**	**35**	**92**		**10%**	**122**	**106**	**16%**	**14%**	**132**	**21%**	**77%**	**19.0**	**101**	**$22**

McMahon,Ryan

Age: 29 Pos: 3B 2B | Bats: L Ht: 6' 2" Wt: 219

Health	A	LIMA Plan	B
PT/Exp	A	Rand Var	-1
Consist	A	MM	4125

Consistency, thy name is Ryan. There's real value in that, just as there's value in knowing you can only rely on him producing at Coors (.835/.661 career home/road OPS) against RHP (.779/.683 career vR/vL OPS). If he ever leaves COL, all bets are off... but he's signed through 2027, so this forecast seems safe.

Yr	Tm	PA	R	HR	RBI	SB	BA	xHR	xSB	xBA	OBP	SLG	OPS+	vL+	vR+	bb%	ct%	Eye	G	L	F	h%	HctX	QBaB	Brl%	PX	xPX	HR/F	xHR/F	Spd	SBA%	SB%	RAR	BPX	R$
19	COL	539	70	24	83	5	250	20	3	246	329	450	108	109	106	10	67	0.35	51	21	28	32	102	ADb	9%	119	112	27%	22%	78	5%	83%	-5.4	30	$15
20	COL	193	23	9	26	0	215	9	1	214	295	419	95	97	93	9	62	0.27	50	15	35	29	100	BCc	11%	131	158	24%	24%	106	2%	0%	-7.8	16	$9
21	COL	596	80	23	86	6	254	21	4	254	331	449	107	90	114	10	72	0.40	39	24	38	31	114	BBc	7%	122	139	16%	15%	87	6%	75%	10.3	131	$18
22	COL	597	67	20	67	7	246	21	6	244	327	414	105	90	111	10	70	0.38	45	23	33	31	121	ACb	11%	114	133	17%	17%	87	7%	70%	1.9	69	$17
23	COL	627	80	23	70	5	240	27	9	241	322	431	103	77	113	11	64	0.34	43	23	34	33	113	BCc	11%	133	140	19%	23%	91	7%	50%	10.6	54	$14
1st Half		344	45	13	43	4	263	16	6	252	346	477	113	94	121	11	65	0.36	43	24	34	36	115	ACc	13%	147	140	19%	24%	103	8%	57%	12.3	118	$20
2nd Half		283	35	10	27	1	211	11	3	225	293	375	90	55	103	11	63	0.33	44	23	33	29	111	CDd	10%	114	141	19%	21%	76	5%	33%	-5.5	-32	$7
24	**Proj**	**595**	**74**	**22**	**71**	**5**	**244**	**24**	**6**	**240**	**325**	**429**	**103**	**83**	**111**	**10**	**67**	**0.35**	**44**	**23**	**34**	**32**	**114**		**10%**	**123**	**138**	**19%**	**20%**	**84**	**6%**	**58%**	**12.7**	**53**	**$19**

McNeil,Jeff

Age: 32 Pos: 2B RF LF | Bats: L Ht: 6' 1" Wt: 195

Health	B	LIMA Plan	A
PT/Exp	A	Rand Var	0
Consist	F	MM	1445

Expected to be ready for spring training after late September UCL tear. Otherwise, the "wet noodling" trend in his bat accelerated in 2023—really, a 1% barrel rate? Rest of batted-ball metrics are just as Liliputian. Sure, elite contact rate keeps a certain BA floor intact, but hard contact? Nope. Value now tied to PA volume, so hope the elbow is healed.

Yr	Tm	PA	R	HR	RBI	SB	BA	xHR	xSB	xBA	OBP	SLG	OPS+	vL+	vR+	bb%	ct%	Eye	G	L	F	h%	HctX	QBaB	Brl%	PX	xPX	HR/F	xHR/F	Spd	SBA%	SB%	RAR	BPX	R$
19	NYM	567	83	23	75	5	318	18	8	297	384	531	127	115	130	6	85	0.47	43	22	35	34	111	CCa	5%	107	94	15%	12%	107	7%	45%	32.9	270	$23
20	NYM	209	19	4	23	0	311	5	2	280	383	454	111	97	118	10	87	0.83	44	24	32	34	109	CCc	2%	81	81	8%	10%	109	3%	0%	5.5	264	$15
21	NYM	426	48	7	35	3	249	9	3	256	317	358	93	86	95	7	85	0.50	47	20	33	28	100	CCc	4%	62	70	6%	8%	111	3%	100%	-8.4	146	$6
22	NYM	589	73	9	62	4	326	9	7	282	382	454	118	106	123	7	89	0.66	41	24	35	36	96	CCb	3%	82	68	5%	5%	118	2%	100%	32.9	245	$27
23	NYM	648	75	10	55	10	270	6	15	260	333	378	97	101	95	6	89	0.60	42	20	38	29	75	DCd	1%	57	53	5%	3%	129	6%	100%	7.7	193	$15
1st Half		336	34	3	24	4	258	2	6	252	332	332	91	86	92	7	87	0.63	41	23	36	29	71	DCc	2%	42	45	3%	2%	119	4%	100%	-2.1	125	$7
2nd Half		312	41	7	31	6	282	3	8	269	334	425	103	112	97	5	91	0.56	42	18	40	29	79	DCf	1%	72	61	7%	3%	130	8%	100%	8.2	254	$18
24	**Proj**	**560**	**66**	**9**	**52**	**7**	**281**	**8**	**9**	**266**	**342**	**395**	**101**	**100**	**101**	**6**	**88**	**0.58**	**43**	**21**	**36**	**31**	**88**		**2%**	**65**	**64**	**5%**	**5%**	**120**	**5%**	**92%**	**14.5**	**211**	**$20**

Mead,Curtis

Age: 23 Pos: 3B | Bats: R Ht: 6' 2" Wt: 171

Health	A	LIMA Plan	C
PT/Exp	D	Rand Var	0
Consist	A	MM	3333

1-5-.253 in 92 PA at TAM. Bat-first prospect who struggled out of spring training and then suffered a May wrist injury that dampened his numbers. Rebounded in 2nd half (.336/.439/.604) to earn callup. Pure hitter with ct% upside, peppers from the gaps to the foul lines with hard contact. Plus HR power, coupled with innate backspin off the bat. (CB)

Yr	Tm	PA	R	HR	RBI	SB	BA	xHR	xSB	xBA	OBP	SLG	OPS+	vL+	vR+	bb%	ct%	Eye	G	L	F	h%	HctX	QBaB	Brl%	PX	xPX	HR/F	xHR/F	Spd	SBA%	SB%	RAR	BPX	R$
19																																			
20																																			
21	aaa																																		
22	a/a	308	31	9	36	5	249		4		313	423	104			9	74	0.36				31				128				80	11%	69%		145	$7
23	TAM *	351	41	8	36	3	246	1	8	246	314	397	97	108	82	9	76	0.41	42	19	39	30	70	FCf	3%	97	40	4%	4%	137	6%	55%	4.1	146	$5
1st Half		103	10	1	12	1	207		1	239	266	338	83	0	0	7	73	0.30	44	20	36	27	0		0%	92	-21	0%		125	5%	100%	-3.7	71	-$
2nd Half		249	31	6	25	2	262	1	6	252	334	423	102	108	81	10	77	0.46	42	19	39	32	71	FCf	3%	99	40	4%	4%	140	6%	48%	3.7	179	$
24	**Proj**	**315**	**34**	**9**	**35**	**4**	**258**	**8**	**6**	**256**	**336**	**441**	**107**	**121**	**98**	**9**	**76**	**0.40**	**41**	**19**	**40**	**31**	**64**		**3%**	**114**	**36**	**11%**	**9%**	**123**	**7%**	**68%**	**8.8**	**138**	**$1**

Meadows,Austin

Age: 29 Pos: OF | Bats: L Ht: 6' 3" Wt: 225

Health	F	LIMA Plan	D+
PT/Exp	D	Rand Var	-5
Consist	C	MM	3221

One-time top prospect's season wrecked by mental health/anxiety issues. Two big years in his past include favorable power and Statcast metrics, but his potential return remains up in the air. Still on the short side of 30 years old, but everything starts with his well-being. Check back in March to see if he has re-entered in the playing-time picture.

Yr	Tm	PA	R	HR	RBI	SB	BA	xHR	xSB	xBA	OBP	SLG	OPS+	vL+	vR+	bb%	ct%	Eye	G	L	F	h%	HctX	QBaB	Brl%	PX	xPX	HR/F	xHR/F	Spd	SBA%	SB%	RAR	BPX	R$
19	TAM	591	83	33	89	12	291	34	11	270	364	558	128	116	132	9	75	0.41	34	23	43	33	118	BBc	13%	137	139	19%	20%	107	13%	63%	28.6	233	$2
20	TAM	152	19	4	13	2	205	5	2	194	296	371	89	51	102	11	62	0.34	26	20	54	29	93	BAd	7%	119	122	9%	11%	95	9%	67%	-5.9	-8	$
21	TAM	591	79	27	106	4	234	20	3	245	315	458	106	77	120	10	76	0.48	29	19	53	25	110	BAd	9%	127	130	13%	9%	74	6%	57%	4.5	200	$1
22	DET *	183	11	1	13	0	220	3	2	219	300	292	84	79	102	10	84	0.73	37	19	44	26	110	CBc	6%	46	80	0%	6%	119	2%	0%	-6.7	110	-$
23	DET	21	0	0	2	0	238	0	0	139	238	286	71	112	55	0	86	0.00	50	11	39	28	97	BBf	0%	35	35	0%	0%	98	0%	0%	-0.9	7	-$
1st Half		21	0	0	2	0	238	0	0	139	238	286	72	113	55	0	86	0.00	50	11	39	28	97	BBf	0%	35	35	0%	0%	98	0%	0%	-1.2	7	-$1
2nd Half																									0%										
24	**Proj**	**245**	**27**	**9**	**27**	**2**	**229**	**9**	**3**	**237**	**314**	**416**	**100**	**74**	**111**	**10**	**75**	**0.46**	**31**	**20**	**49**	**27**	**109**		**8%**	**111**	**114**	**11%**	**11%**	**97**	**7%**	**57%**	**1.9**	**105**	**$**

Meadows,Parker

Age: 24 Pos: CF | Bats: L Ht: 6' 5" Wt: 205

Health	A	LIMA Plan	C+
PT/Exp	A	Rand Var	0
Consist	A	MM	2513

3-13-.240 in 145 PA at DET. Earned a late-season callup with solid AAA year. Pull hitter who tends to chase out of the zone too much. Solid hand/eye limited his whiffs in MiLB. Safe bet for double-digit HR, but additional upside tied to SB. Might be challenged to get on base, but glove carries profile to regular reps so should get chances. (CB)

Yr	Tm	PA	R	HR	RBI	SB	BA	xHR	xSB	xBA	OBP	SLG	OPS+	vL+	vR+	bb%	ct%	Eye	G	L	F	h%	HctX	QBaB	Brl%	PX	xPX	HR/F	xHR/F	Spd	SBA%	SB%	RAR	BPX	R$
19																																			
20																																			
21																																			
22	aa	461	45	10	35	12	234		11		294	380	95			8	77	0.37				28				90				136	14%	84%		131	$1
23	DET *	634	72	14	57	21	215	3	22	224	286	365	89	99	94	9	70	0.33	35	23	42	28	96	CBb	9%	96	101	8%	8%	144	18%	86%	-5.0	68	$1
1st Half		331	35	6	26	7	214		8	227	270	348	85	0	0	7	69	0.25	44	20	36	29	0		0%	90	-21	0%		132	14%	76%	-8.6	21	$
2nd Half		303	37	8	31	13	216	3	13	229	302	385	93	98	93	11	70	0.41	35	23	42	28	96	CBb	9%	103	101	8%	8%	151	20%	93%	0.3	111	$1
24	**Proj**	**420**	**46**	**9**	**36**	**13**	**231**	**9**	**14**	**226**	**305**	**375**	**93**	**96**	**92**	**9**	**73**	**0.35**	**35**	**23**	**42**	**30**	**86**		**8%**	**88**	**91**	**7%**	**8%**	**148**	**15%**	**88%**	**0.0**	**97**	**$1**

Meckler,Wade

Age: 24 Pos: OF | Bats: L Ht: 5' 10" Wt: 178

Health	A	LIMA Plan	D
PT/Exp	F	Rand Var	-2
Consist	F	MM	1421

0-4-.232 in 64 PA at SF. High-OBP hitter struggled with contact in first taste of big-league pitching. But he put up a dazzling .371/.456/.510 at three minor league levels in his first full pro season out of Oregon State. Given his rough debut, expect more MiLB time. But he's a very worthy choice in OBP keeper leagues.

Yr	Tm	PA	R	HR	RBI	SB	BA	xHR	xSB	xBA	OBP	SLG	OPS+	vL+	vR+	bb%	ct%	Eye	G	L	F	h%	HctX	QBaB	Brl%	PX	xPX	HR/F	xHR/F	Spd	SBA%	SB%	RAR	BPX	R
19																																			
20																																			
21																																			
22																																			
23	SF *	328	42	3	29	8	288	0	13	262	373	373	102	110	74	12	72	0.48	43	37	20	39	66	FDc	0%	57	46	0%	0%	144	10%	71%	9.1	7	$
1st Half		92	18	1	12	2	358		3	250	447	446	122	0	0	14	84	1.02	44	20	36	42	0		0%	58	-21	0%		105	9%	69%	7.9	161	$
2nd Half		237	25	2	17	6	266	0	10	245	351	351	95	110	73	12	67	0.40	43	37	20	39	62	FDc	0%	57	46	0%	0%	156	11%	73%	2.0	-46	$
24	**Proj**	**210**	**27**	**2**	**17**	**4**	**263**	**2**	**8**	**237**	**362**	**358**	**99**	**148**	**91**	**11**	**75**	**0.50**	**45**	**24**	**31**	**34**	**86**		**3%**	**61**	**41**	**5%**	**5%**	**139**	**9%**	**67%**	**1.9**	**37**	**$**

ROD TRUESDELL

Melendez Jr.,MJ

Age: 25	Pos: RF LF		Health	A	LIMA Plan	B
Bats: L	Ht: 6' 1"	Wt: 190	PT/Exp	A	Rand Var	-2
			Consist	C	MM	3215

Three reasons his value will rise in 2024... 1) xHR validated by surging QBaB + elite xPX; 2) Late ct% gains give BA hope; 3) Huge overall skills bump in second half. Loss of catcher eligibility, xBA, deepening struggles vL all are opposing forces, but that 2022 vL+ suggests the latter can be solved. UP: .260 BA, 25 HR

Yr	Tm	PA	R	HR	RBI	SB	BA	xHR	xSB	xBA	OBP	SLG	OPS+	vL+	vR+	bb%	ct%	Eye	G	L	F	h%	HctX	QBaB	Brl%	PX	xPX	HR/F	xHR/F	Spd	SBA%	SB%	RAR	BPX	R$
19																																			
20																																			
21	a/a	505	73	29	79	2	251		5		336	500	115			11	73	0.47				28				143				98	8%	25%		227	$16
22	KC *	619	61	19	65	4	205	21	6	232	300	368	95	118	94	12	71	0.47	39	20	41	25	110	BBd	11%	110	122	13%	15%	101	5%	55%	-11.2	100	$7
23	KC	602	65	16	56	6	235	24	14	225	316	398	97	80	103	10	68	0.36	36	20	44	31	116	ABc	11%	109	150	10%	15%	134	7%	60%	3.9	79	$10
1st Half		319	33	6	31	4	210	12	8	201	295	338	87	94	83	11	67	0.35	35	18	47	29	107	AAc	11%	90	150	7%	13%	136	8%	67%	-8.8	7	$5
2nd Half		283	32	10	25	2	262	12	6	250	339	464	109	57	121	10	70	0.38	37	23	40	34	127	ABb	12%	129	150	14%	17%	127	6%	50%	8.3	154	$12
24	Proj	560	63	17	60	4	246	23	9	231	328	418	102	96	104	11	70	0.42	37	21	42	32	115		11%	110	139	12%	15%	112	6%	51%	9.0	117	$12

Meneses,Joey

Age: 32	Pos: DH		Health	A	LIMA Plan	B
Bats: R	Ht: 6' 3"	Wt: 215	PT/Exp	A	Rand Var	-3
			Consist	A	MM	1225

Flash of impact production in 2022 rookie season did not hold. Blame QBaB erosion, as he lost two mph of exit velocity and his barrel rate was sliced in half. Groundball lean, xHR confirm that we can't bank on double-digit homers. That leaves batting average, and xBA suggests no reason for optimism there, either. DN: .250 BA, <10 HR

Yr	Tm	PA	R	HR	RBI	SB	BA	xHR	xSB	xBA	OBP	SLG	OPS+	vL+	vR+	bb%	ct%	Eye	G	L	F	h%	HctX	QBaB	Brl%	PX	xPX	HR/F	xHR/F	Spd	SBA%	SB%	RAR	BPX	R$
19																																			
20																																			
21	a/a	351	30	9	47	0	227		1		264	407	92			5	72	0.18				29				121				84	2%	0%		85	$3
22	WAS *	633	64	25	72	2	252	10	2	256	292	423	101	152	122	5	72	0.20	45	26	30	31	113	ACa	10%	112	110	25%	20%	86	1%	100%	-5.9	55	$17
23	WAS	657	71	13	89	0	275	10	6	250	321	401	98	104	96	6	79	0.29	49	20	31	33	107	BCc	5%	79	76	9%	7%	106	0%	0%	8.3	82	$17
1st Half		330	30	2	39	0	284	4	4	238	324	371	95	94	95	6	78	0.28	51	20	30	36	93	BCf	6%	62	56	3%	6%	115	0%	0%	-2.7	36	$11
2nd Half		327	41	11	50	0	266	7	2	264	318	432	101	117	96	6	79	0.31	46	21	33	30	122	BCc	5%	97	95	14%	9%	93	0%	0%	0.3	132	$19
24	Proj	525	51	10	49	1	259	14	3	245	303	380	94	107	88	6	75	0.24	47	22	31	32	111		7%	80	91	9%	13%	98	1%	72%	-2.4	79	$13

Merrifield,Whit

Age: 35	Pos: 2B LF		Health	A	LIMA Plan	C+
Bats: R	Ht: 6' 1"	Wt: 195	PT/Exp	A	Rand Var	-2
			Consist	B	MM	1335

Seemingly a low-risk $20 investment, but warning signs abound. His speed no longer is unique (2Bmen with 20+ SB nearly doubled from 2022 to 2023) and his SB% is tanking. Can't buy him for BA either, as back-to-back mediocre xBA and second-worst exit velocity in majors point to downside there, too. Bid, but don't look here for profit.

Yr	Tm	PA	R	HR	RBI	SB	BA	xHR	xSB	xBA	OBP	SLG	OPS+	vL+	vR+	bb%	ct%	Eye	G	L	F	h%	HctX	QBaB	Brl%	PX	xPX	HR/F	xHR/F	Spd	SBA%	SB%	RAR	BPX	R$
19	KC	735	105	16	74	20	302	17	27	276	348	463	112	113	111	6	81	0.36	38	29	33	35	108	CBa	4%	83	95	9%	9%	163	16%	67%	17.5	207	$29
20	KC	265	38	9	30	12	282	7	8	275	325	440	101	101	101	5	87	0.36	37	26	37	30	83	DBb	5%	79	78	11%	9%	96	23%	80%	2.3	200	$34
21	KC	720	97	10	74	40	277	11	26	263	317	395	98	98	98	6	84	0.39	41	24	35	32	90	DCb	3%	70	85	5%	6%	123	25%	91%	7.9	169	$37
22	2 AL	550	70	11	58	16	250	10	12	250	298	375	95	100	94	7	83	0.45	41	20	39	28	91	DBc	4%	80	103	7%	6%	100	17%	76%	2.8	148	$18
23	TOR	592	66	11	67	26	272	7	24	250	318	382	95	93	96	6	82	0.36	40	22	37	32	84	DBc	2%	66	55	7%	4%	103	24%	72%	10.9	86	$20
1st Half		304	32	2	30	18	282	3	15	255	339	361	96	95	96	7	81	0.42	38	27	35	34	80	DCc	3%	56	53	3%	4%	107	28%	75%	3.1	61	$17
2nd Half		288	34	9	37	8	263	4	8	246	295	404	94	92	95	5	82	0.29	43	17	40	29	89	DBc	2%	77	56	10%	4%	97	18%	67%	1.2	114	$18
24	Proj	525	64	9	57	19	260	8	17	250	304	372	93	92	93	6	83	0.37	40	22	38	30	89		3%	67	75	6%	5%	101	21%	71%	2.8	129	$21

Mervis,Matt

Age: 26	Pos: 1B		Health	A	LIMA Plan	D
Bats: L	Ht: 6' 4"	Wt: 225	PT/Exp	B	Rand Var	+1
			Consist	B	MM	3113

3-11-.167 in 99 PA at CHC. Big-bodied, 1B-only prospect put up big numbers in AAA. However, whiff rate and chase rate backed up significantly, erasing positive 2022 gains. Hard-hit data darling continued mashing in big league stint—at least when contact was made. Plus power plays, especially with extreme pull approach. Base clogger. (CB)

Yr	Tm	PA	R	HR	RBI	SB	BA	xHR	xSB	xBA	OBP	SLG	OPS+	vL+	vR+	bb%	ct%	Eye	G	L	F	h%	HctX	QBaB	Brl%	PX	xPX	HR/F	xHR/F	Spd	SBA%	SB%	RAR	BPX	R$
19																																			
20																																			
21	aaa																																		
22	a/a	440	48	18	57	1	234		1		284	434	102			6	77	0.29				26				127				88	1%	100%		169	$9
23	CHC *	504	57	16	61	1	209	4	3	223	289	362	89	50	78	10	66	0.34	47	19	34	28	117	ADd	14%	103	139	15%	20%	78	2%	52%	-12.4	-18	$5
1st Half		238	28	8	33	0	202	4	1	232	278	355	87	50	79	10	71	0.37	47	19	34	25	125	ADd	14%	94	139	15%	20%	87	0%	0%	-8.1	25	$3
2nd Half		266	29	8	28	1	215		2	213	298	368	90	0	0	11	62	0.31	44	20	36	31	0		0%	112	-21	0%		86	3%	52%	-6.3	-43	$5
24	Proj	315	35	11	41	1	219	15	2	233	296	387	94	75	98	9	70	0.33	45	19	36	27	113		13%	109	125	15%	20%	91	2%	62%	-3.2	59	$7

Meyers,Jake

Age: 28	Pos: CF		Health	C	LIMA Plan	D
Bats: R	Ht: 6' 0"	Wt: 200	PT/Exp	B	Rand Var	+2
			Consist	C	MM	2211

First extended look in majors did not go well. That second half shows his at-bats dried up as the season went along, which should reinforce why he shouldn't be on your radar, either. In case you aren't convinced, poor batted-ball quality and holes in swing make him a drag in BA and HR, and a sub-.300 OBP zaps impact of decent wheels.

Yr	Tm	PA	R	HR	RBI	SB	BA	xHR	xSB	xBA	OBP	SLG	OPS+	vL+	vR+	bb%	ct%	Eye	G	L	F	h%	HctX	QBaB	Brl%	PX	xPX	HR/F	xHR/F	Spd	SBA%	SB%	RAR	BPX	R$
19	aa	99	8	1	5	3	193		4		273	241	71			10	75	0.44				25				21				139	24%	45%		-70	-$3
20																																			
21	HOU *	451	57	17	62	10	270	6	8	248	313	451	105	122	93	6	71	0.22	43	24	33	34	96	CDb	10%	113	117	19%	19%	95	13%	73%	5.9	58	$17
22	HOU *	319	29	5	26	3	229	2	5	226	283	337	88	80	83	7	69	0.24	54	21	25	31	77	DDc	4%	77	64	4%	8%	130	5%	76%	-6.1	-28	$2
23	HOU	341	42	10	33	5	227	10	6	230	296	382	92	106	88	8	72	0.30	42	17	40	28	85	DCf	6%	100	92	11%	11%	106	9%	71%	-1.7	54	$4
1st Half		227	28	6	22	4	225	7	5	241	313	380	95	97	94	10	71	0.37	46	20	34	29	89	DCd	8%	102	92	13%	15%	115	9%	80%	-0.9	71	$4
2nd Half		114	14	4	11	1	229	3	2	207	263	385	88	112	74	4	73	0.14	36	12	53	28	78	DBf	8%	96	91	10%	7%	91	10%	50%	-2.6	25	-$2
24	Proj	210	24	5	21	3	234	5	4	222	293	363	90	100	85	7	71	0.24	45	19	36	31	83		6%	84	86	10%	11%	98	8%	69%	-2.4	21	$5

Miller,Owen

Age: 27	Pos: 2B 1B 3B		Health	A	LIMA Plan	D
Bats: R	Ht: 6' 0"	Wt: 185	PT/Exp	B	Rand Var	0
			Consist	A	MM	1323

5-27-.261 with 13 SB in 314 PA at MIL. Second straight season that started much better than it ended. That in-year inconsistency makes him a better injury fill-in than a draft-and-hold. 90th percentile sprint speed, decent bat-to-ball skills give him good SB foundation... as long as you don't need to carry the rest of his underwhelming parts.

Yr	Tm	PA	R	HR	RBI	SB	BA	xHR	xSB	xBA	OBP	SLG	OPS+	vL+	vR+	bb%	ct%	Eye	G	L	F	h%	HctX	QBaB	Brl%	PX	xPX	HR/F	xHR/F	Spd	SBA%	SB%	RAR	BPX	R$
19	aa	547	65	10	58	4	261		6		315	380	96			7	81	0.42				30				65				98	7%	44%		89	$10
20																																			
21	CLE *	399	34	9	33	2	223	4	2	228	270	347	85	72	78	6	69	0.20	54	20	25	30	81	DDc	6%	85	80	11%	11%	99	3%	100%	-20.4	-50	$2
22	CLE	472	53	6	51	2	243	7	3	246	301	351	92	87	95	7	78	0.34	43	23	34	30	85	DCf	3%	78	66	5%	6%	100	2%	100%	-13.9	69	$8
23	MIL *	424	37	8	39	14	251	5	10	245	289	370	90	91	92	5	79	0.25	42	21	38	30	100	DCd	3%	76	95	6%	6%	85	18%	87%	-5.7	46	$8
1st Half		235	25	4	22	9	286	4	7	255	328	409	101	101	100	5	80	0.28	43	21	37	34	105	DCd	4%	79	94	6%	6%	92	19%	82%	2.6	89	$10
2nd Half		189	12	4	17	5	207	1	3	230	246	322	77	55	69	5	77	0.22	39	20	41	25	89	CBc	2%	73	95	4%	4%	85	15%	100%	-9.4	11	$0
24	Proj	280	27	4	27	9	240	5	4	239	284	349	87	82	89	6	77	0.27	44	21	35	30	90		3%	73	82	6%	6%	93	18%	84%	-2.0	40	$8

Miranda,Jose

Age: 26	Pos: 3B		Health	C	LIMA Plan	D+
Bats: R	Ht: 6' 2"	Wt: 210	PT/Exp	A	Rand Var	+5
			Consist	D	MM	1033

3-13-.211 in 152 PA at MIN. Strong rookie year had fantasy managers biting (163 ADP). That hope was wiped away after mid-season shoulder injury sent him to shelf. Sure, hit rate recovery will help, but it won't offset mediocre batted-ball quality, low swing plane, and awful xPX. As cousin Lin Manuel Miranda might say, he's throwing away his shot.

Yr	Tm	PA	R	HR	RBI	SB	BA	xHR	xSB	xBA	OBP	SLG	OPS+	vL+	vR+	bb%	ct%	Eye	G	L	F	h%	HctX	QBaB	Brl%	PX	xPX	HR/F	xHR/F	Spd	SBA%	SB%	RAR	BPX	R$
19	aa																																		
20																																			
21	a/a	569	75	23	72	2	306		3		347	490	115			6	84	0.40				33				98				81	5%	25%		208	$24
22	MIN *	572	51	16	73	1	257	15	1	255	299	412	101	115	102	5	80	0.29	42	20	38	30	121	BCf	6%	101	101	11%	11%	71	2%	50%	3.3	117	$14
23	MIN *	323	28	5	28	1	206	2	2	237	254	288	74	77	77	6	80	0.33	49	20	31	24	92	CCf	4%	47	58	8%	6%	86	1%	100%	-12.5	0	-$1
1st Half		315	28	5	28	1	208	2	2	239	257	292	75	89	78	6	80	0.33	49	21	31	24	94	CCf	5%	49	60	9%	6%	84	2%	100%	-15.8	0	$0
2nd Half		8	0	0	0	0	125	0	0	131	125	125	34	0	68	0	88	0.00	57	14	29	14	51	FCf	0%	0	15	0%	0%	110	0%	0%	-1.0	-54	-$10
24	Proj	280	30	7	32	1	259	6	1	255	311	391	96	107	93	6	82	0.34	46	21	33	29	105		5%	76	76	10%	8%	86	3%	43%	1.5	112	$8

STEPHEN NICKRAND

Mitchell,Garrett

Age: 25 Pos: CF | Bats: L Ht: 6' 3" Wt: 215
Health F | PT/Exp F | Consist D
LIMA Plan D | Rand Var +1 | MM 1503

3-7-.246 in 73 PA at MIL. Torn shoulder labrum, April surgery filled the meat of this season, sandwiched between 62 early PA and 11 to close the year. Batted-ball skills didn't support the early SLG, and contact rate issues continued. This isn't the profile of a breakout waiting to happen, but modest power/speed combo could net a few bucks.

Yr Tm	PA	R	HR	RBI	SB	BA	xHR	xSB	xBA	OBP	SLG	OPS+	vL+	vR+	bb%	ct%	Eye	G	L	F	h%	HctX	QBaB	Brl%	PX	xPX	HR/F	xHR/F	Spd	SBA%	SB%	RAR	BPX	R$
19																																		
20																																		
21 aa	143	12	2	8	4	161		3		244	224	64			10	64	0.30				23				40				108	16%	78%		-227	-$3
22 MIL *	325	38	5	32	19	253	2	12	196	308	365	95	140	117	7	62	0.21	39	21	39	39	120	ADa	10%	95	152	15%	15%	121	25%	94%	0.8	-72	$13
23 MIL *	106	12	3	7	3	215	2	4	220	277	362	87	130	102	8	66	0.25	38	26	36	29	74	DFf	10%	89	101	21%	14%	141	18%	76%	-1.7	-18	-$2
1st Half	62	9	3	6	1	259	1	1	226	306	466	106	136	103	6	59	0.17	36	30	33	39	70	DFf	9%	136	100	27%	9%	136	7%	100%	1.8	-4	-$6
2nd Half	44	3	0	1	2	149	0	2	157	236	209	60	0	93	10	76	0.48	50	0	50	20	52	DFf	17%	36	104	0%	0%	122	38%	68%	-3.3	-29	-$9
24 Proj	**350**	**40**	**6**	**28**	**13**	**234**	**6**	**10**	**215**	**295**	**327**	**85**	**92**	**85**	**8**	**70**	**0.29**	**38**	**27**	**36**	**32**	**90**		**9%**	**56**	**121**	**8%**	**8%**	**139**	**17%**	**85%**	**-4.7**	**-110**	**$7**

Monasterio,Andruw

Age: 27 Pos: 3B 2B | Bats: R Ht: 6' 0" Wt: 185
Health A | PT/Exp A | Consist C
LIMA Plan D | Rand Var 0 | MM 1403

3-27-.259 with 7 SB in 315 PA at MIL. If he hit the weight room a little harder, that A-grade launch angle could pay off. As it is, though, all the lazy flyballs put a hard lid on his BA. His path to profit is in his wheels, but he's only just now inching into a trustworthy SB%. Still, walk rate growth and a repeat of near-80% SB% suggests... UP: 20 SB

Yr Tm	PA	R	HR	RBI	SB	BA	xHR	xSB	xBA	OBP	SLG	OPS+	vL+	vR+	bb%	ct%	Eye	G	L	F	h%	HctX	QBaB	Brl%	PX	xPX	HR/F	xHR/F	Spd	SBA%	SB%	RAR	BPX	R$
19 aa	270	20	1	10	5	213		6		275	250	73			8	76	0.35				28				24				104	16%	43%		-104	-$
20																																		
21 a/a	412	54	6	45	5	245		6		311	368	93			9	65	0.27				36				93				101	10%	53%		-58	$
22 a/a	412	45	6	29	10	211		9		278	307	83			9	70	0.32				28				73				99	18%	62%		-34	$
23 MIL *	478	56	6	40	15	245	6	17	228	326	337	90	105	87	11	76	0.50	33	26	41	31	99	CAc	6%	61	95	3%	7%	125	15%	77%	-1.2	43	$
1st Half	218	27	4	18	10	226	1	8	229	336	334	92	136	78	14	73	0.62	38	24	38	29	70	CAd	6%	70	82	8%	8%	102	20%	80%	-2.3	39	$
2nd Half	260	29	2	22	5	260	4	8	229	323	340	90	95	88	8	77	0.38	32	26	42	33	106	CAc	5%	54	98	3%	5%	135	10%	71%	-3.5	39	$
24 Proj	**315**	**36**	**4**	**25**	**8**	**233**	**5**	**8**	**219**	**309**	**326**	**87**	**106**	**78**	**9**	**73**	**0.38**	**34**	**25**	**41**	**31**	**92**		**6%**	**64**	**92**	**5%**	**6%**	**125**	**14%**	**68%**	**-4.6**	**-8**	**$**

Moncada,Yoán

Age: 29 Pos: 3B | Bats: B Ht: 6' 2" Wt: 225
Health F | PT/Exp A | Consist D
LIMA Plan C+ | Rand Var -4 | MM 3225

11-40-.260 in 357 PA at CHW. BPX tells a stark story: This is a stagnant, mediocre skill set. That's at least in part due to another metric—the Health grade. Back woes felled him this time around. Healthy late, he'll hang his hat on a strong finish (.825 OPS in Aug/Sept). But note this: His only really good season is about to age out of this book.

Yr Tm	PA	R	HR	RBI	SB	BA	xHR	xSB	xBA	OBP	SLG	OPS+	vL+	vR+	bb%	ct%	Eye	G	L	F	h%	HctX	QBaB	Brl%	PX	xPX	HR/F	xHR/F	Spd	SBA%	SB%	RAR	BPX	R$
19 CHW *	581	88	27	84	10	317	28	11	264	365	551	127	118	130	7	70	0.25	42	23	35	41	96	ACa	12%	135	103	20%	23%	125	9%	77%	35.2	159	$2
20 CHW	231	28	6	24	0	225	6	3	213	320	385	94	92	94	12	64	0.39	40	22	37	32	86	CCf	6%	103	101	13%	13%	144	0%	0%	-4.8	32	$
21 CHW	616	74	14	61	3	263	17	3	247	375	412	108	95	113	14	70	0.54	44	27	30	35	116	BCc	8%	102	96	13%	16%	87	3%	60%	15.5	62	$1
22 CHW *	456	44	13	54	2	213	14	1	216	271	358	89	110	83	7	71	0.27	39	17	43	27	95	CBc	10%	101	102	10%	11%	66	3%	61%	-11.1	0	$
23 CHW *	405	43	12	43	1	267	11	2	248	311	432	101	104	98	6	67	0.19	42	26	32	37	90	BCb	10%	115	105	15%	15%	83	1%	100%	10.6	0	$
1st Half	164	20	5	16	1	253	2	2	246	298	413	97	85	90	6	70	0.21	52	19	29	33	55	CCc	6%	106	42	10%	7%	99	3%	100%	0.2	32	$
2nd Half	241	23	8	28	0	276	9	1	257	320	446	103	115	104	6	65	0.18	35	32	33	39	116	BBa	13%	122	153	19%	21%	75	0%	0%	5.4	-14	$
24 Proj	**455**	**50**	**14**	**51**	**2**	**252**	**15**	**3**	**239**	**314**	**413**	**100**	**105**	**98**	**8**	**68**	**0.27**	**41**	**24**	**35**	**34**	**96**		**10%**	**110**	**104**	**14%**	**15%**	**84**	**2%**	**75%**	**6.9**	**21**	**$1**

Mondesi,Adalberto

Age: 28 Pos: SS | Bats: B Ht: 6' 1" Wt: 200
Health F | PT/Exp F | Consist D
LIMA Plan D+ | Rand Var | MM 2503

Missed another entire season following ACL tear and subsequent May 2022 surgery. That's no typo—that surgery was two years ago. Given that speed drove most of his value before the injury, a knee not healing properly is NOT a good sign. Wait until he shows that he's all the way back before investing.

Yr Tm	PA	R	HR	RBI	SB	BA	xHR	xSB	xBA	OBP	SLG	OPS+	vL+	vR+	bb%	ct%	Eye	G	L	F	h%	HctX	QBaB	Brl%	PX	xPX	HR/F	xHR/F	Spd	SBA%	SB%	RAR	BPX	R$
19 KC *	488	62	10	64	45	258	14	31	226	293	418	98	88	103	5	67	0.15	47	19	34	37	88	CCd	9%	95	82	9%	14%	152	55%	85%	-5.2	4	$2
20 KC	233	33	6	22	24	256	8	19	216	294	416	94	136	80	5	68	0.16	49	13	39	35	100	DCf	7%	101	102	11%	15%	160	67%	75%	-4.2	52	$4
21 KC *	201	25	8	21	19	209	7	10	218	241	392	87	113	93	4	67	0.13	43	14	43	27	105	CBf	13%	118	146	18%	21%	115	70%	89%	-5.8	31	$
22 KC	54	3	0	3	5	140	1	3	132	204	140	49	14	57	7	60	0.20	52	12	36	23	79	FFf	3%	0	115	0%	11%	102	45%	100%	-4.1	-386	-$
23																																		
1st Half																																		
2nd Half																																		
24 Proj	**280**	**37**	**6**	**32**	**15**	**239**	**12**	**19**	**216**	**275**	**386**	**91**	**105**	**86**	**4**	**67**	**0.14**	**48**	**14**	**38**	**33**	**93**		**7%**	**99**	**112**	**9%**	**17%**	**135**	**36%**	**78%**	**-2.0**	**25**	**$**

Moniak,Mickey

Age: 26 Pos: CF | Bats: L Ht: 6' 2" Wt: 195
Health C | PT/Exp B | Consist C
LIMA Plan C | Rand Var -5 | MM 4403

14-45-.280 with 6 SB in 323 PA at LAA. PRO: Took a big step up in batted-ball skills, with solid barrel rate; FB tilt point to power upside. CON: Awful plate skills are getting even worse; skills overall crashed in 2nd half; fortunate hit rate propped up BA (see xBA); still floundered vL. Unless plate skills improve, stat regression is all but assured.

Yr Tm	PA	R	HR	RBI	SB	BA	xHR	xSB	xBA	OBP	SLG	OPS+	vL+	vR+	bb%	ct%	Eye	G	L	F	h%	HctX	QBaB	Brl%	PX	xPX	HR/F	xHR/F	Spd	SBA%	SB%	RAR	BPX	R$
19 aa	495	58	11	62	14	241		12		288	421	98			6	73	0.24				31				99				140	18%	81%		104	$
20 PHI	18	3	0	0	0	214	0	0	169	389	214	80	0	98	22	57	0.67	63	25	13	38	58	CFf		0	-26	0%	0%	121	0%	0%	-0.8	-352	-
21 PHI *	425	33	13	49	4	208	1	6	203	255	364	85	0	63	6	67	0.19	59	6	35	27	76	CFc	6%	96	154	17%	17%	130	8%	62%	-18.8	-4	
22 2 TM *	232	25	8	19	4	205	3	5	201	237	366	86	33	78	4	65	0.12	38	15	48	27	63	FBf	8%	116	80	10%	10%	121	22%	53%	-8.6	0	
23 LAA *	457	51	19	59	7	271	16	10	232	292	479	105	74	118	3	65	0.09	31	24	45	38	97	CAb	13%	139	133	16%	18%	127	13%	63%	12.7	57	$
1st Half	253	34	14	38	3	277	8	5	236	297	542	115	14	147	3	67	0.09	22	19	58	35	103	CAa	17%	164	174	20%	18%	124	11%	60%	11.0	164	$
2nd Half	204	17	5	21	4	264	8	5	217	289	401	93	83	96	3	61	0.08	37	27	36	41	91	CBc	11%	104	106	12%	19%	118	14%	67%	-0.4	-100	
24 Proj	**385**	**40**	**15**	**43**	**6**	**235**	**17**	**8**	**219**	**273**	**422**	**95**	**61**	**102**	**4**	**66**	**0.12**	**35**	**20**	**45**	**32**	**83**		**11%**	**124**	**113**	**13%**	**16%**	**131**	**15%**	**62%**	**-2.0**	**13**	**$**

Montero,Elehuris

Age: 25 Pos: 1B | Bats: R Ht: 6' 3" Wt: 235
Health A | PT/Exp A | Consist B
LIMA Plan C+ | Rand Var -3 | MM 4015

11-39-.243 in 307 PA at COL. Power prospect definitely hits the ball hard. But as QBaB shows, he needs a swing-path adjustment to realize his HR potential. In a small Sept sample, though, he showed it (6 HR, 39/42 G/F ratio). Shaky an declining plate skills aren't encouraging, but if he can build on those late gains... UP: 30 HR

Yr Tm	PA	R	HR	RBI	SB	BA	xHR	xSB	xBA	OBP	SLG	OPS+	vL+	vR+	bb%	ct%	Eye	G	L	F	h%	HctX	QBaB	Brl%	PX	xPX	HR/F	xHR/F	Spd	SBA%	SB%	RAR	BPX	R$
19 aa	236	20	6	15	0	170		1		210	278	68			5	65	0.15				23				69				98	3%	0%		-152	
20																																		
21 a/a	467	45	20	57	0	248		1		306	443	103			8	73	0.31				29				113				94	0%	0%		108	
22 COL *	454	45	15	50	2	244	5	3	235	281	414	98	113	90	5	70	0.17	37	22	41	31	103	BCd	9%	119	127	13%	10%	101	5%	49%	-6.7	62	
23 COL *	457	58	21	66	0	260	6	5	236	298	465	104	93	100	5	67	0.16	45	18	38	34	110	CCf	7%	132	125	17%	9%	114	1%	0%	10.0	68	$
1st Half	233	27	11	35	0	259	1	2	238	289	456	102	72	76	4	69	0.13	47	17	36	33	101	CCd	5%	121	81	9%	4%	113	0%	0%	2.3	61	$
2nd Half	224	31	10	32	0	262	5	2	236	308	475	106	109	111	6	64	0.19	44	18	38	36	112	CDf	8%	145	151	21%	12%	108	2%	0%	4.5	71	$
24 Proj	**525**	**60**	**22**	**67**	**1**	**246**	**12**	**4**	**233**	**293**	**434**	**100**	**103**	**97**	**5**	**68**	**0.18**	**42**	**19**	**39**	**32**	**106**		**8%**	**122**	**124**	**16%**	**9%**	**97**	**2%**	**27%**	**2.1**	**50**	**$**

Morel,Christopher

Age: 25 Pos: DH OF | Bats: R Ht: 5' 11" Wt: 145
Health A | PT/Exp A | Consist C
LIMA Plan C+ | Rand Var -1 | MM 4425

26-70-.247 with 6 SB in 429 PA at CHC. Despite mid-year slump, a solid growth season. Top-drawer power skills belie his diminutive stature, with an elite exit velocity/barrels combo. Took a step up in SB success also, opening up anothe potential path to value. Ready to break out? Poor contact rate says not yet. But keep an eye on 2025.

Yr Tm	PA	R	HR	RBI	SB	BA	xHR	xSB	xBA	OBP	SLG	OPS+	vL+	vR+	bb%	ct%	Eye	G	L	F	h%	HctX	QBaB	Brl%	PX	xPX	HR/F	xHR/F	Spd	SBA%	SB%	RAR	BPX	R$
19																																		
20																																		
21 a/a	438	48	14	49	13	197		10		259	359	85			8	64	0.23				27				107				116	20%	80%		-15	$
22 CHC *	539	69	20	60	12	237	21	19	236	300	429	103	88	111	8	65	0.26	50	18	33	32	104	CDd	14%	139	110	21%	27%	163	19%	53%	-8.2	128	$
23 CHC *	555	82	33	90	9	252	24	15	248	316	513	113	120	109	9	64	0.26	42	17	41	33	109	ACf	16%	170	133	25%	23%	147	11%	73%	22.0	196	$
1st Half	295	51	22	57	4	274	11	8	257	332	579	125	94	141	8	63	0.24	45	11	43	35	116	BCf	16%	197	156	33%	24%	151	10%	63%	15.4	264	$
2nd Half	260	31	11	33	5	226	13	7	237	304	436	100	137	88	9	65	0.29	40	21	39	30	104	ACd	16%	141	116	19%	22%	140	11%	83%	-2.0	118	$
24 Proj	**525**	**70**	**27**	**70**	**11**	**235**	**28**	**15**	**241**	**301**	**468**	**106**	**102**	**106**	**8**	**64**	**0.25**	**45**	**17**	**38**	**31**	**107**		**15%**	**154**	**124**	**23%**	**24%**	**139**	**15%**	**67%**	**6.9**	**131**	**$**

ROD TRUESDELL

Moreno,Gabriel

Age: 24	Pos: CA		Health	A	LIMA Plan	B
Bats: R	Ht: 5' 11"	Wt: 195	PT/Exp	B	Rand Var	0
			Consist	D	MM	1245

That 2nd half will put him on some breakout radars. However, hope for more power dashed by swing plane, mediocre batted ball quality, and tempering xPX. Late plate discipline gains back batting average potential. A full season's worth of PA more likely to net step forward than a full breakout given work-in-progress power. For now... UP: .300+ BA

Yr	Tm	PA	R	HR	RBI	SB	BA	xHR	xSB	xBA	OBP	SLG	OPS+	vL+	vR+	bb%	ct%	Eye	G	L	F	h%	HctX	QBaB	Brl%	PX	xPX	HR/F	xHR/F	Spd	SBA%	SB%	RAR	BPX	R$
19																																			
20																																			
21	a/a	147	24	7	38	1	332		2		385	567	131			8	81	0.44				37				128				92	8%	28%		273	$8
22	TOR *	329	38	4	38	6	289	1	6	250	336	374	101	101	105	7	81	0.38	57	18	25	35	64	BDd	2%	61	26	7%	7%	112	8%	83%	8.1	79	$11
23	ARI	380	33	7	50	6	284	8	7	270	339	408	102	121	93	8	78	0.39	55	23	22	35	100	BFc	5%	77	63	12%	13%	100	8%	75%	15.0	75	$10
1st Half		221	16	2	26	4	271	4	4	244	308	350	90	128	71	6	76	0.25	58	21	22	35	93	BFc	4%	56	56	6%	11%	94	7%	100%	2.0	-32	$3
2nd Half		159	17	5	24	2	304	4	4	306	384	493	118	110	121	11	80	0.63	50	27	22	35	110	BFb	5%	108	72	20%	16%	109	9%	50%	11.7	232	$7
24	**Proj**	**490**	**55**	**9**	**64**	**7**	**290**	**9**	**9**	**271**	**347**	**416**	**105**	**111**	**102**	**8**	**80**	**0.44**	**55**	**22**	**23**	**35**	**87**		**4%**	**78**	**50**	**11%**	**11%**	**103**	**8%**	**68%**	**22.6**	**132**	**$17**

Mountcastle,Ryan

Age: 27	Pos: 1B DH		Health	B	LIMA Plan	B
Bats: R	Ht: 6' 4"	Wt: 230	PT/Exp	A	Rand Var	0
			Consist	A	MM	3235

18-68-.270 in 470 PA at BAL. Month-long bout with vertigo cut into counting stats. 1st half xPX paired with impactful batted ball quality points to possible return to 30 HR, especially if vR rebounds. Just plan to surround him with some BA padding, since low-contact approach, shoddy xBA history give little hope for movement there.

Yr	Tm	PA	R	HR	RBI	SB	BA	xHR	xSB	xBA	OBP	SLG	OPS+	vL+	vR+	bb%	ct%	Eye	G	L	F	h%	HctX	QBaB	Brl%	PX	xPX	HR/F	xHR/F	Spd	SBA%	SB%	RAR	BPX	R$
19	aaa	540	66	22	68	2	281		2		307	466	107			4	73	0.14				35				105				89	3%	60%		48	$15
20	BAL	140	12	5	23	0	333	5	2	230	386	492	117	86	126	8	76	0.37	44	19	37	41	107	CCf	7%	88	91	14%	14%	116	2%	0%	5.6	112	$13
21	BAL	586	77	33	89	4	255	29	4	248	309	487	109	115	106	7	70	0.25	35	22	43	30	97	CBd	12%	139	125	20%	18%	92	6%	57%	7.5	131	$20
22	BAL	609	62	22	85	4	250	33	3	242	305	423	103	97	105	7	72	0.28	37	22	41	31	111	ABb	15%	117	138	13%	20%	80	4%	80%	4.7	79	$18
23	BAL *	527	68	19	72	3	259	23	6	244	315	425	101	142	87	8	73	0.31	44	20	37	32	101	ACc	12%	101	120	15%	19%	96	3%	75%	11.3	71	$15
1st Half		298	37	12	42	2	222	16	2	239	261	399	90	138	73	5	73	0.20	40	19	41	26	102	ABc	15%	105	144	15%	21%	94	4%	100%	-7.8	57	$12
2nd Half		229	31	7	30	1	309	7	3	247	385	462	114	145	106	11	74	0.48	48	21	31	39	99	ADc	8%	94	88	16%	16%	101	3%	50%	11.6	89	$14
24	**Proj**	**560**	**69**	**25**	**80**	**3**	**259**	**26**	**5**	**250**	**316**	**454**	**106**	**122**	**98**	**8**	**73**	**0.31**	**41**	**21**	**38**	**31**	**103**		**12%**	**118**	**118**	**17%**	**18%**	**95**	**4%**	**65%**	**13.3**	**86**	**$21**

Moustakas,Mike

Age: 35	Pos: 3B 1B		Health	F	LIMA Plan	D
Bats: L	Ht: 6' 0"	Wt: 225	PT/Exp	B	Rand Var	-3
			Consist	A	MM	2213

Ignored by market after rough 2022 (642 ADP), those who took the plunge got a few decent bounceback stats. But this isn't a different player than the 2020-2022 version. QBaB was unconvinced and mediocre vR+ will keep at-bats at risk. First half hit rate offered false hope; as that dips to prior norm, BA will fall with it.

Yr	Tm	PA	R	HR	RBI	SB	BA	xHR	xSB	xBA	OBP	SLG	OPS+	vL+	vR+	bb%	ct%	Eye	G	L	F	h%	HctX	QBaB	Brl%	PX	xPX	HR/F	xHR/F	Spd	SBA%	SB%	RAR	BPX	R$
19	MIL	584	80	35	87	3	254	31	1	277	329	516	117	122	114	9	81	0.54	36	19	45	25	117	BBf	10%	127	129	18%	16%	76	2%	100%	12.5	259	$18
20	CIN	163	13	8	27	1	230	6	0	256	331	468	106	85	114	11	74	0.50	36	20	44	25	114	CBc	10%	137	123	17%	13%	59	3%	100%	-1.6	192	$9
21	CIN	206	21	6	22	0	208	5	0	232	282	372	90	45	101	9	75	0.39	36	19	46	24	83	CAf	0%	104	64	9%	8%	56	0%	0%	-6.9	73	-$1
22	CIN	285	30	7	25	2	214	7	1	200	295	345	91	79	94	8	70	0.32	35	15	50	28	95	CAf	6%	95	87	8%	8%	75	3%	100%	-6.8	-3	$1
23	2 TM	386	43	12	48	0	247	10	2	228	293	392	93	73	99	6	73	0.24	34	21	45	31	98	CAf	6%	89	105	10%	8%	83	0%	0%	1.0	7	$7
1st Half		158	22	5	19	0	259	4	1	235	348	422	105	94	108	12	67	0.42	26	28	46	35	93	BAd	8%	112	105	12%	9%	73	0%	0%	2.8	18	$1
2nd Half		228	21	7	29	0	240	6	1	221	254	373	85	59	91	2	77	0.08	38	17	44	28	100	CBf	5%	77	104	9%	8%	86	0%	0%	-7.8	4	$5
24	**Proj**	**280**	**31**	**9**	**33**	**1**	**233**	**8**	**1**	**225**	**294**	**386**	**93**	**75**	**99**	**7**	**73**	**0.30**	**34**	**19**	**46**	**29**	**96**		**5%**	**97**	**96**	**10%**	**9%**	**74**	**1%**	**100%**	**-0.6**	**38**	**$7**

Mullins II,Cedric

Age: 29	Pos: CF		Health	B	LIMA Plan	B
Bats: L	Ht: 5' 8"	Wt: 175	PT/Exp	A	Rand Var	+3
			Consist	C	MM	2425

15-74-.233 with 19 SB in 455 PA at BAL. Step backwards driven by sharp dips in BA and SB. Mid-season groin strain explains the Spd dip, but not the longer trend—prior impact speed now on a two-year nosedive. xBA, xHR also in freefalls, so that 2021 is a clear outlier now. This projection is a reasonable baseline now; still a $20+ asset.

Yr	Tm	PA	R	HR	RBI	SB	BA	xHR	xSB	xBA	OBP	SLG	OPS+	vL+	vR+	bb%	ct%	Eye	G	L	F	h%	HctX	QBaB	Brl%	PX	xPX	HR/F	xHR/F	Spd	SBA%	SB%	RAR	BPX	R$
19	BAL *	580	68	9	38	28	188	1	20	211	249	279	73	34	50	7	80	0.41	53	8	39	22	52	DBf	2%	47	18	0%	5%	120	31%	78%	-38.8	41	$9
20	BAL	153	16	3	12	7	271	2	7	229	315	407	96	65	106	5	74	0.22	43	22	35	35	64	FCf	3%	73	44	9%	6%	152	24%	78%	-1.2	44	$14
21	BAL	674	91	30	59	30	291	23	26	270	360	518	121	107	128	9	79	0.47	39	20	41	32	107	CCd	8%	125	109	15%	12%	137	22%	79%	37.4	296	$37
22	BAL	670	89	16	64	34	258	13	26	237	318	403	102	81	111	7	79	0.37	39	18	44	30	93	CBf	5%	92	92	8%	6%	120	27%	77%	8.3	148	$32
23	BAL *	486	52	16	76	19	223	10	14	232	294	398	94	95	99	9	76	0.42	35	16	49	26	93	CAf	6%	103	83	10%	7%	93	23%	82%	1.8	121	$13
1st Half		268	29	9	41	13	240	5	11	240	334	428	104	108	106	12	78	0.64	36	15	49	27	89	CAd	6%	106	70	10%	6%	116	25%	81%	6.5	207	$16
2nd Half		218	24	7	35	6	204	5	4	222	245	363	82	73	91	5	74	0.21	35	16	49	24	98	CAf	6%	100	98	11%	8%	69	20%	83%	-6.8	25	$7
24	**Proj**	**560**	**68**	**18**	**70**	**24**	**240**	**13**	**19**	**237**	**302**	**410**	**98**	**87**	**102**	**8**	**77**	**0.36**	**38**	**17**	**45**	**28**	**92**		**6%**	**100**	**86**	**10%**	**7%**	**105**	**24%**	**80%**	**5.1**	**135**	**$23**

Muncy,Max

Age: 33	Pos: 3B		Health	B	LIMA Plan	B+
Bats: L	Ht: 6' 0"	Wt: 215	PT/Exp	A	Rand Var	+2
			Consist	D	MM	4125

The bounceback we were expecting. Can it stick? PRO: Highest exit velocity + launch angle of career; 30+ HR fully supported by xHR. CON: Sliding vL+ puts everyday work at risk; chronically low hit rate cemented in profile, so we have to use actual BA as barometer. In short, buy the pop, but don't expect BA to get out of mud.

Yr	Tm	PA	R	HR	RBI	SB	BA	xHR	xSB	xBA	OBP	SLG	OPS+	vL+	vR+	bb%	ct%	Eye	G	L	F	h%	HctX	QBaB	Brl%	PX	xPX	HR/F	xHR/F	Spd	SBA%	SB%	RAR	BPX	R$
19	LA	589	101	35	98	4	251	31	3	262	374	515	123	124	122	15	69	0.60	38	23	39	29	110	BBb	12%	146	150	27%	23%	82	3%	80%	14.7	193	$20
20	LA	248	36	12	27	1	192	14	1	217	331	389	96	104	91	16	70	0.65	44	14	42	21	118	CBd	12%	107	168	20%	23%	86	2%	100%	-8.4	108	$11
21	LA	592	95	36	94	2	249	40	0	279	368	527	123	131	120	14	76	0.69	38	21	41	26	122	ABc	16%	153	154	23%	26%	67	2%	67%	29.4	292	$20
22	LA	565	69	21	69	2	196	25	1	226	329	384	101	95	103	16	70	0.64	31	19	50	23	125	BAc	13%	128	184	13%	15%	76	1%	100%	-5.3	128	$7
23	LA	579	95	36	105	1	212	34	3	246	333	475	110	86	120	15	68	0.56	33	17	49	23	105	AAc	15%	157	148	22%	21%	70	2%	33%	16.3	182	$17
1st Half		272	42	18	48	1	189	17	2	233	320	454	106	84	115	16	65	0.53	34	15	51	19	107	BAc	16%	162	167	24%	22%	64	5%	33%	1.5	154	$15
2nd Half		307	53	18	57	0	231	17	1	257	345	494	113	88	125	14	71	0.58	33	19	48	25	103	AAd	13%	153	132	20%	19%	80	0%	0%	11.0	218	$23
24	**Proj**	**560**	**88**	**31**	**91**	**2**	**220**	**32**	**2**	**245**	**342**	**463**	**110**	**98**	**115**	**15**	**70**	**0.59**	**34**	**18**	**47**	**24**	**113**		**14%**	**145**	**158**	**20%**	**20%**	**74**	**2%**	**60%**	**18.6**	**187**	**$19**

Murphy,Sean

Age: 29	Pos: CA		Health	A	LIMA Plan	B
Bats: R	Ht: 6' 3"	Wt: 228	PT/Exp	A	Rand Var	0
			Consist	B	MM	4145

Missed five games with a hamstring issue in late June; never went on the IL but could the 2nd half swoon be related? Still a lot to like as exit velocity and Brl% jumped, three-year climb in xBA puts BA spike on table, and xPX and HctX were career highs. If the hammy is to blame, there's more CA1 goodness in store.

Yr	Tm	PA	R	HR	RBI	SB	BA	xHR	xSB	xBA	OBP	SLG	OPS+	vL+	vR+	bb%	ct%	Eye	G	L	F	h%	HctX	QBaB	Brl%	PX	xPX	HR/F	xHR/F	Spd	SBA%	SB%	RAR	BPX	R$
19	OAK *	191	33	11	31	0	253	3	1	281	320	512	115	103	135	9	70	0.33	46	27	27	30	85	BDb	8%	147	99	40%	30%	89	3%	0%	5.6	159	$4
20	OAK	140	21	7	14	0	233	7	1	233	364	457	109	99	113	17	68	0.65	43	18	39	28	94	ABc	13%	134	109	23%	23%	101	0%	0%	5.1	184	$7
21	OAK	448	47	17	59	0	216	19	0	237	306	405	98	86	103	9	71	0.35	39	20	41	26	99	CBc	11%	120	115	15%	17%	64	0%	0%	-0.6	73	$5
22	OAK	611	67	18	66	1	250	23	1	260	332	426	107	119	103	9	77	0.45	42	20	38	29	108	CCd	11%	118	104	11%	15%	83	1%	100%	16.3	162	$14
23	ATL	438	65	21	68	0	251	24	2	265	365	478	115	119	114	11	74	0.50	41	21	38	29	116	ACc	16%	135	124	20%	23%	73	0%	0%	23.2	171	$13
1st Half		253	37	14	48	0	295	16	1	285	391	558	130	141	126	11	73	0.47	38	24	39	34	131	ACc	18%	159	148	23%	26%	75	0%	0%	23.6	239	$20
2nd Half		185	28	7	20	0	190	8	1	237	330	366	94	83	97	13	74	0.55	46	16	38	21	96	BCc	13%	103	90	16%	19%	85	0%	0%	-1.1	111	$2
24	**Proj**	**490**	**68**	**24**	**66**	**0**	**258**	**24**	**2**	**260**	**360**	**481**	**115**	**113**	**116**	**11**	**74**	**0.47**	**42**	**20**	**38**	**30**	**106**		**13%**	**135**	**110**	**20%**	**20%**	**74**	**0%**	**62%**	**28.8**	**150**	**$18**

Naylor,Bo

Age: 24	Pos: CA		Health	A	LIMA Plan	C+
Bats: L	Ht: 6' 0"	Wt: 205	PT/Exp	A	Rand Var	+2
			Consist	C	MM	4225

11-32-.237 with 5 SB in 230 PA at CLE. Former 9D prospect showed those flashes in rookie year, including monstrous Sept (1.124 OPS, 85% ct% in 68 PA). There's work to be done, since exit velocity and Brl% are subpar and southpaws have his number. But among young backstops, he's one of the better growth stocks in game.

Yr	Tm	PA	R	HR	RBI	SB	BA	xHR	xSB	xBA	OBP	SLG	OPS+	vL+	vR+	bb%	ct%	Eye	G	L	F	h%	HctX	QBaB	Brl%	PX	xPX	HR/F	xHR/F	Spd	SBA%	SB%	RAR	BPX	R$
19																																			
20																																			
21	aa	343	33	8	36	8	171		4		243	292	74			9	61	0.25				25				90				92	13%	100%		-138	$0
22	CLE *	477	48	14	45	13	214	0	10	198	302	378	96	0	0	11	66	0.38	0	33	67	29	97	AAa		122	69	0%	0%	99	16%	75%	2.3	59	$10
23	CLE *	483	64	20	65	6	221	7	6	241	328	423	102	89	116	14	73	0.59	31	19	50	25	75	CAd	8%	123	99	15%	10%	76	7%	74%	15.6	154	$10
1st Half		293	38	10	35	1	201	0	3	253	310	362	92	108	62	14	71	0.54	38	29	33	24	14	CCc	5%	99	15	14%	0%	91	4%	38%	-0.8	68	$7
2nd Half		190	26	10	30	5	253	7	3	272	358	519	118	87	129	14	77	0.68	30	18	53	27	90	CAd	9%	157	113	15%	11%	75	11%	100%	13.9	300	$12
24	**Proj**	**455**	**53**	**18**	**55**	**10**	**237**	**5**	**8**	**239**	**332**	**438**	**106**	**102**	**107**	**12**	**69**	**0.46**	**33**	**22**	**45**	**29**	**60**		**7%**	**130**	**74**	**15%**	**4%**	**81**	**11%**	**83%**	**18.5**	**104**	**$16**

STEPHEN NICKRAND

Naylor,Josh

Age: 27 Pos: 1B DH | Bats: L Ht: 5' 11" Wt: 250
Health D | PT/Exp A | Consist C | LIMA Plan B+ | Rand Var -4 | MM 2055

Missed a month with a strained oblique. Otherwise, superb from May on, including post-injury (sans a bit of power). With terrific hard contact skills + vL gains, fine BA is cemented in profile now. New shift rules helped. While power isn't explosive, with his foundational contact rate and prime age, he could take another small next step.

Yr	Tm	PA	R	HR	RBI	SB	BA	xHR	xSB	xBA	OBP	SLG	OPS+	vL+	vR+	bb%	ct%	Eye	G	L	F	h%	HctX	QBaB	Brl%	PX	xPX	HR/F	xHR/F	Spd	SBA%	SB%	RAR	BPX
19	SD *	522	65	15	62	2	257	6	0	261	321	420	103	94	100	9	80	0.46	53	17	30	30	114	BFf	6%	91	89	14%	11%	49	3%	63%	-11.1	93
20	2 TM	103	13	1	6	1	247	1	1	269	291	330	82	156	76	5	88	0.42	53	22	25	27	100	CDd	4%	41	44	5%	5%	92	4%	100%	-6.0	88
21	CLE	249	28	7	21	1	253	7	0	254	301	399	96	70	111	6	81	0.31	49	19	32	29	93	BDf	7%	85	84	12%	12%	60	2%	100%	-3.4	85
22	CLE	498	47	20	79	6	256	18	2	277	319	452	109	72	122	8	82	0.48	49	17	34	27	126	BCf	9%	118	89	16%	14%	45	6%	86%	10.5	186
23	CLE	495	52	17	97	10	308	17	7	284	354	489	115	111	116	7	85	0.49	43	20	37	33	116	CCd	8%	101	94	12%	12%	48	10%	77%	31.9	179
1st Half		300	31	10	60	5	297	11	3	273	337	471	111	91	117	6	82	0.37	41	21	38	33	116	BBc	10%	100	100	11%	12%	52	8%	83%	11.3	139
2nd Half		195	21	7	37	5	324	6	4	301	379	517	121	130	115	8	89	0.79	46	19	35	33	117	CDd	6%	103	84	13%	11%	50	13%	71%	13.6	257
24	**Proj**	**560**	**60**	**19**	**90**	**9**	**284**	**18**	**5**	**277**	**337**	**458**	**109**	**100**	**113**	**7**	**84**	**0.48**	**47**	**19**	**34**	**31**	**114**		**8%**	**98**	**87**	**13%**	**12%**	**45**	**8%**	**78%**	**21.2**	**173**

Neto,Zach

Age: 23 Pos: SS | Bats: R Ht: 6' 0" Wt: 185
Health C | PT/Exp D | Consist A | LIMA Plan C+ | Rand Var 0 | MM 2225

9-34-.225 with 5 SB in 329 PA at LAA. The 13th overall draft choice in 2022, he spent two separate months on the IL (oblique strain, lower back pain), and the back bothered him in between, so it's fair to mulligan that 2nd half collapse. Fared well early and the power emerged. BA may take awhile to arrive, but... UP: 20+ HR

Yr	Tm	PA	R	HR	RBI	SB	BA	xHR	xSB	xBA	OBP	SLG	OPS+	vL+	vR+	bb%	ct%	Eye	G	L	F	h%	HctX	QBaB	Brl%	PX	xPX	HR/F	xHR/F	Spd	SBA%	SB%	RAR	BPX
19																																		
20																																		
21																																		
22	aa	127	15	3	15	3	267		3		298	398	99			4	73	0.16				35				97				89	18%	54%		24
23	LAA *	374	49	13	43	7	241	11	6	243	294	415	97	106	90	7	72	0.27	38	21	42	29	93	CBf	9%	111	117	10%	12%	90	9%	88%	4.7	75
1st Half		230	32	9	30	7	278	7	5	272	330	470	109	112	104	7	77	0.33	41	23	36	32	103	CCc	9%	115	131	12%	14%	89	12%	100%	8.5	154
2nd Half		144	17	5	14	0	184	4	2	198	241	336	78	97	69	7	65	0.22	33	16	51	24	77	CAf	8%	105	91	8%	10%	106	4%	0%	-7.4	-25
24	**Proj**	**525**	**69**	**16**	**64**	**9**	**250**	**18**	**11**	**237**	**330**	**401**	**100**	**118**	**96**	**7**	**74**	**0.29**	**38**	**21**	**41**	**31**	**97**		**8%**	**97**	**107**	**10%**	**12%**	**95**	**10%**	**67%**	**3.8**	**39**

Newman,Kevin

Age: 30 Pos: 3B | Bats: R Ht: 6' 0" Wt: 195
Health D | PT/Exp B | Consist C | LIMA Plan D | Rand Var +1 | MM 1331

3-28-.253 with 8 SB in 253 PA at CIN. Missed time in 2nd half with a strained oblique. Reliable-but-weak contact is his thing, which results in a steady-but-empty skill set. Released in Sept by CIN, he could find a home as a utility player who hits lefties a little. But it's not like those guys are hard to find, and at 30, we've seen his "upside" already.

Yr	Tm	PA	R	HR	RBI	SB	BA	xHR	xSB	xBA	OBP	SLG	OPS+	vL+	vR+	bb%	ct%	Eye	G	L	F	h%	HctX	QBaB	Brl%	PX	xPX	HR/F	xHR/F	Spd	SBA%	SB%	RAR	BPX
19	PIT *	565	65	12	65	16	302	7	21	281	342	435	108	101	113	6	87	0.46	49	22	28	33	80	DDb	2%	63	50	10%	6%	151	16%	64%	7.2	207
20	PIT	172	12	1	10	0	224	1	1	236	281	276	74	100	67	7	87	0.57	49	21	30	25	96	DDf	1%	31	74	2%	2%	114	2%	0%	-9.8	84
21	PIT	554	50	5	39	6	226	4	6	258	265	309	79	82	77	5	92	0.66	44	20	36	24	83	FDf	2%	45	50	3%	2%	119	6%	86%	-28.4	200
22	PIT *	359	35	2	28	8	277	2	7	263	314	368	97	117	87	5	83	0.32	43	26	31	33	75	DCc	2%	64	45	3%	3%	112	11%	80%	-2.3	103
23	CIN *	294	31	3	30	8	238	3	6	266	291	333	85	110	78	7	83	0.44	45	24	31	28	96	DCc	3%	62	66	5%	5%	84	13%	89%	-4.0	82
1st Half		214	24	3	26	6	262	2	5	274	319	377	95	125	76	8	85	0.57	44	23	33	29	93	DCc	3%	71	65	5%	4%	83	13%	86%	0.2	143
2nd Half		80	7	0	4	2	175	0	2	259	215	217	58	63	103	5	77	0.22	48	31	21	23	115	CFa	0%	35	74	0%	0%	99	13%	100%	-6.2	-82
24	**Proj**	**175**	**17**	**2**	**14**	**4**	**236**	**1**	**3**	**259**	**291**	**322**	**84**	**85**	**83**	**6**	**83**	**0.36**	**45**	**25**	**31**	**27**	**93**		**2%**	**55**	**60**	**4%**	**2%**	**100**	**11%**	**86%**	**-3.7**	**74**

Nimmo,Brandon

Age: 31 Pos: CF | Bats: L Ht: 6' 3" Wt: 206
Health C | PT/Exp A | Consist A | LIMA Plan B+ | Rand Var -1 | MM 3335

Late-peaking CF stalwart finally displayed those power skills, fully supported by xHR, xPX and xHR/F, with the possibility of even more in the tank. BA/OBP skills intact despite slight drop in contact. xSB/Spd hint that a green light ANY green light - might yield bags, despite inept (unrefined?) SB%. Intriguing possibility - not to bid on, just to ponder

Yr	Tm	PA	R	HR	RBI	SB	BA	xHR	xSB	xBA	OBP	SLG	OPS+	vL+	vR+	bb%	ct%	Eye	G	L	F	h%	HctX	QBaB	Brl%	PX	xPX	HR/F	xHR/F	Spd	SBA%	SB%	RAR	BPX
19	NYM *	295	42	9	34	5	212	5	3	226	356	386	103	166	93	18	65	0.65	39	23	38	28	81	BCc	7%	110	103	16%	10%	95	6%	100%	2.2	59
20	NYM	225	33	8	18	1	280	8	6	263	404	484	118	85	130	15	77	0.77	47	20	32	33	67	CDd	8%	107	70	17%	17%	153	4%	33%	7.3	280
21	NYM *	418	54	8	28	5	278	6	10	251	378	413	109	112	117	14	77	0.69	47	22	30	34	106	CDd	4%	81	72	11%	8%	138	7%	56%	9.3	162
22	NYM	673	102	16	64	3	274	19	14	263	367	433	113	110	115	11	80	0.61	51	18	32	32	105	CDd	7%	97	93	11%	13%	153	3%	60%	21.3	228
23	NYM	682	89	24	68	3	274	25	15	256	363	466	113	100	119	11	75	0.51	41	20	39	33	117	ACd	10%	112	125	14%	14%	137	3%	50%	31.9	200
1st Half		372	49	12	40	3	279	12	9	254	372	458	114	110	115	11	73	0.47	43	22	34	35	113	ACd	9%	104	119	15%	15%	136	4%	75%	16.8	150
2nd Half		310	40	12	28	0	267	13	5	257	352	476	112	91	125	11	78	0.56	38	17	45	31	122	ABd	10%	120	132	13%	14%	132	3%	0%	13.1	254
24	**Proj**	**665**	**93**	**21**	**63**	**4**	**271**	**21**	**14**	**256**	**366**	**450**	**112**	**103**	**116**	**12**	**77**	**0.57**	**44**	**20**	**36**	**32**	**109**		**8%**	**105**	**106**	**13%**	**13%**	**142**	**4%**	**53%**	**29.1**	**204**

Noda,Ryan

Age: 28 Pos: 1B | Bats: L Ht: 6' 3" Wt: 217
Health B | PT/Exp A | Consist C | LIMA Plan C+ | Rand Var -4 | MM 4205

PRO: Carried patience and good power skills to the majors; held his own against portsiders. CON: Strikes out in darn-near half his trips up, thus falling short of power potential that QBaB and Brl% clearly point to, with awful BA dragging value down like an anchor. In OBP leagues, though, he's a little-known name with sneaky peak-age value.

Yr	Tm	PA	R	HR	RBI	SB	BA	xHR	xSB	xBA	OBP	SLG	OPS+	vL+	vR+	bb%	ct%	Eye	G	L	F	h%	HctX	QBaB	Brl%	PX	xPX	HR/F	xHR/F	Spd	SBA%	SB%	RAR	BPX
19																																		
20																																		
21	aa	430	49	20	52	2	199		2		286	391	93			11	61	0.31				26				130				88	3%	63%		-8
22	aaa	511	46	15	48	11	188		8		263	323	83			9	57	0.24				29				114				86	16%	69%		-117
23	OAK	495	63	16	54	3	229	18	6	214	364	406	105	101	106	16	58	0.45	37	23	40	35	93	BBc	13%	138	133	17%	19%	100	3%	75%	11.5	21
1st Half		302	38	8	32	2	229	11	5	212	384	400	107	95	109	19	58	0.57	31	25	44	36	86	BBd	14%	137	135	13%	18%	105	3%	67%	4.4	54
2nd Half		193	25	8	22	1	229	7	2	216	332	416	101	105	99	11	58	0.29	46	21	33	34	102	ACa	12%	140	131	25%	22%	94	2%	100%	-0.2	-18
24	**Proj**	**525**	**60**	**20**	**56**	**6**	**221**	**20**	**7**	**209**	**337**	**396**	**101**	**102**	**100**	**13**	**58**	**0.35**	**40**	**22**	**37**	**33**	**96**		**13%**	**133**	**133**	**20%**	**20%**	**91**	**6%**	**72%**	**2.1**	**-37**

Nootbaar,Lars

Age: 26 Pos: CF RF LF | Bats: L Ht: 6' 3" Wt: 210
Health B | PT/Exp A | Consist B | LIMA Plan B | Rand Var -1 | MM 3435

BA rebounded to where xBA said it should, and suddenly these numbers look pretty good. GB lean puts a lid on the lo[ng] balls at about where they stand. But you can rely on the plate skills to keep him on the basepaths, where he runs enough to add some value there, too. Not a sexy pick, but now a reliable, mid-tier stat stuffer.

Yr	Tm	PA	R	HR	RBI	SB	BA	xHR	xSB	xBA	OBP	SLG	OPS+	vL+	vR+	bb%	ct%	Eye	G	L	F	h%	HctX	QBaB	Brl%	PX	xPX	HR/F	xHR/F	Spd	SBA%	SB%	RAR	BPX
19	aa	106	10	0	3	1	245		2		339	281	86			12	75	0.56				33				22				134	6%	44%		-56
20																																		
21	STL *	252	29	9	28	3	244	3	5	221	317	396	98	118	98	10	75	0.43	46	15	39	29	88	CDf	5%	81	67	16%	10%	108	13%	37%	-5.4	69
22	STL *	416	61	16	49	5	216	12	5	256	325	425	106	118	110	14	74	0.61	44	17	39	25	114	BCf	12%	134	131	16%	14%	113	6%	84%	3.8	228
23	STL	503	74	14	46	11	261	17	11	260	367	418	107	86	114	14	77	0.73	50	19	31	31	113	CDf	9%	95	108	14%	17%	106	8%	92%	17.3	164
1st Half		227	31	5	23	5	255	6	5	249	358	380	101	88	105	14	77	0.71	54	18	28	31	112	CFf	8%	77	102	12%	15%	93	9%	83%	3.5	93
2nd Half		276	43	9	23	6	265	10	7	267	373	449	111	83	122	15	77	0.74	46	19	34	31	114	CDf	9%	109	113	15%	16%	120	8%	100%	12.2	221
24	**Proj**	**525**	**73**	**18**	**50**	**11**	**246**	**17**	**10**	**252**	**345**	**423**	**105**	**97**	**108**	**13**	**76**	**0.63**	**47**	**18**	**35**	**29**	**110**		**9%**	**104**	**110**	**15%**	**14%**	**115**	**10%**	**80%**	**16.1**	**147**

O'Hearn,Ryan

Age: 30 Pos: 1B RF | Bats: L Ht: 6' 3" Wt: 220
Health A | PT/Exp C | Consist D | LIMA Plan C | Rand Var -5 | MM 3333

14-60-.289 with 5 SB in 368 PA at BAL. DFA'd by two different teams during the winter, he responded with a career season at age 29. Mind you, there are still holes in his game; iffy plate skills add volatility and put BA at risk, and the power skills are solid but not truly elite. But hey, he has a career again, with this... UP: 20 HR

Yr	Tm	PA	R	HR	RBI	SB	BA	xHR	xSB	xBA	OBP	SLG	OPS+	vL+	vR+	bb%	ct%	Eye	G	L	F	h%	HctX	QBaB	Brl%	PX	xPX	HR/F	xHR/F	Spd	SBA%	SB%	RAR	BPX
19	KC *	512	47	20	58	0	209	15	1	234	289	397	95	71	93	10	71	0.38	46	18	36	25	103	BCc	9%	107	97	17%	18%	81	1%	0%	-17.7	52
20	KC	132	7	2	18	0	195	4	0	199	303	301	80	109	77	14	67	0.49	46	21	33	27	113	BCb	6%	77	131	8%	16%	74	0%	0%	-8.7	-68
21	KC *	332	38	16	46	2	240	8	2	237	284	432	98	54	93	6	71	0.21	43	20	38	28	98	BBc	8%	110	85	14%	13%	104	3%	100%	-3.8	65
22	KC	145	14	1	16	0	239	4	1	245	290	321	86	72	88	6	74	0.23	42	30	27	32	116	ACb	7%	61	104	4%	15%	98	0%	0%	-4.2	-41
23	BAL *	419	55	16	68	5	285	15	6	262	315	479	108	106	110	4	75	0.17	43	20	36	35	111	ACc	10%	119	114	14%	15%	99	7%	83%	17.8	118
1st Half		175	24	8	29	0	279	7	2	249	319	499	112	68	119	6	70	0.20	41	18	41	35	111	ABb	14%	139	135	17%	20%	106	3%	0%	5.1	132
2nd Half		244	31	8	39	5	289	8	4	270	313	466	105	117	104	3	78	0.15	45	21	34	34	112	ACc	8%	106	104	13%	13%	94	10%	100%	6.3	114
24	**Proj**	**420**	**51**	**15**	**63**	**3**	**258**	**15**	**4**	**252**	**303**	**431**	**101**	**85**	**103**	**6**	**73**	**0.22**	**43**	**22**	**34**	**32**	**110**		**9%**	**107**	**108**	**15%**	**15%**	**93**	**4%**	**85%**	**5.0**	**59**

ROD TRUESDELL

O'Hoppe,Logan

Age: 24 Pos: CA	Health F	LIMA Plan B
Bats: R Ht: 6' 2" Wt: 185	PT/Exp D	Rand Var +2
	Consist A	MM 3013

Showed flashes before and after labrum tear, including top-tier QBaB and .879 OPS in September. 2nd half hit rate cratered BA but should rebound. The rub: This 200-AB sample can't ignore the absence of power in minors. Accepting xHR as the (quite fine) starting point still gives room for profit potential in a best-case scenario.

Yr	Tm	PA	R	HR	RBI	SB	BA	xHR	xSB	xBA	OBP	SLG	OPS+	vL+	vR+	bb%	ct%	Eye	G	L	F	h%	HctX	QBaB	Brl%	PX	xPX	HR/F	xHR/F	Spd	SBA%	SB%	RAR	BPX	R$
19																																			
20																																			
21	a/a	77	6	3	7	0	248		0		269	398	92			3	81	0.15				27				76				98	0%	0%		77	-$1
22	LAA *	423	47	18	52	5	236	0	8	237	324	415	105	112	83	11	77	0.56	36	18	45	26	30	DAc		105	54	0%	0%	121	8%	50%	9.1	179	$11
23	LAA	199	23	14	29	0	236	11	2	248	296	500	109	125	103	7	74	0.29	38	14	48	24	118	BAc	16%	145	136	22%	17%	96	3%	0%	7.8	196	$3
1st Half		59	5	4	13	0	283	4	1	202	339	547	121	167	107	7	72	0.27	41	10	49	32	120	AAc	13%	151	146	21%	21%	113	0%	0%	4.3	207	-$5
2nd Half		140	18	10	16	0	217	8	1	255	279	481	103	106	101	7	74	0.30	36	16	48	21	117	BAb	17%	143	133	22%	17%	100	4%	0%	2.2	207	$2
24	**Proj**	**420**	**47**	**20**	**61**	**2**	**246**	**23**	**6**	**230**	**318**	**440**	**104**	**125**	**97**	**9**	**75**	**0.38**	**38**	**15**	**46**	**28**	**118**		**12%**	**109**	**138**	**15%**	**17%**	**83**	**5%**	**43%**	**13.7**	**196**	**$11**

O'Neill,Tyler

Age: 29 Pos: LF	Health F	LIMA Plan C+
Bats: R Ht: 5' 11" Wt: 200	PT/Exp B	Rand Var +2
	Consist C	MM 3323

9-21-.231 with 5 SB in 266 PA at STL. Got in skipper's doghouse early and barely climbed out. Low hit rate in 2nd half hid reasons for hope, including legit gains in batted ball quality and huge jump in contact. However, aggregate trends in vR+, Spd, and xPX can't be overlooked. A moderate multi-category play...when lefties are on mound.

Yr	Tm	PA	R	HR	RBI	SB	BA	xHR	xSB	xBA	OBP	SLG	OPS+	vL+	vR+	bb%	ct%	Eye	G	L	F	h%	HctX	QBaB	Brl%	PX	xPX	HR/F	xHR/F	Spd	SBA%	SB%	RAR	BPX	R$
19	STL *	337	42	15	38	3	236	5	2	213	283	413	96	91	101	6	62	0.17	38	23	40	33	100	CAd	7%	111	108	14%	14%	96	4%	100%	-3.0	-70	$6
20	STL	157	20	7	19	3	173	7	2	221	261	360	82	60	88	10	69	0.35	43	15	41	19	92	CBf	8%	110	115	18%	18%	94	14%	75%	-10.2	52	$6
21	STL	537	89	34	80	15	286	39	13	254	352	560	125	140	122	7	65	0.23	36	23	41	37	114	AAc	18%	176	153	26%	30%	120	15%	79%	31.0	208	$30
22	STL	383	56	14	58	14	228	15	11	229	308	392	99	110	96	10	69	0.37	42	20	38	29	97	BCd	11%	109	119	16%	17%	108	20%	78%	-0.5	62	$14
23	STL *	295	29	9	23	5	225	11	4	237	306	383	94	107	93	10	71	0.41	43	19	38	28	105	BBd	12%	103	106	14%	17%	85	8%	100%	1.0	57	$2
1st Half		99	12	2	6	1	228	4	1	207	283	337	85	73	88	7	63	0.21	40	24	36	34	89	BCb	14%	83	104	10%	19%	94	5%	100%	-2.1	-132	-$7
2nd Half		196	17	7	17	4	223	7	3	252	318	408	98	120	97	12	76	0.58	44	17	39	25	115	BBf	12%	113	107	16%	16%	84	9%	100%	2.3	161	$3
24	**Proj**	**420**	**53**	**16**	**47**	**10**	**232**	**19**	**8**	**235**	**307**	**411**	**98**	**105**	**96**	**9**	**69**	**0.33**	**41**	**20**	**39**	**29**	**103**		**13%**	**116**	**117**	**16%**	**19%**	**93**	**12%**	**85%**	**4.1**	**68**	**$14**

Ohtani,Shohei

Age: 29 Pos: DH	Health A	LIMA Plan C
Bats: L Ht: 6' 4" Wt: 210	PT/Exp A	Rand Var -4
	Consist F	MM 5455

Three straight $30+ returns make him firmly elite at the dish, and he hasn't reached his ceiling yet. xHR puts 50 homers in play, and 30-point jump in xBA validates that he can flirt with a .300 BA again. Went under knife for elbow surgery at end of year, but expected to be ready to hit by spring. If that's the case... UP: .300 BA, 50 HR

Yr	Tm	PA	R	HR	RBI	SB	BA	xHR	xSB	xBA	OBP	SLG	OPS+	vL+	vR+	bb%	ct%	Eye	G	L	F	h%	HctX	QBaB	Brl%	PX	xPX	HR/F	xHR/F	Spd	SBA%	SB%	RAR	BPX	R$
19	LAA	423	51	18	62	12	286	19	12	276	343	505	117	110	119	8	71	0.30	50	26	24	36	123	ADa	12%	121	111	26%	28%	141	15%	80%	10.2	156	$17
20	LAA	175	23	7	24	7	190	8	4	228	291	366	87	82	89	13	67	0.44	50	17	33	23	93	CDd	11%	108	109	21%	24%	87	21%	88%	-6.7	36	$13
21	LAA	639	103	46	100	26	257	53	26	270	372	592	133	133	132	15	65	0.51	38	21	41	30	120	ABc	22%	208	162	33%	38%	147	23%	72%	36.0	392	$36
22	LAA	666	90	34	95	11	273	47	13	269	356	519	124	110	131	11	73	0.45	42	20	38	32	121	ACc	17%	156	142	21%	29%	109	12%	55%	25.9	245	$32
23	LAA	594	102	44	95	20	304	48	24	299	412	654	145	120	155	15	71	0.64	42	18	39	35	124	ACc	20%	200	145	31%	34%	139	16%	77%	77.1	425	$36
1st Half		372	61	31	68	11	306	32	14	305	390	670	145	142	146	12	74	0.54	43	16	41	33	125	ACc	18%	197	152	31%	32%	140	16%	73%	43.2	436	$49
2nd Half		222	41	13	27	9	301	15	10	286	450	624	145	84	170	21	66	0.78	41	23	36	39	124	ACc	22%	206	131	32%	37%	129	15%	82%	27.3	396	$22
24	**Proj**	**630**	**102**	**40**	**101**	**21**	**282**	**47**	**21**	**279**	**389**	**588**	**134**	**111**	**145**	**15**	**69**	**0.56**	**42**	**20**	**38**	**33**	**121**		**19%**	**184**	**141**	**28%**	**33%**	**123**	**16%**	**74%**	**60.1**	**336**	**$40**

Olivares,Edward

Age: 28 Pos: LF DH	Health D	LIMA Plan C+
Bats: R Ht: 6' 2" Wt: 190	PT/Exp B	Rand Var 0
	Consist B	MM 3343

12-36-.263 with 11 SB in 385 PA at KC. Mini-breakout: fact or fluke? PRO: xBA gives batting average solid floor; 2nd-half power had backing of jumps in HctX and xPX. CON: Mediocre QBaB; only league average against righties; staying healthy remains an obstacle. For profit, look for alternatives once bidding hits double-digits.

Yr	Tm	PA	R	HR	RBI	SB	BA	xHR	xSB	xBA	OBP	SLG	OPS+	vL+	vR+	bb%	ct%	Eye	G	L	F	h%	HctX	QBaB	Brl%	PX	xPX	HR/F	xHR/F	Spd	SBA%	SB%	RAR	BPX	R$
19	aa	525	73	14	66	30	254		21		307	397	97			7	78	0.35				30				77				99	34%	73%		70	$22
20	2 TM	101	9	3	10	0	240	2	2	237	267	375	85	69	94	4	74	0.16	48	23	30	29	79	FDf	6%	71	65	14%	10%	139	10%	0%	-6.9	16	$2
21	KC *	387	52	15	37	10	254	4	12	253	303	425	100	74	112	7	80	0.36	47	17	36	28	105	CDf	6%	90	117	17%	13%	142	19%	61%	-1.3	196	$13
22	KC *	256	31	4	21	3	261	5	5	258	303	377	96	127	96	6	78	0.27	46	25	29	32	111	BDd	6%	81	91	11%	14%	112	12%	43%	-2.6	86	$4
23	KC *	439	53	14	44	14	266	14	15	269	307	455	104	115	99	5	81	0.31	43	17	40	30	106	CCf	8%	107	106	10%	12%	117	21%	68%	10.9	207	$13
1st Half		236	30	6	15	8	255	9	9	265	309	431	101	92	106	6	81	0.33	41	20	39	29	93	CCf	9%	96	94	9%	13%	145	22%	73%	1.7	214	$7
2nd Half		203	23	8	29	6	279	5	6	269	318	482	108	163	90	5	81	0.30	46	14	40	31	127	CCf	7%	120	124	13%	11%	97	21%	63%	6.4	218	$13
24	**Proj**	**385**	**47**	**13**	**40**	**10**	**268**	**13**	**12**	**264**	**318**	**441**	**104**	**113**	**99**	**6**	**80**	**0.29**	**45**	**19**	**36**	**31**	**108**		**7%**	**101**	**103**	**12%**	**12%**	**114**	**18%**	**62%**	**7.5**	**163**	**$16**

Olson,Matt

Age: 30 Pos: 1B	Health A	LIMA Plan C
Bats: L Ht: 6' 5" Wt: 225	PT/Exp A	Rand Var -2
	Consist F	MM 5255

Joins Judge and Stanton as only bats with 50+ HR, 130+ RBI seasons in past 10 years. Sure, HR/F was overstated, so we can't expect quite the same level of power. But xBA validates batting average rebound, and if that late contact rate holds, a full-season .300 BA is in play. Ace-like durability confirms he's firmly elite now.

Yr	Tm	PA	R	HR	RBI	SB	BA	xHR	xSB	xBA	OBP	SLG	OPS+	vL+	vR+	bb%	ct%	Eye	G	L	F	h%	HctX	QBaB	Brl%	PX	xPX	HR/F	xHR/F	Spd	SBA%	SB%	RAR	BPX	R$
19	OAK *	570	75	37	92	0	262	38	-	269	330	531	119	107	131	9	72	0.37	31	24	45	29	125	AAc	15%	145	161	24%	25%	76	0%	0%	9.5	174	$18
20	OAK	245	28	14	42	1	195	13	1	220	310	424	97	91	99	14	63	0.44	35	21	44	23	110	AAd	13%	136	143	24%	22%	88	2%	100%	-11.5	72	$14
21	OAK	673	101	39	111	4	271	35	2	279	371	540	125	131	121	13	80	0.78	40	16	44	28	119	ABf	13%	145	128	19%	17%	76	3%	80%	33.5	335	$28
22	ATL	699	86	34	103	0	240	34	0	262	325	477	114	105	117	11	72	0.44	39	19	42	28	124	ABf	13%	161	132	18%	18%	60	0%	0%	9.7	207	$21
23	ATL	720	127	54	139	1	283	48	7	284	389	604	135	108	145	14	73	0.62	39	18	44	30	125	ABc	16%	180	153	28%	25%	103	1%	100%	70.2	343	$37
1st Half		374	65	28	68	1	252	27	3	272	356	576	128	87	143	13	68	0.49	36	17	47	28	114	ABd	20%	196	165	27%	26%	96	1%	100%	24.4	307	$36
2nd Half		346	62	26	71	0	317	21	4	297	425	634	143	131	147	16	78	0.84	42	19	40	33	139	ABc	13%	165	142	29%	23%	108	0%	0%	43.8	389	$42
24	**Proj**	**665**	**105**	**44**	**119**	**1**	**274**	**40**	**3**	**274**	**372**	**558**	**128**	**114**	**133**	**13**	**74**	**0.58**	**39**	**18**	**43**	**30**	**125**		**15%**	**163**	**143**	**24%**	**22%**	**85**	**1%**	**88%**	**53.4**	**292**	**$34**

Outman,James

Age: 27 Pos: CF	Health A	LIMA Plan B
Bats: L Ht: 6' 3" Wt: 215	PT/Exp A	Rand Var -3
	Consist B	MM 3305

Power/speed combo netted fantasy managers big profit on his 511 ADP. However, there's more work to do. xHR, xHR/F and xBA point to significant regression off that big 2nd half, and overall exit velocity ranked in the game's 22nd percentile. Add in his poor ct% and expect pullback in his sophomore campaign.

Yr	Tm	PA	R	HR	RBI	SB	BA	xHR	xSB	xBA	OBP	SLG	OPS+	vL+	vR+	bb%	ct%	Eye	G	L	F	h%	HctX	QBaB	Brl%	PX	xPX	HR/F	xHR/F	Spd	SBA%	SB%	RAR	BPX	R$
19																																			
20																																			
21	aa	178	28	6	17	1	236		2		286	404	95			7	64	0.19				33				115				106	8%	37%		-15	$2
22	LA *	529	66	22	66	8	233	0	8	238	294	433	103	70	211	8	61	0.22	33	33	33	34	221	ABa		157	194	50%	0%	103	12%	62%	1.2	55	$15
23	LA	567	86	23	70	16	248	20	17	219	353	437	108	90	114	12	63	0.38	38	21	41	35	74	CBf	11%	125	102	18%	16%	117	12%	84%	18.6	39	$19
1st Half		283	39	9	36	8	232	9	8	202	314	404	98	100	98	9	61	0.26	36	18	45	34	77	CAf	10%	121	106	13%	13%	120	13%	89%	1.5	-14	$14
2nd Half		284	47	14	34	8	266	10	8	237	391	472	117	81	133	16	64	0.52	39	25	37	35	71	DCc	12%	130	99	25%	18%	104	11%	80%	15.9	93	$23
24	**Proj**	**560**	**81**	**19**	**66**	**12**	**235**	**19**	**12**	**213**	**327**	**402**	**100**	**82**	**107**	**10**	**62**	**0.31**	**38**	**22**	**40**	**34**	**73**		**11%**	**118**	**102**	**15%**	**15%**	**113**	**11%**	**73%**	**5.8**	**42**	**$19**

Ozuna,Marcell

Age: 33 Pos: DH	Health D	LIMA Plan B
Bats: R Ht: 6' 1" Wt: 225	PT/Exp A	Rand Var 0
	Consist D	MM 4145

First 40-HR season on back of nifty batted ball components and career-high xPX. Fifty-point BA jump screams regression, but xBA thinks otherwise. Only nit to pick is long history of inconsistency, since he's never posted back-to-back 30+ HR seasons due to shaky health. That risk means you should cap investment at $20.

Yr	Tm	PA	R	HR	RBI	SB	BA	xHR	xSB	xBA	OBP	SLG	OPS+	vL+	vR+	bb%	ct%	Eye	G	L	F	h%	HctX	QBaB	Brl%	PX	xPX	HR/F	xHR/F	Spd	SBA%	SB%	RAR	BPX	R$
19	STL	549	80	29	89	12	243	30	6	275	330	474	111	105	112	11	76	0.54	41	23	35	26	127	ACc	12%	118	119	22%	23%	77	11%	86%	0.9	178	$19
20	ATL	267	38	18	56	0	338	20	0	283	431	636	142	173	133	14	74	0.63	37	23	40	39	138	ABd	15%	166	146	26%	29%	68	0%	0%	33.8	312	$38
21	ATL	208	21	7	26	0	213	8	0	233	288	356	89	82	91	9	76	0.41	37	23	41	24	87	BBd	10%	81	80	12%	14%	48	0%	0%	-10.3	4	$0
22	ATL	507	56	23	56	2	226	28	1	240	274	413	97	70	108	6	74	0.25	38	19	43	26	108	BBf	10%	118	121	15%	18%	50	3%	67%	-12.5	69	$10
23	ATL	592	84	40	100	0	274	43	2	283	346	558	123	132	120	10	75	0.43	40	20	41	29	126	ABc	17%	161	157	25%	27%	65	0%	0%	41.5	243	$25
1st Half		269	35	16	39	0	247	19	1	256	327	481	111	122	106	10	76	0.48	45	17	38	26	114	ABc	15%	127	123	23%	27%	67	0%	0%	4.9	171	$15
2nd Half		323	49	24	61	0	296	24	1	302	362	622	133	143	131	9	74	0.38	36	22	43	32	137	ABc	18%	190	186	26%	26%	66	0%	0%	28.0	311	$34
24	**Proj**	**525**	**68**	**30**	**80**	**1**	**264**	**33**	**1**	**265**	**331**	**503**	**114**	**109**	**116**	**9**	**75**	**0.38**	**38**	**20**	**41**	**29**	**117**		**14%**	**138**	**136**	**20%**	**23%**	**54**	**1%**	**76%**	**22.7**	**170**	**$22**

STEPHEN NICKRAND

Palacios,Joshua

Age: 28 Pos: RF LF | Bats: L Ht: 6' 1" Wt: 200

Health A | PT/Exp C | Consist C | LIMA Plan D | Rand Var 0 | MM 2333

10-40-.239 with 5 SB in 264 PA at PIT. Called up May 9 and got first long MLB look on strong side of platoon. In 2nd half, traded ct% for barrels and power output perked up. If he can keep up SB%, he'll chip in some bags, too, despite average speed. But all this requires PT, and that may go to those with more youth and/or higher ceilings.

Yr	Tm	PA	R	HR	RBI	SB	BA	xHR	xSB	xBA	OBP	SLG	OPS+	vL+	vR+	bb%	ct%	Eye	G	L	F	h%	HctX	QBaB	Brl%	PX	xPX	HR/F	xHR/F	Spd	SBA%	SB%	RAR	BPX
19	aa	328	40	7	36	14	255		10		349	402	104			13	73	0.54				33				89				104	22%	72%		81
20																																		
21	TOR *	100	13	0	6	1	206	1	2	175	266	227	68	109	61	7	67	0.24	54	17	29	31	84	CFc	4%	19	41	0%	14%	105	12%	27%	-7.7	-265
22	WAS *	367	38	6	32	14	226	0	13	237	274	318	84	112	66	6	76	0.28	50	22	28	28	31	FFf		61	17	0%	0%	98	29%	59%	-14.7	-7
23	PIT *	385	44	16	60	9	256	10	8	272	297	439	100	90	95	6	80	0.30	48	19	33	28	103	BDd	10%	97	96	16%	16%	98	12%	87%	7.3	143
1st Half		191	21	4	26	5	272	2	4	296	309	414	99	78	93	5	87	0.43	53	21	26	29	105	BFd	4%	78	60	5%	10%	87	12%	100%	3.5	179
2nd Half		195	23	12	34	4	240	8	4	254	286	464	101	94	97	6	73	0.24	45	18	37	26	97	BDd	13%	120	122	22%	20%	115	13%	75%	2.5	129
24	Proj	**280**	**33**	**10**	**34**	**8**	**239**	**7**	**7**	**248**	**294**	**398**	**95**	**92**	**96**	**7**	**76**	**0.29**	**48**	**19**	**33**	**28**	**100**		**10%**	**91**	**97**	**15%**	**11%**	**109**	**18%**	**67%**	**-1.4**	**41**

Palacios,Richie

Age: 27 Pos: OF | Bats: L Ht: 5' 10" Wt: 180

Health A | PT/Exp A | Consist B | LIMA Plan D | Rand Var +5 | MM 2331

6-16-.258 in 102 PA at STL. Small-sample HR binge a surprise, as BA/OBP has been main calling card in minors. Legit age-related power growth? xPX says maybe, but GB% is still a big problem, and HR/F looks unsustainable. PA only came his way as squad played out string; could struggle to find bigger role on would-be contender.

Yr	Tm	PA	R	HR	RBI	SB	BA	xHR	xSB	xBA	OBP	SLG	OPS+	vL+	vR+	bb%	ct%	Eye	G	L	F	h%	HctX	QBaB	Brl%	PX	xPX	HR/F	xHR/F	Spd	SBA%	SB%	RAR	BPX
19																																		
20																																		
21	a/a	400	54	5	36	15	254		10		335	394	100			11	77	0.53				32				94				103	19%	81%		146
22	CLE *	315	26	2	30	9	218	1	7	225	274	306	82	93	80	7	75	0.31	46	21	34	28	60	DCf	1%	64	26	0%	3%	103	16%	78%	-10.8	-3
23	STL *	521	58	11	54	8	205	3	11	243	283	326	83	156	101	10	82	0.62	53	13	34	23	100	CDd	7%	72	124	21%	11%	92	13%	52%	-15.9	129
1st Half		283	31	3	24	4	166		6	225	249	247	68	0	0	10	76	0.47	44	20	36	20	0		0%	55	-21	0%		96	16%	44%	-19.3	4
2nd Half		238	27	8	30	4	252	3	5	276	325	421	101	155	100	10	89	1.00	53	13	34	25	108	CDd	7%	88	124	21%	11%	92	11%	62%	3.3	271
24	Proj	**175**	**19**	**4**	**18**	**4**	**222**	**3**	**4**	**252**	**296**	**367**	**91**	**79**	**93**	**9**	**80**	**0.50**	**50**	**16**	**34**	**25**	**89**		**5%**	**86**	**85**	**10%**	**8%**	**102**	**15%**	**71%**	**-1.9**	**103**

Paredes,Isaac

Age: 25 Pos: 3B 1B | Bats: R Ht: 5' 11" Wt: 213

Health A | PT/Exp A | Consist B | LIMA Plan B+ | Rand Var 0 | MM 3035

xHR doesn't buy power, but it didn't last year, either. All 31 HR were same flavor—left or left-center. Such a conscious effort to pick spots, pull like hell could be more sustainable than meets the eye. Even if homers dip, xBA says there's BA upside here, especially with RHP solved. A solid investment, with potential in-season MI eligibility as bonus.

Yr	Tm	PA	R	HR	RBI	SB	BA	xHR	xSB	xBA	OBP	SLG	OPS+	vL+	vR+	bb%	ct%	Eye	G	L	F	h%	HctX	QBaB	Brl%	PX	xPX	HR/F	xHR/F	Spd	SBA%	SB%	RAR	BPX
19	aa	534	64	13	67	5	286		5		360	424	109			10	87	0.93				30				68				94	5%	62%		204
20	DET	108	7	1	6	0	220	1	0	212	278	290	75	118	67	7	76	0.33	47	21	32	28	57	DDf	0%	46	36	4%	4%	90	0%	0%	-6.7	-56
21	DET *	385	41	10	41	0	240	1	4	245	353	394	103	96	79	15	82	0.96	37	21	43	26	106	DAf	2%	80	93	4%	4%	130	0%	0%	5.0	238
22	TAM *	485	59	23	58	0	208	11	1	247	296	422	102	118	100	11	79	0.60	42	12	45	21	97	CBf	7%	128	96	17%	9%	71	2%	0%	-0.5	217
23	TAM	571	71	31	98	1	250	14	2	273	352	488	114	104	118	10	79	0.56	32	21	47	26	105	CAd	6%	129	111	17%	8%	69	1%	100%	25.6	221
1st Half		290	40	14	53	0	267	6	2	268	372	494	119	103	124	11	80	0.62	35	19	46	28	102	CAd	5%	125	90	15%	7%	89	0%	0%	12.9	250
2nd Half		281	31	17	45	1	233	8	1	277	331	482	110	106	111	10	78	0.50	28	24	48	23	108	CAc	7%	133	133	18%	9%	56	2%	100%	5.8	204
24	Proj	**560**	**67**	**24**	**80**	**1**	**251**	**16**	**3**	**254**	**346**	**448**	**109**	**113**	**107**	**11**	**80**	**0.61**	**36**	**19**	**45**	**27**	**99**		**5%**	**108**	**99**	**14%**	**9%**	**67**	**1%**	**54%**	**18.4**	**209**

Pasquantino,Vinnie

Age: 26 Pos: 1B | Bats: L Ht: 6' 4" Wt: 245

Health F | PT/Exp B | Consist B | LIMA Plan A+ | Rand Var +4 | MM 3255

Encore to rookie splash was going swimmingly before June 9 labrum tear ended season. If surgery puts history of shoulder pain to rest, maybe pace from spectacular April (5 HR, .319 xBA) can be sustained. Can't ignore injury risk, but ingredients (ct%, HctX, launch angle) are there for... UP: .280 BA, 25 HR

Yr	Tm	PA	R	HR	RBI	SB	BA	xHR	xSB	xBA	OBP	SLG	OPS+	vL+	vR+	bb%	ct%	Eye	G	L	F	h%	HctX	QBaB	Brl%	PX	xPX	HR/F	xHR/F	Spd	SBA%	SB%	RAR	BPX
19																																		
20																																		
21	aa	224	28	8	33	2	273		1		352	472	113			11	86	0.87				29				110				80	4%	100%		308
22	KC *	584	55	19	66	3	255	11	3	263	328	419	106	120	117	10	85	0.73	41	19	40	27	138	ACc	9%	94	135	11%	12%	82	3%	70%	9.0	214
23	KC	259	24	9	26	0	247	7	1	284	324	437	104	94	107	10	87	0.81	36	22	43	25	139	CBc	7%	104	118	11%	8%	64	0%	0%	6.4	250
1st Half		259	24	9	26	0	247	7	1	284	324	437	104	94	108	10	87	0.81	36	22	43	25	139	CBc	8%	104	118	11%	8%	64	0%	0%	2.5	250
2nd Half																									0%									
24	Proj	**560**	**60**	**19**	**69**	**3**	**260**	**18**	**2**	**278**	**340**	**446**	**108**	**102**	**110**	**10**	**86**	**0.82**	**38**	**21**	**41**	**27**	**139**		**8%**	**103**	**125**	**11%**	**10%**	**73**	**2%**	**92%**	**17.2**	**264**

Pederson,Joc

Age: 32 Pos: DH LF | Bats: L Ht: 6' 1" Wt: 220

Health B | PT/Exp A | Consist D | LIMA Plan B | Rand Var +1 | MM 3233

Missed three weeks after being hit on hand with pitch in mid-May bunt attempt. Otherwise, a typical year of steady HR vR, sitting vL. Signs of age-related power decline are faint; exit velocity, launch angle, xPX are all still rock solid. That should be enough for at least another year in familiar strong-side platoon role, yielding similar results.

Yr	Tm	PA	R	HR	RBI	SB	BA	xHR	xSB	xBA	OBP	SLG	OPS+	vL+	vR+	bb%	ct%	Eye	G	L	F	h%	HctX	QBaB	Brl%	PX	xPX	HR/F	xHR/F	Spd	SBA%	SB%	RAR	BPX
19	LA	514	83	36	74	1	249	26	3	271	339	538	121	70	126	10	75	0.45	42	17	41	25	118	ABd	10%	141	124	26%	19%	108	2%	50%	8.2	252
20	LA	137	21	7	16	1	190	7	1	238	285	397	90	96	90	8	72	0.32	48	15	36	20	107	ACc	10%	114	126	23%	23%	87	4%	100%	-6.1	92
21	2 NL	481	55	18	61	2	238	21	4	235	310	422	101	99	101	8	73	0.33	39	19	42	29	101	BCf	10%	108	118	14%	16%	100	5%	40%	-12.1	100
22	SF	433	57	23	70	3	274	24	6	262	353	521	124	104	127	10	74	0.42	36	19	45	32	129	ABf	15%	154	157	18%	19%	119	5%	60%	18.2	259
23	SF	425	59	15	51	0	235	18	4	244	348	416	104	82	107	13	75	0.64	39	19	42	27	128	ABd	12%	103	138	13%	16%	101	0%	0%	7.7	150
1st Half		189	32	8	30	0	252	10	2	244	381	458	115	86	118	16	73	0.69	40	18	41	30	128	ACd	15%	113	146	17%	21%	111	0%	0%	5.3	175
2nd Half		236	27	7	21	0	222	8	2	243	322	384	95	79	98	12	77	0.60	39	19	42	26	129	ABc	10%	95	132	11%	12%	93	0%	0%	-3.9	136
24	Proj	**420**	**58**	**18**	**57**	**1**	**243**	**20**	**4**	**247**	**338**	**448**	**108**	**90**	**111**	**11**	**74**	**0.50**	**39**	**19**	**42**	**28**	**123**		**12%**	**118**	**138**	**16%**	**17%**	**107**	**2%**	**56%**	**9.2**	**173**

Peguero,Liover

Age: 23 Pos: SS 2B | Bats: R Ht: 6' 2" Wt: 200

Health A | PT/Exp B | Consist C | LIMA Plan C | Rand Var +1 | MM 2533

7-26-.237 with 6 SB in 213 PA at PIT. Some rough edges, as you might expect at age 22 with just 30 PA of AAA experience. Struck out one-third of the time in MLB, ground ball rate dims enthusiasm over rising power, and while he can steal a base, lack of walks may limit chances. Might have a 20/20 season in him at some point, but not yet.

Yr	Tm	PA	R	HR	RBI	SB	BA	xHR	xSB	xBA	OBP	SLG	OPS+	vL+	vR+	bb%	ct%	Eye	G	L	F	h%	HctX	QBaB	Brl%	PX	xPX	HR/F	xHR/F	Spd	SBA%	SB%	RAR	BPX
19																																		
20																																		
21																																		
22	PIT *	508	44	6	40	19	220	0	17	262	254	316	81	140	71	4	75	0.18	100	0	0	28	328	AF		67	-14	0%		132	27%	74%	-26.4	14
23	PIT *	553	63	17	57	23	234	4	22	255	288	387	92	106	80	7	74	0.30	52	19	29	28	93	CFf	5%	91	79	18%	11%	133	24%	81%	-1.4	96
1st Half		309	42	9	29	16	241		12	268	306	409	98	0	0	9	80	0.46	44	20	36	27	0		0%	100	-21	0%		110	28%	83%	0.8	182
2nd Half		246	24	9	30	8	234	4	10	229	279	380	89	105	80	6	68	0.20	52	19	29	30	85	CFf	5%	85	79	18%	11%	159	19%	79%	-4.6	11
24	Proj	**350**	**36**	**12**	**34**	**14**	**230**	**3**	**13**	**251**	**278**	**391**	**92**	**113**	**81**	**6**	**74**	**0.25**	**52**	**19**	**29**	**28**	**77**		**5%**	**95**	**71**	**17%**	**5%**	**132**	**25%**	**79%**	**-1.9**	**55**

Peña,Jeremy

Age: 26 Pos: SS | Bats: R Ht: 6' 0" Wt: 202

Health A | PT/Exp A | Consist A | LIMA Plan B | Rand Var -1 | MM 2335

Dodged IL for neck and hamstring woes, but 2nd half suggests they conspired to produce power outage. Launch angle was an accomplice, too, so rebound cannot be assumed. SB% also tanked, bigger bases be damned, even as raw skil persisted. It sums up to a solid across-the-board contributor, but temper 2022 optimism.

Yr	Tm	PA	R	HR	RBI	SB	BA	xHR	xSB	xBA	OBP	SLG	OPS+	vL+	vR+	bb%	ct%	Eye	G	L	F	h%	HctX	QBaB	Brl%	PX	xPX	HR/F	xHR/F	Spd	SBA%	SB%	RAR	BPX
19																																		
20																																		
21	aaa	126	15	7	13	3	234		3		258	454	98			3	66	0.10				29				132				121	19%	74%		54
22	HOU	555	72	22	63	11	253	17	10	253	289	426	101	114	96	4	74	0.16	46	21	33	30	93	CDf	10%	109	92	17%	13%	119	11%	85%	1.4	100
23	HOU	631	81	10	52	13	263	10	19	257	324	381	96	112	89	7	78	0.33	54	19	27	32	95	CFc	4%	75	60	8%	8%	122	14%	59%	5.3	82
1st Half		321	40	9	30	8	247	7	10	263	302	399	96	113	89	5	75	0.23	50	22	28	30	90	CFc	6%	94	81	15%	11%	107	20%	57%	-5.0	71
2nd Half		310	41	1	22	5	281	2	9	250	346	363	96	112	89	8	80	0.47	58	17	25	35	100	CFd	2%	56	40	2%	4%	132	9%	63%	0.9	89
24	Proj	**630**	**82**	**16**	**61**	**12**	**257**	**12**	**16**	**247**	**303**	**392**	**95**	**110**	**90**	**5**	**75**	**0.22**	**51**	**20**	**29**	**32**	**95**		**6%**	**83**	**71**	**12%**	**9%**	**118**	**12%**	**67%**	**2.4**	**84**

KRIS OLSON

Peralta,David

Age: 36 Pos: LF
Bats: L Ht: 6'1" Wt: 210

Health	B	LIMA Plan	D+
PT/Exp	A	Rand Var	+2
Consist	A	MM	2243

October flexor tendon repair revealed that he had been playing through the injury since the All Star break. Explains 2nd half malaise and .190 Sept BA. Still makes hard contact, but reverting to elevated GB% makes clearing fences a stretch. Even if strong-side-platoon days may be ending, there could still be roster spot with his name on it.

Yr	Tm	PA	R	HR	RBI	SB	BA	xHR	xSB	xBA	OBP	SLG	OPS+	vL+	vR+	bb%	ct%	Eye	G	L	F	h%	HctX	QBaB	Brl%	PX	xPX	HR/F	xHR/F	Spd	SBA%	SB%	RAR	BPX	R$
19	ARI	423	48	12	57	0	275	10	2	274	343	461	111	98	116	8	77	0.40	51	21	28	33	116	BDd	5%	105	89	15%	12%	105	0%	0%	12.6	159	$9
20	ARI	218	19	5	34	1	300	5	1	251	339	433	103	82	109	6	78	0.29	49	22	29	37	106	CDf	5%	77	67	11%	11%	104	2%	100%	2.2	72	$18
21	ARI	538	57	8	63	2	259	8	5	269	325	402	100	100	100	9	81	0.50	55	19	26	30	107	BFd	5%	83	56	8%	8%	118	2%	67%	-0.1	173	$10
22	2 TM	490	39	12	59	1	251	14	3	248	316	415	104	65	110	8	74	0.36	36	23	41	31	108	BBd	9%	115	127	9%	10%	86	4%	25%	3.6	114	$9
23	LA	422	47	7	55	4	259	9	4	268	294	381	92	91	92	5	82	0.28	48	22	30	30	112	CDc	5%	76	90	7%	9%	82	5%	80%	0.3	86	$9
1st Half		211	21	5	29	1	286	5	3	270	322	413	101	116	100	6	83	0.36	49	22	28	32	120	ADb	6%	69	83	11%	11%	102	4%	50%	4.4	114	$6
2nd Half		211	26	2	26	3	232	3	2	265	265	348	83	80	83	4	80	0.21	47	21	32	28	103	CDd	4%	82	97	4%	6%	68	8%	100%	-5.1	61	$4
24	**Proj**	**280**	**29**	**5**	**36**	**2**	**257**	**6**	**2**	**260**	**306**	**396**	**96**	**84**	**98**	**6**	**79**	**0.33**	**46**	**21**	**32**	**31**	**109**		**6%**	**88**	**94**	**8%**	**9%**	**86**	**4%**	**70%**	**2.2**	**107**	**$5**

Peraza,Oswald

Age: 24 Pos: 3B
Bats: R Ht: 6'0" Wt: 200

Health	A	LIMA Plan	C
PT/Exp	A	Rand Var	+4
Consist	B	MM	1403

2-14-.191 with 4 SB in 191 PA at NYY. Lost spring SS battle, struggled in April, July MLB cameos, then showed faint signs of life in final six weeks once given 3B job. 14 HR in 63 AAA games hints at power he's yet to tap in MLB, due in part to GB%. SB technique needs work, too. Sometimes things gel quickly, but more growing pains seem likely.

Yr	Tm	PA	R	HR	RBI	SB	BA	xHR	xSB	xBA	OBP	SLG	OPS+	vL+	vR+	bb%	ct%	Eye	G	L	F	h%	HctX	QBaB	Brl%	PX	xPX	HR/F	xHR/F	Spd	SBA%	SB%	RAR	BPX	R$
19																																			
20																																			
21	a/a	375	46	11	35	18	266		15		308	409	98			6	73	0.22				34				86				105	31%	65%		15	$16
22	NYY *	469	50	16	39	27	229	1	17	239	281	373	93	96	122	7	72	0.26	58	15	28	28	94	FFf	3%	96	42	9%	9%	98	33%	83%	-5.6	28	$18
23	NYY *	473	49	12	40	15	211	4	17	237	268	339	83	50	81	7	74	0.29	50	19	32	26	88	CCf	4%	77	58	5%	10%	124	23%	67%	-11.5	32	$6
1st Half		204	23	9	22	10	226	0	8	270	268	395	91	78	67	5	79	0.27	54	19	27	24	74	CDf	0%	87	47	0%	0%	111	30%	75%	-4.4	111	$7
2nd Half		269	26	3	18	6	200	3	8	215	268	295	76	36	83	9	69	0.31	48	19	33	27	88	CCf	5%	68	62	6%	9%	128	17%	57%	-13.7	-36	$1
24	**Proj**	**350**	**38**	**5**	**30**	**14**	**234**	**5**	**16**	**218**	**316**	**324**	**88**	**69**	**95**	**7**	**73**	**0.27**	**49**	**19**	**33**	**31**	**82**		**3%**	**59**	**56**	**7%**	**7%**	**119**	**20%**	**72%**	**-7.3**	**23**	**$11**

Perdomo,Geraldo

Age: 24 Pos: SS 2B
Bats: B Ht: 6'2" Wt: 203

Health	A	LIMA Plan	D+
PT/Exp	A	Rand Var	-3
Consist	C	MM	1403

1st half prompted many to muse, "Maybe he's more than utility guy." After 2nd half? "Nah, we were right all along." Strong walk rate says he won't be total lineup drag, but QBaB screams 5 April-May HR were fluky, and xBA sets BA expectations. Has some wheels, so value could come that way, but to stick as full-timer he'll have to do more.

Yr	Tm	PA	R	HR	RBI	SB	BA	xHR	xSB	xBA	OBP	SLG	OPS+	vL+	vR+	bb%	ct%	Eye	G	L	F	h%	HctX	QBaB	Brl%	PX	xPX	HR/F	xHR/F	Spd	SBA%	SB%	RAR	BPX	R$
19																																			
20																																			
21	ARI *	366	38	4	23	5	202	1	9	168	282	297	80	111	109	10	71	0.38	33	13	54	28	46	DBf	4%	58	51	0%	8%	144	13%	47%	-20.8	-19	$0
22	ARI	500	58	5	40	9	195	4	8	220	285	262	77	79	77	10	76	0.49	47	21	32	24	75	FDf	2%	44	63	5%	4%	108	9%	82%	-27.2	-17	$3
23	ARI	495	71	6	47	16	246	3	18	229	353	359	97	78	100	13	79	0.74	38	19	43	30	79	FCf	1%	69	72	4%	2%	130	14%	80%	5.4	136	$11
1st Half		252	37	5	33	9	284	2	9	251	389	433	112	103	114	14	79	0.79	39	20	41	34	83	FCf	2%	92	81	7%	3%	117	14%	82%	10.7	200	$15
2nd Half		243	34	1	14	7	206	1	9	204	316	281	81	55	86	13	78	0.70	38	18	45	26	75	FBf	0%	44	61	1%	1%	147	14%	78%	-8.4	75	$2
24	**Proj**	**350**	**47**	**3**	**30**	**10**	**227**	**3**	**10**	**216**	**323**	**310**	**87**	**77**	**90**	**12**	**77**	**0.57**	**42**	**20**	**39**	**29**	**77**		**1%**	**52**	**67**	**3%**	**4%**	**120**	**13%**	**78%**	**-4.5**	**54**	**$9**

Pereira,Everson

Age: 23 Pos: LF
Bats: R Ht: 6'0" Wt: 191

Health	A	LIMA Plan	D
PT/Exp	D	Rand Var	0
Consist	A	MM	2403

0-10-.151 with 4 SB in 103 PA at NYY. Earned Sept promotion by terrorizing AAA pitching (.937 OPS, 99th percentile exit velocity) for 35 games. But penchant for swinging outside strike zone, missing a lot was exposed in first MLB action. To be sure, he's got plenty of time to hone approach, but 20/20 potential may be more of a 2025 thing.

Yr	Tm	PA	R	HR	RBI	SB	BA	xHR	xSB	xBA	OBP	SLG	OPS+	vL+	vR+	bb%	ct%	Eye	G	L	F	h%	HctX	QBaB	Brl%	PX	xPX	HR/F	xHR/F	Spd	SBA%	SB%	RAR	BPX	R$
19																																			
20																																			
21																																			
22	aa	120	16	4	10	2	244		3		288	410	99			6	63	0.17				35				117				139	15%	41%		0	$1
23	NYY *	431	47	14	59	12	237	1	11	227	295	401	95	55	59	8	61	0.21	47	23	30	35	104	ACc	8%	120	83	0%	6%	108	15%	85%	3.1	-29	$10
1st Half		180	19	8	25	6	261		6	239	324	477	110	0	0	9	63	0.25	44	20	36	37	0		0%	151	-21	0%		108	20%	72%	6.2	82	$7
2nd Half		251	28	6	36	7	224	1	6	214	280	358	86	55	59	7	61	0.20	47	23	30	34	103	ACc	8%	101	83	0%	6%	108	13%	100%	-3.5	-96	$10
24	**Proj**	**280**	**33**	**5**	**33**	**7**	**243**	**5**	**8**	**208**	**309**	**359**	**92**	**99**	**89**	**7**	**62**	**0.20**	**47**	**23**	**30**	**37**	**93**		**7%**	**85**	**75**	**10%**	**10%**	**125**	**14%**	**73%**	**-2.3**	**-13**	**$9**

Perez,Salvador

Age: 34 Pos: CA DH 1B
Bats: R Ht: 6'3" Wt: 255

Health	D	LIMA Plan	B+
PT/Exp	A	Rand Var	+1
Consist	B	MM	3135

Smattering of ticky-tack injuries (blurred vision, hamstring, hand, finger, concussion) likely caused 2nd half HR outage, but to extent his age-related power decline is upon us, it's graceful. If he logs another 50-plus games at 1B/DH, he's a good bet to yet again outpace most catching peers in HR, RBI, as long as health luck holds.

Yr	Tm	PA	R	HR	RBI	SB	BA	xHR	xSB	xBA	OBP	SLG	OPS+	vL+	vR+	bb%	ct%	Eye	G	L	F	h%	HctX	QBaB	Brl%	PX	xPX	HR/F	xHR/F	Spd	SBA%	SB%	RAR	BPX	R$
19																																			
20	KC	156	22	11	32	1	333	12	0	302	353	633	131	117	135	2	76	0.08	36	27	37	38	131	ABb	14%	168	175	26%	28%	62	3%	100%	16.9	252	$23
21	KC	665	88	48	121	1	273	47	0	270	316	544	118	134	112	4	73	0.16	37	23	40	30	130	ABd	16%	152	153	26%	26%	54	1%	100%	32.9	150	$29
22	KC	473	48	23	76	0	254	27	0	250	292	465	107	118	103	4	76	0.17	36	18	46	29	113	AAc	11%	132	131	15%	17%	71	0%	0%	12.5	131	$15
23	KC	578	59	23	80	0	255	23	0	247	292	422	97	90	100	3	75	0.14	36	23	41	30	109	BBc	9%	97	112	14%	14%	45	0%	0%	11.4	0	$14
1st Half		317	36	15	40	0	253	14	0	252	290	451	102	75	112	3	74	0.13	34	21	44	29	107	ABc	10%	116	110	15%	14%	56	0%	0%	5.9	57	$15
2nd Half		261	23	8	40	0	257	9	0	242	295	386	92	116	86	4	76	0.15	39	25	37	31	112	BCd	7%	74	115	12%	13%	43	0%	0%	1.3	-61	$10
24	**Proj**	**525**	**55**	**22**	**82**	**0**	**257**	**27**	**0**	**249**	**295**	**436**	**100**	**104**	**99**	**4**	**75**	**0.15**	**38**	**22**	**40**	**30**	**116**		**11%**	**106**	**130**	**15%**	**18%**	**52**	**0%**	**100%**	**13.4**	**74**	**$19**

Peterson,Jace

Age: 34 Pos: 3B 2B
Bats: L Ht: 6'0" Wt: 215

Health	C	LIMA Plan	D
PT/Exp	A	Rand Var	+3
Consist	B	MM	1411

Fate—and sage decision to sign with talent-poor OAK—again brought more PA than skills warrant; playoff roster snub showed standing with "real" ARI team. Still, SB% is no joke, defensive versatility could get him more work, and in deep leagues, maybe that equates to cheap end-game speed. But grasp on MLB roster spot will remain tenuous.

Yr	Tm	PA	R	HR	RBI	SB	BA	xHR	xSB	xBA	OBP	SLG	OPS+	vL+	vR+	bb%	ct%	Eye	G	L	F	h%	HctX	QBaB	Brl%	PX	xPX	HR/F	xHR/F	Spd	SBA%	SB%	RAR	BPX	R$
19	BAL *	467	55	9	44	13	236	2	9	257	300	373	93	99	77	8	78	0.41	43	25	32	28	95	CCb	4%	74	97	8%	8%	94	17%	73%	-22.1	67	$9
20	MIL	61	6	2	5	1	200	2	1	181	393	356	99	52	102	25	56	0.75	54	15	31	30	86	BDa	8%	110	117	25%	25%	103	5%	100%	-0.8	-28	$0
21	MIL *	362	43	9	42	11	233	6	6	228	326	371	96	85	101	12	70	0.46	41	23	35	30	71	CCd	5%	88	77	9%	9%	91	13%	91%	-1.8	15	$9
22	MIL	328	44	8	34	12	236	8	7	240	316	382	99	101	99	10	70	0.39	45	23	32	31	96	CDd	7%	102	119	12%	12%	95	16%	92%	-1.4	48	$10
23	2 TM	430	35	6	37	15	211	8	13	213	304	307	83	66	86	11	73	0.47	42	20	39	27	78	DCd	5%	57	97	6%	8%	115	15%	88%	-9.1	-11	$4
1st Half		273	24	5	22	9	209	6	8	212	300	314	84	53	91	11	73	0.45	43	18	39	26	81	DBf	6%	61	98	7%	9%	114	14%	90%	-7.8	-4	$3
2nd Half		157	11	1	15	6	215	2	5	215	310	296	82	109	79	12	73	0.49	39	24	37	29	73	DCc	3%	50	95	3%	6%	103	17%	86%	-4.5	-46	-$1
24	**Proj**	**245**	**25**	**4**	**24**	**9**	**224**	**5**	**6**	**226**	**312**	**338**	**89**	**87**	**90**	**11**	**72**	**0.44**	**42**	**22**	**36**	**29**	**82**		**5%**	**72**	**99**	**7%**	**9%**	**98**	**16%**	**88%**	**-1.6**	**6**	**$7**

Pham,Tommy

Age: 36 Pos: LF DH
Bats: R Ht: 6'1" Wt: 223

Health	B	LIMA Plan	B
PT/Exp	A	Rand Var	0
Consist	B	MM	3335

Took late-career renaissance up a notch. Statcast metrics suggest decent BA, high-teens HR could last (and latter might even be higher but for ground ball rate). No need to banish to weak-side platoon, either. But please, do note xSB, Spd, 2021-22 success rate, and advancing age—unless bases are getting even bigger, some pullback likely.

Yr	Tm	PA	R	HR	RBI	SB	BA	xHR	xSB	xBA	OBP	SLG	OPS+	vL+	vR+	bb%	ct%	Eye	G	L	F	h%	HctX	QBaB	Brl%	PX	xPX	HR/F	xHR/F	Spd	SBA%	SB%	RAR	BPX	R$
19	TAM	654	77	21	68	25	273	23	17	281	369	450	113	131	105	12	78	0.66	53	22	25	32	118	AFc	8%	95	95	19%	21%	106	16%	86%	11.6	178	$25
20	SD	125	13	3	12	6	211	5	3	223	312	312	83	126	66	12	75	0.56	62	13	24	25	145	AFd	7%	54	101	15%	25%	99	18%	100%	-6.2	0	$8
21	SD	561	74	15	49	14	229	17	12	244	340	383	99	94	101	14	73	0.61	48	20	32	28	111	ADd	10%	95	116	14%	15%	104	13%	70%	-4.6	112	$13
22	2 TM	622	89	17	63	8	236	17	7	227	312	374	97	110	93	9	70	0.34	48	18	34	31	117	ADd	8%	96	99	13%	13%	95	7%	73%	-2.6	17	$16
23	2 NL	481	55	16	68	22	256	19	15	276	328	446	106	106	105	10	75	0.44	49	22	29	31	129	ADc	11%	116	114	17%	20%	85	22%	88%	16.3	143	$17
1st Half		207	24	9	34	9	295	11	6	291	362	530	122	127	118	10	74	0.45	45	24	30	35	135	ADc	15%	144	143	21%	26%	77	20%	90%	16.4	207	$15
2nd Half		274	31	7	34	13	226	8	9	265	303	383	93	85	96	10	76	0.44	51	20	28	27	124	AFd	8%	95	93	13%	15%	93	25%	87%	-0.7	100	$14
24	**Proj**	**455**	**57**	**14**	**55**	**13**	**245**	**16**	**11**	**255**	**326**	**409**	**101**	**106**	**98**	**11**	**74**	**0.45**	**49**	**20**	**30**	**30**	**123**		**10%**	**102**	**108**	**15%**	**18%**	**87**	**14%**	**81%**	**8.3**	**101**	**$17**

RIS OLSON

Pillar,Kevin

Age: 35 Pos: LF
Bats: R Ht: 6'0" Wt: 200

Health	F	LIMA Plan	D+
PT/Exp	D	Rand Var	+1
Consist	A	MM	2231

Made it back from shoulder fracture that cost him most of 2022, though hard to see what'd elevate him beyond weak-side platoon/defensive replacement. Some might think 2nd half jeopardizes even that, but xBA says he deserved better. No longer a "pillar"; he's more like a deep-league sconce—moderately appealing and marginally useful.

Yr	Tm	PA	R	HR	RBI	SB	BA	xHR	xSB	xBA	OBP	SLG	OPS+	vL+	vR+	bb%	ct%	Eye	G	L	F	h%	HctX	QBaB	Brl%	PX	xPX	HR/F	xHR/F	Spd	SBA%	SB%	RAR	BPX	R$
19	2 TM	645	83	21	88	14	259	17	11	276	287	432	100	114	93	3	85	0.20	44	20	36	27	110	DBc	5%	86	71	11%	9%	106	15%	74%	-2.9	185	$2
20	2 TM	223	34	6	26	5	288	7	6	266	336	462	106	126	93	6	80	0.32	41	24	35	34	119	CCc	5%	93	106	10%	12%	146	13%	71%	2.0	212	$2
21	NYM	347	40	15	47	4	231	10	6	232	277	415	95	92	96	3	75	0.14	35	19	46	26	98	DAd	7%	102	99	13%	9%	129	10%	57%	-10.4	112	$
22	LA *	172	22	6	20	1	205	1	2	239	255	361	87	163	0	6	79	0.31	50	13	38	23	215	CCa	13%	92	204	0%	33%	114	6%	43%	-6.0	131	$
23	ATL	206	29	9	32	4	228	6	3	256	248	416	90	99	79	3	75	0.12	35	24	41	26	109	CAd	8%	112	113	15%	10%	88	16%	80%	-2.2	79	$
1st Half		107	16	6	17	3	255	4	2	266	280	490	106	120	82	4	75	0.15	30	24	46	29	118	CAf	11%	139	153	17%	11%	99	17%	100%	2.8	171	$
2nd Half		99	13	3	15	1	200	2	1	247	212	337	74	71	76	2	75	0.08	40	25	36	24	100	CBc	5%	83	72	12%	8%	80	14%	50%	-5.2	-14	-$
24	Proj	**210**	**28**	**8**	**30**	**3**	**224**	**10**	**3**	**250**	**259**	**395**	**90**	**95**	**85**	**4**	**77**	**0.17**	**37**	**22**	**40**	**25**	**107**		**7%**	**99**	**100**	**13%**	**15%**	**95**	**12%**	**68%**	**-3.7**	**99**	**$**

Polanco,Jorge

Age: 30 Pos: 2B
Bats: B Ht: 5'11" Wt: 208

Health	F	LIMA Plan	B
PT/Exp	A	Rand Var	-2
Consist	B	MM	3225

14-48-.255 with 4 SB in 343 PA at MIN. Began year on IL (knee), then hamstring laid him low twice, once for seven weeks. Got on roll in Aug, showing that power, patience are still there, though now more reason to think ct% is gone for good. If he can stay on field, 20+ HR is still in reach... but there's more doubt about that than there used to be.

Yr	Tm	PA	R	HR	RBI	SB	BA	xHR	xSB	xBA	OBP	SLG	OPS+	vL+	vR+	bb%	ct%	Eye	G	L	F	h%	HctX	QBaB	Brl%	PX	xPX	HR/F	xHR/F	Spd	SBA%	SB%	RAR	BPX	R$
19	MIN	704	107	22	79	4	295	25	8	267	356	485	116	101	122	9	82	0.52	29	26	44	33	112	CAb	7%	97	132	10%	11%	121	4%	57%	24.6	222	$2
20	MIN	226	22	4	19	4	258	4	3	243	304	354	87	105	81	6	83	0.37	36	25	39	29	82	DBc	3%	53	75	6%	6%	89	11%	67%	-6.1	64	$1
21	MIN	644	97	33	98	11	269	30	8	273	323	503	114	109	116	7	80	0.38	32	23	45	29	109	CAd	10%	128	117	16%	14%	78	12%	65%	21.2	235	$2
22	MIN	445	54	16	56	3	235	20	3	236	346	405	106	84	118	14	75	0.67	30	22	48	27	108	CAc	10%	109	120	12%	15%	73	5%	50%	10.3	134	$1
23	MIN *	378	41	15	49	4	250	18	3	241	329	437	104	111	106	10	70	0.39	29	25	47	32	86	CAc	14%	122	116	14%	18%	76	4%	100%	14.2	75	$
1st Half		136	12	5	16	1	240	8	1	256	282	427	97	130	94	6	73	0.22	33	23	43	29	82	DAc	14%	121	96	13%	21%	73	4%	100%	0.7	89	-$
2nd Half		243	29	10	33	3	256	10	3	232	355	444	108	103	114	13	67	0.47	25	25	49	33	89	BAb	13%	122	130	15%	16%	85	4%	100%	9.6	75	$1
24	Proj	**455**	**55**	**18**	**60**	**5**	**247**	**21**	**4**	**241**	**327**	**433**	**104**	**99**	**106**	**10**	**72**	**0.42**	**30**	**24**	**46**	**30**	**96**		**11%**	**117**	**116**	**13%**	**16%**	**79**	**6%**	**74%**	**13.5**	**123**	**$1**

Pratto,Nick

Age: 25 Pos: 1B OF
Bats: L Ht: 6'1" Wt: 215

Health	B	LIMA Plan	D
PT/Exp	A	Rand Var	-3
Consist	C	MM	3203

7-35-.232 in 345 PA at KC. Left off Opening Day roster, but got quick call, and favorable h% made it seem like he'd arrived (.295 BA in April/May). But poor contact rate eventually caught up with him, late July groin injury sent him to the mat, and he looked lost in 2nd half. Until he shows signs of closing holes in bat, best to pass.

Yr	Tm	PA	R	HR	RBI	SB	BA	xHR	xSB	xBA	OBP	SLG	OPS+	vL+	vR+	bb%	ct%	Eye	G	L	F	h%	HctX	QBaB	Brl%	PX	xPX	HR/F	xHR/F	Spd	SBA%	SB%	RAR	BPX	R$
19																																			
20																																			
21	a/a	508	74	25	74	9	232		9		328	487	112			12	63	0.38				31				173				113	14%	62%		192	$
22	KC *	518	51	16	47	5	180	6	4	180	263	335	85	93	93	10	59	0.27	33	14	53	26	78	DAf	13%	124	139	14%	12%	86	7%	67%	-20.5	-59	
23	KC *	466	42	9	46	1	209	8	3	199	277	326	82	95	88	8	57	0.22	37	27	37	34	80	CCd	8%	98	100	11%	13%	78	2%	50%	-11.7	-175	
1st Half		308	31	6	29	1	225	6	3	226	299	360	90	103	102	10	62	0.28	37	29	34	34	97	CCc	10%	106	112	12%	15%	84	3%	50%	-7.2	-71	
2nd Half		158	12	3	17	0	179	1	1	146	234	264	67	63	66	7	48	0.14	37	21	42	34	49	DBf	5%	77	71	9%	5%	82	0%	0%	-11.5	-379	
24	Proj	**315**	**32**	**9**	**33**	**2**	**207**	**7**	**3**	**185**	**284**	**348**	**87**	**89**	**86**	**9**	**57**	**0.24**	**35**	**20**	**45**	**33**	**73**		**9%**	**112**	**108**	**12%**	**10%**	**88**	**5%**	**64%**	**-7.9**	**-120**	

Profar,Jurickson

Age: 31 Pos: LF
Bats: B Ht: 6'0" Wt: 184

Health	A	LIMA Plan	D+
PT/Exp	A	Rand Var	+1
Consist	B	MM	1331

Missed Opening Day due to signing late, visa issue; once on field, there was no sign of Coors boost. By Aug, COL lost interest, SD took him in, but story stayed same: decent plate skills, no "sizzle"—either from lackluster power or moribund running game. Next step is likely reserve role, where HR, SB totals might be mired in single digits for good.

Yr	Tm	PA	R	HR	RBI	SB	BA	xHR	xSB	xBA	OBP	SLG	OPS+	vL+	vR+	bb%	ct%	Eye	G	L	F	h%	HctX	QBaB	Brl%	PX	xPX	HR/F	xHR/F	Spd	SBA%	SB%	RAR	BPX	R$
19	OAK	518	65	20	67	9	218	17	5	277	301	410	98	116	92	9	84	0.64	41	22	37	22	109	CCd	7%	93	98	14%	12%	82	9%	90%	-17.2	200	$
20	SD	202	28	7	25	7	278	5	5	276	343	428	102	100	103	7	84	0.54	44	25	31	30	99	CCf	3%	74	58	15%	11%	100	14%	88%	-0.4	176	$
21	SD	411	47	4	33	10	227	4	10	239	329	320	89	65	96	12	82	0.75	42	21	37	27	78	DBf	3%	57	53	4%	4%	117	13%	67%	-13.3	127	
22	SD	658	82	15	58	5	243	11	7	268	331	391	102	103	102	11	82	0.71	44	22	34	27	106	CCd	4%	94	86	9%	7%	110	4%	83%	6.5	210	$
23	2 NL	520	55	9	46	1	242	7	4	255	321	368	94	104	90	10	80	0.56	40	23	37	28	109	DBd	4%	77	96	6%	5%	97	1%	100%	0.3	118	
1st Half		336	36	6	31	1	245	4	3	265	327	384	98	106	94	11	79	0.56	40	25	35	29	113	DCd	4%	87	106	7%	5%	100	1%	100%	1.8	136	
2nd Half		184	19	3	15	0	236	2	1	236	310	339	88	101	83	8	83	0.54	41	19	41	27	100	CBd	3%	62	79	5%	4%	95	0%	0%	-3.1	104	
24	Proj	**245**	**29**	**5**	**22**	**2**	**240**	**4**	**3**	**255**	**322**	**367**	**94**	**98**	**93**	**10**	**82**	**0.61**	**42**	**22**	**37**	**27**	**101**		**4%**	**76**	**82**	**7%**	**5%**	**103**	**5%**	**77%**	**0.3**	**149**	

Rafaela,Ceddanne

Age: 23 Pos: CF
Bats: R Ht: 5'8" Wt: 145

Health	A	LIMA Plan	C+
PT/Exp	B	Rand Var	0
Consist	A	MM	2533

2-5-.241 in 89 PA at BOS. Called up to MLB after big second half in AAA. Undersized and short-levered yet packs a soli punch. High swing% hitter who spoils lots of pitches but expands zone. All-fields approach with surprising oppo pop. Defensive skills carry profile to immediate CF reps, and plus run tool should pad SB. (CB)

Yr	Tm	PA	R	HR	RBI	SB	BA	xHR	xSB	xBA	OBP	SLG	OPS+	vL+	vR+	bb%	ct%	Eye	G	L	F	h%	HctX	QBaB	Brl%	PX	xPX	HR/F	xHR/F	Spd	SBA%	SB%	RAR	BPX	R$
19																																			
20																																			
21																																			
22	aa	295	31	8	35	10	246		9		274	412	97			4	76	0.16				30				106				118	28%	64%		124	
23	BOS *	551	69	17	62	29	265	1	32	269	295	442	100	87	92	4	73	0.16	42	27	31	33	53	DDf	5%	112	38	12%	6%	149	42%	65%	6.7	136	$
1st Half		271	31	5	27	22	252		18	242	279	375	90	0	0	4	76	0.15	44	20	36	32	0		0%	82	-21	0%		107	58%	68%	-5.2	32	$
2nd Half		280	37	12	34	7	277	1	12	279	309	507	110	86	91	4	71	0.16	42	27	31	35	52	DDf	5%	143	38	12%	6%	168	23%	57%	9.5	214	$
24	Proj	**315**	**37**	**6**	**36**	**13**	**259**	**4**	**15**	**257**	**292**	**400**	**95**	**90**	**97**	**4**	**74**	**0.16**	**42**	**27**	**31**	**33**	**47**		**5%**	**91**	**34**	**9%**	**6%**	**147**	**31%**	**66%**	**-0.4**	**133**	**$**

Raleigh,Cal

Age: 27 Pos: CA
Bats: R Ht: 6'3" Wt: 235

Health	A	LIMA Plan	B
PT/Exp	A	Rand Var	0
Consist	B	MM	4125

Ended 2022 with broken thumb, torn ligament in left hand, requiring surgery, but no real sign of lingering impact. Sure power skills weren't nearly as elite, and launch angle fluctuated more, but as xHR shows, 30 HR is legit, even as strikeouts will make it hard for him to hit .240. Account for that in roster build, and Big Dumper'll do you just fine.

Yr	Tm	PA	R	HR	RBI	SB	BA	xHR	xSB	xBA	OBP	SLG	OPS+	vL+	vR+	bb%	ct%	Eye	G	L	F	h%	HctX	QBaB	Brl%	PX	xPX	HR/F	xHR/F	Spd	SBA%	SB%	RAR	BPX
19	aa	159	16	7	16	0	217		0		287	403	95			9	63	0.26				29				115				96	0%	0%		-22
20																																		
21	SEA *	334	31	8	39	2	224	3	2	239	265	399	91	79	72	5	73	0.21	36	18	45	28	65	CBf	7%	120	78	5%	8%	69	8%	47%	-5.4	88
22	SEA *	444	48	28	65	1	210	26	1	243	281	477	107	103	112	9	67	0.30	28	16	56	23	108	AAc	15%	183	157	19%	18%	82	1%	100%	9.9	203
23	SEA	569	78	30	75	0	232	30	3	242	306	456	104	85	108	9	69	0.34	31	20	49	27	99	BAf	13%	138	135	17%	17%	86	0%	0%	20.1	121
1st Half		272	36	11	33	0	224	14	2	231	298	411	97	81	100	10	72	0.37	36	18	46	27	93	CAf	13%	113	120	14%	17%	99	0%	0%	3.3	96
2nd Half		297	42	19	42	0	240	17	1	251	313	498	110	87	116	9	67	0.32	27	22	51	28	105	BAd	13%	161	150	21%	18%	77	0%	0%	13.0	146
24	Proj	**525**	**64**	**29**	**69**	**1**	**225**	**29**	**2**	**240**	**292**	**464**	**104**	**93**	**107**	**9**	**69**	**0.30**	**31**	**18**	**51**	**26**	**98**		**13%**	**152**	**136**	**17%**	**17%**	**77**	**1%**	**62%**	**16.0**	**125**

Raley,Luke

Age: 29 Pos: RF 1B
Bats: L Ht: 6'4" Wt: 235

Health	A	LIMA Plan	C
PT/Exp	B	Rand Var	-2
Consist	B	MM	4303

1st half power show put him in heady company, but couldn't keep up pace, even as team hid him from LHP. Nagging injuries (knee, neck) may have played role, but more likely just a good run, given persistent ct% woes. xSB mostly validates SB, and Spd, SB% suggests opps could keep coming. Pay for 15/10, and hope BA stays above water.

Yr	Tm	PA	R	HR	RBI	SB	BA	xHR	xSB	xBA	OBP	SLG	OPS+	vL+	vR+	bb%	ct%	Eye	G	L	F	h%	HctX	QBaB	Brl%	PX	xPX	HR/F	xHR/F	Spd	SBA%	SB%	RAR	BPX
19	aaa	132	23	6	17	3	267		2		299	448	103			4	63	0.12				38				116				100	11%	100%		-59
20																																		
21	LA *	360	43	15	48	5	217	3	4	229	257	388	89	8	95	5	65	0.15	55	18	28	28	84	CFf	12%	111	91	18%	27%	80	13%	58%	-16.9	-54
22	TAM *	317	32	9	36	5	216	2	5	167	278	345	88	101	79	8	58	0.20	41	11	49	34	73	CBd	13%	104	80	6%	11%	103	11%	64%	-9.7	-128
23	TAM	406	56	19	49	14	249	20	12	240	333	490	112	100	114	7	64	0.22	42	13	45	33	95	BBf	13%	165	118	19%	20%	104	19%	82%	13.1	129
1st Half		224	44	14	35	9	281	14	7	268	363	587	130	105	133	8	65	0.23	40	16	44	36	113	BBc	18%	203	154	26%	26%	106	22%	82%	15.7	250
2nd Half		182	12	5	14	5	211	6	4	199	297	373	90	95	90	7	63	0.20	44	10	46	30	73	CBf	7%	117	75	11%	13%	97	15%	83%	-4.6	-29
24	Proj	**385**	**47**	**15**	**46**	**10**	**233**	**17**	**9**	**208**	**315**	**414**	**100**	**84**	**103**	**7**	**62**	**0.20**	**44**	**13**	**44**	**33**	**83**		**12%**	**129**	**95**	**15%**	**18%**	**101**	**14%**	**77%**	**-0.3**	**-5**

KRIS OLSON

Ramírez,Harold

Age: 29	Pos: DH		Health	C	LIMA Plan	B
Bats: R	Ht: 5' 10"	Wt: 232	PT/Exp	A	Rand Var	-5
			Consist	B	MM	1133

Last two seasons of mid-range value almost entirely due to inflated BA. If regression suggested by xBA kicks in, all those lost hits would have cascading effect on OBP, R, and RBI. Even recent dominance vL has been driven by 43% hit rate. All of this makes him a very risky investment; don't be the one burned by... DN: Repeat of 2021

Yr	Tm	PA	R	HR	RBI	SB	BA	xHR	xSB	xBA	OBP	SLG	OPS+	vL+	vR+	bb%	ct%	Eye	G	L	F	h%	HctX	QBaB	Brl%	PX	xPX	HR/F	xHR/F	Spd	SBA%	SB%	RAR	BPX	R$
19	MIA *	560	71	14	62	3	282	11	4	271	312	433	103	92	103	4	79	0.21	57	20	23	34	95	CFb	6%	82	63	14%	14%	102	4%	57%	-7.8	78	$14
20	MIA	11	2	0	1	0	200	0	0	176	273	200	63	65	60	9	80	0.50	50	13	38	25	81	FCf		0	161	0%	0%	87	33%	0%	-1.3	-132	-$2
21	CLE	361	33	7	41	3	268	8	2	260	305	398	97	105	92	4	83	0.25	53	17	30	30	120	ADd	6%	77	92	8%	9%	73	5%	75%	-9.3	104	$8
22	TAM	435	46	6	58	3	300	7	5	253	343	404	106	122	99	4	82	0.26	53	19	28	35	104	CFd	5%	72	76	6%	7%	87	7%	38%	0.4	79	$16
23	TAM	434	58	12	68	5	313	11	8	262	353	460	111	130	102	5	80	0.28	55	17	29	37	95	CDd	5%	83	60	13%	12%	103	7%	63%	18.1	107	$18
1st Half		242	32	9	35	4	284	8	5	264	326	458	107	143	95	6	78	0.28	51	18	31	33	82	BDc	6%	98	64	16%	15%	110	8%	80%	4.6	129	$15
2nd Half		192	26	3	33	1	349	4	3	258	385	463	115	118	113	4	83	0.28	59	15	26	41	111	CFd	3%	67	56	8%	10%	88	5%	33%	8.9	86	$13
24	Proj	420	49	9	59	4	288	10	5	259	327	416	102	113	97	4	81	0.25	55	17	28	33	103		5%	77	69	10%	11%	82	6%	52%	6.3	95	$14

Ramírez,José

Age: 31	Pos: 3B DH		Health	A	LIMA Plan	C
Bats: B	Ht: 5' 9"	Wt: 190	PT/Exp	A	Rand Var	0
			Consist	A	MM	3455

Before getting worried about R$ drop, note his 2nd half RBI. He hit just .147/.304/.213 with runners in scoring position in 2nd half; teammates didn't help as only 92 of his 337 PA were with RISP. This shouldn't happen again. Trends in Brl%, xPX might be more legitimate concerns, but plate skills still solid and will help boost R$ rebound.

Yr	Tm	PA	R	HR	RBI	SB	BA	xHR	xSB	xBA	OBP	SLG	OPS+	vL+	vR+	bb%	ct%	Eye	G	L	F	h%	HctX	QBaB	Brl%	PX	xPX	HR/F	xHR/F	Spd	SBA%	SB%	RAR	BPX	R$
19	CLE	542	68	23	83	24	255	20	14	273	327	479	112	110	112	10	85	0.70	33	21	46	26	118	CAc	6%	109	114	12%	10%	94	24%	86%	6.6	278	$23
20	CLE	254	45	17	46	10	292	14	7	285	386	607	132	184	113	12	80	0.72	30	19	51	30	108	CAc	10%	163	134	19%	16%	101	20%	77%	20.9	432	$42
21	CLE	636	111	36	103	27	266	29	17	287	355	538	123	120	124	11	84	0.83	36	19	45	26	137	BAf	11%	136	125	17%	14%	102	20%	87%	40.9	388	$37
22	CLE	685	90	29	126	20	280	20	16	279	355	514	123	102	130	10	86	0.84	32	17	51	28	110	CAf	7%	133	100	11%	7%	103	16%	74%	41.2	362	$39
23	CLE	691	87	24	80	28	282	23	25	285	356	475	113	103	118	11	88	1.00	35	22	43	29	114	BAc	7%	98	98	10%	10%	113	19%	82%	42.1	314	$29
1st Half		354	51	13	52	9	293	13	10	288	362	511	120	90	132	11	89	1.06	32	21	47	30	108	BAd	8%	110	106	10%	10%	112	14%	69%	21.7	357	$30
2nd Half		337	36	11	28	19	270	10	14	283	350	437	106	114	101	11	87	0.95	38	24	39	28	121	BBc	6%	86	90	11%	10%	108	23%	90%	12.2	264	$25
24	Proj	665	91	26	95	27	280	24	21	277	358	487	116	109	119	11	86	0.89	34	20	45	29	117		8%	109	104	11%	10%	106	19%	82%	41.5	335	$37

Ramos,Heliot

Age: 24	Pos: OF		Health	C	LIMA Plan	D
Bats: R	Ht: 6' 1"	Wt: 188	PT/Exp	B	Rand Var	-4
			Consist	D	MM	2301

1-2-.179 in 60 PA at SF. Showed small signs of progress in 2nd half, but for the most part, development has been slow and discouraging. Can see why SF hasn't given him many PA: not much use for a guy whose two best skills are 1) hitting a lot of ground balls, and 2) running fast and often while being pretty lousy at actually stealing bases.

Yr	Tm	PA	R	HR	RBI	SB	BA	xHR	xSB	xBA	OBP	SLG	OPS+	vL+	vR+	bb%	ct%	Eye	G	L	F	h%	HctX	QBaB	Brl%	PX	xPX	HR/F	xHR/F	Spd	SBA%	SB%	RAR	BPX	R$
19	aa	105	13	3	15	2	244		3		318	416	102			10	65	0.31				35				113				111	22%	40%		19	$0
20																																			
21	a/a	481	50	9	43	11	218		8		270	341	84			7	66	0.21				31				88				102	15%	78%		-69	$7
22	SF *	475	41	6	27	4	176	1	7	189	224	253	68	49	0	6	70	0.21	64	7	29	24	87	CFf	7%	58	39	0%	25%	106	13%	35%	-35.3	-93	-$5
23	SF *	306	35	8	33	6	233	2	9	210	290	392	93	79	50	7	66	0.23	50	9	41	33	76	CCd	14%	112	89	7%	14%	133	17%	57%	-2.0	29	$4
1st Half		96	8	1	9	4	206	1	4	200	248	285	73	66	69	5	73	0.21	50	13	38	27	116	FCc	11%	55	151	0%	17%	111	32%	64%	-5.2	-61	-$7
2nd Half		210	27	7	23	2	245	1	5	213	309	443	102	92	42	8	62	0.24	50	6	44	36	44	ABf	17%	145	35	13%	13%	138	9%	47%	2.8	82	$7
24	Proj	245	26	5	23	5	229	5	6	193	282	354	87	94	64	7	67	0.22	50	8	42	32	73		7%	88	81	8%	8%	115	16%	56%	-4.9	-19	$6

Realmuto,J.T.

Age: 33	Pos: CA		Health	A	LIMA Plan	C+
Bats: R	Ht: 6' 1"	Wt: 212	PT/Exp	A	Rand Var	0
			Consist	B	MM	3435

While power skills mostly held steady, all it took to undo career-best R$ was 24 points of BA (caused by dip in ct%, rise in FB%) and 21 RBI (.782 OPS with runners in scoring position in 2022, .611 in 2023). The former was skills, latter was random fluctuation, but most likely outcome for both is mild rebound. Let regression lead you to profit.

Yr	Tm	PA	R	HR	RBI	SB	BA	xHR	xSB	xBA	OBP	SLG	OPS+	vL+	vR+	bb%	ct%	Eye	G	L	F	h%	HctX	QBaB	Brl%	PX	xPX	HR/F	xHR/F	Spd	SBA%	SB%	RAR	BPX	R$
19	PHI	592	92	25	83	9	275	22	7	272	328	493	114	118	111	7	77	0.33	39	23	38	32	122	BBb	9%	117	118	16%	14%	111	8%	90%	21.0	189	$21
20	PHI	195	33	11	32	4	266	13	3	244	349	491	112	142	100	8	72	0.33	48	14	38	31	110	BCd	14%	124	121	23%	28%	90	10%	80%	7.8	136	$23
21	PHI	537	64	17	73	13	263	16	13	249	343	439	107	99	111	9	73	0.37	46	20	33	33	107	BCc	9%	107	98	15%	14%	131	12%	81%	16.5	138	$19
22	PHI	562	75	22	84	21	276	23	15	266	342	478	116	113	117	7	76	0.34	44	20	36	32	115	BCc	11%	125	112	16%	16%	122	16%	95%	31.0	203	$31
23	PHI	538	70	20	63	16	252	24	17	247	310	452	104	113	100	7	72	0.25	38	20	42	31	96	BBc	11%	124	112	13%	16%	127	18%	76%	17.9	139	$17
1st Half		293	33	9	32	10	244	11	9	255	304	455	104	115	99	7	73	0.28	38	19	43	30	93	CBd	11%	131	109	11%	13%	121	23%	77%	7.6	175	$14
2nd Half		245	37	11	31	6	260	13	6	238	318	448	104	110	102	6	70	0.23	37	21	42	32	99	ABc	12%	115	116	16%	19%	110	14%	75%	7.4	75	$16
24	Proj	525	73	21	72	13	262	23	14	251	326	460	108	111	106	7	73	0.29	41	20	39	32	105		11%	119	111	15%	17%	117	13%	79%	23.6	145	$24

Refsnyder,Rob

Age: 33	Pos: LF		Health	C	LIMA Plan	D
Bats: R	Ht: 6' 0"	Wt: 205	PT/Exp	C	Rand Var	+1
			Consist	C	MM	1221

Keeps pulling rabbits out of his hat, first with perfect storm of high h% and power surge in 2022, then with nearly as many SB in 2023 (7) as in entire MLB career prior (10). HR already gone, steals will likely fade with PA. So here's his best remaining trick: he's played for six teams and can help you get lower rarity score on Immaculate Grid.

Yr	Tm	PA	R	HR	RBI	SB	BA	xHR	xSB	xBA	OBP	SLG	OPS+	vL+	vR+	bb%	ct%	Eye	G	L	F	h%	HctX	QBaB	Brl%	PX	xPX	HR/F	xHR/F	Spd	SBA%	SB%	RAR	BPX	R$
19	aaa	327	33	9	35	0	257		2		314	411	100			8	62	0.22				38				106				97	3%	0%		-67	$4
20	TEX	34	4	0	1	0	200	0	0	170	265	233	66	82	41	6	63	0.18	45	20	35	32	103	ABa		32	98	0%	0%	95	0%	0%	-2.8	-312	-$3
21	MIN *	232	30	5	22	1	246	5	0	235	330	380	97	107	80	11	72	0.45	42	23	35	32	101	CCc	7%	88	125	6%	14%	76	2%	100%	-0.6	27	$2
22	BOS *	346	46	10	39	3	274	7	3	254	345	456	114	141	113	10	67	0.33	37	28	35	38	110	BCa	11%	143	144	16%	18%	86	5%	77%	12.0	103	$11
23	BOS	242	31	1	28	7	248	4	8	243	365	317	93	112	64	14	77	0.70	43	27	30	32	84	CCc	4%	48	69	2%	9%	116	12%	78%	0.1	32	$3
1st Half		153	17	1	21	6	270	2	6	259	395	357	103	126	72	14	74	0.64	42	33	25	36	74	CCa	5%	60	57	4%	9%	121	12%	100%	3.0	36	$2
2nd Half		89	14	0	7	1	211	1	2	213	315	250	76	91	47	14	82	0.86	44	17	38	26	100	CCf	3%	31	86	0%	4%	96	12%	33%	-4.4	32	-$5
24	Proj	245	33	4	26	4	248	6	4	239	346	361	97	111	81	12	73	0.50	41	25	34	32	98		7%	78	106	7%	11%	92	8%	64%	1.4	40	$7

Rendon,Anthony

Age: 34	Pos: 3B		Health	F	LIMA Plan	D+
Bats: R	Ht: 6' 1"	Wt: 200	PT/Exp	D	Rand Var	0
			Consist	A	MM	2231

If it's "Fool me once, shame on you; fool me twice, shame on me," then logical next step is "Fool me thrice, can't you see that I need help??" Even if you're willing to brave health risk, after three seasons of small-sample, injury-marred data, we don't even know if he's the same hitter. Looks more like Cristian Pache right now. (No offense intended.)

Yr	Tm	PA	R	HR	RBI	SB	BA	xHR	xSB	xBA	OBP	SLG	OPS+	vL+	vR+	bb%	ct%	Eye	G	L	F	h%	HctX	QBaB	Brl%	PX	xPX	HR/F	xHR/F	Spd	SBA%	SB%	RAR	BPX	R$
19	WAS	646	117	34	126	5	319	36	5	296	412	598	140	146	137	12	84	0.93	33	21	46	33	130	BAb	12%	136	160	16%	17%	96	3%	83%	59.7	374	$33
20	LAA	232	29	9	31	0	286	8	1	270	418	497	122	131	117	16	84	1.23	35	21	44	30	146	BAb	6%	108	119	13%	12%	105	0%	0%	12.4	348	$18
21	LAA	249	24	6	34	0	240	5	0	245	329	382	98	87	103	12	81	0.71	31	22	47	27	99	CAb	6%	84	97	7%	6%	69	0%	0%	0.5	146	$2
22	LAA	193	15	5	24	2	229	6	1	252	326	380	100	122	91	12	79	0.66	35	23	42	26	114	BAc	8%	99	106	9%	11%	73	4%	100%	0.7	148	$1
23	LAA	183	23	2	22	2	236	4	2	229	361	318	92	98	90	14	82	0.93	35	22	43	28	99	BBd	5%	50	81	4%	7%	73	3%	100%	0.3	64	$1
1st Half		176	23	2	22	2	238	3	2	232	358	322	93	94	92	14	83	0.96	35	21	44	27	99	BBc	4%	51	83	4%	6%	73	4%	100%	-1.7	89	$0
2nd Half		7	0	0	0	0	200	1	0	185	429	200	85	167	0	29	40	0.67	50	50	0	50	81	AAf	13%	0	-21	0%		94	0%	0%	-0.2	-546	-$9
24	Proj	245	29	6	34	2	252	7	1	252	358	401	104	106	103	13	82	0.84	34	22	44	28	112		7%	87	104	8%	9%	80	2%	98%	6.4	182	$8

Renfroe,Hunter

Age: 32	Pos: RF		Health	B	LIMA Plan	B
Bats: R	Ht: 6' 1"	Wt: 230	PT/Exp	A	Rand Var	0
			Consist	B	MM	4125

Salary, August swoon (.590 OPS) landed him on waivers, Sept collapse (.432 OPS) got him released. Late hamstring woes may have contributed to weak 2nd half, but even 1st half power metrics were down from recent levels. 3-year HR/xHR trends urge caution and fits the profile for "old player skills decline faster" so wise to hedge your bets.

Yr	Tm	PA	R	HR	RBI	SB	BA	xHR	xSB	xBA	OBP	SLG	OPS+	vL+	vR+	bb%	ct%	Eye	G	L	F	h%	HctX	QBaB	Brl%	PX	xPX	HR/F	xHR/F	Spd	SBA%	SB%	RAR	BPX	R$
19	SD	494	64	33	64	5	216	28	2	236	289	489	108	126	101	9	65	0.30	36	16	48	25	106	BAd	12%	159	144	24%	20%	75	6%	100%	-7.2	111	$11
20	TAM	139	18	8	22	2	156	7	1	227	252	393	86	105	75	10	70	0.38	42	10	48	14	98	BBf	9%	137	124	20%	17%	70	9%	100%	-8.4	124	$5
21	BOS	572	89	31	96	1	259	32	1	260	315	501	112	120	107	8	75	0.34	39	18	43	29	110	BBf	14%	141	114	18%	19%	66	3%	33%	12.4	192	$20
22	MIL	522	62	29	72	1	255	25	2	256	315	492	114	118	113	7	74	0.32	36	17	46	28	115	BBf	11%	147	131	18%	15%	85	2%	50%	14.5	200	$18
23	2 TM	548	60	20	60	0	233	15	1	243	297	416	97	92	99	8	75	0.35	43	17	40	27	98	CBf	6%	113	87	13%	10%	65	0%	0%	2.0	100	$9
1st Half		319	39	14	40	0	246	12	1	250	292	448	101	97	103	6	77	0.28	39	17	44	28	116	BBf	8%	119	102	14%	12%	66	0%	0%	2.1	129	$15
2nd Half		229	21	6	20	0	214	2	1	234	306	368	91	87	93	11	72	0.45	48	18	34	27	72	DCf	3%	103	63	12%	4%	71	0%	0%	-3.6	57	$0
24	Proj	490	59	22	62	1	235	17	1	245	302	438	102	104	101	8	74	0.35	41	17	42	27	100		9%	125	103	16%	12%	69	1%	67%	5.6	133	$14

RANDON KRUSE

Rengifo,Luis

Age: 27 Pos: 2B SS 3B OF | Bats: R Ht: 5'10" Wt: 195

Health	B	LIMA Plan	B
PT/Exp	A	Rand Var	-3
Consist	B	MM	2335

Ruptured biceps tendon ended season in Sept., cutting short another year of growth. Restored bb%, paired it with above-average ct% while hitting ball harder than ever and raising vR+ to acceptable level. 2nd half BA was more luck than skill; plus power that emerged had more support. Position versatility alone is enough to merit an extra buck.

Yr	Tm	PA	R	HR	RBI	SB	BA	xHR	xSB	xBA	OBP	SLG	OPS+	vL+	vR+	bb%	ct%	Eye	G	L	F	h%	HctX	QBaB	Brl%	PX	xPX	HR/F	xHR/F	Spd	SBA%	SB%	RAR	BPX	R$
19	LAA *	523	54	11	42	4	234	9	10	241	304	362	92	85	99	9	74	0.39	48	22	30	29	83	CCc	6%	73	50	9%	11%	132	10%	32%	-19.1	56	$5
20	LAA	106	12	1	3	3	156	1	3	190	269	200	62	46	71	13	71	0.54	59	14	27	21	83	DFf	2%	26	55	6%	6%	113	15%	75%	-8.8	-124	-$1
21	LAA *	408	50	11	38	9	229	6	9	240	267	361	86	72	78	5	80	0.25	48	17	35	26	95	DCf	6%	72	77	13%	13%	113	18%	60%	-14.1	85	$8
22	LAA *	617	55	19	60	7	259	15	10	259	288	418	100	127	89	4	82	0.22	47	18	35	29	86	CCf	5%	93	67	12%	10%	130	8%	61%	6.5	169	$17
23	LAA	445	55	16	51	6	264	13	12	258	339	444	107	125	99	9	79	0.50	47	17	36	30	107	CCd	8%	96	98	14%	11%	137	9%	60%	17.3	196	$12
1st Half		229	27	4	21	5	204	4	7	235	293	303	82	81	82	10	79	0.53	48	19	34	24	106	CCf	4%	57	81	7%	7%	109	16%	56%	-8.1	54	$1
2nd Half		216	28	12	30	1	326	9	5	283	389	591	132	171	117	9	80	0.46	46	15	39	36	108	BCc	12%	137	115	20%	15%	149	2%	100%	24.0	332	$17
24	Proj	525	61	18	55	7	257	15	12	252	318	423	102	116	95	7	79	0.39	48	17	35	29	98		7%	91	84	13%	11%	122	9%	62%	11.2	162	$14

Reynolds,Bryan

Age: 29 Pos: LF | Bats: B Ht: 6'3" Wt: 205

Health	A	LIMA Plan	B+
PT/Exp	A	Rand Var	0
Consist	C	MM	3445

1st half HR output came in well under xHR, xHR/F, while mid-June back injury led to awful July (.200 BA, .247 xBA, 61 xPX, 0% SBA%), so season could have been even better. New SB rules turned him into five-category asset, exit velocity rose for third straight year... it's possible we haven't seen his best yet. UP: 30 HR, 15 SB.

Yr	Tm	PA	R	HR	RBI	SB	BA	xHR	xSB	xBA	OBP	SLG	OPS+	vL+	vR+	bb%	ct%	Eye	G	L	F	h%	HctX	QBaB	Brl%	PX	xPX	HR/F	xHR/F	Spd	SBA%	SB%	RAR	BPX	R$
19	PIT *	601	91	20	77	5	315	19	10	275	375	513	123	105	128	9	75	0.39	46	24	30	39	111	BCa	7%	111	108	14%	17%	129	5%	56%	40.1	178	$2
20	PIT	207	24	7	19	1	189	8	2	230	275	357	84	82	84	10	69	0.37	44	22	34	23	105	CCc	10%	97	116	16%	18%	128	5%	50%	-12.1	60	$
21	PIT	646	93	24	90	5	302	29	10	281	390	522	125	125	126	12	79	0.63	39	26	36	35	111	BCc	10%	122	109	15%	18%	130	4%	71%	43.8	296	$2
22	PIT	614	74	27	62	7	262	22	11	258	345	461	114	110	116	9	74	0.40	43	22	35	31	96	BCc	8%	121	106	19%	16%	127	6%	70%	18.8	176	$2
23	PIT	640	85	24	84	12	263	29	11	274	330	460	108	98	112	8	76	0.38	43	24	33	31	100	ACc	11%	114	106	16%	20%	101	9%	92%	23.7	157	$2
1st Half		298	38	8	40	8	275	14	6	278	346	466	111	92	119	10	79	0.50	40	24	36	32	109	ABc	14%	115	109	10%	18%	97	11%	100%	14.1	204	$1
2nd Half		342	47	16	44	4	253	15	5	270	316	455	104	101	106	7	74	0.30	46	24	30	29	92	BDc	9%	114	104	23%	22%	107	6%	80%	7.8	125	$2
24	Proj	665	90	27	83	10	267	28	11	269	341	468	111	104	114	9	75	0.40	43	24	33	31	101		10%	116	107	18%	19%	117	7%	83%	28.1	179	$2

Riley,Austin

Age: 27 Pos: 3B | Bats: R Ht: 6'3" Wt: 240

Health	A	LIMA Plan	D+
PT/Exp	A	Rand Var	-1
Consist	A	MM	4245

Excellent health, consistent skills have made him one of the least risky $30 players around, and 2nd half saw him set new highs in HctX, Brl%, PX, and xPX. RBI total was held back by .199 BA, .743 OPS with RISP; career marks aren't great (.247 BA, .814 OPS), but suggest production should bounce back. If 2nd half xHR pace holds up... UP: 50 HR

Yr	Tm	PA	R	HR	RBI	SB	BA	xHR	xSB	xBA	OBP	SLG	OPS+	vL+	vR+	bb%	ct%	Eye	G	L	F	h%	HctX	QBaB	Brl%	PX	xPX	HR/F	xHR/F	Spd	SBA%	SB%	RAR	BPX	R$
19	ATL *	488	75	30	85	0	244	17	1	248	296	505	111	137	93	7	67	0.22	26	25	49	29	97	BAd	14%	152	160	22%	21%	75	2%	0%	-6.4	96	$1
20	ATL	206	24	8	27	0	239	10	1	247	301	415	95	103	92	8	74	0.33	42	24	35	28	101	ACd	10%	97	90	17%	21%	105	0%	0%	-6.4	88	$1
21	ATL	662	91	33	107	0	303	32	2	264	367	531	123	102	130	8	72	0.31	38	25	37	38	103	BBd	13%	138	111	21%	20%	94	1%	0%	41.5	162	$3
22	ATL	693	90	38	93	2	273	44	2	279	349	528	124	152	115	8	73	0.34	38	24	39	32	125	ACd	16%	167	150	22%	25%	78	1%	100%	32.6	228	$2
23	ATL	715	117	37	97	3	281	38	9	262	345	516	117	127	115	8	73	0.34	41	19	40	33	123	ACd	14%	137	138	19%	20%	113	2%	75%	42.2	193	$2
1st Half		367	57	15	43	2	270	15	4	252	335	457	108	119	106	9	74	0.36	43	20	38	32	112	ACf	11%	112	112	16%	16%	95	2%	100%	11.1	118	$2
2nd Half		348	60	22	54	1	294	24	5	272	356	577	126	136	124	8	72	0.32	40	17	43	34	134	ABc	17%	165	168	22%	24%	125	2%	50%	26.7	271	$3
24	Proj	700	108	38	103	2	280	41	5	264	346	519	119	129	116	8	72	0.32	39	21	40	33	119		14%	144	139	20%	22%	92	2%	68%	43.8	195	$3

Rivas III,Alfonso

Age: 27 Pos: 1B | Bats: L Ht: 5'11" Wt: 190

Health	A	LIMA Plan	D
PT/Exp	C	Rand Var	+1
Consist	B	MM	3313

3-15-.229 in 123 PA at SD/PIT. Two mediocre seasons with CHC put him on journeyman nomad path, eventually landed him in PIT, where big boost in FB%, HctX, and PX/xPX was the result. But sample size is small, and previous power skills were awfully weak. This is not a skill set you want in your 1B slot. End-game desperation dice roll.

Yr	Tm	PA	R	HR	RBI	SB	BA	xHR	xSB	xBA	OBP	SLG	OPS+	vL+	vR+	bb%	ct%	Eye	G	L	F	h%	HctX	QBaB	Brl%	PX	xPX	HR/F	xHR/F	Spd	SBA%	SB%	RAR	BPX
19	aaa	34	2	1	4	0	362		0		392	544	130			5	75	0.20				47				98				121	0%	0%		96
20																																		
21	CHC *	270	22	4	25	0	247	1	2	200	326	342	92	88	117	10	70	0.39	50	18	32	34	61	CCa	4%	69	41	11%	11%	113	1%	0%	-8.4	-35
22	CHC *	387	36	4	31	6	233	4	7	211	304	309	87	27	97	9	65	0.29	49	26	25	35	69	DFd	4%	58	50	8%	10%	124	7%	86%	-15.1	-124
23	2 NL *	358	39	8	38	6	229	3	5	232	308	393	95	57	107	10	67	0.35	37	22	41	31	95	CCf	7%	117	126	10%	10%	90	8%	100%	-1.2	46
1st Half		225	27	5	21	4	223	0	4	222	306	358	91	271	85	11	69	0.39	40	20	40	30	56	DDf	0%	93	-21	0%	0%	108	8%	100%	-4.1	21
2nd Half		133	11	4	16	2	242	3	2	249	314	455	104	45	108	9	64	0.30	37	22	41	34	94	CCf	7%	163	137	11%	11%	87	8%	100%	1.7	125
24	Proj	280	27	5	28	3	237	5	4	226	322	374	96	40	105	10	66	0.32	42	24	35	34	84		6%	101	102	9%	8%	93	5%	87%	-0.7	-7

Rivera,Emmanuel

Age: 28 Pos: 3B | Bats: R Ht: 6'2" Wt: 225

Health	A	LIMA Plan	D+
PT/Exp	B	Rand Var	0
Consist	A	MM	1233

4-29-.261 in 283 PA at ARI. Promise of 2022's HR/F uptick gave way to disappointing 2023 campaign, including 2nd hal slump that got him demoted for three weeks. HctX, QBaB, and xPX all suggest power skill stayed mostly intact, but 81 PX over 740 career PA doesn't exactly scream impending breakout.

Yr	Tm	PA	R	HR	RBI	SB	BA	xHR	xSB	xBA	OBP	SLG	OPS+	vL+	vR+	bb%	ct%	Eye	G	L	F	h%	HctX	QBaB	Brl%	PX	xPX	HR/F	xHR/F	Spd	SBA%	SB%	RAR	BPX
19	aa	519	53	6	52	5	245		5		278	325	83			4	84	0.28				28				43				105	6%	71%		41
20																																		
21	KC *	386	49	14	47	4	244	1	3	280	294	421	98	86	91	7	75	0.28	48	29	23	29	129	ADd	1%	105	105	6%	6%	95	5%	100%	-1.4	108
22	2 TM *	439	53	14	43	2	234	13	4	246	285	403	97	110	94	6	75	0.28	49	16	35	28	119	BCd	9%	109	119	14%	15%	117	4%	44%	-7.5	128
23	ARI *	402	45	6	43	2	255	5	5	255	309	371	93	96	89	7	79	0.37	43	24	33	31	108	BCc	6%	72	101	6%	7%	111	2%	100%	0.4	79
1st Half		225	33	2	30	1	295	3	3	273	324	401	99	113	93	4	82	0.24	44	26	31	35	122	ACc	7%	70	103	3%	8%	127	2%	100%	3.3	121
2nd Half		176	12	4	13	1	201	3	1	231	290	328	84	67	85	11	74	0.48	43	21	36	24	89	BCb	5%	76	98	10%	10%	87	3%	100%	-5.4	21
24	Proj	350	38	8	36	2	239	8	4	248	294	369	91	95	89	7	77	0.33	46	22	33	29	112		6%	80	107	9%	10%	89	3%	81%	-1.7	83

Rizzo,Anthony

Age: 34 Pos: 1B | Bats: L Ht: 6'3" Wt: 240

Health	C	LIMA Plan	B
PT/Exp	A	Rand Var	-2
Consist	A	MM	3035

Undiagnosed concussion on pickoff play on May 28 changed course of season: .304 BA, .881 OPS before; .172, .496 after. Sticking with that split, was on pace for 25-30 HR prior to injury. Add in 2022's 43-point gap between BA/xBA, and he could be nicely undervalued this spring. Good bet to rebound to at least the $15 level of past 3.5 seasons.

Yr	Tm	PA	R	HR	RBI	SB	BA	xHR	xSB	xBA	OBP	SLG	OPS+	vL+	vR+	bb%	ct%	Eye	G	L	F	h%	HctX	QBaB	Brl%	PX	xPX	HR/F	xHR/F	Spd	SBA%	SB%	RAR	BPX
19	CHC	613	89	27	94	5	293	21	3	300	405	520	128	112	132	12	83	0.83	43	25	32	31	107	CCb	7%	109	95	20%	15%	77	4%	71%	30.7	252
20	CHC	243	26	11	24	3	222	6	2	267	342	414	100	80	106	12	81	0.74	38	24	38	22	116	CBd	7%	94	99	18%	10%	65	6%	75%	-6.7	180
21	2 TM	576	73	22	61	6	248	18	4	264	344	440	108	123	101	9	82	0.60	41	19	40	26	108	BBd	8%	100	88	13%	11%	84	5%	75%	2.7	212
22	NYY	548	77	32	75	6	224	26	5	267	338	480	116	125	112	11	78	0.57	33	18	49	22	111	BAf	11%	148	139	18%	14%	71	8%	55%	9.1	262
23	NYY	421	45	12	41	0	244	10	3	241	328	378	96	111	92	8	74	0.36	33	26	41	30	87	BBb	7%	81	91	11%	9%	64	3%	0%	0.1	0
1st Half		328	39	11	37	0	267	10	3	251	360	425	107	128	102	10	75	0.43	31	26	43	32	92	BAb	9%	94	104	12%	11%	67	3%	0%	3.5	57
2nd Half		93	6	1	4	0	170	1	0	212	215	227	60	64	59	4	72	0.16	40	25	35	23	69	BCc	1%	38	47	5%	5%	74	0%	0%	-8.4	-179
24	Proj	525	67	23	61	3	250	15	4	252	333	433	105	115	102	8	77	0.39	37	23	41	28	94		7%	103	93	15%	10%	67	4%	52%	7.4	77

Robert Jr.,Luis

Age: 26 Pos: CF | Bats: R Ht: 6'2" Wt: 220

Health	D	LIMA Plan	C+
PT/Exp	A	Rand Var	0
Consist	D	MM	4435

Finally delivered elite value, but even in mostly healthy season, missed six days with mid-Aug finger sprain, final wee with knee injury. And while he's teased some incredible upside over the years—.300+ BA here, 40ish HR there, 30-SB pace—has yet to put it all together at once. With injury risk still high and slight regression likely, gotta play it cool.

Yr	Tm	PA	R	HR	RBI	SB	BA	xHR	xSB	xBA	OBP	SLG	OPS+	vL+	vR+	bb%	ct%	Eye	G	L	F	h%	HctX	QBaB	Brl%	PX	xPX	HR/F	xHR/F	Spd	SBA%	SB%	RAR	BPX
19	a/a	449	79	23	61	25	288		20		322	535	119			5	72	0.18				35				135				132	38%	75%		170
20	CHW	225	33	11	31	9	233	14	6	218	302	436	98	105	96	9	64	0.27	37	20	43	31	77	CBd	13%	129	120	20%	25%	104	22%	82%	-1.9	40
21	CHW *	329	45	14	45	7	327	16	5	277	364	544	125	168	119	5	76	0.25	37	26	37	39	111	ACc	13%	130	116	16%	20%	107	9%	88%	25.8	208
22	CHW	401	54	12	56	11	284	17	8	260	319	426	106	127	100	4	80	0.22	45	22	33	33	107	BCc	9%	89	97	12%	17%	92	14%	79%	10.0	97
23	CHW	590	90	38	80	20	264	36	16	268	315	542	117	128	114	5	68	0.17	36	20	44	32	93	CBd	15%	177	127	23%	22%	97	22%	83%	30.6	204
1st Half		344	59	24	46	8	276	23	7	276	337	575	125	156	116	6	68	0.20	38	19	43	33	93	CBd	16%	190	121	26%	25%	91	14%	80%	22.4	236
2nd Half		246	31	14	34	12	247	13	9	256	285	498	106	83	111	4	69	0.14	34	20	45	30	94	BBc	15%	159	134	19%	18%	107	34%	86%	5.5	161
24	Proj	525	74	26	71	18	266	28	14	257	310	489	110	123	106	5	71	0.18	39	20	40	32	98		13%	140	118	18%	20%	102	20%	82%	19.6	161

BRANDON KRUSE

Robles,Victor

Age: 27	Pos: CF		Health	F	LIMA Plan	C
Bats: R	Ht: 6'0"	Wt: 195	PT/Exp	C	Rand Var	-5
			Consist	C	MM	1413

Sample is limited due to back injury that shut him down June 20, but improved OBP came with bb%, ct% growth. And while there will be some pullback via xBA and h%, getting on base is paramount given his elite Spd, SBA%, and SB%. There's no question the bat has disappointed, but with health, the wheels still simmer with upside.

Yr	Tm	PA	R	HR	RBI	SB	BA	xHR	xSB	xBA	OBP	SLG	OPS+	vL+	vR+	bb%	ct%	Eye	G	L	F	h%	HctX	QBaB	Brl%	PX	xPX	HR/F	xHR/F	Spd	SBA%	SB%	RAR	BPX	R$
19	WAS	617	86	17	65	28	255	15	23	248	326	419	103	103	102	6	74	0.25	41	23	37	31	64	FBc	5%	95	57	12%	10%	130	25%	76%	-0.3	96	$23
20	WAS	189	20	3	15	4	220	2	4	216	293	315	81	107	70	5	68	0.17	35	30	35	30	63	FAc	2%	60	62	8%	5%	121	11%	80%	-12.1	-116	$8
21	WAS *	461	48	5	25	13	218	5	11	230	289	339	86	78	86	9	71	0.35	36	25	39	29	70	FBf	3%	89	80	2%	6%	107	19%	65%	-17.1	31	$6
22	WAS	407	42	6	33	15	224	5	15	204	273	311	83	105	71	4	72	0.16	40	21	39	30	67	FCf	3%	59	53	6%	5%	148	21%	79%	-15.3	-38	$8
23	WAS	126	15	0	8	8	299	1	7	249	385	364	102	117	95	9	83	0.61	53	18	29	36	106	FDf	2%	43	63	0%	4%	124	22%	89%	4.0	86	$2
1st Half		126	15	0	8	8	299	1	7	249	385	364	103	118	95	9	83	0.61	53	18	29	36	106	FDf	2%	43	63	0%	4%	124	22%	89%	3.7	89	$0
2nd Half																									0%										
24	Proj	420	50	4	32	19	247	6	16	229	324	341	91	103	86	7	75	0.30	42	23	35	32	79		3%	63	65	4%	6%	117	20%	80%	-3.1	19	$11

Rocchio,Brayan

Age: 23	Pos: SS		Health	A	LIMA Plan	D
Bats: B	Ht: 5'10"	Wt: 150	PT/Exp	A	Rand Var	+3
			Consist	C	MM	1331

0-8-.247 in 86 PA at CLE. Better real life prospect than fantasy; packed with baseball smarts. Solid hand/eye skills limits whiffs despite a high chase rate. Better from left-hand side, he sprays the ball well across the diamond with surprising pull pop for small, compact player. Also a plus runner with 20+ SB potential if SB% improves. (CB)

Yr	Tm	PA	R	HR	RBI	SB	BA	xHR	xSB	xBA	OBP	SLG	OPS+	vL+	vR+	bb%	ct%	Eye	G	L	F	h%	HctX	QBaB	Brl%	PX	xPX	HR/F	xHR/F	Spd	SBA%	SB%	RAR	BPX	R$
19																																			
20																																			
21	aa	195	28	5	25	6	275		6		315	457	106			6	76	0.25				34				110				115	24%	58%		150	$7
22	a/a	546	55	12	43	9	215		10		266	335	85			7	77	0.31				25				80				93	17%	48%		59	$7
23	CLE *	599	66	5	54	18	235	0	21	271	299	336	86	59	96	8	82	0.49	60	18	22	28	85	DFd	0%	65	47	0%	0%	128	19%	69%	-6.4	125	$10
1st Half		319	33	1	29	12	230	0	11	268	296	317	84	136	46	9	84	0.57	77	8	15	27	79	DFf	0%	56	-1	0%	0%	131	19%	84%	-8.9	132	$8
2nd Half		280	33	4	25	6	242	0	9	271	302	357	89	54	110	8	79	0.42	55	21	24	29	85	DFb	0%	76	63	0%	0%	123	19%	50%	-6.4	118	$9
24	Proj	210	24	1	19	5	235	1	6	254	288	316	83	54	104	7	79	0.38	55	21	24	29	77		1%	57	57	2%	2%	127	18%	59%	-5.0	105	$5

Rodgers,Brendan

Age: 27	Pos: 2B		Health	F	LIMA Plan	B
Bats: R	Ht: 6'0"	Wt: 204	PT/Exp	B	Rand Var	-4
			Consist	B	MM	2335

Mostly a wasted season caused by shoulder injury suffered during spring training. What we did see wasn't too far off from past track record, though xPX and xHR/F suggest there's room for improved results. Still in prime of career, so with a tick up in FB%, power potential could finally show up. But Health grade is real, also.

Yr	Tm	PA	R	HR	RBI	SB	BA	xHR	xSB	xBA	OBP	SLG	OPS+	vL+	vR+	bb%	ct%	Eye	G	L	F	h%	HctX	QBaB	Brl%	PX	xPX	HR/F	xHR/F	Spd	SBA%	SB%	RAR	BPX	R$
19	COL *	234	31	7	21	0	284	1	2	254	325	436	105	66	74	6	75	0.24	49	22	29	35	79	CDf	4%	87	66	0%	7%	128	0%	0%	3.1	74	$3
20	COL	21	1	0	2	0	95	0	0	165	95	143	32	43	22	0	71	0.00	73	0	27	13	39	FFf		41	23	0%	0%	94	0%	0%	-3.4	-200	-$4
21	COL	415	49	15	51	0	284	13	1	267	328	470	110	134	101	5	78	0.23	51	20	29	33	122	CDd	6%	105	97	17%	15%	97	0%	0%	9.5	142	$13
22	COL	581	72	13	63	0	266	15	5	269	325	408	104	126	92	8	81	0.46	52	21	27	31	124	BFc	7%	91	93	11%	13%	121	0%	0%	7.0	172	$15
23	COL	192	21	4	20	0	258	6	2	241	313	388	95	91	97	6	77	0.27	53	17	30	32	105	CFd	11%	79	101	10%	15%	104	0%	0%	1.1	57	$1
1st Half																									0%										
2nd Half		192	21	4	20	0	258	6	2	241	313	388	0	91	97	6	77	0.27	53	17	30	32	105	CFd	11%	79	101	10%	15%	104	0%	0%	0.6	57	$3
24	Proj	525	63	13	58	0	273	15	3	257	323	420	102	112	98	6	78	0.28	52	20	29	33	111		8%	89	93	12%	13%	97	0%	100%	13.9	112	$17

Rodríguez,Endy

Age: 24	Pos: CA		Health	A	LIMA Plan	B
Bats: B	Ht: 6'0"	Wt: 170	PT/Exp	C	Rand Var	0
			Consist	F	MM	2433

3-13-.220 in 204 PA at PIT. Highly-regarded CA prospect reached majors in mid-July. Solid ct%, Eye show he wasn't lost at highest level, but to really catch attention of fantasy managers, he'll need to bring PX closer to xPX with improved Brl% and exit velocity. Don't buy a breakout, but first sample was more encouraging than it may appear.

Yr	Tm	PA	R	HR	RBI	SB	BA	xHR	xSB	xBA	OBP	SLG	OPS+	vL+	vR+	bb%	ct%	Eye	G	L	F	h%	HctX	QBaB	Brl%	PX	xPX	HR/F	xHR/F	Spd	SBA%	SB%	RAR	BPX	R$
19																																			
20																																			
21																																			
22	a/a	153	20	6	28	1	321		1		378	561	133			8	81	0.48				36				158				87	3%	100%		328	$6
23	PIT *	503	66	7	40	3	226	5	8	236	293	337	86	51	97	9	78	0.44	34	24	42	27	97	CBd	5%	67	116	5%	9%	131	3%	100%	-1.3	93	$4
1st Half		271	33	4	24	3	221		5	243	286	326	84	0	0	8	81	0.48	44	20	36	26	0		0%	62	-21	0%		134	5%	100%	-3.5	111	$3
2nd Half		232	33	4	17	0	232	5	3	233	301	350	88	50	96	9	76	0.41	34	24	42	29	94	CBd	5%	73	116	5%	9%	133	0%	0%	-0.5	75	$3
24	Proj	420	56	9	51	2	240	11	4	254	303	393	96	83	100	9	79	0.44	34	24	42	28	85		5%	96	104	7%	9%	107	3%	100%	8.0	185	$11

Rodríguez,Julio

Age: 23	Pos: CF		Health	A	LIMA Plan	D+
Bats: R	Ht: 6'3"	Wt: 228	PT/Exp	A	Rand Var	+1
			Consist	C	MM	4445

Has started each of his big-league seasons slowly, making it all the more impressive that he's returned $35 in each campaign. 2nd half shows the upside, as elite exit velocity and above-average Brl% overcame his high GB%. Aggressiveness on basepaths means a 30 HR/30 SB repeat is holding firm, and another step forward is possible.

Yr	Tm	PA	R	HR	RBI	SB	BA	xHR	xSB	xBA	OBP	SLG	OPS+	vL+	vR+	bb%	ct%	Eye	G	L	F	h%	HctX	QBaB	Brl%	PX	xPX	HR/F	xHR/F	Spd	SBA%	SB%	RAR	BPX	R$
19																																			
20																																			
21	aa	198	29	6	22	13	325		8		408	479	122			12	75	0.56				41				95				92	26%	75%		115	$13
22	SEA	560	84	28	75	25	284	26	22	262	345	509	121	116	122	7	72	0.28	46	18	36	35	108	ACd	13%	146	121	21%	20%	137	23%	78%	32.0	210	$35
23	SEA	714	102	32	103	37	275	29	29	266	333	485	111	113	111	7	73	0.27	48	19	34	33	115	ADd	12%	127	103	20%	18%	98	28%	79%	32.9	139	$35
1st Half		364	49	13	43	19	246	13	15	245	308	413	99	93	100	7	72	0.27	47	19	34	31	118	ACc	10%	103	93	16%	16%	95	29%	79%	2.6	46	$27
2nd Half		350	53	19	60	18	306	16	15	288	360	559	124	135	121	6	75	0.26	48	18	34	36	112	ADd	14%	150	113	23%	20%	102	27%	78%	27.9	232	$44
24	Proj	665	99	31	94	35	285	29	28	262	348	497	116	116	116	8	73	0.30	47	18	35	34	112		13%	129	111	20%	19%	111	26%	78%	37.9	170	$43

Rogers,Jake

Age: 29	Pos: CA		Health	F	LIMA Plan	C+
Bats: R	Ht: 6'1"	Wt: 201	PT/Exp	C	Rand Var	+3
			Consist	C	MM	4413

Recorded highest PA total of career after Tommy John surgery cost him all of 2022, and quietly put together impressive season from power perspective. QBaB, xPX suggest he's capable of repeating it, and quality of contact should keep BA from totally bottoming out despite undesirable ct%. Absorb the BA, take the counting stats.

Yr	Tm	PA	R	HR	RBI	SB	BA	xHR	xSB	xBA	OBP	SLG	OPS+	vL+	vR+	bb%	ct%	Eye	G	L	F	h%	HctX	QBaB	Brl%	PX	xPX	HR/F	xHR/F	Spd	SBA%	SB%	RAR	BPX	R$
19	DET *	412	52	17	54	0	199	3	1	207	287	391	94	138	50	11	63	0.33	37	17	46	26	62	FAf	5%	119	99	15%	11%	99	0%	0%	-0.3	0	$3
20																																			
21	DET	127	17	6	17	1	239	5	3	226	306	496	110	124	102	9	59	0.24	20	32	48	34	80	CAd	11%	175	133	19%	16%	183	4%	100%	4.0	196	$1
22																																			
23	DET	365	47	21	49	1	221	19	2	235	286	444	99	116	92	8	64	0.24	37	21	42	27	92	BBd	12%	143	151	23%	21%	77	3%	50%	7.4	43	$7
1st Half		172	23	11	26	0	203	9	1	241	304	473	106	149	86	12	59	0.34	40	20	40	25	110	BCc	16%	193	203	31%	26%	76	3%	0%	4.0	139	$3
2nd Half		193	24	10	23	1	235	10	1	230	269	421	93	86	96	4	69	0.12	35	22	43	28	77	BBf	9%	109	115	18%	18%	91	3%	100%	0.8	-4	$6
24	Proj	385	51	20	52	2	225	19	4	230	292	455	102	125	92	8	63	0.24	31	24	45	29	82		11%	153	137	21%	19%	128	3%	78%	10.4	95	$12

Rojas,Johan

Age: 23	Pos: CF		Health	A	LIMA Plan	C+
Bats: R	Ht: 6'1"	Wt: 165	PT/Exp	C	Rand Var	-2
			Consist	D	MM	1513

2-23-.302 with 14 SB in 164 PA at PHI. Called up following All-Star break and made impact debut with impressive Spd, SBA%. BA was propped up by 41 h% in majors, and dismal Eye, QBaB call into question whether he'll get on base enough to take advantage of speed over larger sample. End-game speculation, just be willing to cut bait quickly.

Yr	Tm	PA	R	HR	RBI	SB	BA	xHR	xSB	xBA	OBP	SLG	OPS+	vL+	vR+	bb%	ct%	Eye	G	L	F	h%	HctX	QBaB	Brl%	PX	xPX	HR/F	xHR/F	Spd	SBA%	SB%	RAR	BPX	R$
19																																			
20																																			
21																																			
22	aa	250	30	3	11	20	222		16		269	321	84			6	79	0.31				27				58				159	45%	82%		86	$8
23	PHI *	503	69	10	59	38	283	0	38	257	319	430	102	106	104	5	77	0.23	46	21	34	35	78	FDf	1%	89	44	6%	0%	174	41%	79%	14.2	154	$24
1st Half		307	40	6	31	21	276		22	251	319	412	100	0	0	6	79	0.30	44	20	36	33	0		0%	80	-21	0%		154	40%	70%	4.0	139	$23
2nd Half		196	29	4	28	17	295	0	14	258	317	459	105	105	103	3	74	0.12	46	21	34	38	75	FDf	1%	105	44	6%	0%	168	42%	95%	8.9	143	$19
24	Proj	350	47	4	33	28	243	2	25	230	296	354	89	88	90	5	73	0.19	46	21	34	32	68		1%	73	40	4%	2%	176	42%	84%	-3.2	119	$17

AN MARCUS

Rojas,Josh

Age: 30 Pos: 2B 3B
Bats: L Ht: 6' 1" Wt: 207

Health	B	LIMA Plan	D
PT/Exp	A	Rand Var	0
Consist	B	MM	1321

4-40-.245 with 12 SB in 350 PA at ARI/SEA. SB have been the primary draw, but dips in OBP, Spd, SBO% left production lacking even with perfect SB%. Prognosis for rebound isn't strong, as growth in Eye, ct% also fell away, while lack of quality of contact and defensive value suggest PA will continue to decline. Look elsewhere for steals.

Yr Tm	PA	R	HR	RBI	SB	BA	xHR	xSB	xBA	OBP	SLG	OPS+	vL+	vR+	bb%	ct%	Eye	G	L	F	h%	HctX	QBaB	Brl%	PX	xPX	HR/F	xHR/F	Spd	SBA%	SB%	RAR	BPX	R$
19 ARI *	616	82	18	76	28	265	5	22	270	338	450	109	108	79	10	78	0.50	44	23	33	31	111	CCc	6%	99	139	6%	16%	105	28%	67%	-6.0	163	$2
20 ARI	70	9	0	2	1	180	1	1	185	257	180	58	65	52	10	74	0.44	50	20	30	24	89	DFf	0%	0	98	0%	7%	113	11%	50%	-6.7	-192	-$
21 ARI	546	69	11	44	9	264	10	9	251	341	411	103	105	103	11	72	0.42	49	23	28	35	86	CDb	5%	99	90	11%	10%	114	9%	69%	9.9	88	$1
22 ARI	510	66	9	56	23	269	11	14	248	349	391	105	93	108	11	78	0.56	42	23	35	33	102	CCd	4%	84	110	7%	9%	93	18%	88%	12.7	103	$2
23 2 TM *	402	52	5	44	13	235	4	8	226	293	322	84	76	89	7	74	0.32	40	23	37	30	80	DCd	4%	60	71	5%	5%	79	14%	100%	-6.3	-50	$
1st Half	240	26	0	28	6	222	2	4	228	291	289	79	75	84	9	72	0.35	43	25	32	31	82	DDd	3%	58	77	0%	5%	81	11%	100%	-8.2	-79	$
2nd Half	162	26	4	16	7	254	3	5	224	295	367	90	76	97	6	77	0.26	37	20	43	30	76	CBc	5%	64	63	10%	7%	90	18%	100%	-1.0	4	$
24 Proj	245	33	4	26	9	254	5	6	236	319	364	94	87	96	9	76	0.40	42	22	35	32	88		4%	72	87	7%	8%	94	16%	88%	3.1	41	$

Rojas,Miguel

Age: 35 Pos: SS
Bats: R Ht: 6' 0" Wt: 188

Health	B	LIMA Plan	D+
PT/Exp	A	Rand Var	+3
Consist	B	MM	1333

Surprising jumps in HctX, xPX give impression there might still be some value here. However, consistently declining OPS+, minuscule barrel rate, and advanced age suggest results won't get better, while xHR splashes cold water on 2H power surge. Even above-average Spd is overshadowed by subpar SB%, leaving more empty PA as likely outcome.

Yr Tm	PA	R	HR	RBI	SB	BA	xHR	xSB	xBA	OBP	SLG	OPS+	vL+	vR+	bb%	ct%	Eye	G	L	F	h%	HctX	QBaB	Brl%	PX	xPX	HR/F	xHR/F	Spd	SBA%	SB%	RAR	BPX	R$
19 MIA	526	52	5	46	9	284	6	9	275	331	379	98	105	95	6	87	0.52	47	24	30	32	107	CDb	3%	54	65	4%	5%	105	10%	64%	-5.6	137	$1
20 MIA	143	20	4	20	5	304	2	4	292	392	496	118	186	90	11	86	0.89	41	25	35	33	107	CCc	1%	103	91	11%	5%	106	15%	83%	8.7	324	$1
21 MIA	539	66	9	48	13	265	6	11	265	322	392	98	120	89	7	85	0.50	45	21	34	30	86	DCc	3%	73	59	6%	4%	123	12%	81%	-2.9	196	$1
22 MIA	507	34	6	36	9	236	5	8	255	283	323	86	79	88	5	87	0.43	47	21	32	26	79	DCc	2%	53	41	5%	4%	109	10%	75%	-19.6	121	$
23 LA	423	49	5	31	8	236	4	10	254	290	322	83	99	75	6	88	0.54	45	19	35	26	101	CCd	3%	49	71	4%	3%	116	11%	73%	-9.3	139	$
1st Half	192	19	0	7	5	230	2	5	258	271	281	76	65	81	6	85	0.42	48	23	29	27	105	CCc	3%	38	61	0%	4%	103	14%	83%	-8.6	57	-$
2nd Half	231	30	5	24	3	242	2	6	250	306	357	90	125	69	7	89	0.68	43	16	41	25	96	DCd	3%	58	79	7%	3%	127	9%	60%	-4.8	204	$
24 Proj	385	39	4	29	6	235	4	8	254	291	324	84	99	78	6	87	0.53	45	20	34	26	93		3%	52	63	4%	4%	108	9%	68%	-7.9	155	$

Rooker,Brent

Age: 29 Pos: DH RF LF
Bats: R Ht: 6' 4" Wt: 225

Health	A	LIMA Plan	C+
PT/Exp	A	Rand Var	-2
Consist	C	MM	5215

Spike in FB% recharged lagging career, and QBaB, xPX, and xHR/F all confirm there is elite power in his bat. Simultaneously, heavy FB and ct%-lite approach makes his path to a repeat narrow, as 2nd half xBA highlights the downside. Split the difference for 2024 by accounting for a BA ding while penciling in a handsome HR total.

Yr Tm	PA	R	HR	RBI	SB	BA	xHR	xSB	xBA	OBP	SLG	OPS+	vL+	vR+	bb%	ct%	Eye	G	L	F	h%	HctX	QBaB	Brl%	PX	xPX	HR/F	xHR/F	Spd	SBA%	SB%	RAR	BPX	R$
19 aaa	256	33	11	38	2	248		1		332	464	110			11	53	0.27				41				167				85	3%	100%		-11	
20 MIN	21	4	1	5	0	316	1	0	324	381	579	127	99	140	0	74	0.00	36	43	21	38	107	CFf	14%	164	134	33%	33%	97	0%	0%	0.7	228	
21 MIN *	462	54	23	52	1	201	11	2	225	278	418	96	95	94	9	59	0.26	36	25	39	27	90	ACc	13%	153	123	20%	24%	89	3%	23%	-8.9	31	
22 2 TM *	368	40	13	49	3	204	1	3	228	262	392	93	62	36	7	60	0.20	48	19	33	29	126	CCb	5%	159	93	0%	14%	77	10%	52%	-9.4	28	
23 OAK	526	61	30	69	4	246	29	5	233	329	488	111	118	108	9	63	0.28	34	19	47	32	96	AAb	16%	161	153	22%	21%	93	3%	100%	20.7	104	$
1st Half	277	30	14	41	1	243	12	2	242	339	477	112	126	105	12	65	0.39	39	19	42	31	98	ABb	13%	153	140	21%	18%	85	1%	100%	9.4	125	$
2nd Half	249	31	16	28	3	250	17	4	224	317	500	110	110	110	7	60	0.19	27	20	53	34	95	AAc	18%	170	167	22%	23%	107	5%	100%	7.8	89	$
24 Proj	525	62	27	64	4	229	25	5	226	316	451	105	108	103	9	60	0.25	34	22	45	32	94		15%	160	143	21%	20%	93	4%	74%	4.9	62	$

Rosario,Amed

Age: 28 Pos: SS 2B
Bats: R Ht: 6' 2" Wt: 190

Health	A	LIMA Plan	B
PT/Exp	A	Rand Var	0
Consist	A	MM	1545

Disappointing season or a lesson in managing expectations? Excellent Spd and SB% remained; unfortunately, so did modest SBA%, even with rule changes. Poor Brl%, high GB% sabotage any potential of a power breakout, while limite BB%, OBP keep run-scoring potential in check. Pay for double-digit SB and a decent BA floor, nothing more.

Yr Tm	PA	R	HR	RBI	SB	BA	xHR	xSB	xBA	OBP	SLG	OPS+	vL+	vR+	bb%	ct%	Eye	G	L	F	h%	HctX	QBaB	Brl%	PX	xPX	HR/F	xHR/F	Spd	SBA%	SB%	RAR	BPX	R$
19 NYM	655	75	15	72	19	287	13	22	266	323	432	104	123	98	5	80	0.25	48	22	29	34	92	BDb	4%	75	65	10%	9%	149	18%	66%	0.8	133	$
20 NYM	147	20	4	15	0	252	3	2	231	272	371	85	101	73	3	76	0.12	58	16	27	30	68	DFc	4%	62	40	14%	10%	152	3%	0%	-5.0	32	
21 CLE	588	77	11	57	13	282	9	15	255	321	409	100	114	94	5	78	0.26	51	21	28	34	92	CFd	3%	74	58	9%	7%	157	9%	100%	4.0	119	$
22 CLE	670	86	11	71	18	283	13	28	266	312	403	101	112	98	4	83	0.23	52	20	27	33	95	CFd	4%	71	71	8%	9%	187	13%	82%	2.2	183	$
23 2 TM	545	70	6	58	15	263	8	21	258	305	378	93	104	87	5	81	0.29	48	21	31	32	96	CDd	3%	68	72	5%	6%	169	13%	88%	2.8	143	$
1st Half	334	38	1	26	8	259	4	12	244	305	346	89	108	83	6	79	0.30	47	22	31	33	90	CDc	2%	54	68	1%	5%	172	10%	100%	-4.0	82	$
2nd Half	211	32	5	32	7	269	4	8	277	303	428	99	100	97	4	84	0.27	49	19	32	30	105	CDd	5%	86	77	9%	7%	152	20%	78%	1.5	211	$
24 Proj	525	70	9	60	14	268	9	19	261	303	396	96	105	91	4	81	0.25	50	20	30	32	95		4%	73	68	7%	8%	147	14%	83%	6.2	152	$

Rosario,Eddie

Age: 32 Pos: LF
Bats: L Ht: 6' 1" Wt: 180

Health	D	LIMA Plan	B
PT/Exp	A	Rand Var	-1
Consist	D	MM	2235

Blurriness in right eye plagued him in 2022. Hot start backed by career-high Brl%, PX suggest power upside remains high after fixing vision issue. There's a catch, however, as pitchers attacked his diminished ct% with more velocity in 2nd half, and decline in production followed. Combine that with advanced age, and there's reason to be cautious.

Yr Tm	PA	R	HR	RBI	SB	BA	xHR	xSB	xBA	OBP	SLG	OPS+	vL+	vR+	bb%	ct%	Eye	G	L	F	h%	HctX	QBaB	Brl%	PX	xPX	HR/F	xHR/F	Spd	SBA%	SB%	RAR	BPX
19 MIN	590	91	32	109	3	276	31	2	278	300	500	111	107	111	4	85	0.26	37	20	42	28	114	CBd	9%	104	120	16%	15%	86	3%	75%	2.1	211
20 MIN	231	31	13	42	3	257	10	3	258	316	476	105	70	117	8	84	0.56	35	18	47	25	103	CBf	6%	103	135	16%	12%	99	8%	75%	-0.3	264
21 2 TM *	464	47	17	73	11	246	14	8	268	291	425	98	89	107	6	84	0.40	37	23	40	26	108	CBf	6%	93	110	11%	11%	99	15%	79%	-5.1	208
22 ATL *	306	30	5	27	3	212	6	2	212	263	320	83	68	85	6	71	0.24	39	20	41	28	82	CBd	5%	81	91	7%	8%	100	5%	100%	-10.4	-17
23 ATL	516	64	21	74	3	255	19	7	259	305	450	103	95	104	7	74	0.28	40	22	38	30	103	CBd	9%	114	106	16%	14%	105	6%	43%	9.1	129
1st Half	271	36	14	40	1	263	11	5	269	314	498	111	151	106	7	74	0.29	40	21	39	30	115	BBc	12%	136	127	19%	15%	118	7%	25%	8.4	204
2nd Half	245	28	7	34	2	247	8	3	250	295	396	94	37	102	6	75	0.26	40	23	36	30	90	CCd	7%	91	83	11%	13%	93	6%	67%	-0.9	54
24 Proj	490	57	17	67	5	243	16	6	248	290	411	96	81	99	6	76	0.28	39	21	39	29	98		7%	99	102	12%	12%	96	7%	68%	1.9	108

Ruiz,Esteury

Age: 25 Pos: CF
Bats: R Ht: 6' 0" Wt: 169

Health	B	LIMA Plan	D
PT/Exp	A	Rand Var	0
Consist	C	MM	1525

Month-long absence caused by shoulder injury cost him chance at being MLB SB leader, but elite Spd and outrageous SBA% keep that outcome in play. Scouts have suggested more power is on the way, and .492 SLG across 62 PA paire with .295 xBA in Sept gives glimpse of potential. That's enough to go an extra dollar.

Yr Tm	PA	R	HR	RBI	SB	BA	xHR	xSB	xBA	OBP	SLG	OPS+	vL+	vR+	bb%	ct%	Eye	G	L	F	h%	HctX	QBaB	Brl%	PX	xPX	HR/F	xHR/F	Spd	SBA%	SB%	RAR	BPX
19																																	
20																																	
21 aa	332	40	7	32	28	214		18		267	338	83			7	74	0.28				27				78				102	54%	78%		15
22 2 NL *	520	82	11	47	60	266	0	41	246	334	407	105	65	61	9	75	0.40	48	19	33	34	35	FAf	4%	98	13	0%	0%	120	59%	77%	7.4	114
23 OAK	490	47	5	47	67	254	6	45	250	309	345	89	99	85	4	78	0.20	48	22	30	32	53	FDf	3%	62	41	5%	6%	116	67%	84%	-3.0	21
1st Half	356	32	1	33	42	258	3	30	252	312	331	88	104	83	4	80	0.22	50	21	28	32	50	FDf	2%	53	33	1%	4%	124	56%	84%	-6.2	36
2nd Half	134	15	4	14	25	244	3	14	242	301	382	92	91	93	5	72	0.18	41	25	34	31	59	FCf	4%	86	64	14%	10%	101	97%	83%	-1.4	0
24 Proj	525	57	9	48	71	249	5	48	242	320	361	93	96	91	7	75	0.28	45	23	32	32	55		3%	74	52	8%	5%	99	64%	81%	0.2	49

Ruiz,Keibert

Age: 25 Pos: CA
Bats: B Ht: 6' 0" Wt: 225

Health	A	LIMA Plan	B+
PT/Exp	A	Rand Var	+2
Consist	C	MM	1145

Jump in HR, RBI, and R production makes this look like breakout season, but PX and QBaB were virtually identical to 2022. Increased volume can partially explain the rise in raw stats, and xHR/F, xHR both suggest luck played significa role as well. There are worse options at the position, but don't count on another bump in counting stats.

Yr Tm	PA	R	HR	RBI	SB	BA	xHR	xSB	xBA	OBP	SLG	OPS+	vL+	vR+	bb%	ct%	Eye	G	L	F	h%	HctX	QBaB	Brl%	PX	xPX	HR/F	xHR/F	Spd	SBA%	SB%	RAR	BPX
19 a/a	338	32	5	28	0	236		1		289	312	83			7	92	0.97				24				35				95	0%	0%		156
20 LA	8	1	1	1	0	250	1	0	264	250	625	116	0	116	0	63	0.00	20	20	60	25	51	CAf	20%	214	123	33%	33%	98	0%	0%	0.3	212
21 2 NL *	403	48	20	60	0	280	2	0	274	332	513	116	103	102	7	88	0.64	42	15	43	27	105	DAc	3%	118	64	9%	6%	76	0%	0%	22.9	327
22 WAS	433	33	7	36	6	251	8	3	264	313	360	95	82	99	7	87	0.60	40	23	37	27	106	CBb	4%	69	92	5%	6%	62	7%	86%	1.8	134
23 WAS	562	55	18	67	1	260	14	2	277	308	409	98	98	97	6	89	0.53	39	22	39	26	110	CBd	6%	76	87	10%	8%	65	2%	50%	12.8	175
1st Half	284	23	9	30	0	229	10	1	276	285	370	90	100	85	6	91	0.70	39	22	39	22	119	CBc	8%	69	91	10%	11%	62	0%	0%	-1.8	186
2nd Half	278	32	9	37	1	291	4	2	276	331	448	105	97	109	5	87	0.43	38	22	40	31	101	DBf	3%	84	83	10%	4%	76	3%	50%	12.2	175
24 Proj	525	52	14	60	2	261	11	2	268	315	397	98	94	99	6	88	0.57	40	21	39	27	107		4%	73	85	8%	7%	67	3%	74%	12.2	188

DAN MARCUS

Rutschman,Adley

Age: 26	Pos: CA DH		Health	A	LIMA Plan	B+
Bats: R	Ht: 6'2"	Wt: 220	PT/Exp	A	Rand Var	-1
			Consist	A	MM	3155

First full season in the majors was a success, highlighted by elite Eye as well as rare volume at CA position thanks to time at DH. Combination of average FB%, HR/F continues to keep power numbers in check, so next step will require improvement in exit velocity, Brl%. As is, he's an elite option at the position and still has the potential to grow.

Yr Tm	PA	R	HR	RBI	SB	BA	xHR	xSB	xBA	OBP	SLG	OPS+	vL+	vR+	bb%	ct%	Eye	G	L	F	h%	HctX	QBaB	Brl%	PX	xPX	HR/F	xHR/F	Spd	SBA%	SB%	RAR	BPX	R$
19																																		
20																																		
21 a/a	511	65	19	56	2	249		3		336	428	105			12	79	0.61				28				100				95	4%	40%		185	$12
22 BAL *	531	76	15	48	4	250	14	3	275	351	436	111	77	126	13	79	0.75	38	23	38	29	107	CBc	8%	124	114	11%	12%	90	3%	100%	22.9	248	$14
23 BAL	687	84	20	80	1	277	22	6	274	374	435	110	121	106	13	83	0.91	42	23	35	31	101	CCc	8%	88	88	12%	13%	83	1%	33%	39.8	196	$20
1st Half	353	38	11	35	0	268	10	3	263	374	415	108	115	105	15	83	1.04	41	23	36	29	96	CCc	7%	78	101	12%	11%	83	1%	0%	15.4	186	$14
2nd Half	334	46	9	45	1	287	12	3	285	374	457	112	127	107	12	82	0.78	44	24	33	32	106	CCc	8%	99	76	11%	15%	86	2%	50%	20.1	218	$21
24 Proj	665	89	21	79	3	273	21	5	274	368	448	112	105	114	13	81	0.78	41	23	36	31	104		8%	102	97	12%	13%	79	2%	64%	39.8	217	$21

Sabol,Blake

Age: 26	Pos: CA LF		Health	A	LIMA Plan	D
Bats: L	Ht: 6'4"	Wt: 215	PT/Exp	B	Rand Var	-2
			Consist	A	MM	4301

Lack of ability to make consistent contact marred first opportunity in majors and draws his future into question -- xBA illustrates risk that BA might tumble further. Pile on defensive concerns at catcher and struggles vL (44% ct%!), and even decent HR output, backed by xHR and xHR/F, won't be enough to make him relevant in most formats.

Yr Tm	PA	R	HR	RBI	SB	BA	xHR	xSB	xBA	OBP	SLG	OPS+	vL+	vR+	bb%	ct%	Eye	G	L	F	h%	HctX	QBaB	Brl%	PX	xPX	HR/F	xHR/F	Spd	SBA%	SB%	RAR	BPX	R$
19																																		
20																																		
21																																		
22 a/a	484	48	11	49	7	230		6		290	376	94			8	67	0.25				32				109				107	9%	74%		17	$9
23 SF	344	36	13	44	4	235	13	7	208	301	394	95	53	102	7	62	0.21	43	19	38	33	76	DCf	11%	108	120	18%	18%	123	8%	67%	3.6	-39	$6
1st Half	218	25	8	28	2	250	7	4	214	313	413	100	39	110	8	63	0.22	42	20	38	36	81	CCc	11%	114	121	17%	15%	127	6%	67%	4.0	-11	$7
2nd Half	126	11	5	16	2	211	6	3	197	280	360	86	80	87	7	61	0.18	44	18	38	29	67	DBf	11%	98	119	19%	23%	117	11%	67%	-2.1	-93	-$1
24 Proj	210	21	9	25	3	218	9	4	219	290	398	94	67	99	8	64	0.23	43	19	38	29	73		11%	120	120	18%	20%	120	9%	71%	1.3	-29	$5

Sanchez,Gary

Age: 31	Pos: CA		Health	B	LIMA Plan	C+
Bats: R	Ht: 6'2"	Wt: 230	PT/Exp	B	Rand Var	0
			Consist	B	MM	4223

19-47-.217 in 267 PA at NYM/SD. Jammed lots of positives into season cut short by fractured wrist, as FB% and HR/F returned to near-peak marks. The intrigue comes from best ct% (72%) since 2017 and a .248 MLB xBA that suggests he's more than a punt-BA backstop. Note limited sample, but there's a path to profit in middle rounds.

Yr Tm	PA	R	HR	RBI	SB	BA	xHR	xSB	xBA	OBP	SLG	OPS+	vL+	vR+	bb%	ct%	Eye	G	L	F	h%	HctX	QBaB	Brl%	PX	xPX	HR/F	xHR/F	Spd	SBA%	SB%	RAR	BPX	R$
19 NYY	446	62	34	77	0	232	36	0	252	316	525	116	106	119	9	68	0.32	32	20	48	24	100	AAd	19%	156	140	26%	28%	75	1%	0%	10.5	152	$12
20 NYY	178	19	10	24	0	147	10	0	200	253	365	82	79	82	10	59	0.28	38	16	46	16	99	AAd	17%	143	147	24%	24%	61	0%	0%	-7.6	-32	$2
21 NYY	440	54	23	54	0	204	21	0	228	307	423	100	114	95	12	68	0.43	36	18	46	23	86	BAc	14%	131	103	19%	17%	79	0%	0%	2.2	108	$5
22 MIN	471	42	16	61	2	205	25	0	220	282	377	93	78	99	8	68	0.29	44	15	42	26	122	BCf	13%	127	136	13%	21%	53	2%	100%	-3.5	24	$5
23 2 NL *	360	38	20	55	1	198	17	2	220	273	414	94	133	94	9	67	0.31	39	14	47	23	110	BBd	15%	134	136	23%	21%	80	1%	100%	2.2	68	$4
1st Half	204	19	8	29	1	180	5	1	195	274	328	82	112	94	11	60	0.33	41	19	40	25	101	BCd	12%	101	133	26%	19%	78	2%	100%	-4.5	-107	$0
2nd Half	156	19	12	26	0	220	12	1	259	288	525	110	149	94	7	75	0.29	38	10	51	20	123	BAd	17%	169	138	22%	22%	87	0%	0%	4.6	275	$6
24 Proj	420	46	25	62	1	229	25	1	238	308	466	106	120	101	9	70	0.34	40	15	45	26	110		15%	143	132	20%	21%	67	1%	95%	14.7	89	$13

Sánchez,Jesús

Age: 26	Pos: RF		Health	B	LIMA Plan	B
Bats: L	Ht: 6'3"	Wt: 222	PT/Exp	A	Rand Var	-3
			Consist	D	MM	4235

Began translating significant raw power into production, which should buy him more time to deliver on potential that xHR and xHR/F suggest is there. Two things have held him back from true breakout: bloated GB% and limited PA vL, with neither looking likely to change. Still, improvement seems likely, and real leap could come with increased FB%.

Yr Tm	PA	R	HR	RBI	SB	BA	xHR	xSB	xBA	OBP	SLG	OPS+	vL+	vR+	bb%	ct%	Eye	G	L	F	h%	HctX	QBaB	Brl%	PX	xPX	HR/F	xHR/F	Spd	SBA%	SB%	RAR	BPX	R$
19 a/a	454	49	12	63	5	245		6		310	369	94			9	74	0.36				31				67				103	8%	54%		0	$8
20 MIA	29	1	0	2	0	40	1	0	138	172	80	34	0	45	14	56	0.36	57	14	29	7	97	ADf	7%	44	80	0%	25%	97	0%	0%	-4.5	-324	-$5
21 MIA *	402	46	22	61	1	271	14	4	255	326	510	115	109	112	7	70	0.27	45	21	34	33	108	BDc	13%	137	141	27%	27%	133	2%	45%	12.5	173	$13
22 MIA *	516	59	17	55	4	225	13	4	230	286	386	95	43	108	8	71	0.29	47	17	37	28	90	BCf	9%	108	94	16%	16%	102	5%	76%	-4.9	59	$9
23 MIA	402	43	14	52	3	253	18	5	269	327	450	106	76	110	9	70	0.36	49	24	26	32	108	BFd	12%	127	98	21%	27%	100	4%	75%	11.2	118	$9
1st Half	178	20	7	25	3	247	8	2	274	315	451	105	123	103	8	70	0.31	53	23	25	31	106	BDc	12%	136	84	25%	29%	75	8%	100%	3.9	114	$4
2nd Half	224	23	7	27	0	258	10	3	265	336	449	106	56	116	10	70	0.39	47	25	28	33	110	BFf	12%	121	109	18%	26%	124	2%	0%	6.0	136	$7
24 Proj	490	54	20	63	3	248	24	6	256	316	449	105	74	111	9	71	0.32	48	21	31	31	102		11%	124	104	20%	24%	108	4%	69%	10.4	104	$16

Santana,Carlos

Age: 38	Pos: 1B		Health	A	LIMA Plan	B+
Bats: B	Ht: 5'11"	Wt: 215	PT/Exp	A	Rand Var	0
			Consist	B	MM	2235

Despite posting highest BA, SLG, and HR total since 2019, Father Time appears to be catching up. Shift rule changes helped h% climb, explaining jump in BA. Meanwhile, gulf between HR, xHR and HR/F, xHR/F can be explained by dipping exit velocity and launch angle. What has been a gentle decline could suddenly speed up to... DN: 10 HR

Yr Tm	PA	R	HR	RBI	SB	BA	xHR	xSB	xBA	OBP	SLG	OPS+	vL+	vR+	bb%	ct%	Eye	G	L	F	h%	HctX	QBaB	Brl%	PX	xPX	HR/F	xHR/F	Spd	SBA%	SB%	RAR	BPX	R$
19 CLE	686	110	34	93	4	281	28	2	276	397	515	126	136	121	16	81	1.00	45	17	38	29	121	ACd	10%	114	112	19%	16%	74	2%	100%	30.0	267	$24
20 CLE	255	34	8	30	0	199	10	0	231	349	350	93	99	89	18	79	1.09	43	18	40	21	109	CCf	7%	79	106	12%	15%	70	0%	0%	-13.1	160	$9
21 KC	659	66	19	69	2	214	22	0	235	319	342	91	98	88	13	82	0.84	46	18	37	23	113	BCf	7%	66	97	11%	13%	59	1%	100%	-23.5	100	$6
22 2 AL	506	52	19	60	0	202	19	0	239	316	376	98	111	93	14	80	0.81	39	17	44	21	122	BBf	10%	103	122	13%	13%	54	0%	0%	-11.5	162	$5
23 2 NL	619	78	23	86	6	240	15	4	270	318	429	102	109	99	11	81	0.63	44	18	38	26	106	CCf	7%	106	88	13%	9%	64	4%	100%	7.3	182	$16
1st Half	314	36	9	43	6	245	6	4	270	322	414	101	113	96	11	80	0.60	41	21	38	28	98	CCf	5%	102	88	11%	7%	57	8%	100%	2.4	154	$15
2nd Half	305	42	14	43	0	235	9	1	266	315	445	103	104	102	11	82	0.65	46	15	38	24	115	CCf	8%	110	89	16%	10%	78	0%	0%	2.6	221	$16
24 Proj	490	59	18	63	2	235	15	2	255	332	413	102	110	99	13	81	0.76	43	17	39	25	113		8%	98	100	13%	11%	64	2%	100%	7.7	174	$14

Santander,Anthony

Age: 29	Pos: RF DH		Health	B	LIMA Plan	B
Bats: B	Ht: 6'2"	Wt: 235	PT/Exp	A	Rand Var	-2
			Consist	A	MM	4135

Perfected profile for elite HR production from both sides of the plate, combining high FB% and launch angle with above-average exit velocity. Skills cast doubt on BA bump, as h% was personal outlier, while ct% is settling into average range at best. Proven power bat in the middle rounds, but more likely to plateau than grow.

Yr Tm	PA	R	HR	RBI	SB	BA	xHR	xSB	xBA	OBP	SLG	OPS+	vL+	vR+	bb%	ct%	Eye	G	L	F	h%	HctX	QBaB	Brl%	PX	xPX	HR/F	xHR/F	Spd	SBA%	SB%	RAR	BPX	R$
19 BAL *	608	69	24	80	3	246	17	4	245	282	431	99	113	103	5	78	0.23	39	18	43	28	102	BBd	8%	99	110	16%	13%	85	6%	43%	-17.7	96	$13
20 BAL	165	24	11	32	0	261	8	0	308	315	575	118	85	126	6	84	0.40	24	27	50	25	124	CAc	10%	159	129	17%	13%	69	4%	0%	4.4	388	$16
21 BAL	438	54	18	50	1	241	15	0	251	286	433	99	95	101	5	75	0.23	34	23	43	28	110	BAd	0%	115	109	13%	11%	59	2%	50%	-3.7	88	$8
22 BAL	647	78	33	89	0	240	31	1	254	318	455	110	128	102	9	79	0.45	31	19	50	25	120	BAf	12%	125	139	15%	14%	67	1%	0%	7.8	186	$19
23 BAL	656	81	28	95	5	257	26	5	247	325	472	109	107	109	8	74	0.36	35	15	50	30	117	BAf	10%	132	125	13%	12%	72	4%	83%	23.3	154	$20
1st Half	334	41	14	47	2	265	14	2	244	326	477	110	121	106	8	74	0.35	32	16	52	31	110	BAf	10%	130	116	12%	12%	82	3%	100%	10.9	157	$20
2nd Half	322	40	14	48	3	249	12	3	249	323	467	107	93	111	9	74	0.38	38	14	48	29	125	AAd	10%	135	134	14%	12%	66	6%	75%	7.0	161	$20
24 Proj	595	75	28	85	3	249	25	3	252	314	465	107	107	107	8	76	0.35	34	18	48	28	117		9%	128	126	14%	12%	65	3%	63%	14.3	164	$21

Schanuel,Nolan

Age: 22	Pos: 1B		Health	A	LIMA Plan	D+
Bats: L	Ht: 6'4"	Wt: 220	PT/Exp	F	Rand Var	0
			Consist	F	MM	0433

1-6-.275 in 132 PA at LAA. Started the year in college, drafted in July and a starting MLB 1B by August. Long-levered singles hitter with goofy, upright setup and swing to match. Lawn-sprinkler approach (covers the entire field), is selective with excellent hand/eye and elite OBP skills. Strong-bodied, but needs to rework swing to hit 10+ HR. (CB)

Yr Tm	PA	R	HR	RBI	SB	BA	xHR	xSB	xBA	OBP	SLG	OPS+	vL+	vR+	bb%	ct%	Eye	G	L	F	h%	HctX	QBaB	Brl%	PX	xPX	HR/F	xHR/F	Spd	SBA%	SB%	RAR	BPX	R$
19																																		
20																																		
21																																		
22																																		
23 LAA *	204	30	2	15	1	284	1	4	275	398	360	103	86	103	16	83	1.09	49	28	22	33	56	DDb	2%	44	24	5%	5%	116	1%	100%	6.4	121	$2
1st Half																								0%										
2nd Half	204	30	2	15	1	284	1	4	275	398	360	0	86	103	16	83	1.09	49	28	22	33	56	DDb	2%	44	24	5%	5%	116	1%	100%	3.7	125	$5
24 Proj	350	45	3	24	2	256	4	5	257	376	333	97	86	100	14	85	1.09	44	25	30	29	72		2%	44	22	5%	5%	117	1%	100%	1.4	113	$8

AN MARCUS

Schmitt,Casey

Age: 25	Pos: SS 3B	Health	A	LIMA Plan	D
Bats: R	Ht: 6'2" Wt: 215	PT/Exp	C	Rand Var	0
		Consist	D	MM	2121

5-30-.206 in 277 PA at SF. Though he reached majors on basis of his glove, he delivered at the plate early on (.325 BA in May). Ultimately, struggles to make consistent hard contact caught up to him, aligning small-sample-size results wit scouting reports. Defense could keep him around for a long time, but lacks standout skill to excel in fantasy.

Yr	Tm	PA	R	HR	RBI	SB	BA	xHR	xSB	xBA	OBP	SLG	OPS+	vL+	vR+	bb%	ct%	Eye	G	L	F	h%	HctX	QBaB	Brl%	PX	xPX	HR/F	xHR/F	Spd	SBA%	SB%	RAR	BPX
19																																		
20																																		
21																																		
22	a/a	139	9	2	13	1	287		1		309	428	104			3	71	0.10				39				110				95	3%	100%		24
23	SF *	487	47	7	52	4	224	7	4	233	261	334	81	83	76	5	74	0.19	39	22	38	29	87	CBf	7%	76	75	7%	10%	74	6%	65%	-14.8	-29
1st Half		293	29	3	36	4	251	3	4	228	278	342	85	108	74	4	76	0.16	42	20	38	32	84	CBd	7%	67	71	5%	7%	81	8%	80%	-7.5	-39
2nd Half		194	18	5	16	0	181	3	1	238	234	321	75	62	79	6	72	0.25	36	25	40	22	91	DBf	6%	89	81	9%	9%	82	3%	0%	-10.8	0
24	**Proj**	**245**	**21**	**5**	**24**	**2**	**243**	**6**	**2**	**236**	**285**	**380**	**91**	**91**	**91**	**4**	**72**	**0.16**	**38**	**23**	**39**	**32**	**88**		**6%**	**94**	**77**	**8%**	**9%**	**73**	**4%**	**69%**	**-1.9**	**0**

Schneider,Davis

Age: 25	Pos: 2B	Health	A	LIMA Plan	D+
Bats: R	Ht: 5'10" Wt: 190	PT/Exp	C	Rand Var	0
		Consist	D	MM	5323

8-20-.276 in 141 at TOR. Former 28th-round pick spent minor-league career in anonymity, but introduced himself quickly upon reaching majors. Track record of high bb%, power production suggest HR and OBP totals are legit, while low ct% hints that BA will fall closer to .240. Even with signs of promise, be wary of limited track record.

Yr	Tm	PA	R	HR	RBI	SB	BA	xHR	xSB	xBA	OBP	SLG	OPS+	vL+	vR+	bb%	ct%	Eye	G	L	F	h%	HctX	QBaB	Brl%	PX	xPX	HR/F	xHR/F	Spd	SBA%	SB%	RAR	BPX
19																																		
20																																		
21																																		
22	a/a	250	28	6	22	8	227		6		301	372	95			10	67	0.33				31				105				116	16%	87%		31
23	TOR *	496	64	23	63	7	240	7	9	247	344	478	112	175	114	14	67	0.47	21	27	52	30	96	BAa	18%	160	167	21%	18%	99	8%	67%	24.8	189
1st Half		265	28	11	28	5	211		5	236	302	400	96	0	0	12	66	0.38	44	20	36	27	0		0%	129	-21	0%		86	13%	67%	-0.5	57
2nd Half		232	36	12	35	2	277	7	4	273	393	575	131	174	113	16	68	0.59	21	27	52	35	98	BAa	18%	198	167	21%	18%	108	5%	67%	21.7	343
24	**Proj**	**315**	**40**	**15**	**37**	**3**	**232**	**15**	**7**	**238**	**346**	**477**	**113**	**145**	**93**	**12**	**63**	**0.39**	**21**	**27**	**52**	**31**	**88**		**16%**	**171**	**150**	**17%**	**16%**	**108**	**6%**	**68%**	**12.5**	**147**

Schwarber,Kyle

Age: 31	Pos: LF DH	Health	B	LIMA Plan	B+
Bats: L	Ht: 6'0" Wt: 229	PT/Exp	A	Rand Var	+5
		Consist	B	MM	5125

Cemented himself as one of the elite power hitters by repeating high FB% from 2022 while maintaining standout Brl%, HR/F. The tradeoff comes with BA damage, and SB mysteriously came and went to further dent R$ return. Power profile keeps him in conversation as early-round pick, but it will take some planning to work around deficiencies.

Yr	Tm	PA	R	HR	RBI	SB	BA	xHR	xSB	xBA	OBP	SLG	OPS+	vL+	vR+	bb%	ct%	Eye	G	L	F	h%	HctX	QBaB	Brl%	PX	xPX	HR/F	xHR/F	Spd	SBA%	SB%	RAR	BPX
19	CHC	610	82	38	92	2	250	40	2	263	339	531	120	105	123	11	71	0.45	38	20	42	28	102	ABc	15%	154	140	24%	25%	74	4%	40%	11.2	193
20	CHC	224	30	11	24	1	188	11	1	220	308	393	93	78	99	13	65	0.45	51	15	35	22	108	ADd	11%	124	128	26%	26%	84	2%	100%	-6.9	60
21	2 TM	471	76	32	71	1	266	33	0	263	374	554	127	107	137	14	68	0.50	38	21	41	31	109	ABc	18%	174	136	29%	29%	67	2%	50%	22.2	235
22	PHI	669	100	46	94	10	218	50	5	246	323	504	117	96	128	13	65	0.43	33	16	51	24	110	AAd	20%	192	181	24%	26%	75	8%	91%	13.2	224
23	PHI	720	108	47	104	0	197	43	2	237	343	474	111	102	116	18	63	0.59	34	16	49	21	101	AAf	16%	176	148	26%	23%	55	1%	0%	19.1	168
1st Half		365	51	22	47	0	188	19	1	238	326	446	106	112	102	16	65	0.55	35	17	47	20	99	ABf	15%	160	140	24%	20%	63	1%	0%	-2.0	146
2nd Half		355	57	25	57	0	206	24	1	238	361	504	117	92	131	19	61	0.62	34	15	52	22	102	AAf	17%	195	157	27%	26%	58	1%	0%	10.0	214
24	**Proj**	**665**	**102**	**45**	**98**	**3**	**225**	**44**	**3**	**244**	**348**	**505**	**117**	**101**	**125**	**15**	**65**	**0.52**	**36**	**17**	**48**	**26**	**105**		**17%**	**177**	**154**	**26%**	**25%**	**67**	**3%**	**65%**	**31.4**	**197**

Seager,Corey

Age: 30	Pos: SS	Health	D	LIMA Plan	C
Bats: L	Ht: 6'4" Wt: 215	PT/Exp	A	Rand Var	-3
		Consist	F	MM	4255

Consolidation of BA and HR skills suggested in last year's book came to fruition, and end result was an elite fantasy season. Even if h% corrected a bit too much, solid ct% and exit velocity will keep excellent BA floor, while xHR, xHR/ predict another 30-HR season. Has the profile of a four-category stud and potential first-round pick.

Yr	Tm	PA	R	HR	RBI	SB	BA	xHR	xSB	xBA	OBP	SLG	OPS+	vL+	vR+	bb%	ct%	Eye	G	L	F	h%	HctX	QBaB	Brl%	PX	xPX	HR/F	xHR/F	Spd	SBA%	SB%	RAR	BPX
19	LA	541	82	19	87	1	272	21	1	278	335	483	113	98	120	8	80	0.45	39	22	39	31	117	CCc	7%	117	130	12%	14%	87	1%	100%	6.8	215
20	LA	232	38	15	41	1	307	18	1	297	358	585	125	108	133	7	83	0.46	38	23	39	31	174	ACb	16%	137	171	22%	26%	99	2%	100%	17.9	344
21	LA	409	54	16	57	1	306	18	3	283	394	521	126	125	126	12	81	0.73	46	21	33	34	136	ACc	12%	117	125	16%	19%	108	2%	50%	29.9	296
22	TEX	663	91	33	83	3	245	35	2	278	317	455	109	107	110	9	83	0.56	40	21	39	25	134	ACc	10%	117	143	17%	18%	79	2%	100%	13.2	231
23	TEX	536	88	33	96	2	327	34	4	314	390	623	138	119	147	9	82	0.56	40	20	40	35	161	ACb	15%	164	165	21%	22%	85	2%	67%	69.0	368
1st Half		237	34	10	49	1	351	12	2	320	418	606	140	125	147	11	80	0.61	38	27	35	40	173	ACa	19%	155	176	17%	20%	79	3%	50%	30.2	329
2nd Half		299	54	23	47	1	309	22	2	311	368	636	136	113	146	8	83	0.51	41	15	44	30	151	ACb	13%	170	157	23%	22%	95	1%	100%	31.9	404
24	**Proj**	**560**	**87**	**30**	**90**	**2**	**301**	**32**	**4**	**295**	**368**	**554**	**126**	**114**	**132**	**9**	**82**	**0.56**	**41**	**21**	**39**	**32**	**148**		**13%**	**139**	**152**	**19%**	**20%**	**86**	**2%**	**75%**	**50.3**	**317**

Segura,Jean

Age: 34	Pos: 3B	Health	D	LIMA Plan	D+
Bats: R	Ht: 5'10" Wt: 220	PT/Exp	A	Rand Var	+5
		Consist	C	MM	0321

Didn't close the season on a big-league roster after disastrous 1st half. Climbing GB% and lack of quality of contact mean double-digit HR won't likely return, and even with ct% intact, xBA shows BA floor crashing. Still capable of providing some SB, but the rest of the profile is on shaky ground.

Yr	Tm	PA	R	HR	RBI	SB	BA	xHR	xSB	xBA	OBP	SLG	OPS+	vL+	vR+	bb%	ct%	Eye	G	L	F	h%	HctX	QBaB	Brl%	PX	xPX	HR/F	xHR/F	Spd	SBA%	SB%	RAR	BPX
19	PHI	618	79	12	60	10	280	13	8	291	323	420	103	126	95	5	87	0.41	52	21	27	30	100	CDc	3%	72	61	9%	9%	105	8%	83%	-8.2	185
20	PHI	217	28	7	25	2	266	6	5	240	347	422	102	108	99	11	77	0.51	48	18	34	31	96	CCf	6%	80	64	14%	12%	146	7%	50%	-0.9	148
21	PHI	567	76	14	58	9	290	12	8	275	348	436	108	120	102	7	85	0.50	52	19	29	32	100	CDd	6%	79	68	11%	10%	106	8%	75%	15.1	192
22	PHI *	420	47	10	35	14	266	7	11	248	317	368	97	120	95	7	83	0.43	57	16	27	30	96	CFf	4%	58	57	13%	9%	92	17%	70%	-4.2	72
23	MIA	326	25	3	21	6	219	5	8	237	277	279	76	72	76	7	84	0.47	59	15	26	25	96	CFf	4%	31	52	5%	8%	128	10%	75%	-12.0	57
1st Half		246	18	2	14	5	199	3	5	234	261	252	70	70	70	7	83	0.45	58	16	26	23	97	CFf	3%	29	50	4%	6%	99	12%	71%	-15.2	7
2nd Half		80	7	1	7	1	280	2	2	241	325	360	93	78	97	6	88	0.56	60	12	28	31	92	CFf	4%	36	56	6%	11%	140	4%	100%	0.1	132
24	**Proj**	**245**	**25**	**3**	**21**	**5**	**261**	**4**	**6**	**245**	**316**	**345**	**91**	**96**	**89**	**7**	**85**	**0.47**	**57**	**16**	**28**	**30**	**96**		**4%**	**45**	**58**	**6%**	**7%**	**117**	**10%**	**75%**	**-0.7**	**104**

Semien,Marcus

Age: 33	Pos: 2B	Health	A	LIMA Plan	A
Bats: R	Ht: 6'0" Wt: 195	PT/Exp	A	Rand Var	-1
		Consist	D	MM	3335

Rode mega-PA volume to third consecutive $30 season. However... 2nd half power outburst wasn't backed by xHR or xHR/F; SBA% plunge puts future SB at risk despite solid Spd and SB%. BPX says skills are firmly intact, but don't ignore the flaws as small warts tend to snowball in the mid-30s.

Yr	Tm	PA	R	HR	RBI	SB	BA	xHR	xSB	xBA	OBP	SLG	OPS+	vL+	vR+	bb%	ct%	Eye	G	L	F	h%	HctX	QBaB	Brl%	PX	xPX	HR/F	xHR/F	Spd	SBA%	SB%	RAR	BPX
19	OAK	747	123	33	92	10	285	32	16	290	369	522	123	129	120	12	84	0.85	41	20	39	30	122	CBc	9%	114	105	15%	15%	135	9%	56%	35.2	352
20	OAK	236	28	7	23	4	223	7	4	225	305	374	90	103	86	11	76	0.50	33	20	47	26	86	DAf	5%	85	111	9%	9%	123	7%	100%	-4.9	132
21	TOR	724	115	45	102	15	265	30	9	272	334	538	120	106	125	9	78	0.45	31	21	48	28	114	BAc	10%	150	144	18%	12%	97	10%	94%	38.9	308
22	TEX	724	101	26	83	25	248	22	24	249	304	429	104	106	103	7	82	0.44	34	19	47	27	106	CAc	7%	105	116	10%	9%	140	21%	76%	14.2	241
23	TEX	752	122	29	100	14	276	22	18	268	348	478	113	108	114	10	84	0.65	34	20	47	29	117	CAc	7%	108	125	11%	8%	123	9%	82%	45.0	282
1st Half		396	67	11	56	8	287	10	9	267	351	462	111	110	112	9	84	0.64	34	21	45	32	119	CAc	5%	99	127	8%	7%	121	9%	89%	20.1	261
2nd Half		356	55	18	44	6	263	12	8	270	346	495	114	105	117	10	83	0.67	34	18	48	27	115	CAb	8%	119	122	14%	10%	119	9%	75%	17.2	304
24	**Proj**	**700**	**104**	**25**	**90**	**13**	**264**	**23**	**17**	**255**	**333**	**450**	**107**	**105**	**108**	**9**	**82**	**0.55**	**34**	**20**	**47**	**29**	**112**		**7%**	**103**	**123**	**10%**	**9%**	**111**	**9%**	**81%**	**28.1**	**274**

Senzel,Nick

Age: 29	Pos: 3B LF	Health	F	LIMA Plan	D+
Bats: R	Ht: 6'1" Wt: 205	PT/Exp	C	Rand Var	0
		Consist	A	MM	1321

13-42-.236 with 7 SB in 330 PA at CIN. In what has become a common refrain, was limited by injuries (toe, knee). A face value, looks like the power is back, but xHR, xPX, xHR/F all say "Not so fast." In fact, "x" stats say that last two years produced nearly identical skills, none of which are roster-worthy for 2024.

Yr	Tm	PA	R	HR	RBI	SB	BA	xHR	xSB	xBA	OBP	SLG	OPS+	vL+	vR+	bb%	ct%	Eye	G	L	F	h%	HctX	QBaB	Brl%	PX	xPX	HR/F	xHR/F	Spd	SBA%	SB%	RAR	BPX
19	CIN *	447	61	13	44	14	254	14	14	243	309	419	101	126	94	7	72	0.28	48	19	33	32	100	CCc	8%	95	77	13%	16%	146	19%	74%	1.2	85
20	CIN	77	8	2	8	2	186	2	1	252	247	357	80	46	101	8	79	0.40	38	20	43	21	119	CBc	4%	106	143	8%	8%	86	27%	67%	-5.2	168
21	CIN *	161	22	1	10	2	250	2	5	263	314	326	88	101	85	8	87	0.74	46	24	30	28	100	CCc	4%	45	59	3%	7%	124	17%	29%	-6.2	158
22	CIN	411	45	5	25	8	231	7	8	237	296	306	85	83	86	7	80	0.39	46	23	31	28	88	CCc	3%	51	74	5%	8%	105	13%	62%	-13.7	28
23	CIN *	393	55	14	44	8	224	7	8	236	286	375	90	136	68	8	74	0.33	42	19	39	26	90	CBd	5%	88	89	15%	8%	107	12%	80%	-3.1	61
1st Half		250	29	6	30	5	234	3	5	229	311	353	91	138	75	10	74	0.43	40	22	39	29	72	DBd	4%	76	78	9%	5%	98	10%	82%	-1.7	25
2nd Half		143	26	8	14	4	209	4	4	249	242	411	88	134	49	4	75	0.18	46	15	38	22	120	CCc	6%	107	107	25%	13%	126	21%	78%	-3.2	118
24	**Proj**	**245**	**34**	**6**	**22**	**6**	**230**	**6**	**6**	**238**	**286**	**354**	**88**	**112**	**74**	**7**	**77**	**0.33**	**45**	**20**	**35**	**27**	**98**		**5%**	**72**	**86**	**10%**	**9%**	**107**	**15%**	**77%**	**-3.2**	**80**

DAN MARCUS

Sheets,Gavin

Age: 28 Pos: RF 1B	Health A	LIMA Plan D+	
Bats: L Ht: 6' 5" Wt: 230	PT/Exp B	Rand Var +4	
	Consist B	MM 2203	

Solid ct%, high FB% give him decent base for power, but rest of skills (HctX, Brl%, xHR/F) all show that he doesn't hit the ball consistently hard enough to take advantage. Even usefulness vR faded in 2023, with .349 SLG and 76 PX across 324 PA. There are better options for fantasy managers and big-league teams... DN: <250 PA

Yr Tm	PA	R	HR	RBI	SB	BA	xHR	xSB	xBA	OBP	SLG	OPS+	vL+	vR+	bb%	ct%	Eye	G	L	F	h%	HctX	QBaB	Brl%	PX	xPX	HR/F	xHR/F	Spd	SBA%	SB%	RAR	BPX	R$
19 aa	517	55	17	82	3	256		3		332	404	102			10	76	0.48				30				78				89	3%	73%		59	$12
20																																		
21 CHW *	424	48	19	66	1	241	8	0	236	302	437	102	37	124	8	72	0.31	45	17	38	29	117	BCd	10%	118	110	24%	17%	54	2%	37%	0.0	65	$9
22 CHW *	448	38	16	57	0	238	11	1	228	286	409	98	65	105	6	77	0.30	40	15	45	27	98	CBd	7%	109	103	11%	8%	82	0%	0%	-2.9	124	$8
23 CHW	344	24	10	43	1	203	7	1	215	267	331	82	14	86	8	79	0.42	38	16	47	23	86	CBf	5%	72	96	9%	6%	70	1%	100%	-9.6	43	$1
1st Half	197	17	8	25	0	224	6	1	221	305	385	95	0	98	10	80	0.57	37	16	48	24	90	CBf	7%	83	96	12%	9%	79	0%	0%	-1.7	114	$1
2nd Half	147	7	2	18	1	175	2	1	203	218	263	65	20	70	6	77	0.26	39	16	45	21	82	CBf	3%	57	95	4%	4%	77	4%	100%	-10.4	-32	-$6
24 Proj	**350**	**29**	**11**	**47**	**1**	**218**	**10**	**1**	**221**	**279**	**366**	**88**	**40**	**93**	**8**	**77**	**0.36**	**40**	**16**	**44**	**25**	**94**		**5%**	**87**	**100**	**10%**	**9%**	**75**	**2%**	**84%**	**-6.2**	**60**	**$3**

Short,Zack

Age: 29 Pos: 2B SS 3B	Health A	LIMA Plan D	
Bats: R Ht: 5' 10" Wt: 180	PT/Exp B	Rand Var 0	
	Consist B	MM 3201	

7-33-.204 with 5 SB in 253 PA at DET. Across three partial seasons and 450 PA in majors, has 13 HR and 8 SB, suggesting there's something to the profile. Skills say otherwise, as career 89 PX, 77 Spd are subpar, .190 xBA is awful, and .266 OBP will limit SB upside. At his age, sub-Mendoza skills won't be suddenly finding new life.

Yr Tm	PA	R	HR	RBI	SB	BA	xHR	xSB	xBA	OBP	SLG	OPS+	vL+	vR+	bb%	ct%	Eye	G	L	F	h%	HctX	QBaB	Brl%	PX	xPX	HR/F	xHR/F	Spd	SBA%	SB%	RAR	BPX	R$
19 a/a	223	25	5	19	2	203		3		297	354	90			12	62	0.35				30				105				115	8%	43%		-30	-$1
20																																		
21 DET *	366	45	13	43	3	171	4	2	186	280	329	84	76	68	13	64	0.43	27	17	56	21	82	CAf	5%	103	133	10%	7%	90	5%	70%	-14.8	-15	$0
22 DET *	527	52	6	40	8	169	0	9	94	260	265	74	28	0	11	61	0.31	0	0	100	26	89	AAa	33%	87	235	0%	0%	103	13%	56%	-31.0	-103	-$3
23 DET *	346	29	10	40	6	186	8	5	194	280	322	82	93	81	11	65	0.38	35	16	49	25	82	DAf	9%	93	102	9%	11%	78	10%	82%	-7.9	-54	$1
1st Half	212	21	7	25	2	188	6	3	190	274	326	82	98	86	11	65	0.34	32	17	51	25	76	DAf	13%	93	114	10%	15%	94	7%	56%	-8.8	-57	-$1
2nd Half	134	8	3	15	4	184	2	3	200	290	316	82	89	75	13	67	0.45	37	16	47	25	89	DAf	5%	94	89	9%	6%	76	14%	100%	-4.3	-25	-$3
24 Proj	**175**	**16**	**5**	**18**	**3**	**194**	**3**	**3**	**191**	**286**	**338**	**86**	**92**	**81**	**12**	**64**	**0.38**	**32**	**16**	**52**	**27**	**83**		**7%**	**103**	**113**	**10%**	**6%**	**88**	**10%**	**77%**	**-2.7**	**-50**	**$3**

Siri,Jose

Age: 28 Pos: CF	Health B	LIMA Plan C	
Bats: R Ht: 6' 2" Wt: 175	PT/Exp B	Rand Var +3	
	Consist B	MM 4513	

Season was bookended by Apr hamstring, Sept hand injuries that took away PA. Also sat occasionally due to abysmal plate discipline—awful July/Aug (56% ct%) likely played role in in-season HR drop, and 2nd half Eye, BPX cast doubt on future growth. But behind poor plate skills are excellent power and speed metrics, so keep him on your radar.

Yr Tm	PA	R	HR	RBI	SB	BA	xHR	xSB	xBA	OBP	SLG	OPS+	vL+	vR+	bb%	ct%	Eye	G	L	F	h%	HctX	QBaB	Brl%	PX	xPX	HR/F	xHR/F	Spd	SBA%	SB%	RAR	BPX	R$
19 a/a	506	48	10	46	22	214		16		273	326	83			7	58	0.19				34				80				103	28%	71%		-200	$10
20																																		
21 HOU *	428	56	15	56	19	253	5	15	189	284	433	99	147	123	4	58	0.11	34	14	52	39	82	BBa	17%	137	150	27%	33%	137	29%	80%	-2.1	-15	$18
22 2 AL *	400	63	12	37	15	214	7	14	218	261	373	90	66	93	6	64	0.18	43	21	36	30	66	DBd	6%	117	72	10%	10%	163	22%	88%	-6.8	41	$11
23 TAM	364	58	25	56	12	222	22	11	239	267	494	104	86	109	5	62	0.15	39	16	45	27	83	CCd	13%	180	132	27%	23%	129	26%	80%	5.3	150	$12
1st Half	193	33	16	37	7	229	14	6	256	281	549	114	113	113	7	63	0.22	39	14	47	25	85	CCd	18%	201	133	30%	26%	128	29%	78%	6.2	250	$16
2nd Half	171	25	9	19	5	215	8	5	222	251	436	93	59	105	4	60	0.09	40	18	42	30	80	CBd	8%	156	132	23%	20%	131	23%	83%	-2.6	39	$6
24 Proj	**420**	**62**	**21**	**53**	**15**	**231**	**21**	**14**	**223**	**277**	**446**	**99**	**78**	**107**	**5**	**61**	**0.15**	**41**	**18**	**41**	**32**	**76**		**10%**	**150**	**108**	**21%**	**21%**	**125**	**25%**	**81%**	**2.9**	**50**	**$18**

Slater,Austin

Age: 31 Pos: CF LF	Health C	LIMA Plan D	
Bats: R Ht: 6' 1" Wt: 204	PT/Exp C	Rand Var -3	
	Consist B	MM 3321	

5-20-.270 with 2 SB in 207 PA at SF. Hamstring issue plagued him for first month, may have impacted running game, and ended year with elbow surgery for discomfort that has nagged him last couple seasons. So there are valid reasons to consider giving him a pass on down year. Limitations vR still likely to limit overall value though.

Yr Tm	PA	R	HR	RBI	SB	BA	xHR	xSB	xBA	OBP	SLG	OPS+	vL+	vR+	bb%	ct%	Eye	G	L	F	h%	HctX	QBaB	Brl%	PX	xPX	HR/F	xHR/F	Spd	SBA%	SB%	RAR	BPX	R$
19 SF *	467	55	13	55	5	245	8	6	246	337	410	103	117	92	12	65	0.40	52	25	23	34	102	CFb	10%	107	113	20%	32%	111	6%	69%	4.4	22	$9
20 SF	104	18	5	7	8	282	5	6	266	408	506	121	147	98	15	74	0.73	40	29	32	33	94	CCb	14%	114	120	25%	25%	151	26%	89%	6.0	264	$16
21 SF	306	39	12	32	15	241	12	9	255	320	423	102	122	69	9	69	0.33	51	24	26	30	82	DDb	9%	113	88	25%	25%	96	23%	88%	1.0	65	$12
22 SF	325	49	7	34	12	264	10	10	243	366	408	110	115	101	12	68	0.45	52	22	26	36	92	CFa	10%	108	92	15%	21%	125	14%	92%	9.7	76	$12
23 SF *	230	27	6	24	3	267	8	5	227	338	395	100	108	85	10	67	0.32	49	21	29	37	84	BDc	12%	90	82	14%	22%	106	8%	57%	4.2	-18	$4
1st Half	102	12	3	15	3	324	2	4	223	382	435	112	127	107	9	68	0.30	52	21	27	45	86	BDf	6%	72	66	14%	14%	112	15%	57%	5.1	-57	$1
2nd Half	128	15	3	9	0	221	6	1	228	313	363	91	100	45	10	66	0.34	47	22	31	31	83	ADc	15%	104	94	13%	26%	102	0%	0%	-1.3	7	-$3
24 Proj	**210**	**28**	**6**	**22**	**5**	**249**	**8**	**5**	**239**	**337**	**397**	**101**	**109**	**85**	**11**	**68**	**0.37**	**50**	**22**	**28**	**34**	**87**		**11%**	**101**	**89**	**16%**	**22%**	**100**	**11%**	**78%**	**3.6**	**34**	**$7**

Smith,Dominic

Age: 29 Pos: 1B	Health B	LIMA Plan B	
Bats: L Ht: 6' 0" Wt: 239	PT/Exp A	Rand Var 0	
	Consist C	MM 2025	

Finally got a shot at full-time work that he was blocked from in NY, but this career-high PA didn't yield all that much. Career-best ct% and Eye were encouraging and give him decent BA floor, but power was still lacking. Even with 2nd half improvement, ceiling looks to be 15-20 HR. That's a tough sell for 1B-only eligibility.

Yr Tm	PA	R	HR	RBI	SB	BA	xHR	xSB	xBA	OBP	SLG	OPS+	vL+	vR+	bb%	ct%	Eye	G	L	F	h%	HctX	QBaB	Brl%	PX	xPX	HR/F	xHR/F	Spd	SBA%	SB%	RAR	BPX	R$
19 NYM	197	35	11	25	1	282	8	1	274	355	525	122	122	121	10	75	0.43	40	23	37	32	96	CBc	8%	129	89	22%	16%	78	6%	33%	4.6	178	$5
20 NYM	199	27	10	42	0	316	12	0	308	377	616	132	117	137	7	75	0.31	41	26	33	38	114	BCb	13%	183	142	22%	27%	52	0%	0%	11.9	304	$24
21 NYM	493	43	11	58	2	244	14	0	240	304	363	92	107	86	6	75	0.29	38	26	36	30	107	CBb	6%	74	107	9%	12%	60	3%	67%	-17.1	-27	$7
22 NYM *	385	36	6	40	2	202	4	1	221	260	311	81	78	80	7	75	0.31	47	16	36	25	83	BCd	7%	78	81	0%	11%	69	4%	66%	-22.8	0	$0
23 WAS	586	57	12	46	1	254	14	4	245	326	366	94	79	101	8	83	0.52	42	20	37	29	88	DCd	7%	63	94	7%	9%	83	1%	50%	-4.6	86	$9
1st Half	326	31	4	19	0	264	6	3	233	331	339	92	91	92	8	84	0.54	44	20	36	30	83	DCc	5%	41	82	4%	7%	103	0%	0%	-4.8	61	$5
2nd Half	260	26	8	27	1	241	9	2	259	319	401	97	55	109	8	81	0.49	41	20	39	27	96	DCd	8%	91	111	11%	12%	64	3%	50%	-2.2	132	$7
24 Proj	**525**	**54**	**14**	**56**	**2**	**242**	**17**	**3**	**245**	**312**	**383**	**95**	**86**	**98**	**8**	**79**	**0.38**	**42**	**20**	**38**	**28**	**93**		**7%**	**84**	**98**	**10%**	**12%**	**66**	**2%**	**56%**	**-2.6**	**72**	**$12**

Smith,Josh H.

Age: 26 Pos: SS 3B LF	Health A	LIMA Plan D	
Bats: L Ht: 5' 10" Wt: 172	PT/Exp C	Rand Var +5	
	Consist C	MM 1201	

Spent full year in majors, but difficult to judge due to sporadic playing time. Brl%, xPX stand out as significant leaps forward from initial MLB sample, and Spd hints at SB return if light turns green again. Next step will require maintaining 2nd half ct% growth, tapping into power upside. Still young enough to get there; could be worth a flyer.

Yr Tm	PA	R	HR	RBI	SB	BA	xHR	xSB	xBA	OBP	SLG	OPS+	vL+	vR+	bb%	ct%	Eye	G	L	F	h%	HctX	QBaB	Brl%	PX	xPX	HR/F	xHR/F	Spd	SBA%	SB%	RAR	BPX	R$
19																																		
20																																		
21 aa	117	10	2	8	6	260		4		353	376	100			13	78	0.65				31				70				94	24%	72%		85	$2
22 TEX *	494	50	5	43	9	208	3	12	208	287	290	82	66	81	10	74	0.42	34	24	42	27	75	DAf	2%	57	82	3%	4%	121	14%	54%	-19.4	-3	$4
23 TEX	232	29	6	15	1	185	8	4	220	304	328	86	93	85	11	72	0.45	45	15	40	22	115	CCc	10%	89	144	11%	14%	129	2%	100%	-5.1	75	-$2
1st Half	129	19	3	6	1	217	4	3	198	352	340	95	130	91	12	66	0.39	43	16	41	30	106	CBb	9%	84	154	10%	14%	145	3%	100%	-2.3	0	-$5
2nd Half	103	10	3	9	0	146	4	1	242	245	315	76	73	76	11	79	0.58	46	14	39	15	126	CCd	13%	93	134	11%	14%	107	0%	0%	-5.7	161	-$7
24 Proj	**245**	**27**	**5**	**19**	**4**	**221**	**7**	**5**	**218**	**325**	**340**	**91**	**83**	**93**	**11**	**74**	**0.48**	**41**	**18**	**41**	**28**	**101**		**7%**	**74**	**118**	**7%**	**10%**	**106**	**9%**	**66%**	**-2.7**	**60**	**$5**

Smith,Kevin

Age: 27 Pos: SS	Health B	LIMA Plan D	
Bats: R Ht: 6' 0" Wt: 190	PT/Exp B	Rand Var -1	
	Consist D	MM 2201	

5-11-.185 with 1 SB in 146 PA at OAK. Issues with poor Eye remained, resulting in more PA at AAA than in MLB. And while 2nd half Brl%, xPX were positives, BA continues to be so poor that HR, SB can't redeem him. Best shot at value comes from vL+, which matches work in AAA for 2022-23, but that skill means nothing if he's stuck in minors.

Yr Tm	PA	R	HR	RBI	SB	BA	xHR	xSB	xBA	OBP	SLG	OPS+	vL+	vR+	bb%	ct%	Eye	G	L	F	h%	HctX	QBaB	Brl%	PX	xPX	HR/F	xHR/F	Spd	SBA%	SB%	RAR	BPX	R$
19 aa	457	47	18	58	11	205		9		252	395	90			6	62	0.17				28				125				95	24%	62%		-26	$7
20																																		
21 TOR *	430	58	20	61	16	245	2	12	185	319	485	110	75	18	10	69	0.35	19	0	81	30	107	CAb	14%	152	192	6%	12%	124	21%	82%	12.9	212	$18
22 OAK *	498	32	8	38	7	184	4	5	174	220	287	72	106	55	4	61	0.12	41	13	46	28	66	DCf	8%	88	105	4%	9%	102	10%	85%	-29.8	-145	-$2
23 OAK *	323	37	13	36	6	208	5	6	200	238	365	82	105	59	4	63	0.11	43	14	43	28	75	DCf	9%	106	122	14%	14%	89	17%	69%	-9.0	-93	$3
1st Half	181	21	8	19	5	192	4	4	197	223	353	79	122	56	4	62	0.11	45	13	42	26	66	DDf	8%	108	108	16%	16%	97	22%	79%	-9.1	-100	$1
2nd Half	142	16	5	17	1	228	1	2	204	258	380	86	80	68	4	65	0.11	38	17	46	31	99	DBa	13%	105	156	9%	9%	92	8%	46%	-4.4	-64	$0
24 Proj	**210**	**22**	**5**	**23**	**2**	**220**	**6**	**4**	**189**	**265**	**346**	**84**	**109**	**68**	**5**	**64**	**0.15**	**41**	**14**	**45**	**32**	**78**		**9%**	**92**	**124**	**9%**	**11%**	**95**	**8%**	**62%**	**-5.4**	**-46**	**$4**

AN MARCUS

Smith,Pavin

Age: 28 Pos: DH RF | Bats: L Ht: 6' 2" Wt: 208

Health A | PT/Exp A | Consist B | LIMA Plan D+ | Rand Var +2 | MM 2321

.188-7-30 in 228 PA at ARI. Got off to nice start (.873 OPS through 5/10) but fell off cliff and spent nearly all of 2nd hal in AAA. Plate skills, especially bb%, have held up pretty well, but futility vL and modest power make for murky PT outlook. Tack on downward xBA trend, and upside is very limited.

Yr	Tm	PA	R	HR	RBI	SB	BA	xHR	xSB	xBA	OBP	SLG	OPS+	vL+	vR+	bb%	ct%	Eye	G	L	F	h%	HctX	QBaB	Brl%	PX	xPX	HR/F	xHR/F	Spd	SBA%	SB%	RAR	BPX
19	aa	497	58	11	63	2	282		6		364	457	114			11	85	0.87				31				86				127	2%	63%		270
20	ARI	44	7	1	4	1	270	1	1	269	341	405	99	112	96	11	78	0.63	45	32	23	32	92	CDf	6%	58	46	14%	14%	146	8%	100%	0.1	112
21	ARI	545	68	11	49	1	267	13	5	253	328	404	101	83	107	8	79	0.40	47	21	32	32	111	CDf	5%	81	94	9%	10%	126	1%	100%	-2.6	135
22	ARI	277	24	9	33	1	220	11	1	210	300	367	94	81	99	10	73	0.42	43	14	43	27	82	CBf	10%	96	92	12%	14%	95	2%	100%	-4.0	62
23	ARI *	492	51	11	58	2	213	7	4	229	311	334	88	64	93	12	76	0.58	43	19	38	26	108	BCc	8%	72	101	13%	13%	80	2%	68%	-8.9	39
1st Half		247	29	7	32	1	182	7	2	236	299	312	84	64	94	14	78	0.76	42	20	38	20	113	BBc	8%	72	105	13%	13%	74	3%	50%	-8.9	79
2nd Half		245	23	4	26	1	244	0	3	206	323	357	92	0	81	11	74	0.44	80	0	20	31	60	CFd	0%	72	-21	0%	0%	104	2%	100%	-1.6	21
24	**Proj**	**245**	**26**	**7**	**28**	**1**	**233**	**7**	**2**	**240**	**318**	**385**	**97**	**78**	**102**	**11**	**76**	**0.51**	**44**	**19**	**37**	**27**	**104**		**7%**	**90**	**97**	**12%**	**12%**	**109**	**2%**	**78%**	**-0.2**	**85**

Smith,Will

Age: 29 Pos: CA | Bats: R Ht: 5' 10" Wt: 195

Health A | PT/Exp A | Consist A | LIMA Plan B | Rand Var 0 | MM 3335

Looked like his usual self in 1st half with bb%, ct%, power in peak form. Took a pitch to the elbow in July (no IL time) and skills became more volatile after that, sliding a bit overall. Track record of consistent production and volume suggest he's probably good for a few more HR in 2024, and still an upper-tier catcher with a rock-solid floor.

Yr	Tm	PA	R	HR	RBI	SB	BA	xHR	xSB	xBA	OBP	SLG	OPS+	vL+	vR+	bb%	ct%	Eye	G	L	F	h%	HctX	QBaB	Brl%	PX	xPX	HR/F	xHR/F	Spd	SBA%	SB%	RAR	BPX
19	LA *	447	65	30	81	3	236	10	2	248	315	515	115	95	140	10	72	0.41	29	17	54	25	111	BAb	11%	147	168	23%	15%	94	3%	100%	12.9	211
20	LA	137	23	8	25	0	289	6	0	301	401	579	130	110	138	15	81	0.91	24	27	49	30	133	BAb	13%	153	161	17%	13%	87	0%	0%	13.2	408
21	LA	501	71	25	76	3	258	22	3	258	365	495	118	100	126	12	76	0.57	31	22	46	28	115	BAc	11%	131	140	17%	15%	104	2%	100%	25.8	242
22	LA	578	68	24	87	1	260	28	3	264	343	465	114	127	110	10	81	0.58	32	21	47	28	116	BAc	11%	119	144	12%	14%	98	1%	100%	25.5	241
23	LA	554	80	19	76	3	261	18	7	254	359	438	109	108	109	11	81	0.71	37	19	44	29	117	BBc	7%	96	122	11%	11%	107	2%	100%	25.9	204
1st Half		265	39	12	41	1	276	10	3	273	396	495	122	128	120	16	84	1.17	40	17	43	28	120	BBc	8%	111	131	15%	13%	97	1%	100%	20.0	311
2nd Half		289	41	7	35	2	248	8	4	237	325	388	96	93	98	8	78	0.41	35	20	45	29	115	CBc	5%	82	113	8%	9%	116	3%	100%	3.9	114
24	**Proj**	**560**	**81**	**24**	**86**	**3**	**260**	**22**	**5**	**256**	**352**	**459**	**111**	**108**	**112**	**11**	**80**	**0.60**	**34**	**20**	**46**	**28**	**117**		**9%**	**110**	**134**	**13%**	**12%**	**98**	**2%**	**100%**	**29.9**	**224**

Soderstrom,Tyler

Age: 22 Pos: DH | Bats: L Ht: 6' 2" Wt: 200

Health A | PT/Exp C | Consist A | LIMA Plan D+ | Rand Var +2 | MM 1105

3-7-.160 in 138 PA at OAK. Showed off plus power at AAA, but it didn't carry over to majors, where he hit everything o the ground. Free-swinging ways led to awful BA that can't just be chalked up to low h%. Plenty of long-term appeal, bu it will take time, and loss of CA-eligibility in many leagues (at least at start of year) further clouds draftability.

Yr	Tm	PA	R	HR	RBI	SB	BA	xHR	xSB	xBA	OBP	SLG	OPS+	vL+	vR+	bb%	ct%	Eye	G	L	F	h%	HctX	QBaB	Brl%	PX	xPX	HR/F	xHR/F	Spd	SBA%	SB%	RAR	BPX
19																																		
20																																		
21																																		
22	a/a	177	12	5	21	0	222		2		252	335	83			4	69	0.13				29				69				121	3%	0%		-69
23	OAK *	459	38	14	43	1	183	4	2	215	230	319	75	64	64	6	68	0.19	55	14	30	23	89	BDf	6%	89	73	12%	16%	90	1%	100%	-14.0	-61
1st Half		278	25	10	34	1	195		2	231	230	367	82	0	0	4	67	0.14	44	20	36	25	0		0%	114	-21	0%		101	2%	100%	-7.5	-4
2nd Half		181	12	4	9	1	163	4	2	186	228	243	64	63	64	8	69	0.27	55	14	30	21	91	BDf	6%	49	73	12%	16%	98	3%	100%	-10.2	-139
24	**Proj**	**455**	**33**	**9**	**43**	**1**	**219**	**14**	**5**	**203**	**272**	**315**	**81**	**65**	**83**	**6**	**68**	**0.22**	**51**	**18**	**30**	**30**	**82**		**5%**	**61**	**66**	**11%**	**16%**	**94**	**2%**	**57%**	**-17.5**	**-77**

Solano,Donovan

Age: 36 Pos: 1B 2B | Bats: R Ht: 5' 8" Wt: 210

Health D | PT/Exp A | Consist A | LIMA Plan D+ | Rand Var -2 | MM 1133

Provided some deep-league value once again with multi-position eligibility and a LD stroke that continued to yield high BA. Career-high PA will be tough to duplicate, however, and ct% dip suggests even the empty BA is no sure thing at this stage of his career. Can still be useful as a deep league filler, but only if you're in a pinch.

Yr	Tm	PA	R	HR	RBI	SB	BA	xHR	xSB	xBA	OBP	SLG	OPS+	vL+	vR+	bb%	ct%	Eye	G	L	F	h%	HctX	QBaB	Brl%	PX	xPX	HR/F	xHR/F	Spd	SBA%	SB%	RAR	BPX
19	SF *	321	35	5	34	0	307	5	2	280	343	419	105	117	107	5	79	0.26	37	34	29	37	104	CBb	4%	64	77	8%	10%	104	1%	0%	-0.4	41
20	SF	203	22	3	29	0	326	4	1	265	365	463	110	113	108	5	79	0.26	36	28	36	40	110	CBc	5%	86	90	5%	7%	97	0%	0%	7.2	112
21	SF	344	35	7	31	2	280	8	0	261	344	404	103	112	97	7	81	0.43	40	26	34	33	98	CCb	7%	74	98	8%	9%	70	2%	100%	-2.2	81
22	CIN *	334	23	5	26	0	283	6	0	261	327	391	102	108	100	6	78	0.31	45	27	28	35	113	CCb	6%	79	87	7%	10%	52	0%	0%	-0.1	21
23	MIN	450	43	5	38	0	282	9	2	252	369	391	104	101	105	9	75	0.40	41	27	33	37	110	BCa	6%	78	97	5%	9%	71	0%	0%	7.2	7
1st Half		227	18	3	19	0	265	5	1	265	366	378	102	101	102	12	74	0.52	40	30	30	34	116	BCa	6%	80	87	7%	11%	65	0%	0%	0.0	25
2nd Half		223	25	2	19	0	298	5	1	240	372	404	105	100	107	7	75	0.28	42	23	35	39	104	BCa	6%	75	107	4%	10%	78	0%	0%	2.4	-7
24	**Proj**	**350**	**32**	**5**	**30**	**0**	**278**	**7**	**1**	**254**	**342**	**389**	**100**	**102**	**99**	**7**	**76**	**0.30**	**41**	**27**	**32**	**35**	**108**		**6%**	**77**	**94**	**6%**	**9%**	**66**	**0%**	**86%**	**4.4**	**28**

Soler,Jorge

Age: 32 Pos: DH RF | Bats: R Ht: 6' 4" Wt: 235

Health D | PT/Exp A | Consist D | LIMA Plan B | Rand Var 0 | MM 4025

Both health and power returned prior to Sept oblique strain, he mashed vL, and ct%, BA rebounds were an added bonus. xBA and xHR show the gains came with full skill support, though recent history says odds are against the form holding firm. As long as health cooperates, should again be a premier power source.

Yr	Tm	PA	R	HR	RBI	SB	BA	xHR	xSB	xBA	OBP	SLG	OPS+	vL+	vR+	bb%	ct%	Eye	G	L	F	h%	HctX	QBaB	Brl%	PX	xPX	HR/F	xHR/F	Spd	SBA%	SB%	RAR	BPX
19	KC	676	95	48	117	3	265	51	1	270	354	569	128	121	129	11	70	0.41	39	20	41	30	113	ABc	17%	168	140	28%	30%	70	3%	75%	26.4	215
20	KC	172	17	8	24	0	228	10	0	222	326	443	102	94	103	11	60	0.32	38	23	39	32	102	ABd	19%	151	159	23%	29%	68	0%	0%	-1.0	16
21	2 TM	594	74	27	70	0	223	33	0	234	316	432	103	115	98	11	72	0.47	42	15	43	25	110	ABd	13%	126	122	17%	20%	75	0%	0%	-10.3	146
22	MIA	305	32	13	34	0	207	14	1	227	295	400	98	115	94	10	67	0.34	42	18	40	26	116	ACf	12%	138	133	18%	19%	58	3%	0%	-8.2	59
23	MIA	580	77	36	75	1	250	35	2	260	341	512	116	146	107	11	72	0.47	36	18	46	28	126	AAc	15%	153	156	21%	21%	60	1%	100%	27.8	189
1st Half		339	44	22	47	1	241	22	1	264	339	514	117	164	104	12	73	0.51	35	17	47	25	125	BAc	16%	155	152	21%	21%	60	1%	100%	10.1	221
2nd Half		241	33	14	28	0	262	13	1	254	344	510	115	123	113	11	70	0.41	36	19	45	31	127	ABb	14%	150	162	21%	19%	72	0%	0%	8.7	164
24	**Proj**	**560**	**71**	**32**	**71**	**0**	**241**	**31**	**1**	**247**	**329**	**481**	**111**	**128**	**106**	**11**	**70**	**0.41**	**39**	**18**	**43**	**28**	**119**		**14%**	**148**	**146**	**21%**	**21%**	**62**	**1%**	**33%**	**16.6**	**142**

Sosa,Edmundo

Age: 28 Pos: 3B | Bats: R Ht: 6' 0" Wt: 210

Health A | PT/Exp C | Consist B | LIMA Plan D+ | Rand Var 0 | MM 2323

Hard to tell, but speed is his primary asset. Of course, if you don't get on base or get a green light, that asset has no value. Bumps in FB%, HR/F helped him get to double-digit HR for first time, but still not enough pop to make him dra worthy. These are the skills of a utility infielder, and one without dual eligibility in many leagues now.

Yr	Tm	PA	R	HR	RBI	SB	BA	xHR	xSB	xBA	OBP	SLG	OPS+	vL+	vR+	bb%	ct%	Eye	G	L	F	h%	HctX	QBaB	Brl%	PX	xPX	HR/F	xHR/F	Spd	SBA%	SB%	RAR	BPX
19	STL *	476	58	13	49	3	254	0	6	288	276	387	92	0	100	3	77	0.13	50	33	17	31	88	FFd	0%	69	5	0%	0%	121	6%	43%	-16.2	22
20																																		
21	STL	325	39	6	27	4	271	7	12	248	346	389	101	93	104	5	78	0.27	52	21	27	33	78	DFf	4%	63	66	10%	11%	183	9%	50%	-3.9	115
22	2 NL	190	26	2	21	6	227	3	6	241	275	369	91	100	83	3	72	0.10	46	21	33	31	98	DCd	5%	102	99	5%	7%	159	20%	86%	-6.7	79
23	PHI	299	34	10	30	4	251	9	5	250	293	427	98	107	91	3	73	0.11	42	20	37	31	82	DCc	7%	107	97	13%	12%	103	10%	67%	0.1	64
1st Half		180	17	5	17	2	243	4	3	242	263	393	90	92	88	2	75	0.07	43	19	38	30	77	CCf	6%	93	83	10%	8%	107	13%	50%	-5.1	36
2nd Half		119	17	5	13	2	264	4	2	263	339	481	111	128	96	5	72	0.17	41	22	37	32	91	DCa	8%	132	120	18%	14%	95	7%	100%	2.6	114
24	**Proj**	**280**	**37**	**7**	**30**	**5**	**251**	**7**	**7**	**246**	**307**	**406**	**98**	**106**	**92**	**4**	**74**	**0.14**	**45**	**21**	**34**	**32**	**89**		**6%**	**96**	**97**	**11%**	**10%**	**114**	**12%**	**65%**	**-0.5**	**81**

Sosa,Lenyn

Age: 24 Pos: 2B | Bats: R Ht: 6' 0" Wt: 180

Health A | PT/Exp B | Consist C | LIMA Plan D+ | Rand Var +2 | MM 2023

6-14-.201 in 173 PA at CHW. Power took a step forward, but that was only sign of growth as he bounced between AA and majors. Meanwhile, ct% slipped, lack of plate patience continued to drag OBP, and he owns a sub-.500 OPS in 15 career PA vR. Decent power isn't enough to overcome shortcomings elsewhere.

Yr	Tm	PA	R	HR	RBI	SB	BA	xHR	xSB	xBA	OBP	SLG	OPS+	vL+	vR+	bb%	ct%	Eye	G	L	F	h%	HctX	QBaB	Brl%	PX	xPX	HR/F	xHR/F	Spd	SBA%	SB%	RAR	BPX
19																																		
20																																		
21	aa	119	9	1	7	0	198		1		211	261	65			2	74	0.06				26				45				95	5%	0%		-131
22	CHW *	546	55	19	54	2	250	2	7	225	289	400	98	0	67	5	79	0.26	57	9	35	28	75	CFf	9%	89	51	13%	25%	117	6%	31%	1.7	124
23	CHW *	474	40	19	44	0	218	6	3	241	248	391	87	100	69	4	73	0.14	40	21	39	26	104	CCf	8%	105	138	13%	13%	84	3%	0%	-5.8	36
1st Half		227	19	9	19	0	221	2	1	227	252	404	90	74	42	4	75	0.16	38	14	48	25	97	DBf	6%	113	139	4%	8%	93	3%	0%	-4.5	96
2nd Half		247	21	10	25	0	216	4	2	248	245	380	84	113	89	4	71	0.13	41	26	33	26	108	CCc	9%	97	137	21%	17%	91	2%	0%	-6.9	-4
24	**Proj**	**350**	**31**	**13**	**32**	**0**	**227**	**15**	**3**	**239**	**256**	**382**	**88**	**112**	**77**	**4**	**75**	**0.17**	**40**	**21**	**39**	**26**	**104**		**8%**	**92**	**138**	**13%**	**15%**	**92**	**4%**	**16%**	**-5.3**	**42**

BRIAN RUDD

Soto,Juan

Age: 25 Pos: LF — Health A — LIMA Plan C
Bats: L Ht: 6' 2" Wt: 224 — PT/Exp A — Rand Var +1
Consist F — MM 4255

Bounceback from down 2022 included massive September (.340 BA, 10 HR, 6 SB). xBA gives the BA rebound plenty of legs as h% snapped back, hard contact returned in 2nd half, and modest running game reappeared despite Spd decline. Current GLF caps the longball totals, but if second-half tilt takes one more step... UP: 40 HR

Yr	Tm	PA	R	HR	RBI	SB	BA	xHR	xSB	xBA	OBP	SLG	OPS+	vL+	vR+	bb%	ct%	Eye	G	L	F	h%	HctX	QBaB	Brl%	PX	xPX	HR/F	xHR/F	Spd	SBA%	SB%	RAR	BPX	R$
19	WAS	659	110	34	110	12	282	39	9	280	401	548	131	118	137	16	76	0.82	42	21	37	32	108	ACc	12%	138	139	22%	25%	103	7%	92%	42.1	293	$29
20	WAS	196	39	13	37	6	351	15	4	335	490	695	157	158	155	21	82	1.46	52	20	29	36	139	AFd	18%	179	140	36%	42%	83	12%	75%	31.6	556	$36
21	WAS	654	111	29	95	9	313	30	10	285	465	534	137	119	148	22	81	1.56	53	19	29	34	130	ADd	13%	113	99	24%	25%	100	6%	56%	61.2	358	$34
22	2 NL	663	93	27	62	6	242	32	6	273	401	452	121	98	134	20	82	1.41	47	16	37	25	105	ADf	13%	120	107	17%	20%	94	4%	75%	32.5	324	$19
23	SD	708	97	35	109	12	275	37	12	284	410	519	127	110	134	19	77	1.02	51	17	32	30	129	ADf	13%	137	120	24%	26%	77	8%	71%	58.0	289	$29
1st Half		368	46	15	46	6	277	16	6	273	424	502	127	98	140	21	74	1.01	52	17	31	33	117	AFf	12%	137	105	22%	24%	80	7%	75%	28.9	264	$25
2nd Half		340	51	20	63	6	272	21	7	293	395	538	126	123	127	17	80	1.04	50	16	34	27	143	ADd	14%	137	134	26%	28%	83	9%	67%	26.7	329	$33
24	**Proj**	**665**	**100**	**33**	**96**	**10**	**284**	**36**	**11**	**285**	**424**	**526**	**130**	**113**	**138**	**20**	**79**	**1.19**	**50**	**17**	**33**	**30**	**124**		**13%**	**131**	**117**	**23%**	**25%**	**83**	**7%**	**70%**	**61.1**	**329**	**$30**

Springer,George

Age: 34 Pos: RF DH — Health C — LIMA Plan B+
Bats: R Ht: 6' 3" Wt: 220 — PT/Exp A — Rand Var 0
Consist C — MM 2335

First 20/20 season with career-best SB thanks to highest PA total since 2016 and greener light on basepaths. Some warning signs, however, as power skills (xPX, xHR/F) didn't recover from 2022's rut, and it's tough to expect this amount of volume again given age, health history. Be cautious paying for a repeat.

Yr	Tm	PA	R	HR	RBI	SB	BA	xHR	xSB	xBA	OBP	SLG	OPS+	vL+	vR+	bb%	ct%	Eye	G	L	F	h%	HctX	QBaB	Brl%	PX	xPX	HR/F	xHR/F	Spd	SBA%	SB%	RAR	BPX	R$
19	HOU	556	96	39	96	6	292	37	7	289	383	591	135	126	137	12	76	0.59	45	20	36	31	119	BCd	14%	146	127	30%	28%	113	5%	75%	40.2	307	$26
20	HOU	220	37	14	32	1	265	14	5	276	359	540	119	106	124	11	80	0.63	36	21	43	26	118	CAd	12%	132	112	21%	21%	148	5%	33%	7.4	372	$22
21	TOR	341	59	22	50	4	264	19	3	273	352	555	125	128	123	11	74	0.47	33	21	47	29	103	BAc	15%	168	137	21%	18%	100	6%	80%	19.5	315	$14
22	TOR	579	89	25	76	14	267	20	13	270	342	472	115	110	117	9	81	0.54	44	18	38	29	113	CCd	8%	117	89	16%	13%	126	11%	88%	21.6	255	$27
23	TOR	681	87	21	72	20	258	19	18	256	327	405	100	96	101	9	80	0.48	44	20	35	29	108	CCc	8%	82	92	12%	11%	98	14%	80%	12.4	118	$21
1st Half		358	49	12	35	13	270	12	12	262	332	420	103	85	107	8	82	0.49	48	19	34	30	112	CCc	9%	79	88	13%	13%	115	16%	87%	7.4	157	$24
2nd Half		323	38	9	37	7	244	7	7	250	322	387	96	105	93	10	77	0.47	40	22	38	29	104	CBc	6%	86	96	11%	8%	79	12%	70%	-0.6	79	$16
24	**Proj**	**560**	**82**	**21**	**71**	**15**	**261**	**21**	**12**	**256**	**338**	**437**	**106**	**105**	**107**	**10**	**78**	**0.50**	**42**	**20**	**38**	**30**	**109**		**9%**	**99**	**101**	**14%**	**14%**	**97**	**12%**	**81%**	**16.7**	**200**	**$25**

Stanton,Giancarlo

Age: 34 Pos: DH RF — Health F — LIMA Plan C+
Bats: R Ht: 6' 6" Wt: 245 — PT/Exp A — Rand Var +5
Consist A — MM 4013

More injuries; this time an April hamstring strain that cost him six weeks. One of the worst BAs in majors didn't get much help from h%, though xBA is spiraling toward scary lows. There's still plenty of pop—2nd half HR came with full support from Brl%, xPX—but age/health combo with little BA upside make this an alarming floor to fade.

Yr	Tm	PA	R	HR	RBI	SB	BA	xHR	xSB	xBA	OBP	SLG	OPS+	vL+	vR+	bb%	ct%	Eye	G	L	F	h%	HctX	QBaB	Brl%	PX	xPX	HR/F	xHR/F	Spd	SBA%	SB%	RAR	BPX	R$
19	NYY	72	8	3	13	0	288	4	-	218	403	492	124	147	116	17	59	0.50	44	22	33	44	86	ADf	25%	138	116	25%	33%	73	0%	0%	3.2	19	-$1
20	NYY	93	12	4	11	1	250	5	1	268	387	500	118	97	124	16	64	0.56	47	27	27	33	123	ADc	18%	175	86	31%	38%	66	8%	50%	2.9	208	$5
21	NYY	579	64	35	97	0	273	31	0	241	354	516	119	121	119	11	69	0.40	45	19	37	33	118	ACf	16%	144	113	27%	24%	65	0%	0%	18.7	135	$21
22	NYY	451	53	31	78	0	211	28	0	230	297	462	108	91	113	11	66	0.36	47	15	39	23	112	ACd	19%	163	125	30%	27%	70	0%	0%	-2.0	131	$11
23	NYY	415	43	24	60	0	191	24	0	218	275	420	95	126	87	10	67	0.33	43	13	44	21	113	ACf	16%	142	132	22%	22%	51	0%	0%	-6.7	61	$5
1st Half		139	14	7	19	0	195	8	0	226	259	398	90	111	85	7	73	0.26	45	13	42	21	115	ACf	16%	118	108	18%	21%	61	0%	0%	-6.0	64	-$3
2nd Half		276	29	17	41	0	189	16	0	214	283	432	97	133	88	12	63	0.36	42	12	46	21	112	ACf	16%	156	147	24%	23%	56	0%	0%	-5.8	71	$10
24	**Proj**	**420**	**46**	**25**	**67**	**0**	**211**	**24**	**0**	**226**	**296**	**443**	**101**	**111**	**99**	**11**	**67**	**0.35**	**45**	**15**	**40**	**24**	**113**		**17%**	**143**	**124**	**25%**	**24%**	**60**	**0%**	**0%**	**1.4**	**100**	**$11**

Steer,Spencer

Age: 26 Pos: 1B 3B LF — Health A — LIMA Plan B
Bats: R Ht: 5' 11" Wt: 185 — PT/Exp A — Rand Var -3
Consist C — MM 3325

Grabbed full-time gig on Opening Day and never looked back in surprise rookie season. Efficiency on basepaths drove the SB spike, and while underlying ct% and xPX backed the 1st half production, both dipped a bit down the stretch. Sophomore returns may not be quite as fruitful, but if he keeps everyday role, they'll get close.

Yr	Tm	PA	R	HR	RBI	SB	BA	xHR	xSB	xBA	OBP	SLG	OPS+	vL+	vR+	bb%	ct%	Eye	G	L	F	h%	HctX	QBaB	Brl%	PX	xPX	HR/F	xHR/F	Spd	SBA%	SB%	RAR	BPX	R$
19																																			
20																																			
21	aa	264	32	10	30	3	204		2		249	374	85			6	67	0.18				26				109				105	7%	100%		-4	$2
22	CIN *	571	66	20	59	3	226	2	5	249	289	403	98	142	76	8	75	0.35	43	19	38	27	71	DCf	5%	118	83	8%	8%	94	6%	38%	-10.3	134	$10
23	CIN	665	74	23	86	15	271	20	16	256	356	464	112	125	107	10	76	0.49	38	19	43	32	100	CBd	7%	116	106	12%	10%	110	10%	83%	30.0	189	$23
1st Half		345	43	14	50	9	283	11	9	264	374	502	120	133	115	12	78	0.61	33	19	47	32	111	BAc	7%	125	118	13%	10%	111	12%	82%	20.2	257	$27
2nd Half		320	31	9	36	6	260	9	7	247	338	425	103	117	97	9	74	0.39	42	19	38	32	88	CCf	6%	106	93	11%	11%	108	9%	86%	5.7	114	$15
24	**Proj**	**560**	**66**	**19**	**68**	**8**	**260**	**16**	**9**	**243**	**336**	**437**	**106**	**136**	**96**	**9**	**74**	**0.37**	**40**	**19**	**41**	**32**	**87**		**7%**	**111**	**95**	**12%**	**10%**	**104**	**8%**	**76%**	**13.1**	**132**	**$21**

Stephenson,Tyler

Age: 27 Pos: CA DH — Health D — LIMA Plan C+
Bats: R Ht: 6' 4" Wt: 225 — PT/Exp A — Rand Var +5
Consist D — MM 2235

Mediocre results despite a bunch of PA for the position. xBA continued its downward trend, which casts doubt on BA rebound, while GB% lean and another year of mediocre PX/xPX hinder the power outlook. There's value in the volume—he played 51 games at DH/1B—but these are skills of a middling catcher in a strengthening market.

Yr	Tm	PA	R	HR	RBI	SB	BA	xHR	xSB	xBA	OBP	SLG	OPS+	vL+	vR+	bb%	ct%	Eye	G	L	F	h%	HctX	QBaB	Brl%	PX	xPX	HR/F	xHR/F	Spd	SBA%	SB%	RAR	BPX	R$
19	aa	347	42	6	40	0	266		1		339	387	100			10	78	0.50				33				71				96	0%	0%		67	$5
20	CIN	20	4	2	6	0	294	1	0	225	400	647	139	84	196	10	47	0.22	38	25	38	50	71	BBa	13%	268	161	67%	33%	111	0%	0%	2.1	232	$1
21	CIN	402	56	10	45	0	286	8	1	271	366	431	109	111	109	10	79	0.55	50	25	25	34	96	CDc	5%	89	67	14%	11%	96	0%	0%	16.6	142	$11
22	CIN	183	24	6	35	1	319	4	1	261	372	482	121	119	121	7	72	0.26	41	29	30	42	101	CCa	7%	113	97	17%	11%	95	2%	100%	13.4	72	$8
23	CIN	517	59	13	56	0	243	14	5	241	317	378	95	108	90	9	71	0.35	49	23	29	32	98	BDc	8%	87	95	14%	15%	109	1%	0%	7.8	21	$8
1st Half		317	38	7	35	0	258	7	4	242	334	382	98	96	99	10	70	0.35	45	27	29	35	84	CCc	8%	81	87	12%	12%	105	1%	0%	5.6	-11	$11
2nd Half		200	21	6	21	0	220	7	2	238	290	374	90	126	76	9	73	0.34	55	17	29	27	119	ADb	7%	94	108	16%	18%	113	0%	0%	-0.5	64	$1
24	**Proj**	**455**	**56**	**13**	**60**	**1**	**255**	**12**	**3**	**253**	**327**	**405**	**100**	**110**	**96**	**9**	**73**	**0.36**	**47**	**24**	**29**	**32**	**102**		**7%**	**95**	**94**	**15%**	**14%**	**100**	**1%**	**68%**	**13.2**	**63**	**$14**

Stewart,D.J.

Age: 30 Pos: RF — Health A — LIMA Plan D
Bats: L Ht: 6' 0" Wt: 210 — PT/Exp C — Rand Var +1
Consist B — MM 4011

11-26-.238 in 184 PA at NYM. Called up in July and raked in August (.303 BA, 8 HR) before cooling off in Sept. Plus power is nice, but Mendoza-level BA isn't going anywhere due to FB approach and brutal ct%, and career .612 OPS vL limits him to a platoon. Expecting more months like August is more wishcasting than forecasting.

Yr	Tm	PA	R	HR	RBI	SB	BA	xHR	xSB	xBA	OBP	SLG	OPS+	vL+	vR+	bb%	ct%	Eye	G	L	F	h%	HctX	QBaB	Brl%	PX	xPX	HR/F	xHR/F	Spd	SBA%	SB%	RAR	BPX	R$
19	BAL *	418	53	15	58	5	244	4	6	248	330	434	106	104	93	11	76	0.55	48	14	37	28	92	CCf	7%	103	87	11%	11%	81	12%	43%	-6.8	137	$9
20	BAL	112	13	7	15	0	193	5	0	208	355	455	107	70	115	18	57	0.53	41	16	43	23	88	CCf	19%	174	121	33%	24%	94	0%	0%	-0.8	132	$4
21	BAL	318	39	12	33	0	204	12	0	201	324	374	96	73	100	14	67	0.49	35	16	49	25	85	CAf	9%	108	112	14%	14%	78	0%	0%	-6.7	31	$1
22	BAL *	98	10	4	9	1	179	0	1	108	252	325	82	0	0	9	58	0.23	0	0	100	25	0	FA		109	-14	0%	0%	92	5%	100%	-3.9	-110	-$3
23	NYM *	394	41	19	50	1	195	10	2	227	271	400	91	80	126	9	66	0.31	38	18	43	23	101	CBf	13%	131	140	24%	22%	54	3%	50%	-5.5	18	$4
1st Half		210	20	8	24	0	153		1	215	240	309	75	0	0	10	67	0.34	44	20	36	17	0		0%	96	-21	0%		83	0%	0%	-11.2	-36	-$4
2nd Half		184	21	11	26	1	244	10	1	250	333	506	114	79	125	9	65	0.27	38	18	43	30	100	CBf	13%	173	140	24%	22%	57	5%	50%	5.4	125	$8
24	**Proj**	**210**	**25**	**11**	**27**	**1**	**208**	**10**	**1**	**227**	**317**	**431**	**103**	**79**	**109**	**12**	**66**	**0.40**	**40**	**16**	**43**	**25**	**92**		**13%**	**144**	**120**	**21%**	**18%**	**74**	**3%**	**46%**	**1.2**	**72**	**$5**

Story,Trevor

Age: 31 Pos: SS — Health F — LIMA Plan C+
Bats: R Ht: 6' 2" Wt: 213 — PT/Exp B — Rand Var +2
Consist C — MM 4415

3-14-.203 with 10 SB in 168 PA at BOS. Elbow surgery in January pushed debut to August, so small sample caveats apply. Turned running game up a notch, but worrisome declines in both power (xPX) and BA skills (ct%, xBA) continued. Track record is there, so next chapter could be a 20/20 season, but it'll come with BA pain.

Yr	Tm	PA	R	HR	RBI	SB	BA	xHR	xSB	xBA	OBP	SLG	OPS+	vL+	vR+	bb%	ct%	Eye	G	L	F	h%	HctX	QBaB	Brl%	PX	xPX	HR/F	xHR/F	Spd	SBA%	SB%	RAR	BPX	R$
19	COL	656	111	35	85	23	294	26	22	259	363	554	127	130	125	9	70	0.33	33	24	42	36	107	ABb	9%	147	132	20%	15%	139	19%	74%	31.6	226	$34
20	COL	259	41	11	28	15	289	11	14	242	355	519	116	136	107	9	73	0.38	30	23	48	35	121	BAc	9%	129	146	13%	13%	169	28%	83%	13.9	268	$40
21	COL	595	88	24	75	20	251	24	17	250	329	471	110	133	101	9	74	0.38	37	19	44	30	115	BBd	10%	132	135	14%	14%	131	20%	77%	12.8	227	$24
22	BOS	396	53	16	66	13	238	17	8	229	303	434	104	119	100	8	66	0.26	36	19	45	32	95	CAf	11%	147	121	15%	16%	99	16%	100%	5.4	100	$16
23	BOS *	212	17	6	20	11	208	4	8	211	258	355	83	84	75	6	64	0.19	40	18	42	29	83	CBd	10%	111	109	7%	9%	89	38%	78%	-4.5	-46	$1
1st Half																									0%										
2nd Half		212	17	6	20	11	208	4	8	211	258	355	0	84	75	6	64	0.19	40	18	42	29	83	CBd	10%	111	109	7%	9%	90	38%	78%	-7.9	-50	$5
24	**Proj**	**525**	**69**	**18**	**65**	**21**	**245**	**19**	**18**	**232**	**310**	**432**	**102**	**117**	**96**	**8**	**69**	**0.28**	**36**	**20**	**44**	**32**	**102**		**10%**	**125**	**126**	**13%**	**13%**	**113**	**23%**	**80%**	**10.3**	**125**	**$23**

ORBIN YOUNG

Stott,Bryson

Age: 26 Pos: 2B | Bats: L Ht: 6' 3" Wt: 200

Health	A	LIMA Plan	B
PT/Exp	A	Rand Var	-1
Consist	B	MM	1435

Parlayed strong rookie-year finish into sophomore surge, much of which was skill supported. Encouraging ct% bump drove BA/xBA growth and near-flawless SB% should keep the light green, though Brl% and xHR hint this might be his power ceiling. Taking the slight under on BA, HR, and SB repeats still leaves a well-rounded product at prime age.

Yr Tm	PA	R	HR	RBI	SB	BA	xHR	xSB	xBA	OBP	SLG	OPS+	vL+	vR+	bb%	ct%	Eye	G	L	F	h%	HctX	QBaB	Brl%	PX	xPX	HR/F	xHR/F	Spd	SBA%	SB%	RAR	BPX
19																																	
20																																	
21 a/a	375	36	8	27	4	265		4		323	396	99			8	71	0.29				35				87				100	6%	64%		0
22 PHI *	504	65	11	54	13	237	8	12	241	295	367	94	105	89	8	78	0.38	46	18	36	28	93	CCf	4%	83	72	8%	7%	121	15%	77%	-7.1	110
23 PHI	640	78	15	62	31	280	10	24	270	329	419	102	98	103	6	83	0.39	46	21	33	32	103	CCc	5%	79	79	9%	6%	112	21%	91%	20.6	154
1st Half	335	35	7	30	14	294	4	13	262	331	416	102	112	99	5	82	0.33	46	21	32	34	91	CCc	4%	68	60	8%	5%	129	17%	93%	11.3	125
2nd Half	305	43	8	32	17	265	6	12	281	326	422	101	82	107	7	84	0.47	47	20	33	29	115	CCc	5%	92	100	10%	8%	97	26%	89%	7.7	193
24 Proj	**630**	**79**	**13**	**63**	**23**	**261**	**11**	**19**	**254**	**315**	**388**	**97**	**98**	**96**	**7**	**81**	**0.40**	**46**	**19**	**34**	**30**	**100**		**5%**	**76**	**79**	**8%**	**7%**	**110**	**17%**	**85%**	**10.8**	**121**

Straw,Myles

Age: 29 Pos: CF | Bats: R Ht: 5' 10" Wt: 178

Health	A	LIMA Plan	C+
PT/Exp	A	Rand Var	0
Consist	B	MM	0515

A one-trick pony who's losing his trick, as SB% fell amid league-wide stolen base surge. There was nothing else to fall back on—couldn't hold 2022's ct% spike, xBA remained stuck in neutral, and posted the lowest xPX of any hitter in majors (min. 400 AB). Hard to see this skill set earning another 500 PA.

Yr Tm	PA	R	HR	RBI	SB	BA	xHR	xSB	xBA	OBP	SLG	OPS+	vL+	vR+	bb%	ct%	Eye	G	L	F	h%	HctX	QBaB	Brl%	PX	xPX	HR/F	xHR/F	Spd	SBA%	SB%	RAR	BPX
19 HOU *	427	59	1	30	21	259	1	22	234	330	317	90	109	95	10	78	0.48	48	23	29	33	86	DDa	1%	34	60	0%	4%	168	22%	78%	-8.9	37
20 HOU	86	8	0	8	6	207	1	4	195	244	256	66	9	99	5	73	0.18	36	22	42	28	79	CBb	2%	41	83	0%	4%	113	47%	75%	-7.0	-112
21 2 AL	638	86	4	48	30	271	3	26	239	349	348	96	81	103	11	79	0.55	41	26	34	34	70	DCa	1%	53	52	3%	2%	139	19%	83%	0.3	81
22 CLE	596	72	0	32	21	221	3	19	232	291	273	80	91	76	9	84	0.62	47	19	34	26	90	CCb	1%	39	57	0%	2%	145	15%	95%	-17.4	103
23 CLE	518	52	1	29	20	238	2	23	236	301	297	81	80	82	8	79	0.43	47	22	31	30	58	DDd	1%	40	27	1%	2%	142	20%	77%	-10.0	32
1st Half	303	33	0	13	10	239	1	14	236	309	301	84	84	84	9	78	0.46	50	20	29	31	50	DDd	1%	42	21	0%	2%	167	15%	83%	-6.1	61
2nd Half	215	19	1	16	10	237	1	9	237	289	289	78	75	80	7	80	0.39	43	24	33	29	69	DCd	0%	37	35	2%	2%	94	26%	71%	-6.6	-21
24 Proj	**455**	**52**	**1**	**29**	**19**	**241**	**2**	**19**	**233**	**306**	**299**	**83**	**79**	**85**	**9**	**80**	**0.48**	**45**	**22**	**33**	**30**	**72**		**1%**	**40**	**44**	**1%**	**2%**	**126**	**20%**	**80%**	**-7.9**	**48**

Suarez,Eugenio

Age: 32 Pos: 3B | Bats: R Ht: 5' 11" Wt: 213

Health	A	LIMA Plan	B
PT/Exp	A	Rand Var	-2
Consist	C	MM	4115

Volume was there (career-high PA), but the homers weren't (fewest HR since 2016, COVID season aside). Sure, xHR says he deserved a few more, but FB%, xPX, and xHR/F all spiraled to new lows in 2nd half. Poor BA is a given with all those Ks, so while track record hints at likely bounceback, further power erosion puts him in the danger zone.

Yr Tm	PA	R	HR	RBI	SB	BA	xHR	xSB	xBA	OBP	SLG	OPS+	vL+	vR+	bb%	ct%	Eye	G	L	F	h%	HctX	QBaB	Brl%	PX	xPX	HR/F	xHR/F	Spd	SBA%	SB%	RAR	BPX
19 CIN	662	87	49	103	3	271	39	4	260	358	572	129	138	125	11	67	0.37	36	22	42	32	108	BAb	14%	166	145	30%	23%	96	3%	60%	31.8	196
20 CIN	231	29	15	38	2	202	14	1	238	312	470	104	98	105	13	66	0.45	35	18	47	22	93	CAc	14%	160	147	24%	23%	61	4%	100%	-1.1	156
21 CIN	574	71	31	79	0	198	32	0	228	286	428	98	84	103	10	66	0.33	36	17	47	23	94	CAc	15%	146	132	20%	20%	56	1%	0%	-6.3	77
22 SEA	629	76	31	87	0	236	36	2	232	332	459	112	128	107	12	64	0.37	34	20	46	31	100	BAb	15%	160	149	19%	22%	100	0%	0%	16.5	134
23 SEA	694	68	22	96	2	232	29	4	218	323	391	97	100	96	10	64	0.33	34	23	43	32	96	BAb	13%	112	128	13%	17%	70	2%	67%	6.4	-32
1st Half	348	32	9	49	1	222	16	2	211	313	357	92	95	91	11	67	0.36	34	21	45	30	104	AAb	12%	92	143	10%	17%	74	2%	50%	-5.9	-46
2nd Half	346	36	13	47	1	243	12	2	225	332	425	102	105	102	10	61	0.30	34	24	41	35	88	BAc	14%	134	111	17%	15%	70	1%	100%	4.0	-11
24 Proj	**595**	**68**	**26**	**86**	**1**	**230**	**29**	**2**	**225**	**321**	**427**	**103**	**106**	**102**	**11**	**64**	**0.34**	**34**	**21**	**44**	**30**	**96**		**14%**	**134**	**134**	**17%**	**19%**	**71**	**1%**	**68%**	**9.6**	**50**

Suwinski,Jack

Age: 25 Pos: CF RF | Bats: L Ht: 6' 2" Wt: 215

Health	A	LIMA Plan	B
PT/Exp	A	Rand Var	0
Consist	B	MM	4305

Strong April and Sept (.293 BA, 10 HR) bookended a .190 BA and 58% ct% from May to Aug. PRO: FB% swing is tailor-made for homers given PX/xPX combo; SB% hints at speed repeat. CON: Brutal ct% locks in poor BA, struggles vL (career .564 OPS) cap playing time. Useful in spots/OBP leagues, but further growth seems unlikely.

Yr Tm	PA	R	HR	RBI	SB	BA	xHR	xSB	xBA	OBP	SLG	OPS+	vL+	vR+	bb%	ct%	Eye	G	L	F	h%	HctX	QBaB	Brl%	PX	xPX	HR/F	xHR/F	Spd	SBA%	SB%	RAR	BPX
19																																	
20																																	
21 aa	420	50	13	42	8	223		10		321	387	97			13	63	0.39				32				113				109	17%	47%		8
22 PIT *	551	66	24	58	5	204	17	4	217	279	397	96	72	113	9	62	0.28	42	15	42	27	100	CBf	12%	146	145	21%	19%	78	6%	73%	-9.9	38
23 PIT	534	63	26	74	13	224	30	12	218	339	454	108	82	117	14	62	0.44	28	19	54	30	86	BAd	16%	159	150	17%	20%	104	11%	87%	14.5	125
1st Half	268	36	17	42	7	231	18	6	224	354	502	117	88	127	16	62	0.50	24	14	61	28	94	AAd	17%	180	180	20%	21%	95	12%	88%	12.2	196
2nd Half	266	27	9	32	6	217	12	6	216	323	407	99	76	107	13	61	0.38	31	23	46	31	78	BAf	14%	138	121	14%	18%	109	11%	86%	0.7	54
24 Proj	**490**	**58**	**24**	**60**	**10**	**216**	**25**	**8**	**219**	**318**	**436**	**103**	**76**	**113**	**12**	**62**	**0.37**	**34**	**18**	**48**	**29**	**91**		**14%**	**152**	**145**	**18%**	**19%**	**95**	**11%**	**82%**	**8.8**	**70**

Suzuki,Seiya

Age: 29 Pos: RF | Bats: R Ht: 5' 11" Wt: 182

Health	B	LIMA Plan	B+
PT/Exp	A	Rand Var	-2
Consist	D	MM	4345

Missed first two weeks (oblique), had neck issues in June, then surged with .349 BA, 12 HR after 8/1. Lofty h% certainly helped, but 2nd half skills took off: ct% spike pushed xBA to elite territory; Brl%, xHR/F say there was plenty of oomph; finally had some SB success. If those gains hold, we could see BA repeat with new highs in HR/SB.

Yr Tm	PA	R	HR	RBI	SB	BA	xHR	xSB	xBA	OBP	SLG	OPS+	vL+	vR+	bb%	ct%	Eye	G	L	F	h%	HctX	QBaB	Brl%	PX	xPX	HR/F	xHR/F	Spd	SBA%	SB%	RAR	BPX
19 for	582	109	17	85	23	312		20		410	474	122			14	85	1.08				34	0			83				91	21%	56%	20.7	233
20 for	488	83	15	73	5	280		7		365	459	109			12	84	0.84				30	0			93				106	7%	55%	9.0	272
21 for	505	75	23	86	8	296		5		393	513	124			14	81	0.84				32	0			118				78	8%	65%	31.7	273
22 CHC	446	54	14	46	9	262	16	12	241	336	433	109	119	105	9	72	0.38	40	20	40	33	101	BCf	11%	117	121	12%	14%	135	13%	64%	8.0	152
23 CHC	583	75	20	74	6	285	21	18	269	357	485	115	115	115	10	75	0.45	43	22	34	35	115	ACc	10%	119	107	15%	16%	146	9%	46%	28.5	214
1st Half	272	25	6	26	1	246	6	6	235	335	386	99	109	95	12	71	0.46	44	21	35	32	117	ACc	9%	93	92	10%	10%	116	8%	17%	-1.1	68
2nd Half	311	50	14	48	5	319	15	11	295	376	570	128	119	131	9	78	0.45	42	24	34	37	113	BCc	12%	140	118	18%	20%	159	9%	71%	29.2	325
24 Proj	**595**	**82**	**25**	**79**	**9**	**284**	**25**	**15**	**271**	**362**	**500**	**118**	**120**	**117**	**11**	**76**	**0.51**	**42**	**22**	**37**	**33**	**109**		**11%**	**126**	**113**	**17%**	**17%**	**129**	**10%**	**57%**	**34.8**	**215**

Swanson,Dansby

Age: 30 Pos: SS | Bats: R Ht: 6' 1" Wt: 190

Health	A	LIMA Plan	B
PT/Exp	A	Rand Var	+1
Consist	A	MM	3325

Predictable fallback from 2022's career year, as h% came back to earth and he barely ran on new team. Uber-consistent combo of BA skills (ct%, xBA), power (Brl%, xPX), and volume (12th-most PA since 2021) bolster an otherwise reliable floor. There is value in knowing you'll get almost exactly what you pay for.

Yr Tm	PA	R	HR	RBI	SB	BA	xHR	xSB	xBA	OBP	SLG	OPS+	vL+	vR+	bb%	ct%	Eye	G	L	F	h%	HctX	QBaB	Brl%	PX	xPX	HR/F	xHR/F	Spd	SBA%	SB%	RAR	BPX
19 ATL	545	77	17	65	10	251	22	10	252	325	422	103	112	101	9	74	0.41	37	26	37	30	109	BBb	10%	96	106	13%	16%	119	11%	67%	-2.9	115
20 ATL	264	49	10	35	5	274	12	3	243	345	464	107	67	116	8	70	0.31	37	24	39	35	110	CBc	11%	120	134	16%	19%	96	8%	100%	7.4	96
21 ATL	653	78	27	88	9	248	27	8	245	311	449	104	104	105	8	72	0.31	40	20	40	30	98	CCc	11%	124	123	16%	16%	109	9%	75%	2.7	138
22 ATL	696	99	25	96	18	277	32	16	239	329	447	110	118	107	7	72	0.27	39	21	40	35	106	BBc	11%	116	127	14%	17%	108	15%	72%	13.7	97
23 CHC	638	81	22	80	9	244	25	12	248	328	416	101	104	100	10	73	0.43	45	20	35	30	104	BCc	11%	103	127	15%	17%	117	6%	90%	12.3	111
1st Half	353	38	9	35	4	256	16	8	247	343	401	102	105	101	11	75	0.49	44	22	34	32	107	BCc	13%	87	138	11%	20%	131	5%	80%	4.2	114
2nd Half	285	43	13	45	5	229	10	4	251	309	435	101	102	100	10	70	0.36	46	18	36	27	100	BCc	9%	125	112	20%	15%	97	8%	100%	2.0	114
24 Proj	**665**	**92**	**25**	**91**	**10**	**253**	**28**	**12**	**244**	**324**	**433**	**104**	**106**	**103**	**9**	**72**	**0.35**	**42**	**21**	**38**	**31**	**104**		**11%**	**112**	**123**	**15%**	**17%**	**101**	**8%**	**78%**	**17.2**	**113**

Tatis Jr.,Fernando

Age: 25 Pos: RF | Bats: R Ht: 6' 3" Wt: 217

Health	F	LIMA Plan	D+
PT/Exp	A	Rand Var	+3
Consist	F	MM	4445

25-78-.257 with 29 SB in 635 PA at SD. Entered year with questions (3-week PED suspension, offseason shoulder/wrist surgeries) and we still have some. PRO: Ran often with plenty of success, career-low h% masked some solid ct% growth. CON: Power was far off from 2021 breakout. Still retains status as a 1st-round building block.

Yr Tm	PA	R	HR	RBI	SB	BA	xHR	xSB	xBA	OBP	SLG	OPS+	vL+	vR+	bb%	ct%	Eye	G	L	F	h%	HctX	QBaB	Brl%	PX	xPX	HR/F	xHR/F	Spd	SBA%	SB%	RAR	BPX
19 SD	372	61	22	53	16	317	20	19	265	379	590	134	176	122	8	67	0.27	47	22	31	42	97	BDd	13%	150	126	32%	29%	177	22%	73%	24.0	219
20 SD	257	50	17	45	11	277	20	8	279	366	571	124	105	132	11	73	0.44	48	16	35	31	162	ADb	19%	161	176	29%	34%	114	22%	79%	12.3	308
21 SD	546	99	42	97	25	282	44	17	281	364	611	134	132	135	11	68	0.41	40	20	40	33	133	ACd	21%	203	172	32%	34%	114	23%	86%	44.6	358
22 aa																																	
23 SD *	672	98	30	88	30	266	31	21	273	329	472	109	123	99	8	76	0.39	47	19	34	30	126	ACc	11%	120	116	17%	21%	92	22%	88%	26.7	168
1st Half	334	53	21	51	15	295	13	11	309	354	565	126	143	111	8	80	0.45	46	22	32	31	131	ACc	9%	148	119	23%	19%	88	23%	84%	26.3	296
2nd Half	338	45	9	37	15	238	18	11	237	305	381	93	103	89	9	73	0.35	48	17	35	30	122	ACc	13%	91	114	12%	23%	100	21%	94%	-0.8	46
24 Proj	**630**	**104**	**33**	**95**	**28**	**274**	**40**	**22**	**268**	**346**	**511**	**118**	**126**	**115**	**10**	**72**	**0.38**	**46**	**19**	**35**	**33**	**130**		**15%**	**143**	**140**	**23%**	**27%**	**105**	**22%**	**85%**	**38.2**	**231**

RYAN BLOOMFIELD

Tauchman,Mike

Age: 33	Pos: CF		Health	A	LIMA Plan	D
Bats: L	Ht: 6' 2"	Wt: 220	PT/Exp	C	Rand Var	0
			Consist	D	MM	2223

8-48-.252 with 7 SB in 401 PA at CHC. High bb% led to strong OBP and leadoff spot vR, but not much else to get excited about. Lack of hard contact, GB tilt cap power potential; xBA says not much room for BA growth; age, Spd suggest we can't count on more than a handful of SB. A decent streamer vs. RHP, but that's about it.

Yr	Tm	PA	R	HR	RBI	SB	BA	xHR	xSB	xBA	OBP	SLG	OPS+	vL+	vR+	bb%	ct%	Eye	G	L	F	h%	HctX	QBaB	Brl%	PX	xPX	HR/F	xHR/F	Spd	SBA%	SB%	RAR	BPX	R$
19	NYY *	403	62	15	58	9	259	8	5	272	344	470	113	136	113	11	74	0.50	42	25	33	31	86	CCa	6%	120	93	21%	13%	89	9%	100%	3.5	163	$13
20	NYY	111	18	0	14	6	242	1	3	235	342	305	86	32	100	13	73	0.54	41	30	29	33	80	DCb	1%	53	59	0%	5%	81	19%	100%	-3.6	-60	$10
21	2 TM *	331	37	6	26	4	185	3	5	205	272	290	77	73	79	11	64	0.33	45	22	32	27	60	CCf	6%	76	66	11%	9%	110	11%	49%	-22.7	-96	-$1
22																																			
23	CHC *	492	74	10	57	8	242	8	7	245	348	361	97	100	101	14	73	0.60	47	24	29	31	87	CDc	5%	79	79	11%	11%	78	6%	88%	3.4	25	$11
1st Half		231	31	4	26	4	234	2	4	237	342	324	91	88	100	14	69	0.54	48	28	24	32	91	DDc	6%	62	87	10%	10%	74	7%	78%	-2.6	-71	$5
2nd Half		261	43	6	31	4	249	6	4	258	360	394	102	110	101	14	76	0.67	47	21	32	30	86	CDc	5%	94	74	11%	11%	86	5%	100%	4.4	118	$13
24	Proj	**315**	**46**	**6**	**36**	**6**	**230**	**6**	**5**	**239**	**331**	**352**	**94**	**84**	**96**	**13**	**71**	**0.50**	**45**	**25**	**30**	**30**	**80**		**5%**	**84**	**74**	**10%**	**9%**	**88**	**8%**	**83%**	**0.5**	**5**	**$5**

Taveras,Leody

Age: 25	Pos: CF		Health	A	LIMA Plan	C+
Bats: B	Ht: 6' 2"	Wt: 195	PT/Exp	A	Rand Var	-1
			Consist	B	MM	2425

Season had ups and downs, but overall a step forward with strong finish (.819 OPS in final 96 PA). Contact rate continued positive trend, leading to substantial jump in BA/xBA, but power metrics were still below average, SBA% decline is somewhat concerning. Entering prime, there's room for more if ct% gains hold and running game returns.

Yr	Tm	PA	R	HR	RBI	SB	BA	xHR	xSB	xBA	OBP	SLG	OPS+	vL+	vR+	bb%	ct%	Eye	G	L	F	h%	HctX	QBaB	Brl%	PX	xPX	HR/F	xHR/F	Spd	SBA%	SB%	RAR	BPX	R$
19	aa	286	30	3	29	10	273		11		330	391	100			8	77	0.38				34				64				134	24%	56%		70	$7
20	TEX	134	20	4	6	8	227	4	6	227	308	395	93	106	86	10	64	0.33	38	29	33	32	91	DCf	6%	113	110	17%	17%	152	27%	100%	-1.2	56	$12
21	TEX *	543	56	16	50	20	192	3	15	223	260	346	83	68	64	8	66	0.27	52	16	32	25	92	DFf	6%	102	95	9%	9%	111	27%	75%	-24.8	0	$9
22	TEX *	554	60	9	52	15	248	6	18	224	288	359	92	90	98	5	72	0.20	42	22	36	33	95	CCf	4%	79	84	6%	8%	137	20%	61%	-7.8	17	$15
23	TEX	554	67	14	67	14	266	13	14	262	312	421	100	86	105	6	77	0.30	44	22	34	32	99	BCc	7%	95	92	10%	10%	107	15%	78%	12.1	111	$17
1st Half		272	41	9	36	9	299	7	10	275	347	478	113	111	114	7	78	0.33	43	24	33	35	104	BCc	7%	103	88	14%	11%	123	17%	75%	14.0	175	$21
2nd Half		282	26	5	31	5	235	6	5	249	279	365	87	62	96	6	76	0.27	46	21	34	29	95	BDd	7%	87	95	7%	9%	94	11%	83%	-3.8	54	$8
24	Proj	**560**	**64**	**12**	**59**	**16**	**255**	**12**	**17**	**242**	**305**	**394**	**96**	**88**	**99**	**7**	**74**	**0.27**	**44**	**22**	**34**	**33**	**96**		**6%**	**89**	**92**	**9%**	**9%**	**117**	**18%**	**72%**	**4.1**	**62**	**$20**

Taylor,Chris

Age: 33	Pos: LF SS 3B		Health	C	LIMA Plan	C
Bats: R	Ht: 6' 1"	Wt: 196	PT/Exp	A	Rand Var	-1
			Consist	C	MM	4403

Lost grip on full-time role, but still provided value with multi-position eligibility and huge jump in SBA%. Profile is sprinkled with yellow flags: recent ct% ensures low BA; power cratered after June IL stint (knee); not at an age where we can bank on SB jump to hold. Power and speed should be there, but floor may be lower than you think.

Yr	Tm	PA	R	HR	RBI	SB	BA	xHR	xSB	xBA	OBP	SLG	OPS+	vL+	vR+	bb%	ct%	Eye	G	L	F	h%	HctX	QBaB	Brl%	PX	xPX	HR/F	xHR/F	Spd	SBA%	SB%	RAR	BPX	R$
19	LA	414	52	12	52	8	262	11	6	254	333	462	110	120	103	9	69	0.32	38	27	35	35	90	DCa	6%	126	106	14%	13%	117	9%	100%	2.3	111	$11
20	LA	214	30	8	32	3	270	10	5	263	366	476	112	90	119	12	70	0.47	46	27	28	34	104	DDb	11%	122	142	23%	29%	134	9%	60%	3.2	180	$20
21	LA	582	92	20	73	13	254	21	13	226	344	438	107	122	101	11	67	0.38	36	22	42	34	86	CBc	10%	119	111	14%	15%	140	9%	93%	8.7	112	$21
22	LA	454	45	10	43	10	221	14	8	208	304	373	96	85	100	10	60	0.28	31	26	43	34	87	CAc	10%	130	119	10%	14%	116	11%	91%	-2.9	3	$8
23	LA	384	51	15	56	16	237	15	13	220	326	420	102	107	97	11	63	0.33	31	25	45	33	73	DAb	10%	127	105	16%	16%	103	20%	84%	6.9	29	$12
1st Half		182	28	11	26	7	206	11	5	226	275	455	100	121	85	8	62	0.22	27	23	50	25	86	CAc	14%	164	141	22%	22%	103	22%	100%	0.4	96	$8
2nd Half		202	23	4	30	9	266	4	8	215	371	387	103	94	109	14	64	0.44	33	27	40	39	61	FAb	6%	92	72	9%	9%	100	19%	75%	4.6	-39	$11
24	Proj	**420**	**54**	**13**	**55**	**12**	**241**	**15**	**11**	**220**	**330**	**412**	**102**	**103**	**101**	**11**	**64**	**0.34**	**33**	**25**	**42**	**34**	**80**		**10%**	**122**	**109**	**13%**	**15%**	**112**	**14%**	**83%**	**7.9**	**40**	**$16**

Taylor,Michael A.

Age: 33	Pos: CF		Health	A	LIMA Plan	C
Bats: R	Ht: 6' 4"	Wt: 215	PT/Exp	A	Rand Var	0
			Consist	A	MM	3413

A HR/SB outburst with mixed signals. PRO: Lofty HR/F came with support from xHR/F; SBA%, SB% soared in 1st half. CON: ct% crashed, dragging down BA/OBP; stopped running in 2nd half, so maybe hamstring was hurting long before Sept IL stint. Power/speed blend gives him plenty of appeal, but poor OBP puts playing time at risk.

Yr	Tm	PA	R	HR	RBI	SB	BA	xHR	xSB	xBA	OBP	SLG	OPS+	vL+	vR+	bb%	ct%	Eye	G	L	F	h%	HctX	QBaB	Brl%	PX	xPX	HR/F	xHR/F	Spd	SBA%	SB%	RAR	BPX	R$
19	WAS *	336	41	9	33	15	226	3	11	224	292	393	95	108	81	8	62	0.24	46	21	33	33	103	ADf	7%	119	141	6%	18%	102	33%	67%	-6.2	-26	$8
20	WAS	99	11	5	16	0	196	7	0	244	253	424	90	91	89	6	71	0.22	43	17	40	22	75	CCf	15%	139	100	20%	28%	73	0%	0%	-4.1	120	$3
21	KC	528	58	12	54	14	244	13	13	218	297	356	90	105	84	6	70	0.23	44	22	34	32	94	CCc	7%	71	89	10%	11%	114	17%	67%	-13.8	-50	$14
22	KC	456	49	9	43	4	254	14	12	205	313	357	95	95	95	8	74	0.32	41	18	42	32	101	DCf	7%	65	114	7%	11%	170	5%	67%	-0.8	52	$10
23	MIN	388	48	21	51	13	220	21	9	234	278	442	98	123	88	7	63	0.20	42	18	40	28	90	DCf	14%	147	135	24%	24%	96	20%	93%	3.3	54	$10
1st Half		229	25	10	24	11	212	12	7	224	260	406	91	91	91	5	63	0.14	43	16	41	28	81	DCf	14%	136	119	19%	23%	86	32%	92%	-3.4	-4	$8
2nd Half		159	23	11	27	2	231	9	2	247	304	497	108	165	82	9	64	0.29	41	20	39	28	104	DCf	14%	163	158	32%	26%	116	6%	100%	4.8	146	$8
24	Proj	**420**	**52**	**16**	**52**	**10**	**234**	**19**	**11**	**222**	**294**	**404**	**96**	**107**	**90**	**7**	**67**	**0.24**	**42**	**19**	**39**	**31**	**96**		**11%**	**108**	**125**	**16%**	**19%**	**111**	**14%**	**80%**	**1.5**	**46**	**$15**

Taylor,Tyrone

Age: 30	Pos: RF LF		Health	D	LIMA Plan	C+
Bats: R	Ht: 6' 0"	Wt: 194	PT/Exp	C	Rand Var	+3
			Consist	B	MM	4333

10-35-.234 with 9 SB in 243 PA at MIL. Elbow issues led to plenty of missed time and poor results in 1st half. Then finished strong with harder 2nd half contact, and was more active and efficient on basepaths. Sub-.300 career OBP may prevent a full-time gig, but xBA offers better and might be worth gambling on one more time.

Yr	Tm	PA	R	HR	RBI	SB	BA	xHR	xSB	xBA	OBP	SLG	OPS+	vL+	vR+	bb%	ct%	Eye	G	L	F	h%	HctX	QBaB	Brl%	PX	xPX	HR/F	xHR/F	Spd	SBA%	SB%	RAR	BPX	R$
19	MIL *	367	33	11	44	4	232	0	3	264	277	387	92	0	166	6	70	0.21	89	11	0	30	54	FFa	0%	95	-36	0%		99	6%	100%	-18.2	0	$4
20	MIL	41	6	2	6	0	237	2	0	266	293	500	105	92	113	5	79	0.25	43	10	47	25	138	CBf	13%	153	165	14%	14%	89	0%	0%	-0.6	308	$0
21	MIL *	302	40	14	50	6	263	9	7	251	321	486	111	114	103	8	76	0.36	41	16	43	30	106	CBd	8%	122	90	15%	11%	142	10%	86%	5.5	242	$11
22	MIL	405	49	17	51	3	233	16	4	248	286	442	103	101	104	5	73	0.22	38	18	44	28	108	CBc	10%	137	145	14%	13%	99	7%	60%	-2.0	148	$9
23	MIL *	295	43	13	43	10	225	10	6	258	254	440	95	98	96	4	75	0.15	34	22	44	26	103	CAc	7%	130	130	13%	13%	90	23%	100%	-1.5	139	$7
1st Half		113	9	2	8	5	159	2	3	209	183	270	62	34	66	3	69	0.10	35	24	42	21	91	CBc	4%	73	129	4%	9%	112	38%	100%	-9.1	-93	-$8
2nd Half		181	34	10	35	6	268	8	4	293	298	549	114	119	113	4	79	0.20	34	21	45	29	110	CAc	8%	162	130	16%	15%	81	20%	100%	8.5	279	$16
24	Proj	**350**	**47**	**14**	**50**	**9**	**233**	**14**	**7**	**248**	**280**	**434**	**98**	**98**	**98**	**5**	**74**	**0.20**	**37**	**20**	**44**	**27**	**105**		**8%**	**123**	**129**	**13%**	**13%**	**89**	**15%**	**93%**	**0.5**	**138**	**$13**

Tellez,Rowdy

Age: 29	Pos: 1B DH		Health	C	LIMA Plan	C+
Bats: L	Ht: 6' 4"	Wt: 255	PT/Exp	A	Rand Var	+2
			Consist	B	MM	3025

13-47-.215 in 351 PA at MIL. A near-.900 OPS through late May quickly took turn for the worse. Missed large chunk of 2nd half with forearm/finger injuries, and six-week HR drought before IL stint says he may have been hurting for a while. Bet on a power rebound, though likely one that falls short of 2022 levels.

Yr	Tm	PA	R	HR	RBI	SB	BA	xHR	xSB	xBA	OBP	SLG	OPS+	vL+	vR+	bb%	ct%	Eye	G	L	F	h%	HctX	QBaB	Brl%	PX	xPX	HR/F	xHR/F	Spd	SBA%	SB%	RAR	BPX	R$
19	TOR *	514	66	27	72	1	249	20	-	257	310	484	110	116	96	8	69	0.28	39	24	38	30	99	BCc	13%	138	114	22%	21%	55	2%	50%	-4.8	74	$12
20	TOR	127	20	8	23	0	283	7	1	288	346	540	118	106	121	9	82	0.55	46	20	34	28	123	BCc	8%	125	97	25%	22%	82	3%	0%	1.7	292	$13
21	2 TM *	383	40	14	45	0	242	13	0	252	298	425	99	99	99	7	77	0.35	41	21	38	27	112	ACf	12%	104	111	12%	15%	85	0%	0%	-6.6	131	$6
22	MIL	599	67	35	89	2	219	31	0	259	306	461	109	90	114	10	77	0.51	39	16	45	22	136	ABf	13%	143	150	19%	17%	43	2%	67%	-1.8	203	$15
23	MIL *	384	29	14	50	0	212	9	0	224	289	369	90	71	94	10	72	0.39	37	20	43	25	97	BBd	9%	92	117	13%	9%	49	0%	0%	-8.3	-4	$3
1st Half		282	23	12	35	0	214	7	0	229	287	393	93	68	98	10	74	0.41	36	19	46	24	94	CBf	9%	99	122	14%	8%	53	0%	0%	-5.2	43	$6
2nd Half		102	6	2	15	0	204	1	0	214	284	301	79	85	82	10	68	0.34	44	24	32	28	114	ACa	9%	69	95	8%	8%	70	0%	0%	-4.6	-111	-$5
24	Proj	**490**	**46**	**22**	**70**	**0**	**221**	**20**	**1**	**245**	**294**	**413**	**97**	**80**	**101**	**10**	**74**	**0.40**	**41**	**20**	**39**	**25**	**115**		**11%**	**113**	**118**	**17%**	**15%**	**61**	**1%**	**51%**	**-0.6**	**64**	**$11**

Thaiss,Matt

Age: 29	Pos: CA		Health	A	LIMA Plan	D
Bats: L	Ht: 6' 0"	Wt: 215	PT/Exp	B	Rand Var	-2
			Consist	B	MM	2201

Full transition to catcher led to more PA, but skills remained underwhelming. Crazy low h% fueled 2nd half BA crash, but even with correction, he'll likely be flirting with Mendoza line again. Decent power gives him some marginal appeal in two-catcher leagues, but only if you have rock solid BA foundation. Rock, as in metamorphic rock.

Yr	Tm	PA	R	HR	RBI	SB	BA	xHR	xSB	xBA	OBP	SLG	OPS+	vL+	vR+	bb%	ct%	Eye	G	L	F	h%	HctX	QBaB	Brl%	PX	xPX	HR/F	xHR/F	Spd	SBA%	SB%	RAR	BPX	R$
19	LAA *	512	56	18	54	1	212	5	-	233	296	375	93	97	98	11	72	0.42	37	22	40	25	107	CBc	6%	92	126	21%	13%	64	1%	100%	0.0	11	$4
20	LAA	25	3	1	1	0	143	0	0	179	280	286	75	196	36	16	62	0.50	46	15	38	17	39	CDf	8%	82	31	20%	0%	94	0%	0%	-1.1	-96	-$3
21	LAA *	422	42	10	40	1	202	0	1	243	270	331	83	159	0	9	70	0.31	33	33	33	26	47	DAf	0%	84	20	0%	0%	89	2%	48%	-13.3	-27	$0
22	LAA *	388	33	8	33	5	194	2	3	214	265	301	80	22	104	9	71	0.33	57	13	30	25	66	CDf	5%	74	34	14%	14%	83	6%	100%	-10.6	-38	$0
23	LAA	307	32	9	31	2	214	10	2	215	319	340	90	74	92	12	68	0.43	43	21	36	28	68	CDf	10%	78	102	14%	15%	77	2%	100%	1.0	-54	$2
1st Half		184	23	4	21	2	263	5	2	234	370	378	102	84	105	13	70	0.51	43	26	31	35	78	BDf	10%	76	73	12%	15%	85	3%	100%	5.6	-21	$3
2nd Half		123	9	5	10	0	142	6	0	177	244	283	71	66	72	10	66	0.33	42	14	44	15	97	CCf	12%	80	146	16%	19%	82	0%	0%	-5.9	-89	-$7
24	Proj	**210**	**20**	**7**	**20**	**1**	**205**	**6**	**1**	**215**	**291**	**350**	**88**	**56**	**94**	**10**	**69**	**0.37**	**47**	**17**	**36**	**26**	**85**		**8%**	**89**	**89**	**15%**	**13%**	**77**	**3%**	**95%**	**-0.6**	**-43**	**$3**

BRIAN RUDD

Thomas,Alek

Age: 24 Pos: CF	Health A	LIMA Plan B	
Bats: L Ht: 5' 11" Wt: 175	PT/Exp A	Rand Var +2	
	Consist B	MM 2545	

9-39-.230 with 9 SB in 402 PA at ARI. Slow start led to AAA demotion in May; just marginal gains upon June return. Some upside if you squint—xBA says BA should improve, SB ceiling exists with greener light—but extreme GB% puts lid on HR outlook and was inept vL. Too young to discard; too many warts for this to materialize quickly.

Yr	Tm	PA	R	HR	RBI	SB	BA	xHR	xSB	xBA	OBP	SLG	OPS+	vL+	vR+	bb%	ct%	Eye	G	L	F	h%	HctX	QBaB	Brl%	PX	xPX	HR/F	xHR/F	Spd	SBA%	SB%	RAR	BPX	R$
19																																			
20																																			
21	a/a	468	55	11	38	8	266		15		318	448	105			7	75	0.30				33				106				145	19%	40%		165	$1
22	ARI *	534	59	10	50	7	236	6	8	261	280	357	90	66	94	6	81	0.31	58	17	25	27	92	CFd	4%	78	69	10%	8%	108	11%	56%	-12.2	110	$1
23	ARI *	521	66	11	58	10	242	8	12	264	281	378	90	59	96	5	78	0.24	56	19	26	29	119	CFf	5%	79	90	12%	11%	131	10%	91%	-2.8	89	$1
1st Half		286	36	5	32	5	248	4	6	267	291	376	91	20	110	6	78	0.27	55	21	24	30	121	CFd	8%	78	90	10%	14%	120	10%	84%	-1.6	79	$1
2nd Half		235	30	6	26	5	234	3	6	262	275	381	89	100	86	4	78	0.20	56	18	26	28	117	CFf	3%	81	91	13%	7%	141	11%	100%	-3.0	100	$
24	**Proj**	**490**	**60**	**10**	**50**	**11**	**253**	**8**	**11**	**263**	**297**	**391**	**94**	**66**	**102**	**5**	**78**	**0.26**	**57**	**18**	**25**	**30**	**108**		**5%**	**81**	**82**	**11%**	**9%**	**132**	**12%**	**86%**	**2.4**	**109**	**$1**

Thomas,Lane

Age: 28 Pos: RF	Health A	LIMA Plan B	
Bats: R Ht: 6' 0" Wt: 191	PT/Exp A	Rand Var -5	
	Consist B	MM 3425	

Thrilling trip aboard the Lane Train thanks to HR/SB outburst, career-high BA, and a ton of volume to let R+RBI thrive. Next ride might be slightly more bumpy: xHR, QBaB hint at HR pullback; ditto for BA repeat given h% spike; and he likely maxed out PA. A strong five-category contributor, no doubt, but you're buying in after a career year.

Yr	Tm	PA	R	HR	RBI	SB	BA	xHR	xSB	xBA	OBP	SLG	OPS+	vL+	vR+	bb%	ct%	Eye	G	L	F	h%	HctX	QBaB	Brl%	PX	xPX	HR/F	xHR/F	Spd	SBA%	SB%	RAR	BPX	R$
19	STL *	333	39	11	46	10	239	2	11	251	303	415	99	164	145	8	68	0.29	47	27	27	31	102	ADc	13%	105	113	50%	25%	133	24%	55%	-11.8	52	$
20	STL	40	5	1	2	0	111	0	0	187	200	250	60	33	67	10	64	0.31	39	13	48	14	67	ABf	4%	100	93	9%	0%	99	0%	0%	-4.7	-48	-$
21	2 NL *	399	49	11	45	8	235	7	10	232	323	404	100	150	84	11	70	0.43	42	19	39	31	122	ACd	7%	110	124	11%	11%	129	14%	60%	-3.8	119	$
22	WAS	548	62	17	52	8	241	15	10	239	301	404	100	104	97	7	73	0.31	45	17	38	30	88	DCf	7%	109	97	12%	11%	128	10%	67%	0.2	128	$1
23	WAS	682	101	28	86	20	268	24	20	255	315	468	107	128	98	5	72	0.20	44	19	37	33	103	CCd	10%	124	111	16%	14%	120	17%	80%	20.1	129	$2
1st Half		351	57	14	44	7	299	11	9	261	348	506	117	151	100	6	72	0.22	46	19	36	38	101	CCd	9%	130	117	17%	13%	128	11%	78%	19.9	157	$3
2nd Half		331	44	14	42	13	234	13	11	249	281	428	96	95	96	5	72	0.19	42	19	39	28	106	CCd	10%	118	105	16%	15%	109	25%	81%	-1.3	96	$2
24	**Proj**	**595**	**79**	**21**	**71**	**19**	**253**	**21**	**17**	**242**	**311**	**432**	**102**	**117**	**95**	**7**	**72**	**0.27**	**44**	**18**	**38**	**32**	**101**		**9%**	**113**	**107**	**14%**	**14%**	**115**	**18%**	**79%**	**9.6**	**115**	**$2**

Thompson,Trayce

Age: 33 Pos: CF	Health C	LIMA Plan F	
Bats: R Ht: 6' 3" Wt: 225	PT/Exp C	Rand Var +4	
	Consist F	MM 3301	

Fun fact: Hit half of his HR (3) in first game of the season. Not-so-fun fact: Only hitter in majors with this bad of a ct%, xBA, and HctX combo (min. 100 PA). Three-month IL stint (oblique) didn't help. And he can't hit lefties. Yet power skills look fine - yay! Contact issues seem insurmountable and at this age, little reason to think much will change.

Yr	Tm	PA	R	HR	RBI	SB	BA	xHR	xSB	xBA	OBP	SLG	OPS+	vL+	vR+	bb%	ct%	Eye	G	L	F	h%	HctX	QBaB	Brl%	PX	xPX	HR/F	xHR/F	Spd	SBA%	SB%	RAR	BPX	R$
19	aaa	359	38	18	42	6	181		6		238	383	86			7	51	0.15				27				146				110	18%	62%		-104	$
20																																			
21	CHC *	387	36	16	47	4	178	4	2	182	255	357	84	247	67	9	53	0.22	35	18	47	27	128	ABa	35%	142	272	50%	50%	79	7%	75%	-18.7	-112	$
22	2 NL *	417	56	22	63	5	241	15	4	243	315	491	114	87	144	10	59	0.26	31	30	39	34	108	ABc	16%	201	167	26%	30%	90	8%	69%	14.3	152	$1
23	2 TM	179	17	6	17	2	163	6	2	156	285	294	79	63	92	13	50	0.31	33	18	49	27	69	BAd	12%	105	124	16%	16%	91	5%	100%	-6.1	-214	-$
1st Half		87	12	5	14	0	155	5	1	167	310	366	93	82	107	17	48	0.41	26	15	59	21	86	AAc	24%	164	236	25%	25%	88	0%	0%	-1.4	-50	-$
2nd Half		92	5	1	3	2	171	1	2	149	261	232	67	29	83	10	51	0.23	38	21	40	32	55	CAd	2%	57	33	6%	6%	95	10%	100%	-5.5	-354	-$
24	**Proj**	**210**	**22**	**7**	**23**	**3**	**203**	**8**	**3**	**178**	**296**	**348**	**88**	**65**	**105**	**11**	**53**	**0.26**	**32**	**23**	**44**	**34**	**84**		**13%**	**118**	**137**	**16%**	**18%**	**93**	**6%**	**83%**	**-3.2**	**-105**	**$**

Toglia,Michael

Age: 25 Pos: 1B	Health A	LIMA Plan D	
Bats: B Ht: 6' 5" Wt: 226	PT/Exp B	Rand Var +3	
	Consist A	MM 2201	

4-9-.163 in in 152 PA at COL. A step back for former first-rounder with unsuccessful MLB stints in May and July/Aug. Another poor BA thanks to prevalent contact issues (65% ct% in MLB), and while he hit 16 HR in 308 AB at AAA, Brl% says the thump hasn't translated to majors. We can only take a wait-and-see approach for so long...

Yr	Tm	PA	R	HR	RBI	SB	BA	xHR	xSB	xBA	OBP	SLG	OPS+	vL+	vR+	bb%	ct%	Eye	G	L	F	h%	HctX	QBaB	Brl%	PX	xPX	HR/F	xHR/F	Spd	SBA%	SB%	RAR	BPX	R$
19																																			
20																																			
21	aa	159	11	4	12	2	199		1		280	360	88			10	63	0.30				29				121				99	7%	100%		4	-$
22	COL *	582	53	21	60	6	206	2	6	220	263	377	91	83	96	7	62	0.21	37	24	39	29	106	CBc	6%	131	112	8%	8%	106	9%	63%	-25.4	7	$
23	COL *	489	50	15	45	3	193	3	5	214	257	335	81	34	86	8	69	0.28	40	18	43	24	106	BBc	5%	91	114	10%	8%	97	5%	55%	-22.0	-7	$
1st Half		309	32	10	33	1	197	0	3	267	263	353	84	27	88	8	70	0.31	36	36	29	24	61	FBd	0%	95	15	0%	0%	98	3%	49%	-13.1	21	$
2nd Half		180	18	4	12	2	187	3	3	193	246	304	74	36	85	7	67	0.24	40	14	45	25	111	ABc	6%	82	132	11%	9%	99	9%	61%	-11.0	-64	-$
24	**Proj**	**210**	**20**	**5**	**19**	**2**	**207**	**3**	**3**	**204**	**272**	**344**	**84**	**60**	**95**	**8**	**66**	**0.24**	**39**	**18**	**43**	**29**	**109**		**6%**	**96**	**124**	**10%**	**6%**	**103**	**7%**	**70%**	**-6.4**	**-12**	**$**

Torkelson,Spencer

Age: 24 Pos: 1B	Health A	LIMA Plan B	
Bats: R Ht: 6' 1" Wt: 220	PT/Exp A	Rand Var 0	
	Consist F	MM 4125	

Looked en route to second straight year of failed prospect hype, then something clicked, as summer HR barrage came with massive gains in Brl% and PX/xPX. Flyball tilt with ct% issues capped BA, though xBA gives a smidge of hope. Tons of pedigree as he enters prime, so if 2nd half skill growth sticks, we could see... UP: .250 BA, 40 HR.

Yr	Tm	PA	R	HR	RBI	SB	BA	xHR	xSB	xBA	OBP	SLG	OPS+	vL+	vR+	bb%	ct%	Eye	G	L	F	h%	HctX	QBaB	Brl%	PX	xPX	HR/F	xHR/F	Spd	SBA%	SB%	RAR	BPX	R$
19																																			
20																																			
21	a/a	364	56	21	52	2	230		2		320	479	110			12	73	0.48				25				145				94	4%	60%		231	$
22	DET *	551	50	11	40	1	198	12	3	210	276	313	84	91	83	10	71	0.37	40	19	41	26	98	BBd	8%	83	93	7%	11%	97	2%	24%	-21.5	0	$
23	DET	684	88	31	94	3	233	33	4	245	313	446	103	112	100	10	72	0.39	35	19	47	27	116	ABd	14%	131	140	15%	16%	78	2%	100%	14.7	132	$
1st Half		349	40	12	42	2	228	12	2	243	312	404	98	111	94	10	74	0.44	34	21	45	27	118	ABd	12%	110	119	12%	12%	73	3%	100%	-2.0	96	$
2nd Half		335	48	19	52	1	237	21	2	249	313	488	108	112	107	9	70	0.34	36	16	48	27	115	ABf	17%	153	163	19%	21%	90	1%	100%	6.2	179	$
24	**Proj**	**665**	**88**	**31**	**89**	**2**	**235**	**28**	**4**	**242**	**316**	**447**	**105**	**112**	**102**	**10**	**71**	**0.38**	**37**	**18**	**45**	**28**	**109**		**12%**	**130**	**124**	**16%**	**15%**	**83**	**2%**	**68%**	**10.8**	**108**	**$**

Torres,Gleyber

Age: 27 Pos: 2B	Health B	LIMA Plan B+	
Bats: R Ht: 6' 1" Wt: 205	PT/Exp A	Rand Var 0	
	Consist B	MM 2235	

A similar follow-up to 2022's step forward; just needed 100 more PA to get there. Jump in ct% was the highlight, which put xBA in lockstep with BA, and 2nd half xPX quashes fears he sold out for it. Tack on a consistent running game, and while it's hard to see a big step forward, this feels like 25/10 production you can confidently bank.

Yr	Tm	PA	R	HR	RBI	SB	BA	xHR	xSB	xBA	OBP	SLG	OPS+	vL+	vR+	bb%	ct%	Eye	G	L	F	h%	HctX	QBaB	Brl%	PX	xPX	HR/F	xHR/F	Spd	SBA%	SB%	RAR	BPX	R$
19	NYY	604	96	38	90	5	278	31	4	270	337	535	121	125	118	8	76	0.37	37	21	42	30	105	CAb	10%	130	116	21%	18%	87	5%	71%	24.2	200	$
20	NYY	160	17	3	16	1	243	4	1	235	356	368	96	96	96	14	79	0.79	42	19	39	29	98	CBb	4%	75	64	7%	10%	88	2%	100%	-1.0	136	
21	NYY	516	50	9	51	14	259	14	10	235	331	366	96	109	90	10	77	0.48	42	22	36	32	81	CBd	8%	67	80	7%	11%	86	14%	70%	-1.4	38	$
22	NYY	572	73	24	76	10	257	25	10	246	310	451	108	116	105	7	75	0.30	36	19	46	30	114	BBc	11%	124	134	13%	14%	107	12%	67%	15.4	169	$
23	NYY	672	90	25	68	13	273	26	17	272	347	453	109	124	105	10	84	0.68	39	21	40	29	112	BBc	8%	94	108	13%	13%	111	11%	68%	33.2	232	$
1st Half		345	44	12	34	7	248	11	10	269	325	412	101	93	103	10	84	0.71	39	22	39	26	91	CBb	8%	84	90	12%	11%	112	14%	58%	4.3	211	$
2nd Half		327	46	13	34	6	300	15	7	275	370	497	117	162	108	10	83	0.65	40	20	41	32	133	BBc	8%	105	127	13%	15%	109	8%	86%	22.7	254	$
24	**Proj**	**630**	**81**	**23**	**71**	**12**	**269**	**25**	**13**	**256**	**337**	**442**	**107**	**119**	**103**	**9**	**80**	**0.51**	**39**	**20**	**41**	**30**	**109**		**9%**	**98**	**111**	**12%**	**13%**	**99**	**10%**	**70%**	**24.4**	**183**	**$**

Tovar,Ezequiel

Age: 22 Pos: SS	Health A	LIMA Plan B	
Bats: R Ht: 6' 0" Wt: 162	PT/Exp A	Rand Var 0	
	Consist B	MM 2425	

Last year, we said "could deliver double-digit HR, SB right out of gate" and he came through despite brutal April (.213 BA, 0 HR/SB). But some reasons for pause: too many Ks to carry plus BA; middling pop per QBaB; low bb%, SB% prevented plus wheels from turning into more bags. Still a pup, but a repeat seems more likely than a step forward.

Yr	Tm	PA	R	HR	RBI	SB	BA	xHR	xSB	xBA	OBP	SLG	OPS+	vL+	vR+	bb%	ct%	Eye	G	L	F	h%	HctX	QBaB	Brl%	PX	xPX	HR/F	xHR/F	Spd	SBA%	SB%	RAR	BPX	R$
19																																			
20																																			
21																																			
22	COL *	336	28	10	32	10	272	1	9	248	311	432	105	153	49	5	76	0.23	50	17	33	33	83	CDd	10%	101	110	13%	13%	130	17%	76%	2.9	124	$
23	COL	615	79	15	73	11	253	15	15	249	287	408	95	95	94	4	71	0.15	43	24	34	33	92	CCc	8%	103	99	11%	11%	133	13%	69%	0.4	64	$
1st Half		303	40	8	41	4	269	7	7	261	307	437	102	105	101	4	72	0.16	40	27	33	35	94	CCc	7%	112	101	12%	10%	136	11%	57%	2.0	104	$
2nd Half		312	39	7	32	7	237	8	8	238	268	380	87	86	88	4	71	0.14	45	20	34	31	91	CCc	9%	95	97	10%	11%	131	16%	78%	-7.3	32	$
24	**Proj**	**595**	**66**	**15**	**65**	**14**	**260**	**16**	**16**	**243**	**296**	**408**	**96**	**97**	**96**	**5**	**72**	**0.17**	**43**	**23**	**34**	**34**	**92**		**8%**	**96**	**99**	**10%**	**11%**	**123**	**15%**	**74%**	**5.1**	**87**	**$**

RYAN BLOOMFIELD

Trejo,Alan

Age: 28 | Pos: 2B 3B | Bats: R | Ht: 6' 2" | Wt: 205 — Health: A | PT/Exp: C | Consist: A | LIMA Plan: D | Rand Var: 0 | MM: 2221

4-26-.232 with 5 SB in 227 PA at COL. Utilityman saw intermittent playing time sandwiched around AAA stint in June. Little reason to think he earns a regular job given dearth of hard contact, middling xBA, and shaky history on the basepaths. Multi-position eligibility just means he can hurt you at multiple spots. Pass.

Yr	Tm	PA	R	HR	RBI	SB	BA	xHR	xSB	xBA	OBP	SLG	OPS+	vL+	vR+	bb%	ct%	Eye	G	L	F	h%	HctX	QBaB	Brl%	PX	xPX	HR/F	xHR/F	Spd	SBA%	SB%	RAR	BPX	R$
19	aa	462	45	16	49	5	255		5		295	419	99			5	76	0.24				30				90				85	9%	54%		56	$9
20																																			
21	COL *	398	40	12	46	1	236	1	4	257	268	444	98	72	85	4	73	0.17	47	16	38	29	84	CCa	3%	133	72	8%	8%	134	7%	26%	-7.2	196	$5
22	COL *	404	39	13	45	2	241	3	3	250	260	401	94	83	110	2	74	0.10	39	24	37	30	70	DCc	5%	110	95	13%	9%	80	8%	32%	-9.5	45	$8
23	COL *	277	29	5	28	6	243	3	6	247	297	359	89	75	95	7	74	0.30	41	25	34	31	80	DBc	4%	78	87	8%	6%	107	13%	73%	-1.6	32	$3
1st Half		169	15	1	15	5	256	1	5	256	294	347	88	71	86	5	74	0.21	38	32	31	34	76	DBb	2%	71	73	0%	4%	115	17%	80%	-1.7	4	-$1
2nd Half		108	14	4	13	1	221	2	2	237	306	379	93	78	106	10	75	0.46	44	18	38	25	85	DCd	7%	90	104	15%	7%	99	8%	50%	-0.8	86	-$2
24	Proj	**210**	**23**	**5**	**23**	**2**	**238**	**4**	**3**	**247**	**288**	**383**	**92**	**77**	**101**	**6**	**74**	**0.24**	**41**	**24**	**35**	**30**	**77**		**5%**	**92**	**93**	**10%**	**7%**	**95**	**10%**	**58%**	**-0.8**	**73**	**$2**

Trevino,Jose

Age: 31 | Pos: CA | Bats: R | Ht: 5' 10" | Wt: 215 — Health: D | PT/Exp: D | Consist: B | LIMA Plan: D | Rand Var: +5 | MM: 1133

A lost year, as May hamstring injury preceded season-ending wrist surgery in July. Take small sample with a grain of salt, but power went from bad to non-existent, which neutralized his ct% gains. Track record of iffy power and xBA, so even with healthy rebound, he doesn't exactly stand out in murky second-catcher pool.

Yr	Tm	PA	R	HR	RBI	SB	BA	xHR	xSB	xBA	OBP	SLG	OPS+	vL+	vR+	bb%	ct%	Eye	G	L	F	h%	HctX	QBaB	Brl%	PX	xPX	HR/F	xHR/F	Spd	SBA%	SB%	RAR	BPX	R$
19	TEX *	278	28	3	28	1	219	2	1	250	243	323	78	122	75	3	78	0.15	46	23	31	27	104	CDd	2%	66	77	7%	7%	84	2%	100%	-8.2	-7	-$1
20	TEX	83	10	2	9	0	250	4	0	280	280	434	95	104	89	4	80	0.20	41	24	35	29	122	CCf	13%	115	128	9%	18%	76	0%	0%	0.0	180	$2
21	TEX *	324	27	6	33	1	238	7	0	253	270	345	84	65	92	4	80	0.22	44	25	31	28	98	CDf	4%	67	77	7%	10%	59	3%	50%	-7.8	0	$2
22	NYY	353	39	11	43	2	248	9	2	241	283	388	95	123	87	4	81	0.24	40	19	41	27	96	CCf	5%	82	88	10%	8%	91	4%	67%	1.2	100	$8
23	NYY	168	15	4	15	0	210	2	0	246	257	312	78	105	68	5	86	0.36	51	19	30	22	88	DDd	3%	52	63	10%	5%	70	0%	0%	-3.9	64	-$2
1st Half		152	14	3	14	0	210	2	0	245	252	301	76	94	69	5	86	0.35	51	19	30	23	88	DCd	3%	48	63	8%	5%	67	0%	0%	-5.3	50	-$5
2nd Half		16	1	1	1	0	214	0	0	224	313	429	100	187	52	7	86	0.50	50	17	33	18	87	FFf	6%	93	63	25%	0%	95	0%	0%	0.1	218	-$8
24	Proj	**280**	**27**	**6**	**29**	**1**	**229**	**6**	**1**	**249**	**263**	**340**	**83**	**92**	**79**	**4**	**82**	**0.24**	**45**	**21**	**33**	**26**	**99**		**5%**	**65**	**83**	**8%**	**8%**	**69**	**2%**	**63%**	**-3.4**	**34**	**$5**

Triolo,Jared

Age: 26 | Pos: 3B | Bats: R | Ht: 6' 3" | Wt: 212 — Health: A | PT/Exp: C | Consist: C | LIMA Plan: D | Rand Var: -3 | MM: 2421

3-21-.298 with 6 SB in 209 PA at PIT. Impressive surface stats in late-season cameo, but fluky h% played a major part. Underlying skills were less convinced, as MLB xBA lagged BA by over 80 points, the strikeouts piled up, and QBaB was mediocre at best. Running game offers path to value, but only in deep-league end games.

Yr	Tm	PA	R	HR	RBI	SB	BA	xHR	xSB	xBA	OBP	SLG	OPS+	vL+	vR+	bb%	ct%	Eye	G	L	F	h%	HctX	QBaB	Brl%	PX	xPX	HR/F	xHR/F	Spd	SBA%	SB%	RAR	BPX	R$
19																																			
20																																			
21																																			
22	aa	468	43	5	25	16	229		14		299	327	89			9	77	0.43				29				67				120	19%	73%		55	$8
23	PIT *	422	57	4	38	13	267	4	18	221	357	372	99	106	107	12	64	0.40	40	28	32	40	82	CCc	6%	84	95	8%	11%	139	14%	74%	7.8	-21	$10
1st Half		170	22	1	15	6	242	0	9	194	326	345	92	90	80	11	63	0.34	55	9	36	38	70	FFf	0%	84	115	0%	0%	152	25%	55%	-3.0	-36	$0
2nd Half		252	35	4	23	7	284	4	7	228	379	391	104	106	109	13	65	0.44	39	30	31	42	84	CCb	6%	84	93	9%	12%	112	9%	100%	8.2	-36	$13
24	Proj	**245**	**29**	**4**	**19**	**8**	**241**	**3**	**9**	**237**	**329**	**358**	**94**	**94**	**94**	**11**	**69**	**0.40**	**39**	**30**	**31**	**33**	**76**		**6%**	**82**	**84**	**8%**	**7%**	**128**	**17%**	**72%**	**0.5**	**0**	**$7**

Trout,Mike

Age: 32 | Pos: CF | Bats: R | Ht: 6' 2" | Wt: 235 — Health: F | PT/Exp: B | Consist: F | LIMA Plan: B+ | Rand Var: 0 | MM: 5445

Status quo through April (.308 BA, 7 HR), then hit .239 until fractured hand effectively ended season in July. Perhaps some chinks in the armor, as PX/xPX wasn't its elite self, which dragged xBA to new lows, and any hope for a handful of SB seems long gone. Most likely bounces back on per-game basis, but just how many games is anyone's guess.

Yr	Tm	PA	R	HR	RBI	SB	BA	xHR	xSB	xBA	OBP	SLG	OPS+	vL+	vR+	bb%	ct%	Eye	G	L	F	h%	HctX	QBaB	Brl%	PX	xPX	HR/F	xHR/F	Spd	SBA%	SB%	RAR	BPX	R$
19	LAA	600	110	45	104	11	291	48	7	290	438	645	150	138	154	18	74	0.92	24	27	49	30	113	AAa	19%	180	172	26%	28%	89	7%	85%	71.6	396	$31
20	LAA	241	41	17	46	1	281	18	3	269	390	603	132	102	142	15	72	0.63	25	24	50	31	123	AAb	14%	174	157	23%	24%	129	3%	50%	19.5	384	$29
21	LAA	146	23	8	18	2	333	8	2	270	466	624	150	104	169	18	65	0.66	42	24	34	46	101	ACb	18%	191	123	31%	31%	116	4%	100%	20.5	335	$6
22	LAA	499	85	40	80	1	283	41	2	280	369	630	141	148	139	11	68	0.39	25	19	57	32	115	AAb	20%	232	160	24%	24%	102	1%	100%	52.5	390	$27
23	LAA	362	54	18	44	2	263	20	4	246	367	490	117	104	122	12	66	0.43	33	24	43	34	107	AAb	16%	145	120	20%	23%	105	2%	100%	20.7	139	$10
1st Half		353	54	18	43	2	260	19	4	248	365	493	118	99	124	13	66	0.44	32	24	43	33	109	AAb	16%	149	122	21%	22%	101	2%	100%	18.4	150	$24
2nd Half		9	0	0	1	0	375	1	0	123	444	375	111	207	0	11	63	0.33	60	20	20	60	51	DAa	17%	0	29	0%	100%	97	0%	0%	0.6	-346	-$8
24	Proj	**490**	**82**	**30**	**73**	**2**	**280**	**32**	**5**	**262**	**394**	**564**	**131**	**111**	**139**	**15**	**67**	**0.52**	**31**	**23**	**45**	**35**	**111**		**17%**	**181**	**140**	**24%**	**25%**	**106**	**1%**	**100%**	**46.4**	**304**	**$25**

Tucker,Kyle

Age: 27 | Pos: RF | Bats: L | Ht: 6' 4" | Wt: 199 — Health: A | PT/Exp: A | Consist: D | LIMA Plan: C | Rand Var: 0 | MM: 4455

If we could draw up the most well-rounded skill set in this book, his might be it. Elite plate skills, xBA firmly back the BA gains; rock-steady SB% says bags will come in bunches; power skills snapped all the way back in 2nd half. A legit 30/30 candidate at peak age, he's among the safest first-rounders in the pool. As the peak crests... UP: 35 HR

Yr	Tm	PA	R	HR	RBI	SB	BA	xHR	xSB	xBA	OBP	SLG	OPS+	vL+	vR+	bb%	ct%	Eye	G	L	F	h%	HctX	QBaB	Brl%	PX	xPX	HR/F	xHR/F	Spd	SBA%	SB%	RAR	BPX	R$
19	HOU *	578	81	29	81	27	229	4	16	238	292	452	103	117	119	8	71	0.31	34	19	47	26	116	ABa	13%	124	176	18%	18%	95	30%	83%	-9.9	115	$23
20	HOU	228	33	9	42	8	268	9	7	266	325	512	111	91	120	8	78	0.39	38	20	42	31	119	BBd	9%	127	125	13%	13%	150	19%	89%	6.1	304	$29
21	HOU	565	83	30	92	14	294	31	10	289	359	557	126	124	127	9	82	0.59	34	22	44	31	132	ABb	12%	141	139	16%	17%	107	12%	88%	41.8	365	$31
22	HOU	606	71	30	107	25	257	30	14	269	330	478	114	103	121	10	83	0.62	34	19	47	26	128	BAc	10%	126	158	14%	14%	75	21%	86%	22.0	259	$33
23	HOU	667	97	29	112	30	284	33	25	288	369	517	121	126	117	12	84	0.87	38	19	42	30	133	BBc	11%	123	131	14%	16%	110	20%	86%	51.2	332	$34
1st Half		341	42	12	51	14	285	14	11	278	361	466	113	123	109	11	85	0.86	41	19	39	30	137	ACb	8%	98	109	12%	14%	96	17%	88%	17.7	261	$29
2nd Half		326	55	17	61	16	283	19	14	297	377	572	128	128	128	13	83	0.88	35	19	46	29	129	CBd	13%	150	156	16%	18%	122	23%	84%	28.5	411	$38
24	Proj	**651**	**93**	**31**	**113**	**27**	**275**	**33**	**20**	**279**	**352**	**515**	**119**	**117**	**120**	**11**	**82**	**0.68**	**36**	**19**	**44**	**29**	**130**		**11%**	**129**	**144**	**15%**	**16%**	**102**	**20%**	**86%**	**42.9**	**316**	**$39**

Turang,Brice

Age: 24 | Pos: 2B SS | Bats: L | Ht: 6' 0" | Wt: 173 — Health: A | PT/Exp: A | Consist: A | LIMA Plan: C+ | Rand Var: 0 | MM: 1505

6-34-.218 with 26 SB in 448 PA at MIL. Carved out strong-side platoon role for much of rookie season. PRO: SB pace is legit given elite raw speed, green light, primo efficiency; plate skills improved in 2nd half. CON: Lack of hard contact caps HR, xBA/BA ceilings; issues vL could block full-time gig. Plenty of time for growth; a speed-only play for now.

Yr	Tm	PA	R	HR	RBI	SB	BA	xHR	xSB	xBA	OBP	SLG	OPS+	vL+	vR+	bb%	ct%	Eye	G	L	F	h%	HctX	QBaB	Brl%	PX	xPX	HR/F	xHR/F	Spd	SBA%	SB%	RAR	BPX	R$
19																																			
20																																			
21	a/a	476	44	5	40	15	222		13		296	307	83			9	78	0.47				28				54				100	22%	60%		23	$8
22	aaa	578	60	9	53	23	233		14		294	325	88			8	74	0.33				30				64				97	18%	91%		-24	$17
23	MIL *	509	53	8	45	27	222	6	24	222	288	320	83	63	83	8	77	0.40	42	19	39	27	81	DCf	3%	57	81	5%	5%	140	26%	87%	-8.6	50	$10
1st Half		256	23	5	27	10	214	3	9	238	265	345	83	23	84	6	75	0.27	41	22	38	27	82	CCf	3%	81	99	6%	6%	128	27%	78%	-7.0	57	$5
2nd Half		253	30	3	18	17	231	4	15	206	312	294	82	84	81	11	80	0.58	43	17	41	28	81	FCf	3%	34	67	4%	6%	151	25%	94%	-3.3	50	$11
24	Proj	**490**	**51**	**7**	**43**	**23**	**227**	**8**	**19**	**213**	**294**	**312**	**83**	**68**	**86**	**9**	**76**	**0.40**	**42**	**19**	**40**	**28**	**81**		**3%**	**53**	**80**	**5%**	**6%**	**131**	**22%**	**86%**	**-6.6**	**21**	**$15**

Turner,Justin

Age: 39 | Pos: DH 1B | Bats: R | Ht: 5' 11" | Wt: 202 — Health: B | PT/Exp: A | Consist: A | LIMA Plan: B+ | Rand Var: 0 | MM: 2245

Late-career revival kept on rolling, though struggled in Sept (.228 BA, 1 HR) after August heel injury. Ironclad ct% and LD% combo led to another solid BA with just enough oomph and volume to drive HR rebound. Just 1B-eligible now and we can't expect another 600+ PA at this age, but these skills show little sign of slowing down.

Yr	Tm	PA	R	HR	RBI	SB	BA	xHR	xSB	xBA	OBP	SLG	OPS+	vL+	vR+	bb%	ct%	Eye	G	L	F	h%	HctX	QBaB	Brl%	PX	xPX	HR/F	xHR/F	Spd	SBA%	SB%	RAR	BPX	R$
19	LA	549	80	27	67	2	290	25	2	283	372	509	122	131	117	9	82	0.58	34	26	40	31	142	BAa	8%	107	151	17%	16%	91	1%	100%	22.3	222	$18
20	LA	175	26	4	23	1	307	9	2	251	400	460	114	97	122	10	83	0.69	34	22	44	35	163	BBa	11%	84	191	7%	16%	117	2%	100%	4.6	224	$16
21	LA	612	87	27	87	3	278	23	2	260	361	471	114	111	115	10	82	0.62	35	21	44	30	135	AAb	8%	101	143	14%	12%	86	2%	100%	19.9	212	$23
22	LA	532	61	13	81	3	278	17	1	265	350	438	112	103	115	9	81	0.56	32	25	43	32	113	BAb	8%	107	116	8%	10%	66	2%	100%	17.5	172	$19
23	BOS	626	86	23	96	4	276	22	5	267	345	455	109	121	105	8	80	0.46	36	23	41	31	100	BBc	6%	101	108	12%	12%	74	3%	80%	25.5	154	$22
1st Half		351	52	13	46	4	277	13	4	274	350	460	111	126	105	9	82	0.56	37	23	40	30	109	BBc	6%	102	125	13%	13%	83	4%	100%	11.4	193	$24
2nd Half		275	34	10	50	0	275	9	1	258	338	449	106	113	104	7	79	0.36	35	22	43	32	89	CAc	5%	100	86	12%	11%	68	1%	0%	5.0	111	$17
24	Proj	**560**	**76**	**19**	**88**	**3**	**279**	**20**	**3**	**262**	**350**	**449**	**110**	**111**	**109**	**9**	**81**	**0.49**	**34**	**23**	**43**	**31**	**112**		**7%**	**99**	**118**	**11%**	**12%**	**74**	**2%**	**82%**	**19.5**	**169**	**$24**

RYAN BLOOMFIELD

Turner,Trea

Age: 31	Pos: SS		Health	A	LIMA Plan	D+
Bats: R	Ht: 6'2"	Wt: 185	PT/Exp	A	Rand Var	+1
			Consist	C	MM	3545

A disappointing 1st half, as ct% and h% dipped below typical levels. Neither fully rebounded in 2nd half, but displayed more power than ever and continued his perfect season on the bases. Overall xBA and ct% trends question a BA rebound, but otherwise, there's plenty of bankable volume for everything else. Partial bounceback likely.

Yr	Tm	PA	R	HR	RBI	SB	BA	xHR	xSB	xBA	OBP	SLG	OPS+	vL+	vR+	bb%	ct%	Eye	G	L	F	h%	HctX	QBaB	Brl%	PX	xPX	HR/F	xHR/F	Spd	SBA%	SB%	RAR	BPX	R$
19	WAS	569	96	19	57	35	298	19	28	276	353	497	118	113	118	8	78	0.38	47	20	33	35	102	BCc	7%	108	87	14%	14%	158	29%	88%	26.0	237	$32
20	WAS	259	46	12	41	12	335	12	14	300	394	588	130	155	122	8	85	0.61	45	21	35	36	126	BCd	10%	124	115	17%	17%	169	23%	75%	25.9	428	$47
21	2 NL	646	107	28	77	32	328	22	27	283	375	536	125	156	114	6	82	0.37	45	21	34	37	116	BCc	7%	112	91	17%	13%	146	21%	86%	50.1	285	$47
22	LA	706	101	21	100	27	298	23	24	267	343	466	115	124	111	6	80	0.34	43	21	36	35	110	CCf	8%	106	114	11%	12%	145	17%	90%	29.1	217	$43
23	PHI	691	102	26	76	30	266	24	27	261	320	459	106	97	110	7	77	0.30	40	21	39	31	109	BCd	8%	112	117	13%	12%	146	19%	100%	26.2	193	$28
1st Half		369	49	8	29	18	249	10	16	232	304	383	94	93	94	7	75	0.29	36	21	42	31	94	BBd	7%	85	111	7%	9%	148	21%	100%	-0.2	96	$21
2nd Half		322	53	18	47	12	286	14	11	293	339	545	119	101	128	6	78	0.31	43	21	36	31	126	BCc	10%	141	123	21%	16%	137	17%	100%	20.8	293	$34
24	Proj	**665**	**104**	**25**	**85**	**26**	**275**	**24**	**25**	**269**	**326**	**468**	**109**	**110**	**108**	**7**	**79**	**0.33**	**42**	**21**	**37**	**31**	**113**		**8%**	**111**	**111**	**14%**	**13%**	**135**	**19%**	**92%**	**30.1**	**237**	**$32**

Urías,Luis

Age: 27	Pos: 2B		Health	D	LIMA Plan	D+
Bats: R	Ht: 5'9"	Wt: 186	PT/Exp	B	Rand Var	+1
			Consist	B	MM	2103

3-18-.194 in 177 PA at MIL/BOS. Opening Day hamstring injury cost him two months; never really got back on track. Power skills took a big hit while ct%, xBA tumbled. Deserves a bit of an injury-related pass, but below-average speed, lackluster BA history, and middling power say a return to 2021 peak is a long shot.

Yr	Tm	PA	R	HR	RBI	SB	BA	xHR	xSB	xBA	OBP	SLG	OPS+	vL+	vR+	bb%	ct%	Eye	G	L	F	h%	HctX	QBaB	Brl%	PX	xPX	HR/F	xHR/F	Spd	SBA%	SB%	RAR	BPX	R$
19	SD *	570	71	17	60	5	248	5	9	254	317	408	100	124	78	9	75	0.41	49	20	31	30	95	CCb	4%	87	89	8%	10%	131	6%	60%	-3.2	111	$11
20	MIL	120	11	0	11	2	239	1	3	218	308	294	80	92	74	8	71	0.31	63	18	18	34	71	CFf	1%	40	23	0%	7%	126	13%	50%	-5.9	-112	$3
21	MIL	567	77	23	75	5	249	19	4	257	345	445	108	109	108	11	76	0.54	41	21	38	28	109	CCf	9%	112	125	16%	13%	93	4%	83%	11.8	181	$16
22	MIL *	501	57	16	48	1	231	15	3	234	313	387	99	105	104	10	75	0.48	37	20	43	27	105	CAc	8%	99	115	12%	11%	95	2%	33%	-2.2	107	$8
23	2 TM *	304	32	6	29	1	190	5	3	189	285	298	79	94	84	11	68	0.41	47	13	41	26	70	DBf	6%	75	81	7%	12%	90	3%	37%	-9.6	-57	-$1
1st Half		108	7	1	8	0	150	1	1	172	219	220	60	68	73	8	67	0.27	48	13	40	21	68	DAf	5%	54	60	6%	6%	94	5%	0%	-8.2	-150	-$1
2nd Half		196	25	5	21	1	213	3	2	198	321	344	90	105	90	14	68	0.50	46	13	41	28	71	DCf	6%	86	94	8%	12%	93	2%	100%	-1.6	-4	$2
24	Proj	**350**	**40**	**9**	**36**	**2**	**235**	**9**	**4**	**215**	**345**	**368**	**98**	**105**	**95**	**11**	**72**	**0.43**	**44**	**16**	**39**	**30**	**86**		**6%**	**85**	**93**	**10%**	**10%**	**92**	**3%**	**53%**	**1.8**	**23**	**$8**

Urías,Ramón

Age: 30	Pos: 3B 2B		Health	B	LIMA Plan	D
Bats: R	Ht: 6'0"	Wt: 190	PT/Exp	A	Rand Var	0
			Consist	A	MM	2223

Unable to sustain 2022 power gains, as groundballs returned and xPX, HR/F nosedived. The BA uptick looks fluky given all that soft contact and subpar ct%, and well, xBA says so. Didn't record a single HR/SB over final 170 PA. Dual eligibility helps and if h% stays inflated and if... nah, it's not worth even trying to dig up positives.

Yr	Tm	PA	R	HR	RBI	SB	BA	xHR	xSB	xBA	OBP	SLG	OPS+	vL+	vR+	bb%	ct%	Eye	G	L	F	h%	HctX	QBaB	Brl%	PX	xPX	HR/F	xHR/F	Spd	SBA%	SB%	RAR	BPX	R$
19	a/a	357	41	7	41	3	223		2		295	348	89			9	74	0.40				28				78				86	5%	73%		22	$3
20	BAL	27	3	1	3	0	360	1	0	298	407	560	128	140	123	7	76	0.33	47	32	21	44	178	ADa	5%	121	144	25%	25%	101	0%	0%	2.7	192	$1
21	BAL *	391	43	10	47	2	261	8	4	244	327	405	101	97	113	9	70	0.33	50	24	26	35	102	BFf	10%	96	89	15%	17%	106	5%	35%	2.9	31	$9
22	BAL	445	50	16	51	1	248	17	3	246	305	414	102	93	105	7	76	0.31	47	18	35	29	112	CCf	10%	104	114	15%	16%	109	1%	100%	3.0	117	$10
23	BAL	396	45	4	42	3	264	8	7	236	328	375	96	88	99	7	72	0.27	53	18	28	36	85	CDc	7%	79	69	5%	11%	120	4%	75%	4.1	11	$7
1st Half		204	23	3	24	3	257	5	3	239	328	383	97	72	113	7	70	0.25	47	22	32	35	99	BCa	11%	96	90	7%	12%	88	8%	75%	-0.6	-4	$3
2nd Half		192	22	1	18	0	271	2	4	231	328	367	94	115	87	7	74	0.28	60	15	25	36	69	CFf	3%	62	48	3%	6%	152	0%	0%	-0.3	25	$2
24	Proj	**315**	**36**	**6**	**35**	**2**	**246**	**7**	**4**	**236**	**312**	**370**	**94**	**89**	**96**	**7**	**73**	**0.30**	**51**	**19**	**30**	**32**	**95**		**8%**	**82**	**86**	**9%**	**11%**	**111**	**3%**	**68%**	**-0.4**	**43**	**$8**

Urshela,Giovanny

Age: 32	Pos: 3B 1B		Health	F	LIMA Plan	C+
Bats: R	Ht: 6'0"	Wt: 215	PT/Exp	B	Rand Var	-3
			Consist	B	MM	1233

Another strong (but empty) BA, which outperformed xBA by an even wider margin than usual. Pelvis fracture in June ended season, but expected to be fully recovered by spring. Doesn't offer much of a ceiling given marginal power and zero running game, but plus ct% and LD stroke should at least yield a bunch of singles again.

Yr	Tm	PA	R	HR	RBI	SB	BA	xHR	xSB	xBA	OBP	SLG	OPS+	vL+	vR+	bb%	ct%	Eye	G	L	F	h%	HctX	QBaB	Brl%	PX	xPX	HR/F	xHR/F	Spd	SBA%	SB%	RAR	BPX	R$
19	NYY	476	73	21	74	1	314	20	1	293	355	534	123	122	123	5	80	0.29	41	25	33	35	122	BCb	7%	117	122	18%	17%	78	2%	50%	22.6	189	$19
20	NYY	174	24	6	30	1	298	6	0	294	368	490	114	89	120	10	83	0.72	41	27	32	33	107	ACb	7%	104	64	14%	14%	76	2%	100%	7.6	252	$17
21	NYY	442	42	14	49	1	267	14	3	248	301	419	99	106	95	5	74	0.18	48	22	30	33	85	CDc	8%	91	82	15%	15%	114	1%	100%	2.8	54	$10
22	MIN	551	61	13	64	1	285	14	4	262	338	429	109	108	108	7	81	0.43	42	23	35	33	117	CCb	7%	90	97	9%	10%	113	1%	100%	17.3	159	$18
23	LAA	228	22	2	24	3	299	3	6	249	329	374	96	117	89	4	83	0.28	48	22	30	35	86	CDb	4%	45	58	4%	5%	120	8%	60%	4.2	54	$4
1st Half		228	22	2	24	3	299	3	6	249	329	374	96	118	90	4	83	0.28	48	22	30	35	86	CDb	4%	45	58	4%	5%	120	8%	60%	1.4	57	$6
2nd Half																									0%										
24	Proj	**385**	**44**	**8**	**49**	**2**	**290**	**9**	**4**	**259**	**331**	**414**	**102**	**107**	**100**	**6**	**80**	**0.32**	**45**	**23**	**32**	**34**	**99**		**6%**	**75**	**79**	**9%**	**10%**	**93**	**3%**	**68%**	**11.1**	**119**	**$15**

Valdez,Enmanuel

Age: 25	Pos: 2B		Health	A	LIMA Plan	D
Bats: L	Ht: 5'9"	Wt: 171	PT/Exp	B	Rand Var	0
			Consist	A	MM	4331

6-19-.266 with 5 SB in 148 PA at BOS. Solid dose of power/speed in limited MLB sample. Above-average pop might not be enough to overcome other flaws: low SB% tracks with minor league numbers; just 2 of his 44 starts were vL; poor defense questions PT outlook. Most signs point to him remaining a part-timer.

Yr	Tm	PA	R	HR	RBI	SB	BA	xHR	xSB	xBA	OBP	SLG	OPS+	vL+	vR+	bb%	ct%	Eye	G	L	F	h%	HctX	QBaB	Brl%	PX	xPX	HR/F	xHR/F	Spd	SBA%	SB%	RAR	BPX	R$
19																																			
20																																			
21	aa	92	9	4	14	0	221		1		307	434	102			11	69	0.40				27				136				87	5%	0%		138	-$
22	a/a	542	62	18	71	5	251		5		309	430	105			8	72	0.30				31				127				84	7%	61%		114	$1
23	BOS *	363	42	13	45	8	236	6	11	243	307	412	98	53	110	9	72	0.37	46	18	36	29	86	CCc	11%	107	102	16%	16%	127	15%	63%	5.9	114	$
1st Half		184	16	7	21	5	216	4	5	234	264	402	91	15	101	6	70	0.22	51	12	37	26	81	DCd	12%	113	110	16%	16%	126	21%	68%	-2.9	86	$
2nd Half		178	25	5	25	3	257	2	5	261	351	424	105	102	129	13	74	0.55	37	29	34	32	95	BCa	9%	100	86	17%	17%	117	10%	56%	4.8	136	$
24	Proj	**210**	**25**	**9**	**27**	**3**	**244**	**9**	**4**	**247**	**315**	**453**	**105**	**78**	**109**	**9**	**72**	**0.36**	**41**	**18**	**41**	**29**	**89**		**10%**	**128**	**96**	**16%**	**16%**	**105**	**11%**	**65%**	**5.8**	**115**	**$**

Vargas,Ildemaro

Age: 32	Pos: 3B		Health	B	LIMA Plan	D+
Bats: B	Ht: 6'0"	Wt: 180	PT/Exp	B	Rand Var	+1
			Consist	B	MM	1251

Puts the ball in play with the best of them (2nd-highest ct% in MLB), but quality of contact was again abysmal. Track record shows we can expect another low h% that leads to a BA well below his xBA with plus speed that doesn't translate to SB. There are far better targets for your late-round dart throws.

Yr	Tm	PA	R	HR	RBI	SB	BA	xHR	xSB	xBA	OBP	SLG	OPS+	vL+	vR+	bb%	ct%	Eye	G	L	F	h%	HctX	QBaB	Brl%	PX	xPX	HR/F	xHR/F	Spd	SBA%	SB%	RAR	BPX	R$
19	ARI *	342	37	7	38	2	283	4	4	299	316	419	102	143	82	5	91	0.51	53	23	25	29	107	CFf	3%	63	60	14%	9%	124	4%	55%	-7.1	226	$
20	3 TM	54	6	1	3	0	196	1	0	233	222	314	71	50	97	4	80	0.20	60	12	29	23	93	DFf	2%	56	74	8%	8%	141	0%	0%	-4.8	72	-$
21	3 NL *	340	32	5	26	2	196	0	2	263	229	298	72	44	72	4	84	0.26	55	20	25	22	114	DFf	2%	61	53	0%	0%	97	5%	65%	-22.9	85	-$
22	2 NL *	516	41	6	38	5	214	3	8	256	251	312	80	100	96	5	86	0.34	48	20	32	24	80	DDf	2%	61	46	7%	5%	125	9%	57%	-28.4	138	$
23	WAS	286	32	4	31	1	252	4	4	282	304	363	91	108	79	7	92	0.95	57	16	27	26	95	DFf	2%	58	42	6%	6%	109	3%	50%	-1.6	229	$
1st Half		81	13	2	11	0	289	2	1	326	325	461	108	111	104	5	96	1.33	59	18	23	28	100	CFc	6%	83	41	12%	12%	112	0%	0%	2.5	343	-$
2nd Half		205	19	2	20	1	237	2	3	261	296	323	84	106	71	7	91	0.88	56	16	28	25	93	DFf	1%	47	43	4%	4%	105	4%	50%	-5.9	179	$
24	Proj	**245**	**26**	**4**	**24**	**1**	**240**	**3**	**3**	**276**	**283**	**353**	**87**	**92**	**84**	**5**	**89**	**0.53**	**54**	**18**	**28**	**26**	**95**		**3%**	**62**	**47**	**6%**	**6%**	**113**	**4%**	**56%**	**-3.6**	**192**	**$**

Vargas,Miguel

Age: 24	Pos: 2B		Health	A	LIMA Plan	D+
Bats: R	Ht: 6'3"	Wt: 205	PT/Exp	A	Rand Var	+2
			Consist	B	MM	2313

7-32-.195 with 3 SB in 303 PA at LA. Broken pinky in spring, HBP (thumb) in April maybe led to slow start, but bb% spike was only sign of growth through July, when he was sent to AAA. Flyball tilt with modest power yielded a low combo of h%, HR/F, and xBA. Age and pedigree still on his side, but 2024 breakout seems unlikely.

Yr	Tm	PA	R	HR	RBI	SB	BA	xHR	xSB	xBA	OBP	SLG	OPS+	vL+	vR+	bb%	ct%	Eye	G	L	F	h%	HctX	QBaB	Brl%	PX	xPX	HR/F	xHR/F	Spd	SBA%	SB%	RAR	BPX	R$
19																																			
20																																			
21	aa	351	48	12	43	5	275		3		325	432	104			7	80	0.38				31				86				92	7%	82%		127	$1
22	LA *	528	62	12	56	10	230	1	11	216	291	365	93	66	62	8	79	0.40	34	14	51	27	148	BAc	9%	88	142	6%	6%	114	14%	64%	-10.3	128	$1
23	LA *	569	66	14	61	8	216	8	11	227	312	376	94	94	90	12	74	0.53	37	16	47	26	89	DBf	6%	100	107	8%	9%	115	8%	81%	0.5	129	$
1st Half		289	34	7	32	3	199	8	6	241	302	374	93	95	92	13	77	0.64	38	16	46	23	95	CBf	6%	102	111	8%	9%	137	8%	60%	-2.9	211	$
2nd Half		280	32	7	29	5	233	0	4	148	322	378	95	67	75	12	70	0.44	20	0	80	30	0	DBf	0%	97	-21	0%	0%	93	7%	100%	2.0	43	$
24	Proj	**280**	**34**	**8**	**31**	**5**	**231**	**7**	**5**	**230**	**309**	**391**	**96**	**97**	**95**	**10**	**76**	**0.47**	**38**	**16**	**46**	**27**	**97**		**6%**	**97**	**100**	**9%**	**8%**	**107**	**9%**	**74%**	**2.5**	**119**	**$**

BRIAN RUDD

Varsho,Daulton

Age: 27	Pos: LF CF		Health	A	LIMA Plan	B+
Bats: L	Ht: 5' 10"	Wt: 207	PT/Exp	A	Rand Var	+1
			Consist	B	MM	3325

Second straight 20+/16 HR/SB season, but fewer counting stats caused R$ to slip (along with global devaluation of SB). Couldn't hold 2022's power skill spike and xBA trend gives pause for BA rebound. Green light bodes well for SB floor, however. Loss of catcher eligibility stings, but power/speed blend keeps him relevant as a mid-tier outfielder.

Yr	Tm	PA	R	HR	RBI	SB	BA	xHR	xSB	xBA	OBP	SLG	OPS+	vL+	vR+	bb%	ct%	Eye	G	L	F	h%	HctX	QBaB	Brl%	PX	xPX	HR/F	xHR/F	Spd	SBA%	SB%	RAR	BPX	R$
19	aa	437	80	16	55	20	289		16		355	502	119			9	83	0.60				31				103				130	23%	78%		274	$21
20	ARI	115	16	3	9	3	188	4	3	218	287	366	87	44	108	10	67	0.36	39	19	42	25	76	FBf	4%	110	87	11%	15%	134	17%	75%	-7.4	80	$4
21	ARI *	399	51	16	52	7	243	12	4	254	307	447	104	111	101	8	76	0.39	36	22	43	28	106	DBf	7%	118	119	12%	13%	95	9%	100%	1.7	181	$11
22	ARI	591	79	27	74	16	235	23	12	241	302	443	105	77	114	8	73	0.32	40	15	44	27	108	DCf	10%	131	158	16%	14%	90	18%	73%	3.6	138	$22
23	TOR	580	65	20	61	16	220	20	15	232	285	389	92	97	90	8	74	0.33	32	20	47	26	89	DAf	7%	99	101	11%	11%	99	19%	70%	-4.5	86	$11
1st Half		331	37	12	29	11	224	10	8	239	290	388	93	78	96	8	75	0.36	34	21	45	26	95	DBf	7%	96	99	12%	10%	80	20%	79%	-3.1	71	$14
2nd Half		249	28	8	32	5	215	9	7	224	278	390	90	118	83	7	73	0.30	31	19	51	26	80	DAd	8%	103	104	10%	11%	119	19%	56%	-5.5	100	$8
24	Proj	595	76	23	71	16	228	23	14	238	294	418	98	92	100	8	74	0.33	35	19	46	27	94		8%	112	117	12%	12%	106	18%	72%	1.4	124	$16

Vaughn,Andrew

Age: 26	Pos: 1B		Health	A	LIMA Plan	B
Bats: R	Ht: 6' 0"	Wt: 215	PT/Exp	A	Rand Var	0
			Consist	A	MM	3135

Through mid-season, it looked like 2022 and 2023 would be mostly comparable years. But took a foul ball off his foot on July 18, and while it did not land him on the IL, it cost some time and his metrics slid after that. Give him a mulligan on that 2nd half and you'll see the growth more clearly. When bidding stops in the mid-teens, go an extra buck.

Yr	Tm	PA	R	HR	RBI	SB	BA	xHR	xSB	xBA	OBP	SLG	OPS+	vL+	vR+	bb%	ct%	Eye	G	L	F	h%	HctX	QBaB	Brl%	PX	xPX	HR/F	xHR/F	Spd	SBA%	SB%	RAR	BPX	R$
19																																			
20																																			
21	CHW	469	56	15	48	1	235	18	1	244	309	396	97	128	84	9	76	0.41	44	20	36	28	110	ACd	11%	97	117	13%	16%	88	2%	50%	-7.4	100	$7
22	CHW	555	60	17	76	0	271	17	1	257	321	429	106	104	107	6	81	0.32	48	18	34	30	111	BDd	8%	98	108	12%	12%	86	0%	0%	8.6	145	$17
23	CHW	615	67	21	80	0	258	21	3	255	314	429	101	86	106	6	77	0.28	44	20	36	30	109	BCd	8%	100	93	13%	13%	86	0%	0%	10.9	100	$15
1st Half		354	40	12	51	0	248	14	2	261	328	446	106	101	108	8	79	0.42	44	16	40	28	113	ACd	10%	116	100	12%	14%	84	0%	0%	2.9	186	$17
2nd Half		261	27	9	29	0	270	7	1	250	295	409	95	66	103	3	75	0.13	44	25	31	33	103	BDf	6%	80	84	16%	12%	88	0%	0%	-1.4	-7	$11
24	Proj	630	71	23	86	0	261	21	2	255	312	433	102	97	104	6	78	0.28	45	20	36	30	109		8%	100	101	14%	13%	84	0%	50%	8.8	101	$21

Vázquez,Christian

Age: 33	Pos: CA		Health	A	LIMA Plan	D
Bats: R	Ht: 5' 9"	Wt: 205	PT/Exp	A	Rand Var	+2
			Consist	B	MM	1123

Started fine (.262 Mar/Apr) but hit a bump (.196 May) and was relegated to a playing time share from that point on. Results only got minimally better in 2nd half. Dormant power skills (xPX, xHR/F) hint at another single-digit HR season, while sizable ct% drop lowers odds of potential BA rebound. Does better as a regular; value him based on his role.

Yr	Tm	PA	R	HR	RBI	SB	BA	xHR	xSB	xBA	OBP	SLG	OPS+	vL+	vR+	bb%	ct%	Eye	G	L	F	h%	HctX	QBaB	Brl%	PX	xPX	HR/F	xHR/F	Spd	SBA%	SB%	RAR	BPX	R$
19	BOS	521	66	23	72	4	276	18	3	270	320	477	110	124	103	6	79	0.33	39	23	38	31	92	BCb	6%	103	100	16%	13%	81	5%	67%	24.3	141	$16
20	BOS	189	22	7	23	4	283	5	4	242	344	457	106	102	108	8	75	0.37	42	20	38	34	94	CBf	5%	100	96	14%	10%	88	14%	57%	6.0	104	$18
21	BOS	498	51	6	49	8	258	7	5	238	308	352	91	75	98	7	82	0.39	41	22	38	30	76	DCd	3%	58	67	4%	5%	74	10%	67%	-3.5	42	$11
22	2 AL	426	41	9	52	1	274	8	2	262	315	399	101	115	96	5	83	0.32	45	23	32	31	94	CCd	5%	82	73	8%	7%	53	5%	20%	7.6	83	$11
23	MIN	355	34	6	32	1	223	4	1	232	280	318	81	105	75	7	75	0.30	43	23	34	28	84	DCf	3%	61	77	7%	5%	65	1%	100%	-3.9	-54	$1
1st Half		187	17	1	17	0	222	2	1	246	299	281	80	98	75	10	74	0.42	38	31	30	29	99	CCd	2%	45	91	3%	5%	67	0%	0%	-4.3	-89	-$5
2nd Half		168	17	5	15	1	225	2	1	223	257	356	83	110	74	4	76	0.18	48	15	38	27	68	DDf	5%	78	63	11%	4%	70	3%	100%	-2.6	-14	$0
24	Proj	280	28	6	29	2	247	4	2	241	295	361	90	102	85	6	78	0.30	43	22	35	30	84		4%	71	75	8%	6%	67	5%	58%	1.5	17	$7

Velázquez,Nelson

Age: 25	Pos: RF		Health	A	LIMA Plan	C
Bats: R	Ht: 6' 0"	Wt: 190	PT/Exp	B	Rand Var	+3
			Consist	C	MM	5333

17-34-.235 BA in 179 PA at CHC/KC. Spent most of 1st half in AAA, but went on power binge with 14 HR in 147 MLB PA after July 31 trade. The ct% is dreadful and xBA confirms he's a BA liability, but the power metrics were off the charts (xPX, Brl%, xHR/F). A high-risk profile with all those Ks, but the reward might be... UP: 40 HR.

Yr	Tm	PA	R	HR	RBI	SB	BA	xHR	xSB	xBA	OBP	SLG	OPS+	vL+	vR+	bb%	ct%	Eye	G	L	F	h%	HctX	QBaB	Brl%	PX	xPX	HR/F	xHR/F	Spd	SBA%	SB%	RAR	BPX	R$
19																																			
20																																			
21	aa	132	14	6	20	4	253		2		296	480	107			6	69	0.20				32				149				94	17%	100%		138	$3
22	CHC *	426	43	15	46	13	196	9	15	203	264	373	90	106	85	8	58	0.22	43	17	41	29	85	CCf	14%	141	144	12%	18%	151	25%	65%	-14.5	31	$7
23	2 TM *	514	67	27	63	6	206	15	7	221	261	414	92	95	132	7	66	0.22	38	14	47	25	93	ABf	21%	134	171	32%	28%	82	11%	63%	-6.6	36	$9
1st Half		255	32	10	26	3	218	2	5	242	277	390	91	81	165	8	66	0.24	48	24	29	29	76	BFc	19%	118	146	50%	33%	83	15%	43%	-6.2	-7	$6
2nd Half		259	35	17	37	3	195	13	3	225	246	439	92	100	126	6	66	0.20	36	12	52	21	97	ABf	22%	150	177	30%	28%	94	7%	100%	-5.3	93	$12
24	Proj	420	49	29	52	9	221	26	8	249	283	496	107	92	115	7	64	0.22	42	17	42	26	90		18%	179	156	28%	25%	110	18%	70%	5.6	58	$15

Verdugo,Alex

Age: 28	Pos: RF		Health	A	LIMA Plan	A
Bats: L	Ht: 6' 0"	Wt: 192	PT/Exp	A	Rand Var	+2
			Consist	A	MM	2255

Previously-stable BA sunk to new lows. A combination of 2nd half misfortune (h%) and skills slide (ct% drop) was behind it, though track record and penchant for outhitting xBA hint at rebound potential. A consistent compiler, but not a HR/SB threat and hasn't shown that his ceiling is any higher. Concerning lefty splits might chip away at high PA total.

Yr	Tm	PA	R	HR	RBI	SB	BA	xHR	xSB	xBA	OBP	SLG	OPS+	vL+	vR+	bb%	ct%	Eye	G	L	F	h%	HctX	QBaB	Brl%	PX	xPX	HR/F	xHR/F	Spd	SBA%	SB%	RAR	BPX	R$
19	LA	377	43	12	44	4	294	10	3	297	342	475	113	117	111	7	86	0.53	49	23	29	32	129	BDc	6%	90	91	14%	12%	95	5%	80%	8.5	219	$10
20	BOS	221	36	6	15	4	308	6	4	271	367	478	112	103	117	8	78	0.38	52	20	27	37	102	CDd	6%	104	82	14%	14%	127	7%	100%	8.7	196	$22
21	BOS	604	88	13	63	6	289	16	7	271	351	426	107	75	123	8	82	0.53	50	22	29	33	103	BDc	7%	80	71	10%	12%	109	5%	75%	14.5	173	$21
22	BOS	644	75	11	74	1	280	17	3	268	328	405	104	97	106	7	85	0.49	46	21	33	31	114	CDc	6%	81	90	7%	10%	85	3%	25%	7.5	162	$20
23	BOS	602	81	13	54	5	264	12	9	277	324	421	102	82	108	7	83	0.48	45	21	34	30	119	BDd	5%	91	90	8%	8%	103	6%	63%	12.0	186	$14
1st Half		344	53	6	34	3	295	7	6	294	363	464	113	91	123	9	85	0.63	45	22	33	33	127	CDc	5%	99	97	7%	8%	113	6%	60%	14.8	261	$20
2nd Half		258	28	7	20	2	223	6	3	254	271	366	86	63	92	6	80	0.34	46	19	35	25	108	BCd	5%	81	81	10%	9%	88	6%	67%	-6.8	96	$4
24	Proj	560	73	14	55	4	269	14	6	274	324	424	103	86	109	7	83	0.46	47	21	32	30	113		6%	90	86	10%	10%	97	5%	64%	11.6	168	$19

Vientos,Mark

Age: 24	Pos: DH		Health	A	LIMA Plan	D+
Bats: R	Ht: 6' 4"	Wt: 185	PT/Exp	A	Rand Var	+2
			Consist	A	MM	3003

9-22-.211 in 233 PA at NYM. Struggled after May call-up, injured wrist in Aug, then showed pulse with regular playing time in Sept (6 HR, 129 xPX in 90 PA). Some thump per power metrics, but too many GBs limit HR ceiling and struggled to make consistent contact. Has long-term potential, but expect some bumps in the road.

Yr	Tm	PA	R	HR	RBI	SB	BA	xHR	xSB	xBA	OBP	SLG	OPS+	vL+	vR+	bb%	ct%	Eye	G	L	F	h%	HctX	QBaB	Brl%	PX	xPX	HR/F	xHR/F	Spd	SBA%	SB%	RAR	BPX	R$
19																																			
20																																			
21	a/a	336	37	17	45	0	227		1		281	440	99			7	62	0.20				31				147				80	3%	0%		15	$5
22	NYM *	448	46	17	50	0	218	2	3	171	278	376	93	113	38	8	61	0.21	50	4	46	31	78	ACf	11%	119	79	9%	18%	107	2%	0%	-13.3	-31	$5
23	NYM *	486	45	19	56	1	224	11	4	235	274	403	92	79	88	6	68	0.21	52	17	32	28	116	ACc	11%	115	110	19%	23%	104	1%	100%	-3.7	39	$6
1st Half		245	23	10	34	0	233	2	1	256	296	417	98	56	69	8	69	0.29	53	25	22	29	124	AFb	16%	117	104	14%	29%	84	0%	0%	-0.5	54	$6
2nd Half		241	22	9	22	1	215	8	3	227	250	389	86	84	92	4	67	0.14	51	15	34	28	112	ACd	9%	113	112	20%	20%	131	2%	100%	-6.9	32	$3
24	Proj	350	35	11	40	0	222	13	3	218	276	371	89	85	91	7	65	0.20	52	19	29	31	117		12%	103	109	18%	21%	110	2%	33%	-8.2	12	$6

Vierling,Matt

Age: 27	Pos: RF LF 3B CF		Health	A	LIMA Plan	B
Bats: R	Ht: 6' 3"	Wt: 205	PT/Exp	A	Rand Var	0
			Consist	B	MM	1325

Modest all-around production in first full season, though it was front-loaded. Contact and power skills both dropped in 2nd half as he hit more GBs, and SB opportunities dried up given feeble success on the basepaths. There's 15/15 potential if raw speed translates to more bags, but more of a streaming option until that happens.

Yr	Tm	PA	R	HR	RBI	SB	BA	xHR	xSB	xBA	OBP	SLG	OPS+	vL+	vR+	bb%	ct%	Eye	G	L	F	h%	HctX	QBaB	Brl%	PX	xPX	HR/F	xHR/F	Spd	SBA%	SB%	RAR	BPX	R$
19																																			
20																																			
21	PHI *	395	38	10	37	9	255	2	10	255	308	385	95	107	127	7	73	0.29	54	25	21	32	115	ADb	4%	77	46	18%	18%	140	11%	79%	-4.1	46	$10
22	PHI *	448	50	7	38	12	239	8	13	239	289	349	90	106	82	7	78	0.33	41	23	36	29	117	ACc	5%	70	91	6%	9%	135	17%	65%	-9.4	86	$10
23	DET	530	63	10	44	6	261	12	18	250	329	388	98	94	99	8	77	0.39	49	21	31	32	103	CDd	5%	76	84	9%	11%	158	9%	50%	5.8	118	$11
1st Half		238	26	7	22	4	275	7	9	255	336	427	105	85	113	8	79	0.40	45	20	35	32	123	BCd	6%	82	122	12%	12%	147	14%	44%	4.2	157	$8
2nd Half		292	37	3	22	2	249	5	8	245	323	356	92	103	88	9	74	0.39	52	21	27	32	87	CDd	4%	70	51	6%	9%	154	4%	67%	-1.0	71	$7
24	Proj	490	56	10	42	9	252	12	15	247	313	374	94	97	92	8	77	0.36	47	22	31	31	109		5%	73	78	9%	11%	130	12%	63%	-1.3	90	$14

CORBIN YOUNG

Villar,David

Age: 27	Pos: 2B		Health	A	LIMA Plan	F
Bats: R	Ht: 6' 1"	Wt: 215	PT/Exp	A	Rand Var	+2
			Consist	B	MM	4201

5-12-.145 in 140 PA at SF. Opened season in starting role, but combination of poor ct% and low h% soon sent him to bench, then AAA. Though power held up well, strikeouts ensure the HR will come with harmful BA, making it tough to hold down regular job. The pop should keep him on deep-league radars, but that's all he has to offer.

Yr	Tm	PA	R	HR	RBI	SB	BA	xHR	xSB	xBA	OBP	SLG	OPS+	vL+	vR+	bb%	ct%	Eye	G	L	F	h%	HctX	QBaB	Brl%	PX	xPX	HR/F	xHR/F	Spd	SBA%	SB%	RAR	BPX	R$
19																																			
20																																			
21	aa	422	56	14	46	4	233		3		300	408	97			9	67	0.29				31				124				85	6%	78%		42	$
22	SF *	513	60	24	72	1	217	6	3	224	297	429	103	137	92	10	62	0.30	37	18	44	29	99	CAa	9%	159	192	20%	14%	94	3%	21%	-0.9	93	$1
23	SF *	456	50	15	45	4	190	6	4	202	262	337	82	53	92	9	63	0.26	34	20	46	26	80	CAc	14%	105	140	14%	17%	69	6%	81%	-13.2	-89	$
1st Half		202	21	7	24	1	185	6	2	223	256	357	84	59	96	9	67	0.29	32	21	47	23	86	CAc	14%	116	149	14%	17%	69	5%	50%	-6.4	0	-$
2nd Half		254	30	7	21	3	194	0	3	181	267	321	79	17	27	9	59	0.24	75	0	25	29	60	FCa	0%	95	-21	0%	0%	88	5%	100%	-8.2	-146	$
24	**Proj**	**140**	**17**	**6**	**16**	**1**	**207**	**5**	**1**	**218**	**299**	**401**	**96**	**93**	**98**	**9**	**63**	**0.28**	**34**	**20**	**46**	**27**	**91**		**12%**	**135**	**166**	**17%**	**13%**	**89**	**4%**	**71%**	**-0.2**	**-5**	**-$**

Vogelbach,Daniel

Age: 31	Pos: DH		Health	B	LIMA Plan	D
Bats: L	Ht: 6' 0"	Wt: 270	PT/Exp	B	Rand Var	-1
			Consist	B	MM	3113

Skills and results nosedived early on, but power stroke eventually returned, finished with a flourish (1.002 OPS in final 79 PA). The 2nd half BA sure looks like an aberration given h% spike and he didn't play vL, but should remain viable power source vR. That keeps him in play as a streaming option, but you'll have to pick your spots.

Yr	Tm	PA	R	HR	RBI	SB	BA	xHR	xSB	xBA	OBP	SLG	OPS+	vL+	vR+	bb%	ct%	Eye	G	L	F	h%	HctX	QBaB	Brl%	PX	xPX	HR/F	xHR/F	Spd	SBA%	SB%	RAR	BPX	R$
19	SEA	558	73	30	76	0	208	25	-	240	341	439	108	84	116	16	68	0.62	33	22	45	23	90	CBc	11%	130	123	21%	18%	33	0%	0%	-6.5	74	$
20	3 TM	136	16	6	16	0	209	5	0	233	331	391	96	46	102	15	71	0.61	46	21	33	24	92	BCc	9%	101	77	22%	19%	43	0%	0%	-2.6	40	$
21	MIL *	316	35	11	29	0	220	6	0	224	351	375	100	50	108	17	72	0.71	44	20	35	27	98	ACc	8%	91	98	16%	11%	50	0%	0%	-6.2	38	$
22	2 NL	461	47	18	59	0	238	19	0	243	360	433	112	58	125	16	70	0.64	38	21	41	29	102	BBc	11%	131	136	16%	17%	31	0%	0%	7.2	103	$
23	NYM	319	33	13	48	0	233	11	0	221	339	404	101	8	107	13	71	0.52	43	18	39	28	110	ABc	9%	101	123	17%	15%	34	0%	0%	4.0	7	$
1st Half		184	18	5	23	0	209	4	0	209	321	342	91	0	97	14	71	0.57	49	16	35	26	93	ACd	5%	84	93	13%	10%	34	0%	0%	-5.3	-32	-$
2nd Half		135	15	8	25	0	265	7	0	240	363	487	115	27	118	12	70	0.46	35	21	44	31	132	ABb	14%	125	165	22%	19%	55	0%	0%	4.6	82	$
24	**Proj**	**280**	**30**	**12**	**39**	**0**	**235**	**10**	**0**	**230**	**348**	**418**	**105**	**48**	**112**	**14**	**70**	**0.57**	**40**	**20**	**40**	**28**	**108**		**10%**	**110**	**127**	**18%**	**16%**	**40**	**0%**	**100%**	**5.2**	**55**	**$**

Volpe,Anthony

Age: 23	Pos: SS		Health	A	LIMA Plan	B
Bats: R	Ht: 5' 11"	Wt: 180	PT/Exp	A	Rand Var	+2
			Consist	A	MM	3425

Lived up to pre-season hype in some ways, but still plenty of work to do. PRO: Plus Spd, green light reveal enticing SB upside; above-average power held firm. CON: Struggled to put ball in play; SB% slipped in 2nd half. VERDICT: Power/speed combo worth investing in, but surround him with strong BA foundation.

Yr	Tm	PA	R	HR	RBI	SB	BA	xHR	xSB	xBA	OBP	SLG	OPS+	vL+	vR+	bb%	ct%	Eye	G	L	F	h%	HctX	QBaB	Brl%	PX	xPX	HR/F	xHR/F	Spd	SBA%	SB%	RAR	BPX	R$
19																																			
20																																			
21																																			
22	a/a	561	65	16	49	38	210		24		280	374	93			9	74	0.37				25				110				106	41%	85%		121	$2
23	NYY	601	62	21	60	24	209	20	21	238	283	383	91	110	85	9	69	0.31	41	22	37	26	95	CCc	9%	109	112	15%	14%	119	24%	83%	-3.1	68	$1
1st Half		312	33	10	29	16	221	11	13	230	296	386	93	109	89	9	67	0.32	42	22	36	29	96	CCb	9%	104	111	15%	16%	138	25%	94%	-2.2	50	$1
2nd Half		289	29	11	31	8	195	9	8	247	270	379	88	112	82	8	71	0.31	40	22	38	23	93	CCc	9%	114	113	15%	13%	102	23%	67%	-9.9	89	$
24	**Proj**	**595**	**65**	**22**	**58**	**30**	**235**	**21**	**25**	**245**	**307**	**418**	**99**	**112**	**96**	**9**	**71**	**0.33**	**41**	**22**	**37**	**29**	**94**		**9%**	**114**	**112**	**15%**	**14%**	**107**	**27%**	**82%**	**8.1**	**92**	**$2**

Votto,Joey

Age: 40	Pos: 1B		Health	F	LIMA Plan	D+
Bats: L	Ht: 6' 2"	Wt: 220	PT/Exp	B	Rand Var	+2
			Consist	D	MM	4213

14-38-.202 in 242 PA at CIN. Shoulder injury kept him out until June and cost him more time later on. Skills have clearly slipped, but ct% improved after bumpy start, and Brl% says the power held firm. Count on missed time and low BA, but still enough thump in this bat to make one final run at double-digit R$, should he decide to return.

Yr	Tm	PA	R	HR	RBI	SB	BA	xHR	xSB	xBA	OBP	SLG	OPS+	vL+	vR+	bb%	ct%	Eye	G	L	F	h%	HctX	QBaB	Brl%	PX	xPX	HR/F	xHR/F	Spd	SBA%	SB%	RAR	BPX	R$
19	CIN	608	79	15	47	5	261	20	3	253	357	411	106	91	112	13	77	0.62	37	25	38	32	110	CBa	7%	86	116	10%	13%	88	3%	100%	-4.7	107	$1
20	CIN	223	32	11	22	0	226	11	0	262	354	446	106	88	112	17	77	0.86	38	22	39	23	113	CBa	9%	117	144	20%	20%	84	0%	0%	-3.9	248	$1
21	CIN *	555	74	36	100	1	260	37	0	278	366	549	126	96	145	14	71	0.58	32	26	42	29	131	AAb	0%	167	173	26%	27%	78	1%	100%	27.6	281	$2
22	CIN	376	31	11	41	0	205	14	0	229	319	370	98	98	97	12	70	0.45	44	18	37	26	103	BBc	11%	118	104	13%	17%	69	0%	0%	-10.7	69	$
23	CIN *	333	31	16	45	0	182	10	1	195	275	378	89	121	96	11	63	0.35	48	11	41	22	85	BCd	11%	128	113	23%	17%	65	0%	0%	-9.0	0	$
1st Half		128	10	5	14	0	129	2	0	134	235	283	71	126	83	12	48	0.27	40	5	55	19	59	BBf	17%	128	129	27%	18%	79	0%	0%	-9.1	-193	-$
2nd Half		205	21	11	31	0	215	8	1	226	301	437	100	118	98	11	72	0.44	49	12	39	23	98	BCc	10%	128	110	22%	16%	67	0%	0%	-0.6	125	$
24	**Proj**	**350**	**36**	**18**	**47**	**0**	**204**	**16**	**1**	**229**	**320**	**426**	**102**	**106**	**101**	**12**	**67**	**0.42**	**42**	**15**	**42**	**24**	**98**		**10%**	**141**	**124**	**21%**	**18%**	**70**	**0%**	**100%**	**0.9**	**76**	**$**

Wade Jr.,LaMonte

Age: 30	Pos: 1B OF		Health	C	LIMA Plan	B
Bats: L	Ht: 6' 1"	Wt: 205	PT/Exp	A	Rand Var	-2
			Consist	D	MM	2325

Improved health and leadoff spot vR led to career-high in PA. Put together big 1st half that was fueled by massive bb% and higher-than-usual h%, both of which proved unsustainable. Dramatic platoon splits (44 of 45 career HR vR) rule out full-time PA, but enough juice to carve out plenty of value in strong-side platoon.

Yr	Tm	PA	R	HR	RBI	SB	BA	xHR	xSB	xBA	OBP	SLG	OPS+	vL+	vR+	bb%	ct%	Eye	G	L	F	h%	HctX	QBaB	Brl%	PX	xPX	HR/F	xHR/F	Spd	SBA%	SB%	RAR	BPX	R$
19	MIN *	404	52	6	28	6	217	2	7	249	335	330	92	42	108	15	81	0.92	45	21	34	25	107	CCd	6%	61	96	13%	13%	112	8%	64%	-19.2	137	$
20	MIN	44	3	0	1	1	231	0	1	203	318	308	83	0	92	9	77	0.44	37	17	47	30	104	DBf		61	107	0%	0%	89	18%	50%	-2.7	12	-$
21	SF *	435	60	20	61	6	244	17	5	248	319	464	108	53	119	10	72	0.40	33	23	44	29	111	CAd	11%	128	138	16%	15%	108	8%	73%	2.5	177	$1
22	SF *	301	35	9	32	1	203	10	1	225	289	353	91	35	104	11	78	0.54	32	19	50	23	80	CAf	10%	92	117	10%	12%	79	1%	100%	-7.3	107	$
23	SF	519	64	17	45	2	256	19	7	245	373	417	108	96	110	15	78	0.80	38	21	41	29	102	CBf	9%	87	108	12%	14%	105	1%	100%	15.9	157	$1
1st Half		300	40	9	27	2	279	11	4	255	416	450	119	99	123	18	77	0.95	43	20	37	33	99	DCf	10%	100	104	13%	16%	101	2%	100%	16.4	196	$1
2nd Half		219	24	8	18	0	228	7	2	233	313	376	93	89	94	11	79	0.59	32	21	47	25	107	CAf	8%	72	112	11%	10%	115	0%	0%	-1.8	118	$
24	**Proj**	**490**	**62**	**18**	**49**	**3**	**245**	**19**	**5**	**241**	**347**	**414**	**104**	**72**	**110**	**12**	**77**	**0.63**	**35**	**21**	**44**	**28**	**99**		**9%**	**93**	**114**	**12%**	**13%**	**97**	**3%**	**80%**	**9.4**	**142**	**$1**

Walker,Christian

Age: 33	Pos: 1B		Health	B	LIMA Plan	B+
Bats: R	Ht: 6' 0"	Wt: 208	PT/Exp	A	Rand Var	+1
			Consist	B	MM	4235

Though power metrics took a slight step back, continued to amass huge volume with plenty of barrels, leading to a near repeat in HR. Provided surprising boost to value with success on the basepaths while also maintaining ct%, xBA gains. Age, track record point to some SB regression, but the rest of his 2023 line looks doable again.

Yr	Tm	PA	R	HR	RBI	SB	BA	xHR	xSB	xBA	OBP	SLG	OPS+	vL+	vR+	bb%	ct%	Eye	G	L	F	h%	HctX	QBaB	Brl%	PX	xPX	HR/F	xHR/F	Spd	SBA%	SB%	RAR	BPX	R$
19	ARI	603	86	29	73	8	259	34	5	248	348	476	114	110	115	11	71	0.43	42	20	38	31	113	ABc	13%	122	127	20%	24%	91	6%	89%	4.0	119	$1
20	ARI	243	35	7	34	1	271	9	2	270	333	459	105	99	107	8	77	0.38	43	23	34	32	140	BCf	6%	114	117	12%	16%	94	4%	50%	-4.3	180	$1
21	ARI	445	55	10	46	0	244	10	1	234	315	382	96	90	98	9	74	0.36	39	22	39	31	107	CBd	6%	89	103	9%	9%	97	0%	0%	-10.7	54	$
22	ARI	667	84	36	94	2	242	36	4	263	327	477	114	118	112	10	78	0.53	38	17	44	25	128	BBd	12%	138	143	18%	18%	92	3%	50%	8.2	245	$2
23	ARI	660	86	33	103	11	258	30	9	270	333	497	113	124	109	9	78	0.49	38	17	45	28	105	CBf	11%	134	117	16%	14%	83	7%	100%	25.5	236	$2
1st Half		344	44	16	54	4	269	14	3	276	334	506	115	117	114	9	81	0.51	37	16	47	29	113	BAd	10%	136	112	13%	12%	71	5%	100%	14.3	261	$2
2nd Half		316	42	17	49	7	245	16	6	263	332	485	111	132	104	10	75	0.47	40	18	42	26	96	DCf	13%	132	122	19%	18%	105	9%	100%	8.8	218	$2
24	**Proj**	**630**	**84**	**29**	**92**	**6**	**251**	**29**	**6**	**259**	**328**	**467**	**109**	**120**	**105**	**10**	**77**	**0.45**	**39**	**18**	**43**	**28**	**112**		**11%**	**124**	**122**	**16%**	**15%**	**85**	**5%**	**78%**	**18.7**	**202**	**$2**

Walker,Jordan

Age: 22	Pos: RF		Health	A	LIMA Plan	B
Bats: R	Ht: 6' 5"	Wt: 220	PT/Exp	A	Rand Var	-1
			Consist	C	MM	3325

16-51-.276 with 7 SB in 465 PA at STL. Didn't hit enough early on to make up for subpar defense, leading to April demotion. Came back with higher FB%/xPX, which bodes well for power outlook, though xBA hints at risk of slight BA regression. Combo of age/pedigree puts breakout in play, but more likely scenario is a small step forward.

Yr	Tm	PA	R	HR	RBI	SB	BA	xHR	xSB	xBA	OBP	SLG	OPS+	vL+	vR+	bb%	ct%	Eye	G	L	F	h%	HctX	QBaB	Brl%	PX	xPX	HR/F	xHR/F	Spd	SBA%	SB%	RAR	BPX	R$
19																																			
20																																			
21																																			
22	aa	494	58	10	40	13	238		11		288	363	92			7	73	0.26				31				90				102	18%	69%		31	$
23	STL *	589	61	19	62	10	260	13	12	242	321	418	101	92	112	8	74	0.35	47	18	35	32	105	BCc	8%	95	92	14%	12%	102	10%	71%	10.4	75	$
1st Half		296	27	9	33	6	258	5	7	243	319	400	98	76	121	8	74	0.34	58	17	26	32	125	AFc	9%	88	69	19%	16%	81	13%	59%	0.5	29	$
2nd Half		293	34	10	29	4	261	8	6	242	328	436	103	97	106	8	74	0.35	40	19	41	32	93	CCc	7%	103	107	12%	10%	125	6%	100%	5.9	125	$
24	**Proj**	**560**	**62**	**20**	**54**	**12**	**251**	**17**	**12**	**246**	**315**	**424**	**101**	**93**	**104**	**7**	**74**	**0.30**	**47**	**18**	**35**	**30**	**106**		**8%**	**105**	**92**	**15%**	**12%**	**105**	**13%**	**73%**	**7.0**	**63**	**$**

BRIAN RUDD

Wallner,Matt

Age: 26 Pos: LF RF | Bats: L Ht: 6'5" Wt: 220
Health A | PT/Exp B | Consist B
LIMA Plan C+ | Rand Var -1 | MM 4115

14-41-.249 in 254 PA at MIN. Bounced between AAA and majors before settling into strong-side platoon by July, thanks to mega-struggles vs LHPs in small sample. Prodigious power from minors didn't skip a beat (Brl%, xHR/F), but it came with a Gallo-ian mass of Ks. A potentially premier power source, but it might come with a mega BA hit.

Yr Tm	PA	R	HR	RBI	SB	BA	xHR	xSB	xBA	OBP	SLG	OPS+	vL+	vR+	bb%	ct%	Eye	G	L	F	h%	HctX	QBaB	Brl%	PX	xPX	HR/F	xHR/F	Spd	SBA%	SB%	RAR	BPX	R$
19																																		
20																																		
21																																		
22 MIN *	584	60	18	69	7	216	2	9	213	307	386	98	48	122	12	56	0.29	53	19	28	35	53	CCf	12%	152	48	22%	22%	104	10%	52%	-6.7	3	$10
23 MIN *	535	75	21	72	2	237	17	6	217	317	441	103	65	133	10	60	0.29	32	20	47	35	89	AAf	19%	153	116	22%	27%	106	2%	67%	11.3	54	$13
1st Half	270	32	8	32	1	252	2	4	230	322	433	103	0	167	9	57	0.24	47	27	27	41	93	ACf	13%	149	63	25%	50%	113	3%	50%	3.8	4	$9
2nd Half	265	43	13	40	1	221	15	3	226	312	452	103	67	128	12	62	0.35	31	19	50	29	93	AAd	19%	157	123	22%	25%	102	2%	100%	3.2	111	$14
24 Proj	490	64	22	65	2	227	26	7	224	339	443	107	57	123	11	60	0.31	40	19	41	32	77		16%	159	93	20%	24%	101	4%	50%	8.5	41	$11

Walls,Taylor

Age: 27 Pos: 3B 2B SS | Bats: B Ht: 5'10" Wt: 185
Health B | PT/Exp A | Consist C
LIMA Plan D+ | Rand Var 0 | MM 1403

Shot out of gate with 7 HR and 15 SB through May, then hit some... walls. July oblique strain cost him six weeks as strikeouts piled up, HR pace predictably slowed, and wasn't as aggressive on basepaths. Smooth enough with the leather to hold down utility role, but SB prowess isn't enough to overcome some glaring holes in BA/HR skills.

Yr Tm	PA	R	HR	RBI	SB	BA	xHR	xSB	xBA	OBP	SLG	OPS+	vL+	vR+	bb%	ct%	Eye	G	L	F	h%	HctX	QBaB	Brl%	PX	xPX	HR/F	xHR/F	Spd	SBA%	SB%	RAR	BPX	R$
19 aa	236	40	5	19	14	252		14		332	445	108			11	72	0.43				32				111				146	44%	59%		167	$8
20																																		
21 TAM *	387	48	8	39	12	212	2	10	211	326	339	91	83	84	15	64	0.47	47	20	33	31	91	CCb	3%	95	118	3%	6%	91	20%	61%	-8.7	-31	$7
22 TAM	465	53	8	33	10	172	9	9	211	268	285	78	75	80	11	71	0.43	37	21	42	22	79	DBd	6%	82	100	7%	8%	111	14%	77%	-22.7	17	$0
23 TAM	349	50	8	36	22	201	5	16	207	305	333	87	105	80	13	70	0.48	35	19	46	26	70	DAf	3%	85	86	8%	5%	116	27%	96%	-1.2	29	$7
1st Half	247	38	7	26	17	213	4	12	218	312	375	94	125	83	12	73	0.51	34	17	50	26	66	CAd	4%	99	87	9%	5%	119	31%	94%	-0.7	114	$13
2nd Half	102	12	1	10	5	172	1	3	184	287	230	70	54	75	14	62	0.42	40	25	36	26	78	DCd	2%	44	83	5%	5%	104	19%	100%	-5.4	-196	-$4
24 Proj	350	46	5	32	16	204	5	13	207	306	309	84	85	84	13	69	0.47	39	21	40	28	78		4%	72	95	6%	6%	112	22%	82%	-6.4	-20	$9

Walsh,Jared

Age: 30 Pos: 1B | Bats: L Ht: 6'0" Wt: 210
Health D | PT/Exp A | Consist F
LIMA Plan D | Rand Var +3 | MM 3003

4-11-.125 in 116 PA at LAA. A total lost season, as migraines/insomnia pushed debut to May, posted one of the lowest contact rates in the game, and was in AAA by June. Still owns 2021's xBA and power skills, but hasn't shown a pulse since and struggles vL cap playing time. Short-lived peak is quickly fading in the rearview.

Yr Tm	PA	R	HR	RBI	SB	BA	xHR	xSB	xBA	OBP	SLG	OPS+	vL+	vR+	bb%	ct%	Eye	G	L	F	h%	HctX	QBaB	Brl%	PX	xPX	HR/F	xHR/F	Spd	SBA%	SB%	RAR	BPX	R$
19 LAA *	505	60	25	57	0	239	3	-	241	303	466	106	104	81	8	61	0.23	39	27	34	33	115	ACc	14%	150	134	7%	20%	75	0%	0%	-2.5	19	$9
20 LAA	108	19	9	26	0	293	7	1	317	324	646	129	101	143	5	85	0.33	48	15	37	27	146	CCc	13%	159	111	28%	22%	142	0%	0%	6.2	480	$14
21 LAA	585	70	29	98	2	277	20	1	269	340	509	117	77	137	8	71	0.32	48	22	30	34	105	BDf	11%	144	97	25%	18%	77	2%	67%	22.2	162	$22
22 LAA	454	41	15	44	2	215	14	2	222	269	374	91	83	94	6	67	0.20	45	18	37	28	102	BCd	9%	112	119	15%	14%	93	3%	67%	-12.1	3	$4
23 LAA *	321	25	9	26	0	143	3	2	144	228	261	67	64	68	10	49	0.21	33	16	51	24	57	DBf	7%	100	98	14%	10%	66	5%	0%	-20.5	-296	-$6
1st Half	115	10	2	10	0	167	0	0	163	279	263	74	103	55	13	56	0.35	33	18	50	28	61	FAf	2%	86	85	5%	0%	73	0%	0%	-7.0	-200	-$9
2nd Half	205	15	8	17	0	132	2	2	129	200	260	62	0	93	8	45	0.15	35	12	53	22	60	CBf	17%	110	126	33%	22%	86	9%	0%	-19.3	-321	-$7
24 Proj	280	27	12	31	0	227	11	2	217	300	409	97	75	104	8	67	0.28	40	17	43	29	85		11%	116	111	16%	15%	87	3%	24%	-1.3	-86	$6

Ward,Taylor

Age: 30 Pos: LF | Bats: R Ht: 6'1" Wt: 200
Health C | PT/Exp A | Consist C
LIMA Plan B | Rand Var +1 | MM 4235

Started to heat up after slow April (.206 BA, 3 HR), then HBP to face knocked him out for season in July. Couldn't hold 2022's raw power spike (Brl%, xPX); BA took a hit thanks to low h%, fewer line drives; new rules didn't translate to SB success. Should be ready by spring and carries rebound potential; just treat 2022 as high-water mark.

Yr Tm	PA	R	HR	RBI	SB	BA	xHR	xSB	xBA	OBP	SLG	OPS+	vL+	vR+	bb%	ct%	Eye	G	L	F	h%	HctX	QBaB	Brl%	PX	xPX	HR/F	xHR/F	Spd	SBA%	SB%	RAR	BPX	R$
19 LAA *	518	66	19	45	7	226	1	7	243	309	412	100	63	95	11	68	0.37	37	26	37	29	98	ACc	11%	116	121	14%	14%	93	12%	52%	-15.3	52	$8
20 LAA	102	16	0	5	2	277	3	3	238	333	383	95	83	103	8	70	0.29	44	29	27	39	95	ACb	5%	74	98	0%	17%	155	8%	100%	-2.1	16	$5
21 LAA *	291	42	10	39	2	262	8	3	264	328	466	109	116	101	9	72	0.35	36	26	38	33	98	CBa	10%	135	113	14%	14%	109	5%	68%	6.9	188	$7
22 LAA	564	73	23	65	5	281	25	9	252	360	473	118	106	123	11	76	0.50	35	22	43	33	118	BBb	13%	119	139	14%	15%	126	5%	63%	26.0	203	$23
23 LAA	409	60	14	47	4	253	13	5	242	335	421	103	121	96	10	78	0.49	41	16	43	29	114	BBc	8%	98	117	12%	11%	86	6%	67%	9.1	125	$10
1st Half	331	46	9	30	3	240	11	5	229	314	373	94	90	96	9	77	0.42	40	17	42	28	115	ABc	8%	79	118	9%	11%	97	6%	60%	-2.2	71	$12
2nd Half	78	14	5	17	1	313	3	1	307	423	641	144	247	99	15	80	0.85	44	12	44	33	112	CBb	11%	185	114	22%	13%	75	5%	100%	10.2	432	$3
24 Proj	525	81	20	76	5	265	20	7	259	355	467	113	138	101	11	76	0.52	40	19	41	31	110		10%	123	119	14%	14%	90	5%	71%	23.8	226	$22

Waters,Drew

Age: 25 Pos: CF RF | Bats: R Ht: 6'2" Wt: 185
Health B | PT/Exp B | Consist A
LIMA Plan C+ | Rand Var -1 | MM 4515

8-32-.228 with 16 SB at KC. Oblique strain cost him nearly two months, then struggled before running game kicked into high gear. Little hope for plus BA given dormant xBA and Ks galore, but xHR says he deserved a few more HR, and 2nd half SB% should keep light green. An enticing power/speed blend worth targeting late.

Yr Tm	PA	R	HR	RBI	SB	BA	xHR	xSB	xBA	OBP	SLG	OPS+	vL+	vR+	bb%	ct%	Eye	G	L	F	h%	HctX	QBaB	Brl%	PX	xPX	HR/F	xHR/F	Spd	SBA%	SB%	RAR	BPX	R$
19 a/a	565	79	6	51	16	306		15		352	449	111			7	68	0.22				44				97				123	15%	71%		7	$20
20																																		
21 aaa	442	57	9	30	23	216		17		283	335	85			9	62	0.24				33				93				104	35%	70%		-108	$12
22 KC *	441	46	11	37	11	219	5	11	215	275	363	90	108	116	7	64	0.22	48	18	34	31	90	FCc	11%	108	101	26%	26%	148	13%	90%	-6.4	14	$8
23 KC *	393	48	9	36	17	235	13	19	221	297	396	94	80	97	8	66	0.25	36	23	40	33	83	CBb	10%	107	110	10%	16%	153	25%	78%	1.7	43	$8
1st Half	161	23	4	15	4	259	5	5	232	305	427	100	73	109	6	65	0.19	41	22	37	37	104	BBa	18%	120	140	14%	23%	122	19%	59%	1.3	32	$2
2nd Half	232	25	5	21	13	218	8	14	214	293	374	90	85	92	9	66	0.30	35	24	42	31	74	CAb	7%	97	98	9%	14%	176	29%	87%	-1.6	54	$9
24 Proj	490	60	16	43	21	234	22	18	229	299	420	99	89	102	8	65	0.24	41	21	38	32	88		12%	125	110	15%	20%	133	25%	82%	4.8	11	$18

Wells,Austin

Age: 24 Pos: CA | Bats: L Ht: 6'2" Wt: 220
Health A | PT/Exp C | Consist A
LIMA Plan D | Rand Var +1 | MM 3201

4-13-.229 in 75 PA at NYY. Bat-first CA who impressed in his debut despite low BA. Will work counts early, prone to chase when behind. Solid hand/eye doesn't crater ct%, though doesn't take a ton of walks. Pull approach, but plus power plays to all fields. Especially wears out the pull side gap with line-drive contact and keeps LHP honest. (CB)

Yr Tm	PA	R	HR	RBI	SB	BA	xHR	xSB	xBA	OBP	SLG	OPS+	vL+	vR+	bb%	ct%	Eye	G	L	F	h%	HctX	QBaB	Brl%	PX	xPX	HR/F	xHR/F	Spd	SBA%	SB%	RAR	BPX	R$
19																																		
20																																		
21																																		
22 aa	233	25	9	32	5	217		3		290	382	95			9	68	0.32				27				110				97	10%	100%		34	$4
23 NYY *	461	40	16	64	5	207	6	4	223	269	382	89	0	111	8	70	0.29	47	11	42	25	116	BCc	14%	117	150	17%	25%	61	7%	82%	0.0	39	$5
1st Half	198	19	8	31	3	210		2	242	287	400	94	0	0	10	68	0.33	44	20	36	26	0		0%	128	-21	0%		78	8%	100%	1.1	64	$4
2nd Half	264	22	8	35	2	208	5	2	224	261	378	86	0	110	7	72	0.26	47	11	42	25	119	BCc	14%	112	150	17%	21%	65	7%	66%	-3.3	50	$5
24 Proj	245	24	9	34	4	213	11	3	221	278	381	90	3	98	9	69	0.31	42	16	42	27	107		13%	109	135	13%	17%	74	8%	92%	1.2	47	$6

Wendle,Joey

Age: 34 Pos: SS | Bats: L Ht: 6'1" Wt: 195
Health D | PT/Exp B | Consist B
LIMA Plan D+ | Rand Var +5 | MM 1433

2-20-.212 with 7 SB in 318 PA at MIA. Missed most of April (oblique), didn't do much in platoon role from there. Gave back 2022's ct% gains, so BA plummet wasn't entirely on career-low h%, while GB% caps what little power upside he still has. He'll steal the occasional bag, but an easy pass with no signs of a turnaround at this age.

Yr Tm	PA	R	HR	RBI	SB	BA	xHR	xSB	xBA	OBP	SLG	OPS+	vL+	vR+	bb%	ct%	Eye	G	L	F	h%	HctX	QBaB	Brl%	PX	xPX	HR/F	xHR/F	Spd	SBA%	SB%	RAR	BPX	R$
19 TAM	263	32	3	19	8	231	2	7	254	293	340	88	49	98	5	80	0.30	44	23	32	28	89	CCc	2%	62	56	5%	3%	122	19%	73%	-12.3	74	$3
20 TAM	184	24	4	17	8	286	4	6	268	342	435	103	90	106	5	79	0.29	49	24	28	34	98	CFf	4%	83	91	11%	11%	122	21%	80%	2.7	132	$20
21 TAM	501	73	11	54	8	265	8	10	259	319	422	102	82	109	6	75	0.25	49	21	30	33	97	CDd	5%	99	79	11%	8%	123	12%	57%	-2.6	119	$15
22 MIA	371	27	3	32	12	259	3	8	265	297	360	93	83	95	4	86	0.30	55	17	28	30	98	CFf	2%	71	58	4%	4%	93	18%	80%	-7.3	128	$9
23 MIA *	355	36	3	25	8	205	4	8	250	234	306	74	86	74	4	77	0.17	55	19	26	26	100	CFc	3%	65	84	3%	7%	123	15%	88%	-15.6	18	$0
1st Half	192	20	2	13	5	246	1	5	247	279	363	88	169	89	4	73	0.17	55	20	25	33	93	CFd	2%	75	81	4%	4%	146	13%	100%	-3.5	25	$0
2nd Half	163	16	1	12	3	156	3	3	253	185	240	57	45	60	3	81	0.17	54	18	27	19	108	CFc	5%	55	87	3%	9%	92	20%	75%	-14.8	7	-$7
24 Proj	315	33	3	26	8	226	4	7	256	265	333	82	76	83	4	80	0.21	53	19	28	27	99		3%	69	76	5%	6%	106	17%	79%	-8.6	67	$7

RYAN BLOOMFIELD

Westburg,Jordan

Age: 25 Pos: 2B 3B | Health A | LIMA Plan B
Bats: R Ht: 6' 3" Wt: 203 | PT/Exp A | Rand Var -1
Consist B | MM 3425

3-23-.260 with 4 SB in 228 PA at BAL. Called up in June, but debut season had little fantasy juice. Positives include above-average xPX that hints at better power output and SB% and Spd that could lead to more opportunities. Shaky BA history, but secondary skills and prospect pedigree/age point to a higher ceiling. But not yet.

Yr	Tm	PA	R	HR	RBI	SB	BA	xHR	xSB	xBA	OBP	SLG	OPS+	vL+	vR+	bb%	ct%	Eye	G	L	F	h%	HctX	QBaB	Brl%	PX	xPX	HR/F	xHR/F	Spd	SBA%	SB%	RAR	BPX
19																																		
20																																		
21	aa	122	11	3	10	2	202		1		268	357	86			8	70	0.30				26				97				114	8%	100%		38
22	a/a	589	62	20	68	8	219		6		278	396	95			8	70	0.27				27				125				89	10%	69%		83
23	BAL *	516	66	14	61	8	247	5	10	249	301	410	97	106	92	7	73	0.28	42	22	36	31	119	BCd	6%	104	127	5%	9%	125	8%	89%	7.6	100
1st Half		310	42	11	41	4	239	0	5	270	294	408	96	192	72	7	74	0.30	53	24	24	29	124	ADb	0%	101	53	0%	0%	103	7%	81%	-1.5	82
2nd Half		206	24	3	20	4	259	5	5	246	306	413	97	101	94	7	71	0.26	40	22	38	35	116	BBd	7%	110	136	6%	10%	134	10%	100%	1.7	107
24	**Proj**	**490**	**55**	**14**	**53**	**8**	**240**	**11**	**8**	**241**	**292**	**405**	**96**	**99**	**93**	**7**	**71**	**0.28**	**40**	**22**	**38**	**31**	**104**		**6%**	**110**	**122**	**11%**	**9%**	**125**	**9%**	**87%**	**5.6**	**83**

Wiemer,Joey

Age: 25 Pos: CF | Health A | LIMA Plan D
Bats: R Ht: 6' 5" Wt: 215 | PT/Exp B | Rand Var +1
Consist A | MM 2303

Flashed HR/SB prowess in 1st half, then cooled and lost PT amid roster crunch. Late-June HBP (hand) may have driven power collapse, as pre-injury xPX, Brl% were very good and had green light on basepaths. Poor ct% cements a low BA/OBP, so while there's a path to a 20 HR/20 SB season, he may not get the chance.

Yr	Tm	PA	R	HR	RBI	SB	BA	xHR	xSB	xBA	OBP	SLG	OPS+	vL+	vR+	bb%	ct%	Eye	G	L	F	h%	HctX	QBaB	Brl%	PX	xPX	HR/F	xHR/F	Spd	SBA%	SB%	RAR	BPX
19																																		
20																																		
21																																		
22	a/a	523	55	15	52	21	207		12		266	360	89			7	64	0.22				29				120				91	25%	86%		-10
23	MIL	410	48	13	42	11	204	14	10	221	283	362	88	110	78	9	68	0.31	47	14	40	26	97	BCf	9%	106	127	13%	14%	92	18%	73%	-9.8	21
1st Half		278	34	11	30	10	209	12	8	222	284	398	93	130	79	9	67	0.30	44	11	45	26	103	BCf	12%	126	163	14%	16%	96	24%	77%	-4.8	68
2nd Half		132	14	2	12	1	195	3	2	219	280	288	77	81	73	9	70	0.34	52	19	29	26	83	BDd	3%	65	55	8%	13%	97	7%	50%	-6.7	-61
24	**Proj**	**315**	**35**	**7**	**31**	**9**	**220**	**9**	**8**	**214**	**294**	**350**	**88**	**102**	**80**	**8**	**67**	**0.28**	**49**	**16**	**35**	**30**	**91**		**7%**	**93**	**98**	**11%**	**14%**	**92**	**16%**	**78%**	**-4.6**	**-8**

Williams,Alika

Age: 25 Pos: SS | Health A | LIMA Plan D
Bats: R Ht: 6' 2" Wt: 180 | PT/Exp D | Rand Var +2
Consist D | MM 1211

0-6-.198 in 112 PA at PIT. Traded from TAM in June, played mostly in August before being optioned in September. Not much here given awful BA track record, absence of any real power skills, and shaky SB efficiency (61% career SB% in minors). Employed for his glove, which only helps sim gamers, and even then not much.

Yr	Tm	PA	R	HR	RBI	SB	BA	xHR	xSB	xBA	OBP	SLG	OPS+	vL+	vR+	bb%	ct%	Eye	G	L	F	h%	HctX	QBaB	Brl%	PX	xPX	HR/F	xHR/F	Spd	SBA%	SB%	RAR	BPX
19																																		
20																																		
21	aaa																																	
22	a/a	43	1	0	3	1	169		1		265	213	68			11	53	0.28				32				57				99	22%	38%		-293
23	PIT *	419	42	9	39	5	221	1	7	249	281	350	86	31	93	8	75	0.34	47	22	31	27	64	FDa	3%	83	42	0%	5%	105	8%	67%	-7.9	57
1st Half		245	27	6	24	5	212		6	254	273	350	85	0	0	8	80	0.42	44	20	36	24	0		0%	81	-21	0%		117	15%	67%	-8.3	132
2nd Half		174	15	3	14	0	234	1	1	222	292	350	87	31	92	8	68	0.26	47	22	31	32	58	FDa	3%	86	42	0%	5%	100	0%	0%	-3.9	-39
24	**Proj**	**210**	**20**	**1**	**18**	**2**	**225**	**1**	**3**	**223**	**292**	**297**	**81**	**37**	**106**	**8**	**73**	**0.32**	**47**	**22**	**31**	**30**	**52**		**3%**	**57**	**38**	**2%**	**2%**	**105**	**5%**	**71%**	**-5.8**	**29**

Winker,Jesse

Age: 30 Pos: DH | Health F | LIMA Plan D
Bats: L Ht: 6' 3" Wt: 215 | PT/Exp B | Rand Var +5
Consist F | MM 1021

1-23-.199 in 197 PA at MIL. Multiple injuries (oblique, neck, back, quadriceps), strict platoon led to another rough season. Power skills (xPX, xHR/F), righty splits, and xBA have quickly spiraled since his peak with CIN, though plate patience (bb%, Eye) remains intact. Health concerns plus scary skills trend equals a scary floor.

Yr	Tm	PA	R	HR	RBI	SB	BA	xHR	xSB	xBA	OBP	SLG	OPS+	vL+	vR+	bb%	ct%	Eye	G	L	F	h%	HctX	QBaB	Brl%	PX	xPX	HR/F	xHR/F	Spd	SBA%	SB%	RAR	BPX
19	CIN	384	51	16	38	0	269	10	2	301	357	473	115	62	122	10	82	0.63	49	26	25	29	117	CDb	4%	99	88	23%	14%	102	2%	0%	2.7	222
20	CIN	183	27	12	23	1	255	10	1	275	388	544	124	116	126	15	69	0.61	48	23	29	29	137	ACb	13%	166	137	40%	33%	77	2%	100%	9.2	260
21	CIN	485	77	24	71	1	305	20	1	306	394	556	130	78	148	11	82	0.71	42	25	33	32	124	BCc	11%	136	112	21%	17%	88	1%	100%	31.4	338
22	SEA	547	51	14	53	0	219	16	0	227	344	344	97	111	92	15	77	0.82	39	21	41	25	97	CBf	8%	77	89	10%	11%	75	0%	0%	-10.3	93
23	MIL *	282	24	4	28	0	203	2	4	219	321	282	82	78	77	15	71	0.60	39	26	35	27	90	CCd	4%	53	85	2%	5%	82	5%	0%	-9.6	-61
1st Half		188	18	3	23	0	214	2	2	218	317	304	85	79	80	13	71	0.52	39	24	36	28	94	CCd	3%	58	98	3%	6%	87	2%	0%	-7.9	-54
2nd Half		94	6	1	5	0	179	1	2	245	330	236	76	0	66	18	70	0.76	35	35	29	24	67	DAd	10%	42	9	0%	20%	91	10%	0%	-6.3	-68
24	**Proj**	**210**	**21**	**4**	**21**	**0**	**225**	**7**	**2**	**241**	**351**	**335**	**94**	**98**	**93**	**15**	**74**	**0.68**	**39**	**27**	**34**	**28**	**94**		**8%**	**69**	**73**	**9%**	**15%**	**83**	**4%**	**5%**	**-3.0**	**67**

Winn,Masyn

Age: 22 Pos: SS | Health A | LIMA Plan B
Bats: R Ht: 5' 11" Wt: 180 | PT/Exp B | Rand Var 0
Consist B | MM 1405

2-12-.172 with 2 SB in 137 PA at STL. Former 2-way player enjoyed solid season at AAA before callup. Hit-over-power profile with plus contact skills. Sprays the ball well to all fields. Hand/eye skills limit whiffs despite heavy chase rate. Avg raw power, plays mostly to pull side. Plus runner who would benefit from more aggressiveness on bases. (CB)

Yr	Tm	PA	R	HR	RBI	SB	BA	xHR	xSB	xBA	OBP	SLG	OPS+	vL+	vR+	bb%	ct%	Eye	G	L	F	h%	HctX	QBaB	Brl%	PX	xPX	HR/F	xHR/F	Spd	SBA%	SB%	RAR	BPX
19																																		
20																																		
21																																		
22	aa	373	40	6	28	17	197		12		257	305	80			7	73	0.30				25				81				95	33%	75%		14
23	STL *	612	78	14	55	14	228	1	21	225	279	345	85	60	65	7	79	0.35	47	13	40	26	80	DCf	2%	63	53	5%	3%	159	13%	81%	-11.2	111
1st Half		344	43	5	23	10	221		13	229	267	306	78	0	0	6	80	0.32	44	20	36	26	0		0%	45	-21	0%		169	14%	90%	-14.3	71
2nd Half		269	35	9	33	4	237	1	7	241	294	399	94	59	65	7	79	0.38	47	13	40	27	80	DCf	2%	88	53	5%	3%	137	10%	66%	-2.6	157
24	**Proj**	**490**	**59**	**9**	**45**	**15**	**230**	**8**	**17**	**219**	**278**	**343**	**85**	**86**	**85**	**7**	**77**	**0.32**	**47**	**13**	**40**	**28**	**72**		**2%**	**68**	**48**	**7%**	**6%**	**125**	**18%**	**76%**	**-7.6**	**78**

Wisdom,Patrick

Age: 32 Pos: 3B | Health B | LIMA Plan C+
Bats: R Ht: 6' 2" Wt: 220 | PT/Exp A | Rand Var -1
Consist B | MM 5213

Strong April (10 HR, 214 xPX) carried the 1st half, then took a dive with June wrist injury and lighter playing time. Power skills are elite per Brl%, xHR/F, but dreadful amounts of contact, xBA dig quite the deep BA hole. Excellent HR source on per-PA basis, but sub-.300 career OBP says inconsistent PT will continue.

Yr	Tm	PA	R	HR	RBI	SB	BA	xHR	xSB	xBA	OBP	SLG	OPS+	vL+	vR+	bb%	ct%	Eye	G	L	F	h%	HctX	QBaB	Brl%	PX	xPX	HR/F	xHR/F	Spd	SBA%	SB%	RAR	BPX
19	TEX *	461	46	22	50	5	191	0	3	239	258	380	88	48	53	8	62	0.23	9	45	45	25	106	AAa	0%	117	123	0%	0%	80	8%	68%	-31.8	-63
20	CHC	2	0	0	0	0	0	0	0	0	0	0	0	0	0	0	100	0.00	0	0	100	0	0	CAa		0	-26	0%	0%	96	0%	0%	-0.3	124
21	CHC *	403	58	30	68	5	223	22	3	220	292	507	110	113	113	9	54	0.21	31	19	49	31	100	AAc	16%	214	181	31%	24%	79	8%	82%	5.5	112
22	CHC	534	67	25	66	8	207	24	6	223	298	426	103	125	94	10	61	0.29	34	17	49	28	97	BAf	15%	174	146	18%	17%	81	11%	67%	-7.2	100
23	CHC	302	43	23	46	4	205	21	5	232	289	500	107	104	110	10	59	0.27	31	17	53	24	98	AAd	20%	200	183	28%	25%	105	11%	67%	5.0	171
1st Half		208	30	14	28	2	196	13	3	223	285	467	103	101	104	11	56	0.27	32	19	49	25	90	AAd	20%	195	177	28%	26%	119	8%	67%	-0.3	139
2nd Half		94	13	9	18	2	226	7	2	252	298	571	117	106	133	9	64	0.27	27	13	60	22	114	AAd	20%	210	193	27%	21%	76	18%	67%	3.1	239
24	**Proj**	**350**	**47**	**24**	**54**	**5**	**211**	**19**	**4**	**227**	**294**	**483**	**106**	**109**	**105**	**10**	**60**	**0.26**	**31**	**16**	**52**	**26**	**101**		**18%**	**187**	**172**	**25%**	**19%**	**78**	**11%**	**69%**	**5.9**	**135**

Wisely,Brett

Age: 25 Pos: 2B | Health A | LIMA Plan D
Bats: L Ht: 5' 10" Wt: 180 | PT/Exp C | Rand Var 0
Consist A | MM 2201

2-8-.175 with 2 SB in 131 PA at SF. Bounced between AAA and MLB multiple times in debut season. Underwhelming ct%, below-average power carried over to majors, and while he had 30+ SB twice in minors, shaky SB% (75%) questions how that will translate. Middling pedigree, sub-.300 OBP further scream utility role.

Yr	Tm	PA	R	HR	RBI	SB	BA	xHR	xSB	xBA	OBP	SLG	OPS+	vL+	vR+	bb%	ct%	Eye	G	L	F	h%	HctX	QBaB	Brl%	PX	xPX	HR/F	xHR/F	Spd	SBA%	SB%	RAR	BPX
19																																		
20																																		
21																																		
22	a/a	496	61	10	41	22	223		21		293	352	91			9	71	0.34				29				92				121	32%	64%		45
23	SF *	384	37	6	29	7	213	3	8	218	298	332	86	86	63	11	66	0.36	38	23	39	30	66	FBf	7%	92	90	7%	10%	90	13%	60%	-8.2	-36
1st Half		218	21	4	20	5	225	2	4	226	301	370	92	95	72	10	65	0.32	37	23	40	32	71	DBf	8%	114	98	9%	9%	88	11%	100%	-2.1	4
2nd Half		166	16	1	9	1	198	0	4	213	295	281	78	79	39	12	67	0.42	40	25	35	28	50	FCf	5%	64	67	0%	0%	105	13%	23%	-8.7	-75
24	**Proj**	**245**	**26**	**6**	**18**	**6**	**224**	**5**	**7**	**215**	**303**	**365**	**92**	**121**	**82**	**10**	**68**	**0.36**	**38**	**19**	**43**	**30**	**58**		**6%**	**98**	**79**	**8%**	**8%**	**103**	**20%**	**57%**	**-1.3**	**-7**

CORBIN YOUNG

Witt Jr.,Bobby

Age: 24 Pos: SS | Bats: R Ht: 6' 1" Wt: 200

Health A | LIMA Plan D+ | PT/Exp A | Rand Var 0 | Consist C | MM 4545

Sophomore slump? Pfft. Went on SB rampage with elite wheels and constant green light. Powered up with Brl% and xPX gains, xHR says he deserved a few more HR, and 2nd half ct%, xBA boons gave the BA jump plenty of legs. Enjoy the first round, Bobby. We think you'll be here a while.

Yr	Tm	PA	R	HR	RBI	SB	BA	xHR	xSB	xBA	OBP	SLG	OPS+	vL+	vR+	bb%	ct%	Eye	G	L	F	h%	HctX	QBaB	Brl%	PX	xPX	HR/F	xHR/F	Spd	SBA%	SB%	RAR	BPX	R$
19																																			
20																																			
21	a/a	537	78	24	76	23	263		17		318	488	111			7	73	0.30				32				138				97	31%	68%		185	$27
22	KC	632	82	20	80	30	254	23	27	237	294	428	102	100	103	5	77	0.22	36	17	46	30	104	BBd	9%	109	94	9%	11%	155	29%	81%	3.6	186	$31
23	KC	694	97	30	96	49	276	36	50	266	319	495	111	116	109	6	81	0.33	38	18	44	30	124	BBc	12%	112	134	13%	16%	171	42%	77%	32.7	282	$37
1st Half		360	44	12	42	23	249	17	22	240	292	417	97	124	88	6	78	0.27	37	19	44	29	119	BBd	11%	91	136	10%	15%	157	38%	79%	-0.6	164	$27
2nd Half		334	53	18	54	26	305	19	26	296	347	578	125	103	129	6	84	0.42	40	18	43	31	130	BBc	12%	134	132	16%	17%	170	47%	74%	24.7	393	$46
24	Proj	**665**	**94**	**31**	**93**	**43**	**270**	**30**	**36**	**262**	**314**	**496**	**111**	**110**	**111**	**6**	**79**	**0.29**	**37**	**18**	**45**	**30**	**117**		**11%**	**123**	**118**	**14%**	**14%**	**141**	**40%**	**76%**	**27.8**	**244**	**$39**

Wong,Connor

Age: 28 Pos: CA | Bats: R Ht: 6' 1" Wt: 181

Health A | LIMA Plan C | PT/Exp B | Rand Var -3 | Consist A | MM 3513

Broke camp with semi-regular gig, held it all year. Third-most SB among catchers—2nd half SBA%, success rate say that should continue—and paired it with decent pop (Brl%, xHR/F). Poor BA a near-given thanks to ct% issues, but looks like double-digit HR/SB threat, which stands out in the catcher pool.

Yr	Tm	PA	R	HR	RBI	SB	BA	xHR	xSB	xBA	OBP	SLG	OPS+	vL+	vR+	bb%	ct%	Eye	G	L	F	h%	HctX	QBaB	Brl%	PX	xPX	HR/F	xHR/F	Spd	SBA%	SB%	RAR	BPX	R$
19	aa	158	15	8	28	2	323		2		363	555	127			6	62	0.17				47				150				93	8%	62%		37	$5
20																																			
21	BOS *	220	20	6	21	5	229	1	4	217	256	383	88	45	187	4	65	0.11	17	33	50	32	133	CDf	17%	113	269	0%	33%	110	17%	82%	-4.2	-19	$2
22	BOS *	396	37	10	35	4	226	2	5	214	269	365	90	47	102	6	70	0.20	64	6	30	29	63	CFf	9%	103	69	10%	20%	104	11%	55%	-4.4	28	$5
23	BOS	403	55	9	36	8	235	13	10	226	288	385	92	68	100	5	64	0.16	43	22	35	34	83	CBd	9%	115	86	11%	16%	138	13%	80%	2.9	7	$7
1st Half		205	30	6	18	1	218	7	2	229	279	394	92	71	100	6	63	0.19	42	20	38	31	79	CBd	9%	138	85	14%	16%	103	6%	50%	-1.1	25	$1
2nd Half		198	25	3	18	7	251	6	9	223	296	377	91	63	99	5	65	0.14	43	24	33	37	87	CCd	9%	92	86	8%	15%	169	19%	88%	1.1	-14	$6
24	Proj	**420**	**49**	**11**	**42**	**9**	**242**	**14**	**9**	**229**	**291**	**396**	**94**	**66**	**104**	**5**	**66**	**0.16**	**43**	**23**	**35**	**34**	**84**		**9%**	**113**	**86**	**12%**	**16%**	**142**	**13%**	**77%**	**4.7**	**9**	**$13**

Wong,Kolten

Age: 33 Pos: 2B | Bats: L Ht: 5' 7" Wt: 185

Health B | LIMA Plan C | PT/Exp A | Rand Var +5 | Consist A | MM 1223

A dud from the get-go (.175 BA, 0 HR/SB in April), which led to reduced role, Aug DFA. More Ks, crazy-low h% drove BA collapse, stopped running when he did get on base, power went from "meh" to "mush". Worth a late flyer given R$ history and decent Sept with LA, but cut bait if he starts slow again.

Yr	Tm	PA	R	HR	RBI	SB	BA	xHR	xSB	xBA	OBP	SLG	OPS+	vL+	vR+	bb%	ct%	Eye	G	L	F	h%	HctX	QBaB	Brl%	PX	xPX	HR/F	xHR/F	Spd	SBA%	SB%	RAR	BPX	R$
19	STL	549	61	11	59	24	285	8	15	258	361	423	108	103	109	9	83	0.57	44	20	36	33	97	DCd	2%	71	83	8%	6%	100	18%	86%	11.8	133	$21
20	STL	208	26	1	16	5	265	2	6	240	350	326	90	86	90	10	83	0.67	50	21	29	31	83	DDf	1%	31	44	2%	5%	137	11%	71%	-6.2	84	$14
21	MIL	492	70	14	50	12	272	9	9	273	335	447	107	107	107	6	81	0.37	42	22	35	31	113	CCc	5%	102	107	11%	7%	90	15%	71%	6.1	188	$18
22	MIL	497	65	15	47	17	251	10	13	266	339	430	109	62	120	9	80	0.52	42	21	37	28	92	DCf	5%	110	109	12%	8%	100	18%	74%	7.2	197	$18
23	2 TM	250	25	4	27	3	183	3	3	206	256	263	71	53	73	7	76	0.34	44	16	40	22	79	FCd	2%	49	72	6%	4%	71	9%	60%	-13.3	-61	-$2
1st Half		162	13	1	13	0	160	2	1	177	241	208	62	39	66	8	74	0.35	48	12	40	21	67	FCd	2%	34	71	2%	5%	79	3%	0%	-12.0	-118	-$10
2nd Half		88	12	3	14	3	225	1	2	243	284	363	87	111	85	6	80	0.31	37	22	41	25	100	DBf	2%	72	74	12%	4%	70	20%	75%	-1.7	43	-$1
24	Proj	**315**	**40**	**8**	**36**	**8**	**248**	**5**	**7**	**242**	**318**	**379**	**96**	**84**	**98**	**8**	**79**	**0.39**	**42**	**20**	**38**	**29**	**92**		**3%**	**76**	**86**	**9%**	**6%**	**82**	**14%**	**72%**	**1.9**	**78**	**$11**

Yastrzemski,Mike

Age: 33 Pos: RF CF | Bats: L Ht: 5' 10" Wt: 178

Health C | LIMA Plan B | PT/Exp A | Rand Var +1 | Consist B | MM 4225

Hot April (.298 BA, 5 HR), but rebound season derailed by IL stints in May, June, AND July (hamstring). Not much movement under the hood: power skills, FB% stroke keep 20+ HR in play; BA lagged middling xBA thanks to low h%; struggled vL. Decent option vs. RHP, but shoot for higher ceilings.

Yr	Tm	PA	R	HR	RBI	SB	BA	xHR	xSB	xBA	OBP	SLG	OPS+	vL+	vR+	bb%	ct%	Eye	G	L	F	h%	HctX	QBaB	Brl%	PX	xPX	HR/F	xHR/F	Spd	SBA%	SB%	RAR	BPX	R$
19	SF *	563	91	28	73	3	264	22	7	253	328	508	116	131	113	9	70	0.32	34	23	43	32	103	BAc	11%	139	142	18%	19%	112	8%	34%	18.3	163	$17
20	SF	225	39	10	35	2	297	12	5	263	400	568	128	130	127	13	71	0.55	39	19	42	37	108	CAf	11%	159	152	17%	21%	147	5%	67%	15.7	344	$25
21	SF	532	75	25	71	4	224	23	2	247	311	457	105	70	117	10	72	0.39	34	19	47	26	89	CAd	10%	140	133	16%	15%	88	4%	100%	1.4	185	$12
22	SF	558	73	17	57	5	214	21	4	233	305	392	99	81	105	11	71	0.43	34	19	46	27	100	BAc	11%	126	123	11%	13%	84	5%	83%	-2.7	117	$9
23	SF	381	54	15	43	2	233	13	4	250	330	445	106	80	113	12	70	0.45	32	22	46	29	96	CAf	10%	139	136	14%	12%	93	5%	50%	9.0	161	$7
1st Half		217	37	10	27	0	259	9	3	255	324	482	110	86	118	8	71	0.32	36	20	43	32	101	BBd	11%	139	129	17%	15%	108	4%	0%	6.7	168	$10
2nd Half		164	17	5	16	2	195	4	2	243	337	391	98	69	107	17	68	0.64	26	24	50	24	90	CAf	9%	138	147	11%	9%	78	5%	100%	1.0	154	-$1
24	Proj	**490**	**68**	**19**	**57**	**4**	**226**	**19**	**5**	**244**	**324**	**436**	**104**	**83**	**111**	**12**	**70**	**0.46**	**32**	**21**	**47**	**28**	**96**		**10%**	**137**	**135**	**13%**	**13%**	**87**	**5%**	**72%**	**8.0**	**162**	**$13**

Yelich,Christian

Age: 32 Pos: LF DH | Bats: L Ht: 6' 3" Wt: 195

Health B | LIMA Plan B | PT/Exp A | Rand Var -1 | Consist B | MM 3445

Yes, it wasn't 2019, but THAT was a rebound we can invest in. BA gains came with xBA support, ct% uptick; green light returned with plenty of success; xHR/F said he squeezed all he could out of low FB%. Back problems resurfaced in Sept, recent track record questions full repeat, but a strong bet to deliver five-category goods.

Yr	Tm	PA	R	HR	RBI	SB	BA	xHR	xSB	xBA	OBP	SLG	OPS+	vL+	vR+	bb%	ct%	Eye	G	L	F	h%	HctX	QBaB	Brl%	PX	xPX	HR/F	xHR/F	Spd	SBA%	SB%	RAR	BPX	R$
19	MIL	580	100	44	97	30	329	41	19	306	429	671	152	130	164	14	76	0.68	43	21	36	36	133	ACc	16%	172	146	33%	31%	113	18%	94%	77.5	389	$42
20	MIL	247	39	12	22	4	205	12	5	234	356	430	104	139	89	19	62	0.61	51	19	30	26	103	ADb	12%	143	112	32%	32%	115	9%	67%	-2.6	144	$16
21	MIL	475	70	9	51	9	248	10	9	245	362	373	101	83	108	15	72	0.62	54	22	24	32	102	BFf	8%	81	84	13%	15%	119	8%	75%	0.1	73	$12
22	MIL	671	99	14	57	19	252	18	21	248	355	383	105	97	108	13	72	0.54	59	18	23	33	106	AFc	8%	90	79	15%	19%	144	11%	86%	12.4	107	$23
23	MIL	632	106	19	76	28	278	21	22	276	370	447	111	85	121	12	75	0.56	57	20	23	34	119	AFb	9%	106	97	20%	22%	101	17%	90%	33.6	143	$28
1st Half		343	59	10	40	18	276	11	14	268	373	441	112	82	122	13	74	0.56	56	19	25	34	123	AFc	10%	103	98	18%	20%	108	20%	90%	16.6	136	$30
2nd Half		289	47	9	36	10	281	9	8	282	367	455	111	89	119	12	75	0.56	59	21	21	34	114	BFb	8%	110	96	23%	23%	96	14%	91%	15.0	154	$23
24	Proj	**630**	**101**	**18**	**70**	**22**	**266**	**20**	**19**	**263**	**366**	**429**	**109**	**94**	**115**	**13**	**73**	**0.57**	**56**	**20**	**24**	**33**	**112**		**9%**	**103**	**94**	**19%**	**21%**	**115**	**14%**	**88%**	**27.5**	**138**	**$29**

Yoshida,Masataka

Age: 30 Pos: LF DH | Bats: L Ht: 5' 8" Wt: 176

Health A | LIMA Plan B+ | PT/Exp A | Rand Var 0 | Consist C | MM 2355

Stateside debut a success with staunch BA, volume to make it count. PRO: Firm support from mirror-image xBA; squeaky clean sheet on basepaths. CON: 2nd half Eye erosion a sign pitchers adjusted; HR ceiling capped by sketchy PX history, GB% stroke. Likely not another level here, but repeat seems doable.

Yr	Tm	PA	R	HR	RBI	SB	BA	xHR	xSB	xBA	OBP	SLG	OPS+	vL+	vR+	bb%	ct%	Eye	G	L	F	h%	HctX	QBaB	Brl%	PX	xPX	HR/F	xHR/F	Spd	SBA%	SB%	RAR	BPX	R$
19	for	585	90	18	83	5	301		6		377	459	116			11	88	1.05				31	0			73				108	3%	80%	15.1	252	$21
20	for	466	54	8	62	7	327		8		410	449	114			12	93	2.11				34	0			61				94	8%	56%	21.1	308	$52
21	for	436	59	13	70	0	316		1		390	478	119			11	94	1.90				31	0			79				90	0%	0%	19.3	338	$18
22	for	476	55	13	86	4	312		3		405	479	125			14	91	1.66				32	0			95				84	3%	100%	29.5	321	$23
23	BOS	580	71	15	72	8	289	16	8	289	338	445	107	100	109	6	85	0.42	55	19	27	32	102	CFd	7%	87	62	12%	13%	95	6%	100%	17.9	182	$20
1st Half		313	41	9	41	4	305	11	5	292	377	477	117	105	121	9	87	0.77	56	16	29	32	112	BFf	7%	91	69	13%	16%	100	4%	100%	14.4	257	$21
2nd Half		267	30	6	31	4	271	5	3	284	292	411	95	93	95	3	82	0.15	53	22	25	31	91	CFd	6%	83	53	11%	9%	91	7%	100%	-2.5	107	$13
24	Proj	**595**	**74**	**15**	**80**	**6**	**292**	**15**	**6**	**286**	**360**	**444**	**110**	**106**	**111**	**9**	**85**	**0.67**	**54**	**19**	**26**	**32**	**99**		**6%**	**85**	**59**	**12%**	**12%**	**92**	**4%**	**93%**	**28.3**	**242**	**$26**

Zavala,Seby

Age: 30 Pos: CA | Bats: R Ht: 5' 11" Wt: 205

Health B | LIMA Plan F | PT/Exp D | Rand Var +5 | Consist D | MM 2101

7-18-.171 in 193 PA at CHW/ARI. Zero production in season that went out with a whimper (Aug oblique strain, Sept DFA). Little reason to think this turns around, as Ks continued to pile up, xBA squashes odds for BA rebound, xPX trend says he's losing thump. Not a take, even in four-catcher leagues. (Even if that's a thing, just don't.)

Yr	Tm	PA	R	HR	RBI	SB	BA	xHR	xSB	xBA	OBP	SLG	OPS+	vL+	vR+	bb%	ct%	Eye	G	L	F	h%	HctX	QBaB	Brl%	PX	xPX	HR/F	xHR/F	Spd	SBA%	SB%	RAR	BPX	R$
19	CHW *	328	38	16	34	1	179	0	1	208	227	368	82	0	25	6	51	0.13	33	33	33	27	0	FAb	0%	143	-36	0%	0%	83	4%	39%	-17.9	-148	$0
20																																			
21	CHW *	271	27	10	28	0	145	3	1	157	206	294	69	80	86	7	45	0.14	38	19	42	25	49	FBd	9%	137	137	23%	14%	84	3%	0%	-17.4	-258	-$5
22	CHW *	362	36	7	30	0	237	4	1	193	310	372	97	91	106	9	55	0.24	28	24	47	41	77	CAc	9%	136	127	4%	7%	95	0%	0%	2.3	-72	$3
23	2 TM *	216	18	8	19	1	171	4	1	203	223	308	72	76	73	6	61	0.17	39	23	37	23	73	DCc	6%	92	101	18%	10%	73	3%	100%	-7.9	-157	-$3
1st Half		131	12	6	15	1	165	4	1	197	214	331	75	74	75	5	57	0.13	44	20	37	22	82	CCb	7%	116	130	23%	15%	75	5%	100%	-5.6	-157	-$5
2nd Half		85	6	2	4	0	179	1	0	226	241	272	69	81	70	8	68	0.26	31	31	39	24	51	DAf	3%	61	42	7%	7%	85	0%	0%	-3.8	-132	-$8
24	Proj	**175**	**16**	**4**	**15**	**0**	**200**	**4**	**1**	**188**	**267**	**319**	**80**	**77**	**81**	**7**	**58**	**0.19**	**34**	**24**	**42**	**31**	**66**		**7%**	**94**	**104**	**11%**	**9%**	**85**	**1%**	**68%**	**-3.7**	**-143**	**$1**

RYAN BLOOMFIELD

THE NEXT TIER — Batters

The preceding section provided player boxes and analysis for 441 batters. As we know, far more than 441 batters will play in the major leagues ir 2024. Many of those additional hitters are covered in the minor league section, but that still leaves a gap: established major leaguers who don't pla enough, or well enough, to merit a player box.

This section looks to fill that gap. Here, you will find "The Next Tier" of batters who are mostly past their growth years, but who are likely to se some playing time in 2024. We are including their 2022-23 statline here for reference for you to do your own analysis. (Years that include MLEs ar marked by an asterisk.) This way, if Dylan Moore starts creating some early-season havoc on the bases, you can be reminded that he's only one yea removed from a 21-steal season with positive speed metrics. Or when Jackie Bradley pops two HRs in one week in June, a quick scan can show tha given his recent-season GB rates and xPX marks, that this too shall pass. Save your FAB.

Batter	Yr	B	Age	Pos	PA	R	HR	RBI	SB	BA	xBA	OPS+	vL+	vR+	bb%	Ct%	Eye	GLF	HctX	PX	xPX	SPD	SBA%	SB%	BPX
Aguilar,Jesus	22	R	32	3	501	39	16	51	1	235	235	94	78	92	6	74	0.24	31/24/45	97	94	120	45	1	100	(
	23*	R	33		339	25	8	31	0	208	189	80	119	63	9	68	0.31	35/19/46	60	65	87	39	0	0	-154
Ahmed,Nick	22	R	32	6	54	7	3	7	0	231	246	99	44	116	4	71	0.13	58/11/31	92	136	131	98	11	0	110
	23	R	33		210	14	2	17	5	212	234	76	54	108	6	74	0.23	41/25/34	93	63	76	86	15	83	-56
Arroyo,Christian	22	R	27	4	300	32	6	36	5	286	275	104	109	96	4	83	0.27	45/25/29	114	82	79	97	8	83	121
	23*	R	28		274	26	3	25	2	207	234	74	75	92	4	77	0.18	45/18/36	92	72	86	85	11	35	4
Barnes,Austin	22	R	32	2	212	31	8	26	2	212	238	100	96	95	13	79	0.73	42/15/43	86	98	70	77	6	67	159
	23	R	33		200	15	2	11	2	180	208	68	36	81	9	76	0.40	50/17/33	87	40	77	77	7	67	-79
Barnhart,Tucker	22	L	31	2	308	16	1	16	0	221	179	78	78	73	8	74	0.34	53/16/30	60	39	25	86	0	0	-10(
	23*	L	32		148	8	1	10	1	195	161	71	101	70	10	58	0.27	46/19/35	31	46	20	92	3	100	-289
Blanco,Dairon	22*	R	29	79	391	34	7	34	25	219	245	82	187	0	5	67	0.14	100/0/0	0	83	-14	134	45	73	-52
	23*	R	30		324	41	5	29	52	259	241	94	110	104	7	74	0.30	49/19/32	88	74	70	171	82	80	89
Bradley,Jackie	22	L	32	8	370	30	4	38	2	203	236	80	75	76	6	78	0.31	51/17/32	93	80	82	65	8	40	3
	23	L	33		113	10	1	6	0	133	198	54	52	55	4	72	0.17	51/13/36	96	57	107	70	0	0	-11
Calhoun,Kole	22	L	34	3	424	36	12	49	3	196	214	83	90	76	6	65	0.20	38/24/38	101	99	121	64	6	60	-9(
	23*	L	35		422	45	12	52	0	218	232	88	90	90	7	74	0.28	34/20/46	84	96	98	72	1	0	3
Calhoun,Willie	22*	L	27	0	307	30	6	27	0	178	203	74	154	62	8	81	0.44	36/14/50	121	65	82	69	0	0	5
	23*	L	28		193	17	6	19	0	231	254	91	13	104	8	85	0.57	38/20/42	96	78	81	72	0	0	14
Caratini,Victor	22	B	28	2	314	26	9	34	0	199	233	91	79	92	10	75	0.46	50/18/31	118	94	85	62	0	0	5
	23	B	29		226	23	7	25	1	259	236	97	82	103	8	78	0.42	53/18/28	91	66	37	82	3	50	2
Carpenter,Matt	22*	L	36	0	242	36	18	47	1	259	285	132	178	145	11	70	0.43	23/24/53	113	213	189	74	4	29	33
	23	L	37		236	18	5	31	1	176	193	87	129	85	17	64	0.61	27/16/57	77	109	117	65	2	100	
Chang,Yu	22*	R	26	6	216	20	4	17	0	199	184	80	67	95	9	65	0.28	42/17/41	81	77	123	117	2	0	-8
	23*	R	27		191	19	8	24	5	185	222	75	93	72	3	70	0.11	43/19/39	113	89	118	109	17	100	-2
Choi,Ji-Man	22	L	31	03	419	36	11	52	0	233	228	103	101	97	14	65	0.47	45/23/32	95	123	115	68	0	0	3
	23*	L	32		179	17	8	19	0	166	228	82	60	92	9	65	0.29	41/20/39	116	125	145	50	0	0	-1
Cruz,Nelson	22	R	42	0	504	50	10	64	4	234	228	92	102	81	10	73	0.41	52/19/28	103	71	88	68	3	100	-2
	23	R	43		152	9	5	23	1	245	228	93	90	97	4	68	0.13	44/21/35	90	97	104	92	3	100	-4
Dickerson,Corey	22	L	33	7	297	28	6	36	0	267	262	99	36	99	4	83	0.25	46/21/33	88	85	64	81	0	0	11
	23	L	34		152	12	2	17	0	250	239	87	86	88	5	81	0.25	46/19/35	98	63	88	97	3	0	4
Dozier,Hunter	22	R	30	5	500	51	12	41	4	236	240	96	104	87	7	73	0.27	42/20/37	91	105	104	133	7	57	10
	23	R	31		91	8	2	9	2	183	195	76	123	58	9	65	0.28	46/15/39	68	78	104	136	11	100	-6
Duffy,Matt	22*	R	31	45	283	16	3	17	0	232	207	81	93	78	6	77	0.30	47/21/33	79	42	64	106	0	0	-3
	23	R	32		209	17	2	16	1	251	240	86	96	76	6	80	0.31	51/21/27	76	48	46	98	2	100	
Gallagher,Cameron	22*	R	29	2	158	8	2	15	0	161	176	67	76	85	6	64	0.18	39/14/46	64	91	66	72	0	0	-11
	23	R	30		149	6	0	7	0	126	166	44	47	42	3	68	0.09	46/15/40	48	39	47	67	0	0	-24
Guillorme,Luis	22	L	27	4	335	33	2	17	1	273	272	98	80	98	10	85	0.74	55/26/19	80	46	54	111	1	100	10
	23*	L	28		201	19	2	13	0	192	228	77	97	82	12	76	0.56	41/23/37	56	58	65	94	0	0	1
Haase,Eric	22	R	29	27	351	41	14	44	0	254	238	106	109	97	7	70	0.25	39/20/41	89	130	90	93	0	0	9
	23*	R	30		321	23	5	27	4	193	202	70	50	80	6	70	0.21	42/21/37	78	52	69	90	8	80	-13
Harrison,Josh	22	R	34	5	425	50	7	27	2	256	237	97	93	92	5	82	0.30	44/17/39	91	73	85	113	3	67	10
	23*	R	35		143	10	3	13	0	195	220	69	58	95	3	76	0.15	49/20/31	83	54	64	71	0	0	-8
Hedges,Austin	22	R	29	2	338	26	7	30	2	163	193	69	71	64	7	73	0.32	38/18/44	70	52	65	68	3	100	-9
	23	R	30		211	14	1	16	1	184	199	63	58	66	5	75	0.23	42/20/38	93	31	56	83	2	100	-13
Higashioka,Kyle	22	R	32	2	248	27	10	31	0	227	243	92	106	81	5	77	0.23	35/22/43	118	96	125	81	2	0	7
	23	R	33		260	24	10	34	0	236	232	94	105	90	5	69	0.19	39/20/41	112	116	143	75	0	0	2
Hosmer,Eric	22	L	32	3	419	38	8	44	0	268	244	101	108	92	9	83	0.58	57/18/25	100	72	71	86	0	0	12
	23	L	33		100	7	2	14	0	234	202	83	71	85	6	73	0.24	57/16/26	48	60	38	88	0	0	-6

THE NEXT TIER — Batters

Batter	Yr	B	Age	Pos	PA	R	HR	RBI	SB	BA	xBA	OPS+	vL+	vR+	bb%	Ct%	Eye	GLF	HctX	PX	xPX	SPD	SBA%	SB%	BPX
Kelly,Carson	22	R	27	2	354	40	7	35	2	211	236	87	84	84	8	78	0.41	41/20/40	100	85	108	83	3	100	76
	23*	R	28		182	16	2	15	1	213	191	78	108	66	9	69	0.31	42/16/41	76	60	57	85	2	100	-104
Maile,Luke	22	R	31	2	206	19	3	17	0	221	203	89	98	81	9	70	0.35	38/18/44	78	83	83	86	0	0	-21
	23	R	32		199	17	6	25	2	235	238	95	102	93	7	73	0.29	43/19/38	97	101	128	72	7	67	32
Mancini,Trey	22	R	30	03	587	56	18	63	0	239	236	101	91	98	9	74	0.39	40/21/39	107	100	125	90	0	0	79
	23	R	31		261	31	4	28	0	234	206	87	88	86	8	67	0.27	48/19/34	83	77	79	73	0	0	-107
Mastrobuoni,Miles	22*	L	26	5	566	62	10	42	16	226	245	88	0	56	8	75	0.33	70/10/20	66	78	60	106	16	81	41
	23*	L	27		299	45	2	13	18	230	227	87	75	85	12	69	0.42	42/28/31	100	66	97	127	25	95	-29
McCann,James	22*	R	32	2	231	22	4	20	3	193	198	73	45	89	6	67	0.18	36/23/40	93	66	107	83	6	100	-134
	23	R	33		226	25	6	26	3	222	244	88	80	97	4	72	0.16	39/22/39	91	104	90	87	10	75	32
McKenna,Ryan	22*	R	25	89	207	26	4	15	2	234	207	90	111	70	6	62	0.19	39/24/37	81	101	120	110	11	37	-72
	23*	R	26		198	32	4	23	6	217	208	82	86	101	7	64	0.20	41/22/37	68	88	74	139	15	100	-64
McKinney,Billy	22*	L	27	7	326	27	6	28	1	180	174	75	78	38	7	59	0.17	39/17/44	35	92	55	102	2	100	-155
	23*	L	28		296	32	12	30	3	213	228	92	99	100	10	69	0.38	42/20/38	100	100	143	97	6	69	25
Mejia,Francisco	22	B	26	2	299	32	6	31	0	242	256	91	117	75	2	78	0.11	37/24/39	78	100	66	72	0	0	62
	23*	B	27		249	30	9	31	0	233	232	91	58	98	3	72	0.13	37/18/46	87	111	95	87	2	0	43
Moore,Dylan	22	R	29	47	254	41	6	24	21	224	199	107	111	95	13	63	0.45	32/18/50	88	125	147	128	39	72	72
	23*	R	30		192	21	7	21	8	196	196	90	107	89	9	60	0.26	29/13/57	90	144	187	99	32	64	18
Murphy,Tom	22	R	31	2	41	9	1	1	0	303	225	127	117	122	20	61	0.62	35/30/35	132	130	210	112	0	0	72
	23	R	32		158	19	8	17	0	290	263	119	117	121	6	70	0.23	45/18/37	116	164	166	73	0	0	164
Myers,Wil	22*	R	31	9	322	30	8	42	2	247	217	96	114	88	7	67	0.23	40/22/38	100	103	120	97	4	67	-17
	23*	R	32		169	13	4	14	2	179	186	70	61	79	8	63	0.23	50/18/33	70	62	85	87	9	67	-193
Narvaez,Omar	22	B	30	2	296	21	4	23	0	206	218	85	81	80	10	78	0.51	36/20/45	83	68	81	56	0	0	21
	23	B	31		146	12	2	7	0	211	222	79	83	79	10	79	0.52	26/23/51	98	54	119	75	0	0	7
Nola,Austin	22	R	32	2	397	40	4	40	2	251	233	92	103	80	9	83	0.57	43/21/37	114	53	89	88	3	67	66
	23*	R	33		182	12	1	9	0	141	176	57	70	56	11	73	0.47	41/17/43	70	30	31	83	0	0	-118
Odor,Rougned	22	L	28	4	472	49	13	53	6	207	221	90	81	86	7	74	0.29	32/19/49	97	98	109	99	7	86	72
	23	L	29		157	21	4	18	2	203	244	89	62	94	11	73	0.46	32/25/43	91	101	109	81	9	67	79
Perez,Carlos	22*	R	31	2	481	36	16	42	0	179	234	79	0	0	5	73	0.20	44/20/36	0	102	-14	82	0	0	41
	23	R	32		189	17	6	20	0	226	229	89	100	75	7	76	0.33	37/21/41	118	72	97	69	0	0	0
Pollock,A.J.	22	R	34	07	527	61	14	56	3	245	252	96	131	79	6	80	0.33	45/19/36	117	91	104	83	4	75	110
	23	R	35		144	15	5	15	0	165	213	71	49	100	6	76	0.28	49/11/41	105	81	96	89	5	0	36
Reyes,Franmil	22*	R	26	0	506	46	15	51	2	222	212	90	89	85	6	65	0.19	48/18/35	103	107	116	96	6	36	-41
	23*	R	27		221	19	6	22	0	168	188	70	77	68	8	61	0.22	54/16/30	67	78	67	84	0	0	-179
Reyes,Pablo	22*	R	28	46	425	38	7	35	9	196	218	77	47	98	6	77	0.27	58/8/33	26	72	-14	107	23	49	38
	23*	R	29		325	41	5	31	11	248	226	89	104	95	9	80	0.47	42/18/40	97	56	91	119	19	71	64
Schoop,Jonathan	22	R	30	45	510	48	11	38	5	202	240	80	71	77	4	78	0.18	46/19/35	86	80	81	74	6	100	24
	23	R	31		151	15	0	7	0	213	213	75	90	62	9	73	0.35	46/21/34	97	52	63	74	0	0	-89
Stallings,Jacob	22	R	32	2	384	25	4	34	0	223	202	83	78	79	8	76	0.35	42/19/39	75	50	81	79	1	0	-48
	23	R	33		276	22	3	20	0	191	202	77	86	75	10	72	0.40	48/15/37	90	71	110	71	0	0	-39
Stubbs,Garrett	22	L	29	2	121	19	5	16	2	264	244	115	165	94	12	72	0.47	42/19/39	73	125	87	130	6	100	176
	23	L	30		125	15	1	12	2	204	182	76	76	76	7	74	0.31	38/12/50	39	51	13	125	7	100	-25
Tapia,Raimel	22	L	28	9	431	47	7	52	8	265	261	95	89	90	4	80	0.20	55/20/26	98	74	53	123	11	80	93
	23*	L	29		283	40	6	20	14	219	225	84	42	99	10	69	0.36	59/17/24	69	62	80	138	27	76	-32
Wallach,Chad	22*	R	30	2	377	22	6	25	1	143	185	59	71	63	6	62	0.16	38/23/38	80	69	149	69	2	100	-217
	23*	R	31		211	21	8	20	1	210	214	88	108	74	8	66	0.25	38/19/43	81	107	114	96	5	36	-18
Wynns,Austin	22*	R	31	2	298	26	5	33	1	262	230	97	80	98	9	77	0.43	46/22/32	77	65	55	91	1	100	21
	23	R	32		145	11	1	10	1	208	199	74	88	68	6	70	0.23	47/18/35	66	54	56	88	3	100	-125
Zunino,Mike	22	R	31	2	123	7	5	16	0	148	182	71	70	67	5	60	0.13	29/17/54	94	118	146	57	0	0	-124
	23	R	32	0	140	11	3	11	0	177	168	79	105	68	11	51	0.25	48/16/37	69	124	90	85	0	0	-171

The following section contains player boxes for every pitcher who had significant playing time in 2023 and/or is expected to get fantasy roster-worthy innings in 2024. You will find some prospects here, but only those who logged MLB innings in 2023 and who we project to play a significant role in 2024. For more complete prospect coverage, see our Prospects section.

Snapshot Section

The top band of each player box contains the following information:

Age as of July 1, 2024.

Throws right (R) or left (L).

Role: Starters (SP) are those projected to face 20+ batters per game; the rest are relievers (RP).

Ht/Wt: Each batter's height and weight.

Type evaluates the extent to which a pitcher allows the ball to be put into play and his ground ball or fly ball tendency. CON (contact) represents pitchers who allow the ball to be put into play a great deal. PWR (power) represents those with high strikeout and/or walk totals who keep the ball out of play. GB are those who have a ground ball rate more than 50%; xGB are those who have a GB rate more than 55%. FB are those who have a fly ball rate more than 40%; xFB are those who have a FB rate more than 45%.

Reliability Grades analyze each pitcher's forecast risk, on an A-F scale. High grades go to those who have accumulated few injured list days (Health), have a history of substantial and regular major league playing time (PT/Exp) and have displayed consistent performance over the past three years, using xERA (Consist).

LIMA Plan Grade evaluates how well that pitcher would be a good fit for a team using the LIMA Plan draft strategy. Best grades go to pitchers who have excellent base skills and had a 2023 dollar value less than $20. Lowest grades will go to poor skills and values more than $20.

Random Variance Score (Rand Var) measures the impact random variance had on the pitcher's 2023 stats and the probability that his 2024 performance will exceed or fall short of 2023. The variables tracked are those prone to regression—H%, S%, HR/F and xERA to ERA variance. Players are rated on a scale of −5 to +5 with positive scores indicating rebounds and negative scores indicating corrections. Note that this score is computer-generated and the projections will override it on occasion.

Mayberry Method (MM) acknowledges the imprecision of the forecasting process by projecting player performance in broad strokes. The four digits of MM each represent a fantasy-relevant skill—ERA, strikeout rate, saves potential and playing time (IP)—and are all on a scale of 0 to 5. For additional information and specifics of MM, see page 60.

Commentaries for each pitcher provide a brief analysis of his skills and the potential impact on performance in 2024. MLB statistics are listed first for those who played only a portion of 2023 at the major league level. Note that these commentaries generally look at performance related issues only. Role and playing time expectations may impact these analyses, so you will have to adjust accordingly. Upside (UP) and downside (DN) statistical potential appears for some players; these are less grounded in hard data and more speculative of skills potential.

Commentaries that end with "(CB)" were written by BaseballHQ.com Director of Prospect Analysis Chris Blessing. As those players still have rookie eligibility and minimal MLB experience, we've decided it is more beneficial to describe the player's scouting attributes than to focus on his statistical or performance history. The author for the balance of any page's commentaries is noted after the final box on each page.

Player Stat Section

The past five years' statistics represent the total accumulated in the majors as well as in Triple-A, Double-A ball and various foreign leagues during each year. All non-major league stats have been converted to a major league equivalent (MLE) performance level. Minor league levels below Double-A are not included.

Nearly all baseball publications separate a player's statistical experiences in the major leagues from the minor leagues and outside leagues. While this may be appropriate for official record-keeping purposes, it is not an easy-to-analyze snapshot of a player's complete performance for a given year.

Bill James has proven that minor league statistics (converted to MLEs), at Double-A level or above, provide as accurate a record of a player's performance as major league statistics. Other researchers have also devised conversion factors for foreign leagues. Since these are adequate barometers, we include them in the pool of historical data for each year.

Team designations: An asterisk (*) appearing with a team name means that Triple-A and/or Double-A numbers are included in that year's stat line. Any stints of less than 10 IP are not included (to screen out most rehab appearances). A designation of "a/a" means the stats were accumulated at both AA and AAA levels that year. "for" represents a foreign or independent league. The designation "2TM" appears whenever a player was on more than one major league team, crossing leagues, in a season. "2AL" and "2NL" represent more than one team in the same league. Players who were cut during the season and finished 2023w as a free agent are designated as FAA (Free agent, AL) and FAN (Free agent, NL).

Stats: Descriptions of all the categories appear in the Encyclopedia.

- The leading decimal point has been suppressed on some categories to conserve space.
- Data for platoons (vL+, vR+), SwK, balls-in-play (G/L/F), HR/F and xHR/F, consistency (GS, APC, DOM, DIS), xWHIP and velocity (Vel) are for major league performance only.
- Formulas that use BIP data, like xERA and BPV, are used for years in which G/L/F data is available. Where feasible, older versions of these formulas are used otherwise.

Earned run average and WHIP are presented first next to each other, then skills-based xERA and xWHIP for comparison. Next is opponents' OPS splits vs. left-handed and right-handed batters (indexed to league average). Batters faced per game (BF/G) provide a quick view of a pitcher's role—starters will generally have levels over 20.

Basic pitching skills are measured by percentage of batters faced: BB% or walk rate, K% or strikeout rate, and K-BB%. xBB% and Swinging strike rate (SwK) are also presented with these basic skills; compare xBB% to BB% and our research shows that SwK serves as a skills-based indicator of K%. Vel is the pitcher's average fastball velocity.

Once the ball leaves the bat, it will either be a (G)round ball, (L)ine drive or (F)ly ball.

Random variance indicators include hit rate (H%)—often referred to as batting average on balls-in-play (BABIP)—which tends to regress to 30%. Normal strand rates (S%) fall within the tolerances of 65% to 80%. The ratio of home runs to fly balls (HR/F) is another sanity check; levels far from the league average of 12% are prone to regression, as is HR/F vs. xHR/F disparity.

In looking at consistency for starting pitchers, we track games started (GS), average pitch counts (APC) for all outings (for starters and relievers), the percentage of DOMinating starts (PQS 4 or 5) and DISaster starts (PQS 0 or 1). The larger the variance between DOM and DIS, the greater the consistency of good or bad performance.

For relievers, we look at their saves success rate (Sv%) and Leverage Index (LI). A Doug Dennis study showed little correlation between saves success and future opportunity. However, you can increase your odds by prospecting for pitchers who have *both* a high saves percentage (80% or better) *and* high skills. Relievers with LI levels over 1.0 are being used more often by managers to win ballgames.

The final section includes several overall performance measures: runs above replacement (RAR), Base performance index (BPX, which is BPV indexed to each year's league average) and the Rotisserie value (R$).

2024 Projections

Forecasts are computed from a player's trends over the past five years. Adjustments were made for leading indicators and variances between skill and statistical output. After reviewing the leading indicators, you might opt to make further adjustments.

Although each year's numbers include all playing time at the Double-A level or above, the 2024 forecast only represents potential playing time at the major league level, and again is highly preliminary.

Note that the projected Rotisserie values in this book will not necessarily align with each player's historical actuals. Since we currently have no idea who is going to close games for the Padres, or whether Ricky Tiedemann is going to break camp with the Blue Jays, it is impossible to create a finite pool of playing time, something which is required for valuation. So the projections are roughly based on a 12-team AL/NL league, and include an inflated number of innings, league-wide. This serves to flatten the spread of values and depress individual player dollar projections. In truth, a $25 player in this book might actually be worth $21, or $28. This level of precision is irrelevant in a process that is driven by market forces anyway. So, don't obsess over it.

Be aware of other sources that publish perfectly calibrated Rotisserie values over the winter. They are likely making arbitrary decisions as to where free agents are going to sign and who is going to land jobs in the spring. We do not make those leaps of faith here.

Bottom line... It is far too early to be making definitive projections for 2024, especially on playing time. Focus on the skill levels and trends, then consult BaseballHQ.com for playing time revisions as players change teams and roles become more defined. A free projections update will be available online in March.

Do-it-yourself analysis

Here are some data points you can look at in doing your own player analysis:

- Variance between vL+ and vR+ (opposition OPS)
- Variance in 2023 HR/F rate from 11-12%
- Variance in HR/F and xHR/F each year
- Variance in 2023 hit rate (H%) from 30%
- Variance in 2023 strand rate (S%) to tolerances (65% - 80%)
- Variance between ERA and xERA each year
- Growth or decline in base performance index (BPX)
- Spikes in innings pitched
- Trends in average pitch counts (APC)
- Trends in DOM/DIS splits
- Trends in saves success rate (Sv%)
- Variance between K% changes and corresponding SwK levels
- Variance between BB% changes and corresponding xBB% levels
- Improvement or decline in velocity

Abbott,Andrew

Age: 25 | Th: L | Role: SP | Ht: 6' 0" | Wt: 180 | Type: Pwr/xFB
Health: A | PT/Exp: D | Consist: B | LIMA Plan: A+ | Rand Var: -2 | MM: 2305

8-6, 3.87 ERA in 109 IP at CIN. Former 2nd-round pick flew up high minors to get first MLB shot and held his own. PRO: Strong off-speed stuff; filthy vL; lauded for acumen. DN: Hit wall in MLB 2nd half; xFB tilt bad fit in homer-happy park; relies on deception over stuff; lots of hard contact. For now, risk outweighs reward.

Yr	Tm	W	Sv	IP	K	ERA	WHIP	xERA	xWHIP	vL+	vR+	BF/G	BB%	K%	K-BB%	xBB%	SwK	Vel	G	L	F	H%	S%	HR/F	xHR/F	GS	APC	DOM%	DIS%	Sv%	LI	RAR	BPX	R$
19																																		
20																																		
21																																		
22	aa	7	0	91	104	5.05	1.44	4.31				19.4	10%	27%	17%							35%	65%									-12.1	105	-$4
23	CIN *	12	0	166	196	3.44	1.19	3.80	1.30	67	110	21.4	10%	26%	17%	8%	11.5%	92.8	29	20	52	29%	78%	11%	10%	21	90	10%	29%			18.2	112	$18
1st Half		8	0	94	118	2.05	0.92	2.38	1.12	48	72	21.9	8%	33%	25%	7%	11.9%	93.0	21	20	59	23%	89%	8%	7%	6	98	17%	0%			26.4	149	$39
2nd Half		4	0	72	78	5.25	1.54	4.83	1.34	77	128	21.1	10%	25%	15%	8%	11.3%	92.7	32	20	49	35%	70%	12%	11%	15	87	7%	40%			-8.2	91	-$1
Proj		**9**	**0**	**174**	**190**	**4.29**	**1.35**	**4.32**	**1.28**	**71**	**112**	**22.1**	**10%**	**26%**	**17%**	**8%**	**11.5%**	**92.8**	**27**	**20**	**53**	**32%**	**73%**	**11%**	**9%**	**33**						**0.9**	**96**	**$4**

Abreu,Bryan

Age: 27 | Th: R | Role: RP | Ht: 6' 1" | Wt: 225 | Type: Pwr
Health: B | PT/Exp: C | Consist: B | LIMA Plan: B+ | Rand Var: -5 | MM: 5420

The anatomy of a future closer... 1) Filthy SwK validates sky-high K%; 2) No lefty/righty risks; 3) Late control issues likely a blip (see xBB%). Sure, that hit/strand rate and HR/F fortune won't align again, so surface stats will take a step backwards. But with opportunity, that easily could be offset by... UP: 30 Sv

Yr	Tm	W	Sv	IP	K	ERA	WHIP	xERA	xWHIP	vL+	vR+	BF/G	BB%	K%	K-BB%	xBB%	SwK	Vel	G	L	F	H%	S%	HR/F	xHR/F	GS	APC	DOM%	DIS%	Sv%	LI	RAR	BPX	R$
19	HOU *	6	2	87	102	6.39	1.53	4.23	1.03	19	80	14.0	15%	27%	12%	9%	19.2%	95.1	50	25	25	33%	57%	0%	1%	0	21			67	0.44	-20.2	92	-$7
20	HOU	0	0	3	3	2.70	2.40	14.18		41	160	5.0	35%	15%	-20%		5.3%	92.9	38	25	38	14%	88%	0%	0%	0	19			0	0.49	0.7	-394	-$8
21	HOU *	3	1	52	56	4.49	1.47	4.07	1.42	107	99	4.9	13%	25%	12%	11%	13.5%	95.7	48	20	32	32%	70%	12%	12%	0	22			17	1.32	-1.4	92	-$4
22	HOU	4	2	60	88	1.94	1.18	2.70	1.12	71	90	4.5	10%	35%	25%	8%	18.1%	97.2	48	20	32	34%	84%	5%	10%	0	19			100	0.82	15.1	174	$7
23	HOU	3	5	72	100	1.75	1.04	3.29	1.18	82	69	4.0	11%	35%	24%	9%	17.3%	97.6	37	23	40	27%	88%	10%	14%	0	17			56	1.04	22.9	152	$13
1st Half		2	2	39	60	3.00	1.13	2.93	1.10	91	87	4.1	10%	38%	28%	8%	17.8%	97.7	40	23	37	32%	79%	17%	15%	0	18			40	0.95	6.4	188	$5
2nd Half		1	3	33	40	0.27	0.94	3.72	1.29	74	44	3.8	12%	31%	20%	9%	16.7%	97.5	34	21	44	22%	100%	3%	13%	0	16			75	1.15	16.5	111	$10
Proj		**3**	**11**	**58**	**74**	**2.74**	**1.10**	**3.16**	**1.17**	**84**	**78**	**4.4**	**10%**	**33%**	**23%**	**10%**	**16.3%**	**97.1**	**41**	**21**	**37**	**30%**	**77%**	**8%**	**13%**	**0**						**11.4**	**148**	**$9**

Adam,Jason

Age: 32 | Th: R | Role: RP | Ht: 6' 3" | Wt: 229 | Type: Pwr/FB
Health: C | PT/Exp: B | Consist: B | LIMA Plan: B+ | Rand Var: -2 | MM: 5421

A profit center on his 358 ADP, and it was no fluke. Whiffs remain at dominant level despite some regression. Leverage decline and resulting lack of save opps in 2nd half came in spite of sharpened command, so stopper goods remain. If late oblique injury doesn't linger and LI returns... UP: 30 Sv

Yr	Tm	W	Sv	IP	K	ERA	WHIP	xERA	xWHIP	vL+	vR+	BF/G	BB%	K%	K-BB%	xBB%	SwK	Vel	G	L	F	H%	S%	HR/F	xHR/F	GS	APC	DOM%	DIS%	Sv%	LI	RAR	BPX	R$
19	TOR	3	0	22	18	2.91	1.15	5.62	1.54	58	95	4.0	11%	20%	9%	12%	11.3%	94.5	25	23	52	25%	75%	3%	6%	0	17			0	1.12	4.3	28	-$1
20	CHC	2	0	14	21	3.29	1.24	3.79	1.28	85	100	4.5	14%	36%	22%	11%	17.7%	94.8	39	14	46	29%	80%	15%	9%	0	20			0	0.41	2.0	140	$0
21	CHC	1	0	11	19	5.91	1.50	3.36	1.15	124	92	4.2	12%	38%	26%	12%	14.2%	93.8	36	14	50	45%	60%	9%	11%	0	18			0	0.46	-2.2	182	-$6
22	TAM	2	8	63	75	1.56	0.76	2.87	1.06	62	69	3.5	7%	32%	25%	5%	18.7%	94.8	46	13	41	20%	86%	9%	8%	0	14			67	1.28	18.8	166	$13
23	TAM	4	12	54	69	2.98	1.01	3.38	1.17	84	87	4.0	9%	31%	22%	8%	15.0%	94.7	41	19	40	25%	77%	14%	19%	0	16			67	0.94	9.0	152	$10
1st Half		2	11	35	45	3.06	1.13	3.51	1.26	90	87	4.1	10%	29%	19%	9%	15.1%	94.3	45	20	35	27%	78%	14%	21%	0	17			69	1.00	5.6	134	$11
2nd Half		2	1	19	24	2.84	0.79	3.13	1.00	75	85	3.6	6%	35%	29%	6%	14.8%	95.3	35	15	50	21%	75%	15%	16%	0	15			50	0.81	3.5	188	$2
Proj		**5**	**10**	**65**	**77**	**3.06**	**1.00**	**3.16**	**1.10**	**90**	**95**	**3.9**	**7%**	**31%**	**24%**	**7%**	**15.6%**	**94.9**	**40**	**16**	**43**	**27%**	**75%**	**12%**	**15%**	**0**						**10.2**	**159**	**$11**

Adon,Joan

Age: 25 | Th: R | Role: SP | Ht: 6' 2" | Wt: 246 | Type:
Health: A | PT/Exp: C | Consist: A | LIMA Plan: C | Rand Var: +1 | MM: 1101

2-4, 6.45 ERA in 52 IP at WAS. Both stats and skills confirm he needed more work in minors. But when early rotation shot came, he couldn't find the plate, and his chance dried up quickly. That volatility makes him a poor bet to emerge as a starter anytime soon. Avoid until his club learns that any path to value here will only be forged by bullpen work.

Yr	Tm	W	Sv	IP	K	ERA	WHIP	xERA	xWHIP	vL+	vR+	BF/G	BB%	K%	K-BB%	xBB%	SwK	Vel	G	L	F	H%	S%	HR/F	xHR/F	GS	APC	DOM%	DIS%	Sv%	LI	RAR	BPX	R$
19																																		
20																																		
21	WAS *	1	0	23	35	5.39	1.57	4.98		204	60	20.5	11%	34%	23%		12.8%	95.1	73	18	9	43%	66%	100%	91%	1	94	0%	0%			-3.2	133	-$7
22	WAS *	3	0	108	90	6.12	1.68	5.57	1.56	125	123	20.2	13%	19%	6%	10%	7.0%	95.0	48	19	33	33%	64%	12%	17%	14	86	7%	57%			-28.7	47	-$17
23	WAS *	5	0	141	114	5.47	1.60	5.62	1.44	118	111	21.5	10%	20%	10%	8%	10.1%	94.5	37	25	37	34%	68%	13%	15%	10	77	0%	50%	0	0.70	-19.7	49	-$15
1st Half		2	0	78	55	5.09	1.66	5.76				23.4	10%	16%	6%							35%	70%	0%		0	0					-7.4	43	-$14
2nd Half		3	0	63	59	5.93	1.52	5.43	1.43	119	112	19.4	10%	21%	11%	8%	10.1%	94.5	37	25	37	32%	63%	13%	15%	10	77	0%	50%	0	0.70	-12.4	57	-$5
Proj		**4**	**0**	**116**	**93**	**4.61**	**1.42**	**4.63**	**1.47**	**103**	**99**	**22.9**	**11%**	**19%**	**8%**	**9%**	**8.8%**	**94.7**	**42**	**23**	**36**	**30%**	**70%**	**11%**	**16%**	**22**						**-4.1**	**45**	**-$5**

Alcantara,Sandy

Age: 28 | Th: R | Role: SP | Ht: 6' 5" | Wt: 200 | Type: Con/GB
Health: B | PT/Exp: A | Consist: B | LIMA Plan: A | Rand Var: 0 | MM: 4100

Rotation anchor's swift fall from perch driven by forearm issues that eventually led to October Tommy John surgery. Slide in strikeouts came in spite of tiny uptick in whiffs, so don't read much into his skills decline. There's injury profit here...in 2025.

Yr	Tm	W	Sv	IP	K	ERA	WHIP	xERA	xWHIP	vL+	vR+	BF/G	BB%	K%	K-BB%	xBB%	SwK	Vel	G	L	F	H%	S%	HR/F	xHR/F	GS	APC	DOM%	DIS%	Sv%	LI	RAR	BPX	R$
19	MIA	6	0	197	151	3.88	1.32	5.11	1.49	100	90	26.2	10%	18%	8%	7%	11.4%	95.6	45	19	36	28%	74%	11%	14%	32	97	25%	28%			15.3	51	$7
20	MIA	3	0	42	39	3.00	1.19	4.08	1.32	119	63	24.6	9%	23%	14%	8%	11.3%	96.5	49	22	29	28%	78%	12%	13%	7	95	29%	29%			7.5	102	$8
21	MIA	9	0	206	201	3.19	1.07	3.44	1.17	96	78	25.4	6%	24%	18%	5%	13.9%	97.9	53	19	28	28%	74%	13%	13%	33	94	48%	18%			27.2	143	$23
22	MIA	14	0	229	207	2.28	0.98	3.18	1.15	79	88	27.7	6%	23%	18%	5%	12.6%	97.9	53	16	31	27%	80%	9%	12%	32	102	56%	13%			47.5	137	$36
23	MIA	7	0	185	151	4.14	1.21	4.01	1.28	96	92	27.2	6%	20%	14%	5%	12.8%	97.8	52	17	31	29%	69%	13%	13%	28	97	32%	25%			4.3	111	$8
1st Half		3	0	108	89	4.93	1.25	4.20	1.33	99	90	26.5	7%	20%	12%	5%	13.3%	97.7	49	20	31	30%	61%	10%	9%	17	94	35%	24%			-8.0	97	$2
2nd Half		4	0	77	62	3.04	1.16	3.74	1.22	94	96	28.3	5%	20%	15%	4%	12.1%	98.1	57	13	30	29%	82%	17%	18%	11	102	27%	27%			12.3	133	$13
Proj		**0**	**0**	**7**	**6**	**3.37**	**1.14**	**3.51**	**1.23**	**96**	**87**	**26.0**	**6%**	**22%**	**15%**	**5%**	**12.7%**	**97.6**	**53**	**17**	**30**	**28%**	**75%**	**13%**	**14%**	**1**						**0.9**	**122**	**-$5**

Alexander,Tyler

Age: 29 | Th: L | Role: RP | Ht: 6' 2" | Wt: 203 | Type: Con/FB
Health: F | PT/Exp: A | Consist: A | LIMA Plan: B | Rand Var: 0 | MM: 2100

Sneaky tripling of skills base suggest he's a bargain-bin play, especially after torn lat ended year early. Here's why you shouldn't follow suit... 1) Jump in strikeouts had no support from still ultra-subpar SwK; 2) Real club didn't trust him with important work; 3) Soft-tossing flyball pitchers don't have long shelf lives.

Yr	Tm	W	Sv	IP	K	ERA	WHIP	xERA	xWHIP	vL+	vR+	BF/G	BB%	K%	K-BB%	xBB%	SwK	Vel	G	L	F	H%	S%	HR/F	xHR/F	GS	APC	DOM%	DIS%	Sv%	LI	RAR	BPX	R$
19	DET *	6	0	153	131	6.25	1.57	6.68	1.18	89	117	20.3	5%	20%	15%	5%	8.8%	90.7	36	26	38	37%	64%	13%	16%	8	71	0%	50%	0	0.59	-32.8	73	-$14
20	DET	2	0	36	34	3.96	1.32	4.20	1.21	72	130	10.9	6%	22%	16%	8%	9.3%	90.6	45	18	37	31%	80%	21%	17%	2	43	0%	50%	0	0.81	2.2	129	$1
21	DET	2	0	106	87	3.81	1.26	4.82	1.27	77	104	11.0	6%	19%	13%	5%	9.0%	90.4	38	18	44	30%	75%	11%	11%	15	40	13%	67%	0	0.56	6.0	93	$0
22	DET	4	0	101	61	4.81	1.32	4.91	1.33	101	114	15.8	6%	14%	8%	6%	7.9%	90.1	35	22	43	29%	69%	13%	14%	17	59	6%	53%	0	0.80	-10.5	56	-$6
23	DET	2	0	44	44	4.50	1.11	4.16	1.06	113	94	7.2	3%	24%	22%	4%	8.1%	89.9	32	18	50	31%	66%	13%	12%	1	27	0%	0%	0	0.52	-0.9	162	-$2
1st Half		2	0	44	44	4.50	1.11	4.16	1.06	114	95	7.2	3%	24%	22%	4%	8.1%	89.9	32	18	50	31%	66%	13%	10%	1	27	0%	0%	0	0.52	-0.9	163	-$1
2nd Half																																		
Proj		**2**	**0**	**58**	**50**	**4.50**	**1.27**	**4.09**	**1.19**	**95**	**114**	**10.2**	**5%**	**21%**	**16%**	**6%**	**8.6%**	**90.3**	**37**	**20**	**43**	**31%**	**71%**	**14%**	**13%**	**1**						**-1.2**	**118**	**-$3**

Allard,Kolby

Age: 26 | Th: L | Role: SP | Ht: 6' 1" | Wt: 195 | Type:
Health: F | PT/Exp: C | Consist: A | LIMA Plan: B | Rand Var: +5 | MM: 2100

Oblique strain followed by shoulder inflammation made this a lost year—which may have been a blessing. Deep woes vR make him unrosterable as a starter. That leaves relief work, during which he's inflicted a 6.68 ERA and 1.50 WHIP in 62 IP during career, with subpar skills. Time for patience is over, we need to see something now.

Yr	Tm	W	Sv	IP	K	ERA	WHIP	xERA	xWHIP	vL+	vR+	BF/G	BB%	K%	K-BB%	xBB%	SwK	Vel	G	L	F	H%	S%	HR/F	xHR/F	GS	APC	DOM%	DIS%	Sv%	LI	RAR	BPX	R$
19	TEX *	11	0	160	121	4.71	1.54	5.36	1.51	100	98	23.3	8%	17%	9%	8%	8.2%	92.5	45	26	29	34%	72%	7%	8%	9	93	11%	44%			-4.0	52	-$3
20	TEX	0	0	34	32	7.75	1.51	5.89	1.57	125	89	13.8	13%	21%	8%	8%	10.0%	91.6	33	19	48	30%	47%	9%	12%	8	60	13%	50%	0	0.60	-13.7	23	-$15
21	TEX	3	0	125	104	5.41	1.28	4.70	1.25	111	103	16.7	6%	19%	14%	6%	9.2%	91.6	39	20	41	29%	65%	18%	16%	17	64	12%	41%	0	0.78	-17.7	101	-$6
22	TEX *	4	1	110	110	4.79	1.31	5.11	1.23	109	145	15.1	9%	24%	15%	7%	11.7%	91.2	28	26	46	28%	72%	32%	18%	0	30			100	0.49	-11.1	59	-$3
23	ATL	0	0	12	13	6.57	1.62	4.79	1.25	74	125	14.0	7%	23%	16%	6%	12.0%	90.5	31	26	44	39%	61%	12%	11%	3	50	33%	33%	0	0.57	-3.4	113	-$8
1st Half		0	0	5	8	0.00	0.86	1.72		68	61	18.0	6%	44%	39%	4%	18.3%	90.5	56	22	22	37%	100%	0%	2%	1	71	100%	0%			2.5	292	-$8
2nd Half		0	0	8	5	10.57	2.09	6.94	1.49	77	156	12.7	8%	13%	5%	9%	8.5%	90.5	23	27	50	40%	50%	13%	13%	2	43	0%	50%	0	0.51	-5.9	13	-$11
Proj		**2**	**0**	**58**	**52**	**4.76**	**1.39**	**4.34**	**1.35**	**120**	**105**	**20.7**	**9%**	**21%**	**12%**	**8%**	**9.3%**	**91.8**	**38**	**21**	**41**	**30%**	**71%**	**15%**	**12%**	**12**						**-3.1**	**79**	**-$5**

STEPHEN NICKRAND

Allen,Logan

Allen,Logan		Health	A	LIMA Plan	A
Age: 25	Th: L Role SP	PT/Exp	D	Rand Var	-1
Ht: 6' 0"	Wt: 170 Type Pwr	Consist	B	MM	3203

7-8, 3.81 ERA in 125 IP at CLE. Soft-tossing lefty's skills have ebbed as he's faced tougher competition, particularly in terms of missing bats, as three-pitch mix lacks a single standout offering. That said, he throws strikes and controls LH bats well. Future may be as a lefty killer, but for now, he's a decent back-of-rotation arm.

Yr Tm	W	Sv	IP	K	ERA	WHIP	xERA	xWHIP	vL+	vR+	BF/G	BB%	K%	K-BB%	xBB%	SwK	Vel	G	L	F	H%	S%	HR/F	xHR/F	GS	APC	DOM%	DIS%	Sv%	LI	RAR	BPX	R$
19																																	
20																																	
21 aa	4	0	60	66	3.40	0.98	3.17				19.0	6%	29%	23%							26%	74%									6.4	146	$4
22 a/a	9	0	134	150	4.45	1.28	3.95				20.4	8%	27%	19%							33%	67%									-7.9	115	$2
23 CLE *	7	0	146	140	3.69	1.37	4.41	1.35	88	106	21.2	9%	22%	13%	8%	11.0%	91.5	43	21	37	32%	77%	12%	12%	24	89	17%	38%			11.6	84	$5
1st Half	3	0	77	79	3.02	1.37	4.17	1.31	100	103	21.6	9%	24%	15%	6%	12.0%	91.9	44	20	36	33%	81%	9%	13%	12	93	17%	42%			12.5	103	$7
2nd Half	4	0	69	61	4.44	1.38	4.68	1.40	75	109	20.7	10%	21%	11%	8%	10.0%	90.9	41	21	38	30%	72%	15%	10%	12	85	17%	33%			-0.9	65	$3
Proj	**9**	**0**	**160**	**161**	**3.83**	**1.26**	**3.79**	**1.26**	**81**	**99**	**20.5**	**8%**	**25%**	**16%**	**8%**	**10.8%**	**91.3**	**42**	**21**	**37**	**30%**	**74%**	**13%**	**12%**	**32**						**9.7**	**113**	**$8**

Alvarado,José

Alvarado,José		Health	D	LIMA Plan	A
Age: 29	Th: L Role RP	PT/Exp	C	Rand Var	-4
Ht: 6' 2"	Wt: 245 Type Pwr/GB	Consist	C	MM	5510

Missed time with two separate bouts of elbow inflammation, often a scary diagnosis. But he closed the season healthy and was reaching 100 mph in the playoffs. When upright, he's dominated now for two seasons, with best skills of career. Was in saves mix early and late, and with his now-established ability to shut down RHB, too... UP: 30 Sv

Yr Tm	W	Sv	IP	K	ERA	WHIP	xERA	xWHIP	vL+	vR+	BF/G	BB%	K%	K-BB%	xBB%	SwK	Vel	G	L	F	H%	S%	HR/F	xHR/F	GS	APC	DOM%	DIS%	Sv%	LI	RAR	BPX	R$
19 TAM	1	7	30	39	4.80	1.87	5.29	1.70	71	113	4.2	18%	27%	8%	12%	12.8%	98.2	48	22	30	37%	74%	9%	10%	1	17	0%	100%	78	1.17	-1.1	19	-$3
20 TAM	0	0	9	13	6.00	1.67	4.41	1.40	35	140	5.0	13%	29%	16%	10%	10.8%	96.9	42	25	33	36%	69%	25%	29%	0	22			0	0.42	-1.7	104	-$8
21 PHI	7	5	56	68	4.20	1.60	4.21	1.67	65	113	3.9	19%	27%	8%	11%	12.8%	99.4	57	21	22	29%	75%	18%	13%	0	16			63	1.29	0.4	30	$0
22 PHI	4	2	51	81	3.18	1.22	2.35	1.11	90	79	3.6	11%	38%	27%	8%	17.5%	99.6	56	20	24	36%	73%	8%	12%	0	15			50	1.10	5.0	195	$3
23 PHI	0	10	41	64	1.74	1.16	2.59	1.12	70	84	4.1	10%	37%	27%	7%	16.2%	98.7	54	21	25	34%	89%	14%	10%	0	18			83	1.03	13.2	199	$6
1st Half	0	6	24	37	1.48	1.11	2.23	1.00	83	87	4.1	7%	37%	30%	7%	16.8%	99.1	56	24	20	36%	92%	18%	15%	0	17			75	1.01	8.6	237	$4
2nd Half	0	4	17	27	2.12	1.24	3.16	1.31	45	80	4.1	15%	37%	22%	6%	15.3%	98.3	51	17	31	30%	85%	9%	5%	0	19			100	1.05	4.6	146	$0
Proj	**2**	**10**	**51**	**74**	**2.94**	**1.16**	**2.53**	**1.13**	**67**	**88**	**3.6**	**11%**	**36%**	**26%**	**9%**	**15.0%**	**98.9**	**54**	**20**	**26**	**33%**	**76%**	**13%**	**10%**	**0**						**8.7**	**184**	**$6**

Alzolay,Adbert

Alzolay,Adbert		Health	F	LIMA Plan	B
Age: 29	Th: R Role RP	PT/Exp	C	Rand Var	-2
Ht: 6' 1"	Wt: 208 Type Pwr	Consist	C	MM	4330

Slider specialist suffered a case of sinistrophobia late, as lefties devoured him. That may be related to the forearm strain that eventually landed him on the IL in Sept, but he's been susceptible to LHB before. Regardless, the forearm was probably a factor in the overall 2nd-half skills decline. Still looks good for saves, but those vL metrics bear watching.

Yr Tm	W	Sv	IP	K	ERA	WHIP	xERA	xWHIP	vL+	vR+	BF/G	BB%	K%	K-BB%	xBB%	SwK	Vel	G	L	F	H%	S%	HR/F	xHR/F	GS	APC	DOM%	DIS%	Sv%	LI	RAR	BPX	R$
19 CHC *	3	0	78	88	5.84	1.52	5.34	1.67	133	109	17.9	13%	26%	13%	10%	11.1%	94.4	32	24	43	32%	66%	25%	18%	2	56	0%	100%	0	0.54	-12.9	60	-$7
20 CHC	1	0	21	29	2.95	1.17	3.59	1.37	90	66	14.5	15%	33%	18%	9%	11.4%	94.7	43	27	30	26%	75%	8%	12%	4	65	25%	0%	0	0.72	3.9	105	$1
21 CHC	5	1	126	128	4.58	1.16	3.74	1.18	128	74	17.9	7%	25%	18%	6%	12.4%	93.9	45	21	34	28%	68%	22%	20%	21	67	29%	38%	100	0.84	-4.9	134	$3
22 CHC	2	0	13	19	3.38	0.83	2.50	0.86	108	68	8.7	4%	37%	33%	5%	16.1%	94.8	40	20	40	30%	60%	8%	11%	0	32			0	1.21	1.0	234	-$2
23 CHC	2	22	64	67	2.67	1.02	3.45	1.11	98	73	4.4	5%	26%	21%	6%	13.8%	95.3	42	22	36	29%	77%	8%	10%	0	17			88	1.14	13.1	157	$15
1st Half	1	4	35	37	2.06	0.89	3.18	1.06	60	85	4.5	5%	28%	24%	5%	14.0%	95.0	47	15	38	27%	79%	6%	5%	0	18			100	1.00	9.8	175	$8
2nd Half	1	18	29	30	3.41	1.17	3.77	1.16	128	57	4.2	6%	25%	19%	6%	13.7%	95.8	37	28	35	32%	74%	11%	16%	0	16			86	1.28	3.3	140	$11
Proj	**2**	**29**	**58**	**61**	**3.39**	**1.19**	**3.46**	**1.19**	**128**	**78**	**6.1**	**8%**	**26%**	**19%**	**6%**	**13.5%**	**95.2**	**42**	**23**	**35**	**30%**	**77%**	**14%**	**13%**	**0**						**6.7**	**132**	**$13**

Anderson,Chase

Anderson,Chase		Health	F	LIMA Plan	C
Age: 36	Th: R Role RP	PT/Exp	C	Rand Var	0
Ht: 6' 1"	Wt: 210 Type Con/FB	Consist	B	MM	0000

1-6, 5.42 ERA in 86 IP at TAM/COL. Purchased by TAM on May 3, gave him 5 IP and said, "Nope." Got a second chance with COL, which went as poorly as expected. There's nothing in these metrics that suggests anything will get better. If you're 36 with a history of ERAs that look like California gas prices, it's time to move on. DN: 0 IP

Yr Tm	W	Sv	IP	K	ERA	WHIP	xERA	xWHIP	vL+	vR+	BF/G	BB%	K%	K-BB%	xBB%	SwK	Vel	G	L	F	H%	S%	HR/F	xHR/F	GS	APC	DOM%	DIS%	Sv%	LI	RAR	BPX	R$
19 MIL	8	0	139	124	4.21	1.27	5.09	1.39	80	118	18.5	8%	21%	12%	7%	11.2%	93.4	35	20	45	28%	73%	13%	11%	27	75	4%	33%	0	0.73	5.1	76	$6
20 TOR	1	0	34	38	7.22	1.63	4.44	1.20	143	126	15.4	6%	25%	18%	9%	12.1%	92.5	37	27	37	37%	64%	29%	25%	7	65	14%	57%	0	0.64	-11.5	142	-$13
21 PHI *	3	0	81	56	6.51	1.60	6.52	1.47	90	143	14.9	9%	16%	6%	8%	10.2%	91.5	36	19	44	31%	64%	15%	15%	9	61	0%	67%	0	0.55	-22.5	8	-$15
22 CIN *	9	1	104	78	5.26	1.47	5.28	1.55	97	101	12.4	10%	17%	7%	12%	9.5%	92.1	52	18	31	30%	68%	16%	11%	7	55	0%	29%	100	0.83	-16.6	36	-$7
23 2 TM *	3	1	117	78	5.31	1.53	5.92	1.45	113	112	19.5	9%	17%	8%	10%	9.5%	93.2	36	21	43	29%	71%	15%	12%	17	76	6%	47%	100	0.74	-14.1	14	-$12
1st Half	2	1	69	47	6.06	1.62	6.70	1.53	125	119	19.0	10%	15%	6%	9%	9.5%	93.2	37	24	39	31%	68%	19%	14%	9	71	0%	44%	100	0.71	-14.6	2	-$16
2nd Half	1	0	48	31	4.25	1.42	4.79	1.59	94	106	20.3	11%	16%	5%	12%	9.5%	93.1	35	17	48	27%	75%	11%	10%	8	83	13%	50%			0.5	32	-$4
Proj	**2**	**0**	**58**	**43**	**5.54**	**1.52**	**5.08**	**1.47**	**113**	**120**	**16.6**	**10%**	**17%**	**7%**	**10%**	**10.5%**	**92.8**	**36**	**22**	**42**	**30%**	**69%**	**15%**	**15%**	**10**						**-8.6**	**35**	**-$9**

Anderson,Tyler

Anderson,Tyler		Health	D	LIMA Plan	C+
Age: 34	Th: L Role SP	PT/Exp	A	Rand Var	-1
Ht: 6' 2"	Wt: 220 Type /xFB	Consist	C	MM	1103

Turned back into a pumpkin after two relatively encouraging seasons. Sure, xERA showed that 2022 was a mirage, but this was worse, as walks reverted to pre-2021 levels. LAA inexplicably gave him 3 years/$39M after 2022 (apparently, wins and ERA are still a big deal in Anaheim), so he'll keep getting run out there. That doesn't mean you have to.

Yr Tm	W	Sv	IP	K	ERA	WHIP	xERA	xWHIP	vL+	vR+	BF/G	BB%	K%	K-BB%	xBB%	SwK	Vel	G	L	F	H%	S%	HR/F	xHR/F	GS	APC	DOM%	DIS%	Sv%	LI	RAR	BPX	R$
19 COL	0	0	21	23	11.76	2.13	5.45	1.44	154	155	21.2	10%	22%	11%	6%	11.4%	91.3	41	26	33	41%	47%	35%	32%	5	86	0%	40%			-18.5	76	-$12
20 SF	4	0	60	41	4.37	1.39	5.89	1.52	119	92	20.0	10%	16%	6%	7%	10.9%	90.2	28	27	44	29%	69%	6%	9%	11	73	9%	36%	0	0.95	0.6	18	$2
21 2 TM	7	0	167	134	4.53	1.25	4.75	1.25	96	103	22.7	5%	19%	14%	4%	12.0%	90.2	35	22	43	30%	69%	12%	10%	31	84	19%	39%			-5.4	96	$2
22 LA	15	0	179	138	2.57	1.00	3.98	1.19	90	86	23.6	5%	20%	15%	5%	12.2%	90.5	40	18	42	26%	78%	6%	7%	28	86	36%	18%	0	0.78	30.8	107	$26
23 LAA	6	0	141	119	5.43	1.49	5.56	1.47	117	107	23.3	10%	19%	9%	8%	13.0%	90.0	31	21	48	31%	66%	10%	10%	25	90	0%	40%	0	0.77	-19.0	40	-$10
1st Half	4	0	80	63	5.20	1.53	5.73	1.48	95	116	23.8	10%	18%	8%	8%	12.0%	89.6	31	21	49	33%	67%	7%	8%	15	92	0%	47%			-8.5	34	-$8
2nd Half	2	0	61	56	5.72	1.43	5.33	1.46	149	98	22.7	11%	21%	10%	8%	14.2%	90.4	31	21	47	29%	64%	13%	14%	10	87	0%	30%	0	0.76	-10.5	48	-$5
Proj	**8**	**0**	**160**	**130**	**4.71**	**1.34**	**4.64**	**1.37**	**113**	**101**	**21.9**	**9%**	**20%**	**11%**	**6%**	**12.6%**	**90.2**	**33**	**21**	**45**	**30%**	**68%**	**10%**	**10%**	**30**						**-7.5**	**64**	**[illegible]**

Armstrong,Shawn

Armstrong,Shawn		Health	D	LIMA Plan	A
Age: 33	Th: R Role RP	PT/Exp	C	Rand Var	-5
Ht: 6' 2"	Wt: 225 Type Pwr/FB	Consist	C	MM	3300

Missed the first two months with a neck injury, then returned with a newfound, seemingly mystical ability to strand runners and to keep the ball in the yard. The former is mostly luck; the latter due to cutting opponent's barrel rate to a mere 3.6%. Without any real changes in pitch makeup, that seems likely to regress, too. In short, heed xERA here.

Yr Tm	W	Sv	IP	K	ERA	WHIP	xERA	xWHIP	vL+	vR+	BF/G	BB%	K%	K-BB%	xBB%	SwK	Vel	G	L	F	H%	S%	HR/F	xHR/F	GS	APC	DOM%	DIS%	Sv%	LI	RAR	BPX	R$
19 2 AL	1	4	58	63	5.74	1.64	5.45	1.44	81	125	4.9	11%	23%	13%	8%	12.5%	93.4	29	25	45	37%	67%	10%	13%	0	21			44	1.07	-8.8	67	-$
20 BAL	2	0	15	14	1.80	0.80	3.76	1.15	85	65	4.1	5%	25%	19%	6%	12.7%	93.7	44	18	38	22%	82%	7%	10%	0	17			0	0.75	4.9	141	$
21 2 AL *	4	2	67	75	5.55	1.53	6.30	1.25	159	93	4.9	8%	26%	17%	8%	14.3%	93.9	32	22	46	36%	70%	21%	17%	0	22			50	0.58	-10.6	67	-$
22 2 TM	2	2	62	66	4.38	1.35	3.56	1.16	121	100	5.4	6%	25%	18%	4%	13.1%	95.5	48	19	34	35%	70%	11%	12%	3	21	0%	67%	67	0.68	-3.1	146	-$
23 TAM	1	0	52	54	1.38	0.90	3.70	1.12	74	67	5.3	5%	26%	21%	5%	13.5%	94.7	38	21	41	27%	87%	4%	4%	6	20	0%	17%	0	0.72	18.9	149	$
1st Half	0	0	16	15	1.15	1.02	4.14	1.21	91	61	5.3	6%	24%	17%	5%	12.1%	94.2	37	19	44	27%	93%	5%	6%	1	21	0%	0%	0	0.57	6.2	122	-$
2nd Half	1	0	36	39	1.49	0.85	3.51	1.09	68	70	5.3	5%	27%	22%	5%	14.2%	94.9	39	22	39	27%	83%	3%	3%	5	20	0%	20%	0	0.79	12.8	163	$
Proj	**2**	**0**	**58**	**62**	**3.28**	**1.21**	**3.69**	**1.18**	**102**	**87**	**4.9**	**7%**	**26%**	**19%**	**6%**	**13.5%**	**94.4**	**37**	**21**	**42**	**32%**	**77%**	**10%**	**10%**	**0**						**7.5**	**131**	**$**

Ashcraft,Graham

Ashcraft,Graham		Health	D	LIMA Plan	B
Age: 26	Th: R Role SP	PT/Exp	B	Rand Var	+1
Ht: 6' 2"	Wt: 240 Type Con	Consist	B	MM	2003

Missed time to calf and toe injuries. Otherwise, skills looked a lot like 2022. And like in 2022, the metrics don't seem to fit his nasty, sinking, 97-mph stuff. Times-through-order stats are telling: 3.13 ERA 1st time through, followed by 4.85 the 2nd, 6.45 the 3rd time through. Converted to SP from relief, those numbers suggest a return to the bullpen in time.

Yr Tm	W	Sv	IP	K	ERA	WHIP	xERA	xWHIP	vL+	vR+	BF/G	BB%	K%	K-BB%	xBB%	SwK	Vel	G	L	F	H%	S%	HR/F	xHR/F	GS	APC	DOM%	DIS%	Sv%	LI	RAR	BPX	R$
19																																	
20																																	
21 aa	7	0	73	66	4.05	1.27	3.51				21.3	8%	22%	14%							31%	68%									1.9	101	$
22 CIN *	8	0	144	106	4.56	1.52	5.01	1.33	80	126	22.4	8%	17%	9%	7%	8.9%	97.2	55	21	25	35%	70%	13%	11%	19	92	21%	53%			-10.5	67	-$
23 CIN	7	0	146	111	4.76	1.37	4.52	1.41	97	114	24.0	8%	18%	9%	7%	10.1%	96.7	48	21	31	29%	69%	17%	14%	26	89	15%	31%			-7.6	70	-$
1st Half	3	0	76	59	6.66	1.59	4.85	1.46	113	119	23.1	9%	17%	8%	8%	10.2%	96.8	48	23	29	33%	60%	18%	15%	15	86	13%	40%			-21.7	56	-$1
2nd Half	4	0	70	52	2.70	1.14	4.16	1.34	82	110	25.3	7%	19%	12%	5%	10.0%	96.5	48	19	34	26%	84%	15%	12%	11	94	18%	18%			14.1	86	$1
Proj	**9**	**0**	**145**	**115**	**4.31**	**1.34**	**4.05**	**1.36**	**93**	**117**	**22.9**	**8%**	**19%**	**11%**	**7%**	**9.8%**	**96.8**	**49**	**21**	**30**	**30%**	**71%**	**14%**	**12%**	**26**						**0.3**	**81**	**$**

ROD TRUESDELL

Assad,Javier

Age: 26 Th: R Role SP
Ht: 6' 1" Wt: 200 Type Con

Health	A	LIMA Plan	C+
PT/Exp	C	Rand Var	-2
Consist	C	MM	2001

5-3, 3.05 ERA in 109 IP at CHC. Shiny surface stats—check out that 2nd half—will make him draft-worthy regardless of role. But 6th-lowest SwK among SP and marginal command out of bullpen give him risk in any job. With normalized hit and strand rates, he's a 4.00-ERA pitcher. That has value, but only if you stick him near the back of your staff.

Yr Tm	W	Sv	IP	K	ERA	WHIP	xERA	xWHIP	vL+	vR+	BF/G	BB%	K%	K-BB%	xBB%	SwK	Vel	G	L	F	H%	S%	HR/F	xHR/F	GS	APC	DOM%	DIS%	Sv%	LI	RAR	BPX	R$
19																																	
20																																	
21 aa	4	0	94	62	5.98	1.69	6.39				19.3	8%	15%	7%							36%	66%									-19.8	32	-$16
22 CHC *	7	0	149	121	2.62	1.27	3.69	1.53	124	81	19.1	9%	20%	11%	9%	10.1%	92.6	39	22	40	30%	83%	9%	9%	8	77	0%	50%	0	0.71	24.8	84	$10
23 CHC *	5	0	126	106	3.08	1.22	3.52	1.38	87	101	14.1	9%	21%	12%	10%	8.4%	92.9	47	19	35	27%	79%	12%	14%	10	54	20%	60%	0	0.55	19.4	82	$9
1st Half	0	0	50	37	4.14	1.43	4.26	1.53	113	111	13.3	11%	18%	7%	9%	8.1%	93.1	42	20	38	30%	72%	10%	15%	1	44	0%	100%	0	0.30	1.2	63	-$8
2nd Half	5	0	76	69	2.38	1.08	3.88	1.31	76	96	15.2	8%	23%	15%	10%	8.5%	92.8	49	18	33	25%	85%	13%	13%	9	59	22%	56%	0	0.70	18.2	107	$19
Proj	5	0	116	92	3.90	1.38	4.36	1.40	109	107	20.7	9%	19%	10%	10%	8.8%	92.8	45	19	36	31%	74%	10%	12%	24						6.1	68	-$1

Bachman,Sam

Age: 24 Th: R Role RP
Ht: 6' 1" Wt: 235 Type Pwr/GB

Health	D	LIMA Plan	D+
PT/Exp	F	Rand Var	-2
Consist	A	MM	1000

1-2, 3.18 ERA in 17 IP at LAA. 9th overall pick in 2021 draft got MLB shot after barely 50 career innings in minors. Extreme groundball lean pairs uniquely with high-90s velocity, but chronic control issues remained so in majors, and lack of third pitch limits speculation appeal to relief role. Check back in a year.

Yr Tm	W	Sv	IP	K	ERA	WHIP	xERA	xWHIP	vL+	vR+	BF/G	BB%	K%	K-BB%	xBB%	SwK	Vel	G	L	F	H%	S%	HR/F	xHR/F	GS	APC	DOM%	DIS%	Sv%	LI	RAR	BPX	R$
19																																	
20																																	
21																																	
22 aa	1	0	45	26	3.54	1.43	4.07				16.0	12%	14%	2%							27%	77%									2.4	42	-$5
23 LAA *	4	1	44	39	5.11	1.46	3.69	1.67	109	84	11.1	14%	18%	4%	11%	11.4%	96.9	59	22	20	26%	64%	0%	2%	0	29			50	0.72	-4.2	73	-$5
1st Half	4	1	42	38	4.89	1.37	3.31	1.66	88	76	11.1	15%	21%	5%	11%	12.5%	96.9	60	21	19	24%	64%	0%	3%	0	27			50	0.75	-2.9	78	-$3
2nd Half	0	0	2	1	10.80	3.60	10.31		271	131	11.0	18%	9%	-9%		4.6%	97.1	50	25	25	52%	67%	0%	0%	0	44			0	0.37	-1.3	-188	-$9
Proj	3	0	44	33	4.36	1.56	4.39	1.64	124	98	13.2	14%	18%	4%	11%	12.5%	96.9	60	21	19	30%	72%	15%	3%	5						-0.2	19	-$6

Baker,Bryan

Age: 29 Th: R Role RP
Ht: 6' 6" Wt: 245 Type Pwr/xFB

Health	A	LIMA Plan	C+
PT/Exp	C	Rand Var	-3
Consist	C	MM	2300

Another pitcher whose stats seemingly make them draftable... until you look under the hood. Flyball pitchers are risky. Those that don't generate many whiffs are risky. As are pitchers coming off friendly hit/strand and hr/f rates. This one fits in all three groups, and xERA validates it. Don't speculate again until skills show more life.

Yr Tm	W	Sv	IP	K	ERA	WHIP	xERA	xWHIP	vL+	vR+	BF/G	BB%	K%	K-BB%	xBB%	SwK	Vel	G	L	F	H%	S%	HR/F	xHR/F	GS	APC	DOM%	DIS%	Sv%	LI	RAR	BPX	R$
19 a/a	3	12	54	58	4.58	1.58	4.06				4.8	17%	24%	8%							30%	71%									-0.5	84	$2
20																																	
21 TOR *	6	11	43	38	1.85	1.03	1.65			66	4.1	11%	23%	11%		21.1%	94.9	0	33	67	22%	83%	0%	0%	0	19			85	0.01	12.8	111	$10
22 BAL	4	1	70	76	3.49	1.23	3.60	1.23	90	85	4.4	9%	26%	17%	8%	11.4%	96.3	42	22	35	32%	71%	5%	6%	2	18	0%	50%	33	1.02	4.1	117	$2
23 BAL	4	0	45	51	3.60	1.27	4.51	1.41	68	99	4.0	13%	27%	15%	8%	10.1%	95.8	35	17	49	28%	74%	8%	7%	0	17			0	1.12	4.1	75	$0
1st Half	3	0	34	43	3.93	1.22	4.29	1.37	71	90	3.8	14%	31%	17%	8%	11.0%	95.6	32	16	53	28%	68%	5%	4%	0	16			0	1.04	1.7	88	-$1
2nd Half	1	0	11	8	2.53	1.41	5.29	1.53	55	122	5.1	11%	17%	7%	8%	7.1%	96.3	42	18	39	27%	92%	15%	17%	0	22			0	1.43	2.4	32	-$5
Proj	5	0	58	64	3.97	1.34	4.27	1.41	83	92	4.2	13%	27%	14%	9%	11.2%	95.9	36	18	46	30%	70%	5%	5%	0						2.6	71	-$1

Bard,Daniel

Age: 39 Th: R Role RP
Ht: 6' 4" Wt: 215 Type Pwr/FB

Health	D	LIMA Plan	D+
PT/Exp	A	Rand Var	-5
Consist	F	MM	0310

Early bouts with anxiety torpedoed skills and reduced leverage, then forearm strain ended year. PRO: Expected walk rate says he can find plate again; one year removed from viable end-game skills. CON: Lucky H% and S% suggest the opposite; dive in swings-and-misses wasn't a one-year blip. Given age, don't bet on much of a rebound. Or any.

Yr Tm	W	Sv	IP	K	ERA	WHIP	xERA	xWHIP	vL+	vR+	BF/G	BB%	K%	K-BB%	xBB%	SwK	Vel	G	L	F	H%	S%	HR/F	xHR/F	GS	APC	DOM%	DIS%	Sv%	LI	RAR	BPX	R$
19																																	
20 COL	4	6	25	27	3.65	1.30	4.08	1.30	109	72	4.6	9%	25%	16%	6%	12.9%	97.1	48	17	35	32%	73%	9%	13%	0	18			100	1.42	2.4	118	$12
21 COL	7	20	66	80	5.21	1.60	4.22	1.37	139	77	4.5	12%	26%	14%	8%	13.4%	97.5	42	26	31	37%	69%	14%	10%	0	18			71	1.07	-7.6	92	$3
22 COL	6	34	60	69	1.79	0.99	3.18	1.25	78	63	4.3	10%	28%	18%	7%	11.8%	98.0	52	18	30	24%	84%	7%	9%	0	17			92	1.56	16.2	126	$23
23 COL	4	1	49	47	4.56	1.70	6.61	2.01	120	96	4.6	21%	20%	-1%	12%	8.1%	94.8	37	18	45	25%	75%	9%	13%	0	19			33	0.68	-1.4	-81	-$6
1st Half	3	0	28	26	1.91	1.45	5.68	1.89	130	70	4.5	20%	21%	2%	10%	8.7%	94.9	41	17	42	22%	90%	7%	13%	0	19			0	0.66	8.5	-44	-$1
2nd Half	1	1	21	21	8.14	2.05	7.96	2.15	96	124	4.8	23%	19%	-4%	12%	7.5%	94.8	32	19	49	28%	60%	10%	13%	0	19			33	0.70	-9.9	-132	-$11
Proj	5	3	58	61	4.90	1.63	5.23	1.76	118	94	4.4	19%	24%	5%	11%	9.8%	96.0	40	20	40	28%	71%	10%	12%	0						-4.1	-14	-$5

Barlow,Scott

Age: 31 Th: R Role RP
Ht: 6' 3" Wt: 210 Type Pwr

Health	A	LIMA Plan	A+
PT/Exp	A	Rand Var	0
Consist	B	MM	4420

Huge step backward just when it looked like he was becoming a solid saves source. Can he bounce back? Big spike in walks fueled the dip, but his xBB% was right in line with prior baseline. More concerning is the three-year erosion of SwK and a FB that's leaking oil. H%/S% say it wasn't this bad, but he'll need opps to turn a profit and LI seems dubious.

Yr Tm	W	Sv	IP	K	ERA	WHIP	xERA	xWHIP	vL+	vR+	BF/G	BB%	K%	K-BB%	xBB%	SwK	Vel	G	L	F	H%	S%	HR/F	xHR/F	GS	APC	DOM%	DIS%	Sv%	LI	RAR	BPX	R$
19 KC	3	1	70	92	4.22	1.44	4.19	1.35	112	88	5.1	12%	30%	18%	8%	14.8%	94.1	40	23	37	35%	72%	9%	11%	0	21			33	1.13	2.5	111	-$1
20 KC	2	2	30	39	4.20	1.20	3.31	1.10	103	85	3.9	7%	31%	24%	7%	17.2%	94.9	47	19	34	34%	69%	16%	21%	0	16			100	0.95	0.9	184	$4
21 KC	5	16	74	91	2.42	1.20	3.68	1.20	93	78	4.3	9%	30%	21%	8%	16.2%	95.4	39	23	38	32%	81%	6%	11%	0	17			73	1.26	16.9	136	$14
22 KC	7	24	74	77	2.18	1.00	3.31	1.17	86	82	4.2	8%	27%	19%	6%	14.6%	93.7	48	16	37	24%	86%	13%	12%	0	17			86	1.46	16.4	134	$20
23 2 TM	2	13	68	79	4.37	1.40	4.05	1.36	108	76	4.7	11%	26%	15%	8%	13.4%	93.1	43	25	32	34%	68%	7%	7%	0	19			81	1.07	-0.3	98	$2
1st Half	2	10	31	43	4.06	1.29	3.26	1.24	131	52	4.4	11%	33%	21%	7%	15.1%	92.7	47	24	29	33%	70%	14%	12%	0	18			83	1.31	1.0	149	$6
2nd Half	0	3	37	36	4.62	1.49	4.74	1.47	89	96	5.1	11%	21%	10%	8%	12.1%	93.4	40	26	34	34%	67%	3%	4%	0	20			75	0.85	-1.3	57	-$4
Proj	3	10	58	68	3.80	1.28	3.55	1.27	101	81	4.4	10%	28%	18%	8%	14.5%	93.9	43	22	34	32%	71%	9%	10%	0						3.8	119	$4

Barria,Jaime

Age: 27 Th: R Role RP
Ht: 6' 1" Wt: 210 Type Con/FB

Health	B	LIMA Plan	C+
PT/Exp	B	Rand Var	+1
Consist	C	MM	1000

Years of overperforming xERA finally caught up with him, and boy, the crash was hard. Skills weren't any better when he was sent to bullpen. Rising flyball rate adds even further risk to completely underwhelming profile. His career is at a crossroads now and leaves no reason to speculate on him anymore.

Yr Tm	W	Sv	IP	K	ERA	WHIP	xERA	xWHIP	vL+	vR+	BF/G	BB%	K%	K-BB%	xBB%	SwK	Vel	G	L	F	H%	S%	HR/F	xHR/F	GS	APC	DOM%	DIS%	Sv%	LI	RAR	BPX	R$
19 LAA *	7	0	132	113	7.17	1.52	6.90	1.35	96	142	19.7	6%	20%	13%	10%	9.6%	91.7	34	19	46	33%	59%	20%	16%	13	79	0%	62%	0	0.81	-43.3	30	-$14
20 LAA	1	0	32	27	3.62	1.11	4.84	1.30	117	64	18.9	7%	20%	14%	6%	10.8%	92.1	34	21	45	27%	70%	7%	5%	5	73	20%	40%	0	0.73	3.3	90	$2
21 LAA *	5	0	106	63	4.32	1.43	5.48	1.43	116	111	19.5	6%	14%	8%	8%	8.4%	93.1	44	23	33	32%	74%	13%	12%	11	71	9%	55%	0	0.80	-0.7	42	-$5
22 LAA	3	0	79	54	2.61	1.03	4.27	1.28	111	82	9.0	6%	17%	11%	6%	11.3%	91.9	41	18	41	23%	83%	11%	14%	1	32	0%	100%	0	0.75	13.3	78	$5
23 LAA	2	0	82	62	5.68	1.47	5.42	1.42	109	120	10.6	8%	17%	9%	8%	10.6%	93.0	36	19	45	29%	68%	17%	14%	6	40	17%	33%	0	0.71	-13.7	53	-$10
1st Half	2	0	49	40	2.92	1.18	4.57	1.35	106	82	12.0	8%	20%	12%	6%	11.3%	92.9	40	21	39	26%	82%	13%	13%	5	44	20%	40%	0	1.02	8.6	80	$3
2nd Half	0	0	33	22	9.82	1.91	6.73	1.52	115	165	9.3	9%	14%	5%	10%	9.6%	93.1	32	16	52	34%	54%	20%	15%	1	35	0%	0%	0	0.40	-22.3	17	-$19
Proj	2	0	58	41	5.51	1.44	4.84	1.38	112	119	11.6	7%	17%	9%	8%	10.0%	92.7	38	19	43	30%	68%	16%	13%	3						-8.5	60	-$8

Bassitt,Chris

Age: 35 Th: R Role SP
Ht: 6' 5" Wt: 217 Type

Health	C	LIMA Plan	C+
PT/Exp	A	Rand Var	0
Consist	A	MM	3203

Pitches better than his expected stats, and does it with aplomb. But pinpoint control is cemented in profile, skills have been firmly above average for a while, and he consistently avoids hard contact. The risk here is durability; he's on the first back-to-back 180+ IP run of career. Repeat is reasonable, but use 160 IP as baseline.

Yr Tm	W	Sv	IP	K	ERA	WHIP	xERA	xWHIP	vL+	vR+	BF/G	BB%	K%	K-BB%	xBB%	SwK	Vel	G	L	F	H%	S%	HR/F	xHR/F	GS	APC	DOM%	DIS%	Sv%	LI	RAR	BPX	R$
19 OAK	10	0	144	141	3.81	1.19	4.42	1.30	92	93	21.9	8%	23%	15%	7%	9.3%	93.5	41	21	38	28%	74%	14%	13%	25	87	24%	36%	0	0.71	12.3	107	$11
20 OAK	5	0	63	55	2.29	1.16	4.46	1.27	104	78	23.7	7%	21%	15%	7%	10.4%	92.9	44	18	38	29%	85%	9%	11%	11	86	27%	18%			16.8	111	$20
21 OAK	12	0	157	159	3.15	1.06	3.81	1.16	85	85	23.6	6%	25%	19%	6%	10.8%	93.0	42	20	38	28%	74%	9%	10%	27	88	44%	15%			21.7	135	$21
22 NYM	15	0	182	167	3.42	1.14	3.58	1.20	105	83	24.8	7%	22%	16%	6%	10.4%	92.9	49	17	34	29%	74%	11%	12%	30	96	37%	17%			12.3	122	$17
23 TOR	16	0	200	186	3.60	1.18	4.13	1.26	113	79	25.0	7%	23%	15%	6%	9.8%	92.0	42	20	38	28%	75%	13%	13%	33	96	36%	21%			18.1	111	$21
1st Half	8	0	100	93	4.06	1.19	4.34	1.32	130	67	24.7	8%	22%	14%	7%	9.9%	91.8	42	20	39	27%	72%	15%	14%	17	93	41%	24%			3.3	96	$16
2nd Half	8	0	100	93	3.14	1.16	3.94	1.21	98	91	25.4	6%	23%	17%	6%	9.7%	92.2	43	21	37	30%	78%	12%	11%	16	98	31%	19%			14.8	127	$24
Proj	13	0	160	150	3.54	1.16	3.70	1.22	105	84	23.7	7%	24%	17%	6%	10.1%	92.5	43	20	37	29%	74%	12%	12%	27						15.5	120	$15

STEPHEN NICKRAND

Baumann,Mike

Age: 28 | Th: R | Role: RP | Ht: 6'4" | Wt: 235 | Type:
Health: A | PT/Exp: C | Consist: A | LIMA Plan: A | Rand Var: -2 | MM: 1100

PRO: Hey, 10 wins out of the bullpen! And a solid ERA, too! CON: Unfortunately, most everything else. Parlayed 1st-half hit rate, 2nd-half strand-rate fortune to those good surface results. The walks spike when he dials it up for Ks, and doesn't miss bats when he tries to throw it over. Heed the wisdom of xERA here, and let others bid on another 10 wins.

Yr Tm	W	Sv	IP	K	ERA	WHIP	xERA	xWHIP	vL+	vR+	BF/G	BB%	K%	K-BB%	xBB%	SwK	Vel	G	L	F	H%	S%	HR/F	xHR/F	GS	APC	DOM%	DIS%	Sv%	LI	RAR	BPX	R$
19 aa	6	1	70	52	3.26	1.14	2.58				21.3	8%	19%	10%							27%	71%									10.7	95	$5
20																																	
21 BAL *	5	0	77	55	5.06	1.38	4.23	1.73	103	144	16.2	12%	17%	5%	12%	8.1%	93.6	37	21	42	27%	65%	13%	25%	0	46			0	0.62	-7.6	48	-$5
22 BAL *	3	1	94	85	4.50	1.45	4.77	1.31	106	119	12.2	8%	21%	13%	8%	6.9%	95.8	51	18	32	34%	70%	8%	12%	4	45	0%	100%	100	0.72	-6.2	81	-$5
23 BAL	10	0	65	61	3.76	1.31	4.74	1.48	92	95	4.6	12%	22%	10%	8%	11.1%	96.5	42	18	40	27%	74%	10%	15%	0	18			0	1.12	4.6	55	$3
1st Half	5	0	41	45	3.92	1.23	4.50	1.49	74	91	4.5	14%	26%	12%	9%	11.5%	96.6	39	16	44	24%	70%	9%	13%	0	19			0	1.03	2.1	59	$3
2nd Half	5	0	23	16	3.47	1.46	5.20	1.47	126	103	4.7	9%	16%	7%	6%	10.3%	96.2	45	19	35	31%	81%	11%	17%	0	17			0	1.27	2.5	46	$2
Proj	5	0	58	47	4.54	1.41	4.53	1.45	110	106	7.0	10%	19%	9%	8%	10.0%	96.2	45	18	37	30%	70%	10%	14%	0						-1.5	53	-$4

Bautista,Félix

Age: 29 | Th: R | Role: RP | Ht: 6'5" | Wt: 190 | Type: #DIV/0!
Health: C | PT/Exp: A | Consist: B | LIMA Plan: | Rand Var: | MM:

Expected to miss all of 2024 after October Tommy John surgery. Such a shame, as his skills reached rarified heights before the elbow started barking in August. Just look at that 1st-half K rate! Here's hoping he returns to something close to this form in 2025, because this was pretty special.

Yr Tm	W	Sv	IP	K	ERA	WHIP	xERA	xWHIP	vL+	vR+	BF/G	BB%	K%	K-BB%	xBB%	SwK	Vel	G	L	F	H%	S%	HR/F	xHR/F	GS	APC	DOM%	DIS%	Sv%	LI	RAR	BPX	R$
19																																	
20																																	
21 a/a	1	9	33	37	1.95	1.08	1.47				4.5	16%	29%	12%							20%	83%									9.5	127	$4
22 BAL	4	15	66	88	2.19	0.93	2.85	1.09	75	76	3.9	9%	35%	26%	6%	15.9%	99.2	43	18	39	24%	83%	13%	10%	0	15			88	1.48	14.4	169	$15
23 BAL	8	33	61	110	1.48	0.92	2.49	0.98	58	67	4.2	11%	46%	35%	6%	21.6%	99.6	36	16	48	30%	88%	9%	9%	0	18			85	1.55	21.5	227	$29
1st Half	3	22	39	79	1.16	0.96	1.91	0.90	56	70	4.2	11%	51%	40%	7%	21.9%	99.2	41	21	38	36%	94%	14%	10%	0	18			81	1.48	15.1	274	$33
2nd Half	5	11	22	31	2.01	0.85	3.49	1.13	61	61	4.4	11%	37%	27%	6%	21.0%	100.1	29	10	62	22%	78%	4%	9%	0	18			92	1.68	6.4	151	$15
Proj																																	

Baz,Shane

Age: 25 | Th: R | Role: SP | Ht: 6'2" | Wt: 190 | Type: Pwr
Health: F | PT/Exp: D | Consist: D | LIMA Plan: A | Rand Var: 0 | MM: 4301

Another Tommy John patient; his was in September 2022. So he should be ready to go by spring training. If we skip over injury-plagued 2022 and back to 2021, you can see the seeds of a top-flight starter beginning to sprout. Certainly, TAM will be careful with his innings, as he'll still be only 25. But well worth a speculative bid.

Yr Tm	W	Sv	IP	K	ERA	WHIP	xERA	xWHIP	vL+	vR+	BF/G	BB%	K%	K-BB%	xBB%	SwK	Vel	G	L	F	H%	S%	HR/F	xHR/F	GS	APC	DOM%	DIS%	Sv%	LI	RAR	BPX	R$
19																																	
20																																	
21 TAM *	7	0	94	119	2.24	0.82	2.11	0.96	115	48	17.0	5%	35%	30%	6%	16.7%	97.0	43	11	46	25%	83%	23%	17%	3	66	33%	33%			23.4	234	$19
22 TAM	1	0	27	30	5.00	1.33	3.62	1.19	88	120	19.5	8%	26%	18%	8%	13.7%	96.0	43	23	34	32%	68%	19%	15%	6	74	33%	33%			-3.4	132	-$5
23																																	
1st Half																																	
2nd Half																																	
Proj	7	0	102	116	3.50	1.13	3.32	1.15			20.6	8%	29%	21%	7%	15.0%	95.0	43	19	38	30%	73%	12%	13%	20						10.4	150	$8

Beck,Tristan

Age: 28 | Th: R | Role: RP | Ht: 6'4" | Wt: 165 | Type: Con/FB
Health: A | PT/Exp: D | Consist: B | LIMA Plan: B | Rand Var: -1 | MM: 1000

3-3, 3.92 ERA in 85 IP at SF. Oft-injured righty accrued plenty of frequent rider miles on the Triple-A Sacramento shuttle, but did okay in his MLB debut at age 27. That said, given a repertoire of average offerings, he's pretty much maxed out his skills. And spot starters/long relievers with a mediocre skill set are a dime a dozen.

Yr Tm	W	Sv	IP	K	ERA	WHIP	xERA	xWHIP	vL+	vR+	BF/G	BB%	K%	K-BB%	xBB%	SwK	Vel	G	L	F	H%	S%	HR/F	xHR/F	GS	APC	DOM%	DIS%	Sv%	LI	RAR	BPX	R$
19																																	
20																																	
21 aa	2	0	19	14	6.75	1.60	6.45				21.1	8%	17%	8%							33%	61%									-5.9	22	-$7
22 a/a	5	0	112	93	5.34	1.44	4.69				20.8	8%	19%	12%							34%	63%									-19.0	82	-$9
23 SF *	6	2	111	88	4.49	1.30	4.61	1.28	110	84	10.9	6%	19%	13%	6%	11.2%	94.7	41	19	40	29%	70%	10%	10%	3	39	33%	33%	67	0.68	-2.1	63	$1
1st Half	2	2	60	43	3.36	1.22	3.94	1.42	112	82	11.0	9%	18%	9%	7%	10.5%	94.5	44	18	38	26%	79%	12%	9%	0	39			100	0.48	7.2	57	$5
2nd Half	4	0	53	46	5.56	1.33	5.04	1.27	110	87	11.1	6%	21%	14%	6%	12.0%	95.1	38	21	42	31%	62%	8%	10%	3	40	33%	33%	0	0.93	-8.1	77	$0
Proj	3	0	58	45	4.58	1.31	4.40	1.32	121	89	12.9	7%	19%	12%	6%	11.4%	94.8	40	19	40	30%	68%	11%	10%	5						-1.8	82	-$4

Bednar,David

Age: 29 | Th: R | Role: RP | Ht: 6'1" | Wt: 250 | Type: Pwr/FB
Health: B | PT/Exp: A | Consist: A | LIMA Plan: C+ | Rand Var: -5 | MM: 4431

PRO: Three-straight sub-3.00 ERAs; splendid K rate backed by consistently elite SwK; big save total cements role. CON: xERA over 3.00 each of those three seasons; xHR/F points to HR regression; skills ebbed noticeably from June on. Given track record, he'll get lots of leeway. But with a FB tilt, there's blow-up risk if the 2nd-half skills trend continues.

Yr Tm	W	Sv	IP	K	ERA	WHIP	xERA	xWHIP	vL+	vR+	BF/G	BB%	K%	K-BB%	xBB%	SwK	Vel	G	L	F	H%	S%	HR/F	xHR/F	GS	APC	DOM%	DIS%	Sv%	LI	RAR	BPX	R$
19 SD *	2	14	69	83	4.30	1.37	4.31	1.31	107	129	5.1	9%	29%	20%	7%	14.8%	95.3	30	22	48	36%	71%	23%	16%	0	15			93	0.62	1.8	118	$5
20 SD	0	0	6	5	7.11	2.05	6.20	1.37	135	129	8.0	6%	16%	9%	6%	13.6%	95.8	36	24	40	44%	67%	10%	19%	0	30			0	0.25	-2.1	74	-$10
21 PIT	3	3	61	77	2.23	0.97	3.26	1.10	73	81	3.9	8%	32%	24%	5%	17.0%	96.8	41	20	39	27%	81%	9%	9%	0	15			60	0.82	15.3	163	$9
22 PIT	3	19	52	69	2.61	1.12	3.12	1.06	78	94	4.7	8%	33%	25%	6%	16.0%	96.5	33	27	40	33%	80%	8%	10%	0	19			83	1.32	8.6	168	$11
23 PIT	3	39	67	80	2.00	1.10	3.83	1.16	82	81	4.2	8%	29%	21%	6%	16.9%	96.6	39	15	46	31%	83%	4%	8%	0	17			93	1.39	19.3	150	$24
1st Half	2	16	31	37	1.44	0.89	3.62	0.98	50	88	3.9	3%	30%	27%	5%	19.1%	96.3	36	12	52	31%	85%	2%	9%	0	16			94	1.36	11.2	196	$20
2nd Half	1	23	36	43	2.50	1.28	4.03	1.32	107	75	4.4	11%	28%	17%	6%	15.2%	96.9	43	17	40	32%	82%	6%	8%	0	18			92	1.41	8.1	112	$17
Proj	3	34	65	80	2.42	1.11	3.30	1.14	84	85	4.1	8%	31%	23%	6%	16.7%	96.6	39	18	43	31%	81%	6%	9%	0						15.4	154	$20

Bello,Brayan

Age: 25 | Th: R | Role: SP | Ht: 6'1" | Wt: 170 | Type: /GB
Health: C | PT/Exp: B | Consist: B | LIMA Plan: A+ | Rand Var: +1 | MM: 3103

Posted above-average skills in 4 of 6 months in 2023, maintaining a strong GB lean and solid K-BB%. Faded in July/Aug, but rebounded in Sept overall, despite allowing 13 runs in last 2 starts, which shot ERA over 4.00. There are still plenty of rough edges—struggles vL, for example—but at 25, he's got potential. Exercise excruciating patience.

Yr Tm	W	Sv	IP	K	ERA	WHIP	xERA	xWHIP	vL+	vR+	BF/G	BB%	K%	K-BB%	xBB%	SwK	Vel	G	L	F	H%	S%	HR/F	xHR/F	GS	APC	DOM%	DIS%	Sv%	LI	RAR	BPX	R$
19																																	
20																																	
21 aa	2	0	65	75	5.09	1.46	4.61				18.6	8%	27%	19%							38%	65%									-6.6	121	-$
22 BOS *	12	0	156	162	3.25	1.31	3.38	1.39	111	116	20.7	9%	25%	16%	9%	11.8%	96.6	56	21	23	33%	75%	2%	9%	11	77	9%	55%	0	0.70	13.8	118	$1
23 BOS	12	0	157	132	4.24	1.34	4.01	1.30	119	93	23.9	7%	20%	13%	8%	11.2%	95.2	56	15	29	31%	73%	17%	16%	28	94	18%	25%			1.7	113	$
1st Half	5	0	73	67	3.08	1.19	3.80	1.28	93	87	23.7	7%	22%	15%	8%	11.7%	95.3	57	14	29	29%	78%	11%	16%	13	95	31%	15%			11.3	125	$1
2nd Half	7	0	84	65	5.25	1.46	4.20	1.32	140	100	24.0	6%	18%	12%	8%	10.8%	95.2	55	16	29	33%	70%	22%	15%	15	93	7%	33%			-9.5	104	$
Proj	11	0	160	139	3.98	1.28	3.61	1.30	112	91	21.1	8%	21%	13%	8%	11.3%	95.5	56	16	28	30%	72%	15%	13%	31						6.9	110	$

Berríos,José

Age: 30 | Th: R | Role: SP | Ht: 6'0" | Wt: 205 | Type:
Health: A | PT/Exp: A | Consist: A | LIMA Plan: B | Rand Var: 0 | MM: 3205

Modern-day innings-eater: IP total would've barely cracked the MLB top 50 a mere decade ago, but he was easily in the top 20 in 2023. That has value, as do consistent skills—ERA has fluctuated, but xERA and other metrics paint a clearer picture. Not a Picasso, mind you, but one of a steady hand that grabs 10 wins and pads innings. More of a Grant Wood.

Yr Tm	W	Sv	IP	K	ERA	WHIP	xERA	xWHIP	vL+	vR+	BF/G	BB%	K%	K-BB%	xBB%	SwK	Vel	G	L	F	H%	S%	HR/F	xHR/F	GS	APC	DOM%	DIS%	Sv%	LI	RAR	BPX	R$
19 MIN	14	0	200	195	3.68	1.22	4.30	1.23	93	95	26.3	6%	23%	17%	5%	11.2%	92.8	42	21	37	31%	74%	12%	14%	32	98	25%	25%			20.3	126	$1
20 MIN	5	0	63	68	4.00	1.32	4.34	1.32	98	92	22.6	10%	25%	15%	8%	12.3%	94.3	40	24	36	31%	73%	13%	14%	12	92	17%	42%			3.5	105	$1
21 2 AL	12	0	192	204	3.52	1.06	3.54	1.12	109	72	24.4	6%	26%	20%	6%	10.2%	94.0	43	23	34	29%	71%	13%	15%	32	95	44%	16%			17.8	149	$2
22 TOR	12	0	172	149	5.23	1.42	4.27	1.23	124	104	23.5	6%	20%	14%	5%	9.9%	94.0	40	20	40	34%	67%	13%	14%	32	85	22%	41%			-26.8	104	-$
23 TOR	11	0	190	184	3.65	1.19	4.01	1.23	104	84	24.4	7%	24%	17%	7%	11.3%	94.0	42	21	37	30%	74%	13%	14%	32	92	28%	25%			15.9	124	$1
1st Half	8	0	101	95	3.74	1.20	3.97	1.24	106	85	24.6	7%	23%	16%	7%	11.1%	93.7	45	20	35	30%	73%	13%	17%	17	91	35%	24%			7.3	122	$1
2nd Half	3	0	89	89	3.55	1.17	4.05	1.21	103	84	24.3	7%	24%	18%	6%	11.5%	94.4	37	23	40	30%	75%	12%	11%	15	92	20%	27%			8.5	127	$1
Proj	11	0	189	181	3.89	1.22	3.75	1.21	108	87	23.4	7%	24%	17%	6%	11.0%	94.0	41	22	37	30%	73%	13%	14%	33						10.2	121	$1

ROD TRUESDELL

Bibee,Tanner

Age: 25	Th: R	Role: SP	Health: B	LIMA Plan: B
Ht: 6' 2"	Wt: 190	Type: Pwr/FB	PT/Exp: D	Rand Var: -2
			Consist: C	MM: 3305

10-4, 2.98 ERA in 142 IP at CLE. Former top prospect looked the part in MLB debut. While stats were made shiny by S%, rest of profile mostly validated that upside. 2nd-half surge in SwK% without control erosion, no worrisome lefty/righty issues (15%+ K-BB% vL/R), and trifecta of putaway pitches all suggest he could be ready for... UP: 200 K

Yr	Tm	W	Sv	IP	K	ERA	WHIP	xERA	xWHIP	vL+	vR+	BF/G	BB%	K%	K-BB%	xBB%	SwK	Vel	G	L	F	H%	S%	HR/F	xHR/F	GS	APC	DOM%	DIS%	Sv%	LI	RAR	BPX	R$
19																																		
20																																		
21																																		
22	aa	6	0	75	70	1.90	0.91	1.89				21.6	5%	25%	20%							26%	81%									19.2	179	$11
23	CLE *	12	0	158	157	2.84	1.16	3.10	1.26	74	100	22.5	8%	24%	16%	8%	11.9%	94.9	37	21	42	29%	78%	8%	8%	25	93	28%	20%			29.0	116	$21
1st Half		7	0	81	83	3.10	1.21	3.18	1.31	85	97	21.8	9%	25%	15%	8%	10.6%	95.3	39	20	41	30%	76%	8%	8%	12	93	17%	33%			12.3	114	$17
2nd Half		5	0	77	74	2.57	1.10	4.17	1.24	63	104	23.8	7%	24%	17%	7%	13.1%	94.6	35	23	42	28%	81%	8%	9%	13	93	38%	8%			16.7	112	$18
Proj		**13**	**0**	**167**	**179**	**3.23**	**1.23**	**3.71**	**1.19**	**78**	**105**	**24.4**	**7%**	**27%**	**19%**	**8%**	**12.1%**	**94.9**	**37**	**22**	**42**	**33%**	**76%**	**8%**	**8%**	**28**						**22.6**	**130**	**$16**

Bido,Osvaldo

Age: 28	Th: R	Role: RP	Health: A	LIMA Plan: C
Ht: 6' 3"	Wt: 175	Type:	PT/Exp: D	Rand Var: 0
			Consist: A	MM: 1101

2-5, 5.86 ERA in 51 IP at PIT. Okay, here goes... His K rate trend is rising and he posted his first sub-5.00 xERA. He has good velocity and finds the plate on occasion. Keeps the ball in the park fairly well and only about 1 out of 3 baserunners end up scoring. Skills were only 34% below league avg last year, which was an improvement. </spin>

Yr	Tm	W	Sv	IP	K	ERA	WHIP	xERA	xWHIP	vL+	vR+	BF/G	BB%	K%	K-BB%	xBB%	SwK	Vel	G	L	F	H%	S%	HR/F	xHR/F	GS	APC	DOM%	DIS%	Sv%	LI	RAR	BPX	R$
19																																		
20																																		
21	a/a	4	0	104	76	5.77	1.53	5.54				19.7	8%	17%	8%							33%	64%									-19.4	44	-$12
22	aaa	3	0	112	93	4.77	1.62	5.41				15.6	13%	19%	5%							31%	74%									-11.0	42	-$11
23	PIT *	5	3	115	95	5.35	1.49	4.65	1.38	118	84	14.1	9%	20%	11%	8%	9.2%	94.7	35	28	36	32%	64%	7%	6%	9	59	11%	56%	100	0.81	-14.4	66	-$8
1st Half		3	0	75	58	5.28	1.50	4.78	1.50	103	88	20.3	10%	18%	7%	7%	7.5%	93.9	38	28	34	32%	65%	5%	6%	4	87	25%	25%			-8.8	58	-$9
2nd Half		2	3	40	36	5.48	1.47	4.40	1.44	127	82	9.0	10%	20%	10%	8%	10.3%	95.1	34	29	37	33%	62%	8%	6%	5	49	0%	80%	100	0.83	-5.6	83	-$3
Proj		**4**	**0**	**102**	**83**	**5.37**	**1.51**	**4.77**	**1.46**	**125**	**83**	**13.6**	**10%**	**19%**	**8%**	**8%**	**9.2%**	**94.7**	**35**	**28**	**36**	**32%**	**65%**	**10%**	**6%**	**12**						**-13.1**	**41**	**-$10**

Bieber,Shane

Age: 29	Th: R	Role: SP	Health: F	LIMA Plan: A
Ht: 6' 3"	Wt: 200	Type:	PT/Exp: A	Rand Var: 0
			Consist: A	MM: 4203

Worst skills of career...can they recover? PRO: Elbow inflammation likely drove it; control and GB profile remain rock solid. CON: Zip in fastball gone; disintegrating SwK inhibits big K% rebound; still waiting on consecutive healthy seasons. There's profit here now, but given injury risk, be cautious in your bidding.

Yr	Tm	W	Sv	IP	K	ERA	WHIP	xERA	xWHIP	vL+	vR+	BF/G	BB%	K%	K-BB%	xBB%	SwK	Vel	G	L	F	H%	S%	HR/F	xHR/F	GS	APC	DOM%	DIS%	Sv%	LI	RAR	BPX	R$
19	CLE	15	0	214	259	3.28	1.05	3.34	1.05	90	86	25.3	5%	30%	25%	6%	14.3%	93.1	44	21	35	31%	76%	16%	17%	33	98	48%	9%	0	0.76	32.5	188	$30
20	CLE	8	0	77	122	1.63	0.87	2.34	0.93	58	75	24.8	7%	41%	34%	8%	18.0%	94.2	48	22	30	29%	88%	15%	21%	12	103	67%	0%			26.9	244	$48
21	CLE	7	0	97	134	3.17	1.21	3.11	1.09	105	78	25.3	8%	33%	25%	6%	16.6%	92.8	44	24	32	34%	78%	15%	17%	16	97	38%	6%			13.1	179	$9
22	CLE	13	0	200	198	2.88	1.04	3.15	1.08	85	88	25.5	5%	25%	20%	5%	14.1%	91.3	48	20	31	30%	76%	10%	13%	31	93	48%	10%			26.8	157	$25
23	CLE	6	0	128	107	3.80	1.23	4.07	1.28	112	81	25.4	6%	20%	14%	6%	10.7%	91.4	47	23	30	30%	72%	12%	13%	21	93	19%	24%			8.4	108	$6
1st Half		5	0	106	85	3.48	1.19	4.15	1.29	108	79	25.6	6%	19%	13%	6%	11.0%	91.3	47	22	31	29%	75%	12%	14%	17	94	18%	24%			11.1	102	$16
2nd Half		1	0	22	22	5.32	1.45	3.69	1.22	135	93	24.3	6%	23%	16%	6%	9.4%	91.5	48	26	26	37%	63%	12%	7%	4	88	25%	25%			-2.7	138	-$6
Proj		**10**	**0**	**160**	**160**	**3.57**	**1.14**	**3.31**	**1.18**	**102**	**80**	**23.8**	**7%**	**25%**	**19%**	**6%**	**12.5%**	**92.1**	**47**	**23**	**30**	**30%**	**72%**	**13%**	**13%**	**27**						**14.9**	**138**	**$15**

Bielak,Brandon

Age: 28	Th: R	Role: RP	Health: A	LIMA Plan: C+
Ht: 6' 2"	Wt: 208	Type:	PT/Exp: C	Rand Var: 0
			Consist: B	MM: 1101

5-6, 3.83 ERA in 80 IP at HOU. Third-straight season of bouncing between minors and majors, and there's little hope he will stick in the latter anytime soon. One appreciable skill is keeping ball on ground, but without strike zone command, it does little to make his profile attractive. Let someone else grasp onto that lone hope.

Yr	Tm	W	Sv	IP	K	ERA	WHIP	xERA	xWHIP	vL+	vR+	BF/G	BB%	K%	K-BB%	xBB%	SwK	Vel	G	L	F	H%	S%	HR/F	xHR/F	GS	APC	DOM%	DIS%	Sv%	LI	RAR	BPX	R$
19	a/a	11	0	123	103	5.22	1.35	4.19				22.3	10%	20%	10%							29%	63%									-10.8	64	$1
20	HOU	3	0	32	26	6.75	1.75	5.98	1.56	92	179	12.3	11%	18%	6%	9%	11.1%	93.3	36	23	41	32%	68%	21%	18%	6	50	0%	67%	0	0.62	-9.1	19	-$10
21	HOU *	5	1	68	64	3.84	1.32	3.84	1.38	85	106	8.3	9%	23%	14%	8%	11.1%	93.8	44	23	33	32%	72%	10%	9%	2	30	0%	50%	50	0.60	3.6	99	$0
22	HOU *	3	0	103	82	3.10	1.40	3.95	1.24	66	127	15.5	10%	19%	9%	9%	8.0%	93.4	51	6	43	31%	79%	13%	15%	0	45			0	0.35	10.9	76	$0
23	HOU *	6	0	135	113	4.47	1.53	5.37	1.50	115	109	21.0	10%	18%	7%	11%	10.1%	92.2	50	17	32	33%	74%	15%	16%	13	93	8%	54%	0	0.80	-2.2	57	-$6
1st Half		4	0	75	56	4.02	1.42	5.50	1.39	129	122	21.1	8%	18%	10%	11%	10.2%	92.1	48	17	34	30%	79%	19%	20%	8	89	0%	63%	0	0.77	2.9	42	$0
2nd Half		2	0	63	57	4.83	1.59	4.91	1.46	98	87	21.3	11%	20%	10%	12%	9.9%	92.2	53	18	29	35%	69%	7%	7%	5	98	20%	40%	0	0.84	-3.9	78	-$5
Proj		**4**	**0**	**73**	**62**	**4.17**	**1.48**	**4.40**	**1.42**	**98**	**115**	**14.8**	**10%**	**20%**	**10%**	**11%**	**10.5%**	**92.7**	**46**	**20**	**34**	**32%**	**74%**	**11%**	**13%**	**10**						**1.4**	**67**	**-$4**

Bird,Jake

Age: 28	Th: R	Role: RP	Health: A	LIMA Plan: B
Ht: 6' 3"	Wt: 200	Type: Con/GB	PT/Exp: C	Rand Var: 0
			Consist: A	MM: 3100

It's an uphill climb for relievers who don't miss bats. In 2023, those with a single-digit SwK had a 4.31 ERA, 1.37 WHIP, and 19% K%. Conversely, double-digit SwK relievers had a 3.87 ERA, 1.26 WHIP, and 26% K%. Until he finds a pitch or two that generate whiffs, he'll be relegated to an unflattering pool of middling middle-men.

Yr	Tm	W	Sv	IP	K	ERA	WHIP	xERA	xWHIP	vL+	vR+	BF/G	BB%	K%	K-BB%	xBB%	SwK	Vel	G	L	F	H%	S%	HR/F	xHR/F	GS	APC	DOM%	DIS%	Sv%	LI	RAR	BPX	R$
19																																		
20																																		
21	a/a	6	0	60	45	4.00	1.53	4.80				6.7	11%	17%	6%							32%	75%									2.0	57	-$3
22	COL *	4	2	74	67	4.19	1.28	3.95	1.44	114	103	5.0	10%	22%	12%	11%	8.3%	95.1	56	20	24	27%	71%	21%	21%	0	20			40	0.71	-2.0	72	-$1
23	COL	3	0	89	77	4.33	1.35	3.93	1.31	85	111	5.4	7%	20%	13%	7%	9.2%	94.5	53	20	27	33%	68%	8%	14%	3	20	0%	67%	0	0.98	0.0	109	-$3
1st Half		2	0	53	52	3.54	1.31	3.63	1.27	81	108	5.6	8%	23%	16%	7%	9.4%	94.3	55	19	26	34%	73%	8%	13%	1	20	0%	100%	0	0.89	5.2	128	$0
2nd Half		1	0	36	25	5.50	1.42	4.40	1.36	94	114	5.2	6%	16%	10%	7%	8.9%	94.7	51	22	27	33%	60%	9%	15%	2	19	0%	50%	0	1.09	-5.2	83	-$7
Proj		**3**	**0**	**58**	**47**	**4.44**	**1.35**	**3.90**	**1.37**	**95**	**110**	**5.5**	**9%**	**19%**	**11%**	**8%**	**8.9%**	**94.7**	**53**	**21**	**26**	**31%**	**68%**	**11%**	**15%**	**0**						**-0.8**	**85**	**-$4**

Blackburn,Paul

Age: 30	Th: R	Role: SP	Health: F	LIMA Plan: B
Ht: 6' 1"	Wt: 196	Type: Con	PT/Exp: B	Rand Var: 0
			Consist: F	MM: 2103

4-7, 4.43 ERA in 104 IP at OAK. Fingernail issue sidelined him for two months. Healthy version hampered by horrible hit rate, but even without it, xERA confirms his results should've been even worse. If you don't get many whiffs, you either need pinpoint control or a heavy groundball tilt. He no longer has either, and you no longer should speculate.

Yr	Tm	W	Sv	IP	K	ERA	WHIP	xERA	xWHIP	vL+	vR+	BF/G	BB%	K%	K-BB%	xBB%	SwK	Vel	G	L	F	H%	S%	HR/F	xHR/F	GS	APC	DOM%	DIS%	Sv%	LI	RAR	BPX	R$
19	OAK *	11	0	145	81	5.56	1.48	5.52	1.44	165	121	22.3	6%	13%	7%	11%	10.3%	90.6	52	26	21	32%	65%	33%	31%	1	56	0%	100%	0	0.99	-18.9	32	-$6
20	OAK	0	0	2	2	27.00	3.00	8.36		162	133	14.0	14%	14%	0%		4.2%	89.9	50	10	40	52%	0%	0%	0%	1	48	0%	100%			-6.5	-47	-$12
21	OAK *	5	0	129	87	5.33	1.69	6.52	1.33	132	114	22.3	6%	15%	9%	10%	6.3%	91.0	50	21	29	38%	70%	21%	12%	9	76	0%	44%			-16.9	46	-$16
22	OAK	7	0	111	89	4.28	1.26	3.92	1.26	110	104	22.2	6%	19%	13%	8%	9.8%	91.7	47	21	32	30%	70%	14%	12%	21	84	24%	24%			-4.3	98	$0
23	OAK *	4	0	121	111	4.70	1.60	5.56	1.36	108	106	20.5	9%	22%	13%	9%	10.4%	91.9	41	23	35	37%	72%	10%	10%	20	89	10%	30%	0	0.80	-5.5	72	-$9
1st Half		1	0	53	47	5.09	1.62	5.80	1.32	109	101	19.7	7%	20%	13%	7%	10.7%	91.5	42	24	34	38%	69%	8%	9%	7	92	14%	14%			-5.0	81	-$12
2nd Half		3	0	68	64	4.39	1.58	4.78	1.42	108	110	21.5	10%	21%	11%	11%	10.3%	92.0	41	23	36	35%	75%	11%	11%	13	88	8%	38%	0	0.82	-0.5	69	-$1
Proj		**6**	**0**	**131**	**105**	**4.86**	**1.47**	**4.33**	**1.36**	**111**	**104**	**20.9**	**8%**	**19%**	**11%**	**10%**	**9.3%**	**91.6**	**44**	**23**	**33**	**33%**	**69%**	**11%**	**11%**	**27**						**-8.6**	**79**	**-$7**

Blanco,Ronel

Age: 30	Th: R	Role: RP	Health: A	LIMA Plan: C+
Ht: 6' 0"	Wt: 180	Type: Pwr/FB	PT/Exp: D	Rand Var: 0
			Consist: B	MM: 1201

2-1, 4.50 ERA in 52 IP at HOU. In back-to-back years, he has cracked Opening Day roster only to pitch his way back to minors. Uses wipeout slider half the time, and SwK confirms arsenal can work in majors...if somebody keeps him in the bullpen. As SP: 4.74 ERA, 22% K%, 2.6 HR/9. As RP: 3.86 ERA, 25% K%, 0.6 HR/9. Let role determine your interest.

Yr	Tm	W	Sv	IP	K	ERA	WHIP	xERA	xWHIP	vL+	vR+	BF/G	BB%	K%	K-BB%	xBB%	SwK	Vel	G	L	F	H%	S%	HR/F	xHR/F	GS	APC	DOM%	DIS%	Sv%	LI	RAR	BPX	R$
19	a/a	5	6	46	43	6.48	1.81	6.76				7.7	12%	20%	8%							36%	67%									-11.3	30	-$5
20																																		
21	aaa	5	22	45	44	3.70	1.10	3.44				4.2	9%	25%	16%							24%	74%									3.1	88	$11
22	HOU *	4	5	53	51	4.09	1.36	4.61	1.47	133	139	4.3	10%	23%	13%	8%	19.2%	95.3	20	40	40	29%	76%	13%	19%	0	17			45	0.54	-0.8	66	$0
23	HOU *	9	0	126	114	4.19	1.37	4.59	1.48	103	116	16.5	12%	23%	11%	8%	16.2%	94.5	35	19	47	26%	76%	18%	13%	7	53	0%	57%	0	0.48	2.2	51	$2
1st Half		4	0	56	55	3.55	1.43	4.61	1.58	103	121	13.2	14%	23%	8%	9%	16.4%	94.7	32	18	50	25%	83%	18%	13%	5	50	0%	60%	0	0.46	5.4	54	$1
2nd Half		5	0	70	59	4.71	1.32	4.57	1.46	106	101	20.7	11%	21%	10%	7%	15.5%	94.1	47	20	33	26%	70%	20%	13%	2	67	0%	50%	0	0.53	-3.2	50	$4
Proj		**6**	**0**	**65**	**61**	**4.29**	**1.34**	**4.60**	**1.43**	**98**	**113**	**7.4**	**11%**	**22%**	**11%**	**10%**	**16.4%**	**94.7**	**32**	**18**	**50**	**27%**	**74%**	**14%**	**12%**	**0**						**0.3**	**52**	**-$1**

STEPHEN NICKRAND

Bradford,Cody

Age: 26	Th: L	Role RP	Health A	LIMA Plan B	
Ht: 6'4"	Wt: 197	Type Con/xFB	PT/Exp D	Rand Var 0	
			Consist A	MM 2100	

4-3, 5.30 ERA in 56 IP at TEX. Discount 2nd-half a bit; ERA was inflated by wonky hit/strand rates. Soft-tosser flashed fine control, but he's missed fewer bats as he's moved up and xFB lean enhances HR risk. Despite low velocity, 4-seamer and change-up were plus offerings; back-of-rotation potential if he can refine a breaking ball.

Yr Tm	W	Sv	IP	K	ERA	WHIP	xERA	xWHIP	vL+	vR+	BF/G	BB%	K%	K-BB%	xBB%	SwK	Vel	G	L	F	H%	S%	HR/F	xHR/F	GS	APC	DOM%	DIS%	Sv%	LI	RAR	BPX	R$
19																																	
20																																	
21 aa	2	0	36	35	4.63	1.44	4.78				22.0	3%	23%	20%							41%	66%									-1.6	233	-$5
22 aa	10	0	120	102	4.66	1.23	4.05				18.7	6%	21%	15%							30%	64%									-10.3	96	$2
23 TEX *	13	0	131	104	4.40	1.23	4.27	1.20	104	110	15.6	5%	22%	17%	6%	10.5%	90.4	32	21	46	30%	67%	14%	15%	8	49	0%	50%	0	0.80	-1.1	99	$7
1st Half	8	0	79	61	2.77	1.05	2.91	1.31	97	117	20.5	7%	20%	13%	5%	12.8%	90.4	24	22	54	25%	78%	10%	17%	4	67	0%	25%	0	0.62	15.3	97	$22
2nd Half	5	0	52	43	6.90	1.50	6.36	1.17	108	107	11.8	3%	19%	16%	6%	9.2%	90.5	36	21	43	38%	55%	16%	14%	4	43	0%	75%	0	0.86	-16.4	133	-$5
Proj	5	0	58	49	4.53	1.34	4.30	1.18	114	110	16.2	4%	21%	16%	6%	10.7%	90.4	31	22	47	35%	68%	8%	15%	9						-1.4	117	-$3

Bradish,Kyle

Age: 27	Th: R	Role SP	Health C	LIMA Plan C+	
Ht: 6'4"	Wt: 220	Type	PT/Exp B	Rand Var -1	
			Consist B	MM 4205	

Didn't quite earn that sub-3.00 ERA (see xERA), but this was a fine growth season. Skills spiked across the board, even moreso in the 2nd half, a sign that it could very well stick. This projection builds in a typical regression to the mean. But if he maintains those 2nd-half gains... UP: 15 wins, another sub-3.00 ERA

Yr Tm	W	Sv	IP	K	ERA	WHIP	xERA	xWHIP	vL+	vR+	BF/G	BB%	K%	K-BB%	xBB%	SwK	Vel	G	L	F	H%	S%	HR/F	xHR/F	GS	APC	DOM%	DIS%	Sv%	LI	RAR	BPX	R$
19																																	
20																																	
21 a/a	6	0	103	102	4.19	1.46	4.77				18.5	10%	23%	13%							33%	74%									0.9	80	-$2
22 BAL *	7	0	147	136	4.18	1.25	3.91	1.32	96	113	20.6	8%	23%	14%	9%	10.4%	94.7	46	21	33	29%	70%	15%	13%	23	87	17%	39%			-3.8	88	$3
23 BAL	12	0	169	168	2.83	1.04	3.46	1.19	84	81	22.4	7%	25%	19%	8%	11.5%	94.8	49	20	31	28%	76%	10%	14%	30	88	40%	13%			31.3	140	$27
1st Half	4	0	78	74	3.58	1.21	3.85	1.23	99	89	21.5	7%	23%	16%	8%	11.1%	94.5	45	22	32	31%	73%	11%	14%	15	86	40%	20%			7.3	126	$10
2nd Half	8	0	91	94	2.18	0.90	3.13	1.16	71	74	23.3	7%	27%	20%	7%	11.8%	95.0	53	18	29	25%	79%	9%	14%	15	90	40%	7%			24.0	155	$33
Proj	12	0	181	179	3.38	1.17	3.43	1.24	93	95	22.5	8%	25%	17%	8%	11.3%	94.8	49	20	31	29%	74%	12%	13%	32						21.2	124	$18

Bradley,Taj

Age: 23	Th: R	Role SP	Health A	LIMA Plan B	
Ht: 6'2"	Wt: 190	Type Pwr/FB	PT/Exp D	Rand Var +2	
			Consist F	MM 2201	

5-8, 5.59 ERA in 105 IP at TAM. Touted prospect hit a wall in 2023. Gopheritis struck suddenly: Between AAA and TAM, he allowed a stunning 32 HR (after just 14 in similar IP in 2022). As K-BB% shows, he still commands top heat. But hitters were sitting on it, as the 4-seamer was his most-hit pitch. Still a pup, but there's more work to do.

Yr Tm	W	Sv	IP	K	ERA	WHIP	xERA	xWHIP	vL+	vR+	BF/G	BB%	K%	K-BB%	xBB%	SwK	Vel	G	L	F	H%	S%	HR/F	xHR/F	GS	APC	DOM%	DIS%	Sv%	LI	RAR	BPX	R$
19																																	
20																																	
21																																	
22 a/a	7	0	134	129	2.31	0.99	2.43				18.2	6%	25%	20%							27%	80%									27.5	150	$18
23 TAM *	7	0	144	162	5.67	1.41	5.44	1.22	91	130	18.4	8%	28%	20%	6%	12.0%	96.2	37	22	41	32%	65%	19%	16%	21	79	14%	33%	0	0.71	-23.7	73	-$7
1st Half	6	0	72	88	6.47	1.47	5.77	1.20	93	126	18.2	8%	27%	19%	6%	12.3%	96.0	35	27	38	36%	59%	17%	12%	12	83	25%	33%			-19.1	94	-$8
2nd Half	1	0	72	74	4.86	1.34	5.10	1.37	90	136	18.6	10%	24%	14%	7%	11.6%	96.3	38	17	45	27%	72%	21%	20%	9	76	0%	33%	0	0.63	-4.7	56	-$1
Proj	4	0	102	102	4.60	1.36	4.10	1.27	90	124	20.6	8%	24%	16%	7%	11.9%	96.2	37	21	42	31%	72%	15%	17%	21						-3.5	104	-$3

Brash,Matt

Age: 26	Th: R	Role RP	Health A	LIMA Plan A	
Ht: 6'1"	Wt: 173	Type Pwr	PT/Exp D	Rand Var 0	
			Consist C	MM 5521	

Four reasons to speculate... 1) Wipeout slider fuels elite Ks with passable walk rate; 2) SwK says 2nd-half K% dip was not earned; 3) Hit rate will certainly normalize; 4) GB lean helps reduce HR threat. If walk rate continues to improve, he's a quintessential LIMA stud. With his LI trend, he could earn a shot to close and ... UP: 30 Sv

Yr Tm	W	Sv	IP	K	ERA	WHIP	xERA	xWHIP	vL+	vR+	BF/G	BB%	K%	K-BB%	xBB%	SwK	Vel	G	L	F	H%	S%	HR/F	xHR/F	GS	APC	DOM%	DIS%	Sv%	LI	RAR	BPX	R$
19																																	
20																																	
21 aa	3	0	55	72	2.39	1.06	2.06				21.3	11%	34%	23%							28%	79%									12.7	154	$5
22 SEA *	4	3	77	97	3.95	1.43	3.80	1.45	98	98	5.3	14%	30%	16%	8%	13.0%	96.9	52	22	27	33%	73%	9%	13%	5	24	0%	60%	75	0.94	0.1	112	-$1
23 SEA	9	4	71	107	3.06	1.33	3.09	1.12	104	75	3.9	9%	35%	25%	8%	16.0%	98.2	46	19	35	40%	77%	5%	9%	0	17			44	1.25	11.1	190	$8
1st Half	4	1	35	60	3.63	1.50	2.71	1.07	116	79	3.9	9%	38%	28%	8%	16.0%	98.0	47	23	30	49%	75%	4%	8%	0	16			20	1.19	3.0	226	$1
2nd Half	5	3	36	47	2.50	1.17	3.45	1.19	93	71	4.0	9%	32%	22%	8%	16.1%	98.4	45	16	38	32%	80%	6%	11%	0	18			75	1.33	8.1	158	$11
Proj	6	12	65	92	3.00	1.27	2.95	1.17	101	78	5.0	11%	34%	24%	9%	15.4%	97.9	47	19	33	35%	77%	7%	10%	0						10.7	165	$10

Brito,Jhony

Age: 26	Th: R	Role SP	Health A	LIMA Plan A+	
Ht: 6'2"	Wt: 160	Type Con	PT/Exp D	Rand Var 0	
			Consist D	MM 2101	

9-7, 4.28 ERA in 90 IP at NYY. Bombed as a SP (6.32 ERA, 62% PQS-DIS), he was sensational when moved to the 'pen (1.43 ERA, 22% K-BB%). Prior MiLB prowess as a starter (see 2022) means it's too soon to stick him in the bullpen. And who knows, perhaps the late-year relief success carries over to starting. UP: 3.75 ERA

Yr Tm	W	Sv	IP	K	ERA	WHIP	xERA	xWHIP	vL+	vR+	BF/G	BB%	K%	K-BB%	xBB%	SwK	Vel	G	L	F	H%	S%	HR/F	xHR/F	GS	APC	DOM%	DIS%	Sv%	LI	RAR	BPX	R$
19																																	
20																																	
21 aa	3	0	48	39	5.74	1.37	5.63				25.3	4%	19%	15%							33%	62%									-8.8	85	-$7
22 a/a	11	0	114	78	3.05	1.20	3.38				17.7	7%	17%	10%							28%	77%									13.0	78	$8
23 NYY *	11	1	127	100	4.73	1.34	4.86	1.34	104	98	16.6	8%	19%	12%	6%	9.6%	96.0	44	16	40	29%	70%	13%	15%	13	58	8%	62%	100	0.77	-6.2	52	$1
1st Half	5	0	73	49	5.49	1.50	5.69	1.52	101	110	19.6	10%	15%	6%	8%	8.8%	95.8	47	13	41	29%	68%	12%	17%	11	74	9%	55%	0	0.75	-10.4	21	-$8
2nd Half	6	1	55	51	3.71	1.12	3.75	1.20	108	81	13.5	6%	23%	17%	5%	10.9%	96.2	40	22	38	28%	73%	15%	11%	2	43	0%	100%	100	0.79	4.2	113	$1
Proj	9	0	102	81	4.15	1.29	4.23	1.30	117	101	20.2	7%	19%	13%	6%	10.0%	96.0	43	18	39	30%	73%	13%	13%	21						2.2	92	$2

Brown,Hunter

Age: 25	Th: R	Role SP	Health A	LIMA Plan A+	
Ht: 6'2"	Wt: 212	Type Pwr/GB	PT/Exp B	Rand Var +5	
			Consist F	MM 4303	

Don't let 5.00+ ERA fool you—there's still a lot to like in these skills. Already owns a solid power/GB base; needs to refine breaking stuff to take the next step in dominance. Relatedly, he allowed more than his share of HR, as hitters started sitting on the fastball. Young enough to adjust, and as xERA shows, he already owns... UP: 3.50 ERA

Yr Tm	W	Sv	IP	K	ERA	WHIP	xERA	xWHIP	vL+	vR+	BF/G	BB%	K%	K-BB%	xBB%	SwK	Vel	G	L	F	H%	S%	HR/F	xHR/F	GS	APC	DOM%	DIS%	Sv%	LI	RAR	BPX	R$
19																																	
20																																	
21 a/a	6	1	101	113	4.20	1.44	4.60				17.9	11%	26%	15%							34%	74%									0.8	91	-$
22 HOU *	11	1	126	136	2.15	1.07	2.02	1.20	62	108	16.4	10%	28%	18%	6%	10.0%	96.6	68	10	22	27%	80%	0%	11%	2	44	100%	0%	100	0.59	28.4	137	$1
23 HOU	11	0	156	178	5.09	1.36	3.51	1.23	98	115	21.5	8%	27%	18%	8%	10.8%	95.8	52	18	29	33%	67%	21%	20%	29	88	24%	28%	0	0.76	-14.5	145	$
1st Half	6	0	91	103	3.76	1.25	3.09	1.20	93	97	23.4	8%	27%	19%	7%	11.0%	96.0	56	22	22	33%	72%	17%	17%	16	96	31%	6%			6.4	155	$1
2nd Half	5	0	65	75	6.96	1.52	4.10	1.26	106	140	19.3	9%	26%	17%	9%	10.6%	95.4	48	13	39	34%	59%	24%	21%	13	79	15%	54%	0	0.73	-21.0	135	-$
Proj	11	0	160	180	4.18	1.26	3.35	1.23	88	103	21.6	9%	28%	19%	8%	10.7%	95.7	51	17	32	31%	70%	15%	20%	30						2.9	139	$

Buehler,Walker

Age: 29	Th: R	Role SP	Health F	LIMA Plan B+	
Ht: 6'2"	Wt: 185	Type	PT/Exp B	Rand Var 0	
			Consist A	MM 4203	

As expected, missed the entire season following August 2022 Tommy John surgery. Before the injury, consistent skills paint a solid mid-rotation SP, if not the staff ace many saw when stats outperformed skills in 2021. The usual caveats about post-TJ seasons apply, but he's clearly worth a flyer.

Yr Tm	W	Sv	IP	K	ERA	WHIP	xERA	xWHIP	vL+	vR+	BF/G	BB%	K%	K-BB%	xBB%	SwK	Vel	G	L	F	H%	S%	HR/F	xHR/F	GS	APC	DOM%	DIS%	Sv%	LI	RAR	BPX	R$
19 LA	14	0	182	215	3.26	1.04	3.45	1.08	81	88	24.6	5%	29%	24%	5%	12.8%	96.6	43	23	35	31%	73%	12%	11%	30	95	43%	13%			28.1	177	$2
20 LA	1	0	37	42	3.44	0.95	3.92	1.17	76	88	18.4	7%	29%	21%	7%	12.8%	96.9	35	23	42	22%	75%	18%	15%	8	75	38%	25%			4.6	142	$
21 LA	16	0	208	212	2.47	0.97	3.56	1.15	82	76	24.7	6%	26%	20%	5%	12.3%	95.4	45	20	35	26%	79%	10%	9%	33	96	45%	12%			46.0	140	$3
22 LA	6	0	65	58	4.02	1.29	3.75	1.21	107	98	22.8	6%	21%	15%	7%	12.0%	95.2	48	20	32	32%	72%	13%	15%	12	87	17%	50%			-0.4	118	-$
23																																	
1st Half																																	
2nd Half																																	
Proj	11	0	145	146	3.48	1.15	3.47	1.18	92	92	22.3	7%	25%	19%	6%	12.4%	95.9	44	21	35	30%	74%	13%	13%	26						15.2	136	$1

ROD TRUESDELL

Burke,Brock

Age: 27	Th: L	Role: RP	Health: C	LIMA Plan: B
Ht: 6' 4"	Wt: 210	Type: Con	PT/Exp: B	Rand Var: +1
			Consist: C	MM: 3201

That 2022 stat line looks like a clear anomaly now, but not so fast. Hints of those skills still remain. Ugly 2nd half was dragged into ditch by inflated H% and hr/f; command was pristine. Pinpoint control backed by xBB%, and he still misses just enough bats to keep hitters guessing. This is the kind of $1 speculation that can round out your staff nicely.

Yr	Tm	W	Sv	IP	K	ERA	WHIP	xERA	xWHIP	vL+	vR+	BF/G	BB%	K%	K-BB%	xBB%	SwK	Vel	G	L	F	H%	S%	HR/F	xHR/F	GS	APC	DOM%	DIS%	Sv%	LI	RAR	BPX	R$
19	TEX *	3	0	81	63	5.83	1.42	4.70	1.60	129	113	20.2	9%	18%	10%	9%	5.3%	91.6	50	18	32	31%	60%	21%	18%	6	79	0%	67%			-13.2	59	-$7
20																																		
21	aaa	1	0	79	79	6.34	1.49	5.52				16.3	9%	23%	14%							34%	59%									-20.3	66	-$13
22	TEX	7	0	82	90	1.97	1.06	3.53	1.15	91	88	6.3	7%	27%	20%	7%	11.4%	95.0	40	17	43	28%	88%	10%	10%	0	26			0	1.06	20.3	137	$11
23	TEX	5	0	60	52	4.37	1.22	4.26	1.16	99	109	4.7	4%	21%	17%	4%	11.3%	94.6	39	21	40	30%	73%	18%	13%	0	17			0	1.17	-0.3	136	$0
1st Half		2	0	33	25	3.24	1.05	4.62	1.20	97	86	5.2	4%	19%	15%	5%	11.7%	94.4	34	19	47	27%	77%	10%	8%	0	20			0	1.28	4.5	109	$0
2nd Half		3	0	26	27	5.81	1.44	3.77	1.11	101	138	4.3	3%	23%	20%	4%	10.8%	94.9	44	23	32	35%	70%	31%	23%	0	15			0	1.07	-4.8	171	-$3
Proj		**4**	**0**	**65**	**62**	**3.75**	**1.18**	**3.62**	**1.15**	**95**	**103**	**6.2**	**5%**	**24%**	**19%**	**5%**	**11.2%**	**94.8**	**40**	**21**	**39**	**30%**	**75%**	**15%**	**15%**	**0**						**4.6**	**136**	**$1**

Burnes,Corbin

Age: 29	Th: R	Role: SP	Health: A	LIMA Plan: C+
Ht: 6' 3"	Wt: 225	Type: Pwr	PT/Exp: A	Rand Var: -2
			Consist: B	MM: 5405

Among SP with 500+ IP since 2020, he's first in both ERA and WHIP, second in lowest exit velocity allowed, and third in K%. That consistency has made him a legit SP1, but recent cracks bear watching. K% erosion worrisome given recent SwK dive, GB% is slowly declining, and xERA summarizes risk. 2nd half was better and hides profit potential.

Yr	Tm	W	Sv	IP	K	ERA	WHIP	xERA	xWHIP	vL+	vR+	BF/G	BB%	K%	K-BB%	xBB%	SwK	Vel	G	L	F	H%	S%	HR/F	xHR/F	GS	APC	DOM%	DIS%	Sv%	LI	RAR	BPX	R$
19	MIL *	1	1	72	91	9.06	1.84	8.03	1.20	167	111	8.4	9%	27%	18%	7%	17.7%	95.2	45	24	31	43%	53%	39%	29%	4	28	0%	75%	100	1.05	-40.5	53	-$19
20	MIL	4	0	60	88	2.11	1.02	2.99	1.11	80	57	20.0	10%	37%	27%	9%	15.0%	96.0	46	19	34	30%	80%	5%	16%	9	84	56%	11%	0	0.84	17.2	187	$25
21	MIL	11	0	167	234	2.43	0.94	2.55	0.94	78	63	23.5	5%	36%	30%	6%	17.5%	96.9	49	21	30	33%	75%	6%	6%	28	93	50%	4%			37.9	224	$32
22	MIL	12	0	202	243	2.94	0.97	2.85	1.06	88	83	24.2	6%	30%	24%	8%	15.5%	96.3	47	20	33	27%	75%	14%	13%	33	99	45%	15%			25.6	175	$29
23	MIL	10	0	194	200	3.39	1.07	3.77	1.26	69	93	24.5	8%	26%	17%	8%	12.5%	95.4	44	22	34	26%	72%	13%	9%	32	96	38%	19%			22.4	120	$25
1st Half		6	0	101	96	4.00	1.13	4.16	1.31	77	97	24.6	8%	23%	15%	7%	12.2%	95.5	41	23	36	26%	69%	13%	10%	17	94	29%	29%			4.2	100	$16
2nd Half		4	0	92	104	2.73	1.00	3.34	1.21	62	90	24.4	8%	28%	20%	8%	12.9%	95.3	48	21	31	25%	77%	13%	8%	15	98	47%	7%			18.3	143	$24
Proj		**11**	**0**	**189**	**226**	**3.12**	**1.09**	**3.01**	**1.13**	**81**	**86**	**20.8**	**8%**	**31%**	**23%**	**8%**	**14.5%**	**95.9**	**46**	**21**	**33**	**30%**	**75%**	**12%**	**11%**	**35**						**28.2**	**161**	**$25**

Butto,José

Age: 26	Th: R	Role: SP	Health: A	LIMA Plan: C+
Ht: 6' 1"	Wt: 202	Type:	PT/Exp: C	Rand Var: -2
			Consist: C	MM: 1101

1-4, 3.64 ERA in 42 IP at NYM. Unheralded two-pitch hurler held own in majors and showed nice flash in Aug (121 BPV in 21 IP). Hope for staying power dashed by struggles throwing ball over plate, which seem to be getting worse. Absence of third pitch, marginal pedigree also suggest his risk/reward profile teeters too far to the former.

Yr	Tm	W	Sv	IP	K	ERA	WHIP	xERA	xWHIP	vL+	vR+	BF/G	BB%	K%	K-BB%	xBB%	SwK	Vel	G	L	F	H%	S%	HR/F	xHR/F	GS	APC	DOM%	DIS%	Sv%	LI	RAR	BPX	R$
19																																		
20																																		
21	aa	3	0	41	44	2.90	1.01	3.03				19.7	5%	28%	23%							29%	77%									6.9	168	$2
22	NYM *	7	0	133	123	3.56	1.23	3.79	1.31	151	190	19.3	8%	23%	15%	5%	12.2%	94.8	19	31	50	30%	75%	25%	10%	1	98	0%	100%			6.7	96	$6
23	NYM *	4	0	133	108	5.01	1.56	5.08	1.54	72	96	20.8	13%	21%	8%	12%	12.1%	93.8	42	18	40	31%	70%	7%	5%	7	82	29%	57%	0	0.73	-11.1	50	-$11
1st Half		1	0	64	45	5.23	1.66	5.63	1.67	80	106	20.5	13%	16%	2%	12%	8.7%	93.3	51	18	31	30%	71%	8%	8%	2	73	0%	100%	0	0.51	-7.1	28	-$15
2nd Half		3	0	71	63	4.65	1.41	4.32	1.45	70	91	21.5	11%	21%	10%	9%	13.6%	94.0	38	18	44	31%	68%	6%	4%	5	86	40%	40%	0	0.84	-2.8	74	$1
Proj		**3**	**0**	**73**	**65**	**4.56**	**1.41**	**4.46**	**1.38**	**97**	**133**	**20.8**	**9%**	**21%**	**12%**	**10%**	**13.6%**	**94.0**	**38**	**18**	**44**	**32%**	**70%**	**10%**	**4%**	**15**						**-2.0**	**70**	**-$5**

Cabrera,Edward

Age: 26	Th: R	Role: SP	Health: D	LIMA Plan: A
Ht: 6' 5"	Wt: 217	Type: Pwr/GB	PT/Exp: C	Rand Var: 0
			Consist: D	MM: 3303

7-7, 4.24 ERA in 100 IP at MIA. Popular breakout play couldn't find plate. Demotion and month-long shoulder IL stint could have contributed, and xBB% suggests control wasn't quite this bad. With health, still has frontline potential, including GB% and plenty of whiffs. Sometimes the best speculations are last year's failed targets. UP: 3.00 ERA, 200 K

Yr	Tm	W	Sv	IP	K	ERA	WHIP	xERA	xWHIP	vL+	vR+	BF/G	BB%	K%	K-BB%	xBB%	SwK	Vel	G	L	F	H%	S%	HR/F	xHR/F	GS	APC	DOM%	DIS%	Sv%	LI	RAR	BPX	R$
19	aa	4	0	40	38	3.78	1.26	4.37				20.5	9%	23%	14%							27%	78%									3.6	67	$0
20																																		
21	MIA *	3	0	82	97	4.50	1.41	4.56	1.62	131	110	19.4	13%	28%	15%	11%	12.7%	96.7	42	25	33	30%	73%	27%	28%	7	69	0%	43%			-2.4	81	-$4
22	MIA *	8	0	108	114	3.08	1.04	2.44	1.34	69	106	18.9	11%	27%	17%	9%	13.7%	96.0	45	16	38	23%	75%	15%	16%	14	87	29%	43%			11.8	110	$11
23	MIA *	10	0	129	142	3.84	1.39	3.74	1.52	79	113	20.1	15%	27%	12%	11%	12.6%	96.2	54	13	32	28%	75%	14%	14%	20	82	5%	15%	0	0.77	7.8	92	$5
1st Half		5	0	67	84	4.70	1.40	3.86	1.43	84	114	20.8	14%	29%	15%	11%	13.3%	96.1	54	14	32	30%	69%	17%	18%	14	87	7%	7%			-3.1	97	$1
2nd Half		5	0	62	58	2.90	1.37	3.37	1.58	69	112	19.9	14%	23%	8%	11%	11.0%	96.6	55	12	33	27%	80%	7%	6%	6	74	0%	33%	0	0.78	10.9	88	$10
Proj		**9**	**0**	**145**	**157**	**3.78**	**1.33**	**3.81**	**1.43**	**82**	**119**	**20.4**	**13%**	**26%**	**13%**	**11%**	**12.3%**	**96.3**	**53**	**14**	**34**	**28%**	**75%**	**15%**	**11%**	**29**						**9.8**	**84**	**$7**

Cabrera,Génesis

Age: 27	Th: L	Role: RP	Health: A	LIMA Plan: B
Ht: 6' 2"	Wt: 180	Type: Pwr/FB	PT/Exp: C	Rand Var: -1
			Consist: A	MM: 2200

Marginally skilled relievers that keep getting leverage work are maddening, since they take opps away from those more deserving. Two straight single-digit K-BB% seasons vR confirm you can't trust him in high-profile role, even if MLB clubs do. History of bad xERAs and worse xWHIP levels seals fate—the genesis of a situational lefty.

Yr	Tm	W	Sv	IP	K	ERA	WHIP	xERA	xWHIP	vL+	vR+	BF/G	BB%	K%	K-BB%	xBB%	SwK	Vel	G	L	F	H%	S%	HR/F	xHR/F	GS	APC	DOM%	DIS%	Sv%	LI	RAR	BPX	R$
19	STL *	5	1	119	107	6.49	1.61	6.11	1.54	157	83	16.0	9%	20%	11%	8%	7.8%	96.3	36	26	38	35%	62%	8%	12%	2	29	0%	100%	50	0.57	-29.2	44	-$13
20	STL	4	1	22	32	2.42	1.16	4.11	1.46	44	100	5.1	17%	33%	17%	12%	14.9%	96.2	34	25	41	18%	87%	17%	18%	0	21			100	0.92	5.6	79	$9
21	STL	4	0	70	77	3.73	1.26	4.24	1.39	105	73	4.2	12%	26%	14%	8%	11.8%	97.7	42	20	38	29%	69%	5%	8%	0	17			0	1.08	4.6	80	$1
22	STL	4	1	45	32	4.63	1.32	4.70	1.48	98	109	5.0	10%	16%	6%	8%	10.2%	96.1	44	21	35	25%	71%	17%	14%	0	19			50	1.04	-3.7	32	-$3
23	2 TM	2	0	56	58	4.04	1.31	4.56	1.35	85	110	3.9	10%	24%	14%	8%	13.5%	95.9	38	18	44	29%	74%	12%	13%	0	16			0	1.01	2.0	90	-$2
1st Half		1	0	29	35	4.91	1.47	4.49	1.40	86	129	4.4	13%	27%	15%	8%	14.4%	95.5	39	17	43	31%	73%	18%	17%	0	18			0	0.79	-2.1	88	-$9
2nd Half		1	0	26	23	3.08	1.14	4.64	1.30	85	92	3.5	7%	21%	14%	6%	12.3%	96.1	37	19	44	28%	75%	6%	10%	0	13			0	1.21	4.1	93	-$1
Proj		**3**	**0**	**58**	**56**	**4.18**	**1.31**	**4.21**	**1.37**	**94**	**101**	**4.2**	**11%**	**24%**	**13%**	**8%**	**12.4%**	**96.4**	**40**	**19**	**41**	**29%**	**71%**	**11%**	**12%**	**0**						**1.0**	**78**	**-$2**

Canning,Griffin

Age: 28	Th: R	Role: SP	Health: F	LIMA Plan: A
Ht: 6' 2"	Wt: 180	Type: Pwr/FB	PT/Exp: C	Rand Var: +1
			Consist: B	MM: 3303

High-skilled 4.00+ ERA pitchers like this is where profit can come in bunches. Swinging of hit rate pendulum in 2nd half inflated his WHIP, but otherwise displayed elite level of whiffs and newfound groundball lean. Flunking health a reminder of risk, but if he can stay upright... UP: 3.60 ERA, 180 K

Yr	Tm	W	Sv	IP	K	ERA	WHIP	xERA	xWHIP	vL+	vR+	BF/G	BB%	K%	K-BB%	xBB%	SwK	Vel	G	L	F	H%	S%	HR/F	xHR/F	GS	APC	DOM%	DIS%	Sv%	LI	RAR	BPX	R$
19	LAA *	6	0	106	111	3.97	1.17	3.61	1.27	92	104	20.2	8%	26%	19%	9%	14.0%	93.9	38	18	44	29%	70%	13%	13%	17	86	35%	29%	0	0.86	7.0	111	$6
20	LAA	2	0	56	56	3.99	1.37	4.81	1.36	100	107	21.6	10%	24%	14%	10%	11.8%	92.8	36	20	43	31%	75%	12%	15%	11	88	9%	36%			3.2	86	$2
21	LAA	5	0	63	62	5.60	1.48	4.88	1.38	108	118	19.8	10%	22%	12%	8%	14.1%	93.6	35	24	41	31%	68%	18%	14%	13	77	15%	62%	0	0.79	-10.3	71	-$7
22																																		
23	LAA	7	0	127	139	4.32	1.24	3.89	1.18	85	113	22.3	7%	26%	19%	6%	13.4%	94.8	43	19	39	31%	71%	16%	15%	22	91	14%	27%	0	0.85	0.1	145	$5
1st Half		6	0	71	71	4.29	1.16	3.91	1.23	87	104	22.8	7%	24%	17%	6%	13.4%	94.7	46	17	36	28%	69%	17%	15%	13	91	15%	31%			0.4	129	$8
2nd Half		1	0	56	68	4.37	1.33	3.87	1.12	83	126	21.8	6%	28%	22%	7%	13.5%	94.9	38	21	42	36%	73%	15%	16%	9	90	11%	22%	0	0.96	-0.2	167	$0
Proj		**8**	**0**	**152**	**162**	**3.93**	**1.25**	**3.76**	**1.22**	**90**	**110**	**22.0**	**8%**	**26%**	**18%**	**8%**	**13.2%**	**94.0**	**39**	**20**	**41**	**30%**	**75%**	**15%**	**15%**	**28**						**7.4**	**124**	**$8**

Cano,Yennier

Age: 30	Th: R	Role: RP	Health: A	LIMA Plan: B+
Ht: 6' 4"	Wt: 185	Type: /xGB	PT/Exp: D	Rand Var: -4
			Consist: D	MM: 5121

One-time Cuban signee went from dud to stud on back of whiff-inducing change-up and slider and dirt-pounding sinker. Late fade will scare some, but K% erosion came in spite of big SwK jump, so don't read much into it. Lightly-used four-seamer (46% whiff%, .222 Slg) another potential weapon. If prior control woes are behind him... UP: 35 Sv

Yr	Tm	W	Sv	IP	K	ERA	WHIP	xERA	xWHIP	vL+	vR+	BF/G	BB%	K%	K-BB%	xBB%	SwK	Vel	G	L	F	H%	S%	HR/F	xHR/F	GS	APC	DOM%	DIS%	Sv%	LI	RAR	BPX	R$
19																																		
20																																		
21	a/a	5	5	71	67	3.95	1.60	4.92				7.5	12%	21%	9%							34%	76%									2.8	73	-$2
22	2 AL *	2	4	59	55	5.61	1.58	5.46	1.66	182	110	5.9	12%	21%	10%	9%	9.9%	95.4	49	24	27	33%	67%	19%	11%	0	30			50	0.44	-12.0	53	-$8
23	BAL	1	8	73	65	2.11	1.00	3.00	1.15	90	76	3.9	5%	23%	18%	6%	12.3%	96.4	58	23	20	29%	81%	10%	11%	0	14			57	1.53	20.0	154	$11
1st Half		1	4	40	37	1.12	0.84	2.49	1.10	93	49	4.4	4%	25%	21%	6%	11.1%	96.0	66	18	16	27%	85%	0%	7%	0	16			67	1.71	16.0	177	$13
2nd Half		0	4	32	28	3.34	1.21	3.64	1.22	88	106	3.5	5%	21%	16%	6%	13.7%	96.9	49	27	24	31%	77%	17%	13%	0	13			50	1.37	4.0	130	$0
Proj		**2**	**24**	**65**	**59**	**3.13**	**1.23**	**3.25**	**1.24**	**100**	**91**	**4.6**	**7%**	**22%**	**16%**	**6%**	**12.7%**	**96.5**	**56**	**23**	**20**	**31%**	**76%**	**12%**	**11%**	**0**						**9.6**	**128**	**$11**

STEPHEN NICKRAND

Carrasco,Carlos

Age: 37	Th: R	Role: SP	Health: F	LIMA Plan: B
Ht: 6' 4"	Wt: 224	Type:	PT/Exp: A	Rand Var: +5
			Consist: C	MM: 2100

Missed time with a sore elbow, then shut it down for the last month with a broken finger. In between... calling it ugly does ugly an injustice. Across the board skills fell off a cliff—BB%, K%, HR rate all took significant steps back. Do we give him an injury mulligan or project a late 30s rebound? Maybe a minor bounceback but not enough to justify innings.

Yr Tm	W	Sv	IP	K	ERA	WHIP	xERA	xWHIP	vL+	vR+	BF/G	BB%	K%	K-BB%	xBB%	SwK	Vel	G	L	F	H%	S%	HR/F	xHR/F	GS	APC	DOM%	DIS%	Sv%	LI	RAR	BPX	R$
19 CLE	6	1	80	96	5.29	1.35	3.73	1.09	111	118	14.8	5%	28%	23%	5%	15.3%	93.5	41	23	36	36%	68%	22%	21%	12	55	42%	25%	50	0.70	-7.7	180	-$1
20 CLE	3	0	68	82	2.91	1.21	3.70	1.23	97	83	23.3	10%	29%	20%	7%	15.4%	93.6	44	22	34	30%	81%	14%	15%	12	92	33%	8%			12.9	137	$16
21 NYM	1	0	54	50	6.04	1.43	4.59	1.29	96	126	19.8	8%	21%	14%	6%	12.9%	93.3	42	21	36	32%	63%	20%	16%	12	74	8%	33%			-11.7	98	-$9
22 NYM	15	0	152	152	3.97	1.33	3.55	1.18	104	108	22.2	6%	24%	17%	6%	13.6%	92.9	46	22	32	34%	73%	12%	14%	29	83	28%	34%			0.0	133	$7
23 NYM	3	0	90	66	6.80	1.70	5.15	1.48	117	129	20.9	9%	16%	7%	9%	11.1%	92.4	45	25	30	34%	63%	20%	19%	20	80	5%	75%			-27.4	44	-$19
1st Half	2	0	53	39	5.94	1.57	5.25	1.55	98	133	21.8	11%	16%	5%	11%	11.0%	92.2	47	20	33	29%	68%	21%	20%	11	85	0%	82%			-10.5	28	-$14
2nd Half	1	0	37	27	8.03	1.89	5.01	1.39	147	126	19.7	7%	15%	8%	7%	11.2%	92.7	43	32	26	40%	58%	17%	19%	9	73	11%	67%			-16.9	68	-$15
Proj	**2**	**0**	**58**	**51**	**4.87**	**1.50**	**4.18**	**1.33**	**111**	**117**	**21.3**	**8%**	**20%**	**12%**	**8%**	**12.4%**	**92.9**	**44**	**25**	**31**	**33%**	**73%**	**18%**	**18%**	**12**						**-3.9**	**89**	**-$7**

Castillo,Luis

Age: 31	Th: R	Role: SP	Health: C	LIMA Plan: C+
Ht: 6' 2"	Wt: 200	Type: Pwr	PT/Exp: A	Rand Var: -1
			Consist: B	MM: 5305

Another fine season, and among the top in innings pitched as a bonus. But a pitch usage change has earned mixed results. He's thrown the 4-seamer more and the change-up less the last two years, and while walks are down, in 2023 it also meant the highest FB/GB ratio in his career and equalled his most HR allowed. That's a trend to watch.

Yr Tm	W	Sv	IP	K	ERA	WHIP	xERA	xWHIP	vL+	vR+	BF/G	BB%	K%	K-BB%	xBB%	SwK	Vel	G	L	F	H%	S%	HR/F	xHR/F	GS	APC	DOM%	DIS%	Sv%	LI	RAR	BPX	R$
19 CIN	15	0	191	226	3.40	1.14	3.43	1.27	89	78	24.4	10%	29%	19%	9%	16.4%	96.5	55	18	27	27%	74%	18%	15%	32	99	28%	16%			26.0	135	$23
20 CIN	4	0	70	89	3.21	1.23	3.01	1.15	106	74	24.3	8%	30%	22%	6%	16.0%	97.5	58	19	22	34%	75%	13%	13%	12	96	25%	0%			10.7	179	$17
21 CIN	8	0	188	192	3.98	1.36	3.67	1.30	101	98	24.3	9%	24%	15%	8%	13.5%	97.3	57	19	25	32%	73%	15%	13%	33	96	30%	24%			6.6	114	$4
22 2 TM	8	0	150	167	2.99	1.08	3.24	1.15	91	83	24.6	7%	27%	20%	6%	13.0%	97.1	47	20	34	29%	75%	10%	11%	25	100	44%	12%			18.1	146	$16
23 SEA	14	0	197	219	3.34	1.10	3.85	1.17	100	81	24.3	7%	27%	20%	6%	15.2%	96.2	39	19	42	28%	76%	13%	14%	33	97	39%	12%			24.2	144	$27
1st Half	5	0	100	114	3.05	1.07	3.74	1.15	99	82	24.0	7%	28%	21%	6%	16.0%	96.1	40	18	42	27%	79%	14%	14%	17	97	41%	12%			15.9	152	$25
2nd Half	9	0	97	105	3.63	1.13	3.97	1.19	102	82	24.6	7%	27%	20%	6%	14.3%	96.3	38	19	43	29%	73%	12%	13%	16	97	38%	13%			8.4	137	$25
Proj	**13**	**0**	**189**	**209**	**3.44**	**1.11**	**3.25**	**1.16**	**97**	**82**	**23.3**	**8%**	**28%**	**21%**	**7%**	**14.6%**	**96.7**	**46**	**19**	**35**	**29%**	**73%**	**13%**	**13%**	**32**						**20.7**	**149**	**$22**

Castro,Miguel

Age: 29	Th: R	Role: RP	Health: D	LIMA Plan: A+
Ht: 6' 7"	Wt: 201	Type: Pwr	PT/Exp: C	Rand Var: -1
			Consist: A	MM: 2201

Tall righty got in the saves mix early, but pitched his way out of it as hit rate normalized and ERA jumped. Basically, though, he just reverted to his career norm. This is not a closer-worthy skill set, as five teams over the last four seasons have learned. Likely to be best known as the guy who gave up Adolis Garcia's World Series Game 1 walk-off.

Yr Tm	W	Sv	IP	K	ERA	WHIP	xERA	xWHIP	vL+	vR+	BF/G	BB%	K%	K-BB%	xBB%	SwK	Vel	G	L	F	H%	S%	HR/F	xHR/F	GS	APC	DOM%	DIS%	Sv%	LI	RAR	BPX	R$
19 BAL	1	2	73	71	4.66	1.42	4.93	1.54	102	91	4.9	13%	22%	9%	10%	12.1%	97.4	49	17	34	28%	70%	14%	13%	0	19			40	0.87	-1.4	52	-$3
20 2 TM	2	1	25	38	4.01	1.66	3.50	1.23	138	97	4.4	11%	33%	22%	9%	14.1%	98.1	51	19	30	43%	81%	21%	15%	0	18			33	1.29	1.3	170	-$1
21 NYM	3	0	70	77	3.45	1.29	4.20	1.49	81	87	4.4	14%	25%	11%	11%	12.8%	98.1	52	16	32	25%	76%	13%	13%	2	18	0%	50%	0	0.84	7.0	64	$1
22 NYY	5	0	29	31	4.03	1.45	3.94	1.39	96	109	3.9	12%	24%	12%	9%	13.0%	97.9	48	21	31	33%	73%	8%	13%	0	15			0	0.84	-0.2	81	-$3
23 ARI	6	7	65	60	4.31	1.18	4.21	1.36	100	83	3.6	9%	22%	13%	7%	11.8%	96.9	44	22	34	26%	66%	13%	12%	0	13			64	1.04	0.1	88	$4
1st Half	4	7	33	26	3.24	1.05	4.42	1.40	100	64	3.6	9%	19%	10%	7%	10.9%	96.7	41	25	34	23%	72%	9%	8%	0	13			78	1.28	4.5	65	$9
2nd Half	2	0	31	34	5.46	1.31	3.98	1.31	102	101	3.5	10%	25%	16%	8%	12.7%	97.0	47	18	35	30%	61%	17%	16%	0	14			0	0.82	-4.4	113	-$3
Proj	**4**	**0**	**65**	**64**	**4.40**	**1.27**	**3.96**	**1.40**	**99**	**88**	**3.8**	**11%**	**24%**	**13%**	**8%**	**12.1%**	**97.2**	**47**	**19**	**34**	**27%**	**68%**	**14%**	**13%**	**0**						**-0.6**	**79**	**-$1**

Cavalli,Cade

Age: 25	Th: R	Role: SP	Health: F	LIMA Plan: C+
Ht: 6' 4"	Wt: 240	Type: Pwr	PT/Exp: D	Rand Var: 0
			Consist: D	MM: 2200

Underwent Tommy John surgery in March and, of course, missed the year. Look for him to return mid-season, or so, in 2024. Given his pre-injury control issues, not to mention the long layoff, he'll be very risky in the short run. But his raw stuff and top-prospect pedigree still gives plenty of hope for long-term success.

Yr Tm	W	Sv	IP	K	ERA	WHIP	xERA	xWHIP	vL+	vR+	BF/G	BB%	K%	K-BB%	xBB%	SwK	Vel	G	L	F	H%	S%	HR/F	xHR/F	GS	APC	DOM%	DIS%	Sv%	LI	RAR	BPX	R$
19																																	
20																																	
21 a/a	4	0	84	87	4.86	1.55	4.35				21.7	13%	24%	11%							34%	68%									-6.2	90	-$7
22 WAS *	6	0	101	91	4.23	1.22	2.84	1.22	105	150	19.5	9%	22%	13%	12%	13.1%	95.6	50	8	42	30%	63%	0%	14%	1	99	0%	0%			-3.3	111	$
23																																	
1st Half																																	
2nd Half																																	
Proj	**3**	**0**	**58**	**55**	**4.17**	**1.39**	**4.30**	**1.40**			**20.5**	**11%**	**23%**	**12%**				**43**	**18**	**39**	**30%**	**74%**	**13%**	**12%**	**12**						**1.1**	**73**	**-$**

Cease,Dylan

Age: 28	Th: R	Role: SP	Health: A	LIMA Plan: B
Ht: 6' 2"	Wt: 195	Type: Pwr/FB	PT/Exp: A	Rand Var: +1
			Consist: A	MM: 3405

Lost a mph-plus off his fastball, and it made him just a skosh more hittable. Really, that was the only significant skills change between this and ace-like 2022, as xERA and BPX validate. It's obvious that 2022 is the outlier stat-wise (thanks, H%/S%) and he'll never be a WHIP monster, but if the heater cooperates, return to 2022-23 xERA is attainable.

Yr Tm	W	Sv	IP	K	ERA	WHIP	xERA	xWHIP	vL+	vR+	BF/G	BB%	K%	K-BB%	xBB%	SwK	Vel	G	L	F	H%	S%	HR/F	xHR/F	GS	APC	DOM%	DIS%	Sv%	LI	RAR	BPX	R$
19 CHW *	9	0	142	143	5.56	1.63	5.65	1.39	120	102	21.8	11%	23%	12%	10%	11.1%	96.5	46	21	34	36%	68%	21%	16%	14	97	14%	36%			-18.4	64	-$
20 CHW	5	0	58	44	4.01	1.44	5.74	1.66	121	101	21.3	13%	17%	4%	12%	9.9%	97.5	40	22	39	24%	81%	18%	18%	12	90	0%	42%			3.2	-2	$
21 CHW	13	0	166	226	3.91	1.25	3.78	1.18	94	88	22.1	10%	32%	22%	8%	15.5%	96.7	33	23	44	33%	72%	11%	12%	32	92	22%	16%			7.2	145	$1
22 CHW	14	0	184	227	2.20	1.11	3.54	1.22	92	74	23.3	10%	30%	20%	8%	15.3%	96.8	39	17	44	27%	85%	8%	8%	32	98	34%	19%			40.1	125	$2
23 CHW	7	0	177	214	4.58	1.42	4.20	1.29	107	92	23.8	10%	27%	17%	9%	14.0%	95.6	36	25	39	35%	69%	10%	10%	33	99	24%	18%			-5.3	114	$
1st Half	3	0	97	115	4.10	1.31	4.05	1.29	102	88	23.3	10%	27%	17%	8%	13.7%	95.5	40	22	38	32%	72%	11%	12%	18	97	17%	22%			2.8	119	$
2nd Half	4	0	80	99	5.15	1.54	4.37	1.30	115	98	24.3	10%	27%	17%	9%	14.4%	95.7	31	29	40	38%	67%	9%	8%	15	101	33%	13%			-8.1	110	$
Proj	**11**	**0**	**181**	**216**	**3.96**	**1.37**	**3.85**	**1.29**	**107**	**91**	**22.2**	**11%**	**28%**	**18%**	**10%**	**14.0%**	**96.3**	**36**	**23**	**41**	**33%**	**74%**	**11%**	**11%**	**34**						**8.2**	**109**	**$**

Cecconi,Slade

Age: 25	Th: R	Role: SP	Health: A	LIMA Plan: A+
Ht: 6' 4"	Wt: 219	Type: Con	PT/Exp: D	Rand Var: +1
			Consist: A	MM: 2001

0-1, 4.33 ERA in 27 IP at ARI. Strike-thrower simply doesn't miss bats the way his big frame and mid-90s heater would suggest. Add in a bit of a flyball lean, and it makes for a lot of long balls allowed. Stuff may ultimately play up more in the bullpen, where he can air out the fastball in short outings paired with a solid slider.

Yr Tm	W	Sv	IP	K	ERA	WHIP	xERA	xWHIP	vL+	vR+	BF/G	BB%	K%	K-BB%	xBB%	SwK	Vel	G	L	F	H%	S%	HR/F	xHR/F	GS	APC	DOM%	DIS%	Sv%	LI	RAR	BPX	R$
19																																	
20																																	
21																																	
22 aa	7	0	131	106	3.77	1.24	4.27				20.5	5%	20%	15%							31%	74%									3.3	104	$
23 ARI *	5	0	144	117	5.12	1.28	4.55	1.21	100	109	19.7	4%	18%	14%	8%	8.1%	94.2	38	20	42	31%	63%	11%	17%	4	60	25%	50%	0	0.66	-14.0	86	-$
1st Half	3	0	75	67	6.06	1.42	5.55				21.3	7%	20%	13%							33%	61%	0%		0	0					-16.0	66	-$1
2nd Half	2	0	71	50	3.96	1.10	3.25	1.26	100	110	18.6	5%	17%	13%	8%	8.1%	94.2	38	20	42	28%	65%	11%	17%	4	60	25%	50%	0	0.66	3.3	116	$
Proj	**4**	**0**	**102**	**76**	**4.26**	**1.20**	**4.13**	**1.25**	**109**	**116**	**20.7**	**5%**	**19%**	**13%**	**8%**	**8.1%**	**94.2**	**38**	**20**	**42**	**30%**	**67%**	**10%**	**15%**	**20**						**0.8**	**95**	**$**

Chafin,Andrew

Age: 34	Th: L	Role: RP	Health: C	LIMA Plan: B
Ht: 6' 2"	Wt: 235	Type: Pwr	PT/Exp: B	Rand Var: 0
			Consist: B	MM: 3310

On his way to another fine season into June, with career-high 8 saves. Then it all fell to pieces. Inexplicably lost both the ability to miss bats and to find the plate for about three months. Was he nursing a hidden injury? We may never know. Track record says he'll rebound, but at 34, the collapse may have cost this lefty a shot at saves going forward.

Yr Tm	W	Sv	IP	K	ERA	WHIP	xERA	xWHIP	vL+	vR+	BF/G	BB%	K%	K-BB%	xBB%	SwK	Vel	G	L	F	H%	S%	HR/F	xHR/F	GS	APC	DOM%	DIS%	Sv%	LI	RAR	BPX	R$
19 ARI	2	0	53	68	3.76	1.33	3.49	1.17	89	95	2.9	8%	30%	22%	7%	15.8%	93.8	43	28	29	36%	75%	15%	17%	0	12			0	1.23	4.8	160	-
20 2 NL	1	1	10	13	6.52	1.66	4.26	1.30	109	125	3.0	11%	29%	18%	10%	10.3%	93.6	41	26	33	39%	64%	22%	19%	0	12			33	1.38	-2.5	126	-
21 2 TM	2	5	69	64	1.83	0.93	3.84	1.22	65	73	3.7	7%	24%	17%	6%	12.1%	92.0	45	16	39	24%	83%	6%	10%	0	13			63	1.14	20.6	117	$
22 DET	2	3	57	67	2.83	1.17	3.29	1.16	95	82	3.8	8%	28%	20%	8%	14.0%	91.6	51	14	35	31%	79%	10%	11%	0	14			75	1.25	8.1	152	
23 2 NL	3	8	51	63	4.73	1.42	4.22	1.38	100	101	3.6	13%	28%	16%	10%	13.0%	92.3	38	24	38	32%	69%	12%	15%	0	15			62	1.07	-2.5	92	-
1st Half	2	8	29	43	2.83	1.26	3.03	1.14	104	76	3.4	10%	35%	25%	9%	16.3%	92.2	39	32	29	37%	79%	11%	17%	0	14			80	1.27	5.3	179	
2nd Half	1	0	23	20	7.15	1.63	5.94	1.72	96	130	3.8	16%	20%	4%	12%	9.4%	92.4	38	16	47	28%	58%	13%	14%	0	16			0	0.82	-7.9	-15	-
Proj	**3**	**2**	**58**	**64**	**3.97**	**1.28**	**3.81**	**1.32**	**90**	**96**	**3.5**	**11%**	**27%**	**16%**	**9%**	**12.7%**	**92.3**	**42**	**20**	**38**	**30%**	**72%**	**11%**	**13%**	**0**						**2.6**	**101**	**-**

ROD TRUESDELL

Chapman,Aroldis

Age: 36	Th: L	Role: RP	Health: D	LIMA Plan: A
Ht: 6' 4"	Wt: 218	Type: Pwr	PT/Exp: B	Rand Var: +1
			Consist: D	MM: 5520

Seems okay to throw out ugly, injury-filled 2022 season now. Still suffers from periodic bouts of wildness; otherwise, rebound was so strong even a sky-high hit rate barely touched him. New groundball tilt adds wrinkle to dominating mix—as long as he can stay upright to use it. It's been almost a decade since he reached 60 IP.

Yr Tm	W	Sv	IP	K	ERA	WHIP	xERA	xWHIP	vL+	vR+	BF/G	BB%	K%	K-BB%	xBB%	SwK	Vel	G	L	F	H%	S%	HR/F	xHR/F	GS	APC	DOM%	DIS%	Sv%	LI	RAR	BPX	R$
19 NYY	3	37	57	85	2.21	1.11	3.08	1.16	61	75	3.9	11%	36%	26%	7%	14.7%	98.4	42	28	30	32%	82%	8%	8%	0	16			88	1.05	16.1	169	$22
20 NYY	1	3	12	22	3.09	0.86	2.50	0.87	38	104	3.5	9%	49%	40%	5%	20.1%	98.1	22	22	56	27%	75%	20%	17%	0	15			60	1.29	2.0	251	$4
21 NYY	6	30	56	97	3.36	1.31	3.14	1.27	66	98	4.0	16%	40%	24%	10%	17.0%	98.5	43	19	38	30%	82%	23%	25%	0	16			88	1.39	6.3	149	$16
22 NYY	4	9	36	43	4.46	1.43	4.72	1.60	70	102	3.7	18%	27%	9%	11%	13.3%	97.7	36	18	46	25%	71%	10%	11%	0	16			100	0.97	-2.2	20	$0
23 2 AL	6	6	58	103	3.09	1.25	2.74	1.20	88	73	4.1	14%	41%	27%	8%	18.1%	99.6	48	21	31	35%	77%	12%	14%	0	17			55	1.26	9.0	182	$8
1st Half	4	2	30	55	2.37	1.22	2.63	1.22	81	63	3.9	16%	44%	28%	8%	18.0%	99.7	47	22	31	36%	78%	0%	3%	0	17			50	1.21	7.3	179	$6
2nd Half	2	4	28	48	3.86	1.29	2.86	1.19	97	84	4.2	13%	39%	26%	6%	18.1%	99.4	48	21	31	34%	75%	22%	24%	0	16			57	1.32	1.6	186	$3
Proj	5	12	51	83	3.36	1.28	2.91	1.26	77	85	3.8	15%	40%	24%	8%	16.7%	98.9	44	21	35	32%	77%	16%	17%	0						6.1	150	$7

Chirinos,Yonny

Age: 30	Th: R	Role: SP	Health: F	LIMA Plan: C+
Ht: 6' 2"	Wt: 225	Type: Con	PT/Exp: D	Rand Var: +1
			Consist: D	MM: 1001

5-5, 5.40 ERA in 85 IP at TAM/ATL. Another example of when the Rays give up on a pitcher, so should you. Sure, 9.27 ERA, 1.79 WHIP post-trade was result of fluky hit and strand rates, but there just aren't any biddable components here anymore. Add in whiffs that are in a precipitous decline, and you've got a low-upside, low-interest arm.

Yr Tm	W	Sv	IP	K	ERA	WHIP	xERA	xWHIP	vL+	vR+	BF/G	BB%	K%	K-BB%	xBB%	SwK	Vel	G	L	F	H%	S%	HR/F	xHR/F	GS	APC	DOM%	DIS%	Sv%	LI	RAR	BPX	R$
19 TAM	9	0	133	114	3.85	1.05	4.10	1.23	78	101	20.4	5%	22%	16%	7%	10.7%	93.9	43	23	33	25%	71%	18%	17%	18	76	33%	22%	0	0.73	10.8	118	$12
20 TAM	0	0	11	10	2.38	1.59	4.97	1.35	83	152	17.3	8%	19%	12%	10%	14.2%	93.4	31	34	34	35%	94%	17%	15%	3	63	0%	100%			2.9	75	-$6
21																																	
22 TAM *	1	0	23	16	2.12	1.18	3.21	1.12	41	102	13.1	8%	17%	10%	6%	9.0%	93.6	73	9	18	27%	86%	0%	17%	1	50	0%	0%	0	0.81	5.3	79	-$2
23 2 TM *	5	0	105	66	5.32	1.42	5.15	1.44	109	113	17.8	7%	14%	7%	8%	8.3%	92.5	46	21	33	30%	65%	16%	16%	9	67	0%	44%	0	0.63	-12.9	35	-$8
1st Half	4	0	74	40	4.01	1.29	3.86	1.53	91	102	18.0	9%	13%	4%	8%	6.9%	92.3	45	18	37	27%	71%	9%	14%	4	69	0%	50%	0	0.62	3.0	45	$2
2nd Half	1	0	31	26	8.51	1.73	4.44	1.28	134	136	17.8	6%	18%	13%	6%	10.4%	92.9	47	26	27	37%	55%	31%	20%	5	65	0%	40%	0	0.64	-15.8	111	-$13
Proj	3	0	73	52	4.68	1.42	4.45	1.37	114	117	20.1	7%	17%	10%	8%	9.4%	92.9	43	22	35	31%	72%	16%	17%	15						-3.1	69	-$6

Civale,Aaron

Age: 29	Th: R	Role: SP	Health: F	LIMA Plan: B+
Ht: 6' 2"	Wt: 215	Type:	PT/Exp: A	Rand Var: -2
			Consist: B	MM: 3203

Getting to the point that when a pitcher gets traded to TAM, it's time to mortgage the farm for him. This example put up consecutive 160+ BPV months after being acquired at trade deadline. Whiffs soared late too (12.9% SwK in Sept). Poor health caps returns, so stop bidding at double-digits; he's had *200* IL days since start of 2021.

Yr Tm	W	Sv	IP	K	ERA	WHIP	xERA	xWHIP	vL+	vR+	BF/G	BB%	K%	K-BB%	xBB%	SwK	Vel	G	L	F	H%	S%	HR/F	xHR/F	GS	APC	DOM%	DIS%	Sv%	LI	RAR	BPX	R$
19 CLE *	10	0	132	104	2.83	1.19	3.59	1.33	91	81	23.0	6%	20%	13%	9%	9.0%	92.6	40	22	37	29%	80%	7%	6%	10	86	40%	40%			27.2	95	$14
20 CLE	4	0	74	69	4.74	1.32	4.07	1.19	91	125	26.0	5%	22%	17%	7%	10.6%	91.8	44	25	31	34%	68%	16%	16%	12	100	17%	42%			-2.6	136	$4
21 CLE	12	0	124	99	3.84	1.12	4.23	1.26	91	107	23.7	6%	20%	14%	8%	9.6%	91.6	45	18	37	25%	74%	17%	15%	21	91	29%	29%			6.6	100	$11
22 CLE	5	0	97	98	4.92	1.19	3.65	1.13	103	102	20.4	5%	24%	19%	7%	10.7%	91.2	41	20	38	31%	61%	13%	11%	20	79	20%	30%			-11.4	141	-$1
23 2 AL	7	0	122	116	3.46	1.16	4.12	1.23	90	88	21.9	7%	23%	17%	6%	10.3%	92.2	39	22	39	30%	73%	9%	8%	23	87	22%	26%			13.2	118	$10
1st Half	2	0	46	35	2.96	1.18	4.68	1.40	88	89	23.8	8%	18%	10%	7%	10.0%	92.5	42	21	38	27%	78%	8%	6%	8	93	13%	25%			7.7	66	$2
2nd Half	5	0	77	81	3.76	1.15	3.82	1.14	92	88	20.9	5%	26%	20%	6%	10.6%	92.1	37	23	40	32%	70%	10%	10%	15	84	27%	27%			5.4	149	$14
Proj	8	0	131	124	3.63	1.17	3.69	1.19	93	99	21.8	6%	24%	17%	7%	10.2%	91.9	41	21	38	30%	74%	12%	11%	24						11.2	125	$9

Clarke,Taylor

Age: 31	Th: R	Role: RP	Health: F	LIMA Plan: B
Ht: 6' 4"	Wt: 217	Type: Pwr/xFB	PT/Exp: C	Rand Var: +4
			Consist: C	MM: 2211

That 2022 BB% told us to pump brakes on BPX breakout, and sure enough, doubling of walk rate drove this disaster. Ballooning hit rate didn't help, but there are just too many warts here. Lefty bats mash him, flyball rate keeps soaring, and xERA has hung around 5.00 for most of career. Even with more leverage, his blowup risk is high.

Yr Tm	W	Sv	IP	K	ERA	WHIP	xERA	xWHIP	vL+	vR+	BF/G	BB%	K%	K-BB%	xBB%	SwK	Vel	G	L	F	H%	S%	HR/F	xHR/F	GS	APC	DOM%	DIS%	Sv%	LI	RAR	BPX	R$
19 ARI *	8	1	123	90	5.59	1.43	5.66	1.42	114	120	16.9	9%	17%	8%	8%	10.4%	93.7	40	17	44	28%	67%	20%	18%	15	66	7%	53%	100	0.76	-16.5	21	-$4
20 ARI	3	0	43	40	4.36	1.29	4.91	1.46	89	104	15.3	11%	22%	10%	9%	9.0%	94.4	43	20	38	25%	73%	17%	19%	5	59	0%	60%	0	0.58	0.5	60	$2
21 ARI	1	0	43	39	4.98	1.52	4.85	1.30	107	104	4.5	7%	20%	13%	7%	10.6%	95.6	36	26	38	37%	68%	8%	12%	0	18			0	1.00	-3.8	89	-$7
22 KC	3	3	49	48	4.04	1.18	3.84	1.08	106	99	4.3	4%	24%	20%	7%	12.9%	95.7	37	19	44	33%	69%	9%	10%	0	18			38	1.02	-0.4	148	$0
23 KC	3	3	59	65	5.95	1.61	4.87	1.31	145	96	4.6	9%	25%	15%	7%	12.9%	94.8	31	19	50	37%	67%	14%	14%	2	18	0%	0%	50	0.90	-11.8	99	-$8
1st Half	1	0	35	39	4.84	1.58	4.76	1.30	128	103	4.8	9%	25%	16%	6%	12.6%	94.8	34	17	49	37%	74%	12%	10%	1	19	0%	0%	0	0.88	-2.2	107	-$10
2nd Half	2	3	24	26	7.61	1.65	5.03	1.32	177	87	4.3	9%	24%	15%	7%	13.3%	94.9	26	23	51	36%	58%	17%	20%	1	17	0%	0%	75	0.92	-9.6	90	-$6
Proj	4	5	65	66	5.02	1.39	4.26	1.29	125	93	4.7	9%	24%	15%	8%	12.0%	95.0	34	21	45	32%	69%	14%	15%	0						-5.5	97	-$3

Clase,Emmanuel

Age: 26	Th: R	Role: RP	Health: A	LIMA Plan: C+
Ht: 6' 2"	Wt: 206	Type: Con/xGB	PT/Exp: A	Rand Var: -2
			Consist: B	MM: 5231

Normalization of hit rate made ERA, WHIP finally seem human. While skills also took step back, the underpinnings of an elite stopper remain. Pinpoint control is part of his DNA, as is extreme GB tilt and zero lefty/righty splits. Sudden drop in strikeouts product of less whiffs, but prior top-shelf SwK says they can come back. Continue to bid confidently.

Yr Tm	W	Sv	IP	K	ERA	WHIP	xERA	xWHIP	vL+	vR+	BF/G	BB%	K%	K-BB%	xBB%	SwK	Vel	G	L	F	H%	S%	HR/F	xHR/F	GS	APC	DOM%	DIS%	Sv%	LI	RAR	BPX	R$
19 TEX *	3	12	63	54	3.78	1.24	3.46	1.24	90	90	4.7	6%	21%	15%	6%	11.3%	99.3	61	20	20	32%	69%	15%	16%	1	16	0%	100%	86	1.00	5.6	119	$6
20																																	
21 CLE	4	24	70	74	1.29	0.96	2.71	1.11	61	69	3.9	6%	27%	21%	5%	17.6%	100.3	68	14	18	29%	88%	6%	7%	0	15			83	1.11	25.6	178	$22
22 CLE	3	42	73	77	1.36	0.73	2.25	0.99	63	58	3.5	4%	28%	25%	4%	17.6%	99.6	64	16	20	24%	84%	8%	9%	0	12			91	1.16	23.4	199	$31
23 CLE	3	44	73	64	3.22	1.16	3.61	1.22	84	82	4.0	5%	21%	16%	5%	14.1%	99.1	55	20	25	31%	73%	7%	11%	0	15			79	1.31	10.0	137	$22
1st Half	1	24	40	36	3.40	1.18	3.59	1.26	89	72	4.1	7%	22%	15%	5%	14.9%	98.7	58	19	23	32%	70%	4%	10%	0	15			80	1.31	4.5	130	$20
2nd Half	2	20	33	28	3.00	1.12	3.62	1.16	78	95	4.0	4%	21%	17%	4%	13.2%	99.6	52	20	28	31%	76%	11%	12%	0	15			77	1.30	5.4	147	$15
Proj	3	38	65	62	2.90	1.05	2.91	1.14	76	77	3.8	5%	24%	19%	5%	15.3%	99.5	59	18	23	30%	73%	8%	10%	0						11.5	159	$21

Clevinger,Michael

Age: 33	Th: R	Role: SP	Health: F	LIMA Plan: A
Ht: 6' 4"	Wt: 215	Type: /xFB	PT/Exp: A	Rand Var: -3
			Consist: A	MM: 2103

Seemingly a step forward, but warning signs abound: 1) SwK decline with no end in sight; 2) Flyball rate keeps soaring; 3) Overall skills consistently subpar. Even if you put lack of durability aside, escalating xERA illustrates his increasing risk. Few sub-4.00 ERA starters have more blowup potential than this one. DN: 5.00 ERA

Yr Tm	W	Sv	IP	K	ERA	WHIP	xERA	xWHIP	vL+	vR+	BF/G	BB%	K%	K-BB%	xBB%	SwK	Vel	G	L	F	H%	S%	HR/F	xHR/F	GS	APC	DOM%	DIS%	Sv%	LI	RAR	BPX	R$
19 CLE	13	0	126	169	2.71	1.06	3.22	1.09	85	74	23.8	7%	34%	26%	8%	15.7%	95.5	41	24	36	32%	77%	10%	12%	21	100	57%	10%			27.8	180	$21
20 2 TM	3	0	42	40	3.02	1.15	4.19	1.29	102	91	20.3	9%	25%	16%	8%	13.3%	95.2	34	27	39	27%	81%	15%	14%	8	81	25%	25%			7.3	97	$9
21																																	
22 SD	7	0	114	91	4.33	1.20	4.58	1.30	100	103	21.1	7%	19%	12%	8%	11.1%	93.5	35	19	46	26%	70%	13%	12%	22	84	18%	41%	0	0.74	-5.1	74	$1
23 CHW	9	0	131	110	3.77	1.23	4.97	1.32	101	94	22.9	7%	20%	13%	6%	10.4%	94.3	31	19	50	29%	73%	8%	9%	24	88	21%	42%			9.1	79	$8
1st Half	3	0	63	53	3.88	1.36	5.42	1.43	107	100	22.8	9%	19%	10%	8%	9.9%	94.0	31	19	50	29%	76%	9%	11%	12	90	8%	42%			3.5	50	$0
2nd Half	6	0	69	57	3.67	1.11	4.58	1.22	97	89	22.9	5%	21%	16%	5%	11.0%	94.6	31	18	51	29%	70%	7%	8%	12	85	33%	42%			5.6	106	$13
Proj	8	0	131	114	4.11	1.25	4.30	1.28	106	99	22.0	7%	21%	14%	7%	11.8%	94.6	33	21	45	29%	71%	10%	11%	24						3.6	89	$4

Cobb,Alex

Age: 36	Th: R	Role: SP	Health: F	LIMA Plan: A+
Ht: 6' 3"	Wt: 205	Type: /xGB	PT/Exp: A	Rand Var: +1
			Consist: B	MM: 4103

Skills and steady stats are low-risk; health is anything but. November hip surgery will impact 2024 readiness and is likely to blame for his dubious 2nd half. Bigger picture, SwK is falling off a cliff and bringing K% down with it. Still has that GB magic, but has yet to throw 150+ IP in three straight seasons. The newest "When he pitches" poster child.

Yr Tm	W	Sv	IP	K	ERA	WHIP	xERA	xWHIP	vL+	vR+	BF/G	BB%	K%	K-BB%	xBB%	SwK	Vel	G	L	F	H%	S%	HR/F	xHR/F	GS	APC	DOM%	DIS%	Sv%	LI	RAR	BPX	R$
19 BAL	0	0	12	8	10.95	1.86	5.49	1.31	130	203	20.0	3%	13%	10%	7%	10.5%	92.3	46	24	30	31%	57%	60%	55%	3	76	0%	67%			-9.8	98	-$9
20 BAL	2	0	52	38	4.30	1.34	4.42	1.39	109	92	22.6	8%	17%	9%	8%	9.8%	92.5	54	24	22	29%	73%	22%	26%	10	81	0%	40%			1.0	75	$0
21 LAA	8	0	93	98	3.76	1.26	3.50	1.25	84	90	21.8	8%	25%	17%	8%	11.3%	92.8	53	23	24	33%	70%	8%	9%	18	88	33%	22%			5.8	126	$4
22 SF	7	0	150	151	3.73	1.30	2.99	1.19	97	92	22.5	7%	24%	17%	7%	10.8%	94.8	62	18	21	35%	72%	10%	11%	28	86	25%	21%			4.4	147	$4
23 SF	7	0	151	131	3.87	1.32	3.63	1.25	103	102	23.1	6%	20%	15%	8%	8.8%	94.6	58	20	22	33%	75%	18%	20%	28	90	21%	39%			8.7	131	$5
1st Half	5	0	84	79	3.12	1.36	3.49	1.22	98	96	24.0	6%	22%	16%	7%	9.2%	94.8	58	20	22	36%	79%	11%	17%	15	92	27%	20%			12.5	144	$10
2nd Half	2	0	68	52	4.79	1.27	3.79	1.28	109	113	22.0	6%	18%	13%	8%	8.2%	94.3	57	20	22	29%	68%	27%	23%	13	87	15%	62%			-3.8	116	$0
Proj	7	0	131	118	3.99	1.30	3.38	1.25	99	98	21.8	7%	22%	15%	8%	9.7%	93.9	57	21	22	32%	72%	17%	17%	25						5.4	126	$3

STEPHEN NICKRAND

Cole,Gerrit

Age: 33	Th: R	Role SP	Health A	LIMA Plan C
Ht: 6' 4"	Wt: 220	Type Pwr/FB	PT/Exp A	Rand Var -3
			Consist A	MM 5405

Another fabulous season, with the top AL innings total as the cherry on top. But yes, there are signs of decline here. Most noticeable is in whiffs, as K% and SwK dropped to—for him—merely okay levels. Caught a HR/F break, or ERA would likely have teased xERA, his highest since 2017. Still reliable, still great, but let's acknowledge his mortality.

Yr Tm	W	Sv	IP	K	ERA	WHIP	xERA	xWHIP	vL+	vR+	BF/G	BB%	K%	K-BB%	xBB%	SwK	Vel	G	L	F	H%	S%	HR/F	xHR/F	GS	APC	DOM%	DIS%	Sv%	LI	RAR	BPX	R$
19 HOU	20	0	212	326	2.50	0.89	2.71	0.93	77	76	24.8	6%	40%	34%	5%	17.6%	97.2	40	20	39	29%	81%	17%	13%	33	102	42%	12%			52.5	231	$46
20 NYY	7	0	73	94	2.84	0.96	3.43	1.04	106	77	24.0	6%	33%	27%	6%	16.0%	96.7	37	20	43	26%	84%	19%	17%	12	100	50%	8%			14.6	189	$33
21 NYY	16	0	181	243	3.23	1.06	3.14	1.00	92	82	24.2	6%	33%	28%	6%	14.9%	97.7	43	16	41	32%	76%	13%	14%	30	99	37%	7%			23.2	201	$28
22 NYY	13	0	201	257	3.50	1.02	2.99	1.02	90	94	24.0	6%	32%	26%	6%	15.0%	97.8	42	17	41	28%	74%	17%	16%	33	99	48%	6%			11.6	184	$24
23 NYY	15	0	209	222	2.63	0.98	3.60	1.13	80	78	24.9	6%	27%	21%	6%	12.4%	96.7	40	21	39	27%	78%	9%	11%	33	100	42%	12%			44.0	151	$40
1st Half	8	0	110	118	2.79	1.14	3.87	1.20	93	84	24.9	7%	26%	19%	6%	12.6%	96.9	36	24	40	30%	79%	9%	11%	18	99	33%	11%			20.9	130	$30
2nd Half	7	0	99	104	2.45	0.81	3.30	1.05	65	72	24.9	4%	28%	24%	6%	12.1%	96.4	44	17	39	24%	76%	10%	11%	15	100	53%	13%			23.1	174	$35
Proj	**15**	**0**	**196**	**234**	**3.01**	**1.01**	**3.03**	**1.04**	**87**	**83**	**23.9**	**6%**	**31%**	**25%**	**6%**	**13.9%**	**97.1**	**41**	**19**	**40**	**29%**	**76%**	**13%**	**13%**	**31**						**31.8**	**178**	**$32**

Contreras,Roansy

Age: 24	Th: R	Role RP	Health A	LIMA Plan B
Ht: 6' 0"	Wt: 175	Type /FB	PT/Exp C	Rand Var +3
			Consist D	MM 2101

3-7, 6.59 ERA in 68 IP at PIT. Well, this wasn't what we expected. He earned it, too, as skills cratered across the board and the life continued to drain from once-electric fastball. Maybe he hid an injury, maybe it was mechanics, or maybe it was all upstairs. Regardless, while he's young enough to work through things, temper 2024 expectations.

Yr Tm	W	Sv	IP	K	ERA	WHIP	xERA	xWHIP	vL+	vR+	BF/G	BB%	K%	K-BB%	xBB%	SwK	Vel	G	L	F	H%	S%	HR/F	xHR/F	GS	APC	DOM%	DIS%	Sv%	LI	RAR	BPX	R$
19																																	
20																																	
21 PIT *	3	0	63	73	2.48	0.94	2.12		90	95	17.0	5%	31%	25%		13.0%	96.4	57	0	43	28%	76%	0%	14%	1	46	0%	0%			13.9	188	$7
22 PIT *	6	0	130	124	3.57	1.25	3.80	1.36	97	104	17.7	10%	23%	14%	7%	13.0%	95.6	36	20	43	28%	76%	11%	14%	18	76	11%	39%	0	0.74	6.3	85	$4
23 PIT *	3	1	103	79	6.15	1.46	5.41	1.50	120	105	16.2	11%	18%	8%	8%	11.7%	94.4	38	21	41	29%	61%	13%	11%	11	60	9%	45%	100	0.62	-23.0	35	-$12
1st Half	3	1	67	53	6.15	1.51	5.29	1.49	117	101	16.3	10%	18%	8%	7%	11.7%	94.4	38	21	41	32%	60%	11%	9%	11	62	9%	45%	100	0.60	-15.1	40	-$12
2nd Half	0	0	35	26	6.15	1.34	5.83	1.44	251	368	16.3	9%	18%	9%	12%	11.4%	93.1	25	25	50	25%	62%	100%	75%	0	35			0	0.95	-7.9	8	-$8
Proj	**3**	**0**	**116**	**103**	**4.83**	**1.27**	**4.25**	**1.33**	**107**	**97**	**16.6**	**9%**	**22%**	**13%**	**8%**	**12.2%**	**94.9**	**37**	**21**	**42**	**28%**	**66%**	**14%**	**11%**	**19**						**-7.2**	**83**	**-$2**

Corbin,Patrick

Age: 34	Th: L	Role SP	Health A	LIMA Plan C+
Ht: 6' 4"	Wt: 222	Type Con	PT/Exp A	Rand Var +1
			Consist A	MM 1003

These days, we laud SPs who burn innings, but do you really want them burned to the ground? Skills eroded further, truly a bad sign as a guy hits his mid-30s, and things only got worse as the season progressed. xERA portends better, but that's a very low bar. Surely, at some point won't they just quit giving him all those innings? Please?

Yr Tm	W	Sv	IP	K	ERA	WHIP	xERA	xWHIP	vL+	vR+	BF/G	BB%	K%	K-BB%	xBB%	SwK	Vel	G	L	F	H%	S%	HR/F	xHR/F	GS	APC	DOM%	DIS%	Sv%	LI	RAR	BPX	R$
19 WAS	14	0	202	238	3.25	1.18	3.65	1.22	67	94	25.3	8%	29%	20%	8%	14.7%	91.9	50	18	33	30%	77%	14%	19%	33	100	30%	27%			31.2	147	$24
20 WAS	2	0	66	60	4.66	1.57	4.56	1.26	101	116	26.8	6%	20%	14%	7%	11.1%	90.2	44	26	31	37%	74%	15%	17%	11	97	18%	45%			-1.7	117	-$6
21 WAS	9	0	172	143	5.82	1.47	4.51	1.35	85	122	24.2	8%	19%	11%	8%	11.6%	92.5	47	22	31	31%	66%	23%	20%	31	89	19%	48%			-32.9	82	-$13
22 WAS	6	0	153	128	6.31	1.70	4.51	1.30	120	126	23.0	7%	18%	11%	7%	9.5%	92.7	44	23	33	38%	66%	16%	20%	31	85	10%	52%			-44.1	88	-$23
23 WAS	10	0	180	124	5.20	1.48	4.97	1.40	95	117	24.7	7%	16%	8%	9%	9.3%	92.1	44	22	34	32%	70%	16%	17%	32	91	13%	50%			-19.3	64	-$10
1st Half	5	0	97	66	4.84	1.54	4.89	1.39	87	115	25.4	7%	15%	9%	8%	9.1%	92.0	45	25	30	34%	72%	15%	16%	17	92	12%	59%			-6.1	69	-$7
2nd Half	5	0	83	58	5.62	1.42	5.06	1.42	104	120	23.9	8%	16%	8%	11%	9.6%	92.1	43	18	39	29%	66%	17%	18%	15	90	13%	40%			-13.2	59	-$1
Proj	**7**	**0**	**145**	**112**	**5.08**	**1.51**	**4.50**	**1.37**	**98**	**119**	**24.0**	**8%**	**18%**	**10%**	**9%**	**10.3%**	**92.0**	**44**	**22**	**35**	**33%**	**71%**	**17%**	**18%**	**26**						**-13.5**	**73**	**-$9**

Cortes,Nestor

Age: 29	Th: L	Role SP	Health F	LIMA Plan B
Ht: 5' 11"	Wt: 210	Type /xFB	PT/Exp A	Rand Var 0
			Consist B	MM 2203

Started late due to hamstring, missed two months with a rotator cuff strain, back for one August start, then returned to the IL for the rest of 2023. But even an injury mulligan is not really a comfort, as bad shoulders can linger. He'd posted two fine seasons before the injury, but there's newfound risk heading into 2024.

Yr Tm	W	Sv	IP	K	ERA	WHIP	xERA	xWHIP	vL+	vR+	BF/G	BB%	K%	K-BB%	xBB%	SwK	Vel	G	L	F	H%	S%	HR/F	xHR/F	GS	APC	DOM%	DIS%	Sv%	LI	RAR	BPX	R$
19 NYY *	7	0	108	103	5.27	1.39	5.02	1.38	131	103	11.3	9%	23%	14%	8%	10.9%	89.6	34	22	44	31%	67%	18%	13%	1	39	0%	100%	0	0.72	-10.2	64	-$2
20 SEA	0	0	8	8	15.26	2.35	7.09	1.67	208	176	8.8	14%	19%	5%	12%	7.9%	88.1	37	19	44	31%	42%	50%	25%	1	33	0%	100%	0	0.51	-10.2	-7	-$15
21 NYY *	3	1	108	117	2.71	1.03	3.16	1.15	94	87	15.4	6%	28%	22%	7%	11.0%	90.7	27	21	51	27%	82%	11%	9%	14	69	21%	14%	100	0.64	20.7	139	$12
22 NYY	12	0	158	163	2.44	0.92	3.67	1.12	49	83	22.0	6%	27%	20%	5%	11.8%	91.8	34	19	47	25%	79%	8%	7%	28	88	36%	18%			29.8	132	$26
23 NYY	5	0	63	67	4.97	1.25	4.74	1.23	71	109	22.2	8%	25%	18%	6%	11.1%	91.6	26	17	57	30%	65%	11%	10%	12	89	17%	25%			-5.0	111	-$1
1st Half	5	0	59	59	5.16	1.30	4.97	1.27	78	111	22.9	8%	23%	16%	6%	10.4%	91.6	26	17	57	31%	64%	10%	9%	11	91	18%	27%			-6.0	98	-$1
2nd Half	0	0	4	8	2.25	0.50	1.78			89	14.0	7%	57%	50%	5%	21.9%	92.7	40	0	60	0%	0%	33%	30%	1	64	0%	0%			1.0	317	-$6
Proj	**10**	**0**	**145**	**146**	**4.02**	**1.17**	**4.01**	**1.20**	**96**	**94**	**21.6**	**7%**	**25%**	**18%**	**7%**	**11.0%**	**91.0**	**30**	**19**	**50**	**29%**	**71%**	**11%**	**10%**	**27**						**5.5**	**116**	**$10**

Cosgrove,Tom

Age: 28	Th: L	Role RP	Health B	LIMA Plan A
Ht: 6' 2"	Wt: 190	Type /FB	PT/Exp D	Rand Var -5
			Consist C	MM 2110

Rookie lefty somehow appeased the hit- and strand-rate gods into gifting an ERA nearly 3 runs below expected. Ironically, skills had exceeded stats in past MiLB seasons, so he actually could "rebound" and no one would know it. But despite H% history, we refuse to believe he's learned the dark art of guiding batted balls into gloves at his whim.

Yr Tm	W	Sv	IP	K	ERA	WHIP	xERA	xWHIP	vL+	vR+	BF/G	BB%	K%	K-BB%	xBB%	SwK	Vel	G	L	F	H%	S%	HR/F	xHR/F	GS	APC	DOM%	DIS%	Sv%	LI	RAR	BPX	R$
19																																	
20																																	
21 aa	1	1	28	26	2.46	1.01	2.39				4.9	6%	24%	18%							27%	78%									6.3	132	$0
22 a/a	8	0	57	67	3.30	1.07	2.64				4.6	12%	30%	18%							23%	75%									4.7	113	$5
23 SD	1	1	51	44	1.75	0.97	4.47	1.38	88	58	3.8	9%	21%	12%	7%	10.9%	91.6	41	14	45	22%	85%	5%	4%	0	16			100	0.75	16.3	76	$6
1st Half	1	0	19	17	0.96	0.54	3.07	1.09	60	40	3.6	5%	27%	22%	6%	12.6%	91.8	45	17	38	14%	89%	6%	7%	0	15			0	0.70	7.8	149	$1
2nd Half	0	1	33	27	2.20	1.22	5.33	1.52	102	67	3.9	11%	19%	8%	7%	10.0%	91.5	39	13	48	25%	84%	4%	3%	0	16			100	0.78	8.6	36	$0
Proj	**2**	**2**	**51**	**45**	**3.36**	**1.18**	**4.20**	**1.34**	**122**	**73**	**4.2**	**9%**	**22%**	**13%**	**7%**	**11.0%**	**91.6**	**41**	**14**	**44**	**27%**	**75%**	**9%**	**7%**	**0**						**6.1**	**84**	**$1**

Coulombe,Daniel

Age: 34	Th: L	Role RP	Health F	LIMA Plan A
Ht: 5' 10"	Wt: 190	Type Pwr	PT/Exp D	Rand Var -3
			Consist D	MM 4310

Threw slider/sweeper breaking-ball combo two-thirds of the time, and it meant the best skills year of long career. Despite little platoon split, arsenal doesn't fit the traditional closer's, and he didn't get a single save after closer Bautista was lost for the season. So while he might grab one here and there, bid the buck instead for a LIMA ace.

Yr Tm	W	Sv	IP	K	ERA	WHIP	xERA	xWHIP	vL+	vR+	BF/G	BB%	K%	K-BB%	xBB%	SwK	Vel	G	L	F	H%	S%	HR/F	xHR/F	GS	APC	DOM%	DIS%	Sv%	LI	RAR	BPX	R$
19 aaa	4	1	37	45	6.35	1.94	8.88				5.7	11%	25%	14%							39%	78%									-8.5	7	-$
20 MIN	0	0	3	3	0.00	1.88	6.86		92	72	6.5	23%	23%	0%		6.0%	89.6	29	43	29	31%	100%	0%	14%	0	25			0	0.31	1.5	-95	-$
21 MIN *	4	2	55	53	3.18	1.21	4.04	1.14	104	99	5.2	5%	24%	19%	6%	11.9%	90.4	42	22	36	33%	78%	14%	14%	1	18	0%	100%	50	0.49	7.4	140	$
22 MIN	0	0	12	9	1.46	1.30	5.60	1.79	63	79	5.3	17%	17%	0%	12%	13.5%	91.2	37	23	40	21%	88%	0%	1%	0	23			0	0.49	3.8	-49	-$
23 BAL	5	2	51	58	2.81	1.11	3.53	1.11	79	85	3.4	6%	28%	22%	8%	13.3%	91.3	44	19	38	32%	77%	8%	11%	0	14			40	1.68	9.7	166	$
1st Half	2	0	29	38	2.20	1.01	3.21	1.03	69	81	3.3	6%	33%	27%	8%	13.1%	91.3	43	15	43	32%	81%	7%	9%	0	14			0	1.79	7.5	199	$
2nd Half	3	2	23	20	3.57	1.24	4.00	1.22	90	91	3.6	5%	21%	16%	7%	13.7%	91.2	45	22	33	32%	73%	9%	14%	0	13			67	1.53	2.1	127	$
Proj	**6**	**2**	**58**	**63**	**3.55**	**1.25**	**3.47**	**1.19**	**98**	**105**	**3.9**	**7%**	**27%**	**19%**	**8%**	**13.1%**	**91.1**	**44**	**20**	**37**	**31%**	**78%**	**16%**	**12%**	**0**						**5.5**	**139**	**$**

Crawford,Kutter

Age: 28	Th: R	Role SP	Health C	LIMA Plan A
Ht: 6' 1"	Wt: 209	Type Pwr/xFB	PT/Exp C	Rand Var -1
			Consist C	MM 3303

PRO: Took a nice little step back up, with solid K-BB rate; no platoon split in larger sample. CON: Skills aren't THAT great, as xERA confirms; extreme FB tilt makes him HR vulnerable; low IP totals, as he rarely gets 20 hitters/game and never made it past the sixth. The latter could improve with a full season in rotation. Decent end-game filler.

Yr Tm	W	Sv	IP	K	ERA	WHIP	xERA	xWHIP	vL+	vR+	BF/G	BB%	K%	K-BB%	xBB%	SwK	Vel	G	L	F	H%	S%	HR/F	xHR/F	GS	APC	DOM%	DIS%	Sv%	LI	RAR	BPX	R$
19 aa	1	0	20	19	5.83	1.99	6.55				19.4	17%	20%	3%							36%	72%									-3.3	40	-$
20																																	
21 BOS *	6	0	98	108	5.51	1.27	4.49		35	260	19.1	6%	27%	21%		15.8%	93.9	11	33	56	34%	58%	20%	29%	1	57	0%	100%			-15.1	137	-$
22 BOS *	4	0	102	95	5.49	1.45	5.37	1.28	139	95	16.2	8%	22%	14%	8%	11.9%	94.6	31	22	47	33%	65%	11%	12%	12	62	0%	33%	0	0.74	-19.2	68	-$
23 BOS	6	0	129	135	4.04	1.11	4.24	1.19	91	91	17.0	7%	26%	19%	6%	13.1%	93.7	35	16	49	28%	67%	10%	11%	23	68	17%	13%	0	0.76	4.7	128	$
1st Half	3	0	57	55	3.92	1.10	4.12	1.17	81	108	14.5	5%	24%	19%	5%	13.5%	94.6	40	16	44	28%	72%	14%	12%	8	56	0%	0%	0	0.76	2.9	138	$
2nd Half	3	0	72	80	4.13	1.11	4.34	1.22	100	79	19.7	8%	27%	19%	6%	12.9%	93.0	31	16	54	28%	64%	7%	11%	15	80	27%	20%			1.8	121	$
Proj	**7**	**0**	**145**	**151**	**4.18**	**1.18**	**3.83**	**1.18**	**108**	**97**	**20.6**	**7%**	**26%**	**19%**	**6%**	**12.9%**	**93.8**	**34**	**17**	**49**	**30%**	**69%**	**11%**	**11%**	**24**						**2.6**	**127**	**$**

ROD TRUESDELL

Cruz,Fernando

Age: 34 | Th: R | Role: RP | Ht: 6' 2" | Wt: 205 | Type: Pwr/xFB
Health: C | PT/Exp: D | Consist: A
LIMA Plan: B | Rand Var: +5 | MM: 4511

First full season in majors went swimmingly, featuring filthy whiff rate (19.8% SwK% in 2nd half!) and solid control foundation obscured by unfavorable H%/S% combo. If he were 10 years younger, this would be a building block reliever. As a late bloomer, he'll need to keep defying expectations. Sneaky $1 play with late-game potential.

Yr Tm	W	Sv	IP	K	ERA	WHIP	xERA	xWHIP	vL+	vR+	BF/G	BB%	K%	K-BB%	xBB%	SwK	Vel	G	L	F	H%	S%	HR/F	xHR/F	GS	APC	DOM%	DIS%	Sv%	LI	RAR	BPX	R$
19																																	
20																																	
21																																	
22 CIN *	4	23	71	71	3.40	1.30	3.66	1.32	62	93	4.5	11%	24%	13%	11%	16.9%	94.3	35	23	42	29%	77%	8%	8%	2	19	0%	0%	74	1.23	5.0	92	$10
23 CIN	1	0	66	98	4.91	1.21	3.62	1.14	99	82	4.8	10%	35%	25%	8%	16.8%	94.4	32	19	50	34%	59%	8%	11%	2	19	0%	0%	0	0.84	-4.7	165	-$2
1st Half	1	0	31	41	4.94	1.29	3.83	1.21	82	100	5.5	10%	31%	21%	9%	13.4%	93.7	39	16	45	35%	61%	6%	10%	0	22			0	0.86	-2.3	146	-$6
2nd Half	0	0	35	57	4.89	1.14	3.45	1.08	116	69	4.3	10%	39%	29%	8%	19.8%	94.8	23	22	55	33%	58%	10%	11%	2	17	0%	0%	0	0.82	-2.4	182	-$2
Proj	3	1	65	92	3.95	1.16	3.35	1.14	100	78	4.7	10%	35%	25%	8%	17.2%	94.4	30	19	51	32%	67%	8%	11%	0						3.0	153	$2

Cuas,Jose

Age: 30 | Th: R | Role: RP | Ht: 6' 3" | Wt: 195 | Type: Pwr
Health: A | PT/Exp: D | Consist: A
LIMA Plan: C+ | Rand Var: 0 | MM: 2201

Former infielder-turned-sidearmer found himself in high-leverage spots in 2nd half, which turned out to be a big blunder. At this point, he's one of those pitchers who simply issues more walks than his xBB% suggests. It's a bugaboo that overshadows hints of hope shown by good SwK and GB%. At age 30, his MLB lifespan could be a short one.

Yr Tm	W	Sv	IP	K	ERA	WHIP	xERA	xWHIP	vL+	vR+	BF/G	BB%	K%	K-BB%	xBB%	SwK	Vel	G	L	F	H%	S%	HR/F	xHR/F	GS	APC	DOM%	DIS%	Sv%	LI	RAR	BPX	R$
19																																	
20																																	
21 a/a	4	3	38	27	2.04	1.28	3.59				6.2	6%	17%	12%							33%	84%									10.4	106	$2
22 KC *	4	4	61	49	2.83	1.46	3.92	1.57	153	89	3.8	12%	19%	7%	8%	10.8%	93.1	49	25	26	31%	81%	7%	6%	0	15			80	1.14	8.5	76	$1
23 2 TM	3	1	65	71	3.99	1.50	4.32	1.43	104	105	4.1	12%	24%	12%	9%	12.9%	92.6	46	21	33	33%	77%	14%	19%	2	16	0%	100%	25	1.08	2.7	78	-$3
1st Half	3	0	34	42	4.54	1.57	4.21	1.31	95	119	4.3	10%	27%	17%	8%	13.1%	92.4	39	24	38	38%	75%	14%	18%	1	17	0%	100%	0	0.77	-0.9	117	-$6
2nd Half	0	1	32	29	3.41	1.42	4.44	1.59	114	89	3.8	14%	21%	7%	11%	12.7%	92.9	54	19	27	28%	79%	13%	19%	1	16	0%	100%	33	1.38	3.6	39	-$3
Proj	3	0	65	61	4.25	1.43	4.10	1.42	114	100	4.3	11%	22%	11%	10%	12.4%	92.8	48	22	30	32%	71%	10%	15%	0						0.6	72	-$4

Cueto,Johnny

Age: 38 | Th: R | Role: SP | Ht: 5' 11" | Wt: 229 | Type: Con
Health: F | PT/Exp: B | Consist: F
LIMA Plan: C+ | Rand Var: +5 | MM: 1000

1-4, 6.02 ERA in 52 IP at MIA. Ten years ago, this pitcher put up a $41 season behind a 2.25 ERA, 0.96 WHIP, and 242 K. Flash forward, and he's on a string of seven straight 4.00+ xERA campaigns and has averaged 86 IP per year during that period. It's fool's gold to hope for another 2022 positive blip, especially as he inches closer to 40.

Yr Tm	W	Sv	IP	K	ERA	WHIP	xERA	xWHIP	vL+	vR+	BF/G	BB%	K%	K-BB%	xBB%	SwK	Vel	G	L	F	H%	S%	HR/F	xHR/F	GS	APC	DOM%	DIS%	Sv%	LI	RAR	BPX	R$
19 SF	1	0	16	13	5.06	1.25	4.92	1.62	149	60	16.8	13%	19%	6%	11%	7.9%	91.3	53	16	30	20%	65%	23%	26%	4	66	0%	25%			-1.1	28	-$4
20 SF	2	0	63	56	5.40	1.37	4.88	1.40	110	93	23.1	9%	20%	11%	9%	8.6%	91.3	41	25	34	30%	63%	14%	14%	12	95	17%	50%			-7.4	71	-$5
21 SF	7	0	115	98	4.08	1.37	4.45	1.25	112	105	22.3	6%	20%	14%	6%	10.5%	91.8	38	26	36	33%	74%	12%	13%	21	85	14%	33%	0	0.77	2.6	100	$0
22 CHW *	8	0	176	115	3.50	1.23	4.00	1.27	108	96	24.5	5%	16%	11%	6%	8.2%	91.4	43	19	38	30%	75%	8%	10%	24	95	17%	13%	0	0.77	10.2	82	$7
23 MIA *	1	0	84	49	8.30	1.63	8.94	1.35	122	111	18.6	7%	18%	11%	6%	9.1%	92.2	33	19	48	29%	59%	22%	16%	10	66	10%	60%	0	0.62	-40.9	-55	-$23
1st Half	0	0	21	6	14.08	2.53	16.25		407	46	19.0	7%	6%	-1%	12%	0.0%	90.5	0	17	83	37%	53%	40%	28%	1	30	0%	100%			-25.7	-215	-$33
2nd Half	1	0	62	43	6.28	1.31	6.40	1.34	111	113	18.4	6%	17%	10%	6%	9.4%	92.3	34	19	46	25%	63%	21%	15%	9	69	11%	56%	0	0.61	-15.0	5	-$8
Proj	2	0	58	38	5.22	1.45	4.79	1.36	127	118	21.6	7%	16%	9%	7%	9.1%	91.8	39	22	40	31%	71%	16%	13%	11						-6.4	63	-$8

Curry,Xzavion

Age: 25 | Th: R | Role: RP | Ht: 6' 0" | Wt: 195 | Type: Con/xFB
Health: A | PT/Exp: C | Consist: C
LIMA Plan: C+ | Rand Var: -3 | MM: 1001

Molding a useful SP out of raw material has been Cleveland's forte, but this is a project. Surface numbers are foundation-level (especially the 1st half), but turn it over, and only hard work confronts you from underneath. He doesn't miss many bats, throw particularly hard, limit flyballs, nor pound the strikezone. The clay is still dry and stiff.

Yr Tm	W	Sv	IP	K	ERA	WHIP	xERA	xWHIP	vL+	vR+	BF/G	BB%	K%	K-BB%	xBB%	SwK	Vel	G	L	F	H%	S%	HR/F	xHR/F	GS	APC	DOM%	DIS%	Sv%	LI	RAR	BPX	R$
19																																	
20																																	
21																																	
22 CLE *	9	0	131	116	3.98	1.26	4.06	1.82	132	111	19.9	8%	22%	13%	12%	9.7%	92.1	30	32	38	29%	72%	7%	5%	2	83	0%	50%			-0.2	82	$4
23 CLE	3	0	95	67	4.07	1.35	5.35	1.40	87	117	9.9	7%	17%	9%	7%	9.4%	92.6	32	22	46	30%	73%	9%	10%	9	37	11%	44%	0	0.50	3.0	53	-$2
1st Half	3	0	43	27	3.38	1.22	5.29	1.35	72	120	8.9	6%	15%	10%	5%	9.3%	92.9	30	24	46	28%	77%	8%	9%	0	33			0	0.42	5.0	61	$0
2nd Half	0	0	52	40	4.64	1.45	5.39	1.44	101	116	10.8	9%	18%	9%	8%	9.6%	92.3	33	21	46	31%	71%	9%	11%	9	40	11%	44%	0	0.57	-2.0	47	-$8
Proj	3	0	87	62	4.62	1.35	4.84	1.37	91	120	11.5	7%	17%	10%	8%	9.4%	92.6	32	22	46	30%	69%	10%	10%	5						-3.2	56	-$5

Darvish,Yu

Age: 37 | Th: R | Role: SP | Ht: 6' 5" | Wt: 220 | Type: Pwr
Health: D | PT/Exp: A | Consist: A
LIMA Plan: A+ | Rand Var: 0 | MM: 4303

Dare you to find a more difficult pitcher to project than this one. Yo-yo ERA, R$ suggest he follows good with great, making 2024 a year for redemption. Working against that pendulum is SwK nosedive, which puts longstanding strikeout contributions at risk, along with age. Take midpoint of last two seasons as baseline and cross fingers and toes.

Yr Tm	W	Sv	IP	K	ERA	WHIP	xERA	xWHIP	vL+	vR+	BF/G	BB%	K%	K-BB%	xBB%	SwK	Vel	G	L	F	H%	S%	HR/F	xHR/F	GS	APC	DOM%	DIS%	Sv%	LI	RAR	BPX	R$
19 CHC	6	0	179	229	3.98	1.10	3.36	1.14	101	83	23.6	8%	31%	24%	6%	14.0%	94.2	45	21	34	28%	72%	23%	19%	31	92	32%	16%			11.6	168	$15
20 CHC	8	0	76	93	2.01	0.96	3.02	1.01	84	70	24.8	5%	31%	27%	4%	15.0%	95.5	43	26	31	31%	82%	9%	11%	12	96	58%	0%			22.9	197	$40
21 SD	8	0	166	199	4.22	1.09	3.74	1.10	99	93	22.7	6%	29%	23%	6%	12.4%	94.5	37	18	45	29%	68%	15%	12%	30	92	33%	20%			0.9	159	$12
22 SD	16	0	195	197	3.10	0.95	3.54	1.08	77	91	25.7	5%	26%	21%	5%	11.8%	95.0	37	19	44	26%	72%	10%	12%	30	99	50%	7%			20.9	146	$28
23 SD	8	0	136	141	4.56	1.30	3.95	1.24	107	92	23.9	7%	25%	17%	7%	11.0%	94.5	42	23	35	32%	68%	14%	10%	24	92	25%	25%			-3.8	124	$3
1st Half	5	0	80	85	4.84	1.23	3.77	1.22	98	100	23.6	8%	26%	18%	7%	11.3%	94.5	44	21	35	31%	63%	13%	12%	14	94	29%	14%			-5.0	134	$5
2nd Half	3	0	56	56	4.15	1.40	4.20	1.27	123	85	24.3	7%	23%	16%	7%	10.4%	94.5	38	27	35	34%	75%	14%	7%	10	90	20%	40%			1.2	112	$2
Proj	10	0	160	174	3.92	1.18	3.46	1.15	102	89	23.3	7%	27%	20%	6%	11.8%	94.7	40	22	38	31%	71%	13%	11%	27						8.0	143	$12

Davies,Zach

Age: 31 | Th: R | Role: SP | Ht: 6' 0" | Wt: 180 | Type:
Health: F | PT/Exp: A | Consist: B
LIMA Plan: C | Rand Var: +5 | MM: 1001

2-5, 7.00 ERA in 82 IP at ARI. Among starters with 80+ IP, his ERA was the third worst in the majors (Wentz, Wainwright). That level of futility won't be a blip, as swinging strikes keep crumbling, control foundation has tons of cracks, and righty bats light him up. He's a first-round talent if you're employing a tanking strategy.

Yr Tm	W	Sv	IP	K	ERA	WHIP	xERA	xWHIP	vL+	vR+	BF/G	BB%	K%	K-BB%	xBB%	SwK	Vel	G	L	F	H%	S%	HR/F	xHR/F	GS	APC	DOM%	DIS%	Sv%	LI	RAR	BPX	R$
19 MIL	10	0	160	102	3.55	1.29	5.30	1.46	99	95	21.7	8%	15%	8%	9%	7.4%	88.5	40	24	36	28%	77%	11%	13%	31	86	6%	32%			18.8	48	$9
20 SD	7	0	69	63	2.73	1.07	4.20	1.25	70	99	23.0	7%	23%	16%	9%	10.4%	88.6	41	22	37	26%	82%	13%	19%	12	88	42%	17%			14.8	113	$26
21 CHC	6	0	148	114	5.78	1.60	5.26	1.53	114	116	20.9	11%	17%	6%	10%	9.2%	88.0	42	25	32	31%	67%	17%	16%	32	81	3%	56%			-27.6	24	-$17
22 ARI	2	0	134	102	4.09	1.30	4.60	1.40	98	105	21.1	9%	18%	9%	10%	8.9%	89.6	43	17	40	27%	74%	13%	14%	27	85	15%	41%			-2.0	55	-$2
23 ARI *	3	0	103	81	6.79	1.69	5.87	1.47	109	118	21.1	10%	19%	9%	12%	8.6%	89.5	44	22	34	36%	59%	11%	13%	18	83	11%	61%			-31.1	50	-$20
1st Half	1	0	49	38	5.71	1.50	4.54	1.47	108	100	21.1	10%	18%	8%	12%	8.8%	90.0	46	21	34	33%	60%	6%	8%	9	84	11%	67%			-8.3	71	-$13
2nd Half	2	0	54	43	7.67	1.85	7.01	1.51	111	133	20.9	10%	17%	7%	11%	8.4%	89.1	43	23	34	38%	59%	17%	19%	9	82	11%	56%			-22.1	33	-$16
Proj	4	0	102	80	5.67	1.55	4.73	1.46	106	116	21.0	10%	18%	8%	11%	8.8%	89.1	43	22	35	32%	65%	12%	15%	21						-16.8	48	-$12

De Los Santos,Enyel

Age: 28 | Th: R | Role: RP | Ht: 6' 3" | Wt: 235 | Type: Pwr
Health: A | PT/Exp: C | Consist: C
LIMA Plan: A+ | Rand Var: -3 | MM: 3301

Steadily increasing leverage like this is a sign of trust by MLB clubs and often a precursor for saves or holds, especially with two-year stats as stable as these. But this was a step backward, as command erosion was fueled by xBB% and SwK givebacks. All told, prior surging skills are still part of his arsenal. At a buck or two, he's a LIMA gem.

Yr Tm	W	Sv	IP	K	ERA	WHIP	xERA	xWHIP	vL+	vR+	BF/G	BB%	K%	K-BB%	xBB%	SwK	Vel	G	L	F	H%	S%	HR/F	xHR/F	GS	APC	DOM%	DIS%	Sv%	LI	RAR	BPX	R$
19 PHI *	5	0	105	82	5.40	1.39	5.35	1.51	243	105	18.4	9%	19%	9%	5%	12.5%	93.3	39	26	35	28%	68%	36%	27%	1	35	0%	100%	0	0.26	-11.5	30	-$4
20																																	
21 2 NL	2	0	35	48	6.37	1.73	4.37	1.28	128	121	5.2	10%	28%	17%	6%	15.5%	94.9	38	22	40	40%	68%	21%	18%	0	21			0	0.46	-9.2	123	-$9
22 CLE	5	1	53	61	3.04	1.07	3.27	1.15	89	82	4.3	8%	28%	20%	5%	14.6%	95.3	40	26	35	29%	72%	7%	14%	0	17			50	0.96	6.1	139	$4
23 CLE	5	0	66	62	3.29	1.14	4.18	1.34	104	71	3.7	10%	24%	14%	8%	12.8%	95.7	40	20	40	27%	72%	6%	9%	0	15			0	1.16	8.4	88	$4
1st Half	3	0	34	31	2.65	1.00	4.10	1.36	94	62	3.9	10%	23%	14%	8%	12.3%	95.6	46	12	42	23%	75%	6%	9%	0	16			0	1.00	7.1	89	$4
2nd Half	2	0	32	31	3.98	1.29	4.25	1.33	117	79	3.6	9%	24%	15%	6%	13.3%	95.8	35	28	37	32%	69%	6%	9%	0	15			0	1.32	1.4	90	-$1
Proj	5	0	65	70	3.90	1.30	3.90	1.30	115	89	4.4	10%	26%	16%	7%	13.9%	95.4	39	22	39	31%	73%	11%	12%	0						3.5	103	$0

STEPHEN NICKRAND

deGrom,Jacob

Age: 36 | Th: R | Role: SP | Ht: 6' 4" | Wt: 180 | Type: Pwr/FB
Health: F | PT/Exp: C | Consist: A | LIMA Plan: A+ | Rand Var: -1 | MM: 5500

Six starts of unparalleled skills, then... devastation. By mid-October, arm felt "close to normal", but rehab from Tommy John surgery still expected to extend into August. May have one last stretch of elite performance in him, but next injury will always be lurking. For 2024, keep expectations low and rest up—risk-reward conundrum returns full force in 2025.

Yr Tm	W	Sv	IP	K	ERA	WHIP	xERA	xWHIP	vL+	vR+	BF/G	BB%	K%	K-BB%	xBB%	SwK	Vel	G	L	F	H%	S%	HR/F	xHR/F	GS	APC	DOM%	DIS%	Sv%	LI	RAR	BPX	R$
19 NYM	11	0	204	255	2.43	0.97	3.18	1.05	82	74	25.1	5%	32%	26%	5%	16.1%	96.9	44	21	35	30%	80%	11%	10%	32	103	66%	13%			52.3	187	$36
20 NYM	4	0	68	104	2.38	0.96	2.77	0.96	85	68	22.3	7%	39%	32%	5%	22.0%	98.6	42	21	37	31%	81%	13%	16%	12	95	50%	8%			17.4	230	$30
21 NYM	7	0	92	146	1.08	0.55	2.00	0.74	61	49	21.6	3%	45%	42%	4%	22.4%	99.3	44	17	39	23%	89%	9%	10%	15	82	80%	0%			36.2	274	$28
22 NYM	5	0	64	102	3.08	0.75	2.13	0.76	73	76	21.7	3%	43%	39%	4%	21.5%	98.9	39	19	42	28%	67%	17%	18%	11	85	45%	9%			7.1	268	$9
23 TEX	2	0	30	45	2.67	0.76	2.69	0.85	61	83	19.2	3%	39%	36%	5%	21.1%	98.8	38	17	45	30%	67%	7%	12%	6	75	50%	0%			6.2	252	$3
1st Half	2	0	30	45	2.67	0.76	2.69	0.85	61	83	19.2	3%	39%	36%	5%	21.1%	98.8	38	17	45	30%	67%	7%	12%	6	75	50%	0%			6.2	253	$5
2nd Half																																	
Proj	**3**	**0**	**44**	**66**	**3.04**	**0.91**	**2.31**	**0.85**	**80**	**81**	**21.0**	**5%**	**40%**	**36%**	**5%**	**21.1%**	**98.6**	**41**	**19**	**40**	**33%**	**70%**	**11%**	**13%**	**8**						**6.9**	**249**	**$4**

DeSclafani,Anthony

Age: 34 | Th: R | Role: SP | Ht: 6' 2" | Wt: 195 | Type: Con
Health: F | PT/Exp: B | Consist: A | LIMA Plan: B | Rand Var: +2 | MM: 3101

"Tony Disco" hustled to 2.13 ERA through six starts, but with little skill support, disco demolition had begun even before toe, shoulder injuries halted good times. Late July flexor strain ended year, leaving us wanting more, more, more. Strand rate may turn, but 4.00+ xERAs say no hot stuff here. You should be dancin'... with someone else.

Yr Tm	W	Sv	IP	K	ERA	WHIP	xERA	xWHIP	vL+	vR+	BF/G	BB%	K%	K-BB%	xBB%	SwK	Vel	G	L	F	H%	S%	HR/F	xHR/F	GS	APC	DOM%	DIS%	Sv%	LI	RAR	BPX	R$
19 CIN	9	0	167	167	3.89	1.20	4.30	1.26	105	85	22.5	7%	24%	17%	7%	10.4%	94.7	43	19	38	29%	75%	16%	13%	31	86	23%	26%			12.7	122	$12
20 CIN	1	0	34	25	7.22	1.69	5.81	1.53	136	106	17.6	10%	16%	6%	12%	9.8%	94.9	39	27	35	33%	60%	18%	20%	7	67	14%	43%	0	0.71	-11.5	25	-$15
21 SF	13	0	168	152	3.17	1.09	4.00	1.21	96	77	21.8	6%	22%	16%	6%	11.5%	94.1	44	19	36	28%	76%	11%	13%	31	83	26%	23%			22.7	118	$21
22 SF	0	0	19	17	6.63	2.00	4.62	1.19	160	148	18.8	4%	18%	14%	7%	10.0%	92.4	44	20	37	45%	71%	15%	15%	5	66	0%	60%			-6.2	128	-$9
23 SF	4	0	100	79	4.88	1.25	4.28	1.24	110	98	22.1	5%	19%	14%	7%	8.9%	93.2	41	24	34	31%	65%	14%	16%	18	82	22%	28%	0	0.87	-6.7	111	-$2
1st Half	4	0	93	72	4.44	1.19	4.18	1.24	107	92	22.7	5%	19%	14%	7%	8.8%	93.1	43	24	33	30%	66%	13%	13%	17	85	24%	29%			-1.2	112	$6
2nd Half	0	0	6	7	11.37	2.21	5.63	1.25	157	168	16.5	6%	21%	15%	8%	9.6%	93.9	25	29	46	45%	55%	27%	41%	1	58	0%	0%	0	1.45	-5.5	119	-$11
Proj	**5**	**0**	**102**	**87**	**4.40**	**1.24**	**3.93**	**1.26**	**111**	**89**	**20.7**	**7%**	**21%**	**14%**	**8%**	**10.0%**	**94.0**	**43**	**22**	**35**	**29%**	**69%**	**14%**	**14%**	**20**						**-0.9**	**104**	**$0**

Detmers,Reid

Age: 24 | Th: L | Role: SP | Ht: 6' 2" | Wt: 210 | Type: Pwr
Health: B | PT/Exp: A | Consist: A | LIMA Plan: A+ | Rand Var: 0 | MM: 3303

Overall, trendy breakout pick didn't deliver, but remove horrid July-Aug stretch (29 ER in 25.1 IP) and you get 3.28 ERA, 1.23 WHIP. 1st half K-BB%, SwK looked like step forward; 2nd half velocity dip hints at hidden injury or need to add stamina, and lefties were surprisingly vexing. Still, 1st half times two—plus better win luck—is a reasonable expectation.

Yr Tm	W	Sv	IP	K	ERA	WHIP	xERA	xWHIP	vL+	vR+	BF/G	BB%	K%	K-BB%	xBB%	SwK	Vel	G	L	F	H%	S%	HR/F	xHR/F	GS	APC	DOM%	DIS%	Sv%	LI	RAR	BPX	R$
19																																	
20																																	
21 LAA *	4	0	83	114	4.14	1.29	4.50	1.49	134	120	17.9	8%	34%	25%	8%	11.6%	92.9	34	21	46	35%	74%	16%	14%	5	76	0%	80%			1.3	132	$1
22 LAA	7	0	129	122	3.77	1.21	4.13	1.28	86	99	21.6	9%	23%	14%	7%	11.6%	93.2	36	22	42	29%	71%	9%	10%	25	87	20%	28%			3.2	89	$5
23 LAA	4	0	149	168	4.48	1.35	4.20	1.28	119	95	23.0	9%	26%	17%	8%	12.3%	94.4	37	23	40	33%	70%	12%	10%	28	93	36%	32%			-2.7	112	$0
1st Half	2	0	82	103	3.72	1.25	3.81	1.20	104	87	23.1	9%	30%	21%	8%	13.8%	94.9	33	26	41	33%	73%	10%	7%	15	94	33%	27%			6.2	138	$8
2nd Half	2	0	66	65	5.43	1.48	4.71	1.39	137	106	22.9	10%	22%	12%	7%	10.6%	93.8	40	20	40	32%	67%	14%	13%	13	92	38%	38%			-9.0	80	-$4
Proj	**8**	**0**	**160**	**182**	**3.86**	**1.24**	**3.64**	**1.24**	**112**	**94**	**20.2**	**9%**	**28%**	**19%**	**8%**	**11.8%**	**94.0**	**37**	**22**	**41**	**31%**	**72%**	**12%**	**10%**	**32**						**9.1**	**120**	**$9**

Díaz,Alexis

Age: 27 | Th: R | Role: RP | Ht: 6' 2" | Wt: 224 | Type: Pwr/FB
Health: B | PT/Exp: B | Consist: A | LIMA Plan: C+ | Rand Var: -3 | MM: 3431

Initially, seemed he'd arrived as top-shelf closer, working around walks, sustaining SwK despite velocity drop, yielding fewer fly balls to limit home park's HR risk. But it all fell apart in 2nd half, leaving job security a bit shaky. Still, track record suggests K% should revert to elite level, and that's probably enough, even if it's a wild ride at times.

Yr Tm	W	Sv	IP	K	ERA	WHIP	xERA	xWHIP	vL+	vR+	BF/G	BB%	K%	K-BB%	xBB%	SwK	Vel	G	L	F	H%	S%	HR/F	xHR/F	GS	APC	DOM%	DIS%	Sv%	LI	RAR	BPX	R$
19																																	
20																																	
21 aa	3	2	43	60	4.78	1.35	3.40				5.1	12%	33%	21%							35%	63%									-2.7	139	-$3
22 CIN	7	10	64	83	1.84	0.96	3.71	1.28	83	54	4.3	13%	33%	20%	8%	17.1%	95.7	30	15	55	19%	86%	7%	9%	0	18			71	1.26	16.7	103	$14
23 CIN	9	37	67	86	3.07	1.19	3.84	1.34	75	87	4.0	13%	30%	17%	11%	15.7%	94.6	38	23	39	28%	75%	7%	6%	0	16			93	1.61	10.4	104	$23
1st Half	3	23	37	58	2.19	1.03	2.97	1.18	73	62	4.0	13%	38%	26%	10%	17.7%	94.8	36	28	36	28%	78%	4%	9%	0	16			96	1.62	9.8	162	$28
2nd Half	6	14	30	28	4.15	1.38	5.02	1.54	79	119	4.1	13%	21%	8%	11%	13.4%	94.4	40	19	42	28%	72%	9%	5%	0	17			88	1.61	0.7	35	$13
Proj	**9**	**32**	**73**	**91**	**3.60**	**1.29**	**3.75**	**1.33**	**91**	**101**	**4.2**	**13%**	**31%**	**18%**	**11%**	**15.5%**	**94.8**	**37**	**21**	**43**	**30%**	**74%**	**9%**	**7%**	**0**						**6.5**	**101**	**$18**

Díaz,Edwin

Age: 30 | Th: R | Role: RP | Ht: 6' 3" | Wt: 165 | Type: Pwr
Health: F | PT/Exp: A | Consist: D | LIMA Plan: B | Rand Var: 0 | MM: 5530

Tore patellar tendon celebrating World Baseball Classic win, which torpedoed season, but we might've seen him in Sept had games mattered. Given fluky nature of injury, additional time to heal, no reason to think we'll be cueing Timmy Trumpet to play "Taps"—or anything other than a triumphant tune heralding the return of relief pitching royalty.

Yr Tm	W	Sv	IP	K	ERA	WHIP	xERA	xWHIP	vL+	vR+	BF/G	BB%	K%	K-BB%	xBB%	SwK	Vel	G	L	F	H%	S%	HR/F	xHR/F	GS	APC	DOM%	DIS%	Sv%	LI	RAR	BPX	R$
19 NYM	2	26	58	99	5.59	1.38	3.19	1.04	91	124	3.8	9%	39%	30%	6%	18.5%	97.5	37	20	44	40%	68%	27%	14%	0	16			79	1.18	-7.7	217	$
20 NYM	2	6	26	50	1.75	1.25	2.45	1.06	85	75	4.2	13%	45%	33%	8%	21.5%	97.8	43	23	34	42%	90%	13%	9%	0	19			67	1.22	8.5	230	$1
21 NYM	5	32	63	89	3.45	1.05	3.24	1.09	76	81	4.1	9%	35%	26%	7%	16.7%	98.8	34	23	43	31%	67%	5%	6%	0	16			84	1.35	6.3	168	$1
22 NYM	3	32	62	118	1.31	0.84	1.60	0.79	57	68	3.9	8%	50%	43%	4%	25.5%	99.1	47	20	33	35%	88%	9%	8%	0	15			91	1.15	20.4	290	$2
23																																	
1st Half																																	
2nd Half																																	
Proj	**3**	**32**	**58**	**94**	**2.74**	**0.97**	**2.27**	**0.93**	**71**	**86**	**3.9**	**8%**	**43%**	**34%**	**6%**	**21.0%**	**98.7**	**41**	**21**	**39**	**32%**	**75%**	**13%**	**8%**	**0**						**11.4**	**230**	**$2**

Domínguez,Seranthony

Age: 29 | Th: R | Role: RP | Ht: 6' 1" | Wt: 225 | Type: Pwr
Health: F | PT/Exp: C | Consist: F | LIMA Plan: B | Rand Var: -2 | MM: 2211

Hung around late innings, even notching two Aug saves fresh off IL (oblique), but skills say such duty not warranted, even if fastball looked the part. K% took a step back, and though xBB% says positive BB% regression due, K-BB% would still be average. Gave back ground balls, too. Other speculative save sources may have better payoff potential.

Yr Tm	W	Sv	IP	K	ERA	WHIP	xERA	xWHIP	vL+	vR+	BF/G	BB%	K%	K-BB%	xBB%	SwK	Vel	G	L	F	H%	S%	HR/F	xHR/F	GS	APC	DOM%	DIS%	Sv%	LI	RAR	BPX	R$
19 PHI	3	0	25	29	4.01	1.46	4.02	1.36	133	67	4.1	11%	26%	15%	8%	14.0%	97.4	55	17	29	34%	76%	16%	11%	0	17			0	1.11	1.5	115	-$
20																																	
21 PHI *	1	0	19	16	9.83	1.89	8.40				5.3	12%	18%	6%		14.3%	95.2	50	0	50	33%	51%	0%	0%	0	14			0	0.35	-13.1	-17	-$1
22 PHI	6	9	51	61	3.00	1.14	3.27	1.24	87	83	3.8	11%	29%	19%	9%	15.1%	98.0	48	19	33	28%	76%	10%	12%	0	15			82	1.39	6.1	127	$
23 PHI	5	2	50	48	3.78	1.40	4.71	1.40	114	88	3.9	10%	21%	12%	8%	13.0%	97.8	42	18	39	31%	78%	12%	12%	0	15			22	1.12	3.4	77	-$
1st Half	1	0	27	28	4.33	1.56	4.35	1.33	142	89	3.9	9%	22%	13%	8%	13.3%	98.1	45	23	32	37%	74%	12%	11%	0	15			0	1.07	0.0	104	-$
2nd Half	4	2	23	20	3.13	1.22	5.13	1.49	88	89	3.9	11%	20%	9%	8%	12.7%	97.5	39	13	48	22%	83%	13%	13%	0	15			33	1.17	3.4	47	$
Proj	**7**	**5**	**65**	**61**	**3.86**	**1.32**	**4.17**	**1.38**	**110**	**92**	**3.9**	**10%**	**23%**	**13%**	**9%**	**13.4%**	**97.8**	**43**	**17**	**40**	**29%**	**75%**	**12%**	**12%**	**0**						**3.8**	**79**	**$**

Doval,Camilo

Age: 26 | Th: R | Role: RP | Ht: 6' 2" | Wt: 185 | Type: Pwr
Health: A | PT/Exp: A | Consist: A | LIMA Plan: C+ | Rand Var: -2 | MM: 5431

Did everything you'd want closer to do—missed even more bats, induced plenty of ground balls, even did better job solving LHB. To extent he had hiccup in 2nd half, unlucky S%, H% had a lot to do with that. Sure, a few more of his rare fly balls may clear fence, but not so many as to be a big problem. Among the safest save sources out there.

Yr Tm	W	Sv	IP	K	ERA	WHIP	xERA	xWHIP	vL+	vR+	BF/G	BB%	K%	K-BB%	xBB%	SwK	Vel	G	L	F	H%	S%	HR/F	xHR/F	GS	APC	DOM%	DIS%	Sv%	LI	RAR	BPX	R$
19																																	
20																																	
21 SF *	8	4	59	73	3.93	1.35	3.79	1.08	104	65	4.3	13%	30%	17%	7%	14.4%	98.7	48	19	32	31%	73%	20%	15%	0	16			50	1.02	2.4	107	$
22 SF	6	27	68	80	2.53	1.24	3.03	1.26	110	71	4.2	10%	28%	17%	8%	14.1%	99.0	56	22	22	31%	81%	11%	11%	0	16			90	1.52	12.0	130	$
23 SF	6	39	68	87	2.93	1.14	3.10	1.19	79	81	4.1	9%	31%	22%	8%	15.5%	99.0	52	18	30	32%	74%	6%	10%	0	17			83	1.81	11.7	163	$
1st Half	2	24	38	53	1.89	1.05	2.86	1.19	76	69	4.1	11%	34%	23%	8%	15.4%	99.2	55	15	30	28%	84%	8%	11%	0	17			92	1.66	11.4	170	$
2nd Half	4	15	30	34	4.25	1.25	3.40	1.18	84	98	4.0	7%	27%	20%	7%	15.5%	98.7	49	20	30	35%	64%	4%	8%	0	16			71	1.99	0.3	157	$
Proj	**5**	**36**	**73**	**90**	**3.08**	**1.22**	**3.04**	**1.22**	**95**	**86**	**4.0**	**10%**	**31%**	**20%**	**8%**	**15.2%**	**98.9**	**53**	**19**	**29**	**32%**	**76%**	**9%**	**9%**	**0**						**11.2**	**146**	**$**

KRIS OLSON

Dunning,Dane

Age: 29 Th: R Role SP	Health C	LIMA Plan B+	
Ht: 6'4" Wt: 225 Type	PT/Exp A	Rand Var -1	
	Consist A	MM 3105	

After deGrom injury opened door, he did reasonable take on Jake in 1st half—minus the Ks. But xERA said that wouldn't last, and reversal of fortunate HR/F led the regression parade. Stable xERA, xWHIP over three years shows he's no great Dane, but more your average mutt, though one who can still fetch a few wins with good enough backing bats.

Yr Tm	W	Sv	IP	K	ERA	WHIP	xERA	xWHIP	vL+	vR+	BF/G	BB%	K%	K-BB%	xBB%	SwK	Vel	G	L	F	H%	S%	HR/F	xHR/F	GS	APC	DOM%	DIS%	Sv%	LI	RAR	BPX	R$
19																																	
20 CHW	2	0	34	35	3.97	1.12	4.11	1.30	103	60	20.3	9%	25%	15%	10%	11.6%	91.9	45	22	33	26%	68%	13%	12%	7	82	29%	29%			2.0	109	$3
21 TEX	5	0	118	114	4.51	1.44	3.89	1.30	108	102	18.9	8%	22%	14%	7%	10.3%	90.4	54	20	26	34%	71%	14%	15%	25	71	12%	36%	0	0.72	-3.6	110	-$4
22 TEX	4	0	153	137	4.46	1.43	3.92	1.35	115	109	23.1	9%	20%	11%	8%	10.4%	89.5	53	18	29	32%	72%	15%	15%	29	88	10%	45%			-9.3	85	-$6
23 TEX	12	0	173	140	3.70	1.26	4.33	1.35	105	88	20.6	8%	19%	12%	7%	10.0%	91.0	46	21	33	29%	74%	12%	12%	26	77	12%	38%	0	0.70	13.4	87	$12
1st Half	7	0	80	51	2.69	1.10	4.35	1.37	86	83	17.9	7%	16%	9%	6%	8.5%	90.6	49	20	31	26%	77%	6%	13%	10	67	10%	40%	0	0.68	16.3	74	$19
2nd Half	5	0	92	89	4.58	1.41	4.30	1.33	118	95	23.5	9%	22%	14%	7%	11.3%	91.3	44	21	34	32%	72%	16%	11%	16	88	13%	38%	0	0.73	-2.8	100	$6
Proj	10	0	167	149	4.11	1.33	3.89	1.32	109	93	20.1	9%	22%	13%	8%	10.4%	90.7	49	20	31	31%	72%	13%	13%	34						4.5	97	$5

Duran,Jhoan

Age: 26 Th: R Role RP	Health A	LIMA Plan B	
Ht: 6'5" Wt: 230 Type Pwr/xGB	PT/Exp B	Rand Var 0	
	Consist F	MM 5531	

Graduated from setup duty to ninth inning and didn't skip a beat. Pick your poison, batter: swing and miss, or beat it into the ground. Four of five blown saves came after two-plus days off; few likely to complain if he worked more often. A bit unlucky with HR/F, and BB% a tad high, but xBB%, 2nd half suggest he'll get that in check, too. Filth personified.

Yr Tm	W	Sv	IP	K	ERA	WHIP	xERA	xWHIP	vL+	vR+	BF/G	BB%	K%	K-BB%	xBB%	SwK	Vel	G	L	F	H%	S%	HR/F	xHR/F	GS	APC	DOM%	DIS%	Sv%	LI	RAR	BPX	R$
19 aa	3	0	37	35	6.68	1.37	4.23				22.1	6%	23%	16%							36%	48%									-9.9	118	-$5
20																																	
21 aaa	0	0	16	19	6.12	2.01	6.12				15.4	18%	25%	6%							40%	68%									-3.7	77	-$9
22 MIN	2	8	68	89	1.86	0.98	2.17	0.99	85	78	4.7	6%	33%	27%	4%	18.5%	100.9	61	17	22	30%	87%	18%	12%	0	18			100	1.34	17.6	214	$11
23 MIN	3	27	62	84	2.45	1.14	2.54	1.17	70	99	4.3	10%	33%	23%	7%	16.9%	101.9	66	12	22	30%	83%	20%	16%	0	17			84	1.27	14.4	185	$17
1st Half	2	12	33	43	1.93	1.04	2.52	1.24	66	85	4.3	12%	33%	22%	7%	18.0%	101.9	69	10	21	25%	87%	21%	16%	0	18			80	1.41	9.7	168	$15
2nd Half	1	15	30	41	3.03	1.25	2.56	1.11	74	117	4.3	8%	33%	25%	7%	15.6%	101.8	63	14	23	36%	79%	19%	16%	0	17			88	1.12	4.7	206	$10
Proj	3	38	65	84	2.78	1.10	2.39	1.11	76	96	5.3	9%	33%	24%	6%	16.9%	101.7	64	14	22	31%	77%	16%	15%	0						12.5	191	$22

Eflin,Zach

Age: 30 Th: R Role SP	Health F	LIMA Plan C+	
Ht: 6'6" Wt: 220 Type Con	PT/Exp A	Rand Var 0	
	Consist A	MM 5203	

Early IL stint (back) reminded us of his fragility; creaky knees didn't send him to IL in 2023, but required maintenance. Otherwise, this was impressive: cutter now entrenched as part of three-pitch mix, helping control artist push beyond pedestrian K%; gave back ground ball gains in 2nd half, but not overly concerning. With health, looks repeatable.

Yr Tm	W	Sv	IP	K	ERA	WHIP	xERA	xWHIP	vL+	vR+	BF/G	BB%	K%	K-BB%	xBB%	SwK	Vel	G	L	F	H%	S%	HR/F	xHR/F	GS	APC	DOM%	DIS%	Sv%	LI	RAR	BPX	R$
19 PHI	10	0	163	129	4.13	1.35	4.83	1.36	113	95	22.0	7%	18%	11%	6%	9.4%	93.6	45	21	35	30%	76%	16%	13%	28	80	21%	43%	0	0.74	7.5	87	$6
20 PHI	4	0	59	70	3.97	1.27	3.45	1.11	125	84	22.3	6%	29%	22%	6%	10.7%	93.9	47	21	31	35%	73%	16%	16%	10	83	30%	10%	0	0.74	3.5	176	$9
21 PHI	4	0	106	99	4.17	1.25	3.83	1.11	102	106	24.6	4%	22%	19%	5%	10.9%	92.6	43	24	33	34%	71%	14%	13%	18	90	28%	22%			1.2	149	$1
22 PHI	3	1	76	65	4.04	1.12	3.78	1.16	115	80	15.7	5%	21%	16%	6%	10.2%	92.8	44	19	37	29%	66%	10%	11%	13	60	23%	23%	100	0.77	-0.7	125	$1
23 TAM	16	0	178	186	3.50	1.02	3.25	1.05	80	95	22.7	3%	26%	23%	5%	11.6%	92.4	50	17	34	31%	69%	12%	14%	31	83	39%	16%			18.3	185	$27
1st Half	9	0	90	91	3.29	1.03	3.27	1.10	72	100	23.7	4%	26%	21%	5%	11.2%	92.3	53	16	32	29%	72%	13%	13%	15	86	40%	13%			11.6	173	$26
2nd Half	7	0	87	95	3.71	1.02	3.24	1.00	88	90	21.7	3%	27%	25%	4%	12.0%	92.6	47	18	36	32%	66%	11%	15%	16	80	38%	19%			6.7	199	$22
Proj	13	0	160	160	3.65	1.09	3.20	1.08	95	92	20.6	4%	26%	21%	5%	11.1%	92.7	47	19	34	31%	71%	13%	14%	30						13.4	166	$17

Elder,Bryce

Age: 25 Th: R Role SP	Health A	LIMA Plan B	
Ht: 6'2" Wt: 220 Type Con	PT/Exp B	Rand Var -1	
	Consist B	MM 2003	

1st half results made us wonder, "Should we be giving Elder more respect?" But it didn't take much—loss of ground ball tilt, bad turn of strand rate—for things to head south. With below-average velocity, SwK, and K%, he needs those grounders to stay somewhere near sea level. Absent that? The ERA and WHIP damage will get old pretty quick.

Yr Tm	W	Sv	IP	K	ERA	WHIP	xERA	xWHIP	vL+	vR+	BF/G	BB%	K%	K-BB%	xBB%	SwK	Vel	G	L	F	H%	S%	HR/F	xHR/F	GS	APC	DOM%	DIS%	Sv%	LI	RAR	BPX	R$
19																																	
20																																	
21 a/a	9	0	94	86	3.49	1.10	2.74				23.1	10%	23%	13%							24%	71%									9.0	95	$9
22 ATL *	8	0	159	130	4.68	1.31	4.22	1.39	102	82	23.4	9%	20%	11%	9%	10.3%	90.8	49	18	32	29%	67%	8%	14%	9	87	44%	33%	0	0.71	-14.0	70	-$2
23 ATL	12	0	175	128	3.81	1.28	4.45	1.43	96	96	23.6	9%	18%	9%	8%	10.3%	89.8	50	20	30	28%	73%	12%	12%	31	92	23%	32%			11.2	66	$10
1st Half	6	0	96	79	2.44	1.13	3.70	1.31	93	83	24.1	7%	20%	13%	8%	11.5%	89.7	56	18	26	27%	82%	11%	12%	16	96	31%	19%			22.4	108	$24
2nd Half	6	0	79	49	5.49	1.46	5.40	1.57	100	116	23.1	10%	14%	4%	9%	8.8%	90.0	44	23	33	29%	64%	13%	13%	15	88	13%	47%			-11.3	16	-$1
Proj	10	0	160	124	4.35	1.34	4.19	1.41	106	104	23.5	9%	19%	9%	9%	10.0%	90.1	49	20	31	29%	70%	13%	12%	28						-0.4	67	$2

Eovaldi,Nathan

Age: 34 Th: R Role SP	Health F	LIMA Plan B	
Ht: 6'2" Wt: 217 Type	PT/Exp A	Rand Var 0	
	Consist A	MM 3203	

After first-rate 1st half, lost seven weeks to forearm strain, but got tuned up in time for post-season run (5-0, 2.95 ERA). If you write off 2nd half to injury, xERA, xWHIP held stable, though losing velocity, SwK with age could bite him, as he's never been K% standout. IL days are part of the package, but another sub-4.00 ERA is doable.

Yr Tm	W	Sv	IP	K	ERA	WHIP	xERA	xWHIP	vL+	vR+	BF/G	BB%	K%	K-BB%	xBB%	SwK	Vel	G	L	F	H%	S%	HR/F	xHR/F	GS	APC	DOM%	DIS%	Sv%	LI	RAR	BPX	R$
19 BOS	2	0	68	70	5.99	1.58	4.89	1.46	126	107	13.1	12%	23%	12%	8%	10.9%	97.5	45	19	36	32%	68%	23%	18%	12	55	8%	58%	0	0.88	-12.3	71	-$8
20 BOS	4	0	48	52	3.72	1.20	3.35	1.05	86	128	22.1	4%	26%	23%	5%	13.8%	97.4	49	21	30	34%	76%	20%	19%	9	83	22%	33%			4.3	188	$9
21 BOS	11	0	182	195	3.75	1.19	3.67	1.09	91	97	23.9	5%	26%	21%	5%	12.9%	96.9	42	23	35	34%	70%	8%	9%	32	91	41%	13%			11.6	161	$14
22 BOS	6	0	109	103	3.87	1.23	3.69	1.12	105	108	23.0	4%	22%	18%	5%	12.7%	95.8	47	16	37	31%	77%	17%	16%	20	87	35%	30%			1.3	147	$3
23 TEX	12	0	144	132	3.63	1.14	3.81	1.30	78	105	23.1	8%	23%	15%	8%	12.0%	95.2	51	17	32	27%	71%	12%	13%	25	89	32%	20%			12.6	110	$15
1st Half	10	0	112	106	2.64	0.99	3.43	1.19	77	90	25.3	6%	25%	18%	7%	12.5%	95.6	52	16	33	27%	76%	8%	11%	17	97	47%	6%			23.4	140	$39
2nd Half	2	0	32	26	7.11	1.67	5.34	1.66	83	151	18.4	14%	18%	4%	12%	10.8%	93.9	49	20	31	29%	61%	23%	21%	8	74	0%	50%			-10.8	7	-$9
Proj	9	0	138	131	3.81	1.26	3.76	1.29	83	109	23.3	8%	23%	15%	8%	12.1%	95.7	48	19	33	30%	73%	13%	16%	24						8.7	108	$7

Estévez,Carlos

Age: 31 Th: R Role RP	Health B	LIMA Plan B+	
Ht: 6'6" Wt: 277 Type Pwr/FB	PT/Exp B	Rand Var 0	
	Consist A	MM 2321	

1st half had a certain sheen, but this wasn't an "all he needed was to escape Coors" success story, as xERA attests. When lucky strand rate abandoned him, rocky ride ensued. Did kick SwK up a bit, and xBB% says he might shave a few walks—but heed xERA history: despite FB velocity, this is not closer material. DN: 4.50 ERA, no more Sv opps

Yr Tm	W	Sv	IP	K	ERA	WHIP	xERA	xWHIP	vL+	vR+	BF/G	BB%	K%	K-BB%	xBB%	SwK	Vel	G	L	F	H%	S%	HR/F	xHR/F	GS	APC	DOM%	DIS%	Sv%	LI	RAR	BPX	R$
19 COL	2	0	72	81	3.75	1.29	4.38	1.24	112	91	4.3	7%	26%	19%	6%	14.4%	97.9	38	20	42	32%	78%	14%	14%	0	17			0	0.93	6.7	131	$1
20 COL	1	1	24	27	7.50	1.75	5.00	1.28	140	132	4.5	8%	23%	16%	6%	11.7%	96.9	31	29	40	40%	61%	19%	17%	0	17			25	1.16	-9.0	113	-$11
21 COL	3	11	62	60	4.38	1.49	4.35	1.28	109	109	4.2	8%	22%	14%	8%	11.7%	97.1	44	21	36	36%	74%	12%	11%	0	16			65	1.32	-0.9	106	$0
22 COL	4	2	57	54	3.47	1.18	4.27	1.33	103	84	3.8	10%	23%	13%	8%	9.9%	97.6	36	19	45	26%	75%	10%	11%	0	16			33	1.01	3.5	76	$2
23 LAA	5	31	62	78	3.90	1.49	4.54	1.32	109	91	4.5	11%	28%	17%	6%	13.6%	97.2	31	22	47	36%	77%	9%	10%	0	18			89	1.21	3.3	102	$11
1st Half	2	21	34	42	1.85	1.26	4.08	1.30	96	77	4.1	11%	30%	18%	6%	13.3%	97.2	33	24	43	31%	90%	8%	9%	0	17			100	1.29	10.4	109	$21
2nd Half	3	10	28	36	6.35	1.76	5.10	1.35	123	107	5.0	11%	26%	15%	5%	13.8%	97.2	29	20	51	41%	65%	10%	10%	0	20			71	1.10	-7.1	95	$1
Proj	5	20	73	82	4.27	1.35	4.01	1.30	104	90	4.1	10%	27%	17%	7%	12.7%	97.3	35	21	44	32%	72%	11%	11%	0						0.5	102	$7

Faedo,Alex

Age: 28 Th: R Role SP	Health C	LIMA Plan B	
Ht: 6'5" Wt: 225 Type /FB	PT/Exp C	Rand Var 0	
	Consist D	MM 2101	

2-5, 4.45 ERA in 65 IP at DET. Showed signs of growth upon joining rotation in May (3.75 xERA in 5 GS) until he hit IL with fingernail issue that recurred in Sept, twice required removal of portion of middle nail. No small matter, as it's integral to change-up with 55% GB%. If he has clipped issue, might he turn corner? We're watching with interest.

Yr Tm	W	Sv	IP	K	ERA	WHIP	xERA	xWHIP	vL+	vR+	BF/G	BB%	K%	K-BB%	xBB%	SwK	Vel	G	L	F	H%	S%	HR/F	xHR/F	GS	APC	DOM%	DIS%	Sv%	LI	RAR	BPX	R$
19 aa	6	0	116	107	5.86	1.41	5.66				22.3	6%	22%	16%							34%	63%									-19.3	78	-$6
20																																	
21																																	
22 DET	1	0	54	44	5.53	1.64	5.25	1.45	123	112	20.3	10%	18%	8%	8%	10.3%	92.8	31	25	44	34%	68%	9%	11%	12	81	8%	50%			-10.4	32	-$10
23 DET *	2	0	98	86	4.36	1.09	3.68	1.29	69	111	16.7	8%	22%	15%	6%	11.0%	92.9	36	18	46	25%	66%	14%	13%	12	69	8%	50%	0	0.73	-0.3	87	$3
1st Half	1	0	48	41	4.89	1.05	4.05	1.15	85	103	16.9	4%	22%	18%	4%	12.9%	93.0	35	20	45	26%	60%	18%	11%	5	79	0%	40%			-3.3	134	-$2
2nd Half	1	0	50	45	3.75	1.12	3.21	1.39	54	115	16.3	10%	23%	13%	8%	9.9%	92.9	37	16	47	23%	72%	12%	13%	7	64	14%	57%	0	0.70	3.6	81	$2
Proj	2	0	87	77	4.43	1.31	4.29	1.29	93	128	20.7	7%	21%	14%	7%	10.9%	92.9	35	19	46	30%	71%	13%	12%	17						-1.1	92	-$3

KRIS OLSON

Fairbanks,Peter

Age: 30	Th: R	Role RP	Health F	LIMA Plan B+
Ht: 6' 6"	Wt: 225	Type Pwr	PT/Exp C	Rand Var -1
			Consist D	MM 5520

In 1st half, had short-but-inevitable IL stints for forearm and hip, and dealt with chronic numbness in fingers, but elite skills when health cooperates make him hard to quit. K% doesn't get much better than 2nd half, and xBB% says he's mastered zone more than it seems. If digits don't get uncomfortably numb, other injuries stay away... UP: 40 Sv

Yr	Tm	W	Sv	IP	K	ERA	WHIP	xERA	xWHIP	vL+	vR+	BF/G	BB%	K%	K-BB%	xBB%	SwK	Vel	G	L	F	H%	S%	HR/F	xHR/F	GS	APC	DOM%	DIS%	Sv%	LI	RAR	BPX	R$
19	2 AL *	4	2	53	74	6.87	1.47	5.46	1.29	65	167	4.6	8%	32%	24%	7%	14.0%	97.4	43	27	30	39%	55%	28%	19%	0	18			40	0.80	-15.5	115	-$6
20	TAM	6	0	27	39	2.70	1.39	3.55	1.25	84	89	4.3	12%	33%	21%	8%	16.9%	97.5	47	19	34	37%	83%	10%	9%	2	18	0%	50%	0	1.02	5.8	152	$10
21	TAM	3	5	43	56	3.59	1.43	3.94	1.28	128	62	4.0	11%	30%	19%	8%	13.7%	97.2	43	20	37	37%	75%	5%	8%	0	16			71	1.23	3.6	125	$0
22	TAM	0	8	24	38	1.13	0.67	1.66	0.75	61	51	3.6	3%	44%	41%	4%	18.2%	99.0	53	18	29	29%	87%	8%	6%	0	15			100	1.34	8.4	283	$4
23	TAM	2	25	45	68	2.58	1.01	2.71	1.14	76	62	3.8	11%	37%	26%	5%	13.6%	98.9	49	21	30	28%	77%	11%	10%	0	15			86	1.29	9.8	183	$14
1st Half		0	9	16	15	1.65	1.04	3.95	1.47	86	51	3.7	12%	23%	11%	6%	8.3%	98.0	56	15	29	20%	88%	8%	8%	0	13			90	1.26	5.4	72	$3
2nd Half		2	16	29	53	3.10	1.00	2.13	0.97	72	70	3.8	10%	45%	35%	4%	15.9%	99.3	43	27	31	34%	70%	13%	12%	0	16			84	1.31	4.4	244	$15
Proj		**3**	**23**	**58**	**82**	**2.84**	**1.05**	**2.62**	**1.10**	**97**	**68**	**3.7**	**10%**	**37%**	**27%**	**6%**	**13.4%**	**98.4**	**47**	**21**	**32**	**29%**	**77%**	**15%**	**9%**	**0**						**10.6**	**182**	**$14**

Falter,Bailey

Age: 27	Th: L	Role RP	Health B	LIMA Plan B
Ht: 6' 4"	Wt: 175	Type Con	PT/Exp C	Rand Var 0
			Consist C	MM 2101

2-9, 5.36 ERA in 81 IP at PHI/PIT. When down year ends on IL for "neck soreness and overall fatigue," name jokes write themselves. Control can sometimes be a curse if you don't generate grounders or strikeouts. Strong 2022 finish was opponent-fueled fool's gold, it turns out; next time, we'll wait for louder breakout signals, which may never come.

Yr	Tm	W	Sv	IP	K	ERA	WHIP	xERA	xWHIP	vL+	vR+	BF/G	BB%	K%	K-BB%	xBB%	SwK	Vel	G	L	F	H%	S%	HR/F	xHR/F	GS	APC	DOM%	DIS%	Sv%	LI	RAR	BPX	R$
19	aa	6	0	78	57	4.94	1.44	5.53				23.8	5%	17%	12%							34%	69%									-4.2	74	-$3
20																																		
21	PHI *	4	0	66	72	3.79	1.12	3.64	1.10	97	98	8.7	5%	28%	22%	6%	10.3%	91.8	36	23	41	31%	70%	13%	9%	1	25	0%	100%	0	0.66	3.8	152	$2
22	PHI *	10	0	131	114	3.18	1.03	3.45	1.16	96	115	17.4	5%	23%	18%	5%	11.2%	91.2	32	24	44	26%	77%	14%	14%	16	65	13%	25%	0	0.68	12.8	131	$14
23	2 NL *	4	0	128	88	5.10	1.47	5.78	1.31	149	105	18.9	6%	17%	12%	6%	8.4%	90.7	40	22	38	31%	71%	17%	13%	14	72	0%	57%	0	0.82	-12.1	30	-$9
1st Half		2	0	68	43	5.65	1.59	6.50	1.44	146	106	20.1	7%	14%	7%	6%	7.9%	90.5	41	22	37	33%	69%	14%	13%	7	83	0%	43%	0	1.04	-11.1	17	-$15
2nd Half		2	0	59	45	4.46	1.33	4.95	1.39	153	105	17.6	8%	18%	10%	6%	9.0%	91.1	40	21	39	28%	73%	20%	13%	7	64	0%	71%	0	0.65	-1.0	46	$0
Proj		**6**	**0**	**116**	**96**	**4.38**	**1.30**	**4.20**	**1.27**	**115**	**98**	**14.7**	**6%**	**20%**	**14%**	**6%**	**9.4%**	**91.1**	**38**	**22**	**40**	**30%**	**71%**	**14%**	**12%**	**15**						**-0.7**	**96**	**$0**

Farmer,Buck

Age: 33	Th: R	Role RP	Health A	LIMA Plan A
Ht: 6' 4"	Wt: 232	Type Pwr/FB	PT/Exp C	Rand Var -3
			Consist C	MM 1210

Has always posed a dilemma to Forecaster writers. Trust us, we want to resist obvious puns, but then it's like, "Oh look, another garden-variety middle relief season." Skills not total manure, but no bumper crop of interesting metrics, either. Sharp rise in fly balls a blight that could wipe out yield. Given age, maybe next year he'll be weeded out?

Yr	Tm	W	Sv	IP	K	ERA	WHIP	xERA	xWHIP	vL+	vR+	BF/G	BB%	K%	K-BB%	xBB%	SwK	Vel	G	L	F	H%	S%	HR/F	xHR/F	GS	APC	DOM%	DIS%	Sv%	LI	RAR	BPX	R$
19	DET	6	0	68	73	3.72	1.27	4.01	1.28	99	99	3.9	8%	25%	17%	9%	13.2%	95.1	47	20	33	31%	74%	13%	19%	1	16	0%	0%	0	1.22	6.5	124	$3
20	DET	1	0	21	14	3.80	1.17	4.61	1.32	105	75	3.9	6%	16%	10%	7%	9.4%	93.3	52	17	30	27%	73%	14%	20%	0	15			0	0.74	1.7	90	-$2
21	DET *	2	8	62	53	5.60	1.60	5.73	1.49	142	109	4.6	12%	19%	8%	10%	11.0%	94.1	37	22	41	32%	68%	20%	19%	0	20			80	0.36	-10.3	40	-$7
22	CIN *	2	3	70	80	4.15	1.36	3.93	1.37	98	79	4.6	12%	27%	15%	9%	13.2%	94.7	43	20	38	31%	72%	5%	8%	0	19			60	1.13	-1.6	96	-$2
23	CIN	4	3	75	70	4.20	1.16	4.72	1.36	100	92	4.4	9%	23%	13%	8%	13.8%	94.0	33	18	49	25%	68%	11%	12%	0	17			33	1.02	1.2	77	$3
1st Half		2	2	41	35	3.54	1.03	4.55	1.27	100	94	4.2	7%	21%	15%	8%	12.2%	93.6	31	21	48	23%	74%	13%	11%	0	16			33	1.01	4.0	93	$3
2nd Half		2	1	34	35	4.98	1.31	4.92	1.46	101	91	4.6	12%	24%	12%	9%	15.6%	94.3	36	14	49	27%	63%	9%	12%	0	18			33	1.04	-2.7	59	-$2
Proj		**2**	**2**	**44**	**42**	**4.60**	**1.33**	**4.37**	**1.39**	**109**	**94**	**4.3**	**11%**	**23%**	**12%**	**9%**	**13.1%**	**94.2**	**37**	**19**	**44**	**29%**	**69%**	**12%**	**14%**	**0**						**-1.4**	**70**	**-$3**

Feltner,Ryan

Age: 27	Th: R	Role SP	Health F	LIMA Plan C
Ht: 6' 4"	Wt: 190	Type Pwr	PT/Exp C	Rand Var 0
			Consist B	MM 1103

Hit in head by liner in May, suffered skull fracture and concussion. Just making it back to MLB four months later was a victory, though elbow issue soon shelved him again. Before injury woes began, signs of progress were faint—even if BB% normalizes and S% helps a bit more, SwK is not pulling its weight. Glad he has health, but not our interest.

Yr	Tm	W	Sv	IP	K	ERA	WHIP	xERA	xWHIP	vL+	vR+	BF/G	BB%	K%	K-BB%	xBB%	SwK	Vel	G	L	F	H%	S%	HR/F	xHR/F	GS	APC	DOM%	DIS%	Sv%	LI	RAR	BPX	R$
19																																		
20																																		
21	COL *	5	0	85	69	4.39	1.45	5.39	1.73	111	191	22.6	8%	19%	11%	12%	12.0%	92.4	10	33	57	32%	75%	25%	12%	2	71	0%	50%			-1.3	52	-$4
22	COL *	9	0	151	128	5.10	1.37	4.72	1.32	110	115	20.4	8%	20%	12%	8%	9.1%	94.2	41	19	39	31%	65%	13%	15%	19	84	16%	58%	0	0.81	-20.9	69	-$5
23	COL	2	0	43	38	5.82	1.68	5.48	1.64	99	100	20.1	14%	19%	5%	8%	8.5%	94.7	44	23	34	34%	63%	4%	7%	10	78	10%	50%			-7.9	8	-$10
1st Half		2	0	35	33	5.86	1.75	5.47	1.68	106	103	20.6	15%	20%	5%	8%	8.9%	94.4	45	22	33	34%	65%	6%	9%	8	80	13%	50%			-6.7	3	-$1
2nd Half		0	0	8	5	5.63	1.38	5.50	1.49	67	91	18.0	8%	14%	6%	8%	6.9%	95.9	37	26	37	31%	55%	0%	0%	2	73	0%	50%			-1.3	28	-$
Proj		**6**	**0**	**131**	**109**	**5.03**	**1.49**	**4.67**	**1.49**	**102**	**102**	**21.4**	**11%**	**19%**	**8%**	**8%**	**9.0%**	**94.3**	**44**	**21**	**36**	**31%**	**67%**	**9%**	**11%**	**26**						**-11.3**	**43**	**-$**

Ferguson,Caleb

Age: 27	Th: L	Role RP	Health F	LIMA Plan A+
Ht: 6' 3"	Wt: 226	Type Pwr	PT/Exp D	Rand Var 0
			Consist A	MM 4410

If he'd never taken left turn at Albuquerque for late Sept outings at Coors (1 IP, 7 ER), he'd have ended with 2.43 ERA. Effective enough vR to avoid specialist tag, and do a bit of opening and closing. Not dominant enough to seize ninth inning outright, but skills solid enough to produce decent ratios, smattering of wins. Helpful in deep leagues..

Yr	Tm	W	Sv	IP	K	ERA	WHIP	xERA	xWHIP	vL+	vR+	BF/G	BB%	K%	K-BB%	xBB%	SwK	Vel	G	L	F	H%	S%	HR/F	xHR/F	GS	APC	DOM%	DIS%	Sv%	LI	RAR	BPX	R$
19	LA *	1	1	61	77	4.02	1.32	3.77	1.47	95	109	4.3	12%	31%	18%	8%	9.8%	94.5	39	25	37	30%	73%	17%	13%	2	18	0%	50%	100	0.51	3.6	104	$
20	LA	2	0	19	27	2.89	1.02	2.66	0.91	87	92	3.6	4%	36%	32%	4%	16.1%	95.5	55	11	34	32%	87%	27%	17%	1	14	0%	0%	0	1.23	3.6	258	$
21																																		
22	LA	1	0	35	37	1.82	1.15	3.72	1.36	99	73	3.8	12%	26%	14%	6%	11.9%	94.9	42	24	34	27%	85%	3%	6%	1	16	0%	0%	0	0.60	9.2	81	$
23	LA	7	3	60	70	3.43	1.44	3.59	1.25	101	96	4.0	9%	26%	17%	6%	11.9%	95.9	49	24	27	37%	77%	9%	6%	7	16	0%	86%	38	1.22	6.7	137	$
1st Half		4	2	30	33	3.00	1.23	3.45	1.26	68	94	3.8	9%	26%	17%	6%	12.0%	95.9	55	17	28	32%	77%	9%	6%	1	15	0%	100%	67	1.26	4.9	138	$
2nd Half		3	1	30	37	3.86	1.65	3.72	1.25	136	99	4.1	9%	26%	18%	6%	11.8%	95.8	44	31	25	43%	77%	9%	5%	6	16	0%	83%	20	1.19	1.8	139	$
Proj		**4**	**2**	**58**	**68**	**3.37**	**1.28**	**3.41**	**1.27**	**95**	**87**	**3.8**	**11%**	**29%**	**18%**	**7%**	**11.4%**	**95.4**	**45**	**25**	**30**	**32%**	**75%**	**10%**	**7%**	**0**						**6.8**	**123**	**$**

Finnegan,Kyle

Age: 32	Th: R	Role RP	Health B	LIMA Plan B+
Ht: 6' 2"	Wt: 197	Type Pwr	PT/Exp A	Rand Var 0
			Consist B	MM 3231

Lost closer role for a stretch before injury reopened door. Upping splitter usage was smart, it's by far his best pitch, though plethora of hard contact on four-seam, slider likely to keep grasp on ninth tenuous. 2nd half skills offer glimmer of hope he's tweaked pitch mix titration enough to get by, but arm with more complete arsenal could bypass him, too.

Yr	Tm	W	Sv	IP	K	ERA	WHIP	xERA	xWHIP	vL+	vR+	BF/G	BB%	K%	K-BB%	xBB%	SwK	Vel	G	L	F	H%	S%	HR/F	xHR/F	GS	APC	DOM%	DIS%	Sv%	LI	RAR	BPX	R$
19	a/a	3	14	52	55	2.98	1.36	3.72				5.2	10%	25%	16%							33%	79%									9.8	107	$
20	WAS	1	0	25	27	2.92	1.38	4.17	1.41	82	90	4.3	12%	25%	13%	8%	12.2%	95.1	51	22	28	31%	81%	11%	15%	0	17			0	1.13	4.7	88	-$
21	WAS	5	11	66	68	3.55	1.48	4.54	1.42	98	104	4.3	12%	23%	12%	7%	11.2%	95.6	48	17	35	32%	81%	14%	11%	0	18			79	1.18	5.9	74	$
22	WAS	6	11	67	70	3.51	1.14	3.33	1.21	76	108	4.1	8%	26%	18%	6%	13.2%	97.1	48	20	32	28%	75%	16%	15%	0	16			73	1.25	3.8	128	$
23	WAS	7	28	69	63	3.76	1.30	4.09	1.33	94	105	4.3	8%	22%	14%	7%	11.5%	97.3	47	21	32	29%	77%	18%	16%	0	17			78	1.46	4.9	99	$1
1st Half		3	11	35	33	3.34	1.37	4.25	1.37	85	115	4.5	10%	22%	13%	8%	10.9%	97.2	45	21	34	31%	81%	15%	14%	0	18			69	1.50	4.3	88	$
2nd Half		4	17	34	30	4.19	1.22	3.92	1.29	104	96	4.1	7%	21%	14%	5%	12.1%	97.4	49	21	29	28%	72%	21%	18%	0	16			85	1.42	0.6	111	$1
Proj		**6**	**26**	**65**	**63**	**3.63**	**1.32**	**3.83**	**1.32**	**94**	**104**	**4.3**	**9%**	**23%**	**14%**	**7%**	**11.7%**	**96.9**	**48**	**20**	**32**	**30%**	**78%**	**16%**	**15%**	**0**						**5.6**	**100**	**$1**

Flaherty,Jack

Age: 28	Th: R	Role RP	Health F	LIMA Plan B
Ht: 6' 4"	Wt: 225	Type Pwr	PT/Exp C	Rand Var +2
			Consist A	MM 3303

Deadline deal to BAL didn't go as planned, as H%, HR/F conspired to offset reining in of 1st half wildness, and while he dodged IL, did battle hip discomfort, "general soreness." And LHB gave him increasing fits as season wore on. That said, if 2nd half was a step back towards 2021 skill level, sub-4.00 ERA not out of question. But body has to cooperate.

Yr	Tm	W	Sv	IP	K	ERA	WHIP	xERA	xWHIP	vL+	vR+	BF/G	BB%	K%	K-BB%	xBB%	SwK	Vel	G	L	F	H%	S%	HR/F	xHR/F	GS	APC	DOM%	DIS%	Sv%	LI	RAR	BPX	R$
19	STL	11	0	196	231	2.75	0.97	3.59	1.15	81	76	23.4	7%	30%	23%	7%	14.2%	93.9	40	22	38	25%	79%	14%	13%	33	96	42%	12%			42.5	153	$3
20	STL	4	0	40	49	4.91	1.21	3.53	1.23	106	76	18.9	9%	29%	19%	8%	14.7%	93.6	43	32	26	29%	63%	23%	22%	9	80	22%	22%			-2.3	137	$
21	STL	9	0	78	85	3.22	1.06	3.86	1.21	82	93	18.9	8%	26%	18%	9%	12.3%	93.3	39	23	38	25%	77%	16%	19%	15	80	33%	27%	0	0.72	10.1	123	$
22	STL *	3	0	65	58	3.42	1.32	3.72	1.55	121	105	16.9	10%	21%	11%	11%	10.7%	93.1	42	25	33	30%	76%	12%	13%	8	74	13%	38%	0	0.82	4.4	84	-$
23	2 TM	8	0	144	148	4.99	1.58	4.40	1.39	117	105	22.4	10%	23%	13%	9%	11.0%	93.0	43	26	32	36%	70%	13%	13%	27	91	11%	30%	0	0.78	-11.7	85	-$
1st Half		5	0	86	84	4.60	1.56	4.38	1.49	110	100	23.7	12%	22%	10%	11%	10.4%	92.7	47	25	28	34%	70%	9%	11%	16	97	13%	25%			-2.9	60	-$
2nd Half		3	0	58	64	5.55	1.61	4.44	1.25	129	112	20.8	7%	24%	16%	7%	12.0%	93.4	37	26	37	39%	70%	16%	15%	11	83	9%	36%	0	0.77	-8.8	123	-$
Proj		**10**	**0**	**145**	**153**	**4.38**	**1.34**	**3.80**	**1.29**	**105**	**96**	**19.4**	**9%**	**25%**	**16%**	**9%**	**11.9%**	**93.2**	**41**	**26**	**34**	**32%**	**70%**	**14%**	**16%**	**29**						**-0.9**	**105**	**$**

KRIS OLSON

Floro,Dylan

Age: 33	Th: R	Role: RP	Health: C	LIMA Plan: B
Ht: 6' 2"	Wt: 203	Type: /GB	PT/Exp: B	Rand Var: +4
			Consist: A	MM: 4210

Bad fortune on H%, S% first got him traded, then released, even though xERA, K-BB% were both career-best marks. High GB%, low BB% continue to be enough to offset lack of Ks; main knock against him has been shaky command vL (career 9% K-BB%), which results in occasional flare-ups. Skills should lead to slight rebound.

Yr	Tm	W	Sv	IP	K	ERA	WHIP	xERA	xWHIP	vL+	vR+	BF/G	BB%	K%	K-BB%	xBB%	SwK	Vel	G	L	F	H%	S%	HR/F	xHR/F	GS	APC	DOM%	DIS%	Sv%	LI	RAR	BPX	R$
19	LA	5	0	47	42	4.24	1.29	4.21	1.30	123	75	4.0	7%	21%	14%	6%	13.1%	93.9	51	20	28	32%	68%	10%	11%	0	15			0	1.14	1.5	111	$0
20	LA	3	0	24	19	2.59	1.11	3.58	1.19	63	95	3.9	4%	19%	15%	5%	10.2%	93.4	56	24	20	31%	77%	7%	9%	0	15			0	0.79	5.6	136	$5
21	MIA	6	15	64	62	2.81	1.22	4.09	1.32	89	69	4.0	9%	23%	14%	6%	10.5%	93.7	49	20	31	30%	76%	4%	11%	0	16			71	1.20	11.5	98	$11
22	MIA	1	10	54	48	3.02	1.17	3.75	1.23	111	75	3.9	7%	22%	15%	5%	9.8%	92.6	45	21	34	30%	76%	8%	8%	0	15			71	0.94	6.3	110	$4
23	2 TM	5	7	57	58	4.76	1.54	3.47	1.24	135	82	4.0	7%	23%	17%	6%	9.7%	92.6	54	25	21	40%	68%	9%	5%	0	16			70	1.18	-3.0	140	-$2
1st Half		3	7	33	34	4.13	1.41	3.21	1.20	124	81	3.7	7%	25%	18%	7%	9.1%	93.0	55	26	19	38%	70%	11%	3%	0	14			78	1.43	0.8	152	$2
2nd Half		2	0	24	24	5.63	1.71	3.83	1.28	151	83	4.4	7%	22%	15%	6%	10.3%	92.1	53	24	23	42%	65%	6%	6%	0	18			0	0.83	-3.8	127	-$6
Proj		5	5	58	57	3.94	1.30	3.49	1.26	114	72	3.9	8%	24%	16%	6%	10.3%	92.9	51	23	26	33%	69%	7%	7%	0						2.8	122	$1

Foley,Jason

Age: 28	Th: R	Role: RP	Health: A	LIMA Plan: A
Ht: 6' 4"	Wt: 215	Type: Con/GB	PT/Exp: C	Rand Var: -4
			Consist: C	MM: 3010

Except for one-week stretch in mid-Aug, saves were all of one-game fill-in variety, but LI suggests he's not far off from full-time opps. Skills paint a cloudier outlook: 2nd half xERA, xWHIP weren't closer-worthy, and reflect BB%, K% marks that were more in line with underlying indicators. With regression likely, any hold on 9th inning could prove tenuous.

Yr	Tm	W	Sv	IP	K	ERA	WHIP	xERA	xWHIP	vL+	vR+	BF/G	BB%	K%	K-BB%	xBB%	SwK	Vel	G	L	F	H%	S%	HR/F	xHR/F	GS	APC	DOM%	DIS%	Sv%	LI	RAR	BPX	R$
19																																		
20																																		
21	DET *	1	2	47	33	5.20	1.66	5.94	1.60	56	127	4.9	12%	16%	3%	12%	7.1%	95.8	55	19	26	31%	72%	13%	7%	0	18			67	0.44	-5.4	23	-$9
22	DET	1	0	60	43	3.88	1.38	3.67	1.22	121	86	4.3	4%	17%	13%	5%	8.2%	96.3	57	18	25	36%	70%	4%	9%	0	16			0	0.67	0.7	117	-$5
23	DET	3	7	69	55	2.61	1.16	3.54	1.25	114	69	3.9	5%	20%	14%	6%	8.2%	97.3	57	20	23	31%	77%	4%	10%	0	15			78	1.23	14.7	125	$7
1st Half		2	3	37	33	2.17	1.04	3.07	1.17	97	67	3.9	5%	23%	18%	6%	7.4%	97.1	61	18	21	31%	77%	0%	7%	0	15			60	1.50	10.0	154	$7
2nd Half		1	4	32	22	3.13	1.29	4.12	1.33	133	73	3.9	6%	17%	11%	6%	9.1%	97.5	53	21	26	32%	77%	8%	12%	0	15			100	0.91	4.7	93	$1
Proj		2	10	58	43	3.52	1.34	3.81	1.34	137	80	4.2	7%	18%	11%	6%	8.4%	97.1	56	19	24	32%	74%	9%	9%	0						5.7	92	$2

France,J.P.

Age: 29	Th: R	Role: SP	Health: A	LIMA Plan: A+
Ht: 6' 0"	Wt: 216	Type:	PT/Exp: D	Rand Var: -1
			Consist: A	MM: 2101

11-6, 3.83 ERA in 136 IP at HOU. Former 14th-round pick was viewed as replacement-level arm prior to debut, and while S%, run support helped him generate solid fantasy value, 4.90 MLB xERA reinforces pre-call-up assessment. BB% growth was nice step, but with low K%, only average GB%, there's just not enough skill here for staying power as SP.

Yr	Tm	W	Sv	IP	K	ERA	WHIP	xERA	xWHIP	vL+	vR+	BF/G	BB%	K%	K-BB%	xBB%	SwK	Vel	G	L	F	H%	S%	HR/F	xHR/F	GS	APC	DOM%	DIS%	Sv%	LI	RAR	BPX	R$
19																																		
20																																		
21	a/a	9	0	116	127	4.15	1.38	4.41				19.5	11%	26%	15%							32%	73%									1.6	89	$2
22	aaa	3	3	112	109	3.85	1.41	4.49				14.0	10%	23%	13%							31%	76%									1.6	76	-$1
23	HOU *	13	0	156	122	3.64	1.32	4.23	1.41	91	108	22.3	8%	17%	9%	8%	9.3%	93.1	43	20	37	29%	76%	12%	14%	23	92	17%	35%	0	0.87	13.3	65	$10
1st Half		5	0	80	65	2.94	1.17	3.30	1.42	74	110	21.4	10%	20%	10%	10%	10.0%	93.4	46	17	36	25%	80%	13%	13%	10	92	10%	30%			13.8	77	$15
2nd Half		8	0	76	57	4.38	1.47	5.09	1.41	103	107	23.7	8%	17%	9%	8%	8.9%	92.9	40	22	38	32%	74%	11%	14%	13	92	23%	38%	0	0.95	-0.5	60	$8
Proj		9	0	116	102	4.19	1.36	4.29	1.38	91	103	20.7	10%	21%	12%	9%	9.3%	93.1	43	20	37	30%	72%	11%	14%	23						1.9	75	$1

Freeland,Kyle

Age: 31	Th: L	Role: SP	Health: D	LIMA Plan: C+
Ht: 6' 4"	Wt: 204	Type: Con	PT/Exp: A	Rand Var: 0
			Consist: A	MM: 1003

Maybe someday he'll pen a memoir explaining how a soft-tosser who puts way too many balls in play survived all these years at Coors—for now, writing might be on the wall after worst MLB-only xERA, K% of career. Mid-July shoulder injury didn't help, but 1st half wasn't much better. COL is contractually obligated to pitch him; be thankful you aren't.

Yr	Tm	W	Sv	IP	K	ERA	WHIP	xERA	xWHIP	vL+	vR+	BF/G	BB%	K%	K-BB%	xBB%	SwK	Vel	G	L	F	H%	S%	HR/F	xHR/F	GS	APC	DOM%	DIS%	Sv%	LI	RAR	BPX	R$
19	COL *	3	0	136	100	7.40	1.68	6.80	1.45	103	126	21.8	9%	16%	7%	8%	9.9%	91.9	47	21	33	34%	59%	22%	18%	22	81	9%	59%			-48.4	13	-$22
20	COL	2	0	71	46	4.33	1.42	4.72	1.42	113	101	23.4	8%	15%	8%	8%	9.4%	91.9	52	23	25	31%	73%	16%	17%	13	86	0%	46%			1.1	64	-$2
21	COL	7	0	121	105	4.33	1.42	4.35	1.30	109	109	22.4	7%	20%	13%	7%	9.2%	91.4	45	21	34	32%	75%	16%	13%	23	82	22%	35%			-0.9	96	-$2
22	COL	9	0	175	131	4.53	1.41	4.44	1.32	134	107	24.7	7%	17%	10%	8%	9.4%	90.0	42	23	36	32%	70%	10%	15%	31	92	13%	39%			-12.2	75	-$4
23	COL	6	0	156	94	5.03	1.47	5.34	1.40	89	123	23.3	6%	14%	8%	6%	8.2%	88.8	40	20	40	31%	71%	14%	14%	29	83	10%	59%			-13.4	56	-$10
1st Half		4	0	90	60	4.88	1.42	5.23	1.42	96	114	22.7	8%	16%	8%	7%	8.2%	88.4	40	20	40	30%	70%	13%	13%	17	84	18%	47%			-6.1	53	-$4
2nd Half		2	0	65	34	5.23	1.55	5.51	1.37	80	136	24.3	4%	12%	7%	6%	8.2%	89.3	40	21	39	33%	72%	15%	15%	12	82	0%	75%			-7.3	61	-$7
Proj		6	0	152	103	4.89	1.47	4.62	1.36	102	119	23.0	7%	16%	9%	7%	8.8%	90.0	43	21	36	32%	71%	14%	15%	28						-10.6	69	-$9

Fried,Max

Age: 30	Th: L	Role: SP	Health: F	LIMA Plan: A
Ht: 6' 4"	Wt: 190	Type: /xGB	PT/Exp: A	Rand Var: -2
			Consist: A	MM: 5203

First-start hamstring injury derailed him, but it was May forearm strain that really cut into value, shelving him for nearly three months. Fortunately, metrics showed no signs of ill effect before or after, which has largely been the case for previous injuries as well. Dependable skills, unreliable body; to be fair, that can probably be said of most of us.

Yr	Tm	W	Sv	IP	K	ERA	WHIP	xERA	xWHIP	vL+	vR+	BF/G	BB%	K%	K-BB%	xBB%	SwK	Vel	G	L	F	H%	S%	HR/F	xHR/F	GS	APC	DOM%	DIS%	Sv%	LI	RAR	BPX	R$
19	ATL	17	0	166	173	4.02	1.33	3.54	1.21	86	103	21.3	7%	25%	18%	7%	11.9%	93.8	54	24	22	34%	74%	20%	16%	30	81	17%	23%	0	0.80	9.9	144	$12
20	ATL	7	0	56	50	2.25	1.09	3.85	1.31	94	81	20.4	8%	22%	14%	8%	11.8%	93.0	53	19	28	27%	80%	5%	10%	11	82	36%	18%			15.2	105	$24
21	ATL	14	0	166	158	3.04	1.09	3.47	1.18	98	81	23.8	6%	24%	18%	6%	11.7%	93.9	52	21	28	29%	75%	12%	13%	28	91	36%	18%			25.0	136	$22
22	ATL	14	0	185	170	2.48	1.01	3.18	1.11	75	84	24.4	4%	23%	19%	6%	12.6%	93.9	51	19	30	29%	78%	8%	8%	30	94	33%	7%			34.1	149	$27
23	ATL	8	0	78	80	2.55	1.13	3.12	1.15	81	88	22.2	6%	26%	20%	8%	12.0%	93.9	58	17	25	31%	81%	13%	10%	14	89	29%	21%			17.1	164	$10
1st Half		2	0	26	25	2.08	1.08	3.19	1.18	85	81	20.6	6%	24%	18%	7%	13.6%	93.5	61	13	26	29%	85%	11%	8%	5	84	40%	20%			7.2	156	$0
2nd Half		6	0	52	55	2.79	1.16	3.08	1.14	76	91	23.1	6%	26%	21%	8%	11.2%	94.1	56	19	25	32%	80%	14%	11%	9	92	22%	22%			9.8	169	$13
Proj		13	0	152	149	2.95	1.11	3.10	1.16	86	86	22.0	6%	25%	19%	8%	12.1%	93.8	55	18	27	30%	76%	11%	11%	27						25.8	150	$20

Fujinami,Shintaro

Age: 30	Th: R	Role: RP	Health: A	LIMA Plan: C+
Ht: 6' 0"	Wt: 180	Type: Pwr/FB	PT/Exp: A	Rand Var: +5
			Consist: D	MM: 1301

Stateside debut could not have gone worse, as S% abandoned him, added more than two runs to ERA. That said, xERA, xWHIP aren't anything to hang his hat on, and K-BB% shows skills were shaky even before he arrived. 2nd half move to BAL and bullpen helped him settle in a bit, but H% made WHIP look better than it was. Hard to see a path to value.

Yr	Tm	W	Sv	IP	K	ERA	WHIP	xERA	xWHIP	vL+	vR+	BF/G	BB%	K%	K-BB%	xBB%	SwK	Vel	G	L	F	H%	S%	HR/F	xHR/F	GS	APC	DOM%	DIS%	Sv%	LI	RAR	BPX	R$
19	for	3	0	79	71	4.67	1.59	4.47				23.2	12%	20%	9%							35%	69%									-1.6	80	-$5
20	for	4	0	98	108	3.99	1.52	4.25				15.2	15%	25%	11%							32%	75%									5.6	91	$5
21	for	5	0	88	95	5.21	1.89	5.69				14.3	18%	23%	5%							35%	73%									-10.2	67	-$14
22	for	7	0	107	109	3.45	1.26	3.75				17.5	10%	25%	15%							29%	77%									6.9	90	$5
23	2 AL	7	2	79	83	7.18	1.49	4.94	1.49	95	108	5.6	13%	23%	11%	11%	12.8%	98.4	40	18	41	31%	50%	10%	12%	7	22	0%	71%	33	1.13	-27.7	56	-$10
1st Half		4	0	42	43	9.57	1.84	5.84	1.63	110	119	7.4	14%	21%	6%	12%	12.6%	97.9	38	21	42	36%	45%	9%	13%	7	29	0%	71%	0	1.41	-27.3	9	-$23
2nd Half		3	2	37	40	4.42	1.09	3.98	1.30	75	96	4.1	10%	27%	17%		13.1%	99.2	43	15	41	25%	61%	11%	10%	0	17			40	0.91	-0.4	111	$4
Proj		5	0	65	69	5.01	1.49	4.53	1.49	95	108	7.6	14%	24%	11%	12%	12.9%	98.6	41	17	41	31%	67%	9%	12%	0						-5.5	52	-$6

Fulmer,Michael

Age: 31	Th: R	Role: RP	Health: F	LIMA Plan:
Ht: 6' 3"	Wt: 224	Type:	PT/Exp: B	Rand Var:
			Consist: A	MM:

Underwent UCL revision surgery in Oct and is expected to miss entire 2024 season, just five years after Tommy John surgery caused him to miss all of 2019. Forearm pain likely reason BB% blew up in 2nd half, but even in 1st half or healthy 2022, wasn't able to repeat magic formula (fewer walks, more GB%, success vL) that led to prior success.

Yr	Tm	W	Sv	IP	K	ERA	WHIP	xERA	xWHIP	vL+	vR+	BF/G	BB%	K%	K-BB%	xBB%	SwK	Vel	G	L	F	H%	S%	HR/F	xHR/F	GS	APC	DOM%	DIS%	Sv%	LI	RAR	BPX	R$
19																																		
20	DET	0	0	28	20	8.78	2.06	6.21	1.50	98	194	13.6	9%	15%	6%	12%	7.8%	93.1	36	28	36	39%	61%	22%	18%	10	53	0%	80%			-14.8	29	-$22
21	DET	5	14	70	73	2.97	1.28	3.87	1.19	77	108	5.7	7%	25%	18%	8%	13.6%	95.7	45	21	34	33%	80%	10%	12%	4	23	0%	50%	78	1.31	11.1	135	$9
22	2 AL	5	3	64	61	3.39	1.37	4.38	1.36	133	76	4.1	10%	22%	12%	9%	12.3%	94.4	35	24	40	32%	76%	5%	8%	0	16			43	1.23	4.5	68	$1
23	CHC	3	2	57	65	4.42	1.33	4.14	1.36	118	88	4.1	12%	27%	16%	9%	14.3%	94.5	39	22	39	30%	70%	13%	11%	1	16	0%	100%	40	0.94	-0.6	92	-$2
1st Half		0	1	36	39	4.79	1.32	4.08	1.31	125	88	3.9	10%	27%	17%	8%	14.2%	94.4	37	23	40	31%	65%	11%	11%	0	15			33	0.85	-2.0	102	-$7
2nd Half		3	1	21	26	3.80	1.36	4.24	1.45	108	88	4.4	14%	28%	14%	10%	14.4%	94.6	41	20	39	28%	77%	15%	11%	1	18	0%	100%	50	1.11	1.4	77	$0
Proj																																		

BRANDON KRUSE

Gallegos,Giovanny

Age: 32 | Th: R | Role: RP | Ht: 6' 2" | Wt: 215 | Type: Pwr/xFB
Health: B | PT/Exp: A | Consist: A
LIMA Plan: A+ | Rand Var: 0 | MM: 4420

CON: Worst ERA, xERA since his rookie debut in 2017; xERA, xWHIP, vL+, K-BB% all show signs of gradual decline. PRO: LI indicates it hasn't hurt his bullpen standing; 2nd half skill rebound was hidden by high H%. VERDICT: Pros give hope for catching modest rebound at a discount, as he never seems to be too far from save opps.

Yr Tm	W	Sv	IP	K	ERA	WHIP	xERA	xWHIP	vL+	vR+	BF/G	BB%	K%	K-BB%	xBB%	SwK	Vel	G	L	F	H%	S%	HR/F	xHR/F	GS	APC	DOM%	DIS%	Sv%	LI	RAR	BPX	R$
19 STL	3	1	74	93	2.31	0.81	3.44	1.04	68	76	4.2	6%	33%	28%	5%	16.7%	93.7	34	19	47	23%	80%	11%	12%	0	17			25	0.94	20.0	178	$12
20 STL	2	4	15	21	3.60	0.87	2.91	1.00	55	69	3.6	7%	37%	30%	4%	21.0%	93.7	42	19	39	27%	58%	8%	15%	0	14			100	1.17	1.6	206	$7
21 STL	6	14	80	95	3.02	0.88	3.51	1.07	75	75	4.2	6%	31%	24%	6%	16.6%	94.5	33	20	47	25%	68%	7%	9%	0	17			64	1.37	12.3	156	$18
22 STL	3	14	59	73	3.05	1.02	3.67	1.10	104	69	4.1	8%	31%	23%	6%	18.0%	94.4	27	18	55	28%	74%	8%	11%	0	17			70	1.38	6.7	145	$10
23 STL	2	10	55	59	4.42	1.20	4.13	1.13	115	95	4.1	5%	26%	21%	6%	17.7%	93.8	35	19	46	31%	71%	15%	13%	0	16			63	1.44	-0.6	150	$3
1st Half	1	8	33	32	4.64	1.12	4.36	1.20	125	84	4.3	6%	24%	18%	6%	17.3%	93.8	31	22	47	26%	67%	16%	14%	0	16			67	1.57	-1.2	121	$2
2nd Half	1	2	22	27	4.09	1.32	3.79	1.05	100	110	3.8	4%	28%	24%	6%	18.3%	93.7	41	14	44	37%	76%	14%	12%	0	15			50	1.29	0.7	196	-$2
Proj	**3**	**11**	**58**	**68**	**3.60**	**1.07**	**3.39**	**1.07**	**96**	**89**	**3.9**	**6%**	**30%**	**24%**	**6%**	**17.5%**	**94.0**	**34**	**18**	**48**	**30%**	**72%**	**12%**	**12%**	**0**						**5.2**	**163**	**$7**

Gallen,Zac

Age: 28 | Th: R | Role: SP | Ht: 6' 2" | Wt: 189 | Type: Pwr
Health: C | PT/Exp: A | Consist: B
LIMA Plan: C+ | Rand Var: -1 | MM: 4305

Has settled in as strong #2 SP who'll flash ace upside over short stretches (2.83 xERA in 2nd half of 2022), but 3.40 xERA in 2022-23 looks like truer representation of his skill. Difference-makers these last two seasons have been health, fine-tuning BB%, and team improvement (wins). Can't fully control two of those factors, so don't go all-in on repeat.

Yr Tm	W	Sv	IP	K	ERA	WHIP	xERA	xWHIP	vL+	vR+	BF/G	BB%	K%	K-BB%	xBB%	SwK	Vel	G	L	F	H%	S%	HR/F	xHR/F	GS	APC	DOM%	DIS%	Sv%	LI	RAR	BPX	R$
19 2 NL *	12	0	172	190	2.54	1.01	2.51	1.32	88	87	22.7	8%	29%	21%	7%	13.2%	92.9	39	24	37	26%	81%	11%	11%	15	92	27%	7%			41.8	130	$28
20 ARI	3	0	72	82	2.75	1.11	3.64	1.21	86	82	24.3	9%	28%	20%	8%	12.3%	93.3	46	22	33	28%	82%	15%	15%	12	93	33%	8%			15.1	140	$20
21 ARI	4	0	121	139	4.30	1.29	4.01	1.26	97	100	22.7	9%	27%	17%	8%	9.9%	93.4	44	19	37	30%	72%	16%	13%	23	91	17%	30%			-0.5	120	$1
22 ARI	12	0	184	192	2.54	0.91	3.17	1.12	68	89	23.0	7%	27%	20%	6%	10.5%	94.2	46	18	36	24%	76%	9%	12%	31	95	45%	26%			32.3	144	$30
23 ARI	17	0	210	220	3.47	1.12	3.61	1.14	94	87	24.9	6%	26%	20%	7%	11.8%	93.6	42	23	35	31%	72%	11%	14%	34	96	50%	24%			22.3	152	$28
1st Half	10	0	111	120	3.15	1.08	3.66	1.11	88	83	24.8	5%	27%	22%	7%	13.6%	93.5	38	24	39	31%	73%	8%	9%	18	94	50%	22%			16.2	158	$33
2nd Half	7	0	99	100	3.83	1.17	3.54	1.17	102	93	24.9	6%	25%	19%	7%	9.8%	93.6	46	22	31	30%	72%	15%	20%	16	97	50%	25%			6.1	146	$19
Proj	**13**	**0**	**181**	**195**	**3.42**	**1.12**	**3.34**	**1.16**	**91**	**90**	**23.3**	**7%**	**27%**	**20%**	**8%**	**11.1%**	**93.6**	**44**	**21**	**35**	**29%**	**74%**	**13%**	**14%**	**31**						**20.2**	**142**	**$2**

García,Luis H.

Age: 27 | Th: R | Role: SP | Ht: 6' 1" | Wt: 244 | Type: Pwr/FB
Health: F | PT/Exp: A | Consist: A
LIMA Plan: B | Rand Var: -1 | MM: 3201

Underwent Tommy John surgery after just six starts, and is expected to be out until at least midseason 2024. Not a lot to glean from such a small sample, but SwK was at level he also owned in 1st half of 2022. Keep expectations low for return—target dates have a way of shifting, and rotation spots are rarely as secure as they may seem.

Yr Tm	W	Sv	IP	K	ERA	WHIP	xERA	xWHIP	vL+	vR+	BF/G	BB%	K%	K-BB%	xBB%	SwK	Vel	G	L	F	H%	S%	HR/F	xHR/F	GS	APC	DOM%	DIS%	Sv%	LI	RAR	BPX	R$
19																																	
20 HOU	0	0	12	9	2.92	0.97	4.87	1.48	142	28	9.8	10%	18%	8%	11%	11.3%	94.0	41	21	38	19%	73%	8%	13%	1	41	0%	0%	0	0.67	2.3	44	-$
21 HOU	11	0	155	167	3.30	1.17	3.97	1.21	113	73	21.1	8%	26%	18%	8%	13.8%	93.3	38	21	41	29%	77%	11%	12%	28	83	25%	14%	0	0.74	18.4	123	$1
22 HOU	15	0	157	157	3.72	1.13	3.93	1.20	104	90	23.0	7%	24%	17%	7%	13.7%	94.0	38	19	44	27%	73%	12%	11%	28	88	14%	14%			4.9	116	$1
23 HOU	2	0	27	31	4.00	1.30	4.28	1.24	118	89	19.2	9%	27%	18%	7%	14.5%	92.8	26	29	44	33%	72%	9%	11%	6	78	33%	50%			1.1	112	-$
1st Half	2	0	27	31	4.00	1.30	4.28	1.24	119	89	19.2	9%	27%	18%	7%	14.5%	92.8	26	29	44	33%	72%	9%	11%	6	78	33%	50%			1.1	113	-$
2nd Half																																	
Proj	**6**	**0**	**73**	**75**	**3.82**	**1.16**	**3.78**	**1.22**	**112**	**86**	**20.7**	**8%**	**26%**	**18%**	**8%**	**14.1%**	**93.3**	**32**	**24**	**43**	**29%**	**70%**	**11%**	**11%**	**14**						**4.5**	**112**	**$**

García,Yimi

Age: 33 | Th: R | Role: RP | Ht: 6' 1" | Wt: 230 | Type: Pwr
Health: B | PT/Exp: B | Consist: A
LIMA Plan: A+ | Rand Var: +4 | MM: 4311

While unlucky H%, HR/F obscured how good he was in 1st half, 2nd half made it abundantly clear, as BB%, K-BB%, and SwK all reached peak marks. Also posted career-best 33% K% vL for the season. LI says he's not far from another shot at saves, and never hurts to have previous closing experience on résumé. With the right breaks... UP: 25 Sv

Yr Tm	W	Sv	IP	K	ERA	WHIP	xERA	xWHIP	vL+	vR+	BF/G	BB%	K%	K-BB%	xBB%	SwK	Vel	G	L	F	H%	S%	HR/F	xHR/F	GS	APC	DOM%	DIS%	Sv%	LI	RAR	BPX	R$
19 LA	1	0	62	66	3.61	0.87	4.37	1.16	91	88	3.9	6%	27%	21%	6%	12.4%	94.2	30	14	56	19%	74%	17%	11%	0	16			0	0.63	6.9	136	$
20 MIA	3	1	15	19	0.60	0.93	3.40	1.14	87	43	4.3	8%	32%	23%	7%	12.4%	94.5	42	25	33	28%	93%	0%	12%	0	17			50	0.97	7.1	163	$
21 2 TM	4	15	58	60	4.21	1.16	3.90	1.21	117	78	3.8	8%	25%	18%	5%	13.0%	95.9	40	25	35	29%	68%	15%	19%	0	15			83	1.38	0.4	121	$
22 TOR	4	1	61	58	3.10	1.05	3.92	1.18	102	79	4.0	6%	23%	17%	7%	10.9%	94.7	40	14	46	27%	74%	8%	8%	0	17			20	1.25	6.5	119	$
23 TOR	3	3	66	79	4.09	1.24	3.25	1.09	92	101	3.9	5%	28%	23%	8%	14.1%	95.8	46	25	30	36%	70%	15%	13%	0	15			43	1.26	2.0	183	$
1st Half	2	0	35	42	4.93	1.50	3.39	1.15	121	99	4.2	6%	27%	21%	8%	13.0%	95.8	48	27	25	40%	70%	20%	14%	0	17			0	1.12	-2.6	172	-$
2nd Half	1	3	31	37	3.16	0.96	3.11	1.01	58	106	3.5	4%	29%	25%	6%	15.5%	95.9	42	22	36	30%	70%	11%	11%	0	13			60	1.41	4.5	195	$
Proj	**3**	**6**	**65**	**72**	**3.54**	**1.12**	**3.29**	**1.11**	**97**	**92**	**3.7**	**6%**	**28%**	**22%**	**7%**	**13.3%**	**95.5**	**41**	**22**	**37**	**30%**	**74%**	**14%**	**13%**	**0**						**6.4**	**156**	**$**

Garrett,Braxton

Age: 26 | Th: L | Role: SP | Ht: 6' 2" | Wt: 202 | Type:
Health: B | PT/Exp: B | Consist: B
LIMA Plan: B+ | Rand Var: 0 | MM: 4205

Added cutter to repertoire in May, but it, along with two other best strikeout pitches (slider, change-up), lost effectiveness in 2nd half. With no reported injuries, likely explanation is fatigue as he surpassed previous career high in IP, and Aug/Sept skills suggest same (18% K%, 8.5% SwK). If accurate assessment... UP: 3.15 ERA, 200 K

Yr Tm	W	Sv	IP	K	ERA	WHIP	xERA	xWHIP	vL+	vR+	BF/G	BB%	K%	K-BB%	xBB%	SwK	Vel	G	L	F	H%	S%	HR/F	xHR/F	GS	APC	DOM%	DIS%	Sv%	LI	RAR	BPX	R$
19																																	
20 MIA	1	0	8	8	5.87	1.70	4.54	1.56	124	136	17.0	15%	24%	9%	12%	8.8%	89.7	62	10	29	27%	80%	50%	43%	2	69	0%	50%			-1.3	57	-$
21 MIA *	6	0	121	104	4.77	1.49	4.89	1.53	134	109	20.1	10%	20%	10%	8%	9.6%	90.0	38	34	27	32%	70%	11%	11%	7	76	14%	43%	0	0.67	-7.5	64	-$
22 MIA *	5	0	123	114	3.50	1.22	3.69	1.17	69	112	20.7	7%	23%	16%	5%	12.3%	91.2	48	21	31	31%	74%	12%	13%	17	84	18%	24%			7.2	113	$
23 MIA	9	0	160	156	3.66	1.15	3.46	1.13	81	103	21.3	4%	24%	19%	6%	11.4%	90.6	49	22	29	31%	72%	15%	17%	30	80	30%	20%	0	0.76	13.2	158	$1
1st Half	4	0	82	92	3.53	1.13	3.07	1.07	90	98	20.8	5%	28%	23%	5%	13.2%	89.9	49	24	27	33%	73%	17%	20%	15	78	40%	20%	0	0.73	8.1	186	$1
2nd Half	5	0	78	64	3.81	1.17	3.87	1.20	71	109	21.8	4%	20%	15%	7%	9.6%	91.0	49	21	30	30%	72%	14%	14%	15	83	20%	20%			5.0	131	$1
Proj	**9**	**0**	**174**	**165**	**3.62**	**1.25**	**3.49**	**1.20**	**89**	**103**	**20.4**	**6%**	**23%**	**17%**	**7%**	**11.5%**	**90.5**	**46**	**25**	**29**	**32%**	**75%**	**14%**	**15%**	**35**						**15.2**	**130**	**$1**

Gausman,Kevin

Age: 33 | Th: R | Role: SP | Ht: 6' 2" | Wt: 205 | Type: Pwr
Health: B | PT/Exp: A | Consist: A
LIMA Plan: C+ | Rand Var: 0 | MM: 4305

Was scratched from July 15 start with left side discomfort, and although he never went on IL for it, that seems to be dividing line for increase in BB%, FB% that undermined 2nd half WHIP, xERA. 2nd half drop in K may have also been related, but lowest SwK since 2018 didn't really support 1st half K%. Realistic value probably lies between 2022-23 R$.

Yr Tm	W	Sv	IP	K	ERA	WHIP	xERA	xWHIP	vL+	vR+	BF/G	BB%	K%	K-BB%	xBB%	SwK	Vel	G	L	F	H%	S%	HR/F	xHR/F	GS	APC	DOM%	DIS%	Sv%	LI	RAR	BPX	R$
19 2 NL	3	0	102	114	5.72	1.42	4.24	1.24	105	106	14.5	7%	25%	18%	5%	15.5%	94.0	38	27	35	36%	62%	15%	16%	17	54	29%	41%	0	0.79	-15.3	131	-$
20 SF	3	0	60	79	3.62	1.11	3.34	1.06	94	85	20.4	7%	32%	26%	6%	16.0%	95.1	42	22	36	32%	72%	15%	15%	10	81	20%	0%	0	0.71	6.1	191	$
21 SF	14	0	192	227	2.81	1.04	3.42	1.10	83	82	23.5	6%	29%	23%	5%	15.8%	94.6	42	22	36	29%	78%	11%	13%	33	91	48%	18%			34.4	163	$
22 TOR	12	0	175	205	3.35	1.24	3.20	1.00	87	107	23.4	4%	28%	24%	4%	16.0%	95.0	39	25	36	38%	75%	9%	12%	31	90	39%	6%			13.3	185	$
23 TOR	12	0	185	237	3.16	1.18	3.39	1.11	99	85	24.6	7%	31%	24%	6%	13.4%	94.7	43	19	38	34%	77%	11%	14%	31	99	45%	19%			26.7	175	$
1st Half	7	0	110	146	3.04	1.13	3.06	1.04	92	85	24.8	6%	33%	27%	6%	13.2%	94.7	44	20	36	35%	76%	9%	14%	18	101	50%	22%			17.5	201	$
2nd Half	5	0	75	91	3.35	1.25	3.88	1.22	108	86	24.4	9%	29%	20%	6%	13.8%	94.7	40	18	42	32%	79%	12%	14%	13	97	38%	15%			9.2	140	$
Proj	**13**	**0**	**189**	**217**	**3.32**	**1.18**	**3.33**	**1.13**	**96**	**90**	**22.1**	**7%**	**29%**	**22%**	**6%**	**14.7%**	**94.7**	**41**	**21**	**38**	**32%**	**76%**	**11%**	**14%**	**34**						**23.3**	**155**	**$**

Germán,Domingo

Age: 31 | Th: R | Role: SP | Ht: 6' 2" | Wt: 181 | Type: Pwr/FB
Health: F | PT/Exp: B | Consist: B
LIMA Plan: A | Rand Var: +1 | MM: 3301

A lot to recap... April 15: Career-high 11 K; May 16: Ejected, suspended for illegal substance violation; June 28: Perfect game; Aug 2: Agreed to inpatient treatment for alcohol abuse after clubhouse incident. Skills were really turning a corner in July, and this was his best full-season xERA; maybe getting help off field will help him get better on it.

Yr Tm	W	Sv	IP	K	ERA	WHIP	xERA	xWHIP	vL+	vR+	BF/G	BB%	K%	K-BB%	xBB%	SwK	Vel	G	L	F	H%	S%	HR/F	xHR/F	GS	APC	DOM%	DIS%	Sv%	LI	RAR	BPX	R$
19 NYY	18	0	143	153	4.03	1.15	4.20	1.21	103	87	22.0	7%	26%	19%	6%	13.4%	93.6	38	21	41	28%	75%	19%	15%	24	83	25%	13%	0	0.90	8.4	134	$
20																																	
21 NYY	4	0	98	98	4.58	1.18	4.26	1.20	87	104	18.6	7%	24%	17%	6%	14.8%	93.5	42	14	44	29%	67%	14%	13%	18	72	28%	22%	0	0.75	-3.8	126	
22 NYY *	3	0	90	66	3.00	1.05	3.16	1.25	100	102	18.4	6%	19%	13%	6%	11.8%	92.7	40	18	42	25%	77%	12%	10%	14	72	7%	14%	0	0.77	10.8	94	
23 NYY	5	0	109	114	4.56	1.08	3.96	1.23	88	101	22.2	8%	26%	18%	6%	15.1%	92.4	39	20	40	25%	64%	17%	15%	19	83	21%	21%	0	0.74	-3.0	124	
1st Half	5	0	81	78	4.54	1.05	4.15	1.26	82	103	22.1	8%	23%	16%	6%	13.9%	92.5	39	21	40	23%	63%	17%	16%	15	82	27%	27%			-2.1	110	$
2nd Half	0	0	27	36	4.61	1.17	3.42	1.12	103	97	22.4	8%	32%	24%	6%	18.4%	91.9	41	18	41	30%	67%	19%	15%	4	86	0%	0%	0	0.61	-0.9	172	-
Proj	**7**	**0**	**116**	**122**	**4.05**	**1.13**	**3.59**	**1.18**	**95**	**99**	**20.8**	**7%**	**27%**	**19%**	**6%**	**15.1%**	**92.7**	**40**	**18**	**42**	**27%**	**71%**	**16%**	**14%**	**22**						**3.9**	**133**	

BRANDON KRUSE

Gibaut,Ian

Age: 30 | Th: R | Role: RP | Ht: 6' 3" | Wt: 250 | Type: Pwr

Health: A | PT/Exp: D | Consist: F | LIMA Plan: A | Rand Var: -3 | MM: 2210

Basically got to see best-case version of skills in 2nd half as BB% finally moved toward xBB%, and even got some high-leverage work out of it, though that was more about lack of good options in CIN. And R$'s verdict on that 2nd half? Meh. With xERA suggesting regression is next step and vultured wins tough to repeat, value likely to slip back to negative.

Yr Tm	W	Sv	IP	K	ERA	WHIP	xERA	xWHIP	vL+	vR+	BF/G	BB%	K%	K-BB%	xBB%	SwK	Vel	G	L	F	H%	S%	HR/F	xHR/F	GS	APC	DOM%	DIS%	Sv%	LI	RAR	BPX	R$
19 2 AL *	2	4	30	33	6.02	1.83	4.80	1.60	74	123	5.2	18%	23%	6%	11%	11.5%	95.3	43	27	30	36%	65%	9%	15%	0	27			80	0.41	-5.7	86	-$5
20 TEX	0	0	12	14	6.57	1.62	5.14	1.59	89	123	4.2	15%	24%	8%	12%	10.4%	95.3	44	26	29	30%	61%	20%	21%	0	17			0	0.59	-3.2	32	-$9
21 MIN *	1	0	52	45	8.32	1.99	7.80		158	86	7.1	11%	18%	7%	8%	14.4%	94.9	48	19	33	40%	58%	29%	20%	0	35			0	0.18	-25.8	30	-$20
22 2 TM *	3	4	57	62	3.87	1.43	3.96	1.26	113	115	4.8	11%	25%	15%	8%	11.5%	95.9	38	24	39	35%	73%	8%	6%	0	20			50	0.82	0.7	109	-$1
23 CIN	8	3	76	69	3.33	1.28	4.41	1.35	108	80	4.3	9%	22%	13%	6%	12.6%	95.2	40	23	38	30%	78%	10%	9%	0	16			33	1.24	9.3	85	$6
1st Half	8	1	39	32	3.66	1.30	5.06	1.49	123	82	4.4	11%	19%	8%	6%	13.1%	94.9	38	16	46	25%	78%	12%	10%	0	16			20	1.31	3.3	41	$6
2nd Half	0	2	36	37	2.97	1.27	3.74	1.21	97	77	4.2	7%	24%	18%	5%	12.0%	95.5	42	30	29	34%	77%	7%	7%	0	17			50	1.16	6.1	133	$0
Proj	**3**	**1**	**44**	**42**	**4.28**	**1.35**	**4.09**	**1.35**	**116**	**91**	**4.7**	**10%**	**23%**	**13%**	**6%**	**12.2%**	**95.4**	**40**	**24**	**36**	**31%**	**71%**	**12%**	**7%**	**0**						**0.3**	**82**	**-$3**

Gibson,Kyle

Age: 36 | Th: R | Role: SP | Ht: 6' 6" | Wt: 215 | Type: Con

Health: B | PT/Exp: A | Consist: A | LIMA Plan: A+ | Rand Var: 0 | MM: 3105

New career high in wins got buried under another season of subpar ERA, WHIP, and K%, though 2nd half xERA indicates that skills that led to double-digit value in 2021 are still lurking. However, even there, LHB remained an issue (career 7% K-BB%) and HR continued to rain down. He'll get you innings, but he's just not worth much on a per-IP basis.

Yr Tm	W	Sv	IP	K	ERA	WHIP	xERA	xWHIP	vL+	vR+	BF/G	BB%	K%	K-BB%	xBB%	SwK	Vel	G	L	F	H%	S%	HR/F	xHR/F	GS	APC	DOM%	DIS%	Sv%	LI	RAR	BPX	R$
19 MIN	13	0	160	160	4.84	1.44	4.02	1.30	107	100	20.8	8%	23%	15%	9%	13.4%	93.3	51	25	24	34%	70%	20%	20%	29	81	21%	31%	0	0.88	-6.6	115	$2
20 TEX	2	0	67	58	5.35	1.53	4.47	1.43	118	106	25.1	10%	19%	9%	10%	9.6%	92.3	51	27	22	32%	69%	27%	24%	12	95	17%	58%			-7.4	68	-$9
21 2 TM	10	0	182	155	3.71	1.22	4.07	1.34	102	79	24.3	8%	21%	12%	9%	10.8%	92.5	52	19	29	28%	72%	11%	10%	30	93	23%	17%	0	0.78	12.5	91	$11
22 PHI	10	0	168	144	5.05	1.34	3.98	1.25	109	106	23.2	7%	20%	13%	8%	11.3%	91.8	46	20	34	32%	65%	14%	13%	31	88	19%	48%			-22.3	103	-$4
23 BAL	15	0	192	157	4.73	1.32	4.19	1.31	110	96	24.5	7%	19%	13%	8%	11.1%	92.0	49	20	31	31%	66%	13%	15%	33	92	24%	33%			-9.5	101	$4
1st Half	8	0	97	74	4.66	1.38	4.60	1.37	108	96	24.2	8%	18%	10%	9%	9.9%	92.0	45	21	34	32%	66%	8%	13%	17	92	24%	29%			-3.9	78	$4
2nd Half	7	0	95	83	4.81	1.26	3.79	1.25	114	97	24.7	6%	21%	15%	8%	12.4%	92.1	53	19	28	30%	66%	19%	18%	16	92	25%	38%			-5.7	125	$11
Proj	**11**	**0**	**174**	**148**	**4.65**	**1.32**	**3.86**	**1.31**	**110**	**97**	**23.6**	**8%**	**21%**	**13%**	**9%**	**11.2%**	**92.2**	**50**	**21**	**29**	**31%**	**68%**	**15%**	**16%**	**31**						**-6.9**	**100**	**$2**

Gilbert,Logan

Age: 27 | Th: R | Role: SP | Ht: 6' 6" | Wt: 215 | Type: /FB

Health: A | PT/Exp: A | Consist: A | LIMA Plan: C+ | Rand Var: 0 | MM: 3205

Ditched change-up, added splitter, and it immediately became great K pitch (18.8% SwK); then dialed up slider to 19.6% SwK in 2nd half. K% didn't reflect growth as much as it could have, but with elite control already in place, more Ks could take him up another notch. Given strong skill support for 2023, we can speculate on repeat plus... UP: 215 K

Yr Tm	W	Sv	IP	K	ERA	WHIP	xERA	xWHIP	vL+	vR+	BF/G	BB%	K%	K-BB%	xBB%	SwK	Vel	G	L	F	H%	S%	HR/F	xHR/F	GS	APC	DOM%	DIS%	Sv%	LI	RAR	BPX	R$
19 aa	4	0	50	51	4.20	1.19	2.92				22.3	8%	25%	17%							31%	63%									1.9	123	$0
20																																	
21 SEA	6	0	119	128	4.68	1.17	4.21	1.14	92	101	21.0	6%	25%	20%	7%	12.8%	95.3	32	21	46	31%	63%	11%	12%	24	89	25%	17%			-6.0	139	$3
22 SEA	13	0	186	174	3.20	1.18	3.89	1.19	83	108	23.9	6%	23%	16%	7%	11.5%	96.2	37	24	39	30%	77%	9%	11%	32	94	28%	19%			17.6	113	$16
23 SEA	13	0	191	189	3.73	1.08	3.87	1.13	90	95	24.1	5%	25%	20%	5%	12.8%	95.7	41	18	41	29%	72%	13%	12%	32	91	38%	19%			14.2	150	$23
1st Half	5	0	92	93	4.19	1.06	3.82	1.14	90	89	23.3	5%	25%	20%	6%	11.8%	95.3	42	18	40	29%	64%	12%	12%	16	88	38%	25%			1.6	151	$15
2nd Half	8	0	98	96	3.29	1.09	3.92	1.12	90	102	24.9	4%	24%	20%	5%	13.7%	96.1	41	18	41	29%	79%	15%	12%	16	95	38%	13%			12.6	152	$25
Proj	**13**	**0**	**189**	**188**	**3.75**	**1.12**	**3.59**	**1.13**	**89**	**98**	**22.2**	**5%**	**25%**	**20%**	**6%**	**13.2%**	**95.7**	**38**	**20**	**42**	**30%**	**71%**	**12%**	**12%**	**33**						**13.5**	**142**	**$19**

Ginkel,Kevin

Age: 30 | Th: R | Role: RP | Ht: 6' 4" | Wt: 235 | Type: Pwr

Health: A | PT/Exp: D | Consist: C | LIMA Plan: B+ | Rand Var: -5 | MM: 4311

Skills came together for best season of career, though it's important to note that good fortune on H%, S%, HR/F played a role too. xBB% says 2nd half control slippage wasn't as bad as it looked, suggesting outstanding K-BB% could've been even better. Regression will likely push ERA, WHIP higher, but not enough to keep him from saves consideration.

Yr Tm	W	Sv	IP	K	ERA	WHIP	xERA	xWHIP	vL+	vR+	BF/G	BB%	K%	K-BB%	xBB%	SwK	Vel	G	L	F	H%	S%	HR/F	xHR/F	GS	APC	DOM%	DIS%	Sv%	LI	RAR	BPX	R$
19 ARI *	5	13	61	78	1.81	0.98	2.11	1.26	81	62	4.3	10%	34%	24%	9%	14.4%	93.5	34	24	41	25%	89%	8%	9%	0	16			93	1.11	20.2	146	$15
20 ARI	0	1	16	18	6.75	2.13	6.61	1.69	111	144	4.2	16%	23%	6%	11%	14.1%	95.6	27	25	48	40%	71%	13%	13%	0	18			50	1.10	-4.5	-12	-$12
21 ARI	0	0	28	31	6.35	1.55	4.65	1.38	174	92	4.0	11%	24%	13%	10%	11.0%	94.7	42	19	40	32%	65%	22%	16%	0	17			0	0.61	-7.3	85	-$9
22 ARI *	3	10	62	64	2.12	1.18	2.66	1.27	80	97	4.1	9%	26%	17%	6%	11.9%	96.4	49	20	32	31%	82%	4%	7%	0	16			77	1.28	14.0	132	$8
23 ARI	9	4	65	70	2.48	0.98	3.45	1.25	75	75	4.2	9%	28%	19%	9%	13.4%	95.6	50	16	33	25%	75%	6%	13%	0	18			67	0.76	14.9	130	$13
1st Half	3	0	31	28	2.59	1.05	3.52	1.27	83	82	4.6	7%	23%	15%	9%	12.8%	95.6	56	17	27	27%	77%	9%	15%	0	19			0	0.43	6.8	123	$2
2nd Half	6	4	34	42	2.38	0.91	3.39	1.23	68	69	3.9	11%	32%	22%	9%	13.9%	95.5	44	15	41	23%	73%	3%	11%	0	17			67	1.03	8.2	138	$15
Proj	**6**	**8**	**65**	**74**	**2.81**	**1.13**	**3.31**	**1.22**	**89**	**90**	**4.3**	**9%**	**29%**	**19%**	**9%**	**13.4%**	**95.6**	**49**	**16**	**35**	**29%**	**77%**	**8%**	**13%**	**0**						**12.2**	**137**	**$10**

Giolito,Lucas

Age: 29 | Th: R | Role: SP | Ht: 6' 6" | Wt: 245 | Type: Pwr/FB

Health: C | PT/Exp: A | Consist: A | LIMA Plan: A+ | Rand Var: +2 | MM: 3305

A rough two years and 2023 xERA isn't any comfort. 1st half success, 2nd half collapse were both impacted by S%, with walks, HR piling on in 2nd, though xBB%, xHR/F say issues weren't as dire as they seemed. Fading K% driven by slider slippage (20.3% SwK 2019-21, 15.3% 2022-23) has hurt. Take a flyer, keep expectations low.

Yr Tm	W	Sv	IP	K	ERA	WHIP	xERA	xWHIP	vL+	vR+	BF/G	BB%	K%	K-BB%	xBB%	SwK	Vel	G	L	F	H%	S%	HR/F	xHR/F	GS	APC	DOM%	DIS%	Sv%	LI	RAR	BPX	R$
19 CHW	14	0	177	228	3.41	1.06	3.66	1.15	74	96	24.3	8%	32%	24%	6%	15.5%	94.3	36	21	43	28%	74%	14%	12%	29	97	38%	10%			23.8	158	$24
20 CHW	4	0	72	97	3.48	1.04	3.38	1.16	82	73	24.0	10%	34%	24%	6%	17.9%	94.0	41	21	38	27%	70%	13%	12%	12	101	33%	17%			8.6	161	$22
21 CHW	11	0	179	201	3.53	1.10	3.87	1.16	89	92	23.2	7%	28%	21%	6%	15.6%	93.9	33	25	42	28%	75%	14%	10%	31	96	32%	16%			16.3	134	$19
22 CHW	11	0	162	177	4.90	1.44	3.86	1.24	90	128	23.3	9%	25%	17%	7%	12.7%	92.6	39	25	37	35%	69%	14%	13%	30	92	23%	23%			-18.6	113	-$3
23 3 AL	8	0	184	204	4.88	1.31	4.43	1.29	106	110	24.1	9%	26%	17%	8%	12.8%	93.1	36	18	46	29%	71%	18%	16%	33	97	21%	33%			-12.5	109	$2
1st Half	6	0	99	108	3.53	1.18	4.24	1.19	99	99	24.4	7%	26%	19%	7%	12.8%	93.1	33	19	48	29%	77%	12%	14%	17	97	29%	24%			9.8	131	$19
2nd Half	2	0	85	96	6.46	1.47	4.66	1.40	113	128	23.8	12%	25%	14%	8%	12.8%	93.2	40	17	43	28%	64%	25%	19%	16	96	13%	44%			-22.3	84	-$7
Proj	**8**	**0**	**181**	**202**	**4.50**	**1.30**	**3.90**	**1.25**	**98**	**110**	**23.1**	**9%**	**27%**	**18%**	**8%**	**13.6%**	**93.4**	**36**	**20**	**44**	**30%**	**71%**	**15%**	**14%**	**32**						**-4.0**	**114**	**$4**

Glasnow,Tyler

Age: 30 | Th: R | Role: SP | Ht: 6' 8" | Wt: 225 | Type: Pwr

Health: F | PT/Exp: C | Consist: A | LIMA Plan: B | Rand Var: +1 | MM: 5503

Spring training oblique injury delayed debut until late May—after that, return from Tommy John surgery went about as well as it could have, with new career high in IP. However, conundrum remains the same as always: skills are off the charts, but so is injury risk. We've seen the downside; what we hope to see next is... UP: 2nd half x2

Yr Tm	W	Sv	IP	K	ERA	WHIP	xERA	xWHIP	vL+	vR+	BF/G	BB%	K%	K-BB%	xBB%	SwK	Vel	G	L	F	H%	S%	HR/F	xHR/F	GS	APC	DOM%	DIS%	Sv%	LI	RAR	BPX	R$
19 TAM	6	0	61	76	1.78	0.89	2.98	1.05	55	78	19.2	6%	33%	27%	7%	12.1%	97.0	50	16	34	27%	84%	9%	11%	12	75	58%	8%			20.4	190	$11
20 TAM	5	0	57	91	4.08	1.13	3.08	1.06	84	98	21.6	9%	38%	29%	7%	14.5%	97.0	39	23	38	31%	72%	23%	20%	11	88	27%	9%			2.6	204	$16
21 TAM	5	0	88	123	2.66	0.93	2.87	1.04	65	84	24.3	8%	36%	28%	6%	17.5%	97.0	45	18	37	26%	78%	14%	14%	14	96	64%	7%			17.4	192	$13
22 TAM	0	0	7	10	1.35	0.90	2.86		61	91	13.0	8%	38%	31%	7%	14.9%	97.4	36	14	50	25%	100%	14%	24%	2	57	50%	0%			2.2	203	-$4
23 TAM	10	0	120	162	3.53	1.08	2.91	1.09	97	67	23.1	8%	33%	26%	6%	16.8%	96.4	51	17	32	31%	71%	14%	19%	21	91	33%	10%			11.9	194	$16
1st Half	2	0	36	56	4.50	1.33	3.02	1.11	139	66	22.0	10%	36%	27%	7%	18.7%	96.2	43	23	34	37%	71%	21%	25%	7	90	14%	14%			-0.7	193	-$3
2nd Half	8	0	84	106	3.11	0.98	2.86	1.07	79	69	23.6	7%	32%	25%	6%	15.9%	96.5	55	15	31	29%	71%	11%	17%	14	91	43%	7%			12.7	196	$27
Proj	**10**	**0**	**131**	**185**	**3.22**	**1.07**	**2.64**	**1.05**	**91**	**81**	**21.6**	**8%**	**37%**	**28%**	**7%**	**16.0%**	**96.7**	**46**	**19**	**34**	**31%**	**76%**	**18%**	**18%**	**24**						**17.8**	**197**	**$18**

Gomber,Austin

Age: 30 | Th: L | Role: SP | Ht: 6' 5" | Wt: 220 | Type: Con

Health: D | PT/Exp: A | Consist: B | LIMA Plan: C+ | Rand Var: 0 | MM: 1001

Back issues flared up in 2nd half, ended season in late Aug, and may have been related to 2021 stress fracture in lower back. Really though, S% and awful skills finished him off long before then, as steady declines in K%, SwK have taken him from deep-league option to roster poison. Treat DOM%/DIS% like skull and crossbones, warning you to stay away.

Yr Tm	W	Sv	IP	K	ERA	WHIP	xERA	xWHIP	vL+	vR+	BF/G	BB%	K%	K-BB%	xBB%	SwK	Vel	G	L	F	H%	S%	HR/F	xHR/F	GS	APC	DOM%	DIS%	Sv%	LI	RAR	BPX	R$
19 a/a	4	0	50	42	3.41	1.40	4.49				19.2	9%	20%	11%							32%	79%									6.8	73	$0
20 STL	1	0	29	27	1.86	1.17	4.50	1.49	98	68	8.5	13%	23%	10%	10%	10.1%	92.5	49	18	34	25%	85%	4%	5%	4	38	0%	0%	0	1.01	9.3	59	$4
21 COL	9	0	115	113	4.53	1.24	4.23	1.29	91	99	21.2	8%	23%	15%	6%	11.7%	91.6	44	19	37	28%	69%	17%	13%	23	80	30%	26%			-3.7	103	$3
22 COL	5	0	125	95	5.56	1.37	4.32	1.28	88	124	16.0	6%	18%	12%	7%	10.3%	91.0	43	20	37	31%	62%	14%	13%	17	62	12%	47%	0	0.67	-24.5	86	-$9
23 COL	9	0	139	87	5.50	1.49	5.23	1.43	145	111	22.3	7%	14%	7%	8%	8.4%	90.6	42	20	38	31%	67%	15%	14%	27	80	7%	56%			-20.1	52	-$10
1st Half	6	0	84	60	6.64	1.56	5.09	1.43	163	113	22.0	8%	16%	8%	8%	8.5%	90.8	44	21	34	32%	62%	20%	20%	17	80	12%	47%			-23.9	58	-$16
2nd Half	3	0	55	27	3.76	1.38	5.43	1.42	120	109	22.9	6%	12%	6%	6%	8.2%	90.4	38	19	44	30%	77%	9%	8%	10	80	0%	70%			3.9	42	$1
Proj	**7**	**0**	**116**	**85**	**4.76**	**1.38**	**4.53**	**1.36**	**114**	**108**	**20.3**	**7%**	**17%**	**10%**	**7%**	**9.5%**	**90.9**	**42**	**20**	**39**	**30%**	**70%**	**13%**	**13%**	**24**						**-6.3**	**71**	**-$3**

BRANDON KRUSE

Gonsolin,Tony

Age: 30	Th: R	Role: RP	Health: F	LIMA Plan:
Ht: 6' 3"	Wt: 205	Type: #DIV/0!	PT/Exp: A	Rand Var:
			Consist: C	MM:

As expected, regression came knocking, but then BB%, K%, FB% declines decided to crash the party and make everything worse. Elbow inflammation likely played role in 2nd half meltdown—underwent Tommy John surgery at the end of August. Expected to miss all of 2024; skill inconsistency will make him difficult to assess upon return.

Yr Tm	W	Sv	IP	K	ERA	WHIP	xERA	xWHIP	vL+	vR+	BF/G	BB%	K%	K-BB%	xBB%	SwK	Vel	G	L	F	H%	S%	HR/F	xHR/F	GS	APC	DOM%	DIS%	Sv%	LI	RAR	BPX	R$
19 LA *	6	1	82	78	3.83	1.30	3.67	1.38	75	79	14.1	10%	23%	13%	9%	12.3%	93.7	42	15	44	29%	73%	9%	9%	6	63	17%	50%	100	0.65	6.8	87	$3
20 LA	2	0	47	46	2.31	0.84	3.75	1.08	74	67	19.6	4%	26%	22%	5%	14.6%	95.1	34	24	42	26%	73%	4%	9%	8	78	25%	0%	0	0.81	12.3	153	$17
21 LA	4	0	56	65	3.23	1.35	4.69	1.46	90	98	15.9	14%	27%	13%	10%	13.0%	93.8	37	18	45	26%	82%	13%	9%	13	66	15%	23%	0	0.73	7.1	60	$0
22 LA	16	0	130	119	2.14	0.87	3.56	1.20	72	81	20.8	7%	24%	17%	6%	12.6%	93.2	43	18	39	21%	81%	8%	8%	24	84	29%	4%			29.4	114	$26
23 LA	8	0	103	82	4.98	1.22	5.08	1.43	93	103	21.8	9%	19%	10%	8%	10.1%	92.5	36	18	46	24%	64%	14%	15%	20	83	10%	40%			-8.2	55	$1
1st Half	4	0	61	49	3.69	1.11	4.88	1.45	80	84	21.5	10%	19%	9%	7%	9.7%	92.3	39	20	41	23%	69%	8%	10%	12	82	17%	33%			4.8	53	$7
2nd Half	4	0	42	33	6.86	1.38	5.35	1.40	112	132	22.1	8%	19%	10%	8%	10.6%	92.7	32	16	52	26%	58%	20%	20%	8	86	0%	50%			-13.1	57	-$4
Proj																																	

Gonzales,Marco

Age: 32	Th: L	Role: SP	Health: F	LIMA Plan: C+
Ht: 6' 1"	Wt: 205	Type: Con	PT/Exp: A	Rand Var: 0
			Consist: A	MM: 1003

Hit IL in early June with flexor strain, was later shut down due to nerve issue in elbow, and finally underwent surgery on forearm in August. Anticipated he'll be ready for start of 2024. Worst ERA since 2017 might get dismissed as small sample or injury-related, but was more in line with skills than any of his recent work. Beware.

Yr Tm	W	Sv	IP	K	ERA	WHIP	xERA	xWHIP	vL+	vR+	BF/G	BB%	K%	K-BB%	xBB%	SwK	Vel	G	L	F	H%	S%	HR/F	xHR/F	GS	APC	DOM%	DIS%	Sv%	LI	RAR	BPX	R$
19 SEA	16	0	203	147	3.99	1.31	5.12	1.38	108	95	25.5	6%	17%	11%	6%	8.3%	88.9	41	21	38	31%	72%	9%	9%	34	95	26%	32%			12.9	75	$12
20 SEA	7	0	70	64	3.10	0.95	4.02	1.08	97	77	25.2	3%	23%	21%	4%	8.7%	88.2	38	21	41	28%	72%	10%	14%	11	96	55%	18%			11.6	159	$28
21 SEA	10	0	143	108	3.96	1.17	5.00	1.33	83	108	23.4	7%	18%	11%	7%	9.4%	88.4	32	20	48	24%	75%	14%	14%	25	93	16%	36%			5.5	67	$9
22 SEA	10	0	183	103	4.13	1.33	4.91	1.37	116	108	24.5	6%	13%	7%	6%	8.7%	88.5	42	19	39	28%	75%	12%	12%	32	89	13%	53%			-3.7	49	$0
23 SEA	4	0	50	34	5.22	1.46	5.08	1.45	96	108	21.5	8%	16%	7%	6%	9.1%	89.1	41	24	35	32%	65%	9%	11%	10	81	10%	60%			-5.5	47	-$6
1st Half	4	0	50	34	5.22	1.46	5.08	1.45	97	108	21.5	8%	16%	7%	6%	9.1%	89.1	41	24	35	32%	65%	9%	11%	10	81	10%	60%			-5.5	47	-$7
2nd Half																																	
Proj	10	0	131	90	4.30	1.25	4.42	1.32	100	100	22.9	6%	17%	11%	6%	8.9%	88.6	39	21	40	29%	69%	11%	12%	23						0.5	74	$4

Gore,MacKenzie

Age: 25	Th: L	Role: SP	Health: D	LIMA Plan: A+
Ht: 6' 2"	Wt: 197	Type: Pwr	PT/Exp: C	Rand Var: +1
			Consist: A	MM: 3303

Continued on two steps forward, one step back path with promising 1st half that included breakthrough in K%, SwK, followed by 2nd half backslide in K skills and too many fly balls. Horrible vL+ was caused by 45% H%, and xBB% insists control isn't as bad as it looks. Hasn't even pitched full season yet, so keep the faith and be patient.

Yr Tm	W	Sv	IP	K	ERA	WHIP	xERA	xWHIP	vL+	vR+	BF/G	BB%	K%	K-BB%	xBB%	SwK	Vel	G	L	F	H%	S%	HR/F	xHR/F	GS	APC	DOM%	DIS%	Sv%	LI	RAR	BPX	R$
19 aa	2	0	23	22	4.64	1.31	4.22				19.2	8%	23%	15%							31%	67%									-0.4	84	-$3
20																																	
21 a/a	0	0	29	29	4.57	1.66	5.00				16.2	14%	22%	8%							34%	73%									-1.1	75	-$8
22 SD *	4	0	87	85	4.34	1.44	4.50	1.42	89	105	17.7	11%	23%	12%	8%	10.8%	94.7	38	23	39	32%	72%	9%	13%	13	79	31%	31%	0	0.78	-4.0	78	-$4
23 WAS	7	0	136	151	4.42	1.40	4.26	1.31	120	104	21.6	10%	26%	16%	8%	12.7%	95.0	39	21	40	31%	76%	18%	18%	27	91	19%	30%			-1.5	106	$0
1st Half	4	0	88	107	4.48	1.47	3.98	1.29	131	101	22.5	10%	28%	18%	8%	13.3%	95.3	41	23	36	35%	74%	17%	16%	17	95	12%	24%			-1.6	121	$1
2nd Half	3	0	48	44	4.31	1.27	4.78	1.35	97	111	19.9	9%	22%	13%	8%	11.6%	94.6	36	18	47	25%	79%	20%	20%	10	84	30%	40%			0.1	80	$2
Proj	8	0	160	170	4.15	1.28	3.87	1.27	108	106	20.5	9%	26%	17%	8%	11.9%	94.9	38	21	42	29%	75%	18%	17%	32						3.4	109	$6

Graterol,Brusdar

Age: 25	Th: R	Role: RP	Health: D	LIMA Plan: B+
Ht: 6' 1"	Wt: 265	Type: Con/xGB	PT/Exp: C	Rand Var: -5
			Consist: A	MM: 5011

This wasn't a true breakout season, but rather the combo of low H% and ridiculous S%. Despite blazing fastball, SwK regressed and K% remained subpar, leaving elite BB%, GB% to continue doing the heavy lifting. Young enough that strikeout growth is still possible, but gap between stats and skills is likely to leave him overvalued this spring.

Yr Tm	W	Sv	IP	K	ERA	WHIP	xERA	xWHIP	vL+	vR+	BF/G	BB%	K%	K-BB%	xBB%	SwK	Vel	G	L	F	H%	S%	HR/F	xHR/F	GS	APC	DOM%	DIS%	Sv%	LI	RAR	BPX	R$
19 MIN *	8	1	70	59	2.84	1.12	2.60	1.15	100	91	10.6	9%	21%	12%	4%	9.0%	99.0	48	30	22	26%	76%	17%	13%	0	14			100	1.49	14.4	96	$8
20 LA	1	0	23	13	3.09	0.90	3.57	1.24	125	54	3.8	3%	15%	11%	4%	6.5%	99.3	62	16	22	24%	65%	7%	11%	2	13	0%	0%	0	0.84	3.9	112	$2
21 LA *	5	1	52	44	4.99	1.23	3.30	1.39	134	79	4.1	8%	21%	13%	4%	9.0%	100.0	58	23	18	30%	58%	11%	9%	1	15	0%	100%	20	0.93	-4.6	100	-$2
22 LA	2	4	50	43	3.26	0.99	2.94	1.16	109	66	4.3	5%	22%	17%	4%	11.0%	99.7	63	14	23	27%	67%	9%	9%	1	15	0%	100%	80	1.03	4.3	146	$3
23 LA	4	7	67	48	1.20	0.97	3.30	1.24	75	77	3.8	5%	19%	14%	5%	8.1%	98.6	64	13	23	26%	90%	7%	9%	1	14	0%	0%	88	1.05	26.0	128	$14
1st Half	2	4	36	27	2.00	1.22	3.48	1.22	103	91	4.0	4%	18%	14%	4%	7.8%	98.3	62	15	23	33%	86%	8%	8%	1	14	0%	0%	80	0.93	10.4	137	$5
2nd Half	2	3	31	21	0.29	0.67	3.09	1.26	45	57	3.5	5%	19%	14%	5%	8.4%	99.0	67	10	23	17%	100%	5%	9%	0	13			100	1.19	15.6	121	$11
Proj	5	5	65	51	3.08	1.04	3.21	1.25	92	74	4.2	6%	20%	14%	5%	8.8%	99.2	63	15	22	27%	71%	8%	9%	0						10.1	122	$7

Graveman,Kendall

Age: 33	Th: R	Role: RP	Health: D	LIMA Plan: A
Ht: 6' 2"	Wt: 200	Type: Pwr	PT/Exp: B	Rand Var: -5
			Consist: B	MM: 2201

1st half run may have evoked memories of 2021, but xERA, xWHIP, BPX all make case that these were arguably the worst skills of his career. 2nd half BB% was possibly impacted by late-season back, shoulder issues; even so, it's not like he was throwing darts prior to that. Has spent three seasons outperforming xERA—don't bet on a fourth.

Yr Tm	W	Sv	IP	K	ERA	WHIP	xERA	xWHIP	vL+	vR+	BF/G	BB%	K%	K-BB%	xBB%	SwK	Vel	G	L	F	H%	S%	HR/F	xHR/F	GS	APC	DOM%	DIS%	Sv%	LI	RAR	BPX	R$
19																																	
20 SEA	1	0	19	15	5.79	1.23	4.82	1.46	44	127	7.0	10%	19%	9%	12%	7.3%	94.8	48	17	35	26%	52%	11%	10%	2	30	0%	50%	0	1.15	-3.1	59	-$
21 2 AL	5	10	56	61	1.77	0.98	3.06	1.22	103	46	4.2	9%	27%	18%	8%	11.3%	96.6	55	22	23	25%	85%	10%	12%	0	16			67	1.38	17.3	135	$1
22 CHW	3	6	65	66	3.18	1.40	3.52	1.30	105	93	4.4	9%	23%	14%	8%	11.8%	96.5	54	22	24	34%	79%	11%	11%	0	16			50	1.23	6.3	109	$
23 2 AL	5	8	66	66	3.12	1.31	4.64	1.49	86	100	4.1	13%	23%	11%	11%	12.4%	96.0	39	22	39	26%	82%	13%	12%	0	16			67	0.97	9.9	52	$
1st Half	3	6	36	34	3.00	1.11	4.58	1.41	66	93	4.0	11%	23%	12%	8%	11.4%	95.9	41	12	47	22%	80%	11%	13%	0	16			75	1.11	5.9	73	$
2nd Half	2	2	30	32	3.26	1.55	4.74	1.58	106	109	4.3	15%	24%	9%	12%	13.4%	96.0	35	34	30	30%	84%	17%	10%	0	17			50	0.79	4.0	27	$
Proj	5	0	65	67	3.50	1.35	3.96	1.40	103	93	4.2	12%	25%	13%	10%	12.2%	96.2	45	24	32	30%	77%	13%	11%	0						6.6	79	$

Gray,Jonathan

Age: 32	Th: R	Role: SP	Health: C	LIMA Plan: A
Ht: 6' 4"	Wt: 225	Type:	PT/Exp: A	Rand Var: 0
			Consist: B	MM: 3203

Turned in best stretch of career in 1st half, but xERA, xWHIP show it wasn't earned, and he reverted back to frustrating ways in 2nd. On plus side, only spent 4 days on IL at end of year; that it was for forearm tightness is worrying. Leaving Coors has helped (COL: 4.59 ERA, 32% H%; TEX: 4.05, 29%), but he's still a 4.00+ ERA SP.

Yr Tm	W	Sv	IP	K	ERA	WHIP	xERA	xWHIP	vL+	vR+	BF/G	BB%	K%	K-BB%	xBB%	SwK	Vel	G	L	F	H%	S%	HR/F	xHR/F	GS	APC	DOM%	DIS%	Sv%	LI	RAR	BPX	R$
19 COL	11	0	150	150	3.84	1.35	4.02	1.33	108	96	24.5	9%	24%	15%	7%	12.3%	96.1	50	23	26	32%	76%	17%	17%	25	91	28%	32%	0	1.01	12.3	108	$
20 COL	2	0	39	22	6.69	1.44	5.82	1.43	119	99	21.8	6%	13%	6%	7%	9.9%	94.0	37	25	38	31%	54%	11%	13%	8	82	13%	50%			-10.8	43	-$1
21 COL	8	0	149	157	4.59	1.33	4.03	1.29	101	100	22.2	9%	24%	15%	8%	11.5%	94.9	48	18	33	31%	69%	15%	12%	29	87	14%	28%			-6.0	112	$
22 TEX	7	0	127	134	3.96	1.13	3.47	1.18	105	84	21.7	7%	26%	18%	6%	12.2%	96.0	44	21	35	28%	69%	14%	13%	24	86	25%	17%			0.2	130	$
23 TEX	9	0	157	142	4.12	1.29	4.32	1.33	102	96	22.6	8%	22%	13%	6%	12.6%	95.8	40	23	36	30%	72%	13%	12%	29	83	24%	41%			4.1	91	$
1st Half	6	0	87	73	3.21	1.08	4.28	1.32	90	87	23.1	8%	21%	13%	6%	12.4%	95.6	38	23	39	25%	76%	12%	10%	15	86	40%	40%			12.1	86	$1
2nd Half	3	0	70	69	5.25	1.55	4.37	1.34	113	108	22.1	9%	22%	14%	6%	12.9%	95.9	43	24	33	35%	69%	16%	14%	14	79	7%	43%			-7.9	98	-$
Proj	8	0	152	143	4.12	1.28	3.88	1.28	102	93	22.3	8%	23%	15%	7%	12.1%	95.5	43	22	35	30%	71%	13%	13%	28						4.0	104	$

Gray,Josiah

Age: 26	Th: R	Role: SP	Health: A	LIMA Plan: A
Ht: 6' 1"	Wt: 199	Type: Pwr/xFB	PT/Exp: A	Rand Var: -2
			Consist: A	MM: 1205

Growth year? Nope. It was "High S% is a pitcher's best friend" year. Strikeout skills were stagnant (new cutter fizzled at 8.4% SwK, velocity dropped), BB% remains a problem, and high FB% exacerbates both. DOM%/DIS% turned especially ugly in 2nd half, as did xERA, xWHIP. Prospect upside has faded fast; move to pen might help.

Yr Tm	W	Sv	IP	K	ERA	WHIP	xERA	xWHIP	vL+	vR+	BF/G	BB%	K%	K-BB%	xBB%	SwK	Vel	G	L	F	H%	S%	HR/F	xHR/F	GS	APC	DOM%	DIS%	Sv%	LI	RAR	BPX	R$
19 aa	3	0	40	36	3.45	1.23	2.90				18.1	7%	22%	15%							33%	69%									5.2	134	$
20																																	
21 2 NL *	3	0	88	94	4.91	1.21	4.67	1.36	112	113	19.7	10%	27%	17%	8%	14.7%	94.6	31	16	54	24%	69%	19%	15%	13	87	0%	31%	0	0.74	-7.0	64	-$
22 WAS	7	0	149	154	5.02	1.36	4.53	1.33	141	97	23.2	10%	24%	14%	9%	11.6%	94.5	33	18	49	27%	73%	19%	15%	28	93	4%	43%			-19.4	78	-$
23 WAS	8	0	159	143	3.91	1.46	5.10	1.49	102	104	23.3	11%	20%	9%	9%	11.4%	93.4	38	21	41	30%	78%	12%	13%	30	94	10%	43%			8.4	44	$
1st Half	6	0	95	86	3.30	1.38	4.71	1.44	88	109	24.1	11%	21%	11%	9%	12.0%	93.6	43	20	37	30%	81%	12%	12%	17	96	12%	24%			12.1	64	$1
2nd Half	2	0	64	57	4.81	1.57	5.70	1.58	121	95	22.2	13%	20%	7%	10%	10.7%	93.0	31	22	47	30%	73%	11%	14%	13	90	8%	69%			-3.7	14	-$
Proj	8	0	167	160	4.42	1.38	4.56	1.40	109	100	21.1	11%	23%	12%	9%	12.1%	93.8	34	19	46	29%	74%	13%	14%	33						-2.0	63	$

BRANDON KRUSE

Gray,Sonny

Age: 34	Th: R	Role SP	Health D	LIMA Plan C+
Ht: 5' 10"	Wt: 195	Type Pwr	PT/Exp A	Rand Var -3
			Consist A	MM 4203

Really did come into spring training in best shape of his life, and it paid off with most IP, lowest ERA since 2015. But skills were essentially unchanged from previous two seasons, and S%, HR/F boosted ERA nearly a full run—only thing that didn't come together for him was wins. Regression is likely and injury risk remains high; don't pay for a repeat.

Yr Tm	W	Sv	IP	K	ERA	WHIP	xERA	xWHIP	vL+	vR+	BF/G	BB%	K%	K-BB%	xBB%	SwK	Vel	G	L	F	H%	S%	HR/F	xHR/F	GS	APC	DOM%	DIS%	Sv%	LI	RAR	BPX	R$
19 CIN	11	0	175	205	2.87	1.08	3.55	1.26	81	80	22.8	10%	29%	19%	9%	11.8%	93.3	51	18	31	27%	77%	13%	15%	31	94	39%	13%			35.3	135	$24
20 CIN	5	0	56	72	3.70	1.21	3.32	1.26	86	78	21.4	11%	31%	20%	9%	11.6%	93.0	51	26	23	31%	70%	13%	15%	11	88	18%	18%			5.2	141	$14
21 CIN	7	0	135	155	4.19	1.22	3.67	1.22	94	93	22.1	9%	27%	18%	8%	11.0%	92.4	47	21	32	30%	70%	17%	8%	26	86	31%	15%			1.3	132	$6
22 MIN	8	0	120	117	3.08	1.13	3.61	1.21	79	100	20.3	7%	24%	17%	8%	9.5%	92.1	45	20	36	29%	76%	9%	9%	24	78	25%	33%			13.1	119	$10
23 MIN	8	0	184	183	2.79	1.15	3.70	1.24	86	80	23.6	7%	24%	17%	7%	11.7%	92.9	47	22	31	31%	76%	5%	8%	32	88	25%	13%			35.0	127	$23
1st Half	4	0	94	96	2.50	1.26	3.90	1.31	88	84	23.1	9%	24%	15%	8%	11.6%	92.8	48	21	31	32%	80%	4%	10%	17	91	24%	18%			21.2	111	$18
2nd Half	4	0	90	87	3.09	1.03	3.49	1.16	84	75	24.1	5%	24%	19%	6%	11.8%	93.0	47	23	30	29%	70%	7%	7%	15	86	27%	7%			13.9	146	$19
Proj	**9**	**0**	**145**	**148**	**3.43**	**1.17**	**3.43**	**1.23**	**89**	**87**	**21.8**	**8%**	**26%**	**17%**	**8%**	**11.2%**	**92.7**	**47**	**22**	**31**	**30%**	**73%**	**10%**	**9%**	**27**						**16.1**	**126**	**$13**

Greene,Hunter

Age: 24	Th: R	Role SP	Health F	LIMA Plan B
Ht: 6' 5"	Wt: 230	Type Pwr/FB	PT/Exp A	Rand Var +3
			Consist B	MM 4503

Hip pain started in early June, landed him on IL two weeks later, and kept him out of action for two months—2nd half slides in SwK, velocity were likely related. Posted a 3.54 xERA, 9% BB%, 33% K%, and 15.1% SwK in 11 GS prior to injury. Stable xBB%, career 24% K-BB% vL are good signs, and with health, still offers... UP: 3.50 ERA, 225 K

Yr Tm	W	Sv	IP	K	ERA	WHIP	xERA	xWHIP	vL+	vR+	BF/G	BB%	K%	K-BB%	xBB%	SwK	Vel	G	L	F	H%	S%	HR/F	xHR/F	GS	APC	DOM%	DIS%	Sv%	LI	RAR	BPX	R$
19																																	
20																																	
21 a/a	10	0	107	127	4.00	1.30	4.30				21.0	9%	29%	19%							32%	74%									3.5	105	$5
22 CIN	5	0	126	164	4.44	1.21	3.64	1.15	99	107	22.1	9%	31%	22%	8%	15.0%	99.0	29	22	49	30%	70%	16%	14%	24	92	33%	17%			-7.3	138	$3
23 CIN	4	0	112	152	4.82	1.42	4.04	1.21	99	121	22.6	10%	31%	21%	8%	14.1%	98.4	34	19	47	36%	71%	14%	12%	22	95	23%	32%			-6.8	143	-$3
1st Half	2	0	73	100	3.93	1.35	3.96	1.20	84	118	22.7	10%	31%	22%	8%	14.9%	98.6	33	20	48	36%	74%	10%	12%	14	97	21%	29%			3.7	145	$4
2nd Half	2	0	39	52	6.52	1.55	4.20	1.23	126	129	22.5	9%	29%	19%	7%	12.7%	97.9	38	17	45	37%	64%	21%	12%	8	93	25%	38%			-10.4	143	-$6
Proj	**10**	**0**	**145**	**195**	**4.19**	**1.29**	**3.44**	**1.16**	**100**	**111**	**20.8**	**10%**	**33%**	**23%**	**8%**	**14.5%**	**98.4**	**34**	**19**	**47**	**33%**	**72%**	**14%**	**12%**	**29**						**2.4**	**150**	**$7**

Greinke,Zack

Age: 40	Th: R	Role SP	Health F	LIMA Plan B
Ht: 6' 2"	Wt: 200	Type Con	PT/Exp A	Rand Var +2
			Consist A	MM 2001

There has been speculation he'll retire, especially after season with two IL trips (shoulder, elbow) and three-game stint in bullpen. Skills were roughly in line with 2021-22, even if surface stats weren't, but lower IP volume, lack of strikeouts leaves little fantasy value. Root for him to make it to 3,000 K (only needs 21 more), just not while on your roster.

Yr Tm	W	Sv	IP	K	ERA	WHIP	xERA	xWHIP	vL+	vR+	BF/G	BB%	K%	K-BB%	xBB%	SwK	Vel	G	L	F	H%	S%	HR/F	xHR/F	GS	APC	DOM%	DIS%	Sv%	LI	RAR	BPX	R$
19 2 TM	18	0	209	187	2.93	0.98	3.74	1.14	80	86	24.5	4%	23%	19%	6%	10.7%	90.0	45	22	33	28%	74%	11%	12%	33	94	45%	18%			40.5	145	$33
20 HOU	3	0	67	67	4.03	1.13	3.75	1.08	73	112	22.8	3%	25%	21%	8%	10.8%	87.1	41	25	34	33%	66%	9%	17%	12	88	25%	17%			3.5	168	$11
21 HOU	11	0	171	120	4.16	1.17	4.33	1.27	78	110	23.2	5%	17%	12%	8%	9.5%	88.9	44	23	32	27%	71%	17%	13%	29	86	24%	48%	0	0.78	2.3	93	$9
22 KC	4	0	137	73	3.68	1.34	4.72	1.31	103	105	22.5	5%	12%	8%	8%	7.5%	89.2	41	23	35	31%	75%	8%	10%	26	87	12%	46%			4.9	63	-$2
23 KC	2	0	142	97	5.06	1.27	4.52	1.25	123	92	19.8	4%	16%	12%	7%	7.5%	89.7	43	21	36	30%	65%	15%	14%	27	74	7%	52%	0	0.76	-12.8	103	-$5
1st Half	1	0	87	61	5.15	1.29	4.51	1.23	125	92	21.5	4%	17%	13%	6%	7.7%	89.6	43	20	37	31%	64%	14%	15%	17	80	6%	47%			-8.8	111	-$6
2nd Half	1	0	55	36	4.91	1.24	4.54	1.28	122	92	17.5	4%	16%	11%	8%	7.2%	89.9	43	22	35	29%	66%	16%	13%	10	67	10%	60%	0	0.72	-3.9	94	-$3
Proj	**3**	**0**	**102**	**71**	**4.61**	**1.23**	**4.05**	**1.23**	**105**	**100**	**20.3**	**4%**	**17%**	**13%**	**8%**	**8.3%**	**89.3**	**43**	**22**	**35**	**30%**	**67%**	**14%**	**13%**	**20**						**-3.6**	**103**	**-$2**

Grove,Michael

Age: 27	Th: R	Role RP	Health F	LIMA Plan B
Ht: 6' 3"	Wt: 200	Type Pwr	PT/Exp C	Rand Var +5
			Consist D	MM 4301

1st half featured six-week IL stint (groin), two demotions to AAA alongside mediocre skills, terrible luck. Reemerged in 2nd half with K%, SwK blazing and turned xERA, xWHIP around, though H% still refused to cooperate, and lat strain cost him most of Aug/Sept. Sample is small, and vL+ suggests relief role, but he's intriguing enough to speculate on.

Yr Tm	W	Sv	IP	K	ERA	WHIP	xERA	xWHIP	vL+	vR+	BF/G	BB%	K%	K-BB%	xBB%	SwK	Vel	G	L	F	H%	S%	HR/F	xHR/F	GS	APC	DOM%	DIS%	Sv%	LI	RAR	BPX	R$
19																																	
20																																	
21 aa	1	0	71	72	8.00	1.82	7.74				15.7	11%	22%	11%							36%	60%									-32.7	19	-$21
22 LA *	2	0	108	96	3.70	1.24	4.25	1.33	123	96	16.8	8%	22%	14%	6%	10.8%	94.4	40	13	46	29%	76%	13%	7%	6	67	0%	33%	0	0.66	3.5	82	$1
23 LA	2	0	69	73	6.13	1.48	4.12	1.20	135	97	16.8	6%	24%	18%	6%	13.3%	94.8	39	24	37	37%	61%	16%	15%	12	64	0%	33%	0	0.80	-15.3	136	-$10
1st Half	0	0	37	34	7.54	1.59	4.78	1.31	147	106	18.4	7%	20%	13%	7%	10.8%	94.9	38	24	39	36%	55%	17%	16%	7	70	0%	29%	0	0.85	-14.6	97	-$18
2nd Half	2	0	32	39	4.50	1.34	3.41	1.07	126	84	15.1	5%	29%	24%	5%	16.3%	94.7	41	25	34	38%	69%	13%	15%	5	57	0%	40%	0	0.76	-0.7	184	-$1
Proj	**2**	**0**	**87**	**96**	**4.35**	**1.26**	**3.49**	**1.16**	**119**	**81**	**15.1**	**7%**	**27%**	**20%**	**6%**	**14.8%**	**94.7**	**40**	**24**	**36**	**32%**	**70%**	**15%**	**15%**	**12**						**-0.3**	**142**	**-$1**

Hader,Josh

Age: 30	Th: L	Role RP	Health A	LIMA Plan C+
Ht: 6' 3"	Wt: 180	Type Pwr/xFB	PT/Exp A	Rand Var -2
			Consist A	MM 5530

While 2021, 2023 ERAs were very similar, xERA highlights sizable difference due to more walks, fewer K. SwK says lower K% is earned, and though xBB% has long cited better underlying control indicators, he seems resistant to its pull. Setting aside 2020, has steady declines in K-BB%, BPX; he's still elite, but be more cautious as he enters his 30s.

Yr Tm	W	Sv	IP	K	ERA	WHIP	xERA	xWHIP	vL+	vR+	BF/G	BB%	K%	K-BB%	xBB%	SwK	Vel	G	L	F	H%	S%	HR/F	xHR/F	GS	APC	DOM%	DIS%	Sv%	LI	RAR	BPX	R$
19 MIL	3	37	76	138	2.62	0.81	2.57	0.84	82	78	4.7	7%	48%	41%	4%	24.0%	95.6	22	23	55	26%	85%	21%	15%	0	19			84	1.71	17.6	252	$29
20 MIL	1	13	19	31	3.79	0.95	3.54	1.17	96	70	3.7	13%	40%	27%	9%	16.7%	94.6	26	15	59	18%	67%	15%	11%	0	18			87	1.63	1.6	159	$17
21 MIL	4	34	59	102	1.23	0.84	2.54	0.98	52	58	3.7	11%	46%	35%	6%	21.9%	96.4	31	23	46	26%	89%	7%	6%	0	16			97	1.37	22.0	210	$28
22 2 NL	2	36	50	81	5.22	1.28	3.15	1.06	91	103	3.9	10%	37%	27%	8%	16.3%	97.5	29	24	47	37%	63%	15%	15%	0	17			90	1.51	-7.7	184	$11
23 SD	2	33	56	85	1.28	1.10	3.45	1.23	79	67	3.8	13%	37%	24%	8%	16.1%	96.1	35	17	47	28%	92%	6%	5%	0	17			87	1.20	21.2	144	$22
1st Half	0	18	30	45	1.21	0.94	3.22	1.19	45	60	3.8	13%	38%	26%	8%	18.0%	96.1	43	9	48	24%	89%	4%	3%	0	17			86	1.34	11.4	162	$20
2nd Half	2	15	27	40	1.35	1.28	3.69	1.27	139	74	3.8	13%	35%	22%	8%	14.2%	96.2	28	26	46	33%	94%	8%	7%	0	18			88	1.05	9.8	126	$13
Proj	**3**	**35**	**58**	**86**	**2.78**	**1.14**	**3.19**	**1.16**	**90**	**81**	**3.8**	**12%**	**37%**	**26%**	**7%**	**17.9%**	**96.3**	**31**	**21**	**48**	**30%**	**80%**	**11%**	**8%**	**0**						**11.1**	**153**	**$19**

Hall,DL

Age: 25	Th: L	Role RP	Health A	LIMA Plan A
Ht: 6' 2"	Wt: 195	Type Pwr	PT/Exp D	Rand Var 0
			Consist B	MM 5411

3-0, 3.26 ERA in 19 IP at BAL. Was vying for SP role in spring until back injury nixed plans; wound up spending most of 1st half in AAA. (MLB-only 1st half sample was only 3 IP.) Called up in Aug, picked up where he left off, with plenty of K%, but added missing ingredients: control. If he stays in pen, 2nd half BPX says he could be ready for save opps.

Yr Tm	W	Sv	IP	K	ERA	WHIP	xERA	xWHIP	vL+	vR+	BF/G	BB%	K%	K-BB%	xBB%	SwK	Vel	G	L	F	H%	S%	HR/F	xHR/F	GS	APC	DOM%	DIS%	Sv%	LI	RAR	BPX	R$
19																																	
20																																	
21 aa	2	0	33	46	3.23	0.98	2.19				18.0	12%	36%	25%							21%	73%									4.2	138	$0
22 BAL *	4	1	97	125	4.74	1.42	4.15	1.19	139	88	12.1	13%	30%	18%	5%	14.1%	96.3	46	26	28	34%	68%	0%	1%	1	24	0%	0%	100	0.80	-9.2	108	-$4
23 BAL *	4	1	68	79	4.15	1.38	4.14	1.12	72	105	8.2	6%	28%	22%	6%	14.5%	95.6	49	18	33	31%	73%	12%	11%	0	21			50	0.97	1.5	96	-$1
1st Half	0	0	45	48	4.87	1.56	5.03	1.49	113	163	16.4	13%	24%	11%	6%	16.0%	93.2	29	29	43	32%	72%	33%	31%	0	75			0	0.12	-3.0	71	-$10
2nd Half	4	1	26	30	2.51	0.95	1.92	1.15	68	86	4.2	8%	31%	23%	6%	14.1%	96.3	52	16	32	26%	76%	7%	7%	0	18			50	1.02	5.7	161	$7
Proj	**4**	**5**	**73**	**88**	**3.33**	**1.13**	**2.89**	**1.14**	**77**	**102**	**8.1**	**8%**	**31%**	**23%**	**7%**	**14.1%**	**96.3**	**52**	**16**	**32**	**31%**	**72%**	**12%**	**9%**	**0**						**8.9**	**167**	**$6**

Hamilton,Ian

Age: 29	Th: R	Role RP	Health D	LIMA Plan A+
Ht: 6' 1"	Wt: 200	Type Pwr/xGB	PT/Exp D	Rand Var -3
			Consist C	MM 5311

This Hamilton did not throw away his shot, posting elite 1st half xERA in first extended MLB look until mid-May groin injury put him on IL for six weeks. Skills weren't quite as young, scrappy, and hungry in return, and that kept him from room where it happens when it comes to saves. But could be ready to duel for higher-leverage role in 2024.

Yr Tm	W	Sv	IP	K	ERA	WHIP	xERA	xWHIP	vL+	vR+	BF/G	BB%	K%	K-BB%	xBB%	SwK	Vel	G	L	F	H%	S%	HR/F	xHR/F	GS	APC	DOM%	DIS%	Sv%	LI	RAR	BPX	R$
19 aaa	0	3	17	17	11.34	2.07	9.93				5.2	4%	20%	17%							47%	45%									-14.4	81	-$10
20 CHW	0	0	4	4	4.50	2.25	7.94		88	111	5.0	25%	20%	-5%		13.3%	94.3	27	45	27	35%	78%	0%	3%	0	21			0	0.15	0.0	-154	-$8
21 aaa	4	4	59	68	5.30	1.70	5.02				7.0	17%	26%	9%							34%	69%									-7.5	81	-$7
22 MIN *	2	2	51	48	3.39	1.09	2.97	1.78	72	156	5.1	9%	24%	15%	11%	4.8%	93.9	30	40	30	25%	74%	33%	0%	0	42			40	0.35	3.6	96	$1
23 NYY	3	2	58	69	2.64	1.22	3.17	1.29	82	83	6.1	11%	29%	18%	8%	15.7%	95.9	55	23	22	31%	78%	6%	14%	3	25	0%	67%	100	0.89	12.1	131	$4
1st Half	1	1	24	32	1.50	1.17	2.57	1.16	55	100	5.4	9%	33%	24%	6%	16.6%	95.7	55	29	16	34%	89%	11%	24%	1	23	0%	100%	100	0.87	8.4	179	$0
2nd Half	2	1	34	37	3.44	1.26	3.62	1.40	99	71	6.8	12%	26%	14%	9%	15.0%	96.1	55	19	26	30%	71%	5%	10%	2	27	0%	50%	100	0.91	3.7	99	$2
Proj	**4**	**2**	**65**	**75**	**3.28**	**1.20**	**3.00**	**1.24**	**93**	**84**	**5.9**	**10%**	**28%**	**19%**	**8%**	**15.7%**	**96.0**	**55**	**23**	**22**	**31%**	**73%**	**12%**	**15%**	**0**						**8.4**	**140**	**$3**

BRANDON KRUSE

Hancock,Emerson

Hancock,Emerson		Health	C	LIMA Plan	C+
Age: 25 Th: R	Role SP	PT/Exp	D	Rand Var	0
Ht: 6'4" Wt: 213	Type Con	Consist	C	MM	1000

0-0, 4.50 ERA in 12 IP at SEA. Former 1st round pick, spent 2nd full pedestrian season in Double-A prior to late callup. Stuff has continually backed up throughout development and doesn't pile up many whiffs. However, survives despite tight margins by keeping hitters off balance, varying fastballs with a plus change-up and serviceable slider. (CB)

Yr	Tm	W	Sv	IP	K	ERA	WHIP	xERA	xWHIP	vL+	vR+	BF/G	BB%	K%	K-BB%	xBB%	SwK	Vel	G	L	F	H%	S%	HR/F	xHR/F	GS	APC	DOM%	DIS%	Sv%	LI	RAR	BPX	R$
19																																		
20																																		
21	aa	1	0	15	12	3.25	0.97	1.58				19.2	7%	21%	14%							26%	63%									1.9	133	-$4
22	aa	7	0	99	81	3.41	1.14	3.46				18.7	8%	21%	12%							25%	76%									6.8	77	$5
23	SEA *	11	0	110	98	4.51	1.27	3.74	1.43	85	97	19.6	6%	12%	6%	5%	7.7%	92.6	48	15	38	31%	65%	7%	6%	3	65	0%	67%			-2.5	97	$4
1st Half		9	0	72	68	4.44	1.29	3.75				19.8	9%	23%	13%							30%	67%	0%		0	0					-0.9	94	$8
2nd Half		2	0	40	30	4.38	1.15	3.33	1.25	86	97	20.0	5%	19%	14%	5%	7.7%	92.6	48	15	38	30%	61%	7%	6%	3	65	0%	67%			-0.3	115	$0
Proj		3	0	44	28	4.47	1.31	4.49	1.36			21.3	7%	16%	9%				48	15	38	29%	69%	11%	8%	8						-0.7	71	-$4

Harris,Hogan

Harris,Hogan		Health	A	LIMA Plan	C
Age: 27 Th: L	Role RP	PT/Exp	D	Rand Var	+3
Ht: 6'3" Wt: 230	Type Pwr/FB	Consist	F	MM	0101

3-6, 7.14 ERA in 63 IP at OAK. Couldn't settle in as starter (7.80 ERA in 30 IP) or reliever (6.55 ERA in 33 IP) during first partial season in majors. In part, that was due to unfavorable S%, though even without that, xERA and xWHIP tell us there's not much here. 2nd half xBB%, SwK might be seeds of something, but you can wait and see.

Yr	Tm	W	Sv	IP	K	ERA	WHIP	xERA	xWHIP	vL+	vR+	BF/G	BB%	K%	K-BB%	xBB%	SwK	Vel	G	L	F	H%	S%	HR/F	xHR/F	GS	APC	DOM%	DIS%	Sv%	LI	RAR	BPX	R$
19																																		
20																																		
21																																		
22	a/a	2	0	62	69	3.18	1.23	2.88				15.8	12%	27%	15%							28%	76%									6.1	113	$0
23	OAK *	4	0	120	97	6.44	1.60	5.58	1.44	116	111	18.3	10%	20%	10%	8%	9.6%	92.7	40	16	44	31%	61%	12%	12%	6	79	17%	50%	0	0.61	-31.2	39	-$18
1st Half		2	0	69	52	4.33	1.30	3.73	1.54	102	97	17.8	11%	17%	6%	8%	7.7%	92.7	38	15	47	25%	69%	9%	10%	3	79	0%	67%	0	0.60	0.0	60	-$
2nd Half		2	0	51	45	9.33	2.00	8.11	1.57	131	131	18.8	12%	18%	6%	7%	12.0%	92.6	43	18	40	39%	54%	16%	15%	3	79	33%	33%	0	0.63	-31.2	13	-$2
Proj		2	0	73	61	5.29	1.54	4.98	1.51	114	106	18.5	12%	19%	8%	8%	10.5%	92.6	41	16	43	31%	68%	11%	13%	15						-8.6	36	-$9

Harrison,Kyle

Harrison,Kyle		Health	A	LIMA Plan	B
Age: 22 Th: L	Role RP	PT/Exp	D	Rand Var	0
Ht: 6'2" Wt: 200	Type Pwr/xFB	Consist	B	MM	2301

1-1, 4.15 ERA in 34.2 IP at SF. Struggled with control—a sub-60% strike rate at Triple-A. However, high whiff rate made up for it. Low 3/4s delivery and plus-plus extension create significant deception, playing up already plus arsenal. Whiffs are abundant with 4-seam fastball/sinker/sweeper pitch mix. More ready than some rookie SP. (CB)

Yr	Tm	W	Sv	IP	K	ERA	WHIP	xERA	xWHIP	vL+	vR+	BF/G	BB%	K%	K-BB%	xBB%	SwK	Vel	G	L	F	H%	S%	HR/F	xHR/F	GS	APC	DOM%	DIS%	Sv%	LI	RAR	BPX	R$
19																																		
20																																		
21																																		
22	aa	4	0	84	112	3.17	1.19	3.17				18.7	11%	33%	22%							30%	78%									8.3	130	$
23	SF *	2	0	102	127	4.33	1.35	4.15	1.26	144	87	15.7	7%	24%	16%	6%	10.0%	93.6	27	20	54	29%	73%	15%	12%	7	84	14%	57%			0.0	95	-$
1st Half		1	0	54	78	4.52	1.48	4.17				14.6	16%	32%	17%							32%	72%	0%		0	0					-1.3	110	-$
2nd Half		1	0	48	49	4.11	1.19	4.12	1.26	145	88	17.4	8%	24%	16%	6%	10.0%	93.6	27	20	54	27%	73%	15%	12%	7	84	14%	57%			1.3	87	$
Proj		2	0	87	101	3.96	1.30	4.09	1.30	153	90	17.5	11%	28%	17%	7%	10.0%	93.6	27	20	54	30%	74%	12%	11%	15						4.0	94	$

Harvey,Hunter

Harvey,Hunter		Health	F	LIMA Plan	B+
Age: 29 Th: R	Role RP	PT/Exp	C	Rand Var	-2
Ht: 6'2" Wt: 225	Type	Consist	B	MM	4321

Missed only one month with elbow injury, which for him practically qualifies as a healthy season. After career-best K% in 2022, took another step forward by dropping BB% from 12% to 5% against LHB, which led to career-best K-BB%. Injury risk remains a big concern, but improved LI combined with all those career-best skills points to... UP: 30 Sv

Yr	Tm	W	Sv	IP	K	ERA	WHIP	xERA	xWHIP	vL+	vR+	BF/G	BB%	K%	K-BB%	xBB%	SwK	Vel	G	L	F	H%	S%	HR/F	xHR/F	GS	APC	DOM%	DIS%	Sv%	LI	RAR	BPX	R$
19	BAL *	4	1	84	76	6.11	1.55	6.44		90	88	11.1	9%	21%	12%	7%	12.4%	98.4	45	27	27	32%	67%	33%	11%	0	20			50	1.49	-16.6	29	-$
20	BAL	0	0	9	6	4.15	1.15	4.89	1.31	60	115	3.7	5%	16%	11%	6%	11.0%	97.4	39	25	36	25%	75%	20%	16%	0	15			0	1.38	0.3	83	-$
21	BAL	0	0	9	6	4.15	1.27	4.59	1.41	85	113	4.0	8%	17%	8%	6%	5.8%	97.1	48	22	30	28%	70%	13%	7%	0	15			0	1.14	0.1	59	-$
22	WAS	2	0	39	45	2.52	1.14	3.52	1.14	78	97	4.1	8%	29%	21%	6%	12.6%	98.3	39	17	44	33%	77%	2%	7%	0	17			0	0.77	7.0	141	$
23	WAS	4	10	61	67	2.82	0.94	3.34	1.09	89	71	4.1	6%	29%	23%	6%	12.1%	98.3	43	19	38	26%	76%	12%	14%	0	17			67	1.31	11.3	166	$1
1st Half		3	8	37	41	3.16	1.00	3.59	1.20	86	74	4.1	8%	28%	20%	5%	12.6%	98.7	44	19	37	25%	73%	12%	17%	0	17			62	1.49	5.3	139	$1
2nd Half		1	2	24	26	2.28	0.85	2.97	0.92	96	68	4.2	1%	30%	28%	6%	11.4%	97.8	42	19	39	28%	82%	13%	11%	0	18			100	1.02	6.0	212	$
Proj		4	11	65	69	3.36	1.10	3.34	1.12	109	90	4.9	6%	27%	21%	6%	12.0%	98.2	42	19	39	29%	76%	14%	11%	0						7.8	151	$

Heaney,Andrew

Heaney,Andrew		Health	F	LIMA Plan	A+
Age: 33 Th: L	Role RP	PT/Exp	A	Rand Var	0
Ht: 6'2" Wt: 200	Type Pwr/FB	Consist	C	MM	3303

Last year we warned of wide uncertainty bars, and he quickly gave up most of 2022 skill gains. SwK plummeted, which led to corresponding dip in K%, all while posting worst BB% of career. Even highest IP total since 2018 wasn't all that beneficial to his fantasy value. ERA, xERA history both suggest 2023 is truer representation of who he is.

Yr	Tm	W	Sv	IP	K	ERA	WHIP	xERA	xWHIP	vL+	vR+	BF/G	BB%	K%	K-BB%	xBB%	SwK	Vel	G	L	F	H%	S%	HR/F	xHR/F	GS	APC	DOM%	DIS%	Sv%	LI	RAR	BPX	R$
19	LAA	4	0	95	118	4.91	1.29	4.11	1.18	121	98	22.7	7%	29%	22%	7%	14.5%	92.5	34	23	44	33%	69%	18%	16%	18	94	17%	28%			-4.7	148	$
20	LAA	4	0	67	70	4.46	1.23	4.21	1.20	95	97	23.3	7%	25%	18%	6%	13.0%	91.5	39	22	39	31%	67%	12%	17%	12	90	25%	17%			0.0	133	$
21	2 AL	8	0	130	150	5.83	1.32	4.19	1.18	107	108	18.6	7%	27%	20%	7%	13.0%	92.0	33	22	45	32%	61%	18%	14%	23	78	30%	30%	0	0.69	-25.0	133	-$
22	LA	4	0	73	110	3.10	1.09	2.95	0.96	96	102	19.4	6%	35%	29%	6%	17.6%	93.0	35	19	46	33%	83%	18%	15%	14	77	21%	7%	0	0.72	7.8	215	$
23	TEX	10	0	147	151	4.15	1.38	4.51	1.34	109	105	18.9	9%	24%	14%	8%	11.7%	92.5	40	18	42	31%	75%	13%	14%	28	77	21%	29%	0	0.85	3.2	95	$
1st Half		5	0	83	89	4.12	1.28	4.36	1.33	58	109	22.1	10%	25%	15%	8%	12.0%	92.5	37	21	43	28%	74%	15%	13%	16	91	25%	13%			2.2	97	$
2nd Half		5	0	64	62	4.20	1.51	4.72	1.35	143	100	15.9	9%	22%	13%	7%	11.4%	92.7	44	15	41	35%	76%	11%	14%	12	64	17%	50%	0	0.92	1.1	94	$
Proj		8	0	131	147	4.40	1.32	3.79	1.21	112	104	18.1	8%	27%	19%	8%	13.1%	92.4	38	19	43	32%	72%	15%	14%	24						-1.2	128	$

Helsley,Ryan

Helsley,Ryan		Health	F	LIMA Plan	A
Age: 29 Th: R	Role RP	PT/Exp	B	Rand Var	-4
Ht: 6'2" Wt: 230	Type Pwr/FB	Consist	C	MM	4431

Missed games from mid-June to August, and 16 BB% in 11 IP in Sept raises red flag about either health or ongoing control problems. Season-long xBB% should ease concerns about the latter, and elite K%, improving xHR/F have helped minimize the damage of late. Add in recent success in high-leverage situations, and he's a strong option for saves.

Yr	Tm	W	Sv	IP	K	ERA	WHIP	xERA	xWHIP	vL+	vR+	BF/G	BB%	K%	K-BB%	xBB%	SwK	Vel	G	L	F	H%	S%	HR/F	xHR/F	GS	APC	DOM%	DIS%	Sv%	LI	RAR	BPX	R$
19	STL *	4	1	75	65	4.20	1.34	3.96	1.36	100	95	7.6	10%	21%	11%	5%	10.7%	97.8	34	21	46	29%	71%	10%	9%	0	24			50	0.65	2.8	72	$
20	STL	1	1	12	10	5.25	1.33	6.20	1.72	108	101	4.3	15%	19%	4%	9%	14.4%	96.9	33	15	52	17%	69%	18%	13%	0	16			33	0.97	-1.2	-18	-$
21	STL	6	1	47	47	4.56	1.42	4.69	1.50	88	91	4.0	13%	23%	10%	10%	11.8%	97.5	42	26	32	29%	68%	10%	14%	0	16			33	1.03	-1.7	46	-$
22	STL	9	19	65	94	1.25	0.74	2.77	0.98	64	60	4.4	8%	39%	31%	5%	19.2%	99.7	35	14	52	20%	93%	9%	10%	0	18			83	1.49	21.7	191	$2
23	STL	3	14	37	52	2.45	1.06	3.24	1.20	94	55	4.4	12%	36%	24%	7%	16.4%	99.7	41	20	39	29%	76%	3%	7%	0	18			74	1.46	8.5	153	$
1st Half		3	7	25	33	3.24	1.16	3.49	1.23	102	61	4.7	11%	32%	21%	7%	16.1%	99.6	43	19	38	31%	71%	5%	7%	0	19			64	1.48	3.4	144	$
2nd Half		0	7	12	19	0.77	0.86	2.73	1.13	76	43	3.9	14%	44%	30%	8%	17.0%	99.8	33	22	44	22%	90%	0%	7%	0	17			88	1.42	5.1	169	$
Proj		5	27	65	78	3.18	1.14	3.56	1.25	92	75	4.9	11%	30%	19%	7%	14.8%	98.9	38	19	42	28%	74%	8%	9%	0						9.2	120	$1

Hendricks,Kyle

Hendricks,Kyle		Health	F	LIMA Plan	A
Age: 34 Th: R	Role SP	PT/Exp	A	Rand Var	-1
Ht: 6'3" Wt: 190	Type Con	Consist	A	MM	2005

6-8, 3.74 ERA in 137 IP at CHC. Made it back from shoulder injury in late May, and returned to familiar formula of low BB%, high GB%. That's worked for him in the past, but drop in K% has left narrow line between success and failure, and 4.53 MLB xERA for 2023 is a match for disappointing 2021-22 seasons. Even at a cheap cost, probably not worth it.

Yr	Tm	W	Sv	IP	K	ERA	WHIP	xERA	xWHIP	vL+	vR+	BF/G	BB%	K%	K-BB%	xBB%	SwK	Vel	G	L	F	H%	S%	HR/F	xHR/F	GS	APC	DOM%	DIS%	Sv%	LI	RAR	BPX	R$
19	CHC	11	0	177	150	3.46	1.13	4.26	1.22	88	94	24.3	4%	21%	16%	5%	10.5%	86.9	41	24	35	30%	73%	10%	10%	30	90	30%	27%			22.9	122	$
20	CHC	6	0	81	64	2.88	1.00	3.82	1.12	78	93	26.3	3%	20%	18%	5%	12.0%	87.4	47	21	32	28%	77%	13%	13%	12	97	42%	17%			15.8	145	$2
21	CHC	14	0	181	131	4.77	1.35	4.64	1.29	123	99	24.5	6%	17%	11%	5%	9.2%	87.3	43	23	34	31%	69%	16%	13%	32	88	25%	41%			-11.3	87	$
22	CHC	4	0	84	66	4.80	1.29	4.49	1.28	135	86	22.3	7%	19%	12%	8%	10.5%	86.7	36	21	43	29%	68%	14%	13%	16	84	19%	44%			-8.7	79	-$
23	CHC *	8	0	158	108	4.04	1.24	4.00	1.29	83	105	22.1	5%	16%	11%	6%	9.3%	87.7	46	20	34	30%	69%	8%	11%	24	88	25%	21%			5.7	91	
1st Half		5	0	63	37	3.86	1.13	3.01	1.37	68	83	20.6	6%	15%	9%	6%	7.3%	87.3	41	15	44	27%	65%	3%	10%	7	86	14%	29%			3.6	83	$
2nd Half		3	0	95	71	4.15	1.31	4.30	1.25	90	112	24.2	4%	17%	13%	6%	10.1%	87.8	49	21	30	33%	71%	12%	11%	17	89	29%	18%			2.1	114	$
Proj		10	0	167	121	4.16	1.24	4.11	1.26	99	101	22.7	5%	18%	13%	6%	9.7%	87.4	44	21	36	30%	70%	11%	12%	30						3.5	98	$

DAN MARCUS

Hendriks,Liam

Age: 35 | Th: R | Role: RP | Ht: 6'0" | Wt: 235 | Type: #DIV/0!
Health: F | PT/Exp: A | Consist: C | LIMA Plan: | Rand Var: | MM:

Hard to imagine a player with worse luck. After beating offseason cancer diagnosis, returned in late May only to suffer elbow injury that required Tommy John surgery. Won't return until late 2024 at best, and given age and adversity, it's fair to question whether he'll record another save in his career.

Yr	Tm	W	Sv	IP	K	ERA	WHIP	xERA	xWHIP	vL+	vR+	BF/G	BB%	K%	K-BB%	xBB%	SwK	Vel	G	L	F	H%	S%	HR/F	xHR/F	GS	APC	DOM%	DIS%	Sv%	LI	RAR	BPX	R$
19	OAK	4	25	85	124	1.80	0.96	3.27	1.00	93	57	4.4	6%	37%	31%	6%	17.7%	96.5	31	19	49	33%	84%	6%	7%	2	18	0%	100%	78	1.37	28.4	202	$25
20	OAK	3	14	25	37	1.78	0.67	2.48	0.82	77	40	3.8	3%	40%	37%	5%	20.0%	96.1	32	30	38	27%	75%	5%	11%	0	15			93	1.36	8.4	246	$30
21	CHW	8	38	71	113	2.54	0.73	2.55	0.76	60	80	3.9	3%	42%	40%	5%	20.1%	97.7	33	17	51	28%	78%	15%	12%	0	16			86	1.54	15.2	269	$32
22	CHW	4	37	58	85	2.81	1.04	2.94	0.98	91	85	4.1	7%	36%	29%	8%	18.8%	97.6	35	19	47	32%	79%	12%	12%	0	16			90	1.42	8.2	203	$20
23	CHW	2	1	5	3	5.40	1.00	4.58		108	85	4.0	5%	15%	10%	12%	13.8%	95.4	50	13	38	21%	50%	17%	15%	0	17			100	1.42	-0.7	86	-$4
1st Half		2	1	5	3	5.40	1.00	4.58		109	86	4.0	5%	15%	10%	12%	13.8%	95.4	50	13	38	21%	50%	17%	15%	0	17			100	1.42	-0.7	86	-$7
2nd Half																																		
Proj																																		

Henry,Tommy

Age: 26 | Th: L | Role: SP | Ht: 6'3" | Wt: 205 | Type: /FB
Health: D | PT/Exp: C | Consist: C | LIMA Plan: C | Rand Var: -1 | MM: 1001

5-4, 4.15 ERA in 89 IP at ARI. Failed to win Opening Day roster spot, but ended up in big-league rotation for several months anyway until elbow injury ended season in late July. Limited K% carried over from minors, and high FB% casts doubt on sustainability of improved HR/F. Lack of plus skill leaves narrow path for even modest success.

Yr	Tm	W	Sv	IP	K	ERA	WHIP	xERA	xWHIP	vL+	vR+	BF/G	BB%	K%	K-BB%	xBB%	SwK	Vel	G	L	F	H%	S%	HR/F	xHR/F	GS	APC	DOM%	DIS%	Sv%	LI	RAR	BPX	R$
19																																		
20																																		
21	aa	4	0	117	112	5.41	1.51	5.66				22.0	10%	22%	12%							32%	69%									-16.6	52	-$10
22	ARI *	7	0	160	119	3.76	1.29	3.95	1.46	151	108	21.9	9%	18%	9%	8%	11.1%	91.6	39	19	42	28%	74%	17%	12%	9	86	11%	44%			4.2	65	$3
23	ARI *	6	0	111	81	4.43	1.37	4.52	1.47	108	100	22.2	9%	17%	8%	8%	10.4%	90.7	36	20	44	29%	71%	10%	9%	16	82	6%	31%	0	0.84	-1.3	55	-$2
1st Half		6	0	90	66	4.44	1.36	4.80	1.42	113	104	22.2	8%	17%	9%	8%	10.9%	90.8	38	18	44	29%	72%	13%	10%	12	80	8%	42%	0	0.84	-1.3	49	$3
2nd Half		0	0	21	15	4.35	1.40	5.78	1.56	87	90	23.0	11%	16%	5%	9%	9.1%	90.5	31	25	45	31%	66%	0%	5%	4	88	0%	0%			-0.1	10	-$7
Proj		5	0	102	80	4.55	1.40	4.80	1.45	117	102	22.0	10%	19%	9%	8%	10.1%	90.8	35	21	44	30%	69%	8%	8%	19						-2.8	43	-$4

Hentges,Sam

Age: 27 | Th: L | Role: RP | Ht: 6'6" | Wt: 245 | Type: Pwr/xGB
Health: C | PT/Exp: C | Consist: C | LIMA Plan: B | Rand Var: 0 | MM: 5301

Shoulder inflammation cost him first month of season and seemed to plague him after, with sizable dips in SwK, K%. Even so, was trusted in highest-leverage role of career, and xERA, BPX suggest skills otherwise remained sharp. With improved health and H% regression, could be darkhorse for saves.

Yr	Tm	W	Sv	IP	K	ERA	WHIP	xERA	xWHIP	vL+	vR+	BF/G	BB%	K%	K-BB%	xBB%	SwK	Vel	G	L	F	H%	S%	HR/F	xHR/F	GS	APC	DOM%	DIS%	Sv%	LI	RAR	BPX	R$
19	aa	2	0	130	107	7.32	1.99	7.13				24.1	11%	17%	6%							40%	63%									-45.2	35	-$28
20																																		
21	CLE	1	0	69	68	6.68	1.78	4.84	1.39	90	125	10.6	10%	21%	11%	11%	10.4%	94.4	46	19	35	39%	63%	13%	19%	12	42	0%	67%	0	0.49	-20.5	78	-$16
22	CLE	3	1	62	72	2.32	0.97	2.57	1.13	53	87	4.3	8%	29%	22%	6%	14.4%	95.8	61	16	23	27%	77%	9%	13%	0	17			100	0.75	12.6	168	$6
23	CLE	3	0	52	56	3.61	1.36	3.24	1.25	97	84	4.0	8%	25%	17%	8%	11.8%	95.6	59	23	18	36%	72%	7%	15%	0	15			0	1.03	4.6	142	-$1
1st Half		1	0	22	20	2.91	1.06	3.14	1.34	82	71	4.0	9%	23%	14%	7%	11.1%	95.8	64	22	14	25%	73%	13%	10%	0	14			0	1.18	3.8	115	-$4
2nd Half		2	0	31	36	4.11	1.57	3.30	1.20	106	95	4.0	7%	26%	19%	8%	12.2%	95.4	55	24	21	42%	72%	5%	17%	0	16			0	0.93	0.8	162	-$3
Proj		3	0	65	72	3.60	1.24	3.06	1.22	81	89	5.1	8%	27%	19%	8%	11.8%	95.3	56	21	23	32%	72%	12%	15%	0						5.8	145	$1

Hernández,Carlos

Age: 27 | Th: R | Role: RP | Ht: 6'4" | Wt: 245 | Type: Pwr/FB
Health: A | PT/Exp: C | Consist: B | LIMA Plan: B | Rand Var: +2 | MM: 2211

Expected bump in velocity, SwK, and K% followed shift from swingman to full-time reliever, and had 3.57 ERA, 0.98 WHIP with skill support through end of July. But after KC trades gave him save opps, control collapsed and brought everything else down with it. Might get another shot at closing, but overall skill history says be wary.

Yr	Tm	W	Sv	IP	K	ERA	WHIP	xERA	xWHIP	vL+	vR+	BF/G	BB%	K%	K-BB%	xBB%	SwK	Vel	G	L	F	H%	S%	HR/F	xHR/F	GS	APC	DOM%	DIS%	Sv%	LI	RAR	BPX	R$
19																																		
20	KC	0	0	15	13	4.91	1.70	5.21	1.40	151	106	13.4	9%	19%	10%	9%	11.4%	96.2	38	26	36	35%	81%	24%	21%	3	51	0%	67%	0	0.66	-0.8	68	-$9
21	KC *	8	0	113	94	3.93	1.30	3.93	1.47	79	96	15.5	10%	20%	10%	10%	11.4%	97.2	40	20	40	28%	73%	7%	10%	11	60	27%	27%	0	0.65	4.6	71	$3
22	KC *	2	0	106	69	5.62	1.51	5.02	1.61	100	141	11.8	10%	15%	5%	9%	10.8%	96.8	38	21	41	30%	64%	9%	11%	7	38	0%	100%	0	0.99	-21.6	37	-$14
23	KC	1	4	70	77	5.27	1.33	4.49	1.34	80	120	4.5	10%	26%	15%	7%	14.4%	99.1	32	25	43	30%	63%	12%	13%	4	19	0%	25%	40	1.08	-8.1	90	-$4
1st Half		0	0	42	49	4.10	1.03	3.70	1.12	72	88	4.8	7%	29%	23%	6%	15.0%	99.0	33	25	42	30%	60%	7%	8%	4	20	0%	25%	0	0.77	1.2	155	-$1
2nd Half		1	4	28	28	6.99	1.76	5.84	1.65	94	158	4.1	15%	21%	6%	10%	13.8%	99.3	31	25	43	31%	65%	19%	18%	0	17			50	1.41	-9.3	-2	-$8
Proj		2	6	65	67	4.74	1.38	4.27	1.35	83	123	5.8	10%	24%	14%	9%	14.0%	98.3	35	23	42	31%	69%	13%	12%	0						-3.3	81	-$2

Hernandez,Jose

Age: 26 | Th: L | Role: RP | Ht: 6'3" | Wt: 170 | Type: Pwr/FB
Health: C | PT/Exp: D | Consist: A | LIMA Plan: B | Rand Var: +2 | MM: 3300

Rule 5 draft pick started strong, but 2nd half BB% fell in line with minor-league track record, overshadowing previous positive work. xBB% provides some hope he'll improve, but he's yet to own that skill for full season at any level, and is unlikely to see any high-leverage work until he does.

Yr	Tm	W	Sv	IP	K	ERA	WHIP	xERA	xWHIP	vL+	vR+	BF/G	BB%	K%	K-BB%	xBB%	SwK	Vel	G	L	F	H%	S%	HR/F	xHR/F	GS	APC	DOM%	DIS%	Sv%	LI	RAR	BPX	R$
19																																		
20																																		
21																																		
22	aa	3	0	40	39	3.63	1.16	3.72				4.4	10%	24%	14%							25%	77%									1.7	79	-$1
23	PIT	1	0	51	62	4.97	1.36	4.17	1.28	114	101	4.5	10%	28%	18%	7%	12.8%	94.7	39	20	41	32%	68%	16%	15%	0	17			0	0.59	-4.0	123	-$5
1st Half		0	0	27	28	2.63	1.02	3.68	1.14	97	87	4.2	6%	26%	20%	6%	12.8%	94.8	38	26	36	28%	80%	11%	10%	0	16			0	0.55	5.7	145	-$2
2nd Half		1	0	23	34	7.71	1.76	4.74	1.41	129	119	4.8	14%	30%	16%	8%	12.9%	94.5	40	14	46	37%	60%	21%	19%	0	19			0	0.63	-9.7	98	-$9
Proj		2	0	51	59	4.62	1.33	3.89	1.31	110	95	4.5	11%	28%	17%	8%	12.9%	94.6	39	19	42	30%	70%	15%	15%	0						-1.9	106	-$4

Hicks,Jordan

Age: 27 | Th: R | Role: RP | Ht: 6'2" | Wt: 220 | Type: Pwr/xGB
Health: F | PT/Exp: C | Consist: B | LIMA Plan: A | Rand Var: 0 | MM: 5311

Avoided IL for first time since 2019 and was most dominant version of himself since then. SwK was still below peak level, but elite velocity, high GB% keep him viable even as BB% remains a work in progress. Move to TOR didn't provide many save opportunities, but skills, high-leverage experience could coalesce into... UP: 25 Sv

Yr	Tm	W	Sv	IP	K	ERA	WHIP	xERA	xWHIP	vL+	vR+	BF/G	BB%	K%	K-BB%	xBB%	SwK	Vel	G	L	F	H%	S%	HR/F	xHR/F	GS	APC	DOM%	DIS%	Sv%	LI	RAR	BPX	R$
19	STL	2	14	29	31	3.14	0.94	2.86	1.27	106	44	3.8	10%	28%	18%	11%	12.1%	101.2	67	16	16	22%	68%	18%	16%	0	16			93	0.94	4.8	138	$6
20																																		
21	STL	0	0	10	10	5.40	1.50	4.77	1.97	72	79	4.4	23%	23%	0%	12%	8.7%	99.3	71	13	17	22%	60%	0%	0%	0	21			0	0.47	-1.4	-35	-$6
22	STL	3	0	61	63	4.84	1.32	3.61	1.46	111	82	7.5	13%	24%	11%	11%	9.7%	99.4	58	18	24	27%	63%	13%	15%	8	30	0%	38%	0	1.13	-6.6	70	-$4
23	2 TM	3	12	66	81	3.29	1.36	3.29	1.32	90	90	4.4	11%	28%	17%	9%	11.1%	100.2	58	20	22	34%	76%	11%	11%	0	17			80	1.07	8.4	132	$6
1st Half		1	5	34	52	3.93	1.46	3.24	1.34	102	85	4.7	14%	34%	19%	11%	11.6%	100.9	53	23	24	37%	73%	11%	9%	0	20			71	1.01	1.7	136	$0
2nd Half		2	7	31	29	2.59	1.24	3.35	1.29	74	96	4.1	8%	22%	15%	7%	10.3%	99.4	63	17	20	31%	81%	11%	14%	0	15			88	1.13	6.8	128	$6
Proj		3	10	65	70	3.31	1.26	3.24	1.33	92	89	4.7	11%	26%	15%	9%	10.7%	99.9	59	19	22	30%	75%	12%	12%	0						8.2	114	$5

Hill,Rich

Age: 44 | Th: L | Role: RP | Ht: 6'5" | Wt: 221 | Type:
Health: D | PT/Exp: A | Consist: B | LIMA Plan: B | Rand Var: +1 | MM: 1100

K%, SwK each continued to decline, and more balls in play led to career-worst 22 HR, .510 SLG surrendered to RHB. Closed the season as reliever after being traded from SD to PIT, but even role change didn't help (19% K%, 9% K-BB% in 11 IP). At 44, it's hard to see negative trends reversing; as always, age never regresses.

Yr	Tm	W	Sv	IP	K	ERA	WHIP	xERA	xWHIP	vL+	vR+	BF/G	BB%	K%	K-BB%	xBB%	SwK	Vel	G	L	F	H%	S%	HR/F	xHR/F	GS	APC	DOM%	DIS%	Sv%	LI	RAR	BPX	R$
19	LA	4	0	59	72	2.45	1.13	3.36	1.15	70	99	18.6	7%	30%	22%	5%	11.4%	90.3	50	18	32	29%	89%	22%	12%	13	74	15%	23%			14.8	166	$5
20	MIN	2	0	39	31	3.03	1.16	4.86	1.48	71	82	19.5	11%	20%	9%	8%	6.6%	87.7	41	23	37	24%	76%	8%	18%	8	77	13%	13%			6.8	47	$5
21	2 TM	7	0	159	150	3.86	1.21	4.45	1.30	78	102	20.7	8%	23%	14%	6%	10.3%	88.0	35	22	43	28%	73%	11%	11%	31	78	13%	42%	0	0.77	8.0	90	$8
22	BOS	8	0	124	109	4.27	1.30	4.19	1.26	103	105	20.2	7%	21%	14%	5%	9.7%	88.3	40	20	40	31%	70%	10%	14%	26	77	15%	38%			-4.6	97	$1
23	2 NL	8	0	146	129	5.41	1.52	4.94	1.39	103	117	20.6	9%	20%	11%	7%	8.1%	88.1	38	24	38	33%	68%	13%	15%	27	79	7%	56%	0	0.74	-19.5	70	-$10
1st Half		7	0	94	88	4.50	1.38	4.62	1.34	94	110	24.1	9%	22%	13%	7%	8.0%	87.9	36	26	38	32%	70%	11%	14%	17	94	12%	35%			-2.0	85	$5
2nd Half		1	0	52	41	7.05	1.78	5.54	1.48	112	133	16.7	9%	16%	7%	6%	8.3%	88.4	42	21	37	36%	63%	17%	18%	10	62	0%	90%	0	0.71	-17.6	45	-$15
Proj		3	0	58	51	4.85	1.42	4.39	1.36	97	111	18.8	9%	21%	12%	6%	8.8%	88.2	39	22	39	32%	69%	13%	15%	12						-3.8	77	-$5

DAN MARCUS

Hoeing,Bryan

Age: 27	Th: R	Role RP	Health A	LIMA Plan B
Ht: 6'6"	Wt: 210	Type Con	PT/Exp C	Rand Var 0
			Consist B	MM 1000

2-3, 5.48 ERA in 71 IP at MIA. Shifted to full-time work out of bullpen in May, and narrowed pitch mix to sinker, slider in process. Due to lack of swing-and-miss stuff, he's reliant on GB% to be successful, but homer rate has spoiled that plan. If he can stick in majors, role will likely be as a low-leverage reliever, making him safe to ignore on draft day.

Yr Tm	W	Sv	IP	K	ERA	WHIP	xERA	xWHIP	vL+	vR+	BF/G	BB%	K%	K-BB%	xBB%	SwK	Vel	G	L	F	H%	S%	HR/F	xHR/F	GS	APC	DOM%	DIS%	Sv%	LI	RAR	BPX	R$
19																																	
20																																	
21																																	
22 MIA *	10	0	134	66	5.24	1.50	5.44	1.52	141	167	19.3	8%	11%	4%	8%	4.5%	93.1	51	20	29	31%	67%	36%	36%	1	33	0%	100%	0	0.64	-20.9	20	-$10
23 MIA *	3	0	103	81	4.59	1.26	4.49	1.41	132	100	10.5	8%	17%	9%	8%	8.9%	94.1	45	17	38	29%	68%	15%	16%	7	34	14%	57%	0	0.69	-3.2	69	-$1
1st Half	1	0	57	45	3.28	1.23	3.82	1.33	92	109	10.0	7%	20%	12%	8%	9.4%	94.1	47	14	39	29%	77%	11%	13%	5	31	20%	40%	0	0.70	7.3	85	$1
2nd Half	2	0	46	36	6.19	1.30	5.32	1.30	175	90	11.2	6%	19%	12%	9%	8.3%	94.2	43	20	37	29%	57%	20%	20%	2	38	0%	100%	0	0.66	-10.6	52	-$5
Proj	**2**	**0**	**58**	**40**	**4.86**	**1.26**	**4.37**	**1.34**	**133**	**90**	**12.3**	**7%**	**17%**	**10%**	**9%**	**8.7%**	**94.1**	**45**	**17**	**38**	**28%**	**65%**	**13%**	**17%**	**4**						**-3.8**	**76**	**-$4**

Hoffman,Jeff

Age: 31	Th: R	Role RP	Health F	LIMA Plan A
Ht: 6'5"	Wt: 235	Type Pwr/FB	PT/Exp C	Rand Var -5
			Consist B	MM 3410

Enjoyed first healthy season since 2020 and showed significant skill improvement thanks to shift in pitch mix that featured more sliders, jump in fastball velocity. K-BB% was double previous high, and GB% spike helped him correct previous HR problem. Trust in high-leverage situations led to 11 holds, and he's now a darkhorse option for saves.

Yr Tm	W	Sv	IP	K	ERA	WHIP	xERA	xWHIP	vL+	vR+	BF/G	BB%	K%	K-BB%	xBB%	SwK	Vel	G	L	F	H%	S%	HR/F	xHR/F	GS	APC	DOM%	DIS%	Sv%	LI	RAR	BPX	R$
19 COL *	8	0	156	142	7.80	1.69	7.30	1.48	103	152	22.0	9%	20%	11%	8%	9.8%	93.7	35	21	43	34%	58%	24%	20%	15	84	0%	53%			-63.4	15	-$24
20 COL	2	1	21	20	9.28	1.92	5.57	1.40	133	134	6.5	9%	19%	11%	8%	9.3%	94.5	36	25	39	42%	50%	11%	14%	0	25			100	1.07	-12.7	72	-$13
21 CIN *	3	0	89	95	4.17	1.51	5.11	1.50	125	92	11.0	13%	25%	12%	11%	12.4%	94.3	38	24	39	31%	78%	15%	11%	11	44	9%	64%	0	0.44	1.1	63	-$4
22 CIN	2	0	45	45	3.83	1.41	4.95	1.41	106	104	5.6	12%	23%	11%	10%	11.0%	94.3	29	18	53	30%	76%	7%	10%	1	24	0%	0%	0	0.45	0.8	50	-$4
23 PHI	5	1	52	69	2.41	0.92	3.23	1.14	85	58	3.9	9%	33%	24%	6%	16.6%	97.2	43	18	39	25%	76%	7%	8%	0	16			33	1.08	12.4	164	$8
1st Half	1	1	18	26	2.95	1.15	2.92	1.18	98	76	4.5	11%	34%	24%	7%	15.9%	97.0	49	23	28	32%	75%	9%	19%	0	19			100	0.65	3.1	170	-$4
2nd Half	4	0	34	43	2.12	0.79	3.39	1.13	77	49	3.6	8%	33%	24%	6%	17.1%	97.3	39	16	45	21%	76%	6%	4%	0	15			0	1.28	9.3	162	$11
Proj	**4**	**1**	**58**	**68**	**3.61**	**1.22**	**3.70**	**1.28**	**104**	**83**	**5.4**	**11%**	**29%**	**18%**	**8%**	**13.9%**	**95.7**	**39**	**20**	**41**	**29%**	**74%**	**12%**	**11%**	**0**						**5.1**	**111**	**$1**

Holderman,Colin

Age: 28	Th: R	Role RP	Health D	LIMA Plan B
Ht: 6'7"	Wt: 240	Type /GB	PT/Exp D	Rand Var 0
			Consist B	MM 4211

Last name proved prophetic, as he led PIT with 27 holds. Enjoyed moderate skills improvement, decreasing BB% by four percentage points in comparison to 2022 big-league sample, and increased GB% to overcome HR/F regression. Lackluster strikeout skills may limit his ceiling, but can carry value in leagues that reward holds paired with a good ERA.

Yr Tm	W	Sv	IP	K	ERA	WHIP	xERA	xWHIP	vL+	vR+	BF/G	BB%	K%	K-BB%	xBB%	SwK	Vel	G	L	F	H%	S%	HR/F	xHR/F	GS	APC	DOM%	DIS%	Sv%	LI	RAR	BPX	R$
19																																	
20																																	
21 aa	0	4	20	17	3.15	0.98	2.36				7.0	8%	22%	14%							24%	71%									2.8	108	-$2
22 2 NL *	6	3	46	40	3.35	1.11	2.21	1.47	75	85	4.8	10%	22%	12%	11%	10.0%	96.2	45	17	37	25%	69%	0%	7%	0	18			75	0.75	3.5	105	$3
23 PIT	0	2	56	58	3.86	1.34	3.77	1.28	90	96	4.1	8%	24%	16%	8%	10.4%	98.0	53	18	29	34%	72%	9%	13%	0	16			33	1.00	3.3	126	-$2
1st Half	0	1	25	28	3.91	1.46	3.66	1.18	92	117	4.1	6%	25%	19%	6%	11.4%	97.9	50	21	29	38%	76%	14%	17%	0	16			50	0.93	1.3	158	-$8
2nd Half	0	1	31	30	3.82	1.24	3.86	1.37	89	78	4.2	10%	23%	13%	9%	9.6%	98.0	55	16	29	30%	68%	4%	8%	0	16			25	1.06	2.0	100	-$3
Proj	**2**	**3**	**65**	**62**	**3.69**	**1.22**	**3.57**	**1.30**	**85**	**87**	**4.3**	**9%**	**23%**	**15%**	**8%**	**10.3%**	**98.0**	**53**	**18**	**29**	**30%**	**71%**	**9%**	**12%**	**0**						**5.2**	**110**	**$1**

Holmes,Clay

Age: 31	Th: R	Role RP	Health D	LIMA Plan B+
Ht: 6'5"	Wt: 245	Type Pwr/xGB	PT/Exp A	Rand Var -1
			Consist B	MM 5331

Briefly demoted from closer role due to BB% struggles in April (12%), but rebounded from there. Doesn't have dominance of elite closers (2022 SwK% looks like an outlier) and has faded in 2nd half last two years without explanation. Even with shortcomings, elite GB% and HR prevention do a lot to keep him as viable option for saves.

Yr Tm	W	Sv	IP	K	ERA	WHIP	xERA	xWHIP	vL+	vR+	BF/G	BB%	K%	K-BB%	xBB%	SwK	Vel	G	L	F	H%	S%	HR/F	xHR/F	GS	APC	DOM%	DIS%	Sv%	LI	RAR	BPX	R$
19 PIT *	4	1	71	68	6.45	1.80	5.28	1.60	107	93	7.0	16%	21%	4%	12%	9.7%	94.3	60	18	22	34%	63%	17%	19%	0	26			20	0.57	-17.1	61	-$11
20 PIT	0	0	1	1	0.00	1.50	3.77		92	89	6.0	0%	17%	17%		18.2%	92.4	60	20	20	42%	100%	0%	0%	0	22			0	1.12	0.7	180	-$6
21 2 TM	8	0	70	78	3.60	1.17	2.96	1.27	112	63	4.2	10%	27%	17%	8%	11.6%	96.1	69	13	18	29%	70%	16%	16%	0	16			0	1.06	5.7	139	$5
22 NYY	7	20	64	65	2.54	1.02	2.33	1.20	99	63	4.2	8%	25%	17%	7%	13.6%	97.1	76	12	12	27%	75%	10%	8%	0	16			80	1.41	11.2	158	$15
23 NYY	4	24	63	71	2.86	1.17	2.88	1.24	75	83	4.0	9%	27%	18%	7%	11.1%	96.1	65	18	17	31%	75%	7%	9%	0	16			89	1.52	11.5	154	$14
1st Half	4	9	33	41	2.43	1.17	2.89	1.25	79	74	3.9	10%	30%	20%	8%	12.5%	96.3	59	22	19	32%	77%	0%	9%	0	16			82	1.80	7.8	152	$12
2nd Half	0	15	30	30	3.34	1.18	2.87	1.24	73	95	4.0	7%	24%	17%	6%	9.6%	95.9	71	13	15	31%	73%	15%	10%	0	15			94	1.19	3.6	157	$8
Proj	**5**	**30**	**65**	**70**	**3.14**	**1.15**	**2.69**	**1.22**	**89**	**77**	**4.0**	**9%**	**27%**	**19%**	**8%**	**11.2%**	**96.0**	**68**	**15**	**17**	**30%**	**73%**	**12%**	**12%**	**0**						**9.6**	**155**	**$17**

Holton,Tyler

Age: 28	Th: L	Role RP	Health A	LIMA Plan B+
Ht: 6'2"	Wt: 200	Type Con	PT/Exp D	Rand Var -5
			Consist D	MM 3100

Stepped into high-leverage role in 2nd half of first full MLB season and had success by pairing low BB% with improved GB%. SwK% and 2nd half K% bump suggest there might be bit more strikeout upside, though not enough to close gap between ERA/xERA and WHIP/xWHIP. Expect some regression, and don't expect another double-digit R$.

Yr Tm	W	Sv	IP	K	ERA	WHIP	xERA	xWHIP	vL+	vR+	BF/G	BB%	K%	K-BB%	xBB%	SwK	Vel	G	L	F	H%	S%	HR/F	xHR/F	GS	APC	DOM%	DIS%	Sv%	LI	RAR	BPX	R$
19																																	
20																																	
21 a/a	4	1	65	63	6.24	1.57	5.61				11.0	6%	22%	16%							40%	59%									-15.9	107	-$10
22 ARI *	5	1	55	40	3.51	1.15	3.13	1.28	26	112	6.4	7%	18%	11%	8%	13.8%	90.6	30	17	53	27%	71%	6%	5%	0	16			100	0.41	3.1	84	$1
23 DET	3	1	85	74	2.11	0.87	3.69	1.20	49	88	5.5	6%	23%	17%	5%	12.6%	91.5	46	19	36	22%	83%	11%	12%	1	20	0%	0%	50	0.97	23.4	127	$15
1st Half	0	0	44	37	2.06	1.05	3.95	1.33	52	98	6.7	8%	21%	13%	7%	12.6%	91.3	47	22	31	25%	86%	11%	14%	1	25	0%	0%	0	0.78	12.2	95	$4
2nd Half	3	1	42	37	2.16	0.67	3.44	1.06	46	77	4.6	3%	25%	22%	4%	12.6%	91.7	44	15	41	19%	78%	11%	11%	0	17			50	1.12	11.2	161	$12
Proj	**3**	**0**	**58**	**53**	**3.67**	**1.11**	**3.60**	**1.18**	**65**	**106**	**6.4**	**6%**	**23%**	**17%**	**5%**	**12.6%**	**91.5**	**45**	**18**	**37**	**29%**	**70%**	**10%**	**12%**	**0**						**4.7**	**131**	**$1**

Houck,Tanner

Age: 28	Th: R	Role RP	Health F	LIMA Plan B
Ht: 6'5"	Wt: 230	Type Pwr/GB	PT/Exp B	Rand Var +2
			Consist A	MM 3203

Spent off-season recovering from spinal surgery, and just as he began to look more comfortable in June, was struck in face by line drive that required orbital surgery, sidelining him for two months. Despite inconsistent role throughout career, above-average SwK%, GB% are reasons to consider him as late-round dart. UP: 3.50 ERA over 150 IP

Yr Tm	W	Sv	IP	K	ERA	WHIP	xERA	xWHIP	vL+	vR+	BF/G	BB%	K%	K-BB%	xBB%	SwK	Vel	G	L	F	H%	S%	HR/F	xHR/F	GS	APC	DOM%	DIS%	Sv%	LI	RAR	BPX	R$
19 a/a	8	1	109	88	5.50	1.63	5.21				14.7	10%	18%	8%							36%	66%									-13.3	61	-$7
20 BOS	3	0	17	21	0.53	0.88	3.38	1.35	61	59	21.0	14%	33%	19%	12%	12.1%	92.1	47	19	34	16%	100%	9%	16%	3	88	0%	0%			8.2	109	$8
21 BOS *	1	1	90	108	4.22	1.20	3.14	1.11	88	77	15.1	8%	30%	22%	8%	13.7%	94.1	48	20	32	34%	64%	7%	10%	13	64	46%	31%	100	1.11	0.5	150	$0
22 BOS	5	8	60	56	3.15	1.18	3.44	1.30	111	70	7.7	9%	23%	14%	8%	13.3%	94.9	51	23	26	29%	74%	7%	12%	4	29	0%	50%	89	1.05	6.1	100	$5
23 BOS	6	0	106	99	5.01	1.37	4.08	1.36	116	85	22.0	9%	21%	13%	8%	13.1%	93.6	53	19	28	31%	66%	16%	15%	21	83	10%	43%			-8.9	99	-$3
1st Half	3	0	68	64	5.05	1.26	3.90	1.30	110	79	21.9	8%	22%	14%	8%	13.1%	93.6	50	22	28	29%	62%	16%	13%	13	82	15%	31%			-6.0	111	-$2
2nd Half	3	0	38	35	4.93	1.57	4.40	1.45	126	97	22.3	10%	20%	10%	8%	13.3%	93.5	58	15	27	34%	71%	16%	17%	8	85	0%	63%			-2.8	79	-$3
Proj	**7**	**0**	**131**	**128**	**4.01**	**1.30**	**3.62**	**1.31**	**109**	**81**	**14.8**	**9%**	**24%**	**15%**	**8%**	**13.3%**	**93.9**	**53**	**19**	**28**	**31%**	**71%**	**12%**	**14%**	**17**						**5.1**	**108**	**$4**

Houser,Adrian

Age: 31	Th: R	Role SP	Health F	LIMA Plan B
Ht: 6'3"	Wt: 222	Type	PT/Exp A	Rand Var -1
			Consist A	MM 2101

8-5, 4.12 ERA in 111 IP at MIL. Had whirlwind season with multiple injuries and brief demotion to bullpen. K%, K-BB% suggest there was growth in skills in 2nd half, though with no change in underlying indicators, those jumps were better explained simply as fortunate variance. Four consecutive 4.00+ xERA seasons point to continued mediocrity.

Yr Tm	W	Sv	IP	K	ERA	WHIP	xERA	xWHIP	vL+	vR+	BF/G	BB%	K%	K-BB%	xBB%	SwK	Vel	G	L	F	H%	S%	HR/F	xHR/F	GS	APC	DOM%	DIS%	Sv%	LI	RAR	BPX	R$
19 MIL *	8	0	133	136	3.34	1.18	3.55	1.26	109	83	13.7	8%	25%	18%	8%	10.4%	94.4	53	21	26	29%	76%	18%	13%	18	52	11%	39%	0	1.00	19.1	108	$12
20 MIL	1	0	56	44	5.30	1.50	4.20	1.39	137	78	20.5	9%	18%	9%	7%	10.3%	93.4	59	23	19	33%	67%	24%	20%	11	77	18%	55%	0	0.69	-5.9	83	-$10
21 MIL	10	0	142	105	3.22	1.28	4.19	1.49	105	78	21.4	11%	18%	7%	10%	8.0%	93.7	59	20	21	26%	77%	14%	13%	26	84	8%	46%	0	0.80	18.3	52	$10
22 MIL	6	0	103	69	4.73	1.46	4.80	1.51	124	85	20.7	10%	15%	5%	10%	6.8%	94.0	47	23	30	30%	68%	8%	13%	21	84	5%	29%	0	0.74	-9.7	25	-$6
23 MIL *	8	0	128	105	4.03	1.42	4.96	1.31	107	93	20.1	7%	20%	13%	8%	7.9%	92.6	47	18	35	33%	75%	11%	11%	21	81	5%	33%	0	0.71	4.8	74	$0
1st Half	3	0	63	39	3.75	1.55	5.61	1.44	117	99	19.5	8%	15%	7%	8%	7.1%	93.1	50	20	30	34%	79%	11%	8%	8	80	0%	38%	0	0.64	4.5	43	-$4
2nd Half	5	0	65	66	4.29	1.31	4.24	1.25	101	90	21.4	7%	24%	17%	7%	8.4%	92.2	44	16	40	33%	70%	11%	12%	13	82	8%	31%			0.3	126	$7
Proj	**6**	**0**	**102**	**82**	**4.53**	**1.44**	**4.26**	**1.38**	**117**	**91**	**20.0**	**9%**	**19%**	**10%**	**8%**	**8.1%**	**93.2**	**48**	**20**	**32**	**32%**	**70%**	**11%**	**12%**	**22**						**-2.6**	**76**	**-$4**

DAN MARCUS

Hudson,Dakota

Age: 29	Th: R	Role: SP	Health: F	LIMA Plan: D+
Ht: 6' 5"	Wt: 215	Type: Con/GB	PT/Exp: C	Rand Var: 0
			Consist: F	MM: 0001

6-3, 4.98 ERA in 81 IP at STL. Spent 1st half in AAA where month-long IL stint (neck) was sandwiched between 12 starts of soft skills, poor results. Stuck on MLB roster following July call-up, but with almost as many walks as strikeouts (again). Combination of inflated ratios, deflated K% isn't anything you want near your roster.

Yr	Tm	W	Sv	IP	K	ERA	WHIP	xERA	xWHIP	vL+	vR+	BF/G	BB%	K%	K-BB%	xBB%	SwK	Vel	G	L	F	H%	S%	HR/F	xHR/F	GS	APC	DOM%	DIS%	Sv%	LI	RAR	BPX	R$
19	STL	16	1	175	136	3.35	1.41	4.61	1.55	108	90	22.9	11%	18%	7%	10%	10.2%	93.7	57	22	21	28%	81%	20%	20%	32	86	16%	41%	100	0.95	24.9	45	$13
20	STL	3	0	39	31	2.77	1.00	4.13	1.41	66	95	18.9	10%	21%	11%	9%	10.0%	92.9	57	13	31	19%	79%	16%	14%	8	74	25%	38%			8.1	79	$11
21	STL *	2	0	27	13	1.33	0.98	1.50	1.16	82	68	17.0	8%	13%	5%	8%	7.6%	92.1	65	8	27	22%	85%	0%	0%	1	66	0%	0%	0	1.05	9.7	82	$0
22	STL *	9	0	161	92	4.08	1.44	4.14	1.55	103	104	22.8	10%	13%	4%	11%	7.4%	91.8	53	19	28	30%	71%	7%	11%	26	83	12%	54%	0	0.74	-2.3	51	-$3
23	STL *	11	0	129	73	5.54	1.72	6.24	1.57	113	106	20.3	10%	13%	3%	9%	8.6%	91.4	51	21	27	35%	68%	12%	17%	12	73	0%	67%	0	0.98	-19.3	26	-$16
1st Half		5	0	51	30	6.16	2.01	7.84	1.47		34	20.4	7%	13%	6%	9%	2.9%	93.1	29	0	71	42%	69%	0%		0	34			0	1.83	-11.4	29	-$19
2nd Half		6	0	79	43	5.15	1.54	5.11	1.59	114	110	20.3	10%	12%	3%	9%	8.8%	91.4	52	22	26	30%	68%	13%	18%	12	76	0%	67%	0	0.94	-7.9	15	-$1
Proj		**8**	**0**	**102**	**57**	**4.69**	**1.51**	**4.93**	**1.58**	**111**	**109**	**20.6**	**10%**	**13%**	**3%**	**10%**	**8.5%**	**92.3**	**52**	**20**	**28**	**30%**	**70%**	**11%**	**16%**	**21**						**-4.6**	**15**	**-$6**

Hughes,Brandon

Age: 28	Th: L	Role: RP	Health: F	LIMA Plan: B
Ht: 6' 2"	Wt: 215	Type: Pwr	PT/Exp: D	Rand Var: +5
			Consist: D	MM: 3300

Never could shake spring knee injury that eventually led to season-ending surgery in June. In between IL stints, velocity held up and still missed plenty of bats, but some tough luck led to bloated ERA/WHIP. Lost season may push him a little farther away from shot at saves, but he's a good bet to rebound and deliver strong ratios.

Yr	Tm	W	Sv	IP	K	ERA	WHIP	xERA	xWHIP	vL+	vR+	BF/G	BB%	K%	K-BB%	xBB%	SwK	Vel	G	L	F	H%	S%	HR/F	xHR/F	GS	APC	DOM%	DIS%	Sv%	LI	RAR	BPX	R$
19																																		
20																																		
21	aa	0	1	32	34	1.98	1.31	3.78				7.4	11%	26%	15%							31%	90%									9.1	98	-$2
22	CHC *	3	9	76	85	2.37	0.94	2.49	1.18	89	103	4.3	8%	30%	21%	7%	15.4%	93.2	34	22	44	22%	85%	17%	15%	0	17			69	1.17	14.9	127	$12
23	CHC	0	0	14	17	7.24	1.61	4.50	1.41	76	137	3.7	13%	27%	14%	11%	15.9%	93.3	31	31	37	36%	55%	15%	19%	0	14			0	1.14	-4.9	77	-$8
1st Half		0	0	14	17	7.24	1.61	4.50	1.41	76	138	3.7	13%	27%	14%	11%	15.9%	93.3	31	31	37	36%	55%	15%	19%	0	14			0	1.14	-4.9	78	-$13
2nd Half																																		
Proj		**2**	**0**	**51**	**56**	**3.62**	**1.24**	**3.77**	**1.24**	**104**	**108**	**5.4**	**9%**	**27%**	**18%**	**8%**	**15.4%**	**93.2**	**34**	**22**	**44**	**30%**	**75%**	**12%**	**14%**	**0**						**4.4**	**113**	**-$1**

Hurt,Kyle

Age: 26	Th: R	Role: SP	Health: A	LIMA Plan: A+
Ht: 6' 3"	Wt: 215	Type: Pwr	PT/Exp: D	Rand Var: -1
			Consist: F	MM: 5500

0-0, 0.00 ERA in 2 IP at LA. Older prospect finally found strike zone consistently, aiding MiLB breakout. Mid-90s fastball generates significant ride, contributing to 36% whiff rate. Mid-to-high-80s change-up is best secondary offering with natural fade and sudden drop. Improved feel for slider; flashes fringe curve. A fit for multiple MLB roles in 2024. (CB)

Yr	Tm	W	Sv	IP	K	ERA	WHIP	xERA	xWHIP	vL+	vR+	BF/G	BB%	K%	K-BB%	xBB%	SwK	Vel	G	L	F	H%	S%	HR/F	xHR/F	GS	APC	DOM%	DIS%	Sv%	LI	RAR	BPX	R$
19																																		
20																																		
21																																		
22	aa	1	0	31	38	8.87	2.21	6.88				13.0	21%	24%	4%							40%	58%									-18.7	67	-$15
23	LA *	4	0	94	130	4.39	1.30	3.83	0.58			14.4	0%	50%	50%	4%	25.0%	95.7	67	0	33	33%	69%	0%	0%	0	24			0	0.05	-0.6	128	$1
1st Half		2	0	48	72	4.81	1.42	4.93				13.6	9%	35%	26%							40%	70%	0%		0	0					-2.9	139	-$4
2nd Half		2	0	48	58	4.06	1.17	2.71	1.38			16.0	14%	31%	17%	4%	25.0%	95.7	67	0	33	25%	67%	0%	0%	0	24			0	0.05	1.6	119	$3
Proj		**2**	**0**	**44**	**60**	**3.45**	**1.07**	**2.64**	**1.07**			**23.2**	**9%**	**35%**	**27%**		**15.0%**		**47**	**23**	**30**	**30%**	**72%**	**17%**	**15%**	**7**						**4.7**	**188**	**$1**

Iglesias,Raisel

Age: 34	Th: R	Role: RP	Health: D	LIMA Plan: B
Ht: 6' 2"	Wt: 190	Type: Pwr/FB	PT/Exp: A	Rand Var: -3
			Consist: A	MM: 5531

Late start due to spring shoulder injury, but returned with typical skills intact. Minuscule ERA in 2nd half driven by S%, while SwK and K% took slight turns for the worse. xERA says he might be a notch below elite now, but Sv% shows he's still getting it done, and BPX track record says he's safe for at least another year.

Yr	Tm	W	Sv	IP	K	ERA	WHIP	xERA	xWHIP	vL+	vR+	BF/G	BB%	K%	K-BB%	xBB%	SwK	Vel	G	L	F	H%	S%	HR/F	xHR/F	GS	APC	DOM%	DIS%	Sv%	LI	RAR	BPX	R$
19	CIN	3	34	67	89	4.16	1.22	3.83	1.14	105	94	4.1	8%	32%	24%	6%	16.0%	95.5	30	26	44	33%	73%	17%	12%	0	17			85	1.54	2.8	160	$16
20	CIN	4	8	23	31	2.74	0.91	3.02	0.99	74	65	4.1	5%	34%	29%	5%	19.7%	96.2	42	23	36	31%	70%	5%	11%	0	16			80	1.79	4.9	210	$20
21	LAA	7	34	70	103	2.57	0.93	2.67	0.89	89	78	4.2	4%	38%	33%	4%	21.1%	96.4	39	22	39	31%	83%	18%	13%	0	16			87	1.43	14.6	234	$27
22	2 TM	2	17	62	78	2.47	0.97	3.13	1.01	85	78	3.7	6%	32%	26%	5%	17.2%	95.0	34	21	44	30%	78%	8%	13%	0	15			81	1.10	11.5	177	$13
23	ATL	5	33	56	68	2.75	1.19	3.55	1.11	99	80	4.0	6%	29%	23%	5%	16.8%	95.1	43	18	39	33%	83%	12%	11%	0	15			89	1.19	10.9	172	$18
1st Half		3	14	24	31	4.18	1.23	3.27	1.06	113	83	4.0	6%	31%	25%	6%	18.1%	94.8	44	21	35	35%	72%	18%	17%	0	15			88	1.27	0.4	194	$9
2nd Half		2	19	32	37	1.69	1.16	3.76	1.15	91	79	4.0	7%	28%	21%	4%	15.7%	95.3	42	16	41	32%	91%	9%	7%	0	15			90	1.13	10.4	157	$17
Proj		**5**	**34**	**65**	**85**	**3.05**	**1.06**	**2.93**	**1.02**	**94**	**79**	**3.8**	**6%**	**33%**	**27%**	**5%**	**16.5%**	**95.5**	**39**	**20**	**40**	**31%**	**78%**	**14%**	**12%**	**0**						**10.3**	**189**	**$20**

Imanaga,Shota

Age: 30	Th: L	Role: SP	Health: A	LIMA Plan: B+
Ht: 5' 10"	Wt: 176	Type:	PT/Exp: A	Rand Var: -2
			Consist: C	MM: 3203

Had 2.51 ERA over past three seasons in Japan with significant strikeout bump in 2023. Primary concern is that he's been homer-prone—served up the 2nd-most HR in league last year—so landing spot will be important. Upside is probably that of a solid mid-rotation starter, and could fulfill that promise right away.

Yr	Tm	W	Sv	IP	K	ERA	WHIP	xERA	xWHIP	vL+	vR+	BF/G	BB%	K%	K-BB%	xBB%	SwK	Vel	G	L	F	H%	S%	HR/F	xHR/F	GS	APC	DOM%	DIS%	Sv%	LI	RAR	BPX	R$
19	for	13	0	170	176	3.62	1.22	3.93				27.5	10%	26%	15%							26%	78%									18.6	79	$16
20	for	5	0	53	60	4.01	1.35	3.78				24.6	10%	27%	18%							34%	70%									2.9	122	$8
21	for	5	0	120	104	3.82	1.14	4.41				25.0	7%	22%	15%							25%	78%									6.6	69	$6
22	for	11	0	144	125	2.79	1.04	3.37				26.5	6%	22%	16%							24%	83%									20.8	97	$17
23	for	7	0	142	161	3.46	1.15	4.41				26.8	0%	0%	0%							31%	80%									15.2	147	$14
1st Half																																		
2nd Half																																		
Proj		**10**	**0**	**145**	**138**	**3.76**	**1.15**	**3.71**	**1.26**			**22.0**	**8%**	**24%**	**16%**				**44**	**20**	**36**	**27%**	**73%**	**15%**	**12%**	**26**						**10.1**	**111**	**$12**

Irvin,Cole

Age: 30	Th: L	Role: RP	Health: B	LIMA Plan: B
Ht: 6' 4"	Wt: 217	Type: Con	PT/Exp: A	Rand Var: -1
			Consist: B	MM: 2001

1-4, 4.42 ERA in 77 IP at BAL. Allowed 15 ER in first three starts and was sent to AAA for a couple of months. Split time between SP/RP upon return with marginal skills in both roles. Slight uptick in K% was nice and all, but low BB% is only standout skill, while recent xERA history says any bounce back will be a small one.

Yr	Tm	W	Sv	IP	K	ERA	WHIP	xERA	xWHIP	vL+	vR+	BF/G	BB%	K%	K-BB%	xBB%	SwK	Vel	G	L	F	H%	S%	HR/F	xHR/F	GS	APC	DOM%	DIS%	Sv%	LI	RAR	BPX	R$
19	PHI *	8	1	137	87	5.00	1.50	5.95	1.41	123	98	17.9	5%	15%	10%	6%	10.0%	89.8	34	31	34	34%	71%	16%	16%	3	40	33%	67%	100	0.57	-8.4	52	-$4
20	PHI	0	0	4	4	17.18	3.27	5.77		254	158	7.3	5%	18%	14%		7.3%	92.4	41	29	29	61%	45%	20%	23%	0	27			0	0.46	-5.8	146	-$13
21	OAK	10	0	178	125	4.24	1.33	4.90	1.30	106	98	24.0	5%	16%	11%	5%	9.6%	90.7	38	24	38	31%	71%	10%	10%	32	84	19%	44%			0.6	79	$2
22	OAK	9	0	181	128	3.98	1.16	4.34	1.23	92	102	24.7	5%	17%	12%	5%	9.8%	90.6	38	20	42	28%	70%	11%	13%	30	87	30%	40%			-0.2	91	$7
23	BAL *	7	0	127	90	4.66	1.36	5.07	1.27	94	102	16.2	6%	20%	14%	5%	10.0%	92.1	41	21	37	32%	69%	12%	16%	12	53	17%	42%	0	0.56	-5.2	65	-$2
1st Half		7	0	73	44	4.85	1.44	5.50	1.36	93	125	19.5	5%	14%	9%	6%	9.0%	91.7	30	27	43	32%	70%	11%	16%	7	63	0%	57%	0	0.68	-4.7	47	-$1
2nd Half		0	0	54	46	4.41	1.26	4.48	1.25	95	84	13.0	6%	20%	14%	5%	10.9%	92.5	50	17	33	31%	69%	14%	16%	5	47	40%	20%	0	0.49	-0.5	91	-$2
Proj		**4**	**0**	**80**	**57**	**4.41**	**1.32**	**4.33**	**1.28**	**106**	**105**	**14.1**	**5%**	**17%**	**12%**	**5%**	**9.9%**	**91.3**	**40**	**23**	**38**	**31%**	**71%**	**12%**	**14%**	**10**						**-0.8**	**89**	**-$3**

Irvin,Jake

Age: 27	Th: R	Role: SP	Health: A	LIMA Plan: C+
Ht: 6' 6"	Wt: 225	Type: Con	PT/Exp: D	Rand Var: 0
			Consist: B	MM: 1001

3-7, 4.61 ERA in 121 IP at WAS. Called up for debut in early May and held rotation spot the rest of the way. But poor SwK casts doubt he can even repeat the mediocre K%, and BB% went in wrong direction. Ceiling looks severely limited, and DIS% says even in deep leagues, you'll have to be careful when you use him.

Yr	Tm	W	Sv	IP	K	ERA	WHIP	xERA	xWHIP	vL+	vR+	BF/G	BB%	K%	K-BB%	xBB%	SwK	Vel	G	L	F	H%	S%	HR/F	xHR/F	GS	APC	DOM%	DIS%	Sv%	LI	RAR	BPX	R$
19																																		
20																																		
21																																		
22	aa	0	0	74	63	5.60	1.31	4.53				20.4	7%	21%	14%							31%	58%									-14.9	84	-$8
23	WAS *	5	0	144	115	4.84	1.45	5.07	1.47	115	92	21.2	10%	19%	8%	8%	7.3%	94.5	43	18	40	29%	71%	14%	14%	24	90	17%	46%			-9.0	45	-$6
1st Half		3	0	71	53	5.14	1.53	4.93	1.57	107	91	20.5	12%	17%	5%	9%	6.1%	93.7	42	17	42	30%	68%	8%	12%	10	86	20%	50%			-7.1	48	-$9
2nd Half		2	0	73	62	4.54	1.38	4.79	1.41	121	94	22.6	9%	20%	10%	8%	8.2%	95.0	44	18	38	28%	74%	18%	15%	14	92	14%	43%			-1.9	70	$0
Proj		**3**	**0**	**109**	**84**	**4.69**	**1.34**	**4.54**	**1.42**	**113**	**89**	**21.9**	**9%**	**19%**	**9%**	**9%**	**8.3%**	**94.5**	**43**	**18**	**40**	**28%**	**69%**	**13%**	**14%**	**21**						**-4.8**	**59**	**-$5**

BRIAN RUDD

Jameson,Drey

Age: 26	Th: R	Role: RP	Health: D	LIMA Plan:
Ht: 6' 0"	Wt: 165	Type:	PT/Exp: C	Rand Var:
			Consist: A	MM:

3-1, 3.32 ERA in 41 IP at ARI. Demoted to AAA amid pedestrian April, returned to multi-inning relief role before elbow injury in July. Showed ability to miss bats, but BB% spiked and mediocre xERA hardly budged. Eventually had Tommy John surgery in September, so check back in 2025.

Yr Tm	W	Sv	IP	K	ERA	WHIP	xERA	xWHIP	vL+	vR+	BF/G	BB%	K%	K-BB%	xBB%	SwK	Vel	G	L	F	H%	S%	HR/F	xHR/F	GS	APC	DOM%	DIS%	Sv%	LI	RAR	BPX	R$
19																																	
20																																	
21 aa	3	0	47	56	4.22	1.24	3.75				23.9	9%	29%	20%							32%	69%									0.3	121	-$2
22 ARI *	10	0	159	130	4.79	1.37	4.61	1.19	72	104	22.2	7%	20%	13%	6%	12.2%	95.3	56	23	21	33%	67%	14%	20%	4	92	25%	0%			-16.1	81	-$3
23 ARI *	7	1	69	56	4.11	1.43	4.59	1.43	96	109	14.6	10%	21%	11%	8%	13.2%	96.0	46	15	39	31%	73%	13%	20%	3	45	0%	67%	100	0.84	1.8	66	-$1
1st Half	7	1	66	54	4.03	1.40	4.34	1.44	87	109	14.6	10%	19%	10%	8%	13.7%	96.0	44	17	39	31%	73%	12%	20%	3	44	0%	67%	100	0.89	2.5	71	$5
2nd Half	0	0	3	2	6.00	2.00	4.99		184	124	14.0	7%	14%	7%	5%	7.3%	95.9	60	0	40	38%	80%	25%	18%	0	55			0	0.12	-0.6	73	-$8
Proj																																	

Jansen,Kenley

Age: 36	Th: R	Role: RP	Health: C	LIMA Plan: B+
Ht: 6' 5"	Wt: 265	Type: Pwr/xFB	PT/Exp: A	Rand Var: -3
			Consist: B	MM: 3430

One of the slowest to the plate in 2022, we surmised he might be affected by the pitch clock. Instead, he cruised right along, pumping strikes, and velocity surge/SwK say there's plenty left in this tank. But xERA and WHIP hint at decline, which could be clock-related or just Father Time. As long as FBs stay in the park, he's good bet to keep closing.

Yr Tm	W	Sv	IP	K	ERA	WHIP	xERA	xWHIP	vL+	vR+	BF/G	BB%	K%	K-BB%	xBB%	SwK	Vel	G	L	F	H%	S%	HR/F	xHR/F	GS	APC	DOM%	DIS%	Sv%	LI	RAR	BPX	R$
19 LA	5	33	63	80	3.71	1.06	3.79	1.11	83	91	4.2	6%	30%	24%	4%	16.3%	92.0	32	24	43	30%	71%	13%	11%	0	17			80	1.24	6.1	168	$19
20 LA	3	11	24	33	3.33	1.15	3.93	1.15	72	94	3.8	9%	32%	24%	5%	15.7%	92.4	25	25	50	32%	73%	7%	7%	0	17			85	1.39	3.4	150	$19
21 LA	4	38	69	86	2.22	1.04	3.93	1.33	76	61	4.0	13%	31%	18%	6%	15.8%	93.9	37	19	44	23%	81%	6%	7%	0	16			88	1.53	17.4	99	$25
22 ATL	5	41	64	85	3.38	1.05	3.54	1.10	100	75	4.0	8%	33%	24%	5%	12.9%	93.7	30	15	55	28%	73%	10%	8%	0	15			85	1.26	4.7	154	$22
23 BOS	3	29	45	52	3.63	1.28	4.57	1.25	83	104	3.7	9%	28%	19%	5%	13.8%	95.3	23	21	57	32%	75%	8%	8%	0	14			88	1.36	3.9	109	$11
1st Half	2	17	29	35	3.45	1.43	4.44	1.26	86	103	4.2	10%	28%	18%	5%	13.7%	95.4	30	22	48	37%	77%	5%	5%	0	16			85	1.43	3.1	117	$11
2nd Half	1	12	16	17	3.94	1.00	4.74	1.21	78	106	3.0	8%	27%	19%	5%	14.0%	95.2	8	18	74	22%	69%	11%	12%	0	12			92	1.25	0.8	93	$5
Proj	4	30	58	70	3.61	1.21	3.84	1.21	92	90	3.7	10%	30%	20%	5%	14.5%	93.9	29	20	51	31%	74%	9%	8%	0						5.1	121	$14

Javier,Cristian

Age: 27	Th: R	Role: SP	Health: A	LIMA Plan: A
Ht: 6' 1"	Wt: 213	Type: Pwr/xFB	PT/Exp: A	Rand Var: -1
			Consist: C	MM: 2305

Took major step back with mid-season stretch of eight PQS-DISasters in 11 starts. Fastball lost some zip, missed fewer bats, and K% crash allowed FB% tilt to morph into bigger HR problem. Did show signs of life in final month (40/11 K/BB), but forget about a full rebound and use 4.00 ERA as your baseline.

Yr Tm	W	Sv	IP	K	ERA	WHIP	xERA	xWHIP	vL+	vR+	BF/G	BB%	K%	K-BB%	xBB%	SwK	Vel	G	L	F	H%	S%	HR/F	xHR/F	GS	APC	DOM%	DIS%	Sv%	LI	RAR	BPX	R$
19 a/a	6	3	85	115	2.47	1.00	1.64				17.1	13%	35%	22%							22%	79%									21.3	144	$14
20 HOU	5	0	54	54	3.48	0.99	4.58	1.28	109	61	17.8	8%	25%	17%	9%	8.9%	92.3	29	19	52	20%	77%	15%	10%	10	74	0%	30%	0	0.70	6.5	99	$17
21 HOU	4	2	101	130	3.55	1.18	4.21	1.32	103	78	11.8	13%	31%	18%	11%	13.6%	93.6	28	24	49	25%	77%	14%	15%	9	50	44%	11%	50	1.01	8.9	95	$7
22 HOU	11	0	149	194	2.54	0.95	3.52	1.10	85	72	19.5	9%	33%	24%	8%	14.2%	93.9	26	17	57	24%	80%	9%	8%	25	85	24%	24%	0	0.73	26.1	144	$25
23 HOU	10	0	162	159	4.56	1.27	5.07	1.33	110	87	22.2	9%	23%	14%	9%	12.1%	92.8	26	19	56	28%	68%	10%	12%	31	93	10%	35%			-4.5	79	$6
1st Half	7	0	87	78	3.72	1.17	4.91	1.27	110	81	22.4	7%	22%	15%	8%	12.1%	92.6	26	20	54	28%	73%	8%	12%	16	92	13%	25%			6.5	90	$15
2nd Half	3	0	75	81	5.52	1.37	5.24	1.40	111	95	21.9	11%	25%	13%	10%	12.1%	93.0	25	18	57	28%	64%	12%	12%	15	94	7%	47%			-11.0	65	$0
Proj	10	0	174	183	3.96	1.24	4.35	1.32	110	85	21.9	10%	26%	16%	10%	12.5%	93.1	26	20	54	27%	74%	11%	12%	32						7.8	82	$10

Jax,Griffin

Age: 29	Th: R	Role: RP	Health: A	LIMA Plan: A+
Ht: 6' 2"	Wt: 195	Type:	PT/Exp: B	Rand Var: 0
			Consist: C	MM: 4211

Skills looked strong and steady again, as 1st/2nd half ERA spread was just HR/F luck swinging from good to bad. Higher fastball velocity and sweeper usage led to K% spike without sacrificing walks, and it came with elite GB%. Bank on another year of helpful ratios with an outside shot at regular save opps.

Yr Tm	W	Sv	IP	K	ERA	WHIP	xERA	xWHIP	vL+	vR+	BF/G	BB%	K%	K-BB%	xBB%	SwK	Vel	G	L	F	H%	S%	HR/F	xHR/F	GS	APC	DOM%	DIS%	Sv%	LI	RAR	BPX	R$
19 a/a	5	0	128	75	4.06	1.40	4.49				23.5	6%	14%	8%							33%	71%									7.0	67	$0
20																																	
21 MIN *	8	0	124	93	5.82	1.41	5.48	1.38	117	115	20.2	9%	18%	9%	7%	9.9%	92.7	32	16	52	29%	63%	17%	16%	14	77	0%	57%	0	0.65	-23.9	31	-$9
22 MIN	7	1	72	78	3.36	1.05	3.30	1.14	85	86	4.5	7%	27%	20%	5%	13.7%	95.5	47	16	37	28%	71%	10%	12%	0	18			14	1.05	5.4	146	$6
23 MIN	6	4	65	68	3.86	1.18	3.49	1.21	94	82	3.9	7%	25%	18%	5%	12.1%	96.5	56	15	29	31%	68%	9%	8%	0	15			36	1.23	3.8	148	$5
1st Half	4	1	36	35	3.00	1.08	3.50	1.23	73	72	3.8	7%	24%	17%	6%	11.1%	96.2	56	15	29	30%	69%	0%	3%	0	14			20	1.16	5.9	140	$5
2nd Half	2	3	29	33	4.91	1.30	3.49	1.19	119	95	3.9	7%	26%	19%	5%	13.3%	96.7	55	15	30	33%	67%	20%	13%	0	15			50	1.30	-2.1	159	$0
Proj	6	2	73	73	3.56	1.20	3.53	1.19	101	91	5.3	7%	25%	18%	6%	12.5%	95.4	48	15	36	31%	75%	12%	11%	0						6.8	137	$4

Jiménez,Dany

Age: 30	Th: R	Role: RP	Health: F	LIMA Plan: C+
Ht: 6' 1"	Wt: 182	Type: Pwr/xFB	PT/Exp: C	Rand Var: -5
			Consist: B	MM: 1321

Secured Opening Day save, but was soon out with shoulder injury that wiped most of season. Results were solid upon Aug return, but H% luck was on his side, whiffs disappeared, and BB% remained a major issue. Even if he finds himself back in closer role, BPX history and all those walks say he's probably not long for the job.

Yr Tm	W	Sv	IP	K	ERA	WHIP	xERA	xWHIP	vL+	vR+	BF/G	BB%	K%	K-BB%	xBB%	SwK	Vel	G	L	F	H%	S%	HR/F	xHR/F	GS	APC	DOM%	DIS%	Sv%	LI	RAR	BPX	R$
19 aa	2	6	35	37	2.82	1.25	4.04				5.7	10%	26%	16%							28%	86%									7.3	81	$2
20 SF	0	0	1	1	6.75	3.00	17.33		92	86	4.0	38%	13%	-25%		8.1%	93.1	50	0	50	27%	75%	0%	9%	0	19			0	0.22	-0.4	-449	-$8
21 aaa	3	3	46	55	3.24	1.49	4.71				5.1	15%	28%	13%							30%	85%									5.8	77	-$1
22 OAK	3	11	34	34	3.41	1.19	4.47	1.43	92	66	4.3	12%	23%	11%	8%	14.5%	94.0	41	15	44	25%	72%	5%	7%	0	16			79	1.45	2.4	57	$3
23 OAK	0	1	23	21	3.47	1.07	5.40	1.61	59	87	3.8	15%	22%	7%	12%	10.3%	93.3	28	16	56	15%	73%	9%	10%	1	16	0%	0%	50	1.05	2.5	7	-$3
1st Half	0	1	7	4	5.40	1.50	7.77	2.10	34	146	4.3	20%	13%	-7%	12%	7.7%	92.6	35	10	55	12%	75%	18%	19%	0	19			50	1.34	-0.9	-122	-$11
2nd Half	0	0	17	17	2.70	0.90	4.59	1.41	69	59	3.6	13%	27%	14%	12%	11.6%	93.7	24	19	57	17%	71%	5%	5%	1	15	0%	0%	0	0.94	3.4	57	-$3
Proj	3	25	73	76	4.24	1.35	4.55	1.40	112	95	4.5	12%	25%	13%	11%	12.7%	93.8	31	17	52	29%	72%	9%	8%	0						0.8	66	$8

Jiménez,Joe

Age: 29	Th: R	Role: RP	Health: B	LIMA Plan: A+
Ht: 6' 3"	Wt: 277	Type: Pwr/xFB	PT/Exp: C	Rand Var: -3
			Consist: C	MM: 4510

Early results were strong despite 1st half K-BB% taking a step back. Returned to peak form in 2nd half per BPX, when SwK and K% were at all-time highs. xERA history shows he's not without risk, but most signs point to strong ratios, and if late skills hold up, still has a realistic shot at saves.

Yr Tm	W	Sv	IP	K	ERA	WHIP	xERA	xWHIP	vL+	vR+	BF/G	BB%	K%	K-BB%	xBB%	SwK	Vel	G	L	F	H%	S%	HR/F	xHR/F	GS	APC	DOM%	DIS%	Sv%	LI	RAR	BPX	R$
19 DET	4	9	60	82	4.37	1.32	4.11	1.19	107	104	3.9	9%	32%	23%	5%	15.2%	95.2	29	22	49	33%	76%	18%	16%	0	16			64	1.08	1.0	148	$4
20 DET	1	5	23	22	7.15	1.37	4.69	1.23	143	115	4.0	6%	22%	16%	6%	13.1%	94.3	31	26	43	30%	54%	24%	18%	0	16			83	0.92	-7.5	115	-$2
21 DET	6	1	45	57	5.96	1.52	5.26	1.59	106	99	4.0	17%	27%	10%	10%	14.3%	94.7	34	13	53	28%	62%	10%	11%	0	17			50	0.61	-9.5	31	-$5
22 DET	3	2	57	77	3.49	1.09	3.12	0.98	98	78	3.7	6%	33%	28%	4%	15.0%	95.8	33	22	45	35%	69%	6%	10%	0	15			50	0.72	3.3	193	$3
23 ATL	0	0	56	73	3.04	1.15	3.82	1.07	97	95	4.0	6%	31%	25%	5%	15.6%	95.3	28	24	48	33%	82%	13%	13%	0	16			0	0.69	9.0	175	$1
1st Half	0	0	28	32	3.25	1.23	4.69	1.20	78	110	4.1	8%	27%	19%	6%	14.7%	95.0	22	20	58	31%	80%	9%	11%	0	16			0	0.53	3.7	123	-$5
2nd Half	0	0	29	41	2.83	1.08	3.01	0.94	114	80	4.0	4%	34%	30%	5%	16.5%	95.7	34	28	38	35%	85%	19%	16%	0	15			0	0.85	5.3	227	$0
Proj	3	2	58	76	3.79	1.20	3.40	1.10	100	91	3.7	8%	33%	25%	6%	15.2%	95.3	31	21	48	33%	73%	11%	13%	0						3.8	159	$2

Johnson,Pierce

Age: 33	Th: R	Role: RP	Health: F	LIMA Plan: A+
Ht: 6' 2"	Wt: 202	Type: Pwr	PT/Exp: C	Rand Var: +4
			Consist: B	MM: 5510

Started season in COL and delivered saves, but they came with inflated ERA/WHIP. Save opps dried up after July trade to ATL, but SwK soared and he reclaimed GB tilt. Walks are an ongoing concern (though xBB% disagrees), but if he gets another shot at closing, he's an intriguing deep league end-gamer due for better H% fortune.

Yr Tm	W	Sv	IP	K	ERA	WHIP	xERA	xWHIP	vL+	vR+	BF/G	BB%	K%	K-BB%	xBB%	SwK	Vel	G	L	F	H%	S%	HR/F	xHR/F	GS	APC	DOM%	DIS%	Sv%	LI	RAR	BPX	R$
19 for	2	0	59	86	1.71	0.89	1.50				3.8	7%	39%	32%							29%	84%									20.4	213	$9
20 SD	3	0	20	27	2.70	1.20	3.73	1.22	49	105	3.3	11%	34%	23%	7%	16.8%	96.4	30	30	41	31%	82%	11%	11%	0	13			0	0.83	4.3	133	$4
21 SD	3	0	59	77	3.22	1.26	3.87	1.24	97	87	3.9	11%	32%	20%	8%	13.3%	95.5	34	22	43	32%	78%	10%	11%	2	17	0%	100%	0	0.80	7.6	124	$1
22 SD	1	0	14	21	5.02	1.53	3.00	1.26	79	109	4.3	13%	33%	20%	8%	10.7%	94.9	54	20	26	40%	67%	11%	3%	0	19			0	0.86	-1.9	147	-$5
23 2 NL	2	13	63	90	4.02	1.48	3.64	1.23	120	96	4.1	11%	32%	22%	6%	14.8%	96.0	37	28	35	38%	78%	18%	13%	0	16			81	0.95	2.4	147	$2
1st Half	1	13	34	49	6.35	1.74	4.50	1.33	122	121	4.3	13%	31%	18%	8%	13.2%	96.0	27	29	44	41%	67%	18%	13%	0	17			87	0.99	-8.5	107	-$2
2nd Half	1	0	29	41	1.26	1.19	2.61	1.09	117	68	3.9	9%	35%	26%	4%	17.1%	96.0	52	26	23	35%	97%	20%	12%	0	15			0	0.90	10.9	199	$3
Proj	4	2	58	77	3.24	1.17	3.13	1.22	95	75	3.8	11%	33%	22%	6%	14.9%	95.9	40	26	34	30%	74%	12%	11%	0						7.8	138	$4

BRIAN RUDD

Joyce,Ben

Age: 23	Th: R	Role RP	Health C	LIMA Plan C
Ht: 6' 5"	Wt: 225	Type Pwr/FB	PT/Exp F	Rand Var 0
			Consist F	MM 1310

1-1, 5.40 ERA in 10 IP at LAA. Called up in May, but hand/elbow injury after five games cost him three months. Pumps extreme heat with four-seamer, yet it hardly generates whiffs (9.5% SwK) and control struggles from minors (13% career BB%) carried over in tiny sample. Potential high-leverage RP; needs to clear hurdles to get there.

Yr Tm	W	Sv	IP	K	ERA	WHIP	xERA	xWHIP	vL+	vR+	BF/G	BB%	K%	K-BB%	xBB%	SwK	Vel	G	L	F	H%	S%	HR/F	xHR/F	GS	APC	DOM%	DIS%	Sv%	LI	RAR	BPX	R$
19																																	
20																																	
21																																	
22																																	
23 LAA *	1	4	27	31	4.89	1.40	3.08	1.84	60	125	4.4	19%	21%	2%	11%	10.4%	101.0	46	11	43	24%	65%	8%	10%	0	17			80	0.85	-1.9	100	-$4
1st Half	1	4	21	26	4.57	1.37	3.15	1.60	54	156	4.7	18%	29%	11%	7%	10.2%	101.6	50	17	33	24%	68%	25%	13%	0	18			80	0.73	-0.6	103	-$4
2nd Half	0	0	6	5	6.00	1.50	6.26		62	91	3.9	19%	19%	0%	12%	10.5%	100.4	44	6	50	25%	56%	0%	8%	0	16			0	0.94	-1.2	-52	-$8
Proj	2	5	58	64	4.20	1.49	4.70	1.57			5.3	16%	26%	10%		10.0%		40	15	45	30%	73%	7%	8%	0						0.9	36	-$2

Junis,Jakob

Age: 31	Th: R	Role RP	Health D	LIMA Plan A+
Ht: 6' 3"	Wt: 220	Type	PT/Exp B	Rand Var +1
			Consist C	MM 3201

Switched to multi-inning relief role after starting majority of games in 2022. Career-best K-BB% backed by another solid walk rate, velocity uptick, and more whiffs likely due to more sliders (63% usage; 14.6% SwK). Recent BPX shows quality skills are here, but needs better role and more volume to become fantasy viable.

Yr Tm	W	Sv	IP	K	ERA	WHIP	xERA	xWHIP	vL+	vR+	BF/G	BB%	K%	K-BB%	xBB%	SwK	Vel	G	L	F	H%	S%	HR/F	xHR/F	GS	APC	DOM%	DIS%	Sv%	LI	RAR	BPX	R$
19 KC	9	0	175	164	5.24	1.43	4.65	1.33	110	104	24.9	8%	21%	14%	8%	10.0%	91.5	42	23	35	33%	68%	17%	18%	31	94	23%	29%			-15.8	99	-$3
20 KC	0	0	25	19	6.39	1.62	4.88	1.29	141	114	14.3	5%	17%	11%	6%	9.4%	91.0	45	23	32	35%	68%	25%	22%	6	49	0%	83%	0	0.79	-6.1	98	-$12
21 KC *	2	0	59	54	5.61	1.55	6.16	1.21	117	95	11.6	8%	21%	13%	7%	11.0%	90.9	42	22	37	35%	68%	17%	19%	6	39	33%	33%	0	0.60	-9.7	53	-$9
22 SF	5	0	112	98	4.42	1.29	3.87	1.19	122	94	20.8	5%	21%	15%	6%	9.7%	91.9	43	24	33	33%	68%	11%	13%	17	78	12%	35%	0	0.67	-6.2	120	-$2
23 SF	4	1	86	96	3.87	1.29	3.74	1.14	109	103	9.2	6%	26%	21%	5%	11.7%	93.8	43	20	37	35%	75%	13%	13%	4	35	25%	25%	100	0.91	4.9	160	$2
1st Half	3	1	47	53	4.63	1.48	3.99	1.23	111	121	9.3	8%	26%	18%	6%	11.0%	93.9	42	20	37	36%	75%	18%	13%	0	35			100	0.92	-1.7	137	-$4
2nd Half	1	0	39	43	2.97	1.07	3.44	1.03	107	81	9.0	3%	27%	23%	5%	12.6%	93.5	44	19	37	33%	74%	7%	13%	4	34	25%	25%	0	0.89	6.6	190	$3
Proj	4	0	87	88	3.97	1.31	3.67	1.18	114	97	11.0	6%	24%	18%	6%	11.2%	92.5	43	21	36	33%	74%	14%	15%	3						3.8	136	$0

Kahnle,Tommy

Age: 34	Th: R	Role RP	Health F	LIMA Plan A+
Ht: 6' 1"	Wt: 230	Type Pwr/GB	PT/Exp D	Rand Var -5
			Consist D	MM 5510

Biceps injury pushed debut to June after years-long Tommy John battle, then finished year back on IL (shoulder). Fortunate H%, S% hid underlying control issues, yet K% held firm due to deadly change-up (16.8% SwK) used over 75% of the time. Potential middle-relief strikeout source, but health, BB% remain major obstacles.

Yr Tm	W	Sv	IP	K	ERA	WHIP	xERA	xWHIP	vL+	vR+	BF/G	BB%	K%	K-BB%	xBB%	SwK	Vel	G	L	F	H%	S%	HR/F	xHR/F	GS	APC	DOM%	DIS%	Sv%	LI	RAR	BPX	R$
19 NYY	3	0	61	88	3.67	1.06	2.83	1.07	89	79	3.4	8%	35%	27%	6%	18.2%	96.5	50	21	28	30%	71%	23%	18%	0	14			0	1.03	6.3	197	$4
20 NYY	0	0	1	3	0.00	2.00	0.00		207	33	6.0	17%	50%	33%		30.0%	97.6	100	0	0	122%	100%	0%		0	20			0	1.86	0.5	363	-$6
21																																	
22 LA	0	1	13	14	2.84	0.63	2.17	1.05	90	44	3.5	7%	30%	24%	5%	17.2%	95.7	68	4	28	12%	67%	29%	17%	0	13			100	0.88	1.8	185	-$3
23 NYY	1	2	41	48	2.66	1.11	3.68	1.32	86	80	3.9	12%	29%	18%	8%	15.6%	95.1	49	15	36	24%	83%	14%	10%	0	16			50	1.08	8.4	117	$2
1st Half	0	1	12	13	0.00	0.51	3.13	1.01	59	28	3.5	5%	31%	26%	6%	15.3%	94.4	42	12	46	17%	100%	0%	6%	0	15			100	0.93	6.2	180	-$2
2nd Half	1	1	29	35	3.72	1.34	3.91	1.43	96	99	4.1	14%	28%	15%	8%	15.6%	95.2	51	16	33	27%	79%	22%	12%	0	17			33	1.14	2.2	93	-$1
Proj	2	5	44	56	3.70	1.12	2.85	1.15	94	88	3.6	9%	33%	24%	8%	16.6%	95.7	51	18	31	28%	74%	23%	14%	0						3.4	169	$2

Kaprielian,James

Age: 30	Th: R	Role SP	Health F	LIMA Plan C+
Ht: 6' 3"	Wt: 225	Type /xFB	PT/Exp A	Rand Var +3
			Consist B	MM 1100

Rough start (23 ER in 16 IP) sent him to AAA in April; bounced back and forth before shoulder surgery in August. Velocity drop was likely related to injury, yet posted another double-digit BB% and strikeout skills were subpar yet again. xERA/xWHIP history, health issues make him a stay-away on draft day.

Yr Tm	W	Sv	IP	K	ERA	WHIP	xERA	xWHIP	vL+	vR+	BF/G	BB%	K%	K-BB%	xBB%	SwK	Vel	G	L	F	H%	S%	HR/F	xHR/F	GS	APC	DOM%	DIS%	Sv%	LI	RAR	BPX	R$
19 a/a	2	0	33	26	2.03	1.11	2.86				16.3	6%	20%	14%							28%	85%									10.2	108	$1
20 OAK	0	0	4	4	7.36	1.64	6.11		207	63	8.5	12%	24%	12%		15.5%	95.0	36	0	64	24%	75%	29%	33%	0	36			0	0.44	-1.3	66	-$8
21 OAK	8	0	119	123	4.07	1.22	4.48	1.26	119	80	20.9	8%	25%	16%	8%	11.6%	93.0	35	18	47	29%	72%	12%	13%	21	84	14%	33%	0	0.72	2.8	106	$5
22 OAK	5	0	134	98	4.23	1.34	5.02	1.47	100	109	22.2	10%	17%	7%	8%	9.8%	94.1	38	19	44	27%	71%	9%	11%	26	86	8%	42%			-4.3	30	-$3
23 OAK	2	0	61	57	6.34	1.59	5.60	1.48	118	106	20.0	11%	20%	9%	6%	11.8%	92.2	30	20	50	33%	61%	10%	11%	11	78	18%	55%	0	0.78	-15.1	40	-$12
1st Half	2	0	61	57	6.34	1.59	5.60	1.48	119	106	20.0	11%	20%	9%	6%	11.8%	92.2	30	20	50	33%	61%	10%	11%	11	78	18%	55%	0	0.78	-15.1	41	-$16
2nd Half																																	
Proj	2	0	44	37	4.98	1.42	4.71	1.39	119	108	21.6	9%	20%	11%	8%	11.2%	93.0	34	19	47	31%	68%	11%	11%	9						-3.5	61	-$6

Karinchak,James

Age: 28	Th: R	Role RP	Health D	LIMA Plan A+
Ht: 6' 3"	Wt: 215	Type Pwr/xFB	PT/Exp C	Rand Var -1
			Consist A	MM 3400

2-5, 4.15 ERA in 39 IP at CLE. One of the more heavily-used RP through May, but was optioned and recalled multiple times from there. Chronic control problems mixed with concerning decline in strikeout skills (SwK) and growing FB% tilt. There's bounceback potential given 2019-20 BPX, but that peak is quickly fading in the rearview.

Yr Tm	W	Sv	IP	K	ERA	WHIP	xERA	xWHIP	vL+	vR+	BF/G	BB%	K%	K-BB%	xBB%	SwK	Vel	G	L	F	H%	S%	HR/F	xHR/F	GS	APC	DOM%	DIS%	Sv%	LI	RAR	BPX	R$
19 CLE *	1	8	33	63	3.64	1.22	2.69		23	85	4.2	13%	47%	33%		16.0%	97.1	38	31	31	39%	71%	0%	9%	0	19			100	0.09	3.6	185	$3
20 CLE	1	1	27	53	2.67	1.11	2.70	1.09	81	59	4.0	15%	49%	34%	9%	17.9%	95.5	23	31	46	36%	76%	6%	7%	0	17			25	1.01	6.0	198	$7
21 CLE	7	11	55	78	4.07	1.21	3.76	1.31	79	98	3.9	14%	33%	20%	10%	13.5%	95.9	39	20	40	25%	72%	18%	13%	0	17			69	1.43	1.4	115	$7
22 CLE	2	3	39	62	2.08	1.10	3.25	1.17	66	80	4.2	13%	39%	26%	11%	12.9%	95.2	25	24	51	29%	83%	5%	7%	0	19			75	0.85	9.1	143	$3
23 CLE *	2	5	63	84	3.69	1.30	3.16	1.51	113	78	3.8	16%	30%	14%	10%	11.3%	94.8	29	17	54	26%	75%	13%	11%	0	17			71	1.10	5.0	115	$2
1st Half	2	1	34	47	3.79	1.24	3.61	1.44	114	83	3.6	16%	33%	17%	10%	11.7%	95.1	28	16	57	19%	79%	18%	13%	0	16			33	1.28	2.3	95	$0
2nd Half	0	4	29	37	3.58	1.37	2.65	1.47	112	68	4.1	15%	30%	15%	12%	10.5%	94.2	31	21	48	32%	71%	0%	8%	0	20			100	0.61	2.7	138	-$1
Proj	3	0	51	65	3.55	1.21	3.93	1.37	90	86	3.9	14%	32%	18%	11%	12.4%	95.3	29	19	52	26%	73%	9%	11%	0						4.8	85	$0

Keller,Brad

Age: 28	Th: R	Role RP	Health F	LIMA Plan D
Ht: 6' 5"	Wt: 255	Type Pwr/GB	PT/Exp A	Rand Var -1
			Consist B	MM 0000

3-4, 4.57 ERA in 45 IP at KC. Struggled to begin season, shoulder issues kept him in minors after May. Maybe the injury drove career-worst walk rate, subsequent xBB% spike, and more walks than Ks; but still has shaky K-BB% baseline. Introduced new curveball (20% usage, 14.6% SwK), but not enough to warrant intrigue.

Yr Tm	W	Sv	IP	K	ERA	WHIP	xERA	xWHIP	vL+	vR+	BF/G	BB%	K%	K-BB%	xBB%	SwK	Vel	G	L	F	H%	S%	HR/F	xHR/F	GS	APC	DOM%	DIS%	Sv%	LI	RAR	BPX	R$
19 KC	7	0	165	122	4.19	1.35	4.92	1.51	95	94	25.3	10%	17%	7%	8%	8.6%	93.4	50	21	29	29%	70%	10%	13%	28	97	21%	36%			6.4	49	$3
20 KC	5	0	55	35	2.47	1.02	4.26	1.41	79	56	23.9	8%	16%	8%	8%	8.6%	92.8	53	23	25	24%	76%	5%	12%	9	95	44%	22%			13.4	67	$19
21 KC	8	0	134	120	5.39	1.66	4.74	1.44	115	110	23.6	10%	20%	9%	9%	9.5%	93.9	48	23	29	35%	70%	15%	22%	26	90	23%	54%			-18.5	60	-$13
22 KC	6	1	140	102	5.09	1.50	4.46	1.43	106	112	17.6	9%	17%	7%	8%	10.1%	94.1	52	18	30	32%	68%	13%	14%	22	65	14%	55%	100	0.63	-19.3	54	-$10
23 KC *	5	0	65	40	6.38	2.09	6.00	2.14	108	107	12.2	21%	15%	-7%	12%	8.2%	93.2	58	14	28	29%	69%	8%	14%	9	80	11%	33%	0	0.64	-16.3	31	-$18
1st Half	3	0	46	31	4.51	1.92	5.22	2.19	108	107	20.0	22%	14%	-7%	12%	8.3%	93.1	57	14	28	28%	76%	8%	15%	9	93	11%	33%			-1.0	44	-$13
2nd Half	2	0	20	9	9.83	2.21	6.72	2.56	90	113	6.9	26%	10%	-16%	12%	6.7%	94.3	80	0	20	29%	53%	0%	2%	0	23			0	0.05	-13.9	7	-$14
Proj	4	0	58	38	5.78	1.79	5.81	1.87	110	108	12.5	17%	14%	-2%	11%	8.9%	93.4	53	19	28	30%	68%	11%	15%	5						-10.4	-54	-$12

Keller,Mitch

Age: 28	Th: R	Role SP	Health A	LIMA Plan B+
Ht: 6' 2"	Wt: 220	Type Pwr	PT/Exp A	Rand Var 0
			Consist C	MM 3205

Broke out in 1st half, though Ks and GBs fell back and luck factors were unkind in final months. Pitch mix change (new cutter, fewer four-seamers and curves) led to SwK uptick and he threw more strikes, lending credence to BB% gains. Solid overall skill growth makes him a decent mid-rotation arm, assuming volume repeats.

Yr Tm	W	Sv	IP	K	ERA	WHIP	xERA	xWHIP	vL+	vR+	BF/G	BB%	K%	K-BB%	xBB%	SwK	Vel	G	L	F	H%	S%	HR/F	xHR/F	GS	APC	DOM%	DIS%	Sv%	LI	RAR	BPX	R$
19 PIT *	8	0	153	166	5.24	1.53	5.13	1.17	130	121	22.2	8%	25%	17%	6%	12.4%	95.4	39	29	32	38%	66%	13%	9%	11	85	9%	27%			-13.8	102	-$5
20 PIT	1	0	22	16	2.91	1.25	6.24	2.02	112	61	17.4	21%	18%	-2%	12%	7.8%	94.0	44	8	48	10%	87%	16%	20%	5	77	20%	40%			4.1	-68	-$1
21 PIT *	6	0	129	123	5.59	1.74	5.92	1.45	124	114	18.9	11%	21%	10%	8%	8.9%	93.9	40	26	34	38%	68%	9%	11%	23	81	4%	48%			-21.0	68	-$17
22 PIT	5	0	159	138	3.91	1.40	3.93	1.34	107	100	22.2	9%	20%	11%	8%	9.1%	95.1	49	22	29	32%	74%	10%	12%	29	86	21%	41%	0	0.77	1.2	84	-$1
23 PIT	13	0	194	210	4.21	1.25	3.76	1.19	105	88	25.8	7%	25%	18%	6%	10.2%	94.6	44	22	34	32%	70%	14%	13%	32	98	28%	28%			2.8	144	$13
1st Half	9	0	105	118	3.34	1.10	3.41	1.15	94	78	25.4	6%	27%	21%	5%	9.3%	95.0	48	20	32	30%	73%	11%	12%	17	99	41%	24%			12.8	161	$28
2nd Half	4	0	89	92	5.24	1.41	4.19	1.24	117	102	26.2	7%	23%	17%	6%	11.1%	94.2	39	25	36	34%	67%	16%	14%	15	96	13%	33%			-10.0	125	$2
Proj	10	0	189	194	3.98	1.28	3.69	1.26	101	90	21.4	9%	25%	16%	7%	10.0%	94.5	43	24	33	31%	72%	13%	12%	36						8.0	113	$9

CORBIN YOUNG

Kelly,Kevin

Age: 26 Th: R Role: RP
Ht: 6' 2" Wt: 200 Type: Con
Health: B PT/Exp: D Consist: D
LIMA Plan: A Rand Var: -4 MM: 4101

Rule-5 pick was effective cog in seemingly endless TAM RP assembly line, but skills say "not so fast". Mega HR/F luck drove sizable wedge between ERA and xERA, while lack of whiffs says underwhelming K% is here to stay. Combo of groundballs and control keep him relevant in middle relief, but unlikely to ascend much past that.

Yr	Tm	W	Sv	IP	K	ERA	WHIP	xERA	xWHIP	vL+	vR+	BF/G	BB%	K%	K-BB%	xBB%	SwK	Vel	G	L	F	H%	S%	HR/F	xHR/F	GS	APC	DOM%	DIS%	Sv%	LI	RAR	BPX	R$
19																																		
20																																		
21																																		
22	a/a	5	4	58	62	1.95	1.11	2.17				4.8	9%	27%	18%							30%	82%									14.5	144	$7
23	TAM	5	1	67	56	3.09	1.01	3.90	1.23	88	76	4.8	5%	20%	15%	6%	9.6%	90.7	48	19	33	28%	68%	3%	5%	0	19			50	1.11	10.3	120	$7
1st Half		4	1	39	30	2.79	1.09	3.99	1.30	87	81	4.7	6%	19%	13%	8%	9.3%	90.7	48	22	30	29%	71%	0%	2%	0	18			50	1.18	7.3	100	$5
2nd Half		1	0	28	26	3.49	0.92	3.78	1.15	89	70	5.1	4%	22%	18%	4%	10.0%	90.6	48	16	37	26%	63%	7%	7%	0	20			0	1.01	2.9	148	$0
Proj		**4**	**0**	**65**	**56**	**3.50**	**1.08**	**3.57**	**1.20**	**104**	**84**	**4.9**	**6%**	**22%**	**16%**	**6%**	**9.7%**	**90.6**	**48**	**18**	**34**	**28%**	**70%**	**10%**	**5%**	**0**						**6.6**	**124**	**$3**

Kelly,Merrill

Age: 35 Th: R Role: SP
Ht: 6' 2" Wt: 202 Type:
Health: C PT/Exp: A Consist: A
LIMA Plan: B Rand Var: -1 MM: 3205

Near-identical repeat to 2022 breakout, save for three missed starts (calf). This version came with more strikeouts as SwK% reached new heights, and xBB% tempers concerns over the bb% spike. Hard to see another step up—xERA continues to hint at potential pullback—but bankable volume makes him a dependable mid-rotation stabilizer.

Yr	Tm	W	Sv	IP	K	ERA	WHIP	xERA	xWHIP	vL+	vR+	BF/G	BB%	K%	K-BB%	xBB%	SwK	Vel	G	L	F	H%	S%	HR/F	xHR/F	GS	APC	DOM%	DIS%	Sv%	LI	RAR	BPX	R$
19	ARI	13	0	183	158	4.42	1.31	4.69	1.34	101	101	24.3	7%	20%	13%	7%	10.1%	91.9	42	22	36	30%	71%	15%	19%	32	93	22%	41%			2.0	92	$7
20	ARI	3	0	31	29	2.59	0.99	3.91	1.13	73	99	25.0	4%	23%	19%	6%	10.1%	92.1	46	18	37	26%	85%	15%	17%	5	95	40%	40%			7.2	153	$9
21	ARI	7	0	158	130	4.44	1.29	4.36	1.26	90	111	24.7	6%	19%	13%	6%	9.5%	91.8	44	22	34	31%	69%	13%	12%	27	90	22%	26%			-3.5	101	$1
22	ARI	13	0	200	177	3.37	1.14	3.88	1.25	103	85	24.4	8%	22%	14%	6%	10.4%	92.7	43	19	38	27%	74%	10%	12%	33	93	39%	27%			14.8	99	$17
23	ARI	12	0	178	187	3.29	1.19	3.83	1.30	92	90	24.1	10%	26%	16%	7%	12.5%	92.3	45	21	34	28%	77%	13%	12%	30	94	23%	20%			22.8	111	$20
1st Half		9	0	95	98	3.22	1.14	3.77	1.31	83	96	23.8	10%	26%	16%	8%	12.8%	92.6	45	22	33	26%	76%	13%	14%	16	94	25%	13%			13.0	108	$24
2nd Half		3	0	83	89	3.38	1.26	3.89	1.29	104	85	24.4	9%	26%	17%	6%	12.0%	92.0	45	19	35	30%	78%	13%	10%	14	93	21%	29%			9.8	117	$11
Proj		**12**	**0**	**181**	**174**	**3.53**	**1.20**	**3.72**	**1.26**	**94**	**95**	**23.9**	**8%**	**24%**	**16%**	**7%**	**11.2%**	**92.2**	**44**	**20**	**35**	**29%**	**75%**	**13%**	**13%**	**30**						**17.8**	**112**	**$16**

Kershaw,Clayton

Age: 36 Th: L Role: SP
Ht: 6' 4" Wt: 225 Type:
Health: F PT/Exp: A Consist: A
LIMA Plan: C+ Rand Var: -5 MM: 3200

Shoulder woes sidelined him for 6 weeks during the summer leading to November surgery that will sideline him into next summer. Vintage 1st half with elite ratios, but that changed after July IL stint. ERA/WHIP held but velocity sunk, whiffs/Ks tanked, and walk rate spiked. Prime fodder for keeper/dynasty rebuild speculation.

Yr	Tm	W	Sv	IP	K	ERA	WHIP	xERA	xWHIP	vL+	vR+	BF/G	BB%	K%	K-BB%	xBB%	SwK	Vel	G	L	F	H%	S%	HR/F	xHR/F	GS	APC	DOM%	DIS%	Sv%	LI	RAR	BPX	R$
19	LA	16	0	178	189	3.03	1.04	3.55	1.15	84	90	24.3	6%	27%	21%	5%	13.7%	90.4	48	19	33	27%	80%	19%	16%	28	92	50%	14%	0	0.77	32.5	154	$27
20	LA	6	0	58	62	2.16	0.84	3.07	1.02	87	77	22.1	4%	28%	24%	5%	13.0%	91.6	53	16	31	24%	85%	17%	19%	10	89	60%	10%			16.5	192	$30
21	LA	10	0	122	144	3.55	1.02	3.06	1.01	61	95	22.2	4%	30%	25%	6%	17.1%	90.7	49	18	33	31%	70%	15%	15%	22	82	50%	23%			10.7	194	$15
22	LA	12	0	126	137	2.28	0.94	2.99	1.04	88	76	22.4	5%	28%	23%	5%	14.4%	90.8	47	19	33	28%	80%	9%	7%	22	84	27%	9%			26.3	172	$22
23	LA	13	0	132	137	2.46	1.06	3.56	1.22	67	92	21.8	8%	26%	19%	6%	13.6%	90.8	48	19	33	26%	86%	17%	15%	24	85	25%	21%			30.4	135	$23
1st Half		10	0	95	105	2.55	1.05	3.36	1.14	62	90	23.7	6%	28%	21%	5%	14.6%	91.3	47	20	33	28%	83%	15%	15%	16	92	38%	19%			21.0	161	$33
2nd Half		3	0	36	32	2.23	1.10	4.14	1.44	81	97	18.0	11%	22%	11%	9%	10.9%	89.4	48	19	33	19%	94%	23%	13%	8	69	0%	25%			9.4	70	$6
Proj		**3**	**0**	**44**	**40**	**3.43**	**1.23**	**3.79**	**1.32**	**84**	**101**	**21.6**	**9%**	**23%**	**14%**	**6%**	**13.8%**	**90.5**	**48**	**19**	**33**	**28%**	**78%**	**16%**	**14%**	**8**						**4.8**	**100**	**-$1**

Kikuchi,Yusei

Age: 33 Th: L Role: SP
Ht: 6' 0" Wt: 205 Type: Pwr
Health: B PT/Exp: A Consist: A
LIMA Plan: B+ Rand Var: 0 MM: 4305

The strong step forward we were waiting for but thought might never come. Three reasons why it's sustainable: 1) Threw his best pitch (slider, 18% SwK) more often; 2) Walk rate improvements were in line with xBB%; 3) 2nd half BPX says he had no problem managing higher workload and hints that there might even be a higher ceiling.

Yr	Tm	W	Sv	IP	K	ERA	WHIP	xERA	xWHIP	vL+	vR+	BF/G	BB%	K%	K-BB%	xBB%	SwK	Vel	G	L	F	H%	S%	HR/F	xHR/F	GS	APC	DOM%	DIS%	Sv%	LI	RAR	BPX	R$
19	SEA	6	0	162	116	5.46	1.52	5.30	1.41	108	121	22.5	7%	16%	9%	7%	8.9%	92.5	44	21	35	32%	70%	19%	15%	32	85	16%	50%			-18.9	69	-$9
20	SEA	2	0	47	47	5.17	1.30	3.93	1.35	91	92	21.6	10%	24%	14%	9%	12.8%	95.0	52	23	25	31%	59%	9%	9%	9	88	11%	22%			-4.2	100	-$2
21	SEA	7	0	157	163	4.41	1.32	3.92	1.30	66	110	23.0	9%	24%	15%	7%	12.7%	95.2	48	21	30	30%	72%	21%	21%	29	88	24%	28%			-2.9	108	$2
22	TOR	6	1	101	124	5.19	1.50	3.96	1.37	91	127	14.2	13%	27%	15%	9%	13.8%	95.0	44	19	37	30%	73%	24%	22%	20	58	5%	35%	100	0.66	-15.1	90	-$6
23	TOR	11	0	168	181	3.86	1.27	3.91	1.19	89	104	21.9	7%	26%	19%	7%	12.7%	95.1	40	22	38	32%	76%	15%	16%	32	88	22%	28%			9.7	138	$11
1st Half		7	0	88	92	4.08	1.27	4.27	1.23	106	107	21.8	7%	25%	18%	7%	13.0%	95.4	37	20	43	29%	79%	19%	18%	17	89	18%	35%			2.8	123	$11
2nd Half		4	0	79	89	3.63	1.27	3.51	1.15	74	101	21.9	6%	27%	21%	7%	12.4%	94.9	43	25	32	35%	73%	9%	11%	15	87	27%	20%			6.9	156	$11
Proj		**11**	**0**	**167**	**179**	**3.87**	**1.21**	**3.50**	**1.22**	**77**	**99**	**21.8**	**8%**	**27%**	**18%**	**8%**	**12.7%**	**94.9**	**44**	**22**	**34**	**30%**	**73%**	**15%**	**16%**	**31**						**9.4**	**129**	**$12**

Kimbrel,Craig

Age: 36 Th: R Role: RP
Ht: 6' 0" Wt: 215 Type: Pwr/xFB
Health: B PT/Exp: A Consist: B
LIMA Plan: B Rand Var: -1 MM: 4421

Slow start (8.25 ERA through 5/4), but regained primary save share with summer surge. Though favorable H% helped, it was a decent rebound per xERA/xWHIP, as jump in whiffs drove elite K% and velocity held firm. Control issues remain and 2nd half BPX faded, a reminder that in-season consistency might be too much to expect at this point.

Yr	Tm	W	Sv	IP	K	ERA	WHIP	xERA	xWHIP	vL+	vR+	BF/G	BB%	K%	K-BB%	xBB%	SwK	Vel	G	L	F	H%	S%	HR/F	xHR/F	GS	APC	DOM%	DIS%	Sv%	LI	RAR	BPX	R$
19	CHC	0	13	21	30	6.53	1.60	4.62	1.35	114	159	4.2	13%	31%	19%	9%	14.8%	96.2	30	20	50	30%	75%	36%	25%	0	17			81	1.29	-5.2	111	-$1
20	CHC	0	2	15	28	5.28	1.43	3.60	1.34	121	65	3.8	17%	41%	23%	11%	13.3%	96.9	33	22	44	34%	65%	17%	23%	0	17			67	0.65	-1.6	132	-$3
21	2 TM	4	24	60	100	2.26	0.91	2.80	0.99	70	69	3.7	10%	43%	33%	8%	19.0%	96.5	30	22	48	27%	81%	12%	8%	0	16			83	1.53	14.7	204	$2
22	LA	6	22	60	72	3.75	1.32	3.91	1.28	112	81	4.1	11%	28%	17%	8%	12.6%	95.8	40	15	45	33%	72%	6%	11%	0	17			81	0.84	1.6	109	$1
23	PHI	8	23	69	94	3.26	1.04	3.51	1.17	82	84	3.9	10%	34%	24%	7%	14.7%	95.9	34	21	45	25%	76%	14%	12%	0	16			82	1.28	9.1	150	$1
1st Half		5	12	34	54	3.71	1.03	3.09	1.07	77	86	3.8	10%	40%	29%	7%	15.0%	96.0	33	17	50	28%	70%	15%	14%	0	16			100	1.18	2.6	190	$1
2nd Half		3	11	35	40	2.83	1.06	3.95	1.27	86	82	4.1	10%	28%	18%	8%	14.4%	95.7	34	24	42	23%	81%	14%	9%	0	16			69	1.38	6.5	112	$1
Proj		**5**	**20**	**65**	**83**	**3.73**	**1.20**	**3.55**	**1.20**	**97**	**93**	**3.9**	**10%**	**32%**	**21%**	**8%**	**15.4%**	**96.0**	**34**	**21**	**46**	**30%**	**74%**	**13%**	**10%**	**0**						**4.8**	**133**	**$1**

King,Michael

Age: 29 Th: R Role: SP
Ht: 6' 3" Wt: 210 Type: Pwr
Health: F PT/Exp: B Consist: C
LIMA Plan: B+ Rand Var: -3 MM: 4303

Second straight dominant season, this one featured seamless rotation move in Aug (48/9 K/BB, 1.88 ERA last 8 GS). Some S% fortune involved and SwK softened, but Ks kept flowing and "x" ratios held strong. Four-pitch arsenal bodes well if transition sticks, but don't expect this skill level over a full SP workload. Pieces are here for mid-rotation success.

Yr	Tm	W	Sv	IP	K	ERA	WHIP	xERA	xWHIP	vL+	vR+	BF/G	BB%	K%	K-BB%	xBB%	SwK	Vel	G	L	F	H%	S%	HR/F	xHR/F	GS	APC	DOM%	DIS%	Sv%	LI	RAR	BPX	R$
19	NYY *	3	0	41	31	7.04	1.42	5.21		66	54	22.0	5%	18%	13%		2.4%	91.5	38	13	50	34%	50%	0%	0%	0	41			0	0.00	-13.0	82	-$7
20	NYY	1	0	27	26	7.76	1.54	5.05	1.37	125	106	13.4	9%	21%	12%	8%	9.4%	93.1	40	20	40	34%	50%	15%	14%	4	52	0%	25%	0	0.70	-10.9	86	-$1
21	NYY	2	0	63	62	3.55	1.28	4.12	1.31	113	80	12.5	9%	23%	14%	7%	10.8%	94.1	45	24	31	30%	75%	11%	13%	6	46	0%	67%	0	0.69	5.6	98	-$
22	NYY	6	1	51	66	2.29	1.00	2.66	1.08	79	76	5.9	8%	33%	25%	6%	15.1%	95.9	47	25	28	29%	79%	9%	13%	0	23			33	1.72	10.5	175	$6
23	NYY	4	6	105	127	2.75	1.15	3.44	1.15	73	97	8.8	7%	29%	22%	8%	11.8%	94.4	43	22	36	32%	80%	11%	12%	9	34	33%	22%	60	1.31	20.4	161	$14
1st Half		2	5	44	48	2.84	1.13	3.45	1.21	66	99	6.8	8%	26%	19%	8%	11.6%	94.0	50	21	29	30%	77%	9%	11%	0	26			71	1.46	8.1	142	$8
2nd Half		2	1	60	79	2.69	1.16	3.43	1.10	79	97	11.3	7%	32%	25%	7%	11.9%	94.6	37	22	41	33%	83%	12%	13%	9	44	33%	22%	33	1.12	12.3	175	$1
Proj		**9**	**0**	**138**	**155**	**3.43**	**1.19**	**3.32**	**1.18**	**87**	**93**	**21.9**	**8%**	**28%**	**20%**	**8%**	**12.0%**	**94.5**	**44**	**23**	**34**	**31%**	**74%**	**12%**	**13%**	**25**						**15.2**	**143**	**$12**

Kinley,Tyler

Age: 33 Th: R Role: RP
Ht: 6' 4" Wt: 220 Type: Pwr/xFB
Health: F PT/Exp: D Consist: D
LIMA Plan: C+ Rand Var: +3 MM: 1210

Elbow surgery pushed debut to August, when struggles were somehow good enough to land COL closer gig in Sept. Underwhelming small-sample returns were in line with career MLB marks (4.57 xERA, 12% K-BB%), leaving little hope for much growth. Even if he starts in closer role, potential ratio carnage isn't worth the risk.

Yr	Tm	W	Sv	IP	K	ERA	WHIP	xERA	xWHIP	vL+	vR+	BF/G	BB%	K%	K-BB%	xBB%	SwK	Vel	G	L	F	H%	S%	HR/F	xHR/F	GS	APC	DOM%	DIS%	Sv%	LI	RAR	BPX	R$
19	MIA *	3	3	67	61	3.28	1.39	3.44	1.75	101	93	4.2	16%	22%	6%	8%	13.5%	95.0	38	23	40	25%	79%	9%	8%	0	17			60	0.84	10.0	73	$2
20	COL	0	0	24	26	5.32	1.06	4.10	1.40	55	103	4.0	13%	27%	15%	8%	17.0%	95.9	46	15	39	21%	48%	10%	10%	0	15			0	0.68	-2.5	89	-$4
21	COL	3	0	70	68	4.73	1.21	4.49	1.31	96	99	4.2	9%	23%	14%	7%	13.9%	96.0	39	19	42	27%	66%	14%	11%	0	16			0	0.92	-4.1	92	-$2
22	COL	1	0	24	27	0.75	1.13	3.36	1.10	46	106	4.0	6%	27%	21%	6%	16.7%	95.4	39	26	35	34%	93%	0%	4%	0	15			0	1.17	9.5	153	$0
23	COL	0	5	16	17	6.06	1.65	5.43	1.30	120	121	4.2	8%	22%	14%	7%	10.4%	96.5	20	25	55	38%	67%	11%	9%	0	17			71	1.44	-3.5	87	-$6
1st Half																																		
2nd Half		0	5	16	17	6.06	1.65	5.43	1.30	121	122	4.2	8%	22%	14%	7%	10.4%	96.5	20	25	55	38%	67%	11%	9%	0	17			71	1.44	-3.5	87	-$6
Proj		**1**	**9**	**58**	**55**	**4.80**	**1.38**	**4.53**	**1.36**	**107**	**108**	**4.2**	**10%**	**22%**	**13%**	**8%**	**12.1%**	**96.0**	**29**	**23**	**48**	**30%**	**69%**	**12%**	**9%**	**0**						**-3.4**	**68**	**-$2**

RYAN BLOOMFIELD

Kirby,George

Age: 26	Th: R	Role SP	Health A	LIMA Plan C+	
Ht: 6' 4"	Wt: 215	Type Con	PT/Exp B	Rand Var -1	
			Consist A	MM 5205	

Impressive sophomore season came with several signs of growth. MLB-best walk rate came with firm support from xBB%; new split-finger helped drive 2nd half SwK spike; held higher velocity over heavier workload. Already with a strong floor given pinpoint control, he's a bona-fide ace if late whiffs translate to more Ks.

Yr Tm	W	Sv	IP	K	ERA	WHIP	xERA	xWHIP	vL+	vR+	BF/G	BB%	K%	K-BB%	xBB%	SwK	Vel	G	L	F	H%	S%	HR/F	xHR/F	GS	APC	DOM%	DIS%	Sv%	LI	RAR	BPX	R$
19																																	
20																																	
21 aa	1	0	26	25	3.11	1.33	3.52				18.0	6%	23%	17%							37%	74%									3.7	141	-$4
22 SEA *	10	0	158	162	3.25	1.17	3.69	1.07	79	119	20.3	4%	26%	21%	5%	10.4%	95.2	46	16	38	33%	75%	9%	11%	25	84	32%	24%			14.1	173	$13
23 SEA	13	0	191	172	3.35	1.04	3.69	1.08	91	90	24.4	3%	23%	20%	4%	11.5%	96.1	44	19	37	30%	72%	11%	13%	31	91	52%	19%			23.1	162	$26
1st Half	7	0	101	86	3.21	1.04	3.75	1.09	102	80	25.1	2%	21%	19%	4%	10.1%	95.7	46	18	36	30%	73%	10%	12%	16	93	56%	19%			14.0	158	$25
2nd Half	6	0	90	86	3.51	1.04	3.63	1.07	79	103	23.7	3%	24%	21%	4%	13.1%	96.5	42	20	38	30%	71%	11%	13%	15	89	47%	20%			9.1	168	$20
Proj	**12**	**0**	**189**	**176**	**3.19**	**1.01**	**3.24**	**1.05**	**86**	**97**	**23.7**	**3%**	**24%**	**21%**	**4%**	**11.6%**	**96.0**	**44**	**19**	**37**	**30%**	**73%**	**11%**	**12%**	**31**						**26.4**	**165**	**$25**

Kluber,Corey

Age: 38	Th: R	Role SP	Health F	LIMA Plan C+	
Ht: 6' 4"	Wt: 215	Type Con/FB	PT/Exp A	Rand Var +4	
			Consist C	MM 1101	

PRO: Opening Day starter. CON: Everything after that. Gave up 17 ER through four starts, was sent to bullpen in May before June shoulder issue eventually ended season. Gave back all of 2022's BB% gains as Ks and velocity tumbled, and FB% tilt turned into gopheritis. At this age, it's tough to give an injury-related pass.

Yr Tm	W	Sv	IP	K	ERA	WHIP	xERA	xWHIP	vL+	vR+	BF/G	BB%	K%	K-BB%	xBB%	SwK	Vel	G	L	F	H%	S%	HR/F	xHR/F	GS	APC	DOM%	DIS%	Sv%	LI	RAR	BPX	R$
19 CLE	2	0	36	38	5.80	1.65	4.95	1.36	119	102	24.0	9%	23%	14%	8%	13.3%	91.6	40	23	37	39%	65%	10%	17%	7	87	29%	29%			-5.7	96	-$6
20 TEX	0	0	1	1	0.00	1.00	5.41			133	3.0	33%	33%	0%		5.6%	91.7	0	0	100	0%	0%	0%	0%	1	18	0%	0%			0.5	-116	-$6
21 NYY	5	0	80	82	3.83	1.34	4.29	1.32	74	108	21.3	10%	24%	14%	8%	12.9%	90.6	42	20	38	31%	74%	10%	9%	16	84	19%	31%			4.3	94	$0
22 TAM	10	0	164	139	4.34	1.21	4.02	1.11	108	100	22.2	3%	20%	17%	4%	11.8%	88.9	36	22	42	33%	67%	9%	11%	31	79	19%	32%			-7.4	132	$4
23 BOS	3	1	55	42	7.04	1.64	5.91	1.43	136	127	17.1	8%	16%	8%	6%	10.0%	88.2	30	22	48	31%	64%	19%	17%	9	66	0%	67%	100	0.63	-18.3	44	-$12
1st Half	3	1	55	42	7.04	1.64	5.91	1.43	137	127	17.1	8%	16%	8%	6%	10.0%	88.2	30	22	48	31%	64%	19%	17%	9	66	0%	67%	100	0.63	-18.3	44	-$17
2nd Half																																	
Proj	**5**	**0**	**87**	**70**	**5.57**	**1.49**	**4.69**	**1.35**	**120**	**111**	**20.5**	**8%**	**19%**	**11%**	**6%**	**11.7%**	**89.6**	**36**	**22**	**42**	**33%**	**67%**	**14%**	**14%**	**18**						**-13.4**	**72**	**-$9**

Kopech,Michael

Age: 28	Th: R	Role SP	Health F	LIMA Plan C	
Ht: 6' 3"	Wt: 210	Type Pwr/xFB	PT/Exp A	Rand Var 0	
			Consist C	MM 1201	

Some peaks (2.83 ERA in May/June), more valleys (7.00+ ERA in every other month) before season-ending knee surgery in Sept. Couldn't hit water from the boat as BB% and xBB% soared, while mediocre K% hardly budged. Now with two straight seasons of brutal skills as a starter, we'd say the valleys have it.

Yr Tm	W	Sv	IP	K	ERA	WHIP	xERA	xWHIP	vL+	vR+	BF/G	BB%	K%	K-BB%	xBB%	SwK	Vel	G	L	F	H%	S%	HR/F	xHR/F	GS	APC	DOM%	DIS%	Sv%	LI	RAR	BPX	R$
19																																	
20																																	
21 CHW	4	0	69	103	3.50	1.13	3.21	1.06	82	92	6.5	8%	36%	28%	6%	14.7%	97.4	38	19	44	33%	74%	13%	12%	4	26	0%	0%	0	0.95	6.5	189	$4
22 CHW	5	0	119	105	3.54	1.19	4.70	1.44	100	84	19.8	12%	21%	10%	8%	10.1%	94.9	36	16	48	23%	75%	9%	11%	25	80	20%	36%			6.2	45	$5
23 CHW	5	0	129	134	5.43	1.59	5.57	1.63	110	118	19.7	15%	23%	7%	12%	10.7%	95.2	36	17	47	27%	72%	17%	16%	27	81	11%	48%	0	0.71	-17.5	12	-$12
1st Half	3	0	86	97	4.08	1.36	4.75	1.45	101	109	23.3	13%	26%	13%	11%	11.9%	95.7	35	16	48	26%	78%	16%	17%	16	96	19%	50%			2.7	65	$4
2nd Half	2	0	43	37	8.10	2.05	7.46	1.97	124	140	15.6	19%	17%	-2%	12%	8.8%	94.4	36	19	46	29%	65%	19%	14%	11	64	0%	45%	0	0.66	-20.1	-94	-$17
Proj	**5**	**0**	**116**	**118**	**4.95**	**1.47**	**4.70**	**1.48**	**108**	**110**	**20.2**	**13%**	**24%**	**11%**	**11%**	**11.1%**	**95.5**	**36**	**18**	**46**	**29%**	**72%**	**15%**	**14%**	**20**						**-9.0**	**49**	**-$6**

Kremer,Dean

Age: 28	Th: R	Role SP	Health D	LIMA Plan A	
Ht: 6' 2"	Wt: 200	Type /FB	PT/Exp A	Rand Var 0	
			Consist C	MM 1103	

Wins and volume buoyed R$, but ERA took predictable step back with HR/F, S% corrections. More of the same "meh" skills here—K% rise didn't get much support from SwK, continued to struggle vL, middling xERA/xWHIP barely budged. Useful in the right matchups, but hard to see a step forward on the horizon.

Yr Tm	W	Sv	IP	K	ERA	WHIP	xERA	xWHIP	vL+	vR+	BF/G	BB%	K%	K-BB%	xBB%	SwK	Vel	G	L	F	H%	S%	HR/F	xHR/F	GS	APC	DOM%	DIS%	Sv%	LI	RAR	BPX	R$
19 a/a	9	0	106	89	5.06	1.49	5.22				24.1	8%	19%	12%							34%	68%									-7.3	67	-$3
20 BAL	1	0	19	22	4.82	1.45	5.28	1.51	77	113	20.8	14%	27%	12%	12%	10.4%	93.0	31	22	47	33%	63%	0%	14%	4	87	0%	25%			-0.8	49	-$5
21 BAL *	1	0	117	101	6.68	1.55	6.49	1.45	120	134	17.0	9%	20%	11%	10%	8.8%	92.6	30	19	51	32%	62%	20%	16%	13	76	0%	77%			-34.8	28	-$20
22 BAL	8	0	125	87	3.23	1.25	4.37	1.31	102	99	23.3	7%	17%	10%	6%	10.4%	93.2	39	21	39	30%	77%	7%	10%	21	89	24%	38%	0	0.78	11.4	70	$6
23 BAL	13	0	173	157	4.12	1.31	4.45	1.30	109	91	23.0	7%	21%	14%	8%	10.8%	93.9	39	23	38	30%	74%	14%	14%	32	92	22%	28%			4.6	98	$8
1st Half	8	0	91	82	5.04	1.42	4.60	1.26	126	103	23.1	6%	21%	15%	8%	10.6%	94.1	34	25	41	33%	71%	17%	16%	17	91	18%	35%			-8.0	106	$1
2nd Half	5	0	82	75	3.09	1.19	4.28	1.36	89	80	22.8	9%	22%	13%	7%	11.1%	93.7	45	21	34	27%	78%	10%	10%	15	92	27%	20%			12.6	90	$15
Proj	**9**	**0**	**152**	**131**	**4.60**	**1.36**	**4.37**	**1.33**	**107**	**101**	**23.1**	**8%**	**21%**	**12%**	**8%**	**10.3%**	**93.5**	**38**	**21**	**41**	**31%**	**71%**	**13%**	**13%**	**28**						**-5.2**	**82**	**-$1**

Lambert,Peter

Age: 27	Th: R	Role RP	Health F	LIMA Plan C+	
Ht: 6' 2"	Wt: 208	Type Con	PT/Exp F	Rand Var 0	
			Consist C	MM 1001	

3-7, 5.36 ERA in 87 IP at COL. "Lambo" (his nickname) rode more like a Pinto that swerved between multi-inning relief role, rotation gig, and Triple-A before biceps injury ended ride in Sept. Little reason to expect much growth given xERA/injury history, and only has two PQS-DOMinant starts in 32 career tries. Keep this car off the road.

Yr Tm	W	Sv	IP	K	ERA	WHIP	xERA	xWHIP	vL+	vR+	BF/G	BB%	K%	K-BB%	xBB%	SwK	Vel	G	L	F	H%	S%	HR/F	xHR/F	GS	APC	DOM%	DIS%	Sv%	LI	RAR	BPX	R$
19 COL *	5	0	150	99	6.47	1.58	6.20	1.53	135	121	22.1	8%	15%	7%	9%	7.5%	92.7	47	25	28	33%	62%	21%	14%	19	83	5%	74%			-36.4	20	-$16
20																																	
21 COL	0	0	6	3	11.12	2.47	6.44	1.47	220	85	15.0	7%	10%	3%	10%	8.9%	93.6	52	16	32	44%	58%	25%	16%	2	62	0%	100%			-4.8	33	-$9
22																																	
23 COL *	3	0	111	86	5.14	1.42	5.15	1.35	118	118	14.7	7%	19%	11%	8%	9.9%	93.3	42	16	42	30%	68%	16%	16%	11	58	9%	36%	0	0.68	-11.0	48	-$8
1st Half	1	0	48	45	5.90	1.64	6.21	1.47	139	136	10.8	11%	21%	10%	9%	10.1%	94.0	44	12	45	34%	68%	20%	20%	1	40	0%	0%	0	0.60	-9.4	42	-$15
2nd Half	2	0	62	41	4.54	1.25	4.32	1.39	106	107	21.1	7%	16%	9%	8%	9.8%	92.8	41	19	41	28%	68%	13%	14%	10	86	10%	40%			-1.6	55	$0
Proj	**3**	**0**	**116**	**82**	**5.10**	**1.40**	**4.64**	**1.41**	**122**	**115**	**16.8**	**8%**	**17%**	**9%**	**8%**	**9.4%**	**93.2**	**43**	**18**	**39**	**30%**	**67%**	**14%**	**15%**	**20**						**-11.0**	**58**	**-$8**

Lange,Alex

Age: 28	Th: R	Role RP	Health A	LIMA Plan B+	
Ht: 6' 3"	Wt: 202	Type Pwr/GB	PT/Exp B	Rand Var -2	
			Consist D	MM 3420	

Nearly met last year's "UP: 30 Sv", but was pretty lucky to get there. Already-shaky BB% suddenly became the worst in majors (min. 60 IP), as H% kept ERA/WHIP from rising to their "x" counterparts. Combination of Ks and GBs could keep him in ninth; just know this could unravel quickly, and leash may not be as long.

Yr Tm	W	Sv	IP	K	ERA	WHIP	xERA	xWHIP	vL+	vR+	BF/G	BB%	K%	K-BB%	xBB%	SwK	Vel	G	L	F	H%	S%	HR/F	xHR/F	GS	APC	DOM%	DIS%	Sv%	LI	RAR	BPX	R$
19 aa	4	0	56	34	5.56	1.67	5.37				15.8	12%	13%	2%							32%	67%									-7.3	30	-$7
20																																	
21 DET *	3	2	59	59	4.81	1.69	5.34	1.33	98	108	4.8	13%	22%	9%	8%	15.5%	96.4	44	26	30	36%	72%	16%	22%	0	18			50	0.84	-4.0	73	-$7
22 DET	7	0	63	82	3.69	1.25	3.06	1.26	91	88	3.8	11%	30%	19%	11%	19.3%	96.2	56	16	28	31%	72%	12%	11%	0	15			0	1.17	2.1	138	$2
23 DET	7	26	66	79	3.68	1.33	4.11	1.53	92	83	4.3	16%	28%	12%	12%	16.0%	95.8	51	19	31	26%	74%	13%	9%	0	17			81	1.34	5.3	64	$13
1st Half	5	12	35	44	3.89	1.27	3.96	1.45	87	75	4.3	15%	29%	15%	12%	15.6%	95.7	45	23	32	28%	67%	4%	7%	0	18			86	1.47	1.9	84	$12
2nd Half	2	14	31	35	3.45	1.40	4.27	1.63	99	92	4.3	17%	26%	9%	11%	16.4%	96.1	57	14	30	23%	82%	23%	12%	0	17			78	1.19	3.4	42	$9
Proj	**5**	**20**	**58**	**69**	**3.96**	**1.40**	**3.77**	**1.46**	**95**	**92**	**4.5**	**15%**	**28%**	**14%**	**11%**	**16.4%**	**96.1**	**51**	**19**	**30**	**30%**	**74%**	**13%**	**13%**	**0**						**2.6**	**80**	**$7**

Lauer,Eric

Age: 29	Th: L	Role RP	Health C	LIMA Plan B	
Ht: 6' 3"	Wt: 228	Type Pwr/FB	PT/Exp A	Rand Var +2	
			Consist D	MM 1201	

4-6, 6.56 ERA in 47 IP at MIL. Early struggles led to IL stint (shoulder) in May; mostly spent rest of year at Triple-A. Red flags everywhere: velocity was down a couple ticks, which sunk K%; walk rate ballooned; HR/F spike burned him. With health, 2021-22 skills offer mild bounceback hope, but only as a deeper-league streamer.

Yr Tm	W	Sv	IP	K	ERA	WHIP	xERA	xWHIP	vL+	vR+	BF/G	BB%	K%	K-BB%	xBB%	SwK	Vel	G	L	F	H%	S%	HR/F	xHR/F	GS	APC	DOM%	DIS%	Sv%	LI	RAR	BPX	R$
19 SD	8	0	150	138	4.45	1.40	4.83	1.35	120	95	21.7	8%	21%	13%	6%	9.2%	91.9	40	22	38	33%	71%	12%	11%	29	84	10%	34%	0	0.82	1.0	92	$2
20 MIL	0	0	11	12	13.09	2.36	7.29	1.69	117	145	15.3	15%	20%	5%	12%	11.1%	91.6	21	34	45	44%	42%	12%	16%	2	61	0%	100%	0	0.59	-11.7	-26	-$17
21 MIL	7	0	119	117	3.19	1.14	4.32	1.28	88	85	20.4	8%	24%	16%	7%	11.1%	92.6	36	23	41	26%	78%	12%	11%	20	82	35%	20%	0	0.76	15.8	98	$11
22 MIL	11	0	159	157	3.69	1.22	4.16	1.28	90	102	22.8	9%	24%	15%	7%	10.4%	93.4	34	22	44	27%	77%	14%	11%	29	92	21%	31%			5.5	90	$9
23 MIL *	7	0	92	94	6.21	1.82	7.64	1.49	73	149	19.4	11%	20%	9%	9%	9.4%	90.9	25	24	51	37%	72%	22%	16%	9	85	0%	56%	0	0.69	-21.3	23	-$16
1st Half	4	0	49	46	6.30	1.71	7.49	1.46	67	140	20.1	11%	21%	10%	8%	9.5%	90.9	25	25	50	33%	71%	21%	16%	8	85	0%	50%	0	0.68	-11.9	8	-$13
2nd Half	3	0	43	48	6.10	1.95	7.80	1.45	136	225	18.6	12%	24%	12%	11%	8.6%	90.9	22	17	61	41%	73%	27%	17%	1	81	0%	100%			-9.4	41	-$8
Proj	**8**	**0**	**116**	**117**	**4.56**	**1.40**	**4.40**	**1.36**	**92**	**108**	**19.2**	**10%**	**24%**	**13%**	**8%**	**9.9%**	**92.0**	**33**	**23**	**44**	**30%**	**73%**	**14%**	**13%**	**23**						**-3.3**	**75**	**-$1**

RYAN BLOOMFIELD

Lawrence,Justin

Age: 29 Th: R Role RP	Health A	LIMA Plan A	
Ht: 6' 3" Wt: 213 Type Pwr	PT/Exp C	Rand Var -2	
	Consist C	MM 2211	

Grabbed hold of closer role in June, but combo of shaky skills, luck correction, and tough home park eventually got the best of him. Not likely to contribute helpful ratios, as GB% lean probably isn't enough to overcome marginal SwK and high BB%. Odds are, he just blew his only real shot at ninth-inning chances.

Yr	Tm	W	Sv	IP	K	ERA	WHIP	xERA	xWHIP	vL+	vR+	BF/G	BB%	K%	K-BB%	xBB%	SwK	Vel	G	L	F	H%	S%	HR/F	xHR/F	GS	APC	DOM%	DIS%	Sv%	LI	RAR	BPX	R$
19	a/a	1	0	39	25	11.37	2.32	8.42				5.3	16%	12%	-3%							38%	49%									-33.3	-3	-$20
20																																		
21	COL *	7	13	50	39	6.51	1.82	5.80	2.01	103	128	4.6	14%	17%	3%	12%	8.3%	97.4	52	29	19	35%	63%	0%	8%	0	17			62	0.95	-13.8	49	-$4
22	COL *	4	2	73	83	4.65	1.34	3.56	1.36	126	85	4.6	11%	27%	16%	8%	10.2%	95.2	51	22	27	32%	65%	9%	10%	0	20			25	0.95	-6.1	111	-$2
23	COL	4	11	75	78	3.72	1.35	4.11	1.40	94	94	4.7	11%	24%	13%	8%	9.9%	95.4	49	21	31	31%	73%	8%	9%	0	17			61	1.24	5.7	88	$5
1st Half		3	5	43	44	2.93	1.19	3.83	1.42	89	72	4.9	12%	25%	13%	8%	9.4%	95.4	56	16	29	27%	74%	3%	6%	0	17			83	1.05	7.4	91	$8
2nd Half		1	6	32	34	4.78	1.56	4.45	1.38	101	121	4.5	10%	23%	13%	9%	10.4%	95.4	40	26	34	36%	72%	13%	12%	0	17			50	1.44	-1.8	86	-$1
Proj		**5**	**2**	**73**	**69**	**4.88**	**1.48**	**4.30**	**1.50**	**109**	**102**	**4.5**	**13%**	**22%**	**9%**	**8%**	**10.1%**	**95.3**	**47**	**22**	**31**	**31%**	**67%**	**11%**	**9%**	**0**						**-4.9**	**52**	**-$4**

Leclerc,José

Age: 30 Th: R Role RP	Health F	LIMA Plan A+	
Ht: 6' 0" Wt: 195 Type Pwr/xFB	PT/Exp C	Rand Var -5	
	Consist A	MM 2321	

Neck issue bothered him in spring, likely contributing to lower velocity and BB% spike early on. Eventually got on track as 2nd half K-BB%, SwK, and BPX were the best we've seen in years, albeit with a boost from all three luck factors. Susceptible to homers given FB tilt, but four postseason saves could be a precursor to more if late skills hold.

Yr	Tm	W	Sv	IP	K	ERA	WHIP	xERA	xWHIP	vL+	vR+	BF/G	BB%	K%	K-BB%	xBB%	SwK	Vel	G	L	F	H%	S%	HR/F	xHR/F	GS	APC	DOM%	DIS%	Sv%	LI	RAR	BPX	R$
19	TEX	2	14	69	100	4.33	1.33	4.05	1.32	112	77	4.3	13%	33%	20%	10%	14.1%	96.8	35	20	45	32%	69%	10%	9%	3	18	0%	67%	78	0.90	1.5	121	$6
20	TEX	0	1	2	3	4.50	2.00	5.92		121		5.0	20%	30%	10%		12.8%	94.5	0	60	40	43%	75%	0%	1%	0	24			100	0.97	0.0	-25	-$6
21																																		
22	TEX	0	7	48	54	2.83	1.13	4.22	1.28	96	82	5.1	11%	27%	17%	10%	17.6%	96.5	29	17	54	26%	80%	8%	9%	0	20			78	0.92	6.7	92	$3
23	TEX	0	4	57	67	2.68	1.14	4.53	1.35	103	68	4.1	12%	29%	17%	10%	16.7%	95.2	29	14	57	25%	80%	6%	9%	0	17			44	0.94	11.6	88	$4
1st Half		0	1	24	25	3.42	1.35	5.42	1.56	88	88	4.1	15%	25%	10%	11%	15.8%	94.9	25	15	59	25%	79%	9%	6%	0	17			33	0.91	2.7	23	-$6
2nd Half		0	3	33	42	2.16	0.99	3.96	1.20	112	53	4.1	10%	31%	22%	9%	17.4%	95.5	32	13	55	26%	81%	5%	11%	0	17			50	0.96	8.9	135	$5
Proj		**1**	**15**	**65**	**76**	**3.26**	**1.22**	**4.10**	**1.32**	**115**	**78**	**4.1**	**12%**	**29%**	**17%**	**10%**	**17.0%**	**95.8**	**31**	**16**	**53**	**27%**	**78%**	**10%**	**9%**	**0**						**8.6**	**93**	**$7**

Leiter,Mark

Age: 33 Th: R Role RP	Health A	LIMA Plan A+	
Ht: 6' 0" Wt: 210 Type Pwr	PT/Exp C	Rand Var 0	
	Consist B	MM 4311	

Started the season in dominant fashion with huge K% and full support from 1st half xERA. But the latter nearly doubled in 2nd half when whiffs cratered, BB% rose, and hits started falling in. A serviceable deep-league arm, but given age and short track record of success, a 1st half redux and consistent save opps seem unlikely.

Yr	Tm	W	Sv	IP	K	ERA	WHIP	xERA	xWHIP	vL+	vR+	BF/G	BB%	K%	K-BB%	xBB%	SwK	Vel	G	L	F	H%	S%	HR/F	xHR/F	GS	APC	DOM%	DIS%	Sv%	LI	RAR	BPX	R$
19																																		
20																																		
21	a/a	10	0	116	101	5.39	1.38	5.07				19.5	7%	21%	13%							32%	64%									-16.1	70	-$4
22	CHC *	2	3	90	97	4.44	1.20	3.91	1.23	82	110	8.8	9%	27%	18%	8%	12.0%	91.0	49	18	33	29%	68%	18%	15%	4	31	0%	100%	60	1.10	-5.2	99	$0
23	CHC	1	4	64	77	3.50	1.12	3.44	1.22	77	120	3.9	9%	29%	20%	10%	13.2%	91.3	45	23	32	28%	72%	14%	14%	0	15			50	1.17	6.6	142	$4
1st Half		1	3	34	48	2.41	0.86	2.51	1.03	63	101	4.0	8%	36%	29%	10%	14.4%	91.1	50	22	28	25%	77%	15%	24%	0	16			75	1.06	8.0	211	$7
2nd Half		0	1	31	29	4.70	1.40	4.58	1.42	91	139	3.8	10%	21%	11%	10%	11.9%	91.5	41	23	36	30%	69%	13%	8%	0	14			25	1.28	-1.4	70	-$5
Proj		**2**	**3**	**65**	**70**	**3.85**	**1.23**	**3.49**	**1.25**	**89**	**130**	**5.2**	**9%**	**26%**	**17%**	**10%**	**12.7%**	**91.3**	**46**	**22**	**33**	**30%**	**72%**	**14%**	**14%**	**0**						**3.8**	**122**	**$1**

Liberatore,Matthew

Age: 24 Th: L Role RP	Health A	LIMA Plan C+	
Ht: 6' 4" Wt: 200 Type	PT/Exp C	Rand Var -1	
	Consist A	MM 2101	

3-6, 5.25 ERA in 62 IP at STL. Hype surrounding May call-up quickly fizzled with 6.75 ERA and 14% K% in first nine outings, resulting in ticket back to AAA. Returned as RP in Sept with better results, but still wasn't missing bats (8.8% SwK). Has age, pedigree, and handedness on his side but not much else, so expect more growing pains.

Yr	Tm	W	Sv	IP	K	ERA	WHIP	xERA	xWHIP	vL+	vR+	BF/G	BB%	K%	K-BB%	xBB%	SwK	Vel	G	L	F	H%	S%	HR/F	xHR/F	GS	APC	DOM%	DIS%	Sv%	LI	RAR	BPX	R$
19																																		
20																																		
21	aaa	9	0	126	104	3.75	1.20	4.02				23.1	6%	20%	15%							30%	73%									8.0	102	$7
22	STL *	9	0	150	122	4.87	1.41	4.63	1.50	88	142	20.4	8%	19%	11%	11%	8.9%	93.4	38	24	38	32%	67%	12%	13%	7	72	0%	43%	0	0.67	-16.7	70	-$5
23	STL *	7	0	128	114	4.58	1.45	4.41	1.46	70	118	15.6	9%	17%	8%	9%	7.8%	94.3	43	23	34	32%	69%	7%	16%	11	48	9%	64%	0	0.85	-3.9	76	-$3
1st Half		5	0	78	68	4.12	1.37	4.10	1.38	89	125	20.4	9%	20%	11%	11%	7.2%	94.3	43	23	34	32%	71%	5%	17%	7	71	0%	71%	0	0.71	2.1	85	$3
2nd Half		2	0	50	47	5.30	1.56	4.89	1.55	47	111	11.6	13%	21%	8%	8%	8.6%	94.2	44	22	33	32%	67%	10%	14%	4	35	25%	50%	0	0.93	-6.0	65	-$6
Proj		**4**	**0**	**73**	**63**	**4.48**	**1.41**	**4.26**	**1.39**	**72**	**121**	**16.3**	**10%**	**21%**	**11%**	**10%**	**8.2%**	**94.1**	**43**	**23**	**35**	**31%**	**70%**	**11%**	**14%**	**12**						**-1.3**	**71**	**-$4**

Littell,Zack

Age: 28 Th: R Role SP	Health D	LIMA Plan A+	
Ht: 6' 4" Wt: 220 Type Con	PT/Exp C	Rand Var 0	
	Consist A	MM 2103	

Transitioned to SP mid-season and once the kid gloves came off, posted 3.38 ERA in last 11 starts. A few reasons to be wary of fully buying in: IP history questions full workload; SwK, K% were underwhelming; microscopic BB% will be tough to maintain. Still looks like solid deep-league option, but don't count on a ton of volume.

Yr	Tm	W	Sv	IP	K	ERA	WHIP	xERA	xWHIP	vL+	vR+	BF/G	BB%	K%	K-BB%	xBB%	SwK	Vel	G	L	F	H%	S%	HR/F	xHR/F	GS	APC	DOM%	DIS%	Sv%	LI	RAR	BPX	R$
19	MIN *	9	1	100	87	4.08	1.37	4.87	1.26	92	96	8.5	9%	21%	12%	6%	13.6%	93.9	38	28	34	30%	77%	11%	16%	0	19			50	0.81	5.2	59	$4
20	MIN	0	0	6	3	9.95	2.37	7.45	1.67	129	256	5.2	10%	10%	0%	8%	5.1%	94.0	29	25	46	32%	80%	45%	33%	0	20			0	0.29	-4.3	-35	-$12
21	SF	4	2	62	63	2.92	1.14	4.01	1.30	108	79	4.0	10%	25%	15%	7%	13.9%	95.0	47	16	38	26%	79%	12%	14%	2	16	0%	50%	33	1.07	10.2	105	$5
22	SF	3	1	44	39	5.08	1.38	4.23	1.25	104	118	4.9	7%	21%	14%	6%	13.1%	94.5	43	16	40	32%	68%	15%	14%	0	19			100	0.70	-6.1	102	-$5
23	2 AL	3	0	90	74	4.10	1.18	4.24	1.16	92	104	13.5	3%	20%	16%	4%	10.8%	93.9	43	20	38	31%	70%	12%	11%	14	48	21%	21%	0	0.61	2.6	137	$2
1st Half		0	0	15	16	5.26	1.43	4.19	1.25	82	140	5.6	7%	24%	16%	4%	10.6%	94.4	41	24	35	34%	68%	19%	13%	1	21	0%	0%	0	0.37	-1.8	123	-$11
2nd Half		3	0	75	58	3.86	1.13	4.25	1.14	94	97	19.5	2%	19%	16%	5%	10.9%	93.7	43	19	39	31%	70%	11%	10%	13	67	23%	23%	0	0.79	4.4	140	$8
Proj		**6**	**0**	**123**	**105**	**4.11**	**1.25**	**3.99**	**1.26**	**98**	**106**	**20.1**	**7%**	**21%**	**14%**	**6%**	**11.4%**	**94.3**	**43**	**20**	**37**	**30%**	**72%**	**14%**	**13%**	**18**						**3.3**	**105**	**$3**

Lively,Ben

Age: 32 Th: R Role RP	Health D	LIMA Plan C+	
Ht: 6' 4" Wt: 190 Type Con	PT/Exp D	Rand Var +1	
	Consist B	MM 1000	

4-7, 5.38 ERA in 89 IP at CIN. Called up from AAA in May, but missed time with multiple pectoral injuries and COVID. In between IL stints, SwK was weak, xERA ballooned in 2nd half, and was very homer-prone. Nothing in this box hints at another level, so it's best to look elsewhere for your end-game targets.

Yr	Tm	W	Sv	IP	K	ERA	WHIP	xERA	xWHIP	vL+	vR+	BF/G	BB%	K%	K-BB%	xBB%	SwK	Vel	G	L	F	H%	S%	HR/F	xHR/F	GS	APC	DOM%	DIS%	Sv%	LI	RAR	BPX	R$
19	KC *	6	3	74	59	4.73	1.58	5.92		329	134	13.0	9%	18%	9%		11.1%	92.4	20	40	40	33%	75%	50%	57%	0	27			75	0.20	-2.0	36	-$3
20																																		
21																																		
22	aaa	2	0	77	60	5.61	1.73	6.20				19.5	9%	17%	8%							37%	69%									-15.6	45	-$14
23	CIN *	8	0	123	95	5.29	1.37	5.52	1.28	124	96	19.8	7%	21%	14%	8%	9.0%	91.0	40	21	39	29%	68%	19%	15%	12	73	8%	17%	0	0.72	-14.5	42	-$5
1st Half		8	0	73	57	3.57	1.25	4.44	1.37	99	107	21.2	8%	19%	11%	8%	10.4%	90.8	39	20	41	27%	79%	18%	16%	7	80	14%	14%	0	0.79	6.9	58	$11
2nd Half		0	0	50	38	7.82	1.55	7.08	1.33	152	86	18.2	6%	18%	11%	6%	7.4%	91.2	40	23	37	33%	53%	19%	14%	5	66	0%	20%	0	0.66	-21.4	20	-$15
Proj		**3**	**0**	**58**	**45**	**5.32**	**1.51**	**4.66**	**1.37**	**135**	**96**	**17.2**	**8%**	**18%**	**10%**	**8%**	**8.6%**	**91.1**	**40**	**22**	**39**	**32%**	**70%**	**17%**	**15%**	**11**						**-7.1**	**67**	**-$8**

Loáisiga,Jonathan

Age: 29 Th: R Role RP	Health F	LIMA Plan B	
Ht: 5' 11" Wt: 165 Type Con/GB	PT/Exp C	Rand Var -5	
	Consist B	MM 4100	

April elbow injury shelved him for four months, then again in September to end season. Second straight year with a lengthy absence, and while sample was too small to draw firm conclusions, further K% erosion casts additional doubt on return to 2021 form. Just a late-round dart throw with a growing list of questions.

Yr	Tm	W	Sv	IP	K	ERA	WHIP	xERA	xWHIP	vL+	vR+	BF/G	BB%	K%	K-BB%	xBB%	SwK	Vel	G	L	F	H%	S%	HR/F	xHR/F	GS	APC	DOM%	DIS%	Sv%	LI	RAR	BPX	R$
19	NYY *	2	0	51	55	5.41	1.40	5.05	1.39	110	108	10.2	10%	26%	15%	9%	14.4%	96.9	40	24	36	31%	66%	19%	13%	4	39	0%	75%	0	0.67	-5.7	67	-$5
20	NYY	3	0	23	22	3.52	1.22	3.84	1.25	96	103	8.3	7%	22%	15%	6%	10.2%	96.7	51	23	26	30%	76%	18%	19%	3	33	0%	0%	0	1.00	2.6	124	$3
21	NYY	9	5	71	69	2.17	1.02	3.10	1.15	86	66	5.0	6%	24%	19%	5%	13.8%	98.4	61	16	23	29%	80%	7%	6%	0	19			56	1.61	18.3	156	$14
22	NYY	2	2	48	37	4.13	1.29	3.81	1.40	90	82	4.1	9%	18%	9%	6%	12.0%	98.1	60	18	23	29%	68%	9%	8%	0	15			67	1.24	-0.9	73	-$3
23	NYY	0	0	18	6	3.06	0.85	4.54	1.30	97	69	4.1	1%	9%	7%	4%	7.6%	97.8	53	12	35	21%	69%	10%	6%	0	14			0	0.97	2.8	81	-$3
1st Half		0	0	3	1	2.70	0.60	3.85		294	15	4.3	0%	8%	8%	4%	14.3%	96.8	64	9	27	11%	0%	33%	31%	0	9			0	0.74	0.7	102	-$10
2nd Half		0	0	14	5	3.14	0.91	4.70	1.31	64	82	4.0	2%	9%	7%	5%	6.7%	98.0	51	12	37	24%	67%	6%	1%	0	15			0	1.01	2.1	77	-$5
Proj		**3**	**0**	**51**	**43**	**3.78**	**1.23**	**3.50**	**1.28**	**100**	**87**	**5.1**	**7%**	**21%**	**14%**	**6%**	**11.9%**	**97.9**	**56**	**18**	**26**	**30%**	**70%**	**11%**	**8%**	**0**						**3.4**	**114**	**-$1**

BRIAN RUDD

Lodolo,Nick

Age: 26	Th: L	Role SP	Health F	LIMA Plan B
Ht: 6' 6"	Wt: 205	Type Pwr	PT/Exp B	Rand Var +5
			Consist A	MM 5403

Swing-and-miss stuff was on display early, but H%, HR/F misfortune wreaked havoc on ratios. Before they had time to correct, stress reaction in tibia knocked him out in May; August setback ended season. Workload might be managed carefully even if healthy, but keep tabs on progress, as this is a ceiling worth chasing.

Yr Tm	W	Sv	IP	K	ERA	WHIP	xERA	xWHIP	vL+	vR+	BF/G	BB%	K%	K-BB%	xBB%	SwK	Vel	G	L	F	H%	S%	HR/F	xHR/F	GS	APC	DOM%	DIS%	Sv%	LI	RAR	BPX	R$
19																																	
20																																	
21 a/a	2	0	52	70	2.79	1.08	2.82				15.7	6%	34%	29%							35%	76%									9.5	205	$3
22 CIN	4	0	103	131	3.66	1.25	3.13	1.16	51	109	23.2	9%	30%	21%	8%	12.8%	94.2	46	20	34	32%	75%	15%	14%	19	94	42%	16%			4.0	152	$3
23 CIN	2	0	34	47	6.29	1.75	3.66	1.10	96	147	23.7	6%	28%	22%	7%	13.6%	93.3	46	17	37	45%	72%	27%	22%	7	93	14%	29%			-8.3	196	-$9
1st Half	2	0	34	47	6.29	1.75	3.66	1.10	96	148	23.7	6%	28%	22%	7%	13.6%	93.3	46	17	37	45%	72%	27%	22%	7	93	14%	29%			-8.3	197	-$13
2nd Half																																	
Proj	6	0	123	144	3.90	1.21	3.25	1.13	68	106	20.5	7%	29%	22%	8%	13.3%	93.7	46	18	36	31%	76%	20%	19%	24						6.6	160	$6

López,Jorge

Age: 31	Th: R	Role RP	Health C	LIMA Plan B
Ht: 6' 3"	Wt: 200	Type	PT/Exp A	Rand Var +5
			Consist C	MM 3110

Appeared to pick up where he left off with 13 scoreless outings to start year, but things quickly unraveled. Main culprits were K%, GB% plunges; worse luck on H%/S%, HR/F; and stepped away for a few weeks to address mental health issues. Could rebound given 2022 skill growth as RP, but another shot at ninth is in doubt.

Yr Tm	W	Sv	IP	K	ERA	WHIP	xERA	xWHIP	vL+	vR+	BF/G	BB%	K%	K-BB%	xBB%	SwK	Vel	G	L	F	H%	S%	HR/F	xHR/F	GS	APC	DOM%	DIS%	Sv%	LI	RAR	BPX	R$
19 KC	4	1	124	109	6.33	1.47	4.75	1.36	129	100	14.1	8%	20%	12%	8%	9.2%	94.2	46	20	34	32%	61%	21%	23%	18	53	11%	39%	50	0.78	-27.9	92	-$10
20 2 AL	2	0	39	28	6.69	1.49	4.93	1.37	121	101	17.4	7%	16%	9%	10%	8.8%	93.8	49	20	31	32%	57%	18%	21%	6	64	0%	17%	0	0.76	-10.8	77	-$10
21 BAL	3	0	122	112	6.07	1.63	4.51	1.41	129	107	16.8	10%	20%	10%	9%	8.7%	95.2	50	22	28	34%	66%	20%	18%	25	66	12%	56%	0	0.88	-27.0	72	-$18
22 2 AL	4	23	71	72	2.54	1.18	3.36	1.33	98	78	4.4	10%	24%	14%	6%	11.0%	97.7	58	17	26	28%	80%	8%	13%	0	17			79	1.32	12.6	104	$14
23 3 TM	6	3	59	49	5.95	1.51	4.55	1.39	129	115	4.4	8%	18%	10%	6%	10.0%	96.9	48	22	30	32%	65%	21%	15%	0	16			43	0.90	-11.8	78	-$6
1st Half	2	3	27	22	5.00	1.41	4.57	1.40	108	123	4.2	8%	18%	10%	7%	9.1%	97.1	49	20	31	29%	72%	23%	17%	0	15			43	1.16	-2.2	78	-$5
2nd Half	4	0	32	27	6.75	1.59	4.53	1.39	148	109	4.5	8%	19%	10%	6%	10.8%	96.8	47	24	30	34%	60%	20%	14%	0	17			0	0.68	-9.5	79	-$5
Proj	4	2	58	50	4.36	1.35	3.86	1.30	119	101	4.5	8%	21%	13%	8%	10.3%	96.2	50	21	29	30%	73%	20%	16%	0						-0.3	101	-$2

López,Pablo

Age: 28	Th: R	Role SP	Health C	LIMA Plan C+
Ht: 6' 4"	Wt: 225	Type Pwr	PT/Exp A	Rand Var 0
			Consist A	MM 5305

Pushed lengthy history of shoulder issues further into past with second straight year avoiding IL. Skills-wise, this was his best work yet with spikes in velocity, SwK, and K%. Didn't slow down as he pushed past career-high IP, as 2nd half xERA suggests there may still be another level... UP: 15 Wins, 3.00 ERA.

Yr Tm	W	Sv	IP	K	ERA	WHIP	xERA	xWHIP	vL+	vR+	BF/G	BB%	K%	K-BB%	xBB%	SwK	Vel	G	L	F	H%	S%	HR/F	xHR/F	GS	APC	DOM%	DIS%	Sv%	LI	RAR	BPX	R$
19 MIA *	5	0	126	109	5.89	1.38	4.92	1.27	116	84	20.4	7%	21%	14%	7%	10.6%	93.6	48	21	31	33%	59%	15%	16%	21	86	33%	29%			-21.7	78	-$7
20 MIA	6	0	57	59	3.61	1.19	3.78	1.23	99	73	21.8	8%	25%	17%	6%	12.6%	93.7	52	19	29	31%	70%	9%	12%	11	82	45%	27%			6.0	136	$15
21 MIA	5	0	103	115	3.07	1.12	3.32	1.12	92	92	20.9	6%	28%	21%	6%	12.6%	94.0	47	22	31	31%	77%	13%	13%	20	83	35%	20%			15.2	159	$9
22 MIA	10	0	180	174	3.75	1.17	3.56	1.21	107	91	23.0	7%	24%	16%	7%	13.2%	93.6	46	21	33	29%	71%	13%	12%	32	91	38%	19%			4.8	120	$11
23 MIN	11	0	194	234	3.66	1.15	3.37	1.10	102	82	25.0	6%	29%	23%	5%	15.0%	94.8	45	18	36	33%	73%	13%	10%	32	95	38%	16%			16.0	178	$21
1st Half	4	0	102	126	4.24	1.15	3.60	1.13	94	88	24.9	7%	30%	23%	5%	15.1%	94.9	40	18	42	32%	66%	11%	11%	17	95	35%	6%			1.2	166	$14
2nd Half	7	0	92	108	3.03	1.16	3.11	1.06	110	75	25.2	5%	29%	24%	6%	15.0%	94.8	50	19	30	34%	80%	16%	9%	15	94	40%	27%			14.7	193	$24
Proj	12	0	189	210	3.49	1.14	3.16	1.12	101	83	23.8	6%	28%	22%	6%	13.8%	94.3	47	20	33	31%	73%	13%	11%	31						19.4	161	$19

López,Reynaldo

Age: 30	Th: R	Role RP	Health B	LIMA Plan A+
Ht: 6' 1"	Wt: 225	Type Pwr/FB	PT/Exp C	Rand Var -2
			Consist C	MM 4311

Fumbled away shot at closer role with 13 ER in first 15 games, but quickly righted the ship with a sub-2.00 ERA the rest of the way. SwK and K% reached new heights, and while 2nd half S% and HR/F were extremely kind, xBB% shows he can get walks back down. Don't rule out another run at ninth-inning gig.

Yr Tm	W	Sv	IP	K	ERA	WHIP	xERA	xWHIP	vL+	vR+	BF/G	BB%	K%	K-BB%	xBB%	SwK	Vel	G	L	F	H%	S%	HR/F	xHR/F	GS	APC	DOM%	DIS%	Sv%	LI	RAR	BPX	R$
19 CHW	10	0	184	169	5.38	1.46	5.21	1.37	114	107	24.5	8%	21%	13%	7%	11.7%	95.5	35	21	44	32%	68%	14%	14%	33	96	24%	55%			-19.9	83	-$4
20 CHW	1	0	26	24	6.49	1.63	6.15	1.56	102	154	15.1	12%	20%	7%	9%	9.3%	94.2	35	13	53	27%	71%	22%	17%	8	63	0%	63%			-6.6	25	-$10
21 CHW *	5	0	97	95	5.57	1.44	5.30	1.16	96	85	13.7	9%	23%	15%	7%	11.9%	95.8	39	22	39	33%	64%	17%	13%	9	47	0%	33%	0	0.66	-15.5	72	-$8
22 CHW	6	0	65	63	2.76	0.95	3.40	1.08	93	71	4.2	4%	25%	21%	6%	14.4%	97.1	39	22	39	29%	69%	1%	7%	1	16	0%	0%	0	1.02	9.8	146	$7
23 3 AL	3	6	66	83	3.27	1.27	4.07	1.33	85	89	4.1	12%	30%	18%	8%	14.7%	98.3	39	17	44	29%	79%	12%	14%	0	18			50	1.34	8.6	107	$5
1st Half	2	4	35	41	5.14	1.34	4.50	1.37	105	98	4.0	12%	28%	15%	8%	14.5%	98.4	37	16	47	28%	68%	17%	15%	0	17			44	1.36	-3.5	90	-$3
2nd Half	1	2	31	42	1.16	1.19	3.59	1.29	63	79	4.2	12%	33%	20%	7%	14.9%	98.1	42	19	39	31%	92%	4%	14%	0	19			67	1.31	12.1	129	$5
Proj	4	3	65	75	3.59	1.20	3.53	1.18	96	92	5.4	8%	29%	20%	8%	14.2%	97.2	39	20	41	31%	74%	11%	13%	0						6.0	138	$4

Lorenzen,Michael

Age: 32	Th: R	Role SP	Health F	LIMA Plan B+
Ht: 6' 3"	Wt: 217	Type	PT/Exp A	Rand Var -2
			Consist B	MM 2103

Spring groin injury led to rough start, ran off 17-start stretch with 2.73 ERA capped by August no-hitter, then gave up 27 ER over next six outings. Through all the ups and downs, xERA was consistently mediocre, whiffs disappeared, and lost GB% tilt. Just a back-of-rotation arm whose recent H% fortune may dry up.

Yr Tm	W	Sv	IP	K	ERA	WHIP	xERA	xWHIP	vL+	vR+	BF/G	BB%	K%	K-BB%	xBB%	SwK	Vel	G	L	F	H%	S%	HR/F	xHR/F	GS	APC	DOM%	DIS%	Sv%	LI	RAR	BPX	R$
19 CIN	1	7	83	85	2.92	1.15	4.04	1.28	83	88	4.7	8%	25%	17%	8%	14.6%	96.9	44	23	32	28%	79%	13%	10%	0	18			64	1.20	16.3	115	$8
20 CIN	3	0	34	35	4.28	1.40	4.57	1.42	82	106	8.2	12%	24%	12%	11%	15.0%	96.7	48	17	34	31%	70%	9%	10%	2	34	100%	0%	0	1.14	0.7	81	$1
21 CIN	1	4	29	21	5.59	1.38	5.02	1.54	95	87	4.6	11%	17%	6%	8%	12.7%	96.5	45	24	31	28%	58%	7%	4%	0	18			100	1.31	-4.7	25	-$5
22 LAA	8	0	98	85	4.24	1.28	4.08	1.41	109	86	22.8	11%	21%	10%	9%	11.7%	94.3	50	18	32	27%	69%	12%	10%	18	92	17%	22%			-3.3	66	$1
23 2 TM	9	1	153	111	4.18	1.21	4.69	1.38	91	101	21.5	8%	18%	10%	6%	9.9%	94.2	41	20	39	27%	69%	11%	12%	25	82	32%	32%	100	0.69	2.9	69	$8
1st Half	2	0	82	62	4.28	1.17	4.37	1.29	93	99	23.8	6%	19%	13%	6%	9.8%	94.4	41	23	36	28%	67%	12%	15%	14	90	29%	21%			0.5	93	$3
2nd Half	7	1	71	49	4.06	1.25	5.06	1.47	89	104	19.4	9%	17%	8%	7%	10.1%	94.0	41	18	41	26%	71%	10%	10%	11	74	36%	45%	100	0.63	2.4	43	$11
Proj	9	0	131	107	4.28	1.31	4.31	1.40	95	103	21.4	9%	20%	10%	8%	11.0%	95.1	45	19	36	29%	70%	12%	11%	25						0.8	68	$2

Lucchesi,Joey

Age: 31	Th: L	Role SP	Health F	LIMA Plan C+
Ht: 6' 5"	Wt: 225	Type	PT/Exp D	Rand Var -2
			Consist B	MM 1101

4-0, 2.89 ERA in 47 IP at NYM. Returned from Tommy John surgery mostly at AAA, filling in admirably in majors when needed. But skills told different story, as BB% was up, he struggled to miss bats, and HR/F luck played large role. Chances are, MLB opportunities will continue to be sporadic and results won't be as strong.

Yr Tm	W	Sv	IP	K	ERA	WHIP	xERA	xWHIP	vL+	vR+	BF/G	BB%	K%	K-BB%	xBB%	SwK	Vel	G	L	F	H%	S%	HR/F	xHR/F	GS	APC	DOM%	DIS%	Sv%	LI	RAR	BPX	R$
19 SD	10	0	164	158	4.18	1.22	4.38	1.32	86	96	22.9	8%	23%	15%	8%	10.9%	90.2	47	17	36	29%	70%	14%	13%	30	88	27%	33%			6.6	107	$10
20 SD	0	0	6	5	7.94	2.65	5.78	1.35	132	144	10.7	6%	16%	9%	6%	13.8%	90.0	38	38	25	54%	67%	0%	3%	2	41	0%	50%	0	1.18	-2.4	83	-$11
21 NYM	1	0	38	41	4.46	1.17	3.93	1.18	95	97	14.3	7%	26%	19%	8%	10.4%	91.1	40	16	44	31%	63%	9%	12%	8	59	13%	13%	0	0.68	-0.9	133	-$3
22																																	
23 NYM *	10	0	130	89	4.17	1.48	4.77	1.45	63	103	23.3	9%	16%	8%	9%	7.4%	90.0	45	16	39	30%	74%	7%	12%	9	78	11%	56%			2.6	46	-$1
1st Half	7	0	83	59	3.38	1.28	4.00	1.50	54	118	22.5	10%	18%	8%	8%	7.1%	89.9	39	18	42	26%	79%	14%	17%	5	67	20%	80%			9.7	54	$11
2nd Half	3	0	47	30	5.56	1.82	6.12	1.64	75	91	24.4	12%	14%	2%	11%	7.7%	90.2	51	14	36	36%	69%	0%	7%	4	91	0%	25%			-7.2	36	-$8
Proj	5	0	73	58	4.49	1.44	4.60	1.43	90	114	21.2	10%	19%	9%	9%	8.8%	90.2	45	16	39	31%	72%	11%	12%	12						-1.4	59	-$4

Lugo,Seth

Age: 34	Th: R	Role SP	Health D	LIMA Plan B+
Ht: 6' 4"	Wt: 225	Type	PT/Exp B	Rand Var 0
			Consist A	MM 3203

Return to starting role yielded career-high IP and went as well as could be expected, at least on the surface. But he missed a month (calf) and K% continued downward spiral, with weak SwK hinting at further erosion. Consistently strong BB% helps provide solid floor, but if he is starting again, use 4.00 ERA as baseline.

Yr Tm	W	Sv	IP	K	ERA	WHIP	xERA	xWHIP	vL+	vR+	BF/G	BB%	K%	K-BB%	xBB%	SwK	Vel	G	L	F	H%	S%	HR/F	xHR/F	GS	APC	DOM%	DIS%	Sv%	LI	RAR	BPX	R$
19 NYM	7	6	80	104	2.70	0.90	3.17	1.01	71	77	5.1	5%	33%	28%	6%	11.8%	94.4	43	18	39	28%	75%	11%	11%	0	21			55	1.34	17.8	199	$15
20 NYM	3	3	37	47	5.15	1.36	3.30	1.09	114	110	10.0	6%	29%	23%	6%	14.3%	93.4	49	25	27	36%	69%	30%	25%	7	38	29%	29%	60	1.08	-3.2	190	$4
21 NYM	4	1	46	55	3.50	1.29	3.77	1.25	106	88	4.2	10%	28%	18%	6%	13.8%	93.8	42	25	34	32%	78%	15%	13%	0	16			25	1.25	4.4	124	$0
22 NYM	3	3	65	69	3.60	1.17	3.56	1.15	74	109	4.4	7%	25%	19%	8%	9.5%	94.5	46	17	38	30%	75%	13%	12%	0	17			50	0.97	3.0	142	$2
23 SD	8	0	146	140	3.57	1.20	3.88	1.21	100	92	23.2	6%	23%	17%	6%	9.6%	93.4	45	21	34	31%	75%	13%	15%	26	91	31%	31%			13.8	133	$11
1st Half	3	0	58	53	3.59	1.27	3.89	1.19	100	92	22.0	5%	22%	17%	6%	8.2%	93.3	45	24	31	33%	75%	11%	17%	11	87	27%	36%			5.3	136	$3
2nd Half	5	0	89	87	3.55	1.16	3.87	1.22	101	93	24.1	7%	24%	17%	7%	10.6%	93.4	46	19	35	29%	76%	15%	14%	15	95	33%	27%			8.5	132	$16
Proj	9	0	145	135	3.92	1.25	3.76	1.25	99	96	23.4	7%	23%	16%	7%	9.8%	93.7	45	21	34	31%	72%	13%	13%	25						7.2	114	$7

BRIAN RUDD

Luzardo,Jesus

Age: 26 | Th: L | Role: SP | Ht: 6' 0" | Wt: 218 | Type: Pwr
Health: D | PT/Exp: A | Consist: D | LIMA Plan: B | Rand Var: -1 | MM: 4305

Reached new IP heights as he avoided IL for first time in years. Skills held up well: racked up whiffs with slider (22.2% SwK) and change-up (17.5% SwK), walk rate took another step forward, and velocity uptick held all year. With volume now a bit less of a concern, he's approaching high-end SP status. UP: 15 Wins, 3.25 ERA

Yr Tm	W	Sv	IP	K	ERA	WHIP	xERA	xWHIP	vL+	vR+	BF/G	BB%	K%	K-BB%	xBB%	SwK	Vel	G	L	F	H%	S%	HR/F	xHR/F	GS	APC	DOM%	DIS%	Sv%	LI	RAR	BPX	R$
19 OAK *	1	2	43	45	2.96	1.10	2.98	1.04	27	73	13.0	7%	27%	20%	10%	15.2%	96.4	42	15	42	30%	76%	9%	13%	0	29			100	0.85	8.2	144	$2
20 OAK	3	0	59	59	4.12	1.27	3.96	1.22	97	101	20.7	7%	24%	17%	8%	13.0%	95.5	45	24	31	31%	73%	18%	16%	9	78	33%	11%	0	0.70	2.4	130	$6
21 2 TM *	8	0	124	120	6.52	1.62	6.07	1.41	105	123	16.7	11%	22%	10%	9%	13.5%	95.5	38	21	40	34%	62%	18%	16%	18	69	11%	50%	0	0.69	-34.6	46	-$17
22 MIA	4	0	100	120	3.32	1.04	3.22	1.16	84	85	22.2	9%	30%	21%	8%	14.3%	96.1	40	24	36	27%	71%	11%	12%	18	91	39%	17%			8.0	140	$8
23 MIA	10	0	179	208	3.58	1.21	3.78	1.17	81	102	23.2	7%	28%	21%	7%	14.5%	96.8	40	19	41	32%	75%	12%	13%	32	93	41%	22%			16.6	148	$16
1st Half	6	0	97	112	3.53	1.15	3.59	1.12	69	104	23.2	6%	28%	22%	6%	14.8%	96.8	41	19	40	32%	73%	11%	13%	17	95	29%	12%			9.6	165	$20
2nd Half	4	0	82	96	3.64	1.29	4.02	1.24	95	100	23.1	9%	28%	19%	8%	14.3%	96.7	39	19	42	32%	77%	12%	14%	15	92	53%	33%			7.0	130	$12
Proj	**11**	**0**	**181**	**201**	**3.61**	**1.18**	**3.53**	**1.19**	**85**	**96**	**22.5**	**8%**	**28%**	**20%**	**8%**	**14.1%**	**96.2**	**40**	**21**	**39**	**30%**	**74%**	**12%**	**13%**	**32**						**16.0**	**134**	**$16**

Lyles,Jordan

Age: 33 | Th: R | Role: SP | Ht: 6' 5" | Wt: 230 | Type: Con/FB
Health: A | PT/Exp: A | Consist: B | LIMA Plan: C+ | Rand Var: +5 | MM: 1003

PRO: Eats innings. CON: Destroys ratios, returns negative R$, posted league-worst S%, has weak strikeout skills (SwK) that continue to diminish, has spiking xERA, and has more than three times as many disaster starts as dominant outings. "But other than that, Mrs. Lincoln, how was the play?"

Yr Tm	W	Sv	IP	K	ERA	WHIP	xERA	xWHIP	vL+	vR+	BF/G	BB%	K%	K-BB%	xBB%	SwK	Vel	G	L	F	H%	S%	HR/F	xHR/F	GS	APC	DOM%	DIS%	Sv%	LI	RAR	BPX	R$
19 2 NL	12	0	141	146	4.15	1.32	4.63	1.34	121	88	21.4	9%	24%	15%	8%	10.7%	92.6	40	18	41	30%	75%	16%	15%	28	88	11%	29%			6.2	99	$8
20 TEX	1	0	58	36	7.02	1.56	6.13	1.51	112	116	22.2	9%	14%	5%	9%	6.9%	92.2	40	21	39	30%	58%	15%	14%	9	83	0%	67%	0	0.69	-18.3	25	-$19
21 TEX	10	0	180	146	5.15	1.39	4.79	1.32	112	113	24.0	7%	19%	12%	7%	10.6%	92.8	38	23	40	30%	69%	17%	15%	30	93	20%	40%	0	0.76	-19.6	79	-$5
22 BAL	12	0	179	144	4.42	1.39	4.45	1.28	122	103	24.2	7%	19%	12%	8%	9.4%	91.5	40	20	40	32%	72%	11%	14%	32	93	22%	38%			-10.1	86	-$1
23 KC	6	0	178	120	6.28	1.24	5.29	1.35	109	110	24.1	6%	16%	10%	8%	8.9%	91.1	34	18	49	26%	53%	14%	13%	31	91	10%	35%			-42.7	67	-$10
1st Half	1	0	92	64	6.68	1.30	5.56	1.41	115	102	24.6	8%	16%	9%	8%	8.3%	91.1	33	17	50	26%	51%	13%	14%	16	90	6%	31%			-26.5	50	-$15
2nd Half	5	0	86	56	5.86	1.19	5.01	1.28	103	120	23.7	4%	16%	12%	7%	9.5%	91.0	34	19	47	26%	56%	15%	12%	15	92	13%	40%			-16.2	85	$2
Proj	**6**	**0**	**131**	**96**	**5.70**	**1.32**	**4.62**	**1.33**	**112**	**111**	**23.0**	**7%**	**18%**	**11%**	**8%**	**9.3%**	**91.7**	**36**	**19**	**44**	**29%**	**62%**	**15%**	**14%**	**24**						**-22.1**	**72**	**-$8**

Lynch,Daniel

Age: 27 | Th: L | Role: SP | Ht: 6' 6" | Wt: 200 | Type: Con
Health: F | PT/Exp: A | Consist: C | LIMA Plan: C+ | Rand Var: -1 | MM: 1001

3-4, 4.64 ERA in 52 IP at KC. Shoulder injury pushed debut to May, then landed him back on IL in July. Velocity dip was likely related, though he countered with more change-ups (18.6% SwK) to help buoy SwK, which hints at more Ks. Worth monitoring in the end game, though health and BPX history are major concerns.

Yr Tm	W	Sv	IP	K	ERA	WHIP	xERA	xWHIP	vL+	vR+	BF/G	BB%	K%	K-BB%	xBB%	SwK	Vel	G	L	F	H%	S%	HR/F	xHR/F	GS	APC	DOM%	DIS%	Sv%	LI	RAR	BPX	R$
19																																	
20																																	
21 KC *	8	0	125	103	6.09	1.70	6.50	1.47	58	118	20.9	9%	18%	10%	9%	11.6%	93.7	39	24	37	37%	66%	11%	15%	15	84	13%	47%			-28.1	45	-$18
22 KC	4	0	132	122	5.13	1.57	4.49	1.33	124	113	22.2	9%	20%	12%	8%	11.9%	94.0	41	21	37	35%	71%	14%	13%	27	90	7%	30%			-18.8	81	-$12
23 KC *	5	0	75	51	4.48	1.32	4.93	1.41	95	100	20.8	7%	15%	8%	8%	11.5%	92.6	39	16	45	29%	72%	12%	13%	9	90	0%	67%			-1.4	48	-$2
1st Half	4	0	62	45	4.26	1.32	4.83	1.34	128	92	21.5	6%	17%	11%	9%	12.1%	92.8	37	17	45	30%	73%	10%	11%	7	94	0%	57%			0.6	60	$0
2nd Half	1	0	13	6	5.54	1.32	5.41	1.51	45	138	17.9	7%	11%	4%	5%	8.7%	91.6	45	13	42	25%	65%	19%	22%	2	75	0%	100%			-1.9	-4	-$6
Proj	**5**	**0**	**102**	**78**	**4.71**	**1.40**	**4.54**	**1.35**	**118**	**110**	**22.1**	**8%**	**18%**	**11%**	**9%**	**11.9%**	**93.4**	**39**	**20**	**41**	**31%**	**70%**	**12%**	**12%**	**19**						**-4.8**	**71**	**-$5**

Lynn,Lance

Age: 37 | Th: R | Role: SP | Ht: 6' 5" | Wt: 270 | Type: Pwr/FB
Health: D | PT/Exp: A | Consist: B | LIMA Plan: B | Rand Var: +4 | MM: 3303

Continually hammered by longball in one of worst seasons for any 2023 starter. Brutal luck factors, xERA screamed regression in 1st half, but 2nd half K% and BPX tanked despite July trade to LA. Can't be THIS bad again, but late slide at this age suggests even a bounceback to 2022 levels might be wishful thinking.

Yr Tm	W	Sv	IP	K	ERA	WHIP	xERA	xWHIP	vL+	vR+	BF/G	BB%	K%	K-BB%	xBB%	SwK	Vel	G	L	F	H%	S%	HR/F	xHR/F	GS	APC	DOM%	DIS%	Sv%	LI	RAR	BPX	R$
19 TEX	16	0	208	246	3.67	1.22	3.90	1.17	94	88	26.5	7%	28%	21%	7%	12.9%	94.2	40	21	38	34%	73%	10%	12%	33	108	45%	12%			21.4	153	$21
20 TEX	6	0	84	89	3.32	1.06	4.18	1.21	76	103	26.5	7%	26%	19%	7%	11.6%	93.5	36	22	42	26%	76%	14%	11%	13	108	31%	8%			11.7	128	$27
21 CHW	11	0	157	176	2.69	1.07	3.89	1.16	94	71	22.9	7%	28%	21%	8%	12.5%	93.5	38	19	43	28%	81%	10%	8%	28	93	25%	14%			30.4	140	$23
22 CHW	8	0	122	124	3.99	1.13	3.51	1.06	102	95	24.4	4%	24%	21%	6%	13.7%	92.7	42	20	38	31%	71%	14%	12%	21	96	38%	24%			-0.4	162	$6
23 2 TM	13	0	184	191	5.73	1.39	4.57	1.29	122	99	25.3	8%	24%	15%	8%	13.5%	92.2	36	21	43	31%	66%	19%	16%	32	99	22%	31%			-31.8	105	-$5
1st Half	5	0	96	116	6.47	1.50	4.12	1.23	143	88	25.4	8%	27%	19%	7%	14.3%	92.2	39	23	38	36%	61%	21%	18%	17	101	18%	29%			-25.3	137	-$11
2nd Half	8	0	88	75	4.93	1.28	5.07	1.36	100	112	25.1	8%	20%	12%	8%	12.5%	92.3	32	19	48	26%	71%	17%	14%	15	96	27%	33%			-6.4	71	$11
Proj	**11**	**0**	**152**	**158**	**4.43**	**1.23**	**3.82**	**1.21**	**106**	**95**	**23.6**	**8%**	**26%**	**18%**	**8%**	**13.0%**	**92.8**	**37**	**20**	**43**	**29%**	**71%**	**16%**	**13%**	**26**						**-1.9**	**123**	**$7**

Machado,Andrés

Age: 31 | Th: R | Role: RP | Ht: 6' 0" | Wt: 235 | Type: Con
Health: A | PT/Exp: D | Consist: A | LIMA Plan: B | Rand Var: +3 | MM: 2100

4-1, 5.22 ERA in 50 IP at WAS. Bounced between AAA and majors in 1st half with poor results, but saw regular work in Aug/Sept. Control gains supported by xBB% with more whiffs and Ks in 2nd half, but small sample is trumped by years of shaky xERA, BPX. Not worth chasing what's likely to be a low-leverage RP.

Yr Tm	W	Sv	IP	K	ERA	WHIP	xERA	xWHIP	vL+	vR+	BF/G	BB%	K%	K-BB%	xBB%	SwK	Vel	G	L	F	H%	S%	HR/F	xHR/F	GS	APC	DOM%	DIS%	Sv%	LI	RAR	BPX	R$
19 aaa	3	3	76	50	3.51	1.42	4.80				7.4	11%	15%	5%							27%	82%									9.4	28	$1
20																																	
21 WAS *	1	0	52	44	3.82	1.37	4.35	1.42	82	105	4.3	9%	20%	11%	9%	9.9%	94.7	44	20	36	31%	75%	11%	9%	0	16			0	1.14	2.8	76	-$4
22 WAS *	2	0	76	59	4.06	1.41	4.33	1.44	122	86	5.0	10%	18%	9%	7%	11.0%	95.4	43	23	34	31%	73%	11%	14%	0	20			0	0.53	-0.9	66	-$4
23 WAS *	5	3	80	69	5.00	1.33	5.03	1.26	109	120	4.9	6%	21%	14%	6%	11.2%	96.3	42	23	34	32%	67%	24%	21%	0	18			50	0.92	-6.6	86	-$2
1st Half	1	2	37	31	5.93	1.59	6.68	1.27	155	129	5.3	6%	19%	14%	10%	8.8%	96.5	41	30	30	37%	67%	33%	25%	0	21			100	0.81	-7.3	59	-$11
2nd Half	4	1	43	38	4.20	1.11	3.62	1.21	75	117	4.6	6%	23%	17%	5%	12.6%	96.2	43	19	38	28%	66%	19%	19%	0	16			25	0.97	0.7	110	$5
Proj	**3**	**0**	**58**	**48**	**4.33**	**1.35**	**4.17**	**1.32**	**104**	**105**	**4.9**	**8%**	**20%**	**12%**	**8%**	**10.6%**	**95.8**	**43**	**23**	**35**	**31%**	**71%**	**13%**	**17%**	**0**						**0.0**	**87**	**-$4**

Maeda,Kenta

Age: 36 | Th: R | Role: SP | Ht: 6' 1" | Wt: 185 | Type: Pwr/FB
Health: F | PT/Exp: C | Consist: A | LIMA Plan: A | Rand Var: 0 | MM: 4303

Injury-plagued 1st half on heels of Tommy John recovery, but finished both healthy and strong. Effective splitter (18.3% SwK) carried the whiffs, which bodes well for K% repeat. Consistent control, xERA/xWHIP confirm he'll be strong on a per-inning basis, but can't expect a full workload given age, IP history.

Yr Tm	W	Sv	IP	K	ERA	WHIP	xERA	xWHIP	vL+	vR+	BF/G	BB%	K%	K-BB%	xBB%	SwK	Vel	G	L	F	H%	S%	HR/F	xHR/F	GS	APC	DOM%	DIS%	Sv%	LI	RAR	BPX	R$
19 LA	10	3	154	169	4.04	1.07	4.01	1.24	99	72	16.9	8%	27%	19%	6%	15.1%	92.1	41	21	38	26%	67%	15%	10%	26	66	27%	19%	100	0.91	8.8	127	$16
20 MIN	6	0	67	80	2.70	0.75	2.80	0.97	73	64	22.5	4%	32%	28%	5%	18.1%	91.4	49	20	31	22%	73%	19%	19%	11	90	36%	0%			14.4	209	$34
21 MIN	6	0	106	113	4.66	1.30	4.02	1.20	107	97	21.6	7%	25%	18%	7%	14.3%	90.5	38	24	37	33%	68%	14%	12%	21	85	24%	24%			-5.1	126	$0
22																																	
23 MIN	6	0	104	117	4.23	1.17	4.04	1.15	93	102	20.4	7%	27%	21%	7%	13.1%	90.9	33	20	47	30%	70%	13%	12%	20	81	30%	35%	0	0.78	1.3	143	$5
1st Half	1	0	26	26	6.23	1.46	4.66	1.22	120	101	18.8	6%	23%	17%	7%	12.4%	89.9	33	19	47	37%	57%	8%	8%	6	72	17%	67%			-6.1	122	-$11
2nd Half	5	0	78	91	3.56	1.07	3.84	1.13	87	104	21.0	7%	29%	22%	7%	13.4%	91.2	32	20	47	27%	76%	15%	13%	14	85	36%	21%	0	0.79	7.4	150	$17
Proj	**10**	**0**	**152**	**170**	**3.97**	**1.10**	**3.36**	**1.11**	**94**	**92**	**21.2**	**6%**	**28%**	**22%**	**7%**	**14.6%**	**91.0**	**38**	**21**	**41**	**29%**	**69%**	**14%**	**13%**	**28**						**6.6**	**154**	**$13**

Mahle,Tyler

Age: 29 | Th: R | Role: SP | Ht: 6' 3" | Wt: 210 | Type: Pwr/FB
Health: F | PT/Exp: A | Consist: A | LIMA Plan: B | Rand Var: -2 | MM: 3300

Pitched well on surface before Tommy John surgery ended season in May. Sub-indicators (xBB%, SwK) hint early BB% and K% weren't going to last over longer haul, however, and favorable S% drove wedge between ERA and xERA. Likely out for most of 2024, but worth a late-summer stash if rehab looks promising.

Yr Tm	W	Sv	IP	K	ERA	WHIP	xERA	xWHIP	vL+	vR+	BF/G	BB%	K%	K-BB%	xBB%	SwK	Vel	G	L	F	H%	S%	HR/F	xHR/F	GS	APC	DOM%	DIS%	Sv%	LI	RAR	BPX	R$
19 CIN	3	0	130	129	5.14	1.31	4.08	1.23	115	92	22.2	6%	23%	17%	6%	10.0%	93.3	47	22	31	32%	66%	21%	17%	25	88	24%	32%			-10.1	133	-$2
20 CIN	2	0	48	60	3.59	1.15	4.36	1.27	88	92	20.1	10%	30%	19%	8%	14.7%	93.9	29	21	50	27%	73%	10%	12%	9	85	44%	33%	0	0.79	5.1	117	$8
21 CIN	13	0	180	210	3.75	1.23	3.76	1.20	79	111	23.0	8%	28%	19%	8%	12.0%	94.1	42	21	37	31%	74%	14%	11%	33	97	30%	24%			11.4	134	$15
22 2 TM	6	0	121	126	4.40	1.22	4.10	1.24	86	110	21.9	9%	25%	17%	8%	11.8%	93.3	36	18	47	29%	67%	10%	11%	23	91	26%	30%			-6.4	106	$2
23 MIN	1	0	26	28	3.16	1.05	3.78	1.09	62	115	20.4	5%	27%	23%	8%	10.9%	92.7	38	17	45	28%	82%	16%	11%	5	85	0%	0%			3.7	163	-$2
1st Half	1	0	26	28	3.16	1.05	3.78	1.09	62	116	20.4	5%	27%	23%	8%	10.9%	92.7	38	17	45	28%	82%	16%	11%	5	85	0%	0%			3.7	164	-$3
2nd Half																																	
Proj	**1**	**0**	**29**	**33**	**3.80**	**1.16**	**3.61**	**1.18**	**83**	**107**	**20.3**	**8%**	**28%**	**20%**	**8%**	**12.1%**	**93.4**	**37**	**19**	**44**	**29%**	**74%**	**14%**	**12%**	**6**						**1.9**	**134**	**-$3**

CORBIN YOUNG

Manaea,Sean

Age: 32	Th: L	Role: SP	Health: C	LIMA Plan: A+
Ht: 6' 5"	Wt: 245	Type:	PT/Exp: A	Rand Var: 0
			Consist: A	MM: 3203

Spent most of year in bulk relief; ended up with same old mediocre results. Did flash career-high velocity, but it came with fewer whiffs as 2nd half K% fell back to earth and xERA/xWHIP hardly budged. A consistent innings-eater, but without a true plus skill on this page, it's hard to see a major step forward.

Yr Tm	W	Sv	IP	K	ERA	WHIP	xERA	xWHIP	vL+	vR+	BF/G	BB%	K%	K-BB%	xBB%	SwK	Vel	G	L	F	H%	S%	HR/F	xHR/F	GS	APC	DOM%	DIS%	Sv%	LI	RAR	BPX	R$
19 OAK *	7	0	58	63	2.54	0.84	2.14	1.17	74	64	21.1	6%	30%	24%	7%	12.2%	89.8	41	18	41	22%	80%	11%	12%	5	89	60%	20%			14.0	153	$9
20 OAK	4	0	54	45	4.50	1.20	3.93	1.16	106	94	20.2	4%	20%	17%	6%	10.2%	90.4	50	20	29	32%	66%	14%	13%	11	74	27%	27%			-0.3	143	$6
21 OAK	11	0	179	194	3.91	1.23	3.74	1.12	82	101	23.6	5%	26%	20%	5%	13.2%	92.2	42	22	36	33%	73%	14%	14%	32	93	41%	22%			7.8	153	$12
22 SD	8	0	158	156	4.96	1.30	4.10	1.23	86	114	22.4	7%	23%	16%	6%	12.5%	91.2	38	19	43	30%	67%	15%	12%	28	83	25%	29%	0	0.74	-19.2	109	-$2
23 SF	7	1	118	128	4.44	1.24	3.99	1.26	77	106	13.5	8%	26%	17%	6%	11.4%	93.6	41	22	37	31%	67%	12%	13%	10	55	0%	40%	100	0.94	-1.5	122	$4
1st Half	3	0	55	70	5.53	1.32	3.97	1.24	74	122	12.7	10%	29%	19%	7%	11.6%	93.9	35	25	40	33%	60%	14%	17%	6	55	0%	50%	0	0.94	-8.2	132	-$4
2nd Half	4	1	62	58	3.47	1.17	4.00	1.27	80	92	14.3	7%	23%	15%	6%	11.3%	93.4	46	20	34	29%	73%	10%	8%	4	56	0%	25%	100	0.93	6.7	114	$10
Proj	9	0	145	145	4.25	1.22	3.67	1.21	81	103	22.5	7%	25%	17%	6%	11.9%	92.6	42	21	37	30%	69%	13%	13%	26						1.4	124	$7

Manning,Matt

Age: 26	Th: R	Role: SP	Health: F	LIMA Plan: B+
Ht: 6' 6"	Wt: 195	Type: Con/FB	PT/Exp: C	Rand Var: -5
			Consist: F	MM: 1003

Part SP, part human bullseye broke his foot twice off comebackers in April and Sept. Solid on-field results were a complete mirage: already-shaky K% dipped further as he barely missed any bats, H% was extremely kind, and served up more FBs than ever. Heed xERA/xWHIP and leave him for streaming consideration only.

Yr Tm	W	Sv	IP	K	ERA	WHIP	xERA	xWHIP	vL+	vR+	BF/G	BB%	K%	K-BB%	xBB%	SwK	Vel	G	L	F	H%	S%	HR/F	xHR/F	GS	APC	DOM%	DIS%	Sv%	LI	RAR	BPX	R$
19 aa	11	0	135	124	3.63	1.15	2.96				22.4	7%	23%	16%							29%	69%									14.6	114	$13
20																																	
21 DET *	5	0	118	86	7.09	1.58	6.36	1.46	105	108	20.9	8%	16%	8%	7%	7.5%	93.7	44	22	34	33%	57%	10%	13%	18	79	6%	50%			-41.3	25	-$20
22 DET *	3	0	84	66	3.22	1.23	3.38	1.31	94	82	18.9	8%	19%	11%	6%	10.4%	93.2	41	19	40	29%	75%	8%	9%	12	83	42%	50%			7.8	88	$1
23 DET	5	0	78	50	3.58	1.04	5.03	1.38	96	81	21.1	7%	16%	9%	6%	8.4%	93.4	39	15	47	22%	71%	10%	14%	15	79	13%	33%			7.3	62	$6
1st Half	2	0	22	15	4.84	1.21	5.49	1.41	128	84	23.8	7%	16%	8%	7%	7.3%	93.0	36	11	53	25%	65%	11%	11%	4	89	0%	50%			-1.4	52	-$7
2nd Half	3	0	56	35	3.07	0.97	4.84	1.36	85	81	20.1	6%	16%	10%	6%	8.8%	93.6	40	16	44	21%	74%	9%	16%	11	75	18%	27%			8.7	66	$9
Proj	8	0	145	104	4.50	1.23	4.52	1.37	104	92	21.2	8%	18%	10%	7%	8.3%	93.4	40	17	43	27%	67%	11%	13%	28						-3.1	66	$3

Manoah,Alek

Age: 26	Th: R	Role: SP	Health: A	LIMA Plan: C+
Ht: 6' 6"	Wt: 285	Type: Pwr/FB	PT/Exp: A	Rand Var: 0
			Consist: D	MM: 1203

A full-blown disaster from the start, as June demotion to low minors did little to rectify things. Zero signs of solace from the skills: walk rate, xBB% ballooned; whiffs disappeared; spun three times as many DISaster starts as DOMinant ones. Track record offers hope, but even a sub-4.00 ERA seems like an uphill battle at this point.

Yr Tm	W	Sv	IP	K	ERA	WHIP	xERA	xWHIP	vL+	vR+	BF/G	BB%	K%	K-BB%	xBB%	SwK	Vel	G	L	F	H%	S%	HR/F	xHR/F	GS	APC	DOM%	DIS%	Sv%	LI	RAR	BPX	R$
19																																	
20																																	
21 TOR *	12	0	130	150	2.87	0.99	2.37	1.21	98	66	21.5	9%	30%	22%	8%	13.4%	93.4	39	21	41	25%	76%	11%	9%	20	92	50%	20%			22.3	137	$21
22 TOR	16	0	197	180	2.24	0.99	3.81	1.19	98	65	25.4	6%	23%	16%	6%	11.6%	93.6	37	21	42	25%	82%	7%	8%	31	95	35%	10%			41.9	110	$32
23 TOR	3	0	87	79	5.87	1.74	5.87	1.66	120	108	21.8	14%	19%	5%	10%	9.3%	92.8	38	21	41	32%	69%	14%	14%	19	89	16%	47%			-16.6	-2	-$15
1st Half	1	0	58	48	6.36	1.90	6.35	1.74	121	122	21.7	15%	17%	2%	11%	8.8%	92.8	38	22	40	33%	70%	15%	15%	13	89	15%	62%			-14.5	-29	-$23
2nd Half	2	0	29	31	4.91	1.43	4.99	1.49	120	82	22.2	13%	23%	11%	9%	10.4%	92.7	38	19	44	29%	68%	11%	12%	6	90	17%	17%			-2.1	52	-$3
Proj	8	0	131	122	4.43	1.39	4.49	1.42	117	89	21.5	11%	22%	11%	9%	10.8%	93.0	38	20	42	29%	72%	12%	12%	26						-1.6	62	$0

Márquez,Germán

Age: 29	Th: R	Role: SP	Health: F	LIMA Plan: B
Ht: 6' 1"	Wt: 230	Type: Con	PT/Exp: A	Rand Var: +5
			Consist: A	MM: 3100

You're durable until you're not, as the starting pitching adage goes. Underwent Tommy John surgery in May after racking up sixth-most IP from 2017-22. Might be in line for late-2024 return, but not worth stashing given recent trends in SwK, K-BB%, and BPX. Check back next year.

Yr Tm	W	Sv	IP	K	ERA	WHIP	xERA	xWHIP	vL+	vR+	BF/G	BB%	K%	K-BB%	xBB%	SwK	Vel	G	L	F	H%	S%	HR/F	xHR/F	GS	APC	DOM%	DIS%	Sv%	LI	RAR	BPX	R$
19 COL	12	0	174	175	4.76	1.20	3.69	1.16	104	93	25.8	5%	24%	19%	6%	13.0%	95.5	49	22	29	31%	65%	20%	19%	28	93	29%	18%			-5.4	154	$9
20 COL	4	0	82	73	3.75	1.26	4.09	1.28	95	87	26.5	7%	21%	14%	6%	12.6%	95.7	51	23	26	31%	71%	9%	13%	13	94	38%	23%			7.1	112	$12
21 COL	12	0	180	176	4.40	1.27	3.76	1.28	103	86	23.6	8%	23%	15%	8%	12.3%	94.8	52	22	26	30%	68%	16%	14%	32	87	25%	31%			-3.0	112	$7
22 COL	9	0	182	150	5.00	1.37	4.12	1.33	121	103	25.1	8%	19%	11%	6%	10.6%	95.4	48	21	32	30%	67%	17%	14%	31	92	13%	35%			-23.2	83	-$6
23 COL	2	0	20	17	4.95	1.10	3.60	1.15	111	108	20.0	4%	22%	18%	8%	10.9%	95.3	48	21	31	28%	61%	22%	21%	4	76	25%	50%			-1.5	143	-$4
1st Half	2	0	20	17	4.95	1.10	3.60	1.16	112	109	20.0	4%	21%	18%	8%	10.9%	95.3	48	21	31	28%	61%	22%	21%	4	76	25%	50%			-1.5	144	-$6
2nd Half																																	
Proj	2	0	22	19	4.56	1.23	3.58	1.24	107	97	22.9	7%	22%	15%	7%	11.7%	95.4	49	22	29	30%	67%	17%	16%	4						-0.6	121	-$4

Marsh,Alec

Age: 26	Th: R	Role: SP	Health: A	LIMA Plan: B
Ht: 6' 2"	Wt: 220	Type: Pwr	PT/Exp: D	Rand Var: +3
			Consist: B	MM: 2201

3-9, 5.69 ERA in 74 IP at KC. Called up from AAA in June, but gave up 18 ER in first five starts and was whisked away to bullpen. Missed bats thanks to wipeout slider, but control issues from minors (10% career BB%) carried over, and xERA/xWHIP offers little hope for much growth. Shoot your end game shots elsewhere.

Yr Tm	W	Sv	IP	K	ERA	WHIP	xERA	xWHIP	vL+	vR+	BF/G	BB%	K%	K-BB%	xBB%	SwK	Vel	G	L	F	H%	S%	HR/F	xHR/F	GS	APC	DOM%	DIS%	Sv%	LI	RAR	BPX	R$
19																																	
20																																	
21 aa	1	0	26	34	5.79	1.38	4.45				18.3	12%	31%	19%							32%	60%									-4.9	99	-$6
22 a/a	2	0	125	122	6.54	1.58	5.96				20.4	9%	22%	13%							35%	61%									-39.7	58	-$19
23 KC *	8	0	137	142	5.42	1.59	5.57	1.40	130	113	19.6	11%	25%	13%	9%	13.0%	94.2	35	23	42	34%	69%	18%	19%	8	79	0%	63%	0	0.96	-18.5	64	-$11
1st Half	5	0	67	62	5.48	1.68	5.59	1.49	119	221	20.1	11%	21%	9%	12%	7.4%	94.5	15	15	69	36%	68%	22%	19%	1	95	0%	100%			-9.5	64	-$11
2nd Half	3	0	70	80	5.37	1.51	4.55	1.38	132	107	20.0	11%	25%	14%	8%	13.4%	94.2	36	23	41	33%	70%	18%	19%	7	78	0%	57%	0	0.97	-9.0	87	-$2
Proj	4	0	87	90	4.86	1.50	4.28	1.37	142	113	20.3	11%	24%	13%	9%	13.4%	94.2	36	23	41	33%	71%	15%	17%	18						-5.7	78	-$6

Martin,Christopher

Age: 38	Th: R	Role: RP	Health: D	LIMA Plan: A
Ht: 6' 8"	Wt: 225	Type: Con/GB	PT/Exp: C	Rand Var: -5
			Consist: C	MM: 5210

Missed three weeks in April (shoulder), but otherwise familiar story of excellent ratios and few saves to show for it. This version featured fewer Ks—he wasn't able to hold 2022's SwK spike—with another lethal GB%, BB% combo. Luck factors (S%, HR/F) doubt full repeat, but would be a good closer speculation if he was 10 years younger.

Yr Tm	W	Sv	IP	K	ERA	WHIP	xERA	xWHIP	vL+	vR+	BF/G	BB%	K%	K-BB%	xBB%	SwK	Vel	G	L	F	H%	S%	HR/F	xHR/F	GS	APC	DOM%	DIS%	Sv%	LI	RAR	BPX	R$
19 2 TM	1	4	56	65	3.40	1.02	2.96	0.97	77	102	3.7	2%	30%	28%	4%	13.2%	95.7	50	20	30	32%	75%	20%	20%	0	15			67	0.95	7.6	213	$4
20 ATL	1	1	18	20	1.00	0.61	3.14	1.02	47	54	3.5	5%	30%	26%	5%	12.1%	94.1	39	24	37	19%	90%	7%	21%	0	15			100	0.98	7.7	177	$7
21 ATL	2	1	43	33	3.95	1.27	3.99	1.17	108	90	3.9	3%	18%	15%	4%	10.1%	94.8	49	20	31	34%	71%	10%	11%	0	14			20	0.94	1.7	128	-$3
22 2 NL	4	2	56	74	3.05	0.98	2.49	0.87	93	84	3.8	2%	33%	31%	4%	13.4%	95.2	49	19	32	34%	73%	13%	15%	0	14			50	1.06	6.3	242	$5
23 BOS	4	3	51	46	1.05	1.03	3.12	1.13	88	69	3.6	4%	23%	19%	4%	11.7%	95.5	51	28	21	30%	92%	7%	7%	0	13			75	1.17	20.8	153	$9
1st Half	2	1	26	22	1.73	0.96	3.17	1.12	94	59	3.7	3%	22%	19%	4%	12.4%	95.2	51	28	21	29%	83%	6%	6%	0	13			50	1.18	8.3	156	$2
2nd Half	2	2	25	24	0.36	1.11	3.07	1.15	82	81	3.5	5%	24%	19%	4%	11.1%	95.8	51	28	21	32%	100%	7%	8%	0	13			100	1.16	12.4	151	$5
Proj	4	4	58	56	3.01	1.04	2.96	1.07	89	78	3.6	4%	25%	21%	4%	11.7%	95.4	50	24	26	31%	73%	10%	11%	0						9.4	168	$5

Martinez,Nick

Age: 33	Th: R	Role: SP	Health: A	LIMA Plan: A
Ht: 6' 1"	Wt: 200	Type: Pwr	PT/Exp: A	Rand Var: 0
			Consist: B	MM: 4203

Toed the rotation/multi-inning relief line for second straight season. Similar results, but with positive signs as GB% entered elite territory and 2nd half uptick in whiffs and Ks was fueled by more elite change-ups (25% SwK). Fantasy relevance hinges on starting gig, but late skill growth/approach change makes him a fine dart throw.

Yr Tm	W	Sv	IP	K	ERA	WHIP	xERA	xWHIP	vL+	vR+	BF/G	BB%	K%	K-BB%	xBB%	SwK	Vel	G	L	F	H%	S%	HR/F	xHR/F	GS	APC	DOM%	DIS%	Sv%	LI	RAR	BPX	R$
19																																	
20 for	2	0	76	63	5.74	1.73	6.15				20.3	14%	18%	4%							31%	70%									-12.0	27	-$18
21 for	9	0	141	131	1.98	1.16	2.99				26.7	8%	23%	15%							28%	86%									39.7	109	$20
22 SD	4	8	106	95	3.47	1.29	4.01	1.33	103	99	9.5	9%	21%	12%	7%	12.1%	93.4	47	19	34	28%	79%	14%	13%	10	37	20%	40%	89	0.80	6.5	84	$5
23 SD	6	1	110	106	3.43	1.26	3.79	1.32	100	83	7.3	9%	23%	14%	7%	13.0%	93.1	54	18	28	30%	76%	14%	15%	9	28	33%	33%	14	1.15	12.3	112	$7
1st Half	3	1	60	48	4.03	1.31	4.19	1.38	97	89	7.9	8%	19%	11%	6%	12.5%	93.0	56	15	29	29%	72%	13%	16%	4	30	25%	50%	25	1.15	2.3	88	$1
2nd Half	3	0	50	58	2.70	1.20	3.34	1.24	106	77	6.7	9%	28%	19%	8%	13.6%	93.3	50	22	27	30%	82%	15%	13%	5	26	40%	20%	0	1.15	10.1	140	$8
Proj	8	0	138	140	3.72	1.26	3.45	1.27	108	89	20.4	9%	25%	16%	8%	12.9%	93.2	52	19	29	31%	73%	15%	13%	22						10.3	121	$8

RYAN BLOOMFIELD

Matz,Steven

Age: 33	Th: L	Role: SP	Health: F	LIMA Plan: A+
Ht: 6' 2"	Wt: 201	Type:	PT/Exp: B	Rand Var: -1
			Consist: A	MM: 3201

Slow start driven by shaky skills, unkind H%; began to right the ship before August lat strain ended season. Couldn't hold 2022's K% improvement, but in-season uptick in change-ups (16% SwK) with 2nd half control, velocity gains were promising signs. Health, age say not to count on full workload, but can still be effective in spurts.

Yr Tm	W	Sv	IP	K	ERA	WHIP	xERA	xWHIP	vL+	vR+	BF/G	BB%	K%	K-BB%	xBB%	SwK	Vel	G	L	F	H%	S%	HR/F	xHR/F	GS	APC	DOM%	DIS%	Sv%	LI	RAR	BPX	R$
19 NYM	11	0	160	153	4.21	1.34	4.37	1.31	106	103	21.6	8%	22%	15%	7%	10.1%	93.4	47	20	33	31%	74%	17%	18%	30	84	10%	33%	0	0.80	5.8	110	$7
20 NYM	0	0	31	36	9.68	1.70	4.61	1.21	132	146	15.8	7%	25%	18%	7%	10.7%	94.5	33	28	39	36%	50%	38%	25%	6	70	0%	67%	0	0.67	-19.8	138	-$20
21 TOR	14	0	151	144	3.82	1.33	4.08	1.23	100	97	22.3	7%	22%	16%	6%	9.9%	94.5	45	22	32	33%	75%	12%	11%	29	88	17%	31%			8.2	119	$8
22 STL *	5	0	67	70	4.36	1.18	3.85	1.07	109	101	11.7	6%	26%	20%	5%	12.8%	94.6	38	26	35	31%	66%	16%	8%	10	57	20%	20%	0	0.89	-3.2	126	$0
23 STL	4	0	105	98	3.86	1.33	4.13	1.28	81	104	18.0	7%	22%	15%	6%	11.0%	94.2	45	24	32	33%	74%	11%	9%	17	75	24%	35%	0	0.74	6.1	112	$1
1st Half	0	0	64	58	4.92	1.59	4.40	1.36	76	123	16.9	8%	20%	12%	7%	10.2%	93.8	46	27	28	36%	71%	14%	12%	10	70	0%	50%	0	0.71	-4.7	89	-$12
2nd Half	4	0	41	40	2.20	0.93	3.74	1.14	92	73	20.1	5%	25%	20%	5%	12.4%	94.8	43	18	39	26%	80%	7%	6%	7	85	57%	14%	0	0.80	10.8	148	$11
Proj	7	0	116	114	4.02	1.28	3.67	1.20	97	100	20.7	7%	24%	17%	6%	11.2%	94.4	42	23	35	32%	73%	15%	11%	23						4.5	127	$4

Matsui,Yuki

Age: 28	Th: L	Role: RP	Health: A	LIMA Plan: C+
Ht: 5' 8"	Wt: 167	Type: Pwr	PT/Exp: A	Rand Var: -4
			Consist: A	MM: 5520

Closer in Japan, the youngest to reach 200 career saves in Pacific League; led league in each of past two seasons. Excellent strikeout totals with equally shaky walk rates, leading to potential stateside bumps in the road. Landing-spot dependent, but makes for speculative dart throw given ninth-inning track record.

Yr Tm	W	Sv	IP	K	ERA	WHIP	xERA	xWHIP	vL+	vR+	BF/G	BB%	K%	K-BB%	xBB%	SwK	Vel	G	L	F	H%	S%	HR/F	xHR/F	GS	APC	DOM%	DIS%	Sv%	LI	RAR	BPX	R$
19 for	2	38	69	102	2.42	1.05	2.47				3.9	11%	38%	27%							27%	84%									17.8	150	$24
20 for	6	2	85	108	4.73	1.41	4.89				12.8	13%	30%	17%							30%	73%									-2.9	83	$11
21 for	0	24	43	56	0.78	1.16	1.90				4.0	15%	33%	18%							25%	96%									18.5	140	$14
22 for	1	32	51	79	2.40	0.90	1.70				3.6	13%	41%	29%							20%	82%									9.9	161	$18
23 for	2	39	57	68	1.96	1.00	2.38				3.7	8%	35%	27%							28%	86%									16.7	162	$23
1st Half																																	
2nd Half																																	
Proj	3	18	58	83	3.64	1.23	3.10	1.23			4.5	12%	35%	23%				44	20	36	31%	72%	11%	11%	0						4.9	146	$9

May,Dustin

Age: 26	Th: R	Role: SP	Health: F	LIMA Plan: A+
Ht: 6' 6"	Wt: 180	Type:	PT/Exp: D	Rand Var: -5
			Consist: C	MM: 4100

Another tough break, as elbow injury in May and surgery in July ended season. Surface ERA was a H% and HR/F-fueled mirage, as whiffs and Ks plummeted, he kept issuing walks, and vastly outpitched xERA and xWHIP. Might return by summer, but injuries and skill collapse make him a tricky investment.

Yr Tm	W	Sv	IP	K	ERA	WHIP	xERA	xWHIP	vL+	vR+	BF/G	BB%	K%	K-BB%	xBB%	SwK	Vel	G	L	F	H%	S%	HR/F	xHR/F	GS	APC	DOM%	DIS%	Sv%	LI	RAR	BPX	R$
19 LA *	8	0	143	129	3.76	1.17	3.12	1.14	116	64	16.8	6%	23%	17%	6%	9.2%	96.0	44	28	27	32%	67%	7%	13%	4	40	25%	0%	0	0.94	13.1	136	$10
20 LA	3	0	56	44	2.57	1.09	3.98	1.31	108	69	18.7	7%	20%	13%	6%	9.0%	98.1	55	19	26	24%	87%	21%	20%	10	72	0%	40%	0	0.86	13.0	103	$15
21 LA	1	0	23	35	2.74	0.96	2.13	0.95	79	81	18.6	6%	38%	31%	6%	14.7%	98.0	56	24	20	29%	83%	40%	29%	5	74	20%	0%			4.3	238	-$1
22 LA *	3	0	49	56	3.36	1.09	2.68	1.38	75	98	17.4	10%	29%	19%	8%	13.5%	97.7	51	19	29	27%	72%	13%	8%	6	79	17%	33%			3.7	125	$1
23 LA	4	0	48	34	2.63	0.94	4.36	1.41	74	61	20.8	9%	18%	10%	7%	6.7%	97.0	45	20	35	22%	70%	2%	5%	9	82	33%	22%			10.1	64	$5
1st Half	4	0	48	34	2.63	0.94	4.36	1.41	74	61	20.8	9%	18%	10%	7%	6.7%	97.0	45	20	35	22%	70%	2%	5%	9	82	33%	22%			10.1	64	$10
2nd Half																																	
Proj	2	0	29	25	3.39	1.06	3.57	1.28	89	72	21.7	8%	23%	15%	7%	9.4%	97.1	48	22	30	26%	69%	8%	10%	5						3.4	104	-$2

Mayza,Tim

Age: 32	Th: L	Role: RP	Health: C	LIMA Plan: A+
Ht: 6' 3"	Wt: 213	Type: Pwr/xGB	PT/Exp: C	Rand Var: -5
			Consist: A	MM: 5200

Posted a sub-2.25 ERA in every month en route to career year. Heavy sinker usage (77%) drove another elite GB%, though got some help from HR/F to keep homers in check. Continued SwK spiral questions K% uptick, while S% and xERA hint at likely pullback. Doubtful he can enter save conversation.

Yr Tm	W	Sv	IP	K	ERA	WHIP	xERA	xWHIP	vL+	vR+	BF/G	BB%	K%	K-BB%	xBB%	SwK	Vel	G	L	F	H%	S%	HR/F	xHR/F	GS	APC	DOM%	DIS%	Sv%	LI	RAR	BPX	R$
19 TOR	1	0	51	55	4.91	1.40	4.25	1.44	95	102	3.3	12%	24%	12%	11%	14.4%	94.2	53	21	26	29%	69%	22%	22%	0	14			0	1.04	-2.6	84	-$4
20																																	
21 TOR	5	1	53	57	3.40	0.98	2.87	1.10	62	87	3.4	6%	27%	21%	8%	11.4%	94.1	59	18	23	27%	68%	16%	9%	0	14			25	1.00	5.7	171	$4
22 TOR	8	2	49	44	3.14	1.11	2.97	1.18	72	115	3.1	6%	23%	17%	7%	10.1%	93.7	58	22	20	27%	79%	26%	24%	0	12			33	1.25	4.9	135	$4
23 TOR	3	1	53	53	1.52	1.22	3.12	1.22	76	102	3.1	7%	25%	18%	8%	9.5%	93.4	58	23	19	33%	89%	7%	14%	0	12			33	1.26	18.5	144	$5
1st Half	1	1	28	27	1.27	1.16	3.01	1.13	75	93	2.9	4%	24%	19%	6%	9.2%	93.2	56	26	19	35%	88%	0%	12%	0	11			100	1.23	10.7	164	$1
2nd Half	2	0	25	26	1.80	1.28	3.25	1.32	77	113	3.4	10%	25%	16%	9%	9.9%	93.7	62	18	20	31%	90%	15%	16%	0	13			0	1.29	7.8	125	$1
Proj	4	0	58	59	2.61	1.17	3.01	1.21	76	101	3.2	8%	25%	18%	8%	10.7%	93.7	58	21	21	30%	81%	15%	15%	0						12.3	143	$3

McArthur,James

Age: 27	Th: R	Role: RP	Health: D	LIMA Plan: A+
Ht: 6' 7"	Wt: 230	Type: /GB	PT/Exp: D	Rand Var: +3
			Consist: F	MM: 4121

4 Sv, 4.63 ERA in 23 IP at KC. Moved up and down to AAA after May trade; ended season as primary closer. Notable 2nd half growth fueled the ascent with plenty of strikes (xBB%), more Ks, higher velocity, and extreme GB% tilt. Track record has its doubts, but a sneaky closer target if late skills hold.

Yr Tm	W	Sv	IP	K	ERA	WHIP	xERA	xWHIP	vL+	vR+	BF/G	BB%	K%	K-BB%	xBB%	SwK	Vel	G	L	F	H%	S%	HR/F	xHR/F	GS	APC	DOM%	DIS%	Sv%	LI	RAR	BPX	R$
19																																	
20																																	
21 aa	2	0	75	66	4.75	1.39	4.91				16.7	7%	21%	14%							33%	69%									-4.5	80	-$6
22 aa	2	0	57	52	5.48	1.76	6.90				20.1	10%	20%	10%							37%	73%									-10.6	36	-$11
23 KC *	3	5	82	75	5.15	1.33	4.06	1.02	116	73	7.4	2%	26%	23%	4%	11.1%	94.0	59	16	25	32%	61%	13%	14%	2	19	0%	50%	100	1.03	-8.2	91	-$3
1st Half	0	0	38	33	7.98	1.86	6.99	1.52	300	276	9.9	11%	18%	7%	12%	7.5%	93.2	56	22	22	38%	57%	50%	10%	0	40			0	0.02	-17.2	37	-$23
2nd Half	3	5	43	42	2.66	0.87	1.49	1.16	78	60	5.7	6%	26%	20%	4%	11.6%	94.2	59	15	26	24%	70%	7%	14%	2	18	0%	50%	100	1.09	9.0	165	$13
Proj	2	14	65	59	4.01	1.32	3.51	1.32	139	109	9.4	9%	22%	13%	4%	11.6%	94.2	59	15	26	31%	73%	18%	13%	0						2.5	110	$3

McClanahan,Shane

Age: 27	Th: L	Role: RP	Health: F	LIMA Plan:
Ht: 6' 1"	Wt: 200	Type: #DIV/0!	PT/Exp: A	Rand Var:
			Consist: B	MM:

Posted ace-like numbers before August forearm injury led to Tommy John surgery. Some control concerns in 1st half with fewer Ks, but consistently elite sub-indicators (xBB%, SwK) and revamped change-up (28.3% SwK) ease any fear of on-field decline. Expects to miss the 2024 season, but a keeper-worthy stash for 2025.

Yr Tm	W	Sv	IP	K	ERA	WHIP	xERA	xWHIP	vL+	vR+	BF/G	BB%	K%	K-BB%	xBB%	SwK	Vel	G	L	F	H%	S%	HR/F	xHR/F	GS	APC	DOM%	DIS%	Sv%	LI	RAR	BPX	R$
19 aa	1	0	19	19	10.87	2.24	9.63				24.2	6%	20%	13%							48%	50%									-15.0	44	-$11
20																																	
21 TAM	10	0	123	141	3.43	1.27	3.49	1.16	98	92	20.7	7%	27%	20%	6%	15.1%	96.5	45	25	30	34%	77%	14%	17%	25	78	16%	16%			12.7	148	$9
22 TAM	12	0	166	194	2.54	0.93	2.72	1.04	86	78	22.9	6%	30%	24%	6%	16.0%	96.8	50	20	30	26%	79%	16%	14%	28	88	46%	18%			29.2	178	$28
23 TAM	11	0	115	121	3.29	1.18	3.93	1.27	86	94	22.3	9%	26%	17%	6%	16.0%	96.8	44	19	37	28%	78%	13%	13%	21	87	24%	24%			14.8	119	$13
1st Half	11	0	96	101	2.53	1.17	3.97	1.31	95	88	22.9	10%	26%	16%	6%	16.0%	96.7	43	21	37	27%	84%	12%	13%	17	88	29%	24%			21.3	107	$31
2nd Half	0	0	19	20	7.11	1.26	3.78	1.09	51	127	20.0	4%	25%	21%	5%	16.1%	97.4	47	14	39	34%	45%	18%	13%	4	81	0%	25%			-6.5	178	-$8
Proj																																	

McCullers,Lance

Age: 30	Th: R	Role: SP	Health: F	LIMA Plan: A+
Ht: 6' 1"	Wt: 202	Type: Pwr/GB	PT/Exp: C	Rand Var: 0
			Consist: A	MM: 4201

Entered season with forearm injury, had surgery in June without a single inning pitched. Pre-injury profile consisted of regular control problems, tons of groundballs, and solid K% buoyed by slider (16% SwK) and curveball (18% SwK). Likely out until summer with major question marks, yet still a reasonable IL stash.

Yr Tm	W	Sv	IP	K	ERA	WHIP	xERA	xWHIP	vL+	vR+	BF/G	BB%	K%	K-BB%	xBB%	SwK	Vel	G	L	F	H%	S%	HR/F	xHR/F	GS	APC	DOM%	DIS%	Sv%	LI	RAR	BPX	R$
19																																	
20 HOU	3	0	55	56	3.93	1.16	3.46	1.28	91	102	20.6	9%	25%	16%	9%	11.8%	93.8	60	17	23	28%	68%	15%	25%	11	80	36%	36%			3.6	129	$9
21 HOU	13	0	162	185	3.16	1.22	3.53	1.32	95	76	24.4	11%	27%	16%	9%	11.9%	94.0	56	17	27	29%	76%	12%	11%	28	100	21%	21%			22.1	115	$18
22 HOU	4	0	48	50	2.27	1.24	3.59	1.34	80	100	24.4	11%	26%	14%	9%	11.5%	93.1	50	19	31	28%	85%	11%	12%	8	95	25%	13%			10.0	95	$2
23																																	
1st Half																																	
2nd Half																																	
Proj	6	0	87	89	3.58	1.22	3.54	1.37	90	98	24.2	11%	25%	14%	10%	11.7%	93.5	54	18	28	27%	73%	13%	14%	15						8.0	97	$4

CORBIN YOUNG

McGough,Scott

Age: 34	Th: R	Role: RP	Health: B	LIMA Plan: A+
Ht: 5' 11"	Wt: 190	Type: Pwr	PT/Exp: A	Rand Var: +5
			Consist: A	MM: 4310

Returned to majors after eight-year hiatus, briefly held closer gig in June. PRO: Plenty of whiffs behind strong K%; GB% tilt, brutal HR/F luck limit HR concerns. CON: Control issues; 2nd half fade ended with Sept IL stint (shoulder). If healthy and gets the chance, a future stint in ninth could last longer.

Yr	Tm	W	Sv	IP	K	ERA	WHIP	xERA	xWHIP	vL+	vR+	BF/G	BB%	K%	K-BB%	xBB%	SwK	Vel	G	L	F	H%	S%	HR/F	xHR/F	GS	APC	DOM%	DIS%	Sv%	LI	RAR	BPX	R$
19	for	6	11	68	61	3.93	1.52	4.46				4.6	9%	21%	11%							36%	74%									4.8	87	$4
20	for	4	0	46	49	4.86	1.38	4.69				3.9	10%	25%	16%							32%	68%									-2.3	88	$2
21	for	3	31	64	72	3.14	1.17	3.69				3.9	11%	28%	17%							24%	83%									8.9	87	$17
22	for	2	38	53	56	2.94	1.09	3.43				3.8	8%	27%	19%							26%	82%									6.7	109	$18
23	ARI	2	9	70	86	4.73	1.28	3.60	1.26	80	120	4.8	10%	29%	19%	7%	14.6%	93.6	49	20	31	29%	70%	25%	18%	1	20	0%	0%	64	1.13	-3.5	136	$1
1st Half		0	7	43	51	2.93	0.98	3.16	1.22	72	79	4.5	9%	30%	20%	6%	15.4%	93.8	54	16	30	23%	76%	17%	19%	0	18			64	1.21	7.4	151	$10
2nd Half		2	2	27	35	7.57	1.76	4.29	1.33	91	179	5.2	11%	27%	16%	8%	13.6%	93.2	41	25	34	37%	64%	33%	16%	1	22	0%	0%	67	1.01	-10.9	115	-$7
Proj		**3**	**5**	**58**	**67**	**3.66**	**1.21**	**3.32**	**1.22**	**66**	**111**	**4.2**	**9%**	**29%**	**19%**	**8%**	**14.2%**	**93.5**	**47**	**21**	**32**	**30%**	**73%**	**14%**	**18%**	**0**						**4.7**	**136**	**$3**

McKenzie,Triston

Age: 26	Th: R	Role: RP	Health: F	LIMA Plan: A+
Ht: 6' 5"	Wt: 165	Type: Pwr/xFB	PT/Exp: A	Rand Var: -3
			Consist: B	MM: 2201

0-3, 5.06 ERA in 16 IP. Lost season started with March shoulder strain, effectively ended with June elbow strain after just two starts. Returned with a full tick off his fastball in late Sept and BB% collapsed, so while he owns 2022 skills, lingering arm issues like this have "ticking time bomb" vibes.

Yr	Tm	W	Sv	IP	K	ERA	WHIP	xERA	xWHIP	vL+	vR+	BF/G	BB%	K%	K-BB%	xBB%	SwK	Vel	G	L	F	H%	S%	HR/F	xHR/F	GS	APC	DOM%	DIS%	Sv%	LI	RAR	BPX	R$
19																																		
20	CLE	2	0	33	42	3.24	0.90	3.45	1.07	100	68	15.9	7%	33%	26%	7%	13.1%	92.8	40	13	47	22%	75%	17%	20%	6	69	17%	33%	0	0.71	5.0	177	$9
21	CLE *	6	0	142	155	4.66	1.22	3.90	1.35	94	89	19.1	12%	27%	15%	8%	13.1%	92.1	30	22	48	24%	68%	15%	12%	24	79	29%	38%	0	0.74	-7.0	77	$2
22	CLE	11	0	191	190	2.96	0.95	3.74	1.12	85	88	23.9	6%	26%	20%	5%	13.3%	92.5	33	18	49	24%	76%	10%	11%	30	91	40%	3%	0	0.80	23.7	128	$26
23	CLE *	0	0	33	31	5.29	1.41	4.72	1.77	50	112	15.5	18%	22%	4%	12%	11.3%	92.4	34	14	52	25%	68%	4%	9%	4	75	25%	25%			-3.9	48	-$7
1st Half		0	0	21	25	4.33	1.23	4.22	1.22	15	106	17.1	10%	30%	20%	7%	16.4%	92.9	39	13	48	29%	71%	9%	9%	2	86	50%	50%			0.0	102	-$8
2nd Half		0	0	14	6	5.45	1.39	3.76	2.14	68	127	15.0	19%	11%	-9%	12%	4.7%	91.9	29	14	57	16%	63%	0%	9%	2	65	0%	0%			-2.0	14	-$9
Proj		**5**	**0**	**102**	**101**	**3.92**	**1.27**	**4.12**	**1.26**	**114**	**107**	**19.0**	**8%**	**24%**	**16%**	**7%**	**13.2%**	**92.5**	**33**	**18**	**48**	**30%**	**75%**	**12%**	**13%**	**20**						**5.1**	**103**	**$2**

McMillon,John

Age: 26	Th: R	Role: RP	Health: C	LIMA Plan: A+
Ht: 6' 3"	Wt: 230	Type: Pwr	PT/Exp: F	Rand Var: -4
			Consist: F	MM: 3410

0-0, 2.25 ERA in 4 IP at KC. Soared through three levels of minors (2.10 ERA, 91/25 K/BB), but hit IL (forearm) shortly after August call-up. Triple-digit heat, strong SwK says Ks should come in bunches despite awful 18% career BB%. Long-term closer, perhaps, but health/control issues are major obstacles.

Yr	Tm	W	Sv	IP	K	ERA	WHIP	xERA	xWHIP	vL+	vR+	BF/G	BB%	K%	K-BB%	xBB%	SwK	Vel	G	L	F	H%	S%	HR/F	xHR/F	GS	APC	DOM%	DIS%	Sv%	LI	RAR	BPX	R$
19																																		
20																																		
21																																		
22																																		
23	KC *	3	5	26	31	1.15	0.99	1.52	1.27			5.3	12%	33%	21%	6%	25.5%	99.0	20	0	80	24%	91%	25%	22%	0	14			83	0.23	10.3	149	$4
1st Half		0	0	7	5	0.00	0.78	0.88				8.7	5%	24%	19%							24%	100%	0%		0	0					3.9	190	-$7
2nd Half		3	5	19	25	1.59	1.07	1.76	1.31			4.6	14%	34%	21%	6%	25.5%	99.0	20	0	80	25%	88%	25%	22%	0	14			83	0.23	6.4	151	$6
Proj		**5**	**5**	**58**	**74**	**3.92**	**1.29**	**3.58**	**1.36**			**5.4**	**14%**	**31%**	**17%**				**45**	**19**	**36**	**30%**	**71%**	**10%**	**10%**	**0**						**2.9**	**104**	**$3**

Means,John

Age: 31	Th: L	Role: RP	Health: F	LIMA Plan: A+
Ht: 6' 3"	Wt: 235	Type: Con/xFB	PT/Exp: C	Rand Var: -3
			Consist: B	MM: 1003

1-2, 2.66 ERA in 24 IP at BAL. Tommy John recovery pushed debut to Sept, where H% welcomed him back kindly. Can't draw much from tiny sample, but minuscule SwK has to be a concern given concurrent spike in FB%. Return to 2021 line seems like a stretch, and can't count on full season of work.

Yr	Tm	W	Sv	IP	K	ERA	WHIP	xERA	xWHIP	vL+	vR+	BF/G	BB%	K%	K-BB%	xBB%	SwK	Vel	G	L	F	H%	S%	HR/F	xHR/F	GS	APC	DOM%	DIS%	Sv%	LI	RAR	BPX	R$
19	BAL	12	0	155	121	3.60	1.14	5.23	1.33	73	100	20.5	6%	19%	13%	8%	10.2%	91.8	31	19	50	27%	75%	10%	10%	27	86	30%	44%	0	0.88	17.3	83	$15
20	BAL	2	0	44	42	4.53	0.98	4.09	1.11	106	93	17.6	4%	24%	20%	6%	12.8%	93.8	44	11	45	23%	68%	22%	16%	10	75	0%	50%			-0.4	157	$5
21	BAL	6	0	147	134	3.62	1.03	4.32	1.14	87	94	22.7	4%	23%	18%	6%	12.4%	92.8	33	20	47	25%	76%	15%	12%	26	90	31%	31%			11.7	127	$13
22	BAL	0	0	8	7	3.38	1.25	4.06	1.21	73	86	17.0	6%	21%	15%	6%	11.1%	91.8	40	24	36	34%	70%	0%	8%	2	68	0%	0%			0.6	109	-$5
23	BAL *	2	0	47	26	3.51	1.01	2.91	1.38	97	69	18.0	5%	11%	7%	5%	8.0%	91.7	29	15	56	21%	70%	10%	10%	4	85	0%	25%			4.7	57	$1
1st Half																																		
2nd Half		2	0	47	26	3.51	1.01	2.91	1.43	97	69	18.0	7%	15%	7%	5%	8.0%	91.7	29	15	56	21%	70%	10%	10%	4	85	0%	25%			4.7	57	$4
Proj		**6**	**0**	**123**	**94**	**4.06**	**1.24**	**4.39**	**1.26**	**110**	**107**	**20.0**	**6%**	**19%**	**13%**	**6%**	**10.5%**	**92.3**	**36**	**19**	**46**	**29%**	**74%**	**12%**	**12%**	**25**						**4.1**	**92**	**$3**

Medina,Luis

Age: 25	Th: R	Role: SP	Health: B	LIMA Plan: C+
Ht: 6' 1"	Wt: 175	Type: Pwr	PT/Exp: D	Rand Var: +1
			Consist: C	MM: 1201

3-10, 5.42 ERA in 110 IP at OAK. Called up in April and hung around with bad results. Poor BB% is major obstacle—xBB% says it isn't going away—while middling K% seems locked in given subpar SwK. Was a tick better in 2nd half, but just a tick -- not nearly enough to bet on any upside. Was 1 for 17 in PQS-DOMinant starts (those are your odds).

Yr	Tm	W	Sv	IP	K	ERA	WHIP	xERA	xWHIP	vL+	vR+	BF/G	BB%	K%	K-BB%	xBB%	SwK	Vel	G	L	F	H%	S%	HR/F	xHR/F	GS	APC	DOM%	DIS%	Sv%	LI	RAR	BPX	R$
19																																		
20																																		
21	aa	4	0	75	73	4.16	1.51	4.62				21.7	13%	22%	10%							32%	74%									1.0	73	-$4
22	aa	5	0	94	91	4.53	1.41	3.53				16.6	13%	23%	10%							30%	67%									-6.6	91	-$4
23	OAK *	3	0	128	124	5.34	1.52	4.73	1.47	106	109	19.1	12%	21%	10%	10%	11.1%	96.0	44	22	34	32%	66%	13%	12%	17	85	6%	41%	0	0.86	-15.9	70	-$11
1st Half		2	0	68	62	6.24	1.65	5.67	1.63	105	131	18.9	14%	20%	6%	11%	9.5%	96.0	44	20	35	30%	65%	19%	16%	8	87	0%	50%	0	0.85	-16.0	40	-$17
2nd Half		1	0	60	63	4.32	1.38	3.67	1.37	108	84	19.4	10%	24%	14%	8%	12.7%	95.9	43	23	34	33%	68%	6%	8%	9	83	11%	33%	0	0.86	0.1	110	-$1
Proj		**4**	**0**	**116**	**114**	**4.80**	**1.49**	**4.39**	**1.48**	**107**	**103**	**21.0**	**13%**	**23%**	**10%**	**10%**	**11.4%**	**96.0**	**44**	**22**	**34**	**31%**	**69%**	**12%**	**11%**	**24**						**-6.8**	**56**	**-$7**

Megill,Tylor

Age: 28	Th: R	Role: RP	Health: F	LIMA Plan: B
Ht: 6' 7"	Wt: 230	Type:	PT/Exp: C	Rand Var: 0
			Consist: C	MM: 2103

9-8, 4.70 ERA in 126 IP at NYM. Stayed healthy, but tough June stretch sent him to AAA for over a month. Skills took a clear step back: xERA jumped more than two runs; Ks, whiffs collapsed; BB%; xBB% ballooned. Strong Sept (9 ER in 5 GS) was H%/S% mirage, so don't get your hopes up. A streamer at best.

Yr	Tm	W	Sv	IP	K	ERA	WHIP	xERA	xWHIP	vL+	vR+	BF/G	BB%	K%	K-BB%	xBB%	SwK	Vel	G	L	F	H%	S%	HR/F	xHR/F	GS	APC	DOM%	DIS%	Sv%	LI	RAR	BPX	R$
19																																		
20																																		
21	NYM *	6	0	131	148	4.11	1.23	4.32	1.18	138	77	20.4	7%	28%	21%	7%	12.6%	94.7	42	16	41	31%	73%	19%	16%	18	86	22%	28%			2.5	113	$5
22	NYM	4	0	47	51	5.13	1.25	3.59	1.15	120	81	13.3	7%	26%	19%	7%	12.9%	95.8	41	23	36	32%	62%	15%	17%	9	53	44%	33%	0	0.54	-6.8	140	-$3
23	NYM *	9	0	153	116	5.42	1.63	5.79	1.48	109	109	22.0	10%	19%	8%	10%	9.9%	95.0	44	21	35	34%	69%	13%	16%	25	89	8%	48%			-20.7	41	-$14
1st Half		6	0	78	60	5.35	1.66	5.56	1.59	105	114	21.7	12%	17%	5%	12%	9.3%	94.5	44	22	34	33%	69%	12%	17%	15	86	0%	53%			-9.7	43	-$10
2nd Half		3	0	78	56	5.34	1.54	5.75	1.42	114	103	22.7	8%	16%	9%	8%	10.7%	95.6	44	19	36	33%	68%	15%	15%	10	95	20%	40%			-9.7	43	-$5
Proj		**8**	**0**	**138**	**122**	**4.60**	**1.36**	**4.20**	**1.35**	**111**	**91**	**19.3**	**9%**	**21%**	**12%**	**9%**	**11.1%**	**95.1**	**43**	**20**	**37**	**30%**	**70%**	**14%**	**16%**	**28**						**-4.6**	**85**	**-$1**

Merryweather,Julian

Age: 32	Th: R	Role: RP	Health: F	LIMA Plan: A+
Ht: 6' 4"	Wt: 215	Type: Pwr/FB	PT/Exp: D	Rand Var: -1
			Consist: B	MM: 4411

Finally avoided injury bug and racked up strikeouts, though never quite got shot at saves. Uptick in fastball velocity, heavy slider usage (21% SwK) say elite K% can stick, and while walks were an issue, xBB% hints at improvement going forward. A worthy saves flyer if health complies again.

Yr	Tm	W	Sv	IP	K	ERA	WHIP	xERA	xWHIP	vL+	vR+	BF/G	BB%	K%	K-BB%	xBB%	SwK	Vel	G	L	F	H%	S%	HR/F	xHR/F	GS	APC	DOM%	DIS%	Sv%	LI	RAR	BPX	R$
19																																		
20	TOR	0	0	13	15	4.15	1.31	3.70	1.32	43	101	6.9	11%	27%	16%	6%	12.0%	96.7	45	33	21	34%	65%	0%	3%	3	29	0%	33%	0	1.23	0.5	110	-$5
21	TOR	0	2	13	12	4.85	1.31	4.47	1.27	165	86	4.2	7%	22%	15%	5%	10.6%	97.5	41	16	43	27%	77%	25%	19%	1	17	0%	100%	100	0.96	-0.9	103	-$5
22	TOR *	2	0	42	36	4.31	1.22	3.55	1.23	117	118	4.3	8%	21%	14%	4%	11.0%	97.3	48	12	40	29%	66%	12%	16%	1	16	0%	100%	0	0.69	-1.8	93	-$3
23	CHC	5	2	72	98	3.38	1.31	3.70	1.27	91	86	4.4	12%	32%	20%	7%	16.0%	98.1	41	19	40	32%	78%	12%	13%	0	18			50	0.77	8.5	132	$4
1st Half		1	0	35	48	2.86	1.44	3.78	1.23	83	93	4.3	11%	32%	21%	8%	16.9%	97.6	39	23	39	39%	81%	6%	9%	0	17			0	0.42	6.3	145	-$3
2nd Half		4	2	37	50	3.86	1.18	3.62	1.31	100	79	4.4	13%	33%	20%	6%	15.2%	98.7	43	15	42	25%	74%	18%	17%	0	18			50	1.14	2.2	122	$7
Proj		**5**	**5**	**65**	**78**	**3.45**	**1.17**	**3.41**	**1.18**	**92**	**83**	**4.4**	**9%**	**30%**	**21%**	**7%**	**15.9%**	**98.2**	**41**	**18**	**41**	**30%**	**74%**	**11%**	**14%**	**0**						**7.0**	**143**	**$6**

RYAN BLOOMFIELD

Middleton,Keynan

Age: 30 | Th: R | Role: RP | Ht: 6' 3" | Wt: 215 | Type: Pwr
Health: F | PT/Exp: D | Consist: D | LIMA Plan: A+ | Rand Var: +1 | MM: 4300

Might have been on brink of closer gig, but was traded to NYY in July before season-ending shoulder issue in Sept. More change-ups led to elite GB%/K% combo, but injury likely played part in 2nd half BB%, xERA spikes. Flyer-worthy, but with arm injuries in five of last six seasons, can't expect him to last very long.

Yr Tm	W	Sv	IP	K	ERA	WHIP	xERA	xWHIP	vL+	vR+	BF/G	BB%	K%	K-BB%	xBB%	SwK	Vel	G	L	F	H%	S%	HR/F	xHR/F	GS	APC	DOM%	DIS%	Sv%	LI	RAR	BPX	R$
19 LAA	0	0	8	6	1.17	1.43	7.05	2.09	33	88	3.0	21%	18%	-3%	12%	9.1%	94.1	30	25	45	20%	91%	0%	8%	0	13			0	0.95	3.2	-95	-$4
20 LAA	0	0	12	11	5.25	1.50	5.88	1.50	79	129	4.1	11%	21%	9%	7%	12.4%	97.1	22	28	50	30%	69%	11%	5%	0	16			0	0.64	-1.2	30	-$8
21 SEA	1	4	31	24	4.94	1.58	6.13	1.66	105	96	4.4	14%	17%	4%	6%	14.7%	95.4	33	21	46	31%	68%	5%	8%	1	17	0%	100%	100	0.64	-2.6	-14	-$5
22 ARI *	3	1	34	33	3.60	1.00	3.13	1.13	105	123	3.7	7%	25%	18%	4%	17.8%	95.1	27	22	51	23%	72%	20%	15%	0	13			25	1.21	1.5	103	$0
23 2 AL	2	2	51	64	3.38	1.24	3.25	1.27	81	98	4.2	11%	30%	19%	6%	17.7%	95.6	57	16	28	29%	80%	24%	21%	0	17			50	0.72	6.0	145	$1
1st Half	1	2	30	39	2.70	1.13	2.85	1.16	69	94	3.8	9%	32%	23%	5%	19.1%	95.7	58	17	25	29%	83%	22%	18%	0	15			67	0.79	6.0	178	$1
2nd Half	1	0	21	25	4.35	1.40	3.87	1.42	100	104	4.7	13%	28%	15%	8%	15.9%	95.4	54	14	32	28%	76%	25%	24%	0	20			0	0.62	-0.1	98	-$4
Proj	2	0	51	57	3.99	1.22	3.34	1.25	89	95	4.0	10%	28%	18%	7%	16.6%	95.5	51	16	33	30%	70%	13%	16%	0						2.1	131	-$1

Mikolas,Miles

Age: 35 | Th: R | Role: SP | Ht: 6' 4" | Wt: 230 | Type: Con
Health: F | PT/Exp: A | Consist: B | LIMA Plan: B | Rand Var: 0 | MM: 2005

Exhibit A for what luck factors (H%, S%, HR/F) can do to ERA/WHIP, as skills were similar to 2022 minus a few Ks. Elite walk rate is locked in per xBB%, but inability to miss bats puts firm lid on K% and overall ceiling. Now has 200+ IP in two straight years, which just means you're getting a whole bunch of "meh" ratios.

Yr Tm	W	Sv	IP	K	ERA	WHIP	xERA	xWHIP	vL+	vR+	BF/G	BB%	K%	K-BB%	xBB%	SwK	Vel	G	L	F	H%	S%	HR/F	xHR/F	GS	APC	DOM%	DIS%	Sv%	LI	RAR	BPX	R$
19 STL	9	0	184	144	4.16	1.22	4.18	1.23	103	99	23.9	4%	19%	15%	6%	10.2%	93.6	47	23	30	31%	71%	16%	16%	32	90	19%	44%			7.9	119	$9
20																																	
21 STL *	4	0	76	45	4.11	1.28	4.59	1.30	102	90	19.4	5%	14%	9%	5%	7.9%	93.1	49	21	29	29%	72%	15%	15%	9	79	0%	33%			1.5	57	-$2
22 STL	12	0	202	153	3.29	1.03	3.79	1.20	87	94	24.4	5%	19%	14%	6%	8.6%	93.3	45	20	35	26%	73%	12%	12%	32	96	44%	25%	0	0.78	16.9	109	$20
23 STL	9	0	201	137	4.78	1.32	4.86	1.29	108	102	24.6	5%	16%	11%	5%	7.7%	93.0	39	22	39	32%	66%	10%	13%	35	91	17%	43%			-11.2	90	-$1
1st Half	4	0	99	70	4.44	1.38	4.82	1.30	105	104	25.5	5%	16%	11%	6%	7.1%	92.8	38	27	36	33%	69%	8%	12%	17	95	18%	41%			-1.3	86	$0
2nd Half	5	0	102	67	5.12	1.25	4.89	1.27	113	102	23.7	4%	16%	12%	5%	8.2%	93.3	40	17	43	30%	63%	11%	15%	18	88	17%	44%			-9.9	95	$5
Proj	9	0	189	128	4.37	1.25	4.18	1.27	106	100	22.4	5%	17%	12%	6%	8.2%	93.2	43	21	36	30%	68%	12%	14%	34						-1.0	94	$4

Miley,Wade

Age: 37 | Th: L | Role: SP | Ht: 6' 2" | Wt: 220 | Type: Con
Health: F | PT/Exp: B | Consist: C | LIMA Plan: B | Rand Var: -5 | MM: 1003

Two more IL trips (lat, shoulder), yet somehow posted third straight sub-3.40 ERA despite third straight sub-100 BPX. This one was held together with extreme H%/S% fortune, as SwK sunk to career lows, had scary DOM/DIS split, and lost GB% tilt. At 37, expect that ratio inflation is coming... for real this time.

Yr Tm	W	Sv	IP	K	ERA	WHIP	xERA	xWHIP	vL+	vR+	BF/G	BB%	K%	K-BB%	xBB%	SwK	Vel	G	L	F	H%	S%	HR/F	xHR/F	GS	APC	DOM%	DIS%	Sv%	LI	RAR	BPX	R$
19 HOU	14	0	167	140	3.98	1.34	4.60	1.40	86	100	21.8	8%	19%	11%	10%	9.6%	90.5	50	21	30	30%	75%	15%	11%	33	90	12%	48%			10.8	82	$9
20 CIN	0	0	14	12	5.65	1.67	5.05	1.62	34	133	11.2	13%	18%	4%	12%	11.6%	90.2	50	32	18	33%	65%	13%	13%	4	48	0%	75%	0	0.56	-2.1	12	-$9
21 CIN	12	0	163	125	3.37	1.33	4.26	1.33	80	102	24.6	7%	18%	11%	8%	10.5%	89.8	49	23	27	31%	78%	13%	14%	28	93	32%	29%			18.0	84	$10
22 CHC *	2	0	53	37	3.14	1.21	3.32	1.39	49	100	16.5	8%	17%	9%	8%	10.8%	89.0	53	14	33	27%	76%	8%	10%	8	63	25%	50%	0	0.79	5.4	75	-$1
23 MIL	9	0	120	79	3.14	1.14	4.73	1.42	78	96	21.3	8%	16%	8%	8%	8.2%	90.5	46	16	38	24%	79%	12%	12%	23	82	9%	57%			17.7	60	$12
1st Half	5	0	57	34	3.02	1.06	4.84	1.37	84	89	20.5	6%	15%	9%	8%	6.6%	90.0	40	19	41	24%	77%	10%	14%	11	77	9%	55%			9.2	62	$9
2nd Half	4	0	64	45	3.25	1.21	4.62	1.46	71	103	22.0	9%	17%	8%	8%	9.4%	90.9	52	13	35	25%	79%	14%	10%	12	86	8%	58%			8.5	60	$8
Proj	9	0	131	88	3.90	1.34	4.47	1.40	82	109	21.4	8%	16%	8%	8%	9.4%	90.1	48	18	34	30%	74%	11%	12%	25						6.9	62	$2

Miller,Bobby

Age: 25 | Th: R | Role: SP | Ht: 6' 5" | Wt: 220 | Type:
Health: A | PT/Exp: D | Consist: A | LIMA Plan: B | Rand Var: 0 | MM: 4103

11-4, 3.76 ERA in 124 IP at LA. Arrived in May with plenty of hype; mostly delivered despite some early bumps. Really hit stride with 2nd half gains: missed more bats; threw more strikes (xBB%) to back elite BB%; just one DISaster start out of 15. Given pedigree, this could come together quickly... UP: 16 wins, 3.25 ERA.

Yr Tm	W	Sv	IP	K	ERA	WHIP	xERA	xWHIP	vL+	vR+	BF/G	BB%	K%	K-BB%	xBB%	SwK	Vel	G	L	F	H%	S%	HR/F	xHR/F	GS	APC	DOM%	DIS%	Sv%	LI	RAR	BPX	R$
19																																	
20																																	
21																																	
22 a/a	7	0	113	124	3.62	1.08	2.95				18.4	7%	28%	21%							30%	69%									4.8	143	$8
23 LA *	12	0	139	129	3.97	1.11	3.17	1.21	82	95	21.1	6%	24%	17%	6%	12.0%	99.0	48	20	33	28%	66%	11%	10%	22	89	32%	14%			6.3	117	$14
1st Half	5	0	53	45	4.63	1.23	3.34	1.39	86	93	19.7	9%	20%	11%	8%	11.0%	99.0	50	21	29	28%	62%	6%	7%	7	91	29%	29%			-2.0	92	$1
2nd Half	7	0	86	84	3.56	1.03	3.58	1.15	81	97	22.9	5%	24%	19%	6%	12.4%	99.0	47	19	34	28%	70%	13%	12%	15	88	33%	7%			8.2	149	$21
Proj	12	0	160	145	3.58	1.11	3.51	1.21	84	94	21.5	7%	23%	17%	7%	11.8%	99.0	48	20	32	29%	70%	10%	10%	29						14.6	124	$16

Miller,Bryce

Age: 25 | Th: R | Role: SP | Ht: 6' 2" | Wt: 180 | Type: Con/FB
Health: A | PT/Exp: D | Consist: B | LIMA Plan: A | Rand Var: 0 | MM: 2103

8-7, 4.32 ERA in 131 IP at SEA. Called up in May and gave up 4 total ER in first 5 starts, but posted 5.31 ERA from there on. Fastball-heavy approach yielded a ton of strikes, but also a good helping of flyballs and not many Ks. Needs to find reliable out-pitch to take next step, so for now, use xERA/xWHIP as your baseline.

Yr Tm	W	Sv	IP	K	ERA	WHIP	xERA	xWHIP	vL+	vR+	BF/G	BB%	K%	K-BB%	xBB%	SwK	Vel	G	L	F	H%	S%	HR/F	xHR/F	GS	APC	DOM%	DIS%	Sv%	LI	RAR	BPX	R$
19																																	
20																																	
21																																	
22 aa	4	0	52	53	2.90	0.99	1.89				19.9	9%	27%	18%							25%	71%									6.9	136	$3
23 SEA *	8	0	153	134	4.60	1.17	4.16	1.18	124	75	21.0	5%	22%	17%	5%	11.9%	95.1	34	23	44	30%	65%	11%	12%	25	84	24%	28%			-5.0	122	$6
1st Half	5	0	80	70	4.59	1.05	3.40	1.18	93	74	20.7	5%	22%	17%	5%	11.2%	95.0	34	23	43	27%	59%	9%	13%	11	83	55%	27%			-2.6	134	$9
2nd Half	3	0	72	64	4.60	1.30	4.50	1.19	145	77	21.9	5%	21%	16%	5%	12.5%	95.3	33	22	44	33%	70%	12%	12%	14	84	0%	29%			-2.4	122	$3
Proj	8	0	160	138	4.15	1.17	4.03	1.19	127	75	22.0	5%	22%	16%	6%	12.0%	95.2	34	22	44	30%	68%	10%	12%	29						3.5	113	$8

Miller,Mason

Age: 25 | Th: R | Role: RP | Ht: 6' 5" | Wt: 200 | Type: Pwr/xFB
Health: F | PT/Exp: F | Consist: F | LIMA Plan: A+ | Rand Var: -3 | MM: 3401

0-3, 3.78 ERA in 33.1 IP at OAK. Made Apr debut, then UCL strain shelved him until Sept; also missed most of 2022 with shoulder strain. Electric arm that sits high-90s with 4-seam fastball; gyro-slider with devastating, two-plane movement; mixes in hard cutter and occasional change-up. Health is key, but has the stuff to thrive in any role. (CB)

Yr Tm	W	Sv	IP	K	ERA	WHIP	xERA	xWHIP	vL+	vR+	BF/G	BB%	K%	K-BB%	xBB%	SwK	Vel	G	L	F	H%	S%	HR/F	xHR/F	GS	APC	DOM%	DIS%	Sv%	LI	RAR	BPX	R$
19																																	
20																																	
21																																	
22																																	
23 OAK *	1	0	51	62	2.82	0.95	1.70	1.35	77	88	12.7	12%	27%	16%	10%	11.1%	98.4	26	22	52	24%	72%	5%	7%	6	61	33%	17%	0	0.64	9.4	156	$4
1st Half	1	0	32	37	2.81	0.73	1.03	1.04	64	84	18.7	6%	32%	26%	10%	10.7%	98.4	21	25	55	21%	64%	3%	6%	4	92	50%	0%			5.9	200	$3
2nd Half	0	0	19	25	2.84	1.29	2.76	1.43	106	94	8.7	15%	31%	16%	11%	11.8%	98.4	36	18	46	30%	79%	8%	8%	2	41	0%	50%	0	0.53	3.5	135	-$4
Proj	3	0	73	91	3.47	1.19	3.70	1.27	80	108	11.1	12%	31%	20%	10%	10.7%	98.4	29	21	50	29%	73%	8%	8%	3						7.7	109	$

Milner,Hoby

Age: 33 | Th: L | Role: RP | Ht: 6' 3" | Wt: 175 | Type: Con
Health: A | PT/Exp: C | Consist: B | LIMA Plan: A | Rand Var: -5 | MM: 4100

Electric ratios drove plenty of middle-relief value, particularly in 2nd half, but got a ton of help from luck-factor trifecta (H%/S%, HR/F). Skills have far less voltage: strikeout ceiling capped by tiny SwK, sub-90 mph heater; xBB% questions pinpoint control. GBs help and he's dominant vL, but don't be... shocked... if ERA doubles.

Yr Tm	W	Sv	IP	K	ERA	WHIP	xERA	xWHIP	vL+	vR+	BF/G	BB%	K%	K-BB%	xBB%	SwK	Vel	G	L	F	H%	S%	HR/F	xHR/F	GS	APC	DOM%	DIS%	Sv%	LI	RAR	BPX	R$
19 TAM *	3	12	67	74	4.15	1.19	3.78		106	112	5.0	6%	28%	22%		4.3%	87.6	25	42	33	33%	68%	0%	0%	0	18			80	0.75	2.9	142	$
20 LAA	0	0	13	13	8.10	1.43	5.21	1.41	123	121	3.1	10%	22%	12%	7%	6.9%	87.9	38	15	46	25%	50%	28%	24%	0	13			0	1.04	-6.0	73	-$1
21 MIL *	1	5	54	67	3.34	1.08	4.29	0.96	77	158	4.3	2%	32%	30%	5%	10.4%	89.2	25	35	40	34%	80%	32%	24%	0	21			83	0.22	6.1	319	$
22 MIL	3	0	65	64	3.76	1.18	3.29	1.14	94	99	4.1	6%	24%	18%	8%	9.7%	89.0	49	22	29	32%	69%	9%	9%	0	16			0	1.01	1.7	144	$
23 MIL	2	0	64	59	1.82	0.96	3.58	1.17	61	94	3.5	5%	23%	18%	7%	8.5%	88.5	51	15	34	26%	86%	8%	10%	0	14			0	0.88	19.9	144	$
1st Half	0	0	32	27	2.53	1.19	3.87	1.26	98	96	3.3	6%	21%	15%	9%	7.9%	88.1	51	18	31	29%	85%	14%	14%	0	13			0	0.92	7.1	118	-$
2nd Half	2	0	32	32	1.11	0.74	3.31	1.08	16	92	3.6	4%	26%	22%	5%	9.1%	89.0	51	11	38	23%	87%	3%	6%	0	15			0	0.84	12.8	171	$
Proj	2	0	58	52	3.44	1.13	3.38	1.14	75	119	3.9	5%	23%	18%	7%	8.8%	88.7	51	16	34	31%	73%	11%	9%	0						6.4	147	$

RYAN BLOOMFIELD

Minter,A.J.						Health	B	LIMA Plan	A
Age:	30	Th:	L	Role	RP	PT/Exp	B	Rand Var	0
Ht:	6' 0"	Wt:	215	Type	Pwr	Consist	B	MM	4411

Injuries to others brought early 9th inning work, but 1st half H% uptick, S% woes spiked ERA. Turned strand rate luck around afterward; 2nd-half control issues were limited to Sept and one awful outing. Early saves provided most of the value here; bottom line can be volatile. But continued success vR will keep him in high-leverage work.

Yr Tm	W	Sv	IP	K	ERA	WHIP	xERA	xWHIP	vL+	vR+	BF/G	BB%	K%	K-BB%	xBB%	SwK	Vel	G	L	F	H%	S%	HR/F	xHR/F	GS	APC	DOM%	DIS%	Sv%	LI	RAR	BPX	R$
19 ATL *	5	10	54	58	5.97	1.73	6.18	1.64	95	127	4.4	11%	24%	13%	8%	14.3%	96.0	37	29	34	39%	67%	10%	15%	0	16			83	1.14	-9.6	66	-$2
20 ATL	1	0	22	24	0.83	1.11	3.71	1.29	89	78	3.9	11%	28%	18%	8%	13.9%	95.6	49	18	33	27%	96%	6%	8%	0	18			0	0.92	9.7	119	$4
21 ATL	3	0	52	57	3.78	1.22	3.91	1.26	76	96	3.6	9%	26%	17%	6%	14.8%	96.1	45	21	34	32%	68%	4%	7%	0	14			0	1.23	3.1	117	-$1
22 ATL	5	5	70	94	2.06	0.91	2.83	0.95	60	85	3.6	6%	35%	29%	6%	16.6%	96.7	38	17	45	30%	81%	7%	10%	0	15			56	1.16	16.5	200	$12
23 ATL	3	10	65	82	3.76	1.19	3.56	1.14	107	78	3.7	8%	32%	23%	6%	15.0%	95.9	35	22	43	33%	70%	9%	10%	0	15			77	1.05	4.6	157	$6
1st Half	3	10	38	48	5.17	1.10	3.52	1.05	87	87	3.7	6%	32%	26%	6%	15.4%	95.8	30	23	47	33%	53%	9%	10%	0	15			77	1.15	-3.9	174	$7
2nd Half	0	0	26	34	1.71	1.33	3.62	1.26	131	66	3.8	11%	31%	20%	7%	14.4%	96.0	42	21	37	34%	91%	9%	12%	0	16			0	0.90	8.5	134	-$1
Proj	3	4	65	80	3.39	1.23	3.44	1.18	102	85	3.7	9%	30%	21%	6%	15.1%	96.1	39	21	40	33%	74%	8%	10%	0						7.6	143	$4

Mize,Casey						Health	F	LIMA Plan	B
Age:	27	Th:	R	Role	SP	PT/Exp	D	Rand Var	0
Ht:	6' 3"	Wt:	212	Type	Con	Consist	D	MM	3003

Return from June 2022 Tommy John surgery slowed by soreness, fatigue this past summer; 2023 ended up being a blank slate. But former 2018 #1 pick will be 20 months off surgery when spring training begins. Pedigree, BB% / GB% combo from rookie 2021 still speak to some upside. Monitor his spring progress; fine dart throw if healthy.

Yr Tm	W	Sv	IP	K	ERA	WHIP	xERA	xWHIP	vL+	vR+	BF/G	BB%	K%	K-BB%	xBB%	SwK	Vel	G	L	F	H%	S%	HR/F	xHR/F	GS	APC	DOM%	DIS%	Sv%	LI	RAR	BPX	R$
19 aa	6	0	80	63	4.56	1.31	4.14				22.1	6%	19%	13%							33%	66%									-0.5	97	$0
20 DET	0	0	28	26	6.99	1.48	5.20	1.44	145	78	19.0	10%	20%	10%	10%	10.1%	93.7	39	26	35	29%	57%	23%	23%	7	78	0%	71%			-8.9	61	-$12
21 DET	7	0	150	118	3.71	1.14	4.17	1.29	117	80	20.4	7%	19%	13%	8%	9.8%	93.6	48	18	34	26%	74%	16%	19%	30	79	10%	33%			10.3	95	$10
22 DET	0	0	10	4	5.40	1.50	5.84	1.37	82	145	22.5	4%	9%	4%	9%	5.3%	93.5	37	16	47	33%	64%	6%	16%	2	85	0%	100%			-1.8	34	-$6
23																																	
1st Half																																	
2nd Half																																	
Proj	8	0	131	102	4.07	1.21	3.83	1.28	129	94	20.7	6%	20%	13%	8%	9.8%	93.6	48	18	34	29%	70%	14%	17%	25						4.2	102	$5

Montas,Frankie						Health	F	LIMA Plan	B
Age:	31	Th:	R	Role	SP	PT/Exp	A	Rand Var	-5
Ht:	6' 2"	Wt:	255	Type	Pwr	Consist	D	MM	4303

Shoulder woes that plagued him in the 2022 2nd half ended in arthroscopic shoulder surgery the following February; 2023 was lost for all but an inning on the final day of Sept. Previous seasons illustrate his ceiling, backed up by elite SwK, K-BB% at his very best. Workload, IP are in question, but where aren't they? Buy again if he's whole.

Yr Tm	W	Sv	IP	K	ERA	WHIP	xERA	xWHIP	vL+	vR+	BF/G	BB%	K%	K-BB%	xBB%	SwK	Vel	G	L	F	H%	S%	HR/F	xHR/F	GS	APC	DOM%	DIS%	Sv%	LI	RAR	BPX	R$
19 OAK	9	0	96	103	2.63	1.11	3.54	1.16	85	87	24.6	6%	26%	20%	7%	11.7%	96.6	49	22	29	31%	80%	11%	10%	16	93	31%	13%			22.3	155	$13
20 OAK	3	0	53	60	5.60	1.51	4.60	1.32	147	76	21.5	10%	25%	16%	6%	12.1%	95.8	37	26	38	34%	67%	18%	17%	11	83	27%	55%			-7.5	105	-$5
21 OAK	13	0	187	207	3.37	1.18	3.73	1.18	92	89	24.3	7%	27%	19%	6%	14.3%	96.3	43	22	35	31%	75%	11%	14%	32	95	31%	16%			20.7	139	$19
22 2 AL	5	0	144	142	4.05	1.25	3.67	1.21	108	94	22.5	7%	23%	16%	7%	13.3%	95.9	46	20	34	31%	71%	13%	15%	27	86	22%	41%			-1.5	122	$2
23 NYY	1	0	1	1	0.00	2.25	0.00		270	82	7.0	14%	14%	0%	12%	15.4%	94.3	80	20	0	42%	100%	0%		0	26			0	0.83	0.7	-3	-$5
1st Half																																	
2nd Half	1	0	1	1	0.00	2.25	0.00		271	83	7.0	14%	14%	0%	12%	15.4%	94.3	80	20	0	42%	100%	0%		0	26			0	0.83	0.7	-3	-$6
Proj	8	0	131	138	3.76	1.24	3.48	1.20	103	89	22.4	8%	26%	19%	7%	13.0%	94.7	45	22	34	32%	73%	13%	14%	24						9.2	135	$7

Montero,Rafael						Health	D	LIMA Plan	B
Age:	33	Th:	R	Role	RP	PT/Exp	B	Rand Var	+4
Ht:	6' 0"	Wt:	190	Type	Pwr	Consist	C	MM	3301

BPX say skills weren't far off 2022. But ugly 1st half killed late-inning opportunities, fantasy value. Inflated H% was a primary early culprit; regression and 2nd half S% fueled eventual rebound. But HR spike was a season-long problem and xHR/F says it was deserved. Rebound likely, with a wide range of outcomes. Consistency is not his strong suit.

Yr Tm	W	Sv	IP	K	ERA	WHIP	xERA	xWHIP	vL+	vR+	BF/G	BB%	K%	K-BB%	xBB%	SwK	Vel	G	L	F	H%	S%	HR/F	xHR/F	GS	APC	DOM%	DIS%	Sv%	LI	RAR	BPX	R$
19 TEX	2	0	29	34	2.48	0.97	3.34	1.04	48	131	5.1	4%	30%	26%	8%	13.1%	95.8	40	22	38	27%	87%	19%	23%	0	21			0	0.88	7.2	181	$1
20 TEX	0	8	18	19	4.08	1.02	4.57	1.25	73	103	4.2	8%	27%	18%	6%	11.1%	95.5	25	20	55	24%	63%	8%	16%	0	17			100	0.77	0.8	107	$7
21 2 AL	5	7	49	42	6.39	1.54	4.36	1.33	117	99	5.1	8%	19%	11%	7%	11.1%	95.5	55	16	28	36%	57%	9%	7%	0	20			54	1.03	-12.9	96	-$5
22 HOU	5	14	68	73	2.37	1.02	3.14	1.20	72	79	3.8	9%	27%	19%	8%	12.0%	96.3	53	16	31	27%	78%	6%	7%	0	15			88	1.12	13.5	135	$13
23 HOU	3	1	67	79	5.08	1.53	4.19	1.29	106	121	4.4	10%	27%	17%	8%	13.7%	96.0	41	20	39	36%	71%	15%	15%	0	18			17	0.57	-6.2	117	-$6
1st Half	1	1	34	38	7.08	1.72	4.66	1.31	115	143	4.5	9%	24%	15%	7%	13.3%	95.9	37	22	41	39%	62%	16%	14%	0	18			20	0.56	-11.6	107	-$16
2nd Half	2	0	33	41	3.00	1.33	3.70	1.28	99	91	4.2	11%	29%	19%	10%	14.2%	96.0	47	18	35	32%	83%	14%	16%	0	19			0	0.59	5.4	131	$2
Proj	4	0	65	71	4.08	1.28	3.62	1.28	94	96	4.2	10%	26%	17%	8%	12.9%	95.9	47	18	34	31%	71%	13%	12%	0						2.0	117	$0

Montgomery,Jordan						Health	B	LIMA Plan	B
Age:	31	Th:	L	Role	SP	PT/Exp	A	Rand Var	-2
Ht:	6' 6"	Wt:	228	Type		Consist	B	MM	3205

Track record of pitchability with sub-par velocity now firmly entrenched, though this looks like a ceiling. Healthy SwK keeps floor under K%; BB% still his one elite/consistent skill. Value spiked primarily on HR containment, though FB% uptick, xHR/F hints that it won't last. Improved health, IP make free agent valuable in both the real game and ours.

Yr Tm	W	Sv	IP	K	ERA	WHIP	xERA	xWHIP	vL+	vR+	BF/G	BB%	K%	K-BB%	xBB%	SwK	Vel	G	L	F	H%	S%	HR/F	xHR/F	GS	APC	DOM%	DIS%	Sv%	LI	RAR	BPX	R$
19 NYY	0	0	4	5	6.75	1.75	4.05		66	195	9.5	0%	26%	26%		12.2%	91.7	29	36	36	49%	67%	20%	22%	1	41	0%	0%	0	0.75	-1.1	228	-$6
20 NYY	2	0	44	47	5.11	1.30	3.91	1.13	85	106	19.3	5%	24%	20%	6%	13.5%	92.5	43	26	32	35%	64%	17%	15%	10	75	10%	30%			-3.6	163	-$1
21 NYY	6	0	157	162	3.83	1.28	4.06	1.23	83	95	22.0	8%	25%	17%	6%	14.1%	92.5	43	21	36	32%	74%	12%	12%	30	86	23%	30%			8.4	120	$6
22 2 TM	9	0	178	158	3.48	1.09	3.47	1.15	68	98	22.6	5%	22%	17%	6%	13.4%	93.1	48	21	32	29%	72%	13%	13%	32	85	25%	25%			10.7	133	$14
23 2 TM	10	0	189	166	3.20	1.19	4.11	1.25	86	96	24.3	6%	21%	15%	7%	11.7%	93.3	43	22	35	30%	76%	9%	11%	32	91	41%	19%			26.4	114	$19
1st Half	6	0	99	91	3.28	1.24	4.00	1.24	79	101	24.4	6%	22%	16%	7%	10.7%	93.5	46	21	33	32%	76%	9%	13%	17	93	53%	18%			12.8	124	$17
2nd Half	4	0	90	75	3.10	1.14	4.23	1.26	99	91	24.2	6%	21%	15%	8%	12.9%	93.1	40	23	37	29%	77%	9%	10%	15	90	27%	20%			13.7	106	$16
Proj	11	0	181	169	3.63	1.20	3.67	1.21	84	97	22.1	6%	23%	17%	7%	12.9%	93.0	43	22	35	31%	73%	11%	12%	33						15.6	123	$14

Moreta,Dauri						Health	A	LIMA Plan	A+
Age:	28	Th:	R	Role	RP	PT/Exp	D	Rand Var	-1
Ht:	6' 2"	Wt:	185	Type	Pwr/xFB	Consist	F	MM	4310

Late-blooming RP with plus fastball/slider combo with improving K%, GB% and HR containment. 2nd half BB% and vL gains were impressive, as poor S% luck, August IL stint (back) and minor league options impeded a bigger breakout. More of the same makes for intriguing / speculative Sv+Holds upside.

Yr Tm	W	Sv	IP	K	ERA	WHIP	xERA	xWHIP	vL+	vR+	BF/G	BB%	K%	K-BB%	xBB%	SwK	Vel	G	L	F	H%	S%	HR/F	xHR/F	GS	APC	DOM%	DIS%	Sv%	LI	RAR	BPX	R$
19																																	
20																																	
21 CIN *	6	8	59	54	1.34	0.86	2.29		121	22	4.7	5%	25%	20%		10.5%	95.1	22	0	78	22%	97%	14%	12%	0	14			89	0.06	21.3	148	$15
22 CIN *	3	2	66	62	5.18	1.44	6.13	1.23	131	102	4.5	9%	22%	13%	8%	11.7%	96.0	33	18	49	29%	74%	20%	12%	1	18	0%	100%	67	0.37	-9.9	30	-$6
23 PIT	5	1	58	76	3.72	1.09	3.69	1.21	83	82	4.3	10%	32%	22%	8%	13.9%	95.2	40	15	46	29%	66%	7%	11%	0	18			33	0.95	4.3	146	$4
1st Half	4	1	36	47	3.79	1.23	3.86	1.32	107	78	4.2	13%	31%	19%	9%	13.7%	94.8	38	21	41	29%	71%	9%	13%	0	17			33	1.18	2.4	113	$2
2nd Half	1	0	22	29	3.63	0.85	3.45	1.02	43	90	4.7	6%	33%	27%	6%	14.2%	95.8	42	6	53	28%	56%	4%	9%	0	19			0	0.50	1.9	198	$0
Proj	4	1	58	67	3.33	1.04	3.44	1.16	90	93	4.3	8%	30%	22%	8%	13.5%	95.5	39	13	48	27%	72%	10%	10%	0						7.1	142	$5

Morgan,Eli						Health	A	LIMA Plan	B
Age:	28	Th:	R	Role	RP	PT/Exp	C	Rand Var	+1
Ht:	5' 10"	Wt:	190	Type	Pwr/FB	Consist	B	MM	3201

Fun with relievers and small sample volatility. Still owns plus K%, BB% and ability to generate soft contact with three-pitch arsenal. But it was 1st half S% and avoiding HR damage that drove early value—before 2nd half regression of both along with soaring H% crushed him. Skills look unchanged, month-to-month inconsistency holds him back.

Yr Tm	W	Sv	IP	K	ERA	WHIP	xERA	xWHIP	vL+	vR+	BF/G	BB%	K%	K-BB%	xBB%	SwK	Vel	G	L	F	H%	S%	HR/F	xHR/F	GS	APC	DOM%	DIS%	Sv%	LI	RAR	BPX	R$
19 a/a	6	0	107	90	5.28	1.56	5.63				23.4	8%	19%	11%							35%	69%									-10.3	55	-$6
20																																	
21 CLE *	5	0	112	98	5.13	1.29	4.90	1.22	114	106	20.1	7%	21%	14%	6%	11.1%	90.4	29	20	51	30%	65%	15%	15%	18	79	17%	39%			-12.0	68	-$4
22 CLE	5	0	67	72	3.38	0.89	3.55	1.05	89	87	5.1	5%	28%	23%	5%	12.6%	92.2	30	18	51	24%	69%	12%	10%	1	20	0%	0%	0	1.05	4.9	149	$6
23 CLE	5	1	67	75	4.01	1.44	4.16	1.25	82	116	4.9	8%	25%	17%	6%	13.9%	92.6	42	22	36	36%	76%	13%	12%	0	20			33	0.68	2.7	128	-$1
1st Half	3	1	34	33	1.83	1.19	4.29	1.25	94	83	4.7	7%	23%	16%	5%	13.5%	92.4	41	21	39	30%	89%	8%	11%	0	19			100	0.69	10.6	117	$4
2nd Half	2	0	33	42	6.27	1.70	4.01	1.25	73	150	5.1	9%	27%	18%	7%	14.3%	92.7	43	24	33	41%	66%	19%	13%	0	21			0	0.68	-7.9	140	-$7
Proj	4	0	65	68	4.01	1.25	3.85	1.23	83	104	6.4	8%	25%	18%	6%	13.1%	92.0	37	21	42	31%	73%	12%	13%	0						2.5	118	$0

JOCK THOMPSON

Morton,Charlie

			Health B	LIMA Plan A
Age: 40	Th: R	Role SP	PT/Exp A	Rand Var -2
Ht: 6' 5"	Wt: 215	Type Pwr	Consist A	MM 2203

Still healthy and offering value at his age is no small feat; elite K% backed by broad repertoire is intact. But fraying is visible; pitched in traffic all year thanks to wobbly BB% that soared in 2nd half. Limiting HR damage saved him, but xHR/F says he was fortunate. Still an asset in a grim pitching landscape, but with more downside than up.

Yr Tm	W	Sv	IP	K	ERA	WHIP	xERA	xWHIP	vL+	vR+	BF/G	BB%	K%	K-BB%	xBB%	SwK	Vel	G	L	F	H%	S%	HR/F	xHR/F	GS	APC	DOM%	DIS%	Sv%	LI	RAR	BPX	R$
19 TAM	16	0	195	240	3.05	1.08	3.26	1.13	90	75	23.9	7%	30%	23%	6%	13.4%	94.4	48	22	30	31%	74%	10%	11%	33	95	48%	15%			34.9	168	$29
20 TAM	2	0	38	42	4.74	1.39	4.07	1.17	109	100	18.9	6%	25%	19%	5%	12.4%	93.3	42	25	34	37%	67%	11%	13%	9	73	0%	33%			-1.3	153	-$2
21 ATL	14	0	186	216	3.34	1.04	3.22	1.15	79	81	22.9	8%	29%	21%	7%	13.0%	95.3	48	23	29	28%	70%	12%	11%	33	91	33%	18%			21.1	152	$26
22 ATL	9	0	172	205	4.34	1.23	3.50	1.18	111	96	23.5	9%	28%	20%	8%	12.8%	94.9	40	22	39	30%	70%	16%	15%	31	94	32%	29%			-7.9	135	$6
23 ATL	14	0	163	183	3.64	1.43	4.21	1.39	97	97	23.9	12%	26%	14%	9%	13.2%	94.8	43	22	34	33%	76%	9%	13%	30	95	30%	30%			14.0	89	$9
1st Half	8	0	91	105	3.57	1.44	4.01	1.31	99	104	25.1	10%	26%	16%	8%	13.4%	94.9	45	21	33	35%	78%	11%	16%	16	99	25%	25%			8.5	117	$12
2nd Half	6	0	73	78	3.72	1.40	4.49	1.50	95	90	22.4	14%	25%	11%	11%	13.1%	94.6	41	23	36	30%	74%	8%	9%	14	91	36%	36%			5.5	55	$10
Proj	**11**	**0**	**145**	**150**	**3.90**	**1.37**	**3.97**	**1.37**	**100**	**96**	**22.3**	**11%**	**25%**	**14%**	**8%**	**13.0%**	**94.7**	**43**	**23**	**34**	**31%**	**73%**	**11%**	**12%**	**27**						**7.6**	**87**	**$5**

Muller,Kyle

			Health A	LIMA Plan C
Age: 26	Th: L	Role RP	PT/Exp C	Rand Var +3
Ht: 6' 7"	Wt: 250	Type Pwr	Consist D	MM 0101

1-5, 7.60 ERA in 77 IP at OAK. Once-esteemed prospect started season in MLB rotation, gave up just 3 runs in 11 IP over first two starts. But the good news ended there; banished back to AAA before the end of May where he wasn't any better. K%, SwK have fallen off a cliff, bb% is mediocre at best, HR have become a real problem.

Yr Tm	W	Sv	IP	K	ERA	WHIP	xERA	xWHIP	vL+	vR+	BF/G	BB%	K%	K-BB%	xBB%	SwK	Vel	G	L	F	H%	S%	HR/F	xHR/F	GS	APC	DOM%	DIS%	Sv%	LI	RAR	BPX	R$
19 aa	7	0	113	102	5.11	1.64	4.45				23.0	15%	20%	5%							32%	68%									-8.4	69	-$6
20																																	
21 ATL *	7	0	118	113	4.21	1.43	4.19	1.47	77	83	19.3	13%	23%	10%	9%	13.4%	93.4	38	19	43	30%	72%	5%	7%	8	75	25%	13%	0	0.77	0.8	75	-$1
22 ATL *	7	0	149	142	4.62	1.40	4.73	1.55	48	118	24.1	8%	23%	15%	8%	12.0%	94.3	39	32	29	33%	70%	18%	16%	3	78	0%	67%			-11.9	85	-$4
23 OAK *	3	0	139	95	6.98	1.90	7.44	1.56	134	135	19.3	10%	15%	5%	9%	9.7%	93.0	42	22	35	36%	66%	17%	18%	13	69	0%	85%	0	0.74	-45.4	8	-$34
1st Half	2	0	82	56	6.89	1.86	7.15	1.57	127	133	22.6	10%	14%	4%	9%	9.3%	92.9	48	22	30	36%	64%	18%	23%	11	88	0%	82%			-26.0	16	-$30
2nd Half	1	0	59	39	6.83	1.89	7.43	1.67	146	139	16.4	12%	14%	2%	9%	10.3%	94.7	31	22	47	34%	67%	15%	13%	2	49	0%	100%	0	0.69	-18.2	-1	-$18
Proj	**3**	**0**	**87**	**70**	**5.68**	**1.67**	**5.20**	**1.54**	**121**	**117**	**19.7**	**12%**	**18%**	**6%**	**9%**	**10.7%**	**93.9**	**38**	**21**	**41**	**33%**	**68%**	**11%**	**14%**	**19**						**-14.6**	**22**	**-$13**

Muñoz,Andres

			Health F	LIMA Plan A
Age: 25	Th: R	Role RP	PT/Exp C	Rand Var 0
Ht: 6' 2"	Wt: 222	Type Pwr/xGB	Consist C	MM 5530

Still plenty effective, just less bullet-proof after injury-riddled season. Offseason ankle surgery delayed his spring before sprained shoulder shelved him for most of the 1st half. Everything was at least a tick off upon his return, notably bb%, spiking H% and still elite SwK, K-BB%. Should rebound some, but health is now an issue.

Yr Tm	W	Sv	IP	K	ERA	WHIP	xERA	xWHIP	vL+	vR+	BF/G	BB%	K%	K-BB%	xBB%	SwK	Vel	G	L	F	H%	S%	HR/F	xHR/F	GS	APC	DOM%	DIS%	Sv%	LI	RAR	BPX	R$
19 SD *	4	7	60	81	3.38	1.16	2.76	1.30	88	74	4.2	12%	34%	22%	7%	15.6%	99.9	40	24	36	29%	74%	10%	15%	0	19			64	0.95	8.3	135	$7
20																																	
21 SEA	0	0	1	1	0.00	3.00	0.00		138	44	4.0	50%	25%	-25%		5.9%	99.8	100	0	0	0%	100%	0%		0	17			0	0.16	0.4	-448	-$6
22 SEA	2	4	65	96	2.49	0.89	2.16	0.91	63	85	3.9	6%	39%	33%	5%	22.2%	100.2	53	14	33	30%	75%	11%	9%	0	16			50	1.30	11.8	236	$9
23 SEA	4	13	49	67	2.94	1.27	2.91	1.22	90	79	4.1	10%	32%	21%	6%	18.5%	98.9	59	17	24	35%	77%	7%	7%	0	16			81	1.41	8.4	168	$7
1st Half	1	1	13	19	2.77	1.00	2.32	1.03	78	59	3.7	8%	37%	29%	4%	23.2%	99.2	62	14	24	34%	69%	0%	9%	0	15			100	1.26	2.5	228	-$4
2nd Half	3	12	36	48	3.00	1.36	3.15	1.28	95	86	4.2	11%	30%	19%	8%	17.0%	98.9	58	18	24	35%	79%	10%	6%	0	17			80	1.46	5.9	147	$12
Proj	**3**	**27**	**58**	**76**	**2.79**	**1.11**	**2.72**	**1.15**	**79**	**81**	**4.1**	**10%**	**33%**	**24%**	**6%**	**18.9%**	**99.4**	**56**	**17**	**28**	**30%**	**77%**	**11%**	**7%**	**0**						**11.0**	**171**	**$16**

Murphy,Chris

			Health A	LIMA Plan B
Age: 26	Th: L	Role RP	PT/Exp D	Rand Var +2
Ht: 6' 1"	Wt: 175	Type Pwr	Consist C	MM 2201

1-2, 4.91 ERA in 48 IP at BOS. Minor league starter debuted out of the pen in June, with modest results. Whiffed more than a batter an inning in the minors; K% can play at the MLB level. But bb% has always been a tad lofty, GB% inconsistent and needs to show more vR before earning a bigger role. It's a back-end SP ceiling at very best.

Yr Tm	W	Sv	IP	K	ERA	WHIP	xERA	xWHIP	vL+	vR+	BF/G	BB%	K%	K-BB%	xBB%	SwK	Vel	G	L	F	H%	S%	HR/F	xHR/F	GS	APC	DOM%	DIS%	Sv%	LI	RAR	BPX	R$
19																																	
20																																	
21 aa	3	0	33	40	6.22	1.40	4.58				19.9	9%	29%	19%							36%	55%									-7.9	111	-$6
22 a/a	7	0	154	121	4.24	1.32	3.66				21.3	11%	19%	8%							28%	69%									-5.2	71	$0
23 BOS *	3	1	102	98	5.90	1.64	5.74	1.29	91	107	13.0	8%	23%	15%	9%	9.9%	93.9	45	20	35	36%	65%	10%	10%	0	44			100	0.61	-19.7	66	-$15
1st Half	1	0	55	50	6.43	1.75	6.31	1.49	151	24	15.8	11%	20%	9%	10%	11.7%	94.5	54	17	29	37%	64%	14%	16%	0	45			0	0.36	-14.3	50	-$19
2nd Half	2	1	47	47	5.27	1.51	5.06	1.35	77	128	10.6	9%	22%	13%	8%	9.4%	93.8	43	21	37	36%	66%	9%	9%	0	43			100	0.67	-5.4	87	-$4
Proj	**4**	**0**	**73**	**72**	**4.38**	**1.39**	**4.02**	**1.36**	**77**	**123**	**14.2**	**10%**	**24%**	**13%**	**9%**	**9.4%**	**93.8**	**43**	**21**	**37**	**32%**	**71%**	**12%**	**8%**	**9**						**-0.4**	**87**	**-$3**

Musgrove,Joe

			Health F	LIMA Plan B+
Age: 31	Th: R	Role SP	PT/Exp A	Rand Var -2
Ht: 6' 5"	Wt: 230	Type Pwr	Consist A	MM 5303

Fractured toe delayed his season until late April; scuffled early but eventually rounded into form … until sore shoulder ended his season in early August. Broad repertoire, pristine control still intact; K%, GB% had begun to soar in 2nd-half before he went down. Age, track record make him a decent rebound bet. But Health once again is a huge caveat.

Yr Tm	W	Sv	IP	K	ERA	WHIP	xERA	xWHIP	vL+	vR+	BF/G	BB%	K%	K-BB%	xBB%	SwK	Vel	G	L	F	H%	S%	HR/F	xHR/F	GS	APC	DOM%	DIS%	Sv%	LI	RAR	BPX	R$
19 PIT	11	0	170	157	4.44	1.22	4.27	1.23	106	91	22.4	5%	22%	16%	5%	12.2%	92.4	44	20	35	31%	66%	12%	14%	31	83	35%	26%	0	0.80	1.4	126	$9
20 PIT	1	0	40	55	3.86	1.24	3.24	1.16	92	103	20.8	10%	33%	23%	6%	15.0%	92.5	48	20	31	33%	73%	17%	14%	8	84	25%	13%			2.9	172	$3
21 SD	11	0	181	203	3.18	1.08	3.53	1.16	100	76	23.4	7%	27%	20%	6%	13.5%	93.3	44	23	33	28%	76%	14%	14%	31	92	29%	29%	0	0.74	24.4	143	$23
22 SD	10	0	181	184	2.93	1.08	3.41	1.12	89	101	24.7	6%	25%	19%	6%	11.4%	92.9	45	19	36	29%	79%	12%	10%	30	95	40%	17%			23.1	145	$20
23 SD	10	0	97	97	3.05	1.14	3.60	1.15	79	107	23.5	5%	24%	19%	6%	12.1%	93.1	45	22	33	31%	77%	11%	9%	17	92	35%	18%			15.4	148	$12
1st Half	6	0	66	61	3.80	1.27	4.08	1.22	89	109	23.4	6%	22%	16%	6%	11.4%	93.1	44	22	35	33%	73%	10%	9%	12	89	25%	25%			4.4	126	$7
2nd Half	4	0	31	36	1.45	0.87	2.63	1.00	53	105	23.6	4%	31%	26%	6%	13.5%	92.9	49	24	28	27%	92%	15%	9%	5	99	60%	0%			11.0	198	$10
Proj	**12**	**0**	**160**	**174**	**3.22**	**1.08**	**3.10**	**1.11**	**83**	**98**	**22.4**	**6%**	**28%**	**22%**	**6%**	**12.9%**	**92.9**	**46**	**22**	**32**	**30%**	**75%**	**13%**	**11%**	**28**						**21.8**	**159**	**$2**

Nardi,Andrew

			Health B	LIMA Plan A
Age: 25	Th: L	Role RP	PT/Exp D	Rand Var -3
Ht: 6' 3"	Wt: 215	Type Pwr	Consist B	MM 4411

Lefty reliever with fastball/slider combo entered sophomore season with elite K% and little else. But he suddenly began generating more soft contact, more GBs, fewer HR—even whittled down that lofty BB% some. Began dominating vL and vR alike in 2nd half, even as control wavered. LI growth speaks volumes. More of the same brings... UP: 15 saves.

Yr Tm	W	Sv	IP	K	ERA	WHIP	xERA	xWHIP	vL+	vR+	BF/G	BB%	K%	K-BB%	xBB%	SwK	Vel	G	L	F	H%	S%	HR/F	xHR/F	GS	APC	DOM%	DIS%	Sv%	LI	RAR	BPX	R$
19																																	
20																																	
21 aa	1	0	18	16	3.06	1.15	2.89				6.5	13%	22%	10%							21%	79%									2.7	79	-$
22 MIA *	6	9	68	88	3.98	1.30	3.83	1.53	198	145	5.6	11%	31%	20%	8%	13.1%	94.5	22	27	51	32%	73%	22%	22%	0	29			82	0.63	-0.1	114	$
23 MIA	8	3	57	73	2.67	1.15	3.40	1.18	74	99	3.8	9%	31%	22%	6%	14.0%	94.6	44	20	37	30%	83%	14%	11%	0	15			75	1.32	11.8	156	$
1st Half	6	2	36	48	2.97	1.07	3.13	1.06	81	108	3.7	7%	33%	26%	6%	14.3%	94.7	42	20	38	29%	84%	22%	13%	0	14			67	1.17	6.1	189	$1
2nd Half	2	1	21	25	2.14	1.29	3.92	1.37	59	88	4.0	12%	27%	15%	7%	13.5%	94.6	46	19	35	32%	81%	0%	8%	0	17			100	1.59	5.7	101	$
Proj	**8**	**4**	**73**	**86**	**2.65**	**1.16**	**3.36**	**1.24**	**70**	**93**	**4.1**	**10%**	**30%**	**20%**	**7%**	**13.8%**	**94.6**	**45**	**20**	**36**	**29%**	**80%**	**10%**	**10%**	**0**						**15.0**	**130**	**$1**

Nelson,Kyle

			Health D	LIMA Plan A+
Age: 27	Th: L	Role RP	PT/Exp D	Rand Var +3
Ht: 6' 1"	Wt: 175	Type Pwr/FB	Consist A	MM 2300

Soft-tossing lefty produced fine 1st half out of the pen, fueled by suddenly elite control and growing SwK%. But he was hittable throughout, and without good velocity or a GB pitch, his margin for error is slim. FB lean and loss of just a little 2nd half command left him vulnerable vR and to the long ball; unfortunate S% didn't help. Wash, rinse, repeat.

Yr Tm	W	Sv	IP	K	ERA	WHIP	xERA	xWHIP	vL+	vR+	BF/G	BB%	K%	K-BB%	xBB%	SwK	Vel	G	L	F	H%	S%	HR/F	xHR/F	GS	APC	DOM%	DIS%	Sv%	LI	RAR	BPX	R$
19 a/a	3	4	38	44	3.88	1.21	3.83				4.5	10%	29%	19%							28%	75%									2.9	96	$
20 CLE	0	0	1	0	54.00	6.00	18.33		277	246	6.0	17%	0%	-17%		12.0%	90.3	60	20	20	52%	0%	100%	73%	0	25			0	0.02	-4.1	-369	-$1
21 CLE *	0	1	37	33	7.61	1.73	4.57	1.81	99	91	4.8	17%	20%	3%	9%	11.4%	93.0	39	26	35	33%	52%	0%	0%	0	18			100	0.40	-15.2	76	-$1
22 ARI	2	0	37	30	2.19	1.08	4.16	1.37	76	88	3.5	9%	20%	11%	8%	12.1%	91.9	41	22	38	25%	79%	3%	10%	1	14	0%	0%	0	0.93	8.1	64	$
23 ARI	7	0	56	67	4.18	1.30	3.82	1.11	100	116	3.5	6%	28%	22%	5%	15.9%	92.1	37	21	42	34%	77%	19%	15%	2	13	0%	50%	0	0.87	1.1	166	$
1st Half	4	0	32	40	2.84	1.26	3.50	1.11	103	100	3.7	7%	30%	23%	5%	16.7%	92.5	38	24	38	35%	86%	17%	13%	0	13			0	0.92	5.8	171	$
2nd Half	3	0	24	27	5.92	1.36	4.24	1.12	99	134	3.3	5%	26%	21%	6%	15.0%	91.7	36	17	47	34%	65%	21%	17%	2	12	0%	50%	0	0.80	-4.8	162	-$
Proj	**5**	**0**	**58**	**61**	**4.32**	**1.38**	**4.07**	**1.31**	**99**	**113**	**3.7**	**10%**	**25%**	**15%**	**6%**	**14.9%**	**92.0**	**38**	**20**	**42**	**32%**	**73%**	**13%**	**14%**	**0**						**0.0**	**98**	**-$**

JOCK THOMPSON

Nelson,Ryne

Age: 26	Th: R	Role SP	Health A	LIMA Plan C+
Ht: 6' 3"	Wt: 184	Type Con/xFB	PT/Exp C	Rand Var 0
			Consist B	MM 1003

8-8, 5.31 ERA in 144 IP at ARI. PRO: Stayed healthy, ate rotation innings as a strike-throwing rookie; athleticism, 2021 promise still relevant. CON: Mediocre SwK%, K% look lifeless; FB lean hurt in 2nd half, could have been worse all season; beaten up by both LHB, RHB as season progressed. Likely unrosterable on Opening Day; watch from afar.

Yr	Tm	W	Sv	IP	K	ERA	WHIP	xERA	xWHIP	vL+	vR+	BF/G	BB%	K%	K-BB%	xBB%	SwK	Vel	G	L	F	H%	S%	HR/F	xHR/F	GS	APC	DOM%	DIS%	Sv%	LI	RAR	BPX	R$
19																																		
20																																		
21	aa	3	0	77	88	3.61	1.23	4.13				22.3	8%	28%	21%							31%	77%									6.2	113	$2
22	ARI *	11	0	154	121	4.04	1.22	3.94	1.28	74	74	21.5	7%	19%	12%	8%	9.1%	94.9	23	15	62	28%	70%	7%	5%	3	84	67%	33%			-1.3	79	$6
23	ARI *	8	0	167	103	5.01	1.38	5.04	1.42	121	110	21.3	7%	16%	8%	7%	9.3%	94.4	37	19	44	29%	67%	11%	14%	27	81	11%	48%	0	0.75	-13.9	37	-$5
1st Half		5	0	91	64	4.67	1.38	5.20	1.40	116	99	22.8	7%	16%	9%	7%	9.3%	94.5	36	22	42	31%	68%	9%	12%	17	88	12%	41%			-3.7	57	$0
2nd Half		3	0	77	39	5.41	1.38	5.43	1.48	131	131	20.1	7%	12%	5%	8%	9.2%	94.3	37	15	48	28%	66%	15%	17%	10	72	10%	60%	0	0.71	-10.2	11	-$4
Proj		**7**	**0**	**145**	**110**	**4.57**	**1.31**	**4.62**	**1.34**	**115**	**103**	**21.3**	**7%**	**18%**	**11%**	**8%**	**9.3%**	**94.4**	**37**	**18**	**46**	**29%**	**70%**	**11%**	**15%**	**28**						**-4.3**	**71**	**-$1**

Neris,Hector

Age: 35	Th: R	Role RP	Health A	LIMA Plan B+
Ht: 6' 2"	Wt: 227	Type Pwr/xFB	PT/Exp B	Rand Var -5
			Consist B	MM 3400

Skills + fortune = Holds league fantasy gold. Elite K% remained rock solid, mitigated soaring BB%. Able to induce soft contact, taming HR again despite spiking FB%. But it was year-long H%/S% luck that fueled WHIP and otherworldly ERA. Regression is on tap; BPX, age point to risk; xBB% tempers this some. Still a worthy late-inning option.

Yr	Tm	W	Sv	IP	K	ERA	WHIP	xERA	xWHIP	vL+	vR+	BF/G	BB%	K%	K-BB%	xBB%	SwK	Vel	G	L	F	H%	S%	HR/F	xHR/F	GS	APC	DOM%	DIS%	Sv%	LI	RAR	BPX	R$
19	PHI	3	28	68	89	2.93	1.02	3.35	1.16	78	84	4.0	9%	32%	24%	8%	18.0%	94.6	45	19	36	26%	80%	18%	13%	0	17			82	1.54	13.2	163	$19
20	PHI	2	5	22	27	4.57	1.71	4.61	1.42	99	82	4.3	13%	26%	14%	8%	17.8%	94.0	42	29	29	41%	70%	0%	9%	0	17			63	1.19	-0.3	86	$2
21	PHI	4	12	74	98	3.63	1.17	3.53	1.21	109	77	4.2	10%	32%	21%	6%	16.7%	94.4	47	13	40	28%	76%	17%	11%	0	17			63	1.11	5.8	147	$9
22	HOU	6	3	65	79	3.72	1.01	3.25	1.06	77	86	3.8	6%	30%	24%	6%	14.6%	94.4	35	23	43	30%	62%	4%	10%	0	14			43	1.00	2.0	161	$6
23	HOU	6	2	68	77	1.71	1.05	4.25	1.33	69	83	3.8	11%	28%	17%	7%	14.5%	93.0	32	17	52	23%	91%	9%	10%	0	15			67	1.19	22.1	92	$12
1st Half		4	2	34	38	1.07	1.04	3.84	1.32	64	73	3.7	11%	29%	17%	7%	15.5%	92.8	42	16	43	24%	94%	6%	7%	0	14			100	1.31	13.5	106	$10
2nd Half		2	0	35	39	2.34	1.07	4.63	1.34	72	97	4.0	11%	28%	16%	7%	13.7%	93.2	23	18	60	21%	88%	10%	12%	0	17			0	1.07	8.5	80	$5
Proj		**4**	**0**	**58**	**70**	**3.45**	**1.18**	**3.66**	**1.23**	**90**	**91**	**3.9**	**10%**	**30%**	**20%**	**7%**	**15.4%**	**93.8**	**37**	**17**	**47**	**29%**	**75%**	**11%**	**10%**	**0**						**6.3**	**124**	**$2**

Nola,Aaron

Age: 31	Th: R	Role SP	Health A	LIMA Plan B+
Ht: 6' 2"	Wt: 200	Type	PT/Exp A	Rand Var +1
			Consist B	MM 4305

More sub-70% S% illustrates struggles with runners on base (.816 OPS). Also that his command walks a fine line, leaving ERA a big variable. 2022 HR containment vanished; typically elite K%, SwK weren't quite that. Plus skill set still capable of a rebound; buoyed by control, Health, ability to eat innings. Just don't bid on an elite rotation anchor.

Yr	Tm	W	Sv	IP	K	ERA	WHIP	xERA	xWHIP	vL+	vR+	BF/G	BB%	K%	K-BB%	xBB%	SwK	Vel	G	L	F	H%	S%	HR/F	xHR/F	GS	APC	DOM%	DIS%	Sv%	LI	RAR	BPX	R$
19	PHI	12	0	202	229	3.87	1.27	3.79	1.29	96	93	25.1	9%	27%	17%	6%	11.5%	92.9	50	21	30	30%	74%	17%	17%	34	98	32%	26%			15.9	126	$15
20	PHI	5	0	71	96	3.28	1.08	2.97	1.09	92	79	24.1	8%	33%	25%	6%	14.1%	92.4	50	23	28	30%	75%	20%	17%	12	96	42%	8%			10.3	189	$23
21	PHI	9	0	181	223	4.63	1.13	3.48	1.04	93	94	23.4	5%	30%	25%	5%	13.3%	92.7	41	19	41	33%	62%	14%	12%	32	93	34%	22%			-8.2	183	$10
22	PHI	11	0	205	235	3.25	0.96	2.94	0.98	80	91	25.2	4%	29%	26%	4%	13.0%	92.6	44	20	37	30%	69%	10%	11%	32	95	44%	6%			18.2	191	$26
23	PHI	12	0	194	202	4.46	1.15	3.80	1.15	99	94	24.8	6%	25%	20%	5%	12.2%	92.4	43	20	38	30%	66%	16%	13%	32	97	28%	16%			-3.1	150	$14
1st Half		7	0	106	102	4.51	1.12	4.10	1.23	96	93	25.1	7%	24%	17%	6%	12.2%	92.1	40	19	41	27%	64%	14%	13%	17	98	24%	12%			-2.4	122	$15
2nd Half		5	0	88	100	4.40	1.19	3.45	1.07	103	97	24.4	4%	27%	23%	5%	12.2%	92.7	45	20	34	33%	69%	18%	13%	15	96	33%	20%			-0.7	184	$13
Proj		**12**	**0**	**196**	**209**	**3.70**	**1.10**	**3.30**	**1.11**	**94**	**91**	**23.4**	**6%**	**27%**	**21%**	**5%**	**12.7%**	**92.5**	**43**	**20**	**37**	**29%**	**72%**	**15%**	**13%**	**33**						**15.2**	**156**	**$21**

Ober,Bailey

Age: 28	Th: R	Role SP	Health D	LIMA Plan B+
Ht: 6' 9"	Wt: 260	Type /xFB	PT/Exp C	Rand Var 0
			Consist B	MM 3203

8-6, 3.43 ERA in 144 IP at MIN. Avoided IL this year; became rotation mainstay after late April promotion. Soft-tosser relies on deception and pinpoint control to generate big SwK and elite K-BB%. Glaring weakness remains FB% tilt coupled with sub-par velocity; HR issues bit hard in the 2nd half. But it's an attractive floor if health cooperates.

Yr	Tm	W	Sv	IP	K	ERA	WHIP	xERA	xWHIP	vL+	vR+	BF/G	BB%	K%	K-BB%	xBB%	SwK	Vel	G	L	F	H%	S%	HR/F	xHR/F	GS	APC	DOM%	DIS%	Sv%	LI	RAR	BPX	R$
19	aa	3	0	24	28	1.08	0.62	0.59				20.7	2%	34%	31%							22%	89%									10.1	360	$3
20																																		
21	MIN *	4	0	108	113	4.11	1.22	4.66	1.12	116	98	18.3	6%	26%	20%	5%	11.8%	92.4	33	21	46	31%	74%	17%	15%	20	74	10%	35%			2.1	116	$2
22	MIN	2	0	56	51	3.21	1.05	4.20	1.14	101	78	20.6	5%	22%	18%	6%	13.9%	91.6	28	21	51	29%	71%	5%	12%	11	78	18%	27%			5.2	117	$1
23	MIN *	10	0	169	166	3.28	1.06	3.39	1.13	85	101	21.1	5%	25%	20%	6%	14.7%	91.4	34	16	50	28%	75%	11%	12%	26	90	23%	23%			21.8	138	$22
1st Half		7	0	96	91	2.66	0.98	2.55	1.17	76	91	21.5	6%	25%	19%	6%	13.7%	91.4	31	17	51	26%	77%	8%	11%	13	90	31%	15%			19.7	145	$30
2nd Half		3	0	73	74	4.10	1.16	4.48	1.12	97	111	20.7	5%	25%	20%	5%	15.7%	91.4	37	15	48	30%	73%	16%	14%	13	89	15%	31%			2.1	134	$8
Proj		**8**	**0**	**160**	**158**	**3.76**	**1.13**	**3.82**	**1.13**	**96**	**97**	**20.1**	**5%**	**25%**	**20%**	**6%**	**14.0%**	**91.7**	**33**	**18**	**49**	**30%**	**73%**	**11%**	**13%**	**31**						**11.2**	**136**	**$12**

Odorizzi,Jake

Age: 34	Th: R	Role SP	Health F	LIMA Plan B
Ht: 6' 2"	Wt: 190	Type Con/FB	PT/Exp B	Rand Var 0
			Consist A	MM 2101

April shoulder surgery ended season before it began. Broad repertoire and the state of pitching in general will likely earn this five-inning SP another opportunity somewhere, if he wants it. But poorly-trending BPX best tells the story here; bad combination of stuff and pitchability is no longer compelling. Recent IL history keeps it less so.

Yr	Tm	W	Sv	IP	K	ERA	WHIP	xERA	xWHIP	vL+	vR+	BF/G	BB%	K%	K-BB%	xBB%	SwK	Vel	G	L	F	H%	S%	HR/F	xHR/F	GS	APC	DOM%	DIS%	Sv%	LI	RAR	BPX	R$
19	MIN	15	0	159	178	3.51	1.21	4.30	1.25	100	78	21.9	8%	27%	19%	8%	13.1%	92.9	35	21	44	31%	74%	9%	12%	30	93	33%	23%			19.5	123	$17
20	MIN	0	0	14	12	6.59	1.39	4.70	1.23	62	157	15.0	5%	20%	15%	8%	8.8%	93.0	36	24	40	31%	60%	24%	26%	4	71	0%	50%			-3.6	116	-$9
21	HOU	6	0	105	91	4.21	1.25	4.80	1.31	108	93	18.4	8%	21%	13%	8%	10.3%	92.2	35	20	45	28%	71%	12%	12%	23	77	13%	30%			0.7	82	$2
22	2 TM	6	0	106	86	4.40	1.33	4.75	1.32	103	101	20.6	8%	19%	11%	8%	10.7%	92.1	32	22	47	30%	70%	9%	9%	22	82	18%	50%	0	0.76	-5.7	67	-$2
23																																		
1st Half																																		
2nd Half																																		
Proj		**6**	**0**	**94**	**80**	**4.42**	**1.27**	**4.34**	**1.31**	**107**	**98**	**20.5**	**8%**	**21%**	**13%**	**8%**	**11.1%**	**92.3**	**34**	**21**	**46**	**30%**	**68%**	**10%**	**10%**	**19**						**-1.1**	**82**	**$0**

Ohtani,Shohei

Age: 29	Th: R	Role RP	Health B	LIMA Plan B
Ht: 6' 4"	Wt: 210	Type #DIV/0!	PT/Exp A	Rand Var -1
			Consist A	MM 5400

Stellar 1st-half segued into noticeable 2nd-half down-tick that portended what was to come. September Tommy John surgery—his second since arriving in the U.S.—offers slim hope that he could pitch a few 2024 innings, but probably not enough to help your fantasy squad. The pitching side of MLB's most talented player can be ignored on draft day.

Yr	Tm	W	Sv	IP	K	ERA	WHIP	xERA	xWHIP	vL+	vR+	BF/G	BB%	K%	K-BB%	xBB%	SwK	Vel	G	L	F	H%	S%	HR/F	xHR/F	GS	APC	DOM%	DIS%	Sv%	LI	RAR	BPX	R$
19																																		
20	LAA	0	0	2	3	37.80	6.60	65.84		180	129	8.0	50%	19%	-31%		6.3%	93.8	50	25	25	64%	36%	0%	14%	2	40	0%	50%			-6.9	-957	-$14
21	LAA	9	0	130	156	3.18	1.09	3.45	1.16	101	71	23.2	8%	29%	21%	8%	13.4%	95.7	45	20	36	28%	76%	13%	12%	23	88	35%	13%			17.5	148	$16
22	LAA	15	0	166	219	2.33	1.01	2.90	1.02	91	73	23.6	7%	33%	27%	6%	15.4%	97.3	42	20	38	31%	81%	9%	9%	28	94	54%	14%			33.5	187	$29
23	LAA	10	0	132	167	3.14	1.06	3.35	1.22	88	80	23.1	10%	32%	21%	8%	13.5%	96.4	45	18	36	25%	77%	17%	18%	23	91	39%	4%			19.5	142	$20
1st Half		7	0	95	127	3.02	1.04	3.19	1.18	86	78	23.9	10%	33%	23%	8%	14.1%	96.6	44	19	37	25%	77%	16%	14%	16	96	44%	0%			15.4	157	$29
2nd Half		3	0	37	40	3.44	1.12	3.78	1.33	95	86	21.1	11%	27%	16%	7%	12.1%	96.0	48	17	36	23%	77%	19%	25%	7	80	29%	14%			4.0	109	$4
Proj																																		

Olson,Reese

Age: 24	Th: R	Role SP	Health A	LIMA Plan A
Ht: 6' 1"	Wt: 160	Type	PT/Exp D	Rand Var 0
			Consist B	MM 3203

5-7, 3.98 ERA in 104 IP at DET. Rookie was inconsistent early after June callup; ended MLB debut on a plus note—6 earned runs, 35/13 K/BB over 36 IP in his final six starts. 2nd half aided by H% luck; control still a work-in-progress; xHR/F a red flag. But age, SwK, ability to check RHBs are building blocks. Back-end SP growth stock.

Yr	Tm	W	Sv	IP	K	ERA	WHIP	xERA	xWHIP	vL+	vR+	BF/G	BB%	K%	K-BB%	xBB%	SwK	Vel	G	L	F	H%	S%	HR/F	xHR/F	GS	APC	DOM%	DIS%	Sv%	LI	RAR	BPX	R$
19																																		
20																																		
21	aa	2	0	26	17	5.24	1.28	2.95				21.5	12%	16%	4%							25%	56%									-3.2	70	-$5
22	aa	8	0	121	138	4.11	1.24	3.79				18.9	7%	28%	21%							33%	69%									-2.1	133	$4
23	DET *	7	0	142	141	4.62	1.29	4.06	1.26	92	85	18.8	8%	24%	17%	8%	12.2%	94.8	43	21	36	30%	67%	13%	17%	18	83	17%	28%	0	0.76	-5.0	90	$2
1st Half		3	0	65	68	5.69	1.50	5.01	1.35	81	91	17.4	10%	24%	14%	7%	12.0%	95.1	44	21	36	34%	63%	15%	17%	5	80	20%	40%	0	0.74	-10.8	83	-$9
2nd Half		4	0	77	73	3.72	1.11	4.10	1.30	97	83	20.8	8%	23%	15%	8%	12.3%	94.7	42	21	37	26%	71%	13%	17%	13	84	15%	23%	0	0.76	5.8	103	$12
Proj		**8**	**0**	**160**	**154**	**3.98**	**1.19**	**3.77**	**1.27**	**94**	**86**	**20.9**	**8%**	**24%**	**16%**	**8%**	**12.2%**	**94.9**	**43**	**21**	**36**	**29%**	**70%**	**12%**	**17%**	**31**						**6.8**	**107**	**$9**

JOCK THOMPSON

Ortiz,Luis

Age: 25	Th: R	Role SP	Health A	LIMA Plan C
Ht: 6' 2"	Wt: 240	Type	PT/Exp C	Rand Var 0
			Consist F	MM 1003

5-5, 4.78 ERA in 87 IP at PIT. Entered 2023 with speculative upside, finished as a question mark. GB% advanced with more sinkers. But velocity backed up along with effectiveness of once killer 4-seamer/slider combo. BB%, HR% damage spiked; SwK vanished along with promising K-BB%. Has age, Health; needs a reset to rekindle our interest.

Yr Tm	W	Sv	IP	K	ERA	WHIP	xERA	xWHIP	vL+	vR+	BF/G	BB%	K%	K-BB%	xBB%	SwK	Vel	G	L	F	H%	S%	HR/F	xHR/F	GS	APC	DOM%	DIS%	Sv%	LI	RAR	BPX	R$
19																																	
20																																	
21																																	
22 PIT *	5	0	141	131	4.42	1.14	3.37	1.50	106	51	18.6	8%	23%	15%	8%	13.1%	98.5	44	15	41	27%	64%	6%	7%	4	69	25%	25%			-7.9	97	$3
23 PIT *	9	0	145	102	4.87	1.60	5.52	1.64	130	97	20.7	12%	15%	3%	10%	9.8%	96.0	48	20	32	31%	73%	14%	19%	15	81	7%	60%	0	0.75	-9.6	32	-$10
1st Half	4	0	83	54	3.44	1.39	4.47	1.54	149	86	20.7	10%	15%	5%	9%	9.9%	96.1	51	19	31	28%	79%	15%	22%	9	81	11%	67%	0	0.72	9.1	43	$4
2nd Half	5	0	61	48	6.80	1.88	6.94	1.67	106	113	20.6	13%	16%	3%	11%	9.9%	95.9	44	23	33	35%	66%	13%	16%	6	81	0%	50%	0	0.78	-18.7	19	-$11
Proj	**8**	**0**	**131**	**95**	**4.67**	**1.50**	**4.79**	**1.53**	**113**	**92**	**20.9**	**11%**	**17%**	**6%**	**11%**	**9.8%**	**95.9**	**47**	**21**	**32**	**30%**	**72%**	**13%**	**18%**	**27**						**-5.5**	**30**	**-$6**

Ottavino,Adam

Age: 38	Th: R	Role RP	Health A	LIMA Plan A
Ht: 6' 5"	Wt: 246	Type Pwr/GB	PT/Exp B	Rand Var -2
			Consist C	MM 3311

Projected regression landed softly, even with K-BB% retreat and HR/F uptick. GB% rose again, further cutting into LD%, H%--and capping damage to ERA, WHIP. Even found more 9th inning work via injuries, roster upheaval; saves were a personal high. Age will eventually intervene; inconsistency is a red flag. Durability offers short-term optimism.

Yr Tm	W	Sv	IP	K	ERA	WHIP	xERA	xWHIP	vL+	vR+	BF/G	BB%	K%	K-BB%	xBB%	SwK	Vel	G	L	F	H%	S%	HR/F	xHR/F	GS	APC	DOM%	DIS%	Sv%	LI	RAR	BPX	R$
19 NYY	6	2	66	88	1.90	1.31	4.26	1.41	99	75	3.9	14%	31%	17%	10%	11.4%	93.9	40	19	41	30%	89%	8%	8%	0	16			22	1.13	21.3	94	$8
20 NYY	2	0	18	25	5.89	1.58	3.93	1.27	112	100	3.5	11%	29%	19%	7%	9.7%	93.5	48	20	32	40%	63%	13%	16%	0	14			0	0.66	-3.3	144	-$5
21 BOS	7	11	62	71	4.21	1.45	4.50	1.42	106	94	4.0	13%	26%	13%	9%	10.8%	95.0	40	21	39	33%	72%	8%	7%	0	17			65	1.39	0.4	73	$4
22 NYM	6	3	66	79	2.06	0.97	2.72	1.04	120	67	3.9	6%	31%	24%	7%	12.8%	94.4	52	16	32	28%	84%	12%	8%	0	16			50	1.03	15.5	183	$10
23 NYM	1	12	62	62	3.21	1.22	3.87	1.41	105	80	4.0	11%	24%	13%	8%	10.2%	92.6	56	14	30	26%	78%	15%	11%	0	16			80	1.09	8.5	93	$6
1st Half	0	6	34	36	3.97	1.21	3.89	1.38	105	90	3.9	11%	25%	14%	9%	10.8%	92.9	53	13	34	25%	72%	17%	10%	0	16			86	0.96	1.5	99	$0
2nd Half	1	6	28	26	2.28	1.23	3.84	1.44	107	69	4.0	11%	22%	11%	7%	9.5%	92.4	60	15	25	27%	84%	11%	12%	0	15			75	1.25	7.0	86	$4
Proj	**4**	**4**	**65**	**71**	**3.03**	**1.25**	**3.64**	**1.35**	**108**	**80**	**3.8**	**12%**	**27%**	**15%**	**8%**	**10.8%**	**93.6**	**50**	**17**	**33**	**28%**	**79%**	**11%**	**10%**	**0**						**10.5**	**102**	**$4**

Oviedo,Johan

Age: 26	Th: R	Role RP	Health A	LIMA Plan B+
Ht: 6' 5"	Wt: 245	Type Pwr	PT/Exp B	Rand Var -1
			Consist B	MM 1101

Serious elbow injury could cost him most or all of 2024. Too bad; took the ball every turn, BF/G was impressive in first full year in an MLB rotation. Good velocity, SwK, GB% had its moments. But stagnant and sub-par BB% and K% still dominate the sum of these parts. Has yet to step forward; now we'll have to wait a little longer.

Yr Tm	W	Sv	IP	K	ERA	WHIP	xERA	xWHIP	vL+	vR+	BF/G	BB%	K%	K-BB%	xBB%	SwK	Vel	G	L	F	H%	S%	HR/F	xHR/F	GS	APC	DOM%	DIS%	Sv%	LI	RAR	BPX	R$
19 aa	7	0	113	109	6.73	1.74	5.53				22.4	12%	21%	9%							38%	60%									-30.9	69	-$14
20 STL	0	0	25	16	5.47	1.38	5.53	1.51	89	124	22.4	9%	14%	5%	10%	9.2%	94.9	40	27	33	28%	61%	11%	19%	5	89	0%	40%			-3.1	28	-$8
21 STL *	1	0	117	100	5.32	1.53	4.90	1.59	115	94	19.7	12%	20%	7%	10%	11.4%	94.9	48	22	30	31%	66%	14%	17%	13	78	15%	54%	0	0.81	-15.3	56	-$13
22 2 NL *	8	0	118	106	3.95	1.28	4.03	1.33	80	100	13.4	10%	22%	12%	7%	11.4%	96.1	49	14	36	28%	74%	8%	9%	8	47	13%	38%	0	0.70	0.3	72	$3
23 PIT	9	0	178	158	4.31	1.37	4.77	1.46	105	92	24.4	11%	20%	10%	9%	11.5%	95.8	45	19	36	29%	71%	10%	11%	32	93	31%	31%			0.6	60	$2
1st Half	3	0	94	81	4.61	1.43	4.75	1.41	104	96	24.8	9%	19%	10%	8%	11.0%	96.4	46	19	34	32%	68%	8%	9%	17	92	29%	35%			-3.2	74	-$3
2nd Half	6	0	84	77	3.96	1.31	4.79	1.52	107	88	24.0	13%	21%	9%	10%	12.0%	95.3	43	18	39	25%	74%	12%	14%	15	95	33%	27%			3.8	45	$11
Proj	**4**	**0**	**87**	**73**	**4.49**	**1.41**	**4.52**	**1.48**	**107**	**95**	**17.2**	**11%**	**20%**	**8%**	**9%**	**11.5%**	**95.6**	**46**	**19**	**35**	**30%**	**70%**	**10%**	**13%**	**15**						**-1.8**	**49**	**-$4**

Paddack,Chris

Age: 28	Th: R	Role SP	Health F	LIMA Plan B
Ht: 6' 5"	Wt: 217	Type Con	PT/Exp D	Rand Var +5
			Consist B	MM 4201

Made it back for two Sept outings following rehab from 2022 Tommy John surgery. Velocity, SwK%, 8/1 K/BB jump out in the small sample; 15/3 K/BB over 10 minor league innings were similarly encouraging. But this was his second TJS and 2019 is receding further into the rearview. Durability, workload, role are all in question.

Yr Tm	W	Sv	IP	K	ERA	WHIP	xERA	xWHIP	vL+	vR+	BF/G	BB%	K%	K-BB%	xBB%	SwK	Vel	G	L	F	H%	S%	HR/F	xHR/F	GS	APC	DOM%	DIS%	Sv%	LI	RAR	BPX	R$
19 SD	9	0	141	153	3.33	0.98	3.94	1.14	88	81	21.8	5%	27%	21%	4%	12.3%	93.9	40	18	42	26%	75%	15%	13%	26	88	42%	19%			20.4	153	$18
20 SD	4	0	59	58	4.73	1.22	3.87	1.15	117	105	20.4	5%	24%	19%	6%	11.7%	94.2	47	20	33	30%	71%	25%	22%	12	80	8%	17%			-2.0	152	$6
21 SD	7	0	108	99	5.07	1.26	4.12	1.17	83	120	20.0	5%	22%	17%	6%	11.7%	94.9	43	22	35	33%	62%	13%	14%	22	81	14%	36%	0	0.79	-10.7	131	-$2
22 MIN	1	0	22	20	4.03	1.21	3.44	1.05	117	85	18.6	2%	22%	19%	4%	11.7%	93.0	44	24	32	37%	63%	0%	8%	5	73	20%	0%			-0.2	160	-$4
23 MIN	1	0	5	8	5.40	1.40	2.81		135	100	11.0	5%	36%	32%	5%	16.5%	95.6	31	38	31	45%	67%	25%	22%	0	40			0	0.65	-0.7	246	-$5
1st Half																																	
2nd Half	1	0	5	8	5.40	1.40	2.81		136	100	11.0	5%	36%	32%	5%	16.5%	95.6	31	38	31	45%	67%	25%	22%	0	26			0	0.65	-0.7	248	-$6
Proj	**6**	**0**	**102**	**94**	**4.54**	**1.14**	**3.51**	**1.15**	**94**	**109**	**20.5**	**5%**	**23%**	**18%**	**6%**	**11.8%**	**94.5**	**44**	**20**	**36**	**30%**	**64%**	**15%**	**16%**	**20**						**-2.7**	**139**	**$3**

Pallante,Andre

Age: 25	Th: R	Role RP	Health A	LIMA Plan C+
Ht: 6' 0"	Wt: 203	Type Con/xGB	PT/Exp B	Rand Var +5
			Consist A	MM 3001

GB% turned even more elite with fulltime bullpen work. But that's the only plus here and it wasn't enough to save him from his other liabilities. Abysmal K%, and BB% deteriorated further; HR/F turned horrendous. S% regression didn't help, RHBs battered him throughout. A rebound of sorts is likely, but K-challenged profile keeps us away.

Yr Tm	W	Sv	IP	K	ERA	WHIP	xERA	xWHIP	vL+	vR+	BF/G	BB%	K%	K-BB%	xBB%	SwK	Vel	G	L	F	H%	S%	HR/F	xHR/F	GS	APC	DOM%	DIS%	Sv%	LI	RAR	BPX	R$
19																																	
20																																	
21 a/a	4	0	100	71	3.44	1.48	4.55				18.7	9%	16%	7%							33%	77%									10.2	65	-$
22 STL	6	0	108	73	3.17	1.42	3.71	1.42	89	113	9.7	9%	16%	7%	8%	7.6%	95.2	64	19	17	31%	80%	15%	11%	10	37	10%	40%	0	1.07	10.7	68	$
23 STL	4	0	68	43	4.76	1.56	3.82	1.55	93	121	4.9	10%	14%	4%	10%	7.8%	96.1	78	12	10	32%	70%	26%	22%	0	18			0	1.03	-3.6	57	-$
1st Half	2	0	30	27	3.94	1.48	3.47	1.52	88	116	4.6	13%	21%	9%	12%	8.4%	95.9	74	14	12	31%	76%	30%	26%	0	18			0	1.24	1.4	77	-$
2nd Half	2	0	38	16	5.40	1.62	4.14	1.57	99	125	5.1	8%	9%	1%	8%	7.3%	96.3	80	11	9	33%	66%	23%	19%	0	19			0	0.86	-5.1	42	-$
Proj	**4**	**0**	**65**	**43**	**4.07**	**1.52**	**3.71**	**1.50**	**97**	**122**	**6.5**	**10%**	**15%**	**5%**	**10%**	**7.7%**	**95.9**	**75**	**14**	**12**	**32%**	**74%**	**22%**	**19%**	**0**						**2.1**	**65**	**-$**

Paxton,James

Age: 35	Th: L	Role SP	Health F	LIMA Plan A+
Ht: 6' 4"	Wt: 227	Type Pwr	PT/Exp F	Rand Var +1
			Consist F	MM 3301

7-5, 4.50 ERA in 96 IP at BOS. Strained hamstring sidelined him until early May. Despite rust and spotty control, K% and velocity offered early glimpses of his best former self. Balky knee began to rear up in late June, likely factoring into 2nd-half skid before ending his season in early Sept. Age and ongoing IL history say this is as good as it gets.

Yr Tm	W	Sv	IP	K	ERA	WHIP	xERA	xWHIP	vL+	vR+	BF/G	BB%	K%	K-BB%	xBB%	SwK	Vel	G	L	F	H%	S%	HR/F	xHR/F	GS	APC	DOM%	DIS%	Sv%	LI	RAR	BPX	R$
19 NYY	15	0	151	186	3.82	1.28	4.08	1.22	88	101	21.8	9%	29%	21%	7%	14.7%	95.5	38	19	43	32%	76%	14%	12%	29	92	34%	31%			12.7	139	$1
20 NYY	1	0	20	26	6.64	1.48	4.46	1.18	116	118	18.0	8%	29%	21%	6%	14.3%	92.1	32	18	50	38%	58%	14%	16%	5	71	20%	60%			-5.5	151	-$
21 SEA	0	0	1	2	6.75	0.75	0.00			33	5.0	20%	40%	20%		12.5%	94.1	50	50	0	0%	0%	0%		1	24	0%	0%			-0.4	97	-$
22																																	
23 BOS *	9	0	119	120	5.00	1.39	4.88	1.26	107	104	20.1	8%	25%	17%	7%	13.1%	95.3	43	20	37	31%	68%	18%	14%	19	89	32%	37%			-9.9	70	-$
1st Half	6	0	73	80	4.09	1.19	3.34	1.30	109	73	19.6	10%	27%	17%	6%	14.7%	95.7	35	23	42	28%	68%	12%	14%	9	91	56%	11%			2.2	108	$1
2nd Half	3	0	46	40	6.46	1.70	4.95	1.43	107	135	21.5	9%	19%	9%	8%	11.5%	94.8	49	18	34	34%	68%	24%	14%	10	87	10%	60%			-12.1	70	-$
Proj	**7**	**0**	**102**	**106**	**4.18**	**1.30**	**3.76**	**1.26**	**102**	**104**	**20.8**	**9%**	**25%**	**17%**	**8%**	**13.1%**	**95.2**	**42**	**20**	**38**	**31%**	**73%**	**15%**	**13%**	**20**						**1.9**	**114**	**$**

Payamps,Joel

Age: 30	Th: R	Role RP	Health C	LIMA Plan B+
Ht: 6' 2"	Wt: 225	Type	PT/Exp C	Rand Var -4
			Consist B	MM 3111

Poor Sept fueled by H%/S% luck the only blotch on a fine season. Velocity ticked up as SwK, K% moved forward impressively, generating elite K-BB%. GB% remained sturdy again; limited HR damage all year. Worked way into leverage and late-inning work—where he'll likely begin 2024. Rosterable now in Holds leagues.

Yr Tm	W	Sv	IP	K	ERA	WHIP	xERA	xWHIP	vL+	vR+	BF/G	BB%	K%	K-BB%	xBB%	SwK	Vel	G	L	F	H%	S%	HR/F	xHR/F	GS	APC	DOM%	DIS%	Sv%	LI	RAR	BPX	R$
19 ARI *	5	0	84	58	4.47	1.42	4.78		99	94	21.0	6%	16%	10%		7.6%	92.9	10	40	50	33%	70%	0%	22%	0	33			0	0.09	0.4	70	-$
20 ARI	0	0	3	2	3.00	1.67	7.27		28	133	6.5	23%	15%	-8%		5.1%	94.2	13	63	25	24%	80%	0%	32%	0	30			0	0.09	0.5	-163	-$
21 2 AL	1	0	50	38	3.40	1.15	4.62	1.31	75	98	5.5	7%	19%	12%	7%	10.4%	94.7	44	15	41	27%	75%	10%	7%	1	22	0%	100%	0	0.73	5.4	84	-$
22 2 AL	3	0	56	41	3.23	1.37	4.12	1.31	95	112	5.9	7%	17%	10%	9%	10.0%	94.7	53	17	31	31%	81%	13%	14%	0	23			0	0.81	5.0	89	-$
23 MIL	7	3	71	77	2.55	1.05	3.54	1.13	90	80	4.2	6%	27%	21%	8%	11.2%	95.4	46	16	38	29%	82%	11%	8%	0	16			50	1.20	15.6	159	$1
1st Half	2	2	38	42	2.11	1.04	3.31	1.10	83	91	4.3	5%	27%	22%	10%	11.0%	95.4	47	20	34	29%	89%	15%	11%	0	18			67	1.14	10.5	171	$
2nd Half	5	1	32	35	3.06	1.05	3.80	1.18	99	67	4.0	7%	27%	20%	6%	11.6%	95.3	45	12	43	28%	74%	8%	5%	0	15			33	1.26	5.1	148	$
Proj	**5**	**2**	**65**	**60**	**3.26**	**1.16**	**3.73**	**1.22**	**91**	**91**	**4.9**	**7%**	**23%**	**16%**	**8%**	**10.9%**	**95.1**	**46**	**15**	**38**	**29%**	**76%**	**10%**	**8%**	**0**						**8.6**	**121**	**$**

JOCK THOMPSON

Pearson,Nate

Age: 27	Th: R	Role: RP	Health: F	LIMA Plan: C+
Ht: 6'6"	Wt: 255	Type: Pwr/xFB	PT/Exp: F	Rand Var: 0
			Consist: B	MM: 1200

5-2, 4.85 ERA in 43 IP at TOR. Oft-sidelined once-top prospect stayed off the IL, rode MLB-to-AAA shuttle all season. Now anchored in bullpen role, still owns velocity, extension, K%, along with problematic control--note 34/14 K/BB, 1.74 ERA in 21 AAA IP. Big FB% is a red flag. But can health, growth yield power reliever upside? Dart throw.

Yr	Tm	W	Sv	IP	K	ERA	WHIP	xERA	xWHIP	vL+	vR+	BF/G	BB%	K%	K-BB%	xBB%	SwK	Vel	G	L	F	H%	S%	HR/F	xHR/F	GS	APC	DOM%	DIS%	Sv%	LI	RAR	BPX	R$
19	a/a	2	0	82	71	3.65	1.11	2.92				17.0	8%	22%	14%							26%	69%									8.7	99	$3
20	TOR	1	0	18	16	6.00	1.50	6.22	1.73	160	58	16.2	16%	20%	4%	10%	11.1%	96.4	38	17	44	21%	68%	22%	12%	4	65	0%	50%	0	0.62	-3.4	-18	-$7
21	TOR *	2	0	47	56	5.38	1.42	4.56	1.56	116	94	8.3	13%	28%	15%	12%	13.0%	97.9	41	13	46	30%	65%	11%	8%	1	25	0%	100%	0	0.31	-6.5	81	-$6
22																																		
23	TOR *	5	3	65	69	3.78	1.29	3.74	1.36	92	103	4.9	10%	24%	14%	11%	11.0%	97.9	31	19	51	28%	75%	12%	10%	0	21			60	0.62	4.4	90	$2
1st Half		4	1	37	41	3.70	1.15	3.32	1.21	81	105	4.9	8%	27%	19%	9%	12.9%	98.2	31	17	53	30%	71%	10%	7%	0	21			50	0.69	2.9	130	$3
2nd Half		1	2	28	28	3.88	1.48	4.28	1.67	115	100	4.8	16%	23%	7%	12%	7.7%	97.6	30	23	48	25%	78%	16%	16%	0	21			67	0.49	1.6	64	-$2
Proj		3	0	58	59	3.97	1.31	4.38	1.37	99	100	6.4	11%	25%	14%	12%	10.7%	97.8	32	20	48	28%	74%	11%	13%	0						2.6	72	-$2

Peguero,Elvis

Age: 27	Th: R	Role: RP	Health: A	LIMA Plan: A+
Ht: 6'5"	Wt: 208	Type: /xGB	PT/Exp: D	Rand Var: -1
			Consist: B	MM: 3111

Rookie reliever found opportunity, earned leverage work in new home. Improved Whiff% on both sinker and slider as elite GB% became even more so. Sacrificed control in the process, but weak contact generated by moving two-pitch arsenal kept it from becoming a prevailing issue... this time. BB% needs a shave, but age, stuff make him watchable.

Yr	Tm	W	Sv	IP	K	ERA	WHIP	xERA	xWHIP	vL+	vR+	BF/G	BB%	K%	K-BB%	xBB%	SwK	Vel	G	L	F	H%	S%	HR/F	xHR/F	GS	APC	DOM%	DIS%	Sv%	LI	RAR	BPX	R$
19																																		
20																																		
21	LAA *	2	0	28	27	6.31	1.43	4.60		190	209	6.4	8%	22%	14%		1.6%	96.2	38	31	31	34%	55%	0%	1%	0	21			0	0.56	-7.2	88	-$7
22	LAA *	4	5	62	53	3.62	1.18	3.46	1.33	118	140	4.9	7%	21%	14%	6%	12.0%	96.5	51	17	32	29%	71%	21%	18%	0	24			100	0.50	2.7	104	$2
23	MIL	4	1	61	54	3.38	1.22	3.87	1.42	81	86	4.3	10%	21%	11%	8%	14.0%	96.0	56	19	25	27%	73%	10%	11%	0	16			17	1.19	7.2	83	$2
1st Half		1	1	31	26	2.90	1.16	4.15	1.37	61	90	4.4	9%	20%	12%	8%	14.3%	95.6	49	19	32	28%	74%	4%	6%	0	16			50	1.02	5.5	86	-$1
2nd Half		3	0	30	28	3.86	1.29	3.55	1.47	100	83	4.1	12%	23%	11%	8%	13.6%	96.5	64	19	18	27%	72%	21%	19%	0	15			0	1.35	1.8	80	$1
Proj		4	2	65	55	3.33	1.23	3.65	1.38	89	88	4.6	9%	21%	11%	9%	13.9%	96.1	58	19	23	28%	74%	11%	14%	0						8.0	88	$3

Pepiot,Ryan

Age: 26	Th: R	Role: SP	Health: F	LIMA Plan: B+
Ht: 6'3"	Wt: 215	Type: /FB	PT/Exp: C	Rand Var: -4
			Consist: B	MM: 2203

2-1, 2.14 ERA in 42 IP at LA. Legitimate prospect had inside track on Opening Day rotation before oblique injury shelved him in late March; didn't take the mound again until 2nd half. FB% still needs work, but he cut into problematic BB% in small sample despite downtime. Plus change-up fronts promising arsenal. If healthy, buy this growth stock.

Yr	Tm	W	Sv	IP	K	ERA	WHIP	xERA	xWHIP	vL+	vR+	BF/G	BB%	K%	K-BB%	xBB%	SwK	Vel	G	L	F	H%	S%	HR/F	xHR/F	GS	APC	DOM%	DIS%	Sv%	LI	RAR	BPX	R$
19																																		
20																																		
21	a/a	5	0	104	106	4.44	1.24	4.18				16.3	10%	25%	15%							27%	70%									-2.3	79	$1
22	LA *	12	0	128	135	2.49	1.11	2.80	1.58	123	77	18.0	11%	27%	15%	11%	11.3%	94.0	26	16	57	24%	84%	12%	12%	7	82	14%	14%	0	0.68	23.4	103	$17
23	LA *	2	0	66	59	2.85	0.92	3.10	1.08	52	105	17.7	3%	24%	21%	6%	12.8%	94.0	37	17	46	24%	80%	14%	10%	3	82	33%	0%	0	0.62	12.1	158	$7
1st Half																																		
2nd Half		2	0	66	59	2.85	0.92	3.10	1.12	52	106	17.7	4%	23%	19%	6%	12.8%	94.0	37	17	46	24%	80%	14%	10%	3	82	33%	0%	0	0.62	12.1	158	$13
Proj		9	0	145	133	3.68	1.19	4.00	1.22	93	111	20.4	7%	23%	16%	8%	12.1%	94.0	38	18	45	29%	75%	12%	11%	28						11.5	112	$10

Peralta,Freddy

Age: 28	Th: R	Role: RP	Health: D	LIMA Plan: B
Ht: 5'11"	Wt: 199	Type: Pwr/FB	PT/Exp: A	Rand Var: +1
			Consist: A	MM: 5503

As projected, durability was everything. Avoided the IL, bumped up velocity, and just roared following May / June scuffles. 2nd-half control gains were confined to Sept, and overstated as suggested by xBB. But soaring K% backed by elite SwK looks real enough; poor HR luck says results could have been better. If healthy, expect more of the same.

Yr	Tm	W	Sv	IP	K	ERA	WHIP	xERA	xWHIP	vL+	vR+	BF/G	BB%	K%	K-BB%	xBB%	SwK	Vel	G	L	F	H%	S%	HR/F	xHR/F	GS	APC	DOM%	DIS%	Sv%	LI	RAR	BPX	R$
19	MIL	7	1	85	115	5.29	1.46	4.34	1.25	90	114	9.8	10%	30%	20%	6%	13.9%	93.6	32	24	44	37%	68%	15%	15%	8	41	25%	38%	50	0.88	-8.3	134	-$1
20	MIL	3	0	29	47	3.99	1.16	3.22	1.08	77	93	8.3	10%	38%	28%	10%	16.6%	93.0	35	22	43	36%	66%	8%	15%	1	37	0%	100%	0	1.02	1.7	196	$6
21	MIL	10	0	144	195	2.81	0.97	3.52	1.14	75	78	20.7	10%	34%	24%	8%	15.1%	93.4	33	20	47	25%	75%	10%	8%	27	84	30%	15%	0	0.76	26.0	149	$24
22	MIL	4	0	78	86	3.58	1.04	3.64	1.20	71	87	17.6	9%	27%	19%	9%	12.6%	92.7	40	18	42	26%	67%	7%	8%	17	75	29%	24%	0	0.80	3.8	124	$4
23	MIL	12	0	166	210	3.86	1.12	3.48	1.14	90	92	22.7	8%	31%	23%	8%	15.0%	94.5	42	18	40	29%	72%	16%	12%	30	95	20%	23%			9.7	164	$19
1st Half		5	0	87	97	4.67	1.30	4.20	1.29	97	110	23.3	9%	26%	17%	8%	13.3%	94.5	39	20	41	30%	69%	16%	13%	16	95	6%	31%			-3.6	113	$5
2nd Half		7	0	79	113	2.96	0.91	2.76	0.97	82	73	22.0	6%	37%	31%	8%	17.0%	94.5	45	16	39	28%	75%	16%	10%	14	94	36%	14%			13.3	222	$27
Proj		11	0	160	206	3.59	1.10	3.18	1.12	85	90	17.9	9%	33%	24%	8%	14.8%	93.9	39	19	42	29%	72%	13%	10%	28						14.5	160	$19

Pérez,Cionel

Age: 28	Th: L	Role: RP	Health: B	LIMA Plan: B
Ht: 5'11"	Wt: 162	Type: Pwr/GB	PT/Exp: C	Rand Var: -2
			Consist: C	MM: 3111

Hard-throwing lefty gave up 2022 control gains, lost some groundball tilt in the 1st half as RHB feasted; xERA says results could have been worse. Righted the ship afterward as K% returned, GB% spiked and H% regressed. But poor BB% and volatility amp up the risk and is enough to keep us away until something stabilizes.

Yr	Tm	W	Sv	IP	K	ERA	WHIP	xERA	xWHIP	vL+	vR+	BF/G	BB%	K%	K-BB%	xBB%	SwK	Vel	G	L	F	H%	S%	HR/F	xHR/F	GS	APC	DOM%	DIS%	Sv%	LI	RAR	BPX	R$
19	HOU *	3	0	56	44	6.60	1.69	6.27	1.30	127	118	14.0	10%	17%	8%	10%	9.8%	95.3	45	16	39	35%	63%	25%	14%	0	33			0	0.85	-14.5	31	-$10
20	HOU	0	0	6	8	2.84	2.05	5.01	1.71	43	118	4.6	19%	25%	6%	12%	13.3%	95.1	59	24	18	42%	85%	0%	1%	0	18			0	0.65	1.3	13	-$7
21	CIN *	2	2	55	60	5.16	1.59	4.91	1.74	105	112	4.3	14%	25%	10%	12%	11.2%	96.0	52	11	38	33%	69%	20%	13%	0	18			40	0.74	-6.1	76	-$7
22	BAL	7	1	58	55	1.40	1.16	3.53	1.28	77	82	3.5	9%	24%	15%	7%	11.9%	96.9	51	19	30	29%	89%	4%	12%	0	14			100	1.41	18.2	105	$8
23	BAL	4	3	53	44	3.54	1.56	4.51	1.52	81	106	3.8	11%	18%	7%	8%	8.8%	96.6	61	17	23	34%	77%	5%	7%	0	14			100	1.08	5.2	56	-$2
1st Half		2	0	30	22	4.45	1.78	5.26	1.59	98	123	4.4	11%	15%	4%	7%	7.6%	96.6	52	22	26	36%	75%	8%	9%	0	15			0	0.99	-0.4	22	-$11
2nd Half		2	3	23	22	2.35	1.26	3.51	1.44	64	78	3.2	11%	22%	11%	9%	10.2%	96.6	73	9	18	30%	79%	0%	4%	0	12			100	1.17	5.6	101	$2
Proj		5	7	65	57	3.77	1.35	3.79	1.41	82	101	3.8	10%	21%	11%	8%	9.7%	96.7	58	17	25	31%	72%	9%	7%	0						4.5	83	$2

Pérez,Eury

Age: 21	Th: R	Role: SP	Health: B	LIMA Plan: B
Ht: 6'8"	Wt: 220	Type: Pwr/xFB	PT/Exp: D	Rand Var: -2
			Consist: A	MM: 3403

5-6, 3.15 ERA in 91 IP at MIA. Prodigy gave us an immediate glimpse of his future in MLB debut. Control still a work in progress; S%, big FB% hurt in 2nd-half slide. But nagging hip injury that eventually ended his season in September also played a role. Strikeout skills are already elite, as was .214 BAA. If healthy, he's a strong buy.

Yr	Tm	W	Sv	IP	K	ERA	WHIP	xERA	xWHIP	vL+	vR+	BF/G	BB%	K%	K-BB%	xBB%	SwK	Vel	G	L	F	H%	S%	HR/F	xHR/F	GS	APC	DOM%	DIS%	Sv%	LI	RAR	BPX	R$
19																																		
20																																		
21																																		
22	aa	3	0	75	97	4.17	1.14	3.23				17.5	7%	33%	25%							33%	65%									-1.9	158	$1
23	MIA *	8	0	130	155	3.20	1.06	3.26	1.19	87	104	18.6	8%	29%	21%	8%	15.8%	97.6	25	20	55	27%	78%	12%	12%	19	81	32%	26%			18.1	131	$17
1st Half		8	0	78	91	2.48	1.00	2.83	1.15	89	96	18.7	7%	29%	22%	8%	14.3%	97.6	30	23	47	25%	84%	10%	11%	10	79	40%	10%			17.9	137	$27
2nd Half		0	0	51	64	4.29	1.16	3.92	1.15	86	114	18.5	8%	31%	23%	8%	17.4%	97.5	20	16	64	30%	69%	13%	14%	9	83	22%	44%			0.3	124	$1
Proj		10	0	152	178	3.50	1.11	3.81	1.14	87	105	21.4	8%	30%	22%	8%	16.2%	97.6	24	19	57	29%	75%	11%	12%	28						15.6	134	$16

Perez,Martin

Age: 33	Th: L	Role: RP	Health: B	LIMA Plan: C+
Ht: 6'0"	Wt: 200	Type: Con	PT/Exp: A	Rand Var: -1
			Consist: B	MM: 1001

Hitters adjusted to sinker-forward repertoire that fueled career 2022. Regression bit hard beginning in May, was moved to long relief by the end of July. Fared better there (2.70 ERA in 33 IP) with less exposure and fewer BF/G. Aging soft-tosser with entrenched SwK and no plus skills is still an unattractive flyer, even in new pitching paradigm.

Yr	Tm	W	Sv	IP	K	ERA	WHIP	xERA	xWHIP	vL+	vR+	BF/G	BB%	K%	K-BB%	xBB%	SwK	Vel	G	L	F	H%	S%	HR/F	xHR/F	GS	APC	DOM%	DIS%	Sv%	LI	RAR	BPX	R$
19	MIN	10	0	165	135	5.12	1.52	4.94	1.45	77	112	23.0	9%	18%	9%	7%	10.3%	94.1	48	23	29	33%	69%	15%	12%	29	87	21%	55%	0	0.73	-12.5	65	-$5
20	BOS	3	0	62	46	4.50	1.34	5.23	1.52	107	98	21.8	11%	18%	7%	10%	8.7%	92.1	38	26	35	27%	69%	13%	14%	12	86	25%	42%			-0.4	30	$1
21	BOS	7	0	114	97	4.74	1.51	4.56	1.31	92	117	14.1	7%	19%	12%	7%	8.5%	93.0	44	24	33	34%	73%	16%	16%	22	52	9%	45%	0	0.54	-6.6	91	-$6
22	TEX	12	0	196	169	2.89	1.26	3.79	1.31	80	93	25.7	8%	21%	12%	8%	8.6%	92.7	51	19	30	30%	78%	7%	8%	32	93	38%	13%			26.2	92	$16
23	TEX	10	0	142	93	4.45	1.40	5.02	1.45	91	111	17.4	8%	15%	7%	8%	7.6%	91.7	45	19	36	30%	72%	13%	13%	20	64	15%	55%	0	0.75	-2.0	51	-$1
1st Half		7	0	90	60	4.28	1.42	5.10	1.43	101	107	24.4	8%	15%	8%	7%	8.5%	91.6	43	21	37	30%	74%	12%	11%	16	89	19%	50%			0.5	54	$3
2nd Half		3	0	51	33	4.73	1.38	4.89	1.48	86	123	11.5	9%	15%	6%	8%	6.2%	91.8	51	15	34	28%	70%	15%	16%	4	42	0%	75%	0	0.71	-2.5	48	-$1
Proj		7	0	116	86	4.36	1.40	4.43	1.40	90	110	16.0	9%	18%	9%	8%	8.0%	92.3	46	20	33	30%	72%	13%	13%	18						-0.5	64	-$2

OCK THOMPSON

Peterson,David

Age: 28	Th: L	Role: SP	Health: D	LIMA Plan: A+
Ht: 6'6"	Wt: 240	Type: Pwr/GB	PT/Exp: C	Rand Var: +3
			Consist: B	MM: 3301

3-8, 5.03 ERA in 111 IP at NYM. Disappointing season with a cliffhanger twist in four acts: I. Defeat (8 GS, 8.08 ERA); II. Banishment (6 weeks in MiLB); III. Metamorphosis (8 IP, 2.25 ERA as RP); IV. Apotheosis (3.88 ERA, 28.2% K%, 52.8% GB% in 48.2 IP). A faint glimmer of hope, but November hip surgery assures a late start to 2024. Pass.

Yr Tm	W	Sv	IP	K	ERA	WHIP	xERA	xWHIP	vL+	vR+	BF/G	BB%	K%	K-BB%	xBB%	SwK	Vel	G	L	F	H%	S%	HR/F	xHR/F	GS	APC	DOM%	DIS%	Sv%	LI	RAR	BPX	R$
19 aa	3	0	116	106	5.96	1.65	5.72				21.6	8%	20%	13%							39%	64%									-20.8	75	-$12
20 NYM	6	0	50	40	3.44	1.21	4.93	1.52	70	90	20.5	12%	20%	8%	11%	10.8%	92.1	44	19	36	24%	75%	10%	13%	9	81	11%	56%	0	0.79	6.2	40	$13
21 NYM	2	0	67	69	5.54	1.40	3.90	1.34	106	108	19.1	10%	24%	14%	8%	11.5%	92.6	49	23	27	31%	63%	22%	22%	15	75	7%	47%			-10.4	98	-$7
22 NYM *	9	0	132	154	3.99	1.41	4.21	1.27	92	101	16.4	10%	28%	17%	11%	13.0%	93.6	49	24	27	35%	73%	15%	15%	19	67	11%	21%	0	0.77	-0.4	108	$2
23 NYM *	4	0	148	162	5.01	1.62	5.59	1.32	111	113	19.3	10%	26%	16%	9%	12.7%	92.1	55	20	25	36%	72%	21%	21%	21	73	10%	24%	0	0.71	-12.3	75	-$12
1st Half	3	0	86	87	5.89	1.71	6.13	1.44	146	114	22.9	11%	22%	11%	8%	12.0%	92.2	55	22	23	37%	67%	24%	24%	10	88	0%	20%			-16.6	60	-$17
2nd Half	1	0	62	75	3.77	1.48	3.55	1.33	80	113	15.8	11%	28%	17%	9%	13.4%	92.0	54	19	27	35%	79%	19%	19%	11	64	18%	27%	0	0.68	4.3	124	$1
Proj	**6**	**0**	**102**	**109**	**4.12**	**1.38**	**3.64**	**1.35**	**97**	**102**	**20.4**	**11%**	**26%**	**14%**	**9%**	**12.3%**	**92.5**	**51**	**21**	**27**	**31%**	**74%**	**18%**	**19%**	**21**						**2.6**	**101**	**$0**

Pfaadt,Brandon

Age: 25	Th: R	Role: SP	Health: A	LIMA Plan: A
Ht: 6'4"	Wt: 220	Type: /FB	PT/Exp: C	Rand Var: 0
			Consist: F	MM: 2205

3-9, 5.72 ERA in 96 IP at ARI. Highly-touted rookie's first few starts went over like a fart in church (8 HR, 8.37 ERA in 23.2 IP). Sent down for almost two months with a clunker spot start mixed in, but returned a changed man (4.22 ERA, 19.1 K-BB%). Low walk rate, SwK% progress, IP volume provide good foundation to prove he's not some passing fad.

Yr Tm	W	Sv	IP	K	ERA	WHIP	xERA	xWHIP	vL+	vR+	BF/G	BB%	K%	K-BB%	xBB%	SwK	Vel	G	L	F	H%	S%	HR/F	xHR/F	GS	APC	DOM%	DIS%	Sv%	LI	RAR	BPX	R$
19																																	
20																																	
21 aa	1	0	34	30	4.62	1.35	6.61				23.7	5%	21%	16%							30%	81%									-1.5	64	-$5
22 a/a	11	0	169	179	3.20	1.08	3.47				22.8	4%	27%	23%							31%	76%									16.1	184	$18
23 ARI *	9	0	168	140	4.74	1.32	5.13	1.23	117	118	21.1	6%	22%	16%	6%	12.0%	93.6	32	24	44	32%	70%	17%	13%	18	85	22%	44%	0	0.76	-7.9	88	$1
1st Half	5	0	77	68	5.38	1.36	5.52	1.26	152	148	20.0	6%	21%	15%	8%	10.8%	93.6	27	28	46	32%	66%	22%	18%	6	84	0%	83%			-9.9	70	-$3
2nd Half	4	0	82	82	4.13	1.28	4.76	1.19	99	109	22.3	6%	24%	18%	6%	12.5%	93.6	35	22	43	32%	74%	14%	11%	12	86	33%	25%	0	0.74	2.0	107	$9
Proj	**9**	**0**	**181**	**173**	**4.05**	**1.24**	**3.96**	**1.17**	**106**	**102**	**24.0**	**6%**	**23%**	**18%**	**7%**	**11.7%**	**93.6**	**34**	**22**	**44**	**31%**	**74%**	**13%**	**12%**	**31**						**6.2**	**124**	**$8**

Phillips,Connor

Age: 23	Th: R	Role: SP	Health: A	LIMA Plan: C+
Ht: 6'2"	Wt: 190	Type: Pwr/FB	PT/Exp: D	Rand Var: +1
			Consist: B	MM: 1301

1-1, 6.97 ERA in 20.2 IP at CIN. Dominated AA early and earned promotions to AAA, then MLB. Arsenal piles up whiffs, but struggles with BB% and high pitch counts. Sports electric, flat-angled mid-90s fastball with ride/run, varies breakers between sweeper that gets outs and a knee-buckling curve. Walks, inefficiency will hold him back for now. (CB)

Yr Tm	W	Sv	IP	K	ERA	WHIP	xERA	xWHIP	vL+	vR+	BF/G	BB%	K%	K-BB%	xBB%	SwK	Vel	G	L	F	H%	S%	HR/F	xHR/F	GS	APC	DOM%	DIS%	Sv%	LI	RAR	BPX	R$
19																																	
20																																	
21																																	
22 aa	1	0	47	54	4.91	1.75	5.16				18.0	15%	25%	10%							37%	72%									-5.5	86	-$9
23 CIN *	5	1	128	162	4.43	1.42	4.37	1.45	87	118	18.1	14%	27%	14%	10%	9.2%	96.5	34	16	50	33%	72%	18%	14%	5	76	20%	40%			-1.5	102	$0
1st Half	2	0	69	99	3.52	1.34	4.35				19.3	10%	34%	23%							35%	80%	0%		0	0					7.0	125	$6
2nd Half	3	1	61	63	5.07	1.42	3.95	1.52	88	119	17.2	14%	24%	10%	10%	9.2%	96.5	34	16	50	29%	65%	18%	14%	5	76	20%	40%			-5.5	85	$0
Proj	**4**	**0**	**102**	**114**	**4.75**	**1.49**	**4.54**	**1.46**	**93**	**108**	**21.9**	**14%**	**26%**	**12%**	**11%**	**9.2%**	**96.5**	**34**	**16**	**50**	**31%**	**70%**	**10%**	**12%**	**20**						**-5.2**	**56**	**-$6**

Phillips,Evan

Age: 29	Th: R	Role: RP	Health: A	LIMA Plan: B
Ht: 6'2"	Wt: 215	Type: Pwr	PT/Exp: B	Rand Var: -5
			Consist: D	MM: 4331

Answered the call to close with breakout season, fully supported by elite peripherals. BPX reflects many harmonious elements (velocity, command, contact suppression, dominance vL and vR). If we're going to pick nits, strikeout rate merely very good instead of otherworldly, outperformed expected rate stats. Even with regression, a worthwhile arm.

Yr Tm	W	Sv	IP	K	ERA	WHIP	xERA	xWHIP	vL+	vR+	BF/G	BB%	K%	K-BB%	xBB%	SwK	Vel	G	L	F	H%	S%	HR/F	xHR/F	GS	APC	DOM%	DIS%	Sv%	LI	RAR	BPX	R$
19 BAL *	1	1	69	75	5.32	1.61	4.66	1.47	111	108	5.9	12%	24%	12%	10%	12.0%	94.2	38	32	30	36%	66%	9%	11%	0	23			100	0.66	-7.0	90	-$7
20 BAL	1	0	14	20	5.02	1.67	4.27	1.45	68	105	4.9	14%	29%	14%	10%	10.6%	94.6	46	23	31	39%	70%	9%	7%	0	20			0	0.69	-1.0	91	-$6
21 2 TM *	2	1	42	42	5.36	1.49	5.25	1.37	52	106	6.5	11%	23%	11%	4%	11.1%	95.4	51	27	22	31%	68%	11%	9%	0	31			100	0.94	-5.7	58	-$7
22 LA	7	2	63	77	1.14	0.76	2.68	1.01	64	58	3.6	6%	33%	27%	6%	13.1%	96.1	46	17	38	24%	87%	4%	7%	0	14			50	1.12	22.0	181	$15
23 LA	2	24	61	66	2.05	0.83	3.29	1.10	89	56	3.8	6%	28%	23%	5%	13.1%	96.1	43	21	37	23%	82%	11%	11%	0	15			89	1.10	17.2	161	$20
1st Half	1	11	33	39	1.91	0.79	2.92	1.04	77	62	3.6	6%	32%	26%	5%	13.9%	96.1	43	23	35	23%	83%	12%	14%	0	14			92	1.15	9.9	181	$15
2nd Half	1	13	28	27	2.22	0.88	3.73	1.16	101	48	4.0	5%	24%	19%	6%	12.2%	96.1	43	19	39	23%	82%	10%	7%	0	16			87	1.03	7.4	139	$1
Proj	**3**	**27**	**65**	**69**	**3.08**	**1.08**	**3.39**	**1.20**	**112**	**70**	**4.4**	**8%**	**27%**	**19%**	**6%**	**12.9%**	**96.1**	**43**	**20**	**37**	**27%**	**75%**	**11%**	**9%**	**0**						**10.0**	**130**	**$15**

Pivetta,Nick

Age: 31	Th: R	Role: SP	Health: A	LIMA Plan: B+
Ht: 6'5"	Wt: 214	Type: Pwr/FB	PT/Exp: A	Rand Var: +1
			Consist: A	MM: 4305

Used as a traditional SP until May 16 (6.30 ERA, 12.6% K-BB%). Transitioned to mostly multi-inning RP (3.48 ERA, 35.6% K%, 26.6% K-BB% in 72.1 IP), then finished with pitch mix tweak and 5 tantalizing starts (2.37 ERA, 15.7% SwK%, 4.3% BB%). That xBB% progression, velocity/K bump, workhorse frame points to ... UP: 3.25 ERA

Yr Tm	W	Sv	IP	K	ERA	WHIP	xERA	xWHIP	vL+	vR+	BF/G	BB%	K%	K-BB%	xBB%	SwK	Vel	G	L	F	H%	S%	HR/F	xHR/F	GS	APC	DOM%	DIS%	Sv%	LI	RAR	BPX	R$
19 PHI *	9	1	135	138	4.89	1.43	4.85	1.40	114	116	14.7	11%	24%	13%	8%	10.7%	94.6	43	25	32	31%	70%	22%	20%	13	54	15%	46%	100	0.78	-6.3	66	$
20 2 TM	2	0	16	17	6.89	1.53	5.16	1.30	148	109	14.2	8%	24%	15%	8%	10.0%	92.8	28	23	49	34%	60%	17%	18%	2	58	0%	0%	0	0.52	-4.7	100	-$
21 BOS	9	1	155	175	4.53	1.30	4.29	1.29	102	97	21.3	10%	26%	17%	7%	11.1%	94.8	38	19	43	30%	70%	14%	12%	30	89	20%	43%	100	0.82	-5.0	106	$
22 BOS	10	0	180	175	4.56	1.38	4.32	1.32	115	101	23.4	9%	23%	13%	7%	10.5%	93.5	38	20	42	31%	71%	12%	14%	33	93	18%	39%			-13.1	83	-$
23 BOS	10	1	143	183	4.04	1.12	3.60	1.16	107	83	15.4	9%	31%	23%	6%	13.7%	94.7	36	22	42	28%	70%	16%	16%	16	63	38%	31%	50	0.84	5.2	153	$1
1st Half	4	0	64	73	4.92	1.31	4.49	1.34	109	97	13.3	11%	26%	15%	8%	11.5%	94.3	32	24	44	29%	67%	15%	16%	8	56	13%	50%	0	0.90	-4.7	91	$
2nd Half	6	1	79	110	3.32	0.97	2.93	1.00	107	73	18.1	6%	36%	29%	5%	15.8%	95.1	41	19	40	28%	73%	17%	17%	8	71	63%	13%	50	0.77	9.8	207	$2
Proj	**12**	**0**	**181**	**208**	**3.94**	**1.17**	**3.51**	**1.18**	**104**	**89**	**22.0**	**8%**	**29%**	**21%**	**7%**	**14.0%**	**94.6**	**38**	**21**	**41**	**30%**	**71%**	**14%**	**13%**	**33**						**8.7**	**138**	**$1**

Poche,Colin

Age: 30	Th: L	Role: RP	Health: F	LIMA Plan: B+
Ht: 6'3"	Wt: 225	Type: Pwr/xFB	PT/Exp: C	Rand Var: -5
			Consist: A	MM: 3310

Behold, the King of all Vultures! Gaudy win stat aside, rode munificent hit and strand rates in 1st half while rocking some ghastly peripherals and expected stats. Second-half success was more in line with massive improvements in walk, whiff rates. The latter version is worthy of bullpen watchlists; keep an eye on him as roles shift along the way.

Yr Tm	W	Sv	IP	K	ERA	WHIP	xERA	xWHIP	vL+	vR+	BF/G	BB%	K%	K-BB%	xBB%	SwK	Vel	G	L	F	H%	S%	HR/F	xHR/F	GS	APC	DOM%	DIS%	Sv%	LI	RAR	BPX	R$
19 TAM *	7	2	80	113	5.71	1.25	4.14	1.16	82	89	4.6	9%	35%	26%	5%	17.6%	93.0	18	19	62	34%	57%	13%	11%	0	17			29	1.63	-11.8	132	$
20																																	
21																																	
22 TAM	4	7	59	64	3.99	1.16	4.13	1.24	104	95	3.8	9%	26%	17%	6%	13.3%	93.3	32	19	49	26%	74%	14%	11%	0	15			54	1.19	-0.1	105	$
23 TAM	12	1	61	61	2.23	1.09	4.49	1.33	80	79	3.7	10%	25%	15%	8%	13.3%	92.5	34	17	49	26%	82%	5%	5%	0	14			20	1.12	15.8	88	$1
1st Half	6	1	31	23	2.32	1.23	5.88	1.59	103	80	3.8	12%	17%	5%	10%	10.3%	92.5	30	16	54	23%	86%	6%	4%	0	14			25	1.01	7.7	4	$
2nd Half	6	0	30	38	2.12	0.94	3.20	1.06	64	78	3.7	7%	33%	26%	5%	16.6%	92.6	39	19	42	29%	78%	4%	7%	0	14			0	1.25	8.1	179	$1
Proj	**6**	**2**	**58**	**67**	**3.36**	**1.12**	**3.80**	**1.22**	**87**	**88**	**3.8**	**9%**	**29%**	**20%**	**7%**	**14.8%**	**92.8**	**31**	**18**	**51**	**28%**	**74%**	**8%**	**8%**	**0**						**6.9**	**118**	**$**

Pressly,Ryan

Age: 35	Th: R	Role: RP	Health: D	LIMA Plan: B
Ht: 6'2"	Wt: 206	Type: Pwr/GB	PT/Exp: A	Rand Var: 0
			Consist: A	MM: 5430

Still among elite closers, but can he continue to thrive at 35? PRO: First-half performance a virtual carbon-copy of prior years' peripheral excellence; healthy all year. CON: Second-half drop in swinging strike rate, increase in walk rate and xHR/F suggest his stuff wasn't as sharp. Even his lesser self would still qualify as elite--bid confidently.

Yr Tm	W	Sv	IP	K	ERA	WHIP	xERA	xWHIP	vL+	vR+	BF/G	BB%	K%	K-BB%	xBB%	SwK	Vel	G	L	F	H%	S%	HR/F	xHR/F	GS	APC	DOM%	DIS%	Sv%	LI	RAR	BPX	R$
19 HOU	2	3	54	72	2.32	0.90	2.56	1.01	48	96	3.8	6%	34%	29%	5%	18.0%	95.6	51	28	21	28%	81%	22%	20%	0	15			38	1.25	14.7	207	$
20 HOU	1	12	21	29	3.43	1.33	3.25	1.11	97	101	4.0	8%	32%	24%	4%	17.8%	94.7	48	22	30	39%	77%	13%	6%	0	15			75	1.61	2.7	191	$
21 HOU	5	26	64	81	2.25	0.97	2.66	1.00	72	76	3.9	5%	32%	27%	4%	15.2%	95.5	55	17	28	31%	79%	9%	14%	0	15			93	1.40	15.9	207	$
22 HOU	3	33	48	65	2.98	0.89	2.45	1.00	74	72	3.6	7%	36%	29%	7%	18.3%	94.5	46	23	31	27%	69%	13%	14%	0	14			89	1.33	5.9	195	$
23 HOU	4	31	65	74	3.58	1.07	3.24	1.13	87	81	4.1	6%	28%	22%	5%	15.8%	94.7	55	15	31	29%	71%	15%	18%	0	16			84	1.14	6.0	176	$
1st Half	2	17	36	39	2.72	0.88	2.75	1.09	80	65	3.9	5%	28%	23%	5%	16.9%	94.6	64	12	24	26%	72%	13%	17%	0	15			85	1.10	7.2	191	$
2nd Half	2	14	29	35	4.66	1.31	3.84	1.17	96	102	4.4	7%	27%	20%	6%	14.6%	94.9	45	18	37	34%	70%	16%	19%	0	17			82	1.18	-1.2	161	
Proj	**4**	**30**	**58**	**71**	**3.34**	**1.04**	**2.69**	**1.05**	**80**	**83**	**3.8**	**6%**	**32%**	**25%**	**6%**	**16.0%**	**95.0**	**52**	**18**	**30**	**30%**	**72%**	**15%**	**17%**	**0**						**7.1**	**190**	**$**

ALAIN DE LEONARDIS

Priester,Quinn

Age: 23 | Th: R | Role: SP | Ht: 6' 3" | Wt: 195 | Type:
Health: A | PT/Exp: D | Consist: F
LIMA Plan: C+ | Rand Var: +5 | MM: 2001

3-3, 7.74 ERA in 50 IP at PIT. So-so season at Triple-A prior to mid-season callup. Sinker produced lots of groundball contact; 4-seam fastball struggled to miss barrels, but neither brought on whiffs. Rest of arsenal is average and predictable. Lacks overall deception, which heightens blow-up risk in a pitch-to-contact profile. Watch from afar. (CB)

Yr	Tm	W	Sv	IP	K	ERA	WHIP	xERA	xWHIP	vL+	vR+	BF/G	BB%	K%	K-BB%	xBB%	SwK	Vel	G	L	F	H%	S%	HR/F	xHR/F	GS	APC	DOM%	DIS%	Sv%	LI	RAR	BPX	R$
19																																		
20																																		
21																																		
22	a/a	5	0	86	72	2.79	1.17	2.89				20.2	8%	21%	13%							29%	76%									12.5	107	$5
23	PIT *	12	0	158	129	5.44	1.50	4.90	1.60	149	106	21.3	12%	15%	4%	10%	10.0%	93.3	52	20	27	32%	65%	27%	18%	8	87	0%	75%	0	0.71	-21.5	58	-$8
1st Half		7	0	80	65	4.91	1.50	4.60				21.6	10%	19%	9%							33%	67%	0%		0	0					-5.7	72	-$2
2nd Half		5	0	80	64	5.80	1.47	4.96	1.52	149	107	21.5	11%	18%	7%	10%	10.1%	93.3	52	20	27	29%	62%	27%	18%	8	87	0%	75%	0	0.71	-14.6	46	-$2
Proj		6	0	87	67	4.67	1.35	4.09	1.44	123	89	22.0	10%	18%	9%	10%	10.0%	93.3	52	20	27	29%	66%	14%	16%	16						-3.7	63	-$3

Puk,A.J.

Age: 29 | Th: L | Role: RP | Ht: 6' 7" | Wt: 248 | Type: Pwr
Health: D | PT/Exp: B | Consist: D
LIMA Plan: A | Rand Var: +4 | MM: 5411

Shakespeare's Puck is a mischievous sprite deeply involved in the outcomes of the play; so was this one, whose value was in amassing wins and saves. Missed three weeks due to elbow soreness, otherwise posted best skills season to date. Meddlesome hit rate and poor Sv% cost him the closer role, but BPX tells the real story. Flighty, yet powerful.

Yr	Tm	W	Sv	IP	K	ERA	WHIP	xERA	xWHIP	vL+	vR+	BF/G	BB%	K%	K-BB%	xBB%	SwK	Vel	G	L	F	H%	S%	HR/F	xHR/F	GS	APC	DOM%	DIS%	Sv%	LI	RAR	BPX	R$
19	OAK *	6	0	31	37	4.64	1.27	4.50	1.33	117	73	5.1	9%	29%	20%	8%	14.4%	97.1	48	10	41	30%	70%	8%	2%	0	20			0	1.00	-0.5	95	-$1
20																																		
21	OAK *	2	1	64	62	5.94	1.70	6.84	1.29	95	105	7.0	8%	22%	13%	8%	10.3%	95.7	52	26	21	38%	69%	11%	7%	0	20			33	0.57	-13.1	53	-$12
22	OAK	4	4	66	76	3.12	1.15	3.39	1.18	73	105	4.5	8%	27%	19%	6%	13.5%	96.6	43	20	37	29%	77%	11%	13%	0	17			44	1.17	6.9	135	$5
23	MIA	7	15	57	78	3.97	1.18	3.27	1.02	78	105	4.2	5%	32%	27%	5%	15.5%	95.8	44	16	40	35%	74%	17%	16%	0	16			65	1.16	2.5	212	$9
1st Half		3	13	25	28	2.88	1.04	3.63	1.06	77	79	4.1	4%	26%	23%	5%	15.3%	95.7	42	20	38	32%	75%	7%	7%	0	16			87	1.33	4.5	184	$12
2nd Half		4	2	32	50	4.83	1.29	3.00	0.99	79	129	4.3	7%	37%	30%	5%	15.6%	95.9	46	12	42	38%	73%	25%	23%	0	17			25	1.02	-2.0	238	$4
Proj		7	7	73	89	3.69	1.21	3.20	1.11	82	112	4.5	7%	31%	23%	5%	15.1%	96.0	44	16	40	32%	77%	18%	15%	0						5.7	168	$7

Quantrill,Cal

Age: 29 | Th: R | Role: SP | Ht: 6' 3" | Wt: 195 | Type: Con
Health: F | PT/Exp: A | Consist: A
LIMA Plan: C+ | Rand Var: 0 | MM: 1003

4-7, 5.24 ERA in 100 IP at CLE. Oof. Outran peripherals in previous years, but three-year decline in swinging strike, strikeout, K-BB rates accelerated and caught up, driving him off the cliff. Recovered some whiffs in 2nd half, but overall picture was still bad. Missed two months with sore shoulder; even when healthy, it's a game of chicken. xERA tells all.

Yr	Tm	W	Sv	IP	K	ERA	WHIP	xERA	xWHIP	vL+	vR+	BF/G	BB%	K%	K-BB%	xBB%	SwK	Vel	G	L	F	H%	S%	HR/F	xHR/F	GS	APC	DOM%	DIS%	Sv%	LI	RAR	BPX	R$
19	SD *	10	0	140	116	4.95	1.33	4.44	1.30	112	78	19.4	7%	20%	13%	8%	10.4%	94.5	44	21	35	32%	65%	14%	14%	18	77	11%	44%	0	0.83	-7.7	80	$2
20	2 TM	2	1	32	31	2.25	1.22	4.11	1.20	70	114	7.5	6%	23%	17%	8%	10.1%	94.9	44	19	37	31%	89%	12%	15%	3	28	0%	33%	50	1.39	8.7	134	$7
21	CLE	8	0	150	121	2.89	1.18	4.34	1.32	90	93	15.4	8%	20%	12%	8%	9.8%	94.3	43	22	35	27%	80%	11%	10%	22	59	14%	27%	0	0.60	25.5	83	$14
22	CLE	15	0	186	128	3.38	1.21	4.32	1.29	96	101	24.1	6%	17%	11%	7%	8.4%	93.6	42	20	38	28%	76%	10%	12%	32	91	13%	38%			13.5	77	$13
23	CLE *	6	0	124	71	5.53	1.50	5.26	1.49	115	99	22.3	8%	13%	5%	9%	8.3%	93.7	41	23	36	31%	64%	9%	13%	19	90	5%	58%			-18.3	31	-$11
1st Half		3	0	68	37	5.72	1.46	4.96	1.49	119	97	22.3	8%	12%	5%	10%	7.8%	93.7	39	24	37	31%	61%	9%	13%	12	89	0%	58%			-11.6	38	-$12
2nd Half		3	0	56	34	5.30	1.54	5.64	1.52	111	104	22.3	9%	14%	5%	8%	9.2%	93.9	44	20	36	31%	68%	9%	13%	7	92	14%	57%			-6.7	24	-$5
Proj		7	0	131	91	4.35	1.36	4.55	1.39	106	103	23.0	8%	17%	9%	8%	9.0%	94.0	43	21	36	30%	71%	11%	13%	24						-0.4	61	-$1

Quintana,José

Age: 35 | Th: L | Role: RP | Ht: 6' 1" | Wt: 220 | Type:
Health: F | PT/Exp: A | Consist: B
LIMA Plan: B | Rand Var: -3 | MM: 2103

After missing almost four months due to bone graft surgery on his rib, crafty veteran southpaw pitched competently. Velocity, SwK sagged, but makes his living off suppressing quality of contact with effective curveball and change-up. Still, at 35, xERA range is instructive and probably a reasonable expectation. Which makes him more of an end-gamer.

Yr	Tm	W	Sv	IP	K	ERA	WHIP	xERA	xWHIP	vL+	vR+	BF/G	BB%	K%	K-BB%	xBB%	SwK	Vel	G	L	F	H%	S%	HR/F	xHR/F	GS	APC	DOM%	DIS%	Sv%	LI	RAR	BPX	R$
19	CHC	13	0	171	152	4.68	1.39	4.48	1.29	82	107	23.3	6%	20%	14%	8%	8.7%	91.4	44	25	31	34%	68%	12%	13%	31	88	23%	45%	0	0.80	-3.8	110	$4
20	CHC	0	0	10	12	4.50	1.30	3.28	1.14	151	79	10.3	7%	29%	22%	12%	10.9%	91.4	42	35	23	36%	67%	17%	11%	1	46	0%	100%	0	0.61	-0.1	160	-$6
21	2 TM	0	0	63	85	6.43	1.73	4.06	1.32	71	133	10.2	12%	29%	17%	9%	12.5%	91.6	47	21	32	40%	66%	21%	19%	10	43	0%	40%	0	0.82	-16.8	119	-$14
22	2 NL	6	0	166	137	2.93	1.21	3.80	1.26	80	93	21.2	7%	20%	13%	8%	11.0%	91.3	46	22	31	31%	76%	5%	9%	32	85	19%	25%			21.1	98	$11
23	NYM	3	0	76	60	3.57	1.31	4.61	1.35	86	94	24.5	8%	19%	11%	8%	9.3%	90.4	42	23	36	31%	73%	6%	11%	13	95	8%	15%			7.1	80	$0
1st Half																																		
2nd Half		3	0	76	60	3.57	1.31	4.61	1.35	87	95	24.5	8%	19%	11%	8%	9.3%	90.4	42	23	36	31%	73%	6%	11%	13	95	8%	15%			7.1	80	$6
Proj		7	0	145	122	4.06	1.31	4.07	1.33	78	99	18.4	8%	20%	12%	9%	10.1%	91.0	44	23	33	31%	71%	10%	12%	27						4.9	87	$3

Ragans,Cole

Age: 26 | Th: L | Role: SP | Ht: 6' 4" | Wt: 190 | Type: Pwr
Health: B | PT/Exp: C | Consist: F
LIMA Plan: A | Rand Var: 0 | MM: 3303

7-5, 3.47 ERA in 96 IP at TEX/KC. The Cinderella Man of 2023, folks. Started season as a ragged Rangers reliever (5.92 ERA, 9.4 K-BB% in 24.1 IP), finished in Royal fashion as a SP (2.64 ERA, 21.7% K-BB% in 71.2 IP), all while improving on huge off-season velocity bump. Control still wobbly, but if he nears that xBB%... UP: 3.50 ERA, 200 K

Yr	Tm	W	Sv	IP	K	ERA	WHIP	xERA	xWHIP	vL+	vR+	BF/G	BB%	K%	K-BB%	xBB%	SwK	Vel	G	L	F	H%	S%	HR/F	xHR/F	GS	APC	DOM%	DIS%	Sv%	LI	RAR	BPX	R$
19																																		
20																																		
21	aa	3	0	37	27	7.07	1.82	7.56				19.1	12%	16%	3%							33%	66%									-12.8	-7	-$11
22	TEX *	8	0	136	118	3.42	1.21	3.58	1.45	74	119	20.3	8%	21%	13%	9%	11.2%	92.1	36	25	39	29%	75%	12%	8%	9	78	0%	22%			9.1	90	$7
23	2 AL *	9	0	125	140	3.68	1.22	2.98	1.28	96	76	14.0	10%	29%	18%	8%	14.7%	96.6	44	20	36	29%	71%	8%	10%	12	55	42%	8%	0	0.82	10.0	119	$10
1st Half		2	0	39	39	5.65	1.38	4.42	1.46	122	88	7.9	12%	23%	11%	8%	12.1%	96.2	40	19	40	29%	61%	15%	13%	0	24			0	0.86	-6.4	70	-$9
2nd Half		7	0	86	102	2.78	1.14	2.31	1.28	82	73	22.6	11%	29%	19%	7%	15.7%	96.8	46	20	35	29%	75%	5%	9%	12	98	42%	8%			16.4	143	$24
Proj		10	0	160	176	3.98	1.28	3.79	1.34	104	91	23.0	11%	27%	15%	8%	14.5%	95.6	43	20	37	29%	71%	11%	10%	28						6.9	96	$8

Rainey,Tanner

Age: 31 | Th: R | Role: RP | Ht: 6' 2" | Wt: 244 | Type: Pwr/xFB
Health: F | PT/Exp: C | Consist: F
LIMA Plan: B | Rand Var: -5 | MM: 2310

Returned from Tommy John surgery to make a single appearance at season's end. At least we saw big velocity was mostly intact, which bodes well. Wild fluctuations in walk rate have hindered his reliability, though xBB% history shows it should be workable--small samples due to injuries have likely contributed to discordance. With health... UP: 15 Sv

Yr	Tm	W	Sv	IP	K	ERA	WHIP	xERA	xWHIP	vL+	vR+	BF/G	BB%	K%	K-BB%	xBB%	SwK	Vel	G	L	F	H%	S%	HR/F	xHR/F	GS	APC	DOM%	DIS%	Sv%	LI	RAR	BPX	R$
19	WAS *	4	2	66	99	4.20	1.54	4.06	1.49	124	70	4.3	18%	34%	17%	10%	17.7%	97.8	53	18	29	33%	75%	21%	22%	0	17			22	0.71	2.5	113	-$1
20	WAS	1	0	20	32	2.66	0.74	2.74	0.99	59	82	3.8	9%	43%	33%	8%	21.7%	96.6	31	23	46	14%	82%	25%	19%	0	15			0	1.34	4.5	204	$5
21	WAS	1	3	32	42	7.39	1.71	5.72	1.57	116	111	4.0	17%	28%	11%	9%	15.9%	96.4	25	15	60	33%	58%	12%	13%	0	18			50	1.09	-12.2	29	-$9
22	WAS	1	12	30	36	3.30	1.30	4.14	1.25	86	107	4.4	10%	28%	18%	7%	16.5%	97.0	32	18	51	30%	82%	13%	13%	0	18			75	1.30	2.5	109	$2
23	WAS	0	0	1	1	0.00	2.00	7.88		135	46	5.0	20%	20%	0%	9%	11.1%	96.3	33	0	67	35%	100%	0%	0%	0	18			0	0.07	0.5	-79	-$6
1st Half																																		
2nd Half		0	0	1	1	0.00	2.00	7.88		136	46	5.0	20%	20%	0%	9%	11.1%	96.3	33	0	67	35%	100%	0%	0%	0	18			0	0.07	0.5	-79	-$8
Proj		2	2	58	66	4.10	1.37	4.24	1.37	105	104	3.7	12%	27%	15%	8%	16.5%	97.0	34	17	49	30%	75%	13%	14%	0						1.6	82	-$2

Raley,Brooks

Age: 36 | Th: L | Role: RP | Ht: 6' 3" | Wt: 200 | Type: Pwr
Health: D | PT/Exp: C | Consist: B
LIMA Plan: A+ | Rand Var: -5 | MM: 3310

Missed two weeks with left elbow inflammation, otherwise decent follow-up to successful 2022...or was it? PRO: Maintained above-average swinging strike, strikeout rates; repeated excellent quality of contact suppression. CON: Lefties caught up; control skills, velocity faded; outperformed middling x-stats; 3-year BPX dive. Time isn't on his side.

Yr	Tm	W	Sv	IP	K	ERA	WHIP	xERA	xWHIP	vL+	vR+	BF/G	BB%	K%	K-BB%	xBB%	SwK	Vel	G	L	F	H%	S%	HR/F	xHR/F	GS	APC	DOM%	DIS%	Sv%	LI	RAR	BPX	R$
19	for	5	0	181	133	4.82	1.58	5.05				26.5	10%	17%	7%							33%	70%									-7.0	51	-$8
20	2 TM	0	1	20	27	4.95	0.95	3.27	1.08	56	108	4.0	7%	32%	25%	6%	14.3%	90.2	39	24	37	25%	50%	18%	16%	0	16			100	1.10	-1.2	184	-$1
21	HOU	2	2	49	65	4.78	1.20	3.06	1.10	67	106	3.5	8%	32%	24%	8%	14.9%	90.8	45	26	29	34%	62%	18%	22%	0	15			40	1.16	-3.1	174	-$2
22	TAM	1	6	54	61	2.68	0.97	3.21	1.12	69	80	3.7	7%	28%	21%	6%	12.2%	90.7	38	29	34	27%	73%	7%	5%	0	14			67	1.22	8.5	146	$5
23	NYM	1	3	55	61	2.80	1.26	4.15	1.34	99	79	3.6	11%	26%	15%	9%	12.5%	89.9	43	18	39	30%	80%	7%	7%	0	15			50	1.04	10.3	102	$2
1st Half		0	1	30	33	2.43	1.15	3.92	1.22	102	74	3.5	8%	26%	18%	10%	12.9%	90.1	40	18	42	29%	84%	9%	7%	0	15			33	1.00	7.0	132	-$1
2nd Half		1	2	25	28	3.24	1.40	4.44	1.48	97	85	3.7	14%	25%	12%	8%	12.1%	89.8	46	18	35	31%	76%	4%	7%	0	15			67	1.09	3.4	67	-$1
Proj		2	2	58	66	3.69	1.25	3.58	1.27	91	90	3.8	10%	28%	18%	8%	13.0%	90.2	43	22	35	31%	72%	9%	10%	0						4.5	117	$0

ALAIN DE LEONARDIS

Rasmussen,Drew

Age: 28	Th: R	Role: SP	Health: F	LIMA Plan: A+
Ht: 6'1"	Wt: 211	Type: Pwr	PT/Exp: A	Rand Var: -2
			Consist: A	MM: 4201

Was showing career-best skills when he suffered yet another major elbow injury, this time addressed with an internal brace procedure rather than a third Tommy John surgery. ETA is mid-2024, so could still contribute, but it's reasonable to be skeptical of the odds. Given the shortage of quality SPs, worth a roll at the right price.

Yr Tm	W	Sv	IP	K	ERA	WHIP	xERA	xWHIP	vL+	vR+	BF/G	BB%	K%	K-BB%	xBB%	SwK	Vel	G	L	F	H%	S%	HR/F	xHR/F	GS	APC	DOM%	DIS%	Sv%	LI	RAR	BPX	R$
19 aa	1	0	61	66	5.87	1.67	5.27				12.5	13%	24%	11%							36%	65%									-10.3	74	-$9
20 MIL	1	0	15	21	5.87	1.70	3.72	1.34	156	68	5.9	13%	30%	17%	8%	13.2%	97.7	54	24	22	39%	70%	33%	14%	0	25			0	0.52	-2.7	126	-$7
21 2 TM	4	1	76	73	2.84	1.08	3.80	1.26	76	78	8.8	8%	24%	16%	6%	11.2%	97.1	47	23	30	27%	75%	8%	8%	10	34	10%	20%	100	0.83	13.3	110	$7
22 TAM	11	0	146	125	2.84	1.04	3.60	1.17	77	94	20.9	5%	21%	16%	6%	12.6%	95.5	47	19	34	27%	76%	9%	11%	28	80	18%	29%			20.4	124	$17
23 TAM	4	0	45	47	2.62	1.05	3.17	1.15	79	76	22.1	6%	27%	20%	5%	11.2%	95.6	53	21	27	30%	76%	6%	6%	8	85	50%	25%			9.4	159	$4
1st Half	4	0	45	47	2.62	1.05	3.17	1.15	79	77	22.1	6%	27%	20%	5%	11.2%	95.6	53	21	27	30%	76%	6%	6%	8	85	50%	25%			9.4	159	$8
2nd Half																																	
Proj	**5**	**0**	**73**	**72**	**3.53**	**1.21**	**3.44**	**1.25**	**89**	**95**	**20.1**	**8%**	**25%**	**17%**	**6%**	**11.7%**	**95.9**	**50**	**21**	**30**	**31%**	**72%**	**9%**	**8%**	**15**						**7.2**	**122**	**$2**

Ray,Robbie

Age: 32	Th: L	Role: SP	Health: F	LIMA Plan: B
Ht: 6'2"	Wt: 225	Type: Pwr/FB	PT/Exp: A	Rand Var: -3
			Consist: F	MM: 4401

Suffered through one beatdown start before left flexor tendon repair and Tommy John surgery ended season. When healthy, he's an undeniable strikeout machine (3rd most 2016-22) who had been riding a multi-year improvement in control to new skills heights. Expected back mid-year, take the 2nd half K boost, #2 SP metrics are a bonus.

Yr Tm	W	Sv	IP	K	ERA	WHIP	xERA	xWHIP	vL+	vR+	BF/G	BB%	K%	K-BB%	xBB%	SwK	Vel	G	L	F	H%	S%	HR/F	xHR/F	GS	APC	DOM%	DIS%	Sv%	LI	RAR	BPX	R$
19 ARI	12	0	174	235	4.34	1.34	3.90	1.28	85	108	22.6	11%	32%	20%	8%	14.1%	92.4	37	26	37	32%	74%	20%	19%	33	93	18%	12%			3.6	127	$9
20 2 TM	2	0	52	68	6.62	1.90	6.14	1.67	91	135	20.9	18%	27%	9%	12%	13.0%	93.7	24	24	51	34%	71%	19%	18%	11	89	0%	55%	0	0.76	-13.8	4	-$17
21 TOR	13	0	193	248	2.84	1.04	3.46	1.06	82	91	24.2	7%	32%	25%	6%	16.3%	94.8	37	19	44	28%	83%	16%	14%	32	98	38%	22%			34.0	173	$31
22 SEA	12	0	189	212	3.71	1.19	3.61	1.17	93	104	24.2	8%	27%	19%	7%	14.2%	93.4	39	19	42	29%	76%	16%	12%	32	95	31%	19%			5.9	131	$14
23 SEA	0	0	3	3	8.10	2.70	9.82		139	103	19.0	26%	16%	-11%	12%	11.0%	93.0	40	30	30	38%	67%	0%	6%	1	91	0%	100%			-1.5	-225	-$7
1st Half	0	0	3	3	8.10	2.70	9.82		139	103	19.0	26%	16%	-11%	12%	11.0%	93.0	40	30	30	38%	67%	0%	6%	1	91	0%	100%			-1.5	-226	-$13
2nd Half																																	
Proj	**4**	**0**	**73**	**87**	**3.84**	**1.22**	**3.53**	**1.18**	**87**	**105**	**22.1**	**9%**	**30%**	**21%**	**8%**	**14.5%**	**93.6**	**36**	**21**	**43**	**30%**	**76%**	**17%**	**15%**	**13**						**4.4**	**140**	**$2**

Rea,Colin

Age: 34	Th: R	Role: SP	Health: A	LIMA Plan: B
Ht: 6'5"	Wt: 235	Type: Con	PT/Exp: D	Rand Var: +1
			Consist: A	MM: 2101

6-6, 4.55 ERA in 124.2 IP at MIL. See-saw season saw him optioned and recalled four times. Perfectly cromulent, league-average or slightly better skills across the board thanks to beguiling six-pitch mix. If you squint to ignore the elevated HR/F, 2nd half surges in SwK%, xBB%, K-BB% pretty dang decent. Waiver wire consideration.

Yr Tm	W	Sv	IP	K	ERA	WHIP	xERA	xWHIP	vL+	vR+	BF/G	BB%	K%	K-BB%	xBB%	SwK	Vel	G	L	F	H%	S%	HR/F	xHR/F	GS	APC	DOM%	DIS%	Sv%	LI	RAR	BPX	R$
19 aaa	14	0	148	89	5.64	1.78	6.46				26.2	11%	13%	2%							34%	71%									-20.7	12	-$12
20 CHC	1	0	14	10	5.79	1.21	4.72	1.22	52	137	6.9	3%	16%	13%	5%	7.1%	93.0	44	26	30	29%	57%	20%	14%	2	27	0%	100%	0	0.77	-2.3	116	-$5
21 MIL *	4	0	43	32	3.21	1.19	4.06		184	93	21.6	2%	18%	16%		11.0%	92.8	21	16	63	32%	76%	17%	17%	0	91			0	0.52	5.7	185	$0
22																																	
23 MIL *	6	0	143	126	4.36	1.18	4.19	1.30	110	89	19.0	7%	21%	14%	6%	10.6%	92.9	44	19	38	28%	69%	17%	14%	22	78	14%	36%	0	0.72	-0.5	85	$6
1st Half	5	0	83	67	4.03	1.18	3.76	1.33	103	89	19.4	7%	19%	12%	7%	9.4%	92.8	45	18	37	27%	70%	13%	11%	14	81	14%	43%	0	0.77	3.1	81	$9
2nd Half	1	0	60	59	4.81	1.19	4.77	1.18	121	91	18.5	6%	24%	19%	5%	12.4%	93.0	41	20	39	29%	68%	23%	18%	8	74	13%	25%	0	0.65	-3.6	98	$0
Proj	**6**	**0**	**102**	**86**	**4.30**	**1.30**	**4.12**	**1.29**	**118**	**93**	**20.7**	**7%**	**21%**	**13%**	**6%**	**11.7%**	**92.9**	**43**	**19**	**38**	**30%**	**72%**	**14%**	**15%**	**20**						**0.3**	**97**	**$0**

Richards,Trevor

Age: 31	Th: R	Role: RP	Health: C	LIMA Plan: B
Ht: 6'2"	Wt: 205	Type: Pwr/xFB	PT/Exp: B	Rand Var: +3
			Consist: A	MM: 3501

Volatile reliever absolutely ventilated batters with change-up-first, two-pitch mix. However, that fastball-as-secondary (.538 SLG) was easier to hit than your data limit while roaming on vacation with your in-laws. Tantalizing SwK%; H% and S% did him dirty in 2nd half; xBB% says he can find the plate. Are you a gambler? Of course you are!

Yr Tm	W	Sv	IP	K	ERA	WHIP	xERA	xWHIP	vL+	vR+	BF/G	BB%	K%	K-BB%	xBB%	SwK	Vel	G	L	F	H%	S%	HR/F	xHR/F	GS	APC	DOM%	DIS%	Sv%	LI	RAR	BPX	R$
19 2 TM	6	0	135	127	4.06	1.35	5.05	1.42	100	99	19.3	10%	22%	12%	7%	12.3%	90.9	35	22	43	30%	74%	12%	12%	23	76	22%	30%	0	0.78	7.5	70	$4
20 TAM	0	0	32	27	5.91	1.72	5.75	1.37	108	126	16.7	7%	18%	11%	7%	12.3%	90.5	32	25	43	38%	69%	13%	10%	4	64	0%	75%	0	0.71	-5.7	71	-$13
21 3 TM	7	1	64	78	3.50	0.96	3.84	1.16	82	83	4.7	9%	31%	22%	9%	14.7%	92.8	28	22	50	21%	74%	16%	14%	0	20			17	0.87	6.1	131	$8
22 TOR	3	0	64	82	5.34	1.44	4.12	1.32	101	105	4.5	12%	29%	17%	12%	15.4%	93.5	34	19	47	33%	65%	12%	13%	4	19	0%	50%	0	0.67	-10.9	96	-$6
23 TOR	2	0	73	105	4.95	1.35	3.93	1.22	98	103	5.6	11%	33%	22%	8%	17.0%	92.8	32	19	49	33%	68%	15%	12%	3	24	67%	33%	0	0.73	-5.6	143	-$3
1st Half	0	0	41	62	3.29	1.15	3.58	1.12	99	83	6.1	10%	36%	26%	7%	17.9%	92.9	26	20	53	30%	80%	15%	11%	3	26	67%	33%	0	0.59	5.3	167	$1
2nd Half	2	0	32	43	7.11	1.61	4.41	1.35	97	125	5.2	12%	30%	17%	8%	16.1%	92.6	38	18	44	37%	58%	16%	14%	0	22			0	0.87	-10.8	111	-$
Proj	**3**	**0**	**65**	**86**	**4.26**	**1.28**	**3.66**	**1.23**	**91**	**99**	**5.5**	**11%**	**32%**	**21%**	**8%**	**15.5%**	**92.6**	**32**	**20**	**47**	**31%**	**72%**	**15%**	**13%**	**0**						**0.6**	**127**	**-$**

Robertson,David

Age: 39	Th: R	Role: RP	Health: D	LIMA Plan: B+
Ht: 5'11"	Wt: 195	Type: Pwr	PT/Exp: A	Rand Var: -3
			Consist: A	MM: 3321

Does he have one more solid year left in that arm? PRO: Fastball still zippy enough; no discernable platoon split; BPX suggests skills still worthy of later innings. CON: Swinging strike rate withered in 2nd half; walks, both actual and expected, crept up in tandem. Nasty cutter-curveball combo still effective, but... DN: 5 Sv

Yr Tm	W	Sv	IP	K	ERA	WHIP	xERA	xWHIP	vL+	vR+	BF/G	BB%	K%	K-BB%	xBB%	SwK	Vel	G	L	F	H%	S%	HR/F	xHR/F	GS	APC	DOM%	DIS%	Sv%	LI	RAR	BPX	R$
19 PHI	0	0	7	6	5.40	2.10	7.45	1.92	75	174	4.7	18%	18%	0%	12%	11.0%	91.7	33	24	43	35%	77%	11%	11%	0	19			0	1.24	-0.7	-67	-$
20																																	
21 TAM	0	0	12	16	4.50	1.25	3.31	1.11	81	108	4.2	8%	32%	24%	7%	9.6%	92.0	40	27	33	34%	69%	20%	11%	1	17	0%	0%	0	0.87	-0.3	168	-$
22 2 NL	4	20	64	81	2.40	1.16	3.53	1.33	79	88	4.6	13%	31%	17%	8%	14.2%		47	13	40	25%	84%	10%	10%	0	18			71	1.47	12.3	107	$1
23 2 NL	6	18	65	78	3.03	1.19	3.77	1.23	91	88	4.3	9%	29%	20%	8%	13.2%	94.0	43	15	42	30%	79%	10%	11%	0	17			75	1.35	10.5	136	$1
1st Half	3	10	37	44	1.95	1.00	3.25	1.11	77	90	4.4	7%	31%	24%	6%	14.9%	94.0	45	15	40	28%	88%	12%	13%	0	17			77	1.37	10.9	170	$1
2nd Half	3	8	28	34	4.45	1.45	4.47	1.38	112	87	4.3	12%	27%	15%	8%	11.2%		41	15	45	33%	71%	9%	9%	0	17			73	1.32	-0.4	95	$
Proj	**6**	**14**	**73**	**83**	**3.56**	**1.25**	**3.68**	**1.28**	**99**	**92**	**4.5**	**11%**	**28%**	**18%**	**8%**	**12.9%**	**93.0**	**43**	**15**	**42**	**30%**	**74%**	**10%**	**10%**	**0**						**6.8**	**116**	**$**

Rodón,Carlos

Age: 31	Th: L	Role: SP	Health: F	LIMA Plan: B
Ht: 6'3"	Wt: 245	Type: Pwr/xFB	PT/Exp: A	Rand Var: +5
			Consist: C	MM: 3303

What the crap happened here?! Missed 1st half with left forearm and back strains, another two weeks with bum hamstring. When he did pitch, nothing clicked. Broad-based skills collapse—plus terrible S% luck—yielded horrific results. Silver linings: velocity intact; xBB% held; small sample. But...yikes. DN: Same, but over more IP

Yr Tm	W	Sv	IP	K	ERA	WHIP	xERA	xWHIP	vL+	vR+	BF/G	BB%	K%	K-BB%	xBB%	SwK	Vel	G	L	F	H%	S%	HR/F	xHR/F	GS	APC	DOM%	DIS%	Sv%	LI	RAR	BPX	R$
19 CHW	3	0	35	46	5.19	1.44	4.26	1.31	49	101	22.6	11%	29%	18%	9%	12.6%	91.5	43	19	38	36%	65%	11%	13%	7	99	29%	14%			-2.9	127	-$
20 CHW	0	0	8	6	8.22	1.57	5.95	1.45	161	118	8.8	9%	17%	9%	7%	10.5%	92.9	28	24	48	34%	45%	8%	13%	2	33	0%	100%	0	1.90	-3.6	43	-$
21 CHW	13	0	133	185	2.37	0.96	3.20	1.02	82	73	22.3	7%	35%	28%	6%	15.7%	95.4	38	17	45	29%	81%	10%	10%	24	92	42%	21%			30.9	193	$2
22 SF	14	0	178	237	2.88	1.03	3.13	1.04	74	82	22.9	7%	33%	26%	6%	14.6%	95.6	34	21	45	31%	74%	7%	8%	31	96	42%	10%			23.9	173	$2
23 NYY	3	0	64	64	6.85	1.45	5.25	1.38	102	117	20.4	10%	22%	13%	7%	13.0%	95.3	27	20	53	30%	56%	15%	13%	14	81	14%	50%			-20.0	68	-$1
1st Half																																	
2nd Half	3	0	64	64	6.85	1.45	5.25	1.38	103	118	20.4	10%	22%	13%	7%	13.0%	95.3	27	20	53	30%	56%	15%	13%	14	81	14%	50%			-20.0	68	-$
Proj	**10**	**0**	**145**	**165**	**4.22**	**1.22**	**3.78**	**1.22**	**80**	**97**	**20.5**	**9%**	**28%**	**19%**	**7%**	**13.6%**	**94.5**	**34**	**20**	**46**	**30%**	**70%**	**12%**	**11%**	**29**						**2.0**	**121**	**$**

Rodriguez,Eduardo

Age: 31	Th: L	Role: SP	Health: D	LIMA Plan: B
Ht: 6'2"	Wt: 231	Type: Pwr	PT/Exp: A	Rand Var: -2
			Consist: A	MM: 3203

Finger injury cost him five weeks, otherwise returned career-best roto value. Pitcher-friendly home park likely helped him outperform expected stats, but skills—especially command—were solid enough in their own right. Faded down stretch as control eluded him and SwK% slipped. See what laundry he's wearing, bid accordingly.

Yr Tm	W	Sv	IP	K	ERA	WHIP	xERA	xWHIP	vL+	vR+	BF/G	BB%	K%	K-BB%	xBB%	SwK	Vel	G	L	F	H%	S%	HR/F	xHR/F	GS	APC	DOM%	DIS%	Sv%	LI	RAR	BPX	R$
19 BOS	19	0	203	213	3.81	1.33	4.10	1.30	103	93	25.3	9%	25%	16%	8%	12.1%	93.1	48	19	33	32%	75%	13%	15%	34	103	29%	21%			17.5	116	$
20																																	
21 BOS	13	0	158	185	4.74	1.39	3.70	1.15	102	103	21.1	7%	27%	20%	6%	12.1%	92.6	43	22	34	37%	68%	13%	11%	31	85	13%	23%	0	0.79	-9.2	152	$
22 DET *	6	0	106	91	3.58	1.25	3.84	1.37	130	94	21.6	8%	21%	13%	8%	7.8%	91.8	43	19	37	29%	75%	12%	12%	17	86	6%	41%			5.1	82	$
23 DET	13	0	153	143	3.30	1.15	4.11	1.28	74	93	23.9	8%	23%	15%	6%	10.7%	92.2	41	22	37	28%	75%	10%	11%	26	94	42%	23%			19.4	106	$
1st Half	4	0	68	67	2.13	0.98	3.64	1.17	52	84	23.9	6%	25%	19%	6%	11.1%	92.2	43	20	37	26%	83%	9%	10%	11	97	36%	18%			18.4	140	$
2nd Half	9	0	85	76	4.24	1.29	4.50	1.37	88	100	23.9	9%	21%	12%	7%	10.4%	92.3	40	23	37	30%	69%	10%	11%	15	92	47%	27%			1.0	80	$
Proj	**12**	**0**	**152**	**151**	**3.80**	**1.25**	**3.75**	**1.25**	**92**	**96**	**22.5**	**8%**	**24%**	**16%**	**7%**	**10.8%**	**92.3**	**43**	**21**	**36**	**31%**	**73%**	**11%**	**11%**	**28**						**10.0**	**116**	**$**

ALAIN DE LEONARDIS

Rodriguez,Grayson

Age: 24	Th: R	Role: SP	Health: A	LIMA Plan: C+
Ht: 6'5"	Wt: 220	Type: Pwr	PT/Exp: D	Rand Var: 0
			Consist: D	MM: 5305

Fluky HR barrage in May (4.7 HR/9, 33% HR/F) upended strong April (3.11 xERA) and led to 6-week demotion that put him on fantasy waiver wires. Dominant AAA stint sparked a summer run with nearly every facet of his game improved (velocity, SwK, BB%, GB%). Ace elements are all there, just be prepared to pay at the draft table.

Yr Tm	W	Sv	IP	K	ERA	WHIP	xERA	xWHIP	vL+	vR+	BF/G	BB%	K%	K-BB%	xBB%	SwK	Vel	G	L	F	H%	S%	HR/F	xHR/F	GS	APC	DOM%	DIS%	Sv%	LI	RAR	BPX	R$
19																																	
20																																	
21 aa	6	0	81	100	2.71	0.87	1.94				16.7	7%	33%	27%							25%	74%									15.6	176	$13
22 a/a	6	0	77	90	2.51	0.92	1.37				18.1	8%	31%	23%							26%	72%									13.9	170	$10
23 BAL *	11	0	164	175	3.75	1.28	3.95	1.26	113	92	21.7	8%	25%	17%	6%	12.6%	97.4	47	19	34	31%	74%	14%	12%	23	91	30%	30%			11.8	104	$12
1st Half	6	0	78	89	5.32	1.51	5.74	1.34	151	117	21.2	10%	26%	15%	8%	11.5%	96.7	39	25	36	33%	71%	27%	20%	10	89	20%	40%			-9.6	65	-$3
2nd Half	5	0	86	85	2.31	1.06	2.32	1.21	89	74	22.2	7%	25%	18%	5%	13.4%	97.9	53	15	32	29%	78%	4%	7%	13	93	38%	23%			21.3	147	$23
Proj	13	0	181	202	3.18	1.10	3.23	1.18	93	74	22.2	8%	28%	20%	6%	12.5%	97.4	47	19	34	29%	74%	11%	12%	32						25.7	144	$23

Rogers,Taylor

Age: 33	Th: L	Role: RP	Health: D	LIMA Plan: A+
Ht: 6'3"	Wt: 190	Type: Pwr	PT/Exp: A	Rand Var: 0
			Consist: B	MM: 4410

Return to a setup role narrowed his fantasy appeal. L/R split became more extreme than ever, further limiting his viability. Favorable H% and S% rates in 1st half came crashing down, over-correcting to levels similar to 2022. xBB% isn't worried about the BB% hike though it won't matter if SwK and a 9th-inning role don't return.

Yr Tm	W	Sv	IP	K	ERA	WHIP	xERA	xWHIP	vL+	vR+	BF/G	BB%	K%	K-BB%	xBB%	SwK	Vel	G	L	F	H%	S%	HR/F	xHR/F	GS	APC	DOM%	DIS%	Sv%	LI	RAR	BPX	R$
19 MIN	2	30	69	90	2.61	1.00	2.85	0.98	88	82	4.6	4%	32%	28%	4%	11.3%	94.8	51	18	31	32%	80%	15%	15%	0	18			83	1.50	16.1	220	$21
20 MIN	2	9	20	24	4.05	1.50	3.73	1.08	89	111	4.3	4%	26%	22%	4%	11.5%	94.6	42	29	29	43%	75%	11%	15%	0	17			82	1.15	1.0	187	$9
21 MIN	2	9	40	59	3.35	1.14	2.59	0.93	73	95	4.2	5%	36%	31%	4%	13.6%	95.8	50	20	30	38%	74%	14%	11%	0	16			69	1.55	4.6	238	$4
22 2 NL	4	31	64	84	4.76	1.18	3.05	1.07	73	112	4.2	7%	31%	24%	6%	12.9%	94.3	42	20	37	34%	61%	12%	15%	0	16			76	1.36	-6.3	176	$12
23 SF	6	2	52	64	3.83	1.24	3.88	1.31	44	134	3.6	12%	30%	18%	7%	10.5%	93.6	42	17	42	29%	72%	12%	12%	0	14			100	1.00	3.2	116	$3
1st Half	4	1	28	36	2.89	1.07	3.68	1.27	41	119	3.6	11%	31%	20%	8%	11.8%	93.3	42	15	44	23%	81%	15%	15%	0	14			100	0.83	5.0	130	$4
2nd Half	2	1	24	28	4.94	1.44	4.12	1.36	49	151	3.6	12%	28%	16%	6%	9.0%	93.9	41	19	40	34%	66%	9%	9%	0	14			100	1.19	-1.8	99	-$3
Proj	5	5	58	72	3.87	1.24	3.40	1.20	59	116	3.8	10%	30%	21%	6%	11.5%	94.4	43	18	39	32%	71%	11%	12%	0						3.2	142	$3

Rogers,Trevor

Age: 26	Th: L	Role: SP	Health: F	LIMA Plan: B
Ht: 6'5"	Wt: 217	Type: Pwr	PT/Exp: C	Rand Var: 0
			Consist: C	MM: 3201

Suffered a bicep strain four starts into the season and never made it all the way back (two rehab starts) as that injury gave way to a torn lat. An injury washout on the heels of his poor 2022 now makes 2021 but a distant memory. He will be priced to buy once healthy, but there are no guarantees that he returns to starting immediately.

Yr Tm	W	Sv	IP	K	ERA	WHIP	xERA	xWHIP	vL+	vR+	BF/G	BB%	K%	K-BB%	xBB%	SwK	Vel	G	L	F	H%	S%	HR/F	xHR/F	GS	APC	DOM%	DIS%	Sv%	LI	RAR	BPX	R$
19 aa	1	0	26	24	6.99	1.64	5.96				23.2	9%	21%	12%							37%	58%									-8.0	60	-$7
20 MIA	1	0	28	39	6.11	1.61	3.80	1.23	108	120	18.6	10%	30%	20%	8%	13.2%	93.6	47	21	32	40%	65%	21%	11%	7	81	0%	14%			-5.7	156	-$8
21 MIA	7	0	133	157	2.64	1.15	3.63	1.18	92	79	22.0	8%	29%	20%	6%	14.7%	94.6	40	24	36	32%	78%	5%	9%	25	87	40%	16%			26.7	137	$16
22 MIA *	5	0	123	126	5.64	1.48	5.22	1.33	84	124	19.6	9%	24%	15%	7%	11.6%	94.6	42	22	36	35%	64%	13%	14%	23	84	9%	39%			-25.4	79	-$11
23 MIA	1	0	18	19	4.00	1.22	3.95	1.25	67	94	19.8	8%	24%	16%	7%	12.1%	93.0	52	10	38	31%	70%	11%	18%	4	83	25%	25%			0.7	135	-$4
1st Half	1	0	18	19	4.00	1.22	3.95	1.25	67	95	19.8	8%	24%	16%	7%	12.1%	93.0	52	10	38	31%	70%	11%	18%	4	83	25%	25%			0.7	135	-$7
2nd Half																																	
Proj	6	0	102	103	4.02	1.22	3.62	1.24	77	100	20.9	8%	25%	17%	7%	12.5%	93.9	46	17	37	30%	69%	11%	14%	20						3.9	122	$3

Rogers,Tyler

Age: 33	Th: R	Role: RP	Health: A	LIMA Plan: A
Ht: 6'3"	Wt: 181	Type: Con/GB	PT/Exp: B	Rand Var: -3
			Consist: A	MM: 3011

The submarine righty might've been inspired by twin brother Taylor joining the team, flipping his platoon split thanks in part to his best K% in 3 years. Ran hot in the 1st half before regression set in with his H% and S%. HR/F rose as well, but xHR/F wasn't as concerned. His modest K% output means setup will likely remain his home.

Yr Tm	W	Sv	IP	K	ERA	WHIP	xERA	xWHIP	vL+	vR+	BF/G	BB%	K%	K-BB%	xBB%	SwK	Vel	G	L	F	H%	S%	HR/F	xHR/F	GS	APC	DOM%	DIS%	Sv%	LI	RAR	BPX	R$
19 SF *	6	5	80	56	4.75	1.57	4.91	1.14	50	70	5.3	10%	16%	6%	4%	8.2%	82.4	69	16	14	33%	70%	0%	4%	0	15			56	1.17	-2.4	52	-$2
20 SF	3	3	28	27	4.50	1.32	3.58	1.17	100	93	4.2	5%	22%	17%	6%	10.9%	82.5	55	22	22	36%	66%	11%	6%	0	16			50	1.33	-0.2	155	$4
21 SF	7	13	81	55	2.22	1.07	3.77	1.22	63	99	4.1	4%	17%	13%	4%	7.8%	82.7	58	16	26	28%	82%	8%	4%	0	14			68	1.26	20.4	117	$16
22 SF	3	0	76	49	3.57	1.27	3.97	1.36	121	80	4.7	7%	15%	8%	6%	8.6%	83.3	56	18	26	30%	71%	5%	7%	0	17			0	0.95	3.7	72	-$1
23 SF	4	2	74	60	3.04	1.15	4.11	1.28	75	101	4.5	6%	20%	13%	4%	11.1%	82.9	50	17	32	28%	77%	10%	5%	0	17			25	1.28	11.8	109	$6
1st Half	2	2	42	36	1.91	1.02	3.98	1.26	61	87	4.6	6%	21%	15%	4%	11.9%	82.8	50	14	36	26%	83%	5%	1%	0	17			67	1.20	12.6	116	$9
2nd Half	2	0	32	24	4.55	1.33	4.28	1.31	91	121	4.5	6%	17%	12%	5%	10.1%	83.0	51	21	28	31%	70%	17%	11%	0	16			0	1.38	-0.8	102	-$3
Proj	5	2	73	53	3.68	1.22	3.85	1.30	83	102	4.3	6%	18%	12%	5%	9.8%	82.9	53	18	29	30%	71%	10%	6%	0						5.7	98	$2

Rom,Drew

Age: 24	Th: L	Role: RP	Health: A	LIMA Plan: B
Ht: 6'2"	Wt: 170	Type: Pwr	PT/Exp: D	Rand Var: +2
			Consist: B	MM: 2201

1-4, 8.02 ERA in 34 IP at STL. Swingman came over in the Jack Flaherty deal and sputtered upon arrival with hideous H% (39%) and S% (60%) in 8 MLB starts. Sub-90 mph velocity, single-digit SwK, and double-digit BB% is a recipe for disaster. Without improving at least two of three, the bullpen is his eventual home... perhaps in AAA.

Yr Tm	W	Sv	IP	K	ERA	WHIP	xERA	xWHIP	vL+	vR+	BF/G	BB%	K%	K-BB%	xBB%	SwK	Vel	G	L	F	H%	S%	HR/F	xHR/F	GS	APC	DOM%	DIS%	Sv%	LI	RAR	BPX	R$
19																																	
20																																	
21 aa	3	0	40	39	4.06	1.15	4.06				17.6	5%	25%	20%							30%	70%									1.0	124	-$1
22 a/a	8	0	122	119	4.27	1.45	4.65				20.1	8%	23%	15%							36%	72%									-4.5	96	-$2
23 STL *	10	0	131	128	5.54	1.69	5.76	1.51	183	133	20.3	11%	19%	8%	8%	6.7%	89.6	40	17	44	37%	68%	13%	15%	8	84	0%	75%			-19.5	70	-$13
1st Half	5	0	65	59	5.62	1.76	6.07				21.3	10%	19%	10%							39%	68%	0%		0	0					-10.4	66	-$13
2nd Half	5	0	68	69	5.27	1.57	5.17	1.42	184	134	19.8	11%	22%	12%	8%	6.7%	89.6	40	17	44	35%	68%	13%	15%	8	84	0%	75%			-7.9	75	$0
Proj	5	0	73	70	4.93	1.49	4.29	1.33	143	109	19.6	9%	23%	14%	9%	6.7%	89.6	39	17	44	35%	68%	10%	13%	15						-5.4	91	-$5

Romano,Jordan

Age: 31	Th: R	Role: RP	Health: C	LIMA Plan: B
Ht: 6'5"	Wt: 210	Type: Pwr/FB	PT/Exp: A	Rand Var: -4
			Consist: A	MM: 5430

Was sailing along at established skill level when a back issue forced him from the All-Star Game. Hit the IL in late July, but 2nd half results (thanks, H%/S%) papered over the ballooning walk rate and uncharacteristic FB binge. If we get the 1st half pitcher, all is well. But newfound health risk should be baked into the price in the meantime.

Yr Tm	W	Sv	IP	K	ERA	WHIP	xERA	xWHIP	vL+	vR+	BF/G	BB%	K%	K-BB%	xBB%	SwK	Vel	G	L	F	H%	S%	HR/F	xHR/F	GS	APC	DOM%	DIS%	Sv%	LI	RAR	BPX	R$
19 TOR *	2	5	55	63	7.42	1.63	6.72	1.37	86	141	5.9	10%	26%	16%	9%	13.8%	94.6	53	20	28	36%	59%	36%	29%	0	18			100	0.70	-19.6	46	-$8
20 TOR	2	2	15	21	1.23	0.89	2.54	1.06	51	84	3.8	9%	37%	28%	8%	20.7%	96.6	58	16	26	23%	100%	25%	24%	0	16			67	1.80	5.8	209	$7
21 TOR	7	23	63	85	2.14	1.05	3.28	1.15	60	90	4.1	10%	34%	24%	6%	15.2%	97.6	47	13	40	27%	86%	13%	11%	0	17			96	1.14	16.5	161	$20
22 TOR	5	36	64	73	2.11	1.02	3.34	1.16	78	73	4.1	8%	28%	20%	5%	15.1%	96.9	44	17	39	27%	82%	6%	10%	0	16			86	1.58	14.7	140	$23
23 TOR	5	36	59	72	2.90	1.22	4.03	1.24	100	80	4.2	10%	29%	19%	6%	17.7%	96.7	36	18	45	31%	80%	9%	9%	0	16			90	1.53	10.4	127	$19
1st Half	3	24	35	42	3.12	1.18	3.74	1.14	97	86	4.0	7%	29%	22%	5%	17.9%	96.7	38	21	41	33%	78%	11%	8%	0	15			89	1.37	5.2	160	$23
2nd Half	2	12	24	30	2.59	1.27	4.49	1.41	108	73	4.5	14%	29%	16%	8%	17.3%	96.7	34	14	52	28%	83%	7%	11%	0	17			92	1.78	5.2	81	$9
Proj	5	32	58	72	3.15	1.09	3.21	1.12	92	81	4.1	8%	32%	23%	7%	16.6%	97.0	41	18	41	29%	76%	11%	10%	0						8.4	159	$18

Romero,JoJo

Age: 27	Th: L	Role: RP	Health: F	LIMA Plan: A+
Ht: 5'11"	Wt: 200	Type: /GB	PT/Exp: D	Rand Var: -1
			Consist: B	MM: 5210

4-2, 3.68 ERA with 3 Sv in 37 IP at STL. Improved BB% allowed him to carve out a role in July-August before a knee injury ended his season in September. Meager 63% S% undercut the results in majors, but he had a 2.76 xERA. L/R splits remain a dangerous problem despite career-best work vR. Value goes as far as his save opps take him.

Yr Tm	W	Sv	IP	K	ERA	WHIP	xERA	xWHIP	vL+	vR+	BF/G	BB%	K%	K-BB%	xBB%	SwK	Vel	G	L	F	H%	S%	HR/F	xHR/F	GS	APC	DOM%	DIS%	Sv%	LI	RAR	BPX	R$
19 a/a	7	0	114	83	6.97	1.70	6.12				21.6	9%	16%	7%							35%	59%									-34.8	35	-$16
20 PHI	0	0	11	10	7.59	1.41	3.50	1.15	104	120	3.9	4%	21%	17%	6%	14.1%	95.0	50	31	19	37%	43%	17%	16%	0	14			0	1.04	-4.1	152	-$9
21 PHI	0	0	9	8	7.00	1.78	4.72	1.41	107	179	4.0	9%	18%	9%	7%	9.9%	94.5	55	19	26	32%	75%	50%	23%	0	16			0	0.87	-3.0	76	-$8
22 2 NL	0	0	16	17	4.96	1.41	3.51	1.51	88	119	3.9	15%	25%	10%	12%	14.0%	95.4	61	16	24	26%	70%	33%	30%	0	16			0	0.95	-2.0	65	-$6
23 STL *	6	5	58	67	3.47	1.19	3.12	1.14	37	95	5.3	7%	29%	22%	6%	16.0%	94.8	59	22	19	33%	71%	6%	6%	0	20			63	1.24	6.1	145	$5
1st Half	2	2	29	31	3.22	1.35	4.15	1.39	44	118	5.2	12%	26%	14%	12%	9.1%	94.7	58	21	21	30%	81%	25%	21%	0	20			50	0.80	3.9	90	-$1
2nd Half	4	3	29	36	3.72	1.03	2.42	1.01	34	91	5.6	4%	31%	26%	4%	18.0%	94.8	59	22	19	35%	60%	0%	1%	0	20			75	1.36	2.2	222	$7
Proj	6	2	58	60	3.40	1.15	2.81	1.18	50	105	6.5	7%	26%	19%	4%	17.9%	94.8	59	22	19	32%	69%	7%	9%	0						6.7	155	$4

AUL SPORER

Rutledge,Jackson

Age: 25 | Th: R | Role: SP | Ht: 6'8" | Wt: 250 | Type: Con/xFB
Health: C | PT/Exp: F | Consist: F | LIMA Plan: D+ | Rand Var: 0 | MM: 0001

1-1, 6.75 ERA in 20 IP at WAS. Stayed healthy for first time in career. Lacks deception with limited extension despite long frame. Known for mid-90s sinker, incorporated 4-seamer as workhorse pitch, despite lacking profile and performance. Slider misses bats; flashes so-so curve and change-up. Needs a third reliable pitch to remain a SP. (CB)

Yr Tm	W	Sv	IP	K	ERA	WHIP	xERA	xWHIP	vL+	vR+	BF/G	BB%	K%	K-BB%	xBB%	SwK	Vel	G	L	F	H%	S%	HR/F	xHR/F	GS	APC	DOM%	DIS%	Sv%	LI	RAR	BPX	R$
19																																	
20																																	
21																																	
22																																	
23 WAS *	9	0	141	102	4.64	1.39	4.45	1.43	143	99	22.0	7%	14%	7%	8%	9.5%	95.6	26	22	51	28%	69%	11%	13%	4	87	0%	50%			-5.4	50	-$2
1st Half	6	0	74	55	4.15	1.23	3.32				23.1	11%	19%	8%							26%	67%	0%		0	0					1.7	71	$7
2nd Half	3	0	67	47	4.86	1.51	5.34	1.52	144	99	20.7	10%	16%	6%	8%	9.5%	95.6	26	22	51	30%	71%	11%	13%	4	87	0%	50%			-4.3	35	-$3
Proj	**6**	**0**	**102**	**73**	**4.55**	**1.39**	**5.19**	**1.49**	**134**	**87**	**27.0**	**10%**	**17%**	**7%**	**9%**	**9.5%**	**95.6**	**26**	**22**	**51**	**29%**	**70%**	**9%**	**12%**	**14**						**-2.8**	**19**	**-$3**

Ryan,Joe

Age: 28 | Th: R | Role: SP | Ht: 6'2" | Wt: 205 | Type: Pwr/xFB
Health: C | PT/Exp: A | Consist: B | LIMA Plan: B+ | Rand Var: +1 | MM: 4405

Some will see "step backward," but that horrific turn of H%, HR/F rate luck can take credit for "collapse," along with a mid-season groin strain. Fly ball tilt, penchant for hard contact may create some volatility, but there's progress here in SwK, K%, despite 2nd half results. Good chance that ERA is headed back under 4.00. Buy the dip.

Yr Tm	W	Sv	IP	K	ERA	WHIP	xERA	xWHIP	vL+	vR+	BF/G	BB%	K%	K-BB%	xBB%	SwK	Vel	G	L	F	H%	S%	HR/F	xHR/F	GS	APC	DOM%	DIS%	Sv%	LI	RAR	BPX	R$
19																																	
20																																	
21 MIN *	6	0	93	105	4.22	0.89	2.62	1.04	83	69	18.1	5%	31%	25%	4%	12.1%	91.3	28	19	53	24%	57%	12%	15%	5	82	40%	20%			0.5	172	$9
22 MIN	13	0	147	151	3.55	1.10	4.21	1.21	91	97	22.4	8%	25%	17%	6%	12.0%	92.1	28	18	54	26%	73%	9%	10%	27	89	33%	30%			7.6	104	$14
23 MIN	11	0	162	197	4.51	1.17	3.88	1.06	86	114	23.2	5%	29%	24%	5%	14.3%	92.3	32	19	50	32%	69%	15%	12%	29	93	21%	17%			-3.5	175	$1
1st Half	8	0	97	105	3.44	0.97	3.82	1.05	72	95	24.0	4%	27%	23%	4%	13.8%	92.6	34	18	48	28%	70%	10%	9%	16	93	38%	19%			10.6	170	$2
2nd Half	3	0	65	92	6.09	1.46	3.95	1.07	107	140	22.2	7%	32%	25%	6%	14.9%	92.0	27	20	53	38%	67%	21%	16%	13	92	0%	15%			-14.1	185	-$
Proj	**12**	**0**	**174**	**205**	**3.95**	**1.10**	**3.47**	**1.07**	**86**	**105**	**23.4**	**6%**	**30%**	**24%**	**5%**	**14.0%**	**92.2**	**30**	**19**	**52**	**30%**	**70%**	**13%**	**12%**	**29**						**8.1**	**158**	**$1**

Ryu,Hyun-Jin

Age: 37 | Th: L | Role: SP | Ht: 6'3" | Wt: 250 | Type: Con
Health: F | PT/Exp: C | Consist: A | LIMA Plan: B | Rand Var: -2 | MM: 2003

Worked back from Tommy John surgery to return in Aug, made 11 starts, and though results seem promising, S% helped. He's at age where return of velocity is not a given, meaning passable K%, K-BB% could be gone for good, too. Says he plans to finish career with KBO's Hanwha Eagles; by the time you read this, bags could be packed.

Yr Tm	W	Sv	IP	K	ERA	WHIP	xERA	xWHIP	vL+	vR+	BF/G	BB%	K%	K-BB%	xBB%	SwK	Vel	G	L	F	H%	S%	HR/F	xHR/F	GS	APC	DOM%	DIS%	Sv%	LI	RAR	BPX	R$
19 LA	14	0	183	163	2.32	1.01	3.47	1.13	71	87	24.9	3%	23%	19%	6%	11.8%	90.6	50	24	25	29%	82%	13%	12%	29	93	45%	7%			49.3	153	$3
20 TOR	5	0	67	72	2.69	1.15	3.49	1.15	79	87	22.9	6%	26%	20%	8%	12.3%	89.6	51	21	28	32%	80%	12%	10%	12	94	17%	17%			14.6	160	$2
21 TOR	14	0	169	143	4.37	1.22	4.09	1.21	95	99	22.6	5%	20%	15%	6%	10.1%	90.0	47	20	33	30%	68%	14%	14%	31	87	32%	29%			-2.1	119	$
22 TOR	2	0	27	16	5.67	1.33	4.41	1.23	86	128	18.8	4%	14%	11%	8%	7.6%	89.3	46	17	37	31%	61%	15%	15%	6	66	0%	67%			-5.7	93	-$
23 TOR	3	0	52	38	3.46	1.29	4.61	1.34	114	100	20.4	6%	17%	11%	6%	9.5%	88.4	46	22	33	29%	81%	16%	9%	11	75	9%	45%			5.6	86	-$
1st Half																																	
2nd Half	3	0	52	38	3.46	1.29	4.61	1.34	114	101	20.4	6%	17%	11%	6%	9.5%	88.4	46	22	33	29%	81%	16%	9%	11	75	9%	45%			5.6	86	$
Proj	**10**	**0**	**145**	**113**	**4.22**	**1.26**	**3.95**	**1.27**	**99**	**101**	**21.9**	**6%**	**19%**	**13%**	**6%**	**10.6%**	**89.5**	**46**	**22**	**32**	**30%**	**70%**	**13%**	**11%**	**27**						**2.0**	**102**	**$**

Sale,Chris

Age: 35 | Th: L | Role: SP | Ht: 6'6" | Wt: 183 | Type: Pwr/FB
Health: F | PT/Exp: D | Consist: B | LIMA Plan: A | Rand Var: +1 | MM: 5403

No bikes, comebackers involved in two months on IL, just your average shoulder strain. When he pitches, skills are rock solid; it's just that the "when" is "not enough." Could still strike gold if health cooperates, but as age rises, bet gets worse. What's that? He gave up 2 ER in last 16 IP (19/4 K/BB)? Hmm... maybe one last roll of the dice?

Yr Tm	W	Sv	IP	K	ERA	WHIP	xERA	xWHIP	vL+	vR+	BF/G	BB%	K%	K-BB%	xBB%	SwK	Vel	G	L	F	H%	S%	HR/F	xHR/F	GS	APC	DOM%	DIS%	Sv%	LI	RAR	BPX	R$
19 BOS	6	0	147	218	4.40	1.09	2.98	1.00	88	94	24.5	6%	36%	30%	6%	14.6%	93.2	43	21	36	33%	65%	20%	18%	25	99	32%	16%			2.0	218	$1
20																																	
21 BOS *	6	0	62	74	2.77	1.29	4.21	1.11	48	110	19.6	7%	29%	22%	6%	13.0%	93.6	47	21	32	35%	84%	17%	12%	9	82	0%	22%			11.5	136	$
22 BOS	0	0	6	5	3.18	1.06	3.15			109	12.5	4%	20%	16%	6%	4.9%	94.5	50	33	17	31%	67%	0%	5%	2	51	50%	50%			0.6	141	-$
23 BOS	6	0	103	125	4.30	1.13	3.67	1.12	103	96	21.3	7%	29%	23%	6%	13.5%	93.9	37	19	43	30%	66%	13%	14%	20	84	25%	15%			0.5	161	$
1st Half	5	0	59	71	4.58	1.19	3.60	1.11	112	99	22.6	6%	29%	22%	6%	13.4%	94.4	38	23	39	33%	65%	13%	15%	11	87	36%	9%			-1.8	168	$
2nd Half	1	0	44	54	3.92	1.05	3.77	1.14	86	92	19.6	8%	31%	23%	7%	13.7%	93.1	36	14	50	27%	69%	13%	14%	9	79	11%	22%			2.2	154	$
Proj	**8**	**0**	**131**	**167**	**3.61**	**1.11**	**3.08**	**1.06**	**85**	**93**	**21.2**	**7%**	**33%**	**25%**	**6%**	**13.7%**	**93.5**	**40**	**19**	**41**	**31%**	**72%**	**14%**	**14%**	**24**						**11.5**	**177**	**$**

Sánchez,Cristopher

Age: 27 | Th: L | Role: SP | Ht: 6'1" | Wt: 165 | Type: /GB
Health: B | PT/Exp: C | Consist: B | LIMA Plan: A | Rand Var: +2 | MM: 5203

3-5, 3.44 ERA in 99 IP at PHI. Days of riding AAA shuttle may be over, thanks to refined change-up, suddenly elite BB%. Extreme ground ball tilt always a good building block, but other pieces, like rising SwK, are now jelling. Still needs to master RHB (15 of 16 HR)—if that happens, look out. Even without that, a solid back-of-rotation arm.

Yr Tm	W	Sv	IP	K	ERA	WHIP	xERA	xWHIP	vL+	vR+	BF/G	BB%	K%	K-BB%	xBB%	SwK	Vel	G	L	F	H%	S%	HR/F	xHR/F	GS	APC	DOM%	DIS%	Sv%	LI	RAR	BPX	R$
19																																	
20																																	
21 PHI *	6	0	86	88	5.33	1.62	4.56	1.45	103	126	14.6	15%	23%	8%	7%	11.4%	93.9	64	14	22	33%	66%	13%	9%	1	30	0%	100%	0	0.49	-11.3	82	-
22 PHI *	4	1	98	81	4.21	1.30	3.57	1.38	103	103	13.5	9%	20%	11%	8%	8.3%	93.0	54	18	28	30%	67%	15%	17%	3	44	0%	33%	100	0.65	-2.9	88	-
23 PHI *	6	0	151	130	3.89	1.22	4.12	1.11	54	105	21.0	4%	24%	20%	5%	12.3%	92.2	57	17	26	28%	74%	22%	17%	18	77	17%	22%	0	0.71	8.2	81	
1st Half	3	0	71	54	4.35	1.44	4.59	1.54	99	90	21.5	11%	18%	7%	5%	11.2%	92.1	51	17	32	29%	73%	12%	8%	4	74	25%	25%			-0.2	53	-
2nd Half	3	0	80	76	3.49	1.03	3.07	1.11	38	109	21.2	4%	24%	20%	5%	12.5%	92.2	58	17	25	27%	75%	25%	20%	14	78	14%	21%	0	0.70	8.3	174	$
Proj	**9**	**0**	**160**	**150**	**3.88**	**1.20**	**3.28**	**1.20**	**84**	**106**	**20.8**	**6%**	**23%**	**17%**	**6%**	**11.9%**	**92.3**	**55**	**17**	**28**	**30%**	**71%**	**16%**	**15%**	**29**						**8.7**	**139**	**$**

Sánchez,Sixto

Age: 25 | Th: R | Role: SP | Ht: 6'0" | Wt: 234 | Type: Con
Health: F | PT/Exp: F | Consist: F | LIMA Plan: B | Rand Var: 0 | MM: 3100

After he battled shoulder issues for nearly three years, here's what we got: 1 IP at AA-Pensacola (1 H, 1 BB, 2 K). Does that mean he'll come to camp healthy? We've thought that before. Might it be smart to move former top SP prospect to bullpen for good? Perhaps. Stay tuned for spring, when the answers to these mysteries will be revealed. Or not.

Yr Tm	W	Sv	IP	K	ERA	WHIP	xERA	xWHIP	vL+	vR+	BF/G	BB%	K%	K-BB%	xBB%	SwK	Vel	G	L	F	H%	S%	HR/F	xHR/F	GS	APC	DOM%	DIS%	Sv%	LI	RAR	BPX
19 aa	8	0	103	85	3.90	1.29	3.89				23.5	5%	20%	15%							34%	70%									7.8	121
20 MIA	3	0	39	33	3.46	1.21	3.89	1.28	73	99	22.6	7%	21%	14%	5%	12.9%	97.6	58	13	29	30%	73%	9%	11%	7	80	43%	43%			4.8	118
21																																
22																																
23																																
1st Half																																
2nd Half																																
Proj	**4**	**0**	**58**	**49**	**4.43**	**1.29**	**3.72**	**1.30**	**86**	**120**	**21.1**	**7%**	**20%**	**13%**	**6%**	**12.9%**	**97.6**	**54**	**17**	**30**	**31%**	**66%**	**11%**	**10%**	**11**						**-0.7**	**104**

Sandlin,Nick

Age: 27 | Th: R | Role: RP | Ht: 5'11" | Wt: 175 | Type: Pwr/FB
Health: C | PT/Exp: C | Consist: A | LIMA Plan: A+ | Rand Var: -2 | MM: 2301

Odd mishmash of conflicting data points, as velocity went down again, yet SwK ticked up, aided by slightly higher slider usage. Ground ball tilt went away, then went away some more in 2nd half, and HR/F piled on to inflict ERA damage. Unlikely to challenge for 9th-inning duty, and 2nd half casts doubt on "serviceable, trusted reliever" status.

Yr Tm	W	Sv	IP	K	ERA	WHIP	xERA	xWHIP	vL+	vR+	BF/G	BB%	K%	K-BB%	xBB%	SwK	Vel	G	L	F	H%	S%	HR/F	xHR/F	GS	APC	DOM%	DIS%	Sv%	LI	RAR	BPX
19 a/a	1	2	27	33	3.11	1.39	4.42				4.8	14%	29%	15%							28%	87%									4.7	75
20																																
21 CLE	1	0	34	48	2.94	1.13	3.43	1.23	87	75	4.1	12%	34%	22%	9%	12.3%	94.5	42	18	40	29%	75%	7%	9%	0	18			0	0.89	5.5	141
22 CLE	5	0	44	41	2.25	1.16	3.83	1.49	91	70	3.9	13%	23%	9%	8%	12.3%	93.6	56	14	31	23%	82%	6%	7%	0	16			0	1.36	9.3	58
23 CLE	5	0	60	66	3.75	1.03	3.96	1.29	86	92	3.9	10%	28%	18%	8%	14.3%	92.3	41	15	44	20%	74%	19%	16%	0	17			0	1.08	4.3	112
1st Half	4	0	30	30	2.97	0.89	3.72	1.26	54	86	4.0	9%	26%	17%	8%	13.3%	92.4	46	15	39	19%	74%	14%	18%	0	17			0	1.17	5.1	117
2nd Half	1	0	30	36	4.55	1.18	4.21	1.31	112	98	3.9	11%	29%	18%	8%	15.2%	92.2	36	14	50	21%	74%	23%	15%	0	16			0	1.01	-0.8	108
Proj	**5**	**0**	**65**	**71**	**3.96**	**1.28**	**3.97**	**1.34**	**102**	**99**	**4.0**	**11%**	**27%**	**16%**	**9%**	**13.6%**	**93.0**	**42**	**15**	**43**	**28%**	**74%**	**14%**	**13%**	**0**						**3.0**	**97**

KRIS OLSON

Sandoval,Patrick

Age: 27 Th: L Role: SP | Health: C | LIMA Plan: B
Ht: 6' 3" Wt: 190 Type: Pwr | PT/Exp: A | Rand Var: -2
Consist: B | MM: 2203

Steady xERA, xWHIP from 2021-22 gave way as K%, SwK declined, and only S% kept 2nd half from being as bad as it could've been. Oblique issue put him on IL in Sept and may have played role. Thing is, even at his best, was never as good as 2.91 ERA made him look, and platoon splits remain wide. Hard to see much upside here.

Yr Tm	W	Sv	IP	K	ERA	WHIP	xERA	xWHIP	vL+	vR+	BF/G	BB%	K%	K-BB%	xBB%	SwK	Vel	G	L	F	H%	S%	HR/F	xHR/F	GS	APC	DOM%	DIS%	Sv%	LI	RAR	BPX	R$
19 LAA *	4	0	120	127	5.70	1.67	5.61	1.41	135	89	18.0	11%	24%	12%	11%	13.7%	93.0	47	26	27	37%	67%	21%	17%	9	71	11%	56%	0	0.72	-17.8	71	-$11
20 LAA	1	0	37	33	5.65	1.34	4.21	1.30	117	107	17.7	8%	21%	13%	8%	12.9%	92.8	55	18	27	28%	67%	32%	25%	6	66	0%	83%	0	0.87	-5.4	112	-$6
21 LAA	3	1	87	94	3.62	1.21	3.73	1.29	71	93	21.4	10%	26%	16%	8%	15.2%	93.3	51	19	30	28%	74%	16%	12%	14	85	21%	29%	100	0.75	6.9	114	$3
22 LAA	6	0	149	151	2.91	1.34	3.74	1.30	55	102	23.6	9%	24%	14%	7%	13.6%	93.2	47	22	31	33%	79%	6%	11%	27	91	26%	30%			19.5	101	$7
23 LAA	7	0	145	128	4.11	1.51	4.81	1.50	79	102	23.3	11%	20%	8%	8%	12.2%	93.1	47	23	30	32%	74%	9%	11%	28	94	14%	46%			4.0	49	-$3
1st Half	4	0	81	65	4.57	1.49	4.66	1.43	99	100	24.3	9%	18%	9%	8%	12.4%	92.5	49	23	29	34%	69%	8%	11%	15	95	20%	47%			-2.4	69	-$4
2nd Half	3	0	64	63	3.52	1.55	5.02	1.60	54	107	22.2	15%	22%	7%	9%	12.1%	93.8	44	24	32	30%	80%	10%	12%	13	93	8%	46%			6.4	24	$3
Proj	**7**	**0**	**160**	**150**	**4.09**	**1.38**	**4.00**	**1.39**	**82**	**101**	**20.9**	**10%**	**22%**	**12%**	**8%**	**12.7%**	**93.2**	**48**	**22**	**30**	**31%**	**73%**	**13%**	**13%**	**32**						**4.6**	**81**	**$1**

Santos,Gregory

Age: 24 Th: R Role: RP | Health: D | LIMA Plan: A+
Ht: 6' 2" Wt: 190 Type: /GB | PT/Exp: D | Rand Var: 0
Consist: C | MM: 4220

Change of scenery, ditching four-seamer for sinker seemed to finally bring skills into focus (especially BB%), and that was enough to get him shot at closing until elbow inflammation ended season in mid-Sept. K% could stand to be higher, but SwK is optimistic. If he gets a clean bill of health, could be promising second-tier saves option.

Yr Tm	W	Sv	IP	K	ERA	WHIP	xERA	xWHIP	vL+	vR+	BF/G	BB%	K%	K-BB%	xBB%	SwK	Vel	G	L	F	H%	S%	HR/F	xHR/F	GS	APC	DOM%	DIS%	Sv%	LI	RAR	BPX	R$
19																																	
20																																	
21 SF *	1	0	19	16	6.35	1.62	6.14		267	233	5.0	12%	19%	7%		9.4%	97.7	38	0	63	31%	64%	60%	39%	0	18			0	2.37	-5.0	27	-$8
22 SF *	1	1	37	31	4.40	1.43	3.91	1.94	88	88	4.5	13%	20%	6%	11%	9.0%	98.9	75	8	17	28%	70%	0%	2%	0	34			33	0.32	-2.0	69	-$5
23 CHW	2	5	66	66	3.39	1.30	3.46	1.21	78	93	4.8	6%	23%	17%	5%	13.8%	98.7	53	27	21	36%	73%	5%	4%	0	17			56	1.05	7.7	146	$2
1st Half	2	1	43	42	2.95	1.24	3.30	1.19	85	84	4.8	5%	23%	18%	5%	13.8%	98.8	52	29	19	35%	75%	4%	2%	0	17			100	0.93	7.3	150	$2
2nd Half	0	4	24	24	4.18	1.39	3.75	1.24	69	111	4.9	7%	22%	16%	6%	13.9%	98.6	53	23	24	37%	69%	6%	6%	0	18			50	1.24	0.4	139	-$3
Proj	**2**	**16**	**58**	**57**	**3.50**	**1.29**	**3.31**	**1.24**	**71**	**95**	**4.7**	**8%**	**24%**	**16%**	**6%**	**13.8%**	**98.7**	**53**	**25**	**22**	**34%**	**72%**	**7%**	**4%**	**0**						**5.9**	**128**	**$6**

Scherzer,Max

Age: 39 Th: R Role: SP | Health: F | LIMA Plan: B
Ht: 6' 3" Wt: 208 Type: Pwr/xFB | PT/Exp: A | Rand Var: 0
Consist: A | MM: 4303

Signs of age starting to creep in, as this was first-ever xERA over 4.00. K%, SwK, velocity were all lowest since 2014. And yet, even with multiple nagging injuries and three-week IL stint for shoulder strain, K-BB% remained elite, and he delivered more value than most SP. Ace version is likely gone, but sure looks like he's still got plenty left in the tank.

Yr Tm	W	Sv	IP	K	ERA	WHIP	xERA	xWHIP	vL+	vR+	BF/G	BB%	K%	K-BB%	xBB%	SwK	Vel	G	L	F	H%	S%	HR/F	xHR/F	GS	APC	DOM%	DIS%	Sv%	LI	RAR	BPX	R$
19 WAS	11	0	172	243	2.92	1.03	3.04	0.97	100	70	25.7	5%	35%	30%	4%	17.1%	94.9	41	21	38	34%	76%	12%	11%	27	103	52%	7%			33.6	219	$27
20 WAS	5	0	67	92	3.74	1.38	3.86	1.13	119	82	24.6	8%	31%	23%	6%	15.3%	94.7	33	27	40	38%	78%	14%	16%	12	101	25%	33%			5.9	169	$12
21 2 NL	15	0	179	236	2.46	0.86	3.22	0.97	83	72	23.1	5%	34%	29%	6%	16.6%	94.3	34	18	48	26%	80%	12%	12%	30	94	57%	7%			40.0	192	$39
22 NYM	11	0	145	173	2.29	0.91	3.23	0.97	89	75	24.6	4%	31%	26%	5%	15.3%	94.1	31	19	50	29%	80%	7%	10%	23	94	52%	4%			30.1	178	$26
23 2 TM	13	0	153	174	3.77	1.12	4.04	1.17	95	93	23.0	7%	28%	21%	6%	13.9%	93.8	33	18	49	28%	75%	15%	11%	27	91	41%	19%			10.5	139	$18
1st Half	7	0	77	85	3.87	1.20	4.02	1.13	92	106	22.6	6%	27%	21%	5%	14.2%	93.6	33	20	46	32%	75%	13%	12%	14	90	36%	21%			4.3	151	$13
2nd Half	6	0	76	89	3.67	1.04	4.06	1.21	98	78	23.4	9%	29%	20%	6%	13.5%	94.0	33	16	51	23%	75%	16%	11%	13	93	46%	15%			6.2	129	$18
Proj	**10**	**0**	**145**	**165**	**3.73**	**1.12**	**3.56**	**1.11**	**101**	**87**	**24.1**	**7%**	**29%**	**22%**	**6%**	**14.1%**	**94.1**	**33**	**19**	**48**	**30%**	**73%**	**13%**	**12%**	**24**						**10.7**	**148**	**$14**

Schmidt,Clarke

Age: 28 Th: R Role: SP | Health: D | LIMA Plan: A+
Ht: 6' 1" Wt: 200 Type: | PT/Exp: C | Rand Var: 0
Consist: F | MM: 2103

Throwing more IP than previous three years combined likely explains 2nd half velocity drop. Even before that, wasn't able to maintain 2022's K%, SwK gains in return to rotation, and that sent ERA higher, along with H%. With BB% as only plus skill and ongoing issues vL, bullpen still appears to be long-term home. Even there, value is lacking.

Yr Tm	W	Sv	IP	K	ERA	WHIP	xERA	xWHIP	vL+	vR+	BF/G	BB%	K%	K-BB%	xBB%	SwK	Vel	G	L	F	H%	S%	HR/F	xHR/F	GS	APC	DOM%	DIS%	Sv%	LI	RAR	BPX	R$
19 aa	2	0	19	16	3.21	0.96	2.65				23.9	1%	22%	21%							30%	68%									3.0	373	-$2
20 NYY	0	0	6	7	7.11	1.89	5.89	1.66	100	109	11.0	15%	21%	6%	12%	9.5%	95.0	44	17	39	39%	58%	0%	19%	1	42	0%	100%	0	1.18	-2.1	10	-$9
21 NYY *	0	0	41	37	3.32	1.53	6.01	1.64	189	76	17.7	9%	21%	12%	8%	9.1%	93.0	60	20	20	33%	87%	20%	13%	1	72	0%	100%	0	0.48	4.7	46	-$5
22 NYY *	7	2	91	94	3.28	1.18	3.02	1.31	114	77	9.8	9%	26%	17%	6%	12.2%	94.9	42	20	38	30%	73%	9%	11%	3	32	33%	0%	67	1.18	7.7	120	$6
23 NYY	9	0	159	149	4.64	1.35	4.36	1.26	118	94	21.0	7%	21%	15%	6%	10.4%	93.5	44	19	38	33%	70%	13%	12%	32	82	9%	41%	0	0.77	-6.1	116	$1
1st Half	3	0	82	79	4.37	1.42	4.49	1.28	120	95	21.3	7%	22%	15%	6%	10.2%	94.1	43	17	40	34%	73%	11%	13%	17	84	6%	35%			-0.4	113	-$1
2nd Half	6	0	77	70	4.93	1.28	4.22	1.25	116	93	20.8	6%	21%	15%	7%	10.5%	92.7	44	20	35	31%	66%	16%	12%	15	81	13%	47%	0	0.77	-5.7	121	$7
Proj	**7**	**0**	**145**	**131**	**4.33**	**1.34**	**4.02**	**1.29**	**127**	**96**	**20.9**	**8%**	**22%**	**14%**	**7%**	**10.7%**	**93.6**	**44**	**19**	**37**	**31%**	**72%**	**15%**	**11%**	**29**						**0.0**	**100**	**$1**

Scholtens,Jesse

Age: 30 Th: R Role: RP | Health: A | LIMA Plan: C+
Ht: 6' 4" Wt: 230 Type: Con/FB | PT/Exp: D | Rand Var: -1
Consist: B | MM: 1000

1-9, 5.29 ERA in 85 IP at CHW. While he reached All-Star break with 2.96 MLB ERA over 27 IP, it was smoke and mirrors (5.30 xERA), and regression won out in 2nd half. Those 27 IP are probably as good as it'll get for him; he's a 9th-round pick who perservered and made it to the majors at 29. With skills, he'd be a Bull Durham prospect. But here, no.

Yr Tm	W	Sv	IP	K	ERA	WHIP	xERA	xWHIP	vL+	vR+	BF/G	BB%	K%	K-BB%	xBB%	SwK	Vel	G	L	F	H%	S%	HR/F	xHR/F	GS	APC	DOM%	DIS%	Sv%	LI	RAR	BPX	R$
19 aa	5	0	125	104	7.09	1.77	6.70				23.9	8%	18%	10%							39%	60%									-39.8	50	-$20
20																																	
21 aaa	3	0	103	80	4.57	1.38	4.63				20.6	8%	18%	11%							32%	69%									-3.9	69	-$5
22 aaa	4	1	84	72	3.48	1.34	4.35				9.5	8%	21%	12%							31%	78%									5.0	77	$0
23 CHW *	3	1	133	91	5.27	1.50	6.03	1.44	84	133	16.5	8%	15%	7%	9%	8.8%	92.8	41	18	41	31%	70%	13%	11%	11	56	9%	64%	100	0.86	-15.4	25	-$12
1st Half	3	1	76	49	4.41	1.31	4.85	1.44	67	84	16.4	8%	16%	8%	8%	9.7%	92.2	39	14	47	27%	73%	5%	6%	1	41	0%	0%	100	1.03	-0.7	35	-$1
2nd Half	0	0	58	42	6.40	1.75	5.40	1.42	91	153	16.7	7%	16%	8%	10%	8.5%	93.0	42	20	38	36%	68%	17%	14%	10	65	10%	70%	0	0.75	-14.7	61	-$15
Proj	**2**	**0**	**58**	**44**	**5.17**	**1.51**	**4.78**	**1.38**	**86**	**131**	**16.1**	**8%**	**17%**	**10%**	**9%**	**8.9%**	**92.7**	**41**	**18**	**42**	**33%**	**70%**	**12%**	**11%**	**9**						**-6.0**	**66**	**-$8**

Schreiber,John

Age: 30 Th: R Role: RP | Health: D | LIMA Plan: B
Ht: 6' 2" Wt: 210 Type: Pwr | PT/Exp: B | Rand Var: -1
Consist: D | MM: 5411

Maintained 2022's promising K%, GB% breakouts until mid-May shoulder injury took him out for two months; just wasn't the same after that. xBB% offers reassurance on control backslide, though it was especially bad vL (19% BB%). Was working on new cutter with Driveline Baseball immediately after season's end—could be some sleeper upside here.

Yr Tm	W	Sv	IP	K	ERA	WHIP	xERA	xWHIP	vL+	vR+	BF/G	BB%	K%	K-BB%	xBB%	SwK	Vel	G	L	F	H%	S%	HR/F	xHR/F	GS	APC	DOM%	DIS%	Sv%	LI	RAR	BPX	R$
19 DET *	8	4	80	83	3.79	1.27	3.84	1.09	105	116	5.0	9%	25%	16%	8%	12.7%	91.8	37	31	31	30%	74%	27%	18%	0	19			50	0.77	7.1	95	$6
20 DET	0	0	16	14	6.32	1.47	4.96	1.26	136	97	4.7	6%	20%	14%	7%	7.8%	89.8	32	28	40	36%	57%	10%	11%	0	19			0	0.91	-3.6	105	-$9
21 BOS *	3	1	70	56	3.52	1.57	4.83		69	142	9.1	9%	18%	9%		10.7%	92.2	43	43	14	35%	77%	0%	0%	0	56			50	0.51	6.4	73	-$4
22 BOS	4	8	65	74	2.22	0.98	2.86	1.12	97	73	4.0	7%	29%	21%	8%	14.1%	94.0	56	13	31	28%	79%	6%	9%	0	16			80	1.42	14.1	162	$10
23 BOS	2	1	47	53	3.86	1.41	4.34	1.41	133	82	4.4	12%	26%	14%	8%	10.7%	93.0	42	19	39	31%	77%	13%	11%	2	18	0%	100%	33	0.84	2.7	83	-$3
1st Half	1	0	17	21	2.12	1.29	3.13	1.29	83	100	3.9	11%	30%	19%	8%	13.3%	93.0	59	15	26	33%	86%	10%	6%	0	16			0	0.79	4.6	138	-$5
2nd Half	1	1	30	32	4.85	1.48	5.01	1.48	166	74	4.8	13%	24%	11%	8%	9.3%	93.0	34	21	45	30%	72%	14%	12%	2	19	0%	100%	33	0.88	-1.9	53	-$4
Proj	**3**	**4**	**65**	**76**	**3.32**	**1.17**	**3.28**	**1.20**	**122**	**79**	**4.7**	**9%**	**29%**	**20%**	**8%**	**13.5%**	**93.2**	**46**	**18**	**36**	**30%**	**74%**	**11%**	**9%**	**0**						**8.1**	**142**	**$5**

Scott,Tanner

Age: 29 Th: L Role: RP | Health: B | LIMA Plan: B
Ht: 6' 0" Wt: 235 Type: Pwr/GB | PT/Exp: A | Rand Var: -3
Consist: B | MM: 5531

Career bests in BB%, K%, and SwK made him nearly unhittable in 2nd half (0.99 ERA in Aug/Sept), helped net him closer role over final month. Cutting BB% was what really sealed the deal, and xBB% backed it all the way. Lack of name recognition, low Sv total might be enough to keep price reasonable before skills launch him to elite status.

Yr Tm	W	Sv	IP	K	ERA	WHIP	xERA	xWHIP	vL+	vR+	BF/G	BB%	K%	K-BB%	xBB%	SwK	Vel	G	L	F	H%	S%	HR/F	xHR/F	GS	APC	DOM%	DIS%	Sv%	LI	RAR	BPX	R$
19 BAL *	4	7	72	82	4.03	1.44	4.16	1.48	90	133	5.3	11%	27%	15%	12%	15.1%	95.9	50	27	23	34%	73%	27%	21%	0	17			58	0.56	4.2	99	$3
20 BAL	0	1	21	23	1.31	1.06	3.53	1.35	79	61	3.4	12%	27%	15%	12%	13.9%	96.5	58	18	24	24%	90%	8%	12%	0	14			50	1.77	8.0	112	$3
21 BAL	5	0	54	70	5.17	1.57	4.02	1.46	81	103	4.0	15%	28%	13%	11%	15.7%	96.8	51	23	26	34%	68%	17%	16%	0	17			0	1.17	-6.0	80	-$5
22 MIA	4	20	63	90	4.31	1.61	3.57	1.44	109	97	4.3	16%	31%	15%	9%	15.8%	96.9	46	28	26	37%	74%	13%	12%	0	19			74	0.99	-2.6	86	$4
23 MIA	9	12	78	104	2.31	0.99	2.68	1.08	79	69	4.1	8%	34%	26%	5%	18.1%	96.9	51	22	27	30%	77%	6%	5%	0	16			75	1.50	19.5	191	$20
1st Half	4	2	39	56	3.23	1.13	2.72	1.14	76	81	4.0	10%	36%	26%	6%	17.1%	96.1	52	20	28	33%	71%	9%	4%	0	16			50	1.33	5.3	184	$7
2nd Half	5	10	39	48	1.38	0.85	2.64	1.02	83	57	4.3	5%	32%	26%	4%	19.2%	97.6	50	24	26	28%	84%	4%	5%	0	17			83	1.68	14.2	200	$21
Proj	**6**	**32**	**73**	**95**	**2.90**	**1.04**	**2.67**	**1.13**	**77**	**74**	**3.9**	**9%**	**34%**	**25%**	**7%**	**17.1%**	**96.9**	**50**	**23**	**26**	**29%**	**74%**	**11%**	**9%**	**0**						**12.8**	**171**	**$22**

BRANDON KRUSE

Seabold,Connor

Age: 28	Th: R	Role: RP	Health	A	LIMA Plan	C+
Ht: 6' 2"	Wt: 190	Type: Con/xFB	PT/Exp	C	Rand Var	+5
			Consist	C	MM	0000

1-7, 7.52 ERA in 87 IP at COL. Call him Contradiction Connor: He "beat" the H%/S% Regression Monster after 2022, as both of those indicators somehow got worse in 2023. Though he continued to limit free passes, seemingly everyone who got on base scored. And, well ... an MLB team (checks notes) gave him 87 innings. You shouldn't.

Yr Tm	W	Sv	IP	K	ERA	WHIP	xERA	xWHIP	vL+	vR+	BF/G	BB%	K%	K-BB%	xBB%	SwK	Vel	G	L	F	H%	S%	HR/F	xHR/F	GS	APC	DOM%	DIS%	Sv%	LI	RAR	BPX	R$
19 aa	3	0	40	32	2.98	1.32	3.97				23.7	7%	19%	13%							33%	79%									7.5	98	$0
20																																	
21 BOS *	4	0	57	42	4.51	1.34	4.44		265	66	19.8	9%	18%	8%		4.7%	90.4	40	20	40	29%	69%	25%	17%	1	43	0%	100%			-1.7	54	-$4
22 BOS *	8	0	107	88	4.93	1.42	4.99	1.33	190	157	18.8	6%	19%	13%	7%	11.6%	92.2	29	22	49	35%	67%	15%	9%	5	74	0%	60%			-12.6	89	-$5
23 COL *	2	0	119	92	7.72	1.72	7.22	1.38	129	125	15.5	7%	16%	10%	6%	10.4%	92.7	33	20	47	38%	56%	13%	11%	13	58	0%	69%	0	0.50	-50.0	37	-$29
1st Half	1	0	70	51	6.62	1.47	6.05	1.39	119	122	15.7	7%	16%	9%	6%	9.7%	92.6	33	20	47	31%	59%	14%	9%	11	64	0%	64%	0	0.56	-19.7	31	-$17
2nd Half	1	0	50	41	9.26	2.07	8.85	1.32	162	136	15.2	6%	17%	11%	5%	12.5%	92.9	35	20	45	45%	54%	11%	16%	2	45	0%	100%	0	0.37	-30.3	48	-$23
Proj	**2**	**0**	**58**	**45**	**5.79**	**1.60**	**4.96**	**1.34**	**123**	**107**	**17.3**	**7%**	**18%**	**11%**	**6%**	**11.5%**	**92.8**	**34**	**20**	**46**	**36%**	**66%**	**10%**	**13%**	**11**						**-10.5**	**71**	**-$11**

Sears,JP

Age: 28	Th: L	Role: RP	Health	A	LIMA Plan	A+
Ht: 5' 11"	Wt: 180	Type: /xFB	PT/Exp	B	Rand Var	0
			Consist	D	MM	2203

First full season looks passable on the surface, but yellow flags: 1) Dominates neither RHH or LHH; 2) K-BB% is only pedestrian; 3) Extreme FB%/contact profile elevates HR risk; 4) Overall skills took a step back in second half, even though velocity held through a 50+ IP increase. Not a pup; could improve but mostly a deep-league play.

Yr Tm	W	Sv	IP	K	ERA	WHIP	xERA	xWHIP	vL+	vR+	BF/G	BB%	K%	K-BB%	xBB%	SwK	Vel	G	L	F	H%	S%	HR/F	xHR/F	GS	APC	DOM%	DIS%	Sv%	LI	RAR	BPX	R$
19																																	
20																																	
21 a/a	10	1	106	113	4.15	1.25	4.05				17.3	7%	26%	19%							32%	70%									1.6	116	$6
22 2 AL *	7	0	119	99	2.79	1.03	2.64	1.35	98	101	15.8	6%	22%	15%	6%	8.4%	93.2	40	18	41	26%	76%	9%	12%	11	63	0%	45%	0	0.72	17.4	117	$12
23 OAK	5	0	172	161	4.54	1.26	4.89	1.28	126	103	23.0	7%	22%	15%	6%	11.7%	93.1	29	18	53	29%	71%	13%	13%	32	90	19%	31%			-4.5	94	$3
1st Half	1	0	87	85	4.43	1.08	4.60	1.18	101	102	22.3	6%	24%	18%	6%	12.0%	92.9	25	17	58	25%	68%	14%	14%	16	92	25%	31%			-1.1	119	$6
2nd Half	4	0	85	76	4.66	1.46	5.20	1.38	155	104	23.7	9%	20%	11%	8%	11.4%	93.4	33	20	48	32%	73%	12%	11%	16	87	13%	31%			-3.4	69	$2
Proj	**8**	**0**	**160**	**151**	**4.19**	**1.25**	**4.19**	**1.25**	**127**	**102**	**19.7**	**7%**	**23%**	**16%**	**7%**	**11.0%**	**93.2**	**32**	**19**	**50**	**30%**	**72%**	**12%**	**12%**	**32**						**2.6**	**101**	**$6**

Senga,Kodai

Age: 31	Th: R	Role: SP	Health	A	LIMA Plan	C+
Ht: 6' 1"	Wt: 202	Type: Pwr	PT/Exp	A	Rand Var	-3
			Consist	B	MM	3305

The rare East Asia import who met expecations in Year 1. Can he repeat? PRO: Started strong but the took a big step up late (especially walks and K%); handled both-sided hitters; solid GB rate. CON: Quite a bit of S% luck; BB% just okay; MLB xERA/xWHIP show the downside. VERDICT: Solid, but set expectations against 2nd half xERA.

Yr Tm	W	Sv	IP	K	ERA	WHIP	xERA	xWHIP	vL+	vR+	BF/G	BB%	K%	K-BB%	xBB%	SwK	Vel	G	L	F	H%	S%	HR/F	xHR/F	GS	APC	DOM%	DIS%	Sv%	LI	RAR	BPX	R$
19 for	13	0	180	215	3.48	1.32	4.14				28.6	12%	29%	16%							28%	81%									22.8	84	$15
20 for	8	0	99	117	3.27	1.49	3.85				28.4	15%	27%	12%							32%	79%									14.4	105	$19
21 for	10	0	85	85	3.29	1.15	2.51				26.0	10%	25%	15%							28%	71%									10.3	121	$9
22 for	11	0	144	148	2.41	1.19	2.98				26.2	11%	26%	15%							28%	83%									27.7	107	$16
23 NYM	12	0	166	202	2.98	1.22	3.76	1.30	77	93	23.9	11%	29%	18%	10%	13.0%	95.7	45	19	36	29%	80%	12%	13%	29	97	31%	14%			27.8	120	$2
1st Half	6	0	82	101	3.53	1.35	4.06	1.39	82	97	23.7	13%	28%	15%	11%	12.7%	95.9	46	18	36	30%	77%	12%	12%	15	95	27%	20%			8.1	98	$1
2nd Half	6	0	85	101	2.44	1.10	3.48	1.21	72	90	24.2	9%	30%	21%	9%	13.3%	95.5	44	20	37	28%	82%	11%	14%	14	98	36%	7%			19.7	142	$24
Proj	**14**	**0**	**174**	**198**	**3.38**	**1.22**	**3.63**	**1.32**	**78**	**92**	**24.1**	**11%**	**28%**	**17%**	**10%**	**13.0%**	**95.7**	**44**	**19**	**36**	**29%**	**75%**	**10%**	**13%**	**29**						**20.4**	**107**	**$1**

Senzatela,Antonio

Age: 29	Th: R	Role: SP	Health	F	LIMA Plan	C+
Ht: 6' 1"	Wt: 236	Type: Con/GB	PT/Exp	B	Rand Var	+2
			Consist	A	MM	1000

Sprained UCL in May led to mid-season Tommy John surgery; will only see minimal time in 2024 at best. Has a history of very strong GB% paired with outpitching xBB%, but lack of whiffs and Ks along with pitching in an unforgiving home park has led to a "steer clear" sign up to this point. No reason to change that assessment now.

Yr Tm	W	Sv	IP	K	ERA	WHIP	xERA	xWHIP	vL+	vR+	BF/G	BB%	K%	K-BB%	xBB%	SwK	Vel	G	L	F	H%	S%	HR/F	xHR/F	GS	APC	DOM%	DIS%	Sv%	LI	RAR	BPX	R$
19 COL *	12	0	160	85	6.61	1.74	6.66	1.58	124	113	22.8	9%	12%	2%	10%	7.7%	93.7	54	22	24	34%	64%	18%	19%	25	89	8%	68%			-41.5	2	-$1
20 COL	5	0	73	41	3.44	1.21	4.76	1.38	100	94	25.3	6%	14%	8%	8%	8.4%	94.4	51	20	29	27%	76%	13%	14%	12	95	25%	50%			9.2	68	$1
21 COL	4	0	157	105	4.42	1.34	4.27	1.27	108	96	23.9	5%	16%	11%	7%	9.2%	94.6	51	22	27	33%	67%	9%	11%	28	86	14%	39%			-3.1	96	-$
22 COL	3	0	92	54	5.07	1.69	4.38	1.34	122	132	21.7	6%	13%	8%	8%	7.4%	94.2	49	26	25	38%	71%	11%	11%	19	80	5%	58%			-12.5	67	-$1
23 COL	0	0	8	4	4.70	1.17	4.42	1.43	169	76	15.0	7%	13%	7%	10%	8.3%	93.9	54	17	29	19%	83%	43%	44%	2	60	0%	50%			-0.3	60	-$
1st Half	0	0	8	4	4.70	1.17	4.42	1.43	170	77	15.0	7%	13%	7%	10%	8.3%	93.9	54	17	29	19%	83%	43%	44%	2	60	0%	50%			-0.3	60	-$1
2nd Half																																	
Proj	**2**	**0**	**36**	**21**	**5.04**	**1.54**	**4.49**	**1.39**	**116**	**114**	**22.8**	**6%**	**14%**	**7%**	**8%**	**8.0%**	**94.2**	**51**	**23**	**26**	**34%**	**69%**	**13%**	**13%**	**7**						**-3.2**	**64**	**-$**

Severino,Luis

Age: 30	Th: R	Role: SP	Health	F	LIMA Plan	B
Ht: 6' 2"	Wt: 218	Type:	PT/Exp	B	Rand Var	+5
			Consist	C	MM	2101

His back-to-back 190-IP, 220+ K years have now scrolled off this page, which is likely for the best. Yes, 2022—but that's one half-season in the past five, and those skills were still short of the glory days. Lat and oblique injuries book-ended his season; SwK, HR implosions were concerning. Recency bias might be a good thing in this case.

Yr Tm	W	Sv	IP	K	ERA	WHIP	xERA	xWHIP	vL+	vR+	BF/G	BB%	K%	K-BB%	xBB%	SwK	Vel	G	L	F	H%	S%	HR/F	xHR/F	GS	APC	DOM%	DIS%	Sv%	LI	RAR	BPX	R$
19 NYY	1	0	12	17	1.50	1.00	3.59	1.26	61	53	16.0	13%	35%	23%	6%	11.4%	96.1	42	13	46	26%	83%	0%	4%	3	73	33%	0%			4.4	139	-$
20																																	
21 NYY	1	0	6	8	0.00	0.50	2.58		161	23	5.5	5%	36%	32%		13.3%	95.3	42	17	42	18%	100%	0%	2%	0	25			0	0.63	3.2	214	-$
22 NYY	7	0	102	112	3.18	1.00	3.35	1.14	90	85	21.3	7%	28%	20%	7%	12.6%	96.3	44	16	40	25%	75%	14%	11%	19	86	32%	16%			10.0	142	$1
23 NYY	4	0	89	79	6.65	1.65	5.02	1.38	135	115	21.9	8%	19%	11%	6%	9.8%	96.5	42	21	37	34%	65%	21%	17%	18	86	11%	50%	0	0.77	-25.5	79	-$1
1st Half	1	0	40	34	6.30	1.65	5.53	1.46	113	128	23.6	10%	18%	8%	6%	9.2%	96.4	38	20	41	33%	68%	18%	15%	8	87	13%	38%			-9.7	50	-$1
2nd Half	3	0	49	45	6.93	1.64	4.63	1.31	152	105	20.7	7%	20%	13%	6%	10.2%	96.6	45	21	34	36%	63%	24%	18%	10	86	10%	60%	0	0.75	-15.8	104	-$
Proj	**6**	**0**	**116**	**103**	**4.40**	**1.35**	**4.11**	**1.32**	**117**	**95**	**21.1**	**8%**	**21%**	**13%**	**6%**	**10.3%**	**96.5**	**43**	**20**	**37**	**31%**	**72%**	**15%**	**14%**	**23**						**-1.1**	**92**	**-$**

Sewald,Paul

Age: 34	Th: R	Role: RP	Health	B	LIMA Plan	B
Ht: 6' 3"	Wt: 219	Type: Pwr/xFB	PT/Exp	A	Rand Var	-2
			Consist	A	MM	4531

When he moved south to ARI at the deadline, his walk and HR rates took a similar turn. But by that time, was an established Saves source and seasonal line ended up fully acceptable. Extreme FB profile keeps him from the top tier of closers, but the SwK/K% numbers remain elite despite average velocity. No reason he can't run it back.

Yr Tm	W	Sv	IP	K	ERA	WHIP	xERA	xWHIP	vL+	vR+	BF/G	BB%	K%	K-BB%	xBB%	SwK	Vel	G	L	F	H%	S%	HR/F	xHR/F	GS	APC	DOM%	DIS%	Sv%	LI	RAR	BPX	R$
19 NYM *	4	4	71	63	4.51	1.57	5.85	1.09	80	103	5.3	6%	20%	14%	6%	9.7%	91.1	17	21	62	37%	75%	9%	9%	0	19			100	0.61	0.0	73	-$
20 NYM	0	0	6	2	13.50	2.67	8.99	1.84	207	117	7.0	11%	6%	-6%	12%	6.2%	91.8	32	39	29	42%	47%	13%	12%	0	26			0	0.56	-6.7	-111	-$1
21 SEA	10	11	65	104	3.06	1.02	3.28	1.03	90	73	4.3	9%	40%	30%	5%	17.2%	92.4	26	21	53	29%	79%	14%	14%	0	18			69	1.60	9.6	191	$1
22 SEA	5	20	64	72	2.67	0.77	3.42	1.09	85	67	3.7	7%	30%	23%	6%	15.8%	92.6	31	18	51	17%	77%	13%	8%	0	15			80	1.36	10.2	140	$1
23 2 TM	3	34	61	80	3.12	1.15	3.84	1.19	91	83	3.8	10%	32%	22%	6%	14.1%	92.2	32	18	50	29%	79%	11%	9%	0	16			87	1.22	9.1	143	$1
1st Half	2	16	34	47	2.62	0.93	3.32	1.07	69	76	3.7	8%	36%	27%	5%	14.3%	92.0	31	19	50	27%	76%	8%	3%	0	16			84	1.35	7.2	172	$1
2nd Half	1	18	26	33	3.76	1.44	4.56	1.32	122	91	3.9	11%	28%	17%	6%	13.8%	92.4	34	16	50	33%	82%	15%	15%	0	16			90	1.07	1.9	107	$
Proj	**5**	**30**	**73**	**95**	**3.26**	**1.15**	**3.49**	**1.15**	**99**	**83**	**3.9**	**9%**	**33%**	**24%**	**6%**	**15.0%**	**92.3**	**31**	**19**	**51**	**29%**	**79%**	**13%**	**11%**	**0**						**9.5**	**146**	**$1**

Sheehan,Emmet

Age: 24	Th: R	Role: RP	Health	A	LIMA Plan	A
Ht: 6' 5"	Wt: 215	Type: Pwr/xFB	PT/Exp	F	Rand Var	-1
			Consist	F	MM	3403

4-1, 4.92 ERA in 60 IP at LA. Quick riser fared pretty well in MLB debut and finished with a flourish (34/8 K/BB in 22 Sept IP). A classic high-heat, up-in-the-zone guy who gets tons of whiffs and Ks, but big FB% means it comes with HR risk. Realizing xBB potential and improving pitch efficiency the next steps. Talented, but requires patience.

Yr Tm	W	Sv	IP	K	ERA	WHIP	xERA	xWHIP	vL+	vR+	BF/G	BB%	K%	K-BB%	xBB%	SwK	Vel	G	L	F	H%	S%	HR/F	xHR/F	GS	APC	DOM%	DIS%	Sv%	LI	RAR	BPX	R
19																																	
20																																	
21																																	
22																																	
23 LA *	8	1	126	151	3.73	1.05	2.79	1.34	100	93	17.3	10%	26%	15%	8%	14.2%	95.5	33	13	54	22%	70%	13%	11%	11	79	9%	45%	100	0.81	9.3	115	$1
1st Half	6	0	71	87	2.30	0.91	1.86	1.20	68	68	17.7	10%	32%	22%	7%	9.1%	95.7	34	11	55	21%	82%	8%	8%	3	88	0%	33%			17.8	144	$2
2nd Half	2	1	55	64	5.66	1.25	4.14	1.37	110	104	17.1	13%	29%	16%	8%	15.9%	95.4	33	15	53	25%	59%	16%	13%	8	77	13%	50%	100	0.81	-9.0	80	$
Proj	**8**	**0**	**152**	**182**	**4.16**	**1.24**	**3.92**	**1.27**	**103**	**94**	**17.9**	**11%**	**29%**	**19%**	**8%**	**13.4%**	**95.5**	**33**	**16**	**51**	**28%**	**72%**	**13%**	**11%**	**27**						**3.2**	**111**	**$**

BRENT HERSHEY

Shuster,Jared

Age: 25	Th: L	Role: SP	Health: A	LIMA Plan: D+
Ht: 6' 3"	Wt: 210	Type: Con/FB	PT/Exp: D	Rand Var: -1
			Consist: F	MM: 0000

4-3, 5.81 ERA in 53 IP at ATL. Good March, injuries rushed 2020 1st-round pick into MLB rotation with almost predictable results. Soft-tosser's struggles began with advance to AAA in July 2022. K% plunge, BB% spike, HR damage accelerated in ATL; wasn't any better in AAA after June demotion. Avoid until something changes.

Yr	Tm	W	Sv	IP	K	ERA	WHIP	xERA	xWHIP	vL+	vR+	BF/G	BB%	K%	K-BB%	xBB%	SwK	Vel	G	L	F	H%	S%	HR/F	xHR/F	GS	APC	DOM%	DIS%	Sv%	LI	RAR	BPX	R$
19																																		
20																																		
21	aa	0	0	16	14	8.87	1.74	8.83				24.7	7%	19%	12%							35%	55%									-9.2	-6	-$10
22	a/a	7	0	142	121	3.91	1.16	3.79				21.0	7%	21%	14%							27%	71%									1.1	88	$6
23	ATL *	9	0	132	85	5.69	1.70	5.89	1.65	99	110	22.0	11%	13%	2%	9%	9.3%	91.4	36	17	47	32%	68%	9%	10%	11	79	0%	64%			-22.0	25	-$17
1st Half		6	0	75	47	5.01	1.50	4.77	1.62	90	103	21.6	11%	15%	3%	8%	9.4%	91.5	35	17	48	29%	68%	6%	8%	9	81	0%	56%			-6.3	39	-$5
2nd Half		3	0	59	37	6.33	1.88	6.97	1.70	158	145	23.0	13%	14%	1%	11%	8.6%	90.8	38	19	42	35%	68%	27%	21%	2	70	0%	100%			-14.5	10	-$13
Proj		3	0	58	37	5.11	1.53	5.46	1.56	115	126	23.0	11%	15%	4%	9%	9.4%	91.5	35	17	48	30%	69%	9%	7%	11						-5.6	5	-$8

Silseth,Chase

Age: 24	Th: R	Role: SP	Health: C	LIMA Plan: A
Ht: 6' 0"	Wt: 217	Type: Pwr	PT/Exp: D	Rand Var: +1
			Consist: A	MM: 3303

4-1, 3.96 ERA in 52 IP at LAA. 1st-half shuttle yielded inconsistent results; couldn't replicate AAA SP success out of MLB pen despite elite GB%. Then found 2nd-half groove (3.21 ERA, 41 K in 34 IP) as MLB SP despite August concussion that interrupted his roll. BB% needs work but late SwK uptick, GB tilt are optimistic. Growth-stock flyer.

Yr	Tm	W	Sv	IP	K	ERA	WHIP	xERA	xWHIP	vL+	vR+	BF/G	BB%	K%	K-BB%	xBB%	SwK	Vel	G	L	F	H%	S%	HR/F	xHR/F	GS	APC	DOM%	DIS%	Sv%	LI	RAR	BPX	R$
19																																		
20																																		
21																																		
22	LAA *	8	0	112	120	3.25	1.08	3.29	1.39	160	101	19.8	8%	28%	19%	8%	11.4%	95.3	46	23	31	26%	78%	25%	18%	7	72	0%	57%			9.9	109	$10
23	LAA *	8	0	100	98	3.38	1.20	3.20	1.40	92	100	14.8	12%	25%	14%	9%	11.9%	94.9	49	22	29	27%	75%	23%	17%	8	56	13%	13%	0	0.71	11.7	96	$8
1st Half		4	0	54	46	3.77	1.29	3.35	1.47	103	110	13.0	11%	21%	9%	12%	10.0%	94.9	59	16	25	27%	72%	21%	18%	1	40	0%	0%	0	0.64	3.7	84	$2
2nd Half		4	0	46	52	2.92	1.10	3.02	1.26	86	95	18.0	10%	28%	19%	8%	13.2%	94.9	42	26	32	25%	80%	23%	17%	7	76	14%	14%			8.0	114	$9
Proj		10	0	131	136	3.75	1.28	3.72	1.32	91	98	22.0	10%	25%	15%	10%	12.6%	94.9	46	22	32	30%	74%	13%	17%	24						9.3	102	$7

Singer,Brady

Age: 27	Th: R	Role: SP	Health: C	LIMA Plan: B
Ht: 6' 5"	Wt: 215	Type: /GB	PT/Exp: A	Rand Var: +4
			Consist: B	MM: 3103

Couldn't sustain 2022 breakout as previous mojo vR vanished. Struggled with BB% early, K% plummeted, velocity was down all year. 2nd-half yielded positive signs as control returned, SwK ticked up. H%/S% says poor luck was involved throughout. But with GB% as his only consistently plus skill, any rebound from here looks capped.

Yr	Tm	W	Sv	IP	K	ERA	WHIP	xERA	xWHIP	vL+	vR+	BF/G	BB%	K%	K-BB%	xBB%	SwK	Vel	G	L	F	H%	S%	HR/F	xHR/F	GS	APC	DOM%	DIS%	Sv%	LI	RAR	BPX	R$
19	aa	7	0	92	70	4.75	1.46	4.87				24.7	7%	18%	11%							34%	69%									-2.7	68	-$2
20	KC	4	0	64	61	4.06	1.17	3.98	1.31	93	83	21.9	9%	23%	14%	7%	9.8%	93.4	53	17	30	27%	69%	15%	15%	12	89	33%	50%			3.1	110	$11
21	KC	5	0	128	131	4.91	1.55	4.17	1.32	112	97	21.7	9%	22%	13%	8%	10.5%	93.7	50	22	28	36%	70%	13%	14%	27	85	22%	37%			-10.2	102	-$9
22	KC *	11	0	169	158	3.20	1.11	3.45	1.14	103	90	22.1	6%	24%	18%	6%	9.6%	93.8	49	20	31	29%	76%	14%	15%	24	88	42%	21%	0	0.69	16.0	123	$16
23	KC	8	0	160	133	5.52	1.45	4.37	1.33	105	116	24.2	7%	19%	12%	8%	9.8%	92.1	50	20	31	34%	63%	13%	14%	29	90	21%	41%			-23.5	99	-$9
1st Half		5	0	90	74	5.52	1.48	4.67	1.40	111	111	23.4	9%	19%	10%	8%	9.1%	92.4	47	21	32	33%	63%	11%	14%	17	90	12%	47%			-13.1	75	-$8
2nd Half		3	0	70	59	5.53	1.40	4.00	1.23	99	124	25.3	5%	19%	14%	6%	10.8%	91.8	53	18	29	35%	63%	15%	14%	12	90	33%	33%			-10.3	130	-$3
Proj		8	0	160	143	4.47	1.32	3.75	1.28	101	100	23.9	7%	22%	14%	8%	10.1%	92.8	50	20	30	32%	69%	14%	14%	28						-2.9	111	$1

Skubal,Tarik

Age: 27	Th: L	Role: RP	Health: F	LIMA Plan: B+
Ht: 6' 3"	Wt: 240	Type: Pwr	PT/Exp: A	Rand Var: -1
			Consist: B	MM: 5403

Rehab from 2022 flexor tendon surgery kept him out until July; 2nd half DOM%/DIS% worth the wait. Velocity uptick helped broad repertoire play up, as SwK spiked into elite territory. BB%, K% were top-shelf; another GB% spike made HR a non-issue. Pullback is likely. But Health caveat aside, we're buyers. UP: 160 IP, 3.25 ERA.

Yr	Tm	W	Sv	IP	K	ERA	WHIP	xERA	xWHIP	vL+	vR+	BF/G	BB%	K%	K-BB%	xBB%	SwK	Vel	G	L	F	H%	S%	HR/F	xHR/F	GS	APC	DOM%	DIS%	Sv%	LI	RAR	BPX	R$
19	aa	2	0	43	67	3.09	1.19	2.67				19.2	12%	39%	27%							35%	75%									7.5	165	$1
20	DET	1	0	32	37	5.63	1.22	4.58	1.22	48	120	16.8	8%	28%	19%	8%	13.4%	94.5	28	18	54	26%	63%	20%	17%	7	74	14%	43%	0	0.80	-4.6	124	-$4
21	DET	8	0	149	164	4.34	1.26	4.11	1.20	93	107	20.5	7%	26%	18%	7%	12.1%	94.4	39	20	41	29%	76%	20%	20%	29	82	17%	31%	0	0.76	-1.4	129	$5
22	DET	7	0	118	117	3.52	1.16	3.52	1.17	89	94	22.7	7%	25%	18%	6%	12.2%	94.4	46	19	35	31%	71%	8%	10%	21	91	43%	24%			6.5	131	$7
23	DET	7	0	80	102	2.80	0.90	2.66	0.98	49	78	20.7	5%	33%	28%	4%	15.9%	95.8	52	17	31	30%	69%	7%	8%	15	81	53%	7%			15.2	217	$14
1st Half																																		
2nd Half		7	0	80	102	2.80	0.90	2.66	0.98	50	78	20.7	5%	33%	28%	4%	15.9%	95.8	52	17	31	30%	69%	7%	8%	15	81	53%	7%			15.2	218	$28
Proj		10	0	145	172	3.60	1.08	3.14	1.08	66	93	18.9	6%	30%	24%	6%	14.3%	94.9	42	18	40	30%	70%	12%	12%	27						12.9	170	$16

Smith,Drew

Age: 30	Th: R	Role: RP	Health: F	LIMA Plan: B
Ht: 6' 2"	Wt: 190	Type: Pwr/xFB	PT/Exp: C	Rand Var: -2
			Consist: B	MM: 1301

Reliever found early leverage work, courtesy of club injuries and 2021-22 performance—but it diminished as control issues surfaced. Held onto plus K% despite SwK plunge; limited HR damage despite big FB tilt. But he pitched in traffic throughout 2nd half, and xERA says this could have been worse. There are better bullpen flyers.

Yr	Tm	W	Sv	IP	K	ERA	WHIP	xERA	xWHIP	vL+	vR+	BF/G	BB%	K%	K-BB%	xBB%	SwK	Vel	G	L	F	H%	S%	HR/F	xHR/F	GS	APC	DOM%	DIS%	Sv%	LI	RAR	BPX	R$
19																																		
20	NYM	0	0	7	7	6.43	1.14	4.91		60	131	3.6	7%	24%	17%	8%	19.3%	95.2	35	10	55	24%	50%	18%	22%	0	14			0	0.86	-1.7	119	-$7
21	NYM	3	0	41	41	2.40	1.06	4.34	1.31	89	93	5.3	10%	25%	15%	6%	14.3%	95.0	34	20	46	22%	89%	15%	14%	1	20	0%	0%	0	0.72	9.5	86	$2
22	NYM	3	0	46	53	3.33	1.15	3.83	1.16	113	90	4.3	8%	28%	20%	8%	14.2%	95.8	34	15	50	27%	82%	15%	13%	0	18			0	0.96	3.6	132	$0
23	NYM	4	3	56	60	4.15	1.40	4.99	1.43	108	107	3.9	12%	25%	13%	9%	10.8%	95.1	30	18	52	30%	74%	9%	10%	0	17			60	1.04	1.2	62	-$1
1st Half		3	2	28	33	4.23	1.23	4.17	1.28	78	118	3.9	10%	28%	18%	11%	9.1%	95.1	31	19	49	29%	70%	12%	14%	0	17			50	1.27	0.4	110	-$1
2nd Half		1	1	29	27	4.08	1.57	5.84	1.57	138	97	4.0	13%	21%	8%	8%	12.5%	95.0	29	17	54	32%	76%	7%	7%	0	17			100	0.82	0.9	17	-$4
Proj		4	0	65	68	4.00	1.36	4.45	1.37	111	104	4.2	11%	25%	14%	8%	12.2%	95.2	32	18	50	30%	75%	11%	12%	0						2.7	76	-$1

Smith,Will

Age: 34	Th: L	Role: RP	Health: B	LIMA Plan: A
Ht: 6' 5"	Wt: 255	Type: Pwr/xFB	PT/Exp: A	Rand Var: 0
			Consist: A	MM: 3310

Earned keep with 1st-half closer effort, even as regression loomed large in H%, HR/F, dominance vR. The end came abruptly in early August; SwK, K% plunges helped fuel his quick removal from the 9th inning. Free agent will find setup work with someone, but age, handedness, big FB% will likely keep soft-tosser's 9th inning work elusive.

Yr	Tm	W	Sv	IP	K	ERA	WHIP	xERA	xWHIP	vL+	vR+	BF/G	BB%	K%	K-BB%	xBB%	SwK	Vel	G	L	F	H%	S%	HR/F	xHR/F	GS	APC	DOM%	DIS%	Sv%	LI	RAR	BPX	R$
19	SF	6	34	65	96	2.76	1.03	2.95	1.05	52	95	4.1	8%	37%	29%	6%	15.8%	92.7	42	22	36	29%	82%	20%	16%	0	17			89	1.58	14.1	196	$24
20	ATL	2	0	16	18	4.50	0.94	4.12	1.13	102	109	3.4	6%	29%	23%	9%	17.5%	92.6	30	18	53	13%	88%	33%	25%	0	14			0	1.24	-0.1	146	$1
21	ATL	3	37	68	87	3.44	1.13	3.94	1.21	97	92	4.0	10%	31%	21%	7%	14.7%	92.8	31	21	47	27%	77%	14%	10%	0	15			86	1.33	6.9	127	$20
22	2 TM	0	5	59	65	3.97	1.41	4.28	1.28	91	120	4.0	10%	25%	15%	6%	15.4%	92.2	35	20	45	33%	77%	12%	9%	0	15			63	0.85	0.0	98	-$2
23	TEX	2	22	57	55	4.40	1.06	4.33	1.25	61	94	3.8	8%	24%	17%	6%	14.2%	92.4	30	23	47	27%	59%	7%	8%	0	14			81	1.30	-0.5	103	$9
1st Half		1	14	30	33	2.70	0.83	3.94	1.14	51	70	3.8	7%	29%	22%	5%	16.0%	92.8	22	25	53	23%	70%	5%	8%	0	15			93	1.35	6.0	128	$14
2nd Half		1	8	27	22	6.26	1.32	4.79	1.36	68	122	3.8	8%	19%	12%	6%	12.3%	91.9	36	21	43	30%	52%	9%	9%	0	14			67	1.26	-6.5	73	-$1
Proj		3	7	58	63	4.15	1.16	3.79	1.23	75	100	3.8	9%	27%	19%	6%	14.5%	92.4	33	22	45	28%	67%	11%	10%	0						1.3	115	$3

Smith-Shawver,AJ

Age: 21	Th: R	Role: RP	Health: A	LIMA Plan: C+
Ht: 6' 3"	Wt: 205	Type: Pwr/FB	PT/Exp: F	Rand Var: 0
			Consist: F	MM: 1200

1-0, 4.26 ERA in 25.1 IP at ATL. Opened season in High-A, powered through three levels before callup. Four-pitch pitcher will be given chances to start. K% drastically declined vs MLB competition, but mid-90s fastball performed admirably. Hitting the zone, though, is key—slider and curveball strike rates were below 50%. Could take time. (CB)

Yr	Tm	W	Sv	IP	K	ERA	WHIP	xERA	xWHIP	vL+	vR+	BF/G	BB%	K%	K-BB%	xBB%	SwK	Vel	G	L	F	H%	S%	HR/F	xHR/F	GS	APC	DOM%	DIS%	Sv%	LI	RAR	BPX	R$
19																																		
20																																		
21																																		
22																																		
23	ATL *	4	0	73	71	4.10	1.23	3.51	1.48	123	59	16.5	10%	19%	9%	12%	9.3%	94.5	37	8	55	23%	72%	18%	10%	5	76	0%	40%	0	0.64	2.1	74	$1
1st Half		2	0	40	38	4.36	1.26	4.42	1.42	129	75	18.0	11%	23%	12%	12%	11.1%	94.2	34	9	57	25%	73%	19%	9%	3	74	0%	33%	0	0.59	-0.1	59	-$4
2nd Half		2	0	36	33	3.35	1.07	1.93	1.59	115	21	15.5	15%	24%	9%	11%	5.7%	95.2	42	8	50	18%	71%	15%	11%	2	79	0%	50%			4.3	99	$3
Proj		3	0	58	60	4.45	1.37	4.38	1.39	135	73	17.4	11%	25%	13%	12%	11.1%	94.2	34	16	50	30%	71%	11%	8%	10						-0.9	71	-$3

JOCK THOMPSON

Smyly,Drew

Age: 35	Th: L	Role RP	Health D	LIMA Plan B
Ht: 6' 2"	Wt: 188	Type Pwr/FB	PT/Exp A	Rand Var 0
			Consist A	MM 2201

Stayed off the IL for first time since 2016, which just means that he can't blame injuries for this ERA explosion. Fatigue, maybe. Was pretty good in April/May before collapsing over summer. Settled down again in late-season relief role (34% K% in Sept), which may provide a path to extend career... but probably not his relevance to us.

Yr	Tm	W	Sv	IP	K	ERA	WHIP	xERA	xWHIP	vL+	vR+	BF/G	BB%	K%	K-BB%	xBB%	SwK	Vel	G	L	F	H%	S%	HR/F	xHR/F	GS	APC	DOM%	DIS%	Sv%	LI	RAR	BPX	R$
19	2 TM	4	1	114	120	6.24	1.59	5.31	1.44	142	116	20.6	11%	23%	13%	9%	11.0%	91.2	33	22	45	32%	68%	21%	20%	21	85	19%	48%	100	0.73	-24.3	70	-$11
20	SF	0	0	26	42	3.42	1.10	2.97	1.03	37	96	15.9	8%	38%	30%	6%	15.1%	93.8	42	23	35	36%	70%	10%	18%	5	69	20%	20%	0	0.74	3.4	221	$1
21	ATL	11	0	127	117	4.48	1.37	4.55	1.29	117	105	18.8	8%	21%	14%	6%	12.1%	92.1	39	22	39	31%	76%	18%	16%	23	74	4%	26%	0	0.74	-3.3	97	$1
22	CHC	7	0	106	91	3.47	1.19	4.19	1.21	87	105	20.3	6%	20%	15%	5%	12.7%	92.6	40	18	42	29%	77%	12%	12%	22	82	18%	36%			6.5	107	$5
23	CHC	11	0	142	141	5.00	1.43	4.79	1.34	132	104	15.3	9%	23%	14%	8%	11.8%	92.0	35	21	44	32%	70%	14%	11%	23	59	9%	48%	0	0.75	-11.7	87	-$2
1st Half		7	0	86	71	3.96	1.29	5.00	1.34	116	99	23.0	7%	19%	12%	8%	10.4%	91.6	34	20	46	29%	74%	11%	8%	16	87	13%	44%			3.9	78	$9
2nd Half		4	0	56	70	6.59	1.64	4.45	1.35	150	114	10.3	11%	27%	16%	8%	13.8%	92.7	36	23	41	36%	65%	21%	15%	7	40	0%	57%	0	0.75	-15.6	103	-$5
Proj		**5**	**0**	**73**	**73**	**4.54**	**1.43**	**4.24**	**1.31**	**129**	**108**	**11.7**	**9%**	**24%**	**15%**	**8%**	**12.3%**	**92.1**	**37**	**21**	**42**	**32%**	**76%**	**17%**	**14%**	**4**						**-1.9**	**95**	**-$3**

Snell,Blake

Age: 31	Th: L	Role SP	Health D	LIMA Plan C
Ht: 6' 4"	Wt: 225	Type Pwr	PT/Exp A	Rand Var -5
			Consist A	MM 4503

As unusual a season as you'll ever see. Skills-wise, nearly a carbon copy of 2021, just with absurd hit/strand% help. Usually high S% comes with fluky-low HR/F, but not here; obviously this level of S% is unsustainable. And the IP total should be treated as every bit the same. 2022 should be your bid-level baseline.

Yr	Tm	W	Sv	IP	K	ERA	WHIP	xERA	xWHIP	vL+	vR+	BF/G	BB%	K%	K-BB%	xBB%	SwK	Vel	G	L	F	H%	S%	HR/F	xHR/F	GS	APC	DOM%	DIS%	Sv%	LI	RAR	BPX	R$
19	TAM	6	0	107	147	4.29	1.27	3.49	1.16	118	89	19.2	9%	33%	24%	7%	18.2%	95.6	39	25	36	35%	70%	15%	11%	23	82	26%	48%			2.8	162	$5
20	TAM	4	0	50	63	3.24	1.20	3.27	1.17	96	98	18.5	9%	31%	22%	9%	15.6%	95.1	49	23	28	29%	84%	29%	22%	11	79	9%	27%			7.5	162	$13
21	SD	7	0	129	170	4.20	1.32	3.85	1.31	63	101	20.4	13%	31%	18%	10%	13.4%	95.2	40	23	37	31%	71%	14%	19%	27	87	26%	37%			1.1	112	$4
22	SD	8	0	128	171	3.38	1.20	3.41	1.15	91	89	22.3	10%	32%	22%	8%	15.2%	95.9	37	21	43	33%	74%	8%	10%	24	98	21%	13%			9.4	148	$10
23	SD	14	0	180	234	2.25	1.19	3.62	1.35	88	78	23.2	13%	32%	18%	12%	15.6%	95.6	44	21	34	27%	85%	11%	14%	32	99	25%	13%			46.2	111	$31
1st Half		4	0	87	114	3.21	1.21	3.58	1.28	105	85	22.6	12%	31%	20%	12%	15.0%	95.2	41	24	35	28%	79%	15%	18%	16	97	19%	19%			12.1	129	$16
2nd Half		10	0	93	120	1.35	1.17	3.66	1.42	67	72	23.8	15%	32%	17%	12%	16.3%	96.0	48	19	33	25%	90%	6%	11%	16	101	31%	6%			34.1	97	$37
Proj		**11**	**0**	**145**	**190**	**3.30**	**1.24**	**3.36**	**1.28**	**85**	**87**	**21.2**	**12%**	**32%**	**20%**	**11%**	**15.3%**	**95.5**	**43**	**22**	**35**	**29%**	**77%**	**13%**	**15%**	**28**						**18.3**	**125**	**$14**

Soriano,José

Age: 25	Th: R	Role RP	Health D	LIMA Plan B
Ht: 6' 3"	Wt: 168	Type Pwr	PT/Exp F	Rand Var 0
			Consist F	MM 4411

1-3, 3.64 ERA in 42 IP at LAA. Reached majors in June, completing recovery from dual Tommy John surgeries in 2020-21. Those layoffs account for the lack of high-minors data, and give some hope that the evident control issues can be tamed with a little more experience. The Vel, SwK%, and GB% are a starter kit for an impact reliever.

Yr	Tm	W	Sv	IP	K	ERA	WHIP	xERA	xWHIP	vL+	vR+	BF/G	BB%	K%	K-BB%	xBB%	SwK	Vel	G	L	F	H%	S%	HR/F	xHR/F	GS	APC	DOM%	DIS%	Sv%	LI	RAR	BPX	R$
19																																		
20																																		
21																																		
22																																		
23	LAA *	1	1	66	82	4.03	1.40	3.63	1.33	58	117	5.1	12%	30%	18%	9%	15.2%	97.7	51	21	28	32%	72%	15%	19%	0	18			50	1.09	2.5	112	-$
1st Half		0	1	36	46	3.85	1.30	2.59	1.45	69	41	5.6	15%	30%	15%	10%	14.0%	97.9	58	21	21	29%	69%	0%	1%	0	19			100	0.82	2.2	132	-$
2nd Half		1	0	30	36	4.25	1.52	3.95	1.38	55	145	4.9	12%	26%	15%	8%	15.7%	97.7	49	22	29	34%	76%	17%	22%	0	18			0	1.18	0.3	105	-$
Proj		**3**	**1**	**65**	**80**	**3.85**	**1.44**	**3.57**	**1.39**	**57**	**137**	**4.9**	**14%**	**29%**	**15%**	**9%**	**15.7%**	**97.7**	**49**	**22**	**29**	**33%**	**75%**	**14%**	**20%**	**0**						**3.8**	**98**	**-$**

Soroka,Michael

Age: 26	Th: R	Role SP	Health F	LIMA Plan A+
Ht: 6' 5"	Wt: 225	Type Con	PT/Exp D	Rand Var +5
			Consist D	MM 3101

2-2, 6.40 ERA in 32 IP at ATL. Finally completed journey back from August 2020 Achilles' tear that included a complete re-tear of the same tendon in May 2021. Results in majors weren't good, but Triple-A work was credible given the long layoff. Forearm inflammation ended season in early Sept, so it's another winter of health questions.

Yr	Tm	W	Sv	IP	K	ERA	WHIP	xERA	xWHIP	vL+	vR+	BF/G	BB%	K%	K-BB%	xBB%	SwK	Vel	G	L	F	H%	S%	HR/F	xHR/F	GS	APC	DOM%	DIS%	Sv%	LI	RAR	BPX	R$
19	ATL	13	0	175	142	2.68	1.11	3.87	1.27	99	72	24.2	6%	20%	14%	6%	10.7%	92.5	51	23	25	28%	79%	11%	12%	29	88	34%	17%			39.3	113	$2
20	ATL	0	0	14	8	3.95	1.32	4.60	1.64	100	55	19.0	12%	14%	2%	8%	10.6%	92.1	61	24	15	26%	67%	0%	12%	3	66	0%	33%			0.8	11	-$
21																																		
22	aaa	0	0	21	14	8.22	1.51	5.71				18.2	8%	15%	8%							31%	45%									-11.0	29	-$
23	ATL *	6	0	119	106	4.58	1.27	4.09	1.36	114	138	20.3	8%	20%	12%	8%	9.9%	92.9	45	20	35	29%	67%	26%	19%	6	77	0%	67%	0	0.72	-3.7	83	$
1st Half		4	0	71	56	4.43	1.31	4.17	1.39	127	129	20.9	8%	19%	10%	8%	9.2%	93.0	55	16	29	29%	68%	33%	21%	3	87	0%	67%			-0.9	72	$
2nd Half		2	0	51	50	4.57	1.15	3.65	1.23	102	148	20.2	7%	25%	17%	10%	10.5%	92.8	34	26	40	28%	63%	21%	17%	3	69	0%	67%	0	0.65	-1.5	105	$
Proj		**4**	**0**	**87**	**73**	**4.15**	**1.24**	**3.88**	**1.28**	**97**	**106**	**22.5**	**7%**	**21%**	**14%**	**8%**	**10.1%**	**92.8**	**44**	**22**	**34**	**30%**	**69%**	**12%**	**16%**	**16**						**1.9**	**100**	**$**

Soto,Gregory

Age: 29	Th: L	Role RP	Health A	LIMA Plan A+
Ht: 6' 1"	Wt: 234	Type Pwr	PT/Exp A	Rand Var +3
			Consist A	MM 3311

Nothing is at it seems: ERA spiked? Yes, but that was primarily caused by strand rate silliness. Skills surged? Also yes, but that was because moving out of closer role in DET to setup role in PHI, he faced a much higher percentage of lefty batters, who he has a long history of dominating. Moral: How these guys get used is important.

Yr	Tm	W	Sv	IP	K	ERA	WHIP	xERA	xWHIP	vL+	vR+	BF/G	BB%	K%	K-BB%	xBB%	SwK	Vel	G	L	F	H%	S%	HR/F	xHR/F	GS	APC	DOM%	DIS%	Sv%	LI	RAR	BPX	R$
19	DET *	0	0	96	78	6.28	1.77	6.30	1.63	89	129	10.5	12%	18%	6%	9%	8.5%	95.4	48	19	34	35%	66%	14%	18%	7	34	0%	86%	0	0.67	-21.0	33	-$1
20	DET	0	2	23	29	4.30	1.26	3.62	1.37	54	90	3.6	13%	30%	16%	11%	11.4%	97.3	54	20	26	28%	67%	14%	13%	0	15			67	0.69	0.4	112	-$
21	DET	6	18	64	76	3.39	1.35	4.35	1.46	68	93	4.5	14%	28%	13%	8%	13.5%	98.3	45	18	37	27%	78%	12%	12%	0	18			95	1.49	6.9	70	$1
22	DET	2	30	60	60	3.28	1.38	4.22	1.47	107	89	4.1	13%	23%	10%	9%	11.7%	98.4	48	16	36	30%	75%	3%	9%	0	17			91	1.42	5.1	55	$1
23	PHI	3	3	60	65	4.62	1.14	3.76	1.27	58	99	3.6	9%	26%	17%	6%	15.8%	98.3	51	13	35	28%	60%	11%	8%	0	14			50	1.13	-2.2	129	$
1st Half		2	1	31	35	4.31	1.12	3.84	1.33	44	92	3.6	11%	27%	16%	8%	15.3%	98.1	51	12	38	26%	61%	7%	6%	0	15			100	1.24	0.1	114	-$
2nd Half		1	2	29	30	4.97	1.17	3.67	1.20	74	107	3.7	7%	25%	18%	5%	16.5%	98.7	52	15	33	30%	60%	15%	11%	0	13			40	1.00	-2.3	147	-$
Proj		**4**	**3**	**73**	**77**	**3.82**	**1.30**	**3.82**	**1.36**	**71**	**100**	**4.0**	**11%**	**26%**	**14%**	**8%**	**13.8%**	**98.1**	**49**	**15**	**36**	**29%**	**73%**	**11%**	**11%**	**0**						**4.5**	**96**	**$**

Speier,Gabe

Age: 29	Th: L	Role RP	Health B	LIMA Plan A+
Ht: 5' 11"	Wt: 200	Type Pwr/xGB	PT/Exp D	Rand Var +3
			Consist F	MM 5310

Finally got off the Triple-A shuttle with a full year in the majors, and skills say he belongs. Velocity gains were key, as they carried over to slider (45% SwK%). Still looking for an answer vR, which precludes him from save opps, but heavy GB tilt, xBB%, elite 2nd half K%/SwK% all confirm he can stop looking at apartments in Triple-A towns.

Yr	Tm	W	Sv	IP	K	ERA	WHIP	xERA	xWHIP	vL+	vR+	BF/G	BB%	K%	K-BB%	xBB%	SwK	Vel	G	L	F	H%	S%	HR/F	xHR/F	GS	APC	DOM%	DIS%	Sv%	LI	RAR	BPX	R$
19	KC *	1	6	70	69	5.88	1.59	6.04	1.64	124	87	5.6	11%	22%	11%	9%	11.1%	94.5	25	6	69	33%	68%	18%	21%	0	17			75	1.03	-12.0	40	-$
20	KC	0	0	6	6	7.94	2.29	5.59	1.57	25	187	3.8	13%	20%	7%	12%	9.0%	92.1	45	35	20	44%	67%	25%	12%	0	15			0	0.33	-2.4	26	-$1
21	KC *	3	5	54	48	3.05	1.33	4.54	1.10	51	112	4.3	4%	22%	17%	6%	10.5%	93.8	44	26	30	36%	80%	0%	0%	0	15			71	0.64	8.1	144	$
22	KC *	1	0	49	40	9.06	1.84	8.08	1.28	97	84	4.7	7%	18%	11%	10%	7.7%	93.7	46	14	40	39%	52%	9%	7%	1	18	0%	0%	0	0.72	-30.5	24	-$1
23	SEA	2	1	55	64	3.79	1.06	2.73	1.05	72	107	3.1	5%	30%	25%	5%	15.6%	94.6	56	19	25	31%	69%	21%	20%	0	11			100	0.99	3.7	196	$
1st Half		2	0	29	27	4.08	0.98	2.92	1.09	62	102	3.0	4%	25%	21%	4%	12.8%	94.4	57	18	25	29%	58%	11%	16%	0	11			0	0.92	0.9	173	-$
2nd Half		0	1	26	37	3.46	1.15	2.51	1.02	80	116	3.2	7%	35%	28%	5%	18.4%	95.0	55	20	25	33%	80%	33%	25%	0	12			100	1.06	2.8	224	-$
Proj		**2**	**2**	**58**	**64**	**3.63**	**1.17**	**2.87**	**1.11**	**78**	**109**	**3.6**	**6%**	**28%**	**22%**	**5%**	**16.3%**	**94.7**	**56**	**19**	**25**	**32%**	**73%**	**18%**	**21%**	**0**						**5.0**	**172**	**$**

Springs,Jeffrey

Age: 31	Th: L	Role SP	Health F	LIMA Plan A+
Ht: 6' 3"	Wt: 218	Type Pwr	PT/Exp A	Rand Var -5
			Consist B	MM 4400

April Tommy John surgery puts his return timeline into second half, assuming no setbacks. Workload restrictions will likely preclude any meaningful value in 2024, so will have to wait until 2025 to realize the "mid-rotation value" we called for a year ago.

Yr	Tm	W	Sv	IP	K	ERA	WHIP	xERA	xWHIP	vL+	vR+	BF/G	BB%	K%	K-BB%	xBB%	SwK	Vel	G	L	F	H%	S%	HR/F	xHR/F	GS	APC	DOM%	DIS%	Sv%	LI	RAR	BPX	R$
19	TEX	4	0	32	32	6.40	1.89	6.56	1.70	120	116	6.2	15%	21%	6%	9%	12.6%	92.1	23	31	45	36%	67%	9%	8%	0	27			0	0.49	-7.6	-13	-$
20	BOS	0	0	20	28	7.08	1.82	4.18	1.16	122	138	6.2	7%	28%	21%	7%	17.0%	92.1	35	29	35	46%	66%	23%	25%	0	25			0	0.75	-6.6	172	-$
21	TAM	5	2	45	63	3.43	1.10	3.22	1.05	117	87	4.2	8%	35%	27%	7%	16.5%	93.4	34	23	42	29%	80%	21%	14%	0	17			50	1.07	4.6	180	$
22	TAM	9	0	135	144	2.46	1.07	3.48	1.10	107	82	16.6	6%	26%	21%	6%	14.1%	91.5	41	20	40	30%	82%	10%	10%	25	65	12%	8%	0	0.89	25.2	150	$
23	TAM	2	0	16	24	0.56	0.50	2.01	0.89	35	41	18.3	7%	44%	37%	4%	15.6%	91.7	50	15	35	12%	100%	11%	8%	3	70	67%	0%			7.4	236	$
1st Half		2	0	16	24	0.56	0.50	2.01	0.90	35	41	18.3	7%	44%	36%	4%	15.6%	91.7	50	15	35	12%	100%	11%	8%	3	70	67%	0%			7.4	237	$
2nd Half																																		
Proj		**6**	**0**	**58**	**72**	**3.55**	**1.15**	**3.30**	**1.17**	**99**	**84**	**21.1**	**9%**	**32%**	**22%**	**6%**	**14.4%**	**92.0**	**39**	**22**	**40**	**30%**	**73%**	**12%**	**10%**	**11**						**5.6**	**145**	**$**

RAY MURPHY

Steele,Justin

Age: 28	Th: L	Role SP	Health D	LIMA Plan C+
Ht: 6' 2"	Wt: 205	Type Pwr	PT/Exp A	Rand Var -1
			Consist A	MM 4205

Carried over second-half '22 BB% gains, answered workload questions and graduated to ace status. Secret to BB% improvement was just ditching all of his lesser offerings; he's fastball/slider only now. That combo carves up righties, struggles vL look fluky (30% K% vL). Expect R$ to backslide as Wins and ERA normalize, but the skills are legit.

Yr	Tm	W	Sv	IP	K	ERA	WHIP	xERA	xWHIP	vL+	vR+	BF/G	BB%	K%	K-BB%	xBB%	SwK	Vel	G	L	F	H%	S%	HR/F	xHR/F	GS	APC	DOM%	DIS%	Sv%	LI	RAR	BPX	R$
19	aa	0	0	40	35	7.70	1.99	6.92				17.6	12%	18%	6%							40%	60%									-15.8	44	-$13
20																																		
21	CHC *	6	0	85	82	3.33	1.25	3.84	1.38	65	112	11.9	12%	24%	12%	9%	11.8%	93.1	50	20	30	25%	80%	26%	14%	9	48	11%	67%	0	0.90	9.9	71	$4
22	CHC	4	0	119	126	3.18	1.35	3.56	1.30	88	94	21.3	10%	25%	15%	8%	10.7%	92.1	51	21	28	33%	78%	9%	9%	24	85	29%	25%			11.6	108	$3
23	CHC	16	0	173	176	3.06	1.17	3.45	1.14	106	87	23.9	5%	25%	20%	5%	12.0%	91.8	49	22	29	33%	76%	10%	10%	30	89	33%	17%			27.1	158	$23
1st Half		9	0	85	76	2.43	1.03	3.69	1.21	76	83	22.7	6%	22%	17%	6%	11.7%	92.0	51	16	33	29%	76%	4%	7%	15	84	47%	13%			20.1	135	$28
2nd Half		7	0	88	100	3.68	1.31	3.21	1.09	139	92	25.0	5%	27%	22%	5%	12.3%	91.7	48	27	25	37%	76%	17%	13%	15	95	20%	20%			7.1	184	$16
Proj		**12**	**0**	**174**	**175**	**3.65**	**1.23**	**3.41**	**1.22**	**94**	**92**	**23.6**	**8%**	**25%**	**17%**	**6%**	**11.8%**	**92.2**	**50**	**22**	**29**	**31%**	**73%**	**13%**	**11%**	**30**						**14.6**	**131**	**$13**

Stephan,Trevor

Age: 28	Th: R	Role RP	Health A	LIMA Plan A+
Ht: 6' 5"	Wt: 225	Type Pwr/FB	PT/Exp B	Rand Var -1
			Consist C	MM 3311

Gave back 2022's skills breakout (Vel, SwK). Still managed to maintain elite results through 1st half, but then it all unraveled in 2nd half. Such small-sample variance comes with the territory for relievers, and half-season BPX tells us no need to react to that. But slippage off that 2022 BPX peak puts him back in the "good, not great" bucket.

Yr	Tm	W	Sv	IP	K	ERA	WHIP	xERA	xWHIP	vL+	vR+	BF/G	BB%	K%	K-BB%	xBB%	SwK	Vel	G	L	F	H%	S%	HR/F	xHR/F	GS	APC	DOM%	DIS%	Sv%	LI	RAR	BPX	R$
19	aa	2	0	47	48	7.13	1.92	6.51				18.6	12%	21%	9%							41%	62%									-15.3	62	-$11
20																																		
21	CLE	3	1	63	75	4.41	1.41	4.60	1.33	103	111	6.6	11%	27%	16%	8%	13.4%	96.2	33	22	45	29%	78%	19%	17%	0	28			100	0.57	-1.1	92	-$3
22	CLE	6	3	64	82	2.69	1.18	2.93	1.06	104	78	4.0	7%	31%	24%	6%	16.7%	96.6	48	19	33	36%	78%	6%	6%	0	16			60	1.22	10.1	183	$6
23	CLE	7	2	69	75	4.06	1.30	4.16	1.28	89	103	4.1	9%	26%	17%	8%	14.4%	95.0	42	17	41	32%	70%	8%	14%	0	16			20	1.31	2.3	118	$2
1st Half		4	2	36	39	2.75	1.33	4.39	1.27	90	119	4.1	8%	25%	17%	8%	13.6%	94.8	38	16	45	32%	88%	13%	13%	0	16			29	1.45	7.0	117	$4
2nd Half		3	0	33	36	5.51	1.26	3.90	1.29	89	87	4.2	9%	26%	17%	9%	15.4%	95.1	45	19	36	33%	51%	0%	15%	0	16			0	1.15	-4.7	119	-$1
Proj		**6**	**3**	**65**	**74**	**3.86**	**1.27**	**3.73**	**1.27**	**92**	**97**	**4.7**	**10%**	**28%**	**18%**	**8%**	**14.6%**	**95.5**	**41**	**19**	**40**	**31%**	**72%**	**11%**	**14%**	**0**						**3.7**	**116**	**$3**

Stephenson,Robert

Age: 31	Th: R	Role RP	Health D	LIMA Plan A
Ht: 6' 3"	Wt: 205	Type Pwr/xFB	PT/Exp C	Rand Var -1
			Consist B	MM 5520

Latest creation from the Tampa pitching lab: Rays acquired him from Pirates in June, shelved his splitter for a brand-new cutter that he immediately started throwing 70+% of the time. And why throw anything else when batters hit .101 against the cutter? A free agent this winter, his landing spot determines likelihood of... UP: 25 Sv.

Yr	Tm	W	Sv	IP	K	ERA	WHIP	xERA	xWHIP	vL+	vR+	BF/G	BB%	K%	K-BB%	xBB%	SwK	Vel	G	L	F	H%	S%	HR/F	xHR/F	GS	APC	DOM%	DIS%	Sv%	LI	RAR	BPX	R$
19	CIN	3	0	65	81	3.76	1.04	4.03	1.22	100	72	4.6	9%	31%	22%	6%	19.6%	95.0	32	22	46	25%	69%	13%	8%	0	18			0	0.96	6.0	134	$4
20	CIN	0	0	10	13	9.90	1.40	4.54	1.13	170	168	4.3	7%	30%	23%	5%	18.8%	94.8	23	15	62	16%	50%	50%	27%	0	18			0	0.45	-6.7	157	-$10
21	COL	2	1	46	52	3.13	1.30	4.10	1.26	102	94	4.0	9%	26%	17%	6%	12.3%	96.5	38	24	38	32%	80%	11%	13%	0	16			50	0.76	6.4	114	-$1
22	2 NL	2	0	58	55	5.43	1.33	4.33	1.17	112	119	4.3	6%	22%	17%	5%	14.2%	96.9	29	24	47	33%	63%	12%	12%	0	16			0	0.67	-10.5	112	-$6
23	2 TM	3	1	52	77	3.10	0.88	3.03	1.01	99	66	3.4	8%	38%	30%	4%	24.9%	96.9	35	18	48	24%	74%	16%	16%	0	13			17	1.19	8.0	199	$7
1st Half		1	0	26	33	4.56	1.29	4.14	1.31	107	87	3.5	12%	31%	19%	5%	19.1%	96.9	32	23	45	29%	69%	14%	17%	0	13			0	1.11	-0.7	108	-$6
2nd Half		2	1	27	44	1.69	0.49	2.13	0.71	90	44	3.2	3%	47%	44%	4%	31.7%	96.9	38	11	51	16%	89%	17%	15%	0	12			25	1.27	8.7	289	$9
Proj		**3**	**12**	**58**	**76**	**2.93**	**0.95**	**2.92**	**0.99**	**100**	**78**	**3.5**	**6%**	**35%**	**29%**	**5%**	**19.8%**	**96.6**	**35**	**20**	**46**	**28%**	**77%**	**14%**	**14%**	**0**						**10.0**	**191**	**$11**

Stewart,Brock

Age: 32	Th: R	Role RP	Health F	LIMA Plan A+
Ht: 6' 3"	Wt: 215	Type Pwr/FB	PT/Exp F	Rand Var -5
			Consist F	MM 5510

Finally made it back from 2021 Tommy John surgery, complete with a massive Vel spike and eye-popping SwK. That brief taste looks enticing, but the story in this box remains the white space: his return lasted only 29 innings before missing three more months with elbow soreness. For now, he's the fun-to-drive sports car that's always in for repairs.

Yr	Tm	W	Sv	IP	K	ERA	WHIP	xERA	xWHIP	vL+	vR+	BF/G	BB%	K%	K-BB%	xBB%	SwK	Vel	G	L	F	H%	S%	HR/F	xHR/F	GS	APC	DOM%	DIS%	Sv%	LI	RAR	BPX	R$
19	2 TM *	10	0	111	74	10.43	2.18	10.41	1.42	152	144	17.3	10%	13%	3%	8%	9.5%	91.6	36	18	46	38%	56%	26%	20%	0	37			0	0.53	-80.9	-59	-$36
20																																		
21																																		
22																																		
23	MIN	2	1	28	39	0.65	1.08	3.19	1.13	71	78	3.9	10%	36%	26%	5%	20.7%	97.2	37	21	42	32%	97%	4%	6%	0	16			33	1.15	12.6	165	$2
1st Half		2	1	26	35	0.70	1.01	3.32	1.18	77	69	4.0	11%	35%	24%	6%	20.8%	97.2	35	20	45	27%	96%	4%	7%	0	16			33	1.24	11.5	147	$5
2nd Half		0	0	2	4	0.00	2.00	1.72			158	3.3	0%	40%	40%	4%	19.6%	97.2	50	33	17	71%	100%	0%	0%	0	15			0	0.34	1.1	397	-$7
Proj		**4**	**2**	**51**	**75**	**3.52**	**1.26**	**3.06**	**1.11**	**112**	**110**	**5.8**	**10%**	**36%**	**26%**	**6%**	**20.8%**	**97.2**	**35**	**20**	**45**	**36%**	**76%**	**12%**	**10%**	**0**						**5.1**	**173**	**$2**

Stone,Gavin

Age: 25	Th: R	Role SP	Health A	LIMA Plan B
Ht: 6' 1"	Wt: 175	Type	PT/Exp D	Rand Var +5
			Consist F	MM 3201

1-1, 9.00 ERA in 31 IP at LA. Compiled enough frequent flier miles between Triple-A and MLB to earn reward ticket. Average fastball, not enough to get hitters out consistently. Change-up is workhorse offering with fade and late sudden drop; it's a plus-plus pitch. Slider regressed with addition of cutter; one must emerge to stay as a starter. (CB)

Yr	Tm	W	Sv	IP	K	ERA	WHIP	xERA	xWHIP	vL+	vR+	BF/G	BB%	K%	K-BB%	xBB%	SwK	Vel	G	L	F	H%	S%	HR/F	xHR/F	GS	APC	DOM%	DIS%	Sv%	LI	RAR	BPX	R$
19																																		
20																																		
21																																		
22	a/a	8	0	98	117	1.29	1.06	1.99				19.1	8%	31%	22%							31%	88%									32.5	166	$17
23	LA *	8	1	133	122	5.95	1.49	5.29	1.49	123	147	19.8	9%	14%	6%	7%	14.8%	94.3	46	23	31	32%	62%	23%	14%	4	69	0%	75%	100	0.69	-26.5	59	-$11
1st Half		2	0	65	59	8.15	1.89	7.18	1.53	129	195	20.5	12%	19%	8%	8%	15.4%	93.7	39	35	26	38%	57%	8%	8%	3	71	0%	67%			-30.7	33	-$30
2nd Half		6	1	68	64	3.84	1.11	3.49	1.27	118	126	19.1	8%	23%	15%	7%	14.4%	94.7	50	15	35	26%	71%	30%	18%	1	67	0%	100%	100	0.65	4.2	95	$14
Proj		**6**	**0**	**87**	**81**	**4.43**	**1.27**	**3.79**	**1.32**	**102**	**98**	**20.2**	**9%**	**23%**	**14%**	**7%**	**14.4%**	**94.7**	**50**	**15**	**35**	**29%**	**68%**	**14%**	**16%**	**18**						**-1.1**	**100**	**$0**

Strahm,Matt

Age: 32	Th: L	Role RP	Health D	LIMA Plan B+
Ht: 6' 2"	Wt: 190	Type Pwr/xFB	PT/Exp C	Rand Var -1
			Consist B	MM 4311

Another win for the pitching labs, as he ditched his curve for a new slider, which was effective both vL and vR, driving big SwK% and K-BB% gains. Good health as the other key to this revival, as he was able to get back to his do-anything swingman profile. That's got value in real life, and makes for a nice last-guy-on-the-staff in our world as well.

Yr	Tm	W	Sv	IP	K	ERA	WHIP	xERA	xWHIP	vL+	vR+	BF/G	BB%	K%	K-BB%	xBB%	SwK	Vel	G	L	F	H%	S%	HR/F	xHR/F	GS	APC	DOM%	DIS%	Sv%	LI	RAR	BPX	R$
19	SD	6	0	115	118	4.71	1.25	4.26	1.16	106	105	10.6	5%	24%	20%	4%	11.1%	91.5	37	23	41	33%	69%	16%	17%	16	39	13%	25%	0	0.90	-2.9	147	$2
20	SD	0	0	21	15	2.61	0.87	4.19	1.25	57	116	4.4	5%	18%	13%	7%	9.1%	92.9	44	20	36	20%	80%	14%	16%	0	16			0	1.12	4.7	105	$1
21	SD	0	0	7	4	8.10	2.40	5.36	1.28	138	144	6.0	3%	11%	8%	4%	11.0%	93.2	48	31	21	50%	63%	0%	2%	1	23	0%	100%	0	0.41	-3.2	95	-$8
22	BOS	4	4	45	52	3.83	1.23	3.86	1.21	99	92	3.9	9%	27%	18%	6%	10.5%	94.2	37	18	45	31%	72%	9%	11%	0	15			44	1.30	0.8	122	$1
23	PHI	9	2	88	108	3.29	1.02	3.60	1.07	75	92	6.3	6%	31%	25%	5%	13.4%	93.4	33	20	47	29%	73%	11%	10%	10	24	20%	20%	40	1.02	11.3	171	$13
1st Half		4	1	52	68	3.78	1.03	3.45	1.05	88	94	8.8	6%	32%	26%	6%	13.6%	93.3	33	21	46	29%	70%	14%	13%	9	35	22%	22%	33	0.90	3.5	182	$9
2nd Half		5	1	35	40	2.55	0.99	3.81	1.10	59	90	4.4	6%	29%	23%	4%	13.0%	93.6	33	19	48	29%	78%	7%	7%	1	17	0%	0%	50	1.10	7.8	158	$10
Proj		**8**	**2**	**87**	**100**	**3.59**	**1.10**	**3.42**	**1.09**	**85**	**95**	**5.6**	**6%**	**29%**	**23%**	**5%**	**12.3%**	**93.1**	**35**	**20**	**45**	**30%**	**73%**	**12%**	**12%**	**0**						**7.9**	**157**	**$9**

Stratton,Chris

Age: 33	Th: R	Role RP	Health B	LIMA Plan A+
Ht: 6' 2"	Wt: 205	Type Pwr/FB	PT/Exp B	Rand Var -2
			Consist A	MM 3211

Volatility is the norm for RPs, but this veteran is a rare source of stability: ERAs, xERAs live in a very narrow range. Managers (five in last three years!) got the memo, as LI is similarly consistent in a "I trust you, unless there's someone better available" way. SwK% erosion, FB% spike remind us this stability can't last forever, though.

Yr	Tm	W	Sv	IP	K	ERA	WHIP	xERA	xWHIP	vL+	vR+	BF/G	BB%	K%	K-BB%	xBB%	SwK	Vel	G	L	F	H%	S%	HR/F	xHR/F	GS	APC	DOM%	DIS%	Sv%	LI	RAR	BPX	R$
19	2 TM	1	0	76	69	5.57	1.66	5.16	1.44	117	115	9.8	10%	20%	10%	8%	10.8%	92.2	40	26	34	36%	70%	16%	10%	5	39	0%	60%	0	0.53	-9.9	65	-$9
20	PIT	2	0	30	39	3.90	1.30	3.76	1.24	82	93	4.9	10%	30%	20%	8%	15.7%	93.3	47	22	32	34%	72%	12%	16%	0	20			0	1.28	2.0	147	$2
21	PIT	7	8	79	86	3.63	1.30	4.20	1.30	103	82	5.0	10%	26%	16%	8%	12.7%	93.0	41	21	38	31%	76%	11%	11%	0	20			62	0.90	6.2	103	$7
22	2 NL	10	2	63	60	4.26	1.53	4.17	1.32	129	96	4.7	9%	22%	13%	8%	11.9%	92.9	44	21	35	36%	72%	6%	11%	1	18	0%	0%	29	1.08	-2.3	88	-$1
23	2 TM	2	1	83	81	3.92	1.14	4.31	1.25	80	93	5.3	7%	24%	17%	6%	9.9%	93.2	39	16	46	29%	67%	8%	11%	0	21			33	1.02	4.2	115	$3
1st Half		1	0	40	42	4.73	1.20	4.20	1.22	85	100	5.7	7%	25%	18%	6%	10.4%	93.0	38	17	46	32%	60%	6%	12%	0	23			0	0.75	-1.9	127	-$5
2nd Half		1	1	43	39	3.16	1.08	4.42	1.28	75	88	4.9	8%	23%	15%	7%	9.5%	93.4	40	15	45	26%	76%	9%	9%	0	20			50	1.24	6.1	103	$3
Proj		**4**	**2**	**73**	**74**	**3.93**	**1.27**	**3.90**	**1.27**	**96**	**93**	**5.0**	**9%**	**25%**	**16%**	**8%**	**11.4%**	**93.1**	**41**	**19**	**40**	**31%**	**71%**	**9%**	**11%**	**0**						**3.6**	**109**	**$1**

RAY MURPHY

Strider,Spencer

Age: 25 | Th: R | Role: SP | Ht: 6' 0" | Wt: 195 | Type: Pwr
Health: A | PT/Exp: A | Consist: C
LIMA Plan: C+ | Rand Var: +2 | MM: 5505

BPX rates this as a carbon copy of his 2022 coming-out party, although ERA suffered at the hands of the H%- S%- HR/F trifecta. Can't give him a complete pass on that: sample of high-H% years is accumulating, and new FB tilt means HR issues could linger. Best news is that he answered durability questions. Buy for the Ks, expect ERAs in mid-3.00s.

Yr Tm	W	Sv	IP	K	ERA	WHIP	xERA	xWHIP	vL+	vR+	BF/G	BB%	K%	K-BB%	xBB%	SwK	Vel	G	L	F	H%	S%	HR/F	xHR/F	GS	APC	DOM%	DIS%	Sv%	LI	RAR	BPX	R$
19																																	
20																																	
21 ATL *	4	0	66	81	5.90	1.38	4.21		138	66	16.4	11%	29%	18%		13.2%	97.9	25	13	63	33%	57%	20%	4%	0	19			0	1.05	-13.3	105	-$6
22 ATL	11	0	132	202	2.67	0.99	2.60	1.01	78	69	17.0	9%	38%	30%	6%	16.4%	98.2	40	23	37	32%	74%	7%	10%	20	73	35%	10%	0	0.82	21.2	202	$22
23 ATL	20	0	187	281	3.86	1.09	3.10	1.02	89	83	23.8	8%	37%	29%	5%	19.5%	97.3	34	22	44	34%	68%	12%	11%	32	97	50%	16%			10.9	202	$29
1st Half	10	0	98	155	3.66	1.11	3.07	1.01	89	85	23.6	8%	39%	30%	5%	20.2%	97.1	33	20	47	34%	72%	13%	13%	17	100	47%	12%			8.1	209	$29
2nd Half	10	0	88	126	4.08	1.08	3.13	1.03	89	82	24.1	7%	35%	28%	5%	18.8%	97.5	35	24	40	33%	64%	11%	9%	15	94	53%	20%			2.8	198	$26
Proj	**16**	**0**	**181**	**262**	**3.60**	**1.10**	**2.87**	**1.06**	**92**	**84**	**23.2**	**9%**	**37%**	**28%**	**6%**	**18.7%**	**97.5**	**36**	**23**	**42**	**32%**	**70%**	**13%**	**10%**	**31**						**16.2**	**182**	**$25**

Stripling,Ross

Age: 34 | Th: R | Role: RP | Ht: 6' 1" | Wt: 215 | Type: Con
Health: F | PT/Exp: A | Consist: B
LIMA Plan: B | Rand Var: +4 | MM: 3101

We knew that 2022's ratios were out over his skis, but this level of regression was pure whiplash. Held the GB% and BB% gains from last year, but they were overshadowed by an avalanche of LD and HR. Two IL stints for back strain also remind us that health isn't a skill he owns, either. Just not a lot here you can rely on, in either skills or volume.

Yr Tm	W	Sv	IP	K	ERA	WHIP	xERA	xWHIP	vL+	vR+	BF/G	BB%	K%	K-BB%	xBB%	SwK	Vel	G	L	F	H%	S%	HR/F	xHR/F	GS	APC	DOM%	DIS%	Sv%	LI	RAR	BPX	R$
19 LA	4	0	91	93	3.47	1.15	3.66	1.16	93	92	11.6	5%	25%	20%	6%	10.6%	90.5	50	19	31	31%	74%	14%	14%	15	45	13%	27%	0	0.73	11.5	153	$6
20 2 TM	3	1	49	40	5.84	1.50	5.20	1.39	102	137	18.3	8%	18%	10%	7%	7.5%	91.7	40	24	36	30%	69%	23%	23%	9	68	11%	78%	100	0.69	-8.4	69	-$6
21 TOR	5	0	101	94	4.80	1.27	4.66	1.26	102	110	18.0	7%	22%	15%	8%	10.5%	91.9	36	20	45	28%	71%	17%	14%	19	70	11%	37%	0	0.73	-6.6	101	-$2
22 TOR	10	1	134	111	3.01	1.02	3.75	1.13	81	92	16.8	4%	21%	17%	5%	11.5%	91.6	44	17	39	28%	74%	8%	9%	24	64	13%	33%	100	0.98	15.8	132	$1
23 SF	0	0	80	70	6.36	1.35	4.25	1.23	114	109	17.3	4%	18%	14%	6%	10.7%	92.0	44	25	31	32%	67%	22%	21%	11	66	0%	55%	0	0.63	-11.3	119	-$8
1st Half	0	0	37	31	6.51	1.50	4.34	1.32	110	123	15.1	7%	19%	12%	8%	10.2%	91.8	47	26	27	32%	63%	30%	30%	6	60	0%	67%	0	0.58	-10.0	99	-$1
2nd Half	0	0	52	39	4.53	1.24	4.19	1.16	117	98	19.5	2%	18%	16%	5%	11.2%	92.2	42	24	34	31%	70%	17%	16%	5	73	0%	40%	0	0.68	-1.3	134	-$
Proj	**5**	**0**	**102**	**85**	**4.47**	**1.29**	**3.93**	**1.22**	**105**	**109**	**16.6**	**5%**	**20%**	**15%**	**6%**	**10.5%**	**91.8**	**42**	**22**	**35**	**30%**	**73%**	**19%**	**18%**	**17**						**-1.8**	**115**	**-$**

Stroman,Marcus

Age: 33 | Th: R | Role: SP | Ht: 5' 7" | Wt: 180 | Type: /GB
Health: F | PT/Exp: A | Consist: A
LIMA Plan: A | Rand Var: 0 | MM: 3103

August hip injury cost him six weeks, and probably trashed his 2nd half line even before he got shut down. First half was vintage, with copious GBs and just enough K%. Entire five-year scan now no longer shows a 4.00+ ERA in it, underscoring his value as a shock absorber for your rotation. Just beware the trend lines in IP, Vel and SwK.

Yr Tm	W	Sv	IP	K	ERA	WHIP	xERA	xWHIP	vL+	vR+	BF/G	BB%	K%	K-BB%	xBB%	SwK	Vel	G	L	F	H%	S%	HR/F	xHR/F	GS	APC	DOM%	DIS%	Sv%	LI	RAR	BPX	R$
19 2 TM	10	0	184	159	3.22	1.31	4.14	1.33	102	82	24.2	8%	21%	13%	9%	10.6%	92.5	54	20	26	31%	78%	13%	12%	32	95	25%	28%			29.2	104	$1
20																																	
21 NYM	10	0	179	158	3.02	1.15	3.65	1.21	89	88	22.1	6%	22%	16%	6%	11.9%	92.0	51	23	26	29%	77%	13%	16%	33	83	36%	30%			27.6	123	$1
22 CHC	6	0	139	119	3.50	1.15	3.53	1.22	102	86	22.8	6%	21%	15%	7%	9.8%	92.1	52	20	28	28%	73%	14%	13%	25	87	32%	20%			7.9	117	$
23 CHC	10	0	137	119	3.95	1.26	3.83	1.38	77	98	21.3	9%	21%	12%	9%	9.6%	91.6	57	21	22	29%	69%	10%	12%	25	82	24%	28%	0	0.81	6.4	94	$
1st Half	9	0	108	92	2.76	1.09	3.51	1.35	73	79	24.0	9%	21%	13%	8%	10.3%	91.6	60	20	20	26%	75%	8%	11%	18	90	33%	11%			20.9	104	$3
2nd Half	1	0	29	27	8.38	1.90	5.04	1.48	95	146	15.9	10%	19%	8%	11%	7.8%	91.5	50	24	27	40%	55%	15%	15%	7	65	0%	71%	0	0.88	-14.5	59	-$1
Proj	**10**	**0**	**152**	**135**	**3.78**	**1.28**	**3.68**	**1.33**	**86**	**100**	**22.2**	**9%**	**22%**	**13%**	**9%**	**9.7%**	**91.8**	**53**	**22**	**26**	**30%**	**73%**	**14%**	**14%**	**28**						**10.3**	**99**	**$**

Suárez,Ranger

Age: 28 | Th: L | Role: SP | Ht: 6' 1" | Wt: 217 | Type: /GB
Health: D | PT/Exp: A | Consist: A
LIMA Plan: B | Rand Var: 0 | MM: 3203

Elbow strain cost him first six weeks of season, August hamstring strain another couple of starts. He's not the same pitcher as he was in 2021: his sinker is still death to LH batters, vR column shows he hasn't found an answer for that side yet. He's been tweaking arsenal in attempt to solve that, and return to sub-4.00 ERA likely depends on it.

Yr Tm	W	Sv	IP	K	ERA	WHIP	xERA	xWHIP	vL+	vR+	BF/G	BB%	K%	K-BB%	xBB%	SwK	Vel	G	L	F	H%	S%	HR/F	xHR/F	GS	APC	DOM%	DIS%	Sv%	LI	RAR	BPX	R$
19 PHI *	8	0	87	70	4.69	1.40	5.37	1.26	75	110	8.3	6%	19%	13%	9%	10.0%	92.4	55	22	22	32%	72%	18%	17%	0	21			0	1.00	-2.0	64	$
20 PHI	0	0	4	1	20.25	3.50	11.55		152	187	8.7	15%	4%	-12%		8.5%	91.2	45	20	35	47%	38%	14%	13%	0	31			0	0.64	-7.8	-203	-$1
21 PHI	8	4	106	107	1.36	1.00	3.21	1.21	43	80	10.7	8%	26%	18%	8%	11.7%	93.2	59	15	26	26%	88%	6%	6%	12	41	42%	8%	57	1.01	38.0	137	$2
22 PHI	10	0	155	129	3.65	1.33	3.87	1.35	77	106	22.8	9%	19%	11%	8%	9.2%	92.8	55	17	27	30%	75%	12%	12%	29	88	21%	38%			6.1	85	$
23 PHI	4	0	125	119	4.18	1.42	4.20	1.35	83	106	24.5	9%	22%	13%	8%	9.6%	93.1	49	21	31	33%	73%	12%	13%	22	92	23%	32%			2.4	99	-$
1st Half	2	0	56	55	3.67	1.26	3.82	1.27	69	104	23.5	8%	23%	16%	9%	9.5%	93.2	50	20	30	32%	73%	10%	12%	10	93	30%	20%			4.6	122	$
2nd Half	2	0	69	64	4.59	1.54	4.52	1.41	96	109	25.4	10%	21%	11%	8%	9.7%	93.0	47	21	31	34%	72%	12%	11%	12	91	17%	42%			-2.2	79	-$
Proj	**9**	**0**	**160**	**149**	**4.09**	**1.30**	**3.66**	**1.31**	**71**	**102**	**23.3**	**9%**	**23%**	**14%**	**8%**	**10.1%**	**93.0**	**53**	**19**	**28**	**31%**	**70%**	**12%**	**10%**	**28**						**4.7**	**108**	**$**

Suarez,Robert

Age: 33 | Th: R | Role: RP | Ht: 6' 2" | Wt: 210 | Type:
Health: F | PT/Exp: B | Consist: C
LIMA Plan: B | Rand Var: 0 | MM: 3210

Elbow injury cost him entire first half, he returned mid-summer with base skills (Vel, SwK) seemingly intact, but obscured by a really weird H%- S%- HR/F combo. Sample size is sketchy, but GB% bump is a nice addition to this package if it sticks. On the other hand, health is now a concern, but if that checks out... UP: 25 Sv, still.

Yr Tm	W	Sv	IP	K	ERA	WHIP	xERA	xWHIP	vL+	vR+	BF/G	BB%	K%	K-BB%	xBB%	SwK	Vel	G	L	F	H%	S%	HR/F	xHR/F	GS	APC	DOM%	DIS%	Sv%	LI	RAR	BPX	R$
19 for	2	0	80	61	4.61	1.44	5.11				16.2	12%	18%	6%							26%	75%									-1.0	24	-$
20 for	3	25	52	47	2.79	1.19	2.81				4.1	11%	22%	11%							26%	78%									10.7	99	$4
21 for	1	42	62	55	1.44	0.85	1.19				3.7	4%	24%	20%							26%	81%									21.6	197	$2
22 SD	5	1	48	61	2.27	1.05	3.07	1.21	81	80	4.2	11%	32%	21%	8%	12.1%	97.7	43	22	35	25%	83%	11%	10%	0	18			25	1.35	10.0	134	$
23 SD	4	0	28	24	4.23	0.90	3.89	1.36	72	72	4.2	9%	22%	13%	7%	12.5%	97.6	49	22	30	17%	57%	18%	16%	0	17			0	1.28	0.4	89	$
1st Half																																	
2nd Half	4	0	28	24	4.23	0.90	3.89	1.36	72	73	4.2	9%	22%	13%	7%	12.5%	97.6	49	22	30	17%	57%	18%	16%	0	17			0	1.28	0.4	90	$
Proj	**5**	**7**	**58**	**55**	**3.56**	**1.16**	**3.65**	**1.29**	**89**	**88**	**4.5**	**9%**	**24%**	**15%**	**8%**	**12.3%**	**97.6**	**46**	**22**	**32**	**28%**	**72%**	**11%**	**14%**	**0**						**5.5**	**104**	**$**

Swanson,Erik

Age: 30 | Th: R | Role: RP | Ht: 6' 3" | Wt: 222 | Type: Pwr/xFB
Health: D | PT/Exp: C | Consist: C
LIMA Plan: A | Rand Var: -3 | MM: 3310

Somewhat oddly, flipped his pitch mix coming off 2022 career year, favoring splitter over four-seamer. BB% suffered fo the change initially, but snapped back to form in 2nd half (which was interrupted by an IL stint for spinal inflammation). Regardless of pitch mix, this is an elite reliever who can close if called upon. UP: 30 Sv.

Yr Tm	W	Sv	IP	K	ERA	WHIP	xERA	xWHIP	vL+	vR+	BF/G	BB%	K%	K-BB%	xBB%	SwK	Vel	G	L	F	H%	S%	HR/F	xHR/F	GS	APC	DOM%	DIS%	Sv%	LI	RAR	BPX	R$
19 SEA *	1	2	83	75	5.85	1.35	5.78	1.23	121	95	9.4	7%	22%	15%	6%	10.0%	92.7	38	20	42	29%	65%	23%	20%	8	36	0%	63%	100	0.57	-13.7	46	-$
20 SEA	0	0	8	9	12.91	1.70	4.57	1.16	127	169	4.1	5%	24%	19%	6%	13.4%	95.6	29	29	42	39%	20%	30%	25%	0	17			0	1.02	-8.0	151	-$
21 SEA	0	1	35	35	3.31	1.08	4.57	1.21	96	86	4.4	7%	24%	17%	6%	14.0%	94.8	32	15	53	26%	76%	10%	9%	2	17	0%	50%	33	0.93	4.2	112	$
22 SEA	3	3	54	70	1.68	0.91	2.97	0.94	74	78	3.6	5%	34%	29%	5%	15.9%	93.7	33	20	47	31%	85%	5%	5%	1	15	0%	0%	60	1.04	15.2	195	$
23 TOR	4	4	67	75	2.97	1.10	3.81	1.19	82	91	3.8	8%	29%	21%	6%	15.9%	93.8	40	15	46	28%	78%	11%	11%	0	15			67	1.17	11.2	139	$
1st Half	2	1	40	47	3.35	0.99	4.01	1.22	67	97	3.9	10%	30%	20%	6%	15.9%	93.7	34	12	54	22%	74%	12%	11%	0	15			50	1.25	4.9	125	$
2nd Half	2	3	26	28	2.39	1.25	3.51	1.13	106	82	3.6	6%	27%	21%	7%	15.9%	93.9	46	18	35	35%	84%	8%	11%	0	15			75	1.07	6.3	160	$
Proj	**4**	**10**	**58**	**63**	**3.05**	**1.11**	**3.60**	**1.15**	**94**	**88**	**4.1**	**7%**	**28%**	**21%**	**6%**	**14.8%**	**93.9**	**37**	**17**	**46**	**29%**	**78%**	**10%**	**10%**	**0**						**9.1**	**141**	

Syndergaard,Noah

Age: 31 | Th: R | Role: SP | Ht: 6' 6" | Wt: 242 | Type: Con
Health: F | PT/Exp: A | Consist: B
LIMA Plan: B | Rand Var: +5 | MM: 1001

Fall from the heavens for once-mighty Thor now seems complete. Pitch mix was all over the place as he flailed around looking for anything that would get hitters out. Alas, there was no such weapon in his arsenal. Most damning? It was tw of the premier pitch-lab orgs that tried to salvage something, then threw their hands up. Heed their lesson.

Yr Tm	W	Sv	IP	K	ERA	WHIP	xERA	xWHIP	vL+	vR+	BF/G	BB%	K%	K-BB%	xBB%	SwK	Vel	G	L	F	H%	S%	HR/F	xHR/F	GS	APC	DOM%	DIS%	Sv%	LI	RAR	BPX	R$
19 NYM	10	0	198	202	4.28	1.23	3.90	1.20	99	91	25.8	6%	24%	18%	5%	12.9%	97.7	48	20	32	32%	68%	13%	12%	32	97	41%	16%			5.5	142	$
20																																	
21 NYM	0	0	2	2	9.00	1.50	4.08		138	186	4.0	0%	25%	25%		11.5%	94.7	17	33	50	35%	50%	33%	33%	2	13	0%	50%			-1.2	172	-
22 2 TM	10	0	135	95	3.94	1.25	4.34	1.26	107	97	22.6	5%	17%	11%	5%	9.5%	93.8	43	19	38	30%	71%	9%	11%	24	81	13%	29%	0	0.77	0.4	87	
23 2 TM	2	0	89	56	6.50	1.39	5.14	1.33	106	133	21.7	5%	14%	9%	6%	8.4%	92.3	37	23	39	30%	58%	18%	16%	18	78	6%	61%			-23.7	73	-$
1st Half	1	0	55	38	7.16	1.45	4.75	1.26	124	122	20.5	4%	15%	12%	6%	8.9%	92.4	40	26	35	33%	53%	18%	15%	12	74	8%	67%			-19.3	101	-$
2nd Half	1	0	33	18	5.40	1.29	5.80	1.46	61	149	24.2	7%	12%	6%	6%	7.6%	92.1	33	20	47	23%	70%	19%	17%	6	87	0%	50%			-4.4	29	
Proj	**5**	**0**	**102**	**68**	**5.25**	**1.36**	**4.55**	**1.32**	**102**	**124**	**22.5**	**6%**	**16%**	**10%**	**6%**	**9.5%**	**93.8**	**40**	**21**	**39**	**30%**	**67%**	**16%**	**14%**	**19**						**-11.6**	**76**	**-**

RAY MURPHY

Taillon,Jameson

Age: 32 Th: R Role: SP — Ht: 6'5" Wt: 230 Type: Con/FB
Health: D — PT/Exp: A — Consist: B
LIMA Plan: A+ — Rand Var: 0 — MM: 2103

Best part of first half was two weeks on IL with groin strain; everything on the mound was a disaster (almost literally per DIS%). Violent hit/strand% correction in 2nd half undid some of damage. BPX shows full-year skills weren't that different, and the influence a few more BB, FB, and HR can have on a contact-forward skill set.

Yr Tm	W	Sv	IP	K	ERA	WHIP	xERA	xWHIP	vL+	vR+	BF/G	BB%	K%	K-BB%	xBB%	SwK	Vel	G	L	F	H%	S%	HR/F	xHR/F	GS	APC	DOM%	DIS%	Sv%	LI	RAR	BPX	R$
19 PIT	2	0	37	30	4.10	1.13	4.17	1.26	88	93	22.6	5%	19%	14%	4%	12.1%	94.8	50	23	27	28%	66%	13%	16%	7	79	14%	29%			1.9	116	-$1
20																																	
21 NYY	8	0	144	140	4.30	1.21	4.60	1.25	101	95	20.8	7%	23%	16%	6%	12.9%	94.0	33	19	48	28%	70%	12%	10%	29	82	17%	28%			-0.7	103	$6
22 NYY	14	0	177	151	3.91	1.13	3.90	1.15	102	100	22.8	4%	21%	16%	6%	10.6%	94.2	40	21	39	29%	71%	12%	13%	32	88	25%	34%			1.3	124	$12
23 CHC	8	1	154	140	4.84	1.28	4.55	1.25	115	89	21.8	6%	21%	15%	6%	10.0%	93.8	38	19	43	30%	67%	13%	15%	29	84	10%	38%	100	0.77	-9.7	110	$2
1st Half	2	0	64	59	6.93	1.52	5.02	1.30	142	94	20.4	7%	21%	14%	7%	9.1%	93.9	33	21	46	35%	57%	14%	15%	14	78	7%	50%			-20.4	96	-$17
2nd Half	6	1	91	81	3.38	1.10	4.22	1.22	93	88	23.1	6%	22%	16%	5%	10.8%	93.7	42	18	41	27%	77%	13%	15%	15	90	13%	27%	100	0.78	10.7	122	$20
Proj	9	0	152	138	4.47	1.22	4.01	1.22	108	93	20.9	6%	22%	16%	6%	11.0%	94.0	38	19	43	29%	68%	13%	14%	29						-2.7	113	$5

Teheran,Julio

Age: 33 Th: R Role: RP — Ht: 6'2" Wt: 205 Type: Con/FB
Health: F — PT/Exp: F — Consist: A
LIMA Plan: C+ — Rand Var: 0 — MM: 1001

3-5, 4.40 in 72 IP at MIL. Spent '22 knocking around independent and Mexican leagues; now back. Briefly looked like he found something in his travels (2.85 1st half MLB ERA in 41 IP), but further exposure in 2nd half reminded us why we haven't been interested this decade: substandard Vel/SwK, no pinpoint BB% or heavy GB tilt to offset.

Yr Tm	W	Sv	IP	K	ERA	WHIP	xERA	xWHIP	vL+	vR+	BF/G	BB%	K%	K-BB%	xBB%	SwK	Vel	G	L	F	H%	S%	HR/F	xHR/F	GS	APC	DOM%	DIS%	Sv%	LI	RAR	BPX	R$
19 ATL	10	0	175	162	3.81	1.32	5.07	1.48	92	97	22.8	11%	22%	10%	9%	9.7%	89.7	39	21	40	28%	75%	11%	13%	33	92	21%	24%			14.9	56	$10
20 LAA	0	0	31	20	10.05	1.76	6.60	1.62	155	122	14.9	11%	13%	3%	8%	6.5%	89.0	35	25	40	28%	47%	27%	25%	9	57	0%	67%	0	0.70	-21.6	-9	-$24
21 DET	1	0	5	3	1.80	1.40	5.83		126	66	20.0	15%	15%	0%		6.7%	90.2	36	21	43	21%	100%	17%	34%	1	90	0%	100%			1.5	-38	-$5
22																																	
23 MIL *	9	0	127	95	5.25	1.46	5.71	1.26	100	107	20.9	5%	17%	13%	6%	9.3%	89.8	40	19	41	32%	68%	14%	13%	11	77	27%	27%	0	0.68	-14.3	47	-$7
1st Half	6	0	81	60	4.82	1.47	5.81	1.38	101	82	23.2	8%	18%	10%	6%	8.2%	89.5	42	13	45	32%	73%	13%	11%	7	87	43%	14%			-4.9	39	-$2
2nd Half	3	0	46	35	6.00	1.44	5.52	1.31	100	138	17.7	6%	18%	12%	6%	10.7%	90.3	38	25	37	33%	60%	16%	15%	4	68	0%	50%	0	0.60	-9.4	65	-$5
Proj	4	0	73	57	4.92	1.40	4.63	1.40	112	114	18.7	9%	19%	10%	7%	9.2%	89.8	39	21	40	29%	70%	15%	15%	14						-5.3	61	-$5

Thompson,Zack

Age: 26 Th: L Role: SP — Ht: 6'2" Wt: 215 Type: Pwr
Health: A — PT/Exp: D — Consist: F
LIMA Plan: B — Rand Var: +2 — MM: 3203

Started the year in STL bullpen, throwing with the type of control that can only be described as LaLoosh level location. Got sent down, stretched out, eventually looked much better in Aug/Sept rotation audition. Expanded use of cutter gives him a chance to stick as a starter, albeit with a low ceiling unless he figures out another plus pitch.

Yr Tm	W	Sv	IP	K	ERA	WHIP	xERA	xWHIP	vL+	vR+	BF/G	BB%	K%	K-BB%	xBB%	SwK	Vel	G	L	F	H%	S%	HR/F	xHR/F	GS	APC	DOM%	DIS%	Sv%	LI	RAR	BPX	R$
19																																	
20																																	
21 aaa	2	2	93	67	6.91	1.83	6.91				19.7	12%	15%	4%							35%	64%									-30.3	16	-$22
22 STL *	3	1	89	79	3.41	1.10	2.69	1.41	53	85	8.5	9%	23%	14%	6%	7.8%	94.8	54	17	29	25%	71%	11%	10%	1	26	0%	100%	100	0.45	6.1	100	$4
23 STL *	6	0	101	104	5.89	1.73	5.82	1.28	87	110	12.8	9%	25%	16%	8%	9.8%	93.6	44	23	33	36%	67%	13%	15%	9	47	22%	33%	0	0.95	-19.5	63	-$15
1st Half	2	0	46	48	7.73	2.24	7.47	1.88	110	98	11.1	20%	21%	1%	12%	10.3%	94.7	37	41	22	39%	65%	17%	9%	0	19			0	1.32	-19.2	45	-$27
2nd Half	4	0	58	56	4.20	1.26	4.16	1.23	76	112	15.7	7%	24%	17%	7%	9.6%	93.3	45	20	35	32%	70%	13%	16%	9	68	22%	33%	0	0.65	1.0	110	$5
Proj	7	0	123	118	4.45	1.36	3.91	1.33	72	112	20.5	9%	23%	14%	7%	8.9%	93.9	49	19	33	31%	70%	12%	13%	25						-1.8	98	-$1

Tonkin,Michael

Age: 34 Th: R Role: RP — Ht: 6'7" Wt: 220 Type: /FB
Health: B — PT/Exp: D — Consist: A
LIMA Plan: A — Rand Var: -1 — MM: 3200

First time back in MLB since 2017, spending season in pen where being a middle reliever backed by MLB's best offense was a pretty sweet gig (see W column). Actually worked his way into reasonable leverage thanks to early effectiveness, before second half S%-induced collapse. Not likely relevant to us, but kudos for the long road back.

Yr Tm	W	Sv	IP	K	ERA	WHIP	xERA	xWHIP	vL+	vR+	BF/G	BB%	K%	K-BB%	xBB%	SwK	Vel	G	L	F	H%	S%	HR/F	xHR/F	GS	APC	DOM%	DIS%	Sv%	LI	RAR	BPX	R$
19 aaa	3	0	22	18	6.05	1.77	6.87				5.3	15%	18%	3%							30%	72%									-4.2	1	-$6
20																																	
21																																	
22 aaa	5	16	49	54	4.40	1.40	4.26				4.4	9%	26%	17%							36%	69%									-2.6	114	$4
23 ATL	7	1	80	75	4.28	1.09	4.28	1.25	95	84	7.2	7%	23%	16%	6%	11.7%	93.5	38	18	43	25%	66%	14%	11%	0	29			25	0.82	0.6	110	$5
1st Half	4	1	39	32	2.77	0.95	4.27	1.27	66	89	7.9	7%	21%	15%	5%	12.2%	93.4	39	18	43	22%	78%	11%	10%	0	30			33	1.03	7.5	99	$7
2nd Half	3	0	41	43	5.71	1.22	4.28	1.24	118	80	6.7	7%	25%	17%	6%	11.3%	93.7	37	19	43	29%	57%	16%	12%	0	28			0	0.66	-7.0	122	-$1
Proj	5	0	58	54	4.28	1.11	3.88	1.24	99	80	6.3	7%	24%	16%	6%	11.6%	93.6	38	19	43	27%	66%	12%	12%	0						0.3	109	$1

Topa,Justin

Age: 33 Th: R Role: RP — Ht: 6'4" Wt: 200 Type: Con/xGB
Health: F — PT/Exp: D — Consist: F
LIMA Plan: A — Rand Var: -3 — MM: 4111

If you're asking yourself "This guy is 33 years old (and pretty good!), how have I never heard of him?", it's that he's never healthy. From 2015-2022, he threw 150 total IP, with two Tommy John procedures mixed in. Cocktail of Vel, GB% and good BB% are enough to keep him viable; low SwK and Health risk keep us from going over-the-Top(a).

Yr Tm	W	Sv	IP	K	ERA	WHIP	xERA	xWHIP	vL+	vR+	BF/G	BB%	K%	K-BB%	xBB%	SwK	Vel	G	L	F	H%	S%	HR/F	xHR/F	GS	APC	DOM%	DIS%	Sv%	LI	RAR	BPX	R$
19 aa	0	0	24	17	4.75	1.80	5.47				6.2	10%	15%	5%							39%	71%									-0.7	68	-$7
20 MIL	0	0	8	12	2.35	0.91	1.85	0.71	126	63	5.0	0%	40%	40%	5%	14.3%	97.5	56	22	22	38%	83%	25%	26%	0	20			0	0.54	2.0	325	-$3
21 MIL	0	0	3	1	29.70	3.90	10.07		259	177	5.8	4%	4%	0%		3.4%	95.8	43	14	43	54%	18%	22%	9%	0	22			0	0.48	-10.5	-4	-$11
22 MIL *	2	0	28	17	4.64	1.79	5.44	1.63	84	103	5.3	10%	13%	3%	10%	4.8%	95.6	67	22	11	38%	71%	0%	34%	0	18			0	1.03	-2.3	58	-$7
23 SEA	5	3	69	61	2.61	1.14	3.49	1.25	89	82	3.7	6%	22%	15%	5%	8.7%	95.1	57	19	25	30%	79%	8%	7%	0	14			60	1.05	14.7	129	$7
1st Half	1	1	31	27	3.19	1.35	3.71	1.32	90	97	3.9	8%	20%	13%	4%	8.0%	95.1	60	18	22	33%	78%	10%	7%	0	14			50	1.04	4.4	114	-$4
2nd Half	4	2	38	34	2.13	0.97	3.31	1.18	89	71	3.6	5%	23%	18%	6%	9.3%	95.0	53	19	28	27%	80%	7%	7%	0	14			67	1.06	10.3	141	$10
Proj	5	5	65	58	3.38	1.13	3.29	1.22	93	82	3.6	6%	22%	16%	5%	8.8%	95.0	56	19	25	29%	71%	10%	10%	0						7.6	130	$5

Toussaint,Touki

Age: 28 Th: R Role: RP — Ht: 6'3" Wt: 215 Type: Pwr
Health: D — PT/Exp: D — Consist: B
LIMA Plan: C — Rand Var: +1 — MM: 1201

4-7, 4.97 ERA in 87 IP at CLE/CHW. A once highly-touted prospect: throws hard, nice GB tilt, generally tough on same-side batters. But he's never solved lefties, and walks everyone. At 28, it's rather late to hope for the light bulb to click "on". But with four teams in three years, at least he's expanding his Immaculate Grid utility.

Yr Tm	W	Sv	IP	K	ERA	WHIP	xERA	xWHIP	vL+	vR+	BF/G	BB%	K%	K-BB%	xBB%	SwK	Vel	G	L	F	H%	S%	HR/F	xHR/F	GS	APC	DOM%	DIS%	Sv%	LI	RAR	BPX	R$
19 ATL *	5	0	83	81	7.49	1.93	6.61	1.55	159	78	11.6	14%	21%	7%	12%	12.3%	93.5	44	17	39	38%	61%	11%	12%	1	33	0%	100%	0	1.24	-30.6	47	-$17
20 ATL	0	0	24	30	8.88	1.77	4.86	1.48	133	126	17.1	13%	25%	12%	10%	12.6%	94.0	39	30	31	34%	53%	33%	29%	5	70	20%	60%	0	0.72	-13.3	64	-$17
21 ATL *	5	0	77	74	4.46	1.24	3.83	1.38	110	102	16.6	12%	24%	12%	10%	10.4%	92.8	47	18	35	24%	69%	23%	17%	10	75	30%	50%	0	0.72	-1.9	69	$0
22 LAA *	3	0	81	76	4.86	1.51	4.57	1.66	116	68	11.8	15%	22%	7%	12%	11.6%	92.1	54	16	30	28%	70%	12%	7%	2	54	50%	50%	0	0.37	-9.0	59	-$7
23 2 AL *	6	3	126	122	4.70	1.43	3.89	1.61	94	98	13.4	15%	22%	7%	12%	9.8%	93.2	50	19	31	27%	68%	14%	16%	16	80	13%	25%	100	0.69	-5.8	76	-$2
1st Half	2	3	53	50	4.08	1.41	3.36	1.70	108	44	9.3	17%	23%	6%	12%	10.4%	93.4	53	20	27	25%	72%	13%	17%	2	62	0%	0%	100	0.59	1.7	84	-$1
2nd Half	4	0	73	72	5.15	1.45	4.63	1.55	91	105	20.3	14%	22%	9%	11%	9.7%	93.2	49	19	32	28%	66%	14%	15%	14	84	14%	29%	0	0.72	-7.4	46	$1
Proj	6	0	116	111	4.71	1.44	4.44	1.55	109	97	13.6	14%	23%	8%	12%	10.5%	93.1	47	18	34	28%	70%	14%	14%	13						-5.5	39	-$4

Urías,Julio

Age: 27 Th: L Role: SP — Ht: 6'0" Wt: 225 Type: /FB
Health: D — PT/Exp: A — Consist: A
LIMA Plan: A — Rand Var: +1 — MM: 3205

Placed on administrative leave following an early-September arrest on domestic violence charges. While active, he had largely repeated prior skills, but not the results that had been far out in front of those skills. Not clear what future employment opportunities might be, but recent xERAs are always the source of truth.

Yr Tm	W	Sv	IP	K	ERA	WHIP	xERA	xWHIP	vL+	vR+	BF/G	BB%	K%	K-BB%	xBB%	SwK	Vel	G	L	F	H%	S%	HR/F	xHR/F	GS	APC	DOM%	DIS%	Sv%	LI	RAR	BPX	R$
19 LA	4	4	80	85	2.49	1.08	4.14	1.27	89	76	8.8	8%	26%	18%	7%	14.4%	95.2	39	22	39	27%	81%	9%	9%	8	36	38%	25%	80	0.96	19.9	117	$10
20 LA	3	0	55	45	3.27	1.15	5.04	1.36	68	86	20.4	8%	20%	12%	6%	12.5%	94.2	33	22	46	27%	74%	7%	10%	10	80	10%	20%	0	0.74	8.0	72	$10
21 LA	20	0	186	195	2.96	1.02	3.73	1.10	88	80	23.3	5%	26%	21%	4%	11.9%	94.1	40	19	41	29%	75%	9%	10%	32	87	34%	19%			30.0	152	$32
22 LA	17	0	175	166	2.16	0.96	3.76	1.15	79	86	22.2	6%	24%	18%	5%	11.5%	93.1	40	15	45	24%	87%	11%	9%	31	85	29%	23%			39.0	126	$32
23 LA	11	0	117	117	4.60	1.16	4.09	1.15	88	111	23.0	5%	24%	19%	5%	10.8%	92.8	37	18	45	29%	68%	16%	14%	21	88	43%	33%			-3.9	142	$7
1st Half	5	0	58	55	4.94	1.23	4.31	1.19	101	113	22.2	5%	23%	17%	5%	10.7%	93.0	38	18	44	29%	69%	19%	16%	11	86	27%	36%			-4.4	129	$1
2nd Half	6	0	59	62	4.27	1.08	3.88	1.10	74	111	23.8	5%	26%	21%	4%	11.1%	92.5	36	17	47	29%	67%	14%	11%	10	91	60%	30%			0.4	157	$11
Proj	14	0	174	172	3.84	1.12	3.70	1.15	86	100	20.4	6%	25%	19%	5%	11.5%	93.3	38	18	44	29%	72%	13%	11%	34						10.4	136	$17

RAY MURPHY

Uribe,Abner

Age: 24	Th: R	Role: RP	Health: A	LIMA Plan: A+
Ht: 6' 2"	Wt: 200	Type: Pwr	PT/Exp: F	Rand Var: -5
			Consist: F	MM: 5510

1-0, 1 Sv, 1.76 ERA in 31 IP at MIL. Triple-digit flamethrower earned July callup after blowing away AA and AAA batters in first half. Control is a problem, but big K% and GB% tilt kept it survivable. Not allowing a single HR is a pretty good mitigator too. Can't count on that again, but xBB% says walks may be manageable. Closer starter kit.

Yr Tm	W	Sv	IP	K	ERA	WHIP	xERA	xWHIP	vL+	vR+	BF/G	BB%	K%	K-BB%	xBB%	SwK	Vel	G	L	F	H%	S%	HR/F	xHR/F	GS	APC	DOM%	DIS%	Sv%	LI	RAR	BPX	R$
19																																	
20																																	
21																																	
22																																	
23 MIL *	2	8	54	75	1.88	1.16	1.58	1.47	75	60	4.0	16%	31%	15%	11%	12.9%	99.5	53	21	26	25%	83%	0%	10%	0	16			80	0.93	16.2	158	$8
1st Half	1	7	21	35	1.79	1.19	1.80				4.0	17%	39%	22%							26%	87%	0%		0	0					6.6	170	$5
2nd Half	1	1	33	41	1.94	1.14	1.43	1.43	75	60	3.9	15%	31%	16%	11%	12.9%	99.5	53	21	26	25%	81%	0%	10%	0	16			50	0.93	9.6	151	$4
Proj	**2**	**2**	**58**	**82**	**3.24**	**1.29**	**3.07**	**1.38**	**100**	**78**	**4.1**	**16%**	**35%**	**19%**	**12%**	**12.9%**	**99.5**	**53**	**21**	**26**	**30%**	**74%**	**8%**	**9%**	**0**						**7.8**	**115**	**$2**

Urquidy,José

Age: 29	Th: R	Role: SP	Health: F	LIMA Plan: B
Ht: 6' 0"	Wt: 217	Type: Con/FB	PT/Exp: A	Rand Var: 0
			Consist: B	MM: 1003

Got smoked in April, then spent three months on IL with sore shoulder, came back in August and... got smoked some more. Injury was non-surgical, and he did get better in September (and playoffs), so he's got a case to forget 2023 ever happened. But heed xERA history, which says a return to sub-4.00 ERA is a stretch even with a sound shoulder.

Yr Tm	W	Sv	IP	K	ERA	WHIP	xERA	xWHIP	vL+	vR+	BF/G	BB%	K%	K-BB%	xBB%	SwK	Vel	G	L	F	H%	S%	HR/F	xHR/F	GS	APC	DOM%	DIS%	Sv%	LI	RAR	BPX	R$
19 HOU *	9	0	144	153	5.20	1.26	4.76	1.16	70	110	20.2	5%	26%	21%	7%	12.3%	93.3	37	18	45	33%	63%	12%	14%	7	77	29%	29%	0	0.93	-12.4	130	$3
20 HOU	1	0	30	17	2.73	1.01	5.15	1.42	52	114	23.2	7%	15%	8%	5%	10.0%	93.1	36	23	41	21%	81%	11%	12%	5	86	20%	60%			6.3	47	$3
21 HOU	8	0	107	90	3.62	0.99	4.35	1.17	79	97	21.2	4%	21%	17%	4%	12.5%	92.6	32	22	46	25%	71%	12%	11%	20	82	35%	25%			8.6	113	$11
22 HOU	13	0	164	134	3.94	1.17	4.31	1.22	97	109	23.5	6%	20%	14%	5%	10.6%	93.6	36	19	45	28%	74%	13%	13%	28	91	21%	32%	0	0.78	0.5	99	$9
23 HOU	3	1	63	45	5.29	1.43	5.50	1.47	98	113	17.2	9%	16%	7%	8%	12.0%	93.3	36	20	44	29%	67%	12%	10%	10	69	10%	40%	100	0.62	-7.4	37	-$6
1st Half	2	0	28	23	5.20	1.55	5.30	1.38	105	127	20.5	8%	19%	11%	7%	14.1%	93.3	33	22	45	33%	73%	15%	9%	6	85	0%	33%			-3.0	65	-$10
2nd Half	1	1	35	22	5.35	1.33	5.66	1.55	95	101	15.2	10%	14%	5%	8%	10.2%	93.3	39	18	43	26%	62%	10%	10%	4	59	25%	50%	100	0.52	-4.4	17	-$5
Proj	**8**	**0**	**145**	**115**	**4.35**	**1.28**	**4.47**	**1.32**	**93**	**111**	**21.1**	**7%**	**19%**	**12%**	**6%**	**11.9%**	**93.1**	**36**	**20**	**44**	**29%**	**72%**	**13%**	**11%**	**28**						**-0.4**	**78**	**$2**

Valdez,Framber

Age: 30	Th: L	Role: SP	Health: C	LIMA Plan: C+
Ht: 5' 11"	Wt: 239	Type: Pwr/xGB	PT/Exp: A	Rand Var: 0
			Consist: B	MM: 5205

Just missed the 200-IP repeat, but second straight Vel uptick helped nudge him into the 200-K club. Slippage in GB% hurt ERA/WHIP, as FB "spike" (if you can call it that) combined with always-sketchy HR/F to yield more raw HR. His value is rooted in bankable volume and minimal blowup risk, and he's a deity in Quality Start leagues.

Yr Tm	W	Sv	IP	K	ERA	WHIP	xERA	xWHIP	vL+	vR+	BF/G	BB%	K%	K-BB%	xBB%	SwK	Vel	G	L	F	H%	S%	HR/F	xHR/F	GS	APC	DOM%	DIS%	Sv%	LI	RAR	BPX	R$
19 HOU *	9	1	116	124	5.05	1.47	4.31	1.57	87	112	13.8	12%	25%	12%	10%	10.8%	93.0	62	21	17	32%	67%	26%	19%	8	45	25%	50%	100	0.46	-7.7	83	-$1
20 HOU	5	0	71	76	3.57	1.12	2.96	1.11	85	85	26.2	6%	26%	21%	7%	10.5%	93.1	60	21	19	32%	69%	14%	23%	10	95	50%	10%	0	0.77	7.7	178	$18
21 HOU	11	0	135	125	3.14	1.25	3.31	1.37	99	83	26.0	10%	22%	12%	10%	10.7%	92.5	70	15	15	28%	78%	21%	19%	22	95	36%	23%			18.7	103	$12
22 HOU	17	0	201	194	2.82	1.16	2.83	1.25	72	87	26.7	8%	23%	15%	7%	11.6%	94.0	67	17	16	29%	77%	13%	17%	31	97	42%	10%			28.6	132	$24
23 HOU	12	0	198	200	3.45	1.13	3.35	1.22	95	88	26.1	7%	25%	18%	8%	12.0%	95.3	54	20	25	29%	72%	14%	18%	31	96	48%	19%			21.4	141	$23
1st Half	7	0	105	110	2.49	1.05	2.96	1.14	101	80	26.1	6%	26%	21%	8%	11.8%	95.6	57	21	22	30%	79%	11%	20%	16	97	50%	6%			23.9	168	$33
2nd Half	5	0	93	90	4.55	1.22	3.80	1.31	92	99	26.0	8%	23%	15%	7%	12.2%	95.1	52	20	29	28%	65%	16%	17%	15	94	47%	33%			-2.5	113	$11
Proj	**15**	**0**	**196**	**194**	**3.38**	**1.18**	**3.11**	**1.26**	**90**	**89**	**24.1**	**8%**	**25%**	**16%**	**8%**	**11.5%**	**94.2**	**60**	**19**	**21**	**29%**	**74%**	**16%**	**19%**	**32**						**22.8**	**131**	**$2**

Varland,Louie

Age: 26	Th: R	Role: SP	Health: A	LIMA Plan: B+
Ht: 6' 1"	Wt: 205	Type: Con	PT/Exp: C	Rand Var: +1
			Consist: B	MM: 3103

4-3, 4.63 ERA in 68 IP at MIN. Summoned to big-league rotation in late April, pitched decently before gopheritis got him sent back down in June. Returned as a multi-inning RP in Sept callup and was lights-out (17 K/1 BB in 12 IP). So there's impact reliever potential here, but also an intriguing SP as the HR/F normalizes. Buy the skills.

Yr Tm	W	Sv	IP	K	ERA	WHIP	xERA	xWHIP	vL+	vR+	BF/G	BB%	K%	K-BB%	xBB%	SwK	Vel	G	L	F	H%	S%	HR/F	xHR/F	GS	APC	DOM%	DIS%	Sv%	LI	RAR	BPX	R$
19																																	
20																																	
21																																	
22 MIN *	9	0	153	140	3.04	1.26	3.96	1.22	100	114	21.5	7%	22%	15%	5%	9.0%	93.9	36	23	41	31%	80%	13%	13%	5	82	20%	40%			17.5	99	$1
23 MIN *	11	0	151	143	4.29	1.33	4.81	1.17	94	116	19.0	6%	25%	19%	4%	12.9%	95.3	44	16	40	32%	73%	21%	19%	10	64	30%	40%	0	0.79	0.9	90	$5
1st Half	5	0	81	81	5.71	1.44	5.72	1.28	106	121	23.0	8%	23%	15%	5%	12.1%	94.9	43	17	40	33%	65%	21%	18%	10	92	30%	40%			-13.8	67	-$
2nd Half	6	0	70	62	2.63	1.21	3.77	1.22	44	82	15.7	6%	22%	16%	4%	17.3%	97.3	57	9	35	31%	82%	25%	24%	0	25			0	0.83	14.7	120	$1
Proj	**11**	**0**	**160**	**140**	**3.72**	**1.23**	**3.87**	**1.24**	**99**	**109**	**21.3**	**6%**	**22%**	**15%**	**5%**	**12.1%**	**94.9**	**43**	**17**	**40**	**30%**	**74%**	**12%**	**15%**	**30**						**11.9**	**112**	**$1**

Vásquez,Randy

Age: 25	Th: R	Role: SP	Health: A	LIMA Plan: C+
Ht: 6' 0"	Wt: 165	Type:	PT/Exp: D	Rand Var: -1
			Consist: B	MM: 2101

2-2, 2.87 ERA in 38 IP at NYY. Prospect reputed to have plus command, but that supposed strength has eroded as he has climbed the ladder. Only favorable hit/strand% (25/84) saved him from big-league disaster. Not enough Ks for the Vel, too many BB and FB all say not a viable big-league option yet. Needs more minors seasoning.

Yr Tm	W	Sv	IP	K	ERA	WHIP	xERA	xWHIP	vL+	vR+	BF/G	BB%	K%	K-BB%	xBB%	SwK	Vel	G	L	F	H%	S%	HR/F	xHR/F	GS	APC	DOM%	DIS%	Sv%	LI	RAR	BPX	R$
19																																	
20																																	
21 aa	2	0	22	16	4.81	1.51	5.25				23.9	7%	17%	9%							34%	69%									-1.5	62	-$
22 aa	2	0	116	102	4.07	1.33	4.11				19.3	8%	21%	13%							32%	71%									-1.4	88	-$
23 NYY *	5	0	119	114	4.29	1.47	4.76	1.48	98	87	18.2	11%	20%	9%	8%	7.0%	94.4	36	22	42	32%	74%	11%	12%	5	61	0%	20%	0	0.63	0.6	71	-$
1st Half	3	0	74	67	4.91	1.58	5.24	1.49	88	61	21.6	11%	20%	9%	9%	6.5%	94.7	36	18	46	33%	71%	8%	11%	2	85	0%	0%			-5.2	61	-$
2nd Half	2	0	48	47	3.13	1.23	3.63	1.37	102	98	14.8	10%	24%	14%	7%	7.2%	94.3	37	23	40	27%	80%	12%	13%	3	55	0%	33%	0	0.61	7.1	89	$
Proj	**3**	**0**	**73**	**65**	**4.34**	**1.34**	**4.31**	**1.38**	**109**	**106**	**20.8**	**10%**	**21%**	**12%**	**7%**	**7.2%**	**94.3**	**37**	**23**	**40**	**30%**	**70%**	**11%**	**12%**	**14**						**-0.1**	**67**	**-$**

Verlander,Justin

Age: 41	Th: R	Role: SP	Health: F	LIMA Plan: B
Ht: 6' 5"	Wt: 235	Type: /FB	PT/Exp: A	Rand Var: -3
			Consist: C	MM: 2203

Father Time remains undefeated, but he's got a heck of a battle here. Still, you can see the cracks accumulating in SwK, BB%, K%, FB%, DIS%; all summarized in BPX. There's also no evolution in his pitch mix; he's riding his same repertoire as far as it takes him. Pitched to the level of last year's xERA, but bad news if he does that again.

Yr Tm	W	Sv	IP	K	ERA	WHIP	xERA	xWHIP	vL+	vR+	BF/G	BB%	K%	K-BB%	xBB%	SwK	Vel	G	L	F	H%	S%	HR/F	xHR/F	GS	APC	DOM%	DIS%	Sv%	LI	RAR	BPX	R$
19 HOU	21	0	223	300	2.58	0.80	3.18	0.98	74	80	24.9	5%	35%	30%	5%	16.8%	94.7	36	19	45	23%	80%	16%	13%	34	101	59%	6%			52.9	203	$5
20 HOU	1	0	6	7	3.00	0.67	2.73		83	95	21.0	5%	33%	29%		12.3%	94.9	62	0	38	9%	100%	40%	31%	1	73	0%	0%			1.1	213	-$
21																																	
22 HOU	18	0	175	185	1.75	0.83	3.26	1.03	63	78	23.8	4%	28%	23%	5%	12.1%	95.1	38	19	44	25%	83%	6%	9%	28	93	54%	0%			47.9	162	$4
23 2 TM	13	0	162	144	3.22	1.13	4.55	1.27	79	97	24.8	7%	22%	15%	6%	10.4%	94.4	36	20	45	28%	76%	8%	10%	27	96	37%	22%			22.3	101	$2
1st Half	3	0	64	55	3.66	1.19	4.34	1.25	84	101	24.0	6%	21%	15%	8%	10.3%	94.4	42	19	39	29%	74%	11%	9%	11	96	36%	27%			5.3	111	$
2nd Half	10	0	98	89	2.93	1.10	4.68	1.28	76	95	25.3	7%	22%	15%	6%	10.6%	94.3	31	20	49	27%	78%	7%	11%	16	97	38%	19%			17.0	95	$2
Proj	**10**	**0**	**145**	**134**	**4.03**	**1.22**	**4.07**	**1.24**	**90**	**106**	**24.9**	**7%**	**23%**	**16%**	**6%**	**12.2%**	**94.5**	**36**	**19**	**45**	**30%**	**71%**	**10%**	**11%**	**23**						**5.4**	**108**	**$**

Vesia,Alex

Age: 28	Th: L	Role: RP	Health: A	LIMA Plan: B
Ht: 6' 1"	Wt: 209	Type: Pwr/xFB	PT/Exp: C	Rand Var: +1
			Consist: C	MM: 3410

Funky Reliever Sample Sizes, Lesson 392: BPX says skills were right in line with '22, just done in by a flood of hits (especially weird: 42% H% vL). Re-elevated FB% means he's going to continue to be prone to the HR, and backsliding vR likely precludes any hopes of regular 9th-inning work. Another reliever for the "pretty good" pile.

Yr Tm	W	Sv	IP	K	ERA	WHIP	xERA	xWHIP	vL+	vR+	BF/G	BB%	K%	K-BB%	xBB%	SwK	Vel	G	L	F	H%	S%	HR/F	xHR/F	GS	APC	DOM%	DIS%	Sv%	LI	RAR	BPX	R$
19 aa	2	1	17	21	0.00	0.69	0.50				6.7	2%	35%	33%							28%	100%									9.5	513	$
20 MIA	0	0	4	5	18.69	3.23	12.30		171	186	5.4	26%	19%	-7%	12%	12.0%	91.8	20	20	60	36%	45%	33%	23%	0	27			0	0.56	-7.6	-235	-$1
21 LA	3	1	40	54	2.25	0.98	4.30	1.32	63	85	3.9	14%	34%	20%	8%	18.1%	93.9	25	11	64	16%	88%	11%	10%	0	16			50	1.16	9.9	97	$
22 LA	5	1	54	79	2.15	1.12	3.19	1.14	50	87	3.6	11%	35%	24%	7%	15.7%	94.2	35	23	43	32%	81%	4%	9%	0	15			33	0.98	12.2	156	$
23 LA	2	1	50	64	4.35	1.39	4.24	1.16	97	104	3.9	8%	29%	22%	7%	14.5%	94.4	30	18	52	37%	73%	10%	10%	1	15	0%	100%	50	0.92	-0.1	150	-$
1st Half	0	0	19	30	7.58	2.42	4.70	1.32	126	151	4.4	12%	29%	18%	10%	14.7%	94.3	35	23	42	57%	70%	13%	9%	0	18			0	0.76	-7.6	130	-$1
2nd Half	2	1	31	34	2.35	0.75	3.89	1.03	71	67	3.5	4%	30%	25%	5%	14.4%	94.5	25	15	60	21%	79%	9%	10%	1	13	0%	100%	100	1.03	7.5	162	$
Proj	**3**	**1**	**58**	**73**	**3.76**	**1.18**	**3.66**	**1.17**	**80**	**95**	**3.6**	**9%**	**31%**	**22%**	**7%**	**15.6%**	**94.2**	**30**	**18**	**52**	**30%**	**72%**	**10%**	**10%**	**0**						**4.1**	**137**	**$**

RAY MURPHY

Vest,Will

Age: 29	Th: R	Role	RP	Health	D	LIMA Plan	A+
Ht: 6' 0"	Wt: 180	Type		PT/Exp	C	Rand Var	-2
				Consist	B	MM	4210

Non-prospect rose through leverage ladder all year, thrived late in season after missing July with a leg strain. Second straight year of improved skills at big-league level, seen in both improving BB% and K% (see K-BB% trend). BB% gains supported by xBB, K% less so by SwK. Success vs. both sides should keep him in leverage work. Nice Holds play.

Yr Tm	W	Sv	IP	K	ERA	WHIP	xERA	xWHIP	vL+	vR+	BF/G	BB%	K%	K-BB%	xBB%	SwK	Vel	G	L	F	H%	S%	HR/F	xHR/F	GS	APC	DOM%	DIS%	Sv%	LI	RAR	BPX	R$
19 a/a	2	5	35	22	6.55	1.77	7.22				7.0	7%	14%	6%							36%	66%									-8.9	12	-$7
20																																	
21 SEA *	2	2	62	46	6.32	1.60	5.35	1.54	107	112	5.0	10%	17%	7%	9%	10.2%	93.6	43	26	30	34%	60%	6%	7%	0	19			50	1.02	-15.8	52	-$12
22 DET	3	1	63	63	4.00	1.33	3.56	1.25	99	97	4.6	8%	23%	15%	8%	10.9%	95.2	50	23	28	33%	72%	12%	16%	2	18	0%	100%	100	0.69	-0.2	116	-$2
23 DET	2	2	48	56	2.98	1.10	3.54	1.14	87	76	4.1	7%	28%	22%	5%	10.9%	95.3	45	19	36	32%	74%	6%	8%	4	16	0%	75%	40	0.96	8.1	163	$3
1st Half	2	0	30	32	2.73	1.08	3.62	1.20	86	69	4.4	8%	27%	19%	6%	10.5%	95.0	45	21	35	30%	74%	4%	5%	3	17	0%	67%	0	0.87	5.9	140	$0
2nd Half	0	2	19	24	3.38	1.13	3.42	1.04	90	86	3.8	5%	30%	25%	4%	11.5%	95.6	45	16	39	34%	74%	10%	12%	1	15	0%	100%	50	1.08	2.2	202	-$2
Proj	**2**	**2**	**58**	**58**	**3.64**	**1.20**	**3.51**	**1.19**	**96**	**91**	**4.2**	**7%**	**25%**	**18%**	**6%**	**10.8%**	**94.9**	**45**	**21**	**34**	**31%**	**72%**	**10%**	**10%**	**0**						**4.9**	**135**	**$1**

Wacha,Michael

Age: 33	Th: R	Role	SP	Health	F	LIMA Plan	B
Ht: 6' 6"	Wt: 215	Type		PT/Exp	A	Rand Var	-3
				Consist	A	MM	3203

Missed six weeks (shoulder inflammation). Again outpitched peripherals, benefitting from fortuitous H%/S%. It wasn't all luck, as his change-up continues to be elite (20% SwK%; .304 xSLG, 35% usage) and K-BB% was a tick better than average. Expecting ERA to slide toward 4.00 is still prudent, as is setting IP expectations around 130.

Yr Tm	W	Sv	IP	K	ERA	WHIP	xERA	xWHIP	vL+	vR+	BF/G	BB%	K%	K-BB%	xBB%	SwK	Vel	G	L	F	H%	S%	HR/F	xHR/F	GS	APC	DOM%	DIS%	Sv%	LI	RAR	BPX	R$
19 STL	6	0	127	104	4.76	1.56	4.99	1.48	107	120	19.4	10%	19%	9%	8%	10.1%	93.1	48	22	30	32%	76%	22%	22%	24	76	8%	58%	0	0.80	-4.0	58	-$5
20 NYM	1	0	34	37	6.62	1.56	4.53	1.14	112	143	19.5	4%	24%	19%	6%	12.0%	93.6	36	23	41	39%	64%	20%	15%	7	76	0%	71%	0	0.70	-9.1	158	-$11
21 TAM	3	0	125	121	5.05	1.31	4.09	1.19	99	110	18.2	6%	23%	17%	5%	11.8%	93.8	39	25	35	32%	66%	18%	19%	23	68	22%	39%	0	0.76	-12.1	125	-$5
22 BOS	11	0	127	104	3.32	1.12	3.99	1.22	86	107	22.4	6%	20%	14%	6%	10.0%	93.0	41	20	39	27%	77%	12%	16%	23	85	9%	35%			10.2	102	$11
23 SD	14	0	134	124	3.22	1.16	4.50	1.29	90	91	23.0	8%	22%	15%	7%	11.3%	92.0	34	22	43	28%	77%	9%	11%	24	93	29%	25%			18.5	94	$17
1st Half	8	0	86	73	2.84	1.07	4.57	1.30	86	87	22.9	7%	21%	14%	7%	11.1%	91.5	34	21	46	26%	77%	7%	10%	15	92	27%	27%			15.8	89	$23
2nd Half	6	0	49	51	3.88	1.32	4.36	1.29	96	99	23.3	9%	24%	16%	6%	11.7%	92.8	36	26	39	31%	75%	13%	13%	9	93	33%	22%			2.7	106	$8
Proj	**10**	**0**	**131**	**124**	**4.14**	**1.23**	**3.84**	**1.20**	**95**	**106**	**20.4**	**6%**	**23%**	**17%**	**6%**	**11.3%**	**92.9**	**37**	**23**	**39**	**30%**	**72%**	**14%**	**15%**	**26**						**3.0**	**120**	**$6**

Wainwright,Adam

Age: 42	Th: R	Role	RP	Health	D	LIMA Plan	
Ht: 6' 7"	Wt: 230	Type	#DIV/0!	PT/Exp	A	Rand Var	
				Consist	D	MM	

5-11, 7.40 ERA in 101 IP at STL. Unfortunately, the farewell tour didn't go as hoped, as he logged numerous career-worsts. The warning signs were present in the 2022 underlying metrics, so this didn't come as a shock. Regardless, he enjoyed a fine career, finishing with 200 wins, 3.53 ERA, and 2,202 K in 2,668 IP.

Yr Tm	W	Sv	IP	K	ERA	WHIP	xERA	xWHIP	vL+	vR+	BF/G	BB%	K%	K-BB%	xBB%	SwK	Vel	G	L	F	H%	S%	HR/F	xHR/F	GS	APC	DOM%	DIS%	Sv%	LI	RAR	BPX	R$
19 STL	14	0	172	153	4.19	1.43	4.48	1.38	116	94	24.0	9%	21%	12%	8%	8.0%	89.9	49	22	29	32%	74%	15%	14%	31	93	16%	39%			6.6	88	$6
20 STL	5	0	66	54	3.15	1.05	4.21	1.24	92	82	26.2	6%	21%	15%	6%	11.0%	89.3	43	22	34	26%	77%	14%	15%	10	93	40%	20%			10.5	112	$19
21 STL	17	0	206	174	3.05	1.06	3.85	1.23	91	79	25.9	6%	21%	15%	6%	8.5%	89.1	47	22	30	26%	75%	12%	11%	32	96	41%	28%			30.9	113	$29
22 STL	11	0	192	143	3.71	1.28	4.16	1.30	101	97	25.1	7%	18%	11%	7%	7.0%	88.5	43	24	33	31%	73%	8%	11%	32	98	28%	28%			6.1	81	$7
23 STL *	6	0	116	64	7.20	1.85	7.74	1.55	138	127	22.6	8%	11%	3%	10%	5.0%	86.6	40	22	38	36%	63%	14%	16%	21	85	0%	71%			-41.1	-4	-$28
1st Half	4	0	64	34	7.07	1.84	7.61	1.46	157	116	22.8	7%	12%	5%	9%	5.5%	86.9	36	25	40	38%	63%	11%	14%	10	89	0%	70%			-21.5	10	-$24
2nd Half	2	0	53	30	7.35	1.86	6.09	1.59	123	139	22.7	10%	12%	2%	10%	4.4%	86.3	45	20	35	34%	64%	18%	19%	11	82	0%	73%			-19.6	5	-$16
Proj																																	

Waldichuk,Ken

Age: 26	Th: L	Role	SP	Health	A	LIMA Plan	B
Ht: 6' 4"	Wt: 220	Type	Pwr	PT/Exp	B	Rand Var	0
				Consist	F	MM	2203

First full MLB season was a bumpy ride. Abysmal first half was mostly forgotten in the face of broad 2nd-half gains (K-BB%, SwK, xERA, xWHIP). That progress earns him some patience in keeper leagues, but avoid irrational exuberance: per 2nd half BPX, he'll need another step forward just to reach league average.

Yr Tm	W	Sv	IP	K	ERA	WHIP	xERA	xWHIP	vL+	vR+	BF/G	BB%	K%	K-BB%	xBB%	SwK	Vel	G	L	F	H%	S%	HR/F	xHR/F	GS	APC	DOM%	DIS%	Sv%	LI	RAR	BPX	R$
19																																	
20																																	
21 aa	4	0	80	93	4.91	1.39	4.85				21.1	12%	28%	16%							31%	70%									-6.4	77	-$4
22 OAK *	8	0	132	147	2.95	1.08	2.77	1.21	53	126	18.4	8%	29%	21%	7%	12.5%	94.1	35	21	43	29%	76%	12%	14%	7	84	29%	43%			16.6	138	$14
23 OAK	4	1	141	132	5.36	1.56	5.10	1.47	128	112	18.3	11%	21%	10%	9%	11.5%	93.4	40	20	40	32%	69%	14%	13%	22	73	0%	45%	100	0.76	-17.9	53	-$12
1st Half	1	1	66	64	6.78	1.91	5.57	1.56	144	130	17.0	13%	20%	7%	9%	10.8%	93.2	41	22	38	37%	68%	18%	16%	11	67	0%	64%	100	0.76	-20.1	28	-$25
2nd Half	3	0	75	68	4.10	1.25	4.70	1.38	116	93	19.8	9%	22%	12%	8%	12.2%	93.5	39	18	43	27%	71%	11%	11%	11	80	0%	27%	0	0.76	2.2	76	$6
Proj	**7**	**0**	**145**	**147**	**4.43**	**1.36**	**4.13**	**1.34**	**111**	**111**	**20.1**	**10%**	**24%**	**14%**	**9%**	**11.7%**	**93.6**	**39**	**20**	**41**	**30%**	**72%**	**15%**	**13%**	**30**						**-1.9**	**87**	**$0**

Waldron,Matt

Age: 27	Th: R	Role	SP	Health	A	LIMA Plan	C+
Ht: 6' 2"	Wt: 185	Type	Con	PT/Exp	D	Rand Var	+2
				Consist	A	MM	1001

1-3, 4.35 ERA in 41 IP at SD. Knuckleballer logged most of his MLB work late in the season. While he posted a respectable ERA in that tiny MLB sample, it was belied by meager skills and atrocious history. Knuckleballers don't follow our stinkin' rules, but unless he can find a way to miss more bats, he'll likely struggle to stick in the majors.

Yr Tm	W	Sv	IP	K	ERA	WHIP	xERA	xWHIP	vL+	vR+	BF/G	BB%	K%	K-BB%	xBB%	SwK	Vel	G	L	F	H%	S%	HR/F	xHR/F	GS	APC	DOM%	DIS%	Sv%	LI	RAR	BPX	R$
19																																	
20																																	
21 aa	0	0	32	25	7.10	1.74	5.58				20.9	12%	17%	5%							36%	57%									-11.2	58	-$12
22 a/a	5	0	115	79	5.62	1.52	5.23				20.0	7%	16%	8%							34%	63%									-23.5	56	-$13
23 SD *	3	0	134	110	5.51	1.45	5.62	1.35	107	104	20.5	7%	18%	11%	7%	8.5%	91.4	40	18	42	33%	65%	17%	12%	6	84	0%	67%	0	0.78	-19.5	63	-$11
1st Half	1	0	73	62	5.58	1.53	5.78	1.32	95	138	21.1	7%	19%	12%	4%	9.7%	92.4	44	13	44	36%	66%	29%	19%	1	62	0%	100%			-11.2	69	-$13
2nd Half	2	0	64	48	5.23	1.30	5.12	1.31	110	101	20.2	6%	18%	12%	8%	8.4%	91.3	39	19	41	29%	65%	15%	11%	5	87	0%	60%	0	0.78	-7.1	58	-$2
Proj	**2**	**0**	**87**	**67**	**5.29**	**1.45**	**4.57**	**1.37**	**131**	**112**	**20.3**	**8%**	**18%**	**10%**	**8%**	**8.3%**	**91.3**	**39**	**19**	**41**	**32%**	**65%**	**11%**	**10%**	**18**						**-10.3**	**67**	**-$9**

Walker,Ryan

Age: 28	Th: R	Role	RP	Health	A	LIMA Plan	A+
Ht: 6' 2"	Wt: 200	Type	Pwr	PT/Exp	D	Rand Var	-3
				Consist	A	MM	3311

5-3, 3.23 ERA in 61 IP at SF. Solid rookie campaign. Sinker/slider pitcher flipped usage rates in the 2nd half, increasing slider usage from 43% to 55%. That sparked a significant SwK%/K% jump and decrease in GB%. He also handled vL well. If the SwK%/K% sticks and the xBB% manifests, he could become late-inning weapon.

Yr Tm	W	Sv	IP	K	ERA	WHIP	xERA	xWHIP	vL+	vR+	BF/G	BB%	K%	K-BB%	xBB%	SwK	Vel	G	L	F	H%	S%	HR/F	xHR/F	GS	APC	DOM%	DIS%	Sv%	LI	RAR	BPX	R$
19																																	
20																																	
21																																	
22 a/a	7	2	55	51	3.75	1.45	3.61				4.7	12%	22%	10%							33%	72%									1.5	98	$0
23 SF *	6	2	82	96	2.64	1.26	3.59	1.21	96	107	5.3	9%	30%	21%	7%	13.7%	94.9	41	24	35	32%	83%	15%	9%	13	22	0%	38%	67	0.84	17.2	120	$8
1st Half	3	1	42	41	1.75	1.18	3.04	1.30	99	116	5.3	9%	25%	16%	6%	9.1%	95.1	51	21	28	29%	89%	18%	6%	4	21	0%	50%	50	0.71	13.4	111	$8
2nd Half	3	1	40	55	3.57	1.34	3.60	1.19	95	103	5.3	10%	32%	22%	7%	16.0%	94.7	35	25	40	35%	78%	13%	10%	9	22	0%	33%	100	0.91	3.8	149	$4
Proj	**6**	**1**	**73**	**79**	**3.49**	**1.24**	**3.65**	**1.28**	**82**	**93**	**5.3**	**10%**	**27%**	**17%**	**7%**	**13.3%**	**94.9**	**42**	**24**	**35**	**30%**	**75%**	**11%**	**8%**	**0**						**7.5**	**112**	**$4**

Walker,Taijuan

Age: 31	Th: R	Role	SP	Health	D	LIMA Plan	B+
Ht: 6' 4"	Wt: 235	Type		PT/Exp	A	Rand Var	-1
				Consist	B	MM	2103

Maybe early-season forearm tightness was a factor, but he altered pitch mix (more sinkers at expense of four-seam fastball) and velocity dipped, with results deteriorating as the year went on. His K-BB% fell well below-average and SwK%/xBB% say it was deserved. Only one sub-4.00 xERA in this box says rebound potential is modest at best.

Yr Tm	W	Sv	IP	K	ERA	WHIP	xERA	xWHIP	vL+	vR+	BF/G	BB%	K%	K-BB%	xBB%	SwK	Vel	G	L	F	H%	S%	HR/F	xHR/F	GS	APC	DOM%	DIS%	Sv%	LI	RAR	BPX	R$
19 ARI	0	0	1	1	0.00	1.00	4.79			201	4.0	0%	25%	25%		13.3%	93.3	33	0	67	35%	0%	0%	10%	1	15	0%	100%			0.6	188	-$5
20 2 AL	4	0	53	50	2.70	1.16	4.65	1.33	120	68	20.5	8%	22%	14%	9%	8.1%	93.2	39	21	40	26%	85%	13%	15%	11	80	27%	36%			11.5	93	$14
21 NYM	7	0	159	146	4.47	1.18	4.40	1.31	89	98	21.8	8%	22%	14%	7%	10.1%	94.2	42	17	41	26%	67%	14%	14%	29	85	21%	28%	0	0.77	-4.0	93	$5
22 NYM	12	0	157	132	3.49	1.19	3.88	1.26	101	89	22.4	7%	20%	13%	8%	10.4%	93.5	46	20	34	29%	73%	10%	12%	29	86	21%	38%			9.3	100	$11
23 PHI	15	0	173	138	4.38	1.31	4.77	1.45	97	98	23.6	10%	19%	9%	10%	8.7%	92.6	45	19	37	28%	69%	11%	11%	31	92	6%	26%			-1.0	59	$7
1st Half	9	0	89	77	3.93	1.23	4.37	1.37	90	99	21.8	9%	21%	12%	9%	9.0%	93.1	47	18	36	27%	72%	12%	13%	17	85	12%	24%			4.4	84	$14
2nd Half	6	0	83	61	4.86	1.39	5.21	1.53	103	99	25.9	10%	17%	6%	11%	8.4%	92.1	43	20	38	28%	66%	9%	10%	14	100	0%	29%			-5.4	32	$4
Proj	**10**	**0**	**160**	**134**	**4.44**	**1.29**	**4.26**	**1.37**	**101**	**96**	**22.3**	**9%**	**20%**	**11%**	**9%**	**9.2%**	**93.2**	**43**	**19**	**38**	**28%**	**68%**	**12%**	**12%**	**29**						**-2.2**	**75**	**$4**

GREG PYRON

Weathers,Ryan

Age: 24	Th: L	Role: RP	Health: A	LIMA Plan: C
Ht: 6' 1"	Wt: 230	Type: /FB	PT/Exp: C	Rand Var: 0
			Consist: C	MM: 0001

1-8, 6.55 ERA in 58 IP at SD/MIA. Once-pedigreed prospect (7th overall pick in 2018) began 2023 in starting rotation, but spent most of season in minors. Now owns lifetime 5.88 ERA, 8% K-BB% in 156 MLB IP. It's probably too soon to give up on him (especially as a lefty), but shoddy peripherals offer little reason to believe he's close to figuring it out.

Yr Tm	W	Sv	IP	K	ERA	WHIP	xERA	xWHIP	vL+	vR+	BF/G	BB%	K%	K-BB%	xBB%	SwK	Vel	G	L	F	H%	S%	HR/F	xHR/F	GS	APC	DOM%	DIS%	Sv%	LI	RAR	BPX	R$
19																																	
20																																	
21 SD	4	1	95	72	5.32	1.38	4.72	1.35	106	115	13.4	7%	18%	10%	8%	7.8%	94.0	44	19	37	29%	68%	19%	14%	18	54	6%	56%	100	0.64	-12.4	75	-$7
22 SD *	7	0	127	80	5.31	1.64	6.23	1.96		125	17.7	9%	14%	5%	12%	12.4%	93.6	50	21	29	33%	71%	0%	1%	1	89	0%	100%			-21.0	18	-$14
23 2 NL *	6	0	139	116	4.87	1.51	5.25	1.57	123	128	20.0	11%	17%	5%	10%	9.6%	95.1	38	19	43	31%	71%	15%	11%	12	72	0%	83%	0	0.81	-9.3	47	-$8
1st Half	1	0	63	50	5.75	1.67	6.10	1.53	85	131	17.7	11%	18%	7%	9%	9.9%	94.8	40	21	39	33%	68%	14%	12%	9	65	0%	89%	0	0.79	-11.1	33	-$17
2nd Half	5	0	76	66	4.14	1.38	4.54	1.46	178	122	22.8	11%	21%	10%	12%	9.1%	95.6	31	16	53	29%	75%	19%	8%	3	91	0%	67%	0	0.86	1.8	61	$7
Proj	**3**	**0**	**73**	**57**	**5.01**	**1.49**	**4.93**	**1.45**	**132**	**116**	**17.6**	**10%**	**18%**	**9%**	**11%**	**9.1%**	**95.0**	**37**	**18**	**45**	**31%**	**71%**	**13%**	**10%**	**13**						**-6.1**	**45**	**-$7**

Weaver,Luke

Age: 30	Th: R	Role: RP	Health: F	LIMA Plan: B
Ht: 6' 2"	Wt: 183	Type:	PT/Exp: C	Rand Var: +5
			Consist: A	MM: 2201

Logged highest IP total since 2018, as he mostly avoided IL, but pitched so poorly that he was released by CIN and SEA. As has been the case for most of his career, xERA and xWHIP indicate things weren't quite as awful as they seemed. But with three of last four seasons with an ERA in the 6.00s, he's not even stream-worthy.

Yr Tm	W	Sv	IP	K	ERA	WHIP	xERA	xWHIP	vL+	vR+	BF/G	BB%	K%	K-BB%	xBB%	SwK	Vel	G	L	F	H%	S%	HR/F	xHR/F	GS	APC	DOM%	DIS%	Sv%	LI	RAR	BPX	R$
19 ARI	4	0	64	69	2.94	1.07	3.83	1.14	80	91	21.7	5%	27%	21%	7%	11.8%	93.9	41	22	38	30%	76%	9%	13%	12	88	42%	25%			12.4	152	$5
20 ARI	1	0	52	55	6.58	1.56	5.17	1.28	133	105	19.7	8%	23%	16%	8%	11.3%	94.1	32	19	48	37%	61%	13%	13%	12	81	25%	25%			-13.6	110	-$14
21 ARI	3	0	66	62	4.25	1.19	4.35	1.25	116	94	21.2	7%	23%	15%	5%	11.5%	93.7	38	22	40	28%	70%	15%	15%	13	85	15%	31%			0.1	104	-$1
22 2 TM	1	0	36	38	6.56	1.82	4.19	1.25	122	117	6.7	7%	22%	14%	7%	11.1%	94.9	40	30	30	45%	61%	3%	12%	1	28	0%	0%	0	0.25	-11.4	112	-$11
23 3 TM	3	0	124	109	6.40	1.58	4.99	1.33	118	130	19.4	7%	19%	12%	8%	9.6%	94.0	35	25	39	34%	64%	18%	14%	25	78	4%	52%	0	0.71	-31.6	87	-$18
1st Half	1	0	65	55	6.96	1.61	5.12	1.33	116	134	22.7	7%	19%	12%	7%	9.2%	93.8	36	23	41	35%	60%	16%	13%	13	89	8%	62%			-21.0	86	-$21
2nd Half	2	0	59	54	5.80	1.54	4.85	1.33	121	126	16.8	7%	20%	13%	9%	10.1%	94.4	35	28	37	33%	70%	21%	16%	12	69	0%	42%	0	0.67	-10.7	89	-$7
Proj	**2**	**0**	**73**	**69**	**5.77**	**1.50**	**4.25**	**1.27**	**119**	**116**	**14.3**	**8%**	**22%**	**15%**	**8%**	**10.5%**	**94.1**	**37**	**25**	**39**	**35%**	**65%**	**15%**	**14%**	**9**						**-12.9**	**101**	**-$10**

Webb,Logan

Age: 27	Th: R	Role: SP	Health: C	LIMA Plan: C+
Ht: 6' 1"	Wt: 220	Type: Con/xGB	PT/Exp: A	Rand Var: 0
			Consist: A	MM: 5105

Exceeded 200 IP for the first time. Went back to the well with elite BB% and GB% formula and produced highest R$ yet. While he has established a high floor, the low SwK/average K% caps his ceiling and keeps him from joining the truly elite fantasy SP. A full repeat would be a tall order, but any pullback figures to be gentle.

Yr Tm	W	Sv	IP	K	ERA	WHIP	xERA	xWHIP	vL+	vR+	BF/G	BB%	K%	K-BB%	xBB%	SwK	Vel	G	L	F	H%	S%	HR/F	xHR/F	GS	APC	DOM%	DIS%	Sv%	LI	RAR	BPX	R$
19 SF *	3	0	89	82	3.82	1.45	4.65	1.34	92	123	22.3	7%	22%	14%	9%	9.8%	92.9	49	28	23	36%	75%	18%	19%	8	85	13%	38%			7.5	97	-$1
20 SF	3	0	54	46	5.47	1.56	4.49	1.44	109	110	18.9	10%	19%	9%	9%	9.3%	92.7	52	26	22	35%	64%	11%	15%	11	77	9%	55%	0	0.82	-6.8	68	-$7
21 SF	11	0	148	158	3.03	1.11	2.81	1.12	94	75	22.1	6%	27%	20%	6%	12.8%	92.9	61	21	19	31%	74%	13%	12%	26	82	46%	23%	0	0.79	22.5	167	$19
22 SF	15	0	192	163	2.90	1.16	3.31	1.22	105	77	24.6	6%	21%	15%	6%	10.9%	91.9	57	20	24	30%	76%	8%	12%	32	94	41%	13%			25.3	122	$20
23 SF	11	0	216	194	3.25	1.07	2.98	1.12	80	98	25.8	4%	23%	19%	5%	9.3%	92.4	62	17	21	30%	73%	15%	17%	33	96	36%	12%			28.8	169	$27
1st Half	7	0	110	106	3.43	1.12	3.08	1.14	85	100	26.0	5%	24%	19%	5%	9.6%	92.4	61	15	24	30%	74%	18%	20%	17	97	29%	6%			12.3	167	$24
2nd Half	4	0	106	88	3.07	1.02	2.87	1.10	77	96	25.5	2%	22%	19%	5%	9.0%	92.3	63	18	19	30%	71%	12%	12%	16	96	44%	19%			16.5	173	$22
Proj	**12**	**0**	**189**	**172**	**3.39**	**1.16**	**3.03**	**1.17**	**90**	**93**	**23.2**	**5%**	**23%**	**18%**	**6%**	**10.2%**	**92.5**	**59**	**20**	**21**	**31%**	**72%**	**13%**	**14%**	**32**						**21.9**	**150**	**$18**

Wells,Tyler

Age: 29	Th: R	Role: SP	Health: D	LIMA Plan: A+
Ht: 6' 8"	Wt: 255	Type: /xFB	PT/Exp: B	Rand Var: -2
			Consist: B	MM: 1203

7-6, 3.64 ERA in 119 IP at BAL. Logged 5+ IP in each of first 17 starts, though H%/S% provided the ERA/WHIP lipstick. A brutal three-start stretch in July sent him to AAA; arm fatigue slowed his second half recovery. Extreme FB% ups the HR risk, but plus K-BB% should limit damage. With added stamina, 1st half xERA/xWHIP is a reasonable possibility.

Yr Tm	W	Sv	IP	K	ERA	WHIP	xERA	xWHIP	vL+	vR+	BF/G	BB%	K%	K-BB%	xBB%	SwK	Vel	G	L	F	H%	S%	HR/F	xHR/F	GS	APC	DOM%	DIS%	Sv%	LI	RAR	BPX	R$
19																																	
20																																	
21 BAL	2	4	57	65	4.11	0.91	4.08	1.07	65	90	5.1	5%	29%	24%	5%	14.4%	95.2	21	22	57	24%	60%	11%	11%	0	20			57	0.85	1.1	145	$4
22 BAL	7	0	104	76	4.25	1.14	4.56	1.29	81	111	18.4	7%	18%	11%	6%	11.9%	93.6	37	17	47	25%	68%	11%	11%	23	72	4%	43%			-3.7	75	$2
23 BAL *	7	2	135	127	3.95	1.04	3.66	1.23	82	98	14.9	7%	25%	18%	7%	11.6%	92.6	32	13	55	22%	72%	15%	14%	20	76	25%	25%	100	0.82	6.4	81	$13
1st Half	6	0	93	95	3.21	0.88	4.11	1.13	77	93	22.4	6%	27%	21%	7%	12.0%	92.6	33	13	54	21%	78%	15%	14%	15	92	33%	7%	0	0.78	12.9	140	$28
2nd Half	1	2	42	32	5.58	1.40	5.07	1.60	108	114	9.4	13%	18%	6%	8%	10.4%	92.6	32	12	56	24%	66%	15%	15%	5	48	0%	80%	100	0.89	-6.5	25	-$5
Proj	**6**	**0**	**138**	**126**	**4.08**	**1.25**	**4.50**	**1.29**	**95**	**114**	**21.7**	**8%**	**22%**	**14%**	**7%**	**12.0%**	**93.4**	**30**	**16**	**54**	**28%**	**75%**	**12%**	**13%**	**26**						**4.2**	**86**	**$4**

Wentz,Joey

Age: 26	Th: L	Role: RP	Health: C	LIMA Plan: C+
Ht: 6' 5"	Wt: 220	Type: Pwr/FB	PT/Exp: D	Rand Var: +3
			Consist: F	MM: 1100

3-13, 6.90 ERA in 106 IP at DET. 40th overall pick in 2016 MLB draft battled back from 2020 Tommy John surgery and a shoulder injury that cost him a big chunk of 2022. Struggled overall as HR and BB% were problematic. Four-seam fastball was crushed (.317 xBA, .625 xSLG, 42% usage). Future might be as a RP (28% K%, 9% BB% in 25 IP).

Yr Tm	W	Sv	IP	K	ERA	WHIP	xERA	xWHIP	vL+	vR+	BF/G	BB%	K%	K-BB%	xBB%	SwK	Vel	G	L	F	H%	S%	HR/F	xHR/F	GS	APC	DOM%	DIS%	Sv%	LI	RAR	BPX	R$
19 aa	7	0	130	114	6.02	1.46	5.15				22.3	9%	20%	11%							31%	61%									-24.2	53	-$8
20																																	
21 aa	0	0	54	46	4.48	1.50	4.73				18.0	14%	20%	6%							27%	74%									-1.4	47	-$7
22 DET *	4	0	82	69	3.15	1.17	3.02	1.38	76	90	17.2	10%	21%	11%	10%	8.8%	92.4	37	20	43	26%	76%	5%	9%	7	79	14%	29%			8.3	87	$3
23 DET *	5	0	136	127	6.36	1.66	6.63	1.42	107	127	19.7	10%	20%	10%	8%	11.5%	93.4	37	19	44	35%	66%	16%	16%	19	77	11%	53%	0	0.82	-34.0	39	-$20
1st Half	1	0	72	66	6.78	1.63	5.28	1.41	106	123	20.6	9%	20%	11%	8%	10.8%	93.7	38	20	42	34%	62%	16%	16%	15	81	13%	47%	0	0.75	-21.7	68	-$21
2nd Half	4	0	64	61	5.89	1.70	6.61	1.40	111	138	19.3	10%	21%	11%	8%	13.1%	92.8	36	16	48	37%	69%	16%	14%	4	71	0%	75%	0	0.94	-12.4	46	-$6
Proj	**2**	**0**	**58**	**52**	**4.70**	**1.44**	**4.71**	**1.45**	**96**	**111**	**11.6**	**11%**	**21%**	**10%**	**8%**	**11.5%**	**93.0**	**37**	**18**	**45**	**30%**	**72%**	**13%**	**13%**	**3**						**-2.7**	**52**	**-$6**

Wesneski,Hayden

Age: 26	Th: R	Role: RP	Health: A	LIMA Plan: B
Ht: 6' 3"	Wt: 210	Type: Pwr	PT/Exp: C	Rand Var: 0
			Consist: D	MM: 3201

3-5, 4.63 ERA in 89 IP at CHC. Searching for the right mix: Went from 15% SwK% on three pitches to having one pitch >10% (sweeper at 13%). HR shot up as GB% lean vanished. 2nd half K% spiked with more sweepers and velocity, but BB% soared. Most 2nd half outings were out of the pen, so add "Role" to his list of questions to be answered.

Yr Tm	W	Sv	IP	K	ERA	WHIP	xERA	xWHIP	vL+	vR+	BF/G	BB%	K%	K-BB%	xBB%	SwK	Vel	G	L	F	H%	S%	HR/F	xHR/F	GS	APC	DOM%	DIS%	Sv%	LI	RAR	BPX	R$
19																																	
20																																	
21 a/a	10	0	94	88	4.71	1.36	4.76				21.8	7%	22%	15%							33%	68%									-5.1	89	$0
22 CHC *	9	0	144	120	3.46	1.13	3.06	1.11	57	96	19.0	7%	21%	14%	6%	12.3%	92.7	47	11	41	28%	71%	8%	5%	4	83	75%	25%	0	0.73	9.0	104	$10
23 CHC *	4	0	109	105	4.03	1.23	4.44	1.33	133	85	11.4	8%	22%	13%	8%	9.6%	93.8	40	22	38	27%	76%	21%	17%	11	44	9%	45%	0	0.68	4.1	70	$3
1st Half	3	0	70	56	4.26	1.16	4.38	1.33	132	84	16.3	7%	19%	12%	7%	8.6%	93.1	39	23	38	24%	72%	20%	18%	10	64	10%	40%	0	0.63	0.6	58	$3
2nd Half	1	0	40	49	3.63	1.35	4.53	1.31	136	88	7.5	11%	29%	18%	11%	11.4%	95.4	43	22	35	31%	80%	23%	14%	1	27	0%	100%	0	0.71	3.5	93	$0
Proj	**4**	**0**	**73**	**72**	**4.27**	**1.28**	**3.83**	**1.29**	**127**	**92**	**12.3**	**9%**	**24%**	**15%**	**8%**	**10.7%**	**94.1**	**43**	**20**	**38**	**29%**	**72%**	**17%**	**13%**	**5**						**0.5**	**106**	**-$1**

Wheeler,Zack

Age: 34	Th: R	Role: SP	Health: B	LIMA Plan: C+
Ht: 6' 4"	Wt: 195	Type:	PT/Exp: A	Rand Var: -1
			Consist: A	MM: 5305

Avoided IL and posted third consecutive $20 R$ season. Disparity between halves was just H%/S% fluctuations around carbon-copy skills. Career-best SwK suggests another tick of K% upside. As is, only five qualified MLB starting pitchers had a better K-BB% in 2023. Increased FB% means heightened HR vulnerability, but this is still a top-ten SP.

Yr Tm	W	Sv	IP	K	ERA	WHIP	xERA	xWHIP	vL+	vR+	BF/G	BB%	K%	K-BB%	xBB%	SwK	Vel	G	L	F	H%	S%	HR/F	xHR/F	GS	APC	DOM%	DIS%	Sv%	LI	RAR	BPX	R$
19 NYM	11	0	195	195	3.96	1.26	4.22	1.23	102	85	26.7	6%	24%	18%	5%	11.0%	96.7	43	21	35	33%	71%	11%	12%	31	102	45%	19%			13.1	131	$13
20 PHI	4	0	71	53	2.92	1.17	3.67	1.26	90	90	26.2	6%	18%	13%	6%	11.1%	96.9	56	25	19	30%	75%	8%	12%	11	98	27%	18%			13.5	113	$16
21 PHI	14	0	213	247	2.78	1.01	2.98	1.06	82	77	26.5	5%	29%	24%	5%	12.9%	97.1	50	23	28	30%	75%	11%	11%	32	100	63%	6%			39.0	179	$35
22 PHI	12	0	153	163	2.82	1.04	3.11	1.09	88	90	23.3	6%	27%	21%	6%	11.8%	95.8	46	21	33	29%	76%	10%	10%	26	91	38%	8%			21.6	157	$20
23 PHI	13	0	192	212	3.61	1.08	3.61	1.10	97	75	24.6	5%	27%	22%	6%	13.8%	95.6	41	20	39	31%	70%	10%	9%	32	99	44%	13%			17.1	167	$24
1st Half	7	0	98	112	4.03	1.19	3.69	1.11	103	78	24.6	5%	27%	22%	7%	13.5%	95.8	40	23	37	35%	66%	7%	8%	17	101	35%	18%			3.7	167	$17
2nd Half	6	0	94	100	3.17	0.96	3.53	1.08	92	72	24.6	5%	27%	22%	6%	14.2%	95.5	43	18	40	27%	74%	13%	10%	15	97	53%	7%			13.4	169	$25
Proj	**12**	**0**	**174**	**185**	**3.33**	**1.06**	**3.13**	**1.09**	**92**	**80**	**24.0**	**5%**	**27%**	**22%**	**6%**	**13.0%**	**96.1**	**45**	**21**	**34**	**30%**	**71%**	**11%**	**10%**	**28**						**21.4**	**162**	**$22**

GREG PYRON

White,Brendan

Age: 25	Th: R	Role: RP	Health: A	LIMA Plan: B
Ht: 5' 11"	Wt: 185	Type:	PT/Exp: D	Rand Var: +2
			Consist: F	MM: 4200

2-3, 5.09 ERA in 41 IP at DET. Former starting pitcher moved to the bullpen in 2022. Doesn't have elite velocity, but low arm slot helps his stuff play up a bit. K-BB% provokes our initial interest, and SwK/xBB% hint at additional upside in both sides of that calculation. Ability to keep the ball on ground is also a plus. Worth monitoring in Holds leagues.

Yr Tm	W	Sv	IP	K	ERA	WHIP	xERA	xWHIP	vL+	vR+	BF/G	BB%	K%	K-BB%	xBB%	SwK	Vel	G	L	F	H%	S%	HR/F	xHR/F	GS	APC	DOM%	DIS%	Sv%	LI	RAR	BPX	R$
19																																	
20																																	
21																																	
22 aa	6	9	68	59	2.72	0.93	1.73				5.3	6%	23%	17%							25%	70%									10.5	142	$11
23 DET *	5	0	78	83	4.74	1.49	4.97	1.27	106	95	5.4	8%	25%	16%	6%	13.3%	94.2	52	20	29	38%	69%	13%	12%	2	20	0%	50%	0	0.58	-3.9	109	-$5
1st Half	4	0	44	49	5.26	1.74	6.87	1.22	94	135	6.0	7%	24%	17%	5%	14.6%	94.8	61	12	27	43%	72%	33%	16%	1	24	0%	0%	0	0.75	-5.1	93	-$9
2nd Half	1	0	33	35	4.05	1.14	2.45	1.27	113	80	4.7	9%	25%	17%	6%	12.7%	93.9	48	23	29	30%	62%	4%	10%	1	19	0%	100%	0	0.52	1.2	135	-$1
Proj	**3**	**0**	**58**	**57**	**3.96**	**1.25**	**3.52**	**1.23**	**155**	**88**	**5.4**	**7%**	**24%**	**17%**	**7%**	**12.7%**	**93.9**	**46**	**23**	**31**	**32%**	**70%**	**12%**	**9%**	**0**						**2.6**	**122**	**-$1**

White,Owen

Age: 24	Th: R	Role: SP	Health: A	LIMA Plan: C+
Ht: 6' 3"	Wt: 170	Type: Pwr	PT/Exp: D	Rand Var: +5
			Consist: F	MM: 1100

0-1, 11.25 ERA in 4 IP at TEX. Finally got through a season healthy, but struggled to throw strikes. Low-90s fastball did not get many whiffs. Has innate feel for spin with curveball and slider; also added a cutter, which caused as many issues as fastball. With better command, he contributes as starter, but it's not a short runway. (CB)

Yr Tm	W	Sv	IP	K	ERA	WHIP	xERA	xWHIP	vL+	vR+	BF/G	BB%	K%	K-BB%	xBB%	SwK	Vel	G	L	F	H%	S%	HR/F	xHR/F	GS	APC	DOM%	DIS%	Sv%	LI	RAR	BPX	R$
19																																	
20																																	
21																																	
22 aa	3	0	23	19	2.15	1.02	2.30				22.3	4%	21%	17%							28%	79%									5.2	150	-$1
23 TEX *	4	0	114	70	4.58	1.40	4.65	1.44	135	152	17.9	11%	21%	11%	6%	10.3%	93.5	50	17	33	26%	72%	50%	23%	0	34			0	0.30	-3.4	28	-$5
1st Half	2	0	66	45	4.52	1.26	4.05	1.52	181	174	18.0	10%	17%	6%	6%	11.1%	93.9	57	14	29	24%	69%	50%	10%	0	36			0	0.60	-1.5	43	-$2
2nd Half	2	0	48	25	4.55	1.58	5.36	1.75		131	17.6	13%	12%	-1%	6%	9.4%	93.1	40	20	40	28%	75%	50%	36%	0	32			0	0.00	-1.3	12	-$5
Proj	**2**	**0**	**58**	**52**	**4.49**	**1.45**	**4.44**	**1.48**			**20.7**	**12%**	**21%**	**9%**				**45**	**22**	**33**	**29%**	**73%**	**16%**	**12%**	**12**						**-1.2**	**50**	**-$5**

Whitlock,Garrett

Age: 28	Th: R	Role: RP	Health: F	LIMA Plan: A
Ht: 6' 5"	Wt: 225	Type:	PT/Exp: B	Rand Var: +1
			Consist: B	MM: 4211

5-5, 5.15 ERA in 72 IP at BOS. Began 2023 as a starter and moved to bullpen following August return from second IL stint (elbow). Again displayed skills to succeed including elite BB%, ability to miss bats, slight GB lean. What he has not displayed is evidence that he can handle a starter's workload. Intriguing arm regardless of role.

Yr Tm	W	Sv	IP	K	ERA	WHIP	xERA	xWHIP	vL+	vR+	BF/G	BB%	K%	K-BB%	xBB%	SwK	Vel	G	L	F	H%	S%	HR/F	xHR/F	GS	APC	DOM%	DIS%	Sv%	LI	RAR	BPX	R$
19 aa	3	0	71	49	4.12	1.53	5.16				22.1	6%	16%	9%							35%	74%									3.4	66	-$4
20																																	
21 BOS	8	2	73	81	1.96	1.10	3.30	1.10	114	69	6.5	6%	27%	21%	5%	13.2%	96.0	50	20	30	32%	87%	10%	7%	0	25			40	1.20	20.8	165	$12
22 BOS	4	6	78	82	3.45	1.02	3.37	1.07	80	98	10.0	5%	26%	22%	5%	14.2%	95.3	41	20	39	28%	71%	12%	11%	9	38	11%	33%	75	0.95	5.0	157	$7
23 BOS *	6	1	93	91	4.34	1.29	5.02	1.13	104	119	14.1	4%	24%	19%	5%	13.7%	94.0	44	19	37	34%	72%	16%	15%	10	54	20%	20%	50	0.90	-0.1	141	$1
1st Half	5	0	72	64	4.22	1.26	4.98	1.13	121	111	20.9	3%	22%	19%	5%	14.1%	93.6	44	18	38	33%	73%	17%	13%	10	83	20%	20%			1.0	149	$5
2nd Half	1	1	23	27	4.28	1.27	4.31	1.13	62	141	7.3	6%	28%	22%	6%	13.0%	94.9	44	22	35	35%	70%	16%	20%	0	30			50	0.99	0.1	143	-$3
Proj	**6**	**2**	**87**	**90**	**3.56**	**1.15**	**3.41**	**1.12**	**85**	**101**	**9.0**	**6%**	**26%**	**20%**	**5%**	**13.4%**	**94.9**	**43**	**20**	**37**	**31%**	**73%**	**12%**	**13%**	**0**						**8.2**	**151**	**$6**

Wicks,Jordan

Age: 24	Th: L	Role: RP	Health: A	LIMA Plan: A
Ht: 6' 3"	Wt: 220	Type: Con	PT/Exp: D	Rand Var: 0
			Consist: A	MM: 3101

4-1, 4.41 ERA in 34.2 IP at CHC. Command artist relies on design and angles to keep hitters off-balance. It's a heavy fastball/change-up-centric arsenal relying on the 4-seamer up, the cutter in vR and the change-up and sinker staying away. Throws slider and curveball for show but not effect. Seems ready.(CB)

Yr Tm	W	Sv	IP	K	ERA	WHIP	xERA	xWHIP	vL+	vR+	BF/G	BB%	K%	K-BB%	xBB%	SwK	Vel	G	L	F	H%	S%	HR/F	xHR/F	GS	APC	DOM%	DIS%	Sv%	LI	RAR	BPX	R$
19																																	
20																																	
21																																	
22 aa	0	0	28	30	3.66	1.18	3.67				14.0	8%	27%	19%							29%	74%									1.1	106	-$4
23 CHC *	11	0	127	106	3.79	1.21	3.76	1.40	102	101	18.9	7%	16%	9%	9%	10.3%	91.9	47	25	28	28%	72%	16%	14%	7	83	0%	29%			8.5	84	$9
1st Half	4	0	64	61	3.54	1.20	3.72				18.4	8%	24%	16%							29%	75%	0%		0	0					6.3	103	$7
2nd Half	7	0	65	46	3.81	1.17	3.47	1.40	102	102	19.9	8%	18%	10%	9%	10.3%	91.9	47	25	28	26%	71%	16%	14%	7	83	0%	29%			4.2	70	$12
Proj	**10**	**0**	**109**	**88**	**3.73**	**1.23**	**3.82**	**1.33**	**106**	**105**	**19.5**	**8%**	**20%**	**12%**	**9%**	**10.3%**	**91.9**	**47**	**25**	**28**	**28%**	**73%**	**15%**	**12%**	**22**						**8.0**	**87**	**$6**

Williams,Devin

Age: 29	Th: R	Role: RP	Health: A	LIMA Plan: C+
Ht: 6' 2"	Wt: 200	Type: Pwr	PT/Exp: A	Rand Var: -5
			Consist: B	MM: 5530

Finished with fifth most saves in MLB in his first full season as closer. Halted recent velocity decline but didn't really recover, and HR/F regressed to league average as expected. Elite K% and GB tilt overshadow BB% issues, which xBB% scoffs at anyway. Don't count on another sub-2.00 ERA, but he should remain among the best.

Yr Tm	W	Sv	IP	K	ERA	WHIP	xERA	xWHIP	vL+	vR+	BF/G	BB%	K%	K-BB%	xBB%	SwK	Vel	G	L	F	H%	S%	HR/F	xHR/F	GS	APC	DOM%	DIS%	Sv%	LI	RAR	BPX	R$
19 MIL *	7	4	73	83	3.13	1.41	3.77	1.40	107	129	6.6	13%	27%	14%	8%	10.7%	96.2	41	23	36	32%	80%	13%	12%	0	21			100	0.32	12.4	99	$6
20 MIL	4	0	27	53	0.33	0.63	1.40	0.80	48	43	4.5	9%	54%	44%	8%	22.3%	96.5	61	11	28	23%	100%	10%	18%	0	20			0	1.16	13.7	312	$21
21 MIL	8	3	54	87	2.50	1.19	2.99	1.16	93	66	3.9	12%	38%	26%	8%	19.0%	95.4	45	18	37	32%	83%	13%	10%	0	17			50	1.36	11.8	173	$8
22 MIL	6	15	61	96	1.93	1.01	2.34	1.12	89	51	3.7	13%	40%	28%	8%	18.7%	94.0	51	20	29	28%	81%	6%	6%	0	16			88	1.58	15.3	182	$16
23 MIL	8	36	59	87	1.53	0.92	2.81	1.18	65	59	3.8	12%	38%	26%	9%	18.9%	94.2	48	21	31	22%	88%	11%	13%	0	16			90	1.61	20.2	169	$28
1st Half	4	17	30	39	1.52	0.98	3.35	1.33	55	80	3.9	14%	33%	20%	11%	17.2%	94.1	45	23	32	18%	92%	15%	15%	0	16			94	1.63	10.3	119	$22
2nd Half	4	19	29	48	1.55	0.86	2.30	1.04	75	37	3.7	11%	42%	32%	7%	20.7%	94.4	51	19	30	26%	83%	6%	11%	0	15			86	1.59	9.9	222	$23
Proj	**7**	**36**	**58**	**88**	**2.30**	**1.11**	**2.67**	**1.16**	**87**	**64**	**3.9**	**12%**	**39%**	**26%**	**8%**	**19.1%**	**94.5**	**48**	**20**	**32**	**30%**	**82%**	**11%**	**11%**	**0**						**14.5**	**171**	**$23**

Williams,Gavin

Age: 24	Th: R	Role: SP	Health: A	LIMA Plan: A
Ht: 6' 6"	Wt: 238	Type: Pwr	PT/Exp: D	Rand Var: -3
			Consist: A	MM: 3203

3-5, 3.29 ERA in 82 IP at CLE. Top prospect opened 2023 at AA, quickly moved to AAA, and made MLB debut June 21. Flashed big upside in Aug (3.29 xERA, 31% K%/15% SwK, 8% BB in 27 IP) before mid-Sept shutdown. Approach vL needs improvement (only 7% K-BB% vL). Owns frontline SP potential at peak, but will require patience.

Yr Tm	W	Sv	IP	K	ERA	WHIP	xERA	xWHIP	vL+	vR+	BF/G	BB%	K%	K-BB%	xBB%	SwK	Vel	G	L	F	H%	S%	HR/F	xHR/F	GS	APC	DOM%	DIS%	Sv%	LI	RAR	BPX	R$
19																																	
20																																	
21																																	
22 aa	3	0	70	71	2.45	1.02	2.70				16.8	9%	26%	17%							23%	84%									13.1	108	$6
23 CLE *	7	0	143	148	3.00	1.17	3.00	1.40	107	76	20.4	11%	23%	13%	8%	12.4%	95.7	38	23	39	26%	78%	9%	9%	16	87	19%	38%			23.5	105	$15
1st Half	4	0	74	77	2.65	0.99	2.13	1.30	80	31	20.1	10%	27%	17%	4%	9.1%	95.7	32	19	48	22%	78%	7%	2%	2	88	50%	50%			15.3	120	$19
2nd Half	3	0	69	71	3.38	1.36	4.51	1.41	113	82	21.4	11%	24%	13%	9%	12.9%	95.7	39	23	38	30%	78%	10%	10%	14	87	14%	36%			8.2	76	$7
Proj	**7**	**0**	**152**	**149**	**3.64**	**1.25**	**3.92**	**1.33**	**121**	**86**	**21.1**	**10%**	**24%**	**14%**	**10%**	**12.9%**	**95.7**	**39**	**23**	**38**	**29%**	**74%**	**11%**	**9%**	**29**						**12.9**	**88**	**$8**

Williams,Trevor

Age: 32	Th: R	Role: SP	Health: C	LIMA Plan: B
Ht: 6' 3"	Wt: 235	Type:	PT/Exp: A	Rand Var: +1
			Consist: C	MM: 1101

Journeyman found success in 2022 when 21 of 30 appearances came as a reliever, rebuilding Nats decided to see if he could bring that success back to rotation. Answer: Um, no. Velocity, SwK, and K% all tumbled, contributing to career-worst BPX. Recent DOM%/DIS% has been comically awful and hammers the point: this is not a viable starter.

Yr Tm	W	Sv	IP	K	ERA	WHIP	xERA	xWHIP	vL+	vR+	BF/G	BB%	K%	K-BB%	xBB%	SwK	Vel	G	L	F	H%	S%	HR/F	xHR/F	GS	APC	DOM%	DIS%	Sv%	LI	RAR	BPX	R$
19 PIT	7	0	146	113	5.38	1.41	5.26	1.38	125	104	24.5	7%	18%	11%	6%	10.8%	91.3	37	23	40	31%	66%	15%	14%	26	90	19%	31%			-15.6	73	-$5
20 PIT	2	0	55	49	6.18	1.57	4.99	1.37	103	148	22.9	8%	19%	11%	8%	10.9%	91.3	45	20	35	32%	68%	24%	16%	11	92	9%	55%			-11.8	84	-$12
21 2 NL *	6	0	110	102	3.85	1.38	4.60	1.27	109	111	17.1	7%	22%	15%	6%	10.7%	91.1	46	23	31	34%	75%	13%	13%	15	67	20%	40%	0	0.61	5.6	92	$1
22 NYM	3	1	90	84	3.21	1.23	3.99	1.19	126	87	12.4	6%	23%	16%	8%	11.0%	90.9	36	21	42	31%	80%	11%	12%	9	47	11%	56%	50	0.67	8.4	114	$3
23 WAS	6	0	144	111	5.55	1.60	5.40	1.42	118	125	22.0	8%	17%	9%	9%	8.3%	89.3	40	19	41	33%	72%	17%	16%	30	88	0%	53%			-21.7	60	-$15
1st Half	5	0	85	63	4.34	1.42	5.18	1.38	114	111	21.9	7%	17%	10%	8%	8.3%	89.7	39	19	41	30%	78%	16%	14%	17	86	0%	47%			-0.1	68	$0
2nd Half	1	0	59	48	7.28	1.85	5.73	1.46	124	146	22.0	9%	17%	8%	11%	8.3%	88.8	40	19	41	36%	66%	19%	18%	13	89	0%	62%			-21.6	48	-$18
Proj	**4**	**0**	**116**	**98**	**5.19**	**1.53**	**4.53**	**1.35**	**116**	**119**	**20.1**	**8%**	**19%**	**11%**	**8%**	**9.5%**	**90.1**	**41**	**21**	**39**	**33%**	**72%**	**17%**	**15%**	**25**						**-12.4**	**80**	**-$10**

GREG PYRON

Williamson,Brandon

Age: 26 **Th:** L **Role** SP **Ht:** 6'6" **Wt:** 210 **Type** Pwr/FB
Health A | PT/Exp D | Consist B | LIMA Plan B | Rand Var 0 | MM 1201

5-5, 4.46 ERA in 117 IP at CIN. Elite K% at Double-A in 2021 has not yet climbed the ladder with him. Improved change-up (18% SwK, 53% GB%, 17% usage) is promising. However, slider (11% SwK) was only other pitch with a SwK above 8%. Lots of work to be done, but being a southpaw he'll get more time. Patience required in keeper leagues.

Yr	Tm	W	Sv	IP	K	ERA	WHIP	xERA	xWHIP	vL+	vR+	BF/G	BB%	K%	K-BB%	xBB%	SwK	Vel	G	L	F	H%	S%	HR/F	xHR/F	GS	APC	DOM%	DIS%	Sv%	LI	RAR	BPX	R$
19																																		
20																																		
21	aa	2	0	68	84	3.86	1.34	4.28				21.8	8%	30%	22%							37%	74%									3.4	131	-$2
22	a/a	6	0	124	105	4.65	1.68	5.10				20.7	14%	19%	5%							33%	73%									-10.4	56	-$11
23	CIN *	7	0	151	120	4.98	1.44	5.28	1.35	95	103	20.7	8%	20%	12%	8%	9.7%	92.9	37	20	43	30%	70%	12%	12%	23	84	22%	43%			-12.1	46	-$6
1st Half		3	0	78	56	6.09	1.65	6.47	1.55	83	115	20.4	10%	16%	5%	8%	9.7%	92.4	35	22	43	31%	67%	14%	18%	9	82	22%	56%			-16.9	13	-$18
2nd Half		4	0	73	64	3.80	1.21	4.46	1.28	104	97	21.6	7%	21%	14%	7%	9.7%	93.1	39	19	42	29%	73%	11%	9%	14	86	21%	36%			4.8	100	$9
Proj		**4**	**0**	**87**	**80**	**4.52**	**1.36**	**4.39**	**1.36**	**97**	**103**	**20.7**	**10%**	**22%**	**12%**	**8%**	**9.7%**	**92.8**	**37**	**20**	**43**	**30%**	**70%**	**11%**	**12%**	**18**						**-2.1**	**76**	**-$3**

Wilson,Bryse

Age: 26 **Th:** R **Role** RP **Ht:** 6' 1" **Wt:** 250 **Type** Con/FB
Health B | PT/Exp B | Consist B | LIMA Plan B+ | Rand Var -5 | MM 1001

Shifted from starter to multi-inning reliever, tweaked mechanics, and altered pitch mix. ERA and WHIP look improved, but only thanks to H%/S%. Velocity recovered, but SwK/K% remained below par. Leap in FB% adds to HR risk given his HR/F history (lifetime 14% HR/F). As always, xERA highlights true talent level, and this one still isn't pretty.

Yr	Tm	W	Sv	IP	K	ERA	WHIP	xERA	xWHIP	vL+	vR+	BF/G	BB%	K%	K-BB%	xBB%	SwK	Vel	G	L	F	H%	S%	HR/F	xHR/F	GS	APC	DOM%	DIS%	Sv%	LI	RAR	BPX	R$
19	ATL *	11	0	141	116	4.77	1.44	5.14	1.57	149	130	22.2	6%	19%	13%	6%	9.0%	94.7	31	26	43	35%	69%	18%	17%	4	59	0%	50%	0	0.58	-4.6	79	$0
20	ATL	1	1	16	15	4.02	1.72	5.42	1.53	139	99	12.2	12%	21%	8%	8%	9.3%	94.0	42	23	35	35%	80%	12%	24%	2	52	50%	50%	100	0.26	0.8	40	-$5
21	2 NL *	8	0	130	80	5.33	1.51	6.07	1.40	116	113	21.7	7%	14%	7%	6%	9.2%	93.0	37	25	38	32%	69%	16%	16%	16	71	6%	63%			-17.1	24	-$10
22	PIT *	8	0	153	106	4.90	1.34	5.03	1.32	128	108	20.5	6%	17%	11%	7%	8.2%	92.4	43	22	35	30%	68%	15%	14%	20	73	5%	65%	0	0.83	-17.6	56	-$5
23	MIL	6	3	77	61	2.58	1.07	4.68	1.32	106	77	5.9	7%	19%	12%	6%	8.5%	93.3	38	19	44	25%	82%	9%	9%	0	22			75	0.56	16.5	84	$10
1st Half		3	3	39	31	2.77	1.13	4.85	1.34	104	78	5.9	8%	19%	12%	9%	9.1%	93.3	33	22	45	27%	78%	6%	6%	0	22			75	0.46	7.5	73	$6
2nd Half		3	0	38	30	2.39	1.01	4.50	1.30	108	76	5.9	6%	19%	13%	5%	8.0%	93.4	43	15	42	22%	88%	13%	12%	0	21			0	0.67	9.0	96	$6
Proj		**5**	**0**	**65**	**48**	**4.50**	**1.34**	**4.50**	**1.32**	**123**	**98**	**9.4**	**7%**	**18%**	**11%**	**6%**	**8.6%**	**93.1**	**39**	**20**	**41**	**31%**	**70%**	**11%**	**12%**	**0**						**-1.4**	**77**	**-$3**

Wilson,Steven

Age: 29 **Th:** R **Role** RP **Ht:** 6' 3" **Wt:** 221 **Type** Pwr/xFB
Health D | PT/Exp C | Consist C | LIMA Plan C+ | Rand Var -5 | MM 1301

LI improvement shows he climbed the leverage ladder in sophomore season. However, 2022's xERA proved directionally predictive despite continuing to defy storm clouds of xERA in first half. Regression finally bit him hard in small-sample second-half bookended by two IL stints (pectoral, hip). First half is a good baseline, just use xERA rather than ERA.

Yr	Tm	W	Sv	IP	K	ERA	WHIP	xERA	xWHIP	vL+	vR+	BF/G	BB%	K%	K-BB%	xBB%	SwK	Vel	G	L	F	H%	S%	HR/F	xHR/F	GS	APC	DOM%	DIS%	Sv%	LI	RAR	BPX	R$
19	aaa	1	0	35	34	4.24	1.42	4.02				5.9	14%	23%	9%							27%	73%									1.1	67	-$4
20																																		
21	aaa	4	0	40	49	3.09	0.91	2.21				5.3	9%	33%	23%							22%	73%									5.8	139	$3
22	SD	4	1	53	53	3.06	1.06	4.42	1.28	80	92	4.3	9%	25%	15%	8%	13.2%	95.1	24	18	58	23%	78%	9%	6%	1	17	0%	0%	33	0.89	6.0	80	$3
23	SD	1	0	53	57	3.91	1.17	5.01	1.42	92	86	4.2	12%	26%	14%	10%	11.3%	94.5	26	14	61	23%	71%	9%	9%	0	18			0	1.08	2.8	61	-$1
1st Half		1	0	37	40	2.43	1.00	4.41	1.33	63	85	4.2	11%	27%	16%	9%	11.2%	94.6	32	13	56	21%	82%	8%	9%	0	18			0	1.21	8.7	90	$3
2nd Half		0	0	16	17	7.31	1.56	6.41	1.61	148	92	4.3	15%	23%	8%	12%	11.5%	94.3	14	16	70	28%	55%	10%	8%	0	18			0	0.81	-5.9	-4	-$10
Proj		**3**	**0**	**65**	**71**	**4.36**	**1.20**	**4.51**	**1.39**	**111**	**88**	**4.5**	**12%**	**27%**	**15%**	**10%**	**11.7%**	**94.6**	**21**	**15**	**63**	**24%**	**67%**	**10%**	**7%**	**0**						**-0.3**	**62**	**-$**

Winans,Allan

Age: 28 **Th:** R **Role** SP **Ht:** 6' 2" **Wt:** 165 **Type** Con
Health A | PT/Exp D | Consist F | LIMA Plan B | Rand Var 0 | MM 2001

1-2, 5.29 ERA in 32 IP at ATL. Made six starts in 2nd half, allowing 2 ER or fewer in four of them and 13 ER combined in the other two. Blend of good control, bottom-tier velocity, and merely average SwK/K% offers minimal upside, but the floor is fairly steady. Barring skills gains, this profile maxes out as a streamer/matchup play.

Yr	Tm	W	Sv	IP	K	ERA	WHIP	xERA	xWHIP	vL+	vR+	BF/G	BB%	K%	K-BB%	xBB%	SwK	Vel	G	L	F	H%	S%	HR/F	xHR/F	GS	APC	DOM%	DIS%	Sv%	LI	RAR	BPX	R$
19																																		
20																																		
21	aa	1	3	28	24	1.61	0.73	1.08				7.1	8%	24%	16%							16%	87%									9.2	126	$3
22	a/a	1	0	60	47	4.26	1.46	4.84				21.4	7%	18%	12%							35%	71%									-2.2	84	-$6
23	ATL *	10	1	159	124	3.77	1.29	4.13	1.18	133	67	22.6	6%	24%	18%	5%	11.4%	89.8	45	16	38	30%	73%	14%	11%	6	89	33%	33%			11.0	82	$9
1st Half		6	1	87	59	3.45	1.21	3.80				23.5	6%	17%	11%							29%	74%	0%		0	0					9.5	82	$1
2nd Half		4	0	75	65	4.02	1.33	4.30	1.33	134	68	22.1	8%	21%	13%	5%	11.4%	89.8	45	16	38	31%	72%	14%	11%	6	89	33%	33%			2.8	85	$6
Proj		**5**	**0**	**73**	**54**	**4.15**	**1.30**	**4.18**	**1.32**	**132**	**66**	**23.4**	**7%**	**18%**	**11%**	**5%**	**11.4%**	**89.8**	**45**	**16**	**38**	**31%**	**70%**	**10%**	**10%**	**13**						**1.6**	**87**	**-$1**

Winckowski,Josh

Age: 26 **Th:** R **Role** RP **Ht:** 6' 4" **Wt:** 202 **Type**
Health A | PT/Exp C | Consist B | LIMA Plan A+ | Rand Var -3 | MM 3100

Former swingman settled into bullpen role and merited higher leverage outings as the year went on. Kept his GB%-inducing ways, dialed up the velocity and more Ks followed, with no slippage in BB%. Before you get excited about 2nd half K%, SwK gains didn't fully back that. He's found a home in relief, but not back-end material at this point.

Yr	Tm	W	Sv	IP	K	ERA	WHIP	xERA	xWHIP	vL+	vR+	BF/G	BB%	K%	K-BB%	xBB%	SwK	Vel	G	L	F	H%	S%	HR/F	xHR/F	GS	APC	DOM%	DIS%	Sv%	LI	RAR	BPX	R$
19																																		
20																																		
21	a/a	9	0	117	87	4.69	1.38	4.58				20.5	7%	18%	11%							33%	67%									-6.2	75	-$2
22	BOS *	7	0	132	94	4.99	1.44	4.83	1.45	122	120	20.2	8%	17%	9%	8%	7.2%	94.0	52	18	30	32%	66%	14%	14%	14	80	0%	57%	0	0.70	-16.8	60	-$8
23	BOS	4	3	84	82	2.88	1.42	4.00	1.32	81	112	6.1	8%	22%	14%	6%	12.6%	96.3	51	21	28	34%	84%	13%	11%	1	23	0%	0%	43	1.05	15.1	109	$3
1st Half		2	2	47	36	3.28	1.37	4.28	1.37	87	115	6.9	8%	18%	11%	6%	11.6%	95.8	52	20	28	31%	82%	17%	13%	0	24			40	0.98	6.1	87	$0
2nd Half		2	1	38	46	2.39	1.49	3.66	1.27	76	109	5.4	10%	27%	18%	6%	13.6%	96.8	50	22	28	39%	85%	7%	9%	1	22	0%	0%	50	1.12	9.0	138	$3
Proj		**3**	**0**	**58**	**53**	**3.74**	**1.25**	**3.58**	**1.28**	**83**	**103**	**7.7**	**8%**	**22%**	**15%**	**7%**	**11.7%**	**95.9**	**51**	**21**	**28**	**31%**	**72%**	**12%**	**11%**	**0**						**4.2**	**112**	**-$1**

Winn,Keaton

Age: 26 **Th:** R **Role** SP **Ht:** 6' 4" **Wt:** 205 **Type** Con/xGB
Health A | PT/Exp D | Consist A | LIMA Plan B | Rand Var +2 | MM 4100

1-3, 4.68 ERA in 42 IP at SF. Pitched at three MiLB levels in 2022 after missing 2020-21 (COVID, Tommy John surgery). Made MLB debut in June, flashing electric SwK (32% xK%), hefty GB%, and strong xBB%-backed control. Relies heavily on nasty splitter (55% usage, 18% SwK, 67% GB%). If some of that K% upside materializes, could yield profit.

Yr	Tm	W	Sv	IP	K	ERA	WHIP	xERA	xWHIP	vL+	vR+	BF/G	BB%	K%	K-BB%	xBB%	SwK	Vel	G	L	F	H%	S%	HR/F	xHR/F	GS	APC	DOM%	DIS%	Sv%	LI	RAR	BPX	R$
19																																		
20																																		
21																																		
22	aa	2	0	31	20	4.35	1.43	5.26				22.0	5%	15%	11%							34%	72%									-1.5	75	-$5
23	SF *	1	1	100	89	4.85	1.41	4.76	1.20	106	89	16.3	5%	20%	16%	5%	15.2%	95.8	58	13	29	33%	67%	17%	19%	5	66	20%	20%	100	0.60	-6.4	81	-$6
1st Half		0	1	60	54	4.14	1.46	4.45	1.39	89	72	16.1	9%	21%	12%	6%	13.7%	95.8	56	18	26	34%	72%	15%	17%	1	57	0%	0%	100	0.53	1.4	85	-$6
2nd Half		1	0	43	35	5.58	1.26	4.78	1.23	119	101	17.4	5%	20%	15%	4%	16.0%	95.8	59	9	32	31%	59%	18%	20%	4	74	25%	25%	0	0.66	-6.5	94	-$5
Proj		**3**	**0**	**58**	**51**	**3.98**	**1.25**	**3.52**	**1.23**	**119**	**97**	**21.5**	**6%**	**21%**	**15%**	**5%**	**15.2%**	**95.8**	**58**	**12**	**30**	**31%**	**72%**	**14%**	**16%**	**11**						**2.5**	**130**	**-$**

Woo,Bryan

Age: 24 **Th:** R **Role** SP **Ht:** 6' 2" **Wt:** 205 **Type** Pwr/FB
Health B | PT/Exp F | Consist F | LIMA Plan B+ | Rand Var 0 | MM 3303

4-5, 4.21 ERA in 88 IP at SEA. Underwent Tommy John surgery while in college; soared to majors once healthy (skipping AAA). Both SwK and xBB% indicate upside beyond already above-avg K-BB%. Displayed three pitches with a SwK of 13-15%. Started to solve vL in Aug/Sept by featuring cutter more. If that hole is plugged... UP: 3.20 ERA, 185 K's.

Yr	Tm	W	Sv	IP	K	ERA	WHIP	xERA	xWHIP	vL+	vR+	BF/G	BB%	K%	K-BB%	xBB%	SwK	Vel	G	L	F	H%	S%	HR/F	xHR/F	GS	APC	DOM%	DIS%	Sv%	LI	RAR	BPX	R$
19																																		
20																																		
21																																		
22																																		
23	SEA *	7	0	132	145	3.50	1.10	3.10	1.27	125	68	19.1	8%	25%	17%	6%	13.2%	95.1	40	19	41	28%	72%	13%	9%	18	81	17%	17%			13.5	128	$1
1st Half		4	0	67	84	2.87	1.01	2.40	1.06	170	48	18.2	6%	31%	25%	4%	13.7%	95.2	36	19	45	31%	74%	12%	6%	5	80	0%	0%			12.0	190	$1
2nd Half		3	0	65	61	4.15	1.20	4.40	1.35	113	77	21.2	9%	22%	13%	7%	13.0%	95.1	42	19	39	26%	71%	14%	9%	13	81	23%	23%			1.4	88	$6
Proj		**8**	**0**	**152**	**162**	**3.63**	**1.15**	**3.66**	**1.21**	**126**	**59**	**21.6**	**8%**	**27%**	**19%**	**6%**	**13.3%**	**95.1**	**39**	**19**	**42**	**29%**	**73%**	**11%**	**8%**	**28**						**13.2**	**125**	**$1**

GREG PYRON

Wood,Alex

Age: 33	Th: L	Role SP	Health F	LIMA Plan B
Ht: 6' 4"	Wt: 215	Type	PT/Exp A	Rand Var -2
			Consist B	MM 3101

Spent time on IL for eighth consecutive season, missing several weeks in the 1st half (hamstring, back strain). Shifted to bulk RP role for most of 2nd half and ERA/WHIP improved while skills got even worse. Fair to assume injuries played a part, and 2021-22 skills were compelling, so chasing a modest bounceback is reasonable. Keep your IP expectations low.

Yr Tm	W	Sv	IP	K	ERA	WHIP	xERA	xWHIP	vL+	vR+	BF/G	BB%	K%	K-BB%	xBB%	SwK	Vel	G	L	F	H%	S%	HR/F	xHR/F	GS	APC	DOM%	DIS%	Sv%	LI	RAR	BPX	R$
19 CIN	1	0	36	30	5.80	1.40	4.65	1.30	120	124	21.9	6%	20%	14%	8%	11.4%	90.0	38	28	34	30%	69%	30%	21%	7	84	14%	43%			-5.7	99	-$6
20 LA	0	0	13	15	6.39	1.82	5.29	1.34	106	133	7.2	9%	23%	14%	9%	12.8%	91.2	39	17	44	42%	67%	11%	9%	2	31	0%	100%	0	0.68	-3.0	106	-$10
21 SF	10	0	139	152	3.83	1.18	3.34	1.16	93	91	22.5	7%	26%	19%	5%	13.0%	91.8	51	22	27	32%	70%	14%	14%	26	84	31%	23%			7.5	152	$10
22 SF	8	0	131	131	5.10	1.24	3.40	1.14	67	112	21.3	5%	24%	18%	6%	11.6%	92.4	48	21	31	33%	61%	14%	16%	26	86	23%	27%			-18.2	146	-$1
23 SF	5	0	98	74	4.33	1.43	5.03	1.49	92	110	14.8	10%	17%	7%	8%	9.4%	91.5	45	18	37	31%	71%	8%	10%	12	59	0%	50%	0	0.68	0.0	46	-$3
1st Half	3	0	45	46	5.20	1.56	4.82	1.46	86	122	17.3	12%	22%	11%	8%	10.7%	91.6	46	14	40	33%	69%	12%	15%	9	69	0%	33%	0	0.71	-4.8	67	-$8
2nd Half	2	0	53	28	3.59	1.33	5.20	1.51	97	99	13.1	8%	13%	5%	7%	8.3%	91.4	45	21	34	29%	73%	5%	6%	3	52	0%	100%	0	0.66	4.8	29	$0
Proj	6	0	102	89	3.98	1.26	3.90	1.30	89	103	20.7	8%	21%	14%	7%	10.7%	91.6	46	21	33	30%	72%	13%	13%	20						4.4	99	$2

Woodruff,Brandon

Age: 31	Th: R	Role RP	Health F	LIMA Plan
Ht: 6' 4"	Wt: 243	Type #DIV/0!	PT/Exp A	Rand Var
			Consist A	MM

Landed on IL on April 12 (shoulder strain) and didn't return until August. Pitched well when on the mound, but the good feelings didn't last long: underwent October 2023 shoulder surgery to repair the anterior capsule. Will likely miss the entire 2024 season. Also scheduled to be a free agent after 2024, so a lot of question marks about his future.

Yr Tm	W	Sv	IP	K	ERA	WHIP	xERA	xWHIP	vL+	vR+	BF/G	BB%	K%	K-BB%	xBB%	SwK	Vel	G	L	F	H%	S%	HR/F	xHR/F	GS	APC	DOM%	DIS%	Sv%	LI	RAR	BPX	R$
19 MIL	11	0	122	143	3.62	1.14	3.43	1.12	100	74	22.4	6%	29%	23%	5%	12.4%	96.3	45	23	32	33%	71%	12%	12%	22	90	32%	9%			13.2	167	$13
20 MIL	3	0	74	91	3.05	0.99	3.22	1.06	82	83	22.5	6%	31%	25%	6%	13.1%	96.5	49	15	36	28%	75%	14%	15%	13	93	31%	0%			12.7	189	$23
21 MIL	9	0	179	211	2.56	0.96	3.18	1.07	75	80	23.6	6%	30%	24%	5%	13.6%	96.5	41	26	32	28%	79%	13%	11%	30	94	47%	10%			37.7	166	$30
22 MIL	13	0	153	190	3.05	1.07	3.27	1.07	82	99	23.0	7%	31%	24%	6%	14.8%	96.2	38	19	43	30%	77%	11%	11%	27	94	33%	7%			17.3	165	$20
23 MIL	5	0	67	74	2.28	0.82	3.50	1.09	80	69	23.0	6%	29%	23%	5%	13.1%	95.6	36	18	45	21%	83%	13%	7%	11	95	36%	9%			16.9	155	$12
1st Half	1	0	11	12	0.79	0.88	3.44	1.15	80	62	21.0	7%	29%	21%	6%	16.5%	95.9	44	15	41	23%	100%	9%	3%	2	91	0%	0%			4.9	146	-$4
2nd Half	4	0	56	62	2.59	0.81	3.51	1.08	81	71	23.4	6%	29%	24%	5%	12.4%	95.5	35	19	46	21%	78%	13%	8%	9	96	44%	11%			12.0	159	$16
Proj																																	

Wright,Kyle

Age: 28	Th: R	Role RP	Health F	LIMA Plan
Ht: 6' 4"	Wt: 215	Type #DIV/0!	PT/Exp A	Rand Var
			Consist C	MM

Shoulder soreness popped up in January 2023 and lingered all year. When he did pitch, the walks piled up; strikeouts were less frequent and the home run balls flooded the bleachers. He ultimately required October surgery to repair a torn right shoulder capsule and is expected to miss entire 2024 season. Check back in 2025.

Yr Tm	W	Sv	IP	K	ERA	WHIP	xERA	xWHIP	vL+	vR+	BF/G	BB%	K%	K-BB%	xBB%	SwK	Vel	G	L	F	H%	S%	HR/F	xHR/F	GS	APC	DOM%	DIS%	Sv%	LI	RAR	BPX	R$
19 ATL *	11	0	133	112	5.98	1.54	5.46	1.66	134	123	20.7	9%	19%	11%	12%	9.4%	94.6	42	27	32	34%	63%	21%	23%	4	50	0%	75%	0	0.46	-24.1	56	-$7
20 ATL	2	0	38	30	5.21	1.55	5.64	1.67	128	84	21.0	14%	18%	4%	10%	10.0%	94.3	45	23	32	27%	71%	19%	24%	8	80	13%	50%			-3.5	-3	-$7
21 ATL *	10	0	143	114	4.27	1.44	4.59	1.69	171	116	23.5	9%	19%	10%	12%	9.8%	93.2	42	5	53	33%	71%	20%	27%	2	67	0%	50%			0.0	70	-$1
22 ATL	21	0	180	174	3.19	1.16	3.23	1.21	100	83	24.6	7%	24%	16%	6%	12.3%	94.7	56	18	27	29%	76%	14%	16%	30	90	23%	13%			17.2	131	$21
23 ATL	1	0	31	34	6.97	1.84	4.07	1.44	122	119	17.2	11%	22%	11%	8%	10.6%	93.0	60	21	18	40%	63%	28%	29%	7	64	14%	57%	0	0.65	-10.1	92	-$11
1st Half	0	0	19	20	5.79	1.77	4.18	1.44	150	89	18.6	11%	22%	11%	7%	11.2%	93.0	60	20	20	39%	68%	17%	26%	5	73	20%	40%			-3.3	92	-$14
2nd Half	1	0	12	14	8.76	1.95	3.91	1.44	95	181	15.5	11%	23%	11%	8%	9.5%	92.8	61	24	16	40%	57%	50%	36%	2	53	0%	100%	0	0.52	-6.7	95	-$10
Proj																																	

Yamamoto,Yoshinobu

Age: 25	Th: R	Role SP	Health A	LIMA Plan C
Ht: 5' 10"	Wt: 176	Type	PT/Exp A	Rand Var -3
			Consist A	MM 3205

Regarded as quite possibly the best pitcher in the NPB right now. Possesses good command of a four-pitch arsenal that includes a 94-96 mph fastball, splitter, cutter, and curveball. The splitter is his best swing-and-miss pitch and should be above-average in MLB SP right away. Hype machine, landing spot will both influence his draft-day price.

Yr Tm	W	Sv	IP	K	ERA	WHIP	xERA	xWHIP	vL+	vR+	BF/G	BB%	K%	K-BB%	xBB%	SwK	Vel	G	L	F	H%	S%	HR/F	xHR/F	GS	APC	DOM%	DIS%	Sv%	LI	RAR	BPX	R$
19 for	8	0	143	120	2.42	1.07	2.71				27.8	8%	22%	13%							25%	82%									36.7	98	$19
20 for	8	0	127	141	2.73	1.05	2.41				27.3	9%	29%	19%							26%	77%									27.0	135	$48
21 for	18	0	194	195	1.73	0.94	1.94				28.1	7%	27%	20%							26%	85%									60.7	150	$44
22 for	15	0	193	194	2.09	1.03	2.29				28.6	7%	26%	19%							28%	82%									44.8	145	$32
23 for	15	0	157	150	1.57	0.98	1.97				27.2	0%	0%	0%							29%	84%									53.6	174	$37
1st Half																																	
2nd Half																																	
Proj	13	0	174	170	3.48	1.17	3.62	1.22			23.3	7%	25%	17%				44	20	36	30%	72%	9%	10%	30						18.1	123	$17

Yarbrough,Ryan

Age: 32	Th: L	Role RP	Health F	LIMA Plan A+
Ht: 6' 5"	Wt: 205	Type Con	PT/Exp B	Rand Var 0
			Consist B	MM 2001

8-7, 4.52 ERA in 90 IP at KC/LA. Hit in head by line drive on May 7 and missed two months (facial fractures). Groin strain cost him a few weeks during spring training and could explain 1st half skills slippage. 2nd half skills were as good as ever, but his best work over the years has come in bulk relief, where its tough to deliver value for our purposes.

Yr Tm	W	Sv	IP	K	ERA	WHIP	xERA	xWHIP	vL+	vR+	BF/G	BB%	K%	K-BB%	xBB%	SwK	Vel	G	L	F	H%	S%	HR/F	xHR/F	GS	APC	DOM%	DIS%	Sv%	LI	RAR	BPX	R$
19 TAM *	13	0	168	146	4.25	1.04	3.11	1.18	93	84	19.6	4%	23%	19%	6%	10.6%	88.2	44	20	36	29%	61%	10%	10%	14	73	50%	29%	0	0.90	5.2	171	$16
20 TAM	1	0	56	44	3.56	1.19	4.23	1.25	95	92	21.3	5%	19%	14%	5%	13.7%	87.4	42	29	29	30%	72%	10%	13%	9	76	33%	33%	0	0.84	6.2	108	$5
21 TAM	9	0	155	117	5.11	1.23	4.61	1.21	86	106	21.8	4%	18%	14%	6%	9.6%	86.5	36	24	40	30%	62%	13%	11%	21	83	14%	29%	0	0.77	-16.1	103	$0
22 TAM *	5	0	109	81	4.56	1.47	5.28	1.29	74	122	17.3	7%	17%	10%	6%	10.4%	86.8	38	21	41	33%	72%	12%	12%	9	68	33%	22%	0	0.66	-8.0	55	-$6
23 2 TM *	8	2	106	79	4.03	1.16	4.09	1.22	104	98	15.1	4%	18%	14%	5%	11.0%	87.1	39	20	41	30%	69%	11%	12%	9	57	0%	56%	67	0.74	4.0	124	$7
1st Half	1	0	37	22	5.01	1.16	3.69	1.34	106	100	12.1	6%	15%	10%	6%	8.5%	87.5	39	17	45	27%	57%	8%	9%	3	45	0%	67%	0	0.77	-3.1	75	-$6
2nd Half	7	2	69	57	3.50	1.16	4.30	1.14	103	98	17.3	3%	20%	17%	5%	12.2%	87.0	39	21	40	31%	76%	13%	13%	6	65	0%	50%	100	0.72	7.1	175	$16
Proj	6	0	102	76	4.31	1.22	4.13	1.22	95	101	16.8	5%	19%	14%	6%	10.7%	87.0	39	22	40	30%	68%	11%	11%	17						0.3	104	$1

Yates,Kirby

Age: 37	Th: R	Role RP	Health F	LIMA Plan A
Ht: 5' 10"	Wt: 205	Type Pwr/FB	PT/Exp D	Rand Var -4
			Consist F	MM 3500

Finally all the way back from March 2021 Tommy John surgery. Pre-injury velocity intact, but ability to miss bats fell a bit shy of his 2017-19 peak. Fortunate H%/S% masked horrid BB% and FB% lean. If xBB% comes to fruition, it would soften the blow from looming negative regression. Absent that, he'll have a tough time replicating 2023.

Yr Tm	W	Sv	IP	K	ERA	WHIP	xERA	xWHIP	vL+	vR+	BF/G	BB%	K%	K-BB%	xBB%	SwK	Vel	G	L	F	H%	S%	HR/F	xHR/F	GS	APC	DOM%	DIS%	Sv%	LI	RAR	BPX	R$
19 SD	0	41	61	101	1.19	0.89	2.31	0.87	75	60	4.1	5%	42%	36%	6%	16.2%	93.5	48	17	35	36%	88%	5%	8%	0	17			93	1.60	24.8	265	$28
20 SD	0	2	4	8	12.46	2.54	4.86		157	86	4.2	16%	32%	16%	8%	18.8%	93.7	38	31	31	59%	50%	25%	22%	0	17			100	0.80	-4.3	103	-$8
21																																	
22 ATL	0	0	7	6	5.14	1.57	6.51	1.67	52	163	3.7	15%	18%	3%	12%	12.4%	93.4	36	0	64	23%	78%	14%	15%	0	15			0	0.53	-1.0	-23	-$6
23 ATL	7	5	60	80	3.28	1.19	4.09	1.40	77	89	4.2	15%	31%	17%	11%	13.7%	93.7	36	17	47	22%	79%	15%	16%	0	17			63	0.68	7.8	90	$7
1st Half	3	1	32	45	2.84	1.20	4.20	1.31	99	79	4.3	14%	34%	20%	11%	13.3%	93.3	27	15	58	25%	85%	13%	16%	0	18			50	0.63	5.8	109	$3
2nd Half	4	4	29	35	3.77	1.19	3.96	1.51	60	107	4.0	16%	29%	13%	10%	14.0%	94.0	47	19	34	19%	73%	19%	15%	0	17			67	0.74	2.0	69	$6
Proj	5	0	58	76	4.03	1.35	3.79	1.36	90	107	4.3	14%	31%	17%	10%	14.2%	93.7	39	18	44	30%	73%	12%	13%	0						2.1	98	$0

Zerpa,Angel

Age: 24	Th: L	Role RP	Health F	LIMA Plan B
Ht: 6' 0"	Wt: 220	Type Con	PT/Exp D	Rand Var 0
			Consist C	MM 2001

3-3, 4.85 ERA in 43 IP at KC. Didn't throw all spring due to shoulder tendinopathy that sidelined him until July. Made three starts and served as bulk reliever upon return. PRO: GB%, BB%, vL+. CON: Middling K%/SwK, xBB% doesn't support pristine BB%. Struggles vR, albeit in tiny sample, bear watching. Seems destined for 5th SP/swingman role.

Yr Tm	W	Sv	IP	K	ERA	WHIP	xERA	xWHIP	vL+	vR+	BF/G	BB%	K%	K-BB%	xBB%	SwK	Vel	G	L	F	H%	S%	HR/F	xHR/F	GS	APC	DOM%	DIS%	Sv%	LI	RAR	BPX	R$
19																																	
20																																	
21 KC *	0	0	53	49	6.21	1.53	5.49			79	15.4	9%	21%	13%		4.4%	94.1	43	36	21	35%	60%	0%	3%	1	68	0%	0%			-12.8	67	-$11
22 KC *	4	0	84	58	3.42	1.26	3.83	1.52	215	72	15.6	7%	17%	10%	8%	4.4%	94.1	51	16	32	29%	75%	17%	20%	2	53	0%	100%	0	0.84	5.7	75	$0
23 KC *	3	0	79	59	4.50	1.33	4.72	1.21	63	123	13.6	4%	20%	15%	8%	9.2%	94.6	51	17	32	30%	70%	17%	15%	3	47	0%	67%	0	0.80	-1.6	63	-$3
1st Half	0	0	13	9	2.26	1.20	3.55				13.2	12%	18%	6%							23%	89%	0%		0	0					3.4	53	-$8
2nd Half	3	0	66	50	4.87	1.34	4.88	1.31	63	124	13.7	6%	18%	12%	8%	9.2%	94.6	51	17	32	31%	67%	17%	15%	3	47	0%	67%	0	0.80	-4.3	70	$0
Proj	3	0	80	58	4.49	1.28	3.98	1.32	69	124	15.1	7%	18%	11%	8%	9.2%	94.6	51	17	32	30%	67%	14%	13%	11						-1.6	90	-$3

GREG PYRON

THE NEXT TIER — Pitchers

The preceding section provided player boxes and analysis for 399 pitchers. As we know, far more than 399 pitchers will play in the major leagues in 2024. Many of those additional pitchers are covered in the minor league section, but that still leaves a gap: established major leaguers who don't play enough, or well enough, to merit a player box.

This section looks to fill that gap. Here, you will find "The Next Tier" of pitchers who are mostly past their growth years, but who are likely to see some playing time in 2024. We are including their 2022-23 statlines here for reference for you to do your own analysis. (Years that include MLEs are marked by an asterisk.) This way, if Matt Boyd opens some eyes in spring training, you can point to last year's skills to make a case that maybe he deserves a late-draft dart? Or, if Brad Boxberger again gets some chatter as a late-game option for a team in 2024, you can confirm that indeed, the skills dip at his age make a saves resurgence extremely unlikely.

Pitcher	T	Yr	Age	W	Sv	IP	K	ERA	xERA	WHIP	vL+	vR+	BB%	K%	K-BB	xBB%	SwK	G/L/F	H%	S%	BPX
Abreu,Albert	R	22	27	2	0	39	38	3.26	4.14	1.47	90	112	13	22	9	11	10.5	52/19/30	30	83	56
		23	28	2	0	59	61	4.73	4.79	1.47	131	79	13	23	10	10	10.2	46/17/37	29	72	53
Akin,Keegan	L	22	28	3	2	82	77	3.20	3.42	1.09	63	112	6	23	17	4	12.6	49/18/33	28	76	132
		23	29	2	0	24	27	6.85	4.49	1.77	119	115	6	24	18	4	13.1	34/29/38	45	60	140
Alexander,Scott	L	22	33	0	2	17	10	1.04	2.50	0.75	30	100	2	16	14	4	11.7	74/14/12	22	92	145
		23	34	7	1	48	31	4.66	3.98	1.37	76	105	5	15	10	5	9.8	61/20/19	33	64	98
Beeks,Jalen	L	22	29	2	2	61	70	2.80	3.31	1.16	107	92	9	28	19	8	14.6	46/21/34	29	81	135
		23*	30	4	1	70	67	5.21	4.77	1.49	100	96	11	24	14	9	13.1	45/16/39	34	66	81
Bickford,Phil	R	22	27	2	0	61	67	4.72	3.64	1.10	106	103	6	27	21	5	11.5	37/15/48	28	64	151
		23	28	5	1	67	76	4.95	5.10	1.46	85	109	13	25	12	8	13.6	28/23/49	31	68	54
Blach,Ty	L	22*	32	2	1	80	43	5.46	5.38	1.51	78	136	6	15	9	5	9.2	43/19/38	34	64	49
		23*	33	6	0	110	68	5.39	6.55	1.64	111	127	7	14	7	6	7.2	39/28/33	35	70	28
Boxberger,Brad	R	22	35	4	1	64	68	2.95	4.09	1.23	96	90	10	25	15	7	10.0	34/21/45	29	79	90
		23	36	0	2	20	17	4.95	4.88	1.30	98	99	13	20	7	11	8.6	44/20/36	23	65	29
Boyd,Matt	L	22	32	2	0	13	13	1.35	4.05	0.98	45	65	15	25	9	6	13.5	41/21/38	17	85	34
		23	33	5	0	71	73	5.45	4.42	1.32	70	108	8	24	16	7	14.4	39/18/43	31	61	110
Brasier,Ryan	R	22	35	0	1	62	64	5.78	3.74	1.30	128	107	5	24	19	4	13.4	41/19/40	35	57	148
		23	36	3	2	60	56	3.02	3.91	1.02	89	64	8	24	16	6	12.0	44/21/35	26	71	108
Brazoban,Huascar	R	22*	33	3	0	78	84	3.44	3.79	1.32	125	87	15	28	13	12	17.7	49/18/32	29	78	91
		23	34	5	0	59	65	4.14	4.00	1.43	111	83	12	25	13	8	14.5	52/19/29	32	72	91
Bummer,Aaron	L	22	29	2	2	27	30	2.36	2.80	1.50	85	117	9	26	17	11	10.7	64/22/15	38	87	147
		23	30	5	0	58	78	6.79	3.41	1.53	91	96	13	29	16	8	12.1	58/22/20	36	53	115
Chargois,J.T.	R	22	32	2	0	22	17	2.42	3.38	0.94	126	89	6	20	14	5	10.8	60/8/32	22	83	118
		23	33	1	1	42	35	3.61	4.21	1.25	103	87	10	20	10	10	7.8	55/15/30	27	72	71
Cisnero,Jose	R	22	34	1	0	25	23	1.08	4.96	1.36	83	74	18	22	4	11	12.1	37/24/39	24	91	-23
		23	35	3	2	59	70	5.31	4.15	1.48	90	118	9	26	17	7	11.4	44/17/39	35	68	124
Covey,Dylan	R	22	31	0	0	0	0	–	–	–	–	–	–	–	–	–	–	–	–	–	–
		23*	32	2	0	75	51	4.30	5.28	1.58	113	94	9	16	7	8	7.2	54/23/23	32	75	39
Davidson,Tucker	L	22*	27	5	0	133	110	6.26	6.14	1.63	139	112	14	14	-1	11	9.6	44/19/37	33	64	33
		23	28	1	2	51	46	5.96	4.62	1.62	134	107	8	20	12	7	10.9	44/24/32	37	64	87
Devenski,Chris	R	22*	32	2	0	31	27	6.43	5.71	1.32	152	137	1	18	16	5	13.3	42/17/42	31	56	76
		23	33	6	0	42	42	4.46	4.05	1.11	82	95	6	24	18	8	13.7	39/20/41	28	63	129
Diekman,Jake	L	22	36	5	1	58	79	4.99	4.10	1.63	102	121	16	29	14	10	13.7	40/22/38	34	73	69
		23	37	0	0	57	64	3.34	4.48	1.32	90	71	16	26	11	10	10.1	47/17/36	26	75	51
Edwards,Carl	R	22*	31	7	5	77	68	2.35	2.76	1.09	89	97	10	22	12	7	11.0	48/16/37	24	84	93
		23	32	1	2	32	24	3.69	5.21	1.52	126	65	12	17	5	8	9.7	46/24/30	31	74	18
Flexen,Chris	R	22	29	8	2	138	95	3.73	5.11	1.33	90	115	9	16	7	9	10.1	34/20/46	28	76	37
		23	30	2	0	102	74	6.86	5.37	1.67	108	138	8	16	8	8	10.0	39/24/37	33	64	49
Garcia,Luis	R	22	36	4	3	61	68	3.39	3.10	1.21	96	82	7	26	20	8	14.2	53/19/28	34	72	159
		23	37	2	0	60	53	4.07	3.87	1.39	100	93	9	20	11	10	11.4	62/18/20	31	73	97
Gott,Trevor	R	22	30	3	0	46	44	4.14	3.71	1.03	112	83	6	24	17	7	11.3	44/16/40	24	67	126
		23	31	0	1	58	62	4.19	4.29	1.41	124	79	7	24	16	8	9.8	40/22/37	37	71	125
Hand,Brad	L	22	33	3	5	45	38	2.80	4.62	1.33	99	91	12	19	8	9	7.3	40/23/36	28	79	34
		23	34	5	1	54	59	5.53	4.08	1.42	80	130	9	25	16	8	9.2	37/30/33	34	61	105
Hill,Tim	L	22	33	3	0	48	25	3.56	4.02	1.23	76	99	7	13	6	8	7.1	60/17/23	29	69	57
		23	34	1	0	44	26	5.48	4.56	1.65	102	139	7	13	6	6	6.8	61/16/23	34	70	64

THE NEXT TIER — Pitchers

Pitcher	T	Yr	Age	W	Sv	IP	K	ERA	xERA	WHIP	vL+	vR+	BB%	K%	K-BB	xBB%	SwK	G/L/F	H%	S%	BPX
Kelly,Joe	R	22	35	1	1	37	53	6.08	2.93	1.59	97	108	14	31	18	9	13.5	64/13/22	40	60	136
		23	36	2	1	39	60	4.12	2.64	1.19	102	72	11	36	25	6	13.1	58/18/24	34	66	193
Kuhl,Chad	R	22	30	6	0	137	110	5.72	4.94	1.55	120	124	9	18	8	9	10.4	37/24/40	32	67	46
		23	31	0	1	38	31	8.45	6.66	1.96	128	139	15	17	2	12	10.4	31/27/43	34	58	-42
Law,Derek	R	22*	32	3	15	67	53	3.99	4.99	1.51	125	114	9	18	10	8	10.2	47/23/30	34	75	69
		23	33	4	2	55	45	3.60	5.02	1.38	97	92	11	19	8	9	12.2	40/24/36	29	77	40
Leone,Dominic	R	22	31	4	3	49	52	4.01	4.39	1.60	158	91	11	23	13	6	19.0	39/23/38	36	78	77
		23	32	1	1	54	54	4.67	4.94	1.43	129	105	12	23	11	8	16.4	37/19/44	26	78	57
Loup,Aaron	L	22	35	0	1	59	52	3.84	3.90	1.30	90	99	8	20	12	6	11.6	50/22/28	31	71	89
		23	36	2	1	49	45	6.10	4.87	1.75	108	116	9	19	11	5	10.1	47/20/34	39	66	84
Marinaccio,Ron	R	22	28	1	0	44	56	2.05	3.56	1.05	68	83	13	31	18	8	14.5	41/13/46	23	82	102
		23*	29	4	3	63	66	5.45	4.27	1.50	90	100	13	27	14	9	11.9	39/16/45	27	65	72
Maton,Phil	R	22	30	0	0	66	73	3.84	3.67	1.25	108	102	9	26	17	7	14.3	38/24/38	30	75	118
		23	31	4	1	66	74	3.00	3.85	1.12	117	58	9	27	18	7	15.8	43/16/41	28	76	124
McHugh,Collin	R	22	36	3	0	69	75	2.60	3.20	0.94	71	86	5	28	22	6	13.0	40/21/39	28	75	159
		23	37	4	0	59	47	4.30	4.80	1.57	83	121	8	18	9	8	11.0	44/25/31	35	74	68
Miller,Shelby	R	22*	32	2	12	61	65	3.29	2.92	1.21	107	69	10	47	37	6	8.7	15/38/46	30	73	119
		23	33	3	1	42	42	1.71	4.20	0.90	77	57	12	26	14	8	10.3	37/18/44	17	86	75
Moll,Sam	L	22	31	2	0	43	46	2.91	3.87	1.27	73	108	12	25	13	9	10.4	50/16/34	27	82	84
		23	32	2	1	62	68	3.03	3.92	1.24	62	99	11	25	14	7	9.6	51/17/32	29	75	100
Moore,Matt	L	22	34	5	5	74	83	1.95	3.82	1.18	90	77	13	27	15	6	15.1	44/17/39	27	85	87
		23	35	5	0	53	60	2.56	3.94	1.16	119	84	7	28	21	5	14.2	35/20/45	31	85	144
Okert,Steven	L	22	31	5	0	51	63	2.98	3.85	1.17	108	82	12	29	17	8	13.2	35/20/45	25	81	98
		23	32	3	0	59	73	4.45	4.29	1.26	98	101	10	30	20	7	13.5	24/24/53	31	69	117
Pagan,Emilio	R	22	32	4	9	63	84	4.43	3.50	1.37	87	130	9	31	21	6	14.7	40/19/40	34	74	147
		23	33	5	1	69	65	2.99	4.47	0.95	83	68	8	24	16	6	12.6	32/17/51	23	70	99
Peralta,Wandy	L	22	31	3	4	56	47	2.72	3.52	1.05	60	85	8	21	13	8	16.5	54/16/30	26	74	103
		23	32	4	4	54	51	2.83	4.06	1.22	66	102	13	22	9	11	13.5	57/15/27	22	83	59
Plesac,Zach	R	22	28	3	0	132	100	4.31	4.49	1.32	117	94	7	18	11	6	10.6	40/22/38	30	72	78
		23*	29	6	0	118	68	6.67	7.55	1.70	158	108	5	13	9	5	9.6	51/20/29	31	67	-25
Pruitt,Austin	R	22*	33	1	2	77	53	3.80	3.45	1.03	96	102	4	17	13	6	11.9	45/14/40	26	68	119
		23*	34	3	0	65	43	2.84	3.41	1.15	107	82	6	15	9	7	8.8	36/21/43	27	79	77
Ramirez,Erasmo	R	22	33	4	0	86	61	2.92	3.83	1.08	83	105	4	18	14	5	10.7	45/21/34	27	79	108
		23*	34	5	0	83	65	6.45	6.76	1.63	128	112	5	16	11	6	10.0	43/21/35	37	63	52
Ramirez,Nick	L	22*	33	3	16	56	40	2.83	3.53	1.23	0	0	0	0	0		-	-	30	78	93
		23*	34	2	4	64	44	3.05	3.25	1.18	112	73	5	16	11	6	10.3	47/19/34	30	74	104
Sborz,Josh	R	22*	29	4	1	45	54	3.95	3.80	1.30	115	125	11	32	21	10	14.6	30/30/40	30	73	102
		23	30	6	0	52	66	5.50	3.30	1.15	86	93	8	31	23	7	16.5	47/18/35	30	54	169
Shaw,Bryan	R	22	35	6	1	58	52	5.40	4.29	1.44	102	112	10	20	10	8	9.9	50/18/32	30	65	71
		23*	36	2	8	71	59	4.70	3.59	1.35	86	93	9	21	12	10	10.3	40/19/41	27	65	75
Shreve,Chasen	L	22	32	1	0	26	29	6.49	3.93	1.41	123	99	9	25	17	8	12.2	40/21/39	32	58	115
		23	33	1	0	45	45	4.63	4.19	1.34	102	104	7	23	16	7	13.3	45/17/37	33	70	123
Sims,Lucas	R	22	29	1	1	7	5	9.45	5.58	1.65	72	113	19	16	-3	12	7.0	53/21/26	27	36	-73
		23	30	7	3	61	72	3.10	4.93	1.18	95	76	15	28	13	10	14.7	23/16/61	22	76	41
Stanek,Ryne	R	22	31	2	1	55	62	1.15	3.96	1.23	71	85	14	28	14	10	15.9	39/21/40	27	92	69
		23	32	3	0	51	51	4.09	4.98	1.24	84	101	10	24	14	8	15.6	31/14/55	27	73	80
Suter,Brent	L	22	33	5	0	67	53	3.78	4.07	1.20	99	103	8	19	11	8	12.1	45/19/36	27	73	79
		23	34	4	0	69	55	3.38	4.47	1.30	108	79	9	19	10	8	9.5	47/20/33	31	74	74
Urena,Jose	R	22*	31	3	0	118	73	5.54	5.94	1.72	122	97	10	15	5	10	8.9	50/21/29	34	68	30
		23*	32	2	0	134	84	6.71	7.75	1.77	126	135	11	14	3	9	9.5	47/17/35	33	68	-18
VerHagen,Drew	R	22	32	3	0	22	18	6.65	5.83	1.89	130	129	13	17	4	10	12.4	34/25/41	34	69	-11
		23	33	5	0	61	60	3.98	4.66	1.28	102	95	10	22	13	8	13.3	42/14/44	28	74	85
Webb,Jacob	R	22*	29	2	3	37	32	8.11	5.45	1.42	0	0	0	0	0		-	-	33	42	65
		23*	30	2	2	72	73	4.56	4.04	1.46	108	82	13	25	12	7	15.5	37/21/42	30	69	85
Weems,Jordan	R	22*	30	3	16	80	77	4.15	3.99	1.22	89	115	7	25	17	6	13.0	34/18/48	29	70	94
		23*	31	6	6	79	78	3.88	3.42	1.22	107	84	12	26	14	10	11.2	39/17/45	23	73	78
Young,Alex	L	22*	29	4	1	62	59	2.94	4.08	1.36	124	88	9	18	9	7	15.5	54/20/25	34	80	104
		23	30	4	1	54	50	3.86	4.40	1.36	104	99	8	21	13	6	15.1	49/17/34	30	79	98

Five-Year Injury Log

The following chart details the injured list stints for all players during the past five years. Use this as a supplement to our health grades in the player profile boxes as well as the "Risk Management" charts that start on page 270. It's also where to turn when in April you want to check whether, say, a C.J. Cron back injury should be concerning (tip: yes), or where you might realize that Alex Wood has missed 269 days in the past five seasons.

For each injury, the number of days the player missed during the season is listed. A few IL stints are for fewer than 10 days; these are either cases when a player was placed on the IL prior to Opening Day or less than 10 days before the end of the season (only in-season time lost is listed) or when players went on the temporary "COVID-related" list for contact tracing or vaccination side effects.

Abbreviations:
Lt, L = left
Rt, R = right
fx = fractured
R/C = rotator cuff
str = strained
surg = surgery
TJS = Tommy John surgery (ulnar collateral ligament reconstruction)
x 2 = two occurrences of the same injury
x 3 = three occurrences of the same injury

Throughout the spring and all season long, BaseballHQ.com has comprehensive injury coverage.

FIVE-YEAR INJURY LOG — Hitters

Batter	Yr	Days	Injury
Abreu,Jose	23	12	Nerve inflam lower back
Acuna,Ronald	20	11	Strn L wrist
	21	68	Torn ACL R knee
	22	25	Rec fr ACL Surg
Adames,Willy	21	12	Strn L quad
	22	25	Ankle
	23	12	Concussion
Adams,Matt	19	18	L shoulder strain
	20	12	Strn L hamstring
	21	49	Bruised R shin; Strn R elbow
Adams,Riley	23	25	Fx hamate bone L hand
Adell,Jo	23	67	Strained L oblique
Adrianza,Ehire	19	11	Strn ab muscle
	21	7	Covid-19
	22	82	Quad/Covid 19
	23	144	R elbow inflam; strained L should
Aguilar,Jesus	21	9	Inflammation L knee
	22	5	Covid 19
Ahmed,Nick	21	8	Inflam R knee; inflam R shoulder
	22	166	Shoulder/Covid 19
Alberto,Hanser	23	17	Strained R quad
Albies,Ozzie	20	35	Wrist
	22	116	Finger/Foot
	23	14	Strained L hamstring
Alfaro,Jorge	19	8	Concussion
	20	29	Covid-19
	21	34	Strn L hamstring
	22	11	Knee
Alford,Anthony	20	20	Fractured R elbow, Covid-19
	21	9	Strn lower back
	22	18	Hand
Allen,Austin	22	4	Covid 19
Allen,Greg	22	110	Hamstring
	23	51	Strained R hip flexor
Almora,Albert	21	39	Bruised L shoulder
	22	39	Shoulder/Covid 19
Alonso,Pete	21	13	Sprained R hand
	23	10	Sprained L wrist; Fx L hand
Altuve,Jose	19	39	Strn L hamstring
	20	12	Sprained R knee
	21	13	Covid-19
	22	13	Hamstring
	23	72	Fx R thumb; strained L oblique

FIVE-YEAR INJURY LOG — Hitters

Batter	Yr	Days	Injury
Alvarez,Yordan	20	67	Surg repair ligament dam R knee
	21	10	Covid-19
	22	15	Hand/Covid 19
	23	48	Strained R oblique
Anderson,Brian	19	38	Fx L finger
	21	88	Strn L oblique; sublux L shoulder
	22	59	Shoulder/Back/Covid 19
	23	19	Strained lower back
Anderson,Tim	19	34	Sprained R ankle
	20	11	Strn R groin
	21	25	Strn L hamstring x2
	22	82	Hand/Groin
	23	22	Sprained L knee
Andrus,Elvis	19	11	Strn R hamstring
	20	30	Strn lower back
	23	22	Strained L oblique
Andujar,Miguel	19	175	Surg repair torn labrum R shoulder
	21	97	Strn L wrist
Aquino,Aristides	21	59	Fractured hamate bone L hand
	22	51	Calf
Arauz,Jonathan	21	7	Covid-19
	22	53	Finger/Covid 19
Arcia,Orlando	22	23	Hamstring
	23	24	Fx L wrist
Arenado,Nolan	20	9	Bone bruise L shoulder
	23	11	Lower back spasms
Arias,Gabriel	23	6	Fx R wrist
Arozarena,Randy	20	39	Covid-19
	21	5	Covid-19
Arraez,Luis	20	19	Tendinitis L knee
	21	39	Concuss; inflam R shldr; R knee
	22	8	Covid 19
Arroyo,Christian	19	109	Strn R forearm
	20	2	Covid-19
	21	91	Covid; R knee contusion
	22	32	Groin/Covid 19
	23	30	Strained R hamstring
Ashby,Aaron	23	187	Inflammation L shoulder
Astudillo,Willians	19	82	Strn R hamstring
	20	20	Covid-19
Azocar,Jose	23	16	Inflammation R elbow
Baddoo,Akil	21	13	Concussion
	23	28	Strained R quad

FIVE-YEAR INJURY LOG — Hitters

Batter	Yr	Days	Injury
Bader,Harrison	19	11	Strn R hamstring
	21	68	Strn R forearm; fx R side rib
	22	86	Foot
	23	71	Strained L oblique
Bae,Ji-Hwan	23	48	Sprained L ankle
Baez,Javier	21	11	Strn lower back
	22	12	Thumb
Bailey,Patrick	23	8	Concussion
Barnes,Austin	19	11	Strn L groin
Barnhart,Tucker	19	32	Strn R oblique
Barrero,Jose	22	64	Hand
Barreto,Franklin	20	25	Subluxation L shoulder, Covid-19
	21	169	Strn R elbow
Bart,Joey	22	8	Concussion
	23	32	Tight lower back; L groin tightness
Baty,Brett	22	39	Thumb
Bauers,Jake	23	17	L R/C inflammation
Beaty,Matt	19	11	Strn L hip flexor
	22	100	Shoulder
	23	40	Concussion
Bell,Josh	21	7	Covid-19
Bellinger,Cody	21	63	L hamstring strain; fx L fibula
	23	31	Bruised L knee
Belt,Brandon	20	9	Tendinitis R Achilles
	21	57	Str L obliq;R knee infl;Fx L thumb
	22	79	Knee/Covid 19
	23	24	L hamstring inflam; back spasms
Bemboom,Anthony	19	61	Sprained L knee
Benintendi,Andrew	20	47	Strn R ribcage muscle
	21	21	Fx R rib
	22	36	Wrist
Berti,Jon	19	72	Strn L oblique
	20	11	Laceration R index finger
	21	56	Concussion
	22	50	Groin/Covid 19
Betts,Mookie	21	24	Inflammation R hip x2
	22	15	Ribs
Bichette,Bo	20	28	Sprained R knee
	23	29	Strnd R quad; tendinitis R patella
Biggio,Cavan	21	66	Sprain cervical spine;midback tight
	22	22	Covid 19
Blackmon,Charlie	19	12	Strn R calf
	22	11	Knee
	23	65	Fx 5th metacarpal R hand
Blankenhorn,Travis	23	14	Plantar fasciitis L foot
Bleday,J.J.	23	43	Sprained ACL L knee
Bogaerts,Xander	21	10	Covid-19
Bohm,Alec	21	13	Covid-19
	22	4	Covid 19
	23	12	Strained L hamstring
Bolt,Skye	22	102	Knee/Oblique
Bote,David	21	69	Dislocate L shldr; sprain R ankle
	22	82	Shoulder
Bouchard,Sean	22	20	Oblique
	23	138	Ruptured L biceps
Brantley,Michael	20	8	Strn R quad
	21	17	Tightness R ham; sore R knee
	22	47	Shoulder
	23	153	Surgical repair labrum R shoulder
Bregman,Alex	20	20	Sore R hamstring
	21	77	Covid; L quad strain
Bride,Jonah	22	28	Shoulder
Brosseau,Michael	21	13	Strn R oblique
	22	39	Oblique/Ankle
Brown,Seth	21	15	Covid-19
	23	44	Strained L oblique
Bryant,Kris	20	14	Sprained ring finger L hand
	22	127	Foot/Back
	23	79	Fx L index fing; bruised L heel
Burger,Jake	22	28	Hand
	23	11	Strained L oblique
Burleson,Alec	23	13	Fx L thumb
Buxton,Byron	19	73	Concus;L shldr sublux;brse R wrist
	20	12	Inflammation L shoulder
	21	111	Strn R hip; fx L hand
	22	47	Hip
	23	72	Strained R hammy; bruised L ribs
Cabrera,Asdrubal	21	38	Strn R hamstring
Cabrera,Miguel	21	15	Strn L biceps
	22	17	Biceps
Cain,Lorenzo	21	77	Strn R hamstring; Strn L quad
Calhoun,Kole	21	119	Torn menisc R knee; str L hamst x2
	22	18	Heel
Calhoun,Willie	19	27	Strn L quadriceps
	20	27	Strn L hamstring
	21	98	Strn L groin; fx ulna L forearm
	23	37	Strained L quad
Camargo,Johan	19	18	Fx shin R lower leg
	22	36	Knee
Cameron,Daz	20	48	Covid-19
	21	46	Sprained R big toe
	22	17	Covid 19
Campusano,Luis	20	16	Sprained L wrist
	23	96	Sprained L thumb; sprained R ankle
Candelario,Jeimer	19	71	Sprained L thumb; L shldr inflam
	21	4	Covid-19
	22	14	Shoulder
	23	16	Strained lower back
Canha,Mark	19	16	Sprain R wrist
	21	23	Strn L hip
	22	6	Covid 19
Cano,Robinson	19	52	Strn L quadriceps
	20	11	Strn L adductor muscle
Capra,Vinny	22	4	Concussion
Caratini,Victor	19	35	Fx hamate bone L hand
	22	6	Covid 19
Carlson,Dylan	21	10	Sprained R wrist
	22	30	Thumb/Hamstring
	23	79	Strained L oblique; surgery L ankle
Carpenter,Kerry	22	10	Back
	23	42	Tendinitis R shoulder
Carpenter,Matt	19	33	Bruised R foot
	22	61	Foot
	23	18	Inflammation R elbow
Casali,Curt	19	40	Sprained R knee
	21	12	Strn L wrist
	22	46	Oblique/Concussion
	23	71	Bruised L foot
Casas,Triston	23	16	Inflammation R shoulder
Castellanos,Nick	21	14	Sprained R wrist
	22	24	Oblique
Castillo,Welington	19	37	Concussion; Strn L oblique
Castro,Harold	20	31	Strn L hamstring
Castro,Starlin	20	46	Fx R wrist
Castro,Willi	20	1	Sore R shoulder
	22	9	Hamstring
	23	20	Strained L oblique

FIVE-YEAR INJURY LOG — Hitters

Batter	Yr	Days	Injury
Cave,Jake	21	71	Strn lower back
Celestino,Gilberto	22	9	Covid 19
	23	81	Surgery to repair torn UCL L thumb
Chang,Yu	22	29	Covid 19
	23	74	Fx hamate bone L hand
Chapman,Matt	20	17	Strn R hip, Covid-19
	23	18	Sprained R middle finger
Chavis,Michael	19	49	Sprained AC joint L shoulder
	21	19	Strn R elbow
Chirinos,Robinson	20	14	Sprained R ankle
Chisholm,Jazz	21	38	Covid-19; Strn L hamstring
	22	102	Back
	23	71	Turf toe R foot; strained L oblique
Choi,Ji-Man	19	11	Sprained L ankle
	20	16	Strn L hamstring
	21	73	Surge R knee; Strn groin; str L ham
	22	8	Elbow
	23	117	Strnd L ribs; strnd L Achilles tend
Clement,Ernie	21	22	Covid-19
Collins,Zack	22	7	Illness
Conforto,Michael	19	10	Concussion
	20	5	Tightness L hamstring
	21	38	Strn R hamstring
	22	188	Shoulder (unsigned FA)
	23	22	Strained L hamstring
Contreras,Willson	19	42	Strn R foot; Strn R hamstring
	21	24	Sprained R knee
	21	26	Sprained R knee; inflam R hip
	22	22	Ankle
	23	11	Tendinitis L wrist
Cooper,Garrett	19	42	Strn L calf
	20	34	Covid-19
	21	79	Covid; sprain L elbow; lumbar strn
	22	30	Finger/Concussion/Wrist/Covid 19
	23	12	Inner ear infection
Cordero,Franchy	19	176	Sprained R elb; stress reax R elbow
	20	46	Fractured hamate bone R wrist
	22	32	Ankle
Correa,Carlos	19	87	Fx ribs; lower back strain
	21	7	Covid-19
	22	18	Covid 19/Finger
	23	13	Plantar fasciitis L foot
Crawford,Brandon	21	11	Strn L oblique
	22	32	Knee
	23	50	Str R calf;str L/R ham;str L forearm
Crawford,J.P.	19	17	Sprained L ankle
	23	11	Concussion
Cron,C.J.	19	25	R thumb inflammation
	20	49	Sprained L knee
	21	12	Strn lower back
	23	82	Lower back inflammation x2
Cronenworth,Jake	23	38	Fx R wrist
Cruz,Nelson	19	29	L wrist sprain
	21	2	Covid-19
	23	12	Strained R hamstring
Cruz,Oneil	23	176	Fx L ankle
Dahl,David	19	10	Strn abdominal
	20	42	Sore lower back, strnd R shoulder
	21	37	Bruised L rib cage
	23	40	Strained R quad
d'Arnaud,Travis	19	11	TJS
	20	6	Covid-19
	21	102	Sprained L thumb
	23	30	Concussion

FIVE-YEAR INJURY LOG — Hitters

Batter	Yr	Days	Injury
Davis,Henry	22	144	Wrist
	23	26	Strained R hand
Davis,J.D.	21	84	Bruised & sprained R hand
	23	5	Strained L shoulder
Davis,Jonathan	19	28	Sprained R ankle
	20	11	Sprained R ankle
	22	30	Elbow
	23	90	Sprained R knee
Daza,Yonathan	21	40	Covid-19; laceration L thumb
	22	26	Shoulder
DeJong,Paul	20	20	Covid-19
	21	30	Fx rib R side
	23	25	Sore back
DeLuca,Jonny	23	37	Strained R hamstring
Devers,Jose	21	95	Impingement R shoulder
	22	40	Shoulder
Devers,Rafael	22	11	Hamstring
Diaz,Aledmys	19	67	Dizziness; Strn L hamstring
	20	36	Strn R groin
	21	51	Fx L hand
	22	27	Groin
	23	13	Strained L hamstring
Diaz,Elias	19	25	Viral infection
	22	10	Wrist
Diaz,Isan	20	14	Strn L groin
	21	3	Undisclosed inj
Diaz,Yandy	19	91	Strn R ham; bruised L foot
	20	28	Strn R hamstring
	22	2	Covid 19
Dickerson,Corey	19	80	Strn R shoulder; Fx L foot
	21	50	Bruised L foot
	22	35	Calf
	23	44	Strained L calf
Dominguez,Jasson	23	22	Tommy John surgery
Donaldson,Josh	20	27	Strn R calf
	21	12	Strn R hamstring
	22	12	Shoulder
	23	102	Strained R calf; strained R hammy
Donovan,Brendan	23	63	R flexor tendon surgery
Dozier,Hunter	19	22	Bruised chest
	20	18	Covid-19
	21	15	Concussion
Drury,Brandon	22	11	Concussion
	23	34	Bruised L shoulder
Duffy,Matt	19	118	Tightness L hamstring
	21	66	Strn lower back; Covid-19
	22	47	Back/Covid 19
Duggar,Steven	19	67	Strn low back;sprn AC joint L shldr
	22	63	Oblique
Duran,Ezequiel	23	8	Sore R oblique
Duran,Jarren	21	15	Covid-19
	23	42	Torn ligament L big toe + surgery
Duvall,Adam	22	77	Wrist
	23	61	Fx radius bone L wrist
Edman,Tommy	23	26	Inflammation R wrist
Encarnacion,Edwin	19	32	Fx R wrist
Engel,Adam	20	3	Covid-19
	21	119	Strn R hamstring
	22	12	Hamstring
	23	37	Strained L hamstring
Escobar,Alcides	22	21	Hamstring

FIVE-YEAR INJURY LOG — Hitters

Batter	Yr	Days	Injury
Escobar,Eduardo	21	12	Strn R hamstring
	22	11	Oblique
Espinal,Santiago	21	19	Strn R hip flexor
	22	14	Oblique
	23	16	Right hamstring inflam
Espinoza,Anderson	20	68	TJS
Estrada,Thairo	19	22	Strn R hamstring
	22	13	Concussion/Covid 19
	23	45	Sprained L wrist; fx L hand
Fairchild,Stuart	21	20	Covid-19
	23	17	Covid-19; concussion
Farmer,Kyle	19	27	Strn L oblique; concussion
	23	28	Facial laceration; dental injury
Fermin,Freddy	23	24	Fx L index finger
Fletcher,David	20	13	Sprained L ankle
	22	113	Hand/Hip
Fletcher,Dominic	23	29	Fx index finger L hand
Flores,Wilmer	19	59	Fx R foot
	21	22	Strn R hamstring
	23	11	Bruised L foot
Ford,Mike	22	9	Neck
Fraley,Jake	20	6	Strn R quad
	21	89	Covid; Strn L hamstr;inflam R shldr
	22	90	Knee
	23	37	Bruised R wrist; stress fx L 4th toe
France,Ty	21	10	Inflammation L wrist
	22	13	Elbow
Franco,Maikel	21	17	Sprained R ankle
Franco,Wander	21	6	Tightness R hamstring
	22	89	Wrist/Quad
Frazier,Clint	19	12	Sprained L ankle
	21	78	Medical Illness
	22	37	Appendix
Freeman,Tyler	23	12	Strained R shoulder
Friedl,T.J.	22	5	Hamstring
	23	17	Strnd L hammy; strnd L oblique
Fry,David	23	25	Strained L hamstring
Gallagher,Cam	19	25	Strn L oblique
	20	11	Covid-19
	21	54	Concussion; R shldr imping; L knee
	22	51	Hamstring
	23	8	Concussion
Gallo,Joey	19	92	Strn L oblique
	22	4	Covid 19
	23	48	Bruise L foot; strn L ham; strn ribs
Gamel,Ben	20	10	Strn L quad
	21	11	Strn R hamstring
	22	38	Hamstring
Garcia,Adolis	23	11	Strained patellar tendon R knee
Garcia,Aramis	20	68	Torn labrum L hip
	21	9	Medical Illness
	22	90	Finger
Garcia,Avisail	19	11	Strn R oblique muscle
	22	55	Hamstring/Covid 19
	23	131	Strained L hammy; tight low back
Garcia,Leury	20	49	Sprained L thumb
	21	12	Concussion
	22	11	Back
Garcia,Luis (WAS)	21	2	Strn oblique
Garcia,Robel	21	7	Covid-19
Gardner,Brett	19	12	L knee inflammation
Garlick,Kyle	20	13	Strn R oblique
	21	110	Sports hernia; Covid-19
	22	75	Wrist/Ribs/Hamstring/Calf

FIVE-YEAR INJURY LOG — Hitters

Batter	Yr	Days	Injury
Garrett,Stone	23	39	Fx L fibula
Garver,Mitch	19	19	High ankle sprain L ankle
	20	30	Strn R intercostal muscle
	21	69	Surgery groin; lower back tightness
	22	111	Arm/Covid 19
	23	54	Sprained L knee
Gimenez,Andres	20	7	Tight R oblique
Gomes,Yan	21	24	Covid-19; Strn L oblique
	22	17	Oblique
	23	8	Concussion
Gonzalez,Luis	21	45	R shoulder surgery
	22	32	Back
	23	131	Herniated disc surgery
Gonzalez,Oscar	22	32	Abdominal
Gonzalez,Romy	23	118	Inflammation R shoulder x2
Goodrum,Niko	19	38	Strn L groin
	20	11	Strn R oblique
	21	67	Spr L hand; bruised L calf; groin
Gordon,Nick	20	68	Covid-19
	23	135	Fx tibia L leg
Gorman,Nolan	23	29	Strnd R hammy; strnd lower back
Grandal,Yasmani	21	53	Torn tendon L knee
	22	51	Knee/Back
Greene,Riley	23	70	Stress fx L fibula; TJS
Gregorius,Didi	19	72	TJS
	21	52	Covid-19; impingement R elbow
	22	32	Knee
Grichuk,Randal	23	31	Surgery bilateral hernia
Grisham,Trent	21	29	Strn R hamstring; bruised L heel
Grossman,Robbie	22	12	Neck
Guillorme,Luis	21	75	Strn R oblique; Strn L hamstring
	22	29	Groin
	23	59	Strained R calf
Gurriel,Lourdes	19	43	Appendectomy; Strn L quad
	21	3	Covid-19
	22	30	Hamstring
Gurriel,Yulieski	21	12	Strn neck
Haggerty,Sam	20	22	Strn L forearm
	21	116	Inflamed R shoulder
	22	5	Groin
	23	6	Concussion
Hall,Darick	23	74	Sprained R thumb
Hamilton,Billy	21	73	Strn L hamstring; Strn R oblique x2
	23	36	Strained L hamstring
Hampson,Garrett	22	20	Covid 19/Hand
Haniger,Mitch	19	116	Ruptured testicle
	20	67	Strn ab muscle
	22	113	Ankle/Covid 19
	23	108	Fx R ulna; str L oblq; low bk spasm
Happ,Ian	21	12	Bruised ribs
Harper,Bryce	21	14	Bruised L forearm
	22	63	Fx Thumb
	23	34	Tommy John surgery
Harris II,Michael	23	22	Strained lower back
Harrison,Josh	19	91	Strn L ham tendon; L shldr inflam
	21	8	Covid-19
	23	10	Bruised R wrist; stress fx L big toe
Haseley,Adam	19	23	Strn L groin
	20	10	Sprained R wrist
	21	55	Covid-19
Hayes,Ke'Bryan	21	61	Sore L wrist
	22	8	Back
	23	35	Lower back inflammation

FIVE-YEAR INJURY LOG — Hitters

Batter	Yr	Days	Injury
Hays,Austin	20	31	Non-displaced fx rib L side
	21	35	Strn R & L hamstring
Healy,Ryon	19	133	Lower back inflammation
Hedges,Austin	21	9	Concussion
	22	11	Concussion
	23	11	Concussion
Heim,Jonah	21	8	Covid-19
	23	17	Strained tendon L wrist
Heineman,Tyler	22	24	Concussion/Groin
Hermosillo,Michael	19	187	Abdominal muscle injury
	21	9	Strn L forearm
	22	122	Quad
Hernandez,Diego	23	96	Dislocated R shoulder
Hernandez,Enrique	19	23	Sprained L hand
	21	24	Covid; Strn R hamstring
	22	72	Hip/Covid 19
Hernandez,Teoscar	20	10	Strn L oblique
	21	22	Covid-19
	22	24	Oblique
Hernandez,Yadiel	22	50	Calf
Hernandez,Yonny	22	34	Calf
Herrera,Jose	22	6	Covid 19
Herrera,Odubel	19	16	Strn R hamstring
	21	14	Tendinitis L ankle
	22	19	Oblique
Heyward,Jason	21	30	Concus;str L ham;infl L index fing
	22	117	Knee/Covid 19
Hicks,Aaron	19	105	Strn L lower back
	21	127	Sprained L wrist
	23	37	Strained L lat; strained lower back
Higashioka,Kyle	20	25	Strn R oblique
	21	12	Covid-19
	22	3	Covid 19
Hill,Derek	21	31	Sprain R shldr; bruised ribs; L knee
	22	18	Hamstring
Hilliard,Sam	23	76	Bruised R heel
Hiura,Keston	19	12	Strn L hamstring
	21	15	Covid-19
Hoerner,Nico	21	101	Str L forearm;str L ham;str R obliq
	22	15	Ankle
	23	10	strnd L hamstring; bruised L knee
Hoskins,Rhys	20	16	Strn L elbow
	21	38	Strn L groin; ab surgery
	23	187	ACL surgery + recovery
Hosmer,Eric	20	20	Gastritis, fx index finger L hand
	21	8	Covid-19
	22	42	Back
Huff,Sam	21	108	Strn L hamstring
Hummel,Cooper	22	9	Covid 19
Iglesias,Jose	20	12	Strn L quad
	21	11	Strn L hamstring
	22	23	Hand
India,Jonathan	21	3	Undisclosed
	22	52	Hamstring
	23	43	Plantar fasciitis in L foot
Isbel,Kyle	22	5	Covid 19
	23	54	Strained L hamstring
Jackson,Alex	19	26	Sprained L knee
	21	81	Strn L hamstring
	22	121	Finger
Jackson,Drew	22	11	Covid 19

FIVE-YEAR INJURY LOG — Hitters

Batter	Yr	Days	Injury
Jankowski,Travis	19	117	Fx L wrist
	21	6	Covid-19; bruised R foot
	22	46	Hand
	23	19	Strained R hamstring
Jansen,Danny	21	67	Strn R hamstring
	22	70	Finger/Oblique
	23	50	Strained L groin; fx R middle finger
Jeffers,Ryan	22	74	Thumb
Jimenez,Eloy	19	36	Bruise uln nerve R elb;R ankle sprn
	21	117	Surgery - torn L pectoral tendon
	22	74	Hamstring
	23	32	Appendectomy; strained L hammy
Joe,Connor	21	13	Strn R hamstring
	22	10	Oblique
Johnson,Bryce	23	25	Concussion
Jones,Greg	23	17	Strained R hamstring
Jones,Taylor	21	19	Covid-19
	22	81	Back
Judge,Aaron	19	62	Strn L oblique
	20	34	Strn R calf x2
	21	12	Covid-19
	23	64	Strained R big toe; strained R hip
Jung,Josh	23	43	Fx L thumb
Kelenic,Jarred	23	54	Fx L foot
Kelly,Carson	21	52	Fx L big toe; fx R wrist
	22	38	Oblique
	23	75	Fx R forearm
Kepler,Max	20	10	Strn L adductor muscle
	21	30	Covid-19; Strn L hamstring
	22	37	Wrist/Toe/Covid 19
	23	28	Strnd L ham;patella tendnts R knee
Kessinger,Grae	23	14	Covid-19
Kieboom,Carter	20	7	Contusion L wrist
	22	188	R arm, Tommy John surg
	23	39	Tommy John surgery
Kiermaier,Kevin	19	11	Sprained L thumb
	21	23	Strn L quad; Covid-19; spr R wrist
	22	102	Hip
	23	11	Laceration R elbow
Kiner-Falefa,Isiah	19	44	Sprained ligament R middle finger
Kingery,Scott	19	30	Strn R hamstring
	20	15	Back spasms
	21	22	Concussion
Kirilloff,Alex	21	77	Torn ligament R wrist
	22	92	Wrist
	23	73	Rec surg R wrist; str R shldr
Kirk,Alejandro	21	80	Strn L hip flexor
	23	11	Laceration L hand
Knapp,Andrew	21	25	Covid-19; concussion
Knizner,Andrew	23	12	Bruised R groin
Lamb,Jake	19	83	Strn L quad
	21	40	Strn R quad muscle
Larnach,Trevor	22	121	Abdominal/Groin
	23	15	Pneumonia
LaStella,Tommy	19	87	Fx tibia L leg
	21	93	Strn L hamstring
	22	86	Neck/Covid 19/Achilles
Laureano,Ramon	19	38	R lower leg stress reaction
	21	19	Strn R hip
	22	44	Hamstring/Oblique
	23	45	Strained L hamstring
LeMahieu,DJ	20	14	Sprained L thumb, Covid-19
	21	2	Sports hernia
	22	23	Toe

FIVE-YEAR INJURY LOG — Hitters

Batter	Yr	Days	Injury
Leon,Sandy	22	12	Knee
Lewis,Kyle	21	128	Bone brs R knee;torn menisc R kn
	22	103	Concussion/Knee
	23	66	Undisclosed illness
Lewis,Royce	22	132	Knee
	23	117	Rec surg R knee;str L oblq;str L ham
Lindor,Francisco	19	24	Strn R calf
	21	39	Strn R oblique
Locastro,Tim	21	78	Torn ACL R knee
	22	28	Back
	23	118	Back spasms
Long,Shed	20	20	Stress fracture L tibia
	21	114	Stress Fx R shin
Longoria,Evan	19	21	Plantar fasciitis L foot
	20	9	Strn R oblique
	21	83	Sprain R shldr; brse R hand; Covid
	22	68	Thumb/Hamstring/Oblique/Finger
	23	24	Strained lower back
Lopez,Nicky	23	21	Appendectomy
Lopez,Otto	23	63	Strained L oblique
Lowe,Brandon	19	83	Bone bruise R shin
	22	86	Back/Arm
	23	40	Low back inflam; fx patella R knee
Lowrie,Jed	19	164	Sprained L knee capsule
	20	68	Capsule injury L knee
	22	46	Shoulder/Covid 19
Luplow,Jordan	19	28	Strn R hamstring
	21	76	Sprained L ankle
	22	22	Oblique
Lux,Gavin	21	41	Strn L hamstring; sore R wrist
	23	187	ACL recovery
Machado,Manny	23	15	Fx L hand
Madrigal,Nick	20	23	Separated L shoulder
	21	98	Surgery R hamstring
	22	100	Groin/Back
	23	40	Strained R hamstring x2
Maile,Luke	19	53	L oblique strain
	20	68	Fractured R index finger
	22	22	Hamstring
Maldonado,Martin	21	7	Covid-19
Mancini,Trey	20	67	Recovery from colon cancer
Marcano,Tucupita	22	14	Covid 19
	23	70	ACL injury and surgery
Marchan,Rafael	22	68	Hamstring
	23	83	Fx hamate bone R hand
Margot,Manuel	21	21	Strn L hamstring
	22	72	Knee/Hamstring
	23	31	Bone spurs R elbow; surgery
Marisnick,Jake	20	39	Strn L hamstring
	21	29	Strn R hamstring
	22	76	Toe/Thumb
	23	76	Strained L hamstring
Marsh,Brandon	22	10	Knee
	23	15	Bruised L knee
Marte,Ketel	20	14	Inflammation L wrist
	21	77	Strn R & L hamstrings
	22	9	Undisclosed
Marte,Starling	19	11	Bruised abdominal wall
	21	39	Fx rib
	22	26	Hand
	23	73	Migraine; strained R groin
Martinez,J.D.	21	4	Covid-19
	23	32	Tight lower back; L groin tightness
Martini,Nick	19	62	Sprained R knee

FIVE-YEAR INJURY LOG — Hitters

Batter	Yr	Days	Injury
Massey,Michael	23	17	Laceration L index finger
Mateo,Jorge	20	22	Covid-19
	21	10	Strn lower back; Covid-19
Mathias,Mark	21	169	Torn labrum R shoulder
	23	46	Strained R shoulder
Maton,Nick	22	126	Shoulder
McCann,James	21	19	Strn lower back
	22	69	Oblique/Hand
	23	28	Strnd L oblique; sprained R ankle
McCormick,Chas	21	12	Sore L hand
	23	25	Lower back stiffness
McCutchen,Andrew	19	119	Torn ACL L knee
	21	11	Inflammation L knee
	22	14	Covid 19
	23	37	Inflm R elb; L Achilles tend tear
McGuire,Reese	23	41	Strained R oblique
McKinney,Billy	21	7	R hip impingement
	23	42	Back spasms
McKinstry,Zach	21	38	Strn R oblique
	22	9	Neck
McLain,Matt	23	36	Strained R oblique
McMahon,Ryan	19	13	Sprained L elbow
McNeil,Jeff	19	29	Strn L ham; Fx R wrist
	21	36	Strn L hamstring
	23	5	Sprained L elbow
Meadows,Austin	19	20	Sprained R thumb
	20	24	Strn L oblique, Covid-19
	22	140	Achilles/Covid 19/Concussion
	23	179	Anxiety disorder
Mejia,Francisco	19	41	Strn R oblique muscle; sore L knee
	20	31	Thumb
	21	9	L intercostal injury
	22	25	Shoulder/Covid 19
	23	33	Sprained MCL
Mendick,Danny	22	108	Knee
Mercedes,Yermin	22	38	Hand
Meyers,Jake	22	82	Shoulder
Miller,Brad	19	12	Strn R hip flexor
	22	58	Hip/Neck
	23	90	strnd L hamstring; strnd R oblique
Miller,Owen	22	5	Covid 19
Miranda,Jose	23	80	Impingement R shoulder
Mitchell,Garrett	23	163	Sublaxation L shoulder
Molina,Yadier	19	48	Strn tendon R thumb
	20	17	Covid-19
	21	12	Strn tendon R foot
	22	46	Knee
Moncada,Yoan	19	23	Strn R hamstring
	22	56	Hamstring/Oblique
	23	73	Lower back inflammation
Mondesi,Adalberto	19	61	Strn R groin
	21	140	Strn R oblique; L ham; L oblique
	22	166	Knee ACL
	23	187	ACL recovery
Moniak,Mickey	22	94	Hand/Finger
	23	14	Lower back tightness
Moore,Dylan	19	12	Bruised R wrist
	20	22	Concussion, sprained R wrist
	21	25	Strn L calf
	22	30	Oblique/Back
	23	69	Strained L oblique
Moran,Colin	20	5	Concussion
	21	69	Strn L groin; fx L wrist
Moreno,Gabriel	23	22	Inflammation L shoulder

FIVE-YEAR INJURY LOG — Hitters

Batter	Yr	Days	Injury
Mountcastle,Ryan	21	11	Concussion
	22	11	Wrist
	23	35	Vertigo; A/C joint inflam L shldr
Moustakas,Mike	20	15	Bruised L quad, Covid-19
	21	91	Covid-19; bruised R heel
	22	79	Calf/Covid 19/Biceps
	23	10	Strained L forearm extensor
Mullins II,Cedric	23	50	Strained R groin; strained R groin
Muncy,Max	19	16	Fx R wrist
	21	11	Strn R oblique
	22	13	Elbow
	23	12	Strained L hamstring
Munoz,Yairo	20	11	Lower back strain
	21	16	Covid-19
Murphy,Tom	20	68	Fractured metatarsal L foot
	22	156	Shoulder
	23	48	Sprain L thumb; sprain R ankle
Muzziotti,Simon	22	44	Arm
Myers,Wil	20	2	Recovery from bone spur surgery
	21	12	Covid-19
	22	76	Knee/Thumb
	23	37	Covid-19; kidney stones
Naquin,Tyler	19	53	Torn ACL R knee; Strn L calf
	20	18	Hairline fx L big toe
	22	44	Quad/Covid 19
Narvaez,Omar	21	13	Strn L hamstring
	22	26	Quad/Covid 19
	23	60	Strained L calf
Naylor,Josh	21	81	Fx R ankle
	22	20	Covid 19/Ankle
	23	31	Strained R oblique
Neto,Zach	23	68	strnd L oblique; lower back inflam
Nevin,Tyler	23	9	Strained L oblique
Newman,Kevin	19	24	Lacerated R middle finger
	20	9	Bruised peroneal nerve L knee
	22	73	Groin
	23	46	Strained L oblique; gastritis
Nido,Tomas	19	9	Concussion
	20	35	Covid-19
	21	42	Bruised R wrist; sprnd L thumb x2
	22	8	Covid 19
	23	16	Dry eye syndrome
Nimmo,Brandon	19	132	Stiff neck
	21	72	Bruised L index fing; Strn R hamstr
	22	5	Covid 19
	23	3	Sprained R shoulder
Noda,Ryan	23	33	Fractured
Nola,Austin	21	88	Fx L middle finger; sprained L knee
Nootbaar,Lars	23	49	Ab bruise; sore low bk; brse L thmb
Odor,Rougned	19	14	Sprained R knee
	20	10	Infection R eye
	21	14	Covid-19; sprained L knee
O'Hearn,Ryan	20	6	Covid-19
O'Hoppe,Logan	23	120	Torn labrum L shoulder
Ohtani,Shohei	19	41	Recovery from TJS
	23	17	Strained R oblique
Olivares,Edward	22	104	Quad
	23	10	Strained L oblique
Olson,Matt	19	41	R hand surgery
Ona,Jorge	21	169	Strn R elbow
O'Neill,Tyler	19	41	Ulnar nerve subluxation R elbow
	21	24	Strn R groin; fx L middle finger
	22	66	Hamstring/Shoulder
	23	93	strnd lower back; strnd L hammy
Ortega,Rafael	22	25	Finger
Owings,Chris	20	40	Strn L hamstring
	21	134	Spr L thumb;mallet fing inj L thumb
Ozuna,Marcell	19	94	Fx middle finger on R hand
	21	108	Fx L index finger
Pache,Cristian	21	31	Strn L groin; inflammation R ham
	23	99	Torn menisc R knee; sore R elbow
Paredes,Isaac	20	17	Covid-19
	21	30	Strn R hip
Paris,Kyren	23	15	Torn ligament L thumb
Pasquantino,Vinnie	22	18	Arm
	23	115	Torn labrum R shoulder
Pederson,Joc	21	12	Tendinitis L wrist
	22	9	Concussion
	23	32	Bruised R hand; inflam R wrist
Pena,Jeremy	22	12	Thumb
Peralta,David	19	70	R shoulder AC joint inflammation
Peraza,Jose	21	58	Fx R middle finger
Peraza,Oswald	23	12	Sprained R ankle
Perez,Carlos	23	43	Fx L thumb
Perez,Michael	19	34	Strn R oblique
Perez,Roberto	20	21	Strn R shoulder
	21	102	Inflam R shldr; fx finger R hand
	22	155	Hamstring
	23	178	Strained R/C R shoulder
Perez,Salvador	19	187	Recovery from TJS
	20	25	CSC L eye
	22	48	Thumb
	23	7	Concussion
Perkins,Blake	23	38	Strained L oblique
Peterson,Jace	21	40	Covid-19; sprained L thumb
	22	38	Elbow
Pham,Tommy	20	33	Fractured hamate bone R hand
Phillips,Brett	20	8	Covid-19
	21	23	Strn L hamstring; sprained R ankle
Pillar,Kevin	21	14	Multiple facial fractures
	22	129	Shoulder
Pina,Manny	19	17	Strn R hamstring
	20	32	Torn meniscus R knee
Pina,Manuel	21	25	Strn L oblique; fx big toe L foot
	22	168	Wrist
	23	115	Inflammation L wrist
Pinder,Chad	20	15	Strn R hamstring
	21	85	Sprained L knee; Strn R hamstring
	22	10	Covid 19
Pineda,Israel	23	130	Fx R finger
Piscotty,Stephen	19	68	Sprained R knee; R ankle
	21	46	Sprained L wrist x2
	22	62	Calf/Covid 19
Polanco,Gregory	19	127	L shoulder inflammation
	20	5	Covid-19
	21	20	Covid-19; sore R shoulder
Polanco,Jorge	22	48	Knee/Back
	23	85	strnd L hammy x 2; inflam L knee
Pollock,A.J.	19	74	R elbow inflammation
	21	32	L hamstring; R hamstring
	22	11	Hamstring
	23	39	Strnd L oblique; strnd L hamstring
Pratto,Nick	23	43	Strained L groin
Profar,Jurickson	21	22	Covid-19
	22	8	Concussion
Quinn,Roman	19	181	Strn R groin; Strn R oblique
	21	133	Covid-19: torn L Achilles
	22	50	Knee

FIVE-YEAR INJURY LOG — Hitters

Batter	Yr	Days	Injury
Raley,Luke	23	11	Cervical strain
Ramirez,Harold	20	64	Strn L hamstring, Covid-19
	21	21	Strn R hamstring
	22	30	Thumb
Ramirez,Jose	19	31	Fx hamate bone R hand
Ramos,Heliot	23	61	Strained R oblique
Ramos,Henry	23	25	Strained R hip
Ramos,Wilson	21	51	Torn ACL L knee;
Realmuto,J.T.	21	14	Covid-19; bone bruise L wrist
	22	3	Covid 19
Refsnyder,Rob	21	61	Concussion; Strn L hamstr; R elbow
	22	21	Back/Knee
Rendon,Anthony	19	11	Bruised L elbow
	21	98	Groin strain;L ham strn;L knee brse
	22	118	Wrist
	23	116	Str. L groin; bruise L wrist; fx L tibia
Renfroe,Hunter	22	32	Calf/Hamstring
Rengifo,Luis	19	13	Fx hamate bone L hand
	20	9	Strn R hamstring
	23	24	Ruptured L biceps tendon
Reyes,Franmil	21	41	Strn abdominal muscle
	22	27	Hamstring
Reyes,Pablo	23	48	Strained AB muscle; sore L elbow
Reyes,Victor	21	37	Strn intercostal; Strn R groin
	22	52	Quad
Reynolds,Bryan	22	17	Oblique/Covid 19
	23	11	Lower back tightness
Reynolds,Matt	22	18	Hip
Riddle,J.T.	19	75	Strn R forearm
	20	14	Strn ab muscle
Riley,Austin	19	33	Torn LCL R knee
Rios,Edwin	20	16	Strn L hamstring
	21	135	Partially torn R rotator cuff
	22	128	Hamstring
	23	11	Strained L groin
Rivera,Emmanuel	21	36	Fx hamate bone R hand
	22	7	Wrist
Rizzo,Anthony	21	11	Covid-19
	22	12	Illness
	23	61	Concussion
Robert,Luis	21	101	Covid-19; torn flexor tendon R hip
	22	35	Wrist/Eye/Covid 19
	23	7	Sprained MCL L knee
Robertson,Daniel	19	39	Recov R knee surgery (meniscus)
	21	26	Concussion
Robles,Victor	21	12	Sprained R ankle
	23	144	Back spasms x2
Rodgers,Brendan	19	98	R shoulder impingement
	20	29	Strn capsule R shoulder
	21	51	Strn R hamstring
	22	11	Hamstring
	23	124	Torn labrum R shoulder + surgery
Rodriguez,Julio	22	23	Back/Wrist
Rogers,Jake	21	31	Strn pronator R arm
	22	188	Elbow Tommy John
Rojas,Jose	22	16	Covid 19
Rojas,Josh	20	7	Lower back inflammation
	21	20	Dislocated R pinkie finger
	22	33	Oblique
Rojas,Miguel	19	26	Strn R hamstring
	20	17	Covid-19
	21	22	Dislocation index finger L hand
	23	13	Strained L hamstring

FIVE-YEAR INJURY LOG — Hitters

Batter	Yr	Days	Injury
Rooker,Brent	20	16	Fx R forearm
	21	14	Strn neck
Rortvedt,Ben	22	97	Oblique
	23	43	Surg repair aneurysm L shoulder
Rosario,Eddie	19	19	Sprained L ankle
	21	52	Strn abdominal muscle
	22	70	Eye
Rosario,Eguy	23	128	Fx L ankle
Ruf,Darin	21	26	Strn R hamstring
	22	6	Neck
	23	138	Inflm R wrst; lac R kn; fx R kneecap
Ruiz,Esteury	23	30	Subluxation R shoulder
Ruiz,Keibert	22	30	Groin
Sanchez,Gary	19	32	Strn L groin
	21	13	Covid-19
	23	25	Fx R wrist
Sanchez,Jesus	21	52	Covid; Strn R groin
	22	5	Covid 19
	23	17	Strained R hamstring
Sano,Miguel	19	49	Laceration on R heel
	21	15	Strn R hamstring
	22	157	Knee
Santana,Carlos	22	12	Ankle
Santana,Danny	20	48	Strn R forearm
	21	64	Covid; L groin strain; L quad strain
Santander,Anthony	20	24	Strn R oblique
	21	41	Covid; sprained R knee
Schoop,Jonathan	20	16	Sprained R wrist
	22	17	Ankle
Schrock,Max	21	38	Strn L calf
	22	74	Calf
Schwarber,Kyle	21	50	Covid-19; Strn R hamstring
Schwindel,Frank	22	27	Back
Seager,Corey	19	29	Strn L hamstring
	21	76	Fx R hand
	23	48	Strnd L hamstring; sprnd R thumb
Segura,Jean	19	11	Strn L hamstring
	21	30	Strn R quad; Strn L groin
	22	65	Finger
	23	10	Strained L hamstring
Senzel,Nick	20	27	Covid-19
	21	87	Inflammation & surgery L knee
	22	42	Toe/Covid 19
	23	26	Surgery L big toe; sore R knee
Shaw,Travis	19	21	Strn R wrist
	21	66	Dislocated L shoulder
Sierra,Magneuris	20	32	Strn R hamstring
Simmons,Andrelton	19	60	Sprained L ankle
	20	25	Sprained L ankle
	21	13	Covid-19
	22	66	Shoulder
Siri,Jose	23	39	Fx R hand; strained R hamstring
Slater,Austin	20	14	Strn L groin
	21	8	Concussion
	22	28	Hand/Wrist
	23	45	Strained L hamstring x2
Smith,Dominic	19	62	Stress reaction L foot
	22	26	Ankle
Smith,Josh	22	19	Shoulder
Smith,Kevin	22	10	Foot
	23	50	Strained lower back
Smith,Pavin	21	7	Covid-19
Smith,Will	20	24	Neck inflammation, Covid-19
Smith-Njigba,Canaan	22	114	Wrist

FIVE-YEAR INJURY LOG — Hitters

Batter	Yr	Days	Injury
Sogard,Eric	21	11	Bruised L thumb
Solak,Nick	22	18	Foot
Solano,Donovan	21	50	Covid-19; Strn R calf
	22	79	Hamstring
Soler,Jorge	20	15	Strn R oblique
	22	93	Back/Abdominal
	23	12	Strained R oblique
Sosa,Edmundo	20	24	Covid-19
	22	30	Hamstring/Covid 19
Soto,Juan	19	11	Back spasms
	20	12	Covid-19
	21	15	Strn L shoulder
Springer,George	19	31	Strn L hamstring
	21	95	Strn L obliq;str R quad;spr L knee
	22	9	Elbow
Stallings,Jacob	20	1	Concussion
Stanton,Giancarlo	19	164	Sprained PCL R knee
	20	38	Strn L hamstring
	21	15	Strn L quad
	22	42	Achilles/Ankle
	23	47	Strained L hamstring
Stassi,Max	19	27	Sore L knee
	20	17	Strn R quad
	21	43	Concussion; sprained L thumb
	22	14	Covid 19
	23	187	Strained L hip
Stephenson,Tyler	22	122	Collarbone/Hand/Concussion
Stevenson,Andrew	19	16	Back spasms
	21	33	Strn oblique muscle
Stewart,Christin	19	45	Concussion; Strn R quad
Stewart,D.J.	19	50	Concussion; sprained R ankle
	21	10	R Knee osteocondral defect
Story,Trevor	19	13	Sprained R thumb
	21	14	Inflammation R elbow
	22	63	Heel/Hand
	23	132	Recovery from TJS
Strange-Gordon,Dee	19	41	Strn L quad; bruised R wrist
	22	19	Covid 19
Suarez,Eugenio	22	11	Finger
Suzuki,Kurt	22	15	Covid 19
Suzuki,Seiya	22	40	Finger
	23	16	Strained L oblique
Swanson,Dansby	19	34	Bruised R heel
	23	15	Bruised L heel
Tapia,Raimel	19	11	Bruised L hand
	21	21	Sprained big toe R foot
Tatis Jr.,Fernando	19	86	Strn L ham; stress reax low back
	21	36	Covid; L shoulder subluxation x2
	22	131	Wrist
Tauchman,Mike	19	22	Strn L calf
	21	17	Sprained R knee
Taveras,Leody	23	14	Strained L oblique
Taylor,Chris	19	37	Fx L forearm
	22	31	Foot
	23	20	Sore R knee
Taylor,Michael	19	12	Sprained L knee
	22	16	Covid 19
	23	16	Strained R hamstring
Taylor,Tyrone	21	39	Strn R oblique; Strn R shoulder
	22	21	Concussion
	23	76	Sprained R elbow
Tellez,Rowdy	20	21	Knee
	21	5	Strn patella tendon R knee
	23	46	R elbow inflam

FIVE-YEAR INJURY LOG — Hitters

Batter	Yr	Days	Injury
Thaiss,Matt	23	10	Inflammation R shoulder
Thomas,Lane	19	34	Fx R wrist
	20	23	Covid-19
Thompson,Trayce	23	61	Strained L oblique x2
Toro,Abraham	22	11	Shoulder
Torrens,Luis	20	2	Back spasms-lumbar area
	22	20	Shoulder/Covid 19
Torres,Gleyber	20	16	Strn L quad, L hamstring
	21	33	Covid-19; sprained L thumb
Torreyes,Ronald	21	30	Covid-19
Trammell,Taylor	22	46	Hamstring
	23	32	Fx hamate bone R hand
Trevino,Jose	20	16	Sprained L wrist
	21	25	Bruised R forearm
	23	87	Strnd L hamstring; surgery R wrist
Tromp,Chadwick	20	7	Strn R shoulder
	22	54	Quad
Trout,Mike	21	122	Strn R calf muscle
	22	33	Ribs
	23	89	Fx hamate bone L hand
Tsutsugo,Yoshitomo	21	31	Strn R calf
	22	41	Back
Tucker,Cole	20	12	Concussion
	22	5	Covid 19
Tucker,Kyle	21	19	Covid-19
Tucker,Preston	23	45	Plantar fasciitis in right foot
Turner,Justin	20	18	Strn L hamstring
	22	8	Abdominal
Turner,Trea	19	45	Fx R index finger
	21	10	Covid-19
Urias,Luis	20	20	Covid-19
	22	29	Quad
	23	77	Strained L hamstring
Urias,Ramon	22	36	Knee/Oblique
	23	18	Strained L hamstring
Urshela,Giovanny	19	11	Tightness L groin
	20	12	Bone spur R elbow
	21	35	Covid-19; Strn L hamstring
	23	109	Fx L pelvis
VanMeter,Josh	22	25	Finger
Vargas,Ildemaro	20	8	Strn R hamstring
	23	23	Strained L shoulder
Vaughn,Andrew	21	113	Strn lower back; Covid-19
	22	12	Hand
Vavra,Terrin	23	19	Strained R shoulder
Vazquez,Christian	22	2	Covid 19
Velazquez,Andrew	22	25	Knee
Verdugo,Alex	19	56	Strn R oblique muscle
Vientos,Mark	23	11	Tendinitis L wrist
Vierling,Matt	23	14	Sore lower back
Villar,Jonathan	21	13	Strn R calf
	22	12	Mouth
Vogelbach,Dan	21	71	Strn L hamstring
	22	11	Hamstring
Vogt,Stephen	21	7	R hip inflammation
	22	48	Knee
Voit,Luke	19	45	Strn ab muscle; sports hernia
	21	96	Torn menisc L knee; Strn R oblique
	22	17	Biceps
	23	15	Strained neck
Votto,Joey	19	13	Lower back strain
	21	34	Sprained L thumb
	22	69	Shoulder/Covid 19
	23	100	Recovery R/C surgery R shoulder

FIVE-YEAR INJURY LOG — Hitters

Batter	Yr	Days	Injury
Wade,LaMonte	19	57	Dislocated R thumb
	21	30	Strn L oblique
	22	71	Knee
Walker,Christian	21	50	Strn R oblique x2
Walker,Steele	22	6	Covid 19
Wallach,Chad	19	132	Concussion
	20	26	Covid-19
	23	7	Concussion
Walls,Taylor	21	11	R wrist tendonitis
	23	42	Strained L oblique
Walsh,Jared	21	16	Intercostal strain
	22	45	Shoulder
	23	52	Insomnia
Walton,Donnie	22	49	Shoulder
Ward,Taylor	21	2	Strn adductor R groin
	22	20	Hamstring/Undisclosed
	23	65	Facial fractures
Waters,Drew	23	58	Strained L oblique
Wendle,Joe	19	98	Strn L hamstring; Fx L wrist
	22	57	Hamstring
	23	34	Strained right intercostal
White,Eli	21	44	Strn R elbow
	22	118	Wrist
White,Evan	21	125	Covid-19; Strn L hip
	22	148	Hernia
	23	176	Strained L adductor
Williams,Justin	19	187	Fx second metacarpal R hand
	21	16	Strn neck
Williams,Lucas	21	21	Covid-19
Winker,Jesse	19	43	Strn cervical spine
	21	32	Intercostal ligament strain
	22	4	Neck
	23	88	Cervical spine; back spasms
Wisdom,Patrick	22	15	Finger
	23	18	Sprained R wrist
Wong,Kolten	21	44	Strn R calf; Strn L oblique
	22	18	Calf
Wynns,Austin	19	21	Strn L oblique
Yastrzemski,Mike	21	21	Strn L oblique; sprained R thumb
	22	11	Covid 19
	23	57	Strained L hamstring x3
Yelich,Christian	21	47	Covid-19; Strn lower back
Yepez,Juan	22	34	Arm
Zavala,Seby	22	12	Concussion
	23	30	Strained L oblique
Zimmer,Bradley	19	156	Recovery from surgery (July 2018)
Zimmerman,Ryan	19	106	Plantar fasciitis R foot
Zunino,Mike	19	22	Strn L quadriceps
	20	23	Strn L oblique, Covid-19
	22	121	Shoulder

FIVE-YEAR INJURY LOG — Pitchers

Pitchers	Yr	Days	Injury
Abreu,Albert	22	71	Sprained L ankle; inflam R elbow
	23	25	Strained R hamstring
Abreu,Bryan	21	39	Strained R calf
Acevedo,Domingo	23	16	Strained lower back
Adam,Jason	21	3	Undisclosed inj
	23	29	Strained L oblique x2
Adams,Austin	19	60	Strained R shoulder
	20	60	Strained L hamstring
	21	10	Strained R elbow
	22	179	Surgery to repair R flexor tendon
	23	62	Fx R ankle
Akin,Keegan	21	12	Covid-19
	23	55	Lower back pain
Alcala,Jorge	21	19	Tendinitis R biceps
	22	179	R elbow inflammation
	23	139	Stress fx R forearm
Alcantara,Sandy	20	27	Covid-19
	23	27	Strnd R forearm; sprnd UCL R elb
Alexander,Jason	23	101	Strained R/C R shoulder
Alexander,Scott	19	115	L forearm inflam
	21	123	Inflammation L shoulder x2
	23	26	Strained L hamstring x2
Alexander,Tyler	22	47	Sprained L elbow
	23	91	Strained L lat
Allard,Kolby	23	168	Strnd R oblq; nerve inflam L shlder
Allen,Logan	23	10	Inflammation L shoulder
Almonte,Yency	21	32	Covid-19; bruised R hand
	22	53	Tightness R elbow
	23	52	Sprained R knee
Alvarado,Jose	19	75	Strained R oblique muscle
	20	45	Inflammation L shoulder
	21	27	Covid-19; impingement L shoulder
	23	75	L elbow inflammation
Alvarez,Jose	20	16	Testicular contusion
	21	11	Sprained R ankle
	22	109	Sore back; L elbow inflammation
Alzolay,Adbert	21	33	Strn L hamstring; blist R index fing
	22	167	Strained R lat muscle
	23	19	Strained R forearm
Anderson,Chase	19	17	Lacerated R middle finger
	20	17	Strn R oblique
	21	60	Covid-19; tendinitis R triceps
	23	38	Inflammation R shoulder
Anderson,Ian	21	48	Inflammation R shoulder
Anderson,Nick	20	16	Inflam R forearm
	21	165	Sprained R elbow; Strn lower back
	22	159	UCL tear R elb; plant fasciitis R ft
	23	82	Strnd R shldr; strn R pectoral
Anderson,Tyler	19	148	Recovery from L knee surgery
	23	9	Sore L knee
Antone,Tejay	21	99	Inflamm R forearm; surgery R elb
	22	188	Tommy John surg
	23	175	Right elbow pain
Appel,Mark	22	27	R elbow inflammation
Arano,Victor	19	165	R elbow inflammation
	22	83	Sprn R shldr; inflam L knee
	23	187	Impingement R shoulder
Archer,Chris	19	60	R thumb inflammation
	20	67	Recovery from neck surgery
	21	140	Strn R forearm; Strn L hip
	22	41	Tight R pectoral; tight L hip

FIVE-YEAR INJURY LOG — Pitchers

Pitchers	Yr	Days	Injury
Armstrong,Shawn	19	27	Strn R forearm
	20	25	Inflm S.I. joint R shld; sor low back
	21	2	Covid-19
	23	66	Strained neck
Ashby,Aaron	22	46	Inflamed L shldr; inflam R forearm
Ashcraft,Graham	22	33	Sore R biceps
	23	47	Stress reax L big toe; bruised L calf
Avilan,Luis	19	60	Sore L elbow
	20	8	Inflammation L shoulder
	21	154	Tommy John surgery
Bachman,Sam	23	81	Inflammation R shoulder
Baez,Michel	21	169	Tommy John surgery
	22	64	Tommy John surg
Banda,Anthony	19	180	TJS
	21	2	Covid-19
	22	8	Medical illness
Bard,Daniel	23	43	Str R flex;anx disord; fatig R frearm
Barlow,Joe	21	11	Blister R middle finger
	22	72	Blister index finger x2
	23	16	Kidney stones
Barnes,Matt	21	20	Covid-19
	22	66	Inflammation R shoulder
	23	123	Impingement L hip
Barria,Jaime	23	17	Tightness R hamstring
Bassitt,Chris	19	19	R lower leg contusion
	21	30	Head injury
	22	8	Covid-19
Battenfield,Peyton	23	77	Inflammation R shoulder
Bautista,Felix	22	8	Discomfort L knee
	23	38	Torn UCL R elbow
Baz,Shane	22	156	R elbow surgery; Sprnd R elbow
	23	187	Tommy John surgery
Bednar,David	21	5	Strn R oblique
	22	54	inflamed lower back
Bedrosian,Cam	19	33	Strn R forearm
	20	28	Strn R adductor muscle
Beeks,Jalen	20	34	Sprained L elbow
	21	169	Tommy John surgery
	22	29	Tightness lower R leg
Bellatti,Andrew	23	19	R triceps tendinitis
Bello,Brayan	22	20	Strnd L groin
	23	19	R elbow inflam
Bender,Anthony	22	126	Low back sore; Tommy John surg
	23	187	Tommy John surgery
Bergen,Travis	19	81	Strn L shoulder
	21	24	Impingement L shoulder
Bernardino,Brennan	23	8	Covid-19
Betances,Dellin	19	184	R shldr impinge; torn Achilles ten
	20	25	Tight R lat muscle
	21	162	Impingement R shoulder
Bibee,Tanner	23	15	Inflammation R hip
Bickford,Phil	22	11	R shoulder fatigue
	23	21	Lower back tightness
Bieber,Shane	21	95	Strn subscapularis R shoulder
	23	70	Strained R forearm
Blach,Ty	22	17	Strnd L wrist
Black,Ray	20	54	Strn R rotator cuff
Blackburn,Paul	22	60	Inflammation R middle finger
	23	61	Nail avulsion R middle finger
Bleier,Richard	19	36	L shoulder tendinitis
	20	14	Strn L triceps muscle
	22	19	Covid-19
	23	57	Inflammation L shoulder

FIVE-YEAR INJURY LOG — Pitchers

Pitchers	Yr	Days	Injury
Bolanos,Ronald	21	94	Strn flexor R forearm
	22	3	Covid-19
Borucki,Ryan	19	182	Surg remove bone spur R elbow
	21	69	Covid; Strn flex tendon L forearm
	22	86	Blist L hand; Str L flex; Str R ham
Boxberger,Brad	23	127	Strained R forearm x2
Boyd,Matt	21	84	Tendinitis L triceps; Strn L elbow
	22	151	Surgery to repair L flexor tendon
	23	98	Tommy John surgery
Bradish,Kyle	22	36	Inflammation in R shoulder
	23	15	Bruised R foot
Bradley,Archie	21	38	Strn L & R oblique
	22	126	Strnd ab; fx R elbow
Brasier,Ryan	21	154	Strn L calf muscle
Brault,Steven	19	32	Strn L shoulder
	21	132	Strn L lat x2
	22	63	Covid-19; Strnd L shoulder
Brazoban,Huascar	23	44	Strained L hamstring
Brebbia,John	20	67	TJS
	21	81	Tommy John surgery
	23	81	Strained right lat
Brentz,Jake	21	10	Impingement R shoulder
	22	162	Strnd L flexor tendon
	23	187	Tommy John surgery
Brice,Austin	19	79	Gastroenteritis
	20	20	Strn R Lat muscle
Brieske,Beau	22	80	Tendinitis R biceps
	23	101	R ulnar nerve entrapment
Brigham,Jeff	20	56	Covid-19
	21	169	Covid-19
Britton,Zack	20	13	Strn L hamstring
	21	104	Bone spur L elbow; Strn L ham
	22	180	Tommy John surg recovery
Brogdon,Connor	21	37	Covid; tend. R elbow; str R groin
	22	21	Covid-19
Brubaker,JT	21	23	Bilateral adductor strain, R hip
	22	17	Strnd R lat
	23	187	Tommy John surgery
Bubic,Kris	23	170	Tommy John surgery
Buehler,Walker	20	23	Blister R hand
	22	120	Tommy John surg
	23	187	Tommy John surgery
Bukauskas,J.B.	21	48	Strn R flexor
	22	109	Strnd teres major in R shoulder
	23	31	Cervical spine pain
Bumgarner,Madison	20	26	Mid-back strain
	21	44	Inflammation L shoulder
Bummer,Aaron	20	48	Strn L biceps
	21	18	Strn R hamstring
	22	101	Strnd R knee; Strnd R lat
Bundy,Dylan	19	11	R knee tendinitis
	21	23	Strn R ankle
	22	13	Covid-19
Burdi,Nick	23	132	Appendectomy
Burke,Brock	20	67	Torn L labrum surgery
	21	24	Recovery from L shoulder surgery
Burnes,Corbin	19	17	R shoulder irritation
	21	15	Covid-19
Burr,Ryan	19	141	R shldr AC joint inflam; str R elb
	22	26	Strnd R shoulder
Bush,Matt	21	162	Inflamed R shoulder
	22	19	R forearm soreness
	23	61	R/C tendinitis R shoulder

FIVE-YEAR INJURY LOG — Pitchers

Pitchers	Yr	Days	Injury
Cabrera,Edward	22	57	Tendinitis R elbow; Sprnd R ankle
	23	32	Impingement R shoulder
Cabrera,Genesis	22	14	Covid-19
Canning,Griffin	19	55	Inflammation R elbow
	22	188	Sore lower back
	23	27	Strained L groin
Carasiti,Matt	23	59	Inflammation R shoulder
Carlos Mejia,Jean	23	49	Inflammation R shoulder
Carlton,Drew	23	94	Inflammation R elbow
Carrasco,Carlos	19	89	Leukemia
	21	121	Strn R hamstring
	22	20	Strnd L oblique
	23	60	Inflam R elbow
Castano,Daniel	21	74	Impingement L shoulder
	22	71	Concussion
Castellanos,Humberto	22	130	Strnd R elbow
Castillo,Diego	19	19	R shoulder inflam/impingement
	21	28	Covid; inflam R shldr; tight groin
	22	14	Inflammation R shoulder
Castillo,Jose	19	187	Torn L finger tendon
	20	68	Strn lat muscle
	21	169	Tommy John surgery
	23	54	Strained L shoulder
Castillo,Luis M.	22	36	Sore R shoulder
Castro,Anthony	21	73	Strn R forearm; ulnar nerve irritat
	22	12	Covid-19
Castro,Miguel	21	2	Covid-19
	22	80	Strnd R shoulder
Cavalli,Cade	22	40	Inflammation R shoulder
	23	187	Tommy John surgery
Cease,Dylan	21	3	Covid-19
Cederlind,Blake	21	169	Tommy John surgery
	22	188	Tommy John surg
Cessa,Luis	20	15	Covid-19
	22	27	Strnd lower back
Chacin,Jhoulys	19	84	Strn lower back; oblique
	21	13	Covid-19
	22	25	Toe sesamoiditis/inflammation
Chafin,Andrew	20	32	Sprained finger L hand
	22	23	Strnd L groin
Chapman,Aroldis	20	26	Covid-19
	21	13	Impingement L elbow
	22	60	Tndonitis L Achilles; infect low leg
Chargois,J.T.	22	134	Tightness L oblique
	23	59	Strnd R oblique; strnd R ribcage
Chavez,Jesse	19	49	Strn R groin
	20	15	Sprained L big toe
	23	96	Bruised L shin
Chirinos,Yonny	19	48	R middle finger inflammation
	20	54	TJS
	21	169	Tommy John surgery
	22	156	Tommy John surg
	23	43	R elbow inflammation
Cimber,Adam	23	131	Strnd rhomboid; R shldr impinge
Cisnero,Jose	21	3	Laceration R elbow
	22	103	Strnd R shoulder
Civale,Aaron	21	76	Sprained finger R hand
	22	75	Str. L glute R wrist; inflam R 4-arm
	23	54	Strained L oblique
Clarke,Taylor	19	17	Lower L back inflammation
	21	52	Strn teres major muscle R shldr
	22	56	Strnd L oblique x2
	23	15	R elbow inflammation

FIVE-YEAR INJURY LOG — Pitchers

Pitchers	Yr	Days	Injury
Cleavinger,Garrett	21	72	L forearm inflam; R oblique strain
	23	148	Sprained R knee
Clevinger,Mike	19	81	Strn R upper back; sprained R ank
	21	169	Tommy John surgery
	22	57	Sprnd R knee; Str R triceps; covid
	23	57	R wrist tendinitis; R biceps inflam
Clippard,Tyler	21	119	Covid; Strn R shoulder
	22	32	Strnd R groin
Cobb,Alex	19	176	Strn R groin; R hip impinge surg
	20	9	Covid-19
	21	65	Inflammation R wrist; blist R hand
	22	26	Strnd R adductor; Strnd neck
	23	26	Strained L oblique; impinge R hip
Cole,Gerrit	21	14	Covid-19
Cole,Taylor	19	12	Strn R shoulder
Colome,Alex	22	16	R lateral epicondylitis
Coonrod,Sam	20	27	Strn R lat muscle
	21	61	Tendinitis R forearm
	22	134	Sore R shoulder
	23	138	Strained R lat
Corbin,Patrick	21	6	Covid-19
Cortes,Nestor	20	45	Impingement L elbow
	21	9	Covid-19
	22	15	Strnd L groin
	23	112	Strained R/C L shoulder
Cosgrove,Tom	23	16	Strained L hamstring
Coulombe,Daniel	22	151	L hip impingement x2
	23	15	Inflammation L biceps
Cousins,Jake	21	11	Covid-19
	22	116	Effusion R elbow
	23	37	Inflammation R shoulder
Covey,Dylan	23	3	Lower back pain
Cox,Austin	23	24	Sprained ACL L knee
Crawford,Kutter	22	35	Impingement R shoulder
	23	15	Strained L hamstring
Crick,Kyle	19	30	Tight R triceps; surg R index fing
	20	50	Strn R shoulder, lat muscle
	21	26	Covid-19; Strn R triceps
	22	116	R elbow inflammation
Crismatt,Nabil	23	58	Strained L hip
Criswell,Cooper	22	104	Sore R shoulder
Crochet,Garrett	21	12	Strn lower back
	22	188	Tommy John surg
	23	141	TJS recovery; inflam L shoulder
Cronin,Declan	23	15	Blister R hand
Crouse,Hans	22	86	Biceps tendinitis R arm
Crowe,Wil	22	8	Inflammation R elbow
	23	163	Sore R shoulder
Cruz,Fernando	23	35	Covid-19; strained R shoulder
Cueto,Johnny	19	167	TJS
	21	59	Covid; Strn lat muscle; str. R elb
	23	111	R biceps tendinitis; viral infection
Curtiss,John	21	51	Torn UCL R elbow
	22	186	Tommy John surg
	23	50	Bone spurs R elbow
Cyr,Tyler	23	133	Impingement shoulder
Daniel,Davis	23	155	Strained R shoulder
Danish,Tyler	22	54	Strnd R forearm
Danner,Hagen	23	52	Strained L oblique
Darvish,Yu	21	25	Inflam L hip; Strn lower back
	23	36	Inflammation R elbow
Davidson,Tucker	21	93	Inflammation L forearm
Davies,Zach	19	57	Back spasms
	23	88	Strnd L oblique; lower back inflam

FIVE-YEAR INJURY LOG — Pitchers

Pitchers	Yr	Days	Injury
Davies,Zachary	22	37	Inflammation in R shoulder
Davis,Noah	23	33	R elbow inflammation
De Leon,Jose	19	98	TJS
	20	13	Strn R groin
	23	100	Tommy John surgery
De Los Santos,Yerry	22	62	Covid-19; Strnd R lat
deGrom,Jacob	19	11	Sore R elbow
	21	77	Low back tight; tight R forearm
	22	118	Stress FX in scapula in R shoulder
	23	157	Inflammation R elbow
DeJong,Chase	21	16	Inflammation L knee
	22	17	Tendinitis L knee
	23	22	Sprained lumbar spine
Delaplane,Sam	21	108	Tommy John surgery
	22	110	R forearm strain
DeSclafani,Anthony	20	11	Strn R teres major muscle
	21	21	Covid;Fatig R shldr;R ankle inflam
	22	68	Inflammation R ankle
	23	81	R shldr fatigue; strnd flexor R elb
Detmers,Reid	21	23	Covid-19
Detwiler,Ross	22	21	Strnd lower back
Devenski,Chris	20	57	Elbow/undisclosed
	21	125	Sprained UCL R elbow
	23	40	Strained R hamstring
Diaz,Alexis	22	20	Biceps tendinitis R arm
Diaz,Edwin	23	187	R knee ruptured patellar tendon
Diaz,Jhonathan	22	35	Concussion
Diaz,Miguel	19	162	Recov R knee surgery (meniscus)
Dobnak,Randy	21	82	Strn R index finger
	22	164	Sprnd R middle finger
Dominguez,Seranthony	19	117	Torn UCL R elbow
	20	67	TJS
	21	154	Tommy John surgery
	22	22	Strnd R triceps
	23	39	Strained L oblique
Doolittle,Sean	19	15	Tendonitis R knee
	20	31	Inflam R knee, str R oblique
	22	172	Sprnd L elbow
Duarte,Daniel	22	162	Inflammation R elbow
	23	4	Tightness R shoulder
Duffy,Danny	19	59	L shoulder impinge; strn L ham
	21	100	Strn flexor L forearm
	22	188	Strnd L forearm
Dugger,Robert	20	26	Covid-19
	21	2	Covid-19
	22	58	Sore R shoulder
Dunn,Justin	21	100	Inflamed R shoulder x2
	22	139	Covid;subscapularis infl R shldr
	23	187	Strained R/C R shoulder
Dunning,Dane	21	28	Covid-19; impingement R ankle
	22	28	Impingement R ankle
Duplantier,Jon	19	38	R shoulder inflammation
	21	44	Sprained R middle finger
Edwards,C.J.	19	89	Strn R shoulder
	20	50	Strn R forearm
	21	75	Strn L oblique
	23	104	Inflammation R shoulder
Effross,Scott	22	31	Strnd R shoulder
	23	187	Tommy John surgery
Eflin,Zach	19	11	Tightness lower back
	21	59	Covid; patellar tendinitis R knee
	22	87	Covid-19; bruised R knee
	23	13	Lower back tightness
Ellis,Chris	22	167	Inflam R shoulder, surgery

FIVE-YEAR INJURY LOG — Pitchers

Pitchers	Yr	Days	Injury
Emanuel,Kent	21	114	Sore L elbow
	22	121	L elb impinge; Strnd L shoulder
Englert,Mason	23	71	Tightness L hip
Enright,Nic	23	61	Hodgkin's lymphoma
Eovaldi,Nathan	19	92	R elbow surg remve loose bodies
	20	14	Strn R calf
	22	75	Low back inflam; R shldr inflam
	23	38	Strained R forearm
Espino,Paolo	23	19	Strained flexor tendon
Estevez,Carlos	21	23	Strn R middle finger
	22	12	Covid-19
Faedo,Alex	23	35	Blister R middle finger
Fairbanks,Pete	21	57	Strn R/C R shoulder
	22	105	Strnd lower back
	23	31	Inflam L hip:; inflam R forearm
Falter,Bailey	21	32	Covid-19
	23	9	Strained neck
Familia,Jeurys	19	27	Bennett lesion R shoulder
	21	12	Impingement R hip
Farmer,Buck	20	10	Strn L groin
Faucher,Calvin	23	31	Inflam R elbow; tendinitis R biceps
Fedde,Erick	21	38	Covid-19; Strn oblique muscle
	22	25	Inflammation R shoulder
Felipe,Angel	23	49	Sprained R elbow
Feltner,Ryan	23	134	Fx skull; R elbow inflam
Ferguson,Caleb	19	19	Strn L oblique
	20	13	Torn UCL L elbow
	21	169	L elbow TJS
	22	59	Tommy John surg
Festa,Matt	22	16	Sprnd R elbow
Feyereisen,J.P.	21	41	Discomfort R shoulder
	22	128	Impingement R shoulder
	23	187	Labrum + R/C surgery R shoulder
Fiers,Michael	21	159	Strn lower back; Strn R elbow
Finnegan,Kyle	21	17	Strn L hamstring
Flaherty,Jack	21	97	Strn L oblique; Strn R shoulder
	22	144	Rec R shldr surgery; sore R shdlr
Fleming,Josh	21	12	Strn R calf
	22	48	Tightness R oblique
	23	68	Sore L elbow
Floro,Dylan	19	25	Neck inflam; strn L intercostal lig
	22	36	Tendinitis R R/C
Font,Wilmer	20	16	Bruised R shin
Foster,Matt	23	187	Strained R forearm
Freeland,Kyle	19	40	Blister L middle finger
	21	55	Strn L shoulder
	23	31	Strnd R oblique; sublux R shoulder
Fried,Max	19	12	Blister on L index finger
	20	12	Back spasms-lumbar area
	21	34	Blist L index fing;Strn R index fing
	22	8	Concussion
	23	115	Str R ham; str L forarm x2; blister
Fry,Jace	19	11	Sore L shoulder
	20	11	Back spasms-lumbar area
	21	87	Strn lower back
Fulmer,Michael	19	187	Recovery from TJS
	21	43	Strn cervical spine
	23	34	Strained R forearm x2
Funkhouser,Kyle	22	188	Strnd R shoulder
Gallegos,Giovanny	20	16	Strn R groin x2
	23	15	Tendinitis R/C R shoulder
Gallen,Zac	21	67	Fx R forearm;sprn R elb;str R ham

FIVE-YEAR INJURY LOG — Pitchers

Pitchers	Yr	Days	Injury
Garcia,Jarlin	20	18	Covid-19
	21	14	Strn L groin
	23	187	Strained L biceps
Garcia,Luis	22	12	Strnd R oblique; Strnd L groin
	22	12	Strnd R oblique; Strnd L groin
	23	15	Strained L oblique; TJS
	23	154	Tommy John surgery
Garcia,Rico	21	169	Tommy John surgery
	23	34	R biceps tendinitis
Garcia,Rony	21	115	Strn L ab muscle; sprained L knee
	22	98	Sore R shoulder x2
Garcia,Yimi	20	25	Covid-19
	22	15	Strnd lower back
Garrett,Amir	19	17	Strn lat L shoulder
	22	18	Covid-19
	23	29	Valgus extension overload L elbow
Garrett,Braxton	22	24	Strnd R oblique
Garrett,Reed	22	32	Biceps tendinitis R arm
Gausman,Kevin	19	50	R foot plant fasc;tendinitis R shldr
	21	9	Covid-19
German,Domingo	19	26	Strn L hip flexor
	21	47	Inflamed R shoulder
	22	109	Impingement R shoulder
Gibson,Kyle	19	10	Ulcerative colitis
	21	14	Strn R groin
	22	4	Covid-19
Gil,Luis	22	42	Tommy John surg
	23	187	Tommy John surgery
Gilbert,Tyler	21	2	Inflammation L elbow
	22	72	Sprnd L elbow
Gilbreath,Lucas	22	56	Covid-19; Strnd flexor L elbow
	23	187	Tommy John surgery
Giles,Ken	19	9	Inflammation R elbow
	20	55	Strn R forearm x2
	21	169	Tommy John surgery
	22	112	Spr. R mid fing; tight R shldr
Ginkel,Kevin	21	2	Inflammation R elbow
Giolito,Lucas	19	32	Strn L hammy; strn R muscle
	21	13	Strn R hamstring
	22	21	Strnd L abdominal; covid-19
Givens,Mychal	21	20	Strn lower back
	22	19	Covid-19
	23	126	Inflam knee; inflam R shoulder
Glasnow,Tyler	19	121	Strn R forearm
	21	94	Sprained UCL in R elbow
	22	178	Tommy John surg
	23	59	Strained L oblique
Godley,Zack	20	22	Strn flexor mass R elbow
	21	13	Bruised R index finger
Gomber,Austin	20	7	Covid-19
	21	45	L forearm tight stress fx low back
	23	25	Lower back inflammation
Gonsolin,Anthony	21	111	R shoulder inflammation
	22	39	Strnd R forearm
	23	73	Sprained L ankle; TJS
Gonzales,Marco	21	34	Strn L forearm
	23	122	Strained L forearm
Gonzalez,Chi Chi	20	23	Tendinitis R biceps
	21	31	Covid-19; Strn R oblique
Gonzalez,Victor	21	30	Plant fasciitis L ft; inflam R knee
	22	188	L elbow inflammation
Gore,MacKenzie	22	75	L elbow inflammation
	23	24	Blister R index finger
Gose,Anthony	22	98	Strnd L triceps

FIVE-YEAR INJURY LOG — Pitchers

Pitchers	Yr	Days	Injury
Gott,Trevor	19	47	Strn R elbow
	20	16	Inflammation R elbow
	22	59	Strnd R groin; R forearm
	23	22	Back spasms
Graterol,Brusdar	21	56	R forearm strain
	22	62	R shoulder and elbow inflam
Graveman,Kendall	19	187	Recovery from TJS
	20	29	Neck spasms
	21	20	Covid-19
Gray,Jon	19	41	Fractured L foot
	20	27	Inflammation R shoulder
	21	29	Strn R flexor
	22	64	Str L oblq x2; Blist R mid fing
	23	4	Tightness R forearm
Gray,Sonny	20	10	Strn back
	21	52	Strn back; Str R groin; str rib cage
	22	57	Strnd R hamstring; str. pectoral
Green,Chad	22	141	Tommy John surg
	23	156	Tommy John surgery
Greene,Hunter	22	47	Strnd R shoulder
	23	75	Covid-19; R hip pain
Greinke,Zack	21	15	Covid-19
	22	44	Strnd R flexor
	23	31	R shoulder tendinitis; sore R elb
Grove,Michael	22	7	Bruised L knee
	23	93	Strained right groin; tight R lat
Guenther,Sean	21	1	Strn upper back
	22	188	Tommy John surg
Guerra,Deolis	22	188	Tommy John surg
Guerra,Javier	20	16	Covid-19
	21	169	Sprained UCL R elbow
Guerrero,Tayron	19	44	Blister R middle finger
Gustave,Jandel	21	36	Covid-19
	22	110	Strnd R hamstring; sore R forearm
Gutierrez,Vladimir	22	126	Tommy John surg
	23	187	Tommy John surgery
Hader,Josh	21	11	Covid-19
Hamilton,Ian	23	61	Strained R groin
Hammer,JD	21	8	Covid-19
Hancock,Emerson	23	43	Strained R shoulder
Hand,Brad	21	4	Covid-19
	22	11	Tendinitis L elbow
Harris,Will	20	14	Strn R groin
	21	151	Blood clot R arm; TOS surgery
	22	185	Surgery to repair R pec
Harvey,Hunter	20	39	Strn R elbow
	21	143	Strn R triceps
	22	81	Strnd pronatorR forearm
	23	30	Strained R elbow
Harvey,Matt	19	50	Upper back strain
	20	13	Strn R lat muscle
	21	8	Strn R triceps
Head,Louis	22	20	Impingement L shoulder
Heaney,Andrew	19	83	L elbow inflam; L shoulder inflam
	22	95	Inflammation L shoulder
Heasley,Jon	22	21	Tendinitis R shoulder
Helsley,Ryan	19	21	R shoulder impingement
	20	21	Covid-19
	21	31	Stress reaction R elbow
	23	82	Strained R forearm
Hembree,Heath	19	74	Strn R elbow extensor
	20	8	Strn R elbow
	22	22	Strnd R calf

FIVE-YEAR INJURY LOG — Pitchers

Pitchers	Yr	Days	Injury
Hendricks,Kyle	19	17	R shoulder inflammation
	22	95	Strnd R shoulder
	23	57	Surg repair R shoulder capsule
Hendriks,Liam	22	24	Strnd R flexor tendon
	23	175	Tommy John surgery
Henriquez,Ronny	23	44	Inflammation R elbow
Henry,Tommy	23	65	R elbow inflammation
Hentges,Sam	23	37	Inflammation L shoulder
Herget,Jimmy	22	39	Impingement R shoulder
Hernandez,Daysbel	23	62	R forearm inflammation
Hernandez,Elieser	20	27	Strn R late
	21	133	Inflammation R biceps
	22	16	Covid-19
	23	166	Strnd R shoulder; strnd R pectoral
Hernandez,Jonathan	21	169	Tommy John surgery
	22	104	Tommy John surg
Hernandez,Jose	23	34	Strained R calf
Heuer,Codi	22	188	Tommy John surg
	23	187	Tommy John surgery
Hicks,Jordan	19	98	Torn UCL R elbow
	21	136	Inflammation R elbow
	22	57	Sprain flexor R arm; R arm fatigue
Hill,Rich	19	117	Strn L forearm; sprained L knee
	20	16	Shoulder fatigue L shoulder
	21	2	Covid-19
	22	40	Covid-19; Sprnd R knee
Hill,Tim	22	17	InflammationL shoulder
	23	53	Sprained R index finger x2
Hoffman,Jeff	21	56	R shoulder impingement
	22	83	Stiffness R forearm; covid-19
Holderman,Colin	22	51	Impinge R shldr; sore R shoulder
	23	27	Impng R shld;infl R wrist;spr R thm
Holloway,Jordan	20	56	Covid-19
	21	118	Strn R groin
	22	73	R elbow impingement
Holmes,Clay	19	31	R triceps inflammation
	20	63	Strn R forearm
	21	13	Covid-19
	22	13	L lower back spasms
Honeywell,Brent	22	161	Stress reaction R elbow
Houck,Tanner	22	60	Inflamed lower back
	23	68	Facial fractures
Houser,Adrian	21	16	Covid-19
	22	67	Strnd R flexor; Strnd R groin
	23	57	Tightness R groin; R elbow effusion
Howard,Sam	21	61	Tendinitis R knee; Strn R oblique
	22	17	Strndmid-back
Howard,Spencer	20	12	Stiffness R shoulder
	21	12	Covid-19
	22	62	R shoulder impinge; Blist R hand
	23	68	Strained R Lat
Hudson,Dakota	20	11	Strn R forearm
	21	169	Tommy John surgery
	22	16	Strnd neck
Hudson,Daniel	21	43	Covid-19; inflammation R elbow
	22	106	Torn ACL L knee
	23	182	ACL surg L knee; sprnd MCL R knee
Hughes,Brandon	23	145	Inflammation L knee x3
Hunter,Tommy	19	172	R forearm surgery
	21	121	Strn lower back
	22	34	Tight lower back
	23	16	Back spasms
Iglesias,Raisel	23	37	Strained R shoulder
Irvin,Cole	22	21	Sore L shoulder

FIVE-YEAR INJURY LOG — Pitchers

Pitchers	Yr	Days	Injury
Irvin,Jake	23	11	Tendinitis R ankle
Jackson,Jay	21	2	Covid-19
	22	90	Strnd R lat
Jackson,Luke	22	188	Tommy John surg
	23	90	Back spasms; TJS
Jackson,Zach	22	40	Separated L shoulder
	23	137	Strained R flexor tendon
Jacob,Alek	23	73	Sprained UCL right elbow
James,Josh	19	41	Inflammation R shoulder
	20	19	Sore L hip
	21	123	L hip surgery
	22	108	Strnd R lat
Jameson,Drey	23	88	L elbow inflammation
Jansen,Kenley	22	16	Irregular heartbeat
	23	11	Concussion
Jefferies,Daulton	22	133	Strnd cervical spine
Jimenez,Dany	22	86	Strnd R shoulder
	23	110	Strained R shoulder
Jimenez,Joe	21	10	Covid-19
	22	15	Strnd lumbar spine
Johnson,Pierce	21	26	Strn R groin; inflam R triceps tndn
	22	143	R forearm tendinitis
Jones,Damon	22	104	Impingement L shoulder
Joyce,Ben	23	93	Ulnar neuritis R elbow
Junis,Jake	20	26	Lower back spasms/Covid-19
	21	16	Impingement R shoulder
	22	36	Strnd L hamstring
	23	7	Cervical strain
Kahnle,Tommy	20	59	TJS
	21	169	Tommy John surgery
	22	148	Tommy John surg
	23	72	R biceps tendnts; R shlder inflam
Kaprielian,James	21	9	Impingement R shoulder
	22	28	Inflammation AC joint R shoulder
	23	95	Surg repair torn labrum R shoulder
Karinchak,James	22	90	Strnd upper back R side
Kela,Keone	19	79	Shoulder, elbow inflammation
	20	54	Tight R forearm, Covid-19
	21	143	Inflam R shoulder; R forearm
Keller,Brad	20	14	Covid-19
	21	21	Strn R Lat
	23	129	Impinge R shoulder; TOS
Keller,Mitch	20	44	Strn L oblique
	21	3	Covid-19
Kelly,Joe	20	32	Inflammation R shoulder
	21	52	R shoulder inflammation x2
	22	56	Strn L ham; nerve injury R biceps
	23	64	Str R groin; R elbow inflam x2
Kelly,Kevin	23	17	Sprained L ankle
Kelly,Merrill	20	36	Impingement R shoulder
	21	36	Covid-19; undisclosed inj
	23	29	R calf inflammation
Kelly,Michael	23	33	Strained lower back
Kelly,Zack	23	165	R elbow inflam
Kennedy,Ian	20	29	Strn L calf
	21	8	Strn L hamstring
	22	18	R calf inflammation
	23	17	Strained R/C R shoulder
Kershaw,Clayton	19	19	L shoulder inflammation
	20	11	Lower back stiffness
	21	69	L forearm inflammation x2
	22	57	SI joint inflm L shld; Low bck sore
	23	39	Soreness L shoulder

FIVE-YEAR INJURY LOG — Pitchers

Pitchers	Yr	Days	Injury
Keuchel,Dallas	20	13	Back spasms
	23	2	Strained R calf
Kikuchi,Yusei	21	2	Covid-19
	22	24	Strnd cervical spine
Kimbrel,Craig	19	30	R knee inflam; R elbow inflam
King,Michael	21	68	Bruised R middle finger
	22	78	Fx R elbow
Kinley,Tyler	22	119	Torn flex tend, UCL nrve inj R elb
	23	138	Torn flexor R elbow
Kittredge,Andrew	20	48	Sprained UCL R elbow
	22	137	Low back sore; Tommy John surg
	23	141	Tommy John surgery
Kluber,Corey	19	151	Fractured ulna R forearm
	20	63	Torn teres major muscle R shldr
	21	97	Strn R shoulder
	23	104	Inflammation R shoulder
Knebel,Corey	19	187	Recovery from TJS
	20	20	Strn L hamstring
	21	109	Strn R Lat
	22	9	Strnd R lat; covid-19
Knehr,Reiss	23	97	Tommy John surgery
Kopech,Michael	19	187	Recovery from TJS
	21	34	Strn L hamstring
	22	38	Strnd L knee; inflamed R shoulder
	23	23	Inflam R shoulder; inflam R knee
Kranick,Max	22	132	Tommy John surgery
	23	156	Tommy John surgery
Krehbiel,Joey	22	16	InflammationR shoulder
Kremer,Dean	22	57	Strnd L oblique
Kuhl,Chad	19	187	TJS
	21	59	Covid-19; sore R shoulder
	22	27	Strnd R hip flexor; Strnd R triceps
	23	20	Metatarsalgia in right foot
Lakins,Travis	21	79	Stress Fx R elbow
	22	53	InflammationR elbow
Lambert,Jimmy	23	52	R ankle inflam x2
Lambert,Peter	20	68	TJS
	21	169	Tommy John surgery
	22	188	Recovery from Tommy John surg
	23	17	Tendinitis R triceps
Lamet,Dinelson	19	99	Recovery from TJS
	21	101	Strn UCL R elbow; Strn R forearm
	23	28	Lower back stiffness
Lange,Alex	21	23	Strn R shoulder
Lauer,Eric	20	3	Covid-19
	21	12	Covid-19
	22	14	L elbow inflammation
	23	24	Impingement L shoulder
Law,Derek	21	62	Impingement R shoulder
	23	45	Sprained R elbow
Leclerc,Jose	20	60	Strn teres major muscle R shldr
	21	169	Tommy John surgery
	22	74	Tommy John surg
	23	13	Sprained R ankle
Lee,Dylan	23	127	Inflammation L shoulder
Lee,Evan	22	113	Strnd L flexor tendon
Legumina,Casey	23	77	Bruised R ankle; sore R shoulder
Leone,Dominic	22	39	Covid-19; R elbow inflamm
Liberatore,Matthew	23	14	Lower back tightness
Littell,Zack	20	30	Strn L elbow, inflam R elbow
	22	50	Covid-19; Strnd L oblique
	23	22	Fatigue R shoulder
Lively,Ben	23	55	Covid-19; strained R pect muscle
Llovera,Mauricio	22	85	Strnd R flexor tendon

FIVE-YEAR INJURY LOG — Pitchers

Pitchers	Yr	Days	Injury
Loaisiga,Jonathan	19	93	Strn R shoulder
	20	14	Undisclosed medical condition
	21	26	Covid-19; Strn R/C R shoulder
	22	51	Inflammation R shoulder
	23	145	Inflammation R elbow x2
Lodolo,Nick	22	69	Strnd lower back
	23	142	L calf tendinitis
Long,Sam	21	24	Strn lower back
	22	44	Strnd R oblique
Lopez,Jorge	20	6	Covid-19
	21	10	Sprained R ankle
	23	17	Mental health reasons
Lopez,Pablo	19	69	Strn R shoulder
	21	65	Strn R rotator cuff
Lopez,Reynaldo	20	27	Strn R shoulder
	22	13	Strnd lower back
Lorenzen,Michael	21	120	Strn R shoulder; Strn R hamstring
	22	68	Strnd R shoulder
	23	17	Strained L groin
Loup,Aaron	19	176	Strn L elbow
	23	28	Strnd R hamstring; strnd L shldr
Lovelady,Richard	21	19	Sprained UCL L elbow
	23	98	Strained left forearm
Lucchesi,Joey	21	90	Inflammation L elbow; surgery
	22	188	Tommy John surg
Luetge,Lucas	23	33	Inflammation L biceps
Lugo,Seth	19	12	R shoulder tendinitis
	21	61	Recovery from R elbow surgery
	23	34	Strained L calf
Luzardo,Jesus	21	29	Fx L hand
	22	79	Strnd L flexor tendon
Lyles,Jordan	19	29	Strn L ham; Strn L oblique
Lynch,Daniel	22	33	Blister R index finger x2
	23	136	Strained R/C L shoulder
Lynn,Lance	21	27	Strn R trap muscle; inflam R knee
	22	71	Surg repair torn tendon knee
Maeda,Kenta	19	10	Bruised L adductor muscle
	21	49	Strn R adductor; tight R forearm
	22	188	Tommy John surg
	23	57	Strained R triceps
Mahle,Tyler	19	32	Strn L hamstring
	22	71	Strnd R shoulder
	23	153	Posterior impingement R forearm
Manaea,Sean	19	158	R shoulder surgery rehab
Manning,Matt	22	118	InflammationR shoulder
	23	103	Fx toe R foot; fx R foot
Manoah,Alek	21	16	Strn lower back
Mantiply,Joe	21	17	Covid-19
	23	52	Strnd R hammy; inflam L shoulder
Marinaccio,Ron	22	27	InflammationR shoulder
Marquez,German	19	39	R arm inflammation
	23	173	Tommy John surgery
Marte,Jose	21	26	Covid-19
	23	146	Stress reaction R elbow
Martin,Brett	20	26	RC inflam L shoulder, Covid-19
	21	9	Strn lower back
	22	22	Covid-19
	23	187	Recovery from L shoulder surgery
Martin,Chris	20	14	Esophageal constriction
	21	51	Inflam R shoulder; R elbow inflam
	23	19	Inflam R shoulder; viral infection
Martin,Corbin	20	68	TJS
	23	187	Torn latissimus tendon
Martinez,Adrian	23	22	Strained R elbow

FIVE-YEAR INJURY LOG — Pitchers

Pitchers	Yr	Days	Injury
Maton,Phil	23	16	Bruised R elbow
Matz,Steven	19	10	Sore L elbow
	20	15	Impingement L shoulder
	21	18	Covid-19
	22	112	Imping L shldr; torn MCL L knee
	23	50	Strained lat muscle
Matzek,Tyler	22	52	InflammationL shoulder
	23	187	Tommy John surgery
May,Dustin	21	138	Tommy John surgery
	22	153	Tommy John surg
	23	138	Strnd flexor pronator R arm
May,Trevor	22	103	inflammation R triceps
	23	35	Anxiety disorder
Mayers,Mike	19	99	Strn lat R shoulder
	21	3	Covid-19
Mayza,Tim	19	26	Ulnar neuritis L 4arm; TJS
	21	13	Inflammation L elbow
	22	17	Dislocated R shoulder
Mazza,Chris	21	132	Inflamed R shoulder
	22	60	Covid-19
McArthur,James	22	102	Stress reaction R elbow
McClanahan,Shane	21	8	Strn lower back
	22	16	Impingement L shoulder
	23	78	L forearm tight; mid back strain
McCullers,Lance	19	187	Recovery from TJS
	20	10	Neck irritation
	21	24	Sore R shoulder
	22	132	Strnd R forearm
	23	187	Surg R elb bone spur & R flex tear
McFarland,T.J.	19	34	Inflammation L shoulder
	22	20	Covid-19
McGee,Easton	23	156	Strained R forearm
McGee,Jake	19	46	Sprained L knee
	21	3	Covid-19; Strn R oblique
	22	16	Tight lower back
McGough,Scott	23	15	Inflammation R shoulder
McHugh,Collin	19	66	R elbow pain
	21	33	Covid;Strn lower back;R arm fatig
	22	10	Covid-19
	23	47	Hypertrophy R arm; sore R elb; CV
McKay,Brendan	20	19	Sore L shoulder, Covid-19
	22	172	Tommy John surg
McKenzie,Triston	21	8	Fatigue R shoulder
	23	167	Strnd right teres major; sprnd R elb
McMillon,John	23	34	Strained R forearm
Means,John	19	26	Strn L biceps; Strn L shldr
	20	14	Covid-19, L shoulder fatigue
	21	45	Strn L shoulder
	22	176	Strnd L elbow
	23	167	Tommy John surgery
Mears,Nick	22	139	Tommy John surg recovery
	23	69	Strained L oblique
Medina,Luis	23	15	Blister R index finger
Megill,Trevor	21	34	Strn R forearm
	22	29	Strnd L oblique; covid-19
Megill,Tylor	22	127	Tnditis R biceps; Str R shldr; Covid
Melancon,Mark	22	8	Covid-19
	23	187	Strained R elbow + shoulder
Merryweather,Julian	20	8	Tendinitis R elbow
	21	148	Strn L oblique
	22	84	Strain L abdominal
Meyer,Max	22	77	Sprnd R elbow
	23	187	Tommy John surgery

FIVE-YEAR INJURY LOG — Pitchers

Pitchers	Yr	Days	Injury
Middleton,Keynan	19	153	Recovery from TJS
	21	17	Strn R biceps tendon
	22	77	R elb inflam; spr R ank; Sprnd toe
	23	24	Inflammation R shoulder
Mikolas,Miles	20	63	Strn flexor tendon R forearm
	21	142	Rec fr TJS; tightness R forearm
Miley,Wade	20	40	Strn L groin, Strn L shoulder
	21	11	Sprained L foot
	22	138	L elb inflam; Strnd L shoulder
	23	49	Strained left lat; sore L elbow
Miller,Bryce	23	14	Blister R index finger
Miller,Justin	19	88	Low back strain; strn AC R shldr
	21	25	Ulnar nerve irritation R elbow
Miller,Mason	23	119	Sprained R UCL
Miller,Shelby	21	35	Strn lower back
	23	72	Cervical pain
Mills,Alec	21	24	Strn lower back
	22	160	Strnd lower back
Mills,Wyatt	23	18	R elbow inflammation
Milner,Hoby	19	20	Bruised cervical nerve
	20	10	Lower back spasms
Milone,Tom	20	19	Inflammation L elbow
	21	101	Inflamed L shoulder
	22	71	Strnd cervical spine
Minor,Mike	21	2	Impingement R shoulder
	22	77	Sore L shoulder
Minter,A.J.	19	26	L shoulder inflammation x2
	23	17	Inflammation L shoulder x3
Misiewicz,Anthony	21	18	Covid-19; Strn L forearm
	23	39	Concussion; strained R calf
Mize,Casey	22	176	Sprnd R elbow; Tommy John surg
	23	187	Tommy John surgery
Mlodzinski,Carmen	23	21	Sore R elbow
Moll,Sam	22	26	Covid-19; Strnd L shoulder
Montas,Frankie	22	19	Inflammation R shoulder
	23	185	Recovery from surgery R shoulder
Montero,Rafael	20	16	Tendinitis R elbow
	21	38	Discomfort R shoulder
Montes de Oca,Bryce	22	27	Tight L hamstring
	23	187	Tommy John surgery
Montgomery,Jordan	19	172	TJS
	21	15	Covid-19
Moore,Matt	19	178	Recovery meniscus surgery R knee
	21	42	Strn lower back; Covid-19
	23	48	Strained R oblique
Moran,Jovani	23	9	Strained L forearm
Morejon,Adrian	19	55	L shoulder impingement
	21	158	Strn L forearm
	22	92	Covid-19; Tommy John surg
	23	102	Sprained L elbow; inflam R knee
Moreta,Dauri	22	5	Covid-19
Morris,Cody	22	151	Strnd R shoulder
	23	74	Strained right teres major muscle
Morton,Charlie	20	24	Inflammation R shoulder
	23	9	Inflammation R index finger
Munoz,Andres	20	68	TJS
	21	169	Tommy John surgery
	23	61	Strained deltoid muscle R shoulder
Murfee,Penn	23	148	Tommy John surgery
Musgrove,Joe	20	23	Inflam R triceps
	22	7	Covid-19
	23	84	Fx big toe L foot; inflam R shoulder
Mushinski,Parker	22	45	DiscomfortL elbow
	23	54	Muscle spasms lumbar spine

FIVE-YEAR INJURY LOG — Pitchers

Pitchers	Yr	Days	Injury
Nance,Tommy	21	3	Covid-19
	22	36	Covid-19; Strnd R groin
	23	161	Strnd R shoulder; strnd L oblique
Nardi,Andrew	23	29	L triceps inflammation
Naughton,Packy	23	178	Strained L forearm
Nelson,Jimmy	19	126	Labrum surg R shldr; effusn R elb
	20	68	Recovery from lower back surgery
	21	85	Inflam R forearm;Low back str; TJS
	22	188	Tommy John surg
	23	187	Tommy John surgery
Nelson,Kyle	22	61	Covid; low back str; L elb inflam
Nelson,Nick	23	35	Strained L hamstring
Nelson,Ryne	22	18	Inflammation R scapula
Newcomb,Sean	19	7	Concussion
	21	13	Covid-19
	22	33	Sprnd L ankle
	23	16	Strained L knee
Nogosek,Steve	21	48	Impingement R shoulder
	22	28	Strnd L oblique
	23	17	Bone bruise R elbow
Nola,Aaron	21	10	Covid-19
	22	4	Covid-19
Norris,Daniel	20	11	Covid-19
	22	21	Strnd L index finger
Ober,Bailey	22	125	Strnd R groin x2
Oberg,Scott	19	45	Blood clot R arm
	20	68	Strnd low back, blood clot R arm
	21	169	Blood clots R arm
	22	188	Medical illness
O'Day,Darren	19	162	Strn R forearm
	21	133	Strn rotator cuff R shoulder
	22	88	Strnd L calf
Odorizzi,Jake	19	11	Blister R index finger
	20	55	Strn R intercost;brsed chest;R fing
	21	37	Strn R pronator; sore R foot
	22	49	Strnd lower L leg
	23	187	R shoulder fatigue
Ohtani,Shohei	19	41	Recovery from TJS
	23	17	Strained R oblique
Okert,Steven	22	10	Tight L triceps
	23	23	Strained L adductor
Olivarez,Helcris	22	134	Strnd L shoulder
Oller,Adam	22	25	R rib costochondritis
Ort,Kaleb	23	88	R elbow inflammation
Ortega,Oliver	23	40	Strained lower back
Otto,Glenn	22	16	Covid-19
	23	93	Str R shoulder; tight R lat
Overton,Connor	22	123	Stress Fx lower back
	23	171	Strained R elbow
Oviedo,Johan	20	7	Covid-19
Oviedo,Luis	21	47	Strn L quad
	22	15	Sprnd R ankle
Pacheco,Freddy	23	187	Tightness R elbow
Paddack,Chris	21	46	Strn L oblique; inflam R elbow
	22	152	Inflammation R elbow
	23	179	Tommy John surgery
Pagan,Emilio	20	11	Tendinitis R biceps
	22	4	Covid-19
Patino,Luis	21	12	laceration R middle finger
	22	95	Strnd L oblique
Patton,Spencer	22	18	Strnd R oblique

FIVE-YEAR INJURY LOG — Pitchers

Pitchers	Yr	Days	Injury
Paxton,James	19	26	L knee inflammation
	20	39	Strn flexor muscle L forearm
	21	163	Strn L forearm
	22	188	Tommy John surg
	23	65	Strnd R hamstring; inflam R knee
Payamps,Joel	21	3	Covid-19
	22	36	Covid-19
Peacock,Matt	22	19	Covid-19
Pearson,Nate	20	37	Strn flexor tendon R elbow
	21	29	Strn R adductor muscle
	22	185	Medical illness
Peguero,Elvis	23	13	Effusion R elbow
Pena,Felix	19	58	Torn ACL R knee
	21	36	Strn R hamstring
Pepiot,Ryan	23	126	Strained L oblique
Peralta,Freddy	19	17	Sore AC joint R shoulder
	21	16	Inflammation R shoulder
	22	90	Sprnd R lat; fatigue R shoulder
Peralta,Wandy	19	28	Strn R hip flexor
	21	27	Covid-19; Strn lower back
	22	20	TightnessL thoracic spine
	23	11	Strained L triceps
Peralta,Wily	21	11	Blister index finger R hand
	22	29	Strnd L hamstring
Perdomo,Angel	21	70	Strn lower back
	23	49	Sore R elbow
Perdomo,Luis	20	8	R forearm inflam
	22	81	R elbow effusion; Strnd R calf
Perez,Cionel	23	15	Sore left forearm
Perez,Eury	23	10	Inflammation R SI joint in pelvis
Perez,Martin	21	16	Covid-19
Peters,Dillon	20	42	Covid-19
	21	11	Strn lower back
	22	79	Str low back; L elbow inflam
Peterson,David	20	11	Fatigued R shoulder
	21	78	Sore R side
Phelps,David	19	82	Recovery from TJS
	21	134	Strn R lat muscle
Phillips,Evan	20	6	Inflammation R elbow
	21	11	Strn R quad
Pineda,Michael	19	25	R knee tendinitis; strn R triceps
	21	59	Abscess leg;R elb infl;Str L obliqe
	22	88	Fx R mid fing; tightness R triceps
Pivetta,Nick	21	10	Covid-19
Plesac,Zach	21	45	Fx R thumb
	22	30	Fx 5th metacarpal R hand
Poche,Colin	20	68	Torn UCL L elbow
	21	169	Recovery from surgery L elbow
	22	4	Strnd R oblique
Pomeranz,Drew	19	11	Strn L Lat
	20	13	Strn L shoulder
	21	99	Tight L lat; inflam L forearm
	22	188	Surgery L flexor tendon
	23	187	Flexor tendon surgery R elbow
Poncedeleon,Daniel	21	68	Inflamed R shoulder
Pop,Zach	21	18	Inflammation index finger R hand
	23	66	Strained R hamstring
Poppen,Sean	19	30	R elbow contusion
	22	27	Inflammation R shoulder
Poteet,Cody	21	98	Sprained R knee; Strn R MCL
	22	126	Inflammation R elbow
Pressly,Ryan	19	41	Sore R knee
	22	38	Inflamm R knee; neck spasms

FIVE-YEAR INJURY LOG — Pitchers

Pitchers	Yr	Days	Injury
Price,David	19	46	TFCC cyst L wrist; L elb tendinitis
	21	22	Strn R hamstring
	22	48	Covid-19; inflammation L wrist
Pruitt,Austin	20	68	Sore R elbow
	21	107	Recovery from surgery on R elbow
	23	44	Strained R forearm
Puk,A.J.	20	68	Strn L shoulder
	21	51	Strn L biceps
	22	3	Covid-19
	23	24	Nerve irritation in L elbow
Quantrill,Cal	22	4	Covid-19
	23	87	Inflammation R shoulder x2
Quijada,Jose	20	32	Covid-19
	22	50	Strnd R oblique
	23	157	Tommy John surgery
Quintana,Jose	20	57	Laceration R thumb, Strn L lat
	21	22	Inflamed L shoulder
	23	107	Bone graf surgery ribcage
Ragans,Cole	22	19	Strnd L calf
Rainey,Tanner	20	17	Strn flexor muscle R forearm
	21	40	Covid-19; stress reaction R tibia
	22	87	Tommy John surg
	23	184	Tommy John surgery
Raley,Brooks	21	71	Covid-19
	23	17	L elbow inflammation
Ramirez,Erasmo	20	1	Tightness R groin
	21	56	Strn R pectoral muscle
Ramirez,Nick	21	19	Inflamed R/C L shoulder
Ramirez,Noe	19	19	Viral infection
	21	21	Covid-19
Rasmussen,Drew	22	18	Strnd R hamstring
	23	144	Strained R flexor tendon
Ray,Robbie	19	10	Lower R back spasms
	21	12	Bruised R elbow
	23	185	Strained L forearm
Reed,Jake	21	27	Strn R forearm
	22	17	Strnd L oblique
Reid-Foley,Sean	21	78	Inflammation R elbow
	22	161	Partially torn UCLR elbow
	23	21	Strained R lat
Reyes,Alex	22	188	Frayed labrum R shoulder
	23	18	Recovery from torn labrum surgery
Richards,Garrett	19	173	Recovery from TJS
	22	10	Blister index finger
Richards,Trevor	22	17	Strnd neck
	23	16	Inflammation cervical spine
Ridings,Stephen	22	188	Impingement R shoulder
	23	78	Strained R shoulder; sore R lat
Rios,Yacksel	20	45	Inflammation L shoulder
	23	95	Raynaud's syndrome
Roberts,Ethan	22	163	Inflammation R shoulder
	23	187	Tommy John surgery
Robertson,David	19	169	Strn R shoulder
	20	68	TJS
	22	10	Covid-19
Robles,Hansel	22	13	Back spasms
Rodon,Carlos	19	152	L elbow inflammation
	20	52	Sore L shoulder
	21	19	L shoulder fatigue
	22	5	Covid-19
	23	116	Strnd L forearm; strnd L hamstring
Rodriguez,Chris	21	29	Inflammation R shoulder
	22	188	Rec surgery on R shoulder
	23	187	Recovery capsular surg R shoulder

FIVE-YEAR INJURY LOG — Pitchers

Pitchers	Yr	Days	Injury
Rodriguez,Eduardo	20	68	Covid-19, myocarditis
	21	7	Inflammation L elbow
	22	26	Strnd L rib cage
	23	37	Pulley rupture
Rodriguez,Joely	20	37	Strn L lat, str L hamstring
	21	16	Sprained L ankle
	23	145	Str R obliq;L shldr inflam;R hip infl
Rodriguez,Manuel	20	3	Strn R biceps
	22	87	Strnd R elbow
Rodriguez,Wilking	23	187	Strained R shoulder
Rogers,Josh	19	96	Sprained L elbow
	21	3	Strn R hamstring
	22	51	Impingement L shoulder
Rogers,Taylor	21	52	Sprained index finger L hand
Rogers,Trevor	21	13	Strn lower Back; Covid-19
	22	55	Back spasms; Strnd L lat
	23	165	Strained L biceps
Rolison,Ryan	22	188	Recovery R shoulder surgery
	23	142	Strnd L shoulder; surg L shoulder
Romano,Jordan	20	31	Strn R middle finger
	21	9	Ulnar neuritis R elbow
	23	18	Lower back inflammation
Romero,Jhon	22	172	Biceps tendinitis R arm
Romero,JoJo	21	134	Strn L elbow
	22	103	Tommy John surg
	23	29	Tendinitis L patella
Romero,Seth	20	36	Fractured R hand
	22	143	Strnd L calf
Romo,Sergio	22	32	Inflammation R shoulder
Rosario,Randy	20	30	Tightness L forearm
Rosenthal,Trevor	19	44	Viral infection
	21	169	Inflamed R shoulder
	22	80	Strnd L hamstring
Ross,Joe	21	56	Inflammation R elbow; torn UCL
	22	188	Surgery rem bone spurs R elbow
Rucinski,Drew	23	169	Strnd L hamstring; stomach illness
Rucker,Michael	22	14	Turf toe L foot
Ruiz,Jose	20	18	Covid-19
Ryan,Joe	22	21	Covid-19
	23	23	Strained L groin
Ryu,Hyun-Jin	19	23	Strn L groin; neck stiffness
	21	9	Strn R glute; tightness neck
	22	157	Tommy John surg
	23	125	Tommy John surgery
Sadler,Casey	21	84	Inflamed R shoulder
	22	188	Rec R shoulder surgery
Sale,Chris	19	44	L elbow inflammation
	20	67	TJS
	21	143	Covid-19; recovery from TJS
	22	182	Stress Fx R rib cage; fx R wrist
	23	64	Inflammation L shoulder
Sampson,Adrian	19	14	Lower back spasms
	23	71	Torn meniscus R knee
Sanchez,Anibal	19	13	Strn L hamstring
	22	102	Cervical nerve impingement
Sanchez,Cristopher	23	24	Strained L triceps
Sanchez,Miguel	22	109	L elbow pain
Sanchez,Sixto	22	188	Rec from surgery on R shoulder
Sanders,Phoenix	22	16	Lower back spasms
Sandoval,Patrick	21	33	Strn lower back
	23	7	Strained R oblique
Sands,Cole	22	16	Bruised R elbow
	23	32	Impingement R shoulder
Sanmartin,Reiver	23	147	Stress reaction L elbow

FIVE-YEAR INJURY LOG — Pitchers

Pitchers	Yr	Days	Injury
Santana,Dennis	21	3	Covid-19
	22	31	Sprnd L ankle; covid-19
Santillan,Tony	22	114	Strnd lower back
	23	99	Stress fx lower back: strnd R knee
Santos,Gregory	22	47	Strnd R groin
	23	13	Inflammation R elbow
Saucedo,Tayler	22	163	Sore R hip
Sborz,Josh	19	11	Sore lower back
	22	56	Sore R elbow
	23	53	Spr L ank;R tricps tendnts;str L ham
Scherzer,Max	19	42	Inflamed bursa sac back/shoulder
	21	11	Strn R groin
	22	60	Strnd R & L oblique
	23	20	Strained right teres major muscle
Schmidt,Clarke	21	133	Strn extensor R elbow
Scholtens,Jesse	23	9	Strained L calf
Schreiber,John	23	71	Strained right teres major muscle
Scott,Tanner	21	14	Sprained R knee
Scott,Tayler	22	28	Laceration R index finger
Seabold,Connor	22	18	Strnd extensorR forearm
Senzatela,Antonio	19	19	Infected blister on R heel
	21	33	Covid-19; Strn R groin
	22	88	Str low back; infl L shld; ACL L kn.
	23	182	Tommy John surgery
Severino,Luis	19	174	Inflammation R/C R shoulder
	20	67	TJS
	21	169	Tommy John surgery
	22	72	Covid; Strnd R lat
	23	77	Strained R lat; strained L oblique
Sewald,Paul	22	8	Covid-19
Sheffield,Justus	21	57	L forearm strain
Sherfy,Jimmie	21	55	Inflammation R elbow
Sherriff,Ryan	22	120	Strnd biceps; Strnd L shoulder
Silseth,Chase	23	31	Concussion
Sims,Lucas	21	47	Sprained R elbow
	22	170	Lower back spasms
	23	20	Lower back spasms
Singer,Brady	21	35	Covid; R shldr fatigue; R biceps inj
	23	15	Strained lower back
Skubal,Tarik	22	67	Fatigue L arm
	23	97	Flexor tendon surgery L elbow
Smeltzer,Devin	21	128	Inflammation L elbow
Smith,Caleb	19	30	L hip inflammation
	20	39	Covid-19
	22	29	Fx R hand
Smith,Drew	19	187	TJS
	21	59	Impingement R shoulder
	22	55	Strnd R lat
Smith,Joe	19	107	Recovery surgery L Achilles
	21	29	Sore R elbow
	22	18	Tight upper trapezius
Smith,Will	19	11	Concussion
	20	15	Covid-19
	23	13	Concussion
Smyly,Drew	19	16	Tightness L arm
	20	40	Strn L index finger
	21	9	Inflammation L forearm
	22	41	Strnd R oblique
Snead,Kirby	22	6	Covid-19
	23	93	Strained L shoulder
Snell,Blake	19	69	Fx R big toe; loose bodies L elbow
	21	19	Gastroenteritis x2; Str L adductor
	22	38	Strnd L adductor
Song,Noah	23	122	Strained lower back

FIVE-YEAR INJURY LOG — Pitchers

Pitchers	Yr	Days	Injury
Soriano,Jose	21	169	Tommy John surgery
Soroka,Michael	20	56	Torn R Achilles tendon
	21	169	Recovery from R Achilles injury
	22	151	Torn R Achilles
	23	27	Inflammation R forearm
Sousa,Bennett	23	60	Irritated nerve L shoulder
Speier,Gabe	22	19	Covid-19
Springs,Jeffrey	19	77	L biceps tendinitis
	21	47	Sprained R knee
	22	17	Covid-19; tightness lower R leg
	23	168	Tommy John surgery
Stammen,Craig	22	65	Inflammation R shoulder
Stanek,Ryne	19	17	Bruised R hip
	20	32	Covid-19
	23	18	Sprained R ankle
Stashak,Cody	20	25	Lower back inflammation
	21	101	Strn lower back
	22	154	Tndnitis R bicep; impinge R shldr
Staumont,Josh	21	15	Covid-19
	22	66	Biceps tendinitis R arm; Str neck
	23	118	Thoracic outlet syndrome (TOS)
Steckenrider,Drew	19	147	R elbow inflammation
	20	68	Tendinitis R triceps
	21	16	Covid-19
Steele,Justin	21	49	Strn R hamstring
	22	34	Strnd lower back
	23	15	Strained L forearm
Stephens,Jackson	22	9	Concussion
	23	2	Inflammation R elbow
Stephenson,Robert	19	17	Strn cervical spine
	20	28	Strn mid-back
	21	38	Strn lower back
	22	19	Covid-19
	23	16	Inflammation R elbow
Stewart,Brock	23	92	Sore R elbow
Stiever,Jonathan	22	188	Surgical repair R lat
Stout,Eric	22	17	Sore lower back
Strahm,Matthew	19	9	Strn L rib ligament
	20	10	Inflammation R knee
	20	10	Inflammation R knee
	21	155	Rec fr patellar tendon surg R knee
	22	40	Covid-19; bruised L wrist
Strasburg,Stephen	20	45	Carpal tunnel syndrome R hand
	21	144	Inflamed R shoulder; TOS surgery
	22	184	Surgery TOS; stress reaction ribs
	23	187	TOS surgery
Stratton,Chris	19	45	Inflammation R ribcage
Strickland,Hunter	19	121	Strn R lat muscle
	21	9	Covid-19
Strider,Spencer	22	15	Strnd L oblique
Stripling,Ross	19	39	R biceps tendinitis
	21	48	Str flexor R forearm; Str L oblique
	22	15	Strnd R hip
	23	66	Strained lower back x2
Stroman,Marcus	20	19	Strn L calf
	22	42	Covid-19; inflam R shoulder
	23	45	Inflammation R hip
Suarez,Jose	20	20	Covid-19
	23	127	Strained L shoulder
Suarez,Ranger	20	40	Covid-19
	22	17	Lower back spasms
	23	59	Strnd R hamstring; strnd L elbow
Suarez,Robert	22	61	Surg remove loose bodies L knee
	23	113	R elbow inflam

FIVE-YEAR INJURY LOG — Pitchers

Pitchers	Yr	Days	Injury
Suero,Wander	20	13	Covid-19
	21	25	Strn L oblique
	23	16	Lower back tightness
Sulser,Cole	22	63	Strnd R lat
	23	115	Strnd R lat muscle; strnd R should
Suter,Brent	19	158	Recovery from TJS
	23	27	Strained L oblique
Swanson,Erik	20	29	Strn R forearm
	21	40	Strn R groin
	22	28	R elbow inflammation
	23	16	Inflamed thoracic spine
Swarzak,Anthony	19	20	R shoulder inflammation
Syndergaard,Noah	19	15	Strn R hamstring
	20	68	TJS
	21	188	Covid-19; recovery from TJS
	23	54	Blister R index finger
Szapucki,Thomas	22	6	Strain R hip
	23	187	TOS surgery
Taillon,Jameson	19	150	Strn flexor R elbow
	20	68	TJS
	21	10	Tendon injury R ankle
	23	15	Strained L groin
Tarnok,Freddy	23	151	Strained R calf; strained R shoulder
Tate,Dillon	20	34	Bruised R elbow, sprained R fing
	21	20	Strn L hamstring
	23	187	Strained flexor in right forearm
Taylor,Blake	20	12	Sore L elbow
	21	45	Sprained R ankle
	22	102	DiscomfortL elbow
	23	13	Sprained L elbow
Taylor,Josh	20	43	Tendinitis L shldr, Covid-19
	21	10	Covid-19
	22	188	Strnd lower back
	23	128	Impingement L shoulder
Teheran,Julio	20	14	Covid-19
	21	163	Strn R shoulder
	23	53	Impingement R hip
Tepera,Ryan	19	126	R elbow inflammation
	21	17	Laceration R index finger
	23	17	Inflammation R shoulder
Tetreault,Jackson	22	97	Stress fracturescapulaR shoulder
Thielbar,Caleb	21	19	Covid-19; Strn L groin
	22	17	Covid-19; Strnd L hamstring
	23	83	Strained R oblique
Thompson,Keegan	21	14	Inflammation R shoulder
	22	33	Tight lower back
Thompson,Mason	22	83	Biceps tendinitis R arm
	23	16	Bruised L knee
Thompson,Ryan	21	79	Inflamed R shoulder
	22	40	Stress reaction R elbow
	23	14	Strained right lat
Thompson,Zach	22	16	Inflammation w/nerve R forearm
Tonkin,Michael	23	15	Strained neck
Topa,Justin	21	146	Strn R elbow
	22	138	Strnd R forearm; Sprnd L ankle
Toussaint,Touki	21	107	Strn R shoulder
Treinen,Blake	19	12	Strn R shoulder
	22	163	Inflam, tightness R shoulder
	23	187	Labrum + R/C surgery R shoulder
Triggs,Andrew	20	15	R radial nerve irritation
Trivino,Lou	22	16	Covid-19
	23	187	Tommy John surgery

FIVE-YEAR INJURY LOG — Pitchers

Pitchers	Yr	Days	Injury
Turnbull,Spencer	19	34	Strn upr back; R shoulder fatigue
	21	125	Covid-19; Strn R forearm
	22	188	Tommy John surg
	23	109	Cervical neck pain
Uceta,Edwin	21	53	Strn R lower back
	23	114	Sprained L ankle
Uelmen,Erich	23	3	Strained flexor muscle R forearm
Underwood,Duane	21	23	Sore R oblique; inflam R shoulder
	22	54	Strnd R ham; covid-19
Urena,Jose	19	86	Strn L lower back
	20	44	Covid-19
	21	53	Strn R forearm; Strn R groin
Urias,Julio	21	11	Contusion L calf
	23	43	Strained L hamstring
Urquidy,Jose	20	45	Covid-19
	21	80	Sore R shoulder x2
	23	98	Discomfort R shoulder
Valdez,Framber	21	58	Fractured L index finger
Vargas,Carlos	22	106	Tommy John surg
Varland,Gus	23	47	Bruised R hand; inflam R knee
Vasquez,Andrew	22	54	Sprnd R ankle
	23	32	Tight L calf
Velasquez,Vincent	19	18	Strn R forearm
	21	43	Blister R middle finger
	22	57	Strnd L groin; blister R index fing
	23	151	Tommy John surgery
VerHagen,Drew	19	11	Strn R forearm
	22	126	R hip impingement; hip surgery
	23	21	Impingement R hip
Verlander,Justin	20	64	Strn R forearm/TJS
	21	169	Tommy John surgery
	22	18	Strnd R calf
	23	36	Strnd right teres major R shoulder
Vesia,Alex	20	26	Covid-19
Vest,Will	21	9	Covid-19
	22	12	Covid-19
	23	46	Strained R knee
Vieira,Thyago	23	14	Strained R calf
Vincent,Nick	19	62	Strn R pectoral muscle
Voth,Austin	19	43	Sprained AC joint R shoulder
	21	37	Covid-19; broken nose
	23	71	Sore R elbow
Wacha,Michael	19	11	Patellar tendinitis L knee
	20	19	Inflammation R shoulder
	21	20	Strn R hamstring
	22	54	L intercost inflam; inflam R shldr
	23	43	Inflammation R shoulder
Wainwright,Adam	19	10	Strn L hamstring
	21	4	Covid-19
	22	10	Covid-19
	23	58	Strnd L groin; strnd R shoulder
Waites,Cole	23	77	Tommy John surgery
Walker,Josh	23	50	Strained R oblique
Walker,Taijuan	19	186	Recovery from TJS
	21	11	Tightness L oblique
	22	19	Bursitis R shoulder
Ward,Thad	23	74	Inflammation R shoulder
Warren,Art	21	67	Stained L oblique
	22	59	Strnd R flexor pronator
Warren,Austin	21	23	Covid-19
	22	67	Fx nose; Strnd R triceps
	23	33	Recovery from TJS
Watkins,Spenser	22	17	Bruised R elbow
Weathers,Ryan	21	12	Fx R ankle

FIVE-YEAR INJURY LOG — Pitchers

Pitchers	Yr	Days	Injury
Weaver,Luke	19	118	Tightness R forearm
	21	107	Strn R shoulder
	22	66	R elbow inflammation
	23	22	Strained flexor R arm
Webb,Jacob	19	65	R elbow impingement
	20	48	Shoulder
Webb,Logan	21	54	Strn R shoulder
	22	7	Strnd lower back x2
Weber,Ryan	23	122	Strained R forearm
Weems,Jordan	20	11	Shoulder
Wells,Alex	22	141	Strnd L elbow
Wells,Tyler	21	24	Inflammation R shoulder
	22	58	R shoulder inflam; Strnd L obliq
Wendelken,J.B.	20	5	Undisclosed medical condition
	21	59	Strn L oblique
	22	10	Covid-19
Wheeler,Zack	19	15	R shoulder fatigue
	22	36	Tendinitis R forearm; covid-19
White,Mitchell	21	3	Covid-19
	22	18	Covid-19
	23	72	Inflammation R elbow
Whitley,Kodi	20	50	Covid-19
	21	46	Strn lower back
Whitlock,Garrett	21	2	R pectoral strain
	22	53	R hip inflam; R hip impingement
	23	84	Recovery R hip surg; neuritis R elb
Wick,Rowan	20	12	Strn L oblique
	21	132	Strn L oblique
Widener,Taylor	20	20	Strn R ribcage muscle
	21	80	Covid; Strn R groin x2
Wieck,Brad	20	65	Strn R hamstring
	21	72	Irregular heartbeat
	22	188	Strnd L elbow
Wiles,Collin	22	9	Strnd R shoulder
Williams,Devin	21	11	Strn R elbow
Williams,Taylor	21	140	Inflammation R knee
Williams,Trevor	19	34	Strn R side
	21	40	Appendix surgery
Williamson,Brandon	23	11	Covid-19
Wilson,Bryse	21	11	Fatigue R arm; Strn R hamstring
Wilson,Justin	19	67	Sore R elbow
	21	42	Inflam L shldr; Strn R hamstring
	22	165	Sore L elbow
	23	187	Back spasms; TJS
Wilson,Steven	22	19	L hamstring tendinitis
	23	52	Strnd right pectoral; L hip inflam
Winckowski,Josh	22	13	Covid-19
Winder,Josh	22	37	Impingement R shoulder
	23	29	Strained R shoulder
Wingenter,Trey	19	15	Strn R shoulder
	20	68	TJS
	21	169	Tommy John surgery
	23	80	Tendinitis R shoulder
Winkler,Daniel	21	18	Covid; R triceps tendinitis
Winn,Keaton	23	10	Covid-19
Wisler,Matt	21	32	Inflamed R middle finger
	22	37	Strnd neck
Woo,Bryan	23	15	R forearm inflammation
Wood,Alex	19	123	Lower back strain
	20	36	Inflammation R shoulder
	21	36	Covid-19; Strn lower back
	22	36	Impingement L shoulder
	23	38	Strnd lower back; strnd L hammy
Woodford,Jake	23	100	Inflammation R shoulder

FIVE-YEAR INJURY LOG — Pitchers

Pitchers	Yr	Days	Injury
Woodruff,Brandon	19	58	Strn L oblique
	22	32	Sprnd R ankle
	23	118	Inflammation R shoulder
Workman,Brandon	21	6	Covid exposure
Wright,Kyle	23	144	Inflam R shoulder; strnd R shoulder
Yacabonis,Jimmy	22	15	Strnd L groin
	23	22	Strained L quad
Yajure,Miguel	21	84	Sore R forearm
Yarbrough,Ryan	20	10	Tightness L groin
	21	11	Covid-19
	22	39	Strnd L groin; Strnd R oblique
	23	63	Facial bone fx; head injury
Yates,Kirby	20	45	Bone chips R elbow
	21	169	Tommy John surgery
	22	152	Tommy John surg
Ynoa,Huascar	21	93	Fx R Hand
	22	11	Tommy John surg
	23	187	Tommy John surgery
Young,Alex	23	25	Tight L hamstring; Covid-19
Zastryzny,Rob	23	56	Inflammation L forearm
Zerpa,Angel	22	74	Strnd L knee; sore R knee
	23	107	Tendinopathy L shoulder
Zeuch,T.J.	21	12	Tendinitis R shoulder
	22	21	Strnd upper back
Zimmer,Kyle	20	6	Neuritis R elbow
	21	38	Strn lower back; Strn neck
Zimmermann,Bruce	21	91	Tendinitis L biceps tendon
Zuber,Tyler	22	188	Impingement R shoulder
Zuniga,Guillermo	23	37	Strained R forearm

Top 75 Impact Prospects for 2024

by Chris Blessing, Rob Gordon and Jeremy Deloney

Let's be honest, you've come to this part of the *Forecaster* to grab a sneak peek at the rookies you'll be spending most of your FAB on this year. As in past years, in the following pages you'll find skills and narrative profiles of the 75 rookie-eligible prospects most likely to have an impact in 2024.

At the right, we've ranked the Top 40 prospects in terms of projected 2024 Rotisserie value. Beyond those 40, we list 35 more, presented in alphabetical order, who could see time in the majors in 2024, but whose raw skill or later timeline might be less polished or a step below others in terms of potential 2024 impact. Keep in mind, this is just a pre-season snapshot. Prospects develop at different paces and making that one adjustment or finding opportunity when one doesn't seem to exist can make all the difference.

Starting below, many of the 75 has their own narrative capsules, presented in alphabetical order. This year, we've adjusted how we cover these players. If a player got MLB time in 2023 but maintains rookie eligibility, we've included him in the "regular" player box section and here have a note to look for him there. The reasoning behind this section is the same, however—it's a primer on each player's strengths and weaknesses that attempts to balance raw skill, readiness for the majors and likelihood of 2024 playing time.

For even more detail, including profiles of over 900 prospects, statistics and our overall HQ100 top prospect list, see our sister publication, the *2024 Minor League Baseball Analyst*—as well as the weekly scouting reports and minor league information at BaseballHQ.com. Happy Prospecting!

1. Jackson Holliday (SS, BAL)
2. Junior Caminero (3B, TAM)
3. Evan Carter (OF, TEX)
4. Noelvi Marte (3B, CIN)
5. Colt Keith (3B, DET)
6. Wyatt Langford (OF, TEX)
7. Jackson Chourio (OF, MIL)
8. Jordan Lawlar (SS, ARI)
9. Dylan Crews (OF, WAS)
10. Pete Crow-Armstrong (OF, CHC)
11. Ronny Mauricio (IF, NYM)
12. Colton Cowser (OF, BAL)
13. Paul Skenes (RHP, PIT)
14. Kyle Harrison (LHP, SF)
15. Mason Winn (SS, STL)
16. Kyle Manzardo (1B, CLE)
17. Marco Luciano (SS, SF)
18. Mason Miller (RHP, OAK)
19. Jasson Dominguez (OF, NYY)
20. Heston Kjerstad (OF, BAL)
21. Ceddanne Rafaela (SS/OF, BOS)
22. Nolan Schanuel (1B, LAA)
23. Curtis Mead (3B, TAM)
24. Nick Loftin (2B, KC)
25. Jordan Wicks (LHP, CHC)
26. James Wood (OF, WAS)
27. Coby Mayo (3B, BAL)
28. Brayan Rocchio (SS, CLE)
29. Gavin Stone (RHP, LAD)
30. Jace Jung (2B, DET)
31. Marcelo Mayer (SS, BOS)
32. Xavier Edwards (2B, MIA)
33. Mick Abel (RHP, PHI)
34. Justyn-Henry Malloy (OF, DET)
35. Parker Meadows (OF, DET)
36. Michael Busch (IF, LAD)
37. Adael Amador (SS, COL)
38. Austin Wells (C, NYY)
39. Matt Mervis (1B, CHC)
40. Cade Horton (RHP, CHC)

Other considerations (alphabetical order)

Luisangel Acuña (SS, NYM)
Jacob Amaya (SS, MIA)
Edwin Arroyo (SS, CIN)
Tyler Black (2B, MIL)
Ben Brown (RHP, CHC)
Owen Caissie (OF, CHC)
Jake Eder (LHP, CHW)
Yanquiel Fernandez (OF, COL)
Nick Frasso (RHP, LAD)
Robert Gasser (LHP, SD)
Drew Gilbert (OF, NYM)
Emerson Hancock (RHP, SEA)
Tink Hence (RHP, STL)
Brady House (3B, WAS)
Kyle Hurt (RHP, LAD)
Jared Jones (RHP, PIT)
Spencer Jones (OF, NYY)
Brooks Lee (SS, MIN)
Orelvis Martinez (SS, TOR)
Jackson Merrill (SS, SD)
Jacob Misiorowski (RHP, MIL)
Colson Montgomery (SS, CHW)
Connor Norby (2B, BAL)
Connor Phillips (RHP, CIN)
Edgar Quero (C, CHW)
Jeferson Quero (C, MIL)
Jackson Rutledge (RHP, WAS)
Thomas Saggese (IF, STL)
AJ Smith-Shawver (RHP, ATL)
Robby Snelling (LHP, SD)
Drew Thorpe (RHP, NYY)
Ricky Tiedemann (LHP, TOR)
Hurston Waldrep (RHP, ATL)
Owen White (RHP, TEX)
Carson Williams (SS, TAM)

Mick Abel (RHP, PHI) started the Futures Game in 2023 and ended the campaign with a start in Triple-A in September. The 22-year-old is likely to begin 2024 at that level and build off his season in Double-A that saw him post a 4.13 ERA with 132 strikeouts in 113 innings. His plus mid-90s fastball and complement of breaking balls helped him hold hitters to a .192 oppBA.

Luisangel Acuña (SS, NYM) was obtained from the Rangers in the high-profile Max Scherzer trade and is also the brother of Ronald. Though far from the slugger his brother is, the 21-year-old has plus speed as evidenced by his 57 SB in Double-A. He may not have great power, but he gets on base and can play multiple positions, including SS, 2B and CF.

Adael Amador (SS, COL) has rocketed up prospect charts since the beginning of the 2022 season. The 20-year-old SS always had an advanced hit tool, but the uptick in power and ability to control the strike zone has put him on the fast track to Coors Field. Over the past two seasons, Amador has walked more than he's struck out (118 BB/93 K) while launching 24 home runs and 38 SB in 671 AB.

Jacob Amaya (SS, MIA) is covered in the batters player box section, starting on page 81.

Edwin Arroyo (SS, CIN) often gets overlooked in a system blessed with outstanding infielders. The 20-year-old spent most of the 2023 season in High-A, but he continues to make strides in all aspects of the game. He hit .252/.324/.433 with 28 doubles, 13 HR and 29 SB. He is among the best defensive shortstops in the minors and his offensive game should continue to grow.

Tyler Black (3B, MIL) has a legitimate chance to make the Brewers Opening Day lineup even if a roster reset isn't conducted. He has moved exclusively to 3B where his production fits very well. He split the season between Double-A and Triple-A and batted .284/.417/.513 with 18 HR and 55 SB. Known mostly for his consistent OBP, the left-handed hitter increased his HR output in 2023.

Ben Brown (RHP, CHC) comes after hitters with a mid-90s heater with a crossfire delivery and high 3/4 arm slot. While his fastball command isn't great, he has touched 97 and has two average to above breaking balls. Brown was lights-out in a brief stint at Double-A but struggled to the tune of a 5.33 ERA with 6.3 BB/9 at Triple-A Iowa.

Michael Busch (IF, LA) is covered in the batters player box section, starting on page 81.

Owen Caissie (OF, CHC) has plus power, which he was able to get to more consistently in 2023. Caissie's long levers and aggressive approach means there are plenty of swings and misses in his profile. With improved bat-to-ball skills, he would have a chance to hit for average and power despite some hit tool concerns.

Junior Caminero (3B, TAM) is covered in the batters player box section, starting on page 81.

Evan Carter (OF, TEX) is covered in the batters player box section, starting on page 81.

Jackson Chourio (OF, MIL) is an elite prospect who played all of 2023 at age 19. He performed mostly at Double-A before a late promotion to Triple-A. He led the Southern League in hits and was 5th in SB. For the year, he hit .282/.338/.467 with 22 HR and 44 SB. He'll need to hone his aggressiveness at the plate, but he has the skills to be a foundational player.

Colton Cowser (OF, BAL) is covered in the batters player box section, starting on page 81.

Dylan Crews (OF, WAS) was the 2023 Golden Spikes winner as he led LSU to the College World Series championship. Crews is a legit 5-tool talent with plus speed and some of the hardest exit velo in the draft class. There are some concerns about his GB%, but he should be able to tap into more power with some tweaks to his swing mechanics. Crews' ability to get on base is elite.

Pete Crow-Armstrong (OF, CHC) is covered in the batters player box section, starting on page 81.

Jasson Domínguez (OF, NYY) is covered in the batters player box section, starting on page 81.

Jake Eder (LHP, CHW) came over from the Marlins in the Jake Burger trade. Eder had Tommy John Surgery in August of 2021 and then broke his foot and didn't get back on the mound until June of 2023. The rust showed as he walked 36 in 56.2 IP, but also struck out 70. Eder has a low-90s fastball but gets swings and misses because of riding action up in the zone. He also has a plus slider and developing change-up.

Xavier Edwards (2B, MIA) is covered in the batters player box section, starting on page 81.

Yanquiel Fernandez (OF, COL) blasted 25 home runs across three levels, but slumped badly when promoted to Double-A Hartford (.206/.262/.362). Fernandez has some of the best raw power in the system, but an uber aggressive approach led to a 32% K rate at Double-A. Fernandez makes solid contact on pitches in the zone and has exciting upside if he can reduce his chase rate to an acceptable level.

Nick Frasso (RHP, LA) had a breakout in '22 and early success this year at Double-A thrust him into the limelight. He has a plus fastball that sits in the upper-90s, topping at 101 with ride up in the zone. His slider has two-plane break but remains inconsistent. An average change-up leaves him without a plus secondary and a move to relief seems likely.

Robert Gasser (LHP, MIL) could benefit if the Brewers deal RHP Corbin Burnes. The 24-year-old posted the highest K/9 in the Triple-A International League while improving his pitch sequencing. Not blessed with elite velocity, he throws from a lower arm slot and wipes out hitters with his plus slider. His consistency and durability could be the elixir for the Brewers' future rotation needs.

Drew Gilbert (OF, NYM) was a Mets acquisition at the deadline that injected a top prospect into their farm system. In his first full season as a pro—he was a 1st round pick of Houston in 2022—he hit .289/.381/.487 with 18 HR and 12 SB, mostly in Double-A. The left-handed hitter has 20/20 potential and could see big league action due to an aging and mediocre OF in New York (outside of Brandon Nimmo).

Emerson Hancock (RHP, SEA) is covered in the pitchers player box section, starting on page 149.

Kyle Harrison (LHP, SF) is covered in the pitchers player box section, starting on page 149.

Tink Hence (RHP, STL) has emerged as the Cardinals top pitching prospect. The athletic 21-year-old works primarily off a mid-90s fastball that has plenty of late life. He backs up the heater with a plus upper-70s curve ball and an improved low-80s change-up. At 6'1", 185 there are concerns about his durability as a starter, but stuff can be electric.

Jackson Holliday (SS, BAL) quickly established himself as the top prospect in baseball. The 19-year-old has a pretty lefthanded stroke, an advanced understanding of the strike zone, and unrivaled bat-to-ball skills. Holliday is also a plus runner and could put up a 20/20 season once he makes his MLB debut, which should come early in 2024. He's the favorite for 2024 AL ROY.

Cade Horton (RHP, CHC) comes after hitters with an advanced 4-pitch mix, highlighted by a lively mid-90s fastball with nice arm-side run and carry up in the zone. As good as the heater is, his power slider/sweeper has swing-and-miss action. He should find his way into the pitching thin Cubs rotation by mid-season, if not sooner.

Brady House (3B, WAS) was the team's 1st round pick from 2021 and has the makings of an impact 3B at the big-league level. He put together a stellar 2023 campaign, hitting .312/.365/.496 with 12 HR and 9 SB in 340 AB at Double-A. He'll need to continue to focus on his plate approach, but the BA and power should take him far.

Kyle Hurt (RHP, LA) is covered in the pitchers player box section, starting on page 149.

Jared Jones (RHP, PIT) should challenge for a spot in the Pirates rotation, particularly if a few arms are dealt in the offseason. The 22-year-old dominated Double-A (2.23 ERA, 47 K in 44 IP) before a promotion to Triple-A where he missed bats but struggled a bit with command. With a high-90s fastball and two above average breaking balls, he has an excellent repertoire.

Spencer Jones (OF, NYY) has a big, physical 6'6" frame, which generates plus power. Jones' aggressive approach and long levers will make it hard to hit for both average and power in the majors. Jones also has surprising speed for his size and swiped 43 bases to go along with 16 home runs between High-A and Double-A and should be able to stick in CF.

Jace Jung (2B, DET) had a breakout campaign in which he blasted 28 home runs between High-A and Double-A. Jung has worked hard to improve his plate discipline and posted a career best .376 OBP, and as a result, concerns about his funky pre-pitch set up have faded with a .936 OPS at Double-A. A natural 2B, the Tigers had Jung play 3B in the Arizona Fall League.

Colt Keith (3B, DET) emerged as the Tigers top prospect and will likely win a starting role this spring. What position he will play remains to be seen. Keith has worked hard to become a better defender at 3B but his footwork and range remain below-average. Keith had 38 doubles and 28 home runs between Double and Triple-A and has a career .382 OBP.

Heston Kjerstad (OF, BAL) is covered in the batters player box section, starting on page 81.

Wyatt Langford (OF, TEX) could force his way into the big-league lineup early even though the Rangers are the World Series champions. The 4th overall pick from 2023 exploded in his pro debut and reached Triple-A. Given his 30/30 potential and impeccable eye at the plate, he could team with Evan Carter to be a potent Lone Star State outfield.

Jordan Lawlar (SS, ARI) is covered in the batters player box section, starting on page 81.

Brooks Lee (INF, MIN) may not have an obvious path to playing time right now but the Twins could shake things up with a few trades. The 22-year-old was promoted to Triple-A in early August and finished with a strong season. He has the skills to stick at SS, but he will likely see time at multiple positions including 2B and 3B.

Nick Loftin (2B, KC) is covered in the batters player box section, starting on page 81.

Marco Luciano (SS. SF) is covered in the batters player box section, starting on page 81.

Justyn-Henry Malloy (OF, DET) came over from Atlanta in the Joe Jiménez deal. He has great strike zone judgment with a career .410 OBP. Malloy is a below-average defender at both 3B and LF, but the offensively-challenged Tigers will likely figure out a way to get his bat in the lineup on a regular basis. Malloy smoked a career-best 23 home runs and led all minor leaguers with 110 walks.

Kyle Manzardo (1B, CLE) may not have produced as much as expected in 2023 in Triple-A (.236/.337/.464 with 17 HR), but he suffered through a shoulder injury and was traded from Tampa Bay in July. He profiles as a high BA hitter due to his discerning eye, but he showed good power during the year and in the Arizona Fall League. He will compete for a job in Spring Training.

Noelvi Marte (3B, CIN) is covered in the batters player box section, starting on page 81.

Orelvis Martinez (INF, TOR) got off to a very slow start in Double-A in 2023, but eventually turned it around and produced at both the plate and the field. He's hit at least 28 HR in each of the last 3 seasons while also seeing time at all infield positions except 1B. He has elite power potential, but he also gets on base consistently. With Matt Chapman a free agent, Martinez could be a suitable replacement.

Ronny Mauricio (IF, NYM) is covered in the batters player box section, starting on page 81.

Marcelo Mayer (SS, BOS) has Trevor Story and Rafael Devers in front of him, but that doesn't mean he won't have impact potential. The left-handed hitter does everything well except for running. He has a chance to hit for BA with above average power to go along with solid glovework. He ended his season in early August due to inflammation in his non-throwing shoulder but will be ready for spring training.

Coby Mayo (3B/1B, BAL) blasted 29 home runs to go along with 93 walks. The mix of power and plate discipline should play well once he reaches the majors. At this point at the plate, he has nothing left to prove in the minors. The only question is where Mayo would play as he's currently blocked at both 3B and 1B.

Curtis Mead (2B, TAM) is covered in the batters player box section, starting on page 81.

Parker Meadows (OF, DET) is covered in the batters player box section, starting on page 81.

Jackson Merrill (SS, SD) has all the requisite ingredients to be a solid middle infielder for years to come. He's advanced for his age and could work his way into the Padres plans by midseason. The left-handed hitter batted .277/.326/.444 with 15 HR and 15 SB in 466 AB between High-A and Double-A. He's also increasing his versatility by playing 2B and LF.

Matt Mervis (1B, CHC) is covered in the batters player box section, starting on page 81.

Jacob Misiorowski (RHP, MIL) has an opportunity to be a household name in Milwaukee as soon as Opening Day. He resumed throwing in October after being shut down for arm fatigue in August. In his first full season as a pro, he posted the highest K/9 and lowest oppBA in the organization. With a high 90s fastball, knockout slider, and nasty cutter, he has #1 starter potential.

Colson Montgomery (SS, CHW) quietly has the makings of a superstar SS. The 21-year-old doesn't jump out as an elite athlete, but he's one of the better pure hitters in the minors with an advanced understanding of the strike zone. Montgomery missed time at the start of the season with an oblique strain that limited his in-game power, but long term he has the potential to be a .280/.380/.500 middle-of-the-order hitter.

Connor Norby (2B, BAL), despite a smaller frame, hit 40 doubles and 21 home runs for Triple-A Norfolk. Norby spent most of the season playing 2B where he's a solid defender, but also logged 42 games in the OF, giving him much needed positional flexibility. Norby has too much talent to spend another year in the minors.

Connor Phillips (RHP, CIN) is covered in the pitchers player box section, starting on page 149.

Jeferson Quero (C, MIL) spent all 2023 in Double-A and continues to improve in all facets of the game. He is already a standout defender with adept blocking and receiving skills. The 20-year-old hit a career-high 16 HR in 336 AB while batting .262/.339/.440. The right-handed hitter could be a solid fantasy contributor in BA and HR.

Edgar Quero (C, CHW) was a key piece in the Lucas Giolito trade in July. The 20-year-old Quero continues to hold his own against older competition, showing good bat-to-ball skills, though a drop in power once he moved on from the hitter-friendly California League is a bit of a red flag. The trade to the White Sox created a clear path to full-time AB once the organization deems him MLB ready.

Ceddanne Rafaela (SS/OF, BOS) is covered in the batters player box section, starting on page 81.

Bryan Rocchio (SS, CLE) is covered in the batters player box section, starting on page 81.

Jackson Rutledge (RHP, WAS) is covered in the pitchers player box section, starting on page 149.

Thomas Saggese (INF, STL) was part of the Cardinals haul in the Jordan Montgomery trade. Saggese has calmed concerns regarding his aggressive approach as he slashed .306/.374/.530 with 34 doubles and 26 home runs across three levels. Saggese's ability to play multiple positions and make consistent hard contact give him plenty of pathways to playing time.

Nolan Schanuel (1B, LAA) is covered in the batters player box section, starting on page 81.

Paul Skenes (RHP, PIT) may only have pitched 6 2/3 innings in his pro debut after being the #1 overall selection in the draft, but he could get to Pittsburgh very quickly. He has the size and pitch mix to front a big-league rotation. It is tough to find any shortcomings. The 21-year-old has an elite fastball to pair with a double-plus slider while possessing above average control.

AJ Smith-Shawver (RHP, ATL) is covered in the pitchers player box section, starting on page 149.

Robby Snelling (LHP, SD) was sensational in his pro debut, pitching on three levels, including four starts in Double-A as a 19-year-old. He only allowed more than two earned runs in one outing. He led the organization in wins and posted the lowest ERA in the system. Overall, he had a 1.82 ERA and 10.2 K/9. He'll need to polish his change-up, but that shows flashes of being an above average offering.

Gavin Stone (RHP, LA) is covered in the pitchers player box section, starting on page 149.

Drew Thorpe (RHP, NYY) was dominant in his pro debut, going 14-2 with a 2.52 ERA between High-A and Double-A. The 23-year-old has a plus-to-double-plus change-up and attacks hitters with a short arm action that allows his low-90s fastball to play up. An above-average slider rounds out the mix. He commands all three of his offerings and led all minor leaguers with 182 punchouts in just 139.1 IP.

Ricky Tiedemann (LHP, TOR) was named the Pitcher of the Year in the Arizona Fall League after a solid—though injury-riddled—campaign. He started 11 games in Double-A before a late promotion to Triple-A. Simply, the 21-year-old can dominate hitters from both sides. There are no concerns about his durability as he was stretched out in the AFL. He should emerge by mid-2024.

Hurston Waldrep (RHP, ATL) led the Florida Gators to within one win of the 2023 CWS title. The 21-year-old RHP has a strong, athletic frame with a potentially plus three-pitch mix. His fastball sits at 96-98 with excellent ride and arm-side run. Waldrep used a nasty 12-6 curveball in college, but the Braves had him work on refining a mid-80s slider that shows plus potential. His best offering is a plus splitter.

Austin Wells (C, NYY) is covered in the batters player box section, starting on page 81.

Owen White (RHP, TEX) is covered in the pitchers player box section, starting on page 149.

Jordan Wicks (LHP, CHC) is covered in the pitchers player box section, starting on page 149.

Carson Williams (SS, TAM) may be in the right organization for a quick ascension to the big leagues. The 20-year-old was a 1st round pick in 2021 and has already made it to Triple-A. He hit 23 HR and stole 20 bases while batting .257/.356/.497, mostly at High-A. He has some holes in his swing that need to be closed, but he's an all-around talent.

Masyn Winn (SS, STL) is covered in the batters player box section, starting on page 81.

James Wood (OF, WAS) checks all the boxes an organization would want for a future cornerstone player. He has tremendous size (6'6", 240 lbs) and has the athleticism to match. Few can match his premium power, but he also sees a lot of pitches to draw walks and finds pitches to smash. He plays CF now and could play the corners due to his speed and strong arm. He hit 26 HR and 18 SB between High-A and Double-A.

Top Players from East Asia for 2024 and Beyond

by Tom Mulhall

After MLB teams made low-ball offers to Tomoyuki Sugano in 2022, almost ensuring that he would stay in Japan, the Mets made a legitimate offer to Kodai Senga. Both the team and fantasy owners were rewarded with a solid season. Thanks in part to Senga's success, there is almost certain to be a feeding frenzy over Yoshinobu Yamamoto, the best SP in Nippon Professional Baseball (NPB) since, well, arguably forever.

With Japanese teams offering their free agent stars better contracts with opt-out provisions, MLB teams can no longer simply outbid Japanese teams. Still, with labor issues and COVID-19 restrictions now behind us, players from Japan seem anxious to test out MLB. Korean Baseball Organization (KBO) teams will still be easily outbid by MLB teams, making it more appealing for their players to switch leagues. One interesting development is several Japanese high school stars have announced that they may skip the NPB draft and play for an American university. This would allow them to avoid the Japanese posting system entirely. This could be a trend, or perhaps just a bargaining ploy to get leverage with NPB teams.

As always, look for a combination of skill, opportunity, and desire to play in MLB. For Dynasty players, there continues to be many exciting names to follow.

NOTES: For more general background about East Asia baseball style of play and the posting systems, see the Encyclopedia article beginning on page 48. The Sawamura Award for starting pitchers is roughly equivalent to the Cy Young Award but is not given every year. It emphasizes complete games and wins over other stats. Names are sometimes difficult to translate so the official NPB or KBO designation is used. In Korea, surnames are usually listed first and given names second, and that designation is followed here.

Erick Fedde (RHP, NC Dinos, KBO) struggled with health issues throughout his MLB career, and he was non-tendered by the Nationals at the end of 2022. The former first-round pick may have found new life in Korea by becoming only the fourth pitcher in KBO history to win the Triple Crown, leading the league in wins, ERA and strikeouts. Fedde only signed a one-year contract, so at age 30, a return to MLB is not out of the question. It worked for Merrill Kelly.
Probable ETA: 2024

Shota Imanaga (LHP, Yokohama DeNA Baystars, NPB) has had seven solid seasons in eight years. While not quite matching his 2022 career year, he finished 2023 with a 2.80 ERA and an increased K%. His improved fastball in the low to mid 90s is supported by an excellent splitter and change-up, over which he has elite command. At least seven MLB teams have scouted Imanaga and he will almost certainly be posted. His international experience has been successful and he started for the Championship Japanese team in the Gold Medal game. Some of the USA players compared him to Max Fried, which is high praise. Just 30 years old and still in his prime with a lifetime 3.18 ERA and 1.12 WHIP, he could be an acceptable #3 or #4 MLB SP.
Probable ETA: 2024

Kim Hye-seong (2B/SS/OF, Kiwoom Heroes, KBO) is a teammate of the dynamic Lee Jung-hoo, and as such has escaped notice by some. Throwing right but batting left, the 25-year-old is an outstanding defender, being the only player in KBO history to win a Gold Glove at both 2B and SS. Kim has an excellent eye, with a .335 BA and .396 OBP in 2023. And he has some speed, stealing 25, 34, and 46 bases over the past three seasons. Kim could be productive as a utility player or even a starter, depending on where he plays.
Possible ETA: 2025

Lee Jung-hoo (OF, Kiwoom Heroes, KBO) is a hitting machine who won the 2021 KBO batting title with a .360 BA nearly 30 years after his father won it. He followed that up in 2022 with a .349 BA, but only played 85 games in 2023 due to a fractured ankle that required season-ending surgery. With only 6 HR, it looks like the 23 HR he hit in 2022 was an outlier. Once thought to be almost certain to be posted by his last-place team in 2024, his injury may give some MLB teams pause. An MLB team may be willing to take a chance on a good defensive player who might take several years to develop, as did Ha-Seong Kim. But will a player represented by the Boras organization accept such a contract?
Probable ETA: 2024

Raidel Martinez (RHP, Chunichi Dragons, NPB) plays for a terrible team that needs money, so it would seem he's a prime candidate to be posted. However, as a Cuban citizen, he would have to defect to move to MLB. That's unfortunate, as he could be the best closer in Japan and would have an immediate impact in MLB. He lowered an amazing 0.97 ERA in 2022 to a minuscule 0.39 mark in 2023. Martinez has a plus fastball that is consistently in the upper 90s, complemented with a nice splitter. While there have been cracks in the relationship between NPB and the Cuban Federation of Baseball, unless there is a major political shift (globally or personally) it's not likely Martinez will switch leagues.
Possible ETA: 2025

Yuki Matsui (LHP, Tohoku Rakuten Golden Eagles, NPB) has a fastball in the low 90s and at 5' 8" and 163 pounds, he isn't going to overpower hitters. What he does have are excellent off-pitches including a plus slider and a plus forkball. As a result, he has a solid K rate and minimizes home runs, with just 31 in 659.2 lifetime IP.

Control is the question and he struggled with the MLB ball at the WBC. Matsui is an international free agent so a MLB team won't have to pay a posting fee. He seems to project as an above average middle reliever in MLB, rather than a closer. However, he could easily back in to double digit saves in the right situation, and that has some value. A very nice dart throw in the later rounds.
Probable ETA: 2024

Hiroya Miyagi (LHP, Orix Buffaloes, NPB) will soon be out of the shadow of his amazing teammate, Yoshinobu Yamamoto, who should be in MLB in 2024. Miyagi had a slight drop-off to a 3.16 ERA in 2022, but rebounded to a 2.27 ERA and 0.944 WHIP in 2023. He has a fastball in the low-to-mid 90s, supported by excellent off-speed pitches including a wicked forkball. Miyagi is rarely mentioned by touts, so for dynasty players who missed out on Yamamoto and Roki Sasaki, he may be the next best thing.
Possible ETA: 2026

Munetaka Murakami (1B/3B, Tokyo Yakult Swallows, NPB) hit 36, 38, and 39 HR before exploding in 2022 for 56 HR and winning the Triple Crown at age 22. Then Murakami slumped to his worst statistical year since he was a rookie in 2023; only a strong second half still allowed him to finish with 31 HR and a .256 BA. He still was the hard-hit leader in the NPB at 43%. His offensive woes possibly affected his defense and he led all 3B in errors. Murakami signed a three-year deal before the 2023 season that supposedly promises to post him in 2026.
Probable ETA: 2026

Kazuma Okamoto (1B/3B, Yomiuri Giants, NPB) could be the best hitter in Japan other than Murakami. After five straight seasons of 30+ HR, he had his career year in 2023 with 41 HR. It's possible his BA could be a drag, but he's got a good eye with a .356 lifetime OBP. Unfortunately, the Giants have only posted two players in their history so he will probably have to wait until he becomes an international free agent.
Probable ETA: 2027

Yariel Rodriguez (RHP, Chunichi Dragons) is the wildest of wild cards for fantasy owners. The Cuban-born pitcher wants to be a starting pitcher, but excelled in relief in 2022 registering a 1.15 ERA in 54.2 IP with 60 strikeouts. Rodriguez sat out 2023 in order to gain his release, so with only three seasons in the NPB, there isn't much of a record to judge him by. He did pitch well in the WBC. A workout held for MLB teams was heavily attended, so the interest is there. The 26-year-old Rodriguez has a fastball that consistently sits in the upper 90s and touches 100, supported by a good slider. He's an interesting dart throw at the end of your draft.
Probable ETA: 2024

Rintaro Sasaki (1B, likely Vanderbilt University) shocked NPB by announcing he would skip the professional draft and attend college in the U.S. By forgoing the NPB draft, not only does he avoid Japan's onerous posting rules, he is also not subject to MLB's international amateur rules limiting teams to a fixed bonus pool. He could sign with a MLB after his junior year, which is still faster than under NPB posting rules, although he would probably start in the minors. At 6-feet, 250 pounds, Sasaki is a power hitter in the extreme. Although it included so-called "practice games," he set a high school record of 140 HR with a .413/.514/.808 slashline. His OBP shows his good batting eye, and in fact, Sasaki walked twice as often as he struck out. How can you not draft someone nicknamed the "Japanese Prince Fielder"?
Probable ETA (minors): 2027

Roki Sasaki (RHP, Chiba Lotte Marines, NPB) burst on to the scene in 2022 by almost pitching two perfect games in a row, stopped only when his manager took him out after the 8th inning in the 2nd game. Sasaki has an overpowering fastball that's consistently in the high 90s and occasionally touches 100 mph or more. His has a nasty splitter and his other complementary pitches continue to improve. He may need to add some meat to his thin 6'4", 203-pound frame in order to assist with durability, but that's a minor quibble. After 283.2 career IP, his professional ERA sits at an even 2.00 with an eye-popping 0.84 WHIP. Without question the finest young pitcher in Japan. Meet your #1 dynasty pick in any format.
Possible ETA: 2027

Kona Takahashi (RHP, Saitama Seibu Lions, NPB) attended Driveline before the 2023 season, and added 2-3 mph to his fastball. This generated more strikeouts per IP, allowing him to finish second to Yoshinobu Yamamoto in ERA in the Pacific League. After two solid and improving seasons, his team has indicated they may grant his wish and post him if he has another good season.
Possible ETA: 2025

Naoyuki Uwasawa (RHP, Hokkaido Nippon-Ham Fighters, NPB) also attended Driveline but without the same results as Takahashi. Because of his average fastball, he relies on the usual assortment of support pitches including a curve, slider, and change-up. At age 30, the three-time All Star is still in his prime. A very good SP with a lifetime 3.19 ERA, Uwasawa is not quite elite. He projects to be a low-end of the rotation SP, and might be better suited to find success as a long reliever.
Probable ETA: 2024

Yoshinobu Yamamoto (RHP, Orix Buffaloes, NPB) won the Pitching Quadruple Crown (Wins, ERA, Strikeouts and winning percentage) and the Eiji Sawamura Award for the third consecutive season, cementing his reputation as the best SP in NPB. He was the first NPB pitcher to throw a no-hitter in two consecutive seasons since 1941. Yamamoto has a fastball consistently in the mid-90s, with elite command over as many as five off-speed pitches including a knee-buckling curveball. At just 5'8", there are bound to be questions about his durability. However, while his 164 innings in 2023 were slightly down due to illness, the previous two seasons he pitched 193.2 and 193 innings without serious injury. Yamamoto allowed just two home runs the entire 2023 season, and capped it off by throwing a complete game in the championship series with just 1 ER and a playoff record 14 strikeouts. At 27 years old, he is in his absolute prime. Bid with confidence and let your competitors worry about his size and an adjustment period.
Almost definite ETA: 2024

Conclusion

Immediate help: Yoshinobu Yamamoto, Shota Imanaga, Yuki Matsui, Lee Jung-hoo and Naoyuki Uwasawa.

Dynasty help: Roki Sasaki, Munetaka Murakami, followed by a gap, and then Hiroya Miyagi, Kona Takahashi, Kazuma Okamoto, and Kim Hye-seong.

MAJOR LEAGUE EQUIVALENTS

In his 1985 *Baseball Abstract*, Bill James introduced the concept of major league equivalencies. His assertion was that, with the proper adjustments, a minor leaguer's statistics could be converted to an equivalent major league level performance with a great deal of accuracy.

Because of wide variations in the level of play among different minor leagues, it is difficult to get a true reading on a player's potential. For instance, a .300 batting average achieved in the high-offense Pacific Coast League is not nearly as much of an accomplishment as a similar level in the Eastern League. MLEs normalize these types of variances, for all statistical categories.

The actual MLEs are not projections. They represent how a player's previous performance might look at the major league level. However, the MLE stat line can be used in forecasting future performance in just the same way as a major league stat line would.

The model we use contains a few variations to James' version and updates all of the minor league and ballpark factors. In addition, we designed a module to convert pitching statistics, which is something James did not originally do.

Players are listed if they spent at least part of 2022 or 2023 in Triple-A or Double-A and had at least 150 AB or 45 IP within those two levels (players who split a season at both levels are indicated as a/a) in 2023. Major league and Single-A (and lower) stats are excluded. Each player is listed in the organization with which they finished the season. Some players over age 30 with major-league experience have been omitted for space.

These charts also provide the unique perspective of looking at two seasons' worth of data—even when the span is over three years. These are only short-term trends, for sure. But even here we can find small indications of players improving their skills, or struggling, as they rise through more difficult levels of competition. Since players—especially those with any modicum of talent—are promoted rapidly through major league systems, a two-season scan is often all we get to spot any trends. Five-year trends do appear in the *Minor League Baseball Analyst.*

Used correctly, MLEs are excellent indicators of potential. But, just like we cannot take traditional major league statistics at face value, the same goes for MLEs. The underlying measures of base skill—contact rates, pitching command ratios, BPV, etc.—are far more accurate in evaluating future talent than raw home runs, batting averages or ERAs. This chart format focuses more on those underlying gauges.

Here are some things to look for as you scan these charts:

Target players who...

- had a full season's worth of playing time in Double-A and then another full year in Triple-A
- had consistent playing time from one year to the next
- improved their base skills as they were promoted

Raise the warning flag for players who...

- were stuck at the same level both years, or regressed
- displayed marked changes in playing time from one year to the next
- showed large drops in skills from one year to the next

BATTER	yr	b	age	pos	lvl	org	ab	hr	sb	ba	bb%	ct%	px	sx	bpv
Abrams,CJ	22	L	22	SS	aaa	WAS	171	5	10	268	4	79	77	132	26
Abreu,Wilyer	22	L	23	CF	aa	BOS	457	12	21	213	14	63	119	103	10
	23	L	24	LF	aaa	BOS	299	15	5	232	11	72	111	80	26
Acuna,Jose	22	R	20	SS	aa	TEX	152	2	8	187	7	75	59	124	-1
	23	R	21	SS	aa	NYM	510	7	52	269	9	77	65	126	16
Adams,Jordyn	22	R	23	CF	aa	LAA	209	3	9	199	6	61	62	127	-52
	23	R	24	CF	aaa	LAA	415	10	27	216	7	62	105	132	-11
Adams,Riley	22	R	26	C	aaa	WAS	107	3	0	176	6	55	131	14	-58
Adell,Jo	22	R	23	LF	aaa	LAA	155	8	2	182	7	58	193	69	23
	23	R	24	LF	aaa	LAA	278	17	6	222	8	63	150	66	10
Adolph,Ross	22	L	26	LF	aa	HOU	183	3	5	185	14	48	92	109	-71
	23	L	27	LF	aaa	HOU	61	2	0	172	6	37	158	12	-108
Aguilar, Jesus	23	R	33	DH	aaa	ATL	203	3	0	202	10	67	50	17	-65
Aguilar,Ryan	22	L	28	RF	aa	LAA	291	9	6	197	12	54	117	87	-37
	23	L	29	1B	aa	LAA	64	1	1	128	10	38	51	54	-171
Aiello,John	22	B	25	1B	a/a	TOR	309	7	1	240	8	69	91	46	-20
Alcantara,Ismael	22	R	24	CF	aa	LA	34	2	1	191	11	62	140	90	14
	23	R	25	CF	aa	LA	207	2	7	234	6	65	44	84	-67
Alcantara,Sergio	23	B	27	SS	aaa	ARI	336	4	0	194	9	65	60	42	-59
Aldrete,Carter	22	R	25	2B	aa	SF	143	4	1	187	5	65	103	46	-34
	23	R	26	3B	aa	SF	372	9	2	185	6	66	88	44	-40
Alexander,Blaze	22	R	23	SS	a/a	ARI	344	10	6	236	6	66	105	78	-14
	23	R	24	SS	aaa	ARI	247	4	1	226	9	61	81	55	-56
Alexander,C.J.	22	L	26	3B	aa	KC	455	13	11	203	3	72	84	97	-7
	23	L	27	1B	aaa	KC	286	7	3	170	5	63	99	70	-37
Alfaro,Jorge	23	R	30	C	aaa	MIA	254	4	3	222	3	68	85	69	-32
Aliendo,Pablo	23	R	22	C	aa	CHC	321	11	4	198	9	61	130	73	-10
Allen, Greg	23	B	30	CF	aaa	MIL	161	2	17	178	9	67	66	129	-20
Allen,Austin	22	L	28	C	aaa	STL	195	4	0	203	6	64	94	18	-48
	23	L	29	C	aaa	MIA	324	15	0	171	6	68	112	29	-15
Allen,Nick	22	R	24	SS	aaa	OAK	173	1	5	193	8	77	49	80	-13
	23	R	25	SS	aaa	OAK	135	1	7	250	8	86	79	103	55
Almonte, Abraham	22	B	33	LF	aaa	BOS	294	10	3	217	11	67	109	69	-3
	23	B	34	RF	aaa	NYM	134	6	1	134	10	58	87	46	-61
Alu,Jake	22	L	25	3B	a/a	WAS	502	15	11	249	7	76	110	86	33
	23	L	26	3B	aaa	WAS	292	4	11	234	6	80	67	86	16
Alvarez,Andres	22	R	25	3B	aa	PIT	368	12	13	170	10	61	100	106	-20
	23	R	26	SS	aa	PIT	339	6	3	181	7	68	73	61	-37
Alvarez,Armando	22	R	28	3B	aaa	NYY	299	12	3	206	4	69	119	57	-1
	23	R	29	1B	aaa	SF	260	10	5	224	7	76	94	77	19
Alvarez,Francisco	22	R	21	C	a/a	NYM	408	19	0	211	10	65	132	25	-5
Alvarez,Jose	22	R	22	RF	a/a	HOU	95	1	1	204	7	60	53	59	-84
	23	R	23	RF	aa	STL	281	0	4	211	5	79	19	62	-39
Alvarez,Roberto	22	R	23	C	aa	TAM	222	0	1	201	5	77	39	72	-26
	23	R	24	C	a/a	TAM	72	1	0	178	2	64	18	26	-117
Amaya,Jacob	22	R	24	SS	a/a	LA	476	12	4	203	9	72	75	69	-11
	23	R	25	SS	aaa	MIA	484	11	4	211	9	75	75	68	1
Amaya,Miguel	22	R	23	DH	aa	CHC	97	2	0	220	8	66	105	53	-16
	23	R	24	C	a/a	CHC	92	3	1	238	13	61	156	30	4
Amburgey,Trey	22	R	28	LF	aaa	SEA	197	5	1	141	5	56	78	66	-83
Anchia,Jake	22	R	25	C	a/a	SEA	293	2	1	163	4	64	45	37	-87
	23	R	26	C	aa	SEA	237	3	1	144	6	63	71	69	-57
Andujar,Miguel	22	R	27	LF	aaa	NYY	277	9	3	217	4	84	84	67	33
	23	R	28	1B	aaa	PIT	414	10	3	262	7	84	78	50	29
Antico,Mike	22	L	24	CF	aa	STL	240	4	16	165	6	68	64	116	-27
	23	L	25	CF	aa	STL	476	12	35	209	7	69	81	126	-4
Antonini,Aaron	22	L	24	C	aa	STL	64	0	0	131	5	79	30	32	-38
	23	L	25	C	a/a	STL	136	4	2	189	6	61	93	67	-48
Antuna,Yasel	22	B	23	LF	aa	WAS	91	1	1	125	12	61	62	47	-67
	23	B	24	LF	aa	WAS	112	2	3	126	16	63	54	43	-60
Aranda,Jonathan	22	L	24	1B	aaa	TAM	403	12	4	257	7	69	107	73	2
	23	L	25	2B	aaa	TAM	357	18	1	272	11	70	127	36	15
Arauz,Jonathan	22	B	24	2B	aaa	BAL	132	0	1	159	5	81	40	59	-14
	23	B	25	SS	aaa	NYM	352	8	1	179	10	68	70	62	-31
Ardoin,Silas	23	R	23	C	aa	BAL	105	2	2	250	8	63	67	52	-60
Arias,Bryan	22	R	25	1B	aa	HOU	291	4	7	166	8	59	78	68	-62
	23	R	26	1B	a/a	HOU	75	2	4	199	14	68	95	82	3
Arias,Diosbel	22	R	26	2B	a/a	TEX	300	4	1	190	6	70	65	37	-42
	23	R	27	2B	a/a	TEX	396	7	3	219	7	61	90	86	-44
Arias,Gabriel	22	R	22	SS	aaa	CLE	288	8	3	189	5	69	74	62	-35
Armenteros,Lazaro	23	R	24	DH	aa	OAK	330	8	7	200	12	55	121	99	-29
Arruda,J.T.	23	B	26	2B	aa	WAS	376	5	25	192	14	63	65	103	-37
Ashford,Zach	22	L	25	RF	aa	NYM	320	3	6	191	6	69	65	78	-34
Auer,Mason	23	R	22	CF	aa	TAM	454	9	36	176	8	54	93	141	-48
Auerbach,Brett	22	R	24	2B	aa	SF	372	11	8	181	8	58	105	68	-45
	23	R	25	C	aa	SF	163	1	5	130	5	63	24	75	-93
Avans,Drew	22	L	26	CF	aaa	LA	432	4	22	204	7	63	63	147	-40
	23	L	27	CF	aaa	LA	508	8	14	196	9	67	66	83	-35
Avelino,Abiatal	22	R	27	3B	aa	LA	209	5	5	173	4	77	67	86	-1
Aviles Jr.,Luis	22	R	27	3B	a/a	MIA	363	9	9	198	3	66	110	107	-8
	23	R	28	3B	aa	HOU	366	11	18	189	5	62	93	108	-32
Azocar,Jose	22	R	26	CF	aaa	SD	98	3	2	212	4	68	90	42	-34
	23	R	27	CF	aaa	SD	201	3	10	183	2	71	48	89	-46
Bae,Ji-Hwan	22	L	23	2B	aaa	PIT	419	5	20	240	7	79	71	130	27
	23	L	24	2B	aaa	PIT	32	1	1	290	14	65	114	70	3
Bailey,Patrick	23	B	24	C	a/a	SF	105	3	2	232	8	69	63	49	-40
Baker,Darren	23	L	24	2B	aaa	WAS	403	2	13	221	6	78	31	91	-23
Baker,Dru	23	R	23	CF	aa	TAM	115	1	8	245	4	72	68	156	-1
Baker,Luken	22	R	25	1B	aaa	STL	464	12	0	170	5	68	68	19	-56
	23	R	26	1B	aaa	STL	314	21	0	258	11	71	154	21	35
Baldoquin,Roberto	22	R	28	3B	a/a	STL	195	0	1	156	6	76	22	43	-51
Ball,Brycelin	22	L	24	1B	aa	CHC	485	7	1	204	8	71	74	46	-27
	23	L	25	DH	aa	CLE	212	7	0	177	12	60	120	26	-31
Banfield,Will	22	R	23	C	aa	MIA	116	2	0	236	3	76	70	58	-16
	23	R	24	C	aa	MIA	458	17	2	224	4	70	108	65	-3
Banks,Nick	22	L	28	RF	aaa	WAS	272	7	2	200	5	59	100	78	-47
Bannon,Rylan	22	R	26	3B	aaa	ATL	342	10	7	209	12	65	105	87	-4
	23	R	27	3B	aaa	HOU	336	12	7	182	10	66	89	71	-22
Banuelos,David	22	R	26	C	aaa	MIN	181	4	0	151	5	59	86	41	-69
	23	R	27	C	aa	MIN	152	6	1	207	9	43	167	53	-59
Barber,Colin	23	L	23	LF	aa	HOU	270	9	4	211	11	69	103	63	0
Barger,Addison	22	L	23	SS	a/a	TOR	207	9	1	271	7	70	127	37	9
	23	L	24	RF	aaa	TOR	340	6	3	204	9	71	84	47	-15
Barrera,Luis	22	L	27	CF	aaa	OAK	312	4	5	179	4	72	65	108	-16
Barrera,Tres	22	R	28	C	aaa	WAS	177	4	0	192	6	71	76	47	-25
	23	R	29	C	aaa	STL	216	4	1	150	6	71	49	36	-49
Barrero,Jose	22	R	24	SS	aaa	CIN	220	8	4	181	4	53	123	83	-55
	23	R	25	SS	aaa	CIN	291	14	12	206	4	57	152	112	-7
Barreto,Franklin	22	R	26	2B	aaa	HOU	241	4	6	118	7	48	71	92	-107
	23	R	27	RF	aaa	WAS	99	5	1	154	6	64	116	62	-21
Barrosa,Jorge	22	B	21	CF	aa	ARI	434	7	14	226	8	80	78	94	28
	23	B	22	CF	aaa	ARI	412	7	9	221	11	78	67	96	17
Bart,Joey	22	R	26	C	aaa	SF	28	1	0	212	4	73	32	36	-60
	23	R	27	C	aaa	SF	206	3	1	188	9	58	81	39	-71
Basabe,Osleivis	22	R	22	3B	aa	TAM	228	0	10	281	7	87	77	129	64
	23	R	23	SS	aaa	TAM	385	3	11	245	5	80	63	93	10
Bastidas,Jesus	22	R	24	2B	aa	NYY	396	13	8	194	7	66	101	76	-19
	23	R	25	SS	a/a	NYY	397	11	9	203	7	67	82	85	-25
Bates,Parker	23	L	26	LF	aa	KC	257	1	6	183	6	74	30	82	-43
Batten,Matt	22	R	27	SS	aaa	SD	325	6	9	195	7	70	68	89	-22
	23	R	28	SS	aaa	SD	353	7	14	154	8	63	70	97	-47
Baty,Brett	22	L	23	3B	a/a	NYM	362	13	1	254	8	65	119	42	-13
	23	L	24	3B	aaa	NYM	104	6	1	230	10	66	128	41	-1
Bauers,Jake	22	L	27	1B	aaa	NYY	202	5	5	137	11	53	93	70	-68
	23	L	28	LF	aaa	NYY	78	7	4	277	14	73	213	91	118
Beaty, Matt	22	L	29	RF	aaa	SD	126	1	0	172	5	70	26	43	-72
	23	L	30	1B	aaa	KC	154	3	0	205	7	76	70	18	-18
Beavers,Dylan	23	L	22	RF	aa	BAL	134	1	4	287	11	74	78	109	15
Bec,Chris	22	R	27	C	a/a	TOR	106	1	4	157	11	65	44	59	-65
Bechina,Marty	22	R	26	LF	a/a	OAK	303	4	4	152	6	54	72	64	-92
Bechtold,Andrew	22	R	26	C	a/a	MIN	438	11	1	174	8	62	80	35	-58
	23	R	27	3B	aaa	MIN	183	5	0	195	7	61	112	15	-44
Beck,Jordan	23	R	22	LF	aa	COL	192	4	7	225	10	64	119	76	-4
Beer,Seth	22	L	26	1B	aaa	ARI	331	7	0	170	6	75	75	44	-12
	23	L	27	1B	a/a	ARI	377	7	0	200	6	66	78	27	-53
Beesley,Brad	22	R	24	LF	aa	CHC	122	2	6	186	4	65	110	104	-10
	23	R	25	CF	aa	CHC	224	5	15	188	10	59	100	149	-16
Bell,Chad	22	L	25	1B	a/a	NYY	315	11	0	189	8	52	116	25	-75
Beltre,Michael	22	B	27	RF	a/a	NYY	225	6	19	181	10	56	111	136	-27
Bemboom, Anthony	22	L	32	C	aaa	BAL	123	2	0	159	4	71	59	34	-49
	23	L	33	C	aaa	BAL	132	2	1	208	7	73	44	64	-40
Benson,Will	22	L	24	CF	aaa	CLE	316	10	9	213	12	65	117	99	10
	23	L	25	RF	aaa	CIN	97	2	6	161	17	57	109	128	-11
Berglund,Michael	23	L	26	C	aa	CLE	155	4	1	134	12	51	82	29	-94
Bericoto,Victor	23	R	22	RF	aa	SF	186	8	0	213	6	68	123	62	4
Bernabel,Warming	23	R	21	3B	aa	COL	302	5	1	212	3	78	64	47	-13
Berroa,Steward	22	B	23	CF	aa	TOR	55	1	4	145	5	66	35	142	-54
	23	B	24	CF	a/a	TOR	369	5	33	216	11	63	85	116	-22
Berry,Jacob	23	B	22	1B	aa	MIA	113	4	4	225	6	76	93	114	24
Berryhill,Luke	22	R	24	C	aa	HOU	352	8	3	199	10	58	93	58	-52
	23	R	25	C	aaa	HOU	250	5	3	179	12	49	96	97	-71
Bewley,Brhet	22	R	25	2B	aa	KC	111	2	0	178	8	68	66	16	-52
Bigbie,Justice	23	R	24	LF	a/a	DET	294	8	4	291	6	81	76	56	17
Biggers,Jax	22	L	25	3B	aa	TEX	217	1	3	217	5	79	56	75	-5
	23	L	26	2B	a/a	TEX	387	8	9	185	10	67	64	76	-36
Binelas,Alex	22	L	22	3B	aa	BOS	211	7	0	144	7	61	124	48	-26
	23	L	23	1B	aa	BOS	296	13	10	204	7	58	153	117	7
Bissonette,Josh	22	R	26	3B	a/a	PIT	170	0	1	154	9	73	43	46	-43
	23	R	27	3B	aaa	PIT	159	1	0	172	9	75	30	44	-42
Black,Tyler	23	L	23	3B	a/a	MIL	450	14	41	244	13	74	107	147	52
Blanco,Dairon	22	R	29	CF	aaa	KC	366	7	24	218	5	67	84	123	-16
Blankenhorn,Travis	22	L	26	LF	aaa	NYM	329	9	6	198	6	66	100	66	-24
	23	L	27	1B	aaa	WAS	393	16	0	202	8	65	127	39	-9
Bleday,J.J.	22	L	25	CF	aaa	MIA	302	12	1	178	12	61	121	39	-22
	23	L	26	CF	aaa	OAK	108	4	1	242	11	80	105	79	50
Bliss,Ryan	23	R	24	2B	a/a	SEA	540	16	38	240	6	73	94	122	18
Bohanek,Cody	22	R	27	3B	a/a	NYM	239	1	5	128	8	50	64	98	-101
Boldt,Ryan	22	L	28	CF	aaa	TAM	250	4	5	172	4	59	83	102	-57
Bolt,Skye	22	B	28	CF	aaa	OAK	95	2	1	220	4	68	88	43	-36
	23	B	29	LF	aaa	MIL	210	2	2	191	9	62	63	75	-60
Bonifacio,Jorge	22	R	29	LF	aaa	PHI	380	9	5	173	7	59	89	60	-61
	23	R	30	RF	aa	KC	435	13	4	203	8	72	86	78	0

BATTER	yr	b	age	pos	lvl	org	ab	hr	sb	ba	bb%	ct%	px	sx	bpv
Baker,Darren	22	L	23	2B	aa	WAS	169	1	4	257	7	80	49	65	-3
Boswell,Bret	22	L	28	3B	aaa	COL	287	6	3	181	6	60	97	69	-48
	23	L	29	3B	aa	COL	215	4	1	151	8	59	92	67	-51
Bote,David	23	R	30	SS	aaa	CHC	360	7	4	181	8	65	90	57	-34
Bouchard,Sean	22	R	26	LF	aaa	COL	260	11	6	236	8	70	139	124	44
	23	R	27	LF	aaa	COL	54	1	3	169	14	71	44	66	-31
Bowens,TT	23	R	25	1B	aa	BAL	164	5	0	185	9	60	94	27	-54
Bowman,Cooper	23	R	23	2B	aa	OAK	271	5	24	216	9	72	83	134	15
Bracho,Aaron	23	L	22	2B	aa	CLE	367	16	3	224	11	71	101	51	6
Bradley,Bobby	22	L	26	1B	aaa	CLE	167	4	0	124	6	46	127	45	-88
Bradley,Tucker	22	L	24	LF	aa	KC	396	6	12	240	7	77	77	97	15
	23	L	25	LF	a/a	KC	303	4	8	233	9	73	88	94	9
Breaux,Josh	22	R	25	C	a/a	NYY	370	14	1	173	6	63	105	56	-33
	23	R	26	DH	a/a	NYY	135	8	1	207	4	70	120	34	-1
Brennan,Will	22	L	24	CF	a/a	CLE	528	9	13	253	6	84	78	87	39
Brewer,Jordan	22	R	25	RF	aa	HOU	109	1	4	144	5	57	62	92	-83
	23	R	26	1B	aa	HOU	247	6	8	197	8	63	82	85	-37
Bride,Jonah	22	R	27	C	a/a	OAK	134	3	0	253	9	78	111	33	30
	23	R	28	3B	aaa	OAK	259	6	3	210	10	76	83	62	12
Brigman,Bryson	22	R	27	2B	aaa	MIA	382	5	6	192	4	70	57	101	-33
	23	R	28	SS	a/a	LA	278	2	5	209	7	77	38	71	-23
Brito,Juan	23	B	22	2B	a/a	CLE	329	8	3	238	12	78	83	42	15
Brodey,Quinn	22	L	27	RF	a/a	NYM	176	3	6	138	3	52	109	143	-53
Brooks,Trenton	22	L	27	1B	aaa	CLE	293	6	1	195	7	76	83	39	-2
	23	L	28	LF	aaa	SF	430	12	4	213	10	77	89	74	24
Brown,Logan	22	L	26	C	aa	ATL	182	1	0	161	6	69	29	49	-72
Brown,Vaun	23	R	25	CF	aa	SF	190	5	12	189	5	52	130	147	-30
Brujan,Vidal	22	R	24	SS	aaa	TAM	257	4	18	236	7	77	72	144	25
	23	R	25	2B	aaa	TAM	239	7	13	215	8	75	84	106	17
Buchberger,Jacob	23	R	26	3B	aa	STL	397	11	9	183	7	70	70	83	-24
Bunnell,Cade	22	L	25	SS	aa	ATL	146	6	0	255	14	53	191	69	15
	23	L	26	3B	aa	ATL	399	13	6	170	11	45	131	64	-72
Burdick,Peyton	22	R	25	CF	aaa	MIA	364	9	9	170	9	61	103	144	-10
	23	R	26	RF	aaa	MIA	420	16	8	178	8	50	143	86	-40
Burleson,Alec	22	L	24	LF	aaa	STL	432	12	3	259	4	82	79	58	19
Burt,D.J.	22	R	27	3B	a/a	CHW	305	2	26	189	8	75	40	122	-14
Burt,Max	22	R	26	3B	aa	NYY	268	8	13	158	4	61	95	119	-35
	23	R	27	2B	a/a	NYY	323	8	14	184	7	62	80	114	-40
Busch,Michael	22	L	25	2B	a/a	LA	552	21	2	211	7	63	131	57	-8
	23	L	26	3B	aaa	LA	390	19	3	260	10	72	130	71	34
Butler,Lawrence	23	L	23	CF	a/a	OAK	366	8	13	225	6	76	75	103	10
Cabbage,Trey	22	L	25	1B	aa	LAA	113	7	6	258	10	49	208	99	15
	23	L	26	1B	aaa	LAA	418	20	19	239	6	58	149	107	-4
Cabrera,Daniel	22	L	24	RF	aa	DET	355	3	4	169	7	75	52	93	-14
	23	L	25	RF	aa	DET	199	1	2	197	11	80	43	63	-5
Cabrera,Leobaldo	22	R	24	LF	aa	MIN	256	4	4	174	7	60	77	78	-60
Caissie,Owen	23	L	21	RF	aa	CHC	439	15	5	255	12	59	138	59	-10
Calabrese,David	23	L	21	CF	aa	LAA	458	12	10	172	10	61	90	80	-39
Calabuig,Chase	22	L	27	LF	aa	OAK	380	3	2	233	7	81	59	49	3
	23	L	28	LF	aa	OAK	155	2	1	248	7	86	73	75	42
Calhoun, Kole	23	L	36	RF	aaa	LA	232	6	0	220	6	72	98	67	2
Call,Alex	22	R	28	CF	aaa	WAS	257	8	6	222	11	73	108	92	30
	23	R	29	CF	aaa	WAS	40	1	2	202	10	87	64	54	36
Callahan,Austin	23	L	22	3B	aa	CIN	112	1	1	165	1	63	38	47	-101
Camargo, Johan	22	B	29	DH	a/a	PHI	156	1	0	170	8	79	40	29	-27
	23	B	30	SS	aaa	SF	184	5	0	177	7	73	60	12	-38
Camargo,Jair	22	R	23	C	aa	MIN	176	7	3	190	6	57	123	52	-43
	23	R	24	C	aaa	MIN	332	14	1	210	6	57	128	51	-39
Cameron,Daz	22	R	25	CF	aaa	DET	383	6	12	191	6	63	91	117	-25
	23	R	26	CF	aaa	BAL	385	9	15	206	7	71	79	78	-15
Caminero,Junior	23	R	20	3B	aa	TAM	314	16	2	278	7	79	102	60	32
Campbell,Drew	23	L	26	RF	aa	ATL	272	7	8	216	4	65	87	63	-41
Campbell,Noah	22	B	23	LF	aa	MIL	195	1	4	212	10	65	83	80	-28
	23	B	24	LF	a/a	MIL	271	6	4	202	11	66	77	79	-27
Campusano,Luis	22	R	24	C	aaa	SD	319	7	0	215	6	76	70	38	-17
Canario,Alexander	22	R	22	CF	a/a	CHC	375	19	13	198	8	66	144	109	31
	23	R	23	RF	aaa	CHC	145	5	1	223	6	64	125	45	-14
Cannon,Cam	22	R	25	3B	a/a	BOS	144	0	3	183	6	72	43	53	-46
	23	R	26	2B	aa	PHI	155	5	1	171	5	79	92	40	14
Cantrelle,Hayden	22	B	24	2B	aa	SF	92	2	4	153	10	50	117	89	-57
	23	B	25	2B	aa	SF	275	3	11	184	16	68	53	99	-20
Cantu,Michael	22	R	27	C	a/a	SD	98	1	0	132	6	45	47	27	-158
	23	R	28	C	aaa	SD	124	1	0	120	7	46	55	27	-147
Canzone,Dominic	22	L	25	RF	a/a	ARI	386	11	8	224	5	75	96	93	16
	23	L	26	LF	aaa	ARI	257	8	1	266	8	81	93	61	33
Capel,Conner	22	L	25	RF	aaa	OAK	353	5	11	186	7	76	64	87	-3
	23	L	26	CF	aaa	OAK	341	4	9	180	7	71	55	95	-29
Capra,Vinny	22	R	26	SS	aaa	TOR	191	4	4	231	9	82	56	77	17
	23	R	27	SS	aaa	PIT	218	1	4	227	11	79	48	68	-4
Cardenas,Ruben	22	R	25	RF	aaa	TAM	287	10	3	162	7	59	125	86	-21
	23	R	26	RF	aaa	TAM	476	15	5	208	8	62	105	61	-32
Carpenter,Kerry	22	L	25	LF	a/a	DET	358	19	2	249	6	71	152	49	34
	23	L	26	DH	aaa	DET	35	1	0	130	9	61	53	22	-90
Carpio,Luis	22	R	25	2B	aa	DET	243	1	5	172	7	69	56	72	-43
Carreras,Julio	22	R	22	SS	aa	COL	60	0	1	207	5	65	96	133	-14
	23	R	23	SS	a/a	COL	362	5	9	206	7	73	58	79	-20
Carroll,Corbin	22	L	22	CF	a/a	ARI	356	13	18	244	10	67	134	150	41

BATTER	yr	b	age	pos	lvl	org	ab	hr	sb	ba	bb%	ct%	px	sx	bpv
Boone,Trevor	23	R	26	RF	aaa	COL	151	3	1	191	6	49	121	83	-68
Carter,Evan	22	L	20	RF	aa	TEX	21	1	1	376	15	68	144	92	45
	23	L	21	CF	a/a	TEX	411	9	18	252	12	71	77	103	2
Casas,Triston	22	L	22	1B	aaa	BOS	264	7	0	240	10	72	120	35	18
Casey,Donovan	22	R	26	RF	aaa	WAS	287	5	4	169	5	60	72	92	-63
	23	R	27	RF	aa	WAS	231	2	6	164	7	56	45	69	-102
Castanon,Marcos	23	R	24	2B	aa	SD	211	3	0	230	6	72	89	35	-14
Castellano,Angelo	22	R	27	SS	a/a	KC	268	1	4	149	6	74	44	71	-33
	23	R	28	SS	aaa	KC	327	8	7	214	9	79	82	66	19
Castellanos,Pedro	22	R	25	1B	a/a	BOS	467	8	1	227	2	75	84	49	-13
	23	R	26	1B	aa	SD	295	5	1	185	3	73	53	29	-48
Castillo,Diego	22	R	25	SS	aaa	PIT	134	2	1	193	6	72	60	51	-36
	23	R	26	LF	aaa	ARI	454	1	7	236	11	79	53	53	-3
Castillo,Ivan	22	B	27	SS	aaa	KC	392	3	5	183	6	84	52	61	11
Castillo,Moises	22	R	23	SS	aa	CHW	233	2	5	187	9	77	49	78	-9
	23	R	24	SS	aa	CHW	373	4	2	182	8	77	44	39	-28
Castillo,Neyfy	23	R	22	RF	aa	ARI	348	10	13	196	6	60	102	106	-34
Cave,Jake	23	L	31	CF	aaa	PHI	237	10	1	255	7	69	161	62	39
Cedeno,Leandro	22	R	24	1B	a/a	ARI	481	17	1	234	5	69	96	39	-24
Cedrola,Lorenzo	22	R	24	CF	aaa	CIN	475	3	11	230	2	79	48	104	-7
	23	R	25	CF	aaa	NYM	188	4	10	188	8	82	54	114	25
Celestino,Gilberto	23	R	24	CF	aaa	MIN	185	3	3	196	14	76	67	65	8
Cerda,Allan	22	R	23	RF	aa	CIN	207	8	3	168	12	57	130	56	-23
	23	R	24	CF	aa	CIN	155	5	3	156	12	48	128	51	-65
Cespedes,Yoelqui	22	R	25	CF	aa	CHW	458	13	21	199	4	60	113	98	-31
	23	R	26	CF	a/a	CHW	440	7	10	178	6	62	69	70	-60
Chaparro,Andres	22	R	23	3B	aa	NYY	239	15	2	241	7	73	150	45	44
	23	R	24	3B	aaa	NYY	523	18	3	201	8	70	92	63	-9
Chavez,Santiago	22	R	27	C	a/a	MIA	178	2	0	140	4	64	57	35	-80
	23	R	28	C	aaa	MIA	165	1	0	126	7	60	33	33	-108
Cheng,Tsung-Che	23	L	22	SS	aa	PIT	247	3	11	231	6	78	55	100	-1
Chourio,Jackson	22	R	18	CF	aa	MIL	23	0	1	75	6	51	50	69	-119
	23	R	19	CF	a/a	MIL	531	19	35	258	6	78	92	108	34
Cintron,Jancarlos	22	R	28	2B	a/a	ARI	400	3	7	240	3	81	71	86	14
	23	R	29	SS	aa	ARI	71	0	1	162	2	75	27	52	-56
Ciuffo,Nick	22	L	27	C	aaa	CHW	141	3	0	200	3	58	74	15	-97
Clarke,Denzel	23	R	23	CF	aa	OAK	234	7	8	213	10	60	114	128	-8
Clarke,Phil	23	L	25	C	a/a	TOR	216	4	4	218	9	80	60	66	8
Clarke,Philip	22	L	24	C	aa	TOR	248	3	1	183	8	80	42	43	-16
Clarke,Wes	22	R	23	1B	aa	MIL	59	4	0	208	8	58	156	14	-22
	23	R	24	1B	aa	MIL	398	20	4	201	14	56	160	45	-5
Clase,Jonatan	23	B	21	CF	aa	SEA	414	10	47	186	10	62	91	153	-10
Clemens,Kody	22	L	26	2B	aaa	DET	241	8	3	221	5	66	127	115	11
	23	L	27	2B	aaa	PHI	234	12	4	199	10	70	123	95	28
Clement,Ernie	22	R	26	2B	aaa	CLE	80	2	0	172	4	88	58	53	22
	23	R	27	SS	aaa	TOR	287	7	8	272	5	93	72	75	65
Cluff,Jackson	22	L	26	SS	aa	WAS	356	4	6	160	6	58	88	84	-56
	23	L	27	SS	aa	WAS	247	6	12	173	15	58	107	123	-13
Coca,Yeison	22	B	23	3B	a/a	MIL	232	1	7	169	8	62	55	93	-63
Colas,Oscar	22	L	24	RF	a/a	CHW	237	12	1	253	4	67	131	52	-2
	23	L	25	RF	aaa	CHW	213	7	1	218	7	71	96	45	-10
Collins,Isaac	22	B	25	2B	aa	COL	375	3	18	183	8	74	73	133	13
	23	B	26	LF	a/a	MIL	297	7	20	209	15	76	71	102	25
Collins,Zack	22	L	27	1B	aaa	PIT	126	3	2	149	14	60	110	70	-20
	23	L	28	DH	aaa	CLE	419	10	2	183	10	52	113	42	-67
Conine,Griffin	22	L	25	RF	aa	MIA	414	16	1	173	11	48	145	53	-51
	23	L	26	RF	a/a	MIA	372	14	1	204	9	52	132	58	-50
Conley,Cal	23	L	24	SS	aa	ATL	535	2	27	195	8	71	42	100	-36
Conley,Jack	22	R	25	C	a/a	PHI	250	4	2	183	8	67	70	68	-39
Contreras,Mark	22	L	27	CF	aaa	MIN	376	8	14	173	6	59	98	115	-39
	23	L	28	CF	aaa	MIN	340	6	14	204	6	62	73	82	-54
Contreras,William	22	R	25	C	aaa	ATL	48	0	0	251	5	76	51	4	-44
Cook,Billy	23	R	24	RF	aa	BAL	447	17	23	211	7	69	90	103	-7
Cook,Zac	22	L	24	CF	aa	TOR	333	10	9	148	4	49	117	102	-70
	23	L	25	CF	aa	TOR	118	4	7	158	5	49	105	109	-78
Cope,Daniel	22	R	25	C	aa	COL	151	4	1	207	5	68	99	58	-21
	23	R	26	DH	aaa	COL	141	3	0	253	7	64	91	16	-51
Cordero,Franchy	22	L	28	CF	aaa	BOS	117	4	2	253	7	56	169	61	-8
	23	L	29	RF	aaa	NYY	292	8	5	211	10	64	88	72	-28
Corona,Kenedy	23	R	23	CF	aa	HOU	434	16	24	212	8	66	109	109	1
Correa,J.C.	23	R	25	2B	aa	HOU	357	5	5	203	6	84	42	69	3
Cortes,Carlos	22	L	25	LF	a/a	NYM	439	8	0	168	6	65	76	45	-53
	23	L	26	LF	aaa	NYM	369	9	2	176	11	69	78	46	-23
Costes,Marty	22	R	27	LF	aaa	HOU	213	3	6	187	6	72	66	80	-20
	23	R	28	LF	aaa	HOU	167	1	4	187	8	72	61	109	-14
Coulter,Clint	22	R	29	LF	aaa	STL	182	5	0	205	4	77	91	45	5
	23	R	30	RF	aaa	SF	206	3	2	174	5	73	71	75	-15
Cowser,Colton	22	L	22	CF	a/a	BAL	281	12	1	251	10	63	135	54	-2
	23	L	23	CF	aaa	BAL	323	11	6	248	12	63	106	71	-16
Crim,Blaine	22	R	25	1B	a/a	TEX	515	14	2	224	6	78	78	53	4
	23	R	26	1B	aaa	TEX	494	15	1	228	9	74	96	55	7
Crook,Narciso	22	R	27	RF	aaa	CHC	362	11	8	193	6	57	127	105	-25
	23	R	28	LF	aaa	BOS	273	6	7	168	8	48	117	104	-65
Cropley,Tyler	22	R	27	C	aa	KC	92	1	0	123	4	73	62	16	-43
	23	R	28	C	a/a	KC	150	2	0	180	8	68	62	42	-50
Crow-Armstrong,Pete	23	L	21	CF	a/a	CHC	438	13	27	246	7	68	110	143	17
Cruz,Oneil	22	L	24	SS	aaa	PIT	211	5	7	185	9	70	82	121	1

BATTER	yr	b	age	pos	lvl	org	ab	hr	sb	ba	bb%	ct%	px	sx	bpv
Cartaya,Diego	23	R	22	C	aa	LA	354	16	0	171	7	63	105	28	-38
Cruz,Trei	23	B	25	CF	aa	DET	453	9	7	177	12	69	77	86	-13
Cullen,Greg	22	L	26	2B	a/a	BAL	184	5	1	211	11	69	79	51	-22
	23	L	27	3B	a/a	BAL	176	2	3	203	13	65	57	41	-56
Cummings,Cole	23	L	25	LF	aa	SD	294	10	1	199	7	67	92	41	-30
Dahl,David	22	L	28	RF	aaa	WAS	319	6	2	211	6	67	89	72	-24
	23	L	29	RF	aaa	LA	281	6	2	205	6	76	88	47	4
Dalbec,Bobby	22	R	27	1B	aaa	BOS	48	3	1	189	4	65	115	47	-25
	23	R	28	3B	aaa	BOS	413	21	11	210	8	50	158	106	-23
Dalesandro,Nick	22	R	26	C	aa	ARI	280	1	20	205	4	71	41	122	-34
	23	R	27	CF	a/a	ARI	201	0	11	160	6	65	29	115	-69
Daniels,Zach	23	R	24	RF	aa	HOU	309	10	16	236	7	58	123	78	-30
Datres,Kyle	22	R	26	DH	aa	COL	308	9	13	208	6	67	97	92	-12
	23	R	27	2B	a/a	COL	342	9	14	200	9	67	75	100	-25
Davidson,Logan	22	B	25	SS	aa	OAK	424	8	3	192	7	62	82	64	-49
	23	B	26	1B	a/a	OAK	390	5	4	208	6	67	69	54	-45
Davis, Jonathan	22	R	30	CF	aaa	MIL	184	2	8	207	9	67	70	98	-27
	23	R	31	RF	aaa	DET	124	3	3	192	6	68	110	112	7
Davis,Brendon	22	R	25	3B	aaa	DET	503	12	5	186	9	69	94	80	-4
	23	R	26	RF	aaa	DET	135	3	1	134	8	60	101	35	-51
Davis,Brennen	22	R	23	CF	aaa	CHC	141	3	0	151	10	58	78	29	-75
	23	R	24	RF	aaa	CHC	219	2	6	147	6	70	43	71	-51
Davis,Henry	22	R	23	C	aa	PIT	116	2	2	169	7	72	95	77	1
	23	R	24	C	a/a	PIT	196	9	8	265	15	73	115	79	41
Davis,Jaylin	22	R	28	CF	aaa	BOS	340	5	2	164	7	57	85	78	-65
	23	R	29	RF	aaa	NYM	259	7	1	149	9	53	102	56	-71
Dawson,Ronnie	22	L	27	LF	aaa	CIN	393	9	7	205	7	65	93	71	-30
Daza,Yonathan	23	R	29	CF	aaa	COL	164	1	2	225	3	83	49	57	-6
De Goti,Alex	22	R	28	SS	aaa	HOU	494	5	5	180	8	72	60	75	-22
	23	R	29	SS	aaa	MIN	156	1	1	128	12	56	63	56	-82
De La Cruz,Carlos	22	R	23	LF	aa	PHI	151	5	1	232	4	66	135	62	0
	23	R	24	1B	aa	PHI	509	20	2	226	8	64	113	57	-17
De La Cruz,Elly	22	B	20	SS	aa	CIN	190	7	14	274	6	63	167	142	40
	23	B	21	SS	aaa	CIN	158	9	7	258	10	64	172	106	48
De La Cruz,Michael	23	B	30	C	aa	SD	355	5	5	188	8	75	51	63	-24
De La Rosa,Eric	22	R	25	RF	aa	DET	191	2	6	182	5	53	91	142	-60
De Los Santos,Deyvison	22	R	19	3B	aa	ARI	39	1	0	193	7	76	65	23	-22
	23	R	20	3B	aa	ARI	452	12	3	216	4	70	74	70	-29
De Los Santos,Luis	22	R	24	SS	a/a	TOR	421	8	5	210	5	72	71	69	-21
	23	R	25	3B	a/a	TOR	292	6	3	188	8	68	86	58	-23
Dean,Justin	22	R	26	CF	a/a	ATL	328	2	17	189	9	59	66	134	-50
	23	R	27	CF	a/a	ATL	352	6	26	160	13	50	62	116	-87
Dearden,Tyler	22	L	24	LF	aa	BOS	316	5	0	222	9	63	86	30	-48
	23	L	25	LF	a/a	BOS	256	5	0	225	8	68	75	40	-38
Decolati,Niko	22	R	25	RF	aa	COL	141	1	5	163	9	67	51	120	-35
	23	R	26	RF	aa	COL	240	2	8	193	12	65	56	91	-40
Deichmann,Greg	22	L	27	CF	aaa	CHC	257	4	5	156	4	56	70	63	-90
	23	L	28	RF	a/a	OAK	379	9	9	172	6	60	87	111	-44
Del Castillo,Adrian	23	L	24	C	a/a	ARI	357	7	1	206	9	63	85	44	-45
Delgado,Raynel	22	L	22	3B	aa	CLE	210	2	8	198	9	73	52	99	-14
	23	L	23	2B	a/a	CLE	370	6	11	209	10	71	62	82	-22
DeLoach,Zach	22	L	24	RF	aa	SEA	418	9	3	199	10	65	73	74	-36
	23	L	25	RF	aaa	SEA	528	14	5	214	8	59	100	57	-49
Deluca,Jonny	22	R	24	CF	aa	LA	104	5	3	243	5	81	120	127	68
	23	R	25	CF	a/a	LA	279	13	8	246	8	76	125	95	51
DeLuzio,Ben	22	R	28	CF	aaa	STL	364	5	17	197	5	69	63	133	-20
	23	R	29	LF	aaa	BAL	148	2	4	135	6	54	49	90	-105
Devanney,Cam	22	R	25	SS	a/a	MIL	451	15	3	205	7	70	114	55	2
	23	R	26	SS	aaa	MIL	336	8	4	218	9	73	99	64	12
Devers,Jose	22	L	23	2B	aa	MIA	233	1	2	181	4	78	55	126	4
	23	L	24	SS	aa	MIA	373	5	4	243	7	82	70	91	25
Dezenzo,Zachary	23	R	23	3B	aa	HOU	245	11	12	223	7	63	131	108	4
Diaz,Eddy	23	R	23	2B	aa	COL	132	0	1	136	7	73	25	62	-54
Diaz,Isan	22	L	26	2B	aaa	SF	291	12	4	199	8	63	124	83	-7
	23	L	27	2B	aaa	DET	119	5	2	174	8	57	105	75	-48
Diaz,Jordan	22	R	22	DH	a/a	OAK	491	11	0	259	3	82	82	25	10
	23	R	23	3B	aaa	OAK	156	3	0	237	4	78	84	20	-5
Diaz,Lewin	22	L	26	1B	aaa	MIA	325	12	0	195	6	72	107	45	1
	23	L	27	1B	aaa	BAL	414	10	1	203	9	72	69	38	-25
Diaz,Luis Yanel	23	R	24	SS	aa	LA	107	2	4	153	7	60	51	75	-81
Diaz,Yainer	22	R	24	C	a/a	HOU	445	16	1	242	5	78	96	69	22
Diaz,Yusniel	22	R	26	RF	aaa	BAL	247	4	5	191	8	68	57	65	-44
	23	R	27	RF	aa	LA	345	12	5	227	10	72	102	53	7
DiChiara,Sonny	22	R	23	1B	aa	LAA	118	1	1	153	12	47	34	20	-153
	23	R	24	1B	aa	LAA	283	6	0	187	8	53	92	18	-89
Didder,Ray-Patrick	22	R	28	SS	a/a	MIA	390	7	17	181	5	61	61	107	-61
	23	R	29	SS	a/a	SD	320	8	19	168	10	59	87	92	-43
Dingler,Dillon	22	R	24	C	aa	DET	387	9	1	194	7	59	112	77	-35
	23	R	25	C	a/a	DET	281	7	2	189	8	61	107	69	-32
Dini,Nick	22	R	29	C	aaa	NYM	177	6	1	160	6	72	78	47	-19
	23	R	30	C	aaa	TAM	202	6	4	139	11	58	85	73	-54
Dirden,Justin	22	L	25	CF	a/a	HOU	477	15	7	233	6	65	135	97	12
	23	L	26	CF	aaa	HOU	316	7	2	179	7	57	85	78	-64

BATTER	yr	b	age	pos	lvl	org	ab	hr	sb	ba	bb%	ct%	px	sx	bpv
Cruz,Trei	22	B	24	3B	aa	DET	25	0	1	161	12	69	0	52	-83
Downs,Jeter	22	R	24	SS	aaa	BOS	284	10	12	162	8	61	113	124	-10
	23	R	25	SS	aaa	WAS	161	2	7	188	10	65	89	101	-16
Doyle,Brenton	22	R	24	CF	a/a	COL	507	16	13	211	3	64	109	121	-13
	23	R	25	CF	aaa	COL	49	3	1	249	8	58	149	38	-18
Driscoll,Logan	23	L	26	C	a/a	TAM	384	8	3	206	5	64	79	70	-46
Duggar,Steven	23	L	30	LF	aaa	LA	227	6	3	176	10	46	111	60	-88
Dunand,Joe	22	R	27	3B	aaa	ATL	295	4	4	175	8	57	98	91	-48
	23	R	28	1B	aaa	ATL	347	11	2	205	8	59	108	53	-42
Dungan,Clay	22	L	26	2B	aaa	KC	452	4	9	159	5	75	59	107	-8
	23	L	27	2B	aaa	KC	271	2	10	214	10	71	51	87	-25
Dunham,Elijah	22	L	24	LF	aa	NYY	415	13	27	200	9	70	104	124	23
	23	L	25	LF	a/a	NYY	476	12	25	185	9	62	94	106	-26
Dunn,Blake	23	R	25	CF	aa	CIN	295	13	24	284	9	66	117	134	18
Dunn,Jack	22	R	26	CF	a/a	WAS	390	2	7	196	8	72	48	56	-40
	23	R	27	3B	a/a	WAS	322	5	23	199	15	72	50	100	-11
Dunn,Nick	22	L	25	2B	aa	STL	399	3	3	190	7	88	44	67	23
	23	L	26	2B	a/a	STL	457	6	1	249	9	85	51	38	13
Dunn,Oliver	22	L	25	LF	a/a	NYY	80	2	2	227	11	48	190	106	-1
	23	L	26	2B	aa	PHI	417	17	12	228	13	61	140	89	9
Duran,Ezequiel	22	R	23	SS	a/a	TEX	328	10	9	240	4	72	129	84	28
Duran,Jarren	22	L	26	CF	aaa	BOS	279	6	11	229	5	69	103	138	14
	23	L	27	CF	aaa	BOS	41	1	1	164	13	69	112	103	23
Duran,Rodolfo	22	R	24	C	aa	NYY	203	7	0	178	4	69	103	16	-27
	23	R	25	C	aaa	NYY	214	6	1	202	7	70	98	38	-16
Durbin,Caleb	23	R	23	2B	aa	NYY	175	3	17	255	5	94	68	111	76
Duzenack,Camden	22	R	27	LF	aaa	ARI	318	6	5	182	3	71	83	96	-13
	23	R	28	SS	a/a	ARI	276	5	2	226	5	74	70	42	-23
Eaton,Nate	22	R	26	RF	a/a	KC	340	7	13	221	5	74	73	111	0
	23	R	27	CF	aaa	KC	333	9	14	195	5	71	79	95	-12
Eden,Cam	22	R	24	CF	aa	TOR	274	7	20	169	5	55	106	110	-49
	23	R	25	CF	aaa	TOR	393	2	35	205	7	66	49	121	-46
Edwards,Evan	22	L	25	1B	aa	TAM	214	7	4	167	11	48	122	76	-65
	23	L	26	1B	a/a	TAM	338	11	11	198	9	53	120	111	-38
Edwards,Xavier	22	R	23	2B	aaa	TAM	349	3	5	201	8	74	60	71	-15
	23	R	24	2B	aaa	MIA	370	5	23	304	9	91	44	104	50
Eierman,Jeremy	22	R	26	SS	aa	OAK	290	8	2	149	4	57	99	55	-68
	23	R	27	2B	aa	OAK	128	2	3	139	7	58	65	66	-78
Elko,Timothy	23	R	25	1B	aa	CHW	130	5	0	218	2	57	91	20	-90
Ellis,Drew	22	R	27	3B	aaa	SEA	385	11	3	156	10	61	113	60	-28
	23	R	28	3B	a/a	PHI	289	11	2	176	10	67	109	46	-11
Encarnacion,Jerar	22	R	25	RF	a/a	MIA	384	14	4	237	7	62	109	56	-32
	23	R	26	RF	aaa	MIA	434	18	4	185	11	47	147	54	-57
Encarnacion-Strand,Christian	22	R	23	3B	aa	CIN	190	9	1	272	4	68	131	48	0
	23	R	24	1B	aaa	CIN	278	15	1	274	7	70	144	60	30
Engel, Adam	23	R	32	CF	aaa	SEA	317	8	12	158	8	50	104	98	-70
English,Tristin	22	R	25	3B	aa	ARI	230	3	1	207	7	76	54	41	-27
	23	R	26	1B	a/a	ARI	387	12	1	225	7	67	104	34	-20
Enriquez,Roby	22	L	25	RF	aa	ARI	264	4	3	250	4	80	64	63	0
	23	L	26	RF	aa	ARI	155	0	3	200	9	75	54	52	-20
Erro,Alex	23	B	26	C	aa	BOS	28	1	0	242	11	71	70	42	-23
Escobedo,Julian	22	L	24	CF	aa	CLE	377	5	11	178	7	74	62	99	-11
	23	L	25	CF	aa	CLE	118	2	5	187	8	65	106	89	-11
Espino,Sebastian	22	R	22	RF	aa	TOR	354	10	3	148	4	49	137	75	-62
	23	R	23	RF	aa	TOR	221	3	3	175	5	52	82	57	-99
Esplin,Tyler	23	L	24	1B	aa	BOS	68	1	0	241	2	65	130	75	-9
Evans, Phillip	22	R	30	RF	aaa	NYY	361	6	1	173	5	79	53	42	-17
	23	R	31	3B	aaa	ARI	481	5	1	216	9	79	46	46	-12
Fabian,Jud	23	R	23	CF	aa	BAL	238	10	9	148	13	51	126	94	-41
Fabian,Sandro	22	R	24	RF	a/a	TEX	343	9	1	188	4	77	90	64	11
	23	R	25	RF	aaa	TEX	444	16	4	232	3	81	97	65	28
Fairchild,Stuart	22	R	26	RF	aaa	CIN	190	9	5	216	7	62	140	87	1
	23	R	27	LF	aaa	CIN	94	3	2	211	6	64	73	80	-48
Fajardo,Yoyner	23	L	24	LF	aa	MIN	469	6	35	251	7	79	60	115	13
Farmer,Justin	23	R	25	RF	aa	SD	89	0	4	124	3	51	42	110	-122
Feduccia,Hunter	22	L	25	C	a/a	LA	294	10	0	181	7	66	117	33	-15
	23	L	26	C	aaa	LA	319	8	0	221	10	69	84	45	-20
Feliciano,Mario	22	R	24	C	aaa	MIL	285	4	1	217	4	78	56	36	-23
	23	R	25	C	aa	DET	140	0	0	183	5	83	32	21	-24
Fermin,Freddy	22	R	27	C	aaa	KC	296	7	1	202	8	76	85	30	-4
	23	R	28	C	aaa	KC	46	3	0	229	13	77	120	28	39
Fernandez,Juan	22	R	23	1B	a/a	SD	405	1	7	214	5	77	29	66	-35
	23	R	24	3B	aa	SD	364	6	8	216	7	82	53	63	5
Fernandez,Xavier	22	R	27	C	a/a	CHW	287	3	1	194	5	81	46	37	-18
	23	R	28	1B	a/a	CHW	346	11	0	227	7	78	98	17	11
Fernandez,Yanquiel	23	L	20	RF	aa	COL	218	7	0	199	5	66	99	10	-42
Ferrer,Jose	23	R	24	C	a/a	TOR	20	0	0	166	9	38	72	80	-147
Finol,Claudio	22	R	22	2B	aa	PIT	23	0	0	34	8	73	0	0	-91
	23	R	23	3B	aa	PIT	123	2	3	212	10	69	66	66	-32
Fitzgerald,Ryan	22	L	28	3B	aaa	BOS	452	9	4	168	6	64	98	70	-32
	23	L	29	3B	aaa	BOS	322	7	5	204	7	62	121	96	-11
Fitzgerald,Tyler	22	R	25	SS	aa	SF	455	13	14	186	5	56	118	130	-31
	23	R	26	SS	a/a	SF	483	13	23	238	7	67	102	132	5

BATTER	yr	b	age	pos	lvl	org	ab	hr	sb	ba	bb%	ct%	px	sx	bpv
Dixon,Brandon	23	R	31	RF	aaa	SD	239	8	4	174	6	51	101	74	-81
Dominguez,Jasson	23	B	20	CF	a/a	NYY	456	12	32	238	13	68	91	116	5
D'Orazio,Javier	23	R	22	C	aa	ARI	138	1	0	181	2	74	43	40	-52
Dorrian,Patrick	22	L	26	1B	a/a	MIL	314	9	3	154	8	56	109	68	-52
	23	L	27	2B	aaa	MIL	365	15	3	187	6	56	132	53	-42
Florial,Estevan	22	L	25	CF	aaa	NYY	403	11	27	224	9	57	131	115	-11
	23	L	26	CF	aaa	NYY	409	19	17	224	10	56	154	104	-1
Fontana,Shayne	22	L	25	LF	a/a	BAL	194	6	2	196	9	60	97	54	-47
	23	L	26	LF	a/a	BAL	319	4	14	209	8	77	56	93	-2
Ford, Mike	22	L	30	1B	aaa	LAA	113	1	0	163	9	80	54	16	-12
	23	L	31	DH	aaa	SEA	172	7	1	206	9	76	102	49	20
Foscue,Justin	22	R	23	2B	aa	TEX	400	9	2	231	7	81	90	43	25
	23	R	24	2B	aaa	TEX	462	13	9	218	11	82	86	78	46
Fraizer,Matt	22	L	24	CF	aa	PIT	439	4	12	176	5	71	60	130	-18
	23	L	25	RF	aa	PIT	437	6	17	219	7	74	53	106	-13
Franklin V,Jesse	22	L	24	RF	aa	ATL	55	2	1	202	8	63	85	98	-35
	23	L	25	LF	aa	ATL	341	12	17	201	7	59	115	107	-22
Frazier,Clint	22	R	28	LF	aaa	CHC	232	3	3	135	6	50	70	64	-111
	23	R	29	CF	aaa	CHW	260	8	3	172	10	59	107	56	-41
Free,James	22	B	24	C	a/a	CIN	228	6	0	216	4	70	79	18	-43
	23	B	25	DH	aa	CIN	421	14	1	228	9	72	97	35	-2
Freeman,Cole	22	R	28	CF	aaa	WAS	144	1	9	183	4	83	48	142	21
Freeman,Tyler	22	R	23	SS	aaa	CLE	297	4	4	218	5	87	32	64	5
	23	R	24	2B	aaa	CLE	91	1	7	258	11	79	62	117	25
Frelick,Sal	22	L	22	CF	a/a	MIL	413	7	13	286	6	86	66	108	44
	23	L	23	CF	aaa	MIL	158	2	6	209	8	87	45	87	27
Frick,Patrick	22	R	25	2B	aa	SEA	294	1	1	170	7	68	31	66	-67
	23	R	26	2B	aa	SEA	102	0	1	213	3	73	40	64	-49
Friedl,T.J.	22	L	27	LF	aaa	CIN	205	6	7	226	9	71	96	105	11
Fryman,Branden	22	R	24	2B	a/a	NYM	40	0	0	113	0	55	24	42	-145
	23	R	25	SS	a/a	NYM	178	2	3	178	3	66	62	100	-47
Fuentes,Josh	23	R	30	1B	a/a	ATL	247	3	2	179	5	70	48	68	-48
Fulford,Braxton	23	R	25	C	a/a	COL	113	3	1	201	8	65	120	41	-15
Gamboa,Arquimedes	22	B	25	SS	aaa	SF	255	2	4	183	8	68	61	80	-39
	23	B	26	SS	aa	STL	448	6	16	187	11	64	60	110	-38
Gamel,Ben	23	L	31	LF	aaa	SD	273	7	3	185	9	63	86	53	-45
Garcia,David	22	B	22	C	aa	TEX	237	3	0	185	5	69	64	40	-48
	23	B	23	C	aa	TEX	122	2	1	164	12	55	49	49	-99
Garcia,Dermis	22	R	24	1B	aaa	OAK	239	6	2	190	7	59	114	76	-37
	23	R	25	1B	aaa	OAK	171	6	2	189	7	57	112	63	-49
Garcia,Luis	22	L	22	SS	aaa	WAS	185	6	2	267	6	79	91	110	35
	23	L	23	2B	aaa	WAS	97	1	1	223	6	85	66	59	22
Garcia,Maikel	22	R	22	SS	a/a	KC	487	6	24	243	7	78	80	112	25
	23	R	23	SS	aaa	KC	95	1	3	206	10	76	66	51	-6
Garlick,Kyle	23	R	31	1B	aaa	MIN	298	8	1	173	8	51	119	54	-68
Garrett,Stone	22	R	27	RF	aaa	ARI	389	13	8	192	4	66	112	104	-5
Garry,Willie Joe	23	L	23	CF	aa	MIN	106	3	6	220	5	59	139	120	-4
Gasper,Mickey	22	B	27	1B	aa	NYY	214	6	2	202	12	68	97	60	-4
	23	B	28	1B	aa	NYY	224	5	7	186	9	75	56	74	-12
Gauthier,Austin	23	R	24	SS	aa	LA	321	5	11	255	13	80	70	102	35
Gelof,Zack	22	R	23	2B	a/a	OAK	389	10	6	206	7	64	89	79	-33
	23	R	24	2B	aaa	OAK	263	6	11	229	8	62	110	90	-18
Genoves,Ricardo	22	R	23	C	a/a	SF	311	6	0	176	7	65	82	27	-53
	23	R	24	C	aaa	SF	248	3	0	175	8	63	70	30	-65
Gentry,Tyler	22	R	23	RF	aa	KC	274	9	5	268	8	74	106	61	17
	23	R	24	RF	aaa	KC	475	10	9	210	10	71	82	70	-5
Gigliotti,Michael	22	L	26	CF	aa	SF	251	4	16	171	12	63	62	138	-30
	23	L	27	LF	aaa	SF	221	2	4	184	12	70	61	71	-23
Gil,Mateo	23	R	23	3B	a/a	NYM	162	1	2	189	7	65	53	57	-65
Gilbert,Andrew	23	L	23	CF	aa	NYM	347	10	7	239	12	75	83	77	15
Gilliam,Isiah	22	B	26	DH	a/a	CIN	387	14	9	223	8	55	150	105	-11
	23	B	27	DH	a/a	SEA	435	16	16	204	9	52	123	75	-51
Glass,Logan	22	R	21	LF	aaa	CHW	20	1	0	203	0	44	164	85	-66
Glendinning,Robbie	22	R	27	1B	aa	KC	428	10	6	191	9	55	105	75	-56
	23	R	28	DH	a/a	PHI	212	6	0	193	10	56	103	31	-63
Glenn,Jackson	23	R	26	3B	aa	PIT	219	5	3	233	5	77	81	91	10
Glowenke,Jimmy	23	R	24	2B	aa	SF	247	5	5	219	10	72	74	62	-14
Godoy,Jose	22	L	28	C	aaa	PIT	176	3	0	165	5	66	63	22	-66
	23	L	29	C	aaa	BAL	116	2	1	195	7	76	43	48	-30
Gomez,Jose	22	R	26	3B	a/a	LAA	383	4	4	183	4	68	70	69	-39
	23	R	27	3B	a/a	LAA	373	3	8	187	5	68	42	79	-58
Gomez,Moises	22	R	24	RF	a/a	STL	442	21	6	218	6	55	161	79	-14
	23	R	25	RF	aaa	STL	514	19	3	179	4	60	105	71	-46
Gonzales,Nick	22	R	23	2B	aa	PIT	259	4	3	218	10	61	114	75	-18
	23	R	24	2B	aaa	PIT	377	10	3	237	9	66	116	95	5
Gonzalez,Jacob	23	R	25	1B	aa	PIT	308	6	0	205	4	79	51	32	-24
Gonzalez,Norel	22	L	28	DH	a/a	MIA	339	9	1	192	6	68	93	42	-26
	23	L	29	RF	aa	MIA	237	5	1	191	8	68	69	49	-38
Gonzalez,Oscar	22	R	24	RF	a/a	CLE	189	6	0	215	3	81	85	41	12
	23	R	25	RF	aaa	CLE	335	9	1	225	4	70	95	65	-13
Gonzalez,Yariel	22	B	28	SS	a/a	ATL	364	6	4	182	6	72	64	58	-29
Goodman,Hunter	22	R	23	DH	aa	COL	44	1	1	192	4	72	51	40	-51
	23	R	24	LF	a/a	COL	410	25	0	224	6	71	154	15	26
Goodrum,Niko	23	B	31	1B	aaa	BOS	218	5	4	210	15	65	75	74	-26
Gorman,Nolan	22	L	22	2B	aaa	STL	171	10	2	219	5	56	151	68	-23
Gorski,Matt	22	R	25	CF	a/a	PIT	143	3	7	222	7	61	115	137	-8
	23	R	26	CF	a/a	PIT	415	14	17	189	6	69	95	105	-5

BATTER	yr	b	age	pos	lvl	org	ab	hr	sb	ba	bb%	ct%	px	sx	bpv
Fletcher,David	22	R	28	SS	aaa	LAA	49	0	1	137	2	82	12	38	-46
	23	R	29	SS	aaa	LAA	348	3	3	240	4	91	36	67	22
Fletcher,Dominic	22	L	25	CF	a/a	ARI	523	6	5	237	5	74	80	93	1
	23	L	26	CF	aaa	ARI	278	5	3	217	8	73	80	96	2
Flint,Tucker	23	L	22	RF	aa	LAA	433	11	3	205	10	61	100	70	-32
Gray,Tristan	23	L	27	SS	aaa	TAM	468	20	1	177	6	55	134	41	-46
Gregorius, Didi	23	L	33	SS	aaa	SEA	104	2	1	127	4	80	45	79	-8
Grissom,Vaughn	22	R	21	SS	aa	ATL	91	2	6	331	3	83	72	100	28
	23	R	22	SS	aaa	ATL	397	6	10	291	10	81	89	95	44
Groshans,Jordan	22	R	23	SS	aaa	MIA	353	2	2	221	10	79	40	47	-17
	23	R	24	3B	aaa	MIA	460	4	0	207	9	78	47	31	-22
Guldberg,Michael	22	R	23	CF	aa	OAK	166	0	3	222	7	76	36	80	-29
	23	R	24	LF	aa	OAK	127	1	2	176	4	73	48	86	-34
Guthrie,Dalton	22	R	27	CF	aaa	PHI	338	7	13	228	4	73	90	107	7
	23	R	28	CF	aaa	ATL	299	3	5	211	7	68	56	70	-47
Gutierrez,Abrahan	23	R	24	C	aa	PIT	115	2	1	199	10	85	55	29	16
Gutierrez,Kelvin	22	R	28	1B	aaa	BAL	211	4	3	176	6	70	64	83	-30
Guzman,Jeison	22	L	24	SS	aa	KC	69	1	1	199	8	62	75	59	-56
	23	L	25	DH	aa	KC	213	5	3	206	9	55	108	80	-50
Guzman,Jonathan	22	R	23	SS	aa	PHI	404	2	6	138	4	70	36	95	-54
	23	R	24	LF	aa	ARI	29	1	1	249	6	64	34	49	-88
Hackenberg,Adam	22	R	23	C	aa	CHW	42	1	0	132	5	62	56	13	-90
	23	R	24	C	a/a	CHW	340	6	2	221	8	70	64	44	-36
Haggerty,Sam	22	B	28	2B	aaa	SEA	152	3	9	194	6	70	93	130	7
	23	B	29	2B	aaa	SEA	185	5	11	224	8	72	96	119	19
Haley,Jim	22	R	27	1B	aaa	TAM	373	11	10	172	6	57	107	138	-32
	23	R	28	1B	aaa	PHI	364	7	11	189	5	68	73	115	-24
Hall,Darick	22	L	27	1B	aaa	PHI	389	18	4	191	6	69	127	52	9
	23	L	28	1B	aaa	PHI	286	12	0	236	8	71	94	23	-15
Halpin,Petey	23	L	21	CF	aa	CLE	452	8	10	223	9	70	76	91	-12
Hamilton,Caleb	22	R	27	C	aaa	MIN	206	6	1	169	11	60	103	35	-44
	23	R	28	C	aaa	BOS	138	3	0	126	7	52	87	17	-101
Hamilton,David	22	L	25	2B	aa	BOS	463	7	45	207	7	71	72	167	7
	23	L	26	SS	aaa	BOS	393	11	36	203	10	68	90	131	4
Hamilton,Quincy	22	L	24	CF	aa	HOU	126	3	4	159	9	68	67	68	-35
	23	L	25	LF	a/a	HOU	276	9	4	201	9	70	91	43	-15
Handley,Maverick	22	R	24	C	aa	BAL	259	8	4	192	8	72	91	72	2
	23	R	25	C	a/a	BAL	231	3	6	193	11	64	54	68	-57
Hannah,Jameson	22	L	25	CF	aa	COL	99	1	4	226	6	73	60	114	-13
	23	L	26	RF	aaa	COL	60	0	2	207	7	80	11	57	-40
Hardman,Tyler	23	R	24	3B	aa	NYY	283	20	7	203	10	54	188	100	19
Harris II,Michael	22	L	21	CF	aa	ATL	174	4	9	277	7	75	124	128	55
Harris,Brett	22	R	24	3B	aa	OAK	315	6	7	224	6	77	68	88	2
	23	R	25	3B	a/a	OAK	387	5	6	212	7	79	60	81	6
Harris,Dustin	22	L	23	LF	aa	TEX	331	11	12	205	8	75	91	100	19
	23	L	24	LF	a/a	TEX	471	10	27	214	11	69	86	123	5
Harris,Trey	22	R	26	RF	aa	WAS	332	4	5	199	5	73	50	70	-36
	23	R	27	DH	aa	WAS	233	2	3	207	6	70	64	56	-39
Harrison,Monte	22	R	27	CF	aaa	LAA	288	5	14	164	7	50	89	123	-75
	23	R	28	CF	aaa	MIL	269	4	12	157	5	40	96	119	-113
Haseley,Adam	22	L	26	CF	aaa	CHW	418	10	11	175	4	77	71	98	5
	23	L	27	CF	aaa	CHW	280	4	6	202	6	78	49	76	-14
Haskin,Hudson	22	R	23	CF	aa	BAL	387	12	3	220	7	71	103	68	3
	23	R	24	CF	a/a	BAL	103	2	4	233	4	56	97	110	-55
Hassell III,Robert	22	L	21	CF	aa	WAS	108	1	1	201	9	66	60	35	-60
	23	L	22	CF	aa	WAS	414	7	12	207	10	60	74	78	-57
Hatcher,Josh	23	L	25	1B	aa	TEX	180	5	2	213	4	67	74	69	-42
Hauver,Trevor	22	L	24	LF	aa	TEX	61	2	0	177	20	59	143	35	1
	23	L	25	RF	aa	TEX	392	9	1	212	11	60	102	47	-41
Hechavarria, Adeiny	23	R	34	SS	aaa	KC	127	3	0	160	5	70	86	26	-32
Heineman, Tyler	23	B	32	C	aaa	TOR	135	1	3	165	9	66	40	79	-58
Helman,Michael	22	R	26	CF	a/a	MIN	512	11	24	194	7	73	74	126	6
	23	R	27	SS	a/a	MIN	130	4	3	218	4	79	90	86	25
Henderson,Gunnar	22	L	21	SS	a/a	BAL	407	15	15	256	11	69	124	136	41
Henry,Payton	22	R	25	C	aaa	MIA	71	1	0	189	6	53	64	50	-107
	23	R	26	C	aaa	MIL	238	7	0	236	3	69	83	26	-42
Hensley,David	22	R	26	SS	aaa	HOU	379	6	12	224	11	65	100	108	-1
	23	R	27	3B	aaa	HOU	236	4	5	165	12	56	75	87	-65
Hermosillo,Michael	22	R	27	DH	aaa	CHC	20	1	1	313	11	55	258	143	94
	23	R	28	RF	aaa	NYY	207	8	5	165	4	65	87	65	-38
Hernaiz,Darell	22	R	21	SS	aa	BAL	53	1	1	95	6	68	41	81	-55
	23	R	22	SS	a/a	OAK	498	5	8	263	6	83	61	77	20
Hernandez,Diego	22	L	22	CF	aa	KC	124	1	8	253	6	76	43	96	-19
	23	L	23	CF	aa	KC	241	0	13	216	5	70	31	110	-49
Hernandez,Elier	22	R	28	RF	aaa	TEX	319	7	6	211	4	74	86	109	9
	23	R	29	RF	aaa	TEX	554	12	5	219	5	70	83	72	-18
Hernandez,Heriberto	23	R	24	RF	aa	TAM	389	10	5	207	13	59	96	76	-36
Hernandez,Ronaldo	22	R	25	C	aaa	BOS	410	10	0	215	3	74	98	23	-9
	23	R	26	C	aaa	BOS	335	11	1	193	7	76	85	36	-1
Hernandez,Yonny	22	B	24	2B	aaa	ARI	253	0	16	181	7	78	32	157	2
	23	B	25	SS	aaa	LA	322	3	11	202	13	70	48	88	-29
Herrera,Ivan	22	R	22	C	aaa	STL	235	4	3	219	9	76	58	74	-7
	23	R	23	C	aaa	STL	290	7	8	243	15	70	109	78	23
Herrera,Jose	22	B	25	C	aaa	ARI	91	1	0	253	6	86	36	24	-3
	23	B	26	C	aaa	ARI	101	1	0	190	8	76	45	50	-27
Herron,Jimmy	22	R	26	LF	a/a	COL	328	8	8	207	7	76	82	98	16
	23	R	27	LF	aaa	COL	456	12	18	230	7	75	85	101	13

BATTER	yr	b	age	pos	lvl	org	ab	hr	sb	ba	bb%	ct%	px	sx	bpv
Govern,Jimmy	22	R	26	3B	aaa	KC	216	3	2	167	3	73	77	82	-14
	23	R	27	3B	aa	KC	217	2	2	182	4	77	46	85	-18
Gray,Seth	22	L	24	1B	aa	MIN	22	1	0	67	10	49	65	14	-125
	23	L	25	3B	a/a	MIN	289	6	9	207	9	54	77	85	-76
Gray,Tristan	22	L	26	SS	aaa	TAM	458	20	3	170	4	56	139	61	-36
Hicks,Liam	23	L	24	C	aa	TEX	253	2	3	223	12	76	55	50	-10
Higgins, P.J.	22	R	29	C	aaa	CHC	72	1	1	305	9	70	95	29	-16
	23	R	30	C	aaa	CHC	347	6	1	218	7	68	75	50	-38
Hill,Darius	22	L	25	LF	a/a	CHC	528	6	4	244	4	82	66	80	15
	23	L	26	RF	aaa	CHC	334	1	2	211	6	80	50	72	-6
Hill,Derek	22	R	27	CF	aaa	SEA	227	4	5	158	5	61	77	116	-47
	23	R	28	CF	aaa	WAS	322	7	10	240	5	72	84	116	2
Hinds,Rece	22	R	22	RF	aa	CIN	29	2	0	271	0	53	231	83	22
	23	R	23	RF	aa	CIN	412	20	14	240	6	58	170	106	15
Hinojosa,C.J.	22	R	28	SS	aaa	SD	460	8	4	192	5	75	75	62	-11
	23	R	29	2B	aaa	MIA	336	4	3	187	4	78	48	64	-21
Hiraldo,Miguel	23	R	23	2B	aa	TOR	320	10	12	244	6	61	118	69	-26
Hiura,Keston	22	R	26	2B	aaa	MIL	47	4	0	249	11	59	191	25	22
	23	R	27	1B	aaa	MIL	315	17	0	244	6	63	127	22	-25
Hoese,Kody	22	R	25	3B	aa	LA	289	4	1	181	4	69	52	53	-58
	23	R	26	3B	aa	LA	344	9	1	203	5	75	65	47	-22
Holland,Korey	23	R	23	LF	aa	CLE	283	6	10	210	11	59	108	105	-23
Holland,Will	22	R	24	RF	aa	MIN	98	2	7	184	10	54	68	158	-60
	23	R	25	CF	aa	MIN	294	3	20	156	9	61	58	124	-51
Holliday,Jackson	23	L	20	SS	a/a	BAL	217	4	3	281	12	75	75	84	11
Hollis,Connor	22	R	28	3B	a/a	SD	487	5	12	228	8	70	65	81	-25
	23	R	29	SS	a/a	SD	238	2	9	170	8	66	46	88	-54
Holton,Jake	22	R	24	1B	aa	DET	23	0	0	176	3	61	0	45	-133
	23	R	25	1B	aa	DET	379	9	0	203	12	80	61	43	6
Hoover,Connor	22	L	26	3B	aa	SEA	239	3	3	126	8	61	57	66	-72
	23	L	27	2B	a/a	SEA	249	6	5	142	9	56	69	86	-73
Hopkins,T.J.	22	R	25	LF	a/a	CIN	467	17	5	216	7	63	122	61	-19
	23	R	26	RF	aaa	CIN	331	11	1	242	9	65	103	37	-28
Horwitz,Spencer	22	L	25	1B	a/a	TOR	403	9	5	222	10	72	102	75	17
	23	L	26	1B	aaa	TOR	392	7	6	268	11	78	77	51	11
Hostetler,Bennett	23	R	26	1B	aa	MIA	233	10	4	206	10	66	116	51	-7
House,Brady	23	R	20	3B	aa	WAS	139	3	1	311	4	68	103	82	-12
Howell,Korry	22	R	24	CF	aa	SD	146	4	8	196	10	57	126	168	3
	23	R	25	CF	aa	SD	211	3	14	136	8	54	71	140	-67
Huff,Samuel	22	R	24	C	aaa	TEX	246	12	0	198	6	60	114	28	-48
	23	R	25	C	aaa	TEX	272	12	0	240	10	66	124	17	-11
Hulsizer,Niko	22	R	25	RF	a/a	TAM	289	12	11	209	8	50	177	87	-14
	23	R	26	LF	aaa	TAM	392	11	5	162	10	51	121	64	-57
Hummel,Cooper	22	B	28	LF	aaa	ARI	129	3	1	214	8	60	101	84	-36
	23	B	29	1B	aaa	SEA	363	5	15	177	11	60	84	106	-38
Humphreys,Zach	22	R	25	C	aa	LAA	230	5	5	190	12	70	59	73	-24
	23	R	26	C	a/a	LAA	209	2	6	199	8	67	77	74	-30
Hunt,Blake	22	R	24	C	aa	TAM	273	3	1	193	5	69	68	57	-41
	23	R	25	C	a/a	TAM	246	9	1	205	6	70	117	46	1
Hunter Jr.,Torii	22	R	27	LF	a/a	LAA	263	5	13	183	4	57	82	139	-54
Hurst,Scott	22	L	26	CF	aaa	STL	311	6	11	213	9	74	59	88	-9
	23	L	27	LF	aaa	STL	30	0	2	97	9	53	0	69	-148
Hurtubise,Jacob	22	L	25	RF	aaa	CIN	156	1	10	200	9	68	25	125	-50
	23	L	26	LF	a/a	CIN	342	5	29	266	13	77	57	140	24
Iglesias, Jose	23	R	33	SS	aaa	SD	123	2	0	205	4	75	85	54	-8
Infante,Diego	22	R	23	LF	a/a	TAM	159	1	4	215	8	60	71	76	-62
	23	R	24	RF	a/a	TAM	350	9	11	207	5	63	85	73	-45
Isola,Alex	22	R	24	DH	aa	MIN	210	6	0	226	9	75	80	25	-9
	23	R	25	1B	aa	MIN	408	13	3	225	8	70	93	44	-14
Jackson,Alex	22	R	27	C	aaa	MIL	106	1	1	159	7	65	86	58	-38
	23	R	28	C	aaa	TAM	225	10	0	211	5	64	120	42	-24
Jackson,Jeremiah	22	R	22	2B	aa	LAA	307	10	4	174	7	72	93	58	-3
	23	R	23	3B	aa	NYM	440	18	24	222	9	62	112	89	-15
Jimenez,Leo	23	R	22	SS	a/a	TOR	352	6	6	237	8	79	65	81	9
Johnson Jr.,Daniel	22	L	27	DH	a/a	WAS	222	5	1	159	4	59	69	60	-81
	23	L	28	CF	a/a	SD	469	12	19	192	6	72	79	99	-3
Johnson,Bryce	22	B	27	CF	aaa	SF	307	3	17	215	6	63	58	124	-51
	23	B	28	CF	aaa	SF	257	4	11	212	8	65	79	117	-23
Johnson,Ivan	22	B	24	2B	aa	CIN	180	3	3	215	5	57	115	112	-37
	23	B	25	2B	aa	CIN	334	12	14	190	7	64	110	100	-11
Johnston,Troy	22	L	25	1B	a/a	MIA	426	9	3	209	8	73	82	60	-5
	23	L	26	1B	a/a	MIA	512	18	17	256	8	75	111	111	41
Jones,Greg	22	B	24	SS	aa	TAM	319	5	25	188	5	51	111	161	-45
	23	B	25	CF	a/a	TAM	250	7	17	195	6	47	127	137	-54
Jones,Jahmai	22	R	25	2B	aaa	BAL	99	1	1	164	8	73	65	80	-14
	23	R	26	2B	aaa	MIL	354	9	8	216	14	66	113	85	9
Jones,L.J.	23	R	24	DH	aa	STL	256	5	0	177	4	78	57	26	-22
Jones,Nolan	22	L	24	RF	aaa	CLE	214	5	2	211	8	64	93	72	-31
	23	L	25	3B	aaa	COL	149	8	3	294	11	69	164	82	54
Jones,Ryder	22	L	28	3B	aaa	CHW	214	5	0	137	5	53	68	25	-114
Jordan,Blaze	22	R	21	1B	aa	BOS	189	5	0	235	5	84	72	14	11
Jordan,Levi	22	R	27	3B	a/a	CHC	357	8	6	199	5	77	77	89	10
	23	R	28	SS	a/a	CHC	237	1	9	165	10	70	44	113	-31
Jordan,Rowdey	22	B	23	RF	aa	NYM	106	1	1	164	7	63	62	71	-60
	23	B	24	2B	aa	NYM	427	10	26	197	12	68	86	117	2
Joyce,Corey	22	R	24	3B	a/a	DET	72	1	1	279	8	69	94	105	-1
	23	R	25	SS	a/a	DET	284	3	7	178	12	63	73	96	-37
Julien,Edouard	22	L	23	2B	aa	MIN	400	11	12	244	14	64	100	86	-8
	23	L	24	2B	aaa	MIN	133	3	2	240	15	62	123	53	-6
Julks,Corey	22	R	26	3B	aaa	HOU	523	19	13	202	6	69	98	105	1
	23	R	27	LF	aaa	HOU	104	2	4	180	12	72	112	105	34

BATTER	yr	b	age	pos	lvl	org	ab	hr	sb	ba	bb%	ct%	px	sx	bpv
Hickey,Nathan	23	L	24	C	aa	BOS	291	12	2	227	9	65	123	49	-5
Hicklen,Brewer	22	R	26	RF	aaa	KC	480	14	20	189	6	52	146	130	-21
	23	R	27	DH	aaa	PHI	242	7	13	181	9	65	109	134	5
Hicks, John	22	R	33	C	aaa	CHC	357	11	6	182	4	60	126	83	-25
	23	R	34	C	aaa	PHI	180	2	7	150	6	60	71	86	-64
Kaiser,Connor	22	R	26	SS	a/a	SD	187	4	5	142	7	59	73	92	-63
	23	R	27	SS	aaa	COL	307	6	8	183	8	65	77	112	-26
Kapers,Scott	22	R	26	C	aa	TEX	61	2	1	132	6	59	86	92	-53
	23	R	27	C	aa	TEX	233	3	0	163	6	71	69	47	-34
Kavadas,Niko	22	L	24	1B	aa	BOS	81	1	0	186	11	45	97	15	-113
	23	L	25	1B	a/a	BOS	369	16	1	172	15	47	151	34	-48
Keirsey,DaShawn	22	L	25	CF	aa	MIN	425	4	26	210	5	70	71	127	-15
	23	L	26	CF	a/a	MIN	490	10	26	230	7	68	68	114	-23
Keith,Colt	23	L	22	3B	a/a	DET	507	18	2	265	8	74	116	61	27
Kennedy,Buddy	22	R	24	3B	aaa	ARI	330	3	4	194	8	73	54	81	-23
	23	R	25	2B	aaa	OAK	374	2	2	229	10	74	64	76	-6
Kessinger,Grae	22	R	25	SS	aa	HOU	421	10	14	160	9	67	70	98	-24
	23	R	26	SS	a/a	HOU	191	4	1	223	11	68	76	44	-31
Kieboom,Carter	23	R	26	3B	a/a	WAS	152	4	1	214	10	68	78	65	-24
Kingery,Scott	22	R	28	2B	aaa	PHI	301	4	10	168	10	55	81	130	-54
	23	R	29	SS	aaa	PHI	405	8	14	178	7	57	83	113	-57
Kirwer,Tanner	22	R	26	LF	aa	SEA	312	3	14	177	7	61	43	106	-75
	23	R	27	CF	a/a	SEA	181	2	13	156	7	62	43	117	-65
Kjerstad,Heston	23	L	24	RF	a/a	BAL	479	14	4	251	6	76	91	82	17
Knapp, Andrew	22	B	31	C	aaa	SF	208	6	1	168	4	64	109	35	-37
	23	B	32	C	aaa	HOU	313	5	2	165	6	59	71	52	-75
Koch,Grant	23	R	26	C	aaa	PIT	192	3	0	204	6	67	68	42	-52
Kohlwey,Taylor	22	L	28	LF	aaa	SD	501	5	5	196	7	75	60	70	-15
	23	L	29	LF	aaa	SD	428	7	8	179	8	72	62	65	-23
Kokx,Connor	23	R	23	LF	aa	CLE	325	3	25	203	12	70	57	101	-18
Kolozsvary,Mark	22	R	27	C	a/a	CIN	129	2	0	128	8	54	86	37	-86
	23	R	28	C	a/a	MIN	101	2	1	131	4	51	81	50	-107
Koperniak,Matt	22	L	24	LF	a/a	STL	388	7	7	216	6	76	56	79	-15
	23	L	25	LF	a/a	STL	499	11	7	226	7	79	55	62	-4
Koss,Christian	22	R	24	SS	aa	BOS	488	11	11	220	3	69	90	103	-14
	23	R	25	SS	a/a	BOS	248	2	10	196	4	73	67	116	-9
Kreidler,Ryan	22	R	25	SS	aaa	DET	202	5	10	170	10	60	115	132	-7
	23	R	26	SS	aaa	DET	176	6	7	182	10	65	89	71	-27
Kroon,Matt	23	R	27	3B	a/a	PHI	361	8	18	263	8	72	103	105	21
Lamb, Jake	22	L	32	1B	aaa	LA	231	8	1	197	8	57	121	32	-50
	23	L	33	3B	aaa	NYY	291	7	1	209	11	67	77	36	-37
Langeliers,Shea	22	R	25	C	aaa	OAK	353	9	3	201	6	69	88	68	-18
Lantigua,Rafael	22	R	24	2B	a/a	TOR	489	5	10	224	7	75	74	71	-3
	23	R	25	LF	aaa	TOR	465	8	18	247	12	73	90	74	10
Lara,Gilbert	22	R	25	SS	aa	WAS	290	5	0	183	4	65	59	22	-78
	23	R	26	SS	a/a	BAL	124	1	1	146	4	72	31	43	-65
Large,Cullen	22	B	26	RF	aaa	TOR	411	5	5	194	7	64	83	89	-35
Larnach,Trevor	22	L	25	LF	a/a	MIN	44	1	0	154	7	63	25	-1	-115
	23	L	26	RF	aaa	MIN	262	10	1	211	12	57	121	51	-34
Larsen,Jack	22	L	27	RF	aa	SEA	450	6	5	194	9	69	66	92	-24
	23	L	28	LF	aaa	SF	100	0	1	203	14	59	25	33	-103
Lavastida,Bryan	22	R	24	C	a/a	CLE	321	6	4	164	5	71	62	99	-25
	23	R	25	C	a/a	CLE	392	9	12	195	10	75	65	71	-6
Lavigne,Grant	22	L	23	1B	aa	COL	208	3	0	211	8	67	69	57	-41
	23	L	24	1B	aa	COL	445	14	3	205	11	68	95	52	-15
Lawlar,Jordan	22	R	20	SS	aa	ARI	85	2	1	171	7	65	51	81	-61
	23	R	21	SS	a/a	ARI	417	11	23	229	8	73	88	123	18
Leblanc,Charles	22	R	26	3B	aaa	MIA	318	9	4	236	7	62	112	77	-23
	23	R	27	2B	aaa	MIA	305	8	3	202	12	63	86	65	-36
Lee,Brooks	23	B	22	SS	a/a	MIN	501	11	5	234	8	79	89	65	25
Lee,Korey	22	R	24	C	aaa	HOU	404	16	7	184	5	62	122	104	-9
	23	R	25	C	aaa	CHW	334	4	9	221	4	66	64	71	-53
Leon,Pedro	22	R	24	CF	aaa	HOU	413	11	24	176	10	58	120	118	-15
	23	R	25	CF	aaa	HOU	483	14	13	192	8	59	100	83	-40
Leonard,Eddys	23	R	23	SS	a/a	DET	499	12	4	226	6	73	85	49	-9
Lester,Josh	22	L	28	1B	aaa	DET	557	16	4	181	5	70	107	73	0
	23	L	29	3B	aaa	BAL	432	13	1	184	4	64	87	50	-48
Lewis,Brandon	22	R	24	1B	aa	LA	397	17	0	169	4	57	138	35	-40
	23	R	25	1B	aa	LA	337	6	1	167	6	65	61	33	-69
Lewis,Kyle	22	R	27	DH	aaa	SEA	147	7	0	172	9	60	114	28	-40
	23	R	28	DH	aaa	ARI	248	8	0	267	8	69	99	23	-18
Lewis,Royce	22	R	23	SS	aaa	MIN	131	3	8	255	8	72	120	122	38
	23	R	24	3B	a/a	MIN	51	4	3	292	8	62	180	82	34
Leyba,Domingo	22	B	27	2B	a/a	SD	404	6	7	177	8	78	59	74	2
	23	B	28	3B	a/a	PIT	246	6	1	232	8	79	62	37	-6
Liberato,Luis	22	L	27	CF	aaa	SD	329	10	3	174	7	60	129	80	-15
	23	L	28	CF	aaa	SD	230	5	4	173	8	63	84	69	-42
Lindsly,Brady	22	L	24	C	aa	WAS	221	5	0	163	5	60	74	33	-79
	23	L	25	C	a/a	WAS	201	5	3	193	10	59	73	53	-69
Lipcius,Andre	22	R	24	3B	a/a	DET	462	7	9	227	11	78	82	83	28
	23	R	25	1B	aaa	DET	360	6	1	217	9	76	61	47	-11
Lipscomb,LaVictor	23	R	23	3B	aa	WAS	320	9	4	259	3	79	82	68	8
Lockridge,Brandon	22	R	25	CF	aa	NYY	418	10	13	181	6	64	83	103	-34
	23	R	26	CF	a/a	NYY	280	2	28	240	8	67	69	135	-18
Loftin,Nick	22	R	24	CF	a/a	KC	516	9	17	204	6	79	65	106	15
	23	R	25	3B	aaa	KC	315	8	4	218	7	84	64	41	13
Loperfido,Joey	23	L	24	CF	a/a	HOU	433	18	17	232	9	65	118	84	0
Lopes,Tim	22	R	28	2B	aaa	COL	266	5	5	201	4	69	83	104	-15
	23	R	29	2B	aaa	SD	475	7	22	184	7	64	57	92	-53
Lopez,Alejo	22	B	26	2B	aaa	CIN	160	2	1	212	7	84	57	35	8
	23	B	27	2B	aaa	CIN	466	5	10	221	9	79	56	68	2

BATTER	yr	b	age	pos	lvl	org	ab	hr	sb	ba	bb%	ct%	px	sx	bpv
Jung,Jace	23	L	23	2B	aa	DET	183	9	0	242	9	66	129	17	-6
Lopez,Irving	23	L	28	2B	a/a	STL	288	5	0	191	8	72	70	30	-30
Lopez,Johan	22	R	22	SS	a/a	TAM	74	1	1	120	4	61	55	82	-76
	23	R	23	SS	a/a	TAM	104	1	2	158	11	59	65	82	-63
Lopez,Otto	22	R	24	2B	aaa	TOR	340	2	11	254	8	80	65	120	24
	23	R	25	SS	aaa	TOR	318	1	8	205	4	80	32	102	-15
Lowe,Josh	22	L	24	RF	aaa	TAM	302	9	18	255	9	53	173	122	8
Luciano,Marco	23	R	22	SS	a/a	SF	269	10	5	192	12	59	122	61	-23
Lugbauer,Drew	22	L	26	1B	aa	ATL	474	20	0	174	10	47	176	23	-43
	23	L	27	1B	a/a	ATL	322	18	1	212	9	45	195	53	-27
Lugo,Matthew	23	R	22	3B	aa	BOS	289	4	6	224	5	67	98	84	-15
Lukes,Nathan	22	L	28	CF	aaa	TOR	428	8	14	223	7	74	76	90	0
	23	L	29	RF	aaa	TOR	202	3	2	274	5	84	69	58	19
Luplow, Jordan	22	R	29	RF	aaa	ARI	45	3	0	190	2	73	144	30	24
	23	R	30	RF	aaa	TOR	186	5	1	175	8	74	78	41	-11
Lutz,Tristen	22	R	24	LF	aa	MIL	255	8	1	207	8	58	107	24	-55
	23	R	25	DH	aa	MIL	154	5	0	178	11	48	111	22	-87
Machado, Dixon	22	R	30	SS	aaa	SF	461	3	5	203	6	81	47	57	-6
	23	R	31	SS	aaa	HOU	239	4	1	163	11	73	48	38	-35
MacIver,Willie	22	R	26	C	a/a	COL	367	9	5	175	5	65	86	53	-41
	23	R	27	C	aaa	COL	163	2	5	194	9	62	79	98	-40
Madris,Bligh	22	L	26	RF	aaa	TAM	296	7	3	231	7	68	111	87	3
	23	L	27	RF	aaa	HOU	378	10	7	179	10	61	78	88	-45
Maggi, Drew	22	R	33	2B	aaa	PIT	292	0	12	151	7	64	49	107	-57
	23	R	34	3B	aa	PIT	127	0	3	140	5	75	26	72	-48
Mahan,Riley	22	L	26	1B	aa	SF	64	2	1	215	9	40	205	121	-21
	23	L	27	1B	aa	SF	166	5	1	156	4	59	109	85	-41
Maitan,Kevin	22	B	22	3B	aa	LAA	399	8	2	213	6	60	87	49	-60
	23	B	23	1B	aa	LAA	172	1	0	162	9	56	54	22	-107
Maldonado,Nelson	22	R	26	DH	a/a	CHC	373	7	4	208	4	71	93	63	-11
	23	R	27	1B	a/a	CHC	282	5	1	161	9	72	65	36	-28
Malgeri,Ben	23	R	23	CF	aa	DET	344	9	11	200	8	63	100	107	-18
Malloy,Justyn-Henry	22	R	22	LF	a/a	ATL	215	6	2	243	16	67	102	50	-3
	23	R	23	3B	aaa	DET	487	14	3	229	14	66	94	53	-17
Mangum,Jake	22	B	26	CF	a/a	NYM	276	3	9	229	4	74	62	115	-11
	23	B	27	CF	aaa	MIA	473	3	11	242	4	77	64	98	-2
Mann,Devin	22	R	25	2B	a/a	LA	375	11	1	202	9	72	92	51	-2
	23	R	26	3B	aaa	KC	460	12	3	221	10	64	125	56	-6
Manzardo,Kyle	22	L	22	1B	aa	TAM	99	3	1	269	9	77	131	46	48
	23	L	23	1B	aaa	CLE	343	12	1	196	10	74	108	31	14
Marchan,Rafael	22	B	23	C	aaa	PHI	230	3	0	189	5	88	63	23	23
	23	B	24	C	aaa	PHI	175	1	1	245	9	87	65	67	38
Marisnick, Jake	22	R	31	CF	aaa	ATL	96	1	5	186	4	58	53	120	-79
	23	R	32	CF	aaa	LA	120	1	5	195	8	63	85	100	-31
Marlowe,Cade	22	L	25	CF	a/a	SEA	499	14	26	214	7	61	98	117	-28
	23	L	26	CF	aaa	SEA	334	7	18	187	6	62	82	123	-35
Marrero,Elih	22	B	25	C	aa	BOS	246	1	12	171	9	66	49	86	-51
	23	B	26	C	aa	BOS	108	1	6	227	12	65	75	67	-34
Marte,Noelvi	23	R	22	3B	a/a	CIN	339	9	12	244	8	77	87	103	27
Martin,Austin	22	R	23	SS	aa	MIN	336	1	22	194	8	82	38	132	16
	23	R	24	2B	aaa	MIN	205	4	11	214	11	75	67	73	0
Martin,Casey	23	R	24	SS	aa	PHI	217	4	5	155	5	55	76	77	-83
Martin,Jason	22	L	27	RF	aaa	LA	470	19	4	204	7	63	123	72	-11
Martin,Mason	22	L	23	1B	aaa	PIT	481	11	8	172	7	56	128	106	-27
	23	L	24	1B	a/a	PIT	317	13	5	182	13	55	125	57	-35
Martin,Richie	22	R	28	SS	aaa	BAL	292	1	16	181	6	72	65	148	-2
	23	R	29	SS	aaa	WAS	360	2	18	157	8	63	61	106	-51
Martinez,Angel	22	B	20	2B	aa	CLE	82	2	2	219	10	76	114	80	42
	23	B	21	2B	a/a	CLE	525	11	9	220	7	75	68	88	-2
Martinez,Ernesto	23	L	24	1B	aa	MIL	106	2	2	202	10	75	56	56	-15
Martinez,J.P.	22	L	26	CF	a/a	TEX	395	8	23	180	9	61	85	142	-26
	23	L	27	CF	a/a	TEX	300	10	24	229	11	65	121	120	18
Martinez,Orelvis	22	R	21	SS	aa	TOR	433	22	3	169	5	65	124	44	-14
	23	R	22	SS	a/a	TOR	448	22	1	214	10	69	127	49	14
Martinez,Orlando	22	L	24	RF	a/a	LAA	385	6	5	207	5	72	68	76	-24
	23	L	25	RF	a/a	LAA	439	9	5	209	5	74	77	67	-9
Martinez,Pedro	23	B	22	SS	aa	PHI	163	3	6	165	7	62	61	66	-66
Martini, Nick	23	L	33	LF	aaa	CIN	345	10	0	198	9	66	92	42	-29
Martorano,Brandon	22	R	24	C	aa	SF	323	6	8	182	8	57	108	126	-28
	23	R	25	C	aa	SF	205	4	2	161	13	54	67	58	-87
Masterman,Cameron	23	R	24	RF	aa	OAK	150	3	2	202	5	60	73	68	-68
Mastrobuoni,Miles	22	L	27	2B	aaa	TAM	507	10	15	227	8	75	80	106	15
	23	L	28	2B	aaa	CHC	129	1	5	220	14	62	96	128	-8
Matheny,Shane	22	L	26	CF	a/a	SF	362	8	2	186	10	54	94	68	-69
	23	L	27	CF	a/a	SF	439	8	12	181	12	57	83	91	-50
Mathias,Mark	22	R	28	2B	aaa	TEX	199	5	7	229	8	63	89	76	-36
	23	R	29	2B	aaa	SF	168	2	2	214	10	61	61	44	-72
Matijevic,J.J.	22	L	27	1B	aaa	HOU	246	10	6	209	7	64	130	98	7
	23	L	28	1B	aaa	HOU	435	10	5	180	7	63	94	88	-30
Maton,Nick	22	L	25	SS	aaa	PHI	211	3	2	203	9	69	104	68	1
	23	L	26	LF	aaa	DET	140	2	2	231	11	69	90	82	-3
Matos,Luis	23	R	21	CF	a/a	SF	254	8	12	297	8	90	82	90	70
Matthews,Gabe	23	L	26	1B	aa	LAA	158	4	0	194	12	52	81	13	-97
Mauricio,Ronny	22	B	21	SS	aa	NYM	509	18	14	214	3	71	104	86	3
	23	B	22	2B	aaa	NYM	490	14	17	235	5	77	86	88	14

BATTER	yr	b	age	pos	lvl	org	ab	hr	sb	ba	bb%	ct%	px	sx	bpv
Lopez,Irving	22	L	27	3B	a/a	STL	230	1	3	178	6	78	45	59	-20
Mazara,Nomar	22	L	27	RF	aaa	SD	128	4	0	254	8	69	126	32	5
	23	L	28	RF	aaa	WAS	173	3	0	198	9	70	68	41	-32
Mazeika, Patrick	22	L	29	C	aaa	SF	162	2	0	176	6	81	34	19	-28
	23	L	30	C	aaa	LA	182	1	0	154	5	80	31	24	-38
McAfee,Quincy	22	R	25	2B	aa	CIN	254	4	1	174	8	61	77	53	-59
	23	R	26	LF	aa	CIN	317	11	7	199	9	71	105	97	18
McCann,Kyle	22	L	25	C	a/a	OAK	394	11	1	169	7	53	113	46	-65
	23	L	26	C	aaa	OAK	344	8	2	192	6	56	91	53	-73
McCarthy,Jake	22	L	25	CF	aaa	ARI	141	3	6	279	7	81	91	120	47
	23	L	26	RF	aaa	ARI	197	4	9	273	5	82	79	103	32
McCoy,Mason	22	R	27	SS	aaa	SEA	442	12	13	178	6	61	99	114	-27
	23	R	28	SS	aaa	TOR	417	8	15	164	8	56	84	107	-58
McCroskey,David	23	R	23	2B	aa	LAA	129	0	1	192	9	54	23	57	-127
McCullough,Morgan	22	L	25	2B	aa	KC	99	1	1	194	7	67	85	51	-35
	23	L	26	3B	a/a	KC	286	4	7	200	8	64	89	96	-27
McDonald,Mickey	22	L	27	CF	a/a	OAK	272	1	6	198	7	67	48	81	-52
McDonough,Tyler	23	B	24	LF	a/a	BOS	328	4	17	222	7	66	78	129	-17
McDowell,Max	22	R	28	C	aaa	NYY	187	1	2	139	8	66	52	50	-64
	23	R	29	C	a/a	TOR	232	4	0	175	9	62	45	20	-92
McGarry,Alex	22	L	24	1B	a/a	CIN	262	13	6	215	5	65	143	95	13
	23	L	25	1B	a/a	CIN	419	9	9	218	6	64	85	79	-39
McGeary,Haydn	23	R	24	1B	aa	CHC	361	11	3	213	12	67	84	47	-26
McGuire,Shane	23	L	24	C	aa	OAK	330	2	2	182	10	71	44	48	-45
McIlwain,Brandon	22	R	24	CF	aa	NYM	192	3	2	170	6	60	66	60	-76
	23	R	25	CF	a/a	NYM	466	8	15	195	9	69	75	75	-22
McIntosh,Paul	22	R	25	C	aa	MIA	318	9	7	210	11	72	111	96	30
	23	R	26	C	a/a	MIA	237	9	2	200	9	68	70	44	-39
McKenna,Alex	22	R	25	CF	a/a	HOU	367	4	10	176	8	57	74	100	-63
	23	R	26	LF	a/a	HOU	151	3	1	168	9	53	70	74	-92
McKinney,Billy	22	L	28	RF	aaa	OAK	251	5	1	197	7	56	102	87	-51
	23	L	29	1B	aaa	NYY	135	6	2	201	9	68	96	38	-19
McKinstry,Zach	22	L	27	SS	aaa	LA	191	2	0	241	7	78	58	63	-9
McLain,Matt	22	R	23	SS	aa	CIN	371	13	18	196	11	61	134	126	12
	23	R	24	SS	aaa	CIN	144	9	6	283	12	69	166	70	56
Mead,Curtis	22	R	22	3B	a/a	TAM	282	9	5	249	9	74	128	61	36
	23	R	23	3B	aaa	TAM	235	7	3	243	9	76	110	66	32
Meadows,Parker	22	L	23	CF	aa	DET	425	10	12	234	8	77	90	127	35
	23	L	24	CF	aaa	DET	449	11	13	210	8	69	100	121	12
Means,Jake	22	R	26	3B	aa	KC	375	6	6	161	7	64	83	76	-38
	23	R	27	3B	aa	KC	231	4	3	129	7	66	50	51	-63
Meckler,Wade	23	L	23	LF	a/a	SF	231	3	8	301	13	76	63	104	12
Meidroth,Chase	23	R	22	3B	aa	BOS	325	6	7	236	12	75	69	88	6
Mejia,Erick	22	B	28	3B	aaa	SEA	464	8	11	178	6	70	75	91	-19
	23	B	29	3B	aaa	WAS	234	5	5	165	7	68	68	94	-29
Melendez,Raul	23	R	23	3B	aa	ARI	153	7	0	220	4	55	127	64	-47
Mendick,Danny	23	R	30	3B	aaa	NYM	373	6	8	193	7	78	50	73	-11
Mendlinger,Noah	23	L	23	RF	aa	STL	321	3	4	248	11	85	44	58	16
Mendoza,Evan	22	R	26	SS	aaa	STL	360	2	10	182	8	82	37	81	0
	23	R	27	SS	a/a	SD	106	1	3	157	4	75	24	71	-49
Mercado,Oscar	22	R	28	CF	aaa	CLE	167	3	5	197	5	78	60	98	2
	23	R	29	CF	aaa	LA	309	9	17	222	5	69	101	111	1
Merrill,Jackson	23	L	20	SS	aa	SD	187	4	4	242	8	85	80	87	48
Mervis,Matt	22	L	24	1B	a/a	CHC	412	18	1	234	6	77	127	59	40
	23	L	25	1B	aaa	CHC	362	13	1	219	11	67	108	50	-7
Mesa,Victor	23	L	22	CF	aa	MIA	483	14	12	219	6	73	88	90	4
Mesa,Victor Victor	22	R	26	CF	a/a	MIA	301	2	24	172	4	79	28	126	-14
	23	R	27	LF	a/a	MIA	37	1	1	150	3	84	24	95	-7
Meyer,Nick	22	R	25	C	a/a	NYM	246	4	9	175	10	70	59	92	-22
	23	R	26	C	aaa	NYM	230	3	4	160	7	70	32	65	-58
Meyers,Chris	23	L	24	1B	aa	DET	258	6	1	208	4	71	66	43	-39
Mieses,Luis	22	L	22	LF	aa	CHW	97	2	1	248	3	76	77	40	-13
	23	L	23	RF	aa	CHW	458	7	1	195	2	73	66	34	-40
Millas,Drew	22	B	24	C	aa	WAS	152	2	1	181	7	61	57	31	-85
	23	B	25	C	a/a	WAS	278	6	5	244	10	79	74	72	19
Miller,Brian	22	L	27	LF	aaa	MIA	408	4	17	227	6	76	65	146	15
	23	L	28	LF	aaa	MIA	270	1	12	189	7	71	42	99	-37
Miller,Owen	23	R	27	LF	aaa	MIL	106	3	1	223	4	78	90	32	4
Milligan,Cody	22	L	24	CF	aa	ATL	273	1	10	232	8	76	37	102	-20
	23	L	25	CF	aa	ATL	261	2	19	245	11	69	76	140	2
Miranda,Jose	22	R	24	3B	aaa	MIN	86	1	0	202	4	81	103	23	23
	23	R	25	3B	aaa	MIN	161	2	1	202	6	78	45	63	-19
Misner,Kameron	22	L	24	CF	aa	TAM	416	10	22	197	12	55	117	105	-30
	23	L	25	CF	aaa	TAM	421	14	14	178	12	47	157	112	-27
Mitchell,Calvin	22	L	23	RF	aaa	PIT	236	6	5	284	5	82	100	84	44
	23	L	24	LF	aaa	PIT	280	6	4	217	7	64	86	61	-42
Mitchell,Garrett	22	L	24	CF	a/a	MIL	239	3	11	238	7	64	86	126	-20
	23	L	25	CF	aaa	MIL	32	0	2	150	4	77	17	125	-29
Molfetta,Christian	23	R	27	C	aaa	LAA	31	0	0	93	5	64	0	-9	-133
Monasterio,Andruw	22	R	25	SS	a/a	MIL	377	6	10	211	9	70	73	90	-14
	23	R	26	SS	aaa	MIL	140	3	8	217	14	74	63	73	-2
Mondou,Nate	22	L	27	2B	aaa	OAK	385	3	1	194	6	72	71	50	-25
	23	L	28	1B	a/a	CHW	394	10	5	202	10	72	79	45	-13
Moniak,Mickey	22	L	24	CF	a/a	LAA	115	5	3	237	5	71	126	86	21
	23	L	25	CF	aaa	LAA	130	5	1	250	3	67	106	97	-8

BATTER	yr	b	age	pos	lvl	org	ab	hr	sb	ba	bb%	ct%	px	sx	bpv
Mayer,Marcelo	23	L	21	SS	aa	BOS	169	5	3	178	6	70	95	89	-3
Mayo,Coby	22	R	21	3B	aa	BAL	128	4	0	215	6	58	96	32	-67
	23	R	22	3B	a/a	BAL	504	20	4	247	13	68	138	63	28
Montero,Elehuris	23	R	25	1B	aaa	COL	142	10	0	295	5	78	130	21	37
Montes,Coco	22	R	26	2B	a/a	COL	469	12	8	214	6	66	105	109	-6
	23	R	27	2B	aaa	COL	436	14	6	247	7	66	107	76	-11
Montgomery,Colson	22	L	20	SS	aa	CHW	48	2	0	124	3	67	78	31	-53
	23	L	21	SS	aa	CHW	131	3	0	210	12	71	95	71	6
Morales,Jonathan	22	R	27	C	aaa	COL	308	5	0	233	6	78	50	9	-30
	23	R	28	1B	aaa	COL	357	9	1	194	4	82	63	26	-1
Moran, Colin	22	L	30	1B	aaa	CIN	193	5	0	191	6	63	100	14	-49
	23	L	31	3B	aaa	SEA	136	3	0	173	7	67	53	20	-70
Morel,Christopher	22	R	23	CF	aa	CHC	108	4	2	243	5	67	117	96	5
	23	R	24	CF	aaa	CHC	115	7	3	267	9	58	195	113	41
Moreno,Gabriel	22	R	22	C	aaa	TOR	238	3	6	280	7	79	70	72	11
Morgan,Josh	22	R	27	C	aaa	SEA	59	1	0	152	10	67	70	10	-50
	23	R	28	3B	aa	SEA	288	6	1	166	5	64	71	50	-60
Morissette,Cody	23	L	23	2B	aa	MIA	391	12	2	197	6	70	90	68	-14
Moritz,Andrew	22	L	26	LF	aa	ATL	302	1	4	234	8	72	53	79	-27
	23	L	27	LF	aa	ATL	122	1	2	185	8	68	40	91	-49
Morris,PK	23	L	25	1B	aa	TOR	134	2	0	144	13	56	86	44	-65
Morris,Tanner	22	L	24	3B	a/a	TOR	252	4	1	211	12	75	48	44	-21
	23	L	25	2B	aaa	TOR	345	4	1	226	10	72	63	26	-31
Motter, Taylor	22	R	33	2B	aaa	ATL	279	14	1	197	11	66	138	36	10
	23	R	34	1B	aaa	STL	208	5	5	179	7	64	82	77	-41
Mulrine,Anthony	22	R	24	C	a/a	LAA	207	1	1	118	6	63	33	46	-96
	23	R	25	C	a/a	LAA	108	1	0	131	9	67	45	21	-70
Muncy,Max	23	R	21	SS	aa	OAK	202	2	3	259	7	71	88	67	-8
Munguia,Ismael	23	L	25	LF	aa	SF	294	4	13	243	6	82	52	88	11
Murphy,Tanner	23	R	25	RF	a/a	NYM	163	1	7	159	8	43	83	87	-115
Murray,BJ	23	B	23	3B	aa	CHC	452	11	10	225	12	68	106	90	9
Murray,Ethan	22	R	22	SS	aa	MIL	35	1	1	212	13	70	104	81	15
	23	R	23	SS	aa	MIL	351	5	7	216	10	69	65	79	-27
Murray,Tanner	23	R	24	2B	a/a	TAM	196	4	0	204	7	72	99	59	1
Muzziotti,Simon	22	L	24	CF	a/a	PHI	159	4	5	217	8	75	75	124	17
	23	L	25	LF	aaa	PHI	473	5	17	238	6	80	50	84	-2
Myers,Dane	22	R	26	LF	a/a	DET	450	15	14	207	3	65	106	105	-14
	23	R	27	CF	a/a	MIA	374	10	14	257	8	74	74	102	6
Naquin, Tyler	23	L	32	RF	aaa	CHW	245	6	2	186	5	58	80	41	-81
Naranjo,Joe	23	L	22	1B	aa	CLE	288	3	0	182	13	69	52	19	-51
Narvaez,Carlos	23	R	25	C	a/a	NYY	343	9	4	194	12	62	92	44	-41
Navarreto,Brian	22	R	28	C	aaa	MIL	130	3	1	197	5	80	34	50	-28
	23	R	29	C	aaa	MIL	266	5	0	174	6	68	73	41	-43
Navigato,Andrew	22	R	24	2B	aa	DET	361	11	10	203	5	78	81	97	17
	23	R	25	SS	aa	DET	233	7	6	250	5	76	117	82	32
Naylor,Bo	22	L	22	C	a/a	CLE	415	14	13	218	11	67	123	103	21
	23	L	23	C	aaa	CLE	217	9	1	207	14	73	105	49	20
Neslony,Tyler	22	L	28	RF	a/a	CHW	352	9	12	223	6	73	102	91	16
	23	L	29	LF	a/a	CHW	343	9	13	175	9	65	78	66	-39
Nevin,Tyler	22	R	25	3B	aaa	BAL	165	5	2	230	7	74	87	76	7
	23	R	26	1B	aaa	DET	337	9	3	258	7	77	88	79	19
Nido,Tomas	23	R	29	C	aaa	NYM	135	2	0	196	5	73	38	24	-60
Noda,Ryan	22	L	26	1B	aaa	LA	464	15	11	188	9	57	114	75	-39
Noel,Jhonkensy	22	R	21	RF	a/a	CLE	257	9	1	198	7	69	121	75	14
	23	R	22	LF	aaa	CLE	519	19	1	182	7	69	92	34	-24
Noll,Jake	22	R	28	2B	aaa	WAS	390	6	4	194	3	75	78	81	-3
	23	R	29	1B	aaa	WAS	194	4	0	181	5	72	85	22	-28
Norby,Connor	22	R	22	2B	a/a	BAL	291	16	7	262	8	76	135	93	57
	23	R	23	2B	aaa	BAL	565	13	7	239	7	73	88	76	0
Norman,Ben	23	L	25	LF	aa	CHW	170	5	8	165	9	54	91	86	-63
Northcut,Nicholas	22	R	23	3B	aa	BOS	101	3	1	178	3	60	107	51	-51
	23	R	24	3B	a/a	CIN	268	8	0	174	4	53	113	15	-83
Nottingham,Jacob	22	R	27	C	aaa	BAL	301	10	6	172	7	61	101	71	-40
	23	R	28	C	aaa	WAS	197	7	1	163	5	59	108	36	-57
Nunez,Dom	22	L	27	C	aaa	COL	247	3	4	168	6	68	70	74	-36
	23	L	28	C	aaa	PIT	193	3	3	140	11	61	66	67	-59
Nunez,Malcom	22	R	21	1B	a/a	PIT	416	14	3	219	11	73	92	50	4
	23	R	22	1B	aaa	PIT	241	5	0	205	6	72	57	28	-44
Nunez,Nasim	22	B	22	SS	aa	MIA	142	0	16	227	11	72	36	108	-27
	23	B	23	SS	aa	MIA	490	4	39	198	12	76	32	114	-10
Nunez,Rainer	23	R	23	1B	aa	TOR	304	8	0	198	5	68	69	11	-58
Nwogu,Jordan	23	R	24	LF	aa	CHC	324	11	11	160	6	52	94	91	-76
O Hoppe,Logan	22	R	22	C	aa	LAA	360	18	5	234	11	77	109	59	36
O Keefe, Brian	22	R	29	C	aaa	SEA	316	7	1	169	5	65	86	49	-43
	23	R	30	C	aaa	SEA	353	13	1	160	6	62	115	41	-35
Ockimey,Josh	22	L	27	1B	a/a	PHI	395	11	2	174	12	58	109	62	-35
Okey,Chris	22	R	28	C	aaa	CIN	118	2	0	172	5	58	74	100	-66
	23	R	29	C	aaa	LAA	210	4	1	203	4	70	53	52	-53
Oliva,Jared	22	R	27	CF	aaa	PIT	319	4	13	203	5	71	86	127	1
	23	R	28	RF	aaa	LAA	284	5	9	193	6	69	68	107	-23
Ona,Jorge	22	R	25	RF	aa	SD	250	5	0	166	6	50	87	34	-108
	23	R	26	DH	aa	SD	110	2	2	170	6	54	124	58	-53
O'Neill,Matt	23	R	26	C	a/a	NYM	217	4	0	130	10	49	82	23	-108
Ornelas,Jonathan	22	R	22	SS	aa	TEX	525	9	9	247	5	74	60	76	-20
	23	R	23	SS	aaa	TEX	434	6	10	210	10	68	58	88	-30
Ornelas,Tirso	22	L	22	RF	a/a	SD	455	4	4	223	6	77	62	67	-7
	23	L	23	RF	a/a	SD	478	11	6	225	9	74	78	53	-8
Orr,J.D.	22	L	26	LF	a/a	MIA	264	1	27	198	11	73	42	131	-14
	23	L	27	LF	aa	MIA	137	0	9	160	12	65	18	112	-66

BATTER	yr	b	age	pos	lvl	org	ab	hr	sb	ba	bb%	ct%	px	sx	bpv
Montano,Daniel	22	L	23	LF	aa	COL	305	9	3	216	9	65	105	62	-16
	23	L	24	LF	aaa	COL	270	5	1	196	9	65	91	78	-25
Montero,Elehuris	22	R	24	3B	aaa	COL	255	9	2	251	5	73	95	67	1
Ortiz,Jhailyn	22	R	24	RF	aa	PHI	448	12	6	192	6	58	114	91	-37
	23	R	25	1B	a/a	PHI	333	10	1	187	8	58	92	35	-66
Ortiz,Joey	22	R	24	SS	a/a	BAL	539	14	5	230	5	79	91	88	29
	23	R	25	SS	aaa	BAL	349	6	8	256	6	77	83	91	15
Ostberg,Erik	22	L	27	DH	aa	TAM	162	3	2	159	9	55	91	83	-61
	23	L	28	C	aa	TAM	136	3	1	162	6	64	107	60	-26
Outman,James	22	L	25	RF	a/a	LA	473	21	8	227	8	61	151	99	12
Packard,Spencer	23	L	26	LF	aa	SEA	466	10	1	227	9	77	70	36	-7
Padlo,Kevin	22	R	26	3B	aaa	PIT	306	7	8	196	6	65	93	103	-19
	23	R	27	3B	aaa	LAA	333	8	5	196	10	63	100	51	-31
Pages,Andy	22	R	22	RF	aa	LA	487	20	4	198	8	68	125	62	7
	23	R	23	CF	a/a	LA	112	2	5	239	14	65	134	93	25
Pages,Pedro	22	R	24	C	a/a	STL	291	5	1	165	7	60	79	35	-69
	23	R	25	C	aa	STL	424	10	2	210	8	74	77	56	-8
Palacios,Jermaine	22	R	26	SS	aaa	MIN	392	8	7	214	5	68	94	69	-19
	23	R	27	SS	aaa	KC	180	5	2	139	4	61	81	63	-64
Palacios,Joshua	22	L	27	LF	aaa	WAS	296	6	13	228	7	77	64	96	5
	23	L	28	CF	a/a	PIT	112	6	4	293	8	86	100	87	68
Palacios,Richard	22	L	25	LF	aaa	CLE	179	2	7	209	7	70	78	134	0
	23	L	26	CF	aaa	STL	374	5	6	191	11	81	56	60	9
Palensky,Aaron	23	R	25	RF	a/a	NYY	210	7	9	147	12	62	110	113	-4
Palka, Daniel	22	L	31	1B	aaa	NYM	395	15	0	181	7	63	106	28	-39
	23	L	32	1B	aaa	NYM	371	9	2	160	6	65	70	47	-58
Palmegiani,Damiano	23	R	23	3B	a/a	TOR	467	18	5	220	10	63	130	59	-3
Palmeiro,Preston	22	L	27	DH	aa	LAA	407	5	1	193	6	75	72	30	-20
	23	L	28	LF	aaa	LAA	136	1	1	133	8	68	59	47	-47
Palmer,Jaylen	23	R	23	LF	a/a	NYM	190	6	8	145	11	44	111	93	-81
Papierski,Michael	22	B	26	C	aaa	CIN	190	5	0	192	9	75	69	18	-19
	23	B	27	1B	aaa	DET	256	4	0	202	10	70	71	39	-32
Paris,Kyren	22	R	21	2B	aa	LAA	39	2	3	305	15	59	164	83	23
	23	R	22	SS	aa	LAA	415	11	32	225	13	59	106	103	-18
Park,Hoy Jun	22	L	26	3B	aaa	PIT	316	6	9	171	10	63	67	85	-47
	23	L	27	RF	aaa	ATL	317	4	11	206	12	65	61	90	-38
Pasquantino,Vinnie	22	L	25	DH	aaa	KC	264	9	2	216	8	83	102	71	54
Peguero,Liover	22	R	21	SS	aa	PIT	483	6	19	220	4	75	67	119	0
	23	R	22	SS	a/a	PIT	312	10	17	232	8	80	95	110	46
Peraza,Jose	22	R	28	2B	aaa	BOS	237	3	2	182	3	84	57	44	3
	23	R	29	1B	aaa	NYM	134	1	1	181	2	72	43	68	-52
Peraza,Oswald	22	R	22	SS	aaa	NYY	386	15	25	219	6	70	98	104	6
	23	R	23	SS	aaa	NYY	261	10	11	225	7	75	88	104	19
Pereda,Jhonny	22	R	26	C	aaa	SF	206	2	0	204	9	75	53	18	-30
	23	R	27	C	aaa	CIN	231	4	0	248	8	72	72	17	-33
Pereira,Everson	22	R	21	CF	aa	NYY	113	4	2	244	6	63	117	119	-6
	23	R	22	LF	a/a	NYY	303	14	8	264	8	63	140	91	7
Perez, Hernan	22	R	31	2B	aaa	ATL	323	6	14	209	5	70	73	116	-14
	23	R	32	SS	aaa	MIN	204	6	5	201	7	68	79	73	-27
Perez, Michael	22	L	30	C	aaa	NYM	77	1	0	140	9	59	61	7	-93
	23	L	31	C	aaa	NYM	230	5	0	137	8	62	57	17	-82
Perez,Carlos	22	R	26	C	aaa	CHW	418	14	1	188	5	88	71	28	29
	23	R	27	C	aaa	CHW	287	9	0	184	4	83	65	13	-2
Perez,Joe	22	R	23	3B	a/a	HOU	286	5	2	229	7	68	77	44	-36
	23	R	24	RF	a/a	PIT	438	15	4	234	9	67	88	60	-23
Perez,Robert	23	R	23	RF	aa	SEA	450	12	1	199	5	60	97	58	-54
Perez,Wenceel	22	B	23	2B	aa	DET	150	3	3	269	6	83	109	121	72
	23	B	24	2B	a/a	DET	428	6	18	226	10	79	65	121	25
Perkins,Blake	22	B	26	LF	a/a	NYY	329	11	14	190	10	65	106	124	6
	23	B	27	CF	aaa	MIL	156	3	3	243	10	68	109	85	5
Perlaza,Yonathan	22	B	24	RF	aa	CHC	470	14	9	196	8	68	116	89	10
	23	B	25	LF	aaa	CHC	461	13	8	222	10	69	114	83	14
Peroza,Jose	23	R	23	3B	a/a	NYM	379	8	3	209	9	59	108	66	-37
Peters,Tristan	22	L	22	LF	aa	SF	132	1	4	186	8	74	61	97	-8
	23	L	23	LF	aa	TAM	363	5	11	234	8	79	72	105	23
Peterson,Dustin	22	R	28	RF	aaa	PHI	396	6	4	177	6	68	71	67	-36
	23	R	29	RF	aaa	PHI	303	12	1	179	7	64	109	47	-27
Philip,Beau	23	R	25	3B	aa	ATL	226	3	2	173	10	52	76	60	-92
Phillips,Brett	22	L	28	CF	aaa	BAL	65	4	1	209	13	52	176	93	6
	23	L	29	CF	aaa	LAA	213	4	4	166	10	47	76	95	-103
Pinder,Chase	22	R	26	LF	a/a	STL	238	6	3	183	12	70	87	47	-11
	23	R	27	CF	a/a	STL	235	4	5	198	12	65	83	60	-31
Pineda,Israel	22	R	22	C	a/a	WAS	114	6	1	216	8	76	114	40	27
	23	R	23	C	aa	WAS	98	1	0	137	6	61	48	17	-97
Pinto,Rene	22	R	26	C	aaa	TAM	282	9	1	205	5	63	145	60	-2
	23	R	27	C	aaa	TAM	146	6	1	192	4	60	143	47	-21
Piscotty, Stephen	22	R	31	RF	aaa	CIN	109	4	0	213	5	67	91	4	-45
	23	R	32	LF	aaa	CHW	177	4	0	166	8	73	70	24	-29
Plawecki, Kevin	23	R	32	C	aaa	TEX	239	3	0	196	6	74	56	26	-36
Podkul,Nick	22	R	25	1B	aaa	TOR	175	4	2	175	12	60	79	49	-57
	23	R	26	1B	a/a	PHI	190	10	0	233	10	71	131	62	31
Polcovich,Kaden	22	B	23	2B	aa	SEA	451	8	12	188	8	69	71	110	-17
	23	B	24	2B	aa	SEA	131	2	4	138	12	62	68	107	-40
Porter,Logan	22	R	27	1B	a/a	KC	372	6	0	230	11	68	93	21	-25
	23	R	28	C	aaa	KC	379	7	1	175	9	65	67	28	-57
Potts,Hudson	22	R	24	1B	a/a	BOS	274	9	1	196	6	62	132	36	-22
	23	R	25	1B	aa	ATL	238	6	0	137	9	42	138	16	-97
Pozo,Yohel	22	R	25	C	aaa	TEX	253	3	0	243	3	85	71	32	12
	23	R	26	C	aaa	OAK	369	9	1	220	3	87	70	31	20

BATTER	yr	b	age	pos	lvl	org	ab	hr	sb	ba	bb%	ct%	px	sx	bpv
Ortega, Rafael	23	L	32	CF	aaa	NYM	281	5	8	153	11	72	63	67	-17
Prato,Anthony	23	R	25	2B	a/a	MIN	361	8	12	203	13	65	96	82	-10
Pratto,Nick	22	L	24	1B	aaa	KC	303	9	5	179	10	59	102	97	-31
	23	L	25	1B	aaa	KC	111	2	0	144	8	64	75	50	-50
Pries,Micah	22	L	24	1B	aa	CLE	448	13	14	223	6	69	114	114	18
	23	L	25	1B	aaa	CLE	401	9	2	180	8	70	89	61	-12
Prieto,Cesar	22	L	23	3B	aa	BAL	368	3	1	211	3	83	53	41	-8
	23	L	24	2B	a/a	STL	498	7	6	263	4	88	50	61	20
Proctor,Ford	22	L	26	C	aaa	SF	384	6	2	169	9	58	60	31	-91
	23	L	27	3B	aaa	SF	230	3	2	174	11	68	43	48	-56
Qsar,Jordan	22	L	27	LF	a/a	TAM	361	10	7	169	7	44	149	129	-50
	23	L	28	RF	aaa	PHI	233	7	7	187	11	49	128	93	-48
Quero,Edgar	23	B	20	C	aa	CHW	368	5	1	223	13	78	52	25	-10
Quero,Jeferson	23	R	21	C	aa	MIL	335	13	4	227	8	77	84	50	7
Quinn, Roman	22	B	29	CF	aaa	TAM	44	2	1	212	18	53	187	70	21
	23	B	30	CF	aaa	COL	140	1	8	133	8	49	79	112	-88
Quintana,Nick	22	R	25	3B	aa	CIN	189	3	0	188	9	69	75	32	-32
	23	R	26	3B	aa	CIN	111	2	0	110	10	61	72	38	-62
Quiroz, Esteban	22	L	30	2B	aaa	CHC	118	2	0	146	10	61	55	15	-85
	23	L	31	2B	aaa	PHI	325	4	4	165	9	75	56	59	-16
Radcliff,Baron	23	L	24	RF	aa	PHI	224	9	2	182	9	51	127	27	-65
Rafaela,Ceddanne	22	R	22	CF	aa	BOS	284	8	10	246	4	76	106	131	39
	23	R	23	CF	a/a	BOS	444	15	26	269	4	75	112	120	34
Raley,Luke	22	L	28	1B	aaa	TAM	227	8	5	221	7	57	114	79	-41
Ramirez,Agustin	23	R	22	C	aa	NYY	128	2	2	186	6	76	61	70	-12
Ramirez,Micael	23	R	24	C	aa	CLE	114	0	0	160	10	80	24	35	-26
Ramos, Henry	23	B	31	DH	aaa	CIN	280	9	3	230	8	69	97	58	-13
Ramos,Bryan	22	R	20	3B	aa	CHW	80	2	0	191	4	80	73	29	-4
	23	R	21	3B	aa	CHW	291	12	3	236	9	72	89	48	-5
Ramos,Heliot	22	R	23	CF	aaa	SF	427	6	4	179	6	70	61	62	-40
	23	R	24	RF	aaa	SF	227	7	6	246	8	66	115	102	3
Ramos,Jose	23	R	22	CF	aa	LA	416	16	5	217	9	62	98	48	-38
Raposo,Nick	22	R	24	C	aa	STL	204	3	1	192	6	69	93	47	-23
	23	R	25	C	a/a	STL	145	3	0	189	7	80	58	43	-5
Rave,John	22	L	25	CF	a/a	KC	430	8	13	200	8	67	70	94	-31
	23	L	26	CF	a/a	KC	463	7	7	205	9	66	77	69	-33
Ravelo, Rangel	23	R	31	1B	aaa	SD	203	4	0	203	10	75	55	30	-25
Redmond,Chandler	22	L	25	1B	aa	STL	327	10	0	162	6	61	93	50	-55
	23	L	26	1B	aa	STL	453	19	2	196	10	56	123	41	-42
Reed,Buddy	22	B	27	CF	a/a	LA	135	1	6	177	5	57	59	105	-81
	23	B	28	RF	aaa	MIL	113	3	3	155	9	52	115	65	-61
Reetz,Jakson	22	R	26	C	a/a	KC	367	15	1	202	5	66	133	52	-1
	23	R	27	C	aaa	SF	280	9	3	183	7	60	122	50	-31
Remillard,Zach	22	R	28	SS	aaa	CHW	418	6	11	197	7	66	61	90	-43
	23	R	29	3B	aaa	CHW	234	3	10	170	8	73	54	102	-15
Restituyo,Bladimir	23	R	22	CF	aa	COL	430	13	12	242	1	80	79	84	15
Reyes, Franmil	22	R	27	DH	aaa	CLE	32	1	0	226	3	72	104	65	-2
	23	R	28	DH	aaa	WAS	143	4	0	161	8	62	83	44	-55
Reyes, Pablo	22	R	29	2B	aaa	MIL	385	7	9	194	6	76	75	90	6
	23	R	30	2B	a/a	BOS	126	3	4	197	10	69	59	97	-25
Reyes,Ripken	22	B	25	RF	aa	SD	191	0	4	182	9	81	26	95	-6
	23	B	26	2B	aa	SD	409	5	23	204	9	76	46	120	-1
Reyes,Victor	22	B	28	DH	aaa	DET	27	2	1	247	9	91	108	95	97
	23	B	29	RF	aaa	CHW	502	14	2	205	4	69	84	48	-33
Rhodes,John	22	R	22	RF	aa	BAL	90	0	0	157	8	74	39	77	-32
	23	R	23	LF	aa	BAL	408	12	6	194	9	67	96	83	-9
Rice,Benjamin	23	L	24	C	aa	NYY	196	13	5	282	8	74	152	82	61
Richardson,Grant	23	L	24	RF	aa	NYY	53	4	4	292	8	57	166	68	-1
Rincones,Diego	22	R	23	DH	aa	SF	334	7	0	218	3	84	56	19	-6
	23	R	24	RF	aa	DET	182	5	0	202	6	82	64	34	3
Rios,Edwin	22	L	28	3B	aaa	LA	189	5	0	180	5	55	139	37	-47
	23	L	29	3B	aaa	CHC	152	3	0	187	7	54	104	28	-77
Ritter,Luke	22	R	25	3B	a/a	NYM	457	10	6	153	8	55	93	81	-63
	23	R	26	2B	a/a	NYM	369	18	4	188	12	54	125	60	-42
Rivas III,Alfonso	22	L	26	LF	aaa	CHC	94	1	0	229	6	63	75	68	-52
	23	L	27	1B	aaa	SD	208	5	5	229	12	68	104	93	7
Rivas,Leonardo	22	B	25	2B	a/a	CIN	311	5	12	188	8	69	68	92	-25
	23	B	26	SS	aa	SEA	329	3	35	197	14	66	46	116	-33
Rivera,Emmanuel	22	R	26	3B	aaa	KC	75	2	1	239	7	76	94	70	14
	23	R	27	3B	aaa	ARI	112	2	1	243	6	80	92	79	30
Rivera,Laz	22	R	28	2B	aaa	CHW	232	5	5	166	5	66	65	79	-47
	23	R	29	2B	aaa	CHW	147	0	3	166	4	63	46	87	-74
Rivero,Sebastian	22	R	24	C	aa	KC	156	3	1	179	5	74	110	47	10
	23	R	25	C	a/a	CHW	242	3	0	173	4	76	53	37	-34
Rizzo,Joe	22	L	24	3B	aa	SEA	488	14	1	214	6	74	89	48	-4
	23	L	25	3B	a/a	DET	300	6	1	199	6	73	79	43	-17
Roberts,Caleb	22	L	22	C	aa	ARI	31	0	0	269	4	78	69	97	7
	23	L	23	LF	aa	ARI	367	10	7	227	9	65	113	106	3
Roberts,Cody	22	R	26	C	a/a	BAL	266	6	0	209	6	64	96	20	-48
	23	R	27	C	aa	PHI	215	5	1	173	5	71	72	60	-28
Robertson,Daniel	22	R	28	SS	aaa	PHI	197	3	0	150	7	67	77	45	-42
	23	R	29	3B	aaa	ATL	177	2	0	164	8	72	41	43	-47
Robertson,Kramer	22	R	28	SS	aaa	STL	410	6	17	167	10	69	53	98	-28
	23	R	29	3B	aaa	STL	409	2	14	145	10	65	31	84	-69
Robertson,Will	22	L	25	LF	aa	TOR	307	8	1	166	5	64	108	37	-36
	23	L	26	LF	aa	TOR	363	15	7	204	7	65	132	84	5

BATTER	yr	b	age	pos	lvl	org	ab	hr	sb	ba	bb%	ct%	px	sx	bpv
Prato,Anthony	22	R	24	LF	aa	MIN	296	2	6	235	9	72	77	98	-1
Robinson,Errol	22	R	28	3B	aa	STL	119	0	6	177	9	56	35	81	-105
	23	R	29	3B	a/a	STL	255	1	5	162	7	61	34	71	-92
Rocchio,Brayan	22	B	21	SS	a/a	CLE	510	12	9	215	7	77	80	72	11
	23	B	22	SS	aaa	CLE	468	5	18	233	9	84	64	101	38
Rock,Dylan	23	R	25	LF	aa	TOR	117	4	5	174	7	57	99	86	-51
Roden,Alan	23	L	24	RF	aa	TOR	174	5	7	271	10	79	67	87	18
Rodriguez,Alberto	23	L	23	RF	aa	SEA	179	2	4	241	7	66	57	43	-60
Rodriguez,Alfredo	22	R	28	2B	a/a	WAS	150	1	1	153	2	63	49	28	-97
Rodriguez,Carlos	23	L	23	RF	aa	MIL	392	1	10	246	7	85	43	77	13
Rodriguez,Endy	22	B	22	C	a/a	PIT	140	6	1	321	8	81	158	61	87
	23	B	23	C	aaa	PIT	272	4	3	230	9	82	67	92	27
Rodriguez,Gabriel	23	R	21	3B	aa	CLE	250	3	2	175	12	62	60	73	-53
Rodriguez,Johnathan	22	R	23	RF	aa	CLE	107	4	0	175	3	54	164	82	-18
	23	R	24	RF	a/a	CLE	497	22	2	240	9	62	128	55	-13
Rodriguez,Jose	22	R	21	SS	aa	CHW	440	9	28	232	6	83	68	132	40
	23	R	22	2B	a/a	CHW	469	17	22	225	3	75	83	87	1
Rodriguez,Julio	22	R	25	C	aa	STL	218	5	1	175	10	66	68	34	-51
	23	R	26	C	aa	DET	260	10	0	176	8	62	86	22	-58
Rodriguez,Keyber	23	R	23	SS	aa	TEX	153	2	8	205	8	78	66	124	20
Rodriguez,Ramon	22	R	24	C	a/a	BAL	24	1	0	424	0	90	124	25	69
	23	R	25	C	a/a	BAL	153	2	1	190	11	87	42	35	17
Rodriguez,Yorman	22	R	25	1B	aa	SD	491	9	3	214	5	79	64	51	-5
	23	R	26	DH	a/a	SD	202	3	2	190	4	83	50	68	0
Roederer,Cole	22	L	23	LF	aa	CHC	181	5	2	189	5	65	82	49	-47
	23	L	24	LF	a/a	CHC	317	8	7	204	9	62	77	79	-46
Rojas,Johan	22	R	22	CF	aa	PHI	235	3	20	222	6	79	58	170	29
	23	R	23	CF	aa	PHI	320	8	24	274	6	79	90	134	43
Roller,Chris	22	R	26	CF	a/a	CLE	265	2	4	162	7	66	64	82	-44
	23	R	27	CF	aaa	MIL	312	11	13	194	13	55	121	81	-30
Romo,Drew	23	B	22	C	a/a	COL	344	10	4	232	5	80	87	61	18
Rooker,Brent	22	R	28	LF	aaa	KC	308	13	3	212	7	60	174	60	13
Rortvedt,Ben	22	L	25	C	aaa	NYY	154	4	0	173	8	55	116	28	-60
	23	L	26	C	a/a	NYY	108	4	1	230	10	64	116	49	-15
Rosa,Dylan	22	R	26	LF	a/a	DET	164	5	3	143	8	38	129	69	-107
Rosa,Joseph	23	B	26	SS	a/a	BAL	254	2	8	200	10	62	62	90	-54
Rosario,Dalvy	22	R	22	CF	aaa	MIA	21	0	1	339	9	68	86	144	3
	23	R	23	LF	aa	MIA	184	4	8	196	6	71	60	88	-29
Rosario,Eguy	22	R	23	2B	aaa	SD	490	12	12	211	7	73	93	92	9
	23	R	24	3B	aaa	SD	166	3	2	192	6	71	64	61	-31
Rosario,Jeisson	22	L	23	CF	aa	NYY	362	8	9	200	12	74	83	83	11
	23	L	24	RF	aa	NYY	344	8	8	184	15	57	94	55	-51
Rosier,Corey	23	L	24	RF	a/a	BOS	397	5	34	253	6	73	85	149	20
Rucker,Jake	22	R	23	2B	aaa	MIN	26	1	1	88	5	57	47	83	-96
	23	R	24	2B	aa	MIN	420	6	7	202	7	65	71	69	-46
Rudick,Matt	23	L	25	LF	aa	NYM	214	7	10	229	16	76	83	84	31
Ruiz,Agustin	22	L	23	RF	aa	SD	76	1	1	187	10	64	74	95	-33
	23	L	24	RF	aa	NYM	364	14	0	173	9	57	116	50	-44
Ruiz,Esteury	22	R	23	CF	a/a	MIL	437	11	59	273	10	74	102	150	44
	23	R	24	CF	aaa	OAK	20	1	2	312	3	70	106	118	8
Rumfield,T.J.	23	L	23	1B	aa	NYY	297	14	6	190	9	71	110	60	10
Rutherford,Blake	22	L	25	LF	aaa	CHW	439	9	5	203	3	75	75	64	-14
	23	L	26	RF	a/a	WAS	280	9	5	278	6	75	120	78	35
Sabato,Aaron	22	R	23	1B	aa	MIN	84	3	1	140	7	59	121	67	-32
	23	R	24	1B	aa	MIN	272	8	1	179	10	55	129	44	-41
Sabol,Blake	22	L	24	C	a/a	PIT	447	11	7	230	8	67	109	102	4
Saggese,Thomas	22	R	20	2B	aa	TEX	21	1	1	331	3	84	198	133	143
	23	R	21	2B	a/a	STL	555	18	9	261	6	72	104	95	13
Salazar,Cesar	22	L	26	C	a/a	HOU	366	10	5	198	5	76	77	64	-6
	23	L	27	C	aaa	HOU	173	1	2	141	10	76	40	47	-29
Sanchez, Yolmer	22	B	30	2B	aaa	NYM	322	6	3	167	9	63	72	60	-50
	23	B	31	3B	aaa	ATL	377	5	3	174	13	62	57	49	-63
Sanchez,Ali	22	R	25	C	aaa	DET	252	4	1	207	8	65	75	49	-47
	23	R	26	C	aaa	ARI	238	5	0	231	6	78	60	22	-19
Sanchez,Jesus	22	L	25	RF	aaa	MIA	159	4	3	246	8	70	76	65	-20
Sanchez,Jose	23	R	23	3B	aa	WAS	129	2	2	153	9	71	49	56	-39
Sanchez,Lolo	22	R	23	LF	aa	PIT	212	3	5	187	10	79	44	59	-9
	23	R	24	LF	aa	PIT	278	4	5	200	11	82	46	55	3
Sanchez,Yolbert	22	R	25	2B	a/a	CHW	494	2	7	218	5	81	29	50	-27
	23	R	26	3B	aaa	CHW	406	2	4	210	4	78	32	45	-38
Sands,Donny	22	R	26	C	aaa	PHI	201	3	1	239	11	73	60	44	-22
	23	R	27	C	a/a	DET	339	3	1	178	8	71	69	32	-31
Santana,Luis	23	R	24	3B	aa	DET	252	8	1	199	4	74	92	60	-3
Scheffler,Matt	22	R	24	C	aa	SEA	244	1	7	191	10	71	32	108	-37
	23	R	25	C	aa	SEA	216	1	6	162	9	66	29	76	-71
Scheiner,Jake	22	R	27	1B	aa	SEA	477	13	2	181	9	68	100	44	-17
	23	R	28	3B	aaa	SEA	460	17	3	176	9	61	106	62	-32
Schmitt,Casey	22	R	23	3B	a/a	SF	135	2	1	287	3	71	110	62	-3
	23	R	24	SS	aaa	SF	200	2	2	247	5	74	69	61	-19
Schneemann,Daniel	22	L	25	3B	a/a	CLE	387	4	12	155	7	69	43	109	-42
	23	L	26	3B	aaa	CLE	419	8	11	205	9	71	82	74	-8
Schneider,Davis	22	R	23	2B	a/a	TOR	226	6	8	227	10	67	105	121	11
	23	R	24	LF	aaa	TOR	309	15	6	227	13	68	134	61	25
Schobel,Tanner	23	R	22	2B	aa	MIN	177	1	2	191	10	74	40	55	-33
Schuemann,Max	22	R	25	2B	a/a	OAK	325	5	14	202	9	63	73	112	-37
	23	R	26	CF	a/a	OAK	402	5	14	206	10	69	66	111	-18

BATTER	yr	b	age	pos	lvl	org	ab	hr	sb	ba	bb%	ct%	px	sx	bpv
Robinson,Chuckie	22	R	28	C	a/a	CIN	203	4	3	206	4	69	73	61	-37
	23	R	29	C	aaa	CIN	369	9	4	211	5	72	66	55	-30
Schwartz,JT	23	L	24	1B	aa	NYM	245	3	3	263	9	78	72	75	11
Schwarz,JJ	22	R	26	C	a/a	OAK	276	5	1	212	8	64	82	32	-50
	23	R	27	C	a/a	OAK	268	4	0	157	8	65	57	20	-73
Schwecke,Trevor	22	R	25	1B	a/a	TOR	206	4	1	183	6	58	93	88	-52
	23	R	26	RF	a/a	TOR	295	6	9	225	8	70	81	81	-13
Scott,Connor	22	L	23	RF	aa	PIT	380	4	7	205	6	73	82	87	-2
	23	L	24	LF	aa	PIT	260	2	8	173	7	73	65	108	-5
Scott,Stephen	22	L	25	C	aa	BOS	206	4	5	197	12	72	86	90	11
	23	L	26	C	a/a	BOS	340	13	4	196	10	71	103	77	12
Scott,Victor	23	L	22	CF	aa	STL	282	5	32	275	4	82	53	126	20
Seagle,Chandler	22	R	26	C	aa	SD	239	2	1	154	6	62	57	50	-77
	23	R	27	C	a/a	SD	230	2	3	148	3	56	49	60	-109
Seigler,Anthony	23	B	24	C	aa	NYY	205	4	5	139	17	73	48	59	-18
Seise,Chris	23	R	24	3B	aa	TEX	322	3	10	173	6	57	77	77	-74
Selman,Shane	22	R	26	RF	aa	OAK	270	6	1	155	5	57	95	69	-62
Senger,Hayden	22	R	25	C	a/a	NYM	288	3	2	181	4	54	80	72	-87
	23	R	26	C	aa	NYM	261	4	2	154	11	56	70	61	-80
Serretti,Danny	23	B	23	3B	aa	DET	156	1	1	176	11	75	40	31	-34
Serven,Brian	22	R	27	C	aaa	COL	77	3	0	204	9	77	83	30	6
	23	R	28	C	aaa	COL	151	3	0	147	3	62	63	11	-92
Servideo,Anthony	23	L	24	SS	aa	BAL	244	1	5	169	7	51	61	77	-109
Severino, Pedro	22	R	29	C	a/a	MIL	140	3	2	237	4	70	89	60	-22
	23	R	30	C	aaa	SEA	241	6	4	164	5	69	69	74	-36
Severino,Yunior	22	B	23	3B	aa	MIN	143	5	0	220	6	62	122	25	-35
	23	B	24	3B	a/a	MIN	467	24	2	221	7	56	140	51	-33
Shackelford,Aaron	22	L	26	1B	a/a	PIT	413	15	7	177	6	61	125	86	-15
	23	L	27	1B	aaa	PIT	355	9	5	173	10	60	93	80	-39
Shaw, Chris	23	L	30	DH	a/a	CHW	193	8	1	144	11	45	147	35	-70
Shenton,Austin	22	L	24	3B	aa	TAM	195	5	0	185	9	56	105	46	-57
	23	L	25	3B	a/a	TAM	473	21	0	246	12	60	166	26	8
Shewmake,Braden	22	L	25	SS	aaa	ATL	278	5	7	222	6	76	77	104	11
	23	L	26	2B	aaa	ATL	474	11	19	186	5	73	80	119	3
Shrum,Dillan	23	R	25	1B	aa	KC	277	8	1	196	12	55	114	65	-42
Siani,Mike	22	L	23	CF	a/a	CIN	492	11	37	217	9	78	73	131	28
	23	L	24	CF	aaa	STL	409	6	15	180	11	68	59	99	-29
Sierra,Magneuris	22	L	26	CF	aaa	LAA	279	4	12	216	5	77	52	113	-5
	23	L	27	RF	aaa	ATL	193	1	8	170	7	64	38	105	-67
Sikes,Phillip	23	R	24	CF	aa	BOS	414	7	29	188	7	61	81	145	-30
Simon,Ronny	22	B	22	2B	aa	TAM	144	5	8	224	5	80	98	136	50
	23	B	23	2B	a/a	TAM	480	10	22	208	8	71	77	106	-2
Simoneit,Will	22	R	26	C	a/a	OAK	250	3	1	190	9	64	77	54	-44
	23	R	27	1B	aa	OAK	253	4	2	178	6	63	78	71	-52
Simpson,Colin	23	L	27	DH	aa	COL	208	5	0	186	8	62	108	17	-41
Singleton, Jonathan	22	L	31	1B	aaa	MIL	456	14	2	153	13	52	120	57	-49
	23	L	32	1B	aaa	HOU	298	14	1	208	11	66	115	28	-14
Skoug,Evan	22	L	27	C	aa	CHW	215	8	1	173	10	56	140	48	-28
	23	L	28	DH	aaa	CHW	123	3	0	126	9	57	91	35	-70
Slaughter,Jake	22	R	26	3B	aa	CHC	328	12	16	217	6	68	104	98	1
	23	R	27	3B	aaa	CHC	371	12	10	179	7	60	107	74	-35
Smith,Dominic	22	L	27	1B	aaa	NYM	218	6	2	207	7	76	78	64	2
Smith,Kevin	22	R	26	SS	aaa	OAK	332	6	3	185	4	58	84	67	-71
	23	R	27	SS	aaa	OAK	170	8	5	226	4	64	114	76	-21
Smith,Pavin	23	L	27	1B	aaa	ARI	239	4	1	233	10	75	69	55	-6
Smith-Njigba,Canaan	22	L	23	LF	aaa	PIT	184	1	5	233	11	69	92	111	5
	23	L	24	LF	aaa	PIT	389	11	15	234	9	67	104	78	-6
Snyder,Taylor	22	R	28	RF	aaa	COL	129	2	1	141	3	43	83	91	-125
	23	R	29	3B	a/a	CHW	241	5	8	132	8	56	62	81	-83
Soderstrom,Tyler	22	L	21	C	a/a	OAK	170	5	0	222	4	69	69	44	-45
	23	L	22	C	aaa	OAK	306	11	1	192	5	68	104	59	-14
Sogard,Nick	22	B	25	3B	a/a	BOS	402	2	12	210	9	75	60	93	-6
	23	B	26	3B	aaa	BOS	391	5	11	218	9	76	62	104	7
Solak,Nick	22	R	27	LF	aaa	TEX	223	5	3	200	7	71	91	76	-2
	23	R	28	LF	aaa	DET	345	4	2	177	9	72	53	58	-33
Sosa,Andres	23	R	26	C	aa	TOR	127	1	1	189	7	66	81	51	-42
Sosa,Lenyn	22	R	22	SS	a/a	CHW	483	18	2	260	5	80	89	44	18
	23	R	23	2B	aaa	CHW	288	13	0	228	4	71	116	21	-6
Soto,Livan	22	L	22	SS	aa	LAA	456	4	12	230	9	75	44	69	-25
	23	L	23	SS	a/a	LAA	405	7	1	198	9	67	66	49	-44
Soularie,Alerick	23	R	24	RF	aa	MIN	225	7	15	187	11	61	83	101	-37
Sparks,Lamar	23	R	25	RF	aa	MIL	292	7	13	206	10	49	121	113	-48
Stauss,Wade	23	L	24	DH	aa	STL	76	1	0	146	6	47	63	35	-136
Steer,Spencer	22	R	25	3B	a/a	CIN	427	18	3	229	8	75	125	60	35
Stefanic,Michael	22	R	26	2B	aaa	LAA	287	2	2	228	9	90	42	65	33
	23	R	27	2B	aaa	LAA	381	3	5	280	9	89	42	51	23
Stephens,Landon	23	R	25	RF	aa	ATL	341	17	2	172	11	47	172	33	-40
Stevens,Chad	23	R	24	SS	aa	HOU	418	12	17	187	10	50	122	109	-47
Stevenson,Andrew	22	L	28	CF	aaa	WAS	545	10	24	212	5	69	87	131	-4
	23	L	29	CF	aaa	MIN	416	10	27	233	6	69	84	130	-5
Stevenson,Cal	22	L	26	CF	aaa	OAK	257	3	8	198	8	74	47	103	-18
	23	L	27	CF	aaa	PHI	216	6	12	194	15	62	77	82	-35
Stewart, D.J.	22	L	29	RF	aaa	BAL	86	4	1	186	9	59	111	52	-40
	23	L	30	RF	aaa	NYM	188	8	0	153	10	67	95	23	-28

BATTER	yr	b	age	pos	lvl	org	ab	hr	sb	ba	bb%	ct%	px	sx	bpv
Schunk,Aaron	22	R	25	3B	aa	COL	450	9	4	211	4	72	93	62	-8
	23	R	26	3B	aaa	COL	458	9	7	230	5	71	78	72	-22
Stowers,Josh	23	R	26	LF	aa	LA	287	7	9	144	6	62	87	95	-39
Stowers,Kyle	22	L	24	CF	aaa	BAL	349	14	2	212	7	66	145	58	14
	23	L	25	RF	aaa	BAL	233	10	2	190	10	62	111	57	-22
Strahm,Kellen	22	R	25	RF	aa	TEX	354	6	7	213	10	68	66	79	-28
	23	R	26	RF	aa	TEX	438	4	6	195	10	69	49	75	-41
Strumpf,Chase	22	R	24	2B	aa	CHC	393	13	1	178	10	51	137	63	-44
	23	R	25	3B	a/a	CHC	349	13	3	180	12	53	126	68	-41
Stubbs,C.J.	22	R	26	C	aa	HOU	133	7	5	158	7	44	171	130	-31
	23	R	27	C	a/a	HOU	320	10	10	155	8	48	124	86	-68
Sullivan,Brett	22	L	28	C	aaa	SD	421	4	1	187	4	81	58	75	5
	23	L	29	C	aaa	SD	238	4	5	216	7	84	67	64	24
Suozzi,Joe	23	R	25	RF	a/a	NYM	227	5	3	208	9	61	61	74	-64
Suwinski,Jack	22	L	24	RF	a/a	PIT	168	5	1	206	6	57	150	64	-17
Swaggerty,Travis	22	L	25	CF	aaa	PIT	398	5	13	201	9	66	72	121	-23
	23	L	26	CF	aaa	PIT	65	1	2	161	5	67	83	149	-8
Sweeney,Trey	22	L	22	SS	aa	NYY	43	2	1	197	11	74	76	60	-3
	23	L	23	SS	aa	NYY	397	10	16	219	11	74	83	93	14
Swift,Drew	23	R	24	3B	aa	OAK	261	0	3	205	6	69	40	88	-52
Talley,L.J.	22	L	25	1B	a/a	TOR	394	9	8	212	6	74	76	95	-1
	23	L	26	1B	aaa	TOR	187	3	3	170	9	73	51	61	-30
Tapia, Raimel	23	L	29	RF	aaa	TAM	104	3	4	193	10	64	64	68	-51
Tatum, McCarthy	22	R	26	3B	aa	PHI	102	3	2	159	5	65	124	104	3
	23	R	27	LF	aa	PHI	138	2	2	200	4	70	72	44	-38
Tatum,Terrell	23	L	24	CF	aa	CHW	222	2	10	186	12	59	54	106	-62
Taveras,Leody	22	B	24	CF	aaa	TEX	204	4	4	227	4	72	85	99	-3
Tawa,Tim	22	R	23	2B	aa	ARI	218	3	2	152	6	71	47	50	-51
	23	R	24	2B	aa	ARI	434	12	7	202	8	68	86	61	-24
Taylor,Carson	22	B	23	C	aa	LA	269	3	0	207	6	71	51	22	-52
	23	L	24	C	aa	LA	249	8	1	191	8	70	71	50	-29
Taylor,Kennie	22	R	26	LF	aa	MIN	27	0	0	26	10	40	0	0	-218
Taylor,Samad	22	R	24	2B	aaa	TOR	244	7	17	220	8	71	91	133	15
	23	R	25	2B	aaa	KC	335	5	28	249	11	72	84	116	15
Tena,Jose	22	L	21	SS	a/a	CLE	535	10	5	224	3	70	81	87	-20
	23	L	22	SS	a/a	CLE	368	6	12	239	9	64	92	78	-28
Tenerowicz,Robbie	22	R	27	1B	a/a	CIN	193	5	1	206	10	67	97	52	-17
	23	R	28	1B	a/a	SEA	490	12	1	203	7	73	70	38	-25
Teodosio,Bryce	22	R	23	CF	aa	LAA	369	9	17	152	7	49	93	94	-86
	23	R	24	CF	aa	LAA	368	5	11	177	6	56	71	89	-79
Teter,Jacob	23	L	24	1B	aa	BAL	126	1	1	162	8	71	26	38	-66
Thaiss,Matt	22	L	27	C	aaa	LAA	284	6	4	188	8	73	75	82	-8
Thomas,Alek	22	L	22	CF	aaa	ARI	115	2	3	255	6	82	98	93	49
	23	L	23	CF	aaa	ARI	112	2	1	281	6	79	65	83	8
Thomas,Andy	23	L	25	C	aa	SF	381	7	4	193	10	67	71	59	-33
Thomas,Cody	22	L	28	LF	aaa	OAK	35	0	0	130	3	53	105	16	-93
	23	L	29	RF	aaa	OAK	429	10	3	203	4	71	88	77	-13
Thompson,Bubba	22	R	24	CF	aaa	TEX	346	8	30	235	4	68	73	161	-13
	23	R	25	CF	aaa	KC	266	4	18	212	6	72	67	123	-8
Thompson,Sterlin	23	L	22	2B	aa	COL	126	6	2	223	8	75	91	34	1
Tirotta,Riley	23	R	25	3B	aa	TOR	225	6	5	180	10	61	89	75	-41
Toerner,Justin	22	L	26	CF	a/a	STL	277	3	5	157	10	58	65	77	-71
	23	L	27	RF	a/a	STL	163	4	2	117	11	60	69	78	-57
Toglia,Michael	22	B	24	1B	a/a	COL	429	19	5	203	7	63	129	64	-10
	23	B	25	1B	aaa	COL	308	11	2	207	8	72	93	55	-4
Tolbert,Tyler	23	R	25	SS	aa	KC	518	7	36	236	5	74	69	148	6
Tolentino,Milan	23	L	22	SS	aa	CLE	116	0	2	188	11	67	30	57	-69
Tolve,Tyler	23	L	23	C	aa	ATL	193	6	2	216	8	65	94	53	-32
Torkelson,Spencer	22	R	23	1B	aaa	DET	131	3	1	186	11	66	85	38	-34
Toro,Abraham	22	B	26	2B	aaa	SEA	58	1	2	171	9	74	74	76	-3
	23	B	27	3B	aaa	MIL	357	6	5	230	9	74	100	68	14
Torrealba,Eduardo	23	R	24	3B	aa	NYY	132	1	3	172	7	74	38	78	-34
Torrealba,Yorvis	23	R	26	LF	aaa	COL	58	1	2	202	4	75	40	59	-40
Torres,Jose	23	R	24	SS	aa	CIN	294	5	8	160	8	58	70	94	-66
Tostado,Frankie	22	L	24	1B	aa	SF	292	7	2	238	5	71	93	57	-12
	23	L	25	1B	a/a	WAS	454	11	2	199	6	79	67	53	0
Tovar,Ezequiel	22	R	21	SS	a/a	COL	285	9	10	279	5	76	103	105	31
Trammell,Taylor	22	L	25	LF	aaa	SEA	87	3	5	249	7	75	103	88	25
	23	L	26	CF	aaa	SEA	317	13	10	196	10	58	128	67	-23
Trautwein,Mike	23	L	24	C	aa	CIN	136	2	2	201	10	65	75	79	-33
Trenkle,Caeden	23	L	22	CF	aa	OAK	166	1	1	207	5	66	48	81	-62
Tresh,Luca	22	R	22	C	aa	KC	91	3	1	211	8	71	93	47	-9
	23	R	23	C	aa	KC	334	7	1	199	9	78	59	51	-7
Triolo,Jared	22	R	24	3B	aa	PIT	425	5	16	229	9	77	67	112	14
	23	R	25	3B	aaa	PIT	185	1	7	236	13	64	90	113	-11
Tromp,Chadwick	22	R	27	C	aaa	ATL	249	9	0	208	5	73	95	33	-11
	23	R	28	C	aaa	ATL	224	6	0	159	11	69	75	20	-35
Tsutsugo, Yoshitomo	22	L	31	LF	aaa	TOR	123	5	0	229	13	57	133	21	-31
	23	L	32	1B	a/a	SF	223	6	2	194	13	54	102	72	-53
Tucker,Cole	22	B	26	SS	aaa	ARI	151	1	3	148	5	62	39	63	-88
	23	B	27	CF	aaa	COL	268	3	4	215	9	72	65	62	-23
Turang,Brice	22	L	23	SS	aaa	MIL	532	9	23	233	8	74	64	111	-3
Turconi,Michael	23	L	24	SS	aa	TOR	102	2	2	151	11	70	74	75	-12
Turner,Gionti	23	R	23	2B	a/a	TAM	194	1	7	186	7	63	36	81	-80

BATTER	yr	b	age	pos	lvl	org	ab	hr	sb	ba	bb%	ct%	px	sx	bpv
Stokes,Madison	22	R	26	CF	a/a	PHI	162	3	4	131	6	45	106	99	-91
	23	R	27	SS	aa	PHI	358	5	4	174	12	60	84	74	-45
Stovall,Hunter	22	R	26	SS	aa	COL	393	6	6	216	5	74	82	78	-3
	23	R	27	2B	aaa	COL	385	5	8	214	5	82	52	86	7
Stowers,Josh	22	R	25	CF	aa	TEX	356	6	14	168	8	61	85	110	-36
Urena,Richard	22	B	26	3B	aaa	WAS	134	1	1	181	3	74	50	38	-44
Urias,Luis	22	R	25	3B	aa	MIL	27	0	0	112	7	69	28	55	-70
	23	R	26	3B	aaa	MIL	116	3	1	185	10	63	81	45	-46
Valdes,Javier	22	R	24	C	aa	ATL	78	2	1	197	14	69	77	84	-6
	23	R	25	C	aa	ATL	239	6	1	203	14	68	94	43	-9
Valdez,Enmanuel	22	L	24	2B	a/a	BOS	500	18	5	251	8	72	127	68	28
	23	L	25	2B	aaa	BOS	189	7	3	213	12	71	99	87	16
Valenzuela,Sahid	22	B	25	2B	aa	OAK	90	2	0	158	3	78	70	62	-6
	23	B	26	2B	aa	OAK	178	1	2	214	5	81	37	55	-19
Valera,George	22	L	22	RF	a/a	CLE	484	16	2	207	9	66	111	63	-8
	23	L	23	CF	aaa	CLE	256	7	1	170	12	63	82	40	-45
Valera,Leonel	22	R	23	SS	aa	LA	321	10	15	239	6	57	111	140	-26
	23	R	24	SS	aa	KC	286	2	7	185	5	67	53	96	-47
Valerio,Felix	22	R	22	2B	aa	MIL	417	9	21	188	8	78	59	109	9
	23	R	23	2B	aa	MIL	264	5	5	188	5	76	58	90	-11
Vance,Cobie	22	R	25	3B	aa	MIA	395	3	1	198	5	80	47	38	-19
	23	R	26	3B	a/a	MIA	200	2	0	202	6	71	74	25	-36
VanMeter,Josh	22	L	27	2B	aaa	PIT	31	1	0	120	12	62	93	42	-39
	23	L	28	2B	aaa	MIL	141	4	1	151	18	60	78	59	-40
Vargas,Imanol	23	L	25	1B	aa	LA	447	18	0	213	11	54	148	19	-37
Vargas,Miguel	22	R	23	3B	aaa	LA	438	11	9	236	8	79	91	92	37
	23	R	24	2B	aaa	LA	236	7	5	239	11	71	96	64	6
Vaz,Javier	23	L	23	LF	aa	KC	112	1	3	270	9	83	54	91	24
Vazquez,Luis	22	R	23	SS	a/a	CHC	409	6	6	178	4	72	60	78	-30
	23	R	24	SS	a/a	CHC	454	13	7	221	8	69	84	48	-25
Veen,Zac	22	L	21	RF	aa	COL	124	1	3	153	6	66	40	64	-69
	23	L	22	RF	aa	COL	172	2	16	196	9	76	56	117	2
Vega,Onix	22	R	24	DH	aaa	WAS	20	0	0	248	3	66	45	6	-92
	23	R	25	C	a/a	WAS	176	0	1	196	11	73	27	44	-50
Velazquez,Andrew	23	B	29	SS	aaa	ATL	134	2	5	155	8	52	69	99	-87
Velazquez,Nelson	22	R	24	CF	a/a	CHC	203	9	8	187	8	52	167	105	-10
	23	R	25	CF	aaa	KC	314	10	6	192	6	64	95	63	-33
Vellojin,Daniel	22	L	22	C	aa	CIN	94	3	0	164	11	59	96	53	-46
	23	L	23	C	aa	CIN	237	3	2	172	10	70	66	52	-28
Veras,Wilfred	22	R	20	DH	aa	CHW	45	2	0	230	5	66	158	3	3
	23	R	21	RF	aa	CHW	152	5	4	269	4	69	131	85	14
Vientos,Mark	22	R	23	3B	aaa	NYM	378	16	0	223	7	61	123	37	-30
	23	R	24	3B	aaa	NYM	232	10	0	236	8	69	134	32	11
Vilade,Ryan	22	R	23	RF	aaa	COL	368	3	6	205	7	81	49	92	5
	23	R	24	CF	aaa	PIT	440	4	5	227	10	69	62	69	-35
Villar,David	22	R	25	3B	aaa	SF	298	15	1	210	10	62	158	54	14
	23	R	26	3B	aaa	SF	287	10	3	210	9	62	98	57	-36
Vivas,Jorbit	23	L	22	2B	a/a	LA	506	10	19	237	9	84	64	100	38
Voit, Luke	23	R	32	1B	aaa	NYM	156	8	1	177	13	53	153	53	-21
Volpe,Anthony	22	R	21	SS	a/a	NYY	511	16	38	210	9	74	110	144	47
Vosler,Jason	22	L	29	3B	aaa	SF	360	9	2	167	5	64	79	62	-52
	23	L	30	3B	aaa	CIN	313	13	2	173	7	60	115	37	-39
Vukovich,A.J.	22	R	21	LF	aa	ARI	44	1	1	240	1	67	48	46	-75
	23	R	22	CF	aa	ARI	456	14	13	217	6	65	95	101	-19
Waddell,Luke	22	L	24	SS	aa	ATL	162	2	2	233	10	84	58	48	19
	23	L	25	SS	a/a	ATL	476	6	22	234	12	82	45	86	14
Wade,Tyler	22	L	28	CF	aaa	NYY	145	3	10	167	11	67	72	124	-13
	23	L	29	2B	aaa	OAK	340	3	21	196	7	67	55	100	-41
Wagaman,Eric	23	R	26	1B	aa	NYY	122	4	10	263	7	72	91	85	3
Wagner,Max	23	R	22	3B	aa	BAL	111	2	1	221	5	67	88	76	-27
Wagner,Will	22	L	24	2B	aa	HOU	251	4	3	196	8	73	66	83	-13
	23	L	25	2B	a/a	HOU	233	5	3	278	8	74	96	70	10
Walker,Jordan	22	R	20	3B	aa	STL	461	10	13	238	7	73	90	102	8
	23	R	21	RF	aaa	STL	113	3	3	199	9	69	80	53	-23
Wall,Forrest	22	L	27	CF	aaa	SEA	412	3	30	178	5	60	53	129	-65
	23	L	28	CF	aaa	ATL	354	5	35	216	9	67	67	134	-20
Wallace,Cayden	23	R	22	3B	aa	KC	127	2	2	212	7	82	57	86	13
Wallner,Matt	22	L	25	RF	a/a	MIN	458	16	6	215	12	56	153	78	-6
	23	L	26	RF	aaa	MIN	254	7	0	228	10	57	132	55	-28
Walsh,Jared	23	L	30	1B	aaa	LAA	184	5	0	154	10	44	86	22	-127
Walton,Donnie	22	L	28	SS	aaa	SF	122	1	3	185	8	80	76	106	30
	23	L	29	2B	a/a	SF	157	3	2	186	8	79	51	44	-10
Ward,Ryan	22	L	24	LF	aa	LA	459	20	3	207	5	71	109	55	-2
	23	L	25	LF	aaa	LA	538	15	8	189	7	65	95	86	-22
Warmoth,Logan	22	R	27	RF	aaa	TOR	293	5	10	182	8	62	97	100	-28
	23	R	28	3B	aa	SEA	360	5	19	176	9	58	68	86	-68
Warren,Zavier	22	B	23	3B	aa	MIL	92	1	2	203	8	65	56	48	-61
	23	B	24	1B	aa	MIL	377	12	4	195	8	73	80	65	-8
Waters,Drew	22	R	24	CF	aaa	KC	313	6	11	212	6	66	84	134	-15
	23	R	25	CF	aaa	KC	52	1	1	275	7	73	150	112	60
Watson,Zach	22	R	25	CF	aa	BAL	331	6	3	158	4	58	77	89	-72
	23	R	26	CF	aa	BAL	187	5	8	166	5	65	88	110	-25
Weber,Andy	22	L	25	SS	aa	CHC	280	2	4	228	5	68	51	80	-53
	23	L	26	2B	aa	CHC	372	3	3	190	8	71	51	66	-36
Welker,Colton	22	R	25	3B	aaa	COL	37	1	0	256	8	79	68	32	-3
	23	R	26	DH	aaa	SF	135	0	1	185	13	68	28	33	-69
Wells,Austin	22	L	23	C	aa	NYY	211	9	5	217	9	68	110	88	7
Ulrich,Wyatt	22	L	26	CF	aa	SD	43	0	2	154	6	74	0	96	-62
Unroe,Riley	22	B	27	SS	aa	SEA	368	5	15	190	9	70	62	112	-17
	23	B	28	2B	a/a	SEA	320	6	12	179	10	63	66	91	-45
Urbaez,Francisco	22	R	25	2B	aa	CIN	164	2	1	228	8	77	74	66	5
	23	R	26	2B	a/a	CIN	284	5	3	210	8	73	55	47	-31
Westburg,Jordan	22	R	23	SS	a/a	BAL	544	20	8	219	8	70	125	82	22
	23	R	24	SS	aaa	BAL	268	11	4	237	7	73	106	89	18
Whalen,Brady	22	L	24	1B	aa	STL	98	0	3	223	4	76	88	137	26
	23	L	25	1B	aa	SF	143	3	2	222	4	80	78	83	20
Whatley,Matt	22	R	26	C	a/a	TEX	189	2	1	167	5	70	48	64	-50
	23	R	27	C	aaa	TEX	236	4	3	153	5	64	62	69	-62
Whitcomb,Shay	22	R	24	2B	aa	HOU	461	12	13	170	5	57	103	111	-43
	23	R	25	SS	a/a	HOU	538	25	14	194	5	60	117	65	-36
White, Tyler	22	R	32	1B	aaa	ATL	357	11	3	178	12	68	89	62	-11
	23	R	33	1B	aaa	NYM	101	1	0	176	10	69	41	20	-65
White,Eli	23	R	29	CF	aaa	ATL	169	6	9	191	10	54	95	99	-56
Whitefield,Aaron	22	R	26	LF	aa	LAA	301	6	17	197	7	62	93	126	-24
	23	R	27	LF	aa	LAA	105	2	8	149	7	45	104	99	-92
Whiteman,Simon	22	R	25	LF	aa	SF	85	0	3	134	6	58	49	95	-87
	23	R	26	SS	aa	SF	207	1	8	175	10	70	45	96	-33
Wiemer,Joey	22	R	23	RF	a/a	MIL	484	15	21	207	7	64	120	118	4
Williams,Alika	22	R	23	SS	a/a	TAM	38	0	1	169	11	53	57	36	-105
	23	R	24	SS	a/a	PIT	284	9	5	229	8	79	93	69	27
Williams,Carter	23	L	25	RF	aa	SF	172	3	3	193	5	72	49	69	-42
Williams,Chris	22	R	26	1B	a/a	MIN	422	16	1	184	8	59	127	39	-34
	23	R	27	1B	aaa	MIN	309	13	2	178	10	50	140	66	-46
Williams,Donta'	23	L	24	CF	aa	BAL	335	5	18	162	12	62	73	91	-41
Williams,Luke	22	R	26	2B	aaa	MIA	49	1	6	257	10	55	112	113	-36
	23	R	27	SS	aaa	ATL	355	8	19	203	9	68	72	110	-18
Wilson,Cody	23	R	27	CF	aaa	WAS	160	1	8	160	5	53	60	98	-97
Wilson,Ethan	22	L	23	LF	aa	PHI	70	1	1	176	5	66	43	53	-73
	23	L	24	LF	aa	PHI	419	14	9	219	5	70	105	81	2
Wilson,Izzy	22	L	24	RF	a/a	BOS	314	8	8	179	8	65	106	110	-5
Wilson,Marcus	22	R	26	RF	aaa	SEA	293	9	8	154	9	45	155	108	-41
	23	R	27	LF	aaa	BOS	59	1	3	117	8	36	104	108	-121
Wilson,Peyton	23	B	24	2B	aa	KC	489	4	14	250	7	78	70	93	13
Wilson,Weston	22	R	28	3B	aaa	MIL	416	7	10	164	6	59	76	87	-65
	23	R	29	SS	aaa	PHI	460	20	19	190	9	59	119	98	-19
Wilson,William	22	R	24	SS	a/a	SF	224	7	1	173	8	59	102	48	-50
	23	R	25	SS	a/a	SF	443	11	3	186	6	70	71	60	-32
Winaker,Matt	22	L	27	1B	aa	NYM	202	2	1	117	9	64	45	82	-63
Windham,Bryce	22	L	26	C	aa	CHC	253	2	1	145	9	79	39	52	-18
	23	L	27	C	aaa	CHC	186	1	2	221	8	73	43	71	-37
Wingrove,Rixon	23	L	23	1B	aa	PHI	47	1	0	111	10	56	36	0	-125
Winkel,Pat	23	L	23	C	aa	MIN	304	7	2	223	10	67	83	48	-29
WInkler,Jack	23	R	25	1B	aa	OAK	172	2	2	182	8	74	61	70	-16
Winn,Masyn	22	R	20	SS	aa	STL	345	6	17	197	7	73	81	109	8
	23	R	21	SS	aaa	STL	445	12	12	243	6	80	70	123	26
Wisely,Brett	22	L	23	2B	a/a	TAM	451	10	22	223	9	71	92	134	17
	23	L	24	2B	aaa	SF	221	4	5	234	13	66	105	68	-4
Witherspoon,Grant	22	L	26	RF	a/a	TAM	415	10	10	202	7	66	100	97	-12
	23	L	27	RF	a/a	DET	261	6	6	184	10	62	82	81	-41
Wolforth,Garrett	22	B	25	1B	aa	CIN	38	1	0	194	6	56	138	16	-47
	23	R	26	C	aa	HOU	193	3	2	170	4	57	82	55	-81
Womack,Alsander	23	R	24	2B	aa	CHW	380	6	5	211	9	79	41	38	-17
Wong,Connor	22	R	26	C	aaa	BOS	323	9	4	232	5	71	103	54	-6
Wong,Kean	22	L	27	3B	aaa	LAA	497	2	21	181	6	68	36	106	-53
	23	L	28	2B	aaa	CHW	148	4	3	203	9	72	59	57	-25
Wood,James	23	L	21	RF	aa	WAS	323	17	9	235	10	58	177	100	27
Workman,Gage	22	B	23	SS	aa	DET	475	9	21	193	5	53	139	150	-20
	23	L	24	SS	aa	DET	178	5	8	161	12	49	129	144	-32
Wyatt,Logan	23	L	26	1B	aa	SF	206	6	1	214	8	70	89	41	-16
Yang,Eric	22	R	24	C	a/a	CIN	151	2	1	172	8	62	71	47	-62
	23	R	25	C	a/a	CIN	119	1	0	175	8	64	52	19	-79
Yepez,Juan	22	R	24	1B	aaa	STL	188	9	0	211	5	72	118	29	5
	23	R	25	LF	aaa	STL	341	6	1	199	6	75	71	54	-13
Yorke,Nick	23	R	21	2B	aa	BOS	444	11	14	255	8	71	100	120	19
Young,Andy	22	R	28	LF	a/a	WAS	318	9	2	162	8	54	110	34	-68
Young,Chavez	22	B	25	CF	aaa	TOR	214	4	15	194	9	69	63	142	-12
	23	B	26	CF	a/a	PIT	302	4	23	165	10	72	53	102	-18
Young,Jacob	23	R	24	LF	a/a	WAS	221	3	13	259	6	79	65	112	16
Young,Jared	22	L	27	1B	aaa	CHC	400	10	2	170	6	66	91	72	-29
	23	L	28	1B	aaa	CHC	310	12	4	228	9	65	105	76	-13
Young,Wyatt	22	L	23	2B	a/a	NYM	445	5	5	216	9	72	61	79	-18
	23	L	24	SS	a/a	CHC	492	3	12	178	10	72	34	75	-40
Yurchak,Justin	22	L	26	1B	aa	LA	393	6	1	218	8	81	58	35	-2
	23	L	27	1B	aaa	LA	242	4	1	201	10	75	60	44	-18
Zamora,Freddy	22	R	24	SS	aa	MIL	91	1	3	164	4	71	46	80	-46
	23	R	25	SS	aa	MIL	377	5	12	205	9	71	58	88	-23
Zamora,Joshua	23	R	24	2B	aa	MIA	40	1	1	262	4	83	78	45	18
Zavala,Aaron	22	L	22	RF	aa	TEX	112	3	3	226	11	71	106	80	18
	23	L	23	LF	aa	TEX	341	4	5	162	13	48	79	50	-101
Zimmer, Bradley	23	L	31	CF	aaa	BOS	261	5	11	156	7	45	86	121	-98

PITCHER	yr	t	age	lvl	org	ip	era	whip	bf/g	k%	bb%	k-bb	hr/9	h%	s%	bpv
Abbott,Andrew	22	L	23	aa	CIN	91	5.05	1.44	19.4	27	10	17	0.8	35	65	95
	23	L	24	a/a	CIN	56	2.61	0.95	21.2	36	8	28	1.5	24	85	140
Abbott,Cory	23	R	28	aaa	WAS	56	5.75	1.54	18.8	22	15	7	1.4	28	65	47
Abel,Mick	23	R	22	a/a	PHI	116	4.42	1.26	20.7	24	13	11	1.2	24	69	68
Abeyta,Blane	23	R	25	aa	NYY	127	6.91	1.63	22.6	19	9	9	1.4	35	58	40
Acker,Dane	23	R	24	aa	TEX	46	2.93	1.34	16.0	22	13	9	0.8	27	81	71
Acosta,Daison	23	R	25	aa	NYM	36	6.09	1.69	5.6	20	17	4	1.6	29	67	32
Adams,Chance	23	R	29	aaa	COL	34	4.37	1.55	4.8	9	7	3	1.3	31	76	4
Adams,Travis	23	R	23	aa	MIN	111	5.52	1.48	18.4	18	9	9	1.1	32	64	49
Adon,Joan	23	R	25	aaa	WAS	89	4.90	1.58	23.1	17	10	7	1.0	33	71	42
Adon,Melvin	23	R	29	aaa	SF	40	8.38	2.38	6.5	18	19	-1	0.8	41	63	35
Aguiar,Julian	23	R	22	aa	CIN	56	4.75	1.35	21.3	23	5	17	1.2	35	68	101
Albright,Luke	23	R	24	aa	ARI	112	5.27	1.66	20.1	22	13	10	0.7	36	68	70
Alexander,Jason	22	R	29	aaa	MIL	64	3.15	1.36	20.6	14	7	7	0.7	31	79	50
	23	R	30	a/a	MIL	59	7.53	2.07	17.0	10	8	2	0.9	40	63	5
Alexy,A.J.	22	R	24	aaa	TEX	96	5.22	1.64	13.8	19	11	8	1.8	32	74	27
	23	R	25	aaa	CHW	21	13.37	2.71	7.3	14	36	-22	2.0	19	49	6
Allard,Kolby	22	L	25	aaa	TEX	89	4.20	1.31	18.4	24	9	15	1.7	29	75	66
Alldred,Cam	22	L	26	aaa	PIT	67	4.17	1.46	6.8	17	9	8	0.6	33	71	61
	23	L	27	aaa	PIT	107	6.09	1.56	15.1	15	10	5	1.4	31	63	23
Allen,Logan	22	L	24	a/a	CLE	134	4.45	1.28	20.4	27	8	19	1.0	33	67	104
	22	L	25	aaa	COL	53	7.21	1.76	9.0	14	7	7	2.0	36	62	5
Allen,Logan	23	L	25	aaa	CLE	21	3.02	1.25	17.2	25	11	14	0.4	30	76	101
	23	L	26	aaa	SEA	103	5.40	1.72	12.3	18	10	7	1.4	35	71	30
Allgeyer,Nick	22	L	26	aaa	TOR	101	6.53	1.60	12.7	17	9	7	1.8	32	62	19
	23	L	27	aaa	HOU	82	6.44	1.75	16.3	18	13	5	1.7	32	66	22
Alston,Garvin	23	L	26	aa	WAS	60	6.67	1.93	6.5	13	10	3	1.0	38	65	17
Alvarez,Nelson	23	R	25	aa	TAM	37	4.55	1.28	4.5	31	10	21	0.5	34	63	127
Anderson,Aidan	23	R	26	aa	TEX	55	4.19	1.47	7.2	25	9	15	0.4	37	70	102
Anderson,Grant	22	R	25	a/a	TEX	70	3.10	1.23	6.1	25	7	19	0.8	33	78	115
	23	R	26	a/a	TEX	42	3.70	1.22	6.8	29	9	20	1.6	29	78	93
Anderson,Shaun	23	R	29	aaa	PHI	52	5.73	1.69	21.3	11	7	4	2.2	33	73	-15
Andrews,Clayton	23	L	26	aaa	MIL	57	2.84	1.34	4.9	26	13	13	0.7	29	81	90
Andrews,Tanner	23	R	28	aaa	SF	54	6.24	1.87	9.4	16	12	4	0.9	37	66	35
Arias,Dayeison	23	R	26	aa	SEA	52	4.89	1.50	5.5	22	15	7	0.5	30	66	77
Arias,Jaime	22	L	23	a/a	CLE	48	5.73	1.59	14.1	15	7	7	1.1	34	65	38
	23	L	24	a/a	CLE	33	6.57	1.51	18.0	16	11	5	1.6	28	59	18
Armbruester,Justin	22	R	24	aa	BAL	64	3.77	1.06	17.7	20	6	14	2.0	23	76	65
	23	R	25	a/a	BAL	122	4.02	1.42	19.9	17	10	7	1.0	30	74	48
Armstrong,Ivan	23	R	23	aa	LAA	70	5.64	1.74	7.4	21	12	9	1.9	35	73	27
Arrighetti,Spencer	23	R	23	a/a	HOU	126	4.40	1.24	18.3	24	11	14	0.8	28	65	88
Assad,Javier	22	R	25	a/a	CHC	111	2.45	1.21	19.5	20	7	13	0.7	30	83	89
	23	R	26	aaa	CHC	16	3.30	1.20	16.3	18	10	8	0.0	28	70	88
Avila,Nick	23	R	26	aaa	SF	72	3.17	1.38	5.4	17	12	5	0.7	28	79	54
Avila,Pedro	22	R	25	aaa	SD	112	3.67	1.22	15.1	22	9	13	0.9	28	73	83
	23	R	26	aaa	SD	57	6.77	1.68	13.6	15	10	5	1.6	33	62	16
Bachar,Lake	22	R	27	aa	SD	46	6.35	1.57	7.5	17	9	8	1.8	32	63	24
	23	R	28	aa	SD	61	3.19	1.46	6.2	21	10	11	0.7	33	80	72
Backhus,Kyle	23	L	25	a/a	ARI	70	3.36	1.40	5.8	21	10	11	0.6	32	77	75
Baez,Michel	22	R	26	a/a	SD	42	4.84	1.39	4.8	22	11	10	1.0	29	67	66
	23	R	27	a/a	SD	39	6.45	1.80	6.3	12	15	-3	1.3	30	65	9
Bain,Jeff	22	R	26	a/a	ARI	71	3.13	1.12	6.2	21	6	15	1.3	27	79	90
	23	R	27	aa	ARI	56	7.26	1.74	13.5	14	6	8	2.2	36	62	5
Baker,Drew	23	R	23	aa	PHI	41	9.95	2.18	5.0	26	24	3	1.6	35	54	51
Baker,Robbie	23	R	28	aa	MIL	55	6.80	1.81	8.2	18	8	9	3.0	35	71	-12
Balazovic,Jordan	22	R	24	aaa	MIN	72	6.65	1.88	15.4	18	9	9	2.0	38	69	17
	23	R	25	aaa	MIN	47	5.18	1.74	9.8	21	15	6	0.9	34	71	56
Baldonado,Alberto	22	L	29	aaa	WAS	64	4.30	1.29	4.7	23	11	12	0.7	29	67	81
	23	L	30	aaa	WAS	31	3.44	1.49	4.6	17	14	3	0.7	28	78	51
Banda,Anthony	23	L	30	aaa	WAS	66	8.94	2.09	9.8	14	11	4	1.4	40	57	8
Baragar,Caleb	22	L	28	aaa	ARI	48	4.78	1.51	4.8	18	12	6	2.1	27	77	13
	23	L	29	aaa	CLE	33	6.88	1.85	6.7	20	19	0	1.6	29	65	26
Barclay,Edgar	23	L	25	a/a	NYY	79	4.45	1.58	16.6	24	13	12	1.4	33	76	56
Barger,Alec	23	R	25	aa	COL	53	7.74	1.81	5.7	19	13	5	1.3	35	57	35
Barlow,Joe	23	R	28	aaa	KC	44	6.31	1.89	6.5	15	9	6	1.9	37	71	1
Barnett,Mason	23	R	23	aa	KC	34	3.85	1.21	19.7	25	8	16	0.5	31	68	108
Bash,Andrew	22	R	26	a/a	TOR	97	4.55	1.29	11.8	14	9	5	0.4	28	63	59
	23	R	27	a/a	TOR	92	2.77	1.35	10.7	16	12	4	0.9	26	83	48
Battenfield,Peyton	22	R	25	aaa	CLE	155	3.10	1.20	22.3	14	8	6	0.8	26	77	53
	23	R	26	a/a	NYM	67	5.51	1.49	22.4	9	11	-2	1.6	25	67	-6
Bazardo,Eduard	22	R	27	aaa	BOS	58	3.84	1.63	7.0	18	8	10	0.8	37	78	62
	23	R	28	aaa	SEA	49	3.04	1.20	5.4	23	7	16	0.3	32	74	114
Beck,Tristan	22	R	26	a/a	SF	112	5.34	1.44	21	19	7	12	0.8	34	63	74
	23	R	27	aaa	SF	26	6.35	1.55	13	18	13	5	2.6	26	67	-4
Beck,Tyler	23	R	28	a/a	WAS	41	7.35	1.90	7.4	18	14	3	1.6	34	63	17
Beers,Blake	23	R	25	aa	OAK	82	7.86	1.70	21	16	9	7	1.4	35	54	25
Beeter,Clayton	22	R	24	aa	NYY	77	4.78	1.48	13	32	13	19	1.3	35	71	98
	23	R	25	a/a	NYY	133	4.12	1.47	21	24	13	11	1.3	30	76	63
Belge,Jeff	23	L	26	aa	TAM	53	3.80	1.49	5.6	26	14	13	0.4	34	74	98
Bello,Brayan	22	R	23	a/a	BOS	98	2.40	1.04	21	28	9	19	0.5	27	79	126
Benitez,Jorge	23	L	24	aa	SEA	59	2.23	1.32	6.1	26	14	12	0.4	28	84	98
Bennett,Nick	22	L	25	a/a	MIL	126	5.31	1.45	21	19	9	11	1.4	32	66	51
	23	L	26	a/a	MIL	65	4.94	1.54	8.6	19	9	10	1.4	33	71	45
Benschoter,Sam	23	R	25	aa	CIN	125	8.73	1.86	22	20	12	8	2.8	34	57	-8
Bentley,Denny	22	L	24	aa	MIN	38	3.55	1.49	5	23	14	9	0.4	31	76	86
	23	L	25	aa	MIN	44	4.41	1.64	6.8	19	9	10	0.6	37	73	67
Benton,Trey	23	R	25	aa	CLE	47	4.90	2.01	5.4	23	15	8	1.1	41	78	52

PITCHER	yr	t	age	lvl	org	ip	era	whip	bf/g	k%	bb%	k-bb	hr/9	h%	s%	bpv
Bergert,Ryan	23	R	23	aa	SD	44	3.10	1.18	19.5	25	10	16	0.2	30	72	115
Bergner,Austin	22	R	25	a/a	DET	122	3.53	1.18	18.1	19	9	10	1.1	25	74	64
	23	R	26	a/a	DET	75	6.23	1.73	9.2	21	12	9	1.1	36	64	52
Bermudez,Jonathan	22	L	27	aaa	SF	81	8.67	1.86	15.8	16	11	5	2.1	35	55	2
	23	L	28	aa	MIA	95	5.73	1.63	22.3	19	10	9	1.5	34	68	36
Berroa,Prelander	23	R	23	aa	SEA	66	2.93	1.23	6.2	33	13	21	0.3	32	75	135
Bertrand,John	23	L	25	aa	SF	52	5.88	1.73	21.5	14	10	4	0.2	37	63	50
Bettencourt,Trevor	23	R	29	a/a	LA	61	6.60	1.82	6.6	15	10	5	0.7	37	62	37
Biasi,Dante	22	L	25	aa	KC	85	3.99	1.47	16.6	18	13	5	0.6	29	73	59
	23	L	26	aa	KC	69	5.33	1.73	8.7	18	17	1	1.6	28	73	24
Bibee,Tanner	22	R	23	aa	CLE	75	1.90	0.91	21.6	25	5	20	0.5	26	81	162
	23	R	24	aaa	CLE	16	1.66	1.01	20.6	26	13	13	0.0	22	82	118
Bice,Dylan	23	R	26	a/a	MIA	55	5.98	1.70	6.1	17	10	7	2.0	33	70	11
Bido,Osvaldo	22	R	27	aaa	PIT	112	4.77	1.62	15.6	18	13	5	1.3	31	74	38
	23	R	28	aaa	PIT	64	4.94	1.48	14.5	17	11	6	0.9	30	68	46
Bielak,Brandon	22	R	26	aaa	HOU	90	3.03	1.43	16.7	18	11	8	0.5	31	79	68
	23	R	27	aaa	HOU	55	5.40	1.53	18.4	21	8	14	1.0	36	65	74
Bienlien,Michael	23	R	25	aa	DET	33	10.20	1.94	6.8	19	11	7	1.3	39	45	32
Bigge,Hunter	23	R	25	a/a	CHC	56	4.45	1.46	5.7	23	13	9	0.5	31	69	79
Bilous,Jason	22	R	25	a/a	CHW	107	5.99	1.74	15.8	21	15	6	1.2	33	67	49
	23	R	26	aaa	CLE	50	5.92	2.25	6.7	17	21	-4	1.2	35	75	26
Birlingmair,Reid	23	R	27	aa	TEX	30	2.38	1.39	7.5	20	8	11	1.0	32	88	65
Bivens,Spencer	23	R	29	aa	SF	78	5.08	1.62	12.8	16	12	4	0.4	33	67	53
Black,Grant	22	R	28	a/a	STL	79	3.43	1.33	7.3	12	9	3	0.9	27	77	34
	23	R	29	aaa	STL	79	7.16	2.11	9.1	13	12	1	1.5	38	68	-1
Black,Mason	23	R	24	a/a	SF	125	4.07	1.29	17.7	25	10	15	1.0	30	71	86
Blackwood,Nolan	22	R	27	aaa	DET	51	3.99	1.48	5.0	13	9	5	1.4	30	78	18
	23	R	28	aaa	SEA	48	4.58	1.47	5.7	13	8	5	0.2	33	66	59
Blanchard,Jason	22	L	25	aa	SD	15	4.82	1.52	10.9	26	13	13	0.5	35	67	87
	23	L	26	aa	SD	38	8.14	1.99	6.3	21	10	11	1.5	42	60	39
Blanco,Ronel	22	R	29	aaa	HOU	46	3.67	1.28	4.3	24	10	14	1.5	27	79	63
	23	R	30	aaa	HOU	74	3.98	1.29	20.3	20	13	8	1.3	24	74	52
Blewett,Scott	22	R	26	a/a	CHW	123	5.69	1.66	20.4	16	8	7	1.3	35	68	31
	23	R	27	aa	ATL	74	5.68	1.46	18.7	20	10	9	1.0	31	62	56
Bolanos,Ronald	23	R	27	aaa	MIA	67	9.96	2.26	21.3	11	14	-4	1.2	38	54	-5
Bolton,Cody	22	R	24	aaa	PIT	77	3.01	1.28	10.5	21	12	9	0.4	27	76	83
	23	R	25	aaa	PIT	48	4.25	1.31	5.9	18	9	9	0.4	30	66	76
Booser,Cam	22	L	30	aa	ARI	25	6.51	2.03	6.4	19	18	0	1.5	34	70	19
	23	L	31	aaa	BOS	59	5.93	1.56	5.4	18	10	9	2.0	31	67	22
Boushley,Caleb	22	R	29	aaa	MIL	128	3.63	1.34	21.3	14	9	5	0.9	28	76	38
	23	R	30	aaa	MIL	137	6.14	1.64	21.1	14	9	5	1.4	33	65	17
Bowden,Ben	23	L	29	aaa	PHI	53	5.41	1.72	4.9	23	14	9	1.6	34	72	45
Bowlan,Jonathan	23	R	27	a/a	KC	102	6.92	1.79	19.6	16	10	6	1.6	36	64	16
Boyle,Joe	23	R	24	a/a	OAK	118	3.44	1.42	20.0	27	17	10	0.4	28	75	99
Boyle,Michael	23	L	29	a/a	MIN	66	4.38	1.44	5.8	18	14	4	1.5	25	75	32
Boyle,Sean	22	R	26	a/a	NYY	156	4.02	1.22	22.5	21	5	15	1.5	30	73	84
	23	R	27	aaa	NYY	35	7.60	1.82	18.0	18	8	10	1.9	39	60	25
Bracho,Silvino	22	R	30	aaa	ATL	58	3.72	1.36	6.4	23	5	17	0.8	36	74	113
	23	R	31	aaa	CIN	52	6.05	1.56	4.9	17	9	8	3.9	26	79	-41
Bradford,Cody	22	L	24	aa	TEX	120	4.66	1.23	18.7	20	6	14	1.1	30	64	87
	23	L	25	aaa	TEX	75	3.72	1.24	21.8	17	5	12	0.7	31	71	88
Bradley,Taj	22	R	21	a/a	TAM	134	2.31	0.99	18.2	24	5	19	0.7	27	80	137
	23	R	22	aaa	TAM	39	5.88	1.46	16.8	20	11	9	1.8	29	64	31
Branche,Stevie	22	R	25	aa	CIN	36	6.33	2.04	6.3	22	20	2	1.7	33	72	28
	23	R	26	aa	CIN	42	5.83	1.65	6.1	26	19	7	0.6	31	63	84
Bravo,Jose	22	R	25	aa	HOU	109	4.33	1.40	19.2	18	7	11	1.2	32	73	58
	23	R	26	a/a	MIN	36	6.98	1.76	11.8	15	10	6	2.5	33	67	-14
Braymer,Ben	23	L	29	aaa	COL	60	11.57	2.42	19.7	9	11	-2	3.3	39	55	-79
Bremer,Noah	23	R	27	aa	TEX	47	6.96	1.73	15.3	12	11	1	1.5	32	61	1
Brewer,Michael	23	R	23	aa	TEX	43	6.34	1.72	5.6	16	14	2	1.5	30	65	19
Brice,Austin	22	R	30	aaa	PIT	45	6.03	1.54	5.3	19	10	9	1.3	33	62	46
	23	R	31	aaa	MIN	41	7.55	1.93	5.3	17	15	2	0.9	36	60	35
Brigden,Trevor	22	R	27	a/a	TAM	61	2.98	0.99	6.3	28	4	25	1.0	30	75	191
	23	R	28	aaa	TAM	78	3.74	1.33	7.4	23	12	11	1.1	27	75	69
Briggs,Austin	22	L	27	aa	OAK	33	3.89	1.65	5.3	16	13	4	0.9	32	78	42
	23	L	28	aa	OAK	42	5.17	1.82	4.9	18	17	1	0.4	33	70	58
Brink,Jordan	22	R	29	a/a	MIN	30	6.76	1.85	5.2	18	12	6	1.1	37	63	33
	23	R	30	aa	MIN	33	6.83	1.83	5.5	13	15	-2	1.1	31	63	16
Bristo,Braden	22	R	28	aaa	NYY	54	5.10	1.74	6.0	21	13	7	1.1	35	72	48
	23	R	29	aaa	DET	51	8.71	2.02	5.6	18	14	4	2.3	36	59	-2
Brito,Jhony	22	R	24	a/a	NYY	114	3.05	1.20	17.7	17	7	10	0.7	28	77	71
	23	R	25	aaa	NYY	37	5.81	1.63	23.6	17	9	7	1.9	32	70	15
Brito,Raul	23	R	26	aa	SD	41	3.03	1.56	10.6	24	11	13	0.2	38	80	95
Broadway,Taylor	22	R	25	aa	BOS	56	4.78	1.45	5.7	28	6	22	1.4	39	71	121
	23	R	26	a/a	BOS	38	6.50	1.69	6.9	14	9	5	3.0	30	71	-29
Brock,T.J.	23	R	24	aa	TOR	33	7.52	1.71	4.7	31	9	22	2.1	43	59	77
Brown,Aaron	23	R	24	aa	HOU	104	4.68	1.52	17.4	21	8	13	1.2	36	72	65
Brown,Ben	23	R	24	a/a	CHC	94	4.24	1.39	15.3	27	13	14	0.8	31	71	90
Brown,Hunter	22	R	24	aaa	HOU	106	2.39	1.06	17.9	27	10	17	0.4	27	78	122
Brown,Tyler	22	R	24	aa	HOU	65	6.45	1.62	17.0	20	9	12	2.0	35	64	36
	23	R	25	a/a	HOU	57	3.81	1.35	5.5	20	12	8	1.3	26	77	49
Brown,Zack	22	R	28	aaa	MIL	51	4.25	1.32	4.3	19	9	10	0.7	29	68	68
	23	R	29	aaa	CIN	36	8.62	1.89	9.0	6	14	-7	1.2	30	53	-18
Bukauskas,J.B.	22	R	26	aaa	ARI	21	2.16	1.15	4.0	19	4	14	0.3	31	82	124
	23	R	27	aaa	MIL	44	3.97	1.45	5.2	21	7	14	0.7	36	73	87
Burch,Tyler	22	R	25	aa	BAL	45	5.69	1.46	5.8	18	8	10	2.2	30	68	21
	23	R	26	aa	BAL	41	3.81	1.72	7.2	14	12	2	1.1	33	81	23

PITCHER	yr	t	age	lvl	org	ip	era	whip	bf/g	k%	bb%	k-bb	hr/9	h%	s%	bpv
Burgos,Raymond	23	L	25	a/a	SF	60	3.73	1.37	6.8	18	10	7	0.8	29	75	57
Burke,Sean	22	R	23	a/a	CHW	80	4.99	1.47	16	26	9	16	1.3	35	69	79
	23	R	24	aaa	CHW	38	7.96	1.75	19	16	16	0	2.4	27	59	-11
Burnette,Jimmy	23	L	25	a/a	TOR	45	7.98	1.73	4.9	25	16	8	0.8	34	51	71
Burns,Tanner	22	R	24	aa	CLE	90	3.77	1.39	18	20	11	9	1.4	28	79	49
	23	R	25	aa	CLE	88	3.79	1.46	13	18	12	6	1.3	28	79	40
Burrows,Beau	22	R	26	aaa	LA	101	6.03	1.71	15	16	11	5	1.4	34	67	26
	23	R	27	a/a	ATL	77	6.79	1.70	9.4	18	11	7	1.7	33	63	22
Bush,Ky	22	L	23	aa	LAA	103	3.44	1.17	20	20	6	14	1.1	29	75	86
	23	L	24	aa	CHW	69	6.92	1.67	21	18	12	6	2.4	30	64	1
Butto,Jose	22	R	24	a/a	NYM	129	3.18	1.18	19	22	7	15	0.9	29	77	92
	23	R	25	aaa	NYM	91	5.64	1.66	21	17	12	6	1.3	33	68	31
Byrne,Michael	22	R	25	a/a	CIN	64	5.07	1.60	6.8	22	11	11	1.2	35	71	56
	23	R	26	aa	CIN	52	3.43	1.35	7	24	8	16	1.2	33	80	81
Caceres,Kelvin	23	R	23	a/a	LAA	45	4.48	1.37	4.6	29	13	16	0.6	32	67	104
Cachutt,Manuel	23	R	26	aa	CIN	50	5.36	1.50	8.3	14	13	0	2.0	24	71	1
Calvo,Blair	23	R	27	aaa	DET	58	7.65	2.02	5.3	18	16	2	1.0	37	61	37
Camarena,Daniel	23	L	31	aa	SD	71	7.56	1.81	13	12	5	7	1.3	39	58	24
Cameron,Noah	23	L	24	aa	KC	73	6.94	1.70	19	17	8	10	1.6	36	61	30
Cannon,Jonathan	23	R	23	aa	CHW	49	6.17	1.66	20	15	7	8	1.7	35	66	21
Cantillo,Joey	22	L	23	aa	CLE	62	1.99	1.08	17	31	11	20	0.3	28	82	134
	23	L	24	a/a	CLE	120	4.48	1.56	20	23	14	9	1.4	31	75	53
Carver,Ross	23	R	24	aa	CLE	73	7.55	1.62	17	21	12	9	1.3	34	53	48
Case,Brad	22	R	26	a/a	PIT	72	4.65	1.52	8.7	16	8	8	0.7	34	70	54
	23	R	27	a/a	PIT	32	7.86	2.12	9.4	13	12	1	1.6	38	64	-8
Casparius,Ben	23	R	24	aa	LA	72	7.77	1.68	18	20	11	9	2.2	33	57	15
Castaneda,Victor	22	R	24	a/a	MIL	122	4.10	1.38	20	19	10	10	1.2	30	74	55
	23	R	25	a/a	TAM	17	5.54	1.59	8.4	22	13	9	1.6	32	69	44
Castano,Blas	23	R	25	a/a	SEA	81	4.14	1.30	13	19	9	10	0.8	29	69	68
Castano,Daniel	23	L	29	aaa	MIA	63	5.63	1.53	16	15	10	5	1.6	30	67	18
Castillo,Diego	23	R	29	aaa	SEA	48	5.06	1.83	5.2	17	14	3	0.8	35	73	40
Castillo,Jose	22	L	26	aaa	SD	44	2.34	1.36	4.3	26	10	16	0.4	34	84	105
	23	L	27	aaa	MIA	39	8.67	2.00	5.2	19	13	6	1.5	39	56	26
Castillo,Max	22	R	23	a/a	KC	79	3.41	1.20	18	20	8	12	0.7	28	73	86
	23	R	24	aaa	KC	116	4.79	1.32	22	15	5	10	2.1	28	72	28
Cate,Tim	22	L	25	aa	WAS	57	7.29	1.65	23	16	8	7	1.6	34	57	24
	23	L	26	a/a	WAS	44	4.76	1.68	4.7	18	14	4	1.0	32	73	41
Cavalli,Cade	22	R	24	aaa	WAS	97	3.77	1.19	19	21	9	12	0.3	29	67	99
Cecconi,Slade	22	R	23	aa	ARI	131	3.77	1.24	21	19	5	14	1.1	31	74	95
	23	R	24	aaa	ARI	117	5.30	1.31	21	20	6	14	1.2	31	62	73
Cellucci,Brendan	23	L	25	aa	BOS	51	6.66	2.07	6.7	20	13	7	1.5	40	70	28
Cessa,Luis	23	R	31	aaa	WAS	42	10.24	2.10	9.4	15	10	5	2.2	39	52	-12
Chacin,Jose	22	R	25	aa	NYM	103	5.32	1.41	19	18	7	11	1.2	33	64	60
	23	R	26	a/a	NYM	107	5.81	1.43	16	17	7	9	1.9	30	64	26
Chaidez,Adrian	22	R	23	aa	HOU	79	5.82	1.57	16	20	14	6	1.7	29	67	33
	23	R	24	aa	HOU	46	7.34	1.62	11	21	16	5	1.3	29	54	47
Chamberlain,Christian	23	L	24	a/a	KC	58	5.08	1.48	5.5	26	19	7	0.7	26	65	84
Champlain,Chandler	23	R	24	aa	KC	73	4.40	1.33	22	16	8	8	1.3	28	71	43
Charle,Cristian	23	R	23	a/a	MIA	44	3.40	1.28	6.9	22	12	10	2.1	23	86	34
Charles,Wandisson	23	R	27	a/a	BAL	46	5.32	1.45	4.8	26	18	8	0.8	26	63	82
Chentouf,Yaya	22	R	25	aa	DET	59	3.03	1.19	4.8	21	6	15	0.9	30	78	98
	23	R	26	aa	DET	30	9.28	2.44	7.2	12	13	-2	0.9	43	60	5
Church,Marc	23	R	22	a/a	TEX	62	3.63	1.48	6.2	26	13	12	1.0	32	79	76
Clarke,Chris	22	R	23	aa	CHC	98	4.26	1.42	21	17	4	13	0.7	36	71	105
	23	R	24	aaa	CHC	76	4.61	1.50	9.4	17	7	9	0.5	35	68	68
Claudio,Alexander	22	L	30	aaa	NYM	48	3.98	1.38	6.1	15	7	8	1.2	30	75	43
	23	L	31	aaa	MIL	43	5.09	1.90	4	10	7	3	0.2	39	71	31
Clay,Sam	22	L	29	aaa	NYM	43	3.56	1.54	4.7	19	9	10	0.6	35	78	67
	23	L	30	aaa	DET	53	5.92	1.79	5.8	15	13	2	1.3	33	69	21
Clenney,Nolan	23	R	27	a/a	NYM	66	6.19	1.69	8.1	22	11	11	1.3	37	65	54
Cobb,Trey	22	R	28	a/a	NYM	72	3.85	1.30	7.4	18	9	8	0.7	29	71	65
	23	R	29	aaa	PHI	31	7.55	1.89	4.3	17	23	-6	0.7	27	58	48
Cody,Kyle	23	R	29	aaa	TEX	77	6.60	1.78	11	14	8	5	1.8	35	66	2
Coffey,Isaac	23	R	23	aa	BOS	58	4.67	1.30	20	25	9	16	2.0	28	72	58
Cohen,Chase	22	R	25	aa	OAK	58	3.13	1.32	5.5	22	11	11	0.6	29	78	83
	23	R	26	a/a	OAK	56	5.43	1.65	5.5	19	14	5	0.6	33	66	58
Coker,Calvin	23	R	27	aa	OAK	75	3.34	1.47	7	11	8	4	0.4	32	77	43
Coleman,Dylan	23	R	27	aaa	KC	32	4.99	1.70	4.6	24	22	2	0.8	27	71	72
Colina,Edwar	23	R	26	aaa	TEX	31	4.91	1.55	5.2	18	15	3	1.2	27	71	37
Contreras,Efrain	23	R	23	aa	SD	97	5.32	1.45	12	25	11	14	1.3	32	66	67
Contreras,Luis	22	R	26	a/a	MIL	51	4.10	1.42	6.2	27	14	13	0.7	31	72	94
	23	R	27	a/a	MIL	64	5.12	1.51	7.1	26	11	16	1.1	36	68	82
Contreras,Roansy	22	R	23	aaa	PIT	35	2.99	1.20	16	27	9	18	0.8	31	78	108
	23	R	24	aaa	PIT	34	5.28	1.24	17	17	8	9	2.1	24	65	25
Cooke,Connor	23	R	24	a/a	TOR	37	4.37	1.42	5.5	32	9	23	1.0	38	71	117
Cornwell,Alexander	23	L	24	aa	STL	38	2.59	1.16	22	17	5	12	0.4	30	78	101
Correa,Danis	22	R	23	a/a	CHC	58	3.24	1.23	6.2	22	11	11	0.6	27	75	86
	23	R	24	a/a	CIN	32	8.26	1.78	4.9	22	15	7	1.0	35	52	56
Cox,Austin	22	L	25	aaa	KC	148	4.03	1.44	22	12	7	6	0.9	31	74	37
	23	L	26	aaa	KC	48	3.88	1.48	17	14	10	4	2.0	27	84	1
Crismatt,Nabil	23	R	29	aaa	ARI	59	6.69	1.71	12	15	8	7	1.6	35	63	18
Criswell,Cooper	23	R	27	aaa	TAM	86	4.07	1.40	16	18	6	11	0.8	33	72	72
Criswell,Jeff	22	R	23	a/a	OAK	71	3.20	1.22	21	18	7	10	0.5	29	74	81
	23	R	24	aaa	COL	121	7.99	1.81	19	18	12	6	2.7	33	61	-11
Cronin,Declan	22	R	25	a/a	CHW	51	3.57	1.41	4.4	14	8	5	0.7	30	76	44
	23	R	26	aaa	CHW	53	4.24	1.57	5	14	9	5	0.6	33	73	44

PITCHER	yr	t	age	lvl	org	ip	era	whip	bf/g	k%	bb%	k-bb	hr/9	h%	s%	bpv
Crow,Coleman	23	R	22	aa	LAA	24	2.02	0.64	20.7	33	7	26	1.2	14	82	157
Cruz,Jesus	22	R	27	aaa	ATL	29	5.34	1.48	4.5	25	15	11	1.5	28	68	55
	23	R	28	aaa	PHI	35	6.24	1.77	5.7	18	10	8	1.2	37	66	41
Cruz,Omar	22	L	23	aa	PIT	64	4.78	1.39	11.8	20	9	11	1.0	31	67	66
	23	L	24	aa	PIT	48	5.11	1.65	8.0	16	15	1	0.4	31	68	52
Cruz,Steven	22	R	23	aa	MIN	56	4.71	1.53	5.3	24	12	11	0.5	34	68	88
	23	R	24	a/a	KC	51	4.05	1.25	4.8	24	14	10	0.6	25	68	85
Cuevas,Michael	23	R	22	aa	WAS	99	6.98	1.79	19.9	14	10	4	1.1	36	61	23
Curry,Xzavion	22	R	24	a/a	CLE	122	3.84	1.20	19.6	22	7	15	1.2	29	72	85
Curtis,Keegan	22	R	27	a/a	LA	43	6.20	1.62	5.8	17	8	9	1.2	36	62	44
	23	R	28	aaa	LA	34	7.28	1.96	8.2	12	11	1	1.5	36	64	-2
Cushing,Jack	22	R	26	a/a	OAK	132	4.49	1.42	22.4	16	6	10	0.9	33	70	64
	23	R	27	a/a	OAK	125	5.13	1.37	16.9	19	5	14	1.3	33	65	77
Cusick,Ryan	23	R	24	a/a	OAK	99	4.50	1.46	18.5	16	14	3	1.1	26	72	37
Dallas,Chad	23	R	23	aa	TOR	98	4.56	1.32	22.6	22	9	14	1.5	30	70	64
Danielak,Michael	22	R	28	aa	OAK	76	3.81	1.44	7.9	15	8	7	0.8	32	75	49
Danner,Hagen	23	R	25	a/a	TOR	38	3.86	1.07	4.8	28	6	22	2.0	27	76	111
Darnell,Dugan	22	R	25	aa	COL	49	5.71	1.69	5.8	23	14	9	1.8	33	71	38
	23	R	26	a/a	COL	55	4.46	1.54	6.0	20	10	10	2.0	31	79	27
Dashwood,Jack	22	L	25	aa	LAA	61	4.75	1.25	8.0	27	8	19	1.3	31	65	101
	23	L	26	a/a	LAA	30	6.87	1.86	7.4	20	8	11	4.0	35	77	-34
Davidson,Tucker	22	L	26	aaa	ATL	81	5.94	1.57	23.8	22	8	15	1.9	36	67	50
Davila,Garrett	22	L	25	aa	CHW	90	4.91	1.62	13.8	18	11	7	0.7	34	70	52
	23	L	26	a/a	CHW	127	7.48	1.82	20.3	16	11	5	2.0	35	62	4
Davis,Noah	22	R	25	a/a	COL	140	5.58	1.49	22.4	19	9	10	1.7	31	67	36
	23	R	26	aaa	COL	60	4.99	1.55	18.7	12	13	-1	1.3	27	71	15
De Avila,Luis	23	L	22	a/a	ATL	129	3.64	1.36	20.8	21	11	10	0.6	30	74	78
De Geus,Brett	23	R	26	a/a	KC	47	5.47	1.71	7.4	12	8	5	0.9	36	69	26
De Jesus,Angel	22	R	25	aaa	DET	49	4.17	1.14	4.4	17	10	8	0.6	24	63	70
	23	R	26	aa	DET	37	4.92	1.56	5.1	21	13	8	1.6	30	73	39
De Jesus,Enmanuel	22	L	26	aaa	SF	103	4.19	1.57	13.0	20	10	10	0.8	35	74	66
	23	L	27	aaa	MIA	86	5.55	1.88	23.8	11	13	-2	1.0	34	72	10
De Jong,Chase	23	R	30	aaa	PIT	32	4.59	1.99	6.4	14	17	-3	0.3	35	76	39
Deal,Hayden	22	L	28	aa	ATL	59	5.29	1.66	8.5	16	11	5	0.4	35	66	52
	23	L	29	aa	ATL	48	5.13	1.83	7.7	14	12	3	0.5	36	71	40
Del Bonta-Smith,Finn	22	R	25	aa	COL	50	4.42	1.18	5.7	20	6	15	2.2	26	73	62
	23	R	26	aa	COL	45	7.62	1.91	6.1	19	11	8	3.6	34	71	-37
Del Rosario,Yefri	22	R	23	a/a	KC	73	4.16	1.42	6.6	13	8	6	0.8	31	72	42
	23	R	24	aa	KC	52	3.59	1.32	5.5	23	12	12	0.7	29	74	83
Denlinger,Theo	23	R	27	a/a	BOS	49	6.26	1.55	6.2	18	15	3	0.6	29	58	55
Denoyer,Noah	22	R	24	aa	BAL	53	2.62	0.80	13.8	29	5	23	1.5	20	80	147
	23	R	25	aaa	BAL	52	5.90	1.77	9.6	21	16	5	1.3	33	69	40
Diaz,Jhonathan	22	L	26	aaa	LAA	47	4.41	1.34	19.6	18	9	9	0.7	30	67	69
	23	L	27	aaa	LAA	87	4.75	1.53	10.0	17	11	6	1.1	31	71	38
Diaz,Miguel	22	R	28	aaa	DET	65	4.75	1.53	4.9	18	11	7	0.6	33	69	59
	23	R	29	aaa	DET	57	5.81	1.63	5.2	21	11	10	0.4	36	62	73
Diehl,Phillip	22	L	28	aaa	NYM	41	5.77	1.49	4.7	18	10	8	1.6	30	65	31
	23	L	29	aaa	CLE	34	7.26	1.64	6.4	17	14	3	1.6	28	57	21
Dion,Will	23	L	23	aa	CLE	83	3.20	1.27	20.0	22	8	14	0.7	31	77	89
Dipoto,Jonah	22	R	26	aa	KC	65	3.65	1.58	6.8	21	16	5	0.7	30	78	68
	23	R	27	a/a	KC	52	4.03	1.60	5.4	19	14	5	1.3	30	79	36
Dobbins,Hunter	23	R	24	aa	BOS	73	5.15	1.46	24.1	20	8	12	1.2	33	67	62
Dobnak,Randy	23	R	28	aaa	MIN	127	5.48	1.84	19.1	15	11	4	0.8	37	70	34
Dodd,Dylan	22	L	24	a/a	ATL	55	3.75	1.34	23.0	24	7	17	0.7	35	73	104
	23	L	25	aaa	ATL	76	6.47	1.67	21.4	17	9	8	1.6	35	64	25
Dodson,Tanner	23	R	26	a/a	LA	67	5.65	1.74	6.1	14	14	0	0.9	31	68	25
Dombkowski,Nick	23	L	25	a/a	PIT	88	5.14	1.47	11.1	12	7	5	1.5	30	69	18
Dominguez,Johan	23	R	27	aaa	CHW	30	6.24	1.75	17.3	13	11	2	2.5	30	72	-25
Dominguez,Michael	23	R	23	aa	TOR	37	4.64	1.24	18.9	23	14	9	2.9	15	79	14
Donato,Chad	22	R	27	aaa	HOU	126	5.28	1.53	18.9	15	11	4	1.3	29	68	24
	23	R	28	aa	MIN	42	12.73	2.58	17.4	12	11	2	2.7	44	51	-49
Dowdy,Kyle	22	R	29	aaa	CIN	53	5.28	1.84	5.2	18	16	3	0.7	35	71	43
	23	R	30	aaa	BAL	65	5.05	1.82	7.8	18	13	5	0.5	37	71	52
Doxakis,John	22	L	24	aa	TAM	83	5.26	1.41	17.6	17	11	6	0.9	28	63	51
	23	L	25	aaa	TAM	86	6.04	1.52	10.4	19	11	7	1.1	31	61	46
Doyle,Tommy	23	R	27	aaa	COL	37	3.86	1.40	4.7	19	11	7	1.5	27	79	38
Drohan,Shane	23	L	24	a/a	BOS	123	5.81	1.69	20.6	19	13	6	1.6	33	69	27
Duarte,Daniel	23	R	27	aaa	CIN	35	3.57	1.27	4.5	22	12	10	0.0	29	69	97
Dubin,Shawn	22	R	27	aaa	HOU	59	4.73	1.49	11.1	26	12	13	0.4	35	67	93
	23	R	28	aaa	HOU	57	6.80	1.68	12.9	18	14	4	1.1	31	59	39
Dugger,Robert	22	R	27	aaa	CIN	67	5.73	1.70	16.0	15	13	2	1.3	31	68	15
	23	R	28	aaa	TEX	147	4.74	1.61	22.5	17	10	7	1.2	33	73	36
Dunshee,Parker	22	R	27	aaa	OAK	112	7.20	1.63	16.1	13	9	5	2.0	31	59	2
	23	R	28	a/a	SF	67	3.73	1.46	8.5	21	12	8	1.1	30	78	54
Eastman,Colton	22	R	26	a/a	PHI	101	4.93	1.55	17.7	15	15	1	1.1	27	70	32
	23	R	27	aaa	OAK	67	6.21	1.75	14.0	14	12	2	1.1	33	65	23
Eder,Jacob	23	L	25	aa	CHW	47	7.59	1.87	20.1	22	15	7	1.6	36	61	34
Eickhoff,Jerad	22	R	32	aaa	PIT	115	5.53	1.34	17.1	16	7	9	1.2	30	60	49
	23	R	33	aaa	CLE	69	7.56	1.94	23.6	9	11	-2	1.9	34	64	-27
Eisert,Brandon	22	L	24	aaa	TOR	62	3.83	1.22	5.6	25	6	20	1.3	32	74	112
	23	L	25	aaa	TOR	69	4.23	1.36	4.9	21	8	14	1.1	32	72	73
Elder,Bryce	22	R	23	aaa	ATL	105	5.46	1.34	24.3	19	8	11	1.4	30	62	56
Elledge,Seth	22	R	26	aaa	ATL	47	4.99	1.29	4.5	27	9	18	0.7	33	61	104
	23	R	27	aaa	ATL	58	6.15	1.65	6.0	18	10	9	1.4	35	65	36
Emanuel,Kent	22	L	30	a/a	PHI	54	3.24	1.36	20.7	16	3	12	0.7	34	78	101
	23	L	31	aaa	PIT	85	7.72	1.93	20.2	13	6	7	1.6	40	61	13

PITCHER	yr	t	age	lvl	org	ip	era	whip	bf/g	k%	bb%	k-bb	hr/9	h%	s%	bpv
Endersby,Jimmy	23	R	25	aaa	HOU	68	5.48	1.60	8.1	17	13	4	1.7	29	70	20
Enlow,Blayne	22	R	23	aa	MIN	58	3.98	1.50	10	21	10	11	0.5	34	73	79
	23	R	24	a/a	MIN	100	5.29	1.38	16	22	7	15	1.3	33	64	75
Enright,Nic	22	R	25	a/a	CLE	67	2.72	0.96	5.3	28	5	23	0.8	28	76	163
	23	R	26	aaa	CLE	46	5.25	1.50	6.2	20	9	10	2.0	31	72	28
Erceg,Lucas	22	R	27	a/a	MIL	62	4.85	1.79	5.8	20	14	6	0.9	36	74	49
	23	R	28	aaa	MIL	16	7.22	1.71	5.6	18	15	3	1.9	29	61	11
Erla,Mason	22	R	25	aa	LAA	82	4.18	1.36	21	15	5	10	0.9	32	71	65
	23	R	26	a/a	LAA	52	9.17	2.00	19	12	12	1	1.9	36	55	-15
Escobar,Edgar	22	R	25	aa	STL	125	5.10	1.40	19	14	7	7	1.0	30	65	42
	23	R	26	aa	STL	66	4.97	1.55	12	15	12	3	0.9	30	69	37
Espada,Jose	23	R	26	a/a	SD	84	2.65	1.28	9.8	26	12	15	0.7	29	82	96
Espinal,Carlos	22	R	26	a/a	NYY	63	3.71	1.33	7.1	20	13	7	1.0	26	75	56
Espinoza,Anderson	22	R	24	a/a	CHC	71	6.94	1.58	15	21	12	8	1.8	31	59	32
	23	R	25	aaa	SD	133	4.84	1.51	21	17	10	7	0.9	32	69	48
Espinoza,Manuel	23	R	23	aa	CHC	30	7.25	1.87	14	14	10	4	1.6	36	63	8
Estes,Joey	23	R	22	a/a	OAK	139	3.19	1.07	20	20	7	13	1.1	25	75	83
Estrada,Jeremiah	22	R	24	a/a	CHC	26	1.28	1.00	5.3	32	9	23	0.0	30	86	162
	23	R	25	aaa	CHC	30	5.49	1.63	5.2	26	18	8	1.9	27	72	44
Eveld,Tommy	22	R	29	aaa	MIA	36	3.77	1.22	6.4	16	7	9	1.4	26	76	43
	23	R	30	a/a	CIN	33	6.01	1.63	7.4	19	6	13	1.5	38	66	59
Faedo,Alex	23	R	28	a/a	DET	33	4.17	1.17	17	21	6	15	1.3	29	69	89
Falter,Bailey	22	L	25	aaa	PHI	47	1.96	0.70	18	23	3	20	0.8	20	78	189
	23	L	26	aaa	PHI	47	4.66	1.56	19	14	11	3	1.4	29	74	15
Faria,Jake	22	R	29	aaa	MIN	44	7.54	1.96	18	14	13	1	1.6	35	63	-1
	23	R	30	aaa	BOS	62	7.58	1.81	14	13	13	0	1.7	31	60	-1
Farr,Thomas	23	R	24	aa	CIN	49	8.93	1.85	21	8	10	-2	1.9	32	52	-31
Felipe,Angel	22	R	25	a/a	SD	64	3.12	1.29	5.2	26	12	14	0.1	30	74	112
	23	R	26	aaa	OAK	31	4.44	1.45	4.4	27	13	14	0.4	34	68	100
Feltman,Durbin	22	R	25	aaa	BOS	49	8.12	1.67	5.5	20	10	10	2.1	34	53	23
	23	R	26	a/a	OAK	42	2.81	1.13	7.3	20	9	12	0.8	26	79	81
Feltner,Ryan	22	R	26	aaa	COL	53	3.76	1.31	20	20	7	13	0.8	31	73	80
Fenter,Gray	22	R	26	aa	SF	41	5.64	1.75	8.5	21	21	0	0.8	27	68	61
	23	R	27	aa	NYY	42	6.26	1.62	19	22	12	10	1.5	33	64	45
Ferguson,Tyler	22	R	29	a/a	ATL	52	6.30	1.98	4.8	20	19	1	0.2	36	65	64
	23	R	30	aaa	ARI	80	5.31	1.81	7.3	17	15	2	0.5	34	70	49
Fernandez,Junior	22	R	25	aaa	PIT	45	4.86	1.67	4.9	20	11	9	0.7	36	71	62
	23	R	26	aaa	WAS	60	5.61	1.83	5.5	15	11	4	1.6	35	73	10
Fernandez,Pedro	23	R	29	aaa	MIL	68	4.76	1.69	15	14	10	4	2.2	32	80	-6
Fernandez,Ryan	23	R	25	a/a	BOS	53	4.96	1.46	5.7	21	8	13	1.5	34	71	59
Ferrer,Jose A.	23	L	23	aaa	WAS	40	3.96	1.59	5.2	16	11	6	0.9	33	77	42
Festa,David	23	R	23	a/a	MIN	93	4.06	1.39	16	26	10	16	0.8	34	72	96
Festa,Matt	23	R	30	aaa	SEA	34	0.54	0.80	4.4	17	12	5	0.5	13	99	82
Fisher,Andy	23	L	27	aa	CIN	52	3.73	1.32	4.8	17	11	6	1.0	26	75	48
Fisher,Braydon	23	R	23	aa	LA	61	3.47	1.36	6.1	28	14	14	1.5	26	82	71
Fisher,Nate	23	L	27	aaa	CHW	105	7.47	1.90	19	13	11	2	2.4	34	66	-25
Fitterer,Evan	23	R	23	aa	MIA	107	5.05	1.64	21	17	15	3	1.3	29	72	30
Fitts,Richard	23	R	24	aa	NYY	154	4.11	1.27	23	22	7	15	1.4	30	73	78
Fleming,Josh	22	L	26	aaa	TAM	66	3.02	1.41	19	15	5	10	0.5	34	79	72
	23	L	27	aaa	TAM	31	4.59	1.96	11	8	5	3	0.9	40	78	7
Fleming,William	23	R	24	aa	KC	49	4.84	1.47	21	14	8	6	1.1	31	69	35
Flores,Wilmer	22	R	21	aa	DET	85	2.89	1.02	17	23	5	18	0.7	28	74	131
	23	R	22	aa	DET	82	4.21	1.34	19	20	9	11	0.5	31	68	81
Flowers,J.C.	22	R	24	aa	PIT	70	2.80	1.19	8.5	18	8	10	0.6	27	78	74
	23	R	25	aaa	PIT	46	10.70	2.51	8.2	14	16	-2	1.8	41	57	-14
Floyd,Taylor	22	R	25	aa	MIL	23	8.14	2.29	5.6	18	18	0	0.8	40	63	37
	23	R	26	aa	MIN	39	6.04	1.77	6.4	19	11	8	1.3	37	68	37
Fluharty,Mason	23	L	22	aa	TOR	43	4.62	1.63	5.3	24	9	16	1.3	39	75	71
France,J.P.	22	R	27	aaa	HOU	112	3.85	1.41	14	23	10	12	1.1	31	76	69
	23	R	28	aaa	HOU	20	2.36	1.05	16	26	14	12	0.0	22	75	119
Francis,Bowden	22	R	26	aaa	TOR	99	7.86	1.72	12	19	9	10	2.5	34	59	7
	23	R	27	aaa	TOR	27	2.82	1.41	13	29	6	23	2.0	37	93	104
Francisco,Carlos	23	R	24	aa	PHI	31	6.13	1.61	5.8	21	16	5	0.7	31	61	63
Franklin,Kohl	23	R	24	aa	CHC	87	6.33	1.55	18	19	10	9	1.8	32	63	30
Frasso,Nick	23	R	25	a/a	LA	95	4.22	1.37	16	22	8	15	0.4	35	68	100
Fraze,Nick	22	R	25	aa	TOR	60	4.69	1.10	18	17	3	14	1.0	29	59	127
	23	R	26	a/a	TOR	33	6.66	1.70	10	18	15	2	1.7	28	64	17
Freeman,Caleb	22	R	24	aa	CHW	15	8.20	1.79	4.6	19	19	0	0.6	30	51	57
	23	R	25	a/a	CHW	33	3.96	1.87	4.9	19	17	2	1.0	34	81	42
Frias,Luis	22	R	24	aaa	ARI	48	3.17	1.31	7.4	29	10	19	0.8	34	78	113
	23	R	25	aaa	ARI	33	2.66	0.88	4.6	24	6	17	0.6	23	71	125
Frisbee,Matt	22	R	26	aa	SF	141	5.71	1.49	23	17	6	11	1.4	34	64	50
	23	R	27	a/a	SF	49	5.85	1.62	6.8	13	9	4	1.5	32	67	11
Fry,Paul	22	L	30	aaa	ARI	30	3.80	1.42	4.4	16	11	5	0.5	30	73	58
	23	L	31	aaa	TOR	56	4.66	1.63	5.3	19	13	6	1.0	32	73	46
Fulmer,Carson	22	R	29	aaa	LA	58	2.52	1.20	4.8	19	13	6	0.6	23	81	74
	23	R	30	aaa	LAA	41	5.82	2.00	16	13	15	-2	1.2	34	73	6
Fulton,Daxton	22	L	21	aa	MIA	21	2.73	0.76	19	33	8	25	0.8	19	68	158
	23	L	22	aa	MIA	33	5.75	1.61	21	23	12	10	1.1	34	65	59
Funderburk,Kody	22	L	26	aa	MIN	107	2.87	1.36	14	18	9	9	0.6	31	80	70
	23	L	27	a/a	MIN	61	2.51	1.24	5.9	29	11	17	0.1	32	78	124
Gaddis,Hunter	22	R	24	a/a	CLE	122	3.77	1.06	20	27	7	20	1.1	27	68	115
	23	R	25	aaa	CLE	75	6.06	1.62	17	16	10	6	2.0	31	68	8
Gage,Matt	22	L	29	aaa	TOR	43	2.95	1.28	4.3	20	10	10	0.3	30	76	84
	23	L	30	aaa	HOU	38	4.90	1.81	5.2	17	12	5	1.3	36	76	28
Gaither,Ray	23	R	25	aa	HOU	34	3.87	1.74	5.2	20	15	4	1.2	32	81	41
Gallagher,Nick	23	R	28	a/a	CHW	39	7.14	1.62	5.6	20	16	4	0.6	30	53	65

PITCHER	yr	t	age	lvl	org	ip	era	whip	bf/g	k%	bb%	k-bb	hr/9	h%	s%	bpv
Gamboa,Alec	22	L	25	aa	LA	89	5.71	1.50	12.8	15	11	4	1.1	30	63	33
	23	L	26	a/a	LA	77	4.24	1.43	8.9	19	15	4	0.7	27	71	61
Gambrell,Grant	23	R	26	a/a	BOS	97	3.77	1.33	23.8	19	9	10	1.2	29	76	55
Garcia,Bryan	23	R	28	aaa	HOU	49	7.36	2.31	16.7	12	18	-6	1.3	36	69	-2
Garcia,Carlos	22	R	24	a/a	TAM	64	4.01	1.22	6.5	24	10	14	1.0	28	70	85
	23	R	25	a/a	TAM	78	3.75	1.36	8.6	22	13	9	1.0	27	76	66
Garcia,Deivi	22	R	23	a/a	NYY	66	6.81	1.42	14.1	23	10	12	1.7	30	54	53
	23	R	24	aaa	CHW	55	5.54	1.78	7.2	20	15	5	2.1	31	75	15
Garcia,Nick	23	R	24	aa	COL	95	9.86	1.96	17.5	14	9	5	2.8	36	52	-30
Garcia,Oliver	23	R	25	aa	PIT	47	5.57	1.90	5.4	17	16	1	0.7	34	70	44
Garcia,Pedro	22	R	27	a/a	CIN	59	3.70	1.42	5.1	22	10	12	0.8	33	76	73
	23	R	28	a/a	CIN	50	7.48	1.80	4.9	26	19	8	2.8	28	65	14
Garcia,Robert	22	L	26	a/a	MIA	65	4.03	1.34	5.9	20	11	8	0.6	28	70	67
	23	L	27	aaa	MIA	41	3.37	1.51	5.7	27	13	14	1.0	34	81	81
Garcia,Rony	23	R	26	aaa	DET	38	8.91	1.97	6.7	21	14	7	1.6	38	55	30
Garcia,Ryan	23	R	25	aa	TEX	100	7.16	1.71	17.5	20	14	6	1.9	31	61	19
Garrett,Reed	22	R	29	aaa	WAS	48	3.39	1.37	4.8	20	9	10	1.0	30	79	61
	23	R	30	aaa	NYM	36	3.14	1.65	5.2	18	13	6	0.9	33	84	49
Garza,Justin	22	R	28	aaa	CLE	44	4.13	1.19	4.8	22	10	12	1.0	26	68	74
	23	R	29	aaa	BOS	37	5.55	1.63	5.5	15	11	3	1.1	32	67	26
Gasser,Robert	22	L	23	a/a	MIL	48	3.33	1.34	22.3	25	11	14	0.5	31	76	95
	23	L	24	aaa	MIL	136	4.06	1.35	21.9	25	9	17	0.8	34	72	97
Gates,Evan	23	R	25	aa	SF	56	5.45	1.94	6.4	22	12	10	0.5	43	71	71
Gau,Chris	22	R	25	a/a	TAM	58	3.15	1.09	6.0	22	7	15	0.9	27	75	100
	23	R	26	a/a	TAM	55	2.64	1.09	5.4	25	10	15	0.5	26	77	108
Gilbert,Tyler	22	L	29	aaa	ARI	44	6.83	1.83	18.6	9	11	-1	1.7	32	65	-19
	23	L	30	aaa	ARI	76	5.12	1.64	11.3	19	7	11	0.9	38	70	63
Gillaspie,Logan	22	R	25	a/a	BAL	44	4.81	1.41	6.7	21	6	14	0.4	36	64	99
	23	R	26	aaa	BOS	42	4.56	1.51	4.8	16	9	7	1.4	31	74	32
Gillispie,Connor	23	R	26	aa	BAL	117	4.76	1.32	18.0	16	8	8	1.1	29	66	47
Gipson-Long,Sawyer	22	R	25	aa	DET	74	6.12	1.42	21.0	17	5	13	1.3	34	58	77
	23	R	26	a/a	DET	101	4.83	1.25	18.7	24	7	16	1.6	29	67	76
Goldsberry,Blake	23	R	26	aa	COL	45	5.35	1.62	6.1	20	11	9	2.4	31	76	10
Gomez,Cesar	23	R	25	a/a	HOU	49	7.53	2.05	5.6	14	11	3	1.5	39	64	5
Gomez,Michael	22	R	26	a/a	NYY	66	4.90	1.69	6.5	16	12	4	0.6	34	70	48
	23	R	27	aaa	NYY	69	6.06	1.73	6.7	16	14	2	1.0	32	65	33
Gomez,Ofreidy	22	R	27	a/a	PHI	44	5.55	1.87	5.4	21	16	5	0.6	36	70	58
	23	R	28	a/a	BAL	34	7.63	2.02	6.4	18	18	1	0.5	37	60	51
Gomez,Rio	23	L	29	a/a	BOS	79	6.11	1.77	14.0	18	13	5	2.0	32	70	10
Gomez,Yoendrys	23	R	24	aa	NYY	66	4.23	1.39	14.7	24	13	11	0.9	29	71	76
Gonzalez,Chi Chi	22	R	30	aaa	NYY	81	4.70	1.60	19.9	16	9	7	1.0	34	72	39
	23	R	31	aaa	MIA	123	7.49	1.94	24.4	9	6	2	1.9	37	64	-26
Gonzalez,Domingo	23	R	24	aa	ATL	55	5.26	1.61	6.1	27	14	13	0.4	37	65	97
Gonzalez,Wikelman	23	R	21	aa	BOS	49	2.79	1.16	19.5	28	14	14	0.4	25	76	109
Gordon,Colton	23	L	25	a/a	HOU	129	4.33	1.40	18.8	23	10	13	1.2	31	73	68
Gordon,Tanner	22	R	25	aa	ATL	99	6.33	1.64	21.1	19	9	10	1.6	35	64	32
	23	R	26	a/a	COL	142	6.76	1.57	23.1	15	7	8	1.6	34	59	28
Goudeau,Ashton	22	R	30	aaa	COL	65	10.28	2.17	16.3	10	7	2	2.2	40	53	-37
	23	R	31	aaa	DET	62	8.42	2.03	16.8	12	11	0	1.9	36	60	-19
Gowdy,Kevin	22	R	25	aa	TEX	40	9.54	2.09	6.1	13	14	-1	2.1	34	55	-18
	23	R	26	aa	LA	39	6.05	1.62	5.6	19	12	7	1.1	33	63	45
Grace,Regi	23	R	24	aa	MIN	51	4.08	1.27	7.7	22	11	11	0.8	28	69	76
Graceffo,Gordon	22	R	22	aa	STL	95	2.78	0.89	19.6	18	5	13	0.9	22	74	108
	23	R	23	aaa	STL	86	4.68	1.49	17.6	18	11	8	0.8	32	69	56
Gragg,Logan	23	R	25	a/a	STL	126	4.95	1.42	19.8	15	8	7	1.4	30	69	33
Grammes,Conor	23	R	26	aa	ARI	47	3.45	1.62	7.0	24	16	9	0.7	33	80	74
Granillo,Andre	23	R	23	a/a	STL	69	4.52	1.26	5.3	26	12	14	0.9	28	65	90
Green,Haylen	23	L	26	a/a	CHW	40	6.95	1.77	6.1	17	11	6	0.8	36	59	44
Green,Josh	22	R	27	a/a	ARI	61	6.10	1.64	7.2	12	9	3	0.9	33	63	25
	23	R	28	a/a	ARI	68	4.34	1.28	7.2	14	7	7	0.7	29	67	53
Greene,Zach	22	R	26	aaa	NYY	69	3.68	1.30	5.9	27	11	16	1.5	28	78	78
	23	R	27	aaa	NYY	28	6.21	1.77	6.1	15	17	-2	1.0	29	65	29
Griffin,David	22	R	26	a/a	NYM	72	5.84	1.64	15.3	15	9	6	1.2	34	66	28
	23	R	27	a/a	NYM	83	7.39	1.80	17.5	13	10	3	1.6	34	60	3
Groome,Jay	22	L	24	a/a	SD	146	2.95	1.25	20.6	19	9	10	0.8	28	79	72
	23	L	25	aaa	SD	136	6.73	1.87	21.3	18	14	4	1.2	35	65	30
Grove,Michael	22	R	26	a/a	LA	78	3.37	1.17	16.5	22	7	15	1.2	28	77	88
Gudino,Norwith	22	R	27	aaa	SF	49	8.28	1.62	8.4	22	14	8	1.9	30	50	29
	23	R	28	aaa	BOS	55	6.74	1.91	11.8	9	11	-2	0.9	35	64	3
Guenther,Sean	23	L	28	a/a	DET	44	4.57	1.36	5.6	20	6	14	1.7	31	73	59
Guerra,Javier	22	R	27	aaa	TAM	42	1.77	0.91	3.6	26	10	16	0.2	22	80	128
	23	R	28	aaa	TAM	37	4.46	1.37	4.8	19	10	9	1.0	30	69	59
Guerrero,Luis	23	R	23	a/a	BOS	57	2.47	1.19	4.7	24	15	9	0.5	22	81	92
Gusto,Ryan	23	R	24	aa	HOU	62	3.20	1.06	17.2	22	10	12	0.3	24	69	100
Guzman,Carlos	23	R	25	a/a	CHC	78	5.11	1.62	9.6	19	13	7	0.8	33	69	55
Guzman,Jorge	23	R	27	aaa	SF	36	3.24	1.68	6.0	13	16	-4	0.4	29	81	39
Haake,Zach	23	R	27	aa	PHI	54	6.65	1.60	19.9	16	9	7	1.3	33	59	31
Haberer,Jake	23	R	28	aa	SEA	47	4.81	1.51	5.7	16	13	3	0.8	29	69	44
Hagenman,Justin	22	R	26	a/a	LA	65	4.92	1.36	5.9	19	7	12	1.2	32	66	66
	23	R	27	aaa	BOS	86	3.37	1.29	8.6	19	7	12	1.7	28	83	49
Hall,Charles	22	R	28	aa	OAK	34	2.32	1.40	6.3	21	17	5	1.1	23	89	62
	23	R	29	aa	OAK	30	6.39	1.68	8.4	14	20	-5	0.5	25	60	46
Hall,DL	22	L	24	a/a	BAL	83	4.54	1.38	15.2	29	13	17	1.2	31	70	93
	23	L	25	aaa	BAL	49	4.51	1.46	12.3	27	14	13	1.1	30	72	76
Hall,Dylan	23	R	26	a/a	NYM	32	2.80	1.38	6.5	14	9	5	0.5	29	81	51
Hamel,Dominic	23	R	24	aa	NYM	124	4.83	1.47	20.5	26	10	16	0.9	35	68	88

PITCHER	yr	t	age	lvl	org	ip	era	whip	bf/g	k%	bb%	k-bb	hr/9	h%	s%	bpv
Hammer,J. D.	23	R	29	aaa	LAA	38	7.25	2.10	23	8	11	-4	1.3	36	66	-20
Hampton,Aubrey	23	R	22	aa	NYY	61	4.89	1.31	23	24	8	16	1.2	32	66	83
Hancock,Emerson	22	R	23	aa	SEA	99	3.41	1.14	19	20	8	12	1.2	25	76	70
	23	R	24	aa	SEA	98	4.51	1.26	20	23	8	15	0.8	31	65	91
Hanhold,Eric	22	R	29	aaa	PIT	53	3.77	1.53	5.2	15	11	4	0.5	32	75	52
	23	R	30	aaa	SD	54	7.31	1.91	5.1	18	15	3	1.9	33	65	8
Hanifee,Brenan	23	R	25	aaa	DET	91	4.57	1.57	16	16	7	9	0.9	35	72	50
Hanner,Bradley	23	R	24	aa	CLE	66	3.41	1.41	6.8	21	13	8	0.9	28	79	61
Hansen,Austin	23	R	27	aaa	HOU	84	7.07	2.10	12	17	15	2	1.9	36	70	-1
Harding,Houston	23	L	25	aa	LAA	47	8.31	1.94	13	17	14	3	1.6	36	58	15
Harris,Ben	23	L	23	aa	LA	53	5.56	1.56	5.1	28	20	8	0.8	27	64	87
Harris,Hayden	23	L	24	aa	ATL	35	3.65	1.44	6.5	29	12	17	0.3	36	74	115
Harris,Hobie	22	R	29	aaa	MIL	53	2.29	1.22	4	21	15	6	0.9	22	86	65
	23	R	30	aaa	WAS	33	6.49	2.18	6.1	11	12	-2	0.9	39	70	4
Harris,Hogan	22	L	26	a/a	OAK	62	3.18	1.23	16	26	12	14	0.6	28	76	102
	23	L	27	aaa	OAK	57	5.67	1.69	17	16	14	2	1.3	31	69	24
Harrison,Kyle	22	L	21	aa	SF	84	3.17	1.19	19	32	11	21	1.0	30	78	118
	23	L	22	aaa	SF	67	4.42	1.44	14	32	15	17	1.0	32	72	98
Hart,Kyle	22	L	30	a/a	BOS	83	6.28	1.63	15	15	10	5	1.5	32	64	17
	23	L	31	aaa	SEA	90	4.56	1.58	21	17	8	8	0.9	35	73	49
Hart,Zach	23	R	26	aa	CLE	32	6.94	1.84	8.8	16	13	3	2.0	33	66	0
Hartlieb,Geoff	22	R	29	aaa	BOS	61	6.10	1.63	6.8	18	10	8	1.2	34	64	37
	23	R	30	aaa	MIA	46	4.38	1.54	5.8	16	10	7	0.9	33	73	45
Hartwig,Grant	22	R	25	a/a	NYM	28	0.89	0.94	5.9	29	11	18	0.0	23	89	143
	23	R	26	aaa	NYM	30	4.63	1.83	5.9	22	13	9	0.7	39	75	63
Harvey,Joe	23	R	31	aaa	ATL	31	6.80	1.44	5.5	16	15	1	0.9	25	51	43
Hatch,Thomas	22	R	28	aaa	TOR	131	5.87	1.50	20	15	7	8	1.4	33	63	35
	23	R	29	aaa	PIT	48	5.58	1.60	6.9	19	12	7	1.7	31	69	27
Headrick,Brent	23	L	26	aaa	MIN	75	4.81	1.40	17	21	8	13	1.2	32	68	68
Hearn,Taylor	23	L	29	aaa	KC	54	3.90	1.78	6.9	21	14	7	0.5	37	78	67
Heasley,Jon	23	R	26	aaa	KC	96	7.36	1.72	14	15	10	5	1.7	34	59	10
Hecht,Ben	23	R	28	aa	CHC	30	4.20	1.50	5.9	19	20	-1	1.5	19	77	38
Helvey,Clay	22	R	25	aa	SF	30	2.29	1.24	5.3	22	14	8	0.3	25	82	92
	23	R	26	a/a	SF	42	10.38	2.32	6.6	11	18	-7	1.7	35	55	-20
Hence,Markevian	23	R	21	aa	STL	55	5.12	1.44	20	19	8	11	1.1	33	66	62
Henderson,Layne	22	R	26	a/a	HOU	54	3.44	1.18	6.4	26	11	15	0.8	27	73	97
	23	R	27	a/a	DET	61	4.91	1.70	6.6	21	16	5	0.8	32	72	60
Hendrickson,Josh	23	L	26	a/a	PHI	108	6.68	1.89	21	14	10	4	2.4	35	71	-18
Henley,Blair	23	R	26	aa	HOU	108	5.76	1.62	19	18	11	7	0.8	34	64	54
Henriquez,Ronny	22	R	22	aaa	MIN	96	4.96	1.30	17	22	7	15	1.4	31	65	80
	23	R	23	aaa	MIN	57	5.48	1.57	6.8	17	14	3	0.8	30	65	46
Henry,Henry	22	R	24	aa	SD	81	5.01	1.76	11	19	14	5	0.5	35	71	59
	23	R	25	aa	SD	33	6.44	1.92	6.5	13	17	-4	0.3	33	64	40
Henry,Thomas	22	L	25	aaa	ARI	113	3.09	1.22	22	17	8	10	0.6	28	76	75
	23	L	26	aaa	ARI	22	5.56	1.40	23	19	8	11	0.9	32	60	67
Herget,Jimmy	23	R	30	aaa	LAA	34	4.94	1.39	5.8	19	9	9	1.5	29	69	43
Herget,Kevin	22	R	31	a/a	TAM	198	3.12	1.41	20	19	4	14	1.1	35	82	94
	23	R	32	a/a	CIN	96	6.20	1.84	6.6	16	10	6	2.0	35	71	2
Hernandez,Adrian	23	R	23	aa	TOR	50	5.06	1.64	5.9	23	19	3	1.0	27	70	62
Hernandez,Antonio	23	L	24	a/a	WAS	120	4.23	1.47	22	14	5	9	1.5	33	77	40
Hernandez,Cristian	23	R	23	aa	PHI	53	4.35	1.55	6.6	24	10	14	2.0	33	80	44
Hernandez,Jonathan	22	R	26	a/a	TEX	17	2.97	1.55	4.7	20	18	2	0.4	27	81	65
	23	R	27	aaa	TEX	32	1.22	1.21	5.4	19	17	3	0.3	20	91	80
Hernandez,Kenny	22	L	24	aa	ARI	46	5.57	1.78	9.2	16	8	8	1.3	38	71	30
	23	L	25	aa	STL	74	6.08	1.64	22	16	9	7	0.5	36	61	55
Hernandez,Nick	22	R	28	a/a	HOU	66	3.64	1.11	5.1	26	12	14	1.0	23	71	86
	23	R	29	a/a	SD	63	3.77	1.18	5.4	25	8	17	0.5	30	68	110
Herrin,Tim	22	L	26	a/a	CLE	70	3.93	1.27	6.2	28	7	20	0.8	35	71	122
	23	L	27	aaa	CLE	38	3.49	1.17	4.6	22	14	8	0.7	22	72	79
Herz,DJ	23	L	22	aa	WAS	95	4.37	1.45	18	29	14	14	0.6	32	70	101
Hickman,Mason	23	R	25	aa	CLE	56	4.92	1.64	7.2	23	14	9	1.7	31	75	41
Higginbotham,Jake	22	L	26	aa	ATL	52	5.72	1.72	4.9	17	8	9	1.0	38	67	43
	23	L	27	a/a	DET	55	3.57	1.57	6.7	15	10	5	0.6	33	78	46
Hill,Garrett	22	R	26	a/a	DET	71	3.37	1.13	19	26	9	18	0.8	28	72	110
	23	R	27	aaa	DET	47	6.51	2.04	8.8	21	14	7	1.0	41	68	46
Hill,Jamison	23	R	24	aa	ARI	118	4.19	1.41	19	17	14	4	0.7	27	71	53
Hjelle,Sean	22	R	25	aaa	SF	97	4.54	1.56	19	15	8	7	0.8	34	72	47
	23	R	26	aaa	SF	93	6.33	1.65	19	14	10	4	1.1	33	62	23
Hodge,Porter	23	R	22	aa	CHC	82	5.20	1.37	9.8	26	13	13	0.3	31	59	101
Hoeing,Bryan	22	R	26	a/a	MIA	121	4.52	1.46	24	12	8	4	1.0	31	71	28
	23	R	27	aaa	MIA	32	2.64	1.05	18	23	3	19	0.9	30	80	169
Hoffman,Nolan	23	R	26	a/a	BAL	45	3.47	1.46	6	14	7	6	0.2	33	75	62
Hoffmann,Andrew	23	R	23	a/a	KC	126	5.90	1.62	20	19	10	9	1.3	34	65	42
Holder,Jonathan	22	R	29	aaa	CHC	18	10.80	2.49	6.8	15	12	3	1.0	47	54	16
	23	R	30	aaa	LAA	68	5.83	1.80	6.9	18	13	5	1.2	35	73	34
Holman,Grant	23	R	23	aa	OAK	33	5.62	1.44	5.6	26	7	19	1.7	36	65	82
Holmes,Grant	22	R	26	aaa	ATL	37	10.80	2.32	6.8	11	8	3	2.9	41	56	-55
	23	R	27	aaa	ATL	61	4.14	1.47	5.2	23	10	13	0.8	34	73	79
Holub,Blake	23	R	25	aa	DET	41	4.35	1.34	5.7	20	8	12	1.2	31	71	64
Horn,Bailey	23	L	25	a/a	CHC	62	4.34	1.49	5.9	24	12	12	0.6	33	71	82
Houston,Zac	22	R	28	a/a	DET	54	5.92	1.72	5.1	26	16	10	1.4	33	68	60
	23	R	29	a/a	NYY	44	5.37	1.55	5.2	29	16	13	1.2	32	67	81
Hudson,Bryan	22	L	25	a/a	CHC	59	3.48	1.30	6.2	24	10	15	0.6	32	74	98
	23	L	26	aaa	LA	57	2.59	1.37	5.2	29	11	19	0.5	36	82	115
Hudson,Dakota	23	R	29	aaa	STL	48	6.50	2.10	21	12	7	5	0.9	43	69	20
Hunley,Sean	22	R	23	aa	TAM	92	3.22	1.21	14	16	4	12	0.3	32	72	106
	23	R	24	a/a	TAM	114	5.04	1.35	18	18	5	12	1.2	32	65	71

PITCHER	yr	t	age	lvl	org	ip	era	whip	bf/g	k%	bb%	k-bb	hr/9	h%	s%	bpv
Hurt,Kyle	23	R	25	a/a	LA	92	4.48	1.33	14.7	33	11	22	1.1	34	69	111
Hurter,Brant	23	L	25	aa	DET	118	3.83	1.35	18.9	21	7	14	0.5	34	71	97
Imanaga,Shoto	23	R	29	for	JPN	142	3.46	1.15	26.8	29	5	24	1.8	31	80	131
Ingram,Kolton	22	L	26	aa	LAA	62	2.60	0.94	4.7	25	7	18	0.8	24	77	116
	23	L	27	a/a	LAA	63	3.17	1.29	5.8	23	13	10	0.5	27	76	88
Iriarte,Jairo	23	R	22	aa	SD	30	4.44	1.26	9.5	37	13	24	0.6	34	64	138
Irvin,Cole	23	L	29	aaa	BAL	50	5.03	1.50	24.0	10	4	6	1.4	33	70	22
Jackson,Andre	22	R	26	aaa	LA	77	4.14	1.54	16.0	17	14	3	1.0	27	76	45
	23	R	27	aaa	PIT	39	6.02	1.57	10.7	19	14	5	1.2	29	63	40
Jacques,Joe	22	L	27	a/a	PIT	41	3.48	1.34	5.5	14	9	6	0.8	29	76	46
	23	L	28	aaa	BOS	39	2.99	1.33	4.9	16	8	8	1.0	29	82	49
Jameson,Drey	22	R	25	a/a	ARI	134	5.39	1.42	21.9	18	7	11	1.0	33	63	66
	23	R	26	aaa	ARI	28	5.27	1.43	23.8	16	8	8	0.5	32	61	63
Jarvis,Bryce	22	R	25	aa	ARI	108	7.41	1.82	20.1	18	10	7	1.7	36	61	18
	23	R	26	a/a	ARI	107	4.82	1.45	16.9	19	11	9	0.6	32	66	67
Jarvis,Justin	23	R	23	a/a	NYM	120	5.49	1.65	20.7	23	11	11	1.3	36	69	56
Javier,Odalvi	22	R	26	a/a	ATL	61	3.16	1.18	5.2	23	10	13	0.3	28	73	99
	23	R	27	a/a	WAS	52	7.60	2.16	7.4	15	17	-2	1.7	36	67	-1
Jennings,Steven	22	R	24	aa	NYY	68	4.29	1.19	5.9	21	5	16	0.9	31	65	110
	23	R	25	aa	NYY	32	3.42	1.16	6.4	26	10	17	0.6	28	72	107
Jensen,Ryan	22	R	25	aa	CHC	60	3.83	1.33	14.7	19	13	6	0.6	25	72	69
	23	R	26	a/a	SEA	65	5.29	1.79	7.0	21	16	6	0.8	35	70	60
Jensen,Wil	23	R	26	aa	SF	89	3.25	1.54	11.4	19	12	8	1.0	32	83	51
Jimenez,Antonio	23	L	22	aa	TAM	49	2.84	1.31	8.1	22	11	11	1.8	25	89	47
Johnson,M.D.	23	R	26	aa	MIA	115	6.69	1.53	20.1	16	12	4	1.7	28	59	16
Johnston,Kyle	22	R	26	aaa	TOR	64	6.40	1.74	6.0	16	10	6	1.3	35	65	26
	23	R	27	aaa	COL	36	7.09	2.07	6.8	12	16	-3	2.1	32	70	-23
Jones,Jared	23	R	22	a/a	PIT	127	4.40	1.32	20.2	23	9	13	0.9	31	68	80
Jones,Joe	23	R	28	aa	TOR	38	5.94	1.63	5.3	17	15	2	1.1	29	65	36
Jones,Jordan	23	R	26	aa	CLE	63	2.62	1.42	7.2	19	18	1	1.2	20	88	46
Jones,Nick	22	L	23	aa	LAA	35	3.86	1.46	4.8	24	15	9	0.5	30	73	89
	23	L	24	a/a	LAA	41	3.44	1.37	6.1	23	13	11	0.7	29	76	79
Jones,Stephen	22	R	25	aa	COL	58	2.94	1.15	4.9	21	9	12	1.0	25	79	76
	23	R	26	a/a	COL	65	9.41	2.03	6.0	19	11	8	1.7	40	53	21
Joyce,Jimmy	23	R	24	aa	SEA	32	3.80	1.25	18.7	19	7	12	0.3	32	68	97
Juan,Jorge	23	R	24	aa	OAK	35	5.68	1.81	6.2	18	20	-2	0.6	29	68	54
Juarez,Daniel	23	L	23	aa	NYM	42	3.94	1.14	7.9	20	8	12	0.9	26	67	78
Juenger,Hayden	22	R	22	a/a	TOR	90	3.71	1.08	9.3	24	9	15	1.8	22	76	67
	23	R	23	aaa	TOR	76	6.09	1.61	6.2	23	10	13	1.2	37	63	63
Junk,Janson	22	R	26	aaa	LAA	75	4.02	1.26	19.2	18	5	12	0.9	31	70	83
	23	R	27	aaa	MIL	140	4.80	1.54	22.6	13	8	5	1.0	33	71	29
Junker,Cameron	23	R	26	a/a	PIT	58	3.88	1.56	5.5	14	13	1	0.5	30	75	44
Kachmar,Chris	23	R	27	a/a	CHC	67	5.55	1.58	11.8	20	7	12	1.5	36	68	51
Kaminsky,Rob	22	L	28	aa	SEA	38	4.81	1.51	4.2	19	11	8	1.1	31	70	48
	23	L	29	a/a	SEA	39	5.71	1.73	5.9	13	5	8	0.9	39	67	45
Karcher,Ricky	22	R	25	a/a	CIN	58	4.16	1.61	5.0	29	17	13	0.6	35	74	95
	23	R	26	aaa	CIN	61	4.93	1.91	5.7	20	25	-5	0.5	27	73	65
Kauffmann,Karl	22	R	25	a/a	COL	143	5.14	1.58	22.5	17	11	6	1.3	31	70	34
	23	R	26	aaa	COL	93	7.08	1.97	23.5	10	9	1	1.3	37	65	-5
Kay,Anthony	23	L	28	aaa	NYM	42	3.68	1.33	5.5	26	14	13	0.4	30	71	101
Kelley,Trevor	22	R	29	aaa	MIL	35	2.59	1.29	4.2	23	8	15	0.5	33	81	100
	23	R	31	aaa	TAM	34	5.58	1.66	5.7	14	7	6	1.9	33	72	5
Kelly,Antoine	23	L	24	a/a	TEX	60	2.01	1.18	4.9	27	9	18	0.6	30	86	112
Kelly,Michael	22	R	30	aaa	PHI	50	6.10	1.85	5.1	21	11	10	1.6	38	70	34
	23	R	31	a/a	CLE	41	4.09	1.82	5.6	23	14	10	0.7	39	79	68
Kennedy,Brett	22	R	28	a/a	BOS	78	4.43	1.53	13.6	14	9	5	0.9	32	73	32
	23	R	29	aaa	CIN	80	5.27	1.69	21.3	15	9	6	1.3	35	71	26
Kennedy,Nick	22	L	26	a/a	COL	52	7.57	1.92	4.9	12	11	1	1.4	36	61	-2
	23	L	27	aaa	COL	38	6.14	1.95	6.1	10	15	-5	0.6	33	67	19
Kent,Zak	22	R	24	a/a	TEX	111	3.55	1.26	18.9	20	8	11	0.8	29	74	74
	23	R	25	aaa	TEX	34	4.11	1.12	13.4	21	7	13	1.1	26	66	80
Kerr,Ray	22	L	28	aaa	SD	45	4.27	1.77	4.5	26	16	9	0.6	37	76	79
	23	L	29	aaa	SD	36	1.96	1.12	3.9	23	11	12	0.4	25	84	96
Kerry,Brett	22	R	23	aa	LAA	103	4.18	1.37	17.3	23	6	17	1.5	34	75	83
	23	R	24	a/a	LAA	137	4.72	1.35	21.2	18	8	10	1.9	28	72	33
Kilian,Caleb	22	R	25	aaa	CHC	108	4.11	1.57	18.3	21	11	10	0.5	35	74	75
	23	R	26	aaa	CHC	121	4.49	1.38	20.3	15	7	8	1.0	31	70	48
Kilkenny,Mitchell	22	R	25	aa	COL	102	6.20	1.62	18.9	13	7	6	2.2	32	68	-7
	23	R	26	aa	COL	23	8.25	2.15	8.8	11	9	2	0.0	43	57	34
Killgore,Keylan	23	L	27	aa	PHI	56	6.85	1.88	5.7	20	12	8	1.9	37	67	20
Kilome,Franklyn	22	R	27	a/a	WAS	93	6.37	1.66	20.8	18	10	8	1.5	34	64	33
Kingham,Nolan	22	R	26	a/a	ATL	98	5.80	1.53	13.3	14	4	10	1.5	35	65	45
	23	R	27	a/a	ATL	87	5.49	1.77	14.8	13	10	3	0.8	35	69	26
Kitchen,Austin	23	L	26	a/a	COL	62	5.39	1.56	6.1	14	6	8	1.0	35	66	47
Klein,Will	22	R	23	aa	KC	45	9.69	2.21	7.6	19	19	0	0.9	38	54	40
	23	R	24	a/a	KC	65	5.00	1.73	6.0	24	13	12	0.5	39	70	82
Kloffenstein,Adam	22	R	22	aa	TOR	86	5.59	1.57	19.9	19	9	10	1.2	34	66	53
	23	R	23	a/a	STL	128	3.05	1.25	20.0	22	9	13	0.8	29	79	83
Knack,Landon	22	R	25	aa	LA	66	4.77	1.38	16.4	23	9	15	1.1	33	68	80
	23	R	26	a/a	LA	101	2.92	1.29	18.9	19	7	12	0.9	31	81	75
Knehr,Reiss	22	R	26	aaa	SD	89	5.54	1.53	12.1	19	12	7	1.3	30	66	42
	23	R	27	aaa	SD	38	3.13	1.08	8.3	22	6	16	0.9	27	75	101
Knowles,Antonio	23	R	23	aa	LA	41	5.93	1.36	5.0	22	15	6	1.3	23	58	55
Knowles,Lucas	23	L	25	a/a	WAS	55	6.08	1.57	8.1	17	8	9	1.7	33	65	31
Kober,Collin	22	R	28	aa	SEA	48	3.45	1.21	4.4	25	11	14	1.0	26	75	87
	23	R	29	aa	SEA	60	6.48	1.59	6.2	18	8	9	1.6	34	62	34
Kochanowicz,Jack	23	R	23	aa	LAA	71	7.08	1.55	19.4	15	7	9	2.1	32	58	14

PITCHER	yr	t	age	lvl	org	ip	era	whip	bf/g	k%	bb%	k-bb	hr/9	h%	s%	bpv
Koenig,Jared	22	L	28	aaa	OAK	107	3.79	1.28	22	18	6	12	0.7	32	72	84
	23	L	29	a/a	SD	59	3.89	1.84	5.7	19	10	9	1.2	39	82	44
Kolek,Stephen	22	R	25	aa	SEA	145	4.26	1.42	23	18	9	9	0.5	32	70	71
	23	R	26	a/a	SEA	72	3.63	1.17	5.9	22	10	12	0.3	28	68	95
Kollar,Jared	23	R	25	aa	SD	52	5.05	1.64	19	12	8	4	0.9	34	70	26
Komar,Brandon	22	R	23	aa	SD	75	5.77	1.61	21	14	9	6	1.0	34	65	33
	23	R	24	a/a	STL	129	4.79	1.34	22	14	8	6	1.0	29	66	40
Kopps,Kevin	22	R	25	aa	SD	55	4.10	1.46	5.6	21	14	7	0.6	29	72	72
	23	R	26	a/a	SD	73	3.27	1.52	6.9	21	10	11	0.3	35	78	81
Kouba,Rhett	23	R	24	a/a	HOU	128	3.55	1.25	19	23	7	16	1.0	31	75	94
Kowar,Jackson	22	R	26	aaa	KC	84	5.99	1.67	19	17	10	7	1.2	35	65	38
	23	R	27	aaa	KC	46	6.54	1.97	7.4	16	14	2	0.7	37	66	36
Krauth,Nick	23	R	24	a/a	TEX	116	6.53	1.61	19	12	8	4	1.3	33	60	15
Kravetz,Evan	23	L	27	a/a	CIN	62	5.20	1.60	7.6	19	12	7	1.5	31	71	35
Krehbiel,Joey	23	R	31	aaa	BAL	40	4.50	1.80	5.3	12	15	-2	1.5	30	80	1
Kriske,Brooks	23	R	29	aaa	KC	30	6.29	1.76	5.1	25	12	12	1.5	38	66	55
Kristofak,Zac	23	R	26	aa	LAA	42	4.76	1.33	11	15	9	6	0.8	28	64	51
Krook,Matt	22	L	28	aaa	NYY	140	4.59	1.56	21	20	13	7	1.3	31	74	43
	23	L	29	aaa	NYY	34	1.58	1.18	5	31	20	11	0.0	19	85	132
Kuhn,Travis	22	R	24	aa	SEA	60	3.78	1.25	4.9	24	12	12	0.4	28	69	99
	23	R	25	aa	SEA	56	3.25	1.28	4.7	19	9	10	0.3	30	74	83
Kuhnel,Joel	23	R	28	aaa	HOU	45	6.30	1.79	5.5	12	8	4	0.8	37	64	25
Kuhns,Max	23	R	29	a/a	PHI	32	9.65	2.15	5	19	18	1	2.8	33	59	-18
Kuzia,Nick	22	R	26	a/a	DET	58	5.10	1.50	6.1	16	12	5	0.8	30	66	46
	23	R	27	aa	COL	55	7.56	1.73	5.6	14	13	1	1.3	31	56	18
Labaut,Randy	23	L	27	a/a	CLE	61	4.15	1.47	8	15	15	0	0.8	26	73	42
Lamet,Dinelson	22	R	30	a/a	SD	20	1.76	1.30	4.9	25	8	18	0.8	33	91	104
	23	R	31	aaa	BOS	30	3.29	1.23	15	16	7	9	1.4	27	81	46
LaSorsa,Joe	22	L	24	aa	TAM	35	2.87	0.84	6.8	23	2	20	0.6	26	67	267
	23	L	25	a/a	WAS	38	4.26	1.64	7.4	14	8	6	1.4	34	78	23
Latz,Jake	22	L	26	aaa	TEX	53	5.33	1.70	13	19	12	7	1.6	33	73	29
	23	L	27	aaa	TEX	65	4.33	1.47	6.1	24	11	14	0.7	34	71	84
Lauer,Eric	23	L	28	aaa	MIL	45	5.85	1.98	18	24	11	12	1.4	43	73	51
Lavender,Nathan	23	L	23	a/a	NYM	55	3.08	1.23	5.3	34	12	22	1.0	31	79	119
Laweryson,Cody	22	R	23	aa	MIN	61	0.94	0.89	12	26	6	20	0.2	26	91	152
	23	R	24	aaa	MIN	52	4.58	1.51	7.1	19	11	9	1.7	30	76	34
Leahy,Kyle	22	R	25	a/a	STL	146	4.35	1.47	22	17	9	8	1.0	32	72	53
	23	R	26	aaa	STL	84	6.28	1.78	8.4	19	9	9	1.4	38	67	36
Leal,David	22	L	25	aa	OAK	116	4.40	1.33	24	13	3	10	0.7	33	67	108
	23	L	26	aa	OAK	85	5.65	1.56	10	14	6	8	1.1	35	65	41
Leasher,Aaron	22	L	26	aaa	SD	88	3.43	1.35	11	20	9	11	0.7	31	76	74
	23	L	27	a/a	SD	65	5.11	1.68	10	14	16	-3	0.6	28	69	37
Leasure,Jordan	22	R	24	aa	LA	50	3.43	1.12	4.5	26	8	18	1.4	26	77	93
	23	R	25	a/a	CHW	49	4.32	1.36	4.7	31	12	19	1.9	29	77	72
Leban,Zack	22	R	26	aa	MIA	33	7.29	1.48	6.8	23	11	12	1.6	31	51	54
	23	R	27	a/a	MIA	39	6.39	1.83	6.7	18	19	-1	0.8	30	64	47
Ledo,Luis	22	R	27	a/a	LAA	46	3.18	1.24	5.1	19	13	7	1.3	22	81	51
	23	R	28	aaa	LAA	77	5.98	1.87	15	13	15	-1	1.0	33	69	18
Lee,Chase	22	R	24	a/a	TEX	56	3.66	1.31	4.5	24	7	17	0.3	36	71	123
	23	R	25	aaa	TEX	64	4.07	1.52	5.9	25	10	16	1.0	36	76	82
Lee,Jake	23	R	28	a/a	LAA	94	6.75	1.76	12	14	6	8	2.4	35	68	-6
Leftwich,Jack	23	R	25	aa	CLE	78	6.65	1.47	15	17	8	9	1.6	31	57	32
Legumina,Casey	22	R	25	aa	MIN	73	4.71	1.53	11	19	9	10	1.1	33	72	54
	23	R	26	aaa	CIN	33	4.82	1.72	5.8	21	9	12	0.9	40	73	66
Lehman,Taylor	23	L	28	a/a	PHI	54	4.56	1.39	4.6	16	15	2	1.0	24	69	42
Leigh,Zac	23	R	26	aa	CHC	35	4.62	1.31	5.8	29	11	17	1.0	31	66	97
Leiter,Jack	22	R	22	aa	TEX	94	4.93	1.44	17	22	12	10	0.8	31	66	74
	23	R	23	a/a	TEX	87	5.15	1.45	19	26	13	13	1.7	30	69	59
Leverett,Adam	22	R	24	aa	PHI	76	5.65	1.53	11	21	8	13	1.7	34	67	50
	23	R	25	aa	PHI	64	5.03	1.64	8.2	15	10	5	0.7	34	69	41
Liberatore,Matthew	22	L	23	aaa	STL	115	4.54	1.31	22	19	7	12	0.9	31	67	77
	23	L	24	aaa	STL	66	3.96	1.42	22	24	12	12	0.9	31	74	77
Lin,Yu-Min	23	L	20	aa	ARI	61	3.85	1.14	22	23	9	14	0.7	27	67	94
Lindgren,Jeff	22	R	26	a/a	MIA	138	4.70	1.45	22	16	9	7	1.1	31	70	41
	23	R	27	aaa	MIA	88	5.66	1.53	17	12	13	-1	1.7	26	67	0
Lindow,Ethan	22	L	24	aa	PHI	97	4.33	1.28	21	14	5	8	1.1	29	69	51
	23	L	25	aa	SEA	96	5.20	1.51	18	16	8	8	1.6	32	70	29
Lingos,Eli	22	L	26	a/a	CLE	66	2.95	1.04	6.8	17	7	10	0.7	24	75	73
	23	L	27	aaa	COL	51	5.59	1.75	7.3	11	12	-1	1.7	31	72	-9
Liranzo,Jesus	22	R	27	aaa	DET	19	10.14	2.04	4.9	22	14	8	2.1	39	51	17
	23	R	28	a/a	NYY	37	7.73	1.85	6.2	21	14	7	1.4	37	59	39
Little,Brendon	22	L	26	aaa	CHC	51	4.27	1.54	6.2	18	11	7	0.6	33	73	56
	23	L	27	aaa	CHC	74	4.06	1.49	6.4	18	11	6	0.6	31	73	58
Little,Luke	23	L	23	a/a	CHC	49	2.52	1.24	6.5	35	16	20	0.1	29	78	140
Liu,Chih-Jung	23	R	24	aa	BOS	115	6.55	1.73	20	23	12	11	1.8	36	65	39
Lively,Ben	22	R	30	aaa	CIN	77	5.61	1.73	19	18	10	8	1.0	37	69	41
	23	R	31	aaa	CIN	34	5.06	1.39	21	11	9	3	1.7	26	69	5
Lockhart,Lael	23	L	25	a/a	DET	95	4.50	1.47	15	22	12	10	0.8	32	70	70
Loeprich,Conner	22	R	25	aa	BAL	72	4.74	1.47	9.7	20	8	11	1.4	33	72	52
	23	R	26	a/a	BAL	53	5.30	1.40	6.4	19	9	10	1.0	31	63	62
Logue,Zach	22	L	26	aaa	OAK	80	6.13	1.80	22	12	8	4	1.8	35	70	-2
	23	L	27	aaa	DET	91	7.17	1.92	16	15	11	4	1.7	37	65	3
Long,Ryan	23	R	24	aa	BAL	47	7.73	1.65	17	16	8	8	1.5	35	53	29
Lopez,Jacob	23	L	25	a/a	TAM	108	2.81	1.23	17	25	12	13	0.7	27	80	90
Lopez,Jose	22	L	23	a/a	TAM	58	2.31	1.17	5.7	34	14	20	0.1	29	79	145
	23	L	24	aaa	TAM	31	7.41	1.88	5.4	19	12	7	0.8	39	59	47
Lopez,Justin	23	R	23	aa	SD	45	4.98	1.52	5.3	19	14	5	1.0	29	69	49

PITCHER	yr	t	age	lvl	org	ip	era	whip	bf/g	k%	bb%	k-bb	hr/9	h%	s%	bpv
Loutos,Ryan	22	R	23	a/a	STL	50	3.30	1.43	5.8	20	8	12	0.5	35	77	87
	23	R	24	a/a	STL	75	6.23	1.85	7.0	19	10	9	0.7	40	65	56
Lucas,Easton	22	L	26	aa	BAL	58	4.99	1.38	7.6	21	10	11	1.1	30	65	63
	23	L	27	a/a	OAK	48	3.60	1.39	5.6	19	8	11	1.3	31	79	55
Lucchesi,Joey	23	L	30	aaa	NYM	83	4.89	1.57	24.4	16	11	4	1.1	31	71	32
Lugo,Moises	22	R	23	a/a	SD	74	2.70	1.14	7.5	28	11	16	0.5	27	78	113
	23	R	24	aaa	SD	51	4.65	1.45	4.8	27	14	13	0.5	32	67	96
Luna,Carlos	22	R	26	aa	MIL	110	5.65	1.59	17.3	19	8	11	1.4	35	67	47
	23	R	27	a/a	MIN	99	6.76	1.61	17.5	18	6	12	2.8	34	66	12
Luna,Gil	23	L	24	aa	CHW	41	6.54	1.82	4.8	22	22	0	0.8	29	63	63
Lunn,Connor	22	R	24	aa	STL	83	4.84	1.37	16.6	17	5	12	1.0	33	66	77
	23	R	25	aa	STL	130	4.80	1.47	22.3	16	5	11	1.0	35	69	64
Mace,Tommy	23	R	25	aa	CLE	62	6.85	2.00	21.4	14	14	0	1.5	35	68	2
MacGregor,Travis	22	R	25	a/a	PIT	81	5.30	1.54	9.3	22	13	9	0.9	32	66	67
	23	R	26	a/a	PIT	79	4.69	1.69	8.3	18	9	8	0.8	37	73	53
Machado,Andres	22	R	29	aaa	WAS	17	6.60	1.56	5.7	18	7	11	0.0	38	53	90
	23	R	30	aaa	WAS	30	4.62	1.35	5.3	21	5	16	0.3	36	64	119
Maciejewski,Josh	22	L	27	a/a	NYY	39	3.83	1.28	10.7	25	9	16	0.7	32	71	98
	23	L	28	a/a	NYY	44	3.73	1.46	7.1	17	9	8	0.7	33	76	60
Macuare,Angel	23	R	23	a/a	HOU	77	5.29	1.56	17.8	18	8	10	1.6	34	70	38
Madden,Ty	23	R	23	aa	DET	118	3.85	1.38	19.0	24	10	14	1.1	31	76	77
Madison,Ben	23	R	26	aa	SF	33	4.88	1.69	7.9	23	22	1	0.8	26	72	69
Magno,Andrew	23	L	25	a/a	DET	64	2.18	1.34	6.1	24	14	10	0.2	29	84	96
Maldonado,Anthony	22	R	24	a/a	MIA	65	3.12	1.07	6.1	29	8	21	1.1	27	76	117
	23	R	25	aaa	MIA	46	1.99	1.02	5.2	32	12	20	1.0	22	88	114
Marceaux,Landon	23	R	24	aa	NYM	61	6.85	1.86	22.0	14	8	6	1.1	39	63	25
Marciano,Joey	22	L	27	aaa	SF	59	3.97	1.60	4.7	18	12	6	0.7	33	76	54
	23	L	28	aaa	SF	44	7.19	2.14	7.1	18	20	-3	0.9	35	66	37
Margevicius,Nick	22	L	26	aaa	SEA	49	6.81	1.99	7.1	17	7	10	1.2	43	66	44
	23	L	27	a/a	ATL	70	8.42	1.73	15.2	13	6	6	1.6	36	51	14
Marsh,Alec	22	R	24	a/a	KC	125	6.54	1.58	20.4	21	9	12	1.6	35	61	52
	23	R	25	a/a	KC	63	5.11	1.63	20.0	20	11	9	0.7	36	68	65
Martin,Corbin	22	R	27	aaa	ARI	77	5.24	1.47	19.5	18	8	10	1.3	33	67	51
Martin,Riley	23	L	25	a/a	CHC	59	4.39	1.63	6.0	29	16	14	0.8	36	74	92
Martinez,Adrian	22	R	26	aaa	OAK	91	4.33	1.28	20.8	20	7	13	1.5	29	72	67
	23	R	27	aaa	OAK	39	7.25	2.04	14.6	10	10	-1	1.4	37	66	-14
Martinez,Daniel	23	R	25	aa	ATL	30	5.89	1.70	22.8	23	14	9	0.0	37	62	91
Martinez,Jose	22	R	23	a/a	LA	61	4.44	1.39	9.2	14	10	4	0.7	29	68	50
	23	R	24	a/a	STL	60	5.16	1.83	9.0	7	15	-8	0.9	29	73	0
Martinez,Justin	23	R	22	aaa	ARI	50	3.46	1.42	4.5	27	19	8	0.3	26	75	100
Martinez,Marcelo	22	L	26	a/a	KC	110	6.12	1.51	15.9	17	10	8	1.5	31	62	34
	23	L	27	aaa	KC	21	4.79	1.56	10.2	10	5	5	2.4	31	79	-17
Marvel,James	22	R	29	aaa	PHI	94	6.72	1.76	12.7	11	8	3	0.8	36	61	19
	23	R	30	aaa	TEX	24	9.01	2.50	21.3	9	10	-2	0.4	45	61	3
Mata,Bryan	22	R	23	a/a	BOS	74	2.41	1.26	20.2	24	12	13	0.4	28	82	95
	23	R	24	aaa	BOS	27	6.83	2.22	15.1	17	21	-4	0.3	37	67	48
Mateo,Alejandro	23	R	29	a/a	CHW	57	7.32	1.97	6.1	18	13	5	2.2	36	67	-1
Matthews,John	23	R	25	aa	TEX	46	8.50	1.88	6.8	16	16	0	0.8	33	52	36
Mattison,Tyler	23	R	24	aa	DET	34	1.81	1.20	6.2	27	13	14	0.0	28	83	118
Mattson,Isaac	22	R	27	aaa	BAL	19	6.34	1.70	4.6	12	23	-10	2.1	17	68	-5
	23	R	28	aa	MIN	33	3.89	1.30	6.5	24	19	5	0.8	19	72	80
Mauricio,Alex	23	R	27	aa	NYY	50	3.88	1.44	5.9	17	10	7	1.0	30	76	46
Mayberry,Seth	23	R	23	aa	SD	41	5.46	1.71	6.0	25	14	12	1.1	37	70	67
Mazur,Adam	23	R	22	aa	SD	38	4.27	1.49	13.7	23	4	19	0.7	41	72	149
McArthur,James	22	R	26	aa	PHI	57	5.48	1.76	20.1	20	10	10	1.7	37	73	33
	23	R	27	aaa	KC	58	5.35	1.49	9.0	21	11	10	0.9	32	64	64
McCambley,Zach	22	R	23	aa	MIA	94	6.19	1.50	21.4	21	12	9	1.0	31	59	59
	23	R	24	aa	MIA	39	4.26	1.66	7.0	20	12	8	0.2	36	73	75
McCaughan,Darren	22	R	26	aaa	SEA	155	4.09	1.17	22.1	18	6	12	1.0	28	68	80
	23	R	27	aaa	SEA	139	5.58	1.46	23.8	18	6	11	1.7	33	66	44
McDermott,Chayce	23	R	25	a/a	BAL	121	3.45	1.21	18.8	25	14	11	0.6	24	73	90
McDonald,Cole	23	R	26	aa	HOU	48	4.54	1.41	5.8	27	11	16	0.4	35	67	106
McDowell,Theo	23	R	25	aa	TEX	36	8.41	2.13	6.9	19	17	1	1.9	36	62	9
McGarity,Aaron	23	R	28	aaa	NYY	71	5.88	1.40	5.9	19	9	10	1.8	29	62	35
McGarry,Griff	23	R	24	a/a	PHI	61	6.56	1.53	16.7	25	19	6	0.7	27	55	80
McGee,Easton	22	R	25	aaa	TAM	109	5.30	1.36	16.9	15	4	11	1.6	32	66	58
	23	R	26	aaa	SEA	30	2.79	1.16	24.0	17	6	10	0.3	29	75	89
McGreevy,Michael	22	R	22	aa	STL	99	3.32	1.16	19.7	15	5	11	0.8	29	74	84
	23	R	23	a/a	STL	155	3.91	1.39	24.2	16	5	11	0.8	33	74	72
McKay,Tyler	23	R	26	a/a	PHI	56	3.07	1.38	4.9	19	13	6	0.6	28	79	66
McKendry,Evan	22	R	24	a/a	TAM	96	3.74	1.06	16.2	21	3	18	1.3	29	70	163
	23	R	25	aaa	MIL	143	4.70	1.30	21.1	19	8	11	1.8	28	71	41
McKillican,Adam	23	R	25	aa	COL	34	8.38	1.77	6.3	16	10	6	2.0	35	54	5
McLoughlin,Trey	23	R	24	aa	NYM	36	4.07	1.29	5.9	22	7	15	1.0	31	71	84
McMahon,Chris	23	R	24	aa	COL	67	8.00	1.94	21.2	16	8	7	2.5	38	63	-12
McMahon,Hunter	23	R	25	a/a	MIN	73	5.88	1.45	6.6	17	8	9	1.0	32	59	53
McSteen,Jake	23	L	27	aa	ATL	58	5.53	1.69	6.6	16	8	8	1.9	35	73	16
McSweeney,Morgan	22	R	25	a/a	BAL	48	4.02	1.43	5.4	17	12	5	1.2	27	76	37
	23	R	26	aaa	BAL	46	5.97	1.61	4.9	18	15	3	1.2	29	64	35
Mederos,Victor	23	R	22	aa	LAA	92	6.10	1.53	20.0	22	10	12	2.2	31	66	29
Medina,Luis	22	R	23	aa	OAK	94	4.53	1.41	16.6	22	13	9	0.5	30	67	82
	23	R	24	aaa	OAK	18	4.86	1.55	13.3	23	17	6	0.3	29	67	84
Medrano,Ronald	23	R	28	aa	KC	31	6.56	1.74	15.7	14	8	5	0.9	36	62	30
Meeker,James	23	R	28	a/a	MIL	93	3.95	1.42	11.0	16	4	12	1.3	34	77	76
Meis,Justin	23	R	24	aa	PIT	83	5.91	1.69	12.9	16	14	3	1.6	30	69	15
Meisinger,Ryan	22	R	28	aaa	ARI	16	4.89	1.60	5.5	17	9	8	2.1	32	77	13
	23	R	29	a/a	CIN	40	7.65	1.96	5.8	20	18	2	1.8	33	63	18

PITCHER	yr	t	age	lvl	org	ip	era	whip	bf/g	k%	bb%	k-bb	hr/9	h%	s%	bpv
Mejia,Enmanuel	22	R	24	aa	PIT	51	5.59	1.61	5.7	18	13	5	0.9	32	65	48
	23	R	25	a/a	TAM	52	3.99	1.33	5.3	29	13	16	1.0	30	73	91
Mejia,Humberto	22	R	25	aaa	ARI	15	7.92	1.84	7.8	7	5	2	1.7	36	58	-21
	23	R	26	aaa	NYM	35	6.00	1.53	19	16	8	8	2.3	31	68	10
Mejia,Jean Carlos	22	R	26	a/a	MIL	33	2.57	0.90	4.8	24	11	14	0.8	18	76	96
	23	R	27	aaa	MIL	31	4.32	1.38	5.7	20	10	10	0.7	31	69	71
Mejias,Christian	23	R	24	aa	MIL	122	7.27	1.60	20	20	10	9	1.6	33	56	36
Melean,Alejandro	23	R	23	aa	TOR	64	4.92	1.64	11	19	12	7	1.2	33	73	41
Mena,Cristian	23	R	21	a/a	CHW	135	5.01	1.43	21	23	11	12	1.3	31	68	63
Mendez,Josan	23	R	23	aa	MIA	49	4.99	1.57	6.3	16	7	9	1.2	35	70	42
Mengden,Daniel	22	R	29	aaa	KC	109	5.46	1.61	19	14	11	2	1.7	29	70	6
	23	R	30	aaa	WAS	51	8.39	2.26	9.3	13	13	0	1.0	41	62	8
Mercado,Michael	22	R	23	aa	TAM	104	4.43	1.29	18	23	7	16	1.1	32	69	89
	23	R	24	a/a	TAM	64	4.76	1.32	5.1	30	12	18	1.6	29	69	82
Mercedes,Juan	23	R	23	aa	SEA	47	6.65	1.63	17	17	8	9	1.4	35	60	34
Meyer,Max	22	R	23	aaa	MIA	58	3.81	1.02	19	24	8	17	0.7	26	63	113
Middendorf,Ryan	23	R	26	a/a	MIL	60	4.81	1.59	6.3	18	7	11	0.8	37	70	65
Milacki,Bobby	23	R	27	aa	SD	52	5.71	1.59	13	15	8	8	2.7	31	74	-8
Miller,Bobby	22	R	23	a/a	LA	113	3.62	1.08	18	26	6	20	0.8	30	69	130
	23	R	24	aaa	LA	15	5.65	1.16	15	17	9	8	1.2	23	52	49
Miller,Bryce	22	R	24	aa	SEA	52	2.90	0.99	20	26	8	18	0.4	25	71	124
	23	R	25	aa	SEA	21	6.34	1.33	22	17	3	14	2.0	32	57	91
Miller,Erik	22	L	24	a/a	PHI	49	3.55	1.45	6.5	24	14	10	0.7	30	77	80
	23	L	25	a/a	SF	63	2.75	1.27	4.8	28	18	10	0.3	23	78	110
Miller,Ryan	23	R	27	aa	BOS	61	5.23	1.63	6.6	19	7	11	1.5	36	72	46
Miller,Tyson	22	R	27	aaa	TEX	91	4.19	1.47	14	22	9	13	1.1	33	75	67
	23	R	28	aaa	LA	45	3.89	1.44	7.4	20	8	12	0.9	34	75	72
Minnick,Matt	22	L	26	a/a	NYY	63	2.02	0.79	6.3	23	8	14	0.9	16	82	100
	23	L	27	a/a	NYM	31	2.94	1.12	5.9	16	11	6	1.1	21	79	50
Misiewicz,Anthony	22	L	28	aaa	KC	19	3.89	1.11	3.6	18	8	10	1.6	22	72	52
	23	L	29	aaa	NYY	42	4.82	1.53	5.7	20	10	9	1.4	32	72	44
Mlodzinski,Carmen	22	R	23	aa	PIT	106	4.63	1.42	17	20	8	12	0.7	34	67	78
	23	R	24	aaa	PIT	28	3.20	1.46	6	21	10	11	0.6	33	79	75
Molina,Anthony	23	R	21	a/a	TAM	124	4.33	1.47	19	17	6	11	0.9	34	72	66
Montero,Keider	23	R	23	a/a	DET	112	5.20	1.50	21	23	9	14	1.0	35	67	77
Montes De Oca,Christian	23	R	24	aa	ARI	61	4.13	1.26	5.9	18	10	9	0.9	27	69	61
Monteverde,Patrick	23	L	26	a/a	MIA	124	4.87	1.43	23	18	10	8	1.3	29	69	40
Montgomery,Mason	22	L	22	aa	TAM	55	2.20	0.97	19	22	6	16	0.6	25	80	115
	23	L	23	a/a	TAM	127	3.92	1.30	18	24	11	13	1.3	28	75	68
Montilla,Jose	23	R	25	aa	ATL	47	8.81	1.87	11	14	10	4	1.8	36	53	0
Moore,Xavier	23	R	24	aa	BAL	31	7.19	2.11	5.9	23	23	0	0.8	34	65	62
Moreno,Gerson	22	R	27	aa	DET	57	3.64	1.24	4.8	31	14	17	0.7	27	72	110
	23	R	28	aaa	WAS	73	3.54	1.41	5.2	23	17	6	0.7	25	76	75
Moreno,Luis	23	R	24	a/a	NYM	124	5.19	1.58	21	19	12	8	0.8	33	67	57
Moronta,Reyes	23	R	30	aaa	LAA	42	3.53	1.63	5.5	21	20	1	0.7	26	80	63
Morris,Cody	22	R	26	aaa	CLE	16	1.97	0.64	9.3	42	9	33	0.9	14	78	185
	23	R	27	a/a	CLE	41	3.60	1.36	8.2	20	17	3	1.2	20	78	53
Mosqueda,Oddanier	22	L	23	aa	BOS	60	4.43	1.14	5.3	26	8	18	1.2	28	64	100
	23	L	24	aaa	BOS	61	5.73	1.55	5.6	23	14	9	1.5	30	66	46
Mosser,Gabe	22	R	26	aa	SD	25	4.76	1.49	22	10	8	2	1.3	30	71	5
	23	R	27	aa	SD	38	5.86	1.75	17	14	9	5	2.6	33	75	-19
Muckenhirn,Zach	22	L	27	aaa	CHW	55	3.01	1.41	4.9	19	10	9	1.5	29	87	41
	23	L	28	aaa	SEA	49	2.69	1.22	6.6	13	8	5	0.8	26	81	44
Muller,Kyle	22	L	25	aaa	ATL	136	4.31	1.37	25	24	8	16	1.1	33	71	83
	23	L	26	aaa	OAK	62	6.22	1.83	22	14	12	2	1.2	34	67	16
Munoz,Roddery	23	R	23	a/a	WAS	70	6.84	1.77	11	19	15	4	1.6	31	63	27
Munoz,Victor	23	R	23	aa	TAM	80	7.82	1.64	14	16	9	7	1.1	35	51	35
Murdock,Noah	23	R	25	aa	KC	69	6.90	1.75	8.8	18	15	3	0.5	33	58	56
Murphy,Chris	22	L	24	a/a	BOS	154	4.24	1.32	21	19	11	8	0.8	28	69	65
	23	L	25	aaa	BOS	54	6.77	1.85	17	19	12	7	1.2	38	64	38
Murphy,Luke	22	R	23	aa	LAA	46	2.37	1.06	4.9	25	13	11	0.0	23	75	114
	23	R	24	aa	LAA	49	5.56	1.75	5.1	23	12	12	0.8	39	68	70
Murphy,Patrick	23	R	28	aaa	MIN	86	3.93	1.72	9.3	19	13	6	0.7	35	78	55
Murphy,Ryan	23	R	24	aa	SF	108	5.33	1.61	16	19	11	8	1.2	33	69	42
Murray,Jayden	22	R	25	a/a	HOU	110	3.31	1.21	19	18	7	11	1.0	28	76	72
	23	R	26	aaa	HOU	42	8.19	2.22	19	16	14	2	1.7	40	64	3
Mushinski,Parker	22	L	27	aaa	HOU	42	2.56	1.16	4.4	19	11	8	0.6	24	80	76
	23	L	28	aaa	HOU	33	2.86	1.08	4.1	24	8	15	0.6	27	75	105
Myatt,Tanner	23	R	25	a/a	NYY	59	3.15	1.30	5.5	25	17	8	0.6	24	77	87
Myers,Tobias	22	R	24	aaa	CHW	76	7.09	1.97	16	12	12	0	1.7	34	66	-9
	23	R	25	a/a	MIL	142	5.32	1.35	20	25	8	17	2.0	31	67	66
Nail,Brendan	23	L	28	a/a	BOS	54	3.55	1.54	6.9	17	12	5	1.2	30	81	36
Naile,James	22	R	29	aaa	STL	74	3.28	1.48	7.2	14	6	8	0.5	34	78	61
	23	R	30	aaa	STL	59	4.01	1.56	8.3	18	8	10	0.9	35	76	60
Nardi,Andrew	22	L	24	a/a	MIA	53	2.37	0.92	5.4	32	9	23	0.6	25	77	144
Nastrini,Nick	23	R	23	a/a	CHW	116	4.34	1.36	19	24	11	13	1.0	30	70	77
Naughton,Tim	23	R	28	aa	DET	52	5.59	1.54	6.3	19	9	10	0.9	35	64	61
Navarro,Edgar	22	R	24	a/a	CHW	47	3.79	1.50	5.4	22	16	5	0.6	27	75	79
	23	R	25	a/a	CHW	54	3.92	1.50	5.1	15	16	-1	0.2	26	72	59
Neidert,Nick	22	R	26	aaa	MIA	46	2.13	1.15	13	21	5	16	1.1	30	88	109
	23	R	27	aaa	CHC	107	5.71	1.67	18	14	8	6	1.3	35	68	23
Nelson,Nick	23	R	28	a/a	PHI	111	4.97	1.69	22	13	9	4	1.3	34	74	17
Nelson,Ryne	22	R	24	aaa	ARI	136	4.38	1.28	21	18	6	11	1.1	30	69	68
	23	R	25	aaa	ARI	23	3.11	1.09	23	8	7	1	0.8	23	74	27
Newcomb,Sean	22	L	29	aaa	CHC	24	3.65	1.34	8.3	23	18	5	0.4	23	72	89
	23	L	30	aaa	SF	32	3.52	1.57	7.8	21	15	6	0.5	31	78	70

PITCHER	yr	t	age	lvl	org	ip	era	whip	bf/g	k%	bb%	k-bb	hr/9	h%	s%	bpv
Nicolas,Kyle	23	R	24	a/a	PIT	100	6.14	1.67	12.9	22	12	10	1.6	35	66	44
Nikhazy,Doug	23	L	24	aa	CLE	102	6.19	1.87	18.4	22	17	5	1.3	34	68	44
Nogosek,Stephen	22	R	27	aaa	NYM	44	1.95	1.03	5.7	25	8	17	0.4	26	82	121
	23	R	28	a/a	ARI	38	6.57	1.79	6.1	15	18	-2	0.5	30	61	44
Nordlin,Seth	22	R	25	a/a	TEX	78	3.33	1.27	10.0	16	7	9	0.7	30	75	69
	23	R	26	a/a	TEX	99	5.90	1.67	14.0	12	6	6	1.3	35	66	20
Norris,Daniel	23	L	30	aaa	CLE	69	5.96	1.81	14.6	14	10	4	1.7	35	71	4
Nowlin,Jaylen	23	L	22	aa	MIN	39	3.55	1.33	18.1	19	13	6	0.8	26	75	61
Nunez,Andres	22	R	27	aaa	KC	63	3.58	1.36	4.9	19	6	13	0.6	34	74	93
	23	R	28	aaa	BOS	46	6.88	1.91	5.9	12	14	-1	0.7	35	62	23
Nunez,Dedniel	23	R	27	a/a	NYM	57	6.30	1.92	6.8	21	13	8	1.3	39	69	39
Nunez,Juan	23	R	27	aa	TOR	40	4.69	1.70	5.7	25	24	2	0.5	26	72	86
Nutof,Ryan	22	R	27	a/a	CIN	61	3.59	1.67	6.4	20	14	6	0.6	34	79	61
	23	R	28	aaa	CIN	67	5.71	1.63	5.1	15	14	1	1.0	29	65	32
O Brien,Riley	23	R	28	aaa	SEA	55	2.24	1.22	4.4	31	12	18	0.3	30	82	124
Ogle,Braeden	22	L	25	aaa	PHI	37	5.19	1.70	4.7	12	12	0	0.2	33	67	38
	23	L	26	a/a	PIT	37	6.70	2.00	5.2	17	22	-5	1.6	28	69	16
Ohl,Pierson	23	R	24	aa	MIN	87	2.71	1.00	20.8	19	4	15	0.8	27	77	127
Olds,Wyatt	23	R	24	aa	BOS	47	10.10	2.04	10.0	19	20	-1	0.9	33	47	44
Olivero,Deyni	22	R	24	a/a	ARI	125	4.75	1.42	21.2	14	7	7	1.1	31	69	40
	23	R	25	aa	ARI	68	9.39	2.21	20.1	9	10	-1	1.5	39	57	-23
Oller,Adam	23	R	29	aaa	SEA	115	6.19	1.70	21.7	18	9	9	1.8	35	67	25
O'Loughlin,Jack	23	L	23	aaa	DET	88	4.74	1.51	21.2	17	9	8	0.7	33	69	55
Olson,J.B.	22	R	27	a/a	CHW	71	5.85	1.65	6.4	14	10	4	1.5	32	67	14
	23	R	28	aaa	CHW	30	12.41	2.20	10.1	10	9	2	2.6	39	43	-47
Olson,Reese	22	R	23	aa	DET	121	4.11	1.24	18.9	27	7	20	0.9	33	69	121
	23	R	24	aaa	DET	38	6.31	1.74	17.4	22	12	9	1.0	37	64	57
Onyshko,Ben	22	L	26	aa	SEA	55	4.14	1.38	5.4	15	10	5	1.3	27	74	33
	23	L	27	aa	SEA	49	5.72	1.49	7.8	17	9	8	0.7	33	61	56
O'Reilly,John	23	R	28	aaa	PIT	69	6.98	2.13	6.8	12	11	1	1.3	39	68	-2
Ortega,Oliver	22	R	26	aaa	LAA	27	4.97	1.54	5.2	18	6	12	0.9	37	68	72
	23	R	27	aaa	MIN	36	1.83	1.03	5.8	25	7	18	0.7	26	87	117
Ortiz,Luis	22	R	23	a/a	PIT	125	4.41	1.15	19.1	22	7	15	1.2	28	64	90
	22	R	27	aaa	SF	68	4.33	1.26	7.9	20	4	15	0.9	33	67	112
Ortiz,Luis	23	R	28	aaa	PHI	45	5.31	1.31	5.6	18	7	11	0.4	32	57	83
	23	R	24	aaa	PIT	58	5.00	1.46	19.2	17	11	6	1.1	30	68	43
Ortiz-Mayr,Orlando	23	R	26	aa	LA	62	7.06	1.58	21.1	14	7	7	1.6	33	57	20
Orze,Eric	22	R	25	aaa	NYM	48	4.63	1.16	6.0	28	7	21	1.7	29	67	105
	23	R	26	aaa	NYM	61	5.16	1.58	6.9	25	15	10	0.7	33	67	79
Osterberg,Matt	23	L	24	aa	PHI	31	3.98	1.19	20.8	20	5	15	1.1	30	70	99
Otanez,Michel	22	R	25	a/a	NYM	46	4.37	1.72	4.7	23	18	5	0.7	32	75	72
	23	R	26	a/a	ARI	37	5.81	1.62	5.1	29	16	13	0.5	36	62	99
Otto Jr.,Glenn	23	R	27	aaa	SD	35	3.42	1.26	11.0	24	16	9	1.0	22	77	74
Oviedo,Johan	22	R	24	aaa	PIT	62	4.61	1.27	16.9	20	10	10	1.7	26	70	47
Oviedo,Luis	22	R	23	a/a	CLE	60	4.97	1.51	10.1	19	14	5	1.3	27	70	45
	23	R	24	aaa	CLE	63	4.65	1.51	6.5	18	14	4	0.5	29	68	61
Ozuna,Fernery	22	R	27	a/a	TEX	63	4.72	1.38	5.5	21	8	13	0.7	33	66	83
	23	R	28	aaa	TEX	50	6.14	1.65	6.8	16	13	3	2.0	29	68	7
Pacheco,Freddy	22	R	24	a/a	STL	64	2.39	0.90	4.8	27	9	18	0.6	21	76	123
Padilla,Nicholas	22	R	26	a/a	CHW	45	2.15	1.22	5.7	21	14	7	0.2	25	82	88
	23	R	27	aaa	CHW	47	6.21	2.11	5.3	18	18	0	1.2	36	72	27
Palacios,Luis	23	L	23	a/a	MIA	125	5.18	1.37	23.8	15	5	9	2.0	30	69	29
Palencia,Daniel	23	R	23	a/a	CHC	31	6.25	1.27	7.1	24	11	12	0.9	27	49	79
Pannone,Thomas	22	L	28	aaa	BOS	63	5.27	1.47	19.3	20	3	17	1.0	38	65	138
	23	L	29	aaa	MIL	54	3.20	1.28	20.2	18	6	11	1.0	30	79	69
Paredes,Enoli	22	R	27	aaa	HOU	56	2.56	1.20	4.5	28	13	15	0.6	26	81	107
	23	R	28	aaa	HOU	55	4.99	1.60	4.7	21	18	3	1.0	26	70	57
Parke,John	22	L	27	aaa	CHW	135	6.64	1.73	22.0	13	7	6	1.7	36	64	10
	23	L	28	aaa	CHW	43	7.93	2.18	15.4	13	12	1	1.3	40	64	1
Parker,Mitchell	23	L	24	a/a	WAS	126	5.47	1.54	19.7	23	11	12	1.0	34	65	67
Parkinson,David	23	L	28	a/a	PHI	131	4.72	1.65	23.4	18	10	8	1.5	34	76	29
Parrish,Drew	22	L	25	a/a	KC	130	3.99	1.21	19.4	14	9	4	1.1	24	70	40
	23	L	26	a/a	KC	117	7.48	1.91	19.8	13	13	0	2.3	32	65	-25
Parsons,Hunter	23	R	26	a/a	NYM	58	5.16	1.45	6.7	22	11	10	1.3	30	67	56
Parsons,Tommy	22	R	27	aaa	STL	137	4.08	1.17	14.4	15	9	5	1.5	22	72	31
	23	R	28	aaa	STL	74	7.72	1.87	18.3	11	9	3	2.4	34	63	-30
Parsons,Wes	23	R	31	aaa	TOR	83	4.97	1.52	21.2	20	12	7	1.3	30	70	45
Patino,Luis	22	R	23	aaa	TAM	34	4.27	1.31	15.6	21	8	13	1.3	30	71	68
	23	R	24	aaa	CHW	61	6.90	1.78	8.8	14	15	-1	2.2	28	66	-10
Patrick,Chad	23	R	25	a/a	OAK	126	5.06	1.59	20.6	18	9	9	1.0	35	70	51
Peek,Zach	22	R	24	aa	BAL	46	3.63	1.22	16.9	18	7	11	0.6	30	71	79
Peguero,Elvis	22	R	25	aaa	LAA	45	2.42	1.01	4.5	23	6	16	0.3	27	76	126
Peguero,Francis	22	R	27	aa	WAS	57	6.05	1.41	6.9	17	12	6	1.3	27	58	39
	23	R	26	a/a	MIN	45	4.99	1.52	5.7	17	7	9	2.0	32	75	22
Peguero,Joel	22	R	25	aaa	COL	58	4.59	1.65	5.2	15	12	3	1.0	32	74	30
	23	R	26	a/a	WAS	52	5.52	1.83	5.5	13	12	2	0.8	35	70	25
Peluse,Colin	22	R	24	a/a	OAK	123	4.60	1.28	21.1	15	5	10	0.9	31	65	73
	23	R	25	aaa	OAK	65	5.69	1.78	7.1	14	11	2	1.8	33	73	-2
Pena,Malvin	23	R	26	a/a	WAS	67	3.79	1.36	6.7	16	12	4	1.1	26	76	39
Pennington,Walter	22	L	24	aa	KC	62	5.52	1.67	8.4	15	9	5	0.5	36	65	48
	23	L	25	a/a	KC	72	3.49	1.35	6.1	19	11	7	0.6	29	75	67
Pepiot,Ryan	22	R	25	aaa	LA	92	2.11	0.98	18.4	25	8	17	0.8	24	84	114
	23	R	26	aaa	LA	24	4.08	1.19	16.2	22	5	17	1.6	29	73	94
Peralta,Sammy	22	L	24	a/a	CHW	62	3.56	1.25	7.4	24	8	17	0.9	31	74	100
	23	L	25	aaa	CHW	69	5.67	1.45	10.2	18	7	12	1.4	33	63	56
Percival,Cole	23	R	24	aa	LAA	50	7.24	1.82	15.5	16	12	4	0.8	36	59	37
Pereira,Wilfredo	23	R	24	aa	STL	139	4.91	1.39	22.6	14	8	6	1.0	30	66	41

PITCHER	yr	t	age	lvl	org	ip	era	whip	bf/g	k%	bb%	k-bb	hr/9	h%	s%	bpv
Perez,Andrew	22	L	25	aaa	CHW	64	5.20	1.36	4.5	22	9	12	1.8	29	67	49
	23	L	26	a/a	CHW	64	7.40	1.74	7.3	18	11	7	1.2	36	57	37
Perez,Eury	22	R	19	aa	MIA	75	4.17	1.14	17	31	7	24	0.9	33	65	143
	23	R	20	aa	MIA	38	3.30	0.91	18	33	6	27	1.2	25	70	155
Perez,Francisco	22	L	25	aaa	WAS	48	4.84	1.39	4.5	24	15	9	0.5	28	64	85
	23	L	26	a/a	OAK	42	4.02	1.30	5.8	24	11	13	0.6	30	69	87
Perez,Hector	23	R	27	aaa	PHI	65	4.54	1.54	6.7	23	15	8	1.4	29	75	51
Perkins,Jackson	23	R	24	aa	OAK	54	5.69	1.89	21	14	11	3	0.3	38	68	44
Petersen,Michael	23	R	29	a/a	COL	43	4.43	1.77	4.8	17	14	3	0.9	34	76	38
Peterson,David	22	L	27	aaa	NYM	26	4.64	1.73	20	23	8	15	0.3	43	72	99
	23	L	28	aaa	NYM	37	4.94	1.76	24	20	14	6	1.0	35	74	47
Petit,RJ	23	R	24	aa	DET	53	4.26	1.65	6.4	16	7	9	0.9	37	76	49
Peto,Robbie	23	R	25	a/a	LA	37	10.31	2.44	15	16	16	0	2.5	40	60	-26
Pfaadt,Brandon	22	R	24	a/a	ARI	169	3.20	1.08	23	26	4	22	1.1	31	76	167
	23	R	25	aaa	ARI	62	3.22	1.19	21	22	6	17	1.1	30	78	102
Pham,Alex	23	R	24	aa	BAL	62	3.09	1.08	17	18	7	11	0.7	25	73	81
Phillips,Connor	22	R	21	aa	CIN	47	4.91	1.75	18	25	15	10	0.6	37	72	78
	23	R	22	a/a	CIN	107	3.94	1.40	18	30	12	18	1.0	34	75	98
Phillips,Tyler	23	R	26	a/a	PHI	124	5.81	1.72	22	15	10	6	1.1	36	67	32
Pike,Tyler	22	L	28	aa	STL	63	4.06	1.38	7.4	21	10	10	0.8	30	72	74
Pilarski,Jacob	23	R	25	aa	LA	31	7.44	2.16	6.2	13	16	-3	1.1	37	65	10
Pilkington,Konnor	22	L	25	aaa	CLE	58	4.93	1.39	19	19	9	10	1.0	31	66	62
	23	L	26	aaa	ARI	76	7.53	1.97	14	17	16	1	1.4	34	62	17
Pina,Robinson	23	R	25	a/a	LAA	86	4.80	1.57	15	16	13	3	0.6	31	69	49
Pint,Riley	22	R	25	a/a	COL	47	4.60	1.39	4.8	22	14	8	0.8	27	67	70
	23	R	26	aaa	COL	58	6.70	1.79	5.7	23	21	2	0.6	31	61	73
Plassmeyer,Michael	22	L	26	aaa	PHI	129	4.37	1.32	20	19	8	10	1.9	27	75	36
	23	L	27	aaa	PHI	69	5.58	1.60	19	19	10	9	1.4	33	68	38
Plesac,Zach	23	R	28	aaa	CLE	96	6.46	1.64	23	13	11	2	2.8	28	69	-31
Plumlee,Peyton	23	R	26	aa	HOU	47	8.84	1.97	12	19	13	7	1.3	39	54	34
Politi,Andrew	22	R	26	a/a	BOS	70	2.58	1.05	5.4	24	8	16	0.7	26	79	103
	23	R	27	aaa	BOS	60	4.99	1.58	4.9	17	11	7	1.0	33	70	44
Polley,Triston	23	L	27	a/a	TEX	62	5.94	1.61	6.9	16	9	7	1.0	35	63	43
Ponce,Gabriel	22	R	23	a/a	TOR	59	3.73	1.21	6.6	21	12	9	1.1	24	73	64
	23	R	24	a/a	TOR	63	4.40	1.52	7.2	25	15	10	1.0	31	73	70
Ponticelli,Thomas	22	R	25	a/a	CLE	72	3.86	1.37	7.7	17	10	7	0.9	28	74	53
	23	R	26	aaa	CLE	64	4.79	1.74	6.6	16	11	4	1.1	34	74	30
Pop,Zach	22	R	26	aaa	TOR	28	3.09	1.74	5.5	16	10	6	0.0	38	80	64
	23	R	27	aaa	TOR	34	5.57	1.54	4.8	17	8	8	1.1	34	65	45
Pope,Austin	23	R	25	a/a	ARI	68	3.33	1.35	5.9	24	7	16	0.6	35	76	105
Pope,Bryan	23	R	24	aa	STL	32	4.22	1.78	6.1	18	9	9	1.0	39	78	47
Poppen,Sean	23	R	29	aaa	SD	59	5.43	1.85	5.9	14	10	4	0.4	39	69	44
Poulin,PJ	22	L	26	a/a	COL	62	4.34	1.44	4.8	22	9	13	1.2	33	73	67
	23	L	27	aaa	COL	51	5.98	1.96	7.6	11	13	-2	2.1	32	75	-26
Povich,Cade	23	L	23	a/a	BAL	128	5.43	1.40	19	26	12	14	1.1	31	63	79
Powell,Walker	23	R	27	aa	CHC	120	4.22	1.24	19	17	5	12	1.6	29	73	60
Priester,Charles	22	R	22	a/a	PIT	86	2.79	1.17	20	20	8	13	0.4	29	76	97
	23	R	23	aaa	PIT	108	4.37	1.41	21	20	10	10	0.5	32	68	78
Puckett,A.J.	22	R	27	aa	ATL	60	9.00	2.12	9	21	10	11	1.2	45	56	41
	23	R	28	a/a	SEA	65	4.65	1.46	5.9	15	10	6	0.7	31	68	50
Puckett,Brady	23	R	28	a/a	MIA	44	5.79	1.94	6	13	16	-3	1.2	32	72	13
Pushard,Matthew	23	R	26	aa	MIA	30	5.05	1.27	5.9	13	11	2	0.7	25	59	44
Quezada,Andrew	23	R	26	aa	COL	106	7.79	2.02	21	12	9	3	2.2	38	65	-23
Quezada,Johan	22	R	28	a/a	STL	56	4.55	1.75	6.4	19	13	6	0.4	37	73	64
	23	R	29	a/a	MIA	42	5.41	2.07	7.6	15	16	-1	1.3	36	76	15
Quinones,Luis	22	R	25	aa	TOR	71	5.34	1.44	16	23	14	9	0.9	29	63	74
	23	R	26	a/a	TOR	94	5.85	1.30	12	23	10	13	1.9	26	60	47
Ragans,Cole	22	L	25	a/a	TEX	96	2.79	1.10	21	24	7	16	0.8	28	78	106
	23	L	26	aaa	KC	29	4.39	1.43	18	22	13	10	0.6	31	69	78
Ramsey,Lane	22	R	26	aaa	CHW	22	4.99	1.73	5.3	17	17	1	1.2	29	74	29
	23	R	27	aaa	CHW	36	6.40	2.05	5.5	21	17	4	1.2	38	70	38
Rangel,Alan	22	R	25	a/a	ATL	119	6.45	1.72	20	22	10	12	1.3	38	64	53
	23	R	26	a/a	ATL	127	5.70	1.51	21	21	10	12	1.4	33	65	54
Record,Joe	22	R	27	a/a	HOU	61	4.60	1.60	6	19	12	7	0.4	34	70	66
	23	R	28	aaa	HOU	54	3.86	1.42	4.6	18	13	5	0.3	29	72	68
Reed,Jake	22	R	30	aaa	LA	22	2.98	1.25	5	17	8	10	0.4	30	76	81
	23	R	31	aaa	LA	35	8.54	2.00	5.8	14	13	1	1.5	36	57	3
Reyes,Denyi	22	R	26	aaa	BAL	54	7.30	1.64	16	17	3	14	2.3	38	60	74
	23	R	27	aaa	NYM	93	5.66	1.49	20	14	8	6	1.9	30	67	11
Reyes,Gerardo	22	R	29	aaa	LAA	47	3.43	1.49	4.4	21	16	5	0.9	27	80	62
	23	R	30	aaa	LAA	41	6.05	1.72	5.2	22	13	9	1.7	34	69	37
Reyes,Luis	22	R	28	a/a	WAS	123	6.72	1.70	21	16	13	3	1.4	31	62	20
	23	R	29	aaa	WAS	69	5.07	1.75	7	16	16	0	0.6	31	70	45
Reyes,Samuel	22	R	26	a/a	CHC	54	4.66	1.39	8.5	23	10	13	1.4	31	71	61
	23	R	27	a/a	CHC	69	3.36	1.30	8.6	19	11	8	0.7	27	76	66
Reynolds,Sean	23	R	25	a/a	SD	66	4.94	1.62	5.3	21	15	6	0.6	32	69	65
Rice,Jake	22	L	25	aa	ARI	25	8.51	2.06	5.1	14	13	2	2.5	35	63	-26
	23	L	26	aa	ARI	42	7.55	1.73	4.8	24	17	7	0.8	33	54	68
Richardson,Lyon	23	R	23	a/a	CIN	61	4.08	1.40	12	27	14	14	0.3	32	70	104
Riley,Trey	23	R	25	aa	ATL	50	5.20	1.91	5.7	21	19	3	0.4	35	71	67
Rivera,Blake	22	R	24	aa	SF	48	2.81	1.16	6.9	21	12	9	0.3	25	76	88
	23	R	25	aa	SF	47	5.99	2.00	6.2	21	19	1	0.6	35	69	59
Roa,Christian	23	R	24	a/a	CIN	121	5.58	1.67	19	26	17	10	1.7	31	71	52
Roach,Dalton	22	R	26	a/a	STL	101	3.55	1.14	9.8	18	5	13	1.3	27	74	80
	23	R	27	a/a	STL	72	4.57	1.36	6.7	18	9	9	1.7	28	73	34
Robaina,Julio	22	L	21	aa	HOU	82	6.04	1.76	16	19	14	6	1.0	34	66	47
	23	L	22	aa	HOU	116	3.38	1.36	19	21	9	12	0.5	32	75	85

PITCHER	yr	t	age	lvl	org	ip	era	whip	bf/g	k%	bb%	k-bb	hr/9	h%	s%	bpv
Robberse,Sem	23	R	22	a/a	STL	126	3.97	1.27	19.9	21	9	12	1.2	28	73	67
Robbins,Jimmy	23	L	26	a/a	TOR	96	6.02	1.70	17.4	17	15	2	0.9	31	64	38
Roberson,Josh	22	R	26	aa	TAM	35	6.23	1.86	5.3	20	15	5	0.8	37	66	50
	23	R	27	aaa	CHC	40	6.16	1.99	5.3	20	16	4	0.6	39	68	55
Robert,Daniel	22	R	28	aaa	TEX	40	5.83	1.54	4.7	21	15	6	0.6	30	60	68
	23	R	29	aaa	TEX	43	4.97	1.65	6.9	20	13	7	0.7	34	70	58
Roberts,Austin	22	R	24	aa	PIT	49	4.19	1.49	5.7	21	8	12	1.4	34	77	60
	23	R	25	a/a	MIA	73	6.54	1.69	7.5	18	11	8	1.2	35	62	39
Robertson,Nick	22	R	24	a/a	LA	69	3.76	1.25	5.3	25	8	16	0.8	31	72	100
	23	R	25	aaa	BOS	44	3.36	1.12	4.1	26	7	19	1.1	29	75	111
Robinson,Cam	23	R	24	a/a	MIL	52	5.52	1.95	5.1	20	15	5	1.1	37	73	42
Robles,Domingo	22	L	24	aa	STL	110	4.58	1.35	15.3	11	7	5	0.6	30	66	45
	23	L	25	a/a	ATL	131	4.64	1.43	21.5	20	7	13	0.7	35	68	82
Roby,Tekoah	23	R	22	aa	STL	59	4.38	1.17	16.8	25	5	19	0.8	32	63	130
Rock,Joe	23	L	23	a/a	COL	94	5.35	1.51	20.4	21	8	13	1.7	34	69	51
Rodriguez,Carlos	23	R	22	a/a	MIL	131	2.88	1.10	19.8	28	10	17	0.7	26	76	110
Rodriguez,Dereck	22	R	30	aaa	MIN	96	4.86	1.45	17.9	17	8	9	1.1	32	69	47
	23	R	31	aaa	ATL	66	7.09	1.84	9.9	16	12	4	1.3	36	62	21
Rodriguez,Elvin	22	R	24	aaa	DET	100	5.02	1.56	19.1	17	8	9	1.3	34	71	41
	23	R	25	aaa	TAM	45	3.43	1.14	17.8	23	10	13	1.5	24	78	65
Rodriguez,Grayson	22	R	23	a/a	BAL	77	2.51	0.92	18.1	31	8	23	0.2	26	72	155
	23	R	24	aaa	BAL	42	2.01	1.10	20.6	28	11	17	0.7	25	86	106
Rodriguez,Jose	22	R	27	aaa	NYM	76	4.74	1.56	11.9	17	11	6	1.5	31	74	26
	23	R	28	aaa	SEA	81	7.16	1.87	12.3	13	8	5	1.8	37	64	0
Rodriguez,Manuel	23	R	27	aaa	TAM	57	4.16	1.53	5.0	26	10	15	0.3	38	71	103
Rodriguez,Randy	23	R	24	a/a	SF	70	4.83	1.59	7.2	22	18	4	0.4	29	68	75
Rodriguez,Yerry	22	R	25	aaa	TEX	59	3.86	1.52	5.2	22	11	11	1.1	33	78	65
	23	R	26	aaa	TEX	49	5.23	1.46	5.5	24	12	11	1.7	29	69	49
Rogers,Josh	22	L	28	a/a	MIA	71	7.44	1.76	23.3	11	9	2	2.1	32	61	-20
	23	L	29	aaa	COL	105	9.45	2.05	17.1	8	8	0	3.4	34	60	-77
Rom,Drew	22	L	23	a/a	BAL	122	4.27	1.45	20.1	22	8	15	0.8	36	72	88
	23	L	24	aaa	STL	97	4.68	1.55	20.2	23	10	12	0.6	36	70	79
Romero,Jhon	23	R	28	aaa	CLE	49	4.55	1.58	6.4	20	13	6	0.9	31	73	54
Romero,Tommy	22	R	25	aaa	WAS	86	3.37	1.26	12.1	16	9	7	1.6	25	82	33
	23	R	26	aaa	WAS	89	5.90	1.78	11.4	16	15	1	1.2	32	68	27
Rondon,Angel	22	R	25	aaa	SF	53	3.90	1.48	10.9	20	15	5	1.1	27	77	52
Rooney,John	22	L	25	aa	LA	98	6.00	1.57	17.9	18	10	9	1.7	32	66	30
	23	L	26	a/a	LA	70	3.31	1.32	5.5	19	8	12	1.0	31	79	68
Rosenberg,Kenny	22	L	27	aaa	LAA	64	2.79	1.21	18.5	18	10	9	1.1	25	83	58
	23	L	28	aaa	LAA	100	5.29	1.66	22.4	21	10	11	1.4	36	71	47
Roth,Houston	23	R	25	a/a	BAL	81	5.80	1.59	13.7	19	13	6	1.7	29	68	25
Roupp,Landen	22	R	24	aa	SF	27	3.92	1.18	21.7	24	10	14	0.9	26	69	86
	23	R	25	aa	SF	31	2.19	1.16	12.4	28	8	20	0.3	32	81	135
Roycroft,Chris	23	R	26	a/a	STL	53	6.25	1.86	6.7	15	15	1	0.5	35	64	43
Rozek,Aaron	23	L	28	aa	MIN	86	6.33	1.63	14.7	17	8	8	1.5	34	63	29
Ruff,Mike	23	R	25	aa	COL	72	10.71	2.04	13.5	13	13	0	3.3	32	51	-57
Ruiz,Norge	23	R	29	aaa	OAK	46	6.26	1.82	5.6	11	9	2	1.0	36	66	12
Ruppenthal,Matt	22	R	27	a/a	HOU	65	4.87	1.47	6.2	24	15	10	0.5	30	66	87
	23	R	28	a/a	HOU	49	6.57	1.84	6.8	18	14	4	1.2	35	65	30
Rutledge,Jackson	23	R	24	a/a	WAS	121	4.29	1.37	22.1	18	11	7	1.0	28	71	50
Ryan,River	23	R	25	a/a	LA	105	4.32	1.41	17.1	21	10	11	1.0	31	72	64
Ryan,Ryder	22	R	27	aaa	TEX	60	3.39	1.39	5.4	20	10	9	0.9	30	78	65
	23	R	28	aaa	SEA	55	3.68	1.27	4.7	20	9	11	0.6	30	71	79
Saalfrank,Andrew	23	L	26	a/a	ARI	66	2.34	1.21	6.1	27	12	15	0.2	29	80	115
Saenz,Dustin	23	L	24	aa	WAS	73	5.93	1.57	21.4	11	6	5	1.3	33	64	17
Salazar,Eduardo	22	R	24	aa	CIN	127	5.60	1.63	21.0	17	11	6	0.9	33	66	43
	23	R	25	a/a	CIN	48	7.03	1.91	6.3	18	10	8	1.1	40	63	36
Salinas,Royber	23	R	22	aa	OAK	68	5.23	1.30	15.6	27	10	16	0.9	31	60	94
Samaniego,Tyler	23	L	24	aa	PIT	48	7.04	1.80	5.4	19	11	8	0.4	39	58	63
Sammons,Bryan	22	L	27	aa	MIN	50	5.75	1.38	5.7	21	8	13	2.2	29	65	41
	23	L	28	a/a	DET	84	5.55	1.66	19.9	19	11	8	1.6	33	70	28
Sanchez,Aaron	22	R	30	aaa	MIN	63	3.85	1.42	20.6	12	8	4	1.2	29	77	24
	23	R	31	aaa	ARI	90	5.41	1.89	19.3	12	15	-3	1.0	33	72	12
Sanchez,Cristopher	22	L	26	aaa	PHI	58	3.23	1.25	15.8	19	8	11	0.2	31	72	94
	23	L	27	aaa	PHI	51	4.76	1.55	22.4	15	13	2	1.2	28	72	29
Sanchez,Juan	23	L	23	a/a	SF	75	3.26	1.19	6.5	23	10	12	0.5	27	73	92
Sanders,Cam	22	R	26	a/a	CHC	99	4.76	1.30	11.7	21	13	8	0.9	25	65	67
	23	R	27	aaa	CHC	66	5.10	1.67	5.8	25	22	3	0.7	26	69	81
Sands,Cole	22	R	25	aaa	MIN	63	5.08	1.63	14.8	21	8	13	1.0	38	70	66
	23	R	26	aaa	MIN	32	1.44	0.89	6.3	28	8	20	0.5	23	88	132
Santana,Dennis	23	R	27	aaa	NYM	33	4.88	1.94	5.4	21	13	8	1.3	39	78	40
Santillan,Tony	23	R	26	aaa	CIN	32	8.24	2.18	4.6	20	17	3	1.6	39	63	22
Santos,Junior	23	R	22	aa	NYM	97	7.16	1.85	16.2	14	10	5	0.9	37	60	27
Santos,Lisandro	23	L	25	aa	NYY	51	3.23	1.41	6.5	22	16	5	0.6	25	78	73
Santos,Victor	22	R	22	a/a	BOS	147	5.02	1.28	21.6	17	5	12	1.3	31	63	74
Sauer,Matt	23	R	24	aa	NYY	69	4.04	1.25	20.1	25	10	15	1.6	27	74	70
Sawyer,Logan	23	R	31	a/a	STL	54	6.28	1.76	5.6	18	9	8	0.6	39	63	55
Schaller,Reid	23	R	26	aa	WAS	47	5.34	1.35	6.1	24	10	13	1.0	31	61	76
Scherff,Alex	23	R	25	a/a	MIN	60	4.11	1.61	6.1	23	14	9	0.9	33	77	63
Schoenle,Garrett	23	L	25	aa	CHW	104	6.94	1.70	13.8	20	14	6	1.5	32	61	32
Scholtens,Jesse	22	R	28	aaa	SD	84	3.48	1.34	9.5	20	8	12	1.0	31	78	70
	23	R	29	aaa	CHW	48	5.23	1.46	22.9	16	7	9	2.1	30	72	16
Schulfer,Austin	22	R	27	a/a	MIN	57	3.11	1.07	5.1	21	7	14	0.5	27	72	100
	23	R	28	aaa	MIN	57	4.07	1.78	6.4	15	12	3	0.2	36	75	54
Schultz,Andrew	22	R	25	aa	PHI	16	2.36	1.73	5.3	16	19	-3	0.0	29	85	63
	23	R	26	aa	PHI	39	7.48	1.93	5.5	17	17	0	0.9	34	60	39

PITCHER	yr	t	age	lvl	org	ip	era	whip	bf/g	k%	bb%	k-bb	hr/9	h%	s%	bpv
Schultz,Paxton	23	R	25	a/a	TOR	110	5.16	1.62	16	19	12	7	1.2	33	70	42
Schulze,Brett	23	R	26	a/a	PHI	59	4.90	1.51	5.6	25	17	8	0.9	29	68	74
Scolaro,Jonah	23	L	25	aa	CHW	57	4.10	1.34	7	22	14	8	0.9	25	72	66
Scott,Adam	22	L	27	aaa	CLE	76	5.65	1.61	9.1	19	12	7	1.3	32	67	43
	23	L	28	aaa	CLE	47	6.19	2.20	10	14	21	-6	0.6	34	71	34
Scott,Christian	23	R	24	aa	NYM	62	3.10	0.99	20	28	4	24	0.7	30	71	202
Scott,Tayler	22	R	30	aaa	PHI	44	4.61	1.56	5.4	22	7	14	1.1	37	73	71
	23	R	31	aaa	OAK	39	1.49	1.05	4.3	21	8	12	0.2	26	86	104
Seabold,Connor	22	R	26	aaa	BOS	88	3.60	1.23	19	19	5	14	0.7	32	72	102
	23	R	27	aaa	COL	32	8.26	1.92	19	17	5	12	1.0	43	55	60
Sears,JP	22	L	26	aaa	OAK	49	1.27	0.66	14	26	3	23	0.3	21	83	238
Selby,Colin	22	R	25	a/a	PIT	37	2.21	1.21	5.2	23	9	14	0.4	30	83	99
	23	R	26	aaa	PIT	31	4.38	1.45	4.7	23	17	6	0.0	28	66	97
Seminaris,Adam	22	L	24	a/a	LAA	67	4.33	1.60	17	15	9	6	0.6	34	73	49
	23	L	25	a/a	MIL	58	6.58	1.68	20	19	9	10	1.0	37	61	54
Semple,Shawn	23	R	28	a/a	SEA	103	5.61	1.77	19	11	6	5	1.4	36	71	8
Seymour,Carson	23	R	25	aa	SF	114	4.96	1.41	17	19	10	10	0.6	32	64	70
Sharp,Sterling	22	R	27	a/a	BOS	102	6.12	1.77	19	15	10	6	0.9	37	65	34
	23	R	28	aa	BOS	87	7.08	1.86	20	12	10	2	1.6	35	64	-4
Sharpe,Davis	23	R	23	aa	CLE	62	5.15	1.53	6.6	20	6	14	1.3	36	69	67
Sheehan,Emmet	23	R	24	a/a	LA	65	2.63	0.91	16	36	11	24	1.1	20	78	131
Sheffield,Justus	22	L	26	aaa	SEA	103	6.32	1.79	20	15	9	6	1.3	37	66	22
	23	L	27	a/a	ATL	65	9.42	2.16	14	15	15	0	1.4	38	55	9
Shook,TJ	22	R	24	aa	MIL	81	5.77	1.71	20	17	12	5	1.9	32	71	13
	23	R	25	aa	MIL	98	4.97	1.31	16	23	9	14	1.3	30	65	71
Shortridge,Aaron	22	R	25	aa	PIT	56	4.89	1.72	18	12	12	0	0.8	32	72	21
	23	R	26	a/a	PIT	144	6.10	1.73	22	14	9	5	1.3	35	66	19
Shreve,Ryan	23	R	25	aa	STL	72	4.58	1.44	7	16	8	8	1.3	31	72	39
Shugart,Chase	22	R	26	a/a	BOS	64	5.78	1.54	6.2	18	8	10	1.1	35	63	53
	23	R	27	aaa	BOS	46	9.46	2.10	5.7	13	11	3	2.4	38	57	-27
Shuster,Jared	22	L	24	a/a	ATL	142	3.91	1.16	21	22	7	15	1.3	27	71	80
	23	L	25	aaa	ATL	79	5.61	1.83	23	15	12	3	1.1	35	71	23
Sikkema,T.J.	23	L	25	aa	KC	73	6.80	1.50	9.3	15	12	3	1.3	27	55	25
Silseth,Chase	22	R	22	aa	LAA	83	2.09	0.92	21	30	8	22	1.1	23	86	132
	23	R	23	aaa	LAA	47	2.74	1.12	17	23	10	13	0.2	27	74	106
Silven,Yoelvin	22	R	23	aa	CHW	48	7.19	1.70	6	20	8	13	2.5	36	63	21
	23	R	24	aa	CHW	56	8.36	1.77	6.3	19	9	9	2.2	36	55	11
Simpson,Josh	22	L	25	a/a	MIA	70	4.24	1.13	5.6	33	12	21	0.6	28	62	128
	23	L	26	aaa	MIA	35	4.74	1.65	6.3	29	15	14	1.1	37	74	82
Sinclair,Jack	23	R	24	a/a	WAS	46	4.60	1.54	5.6	20	13	7	1.8	29	76	31
Sisk,Evan	22	L	25	a/a	MIN	65	1.44	0.97	5	24	11	14	0.2	22	86	114
	23	L	26	aaa	KC	61	6.93	1.90	5	16	13	2	0.8	36	62	34
Skirrow,Noah	22	R	24	a/a	PHI	121	4.39	1.39	20	21	8	14	1.0	34	70	80
	23	R	25	aaa	PHI	103	6.22	1.86	20	13	11	3	1.7	35	70	-2
Slaten,Justin	22	R	25	aa	TEX	52	6.47	1.84	9.7	21	18	3	0.9	33	64	54
	23	R	26	a/a	TEX	61	3.03	1.14	6.1	28	8	20	1.6	27	83	94
Small,Ethan	22	L	25	aaa	MIL	103	4.58	1.42	16	22	13	9	0.7	30	68	74
	23	L	26	aaa	MIL	51	3.57	1.38	5.6	24	11	12	1.0	30	77	75
Smeltzer,Devin	23	L	28	aaa	MIA	86	7.71	1.99	21	13	12	0	2.3	34	66	-27
Smith,Cade	23	R	24	a/a	CLE	64	4.34	1.39	5.8	29	11	18	1.0	34	71	98
Smith,Chad	22	R	27	aaa	COL	35	3.19	1.15	4.3	21	7	14	1.6	26	81	66
	23	R	28	aaa	OAK	36	6.45	2.00	5	18	16	2	1.1	36	68	32
Smith,Russell	23	L	25	aa	MIL	37	5.53	1.60	7.8	25	11	14	2.1	34	72	42
Smith-Shawver,AJ	23	R	21	a/a	ATL	48	4.01	1.29	16	26	14	12	0.7	26	70	89
Snelten,D.J.	23	L	31	aaa	NYY	36	9.03	2.36	6.2	20	24	-5	1.7	34	62	21
Snider,Collin	22	R	27	aaa	KC	23	5.05	1.48	5	9	15	-5	0.3	25	64	35
	23	R	28	aaa	KC	44	6.51	1.84	5.3	14	15	-1	1.0	32	64	25
Snider,Duncan	23	R	26	aa	SD	47	6.38	1.88	17	12	15	-3	1.0	32	66	11
Solesky,Chase	23	R	26	a/a	CHW	117	6.09	1.80	21	13	11	3	1.5	34	69	6
Solis,Jairo	23	R	24	aaa	HOU	63	7.98	1.97	17	14	11	3	1.7	37	61	-1
Solometo,Anthony	23	L	21	aa	PIT	53	5.21	1.33	18	19	7	12	1.1	31	62	69
Solomon,Peter	22	R	26	aaa	PIT	111	5.71	1.59	18	15	11	4	1.5	30	67	20
	23	R	27	aa	ARI	92	7.34	1.99	18	16	10	7	1.3	41	63	26
Sommer,Tommy	23	L	25	aa	CHW	68	6.89	1.82	20	14	15	-1	2.7	28	69	-26
Soroka,Michael	23	R	26	aaa	ATL	87	3.90	1.19	21	22	8	14	0.6	29	68	94
Spacke,Dylan	22	R	24	aa	BOS	66	6.03	1.66	9.3	16	12	4	1.0	32	64	36
	23	R	25	aa	BOS	52	4.36	1.57	7.6	13	12	1	0.8	30	74	29
Spain,Dylan	23	R	25	aa	COL	33	7.89	1.69	6.8	15	8	7	3.2	31	61	-28
Speas,Alex	23	R	25	a/a	TEX	58	2.96	1.29	4.9	29	16	13	0.3	27	77	110
Spence,Mitch	22	R	24	a/a	NYY	131	4.88	1.45	21	19	7	12	1.1	34	69	64
	23	R	25	aaa	NYY	163	4.87	1.43	24	19	7	11	1.7	31	71	44
Spiers,Carson	22	R	25	a/a	CIN	123	6.15	1.70	21	16	9	8	2.4	33	71	-4
	23	R	26	a/a	CIN	85	4.09	1.46	13	24	12	12	0.8	33	73	77
Stadler,Fitz	23	R	26	aa	TOR	30	4.66	1.73	6	20	14	6	0.7	35	73	56
Stallings,Garrett	22	R	25	aa	BAL	119	6.61	1.53	20	19	5	13	2.3	34	62	43
	23	R	26	a/a	BAL	128	5.95	1.56	20	18	8	10	1.2	35	63	51
Stankiewicz,Teddy	23	R	30	a/a	CIN	72	9.02	2.08	20	10	13	-3	1.9	35	58	-24
Stanley,Hunter	23	R	26	aa	CLE	119	6.43	1.68	21	16	11	5	1.4	33	64	22
Starr,Nick	23	R	27	aa	TEX	49	6.69	1.51	6.5	19	7	12	1.4	35	57	53
Sterner,Justin	22	R	26	a/a	TAM	48	3.91	1.45	5.4	26	11	15	1.1	33	76	82
	23	R	27	a/a	TAM	56	5.63	1.50	7.1	23	9	15	2.2	33	69	45
Stewart,Will	22	L	25	a/a	MIA	97	5.72	1.71	14	16	10	5	0.6	36	65	45
	23	L	26	a/a	MIA	33	3.84	1.89	8.2	12	18	-6	0.3	31	79	37
Stinson,Graeme	23	L	26	aa	TAM	46	6.58	1.72	7.2	20	14	6	1.0	33	62	47
Stockton,Spencer	22	R	26	aa	CIN	49	4.57	1.45	8.4	20	11	9	1.3	30	72	48
	23	R	27	aa	CIN	43	4.51	1.57	6.7	20	12	8	1.8	31	78	30

PITCHER	yr	t	age	lvl	org	ip	era	whip	bf/g	k%	bb%	k-bb	hr/9	h%	s%	bpv
Stone,Gavin	23	R	25	aaa	LA	102	5.02	1.36	20.4	23	10	13	1.1	31	65	72
Stoudt,Levi	22	R	25	a/a	CIN	111	5.50	1.46	19.0	18	7	11	1.3	33	65	54
	23	R	26	aaa	CIN	83	6.46	1.75	15.2	12	13	-1	2.5	28	70	-28
Stout,Eric	22	L	29	aaa	PIT	43	3.25	1.52	6.9	25	17	8	0.8	29	81	76
	23	L	30	aaa	SEA	42	4.11	1.53	8.7	18	11	7	0.6	33	73	61
Stratton,Hunter	22	R	26	aaa	PIT	63	5.93	1.57	5.9	23	14	9	1.0	32	62	64
	23	R	27	aaa	PIT	57	4.69	1.50	5.2	22	13	9	1.2	30	72	57
Strotman,Drew	22	R	26	aaa	TEX	54	5.67	1.68	5.8	20	13	6	0.8	34	66	56
	23	R	27	aaa	SF	98	6.93	1.98	14.7	16	16	0	0.8	36	64	34
Strowd,Kade	23	R	26	aa	BAL	56	6.36	1.77	7.4	20	13	7	1.1	35	65	45
Stuart,Tyler	23	R	24	aa	NYM	35	4.52	1.44	21.3	16	7	10	1.1	33	71	53
Stumpo,Mitchell	23	R	27	a/a	ARI	46	8.54	2.18	5.5	19	19	0	1.6	36	61	19
Suarez,Andrew	23	L	31	aaa	STL	64	4.47	1.68	10.3	17	9	9	0.8	37	74	52
Sublette,Ryan	23	R	25	aa	LA	48	7.56	1.91	5.3	22	21	1	1.4	31	61	43
Sullivan,Billy	22	R	23	aa	PHI	51	4.67	1.70	5.2	27	14	13	0.9	38	74	85
	23	R	24	aaa	OAK	58	4.32	1.58	5.3	17	18	-1	0.1	28	70	68
Sullivan,Sean	23	R	23	aa	PIT	115	4.87	1.44	20.4	16	8	8	1.2	31	69	42
Sulser,Beau	22	R	28	aaa	BAL	58	4.28	1.49	12.6	18	6	12	0.9	36	73	76
	23	R	29	a/a	PIT	41	7.89	1.70	15.5	11	6	4	2.1	34	56	-13
Supak,Trey	23	R	27	a/a	OAK	87	5.26	1.66	10.6	12	8	4	1.1	34	70	18
Swanda,John	23	R	24	a/a	LAA	53	9.87	2.24	12.8	15	15	0	0.5	41	52	34
Swarmer,Matt	22	R	29	aaa	CHC	82	4.14	1.40	16.5	19	10	9	1.0	30	73	57
	23	R	30	aaa	ATL	33	9.75	2.16	8.7	14	16	-2	1.5	36	54	2
Sweet,Devin	22	R	26	aa	SEA	58	5.15	1.35	5.6	23	9	14	1.2	31	64	75
	23	R	27	a/a	OAK	44	2.17	1.07	4.8	25	6	19	0.6	29	83	128
Swiney,Nick	23	L	24	a/a	SF	57	4.72	1.63	8.0	16	12	4	0.8	32	72	40
Szapucki,Thomas	22	L	26	aaa	SF	73	2.90	1.30	12.0	27	10	17	0.5	33	78	109
Tamarez,Misael	22	R	22	a/a	HOU	122	3.88	1.17	17.4	25	12	13	1.2	23	72	79
	23	R	23	aaa	HOU	101	4.81	1.43	16.5	21	12	8	1.5	27	71	44
Tarnok,Freddy	22	R	24	a/a	ATL	108	4.84	1.41	18.3	23	10	13	1.4	31	70	61
Tassin,Bryce	23	R	26	aa	DET	36	5.34	1.78	8.3	14	9	5	0.7	37	70	37
Tavera,Carlos	23	R	25	aa	BAL	81	5.78	1.76	16.2	19	16	3	1.6	30	71	24
Taveras,Diosmerky	23	R	24	aa	HOU	56	5.15	1.59	11.8	20	10	10	1.0	35	69	57
Taveras,Willy	22	R	24	aa	NYM	45	5.04	1.50	8.1	15	4	11	2.1	34	74	47
Taylor,Blake	23	L	28	aaa	HOU	38	5.22	1.91	5.2	11	12	-1	0.5	36	72	23
Taylor,Curtis	23	R	28	a/a	MIN	49	4.77	1.57	6.2	20	12	7	0.7	33	70	60
Teng,Kai-Wei	22	R	24	aa	SF	137	5.57	1.60	21.6	23	14	9	0.8	33	65	69
	23	R	25	a/a	SF	127	4.98	1.48	18.8	25	13	12	0.5	33	65	88
Then,Juan	23	R	23	a/a	SEA	37	8.26	2.13	5.4	14	11	3	0.8	41	59	22
Thomas,Connor	22	L	24	aaa	STL	135	4.91	1.53	21.0	14	6	9	0.8	35	68	58
	23	L	25	aaa	STL	95	5.44	1.80	20.9	12	6	6	0.8	39	70	33
Thomas,Tahnaj	22	R	23	aa	PIT	52	2.85	1.23	5.7	20	9	11	0.6	29	78	84
	23	R	24	aa	PIT	45	6.21	1.79	5.8	10	16	-6	1.2	28	66	3
Thomas,Tyler	22	L	27	a/a	TEX	44	5.97	1.54	7.1	20	13	7	1.6	29	64	40
	23	L	28	a/a	NYM	36	3.19	1.36	6.3	21	10	12	0.2	33	75	93
Thompson,Darrell	23	L	29	a/a	MIL	61	4.73	1.49	5.5	23	12	11	1.4	31	72	55
Thompson,Keegan	23	R	28	aaa	CHC	30	8.39	2.03	7.3	21	16	5	2.1	37	61	13
Thompson,Matthew	23	R	23	aa	CHW	125	5.23	1.64	20.7	20	15	5	1.2	30	70	44
Thompson,Riley	22	R	26	aa	CHC	57	4.13	1.37	12.6	21	12	9	1.1	28	73	62
	23	R	27	aaa	CHC	82	5.66	1.67	14.7	16	14	2	1.4	30	69	24
Thompson,Zach	23	R	30	aaa	TOR	106	5.13	1.58	19.4	13	10	2	1.3	30	70	15
Thompson,Zack	22	L	25	aaa	STL	54	4.27	1.17	11.4	23	8	15	0.8	29	64	99
	23	L	26	aaa	STL	35	8.57	2.33	16.4	18	20	-2	1.1	38	63	26
Thorpe,Andrew	23	R	23	aa	NYY	31	1.69	0.71	21.9	35	5	31	0.9	22	86	226
Tice,Ty	23	R	27	a/a	ATL	55	7.83	2.17	6.1	25	12	12	1.1	47	63	60
Tidwell,Janzen	23	R	22	aa	NYM	35	5.56	1.55	19.2	24	12	12	1.5	33	68	55
Tiedemann,Ricky	23	L	21	a/a	TOR	36	4.56	1.40	12.7	37	13	24	0.2	40	65	145
Tomioka,Shohei	23	R	27	a/a	OAK	58	3.56	1.61	7.0	18	13	5	0.2	33	77	65
Toribio,Noe	22	R	23	a/a	PIT	83	4.33	1.40	9.5	17	11	6	0.5	29	68	65
	23	R	24	a/a	PIT	65	4.14	1.38	7.6	21	12	9	0.9	29	72	64
Torres,Eric	22	L	23	aa	LAA	51	1.49	0.91	4.5	34	10	23	0.5	23	87	153
	23	L	24	a/a	LAA	49	8.41	2.16	6.3	23	22	1	2.3	32	65	15
Toussaint,Touki	22	R	26	aaa	LAA	56	4.97	1.59	11.2	20	13	7	1.4	30	72	41
	23	R	27	aaa	CLE	39	4.12	1.39	8.3	23	15	8	0.7	27	71	76
Trogrlic-Iverson,Nick	23	R	26	aa	STL	66	4.96	1.56	7.1	15	9	5	0.9	33	69	39
Troop,Alex	22	L	26	a/a	WAS	115	5.29	1.42	16.9	21	7	15	1.7	33	68	61
	23	L	27	a/a	WAS	106	6.40	1.70	17.8	16	11	6	1.7	33	66	14
Troye,Christopher	23	R	24	aa	BOS	31	4.65	1.63	5.7	29	20	10	0.0	33	68	115
Tully,Tanner	22	L	28	aaa	CLE	122	4.35	1.43	21.6	14	5	10	0.8	34	70	71
	23	L	29	aaa	NYY	91	6.71	1.93	22.8	14	6	7	1.5	40	67	17
Turner,Matt	23	L	24	aa	CLE	31	5.08	1.67	10.0	15	14	1	0.3	32	68	52
Tyler,Kyle	23	R	27	aa	SEA	135	6.25	1.75	22.8	18	9	9	1.0	38	64	48
Uceta,Edwin	22	R	24	aaa	ARI	50	3.93	1.16	7.1	27	11	15	1.1	25	70	95
Ueckert,Cayne	22	R	26	aaa	CHC	50	7.81	2.16	6.4	20	19	1	2.0	35	66	14
	23	R	27	aa	CHC	40	5.15	1.62	4.9	22	13	9	0.6	35	68	70
Vallimont,Chris	22	R	25	a/a	BAL	104	5.76	1.56	17.5	18	10	8	1.2	32	65	43
	23	R	26	aaa	CLE	87	5.66	1.57	12.7	18	12	5	1.4	30	66	33
Valverde,Alex	22	R	26	aa	NYM	87	5.64	1.57	16.6	21	9	12	1.7	34	68	46
	23	R	27	a/a	SEA	81	5.59	1.64	15.1	15	10	4	1.0	33	67	30
Van Belle,Brian	22	R	26	aa	BOS	80	5.19	1.41	21.2	19	4	15	1.8	34	69	92
	23	R	27	a/a	BOS	142	5.44	1.57	23.1	16	8	8	2.0	32	72	15
Van Loon,Peter	23	R	24	aa	BAL	55	6.97	1.62	13.6	23	10	14	1.9	35	60	45
Van Scoyoc,Connor	23	R	24	aa	COL	43	7.32	1.70	24.4	14	8	6	2.1	34	61	-3
Vanasco,Ricky	23	R	25	a/a	LA	32	3.21	1.29	4.9	28	10	17	1.0	31	79	98
VanWey,Logan	23	R	24	a/a	HOU	32	3.76	1.36	5.4	28	14	14	1.4	27	78	73
Vargas,Carlos	22	R	23	a/a	CLE	35	3.33	1.37	5.5	21	10	11	0.4	32	76	85
	23	R	24	aaa	ARI	43	6.01	1.95	5.4	14	13	1	0.4	37	67	38

PITCHER	yr	t	age	lvl	org	ip	era	whip	bf/g	k%	bb%	k-bb	hr/9	h%	s%	bpv
Vargas,Emilio	22	R	26	a/a	CHW	115	5.38	1.51	19	19	11	8	1.5	31	68	37
Varland,Gus	22	R	26	aa	LA	72	5.96	1.65	7.9	21	10	11	1.4	35	66	47
Varland,Louie	22	R	25	a/a	MIN	127	2.88	1.27	22	22	7	15	0.9	31	81	92
	23	R	26	aaa	MIN	83	4.00	1.42	22	20	7	13	0.8	34	73	79
Vasil,Mike	23	R	23	a/a	NYM	124	4.87	1.28	20	24	9	15	1.1	30	64	81
Vasquez,Randy	22	R	24	aa	NYY	116	4.07	1.33	19	21	8	13	0.8	32	71	80
	23	R	25	aaa	NYY	81	4.95	1.56	21	23	11	12	1.1	34	70	64
Veneziano,Anthony	22	L	25	aa	KC	124	5.62	1.62	21	17	10	7	1.4	33	68	34
	23	L	26	a/a	KC	134	3.99	1.39	22	17	8	8	0.9	31	73	54
Vennaro,Zach	22	R	26	a/a	MIL	55	5.69	1.73	5.1	19	14	4	0.6	34	66	53
	23	R	27	aa	MIL	43	6.59	1.87	4.9	19	18	1	0.2	34	62	65
Vespi,Nick	22	L	27	aaa	BAL	30	0.00	0.60	4	27	5	22	0.0	19	##	196
	23	L	28	aaa	BAL	40	2.55	1.25	4.5	19	8	10	0.6	29	82	76
Vieaux,Cam	22	L	29	aaa	PIT	50	3.39	1.19	5.7	17	8	9	1.2	26	77	55
	23	L	30	aaa	LAA	73	5.72	1.53	6.4	17	12	5	1.2	30	64	34
Vieira,Thyago	23	R	30	aaa	MIL	39	3.91	1.41	5	24	10	14	0.8	33	74	82
Villalobos,Eli	22	R	25	a/a	MIA	80	3.09	1.08	6	27	9	18	1.0	26	76	100
	23	R	26	a/a	MIA	56	5.48	2.08	6.1	16	18	-2	1.6	34	77	8
Vines,Darius	22	R	24	a/a	ATL	142	4.53	1.38	22	22	8	14	1.2	33	70	74
	23	R	25	aaa	ATL	35	2.58	1.30	24	16	9	8	1.3	27	87	43
Vizcaino,Raffi	23	R	28	a/a	ARI	50	5.02	1.64	5.5	23	16	7	1.1	31	71	57
Vodnik,Victor	23	R	24	a/a	COL	55	3.88	1.41	5.6	22	13	9	1.0	28	76	64
Waites,Cole	22	R	24	a/a	SF	29	1.22	1.14	4.6	34	14	20	0.0	28	88	149
	23	R	25	aaa	SF	32	6.06	1.69	4.5	18	18	0	0.7	29	63	52
Waldichuk,Ken	22	L	24	a/a	OAK	97	2.25	1.03	18	29	7	21	0.6	28	81	139
Waldron,Matt	22	R	26	a/a	SD	115	5.62	1.52	20	15	7	8	0.9	34	63	51
	23	R	27	aaa	SD	93	6.02	1.54	20	20	6	13	1.4	36	63	63
Walker,Jeremy	23	R	28	aaa	PHI	69	3.31	1.40	6.2	14	11	2	1.2	26	81	27
Walker,Josh	22	L	28	aaa	NYM	15	6.41	1.76	7.7	27	10	17	1.1	42	64	81
	23	L	29	aaa	NYM	30	1.86	1.18	5.7	26	11	14	0.3	28	84	109
Walkinshaw,Jake	22	R	26	aaa	OAK	19	2.54	1.22	13	11	4	7	0.9	29	84	55
	23	R	27	aa	OAK	34	6.22	1.62	19	11	9	3	1.6	31	64	2
Wallace,Jacob	22	R	24	aa	BOS	58	4.01	1.47	5.3	25	19	6	1.0	24	75	71
	23	R	25	aa	KC	50	4.86	1.86	4.8	18	17	1	0.2	35	72	64
Walsh,Jake	22	R	27	aaa	STL	16	1.07	1.13	4.9	26	10	16	0.4	27	94	110
	23	R	28	aaa	STL	32	5.32	1.68	5.4	17	15	2	1.3	29	71	31
Walston,Blake	22	L	21	aa	ARI	107	4.33	1.32	21	21	7	14	1.0	32	69	84
	23	L	22	aaa	ARI	150	3.77	1.41	21	14	12	2	0.3	28	72	52
Walter,Brandon	22	L	26	a/a	BOS	59	3.90	0.99	20	25	3	22	0.9	30	62	211
	23	L	27	aaa	BOS	94	5.29	1.61	20	16	8	8	1.1	35	68	41
Walters,Jake	23	R	27	a/a	MIA	74	7.45	1.78	15	13	15	-2	1.8	29	60	-2
Walters,Nash	22	R	25	a/a	LAA	55	4.19	1.25	4.4	25	8	17	0.7	32	67	108
	23	R	26	a/a	WAS	42	10.27	1.93	5.4	23	14	9	2.3	37	47	21
Warren,Will	22	R	23	aa	NYY	94	4.13	1.34	22	18	8	10	0.7	31	70	70
	23	R	24	a/a	NYY	131	3.71	1.38	20	23	11	13	1.1	31	77	73
Washington,Mark	22	R	26	a/a	LA	59	3.33	1.26	5.8	18	9	8	0.7	28	75	64
	23	R	27	aaa	LA	47	4.08	1.32	6.5	18	8	9	1.3	29	74	50
Watkins,Spenser	23	R	31	aaa	OAK	71	7.28	2.01	16	13	12	2	0.8	38	63	21
Watson,Daniel	23	R	23	aa	NYY	39	1.88	0.93	4.9	26	11	15	1.2	17	91	89
Watson,Nolan	22	R	25	aa	SD	91	5.86	1.67	14	18	11	8	0.7	36	64	58
	23	R	26	a/a	SD	126	4.97	1.58	21	13	8	4	1.2	32	71	20
Watson,Ryan	22	R	25	a/a	BAL	108	3.50	1.14	16	19	6	13	1.5	27	77	73
	23	R	26	aaa	BAL	89	6.38	1.71	12	16	11	4	1.2	34	63	29
Watson,Troy	23	R	26	a/a	TOR	61	5.24	1.62	6.3	16	13	2	0.6	31	67	45
Way,Beck	23	R	24	aa	KC	81	7.52	1.85	14	16	16	0	1.1	32	59	29
Weathers,Ryan	22	L	23	aaa	SD	123	5.18	1.61	18	14	8	5	1.5	32	72	16
	23	L	24	aaa	MIA	81	3.68	1.39	23	21	11	11	1.0	30	77	65
Webb,Jacob	23	R	24	aa	BOS	59	6.20	1.64	6.4	20	14	6	0.9	32	62	53
Weems,Avery	22	L	25	aa	TEX	91	4.95	1.44	15	21	7	14	1.2	34	68	75
Weigel,Patrick	22	R	28	aaa	SEA	62	3.98	1.44	5	18	13	5	0.7	28	73	59
Weiman,Blake	22	L	27	a/a	SEA	45	4.21	1.07	5.2	19	3	16	1.0	29	63	142
	23	L	28	aaa	SEA	54	5.06	1.58	5.4	18	9	9	1.9	33	74	23
Weiss,Zack	22	R	30	aaa	LAA	50	4.31	1.39	4.9	22	10	12	1.0	32	71	74
	23	R	31	aaa	BOS	42	6.51	1.95	5.9	20	14	6	1.5	38	69	29
Weissert,Greg	22	R	27	aaa	NYY	48	1.87	0.98	4.3	29	10	19	0.6	24	84	127
	23	R	28	aaa	NYY	41	3.31	1.22	4.4	28	11	17	1.2	28	78	91
Wentz,Joey	22	L	25	aaa	DET	49	3.23	1.21	16	21	10	12	0.9	27	77	73
	23	L	26	aaa	DET	30	4.48	1.59	22	21	9	12	0.8	37	73	73
Wesneski,Hayden	22	R	25	aaa	CHC	111	3.84	1.18	19	19	7	12	0.7	28	68	83
	23	R	26	aaa	CHC	20	1.34	1.02	15	29	10	19	0.7	25	93	117
White,Brendan	22	R	24	aa	DET	68	2.72	0.93	5.3	22	6	16	0.3	25	70	129
	23	R	25	aaa	DET	37	4.35	1.63	5.7	24	7	17	0.8	41	75	99
White,Mitchell	22	R	28	aaa	TOR	18	4.96	0.99	23	18	5	13	1.2	24	51	83
	23	R	29	aaa	TOR	57	5.75	1.69	15	19	12	8	1.5	34	69	33
White,Owen	23	R	24	a/a	TEX	110	4.33	1.39	19	14	12	3	1.3	26	73	27
Whitley,Forrest	22	R	25	aaa	HOU	33	6.80	1.72	15	19	15	4	0.5	34	58	64
	23	R	26	aaa	HOU	30	5.75	1.37	16	21	13	8	1.8	25	62	38
Whitley,Kodi	23	R	28	aaa	ATL	58	6.48	1.94	6	17	9	8	1.6	39	69	18
Whitney,Blake	22	R	26	a/a	CHC	69	4.05	1.34	8.2	20	9	12	1.0	31	72	70
	23	R	27	a/a	CHC	73	3.30	1.38	7.9	20	9	11	0.7	32	78	75
Wick,Rowan	23	R	31	aaa	TOR	52	7.35	1.56	5.3	23	13	11	2.4	29	58	24
Wicklander,Patrick	23	L	23	aa	TAM	83	4.22	1.50	16	17	7	10	1.5	33	77	39
Wicks,Jordan	23	L	24	a/a	CHC	92	3.55	1.19	18	22	8	14	1.0	28	74	84
Wilcox,Cole	23	R	24	aa	TAM	108	5.55	1.36	18	19	9	9	1.2	29	60	53
Wilcox,Kyle	23	R	29	a/a	ATL	57	3.32	1.29	4.9	24	17	7	0.4	24	74	91
Wiles,Nathan	23	R	25	a/a	TAM	111	5.63	1.43	17	17	6	11	1.6	32	64	47
Williams,Case	23	R	21	aa	COL	103	8.97	1.98	22	13	10	2	2.7	35	58	-35
Williams,Garrett	22	L	28	a/a	STL	79	4.94	1.45	12.1	21	12	10	0.9	31	67	66
	23	L	29	aaa	OAK	54	4.56	1.90	6.1	20	23	-3	0.1	30	74	76
Williams,Gavin	22	R	23	aa	CLE	70	2.45	1.02	16.8	25	9	16	1.1	23	84	98
	23	R	24	a/a	CLE	61	2.61	1.05	19.7	28	11	18	0.9	24	80	107
Williams,Kendall	23	R	23	a/a	LA	45	4.84	1.47	21.4	16	14	2	0.7	27	67	49
Williamson,Brandon	22	L	24	a/a	CIN	124	4.65	1.68	20.7	19	14	5	0.8	33	73	51
	23	L	25	aaa	CIN	34	6.78	1.97	20.4	14	12	2	2.1	35	70	-15
Willingham,Amos	23	R	25	a/a	WAS	37	2.33	1.28	5.4	20	9	11	0.3	30	82	88
Winans,Allan	22	R	27	a/a	ATL	60	4.26	1.46	21.4	18	6	12	0.7	35	71	77
	23	R	28	aaa	ATL	127	3.39	1.26	22.6	17	7	10	0.8	29	76	68
Winckowski,Josh	22	R	24	aaa	BOS	62	3.98	1.27	19.6	20	7	13	0.5	32	68	93
Winder,Josh	22	R	26	aaa	MIN	16	3.24	1.08	12.5	13	9	5	1.4	20	78	34
	23	R	27	aaa	MIN	32	6.16	1.97	8.6	20	13	8	1.3	40	70	37
Winn,Cole	22	R	23	aaa	TEX	123	5.57	1.60	19.5	18	13	5	0.7	31	65	55
	23	R	24	aaa	TEX	101	7.32	1.96	16.6	17	16	1	1.5	34	64	15
Winn,Keaton	23	R	25	aaa	SF	58	4.97	1.67	15.3	21	10	11	0.9	38	71	63
Wisler,Matthew	23	R	31	aaa	TOR	64	5.02	1.60	5.3	19	11	8	1.1	34	70	48
Wolf,Adam	22	L	26	aa	DET	90	2.89	1.39	10.8	18	9	9	0.5	31	80	71
	23	L	27	aa	DET	86	4.21	1.46	9.2	16	12	5	0.5	30	71	55
Wolf,Jackson	23	L	24	aa	PIT	125	5.32	1.30	19.8	21	7	14	1.4	30	62	70
Wolfram,Grant	22	L	26	aa	TEX	57	4.35	1.64	6.5	21	16	6	0.4	32	73	75
	23	L	27	a/a	TEX	63	4.27	1.22	6.4	24	10	14	0.9	28	67	84
Wong,Jake	23	R	27	a/a	CIN	69	7.39	1.59	9.0	16	11	5	2.8	27	60	-18
Woo,Bryan	23	R	23	aa	SEA	44	2.10	0.89	18.1	32	6	25	0.4	27	77	175
Woodford,Jake	22	R	26	aaa	STL	43	2.94	1.34	16.3	16	9	7	0.3	30	78	69
	23	R	27	a/a	STL	30	2.81	1.09	11.8	22	9	13	1.4	23	83	71
Woods Richardson,Simeon	22	R	22	a/a	MIN	110	2.40	0.97	18.2	23	7	16	0.4	25	76	119
	23	R	23	aaa	MIN	115	4.67	1.48	20.6	17	12	5	0.9	30	69	47
Woods,William	23	R	25	a/a	NYM	54	6.53	1.70	6.4	20	11	10	1.8	35	65	31
Workman,Blake	22	R	25	a/a	ARI	51	3.80	1.28	5.3	21	6	15	1.0	32	74	94
	23	R	26	aa	ARI	30	6.94	1.48	7.6	20	7	13	2.6	31	59	26
Workman,Logan	23	R	25	aa	TAM	64	4.48	1.50	18.4	21	7	14	1.0	36	72	76
Wright,Chris	22	L	24	aa	SF	56	4.14	1.49	5.9	26	14	12	0.7	32	73	86
	23	L	25	a/a	SF	51	5.38	2.05	5.9	24	20	4	0.9	37	75	59
Wynne,Randy	22	R	29	aaa	CIN	134	6.36	1.78	23.8	11	7	4	2.7	34	73	-35
	23	R	30	aaa	CIN	74	7.44	1.77	11.7	11	6	5	4.0	31	71	-69
Yacabonis,Jimmy	22	R	30	a/a	TAM	35	3.30	1.27	5.3	24	11	13	0.2	30	73	98
	23	R	31	a/a	NYM	31	4.18	1.27	5.3	13	11	2	0.6	25	67	44
Yajure,Miguel	22	R	24	aaa	PIT	56	5.89	1.50	15.2	18	9	9	0.9	33	61	53
	23	R	25	aaa	SF	61	6.09	1.60	16.9	19	11	8	1.1	34	62	47
Yamamoto,Jordan	22	R	26	a/a	NYM	50	5.29	1.54	10.4	19	7	11	1.6	34	70	45
Yamamoto,Yoshinobu	23	R	24	for	JPN	157	1.57	0.98	32.5	25	5	20	0.2	31	84	0
Yan,Jefry	22	L	26	aa	MIA	57	5.71	1.84	7.0	27	18	9	0.5	38	67	87
	23	L	27	a/a	MIA	57	5.91	1.85	5.5	29	19	10	0.7	38	67	89
Ynoa,Huascar	22	R	24	aaa	ATL	79	6.97	1.56	19.3	22	11	11	1.8	32	58	35
Yovan,Kenyon	23	R	26	a/a	LAA	57	5.99	1.44	4.8	19	12	7	1.7	27	62	29
Zabala,Aneurys	23	R	27	aaa	DET	67	4.56	1.63	5.6	26	17	9	0.2	34	70	95
Zarbnisky,Braden	23	R	27	a/a	PHI	57	5.38	1.56	5.7	20	11	9	1.9	31	71	31
Zeferjahn,Ryan	23	R	25	aa	BOS	43	6.32	1.87	5.9	27	20	7	1.8	32	70	48
Zerpa,Angel	22	L	23	a/a	KC	73	3.69	1.29	15.8	18	7	11	0.6	31	72	78
	23	L	24	a/a	KC	36	4.09	1.40	17.0	15	10	5	1.1	28	74	36
Zeuch,T.J.	23	R	28	aaa	PHI	76	5.73	1.66	21.3	9	9	1	1.1	32	66	6
Zimmermann,Bruce	22	L	27	aaa	BAL	77	3.89	1.43	23.4	17	5	12	0.8	35	74	79
	23	L	28	aaa	BAL	101	4.96	1.75	22.0	18	9	9	0.4	39	70	64
Zulueta,Yosver	23	R	25	aaa	TOR	64	4.13	1.53	6.2	21	15	7	0.1	32	71	83
Zuniga,Guillermo	22	R	24	aa	LA	56	4.43	1.33	4.9	23	11	12	1.9	26	75	49
	23	R	25	aaa	STL	32	7.20	1.62	4.9	21	13	8	1.4	32	56	41

LEADERBOARDS & INSIGHTS

This section provides rankings of projected skills indicators for 2024. Rather than take shots in the dark predicting league leaders in the exact number of home runs, or stolen bases, or strikeouts, the Forecaster's Leaderboards focus on the component elements of each skill.

For batters, we've ranked the top players in terms of pure power, speed, and batting average skill, breaking each down in a number of different ways. For pitchers, we rank some of the key base skills, differentiating between starters and relievers, and provide a few interesting cuts that might uncover some late round sleepers.

In addition, the section examines some potential gainers/faders for 2024 based on 2023 results and supporting skills (or lack thereof), and a format-specific leaderboard for DFS play.

These are clearly not exhaustive lists of sorts and filters—drop us a note if you see something we should consider for next year's book. Also, the database at BaseballHQ.com allows you to construct your own custom sorts and filters. Finally, remember that these are just tools. Some players will appear on multiple lists—even mutually exclusive lists—so you have to assess what makes most sense and make decisions for your specific application.

Power

Top PX, 400+ AB: Top power skills among projected full-time players.

Top PX, -300 AB: Top power skills among projected part-time players; possible end-game options are here.

Position Scarcity: See which positions have deepest power options.

Top PX, ct% over 75%: Top power skills among the top contact hitters. Best pure power options here.

Top PX, ct% under 70%: Top power skills among the worst contact hitters; free-swingers who might be prone to streakiness and lower BAs.

Top PX, FB% over 40%: Top power skills among the most extreme fly ball hitters. Most likely to convert their power into home runs.

Top PX, FB% under 35%: Top power skills among those with lesser fly ball tendencies. There may be more downside to their home run potential.

Speed

Top Spd, 400+ AB: Top speed skills among projected full-time players.

Top Spd, -300 AB: Top speed skills among projected part-time players; possible end-game options here.

Position Scarcity: See which positions have deepest speed options.

Top Spd, OBP .330 and above: Top speed skills among those who get on base most often. Best opportunities for stolen bases here.

Top Spd, OBP under .300: Top speed skills among those who have trouble getting on base; worth watching if they can improve OB%.

Top Spd, SBA% over 15%: Top speed skills among those who get the green light most often. Most likely to convert their speed into stolen bases.

Top Spd, SBA% under 10%: Top speed skills among those who are currently not running; sleeper SBs here if given more opportunities.

Batting Average

Top ct%, 400+ AB: Top contact skills among projected full-time players. Contact is strongly correlated to higher BAs.

Top ct%, -300 AB: Top contact skills among projected part-time players; possible end-gamers here.

Low ct%, 400+ AB: The poorest contact skills among projected full-time players. Potential BA killers.

Top ct%, bb% over 9%: Top contact skills among the most patient hitters. Best batting average upside here.

Top ct%, bb% under 6%: Top contact skills among the least patient hitters; free-swingers who might be prone to streakiness or lower BAs.

Top ct%, GB% over 50%: Top contact skills among the most extreme ground ball hitters. A ground ball has a higher chance of becoming a hit than a non-HR fly ball so there may be some batting average upside here.

Top ct%, GB% under 40%: Top contact skills from those with lesser ground ball tendencies. These players make contact but hit more fly balls, which tend to convert to hits at a lower rate than GB.

Potential Skills Gainers/Faders

Expected Stats vs. Actual

These charts look to identify upcoming changes in performance by highlighting 2023 results that were in conflict with their corresponding skill indicators as well as our own set of expected statistics (xBA, xHR, xSB for hitters; xW, xERA, xWHIP for pitchers). Use these as a check on recency bias, as players here could compile stats in the upcoming season that look every different than the one just completed. Additional details are provided on the page in which the charts appear.

Pitching Skills

Top K-BB%: Leaders in projected K-BB% rates.

Top BB%: Leaders in fewest projected walks allowed.

Top K%: Leaders in projected strikeout rate.

Top Ground Ball Rate: GB pitchers tend to have lower ERAs (and higher WHIP) than fly ball pitchers.

Top Fly Ball Rate: FB pitchers tend to have higher ERAs (and lower WHIP) than ground ball pitchers.

High GB, Low K%: GB pitchers tend to have lower K rates, but these are the most extreme examples.

High GB, High K%: The best at dominating hitters and keeping the ball down. These are the pitchers who keep runners off the bases and batted balls in the park, a skills combination that is the most valuable a pitcher can own.

Lowest xERA: Leaders in projected skills-based ERA.

Top BPX: Two lists of top skilled pitchers. For starters, those projected to be rotation regulars (160+ IP) and fringe starters with skill (<120 IP). For relievers, those projected to be frontline closers (10+ saves) and high-skilled bullpen fillers (<10 saves).

Risk Management

These lists include players who've accumulated the most days on the injured list over the past five years (Grade "F" in Health) and whose performance was the most consistent over the past three years. Also listed are the most reliable batters and pitchers overall, with a focus on positional and skills reliability. As a reminder, reliability in this context is not tied to skill level; it is a gauge of which players manage to accumulate playing time and post consistent output from year to year, whether that output is good or bad.

Daily Fantasy Indicators

Players splits, teams and park factors designed to give you an edge in DFS.

BATTER SKILLS RANKINGS — Power

Top PX, 400+ AB

NAME	POS	PX
Judge,Aaron	0 9	202
Ohtani,Shohei	0	184
Trout,Mike	8	181
Schwarber,Kyle	0 7	177
Alvarez,Yordan	0 7	175
Olson,Matt	3	163
Martinez,J.D.	0	161
Rooker,Brent	0 7 9	160
Wallner,Matt	7 9	159
Lewis,Royce	5	154
Morel,Christopher	0 O	154
Casas,Triston	3	152
Suwinski,Jack	8 9	152
Harper,Bryce	0 3	152
Raleigh,Cal	2	152
Alonso,Pete	3	151
Gorman,Nolan	0 4	150
Garcia,Adolis	9	149
Jones,Nolan	7 9	149
Soler,Jorge	0 9	148
Jung,Josh	5	147
Hoskins,Rhys	3	145
Muncy,Max	5	145
Burger,Jake	0 5	145
Chapman,Matt	5	145
Riley,Austin	5	144
Tatis Jr.,Fernando	9	143
De La Cruz,Elly	5 6	141
Robert Jr.,Luis	8	140
Henderson,Gunnar	5 6	139
Cruz,Oneil	6	139
Seager,Corey	6	139
Betts,Mookie	4 9	139
Ozuna,Marcell	0	138
Yastrzemski,Mike	8 9	137
Álvarez,Francisco	2	137
Contreras,Willson	0 2	136
Julien,Edouard	0 4	135
Murphy,Sean	2	135
Suarez,Eugenio	5	134

Top PX, 300 or fewer AB

NAME	POS	PX
Gallo,Joey	3 7	190
Schneider,Davis	4	171
Belt,Brandon	0 3	158
Hiura,Keston	0	144
Stewart,D.J.	9	144
Garrett,Stone	7	142
Villar,David	4	135
Jansen,Danny	2	135
Donaldson,Josh	5	134
Garver,Mitch	0 2	134
Adams,Riley	2	130
Valdez,Enmanuel	4	128
Bauers,Jake	3 7 9	126
Larnach,Trevor	7 9	125
Ford,Mike	0	124
Sabol,Blake	2 7	120
Busch,Michael	5	120
Thompson,Trayce	8	118
Kjerstad,Heston	0	118
Walsh,Jared	3	116
Mead,Curtis	5	114
Maton,Nick	4 5	112
Pratto,Nick	3 0	112

Positional Scarcity

NAME	POS	PX
Judge,Aaron	DH	202
Ohtani,Shohei	2	184
Buxton,Byron	3	179
Schwarber,Kyle	4	177
Alvarez,Yordan	5	175
Martinez,J.D.	6	161
Rogers,Jake	CA	153
Raleigh,Cal	2	152
Sanchez,Gary	3	143
Álvarez,Francisco	4	137
Contreras,Willson	5	136
Jansen,Danny	6	135
Murphy,Sean	7	135
Diaz,Yainer	8	134
Gallo,Joey	1B	190
Olson,Matt	2	163
Belt,Brandon	3	158
Casas,Triston	4	152
Harper,Bryce	5	152
Alonso,Pete	6	151
Hoskins,Rhys	7	145
Votto,Joey	8	141
Drury,Brandon	9	134
Noda,Ryan	10	133
Schneider,Davis	2B	171
Gorman,Nolan	2	150
Betts,Mookie	3	139
Julien,Edouard	4	135
Villar,David	5	135
Drury,Brandon	6	134
Lowe,Brandon	7	133
Valdez,Enmanuel	8	128
Wisdom,Patrick	3B	187
Lewis,Royce	2	154
Jung,Josh	3	147
Muncy,Max	4	145
Burger,Jake	5	145
Chapman,Matt	6	145
Riley,Austin	7	144
De La Cruz,Elly	8	141
Henderson,Gunnar	9	139
Donaldson,Josh	10	134
De La Cruz,Elly	SS	141
Henderson,Gunnar	2	139
Cruz,Oneil	3	139
Seager,Corey	4	139
Adames,Willy	5	132
Story,Trevor	6	125
Witt Jr.,Bobby	7	123
McLain,Matt	8	122
Judge,Aaron	OF	202
Gallo,Joey	2	190
Trout,Mike	3	181
Velázquez,Nelson	4	179
Schwarber,Kyle	5	177
Alvarez,Yordan	6	175
Duvall,Adam	7	173
Rooker,Brent	8	160
Wallner,Matt	9	159
Morel,Christopher	10	154
Suwinski,Jack	11	152
Siri,Jose	12	150
Garcia,Adolis	13	149
Jones,Nolan	14	149
Soler,Jorge	15	148
Stewart,D.J.	16	144

Top PX, ct% over 75%

NAME	ct%	PX
Alvarez,Yordan	77	175
Seager,Corey	82	139
Betts,Mookie	82	139
Jansen,Danny	78	135
Diaz,Yainer	79	134
Acuña Jr.,Ronald	80	133
Devers,Rafael	78	132
Soto,Juan	79	131
Freeman,Freddie	82	129
Tucker,Kyle	82	129
Santander,Anthony	76	128
Suzuki,Seiya	76	126
Walker,Christian	77	124
Witt Jr.,Bobby	79	123
Carroll,Corbin	76	123
Ward,Taylor	76	123
Harris II,Michael	78	121
Machado,Manny	80	118
Reynolds,Bryan	75	116
Mead,Curtis	76	114
Albies,Ozzie	81	114
Bellinger,Cody	77	114
Jimenez,Eloy	77	114
Gurriel Jr.,Lourdes	80	111
Arenado,Nolan	84	111
Marte,Ketel	81	111
Meadows,Austin	75	111
Turner,Trea	79	111
Altuve,Jose	82	110
Smith,Will	80	110
Lindor,Francisco	79	110
d'Arnaud,Travis	75	109
Kepler,Max	78	109
Ramírez,José	86	109
Guerrero Jr.,Vladimir	83	108
Paredes,Isaac	80	108
Grichuk,Randal	77	108
Bichette,Bo	78	108
Hays,Austin	75	107
Correa,Carlos	76	107

Top PX, ct% under 70%

NAME	ct%	PX
Judge,Aaron	67	202
Gallo,Joey	51	190
Wisdom,Patrick	60	187
Ohtani,Shohei	69	184
Trout,Mike	67	181
Buxton,Byron	66	179
Velázquez,Nelson	64	179
Schwarber,Kyle	65	177
Duvall,Adam	66	173
Schneider,Davis	63	171
Martinez,J.D.	69	161
Rooker,Brent	60	160
Wallner,Matt	60	159
Belt,Brandon	65	158
Morel,Christopher	64	154
Rogers,Jake	63	153
Suwinski,Jack	62	152
Raleigh,Cal	69	152
Siri,Jose	61	150
Gorman,Nolan	64	150
Garcia,Adolis	67	149
Jones,Nolan	67	149
Soler,Jorge	70	148

Top PX, FB% over 40%

NAME	FB%	PX
Judge,Aaron	45	202
Gallo,Joey	54	190
Wisdom,Patrick	52	187
Trout,Mike	45	181
Buxton,Byron	52	179
Velázquez,Nelson	42	179
Schwarber,Kyle	48	177
Alvarez,Yordan	44	175
Duvall,Adam	55	173
Schneider,Davis	52	171
Olson,Matt	43	163
Martinez,J.D.	40	161
Rooker,Brent	45	160
Wallner,Matt	41	159
Belt,Brandon	49	158
Lewis,Royce	44	154
Rogers,Jake	45	153
Suwinski,Jack	48	152
Raleigh,Cal	51	152
Alonso,Pete	46	151
Siri,Jose	41	150
Gorman,Nolan	49	150
Garcia,Adolis	44	149
Soler,Jorge	43	148
Hoskins,Rhys	45	145
Muncy,Max	47	145
Burger,Jake	40	145
Chapman,Matt	50	145
Stewart,D.J.	43	144
Sanchez,Gary	45	143
Stanton,Giancarlo	40	143
Garrett,Stone	45	142
Votto,Joey	42	141
Robert Jr.,Luis	40	140
Betts,Mookie	47	139
Ozuna,Marcell	41	138
Yastrzemski,Mike	47	137
Álvarez,Francisco	43	137
Villar,David	46	135
Jansen,Danny	50	135

Top PX, FB% under 35%

NAME	FB%	PX
Harper,Bryce	35	152
De La Cruz,Elly	25	141
Henderson,Gunnar	34	139
Contreras,Willson	33	136
Julien,Edouard	24	135
Acuña Jr.,Ronald	33	133
Soto,Juan	33	131
Rodríguez,Julio	35	129
Sánchez,Jesús	31	124
McMahon,Ryan	34	123
Gelof,Zack	34	123
Harris II,Michael	29	121
Contreras,William	30	119
Reynolds,Bryan	33	116
Marsh,Brandon	34	116
Davis,J.D.	30	114
Jimenez,Eloy	31	114
Wong,Connor	35	113
Gurriel Jr.,Lourdes	35	111
Cooper,Garrett	30	111
Altuve,Jose	35	110
Moncada,Yoán	35	110
Gonzales,Nick	31	109

BATTER SKILLS RANKINGS — Speed

Top Spd, 400+ AB

NAME	POS	Spd
Carroll,Corbin	7 8 9	164
Rosario,Amed	4 6	147
De La Cruz,Elly	5 6	144
McCarthy,Jake	9	143
Nimmo,Brandon	8	142
Witt Jr.,Bobby	6	141
Giménez,Andrés	4	140
Kwan,Steven	7	139
Morel,Christopher	0 O	139
Cruz,Oneil	6	137
Turner,Trea	6	135
Garcia,Maikel	5	134
Lux,Gavin	0	134
Friedl,T.J.	7 8	133
Waters,Drew	8 9	133
McLain,Matt	4 6	132
Abrams,CJ	6	132
Thomas,Alek	8	132
Greene,Riley	8	131
Henderson,Gunnar	5 6	131
Turang,Brice	4 6	131
Anderson,Tim	6	130
Vierling,Matt	5 7 8 9	130
Suzuki,Seiya	9	129
Franco,Wander	6	127
Straw,Myles	8	126
McKinstry,Zach	4 5 6 7 9	126
Hoerner,Nico	4 6	126
Lee,Jung-hoo	7	126
Winn,Masyn	6	125
Westburg,Jordan	4 5	125
Cronenworth,Jake	3 4	124
Lawlar,Jordan	6	123
Marsh,Brandon	7 8	123
Ohtani,Shohei	0	123
Tovar,Ezequiel	6	123
Arozarena,Randy	7	123
Rengifo,Luis	4 5 6 O	122
Báez,Javier	6	121
Doyle,Brenton	8	120

Top Spd, 300 or fewer AB

NAME	POS	Spd
Mateo,Jorge	6	144
Adams,Jordyn	O	141
Crow-Armstrong,Pete	8	141
Basabe,Osleivis	6	139
Meckler,Wade	O	139
Mondesi,Adalberto	6	135
Kjerstad,Heston	0	132
Hampson,Garrett	6 8 9	132
Marcano,Tucupita	6	130
Triolo,Jared	5	128
Rocchio,Brayan	6	127
Pereira,Everson	7	125
Monasterio,Andruw	4 5	125
Loftin,Nick	3	124
Batten,Matthew	4	123
Mead,Curtis	5	123
Lopez,Nicky	4 5	122
Caballero,Jose	4 6	122
Abreu,Wilyer	O	121
Barrero,Jose	6	121
Escobar,Eduardo	4 5	120
Edwards,Xavier	4	120
Sabol,Blake	2 7	120

Positional Scarcity

NAME	POS	Spd
Morel,Christopher	**DH**	139
Lux,Gavin	2	134
Kjerstad,Heston	3	132
Ohtani,Shohei	4	123
Lowe,Josh	5	115
Yelich,Christian	6	115
Wong,Connor	**CA**	142
Rogers,Jake	2	128
Sabol,Blake	3	120
Realmuto,J.T.	4	117
Contreras,William	5	113
Rodríguez,Endy	6	107
Jeffers,Ryan	7	105
Moreno,Gabriel	8	103
Cronenworth,Jake	**1B**	124
Loftin,Nick	2	124
Schanuel,Nolan	3	117
Clemens,Kody	4	114
Bellinger,Cody	5	114
Joe,Connor	6	109
Steer,Spencer	7	104
Toglia,Michael	8	103
Biggio,Cavan	9	103
Lowe,Nathaniel	10	103
Rosario,Amed	**2B**	147
Giménez,Andrés	2	140
Peguero,Liover	3	132
McLain,Matt	4	132
Turang,Brice	5	131
McKinstry,Zach	6	126
Dubón,Mauricio	7	126
Hoerner,Nico	8	126
De La Cruz,Elly	**3B**	144
Caminero,Junior	2	136
Garcia,Maikel	3	134
Henderson,Gunnar	4	131
Vierling,Matt	5	130
Triolo,Jared	6	128
Marte,Noelvi	7	128
Castro,Willi	8	127
Berti,Jon	9	126
McKinstry,Zach	10	126
Rosario,Amed	**SS**	147
Mateo,Jorge	2	144
De La Cruz,Elly	3	144
Witt Jr.,Bobby	4	141
Basabe,Osleivis	5	139
Cruz,Oneil	6	137
Turner,Trea	7	135
Mondesi,Adalberto	8	135
Rojas,Johan	**OF**	176
Carroll,Corbin	2	164
Carter,Evan	3	155
Meadows,Parker	4	148
Rafaela,Ceddanne	5	147
McCarthy,Jake	6	143
Nimmo,Brandon	7	142
Adams,Jordyn	8	141
Crow-Armstrong,Pete	9	141
Benson,Will	10	140
Kwan,Steven	11	139
Morel,Christopher	12	139
Mitchell,Garrett	13	139
Meckler,Wade	14	139
Gordon,Nick	15	135
Friedl,T.J.	16	133

Top Spd, .330+ OBP

NAME	OBP	Spd
Carroll,Corbin	352	164
Carter,Evan	350	155
Nimmo,Brandon	366	142
Benson,Will	339	140
Kwan,Steven	350	139
Meckler,Wade	362	139
Caminero,Junior	330	136
Lux,Gavin	337	134
Friedl,T.J.	332	133
McLain,Matt	344	132
Greene,Riley	342	131
Henderson,Gunnar	337	131
Suzuki,Seiya	362	129
Franco,Wander	341	127
Berti,Jon	332	126
Hoerner,Nico	343	126
Lee,Jung-hoo	343	126
Marsh,Brandon	339	123
Ohtani,Shohei	389	123
Mead,Curtis	336	123
Arozarena,Randy	351	123
Caballero,Jose	337	122
Abreu,Wilyer	335	121
Edwards,Xavier	335	120
McNeil,Jeff	342	120
Jones,Nolan	349	119
Jankowski,Travis	337	117
Altuve,Jose	363	117
Schanuel,Nolan	376	117
Reynolds,Bryan	341	117
Yelich,Christian	366	115
Nootbaar,Lars	345	115
Bellinger,Cody	334	114
Donovan,Brendan	358	114
Contreras,William	348	113
Grissom,Vaughn	352	112
Hicks,Aaron	341	112
Rodríguez,Julio	348	111
Madrigal,Nick	331	111
Marte,Ketel	349	111

Top Spd, OBP under .300

NAME	OBP	Spd
Rojas,Johan	296	176
Rafaela,Ceddanne	292	147
Mateo,Jorge	271	144
Wong,Connor	291	142
Adams,Jordyn	249	141
Mitchell,Garrett	295	139
Mondesi,Adalberto	275	135
Gordon,Nick	287	135
Waters,Drew	299	133
Peguero,Liover	278	132
Kjerstad,Heston	299	132
Thomas,Alek	297	132
Moniak,Mickey	273	131
Turang,Brice	294	131
Marcano,Tucupita	295	130
Rogers,Jake	292	128
Rocchio,Brayan	288	127
Butler,Lawrence	276	126
McKinstry,Zach	296	126
Dubón,Mauricio	292	126
Winn,Masyn	278	125
Siri,Jose	277	125
Westburg,Jordan	292	125

Top Spd, SBA% over 15%

NAME	SBA%	Spd
Rojas,Johan	42%	176
Carroll,Corbin	31%	164
Carter,Evan	19%	155
Meadows,Parker	15%	148
Rafaela,Ceddanne	31%	147
Mateo,Jorge	46%	144
De La Cruz,Elly	44%	144
McCarthy,Jake	30%	143
Adams,Jordyn	31%	141
Crow-Armstrong,Pete	32%	141
Witt Jr.,Bobby	40%	141
Benson,Will	20%	140
Giménez,Andrés	20%	140
Morel,Christopher	15%	139
Mitchell,Garrett	17%	139
Basabe,Osleivis	17%	139
Cruz,Oneil	18%	137
Turner,Trea	19%	135
Mondesi,Adalberto	36%	135
Gordon,Nick	17%	135
Garcia,Maikel	23%	134
Friedl,T.J.	20%	133
Waters,Drew	25%	133
Peguero,Liover	25%	132
McLain,Matt	21%	132
Abrams,CJ	41%	132
Hampson,Garrett	16%	132
Turang,Brice	22%	131
Triolo,Jared	17%	128
Marte,Noelvi	21%	128
Castro,Willi	30%	127
Franco,Wander	27%	127
Rocchio,Brayan	18%	127
Chisholm Jr.,Jazz	29%	126
Berti,Jon	26%	126
Straw,Myles	20%	126

Top Spd, SBA% under 10%

NAME	SBA%	Spd
Nimmo,Brandon	4%	142
Meckler,Wade	9%	139
Caminero,Junior	7%	136
Lux,Gavin	7%	134
Kjerstad,Heston	6%	132
Greene,Riley	6%	131
Rogers,Jake	3%	128
Dubón,Mauricio	9%	126
Lee,Jung-hoo	10%	126
Westburg,Jordan	9%	125
Cronenworth,Jake	6%	124
Mead,Curtis	7%	123
Rengifo,Luis	9%	122
Escobar,Eduardo	3%	120
McNeil,Jeff	5%	120
Sabol,Blake	9%	120
Segura,Jean	10%	117
Schanuel,Nolan	1%	117
Reynolds,Bryan	7%	117
Nootbaar,Lars	10%	115
Clemens,Kody	9%	114
Fletcher,Dominic	10%	114
Donovan,Brendan	6%	114
Amaya,Jacob	5%	114
Vargas,Ildemaro	4%	113
Contreras,William	3%	113
Melendez Jr.,MJ	6%	112

BATTER SKILLS RANKINGS— Batting Average

Top ct%, 400+ AB

NAME	ct%	BA
Arraez,Luis	92	328
Kwan,Steven	89	281
Lee,Jung-hoo	88	283
Ruiz,Keibert	88	261
McNeil,Jeff	88	281
Matos,Luis	87	263
Ramírez,José	86	280
Pasquantino,Vinnie	86	260
Bregman,Alex	86	264
Hoerner,Nico	86	280
Yoshida,Masataka	85	292
Franco,Wander	85	282
Brennan,Will	85	272
Arenado,Nolan	84	271
Frelick,Sal	84	256
Naylor,Josh	84	284
Flores,Wilmer	84	268
Díaz,Yandy	83	302
Verdugo,Alex	83	269
Guerrero Jr.,Vladimir	83	273
Merrifield,Whit	83	260
Garcia,Luis	83	274
Benintendi,Andrew	82	272
Tucker,Kyle	82	275
Edman,Tommy	82	258
Betts,Mookie	82	294
Freeman,Freddie	82	326
Semien,Marcus	82	264
Seager,Corey	82	301
Altuve,Jose	82	284
Ramírez,Harold	81	288
Marte,Ketel	81	275
Stott,Bryson	81	261
Rosario,Amed	81	268
Rutschman,Adley	81	273
Santana,Carlos	81	235
Albies,Ozzie	81	277
Turner,Justin	81	279
Cronenworth,Jake	81	250
Bogaerts,Xander	81	288
Bohm,Alec	81	273
Gurriel Jr.,Lourdes	80	277
France,Ty	80	265
LeMahieu,DJ	80	253
Straw,Myles	80	241
Friedl,T.J.	80	255
Acuña Jr.,Ronald	80	304
Abrams,CJ	80	251
Moreno,Gabriel	80	290
Torres,Gleyber	80	269
Marte,Starling	80	264
Machado,Manny	80	275
Smith,Will	80	260
Campusano,Luis	80	256
Paredes,Isaac	80	251
Soto,Juan	79	284
Canha,Mark	79	255
Crawford,J.P.	79	265
Rengifo,Luis	79	257
Witt Jr.,Bobby	79	270
Turner,Trea	79	275
Arcia,Orlando	79	253
Diaz,Yainer	79	265
Lindor,Francisco	79	260
Heim,Jonah	79	250
Kim,Ha-Seong	79	252

Low ct%, 400+ AB

NAME	ct%	BA
Noda,Ryan	58	221
Luciano,Marco	59	205
Wallner,Matt	60	227
Rooker,Brent	60	229
Suwinski,Jack	62	216
Outman,James	62	235
Doyle,Brenton	63	219
De La Cruz,Elly	63	243
Julien,Edouard	63	253
Gorman,Nolan	64	232
Morel,Christopher	64	235
Suarez,Eugenio	64	230
Marsh,Brandon	65	257
Schwarber,Kyle	65	225
Waters,Drew	65	234
Gelof,Zack	65	242
Davis,J.D.	66	247
Chapman,Matt	67	227
McMahon,Ryan	67	244
Judge,Aaron	67	279
Trout,Mike	67	280
Garcia,Adolis	67	241
Jones,Nolan	67	264
Kelenic,Jarred	67	248
McLain,Matt	68	259
Jung,Josh	68	257
Langeliers,Shea	68	220
Hernández,Teoscar	68	261
Montero,Elehuris	68	246
Moncada,Yoán	68	252
Soderstrom,Tyler	68	219
Raleigh,Cal	69	225
Álvarez,Francisco	69	231
Cruz,Oneil	69	249
Burger,Jake	69	256
Story,Trevor	69	245

Top ct%, 300 or fewer AB

NAME	ct%	BA
Vargas,Ildemaro	89	240
Kemp,Tony	87	231
Gurriel,Yulieski	86	251
Segura,Jean	85	261
Schanuel,Nolan	85	256
Espinal,Santiago	84	266
Lopez,Nicky	84	241
Newman,Kevin	83	236
Freeman,Tyler	83	242
Edwards,Xavier	83	263
Burleson,Alec	83	257
Andrus,Elvis	82	255
Rendon,Anthony	82	252
Miranda,Jose	82	259
Profar,Jurickson	82	240
Trevino,Jose	82	229
Loftin,Nick	81	239
Marcano,Tucupita	80	233
Fortes,Nick	80	209
Ibanez,Andy	80	260
Palacios,Richie	80	222
Wong,Kolten	79	248
Peralta,David	79	257
Rocchio,Brayan	79	235
Jankowski,Travis	79	241
Grissom,Vaughn	79	280
Basabe,Osleivis	78	257

Top ct%, bb% over 9%

NAME	bb%	ct%
Kwan,Steven	9	89
Kirk,Alejandro	11	87
Kemp,Tony	11	87
Ramírez,José	11	86
Pasquantino,Vinnie	10	86
Bregman,Alex	13	86
Schanuel,Nolan	14	85
Díaz,Yandy	12	83
Guerrero Jr.,Vladimir	10	83
Tucker,Kyle	11	82
Betts,Mookie	12	82
Rendon,Anthony	13	82
Profar,Jurickson	10	82
Freeman,Freddie	11	82
Semien,Marcus	9	82
Seager,Corey	9	82
Altuve,Jose	10	82
Marte,Ketel	10	81
Rutschman,Adley	13	81
Santana,Carlos	13	81
Bogaerts,Xander	9	81
LeMahieu,DJ	11	80
Acuña Jr.,Ronald	12	80
Torres,Gleyber	9	80
Palacios,Richie	9	80
Machado,Manny	9	80
Smith,Will	11	80
Paredes,Isaac	11	80
Soto,Juan	20	79
Canha,Mark	11	79
Crawford,J.P.	13	79
Jankowski,Travis	12	79
Lindor,Francisco	10	79
Kim,Ha-Seong	10	79
Springer,George	10	78
Kepler,Max	10	78
Devers,Rafael	9	78
Jansen,Danny	9	78
Bell,Josh	11	78
Berti,Jon	9	78

Top ct%, bb% under 6%

NAME	bb%	ct%
Madrigal,Nick	5	90
Vargas,Ildemaro	5	89
Brennan,Will	5	85
Dubón,Mauricio	5	84
Newman,Kevin	6	83
Freeman,Tyler	6	83
Burleson,Alec	6	83
Merrifield,Whit	6	83
Garcia,Luis	5	83
Andrus,Elvis	6	82
Miranda,Jose	6	82
Margot,Manuel	6	82
Trevino,Jose	4	82
Ramírez,Harold	4	81
Rosario,Amed	4	81
Diaz,Aledmys	6	81
Gurriel Jr.,Lourdes	6	80
Urshela,Giovanny	6	80
Abrams,CJ	5	80
Marte,Starling	6	80
Olivares,Edward	6	80
Campusano,Luis	6	80
Wendle,Joey	4	80

Top ct%, GB% over 50%

NAME	GB%	ct%
Madrigal,Nick	57	90
Vargas,Ildemaro	54	89
Yoshida,Masataka	54	85
Segura,Jean	57	85
Frelick,Sal	53	84
Lopez,Nicky	56	84
Díaz,Yandy	52	83
Garcia,Luis	53	83
Andrus,Elvis	52	82
Ramírez,Harold	55	81
Rosario,Amed	50	81
Kiner-Falefa,Isiah	53	81
LeMahieu,DJ	54	80
Allen,Nick	52	80
Moreno,Gabriel	55	80
Marte,Starling	54	80
Palacios,Richie	50	80
Wendle,Joey	53	80
Rocchio,Brayan	55	79
Jankowski,Travis	53	79
Grissom,Vaughn	52	79
Arcia,Orlando	51	79
Basabe,Osleivis	54	78
Thomas,Alek	57	78
Rodgers,Brendan	52	78
Harris II,Michael	51	78
Anderson,Tim	57	78
Berti,Jon	55	78
Diaz,Jordan	51	77
Jimenez,Eloy	51	77
Alu,Jake	53	77
McCarthy,Jake	51	76
Peña,Jeremy	51	75
Gonzalez,Oscar	50	74
Bae,Ji Hwan	62	74
Contreras,William	53	74
Kiermaier,Kevin	55	74
Peguero,Liover	52	74
Urías,Ramón	51	73
Yelich,Christian	56	73

Top ct%, GB% under 40%

NAME	GB%	ct%
Ruiz,Keibert	40	88
Ramírez,José	34	86
Pasquantino,Vinnie	38	86
Bregman,Alex	36	86
Arenado,Nolan	35	84
Frazier,Adam	39	84
Flores,Wilmer	35	84
Edwards,Xavier	40	83
Benintendi,Andrew	39	82
Tucker,Kyle	36	82
Betts,Mookie	31	82
Rendon,Anthony	34	82
Freeman,Freddie	38	82
Semien,Marcus	34	82
Albies,Ozzie	37	81
Turner,Justin	34	81
Cronenworth,Jake	39	81
Friedl,T.J.	37	80
Torres,Gleyber	39	80
Machado,Manny	39	80
Hernández,Kiké	37	80
Smith,Will	34	80
Paredes,Isaac	36	80

POTENTIAL SKILLS GAINERS AND FADERS — Batters

Power Gainers

Batters whose 2023 Power Index (PX) fell significantly short of their underlying power skill (xPX). If they show the same xPX skill in 2024, they are good candidates for more power output.

Power Faders

Batters whose 2023 Power Index (PX) noticeably outpaced their underlying power skill (xPX). If they show the same xPX skill in 2024, they are good candidates for less power output.

PX GAINERS

NAME	PX	xPX
Smith,Josh	90	144
Sosa,Lenyn	86	137
Bregman,Alex	91	128
Bryant,Kris	76	124
Smith,Will	97	122
Isbel,Kyle	90	118
Tellez,Rowdy	94	117
Rodriguez,Endy	67	116
Farmer,Kyle	91	115
Cave,Jake	89	113
Biggio,Cavan	89	110
Donovan,Brendan	71	110
Stallings,Jacob	71	110
Story,Trevor	89	109
Massey,Michael	89	108
Wade,LaMonte	88	108
Maton,Nick	84	106
Garcia,Maikel	57	105
Thaiss,Matt	78	102
Rivera,Emmanuel	64	101
Rodgers,Brendan	80	101
Smith,Pavin	76	101
Call,Alex	63	99
Perez,Carlos	73	97
Peterson,Jace	58	97
Solano,Donovan	78	97
Bader,Harrison	65	96
Profar,Jurickson	78	96
Sheets,Gavin	72	96

PX FADERS

NAME	PX	xPX
Duvall,Adam	192	135
Siri,Jose	182	132
Burger,Jake	166	129
Robert,Luis	178	127
Raley,Luke	167	118
Wallner,Matt	177	116
Drury,Brandon	145	112
Gelof,Zack	156	111
McLain,Matt	142	110
Julien,Edouard	138	109
Candelario,Jeimer	137	107
Jeffers,Ryan	138	103
Lewis,Royce	132	101
Naylor,Bo	143	99
Sanchez,Jesus	128	97
Lowe,Josh	132	93
Marsh,Brandon	129	93
Duran,Jarren	133	89
Renfroe,Hunter	114	87
Davis,J.D.	109	86
Wong,Connor	116	86
Mullins II,Cedric	111	83
Altuve,Jose	117	82
Fairchild,Stuart	115	81
Fraley,Jake	107	80
Kelenic,Jarred	124	80
De La Cruz,Elly	118	79
Crawford,J.P.	107	73
Friedl,T.J.	99	69
Yoshida,Masataka	88	62
Kiermaier,Kevin	93	46

BA Gainers

Batters who had strong Hard Contact Index levels in 2023, but lower hit rates (h%). Since base hits come most often on hard contact, i[illegible] these batters can make hard contact at the same strong rate again in 2024, they may get better results in terms of hit rate, resulting in a batting average improvement.

BA Faders

Batters who had weak Hard Contact Index levels in 2023, but highe[illegible] hit rates (h%). Since base hits come most often on hard contact, i[illegible] these batters only make hard contact at the same weak rate again in 2024, they may get worse results in terms of hit rate, resulting in [illegible] batting average decline.

BA GAINERS

NAME	h%	HctX
Pasquantino,Vinnie	25	138
Canzone,Dominic	24	132
Sanchez,Gary	21	119
O Hoppe,Logan	24	118
Perez,Carlos	26	117
Smith,Josh	22	114
Stanton,Giancarlo	21	113
Donaldson,Josh	12	111
Ruiz,Keibert	26	111
Burleson,Alec	26	109
Jansen,Danny	23	109
Pillar,Kevin	26	109
Smith,Pavin	21	109
D Arnaud,Travis	26	108
Sosa,Lenyn	23	108
Fortes,Nick	24	107
Santana,Carlos	26	106
Paredes,Isaac	26	105
Muncy,Max	23	104
Alonso,Pete	21	103
Alvarez,Francisco	22	103
Adames,Willy	26	101
Schwarber,Kyle	21	101
Rojas,Miguel	26	100
Bader,Harrison	26	98
Carlson,Dylan	26	97
Massey,Michael	26	97
Tellez,Rowdy	25	97
Velazquez,Nelson	22	97
Wiemer,Joey	26	97
Wisdom,Patrick	24	97

BA FADERS

NAME	h%	HctX
Delay,Jason	34	62
McGuire,Reese	37	64
Hampson,Garrett	38	73
Outman,James	35	74
Pratto,Nick	40	79
Castro,Harold	34	82
Triolo,Jared	44	82
Wong,Connor	34	83
De La Cruz,Elly	34	83
Julien,Edouard	38	84
Urias,Ramon	36	84
Marsh,Brandon	40	8[illegible]
Slater,Austin	37	8[illegible]
Urshela,Giovanny	35	8[illegible]
Altuve,Jose	35	8[illegible]
Kelenic,Jarred	36	8[illegible]
Belt,Brandon	37	8[illegible]
Jeffers,Ryan	36	9[illegible]
Moncada,Yoan	35	9[illegible]
Noda,Ryan	35	9[illegible]
Berti,Jon	35	9[illegible]
Lowe,Josh	36	9[illegible]
Lewis,Royce	35	9[illegible]
McLain,Matt	38	9[illegible]
Ramirez,Harold	37	9[illegible]
Duran,Ezequiel	36	9[illegible]
Moniak,Mickey	40	9[illegible]
Benson,Will	39	9[illegible]
Encarnacion-Strand,Chr	34	9[illegible]
Kirilloff,Alex	34	10[illegible]
Montero,Elehuris	36	10[illegible]
Moreno,Gabriel	35	10[illegible]

EXPECTED STATS vs. ACTUAL — Batters

BA Underperformers (min. 250 AB)

NAME	BA	xBA	Diff
Kemp,Anthony	209	256	-47
Alonso,Pete	217	263	-46
Vargas,Miguel	195	234	-39
Schwarber,Kyle	197	235	-38
Wendle,Joe	212	248	-36
Frazier,Adam	240	274	-34
Thomas,Alek	230	263	-33
Muncy,Max	212	243	-31
Burleson,Alec	244	273	-29
Santana,Carlos	240	268	-28
Alvarez,Francisco	209	236	-27
Schmitt,Casey	206	233	-27
Vargas,Ildemaro	252	279	-27
Volpe,Anthony	209	236	-27
Grisham,Trent	198	223	-25
Stanton,Giancarlo	191	216	-25
Wisdom,Patrick	205	230	-25
Bleday,J.J.	195	219	-24
Madrigal,Nick	263	286	-23
Gurriel,Lourdes	261	282	-21
Jansen,Danny	228	249	-21

HR Underperformers

NAME	HR	xHR	Diff
Chapman,Matt	17	28	-11
Judge,Aaron	37	47	-10
Greene,Riley	11	19	-8
Melendez Jr.,MJ	16	24	-8
Acuna,Ronald	41	48	-7
Hernandez,Teoscar	26	33	-7
Suarez,Eugenio	22	29	-7
Freeman,Freddie	29	35	-6
Grisham,Trent	13	19	-6
Tatis Jr.,Fernando	25	31	-6
Witt Jr.,Bobby	30	36	-6
Alvarez,Yordan	31	36	-5
Bailey,Patrick	7	12	-5
Bauers,Jake	12	17	-5
Contreras,William	17	22	-5
France,Ty	12	17	-5
Goldschmidt,Paul	25	30	-5
Harper,Bryce	21	26	-5
Hays,Austin	16	21	-5
Mountcastle,Ryan	18	23	-5
Reynolds,Bryan	24	29	-5

SB Underperformers

NAME	SB	xSB	Diff
Nimmo,Brandon	3	15	-12
Suzuki,Seiya	6	18	-12
Vierling,Matt	6	18	-12
Arozarena,Randy	22	31	-9
Bregman,Alex	3	12	-9
Melendez Jr.,MJ	6	14	-8
Arraez,Luis	3	10	-7
Marte,Ketel	8	15	-7
Anderson,Brian	1	7	-6
Bichette,Bo	5	11	-6
Diaz,Yandy	0	6	-6
Jeffers,Ryan	3	9	-6
Joe,Connor	3	9	-6
Meneses,Joey	0	6	-6
Olson,Matt	1	7	-6
Pena,Jeremy	13	19	-6
Rengifo,Luis	6	12	-6
Riley,Austin	3	9	-6
Rosario,Amed	15	21	-6
Allen,Nick	5	10	-5
Chapman,Matt	4	9	-5

BA Overperformers (min. 250 AB)

NAME	BA	xBA	Diff
Freeman,Freddie	331	301	30
Castro,Willi	257	228	29
Contreras,William	291	262	29
Sabol,Blake	235	206	29
Walker,Jordan	276	247	29
Altuve,Jose	311	283	28
Cabrera,Miguel	257	229	28
Carpenter,Kerry	278	250	28
Jimenez,Eloy	272	244	28
Meneses,Joey	275	247	28
Montero,Elehuris	243	216	27
Naylor,Josh	308	281	27
Hoerner,Nico	283	257	26
O Hearn,Ryan	289	263	26
Belt,Brandon	254	229	25
Merrifield,Whit	272	247	25
Bogaerts,Xander	285	262	23
Duran,Jarren	295	272	23
Estrada,Thairo	271	248	23
Arozarena,Randy	254	232	22
Moustakas,Mike	247	225	22

HR Overperformers

NAME	HR	xHR	Diff
Paredes,Isaac	31	14	17
Friedl,T.J.	18	5	13
Bellinger,Cody	26	18	8
Crawford,J.P.	19	11	8
Santana,Carlos	23	15	8
Bregman,Alex	25	18	7
Flores,Wilmer	23	16	7
Fraley,Jake	15	8	7
Frazier,Adam	13	6	7
Marte,Ketel	25	18	7
Semien,Marcus	29	22	7
Arenado,Nolan	26	20	6
Drury,Brandon	26	20	6
Kim,Ha-Seong	17	11	6
Olson,Matt	54	48	6
Senzel,Nick	13	7	6
Albies,Ozzie	33	28	5
Alvarez,Francisco	25	20	5
Burger,Jake	34	29	5
Carroll,Corbin	25	20	5
Gurriel,Lourdes	24	19	5

SB Overperformers

NAME	SB	xSB	Diff
Ruiz,Esteury	67	45	22
Acuna,Ronald	73	57	16
Abrams,CJ	47	35	12
Lowe,Josh	32	22	10
Lindor,Francisco	31	22	9
Duran,Jarren	24	16	8
Mateo,Jorge	32	24	8
Rodriguez,Julio	37	29	8
Tatis Jr.,Fernando	29	21	8
Blanco,Dairon	24	17	7
Castro,Willi	33	26	7
Fraley,Jake	21	14	7
Kim,Ha-Seong	38	31	7
Pham,Tommy	22	15	7
Stott,Bryson	31	24	7
Caballero,Jose	26	20	6
Carroll,Corbin	54	48	6
Chisholm,Jazz	22	16	6
Edman,Tommy	27	21	6
Marte,Starling	24	18	6
Walls,Taylor	22	16	6

PITCHER SKILLS RANKINGS — Starting Pitchers

Top K-BB%

NAME	K-BB%
deGrom,Jacob	34
Cole,Gerrit	28
Scherzer,Max	28
Strider,Spencer	28
Sale,Chris	26
Glasnow,Tyler	26
Heaney,Andrew	26
Burnes,Corbin	26
Gausman,Kevin	25
Nola,Aaron	25
Rodón,Carlos	25
Ohtani,Shohei	25
Woodruff,Brandon	24
Greene,Hunter	24
Kershaw,Clayton	24
Baz,Shane	24
Paxton,James	23
Alzolay,Adbert	23
Darvish,Yu	22
Ray,Robbie	22
Snell,Blake	22
Javier,Cristian	22
Miller,Bobby	22
Verlander,Justin	22
Kirby,George	21
Musgrove,Joe	21
Castillo,Luis	21
Lodolo,Nick	21
Morton,Charlie	21
McClanahan,Shane	21
Springs,Jeffrey	21

Top BB%

NAME	BB%
Paddack,Chris	4
Pineda,Michael	4
Ryu,Hyun-Jin	4
Kirby,George	4
Greinke,Zack	5
Kershaw,Clayton	5
Falter,Bailey	5
Mikolas,Miles	5
Means,John	5
Gausman,Kevin	5
Irvin,Cole	5
Verlander,Justin	5
Eflin,Zach	5
Hendricks,Kyle	5
Bradley,Taj	5
Urquidy,José	5
deGrom,Jacob	5
Fried,Max	5
Eovaldi,Nathan	5
Stripling,Ross	5
Scherzer,Max	6
Taillon,Jameson	6
Civale,Aaron	6
Chirinos,Yonny	6
Montgomery,Jordan	6
Bieber,Shane	6
Nola,Aaron	6
Ober,Bailey	6
Wheeler,Zack	6
Syndergaard,Noah	6
Kluber,Corey	6

Top K%

NAME	K%
deGrom,Jacob	40
Strider,Spencer	36
Glasnow,Tyler	36
Cole,Gerrit	34
Scherzer,Max	33
Heaney,Andrew	33
Rodón,Carlos	33
Sale,Chris	33
Ohtani,Shohei	33
Burnes,Corbin	33
Snell,Blake	32
Javier,Cristian	32
Greene,Hunter	32
Paxton,James	31
Nola,Aaron	31
Woodruff,Brandon	31
Baz,Shane	31
Lodolo,Nick	31
Ray,Robbie	31
Gausman,Kevin	30
Peralta,Freddy	30
Alzolay,Adbert	30
Hall,DL	30
Pérez,Eury	29
Morton,Charlie	29
Cease,Dylan	29
Castillo,Luis	29
Darvish,Yu	29
Miller,Bobby	28
Kershaw,Clayton	28
Springs,Jeffrey	28

Top Ground Ball Rate

NAME	GB%
Valdez,Framber	66
Cobb,Alex	57
Ashby,Aaron	57
Jameson,Drey	56
Bello,Brayan	56
Webb,Logan	55
Sánchez,Sixto	55
Ashcraft,Graham	55
Hudson,Dakota	54
Wright,Kyle	54
Stroman,Marcus	53
McCullers Jr.,Lance	52
Senzatela,Antonio	52
Alcantara,Sandy	52
Fried,Max	52
Houser,Adrian	52
Dunning,Dane	52
Castillo,Luis	51
Miley,Wade	51
Soroka,Mike	51
Steele,Justin	51
Turnbull,Spencer	51
May,Dustin	51
Alexander,Jason	51
Winckowski,Josh	50
Brown,Hunter	50
Singer,Brady	50
Sandoval,Patrick	50
Anderson,Ian	49
Elder,Bryce	49
McClanahan,Shane	49

Top Fly Ball Rate

NAME	FB%
Javier,Cristian	54
Ryan,Joe	54
Ober,Bailey	51
Patino,Luis	51
Logue,Zach	51
Oller,Adam	51
Gray,Josiah	50
Pepiot,Ryan	50
Winn,Cole	49
McKenzie,Triston	48
Wentz,Joey	48
García,Rony	48
Crawford,Kutter	48
Winder,Josh	47
Wells,Tyler	47
Nelson,Ryne	47
Means,John	47
Liberatore,Matthew	47
Cortes,Nestor	47
Verlander,Justin	46
Kopech,Michael	46
Scherzer,Max	46
Odorizzi,Jake	46
Heasley,Jon	45
Peralta,Freddy	45
Urquidy,José	45
Pérez,Eury	45
Faedo,Alex	45
Hill,Garrett	45
Kaprielian,James	44
Greene,Hunter	44

High GB, Low K%

NAME	GB%	K%
Ashcraft,Graham	55	17
Hudson,Dakota	54	16
Senzatela,Antonio	52	14
Houser,Adrian	52	16
Miley,Wade	51	18
Soroka,Mike	51	18
Alexander,Jason	51	15
Winckowski,Josh	50	15
Elder,Bryce	49	19
Adon,Joan	48	19
Mize,Casey	48	20
Pérez,Martín	47	20
Mikolas,Miles	47	19
Fedde,Erick	47	16
Blackburn,Paul	46	18
Silseth,Chase	45	18
Freeland,Kyle	45	18
Davidson,Tucker	45	19
Castillo,Max	45	19
Wainwright,Adam	45	19
Mills,Alec	44	17
Corbin,Patrick	44	19
White,Mitch	44	19
Chirinos,Yonny	43	19
Otto Jr.,Glenn	43	20
Thompson,Zach	43	18
Greinke,Zack	43	18
Davies,Zach	42	18
Sears,JP	42	18
Quantrill,Cal	42	19
Wilson,Bryse	42	18

High GB, High K%

NAME	GB%	K%
Ashby,Aaron	57	27
Castillo,Luis	51	29
McClanahan,Shane	49	27
Kershaw,Clayton	49	28
Burnes,Corbin	47	33
Gray,Sonny	47	27
Lodolo,Nick	46	31
Kikuchi,Yusei	46	27
Glasnow,Tyler	46	36
Alzolay,Adbert	45	30
Sale,Chris	45	33
Nola,Aaron	45	31
Miller,Bobby	45	28
Musgrove,Joe	45	28
Gallen,Zac	45	27
Baz,Shane	44	31
Hall,DL	44	30
Senga,Koudai	44	27
Morton,Charlie	43	29
deGrom,Jacob	43	40
Megill,Tylor	43	27
Woodruff,Brandon	42	31
Ohtani,Shohei	42	33
Rodriguez,Grayson	41	27
Cole,Gerrit	41	34
Snell,Blake	40	32
Strider,Spencer	40	36
Pérez,Eury	40	29
Luzardo,Jesús	40	28
Gausman,Kevin	40	30
Lynn,Lance	40	26

Lowest xERA

NAME	xERA
deGrom,Jacob	2.16
Strider,Spencer	2.57
Sale,Chris	2.58
Glasnow,Tyler	2.59
Burnes,Corbin	2.60
Cole,Gerrit	2.67
Nola,Aaron	2.68
Baz,Shane	2.70
Ohtani,Shohei	2.71
Kershaw,Clayton	2.75
Gausman,Kevin	2.80
Alzolay,Adbert	2.81
Castillo,Luis	2.81
McClanahan,Shane	2.83
Valdez,Framber	2.84
Scherzer,Max	2.86
Woodruff,Brandon	2.88
Cobb,Alex	2.90
Miller,Bobby	2.91
Heaney,Andrew	2.94
Fried,Max	2.97
Wheeler,Zack	2.98
Rodón,Carlos	2.98
Lodolo,Nick	2.98
Paxton,James	2.99
Musgrove,Joe	3.00
Bieber,Shane	3.01
May,Dustin	3.01
Ashby,Aaron	3.06
Paddack,Chris	3.07
Snell,Blake	3.07

Top BPX, 160+ IP

NAME	BPX
Cole,Gerrit	192
Scherzer,Max	183
Burnes,Corbin	181
Nola,Aaron	179
Gausman,Kevin	179
Woodruff,Brandon	166
Ohtani,Shohei	164
Kirby,George	163
Rodón,Carlos	161
Castillo,Luis	154
Darvish,Yu	153
Musgrove,Joe	151
Ray,Robbie	145
Wheeler,Zack	145
Morton,Charlie	144
Bieber,Shane	143
Fried,Max	142
Montgomery,Jordan	138
Alcantara,Sandy	131
Cortes,Nestor	130
McKenzie,Triston	126
Singer,Brady	125
Giolito,Lucas	124
Valdez,Framber	122
Gilbert,Logan	116
Urías,Julio	116
Berríos,José	115
Bassitt,Chris	115
Bello,Brayan	114
Webb,Logan	112
Wright,Kyle	111

Top BPX, <120 IP

NAME	BPX
Kershaw,Clayton	176
Heaney,Andrew	174
Alzolay,Adbert	167
Baz,Shane	160
Small,Ethan	158
Paxton,James	156
Miller,Bobby	156
Paddack,Chris	150
Civale,Aaron	140
Megill,Tylor	139
Wood,Alex	136
Buehler,Walker	132
Ryu,Hyun-Jin	131
Bradley,Taj	130
Eflin,Zach	129
Strasburg,Stephen	128
Skubal,Tarik	128
Whitlock,Garrett	124
Pérez,Eury	124
Rodriguez,Grayson	122
Stripling,Ross	119
Falter,Bailey	115
Germán,Domingo	114
Means,John	114
White,Owen	113
Hall,DL	111
Jameson,Drey	110
Ober,Bailey	109
Ortiz,Luis	106
Kikuchi,Yusei	103
Garrett,Braxton	103

PITCHER SKILLS RANKINGS — Relief Pitchers

Top K-BB%

NAME	K-BB%
Díaz,Edwin	38
Hader,Josh	33
Alvarado,José	32
Hendriks,Liam	31
Muñoz,Andrés	30
Fairbanks,Peter	29
Pressly,Ryan	28
Martin,Christopher	28
Rogers,Taylor	27
Iglesias,Raisel	27
Kahnle,Tommy	26
Karinchak,James	25
Neris,Hector	25
Gallegos,Giovanny	25
Lee,Dylan	25
Williams,Devin	24
Jiménez,Joe	24
Swanson,Erik	24
Vesia,Alex	24
Duran,Jhoan	24
Anderson,Nick	24
Pagan,Emilio	24
Jansen,Kenley	24
Minter,A.J.	24
Bednar,David	24
Hudson,Daniel	23
Clase,Emmanuel	23
Hentges,Sam	22
Poche,Colin	22
Thielbar,Caleb	22
Bautista,Félix	22

Top BB%

NAME	BB%
Martin,Christopher	2
Mantiply,Joe	5
Clase,Emmanuel	5
Ramirez,Erasmo	5
Clarke,Taylor	6
Akin,Keegan	6
Foley,Jason	6
Anderson,Nick	6
Acevedo,Domingo	6
Alexander,Tyler	6
Cimber,Adam	6
Swanson,Erik	6
Garcia,Yimi	6
Milner,Hoby	6
Lee,Dylan	6
Espino,Paolo	6
Hendriks,Liam	6
Kuhnel,Joel	6
Barria,Jaime	6
Rogers,Taylor	6
Duran,Jhoan	6
Bickford,Phil	6
Morgan,Elijah	6
López,Reynaldo	6
Sadler,Casey	6
Thielbar,Caleb	6
King,John	7
Smeltzer,Devin	7
Iglesias,Raisel	7
Suter,Brent	7
Price,David	7

Top K%

NAME	K%
Díaz,Edwin	46
Hader,Josh	43
Alvarado,José	42
Karinchak,James	38
Hendriks,Liam	38
Williams,Devin	37
Muñoz,Andrés	37
Fairbanks,Peter	36
Pressly,Ryan	36
Vesia,Alex	35
Chapman,Aroldis	34
Kahnle,Tommy	34
Rogers,Taylor	34
Abreu,Bryan	33
Neris,Hector	33
Jiménez,Joe	33
Iglesias,Raisel	33
Jansen,Kenley	33
Moran,Jovani	32
Brash,Matt	32
Bautista,Félix	32
Gallegos,Giovanny	32
Lamet,Dinelson	32
Pagan,Emilio	32
Leclerc,José	32
Rainey,Tanner	32
Díaz,Alexis	32
Bednar,David	31
Poche,Colin	31
Sims,Lucas	31
Lee,Dylan	31

Top Ground Ball Rate

NAME	GB%
Holmes,Clay	70
Britton,Zack	70
Bummer,Aaron	66
Clase,Emmanuel	65
Pallante,Andre	64
King,John	64
Duran,Jhoan	62
Graterol,Brusdar	60
Hill,Tim	60
Tate,Dillon	59
Hentges,Sam	59
Sadler,Casey	58
Hicks,Jordan	58
Doval,Camilo	58
Kelly,Joe	58
Foley,Jason	57
Schreiber,John	56
Suárez,Ranger	56
Mayza,Tim	56
Hernández,Jonathan	56
Sanmartin,Reiver	55
Graveman,Kendall	54
Loáisiga,Jonathan	54
Alvarado,José	54
Muñoz,Andrés	54
Lange,Alex	53
Montero,Rafael	53
López,Jorge	53
Peralta,Wandy	53
Keller,Brad	52
Martin,Brett	52

Top Fly Ball Rate

NAME	FB%
Jackson,Zach	59
Wilson,Steven	58
Díaz,Alexis	54
Wantz,Andrew	52
Morejon,Adrian	52
Poche,Colin	52
Gallegos,Giovanny	52
Morgan,Elijah	51
Hernandez,Elieser	51
Sewald,Paul	50
Jansen,Kenley	50
Rainey,Tanner	49
Leclerc,José	49
Hader,Josh	49
Bellatti,Andrew	49
Thielbar,Caleb	49
Murfee,Penn	49
Sims,Lucas	48
Vesia,Alex	48
Hendriks,Liam	48
Karinchak,James	48
Helsley,Ryan	47
Garcia,Yimi	47
Staumont,Josh	47
Swanson,Erik	47
Pagan,Emilio	47
Jiménez,Joe	47
Richards,Trevor	46
Kimbrel,Craig	46
Okert,Steven	46
Kennedy,Ian	46

High GB, Low K%

NAME	GB%	K%
Britton,Zack	70	20
Pallante,Andre	64	16
King,John	64	18
Graterol,Brusdar	60	21
Hill,Tim	60	18
Tate,Dillon	59	19
Sadler,Casey	58	20
Foley,Jason	57	16
Suárez,Ranger	56	20
Hernández,Jonathan	56	21
Sanmartin,Reiver	55	20
López,Jorge	53	22
Peralta,Wandy	53	20
Keller,Brad	52	18
Martin,Brett	52	19
Kuhnel,Joel	52	22
Rodríguez,Manuel	51	20
Mantiply,Joe	50	22
Woodford,Jake	50	15
Cessa,Luis	49	20
Oviedo,Johan	49	22
Vest,Will	48	20
Crowe,Wil	48	19
Floro,Dylan	48	22
Melancon,Mark	48	18
Santana,Dennis	47	21
Martinez,Nick	47	20
Cimber,Adam	47	20
Suter,Brent	47	21
Cuas,Jose	46	18
Uelmen,Erich	45	19

High GB, High K%

NAME	GB%	K%
Duran,Jhoan	62	30
Kelly,Joe	58	30
Alvarado,José	54	42
Muñoz,Andrés	54	37
Williams,Devin	51	37
Brash,Matt	51	32
Kahnle,Tommy	50	34
Fairbanks,Peter	49	36
Pressly,Ryan	49	36
Abreu,Bryan	49	33
Moran,Jovani	48	32
Antone,Tejay	48	30
Martin,Christopher	48	30
Robertson,David	46	30
Rogers,Taylor	45	34
Bautista,Félix	44	32
Suarez,Robert	44	30
Díaz,Edwin	43	46
Marinaccio,Ron	42	30
Hudson,Daniel	41	30
Neris,Hector	40	33
Minter,A.J.	39	31
Chapman,Aroldis	39	34
Lamet,Dinelson	37	32
Smith,Will	36	31
Bednar,David	36	31
Lee,Dylan	36	31
Kimbrel,Craig	35	30
Helsley,Ryan	35	30
Pagan,Emilio	35	32
Iglesias,Raisel	34	33

Lowest xERA

NAME	xERA
Díaz,Edwin	1.91
Alvarado,José	1.94
Muñoz,Andrés	2.25
Clase,Emmanuel	2.26
Duran,Jhoan	2.29
Pressly,Ryan	2.31
Fairbanks,Peter	2.35
Kahnle,Tommy	2.43
Holmes,Clay	2.46
Hentges,Sam	2.50
Hader,Josh	2.51
Martin,Christopher	2.53
Williams,Devin	2.54
Rogers,Taylor	2.61
Hendriks,Liam	2.65
Kelly,Joe	2.72
Abreu,Bryan	2.79
Bummer,Aaron	2.81
Doval,Camilo	2.84
Neris,Hector	2.85
Iglesias,Raisel	2.86
Brash,Matt	2.86
Stephan,Trevor	2.93
Ottavino,Adam	2.95
Bautista,Félix	2.95
Suarez,Robert	2.95
Moran,Jovani	2.96
Karinchak,James	2.96
King,Michael	2.97
Hudson,Daniel	2.98
Phillips,Evan	3.00

Top BPX, 10+ Saves

NAME	BPX
Díaz,Edwin	253
Muñoz,Andrés	210
Hendriks,Liam	205
Hader,Josh	203
Fairbanks,Peter	203
Rogers,Taylor	194
Pressly,Ryan	192
Clase,Emmanuel	181
Iglesias,Raisel	174
Williams,Devin	159
Holmes,Clay	153
Gallegos,Giovanny	152
Bednar,David	151
Romano,Jordan	149
Puk,A.J.	146
Jansen,Kenley	144
Bautista,Félix	143
Barlow,Scott	139
Adam,Jason	136
Robertson,David	129
Sewald,Paul	129
Helsley,Ryan	121
Doval,Camilo	121
Hughes,Brandon	113
Leclerc,José	111
Díaz,Alexis	108
Kimbrel,Craig	107
Floro,Dylan	106
Finnegan,Kyle	106
Bard,Daniel	105
Domínguez,Seranthony	104

Top BPX, <10 Saves

NAME	BPX
Alvarado,José	222
Martin,Christopher	210
Duran,Jhoan	187
Kahnle,Tommy	183
Hentges,Sam	171
Lee,Dylan	167
Anderson,Nick	165
Neris,Hector	165
Swanson,Erik	160
Pagan,Emilio	155
Jiménez,Joe	155
Hudson,Daniel	150
Stephan,Trevor	149
King,Michael	146
Milner,Hoby	145
Mantiply,Joe	143
McHugh,Collin	143
Chafin,Andrew	142
Ottavino,Adam	142
Smith,Will	142
Vesia,Alex	142
López,Reynaldo	141
Lugo,Seth	141
Kelly,Joe	141
Thielbar,Caleb	141
Brogdon,Connor	138
Karinchak,James	138
Suarez,Robert	137
Lamet,Dinelson	137
Festa,Matt	137
Poche,Colin	132

POTENTIAL SKILLS GAINERS AND FADERS — Pitchers

K% Gainers

From a pitcher's swinging-strike rate (SwK), we can establish a typical range in which we would expect to find their K%. The pitchers on this list posted a 2023 K% that was in the bottom of the expected range based on their SwK. The names above the break line are in the bottom 10% of that range, and are the strongest candidates for K% gains. The names below the break line are in the bottom 25%, and are also good candidates for K% gains.

K% Faders

From a pitcher's swinging-strike rate (SwK), we can establish a typical range in which we would expect to find their K%. The pitchers on this list posted a 2023 K% that was in the top of that expected range based on their SwK. The names above the break line are in the top 10% of that range, and are the strongest candidates for a K% fade. The names below the break line are in the top 25%, and are also good candidates for a K% fade.

BB% Gainers

A pitcher's xBB% is a skills-based representation of what their BB% should be. Assuming the same underlying skills across seasons, a pitcher's actual BB% should move in the direction of their xBB%. Therefore, by ordering pitchers with the biggest gap between actual BB% and xBB% in 2023 in the chart below, we can identify those whose walk rates should improve (Gainers) in 2024.

BB% Faders

A pitcher's xBB% is a skills-based representation of what their BB% should be. Assuming the same underlying skills across seasons, a pitcher's actual BB% should move in the direction of their xBB%. Therefore, by ordering pitchers with the biggest gap between xBB% and actual BB% in 2023 in the chart below, we can identify those whose walk rates should get worse (Faders) in 2024.

K% GAINERS

NAME	SwK	K%
McClanahan, Shane	16.0	26
German, Domingo	15.1	26
Houck, Tanner	13.1	21
Anderson, Tyler	13.0	19
Alcantara, Sandy	12.8	20
Sandoval, Patrick	12.2	20
Carrasco, Carlos	11.1	16
Yarbrough, Ryan	11.0	18
Stripling, Ross	10.7	18
Barria, Jaime	10.6	17
Ober, Bailey	14.6	25
Farmer, Buck	13.8	23
Lynn, Lance	13.5	24
Morton, Charlie	13.2	26
Woo, Bryan	13.2	25
Crawford, Kutter	13.1	26
Paxton, James	13.1	25
Martinez, Nick	13.0	23
Holton, Tyler	12.6	23
Gray, Jon	12.6	22
Gibaut, Ian	12.6	22
Winckowski, Josh	12.6	22
Miller, Bryce	11.9	22
Sears, JP	11.7	22
Montgomery, Jordan	11.7	21
Wentz, Joey	11.5	20
Waldichuk, Ken	11.5	21
Oviedo, Johan	11.5	20
Gray, Josiah	11.4	20
Bello, Brayan	11.2	20
Beck, Tristan	11.2	19
Gibson, Kyle	11.1	19
Littell, Zack	10.8	20
Bieber, Shane	10.7	20

K% FADERS

NAME	SwK	K%
Assad, Javier	8	20.9
Webb, Logan	9	22.8
Brown, Hunter	11	26.8
King, Michael	12	29.5
Bradley, Taj	12	28.0
Senga, Kodai	13	29.1
Irvin, Jake	7	18.7
Houser, Adrian	8	20.0
Hill, Rich	8	19.5
Wilson, Bryse	9	19.4
Davies, Zach	9	19.1
Walker, Taijuan	9	18.8
Cobb, Alex	9	20.3
DeSclafani, Anthony	9	18.9
Lively, Ben	9	20.6
Bird, Jake	9	20.2
Lugo, Seth	10	23.2
Lawrence, Justin	10	23.9
Stratton, Chris	10	24.0
Keller, Mitch	10	25.5
Civale, Aaron	10	23.0
Rodriguez, Eduardo	11	23.0
Urias, Julio	11	24.3
Darvish, Yu	11	24.6
Manaea, Sean	11	25.7
Bradish, Kyle	11	25.0
Abbott, Andrew	11	26.1
Eflin, Zach	12	26.5
Junis, Jakob	12	26.2
Gallen, Zac	12	26.0
Fried, Max	12	25.7
Cole, Gerrit	12	27.0

BB% GAINERS

NAME	xBB%	BB%
Manoah, Alek	9.6	14.2
Kopech, Michael	11.6	15.4
Cabrera, Edward	11.6	15.2
Toussaint, Touki	11.6	14.8
Gibaut, Ian	5.9	8.8
Ragans, Cole	7.6	10.5
McClanahan, Shane	5.9	8.7
Scott, Tanner	5.0	7.8
Ohtani, Shohei	7.6	10.4
Lawrence, Justin	8.3	11.0
Sandoval, Patrick	8.7	11.3
Strider, Spencer	5.0	7.6
Anderson, Tyler	7.6	10.2
Williams, Gavin	8.3	10.7
Waldichuk, Ken	8.7	11.1
Ortiz, Luis	9.6	12.0
Kelly, Merrill	7.2	9.6
Manaea, Sean	6.1	8.4
Woo, Bryan	6.1	8.4
Wood, Alex	7.6	9.8
Gray, Jon	6.1	8.2
Fujinami, Shintaro	10.5	12.6
Rodriguez, Grayson	6.1	8.2
Severino, Luis	6.1	8.2
Greene, Hunter	7.6	9.6

BB% FADERS

NAME	xBB%	BB%
Greinke, Zack	7.6	3.9
DeSclafani, Anthony	7.6	4.8
Fried, Max	8.3	5.8
Kirby, George	4.1	2.5
Littell, Zack	4.8	3.2
Garrett, Braxton	6.1	4.4
Stripling, Ross	6.1	4.2
Gallen, Zac	7.2	5.6
Cobb, Alex	7.6	5.7
Bello, Brayan	8.3	6.7
Lyles, Jordan	8.3	6.0
Gibson, Kyle	8.7	6.8
Williams, Trevor	9.6	8.0

EXPECTED STATS vs. ACTUAL — Pitchers

ERA Underperformers (min. 75 IP)

NAME	ERA	xERA	Diff
Davies,Zachary	7.00	5.04	1.96
Carrasco,Carlos	6.80	5.15	1.65
Brown,Hunter	5.09	3.51	1.58
Bradley,Taj	5.59	4.10	1.49
Weaver,Luke	6.40	4.99	1.41
Peterson,David	5.03	3.64	1.39
Lynn,Lance	5.73	4.58	1.15
Singer,Brady	5.52	4.37	1.15
Stripling,Ross	5.36	4.25	1.11
Pfaadt,Brandon	5.72	4.66	1.06
Houck,Tanner	5.01	4.07	0.94
Lively,Ben	5.38	4.55	0.83
Greene,Hunter	4.82	4.04	0.78
Strider,Spencer	3.86	3.10	0.76
Nola,Aaron	4.46	3.80	0.66
Medina,Luis	5.42	4.78	0.64
Ryan,Joe	4.51	3.88	0.63
Sale,Chris	4.30	3.67	0.63
Glasnow,Tyler	3.53	2.91	0.62
Darvish,Yu	4.56	3.95	0.61
DeSclafani,Anthony	4.88	4.28	0.60

WHIP Underperformers (min. 75 IP)

NAME	WHIP	xWHIP	Diff
Muller,Kyle	1.96	1.55	0.41
Seabold,Connor	1.65	1.36	0.29
Severino,Luis	1.65	1.36	0.29
Wentz,Joey	1.68	1.40	0.28
Weaver,Luke	1.58	1.31	0.27
Peterson,David	1.57	1.31	0.26
Flexen,Chris	1.67	1.42	0.25
Blach,Ty	1.64	1.40	0.24
Carrasco,Carlos	1.70	1.47	0.23
Greene,Hunter	1.42	1.20	0.22
Flaherty,Jack	1.58	1.37	0.21
Davies,Zachary	1.66	1.45	0.21
Williams,Trevor	1.60	1.40	0.20
Blackburn,Paul	1.54	1.34	0.20
Pfaadt,Brandon	1.41	1.22	0.19
Bradley,Taj	1.39	1.20	0.19
Junis,Jakob	1.29	1.13	0.16
Brown,Hunter	1.36	1.21	0.15
Hill,Rich	1.52	1.38	0.14
Stripling,Ross	1.35	1.21	0.14
Cease,Dylan	1.42	1.28	0.14

Wins Underperformers (SP)

NAME	W	xW	Diff
Gray,Sonny	8	16	-8
Detmers,Reid	4	10	-6
Montgomery,Jordan	10	16	-6
Hendricks,Kyle	6	11	-5
Irvin,Jake	3	8	-5
Suarez,Ranger	4	9	-5
Bradish,Kyle	12	16	-4
Burnes,Corbin	10	14	-4
Civale,Aaron	7	11	-4
Cobb,Alex	7	11	-4
Gray,Jonathan	9	13	-4
Gray,Josiah	8	12	-4
Greene,Hunter	4	8	-4
Ober,Bailey	8	12	-4
Sandoval,Patrick	7	11	-4
Sears,JP	5	9	-4
Snell,Blake	14	18	-4
Williams,Gavin	3	7	-4
Williamson,Brandon	5	9	-4
Alcantara,Sandy	7	10	-3
Berrios,Jose	11	14	-3

ERA Overperformers (min. 75 IP)

NAME	ERA	xERA	Diff
Wilson,Bryse	2.58	4.68	-2.10
Miley,Wade	3.14	4.73	-1.59
Holton,Tyler	2.11	3.69	-1.58
Manning,Matt	3.58	5.03	-1.45
Snell,Blake	2.25	3.63	-1.38
Verlander,Justin	3.22	4.55	-1.33
Wacha,Michael	3.22	4.50	-1.28
Curry,Xzavion	4.07	5.35	-1.28
Assad,Javier	3.05	4.30	-1.25
Bibee,Tanner	2.98	4.23	-1.25
Henry,Thomas	4.15	5.36	-1.21
Williams,Gavin	3.29	4.49	-1.20
Clevinger,Michael	3.77	4.97	-1.20
Gray,Josiah	3.91	5.10	-1.19
Winckowski,Josh	2.88	4.00	-1.12
Perez,Eury	3.15	4.26	-1.11
Kershaw,Clayton	2.46	3.56	-1.10
Gibaut,Ian	3.33	4.41	-1.08
France,J.P.	3.83	4.90	-1.07
Quintana,Jose	3.57	4.61	-1.04
Bielak,Brandon	3.83	4.85	-1.02

WHIP Overperformers (min. 75 IP)

NAME	WHIP	xWHIP	Diff
Manning,Matt	1.04	1.36	-0.32
Holton,Tyler	0.87	1.18	-0.31
Miley,Wade	1.14	1.40	-0.26
Wilson,Bryse	1.07	1.31	-0.24
Wells,Tyler	0.99	1.21	-0.22
Gonsolin,Tony	1.22	1.41	-0.19
Farmer,Buck	1.16	1.34	-0.18
Burnes,Corbin	1.07	1.25	-0.18
Ohtani,Shohei	1.06	1.21	-0.15
Lorenzen,Michael	1.21	1.36	-0.15
Tonkin,Michael	1.09	1.24	-0.15
Toussaint,Touki	1.45	1.60	-0.15
Snell,Blake	1.19	1.33	-0.14
Eovaldi,Nathan	1.14	1.28	-0.14
Kershaw,Clayton	1.06	1.20	-0.14
Bradish,Kyle	1.04	1.18	-0.14
Cole,Gerrit	0.98	1.12	-0.14
Assad,Javier	1.23	1.36	-0.13
German,Domingo	1.08	1.21	-0.13
Elder,Bryce	1.28	1.41	-0.13
Verlander,Justin	1.13	1.25	-0.12

Wins Overperformers (SP)

NAME	W	xW	Diff
Strider,Spencer	20	15	5
Gibson,Kyle	15	12	3
Wacha,Michael	14	11	3
Walker,Taijuan	15	12	3
Bassitt,Chris	16	14	2
Gallen,Zac	17	15	2
Lynn,Lance	13	11	2
Musgrove,Joe	10	8	2
Rodriguez,Eduardo	13	11	2
Urias,Julio	11	9	2
Bello,Brayan	12	11	1
Boyd,Matt	5	4	1
Cortes,Nestor	5	4	1
Eflin,Zach	16	15	1
Gomber,Austin	9	8	1

RISK MANAGEMENT

GRADE "F" in HEALTH (R$>0)

Pitchers		Batters
Alcantara,Sandy	Lorenzen,Michael	Albies,Ozzie
Alzolay,Adbert	Maeda,Kenta	Anderson,Brian
Baz,Shane	Manning,Matt	Anderson,Tim
Bieber,Shane	Matz,Steven	Bader,Harrison
Buehler,Walker	McClanahan,Shane	Belt,Brandon
Canning,Griffin	McCullers,Lance	Brantley,Michael
Civale,Aaron	McKenzie,Triston	Bryant,Kris
Clevinger,Michael	Means,John	Buxton,Byron
Cobb,Alex	Merryweather,Julian	Chisholm Jr.,Jazz
Cortes,Nestor	Mikolas,Miles	Cooper,Garrett
Coulombe,Daniel	Miley,Wade	Cron,C.J.
deGrom,Jacob	Miller,Mason	Cruz,Oneil
DeSclafani,Anthony	Mize,Casey	Davis,Henry
Díaz,Edwin	Montas,Frankie	Donaldson,Josh
Domínguez,Serantho	Muñoz,Andres	Duvall,Adam
Eflin,Zach	Musgrove,Joe	Fraley,Jake
Eovaldi,Nathan	Paddack,Chris	Garcia,Avisail
Fairbanks,Peter	Paxton,James	Garver,Mitch
Ferguson,Caleb	Pepiot,Ryan	Haniger,Mitch
Flaherty,Jack	Poche,Colin	Heyward,Jason
Fried,Max	Quintana,José	Hicks,Aaron
Fulmer,Michael	Rasmussen,Drew	Hoskins,Rhys
García,Luis	Ray,Robbie	Jansen,Danny
Germán,Domingo	Rodón,Carlos	Jimenez,Eloy
Glasnow,Tyler	Rogers,Trevor	Kieboom,Carter
Gonsolin,Tony	Romero,JoJo	Kirilloff,Alex
Gonzales,Marco	Ryu,Hyun-Jin	Lewis,Kyle
Greene,Hunter	Sale,Chris	Lewis,Royce
Harvey,Hunter	Scherzer,Max	Longoria,Evan
Heaney,Andrew	Skubal,Tarik	Lowe,Brandon
Helsley,Ryan	Soroka,Michael	Lux,Gavin
Hendricks,Kyle	Springs,Jeffrey	Madrigal,Nick
Hendriks,Liam	Stewart,Brock	Marte,Starling
Hicks,Jordan	Stroman,Marcus	Meadows,Austin
Hoffman,Jeff	Suarez,Robert	Mitchell,Garrett
Houck,Tanner	Topa,Justin	Moncada,Yoán
Jiménez,Dany	Urquidy,José	Mondesi,Adalberto
Johnson,Pierce	Verlander,Justin	Moustakas,Mike
Kahnle,Tommy	Wacha,Michael	O'Hoppe,Logan
King,Michael	Whitlock,Garrett	O'Neill,Tyler
Leclerc,José	Wood,Alex	Pasquantino,Vinnie
		Pillar,Kevin
		Polanco,Jorge
		Rendon,Anthony
		Robles,Victor
		Rodgers,Brendan
		Rogers,Jake
		Senzel,Nick
		Stanton,Giancarlo
		Story,Trevor
		Tatis Jr.,Fernando
		Trout,Mike
		Urshela,Giovanny
		Votto,Joey
		Winker,Jesse

Highest Reliability-Health/Experience/Consistency (Min. Grade BBB)

CA	Rel
Rutschman,Adley	AAA
Maldonado,Martín	AAA
Smith,Will	AAA
Contreras,William	AAB
Langeliers,Shea	AAB
Murphy,Sean	AAB
Raleigh,Cal	AAB
Realmuto,J.T.	AAB
Vázquez,Christian	AAB
Álvarez,Francisco	ABA
Lee,Korey	ABA
Sabol,Blake	ABA
Wong,Connor	ABA
Bethancourt,Christian	ABB
Fortes,Nick	ABB
Thaiss,Matt	ABB

1B/DH	Rel
Vaughn,Andrew	AAA
Meneses,Joey	AAA
Vientos,Mark	AAA
Alonso,Pete	AAB
Bell,Josh	AAB
Bohm,Alec	AAB
France,Ty	AAB
Freeman,Freddie	AAB
Montero,Elehuris	AAB
Paredes,Isaac	AAB
Santana,Carlos	AAB
Miller,Owen	ABA
Toglia,Michael	ABA
Clemens,Kody	ABB
Loftin,Nick	ABB
Mervis,Matt	ABB
Raley,Luke	ABB
Sheets,Gavin	ABB
Ford,Mike	ABB
Hiura,Keston	ABB
LeMahieu,DJ	BAA

2B	Rel
Batten,Matthew	AAA
Garcia,Luis	AAA
McMahon,Ryan	AAA
Rosario,Amed	AAA
Turang,Brice	AAA
Gorman,Nolan	AAB
Edman,Tommy	AAB
Kim,Ha-Seong	AAB
Massey,Michael	AAB
Merrifield,Whit	AAB
Stott,Bryson	AAB
Vargas,Miguel	AAB
Villar,David	AAB
Westburg,Jordan	AAB
Miller,Owen	ABA
Gonzales,Nick	ABA
Valdez,Enmanuel	ABA
Castro,Harold	ABB
Castro,Rodolfo	ABB
Short,Zack	ABB
Estrada,Thairo	BAA
Farmer,Kyle	BAA
McKinstry,Zach	BAA
Urías,Ramón	BAA

3B	Rel
Kiner-Falefa,Isiah	AAA
Henderson,Gunnar	AAA
McMahon,Ryan	AAA
Ramírez,José	AAA
Devers,Rafael	AAA
Garcia,Maikel	AAA
Riley,Austin	AAA
Castro,Willi	AAB
Vierling,Matt	AAB
Kim,Ha-Seong	AAB
Westburg,Jordan	AAB
Bohm,Alec	AAB
Paredes,Isaac	AAB
Busch,Michael	AAB
Peraza,Oswald	AAB
Miller,Owen	ABA
Rivera,Emmanuel	ABA
Short,Zack	ABB

OF	Rel
Kiner-Falefa,Isiah	AAA
Arozarena,Randy	AAA
De La Cruz,Bryan	AAA
Florial,Estevan	AAA
Happ,Ian	AAA
Harris II,Michael	AAA
Kwan,Steven	AAA
Meadows,Parker	AAA
Taylor,Michael A.	AAA
Verdugo,Alex	AAA
Castro,Willi	AAB
Vierling,Matt	AAB
Edman,Tommy	AAB
Merrifield,Whit	AAB
Burleson,Alec	AAB
Smith,Pavin	AAB
Brennan,Will	AAB
Garcia,Adolis	AAB
Gonzalez,Oscar	AAB
Julks,Corey	AAB
Outman,James	AAB
Profar,Jurickson	AAB
Straw,Myles	AAB
Suwinski,Jack	AAB
Taveras,Leody	AAB
Thomas,Alek	AAB
Thomas,Lane	AAB
Varsho,Daulton	AAB
Sabol,Blake	ABA
Doyle,Brenton	ABA
Rafaela,Ceddanne	ABA
Wiemer,Joey	ABA
Raley,Luke	ABB
Sheets,Gavin	ABB
Cabrera,Oswaldo	ABB
Wallner,Matt	ABB
McKinstry,Zach	BAA
Canha,Mark	BAA
Gurriel Jr.,Lourdes	BAA
Brown,Seth	BAA
Conforto,Michael	BAA
Grichuk,Randal	BAA
Peralta,David	BAA

SS	Rel
Rosario,Amed	AAA
Turang,Brice	AAA
Amaya,Jacob	AAA
Henderson,Gunnar	AAA
Mateo,Jorge	AAA
Peña,Jeremy	AAA
Swanson,Dansby	AAA
Volpe,Anthony	AAA
Edman,Tommy	AAB
Kim,Ha-Seong	AAB
Abrams,CJ	AAB
Allen,Nick	AAB
Bogaerts,Xander	AAB
Lindor,Francisco	AAB
Tovar,Ezequiel	AAB
Castro,Rodolfo	ABB
Short,Zack	ABB
Winn,Masyn	ABB
Estrada,Thairo	BAA
Farmer,Kyle	BAA
McKinstry,Zach	BAA
Andrus,Elvis	BAB
Rengifo,Luis	BAB
Adames,Willy	BAB
Arcia,Orlando	BAB
Bichette,Bo	BAB
Rojas,Miguel	BAB

SP	Rel
Berríos,José	AAA
Cease,Dylan	AAA
Cole,Gerrit	AAA
Corbin,Patrick	AAA
Gilbert,Logan	AAA
Gray,Josiah	AAA
Pivetta,Nick	AAA
Yamamoto,Yoshinobu	AAA
Burnes,Corbin	AAB
Lyles,Jordan	AAB
Martinez,Nick	AAB
Nola,Aaron	AAB
Senga,Kodai	AAB
Kirby,George	ABA
Elder,Bryce	ABB
Oviedo,Johan	ABB
Detmers,Reid	BAA
Gausman,Kevin	BAA
Gibson,Kyle	BAA
Kikuchi,Yusei	BAA
Morton,Charlie	BAA
Wheeler,Zack	BAA
Irvin,Cole	BAB
Montgomery,Jordan	BAB
Perez,Martin	BAB
Garrett,Braxton	BBB

(Minimum Grade AAA)

RP	Rel
Doval,Camilo	AAA
Hader,Josh	AAA
Matsui,Yuki	AAA
Soto,Gregory	AAA

RISK MANAGEMENT

GRADE "A" in CONSISTENCY

Pitchers (min 80 IP)	Batters (min 350 AB)
Adon,Joan	Álvarez,Francisco
Bassitt,Chris	Arozarena,Randy
Berríos,José	Bae,Ji Hwan
Bido,Osvaldo	Bregman,Alex
Bieber,Shane	Brown,Seth
Buehler,Walker	Canha,Mark
Cease,Dylan	Chapman,Matt
Cecconi,Slade	Conforto,Michael
Clevinger,Michael	Contreras,Willson
Cole,Gerrit	De La Cruz,Bryan
Corbin,Patrick	Devers,Rafael
Darvish,Yu	Doyle,Brenton
DeSclafani,Anthony	Estrada,Thairo
Detmers,Reid	Garcia,Luis
Dunning,Dane	Garcia,Maikel
Eflin,Zach	Gurriel Jr.,Lourdes
Eovaldi,Nathan	Happ,Ian
Flaherty,Jack	Harris II,Michael
France,J.P.	Henderson,Gunnar
Freeland,Kyle	Hoerner,Nico
Fried,Max	Kirilloff,Alex
Gausman,Kevin	Kwan,Steven
Gibson,Kyle	Lee,Korey
Gilbert,Logan	LeMahieu,DJ
Giolito,Lucas	McKinstry,Zach
Glasnow,Tyler	McMahon,Ryan
Gonzales,Marco	Meadows,Parker
Gore,MacKenzie	Meneses,Joey
Gray,Josiah	Mountcastle,Ryan
Gray,Sonny	Neto,Zach
Greinke,Zack	Nimmo,Brandon
Hendricks,Kyle	O'Hoppe,Logan
Houck,Tanner	Peña,Jeremy
Houser,Adrian	Ramírez,José
Kelly,Merrill	Riley,Austin
Kikuchi,Yusei	Rizzo,Anthony
Kirby,George	Rosario,Amed
Littell,Zack	Rutschman,Adley
Lodolo,Nick	Smith,Will
López,Pablo	Soderstrom,Tyler
Lugo,Seth	Swanson,Dansby
Maeda,Kenta	Taylor,Michael A.
Manaea,Sean	Turang,Brice
Matz,Steven	Turner,Justin
McCullers,Lance	Vaughn,Andrew
Miller,Bobby	Verdugo,Alex
Morton,Charlie	Volpe,Anthony
Musgrove,Joe	Waters,Drew
Odorizzi,Jake	Wong,Connor
Peralta,Freddy	
Pérez,Eury	
Pivetta,Nick	
Quantrill,Cal	
Rea,Colin	
Rodriguez,Eduardo	
Ryu,Hyun-Jin	
Scherzer,Max	
Silseth,Chase	
Snell,Blake	
Steele,Justin	
Stroman,Marcus	
Suárez,Ranger	
Urías,Julio	
Wacha,Michael	
Waldron,Matt	
Webb,Logan	
Wheeler,Zack	
Wicks,Jordan	
Williams,Gavin	
Yamamoto,Yoshinobu	

TOP COMBINATION OF SKILLS AND RELIABILITY

Maximum of one "C" in Reliability Grade

BATTING POWER (Min. 400 AB)

PX 110+	PX	Rel
Schwarber,Kyle	177	BAB
Martinez,J.D.	161	BAC
Rooker,Brent	160	AAC
Wallner,Matt	159	ABB
Morel,Christopher	154	AAC
Casas,Triston	152	AAC
Suwinski,Jack	152	AAB
Raleigh,Cal	152	AAB
Alonso,Pete	151	AAB
Gorman,Nolan	150	AAB
Garcia,Adolis	149	AAB
Burger,Jake	145	BAC
Chapman,Matt	145	BAA
Riley,Austin	144	AAA
De La Cruz,Elly	141	ABC
Henderson,Gunnar	139	AAA
Betts,Mookie	139	BAC
Yastrzemski,Mike	137	CAB
Álvarez,Francisco	137	ABA
Contreras,Willson	136	BAA
Julien,Edouard	135	ABC
Murphy,Sean	135	AAB
Suarez,Eugenio	134	AAC
Drury,Brandon	134	BAC
Langeliers,Shea	134	AAB
Noda,Ryan	133	BAC
Devers,Rafael	132	AAA
Adames,Willy	132	BAB
Hernández,Teoscar	132	BAB
Carpenter,Kerry	129	BAC
Freeman,Freddie	129	AAB
Encarnacion-Strand,C	129	ACB
Rodríguez,Julio	129	AAC
Santander,Anthony	128	BAB
Waters,Drew	125	BBA
Renfroe,Hunter	125	BAB
Walker,Christian	124	BAB
Witt Jr.,Bobby	123	AAC
McMahon,Ryan	123	AAA
Brown,Seth	123	BAA
Happ,Ian	122	AAA
Montero,Elehuris	122	AAB
Arozarena,Randy	121	AAA
Harris II,Michael	121	AAA
Realmuto,J.T.	119	AAB
Contreras,William	119	AAB
Kelenic,Jarred	118	BAC
Mountcastle,Ryan	118	BAA
Outman,James	118	AAB
Reynolds,Bryan	116	AAC
Marsh,Brandon	116	AAC
Davis,J.D.	114	CAB
Volpe,Anthony	114	AAA
Thomas,Lane	113	AAB
Tellez,Rowdy	113	CAB
Swanson,Dansby	112	AAA
Varsho,Daulton	112	AAB
Gurriel Jr.,Lourdes	111	BAA
Turner,Trea	111	AAC
Steer,Spencer	111	AAC
Melendez Jr.,MJ	110	AAC
Smith,Will	110	AAA
Lindor,Francisco	110	AAB
Westburg,Jordan	110	AAB

RUNNER SPEED (Min. 400 AB)

Spd 100+	Spd	Rel
Rosario,Amed	147	AAA
De La Cruz,Elly	144	ABC
McCarthy,Jake	143	AAC
Nimmo,Brandon	142	CAA
Witt Jr.,Bobby	141	AAC
Kwan,Steven	139	AAA
Morel,Christopher	139	AAC
Turner,Trea	135	AAC
Garcia,Maikel	134	AAA
Friedl,T.J.	133	AAC
Waters,Drew	133	BBA
Abrams,CJ	132	AAB
Thomas,Alek	132	AAB
Henderson,Gunnar	131	AAA
Turang,Brice	131	AAA
Vierling,Matt	130	AAB
Franco,Wander	127	CAB
Straw,Myles	126	AAB
McKinstry,Zach	126	BAA
Hoerner,Nico	126	CAA
Lee,Jung-hoo	126	AAC
Winn,Masyn	125	ABB
Westburg,Jordan	125	AAB
Cronenworth,Jake	124	BAB
Marsh,Brandon	123	AAC
Tovar,Ezequiel	123	AAB
Arozarena,Randy	123	AAA
Rengifo,Luis	122	BAB
Báez,Javier	121	AAC
Doyle,Brenton	120	ABA
Edman,Tommy	119	AAB
Peña,Jeremy	118	AAA
Duran,Jarren	117	BBC
Reynolds,Bryan	117	AAC
Isbel,Kyle	117	BBC
Realmuto,J.T.	117	AAB
Taveras,Leody	117	AAB
Thomas,Lane	115	AAB
Yelich,Christian	115	BAB
Nootbaar,Lars	115	BAB
Outman,James	113	AAB
Contreras,William	113	AAB
Melendez Jr.,MJ	112	AAC
Rodríguez,Julio	111	AAC
Harris II,Michael	111	AAA
Bichette,Bo	111	BAB
Lindor,Francisco	111	AAB
Stott,Bryson	110	AAB

OVERALL PITCHING SKILL

BPX 100+	BPX	Rel
Strider,Spencer	182	AAC
Cole,Gerrit	178	AAA
Williams,Devin	171	AAB
Scott,Tanner	171	BAB
Kirby,George	165	ABA
Gallegos,Giovanny	163	BAA
Wheeler,Zack	162	BAA
Burnes,Corbin	161	AAB
López,Pablo	161	CAA
Adam,Jason	159	CBB
Romano,Jordan	159	CAA
Clase,Emmanuel	159	AAB
Ryan,Joe	158	CAB
Nola,Aaron	156	AAB
García,Yimi	156	BBA
Gausman,Kevin	155	BAA
Bednar,David	154	BAA
Hader,Josh	153	AAA
Webb,Logan	150	CAA
Castillo,Luis	149	CAB
Abreu,Bryan	148	BCB
Milner,Hoby	147	ACB
Matsui,Yuki	146	AAA
Sewald,Paul	146	BAA
Doval,Camilo	146	AAA
Minter,A.J.	143	BBB
Gallen,Zac	142	CAB
Gilbert,Logan	142	AAA
Sánchez,Cristopher	139	BCB
Pivetta,Nick	138	AAA
Jax,Griffin	137	ABC
McGough,Scott	136	BAA
Kimbrel,Craig	133	BAB
Valdez,Framber	131	CAB
Garrett,Braxton	130	BBB
Kikuchi,Yusei	129	BAA
Richards,Trevor	127	CBA
Manaea,Sean	124	CAA
Bradish,Kyle	124	CBB
Neris,Hector	124	ABB
Yamamoto,Yoshinobu	123	AAA
Montgomery,Jordan	123	BAB
Leiter,Mark	122	ACB
Floro,Dylan	122	CBA
Martinez,Nick	121	AAB
Jansen,Kenley	121	CAB
Berríos,José	121	AAA
Bassitt,Chris	120	CAA
Detmers,Reid	120	BAA
Barlow,Scott	119	AAB
Morgan,Eli	118	ACB
Stephan,Trevor	116	ABC
Smith,Will	115	BAA
Giolito,Lucas	114	CAA
Keller,Mitch	113	AAC
Winckowski,Josh	112	ACB
Kelly,Merrill	112	CAA
Varland,Louie	112	ACB
Imanaga,Shota	111	AAC

DAILY FANTASY INDICATORS

Top OPS v LHP, 2022-23

Hitter	OPS
Contreras, William	1074
Goldschmidt, Paul	1049
Betts, Mookie	1042
Judge, Aaron	1024
Riley, Austin	1018
Diaz, Yandy	994
Soler, Jorge	993
McCormick, Chas	992
Friedl, T.J.	989
Altuve, Jose	987
Garver, Mitch	976
Martinez, J.D.	961
Jung, Josh	961
Grichuk, Randal	955
Alvarez, Yordan	948
Trout, Mike	941
Burger, Jake	941
Steer, Spencer	938
Robert, Luis	934
Bohm, Alec	932
Jeffers, Ryan	927
Ramirez, Harold	920
Freeman, Freddie	920
Rengifo, Luis	917
Tatis Jr., Fernando	915
Grossman, Robert	914
Bogaerts, Xander	907
Albies, Ozzie	900
Walker, Christian	884
Drury, Brandon	884
Contreras, Willson	882
D Arnaud, Travis	880
Hernandez, Teoscar	880
Mountcastle, Ryan	876
Arozarena, Randy	874
Farmer, Kyle	873
Torres, Gleyber	872
Olivares, Edward	871
Correa, Carlos	870
Moreno, Gabriel	869
Machado, Manny	869

450+ AB, 2022-23

Top OPS v RHP, 2022-23

Hitter	OPS
Judge, Aaron	1087
Alvarez, Yordan	1037
Ohtani, Shohei	1025
Soto, Juan	963
Freeman, Freddie	959
Olson, Matt	949
Trout, Mike	941
Acuna, Ronald	924
Carroll, Corbin	920
Harper, Bryce	914
Seager, Corey	913
Devers, Rafael	896
Betts, Mookie	893
Jones, Nolan	893
Altuve, Jose	893
Ramirez, Jose	892
Chisholm, Jazz	883
Henderson, Gunnar	881
Schwarber, Kyle	874
Harris II, Michael	869
Bregman, Alex	864
Arraez, Luis	858
Outman, James	857
Casas, Triston	856
Tucker, Kyle	855
Naylor, Josh	854
Goldschmidt, Paul	848
Arenado, Nolan	845
Alonso, Pete	844
Diaz, Yandy	843
Nimmo, Brandon	841
Carpenter, Kerry	841
Pederson, Joc	840
Vogelbach, Daniel	835
Fraley, Jake	833
Machado, Manny	832
Suwinski, Jack	832
Rodriguez, Julio	831
Ozuna, Marcell	829
Riley, Austin	827
Lowe, Nate	826

Top L-R Splits, 2022-23

Hitter	OPS vL-vR
Grossman, Robert	348
Contreras, William	330
Castro, Rodolfo	300
Grichuk, Randal	300
McCormick, Chas	282
Jung, Josh	270
Bohm, Alec	268
Trevino, Jose	267
Maldonado, Martin	252
Soler, Jorge	251
Allen, Nick	248
Senzel, Nick	246
Rengifo, Luis	240
Farmer, Kyle	235
Robles, Victor	232
Garver, Mitch	232
Newman, Kevin	230
Friedl, T.J.	227
Jeffers, Ryan	216

Top R-L Splits, 2022-23

Hitter	OPS vR-vL
Vogelbach, Daniel	476
Chisholm, Jazz	373
Sanchez, Jesus	354
Fraley, Jake	341
Sheets, Gavin	333
Kirilloff, Alex	312
Wong, Kolten	306
Abrams, CJ	292
Lowe, Josh	291
Henderson, Gunnar	286
Suwinski, Jack	268
Voit, Luke	262
Brown, Seth	257
Wong, Connor	253
Brennan, Will	239
Belt, Brandon	230
Thomas, Alek	229
Carroll, Corbin	219
Bleday, J.J.	210

Best Parks - LH HR

Ballpark	Factor
CIN	46%
NYY	28%
TEX	26%
CHW	25%
MIL	21%
LA	19%
NYM	18%

Best Parks - RH HR

Ballpark	Factor
CIN	35%
LA	29%
COL	26%
LAA	14%
TEX	13%
CHW	12%
PHI	10%

Worst Parks - LH HR

Ballpark	Factor
KC	-22%
ARI	-21%
SF	-21%
TAM	-18%
TOR	-17%
PIT	-14%
OAK	-13%
STL	-12%

Worst Parks-RH HR

Ballpark	Factor
ARI	-28%
BAL	-27%
PIT	-24%
OAK	-24%
SF	-19%
MIA	-13%
MIN	-11%
STL	-10%

Best Parks - Runs

Ballpark	Factor
COL	35%
BOS	16%
CIN	13%

Best Parks - Ks

Ballpark	Factor
TAM	10%
SEA	8%
MIL	8%
ATL	7%
NYM	7%

Worst Parks - Runs

Ballpark	Factor
SD	-15%
SEA	-12%
TAM	-11%
TOR	-10%
OAK	-9%

Worst Parks - Ks

Ballpark	Factor
COL	-14%
KC	-12%
PIT	-9%
BOS	-8%

Best Parks - BB

Ballpark	Factor
TOR	13%
NYM	12%
MIL	9%
DET	9%

Worst Parks - BB

Ballpark	Factor
STL	-9%
LA	-7%
COL	-5%

Note: for Runs, the best parks for hitters are also the worst for pitchers and vice versa

Consistent Hi-PQS SP

Pitcher	QC*
Cole,Gerrit	55
McKenzie,Triston	53
Verlander,Justin	47
Scherzer,Max	44
Wheeler,Zack	41
Glasnow,Tyler	35
Castillo,Luis	34
Gausman,Kevin	32
Valdez,Framber	32
Nola,Aaron	28
Skubal,Tarik	28
Webb,Logan	28
Darvish,Yu	19
Fried,Max	18
Burnes,Corbin	15
Bieber,Shane	12
Musgrove,Joe	9
Springs,Jeffrey	7

20+ Starts, 2022-23
**Quality-Consistency score*

Consistent Low-PQS SP

Pitcher	QC*
Hutchison,Drew	(267)
Fedde,Erick	(252)
Wilson,Bryse	(250)
Beeks,Jalen	(240)
Cessa,Luis	(238)
Espino,Paolo	(232)
Minor,Mike	(232)
Bumgarner,Madison	(224)
Senzatela,Antonio	(219)
Hudson,Dakota	(216)
Williams,Trevor	(210)
Urena,Jose	(207)
Kuhl,Chad	(206)
Keuchel,Dallas	(200)
Ryu,Hyun-Jin	(200)
Gonzales,Marco	(195)
Flexen,Chris	(195)
Miley,Wade	(194)
Weaver,Luke	(192)
Gomber,Austin	(191)

Most DOMinant SP

Pitcher	DOM
Gallen,Zac	48%
Skubal,Tarik	47%
Scherzer,Max	46%
Verlander,Justin	45%
Cole,Gerrit	45%
Valdez,Framber	45%
Gausman,Kevin	42%
Burnes,Corbin	42%
Castillo,Luis	41%
Wheeler,Zack	41%
Luzardo,Jesus	40%
Darvish,Yu	39%
Webb,Logan	38%
Musgrove,Joe	38%
McKenzie,Triston	38%
Lopez,Pablo	38%
Bieber,Shane	37%
Bassitt,Chris	37%
Nola,Aaron	36%
Glasnow,Tyler	35%

Most DISastrous SP

Pitcher	DIS
Fedde,Erick	67%
Wilson,Bryse	65%
Bumgarner,Madison	62%
Hudson,Dakota	58%
Senzatela,Antonio	57%
Flexen,Chris	55%
Keuchel,Dallas	55%
Miley,Wade	55%
Gonzales,Marco	55%
Williams,Trevor	54%
Kuhl,Chad	53%
Gomber,Austin	52%
Urena,Jose	52%
Carrasco,Carlos	51%
Corbin,Patrick	51%
Odorizzi,Jake	50%
Faedo,Alex	50%
Weaver,Luke	50%
Greinke,Zack	49%
Davies,Zachary	49%

Universal Draft Grid

Most publications and websites provide cheat sheets with ranked player lists for different fantasy draft formats. The biggest problem with these tools is that they perpetrate the myth that players can be ranked in a linear fashion.

Since rankings are based on highly variable projections, it is foolhardy to draw conclusions that a $24 player is better than a $23 player is better than a $22 player. Yes, a first round pick is better than a 10th round pick, but within most rounds, all players are pretty much interchangeable commodities.

But typical cheat sheets don't reflect that reality. Auction sheets rank players by dollar value. Snake draft sheets rank players within round, accounting for position and categorical scarcity. But just as ADPs have a ridiculously low success rate, these cheat sheets are similarly flawed.

We have a tool at BaseballHQ.com called the Rotisserie Grid. It is a chart—that can be customized to your league parameters—which organizes players into pockets of skill, by position. It is one of the most popular tools on the site. One of the best features of this grid is that its design provides immediate insight into position scarcity.

So in the *Forecaster*, we have transitioned to this format as a sort of Universal Draft Grid.

How to use the chart

Across the top of the grid, players are sorted by position. First and third base, and second and shortstop are presented side-by-side for easy reference when considering corner and middle infielders, respectively.

The vertical axis separates each group of players into tiers based on potential fantasy impact. At the top are the Elite players; at the bottom are the Fringe players.

Auction leagues: The tiers in the grid represent rough break-points for dollar values. Elite players could be considered those that are purchased for $30 and up. Each subsequent tier is a step down of approximately $5.

Snake drafters: Tiers can be used to rank players similarly, though most tiers will encompass more than one round. Any focus on position scarcity will bump some players up a bit. In recent years, Catcher has been the only position to exhibit any real positional scarcity effect. As such, one might opt to draft Will Smith (from the Stars tier) before the Gold level Steven Kwan.

To build the best foundation, try to stay balanced in the first 10 rounds of your draft: 2 MI, 2 CI, 3 OF, and 3 SP (likely one closer) is a foundation target that will set you up for maximum flexibility in the mid- and end-games.

The players are listed at the position where they both qualify and provide the most fantasy value. Additional position eligibility (20 games) is listed in parentheses. (NOTE: check out our Multiposition Eligibility Chart on page 280 for additional eligibility detail.) Listings in bold are players with high reliability grades (minimum "B" across the board).

Each player is presented with his 7-character Mayberry score. The first four digits (all on a 0-5 scale) represent skill: power, speed, batting average and playing time for batters; ERA, dominance, saves potential and playing time for pitchers. The last three alpha characters are the reliability grade (A-F): health, experience and consistency.

Within each tier, players are sorted by the first character of their Mayberry score. This means that batters are sorted by power; pitchers by ERA potential. If you need to prospect for the best skill sets among players in a given tier, target those with 4s and 5s in whatever skill you need.

CAVEATS and DISCLAIMERS

The placement of players in tiers does not represent average draft positions (ADP) or average auction values (AAV). It represents where each player's true value may lie. It is the variance between this true value and the ADP/AAV market values—or better, the value that your league-mates place on each player—where you will find your potential for profit or loss.

That means ***you cannot take this chart right into your draft with you***. You have to compare these rankings with your ADPs and AAVs, and build your draft list from there. In other words, if we project Nico Hoerner as a "Elite" level pick but you know the other owners (or your ADPs) see him as a fourth-rounder, you can probably wait to pick him up in round three. If you are in an auction league with owners who overvalue young players and Triston Casas (projected at $21) gets bid past $25, you will likely take a loss should you decide to chase the bidding, especially given the depth of first basemen in in that tier for 2024.

Finally, this chart is intended as a preliminary look based on current factors. For Draft Day, you will need to make your own adjustments based upon many different criteria that will impact the world between now and then. Daily updates appear online at BaseballHQ.com. A free projections update is available in March at **http://www.baseballhq.com/bf2024**

Simulation League Cheat Sheet

Using Runs Above Replacement creates a more real-world ranking of player value, which serves simulation gamers well. Batters and pitchers are integrated, and value break-points are delineated.

Multi-Position Eligibility Chart

The default position eligibility requirements throughout this book is 20 games in the previous season. This chart serves those who play in leagues where the eligibility requirements are 10 or 5 games at a position in the preceeding year.

Playing Time Measurement Charts

Based on foundations discussed on page 31 and expanded on page 70 and following, these charts offer a snapshot view of our new playing time metrics. Charts are presented by position, and include a key for the column headers, so you can identify those players who could be due or playing time changes in 2024.

Universal Draft Grid

TIER	FIRST BASE		THIRD BASE		SECOND BASE		SHORTSTOP	
Elite	Olson,Matt	(5255 AAF)	**Devers,Rafael**	**(4155 AAA)**	Betts,Mookie (o)	(4355 BAC)	Seager,Corey	(4255 DAF)
	Alonso,Pete	**(4145 AAB)**	**Riley,Austin**	**(4245 AAA)**	Albies,Ozzie	(3345 FAD)	Witt Jr.,Bobby	(4545 AAC)
	Freeman,Freddie	**(4355 AAB)**	**Ramírez,José**	**(3455 AAA)**	Arraez,Luis	(1255 BAC)	**Bichette,Bo**	**(3355 BAB)**
	Harper,Bryce	(4255 DAD)					**Lindor,Francisco**	**(3435 AAB)**
	Bellinger,Cody (o)	(3435 CAF)					Franco,Wander	(3555 CAB)
							Turner,Trea	(3545 AAC)
							Abrams,CJ	**(2535 AAB)**
							Hoerner,Nico (4)	(1545 CAA)
Gold	Goldschmidt,Paul	(3335 AAF)	Lewis,Royce	(4445 FFF)	Altuve,Jose	(3455 DAC)	**Henderson,Gunnar (5)**	**(4445 AAA)**
	Guerrero Jr.,Vladimir	(3155 AAD)	Arenado,Nolan	(3155 AAD)	Semien,Marcus	(3335 AAD)	De La Cruz,Elly (5)	(4535 ABC)
	Díaz,Yandy	(2145 BAD)	Machado,Manny	(3245 AAD)	**Torres,Gleyber**	**(2235 BAB)**	**Swanson,Dansby**	**(3325 AAA)**
			Bregman,Alex	**(2145 BAA)**	Giménez,Andrés	(2535 AAF)	**Bogaerts,Xander**	**(2445 AAB)**
							Kim,Ha-Seong (45)	**(1425 AAB)**
Stars	**Walker,Christian**	**(4235 BAB)**	Burger,Jake	(4025 BAC)	Drury,Brandon (3)	(4035 BAC)	**Adames,Willy**	**(4225 BAB)**
	Casas,Triston	(4145 AAC)	Jung,Josh	(4135 BAF)	Marte,Ketel	(3355 CAF)	Cruz,Oneil	(4425 FDF)
	Hoskins,Rhys	(4135 FCB)	Hayes,Ke'Bryan	(3345 CAB)	**Merrifield,Whit (o)**	**(1335 AAB)**	McLain,Matt (4)	(4525 BBF)
	Torkelson,Spencer	(4125 AAF)	Steer,Spencer (3o)	(3325 AAC)	**Stott,Bryson**	**(1435 AAB)**	Story,Trevor	(4415 FBC)
	Mountcastle,Ryan	**(3235 BAA)**	**Bohm,Alec (3)**	**(2245 AAB)**			**Volpe,Anthony**	**(3425 AAA)**
	Vaughn,Andrew	**(3135 AAA)**	**Garcia,Maikel**	**(1535 AAA)**			**Edman,Tommy (4o)**	**(2545 AAB)**
	Lowe,Nathaniel	(3335 AAC)					**Estrada,Thairo (4)**	**(2335 BAA)**
	Turner,Justin	**(2245 BAA)**					**Peña,Jeremy**	**(2335 AAA)**
	Naylor,Josh	(2055 DAC)					**Tovar,Ezequiel**	**(2425 AAB)**
							Rosario,Amed (4)	**(1545 AAA)**
Regulars	**Montero,Elehuris**	**(4015 AAB)**	**Chapman,Matt**	**(4215 BAA)**	**Gorman,Nolan**	**(4215 AAB)**	Taylor,Chris (5o)	(4403 CAC)
	Encarnacion-Strand,Chri	(4135 ACB)	Muncy,Max	(4125 BAD)	**McMahon,Ryan (5)**	**(4125 AAA)**	Correa,Carlos	(3035 BAC)
	Bell,Josh	**(3035 AAB)**	Suarez,Eugenio	(4115 AAC)	Gelof,Zack	(4425 ABD)	Crawford,J.P.	(2235 AAC)
	Abreu,José	(3035 AAC)	**Paredes,Isaac (3)**	**(3035 AAB)**	Julien,Edouard	(4325 ABC)	Neto,Zach	(2225 CDA)
	Kirilloff,Alex (o)	(3243 FCA)	Candelario,Jeimer (3)	(3335 BAF)	Lowe,Brandon	(4323 FAD)	Anderson,Tim	(1545 FAC)
	O'Hearn,Ryan (o)	(3333 ACD)	Flores,Wilmer (3)	(3345 BAD)	India,Jonathan	(3335 CAC)	Berti,Jon (5)	(1533 DAB)
	Pasquantino,Vinnie	(3255 FBB)	**Castro,Willi (o)**	**(2523 AAB)**	Polanco,Jorge	(3225 FAB)		
	Rizzo,Anthony	(3035 CAA)	Caminero,Junior	(2123 ADF)	**Cronenworth,Jake (3)**	**(2435 BAB)**		
	France,Ty	**(2235 AAB)**	Marte,Noelvi	(2533 ADF)	Rodgers,Brendan	(2335 FBB)		
			Urshela,Giovanny (3)	(1233 FBB)	**Garcia,Luis**	**(1245 AAA)**		
					McNeil,Jeff (o)	(1445 BAF)		
Mid-Level	**Raley,Luke (o)**	**(4303 ABB)**	**Wisdom,Patrick**	**(5213 BAB)**	**Westburg,Jordan (5)**	**(3425 AAB)**	**Arcia,Orlando**	**(2235 BAB)**
	Belt,Brandon	(4123 FAF)	Davis,J.D.	(3215 CAB)	**Massey,Michael**	**(2225 AAB)**	**Mateo,Jorge**	**(2513 AAA)**
	Cron,C.J.	(4233 FAC)	Mead,Curtis	(3333 ADA)	Mauricio,Ronny	(2415 AAD)	**McKinstry,Zach (4o)**	**(2415 BAA)**
	Noda,Ryan	(4205 BAC)	Moncada,Yoán	(3225 FAD)	**Bae,Ji Hwan (o)**	**(1423 BBA)**	**Rengifo,Luis (4o)**	**(2335 BAB)**
	Cooper,Garrett	(3033 FAB)	**Kiner-Falefa,Isiah (o)**	**(1333 AAA)**	Donovan,Brendan (o)	(1243 CAB)	Duran,Ezequiel (5o)	(2313 ABC)
	Tellez,Rowdy	(3025 CAB)	**LeMahieu,DJ (3)**	**(1245 BAA)**	Dubón,Mauricio (o)	(1333 AAD)	Mondesi,Adalberto	(2503 FFD)
	Santana,Carlos	**(2235 AAB)**	**Peraza,Oswald**	**(1403 AAB)**	Frazier,Adam	(1343 AAD)	Peguero,Liover (4)	(2533 ABC)
	Smith,Dominic	(2025 BAC)	**Vierling,Matt (o)**	**(1325 AAB)**	Wong,Kolten	(1223 BAC)	**Andrus,Elvis (4)**	**(1233 BAB)**
	Wade Jr.,LaMonte (o)	(2325 CAD)	Madrigal,Nick	(0353 FCD)	Edwards,Xavier	(0403 AAD)	**Turang,Brice (4)**	**(1505 AAA)**
							Winn,Masyn	**(1405 ABB)**
							Báez,Javier	(1415 AAC)
							Caballero,Jose (4)	(1501 ADC)
							Lawlar,Jordan	(1515 ACD)
Bench	Gallo,Joey (o)	(5203 CAC)	**Busch,Michael**	**(4213 AAB)**	Schneider,Davis	(5323 ACD)	Luciano,Marco	(3205 AFF)
	Bauers,Jake (o)	(4213 ACF)	Donaldson,Josh	(4011 FBC)	**Valdez,Enmanuel**	**(4331 ABA)**	Arias,Gabriel (3)	(2113 AAC)
	Votto,Joey	(4213 FBD)	Moustakas,Mike (3)	(2213 FBA)	Diaz,Jordan (5)	(3023 ACB)	Basabe,Osleivis	(2531 ACD)
	Mervis,Matt	**(3113 ABB)**	Rendon,Anthony	(2231 FDA)	**Urías,Ramón (5)**	**(2223 BAA)**	Hampson,Garrett (o)	(2511 ABC)
	Rivas III,Alfonso	(3313 ACB)	Sosa,Edmundo	(2323 ACB)	**Vargas,Miguel**	**(2313 AAB)**	Hernández,Kiké (4o)	(2223 CAC)
	Walsh,Jared	(3003 DAF)	Triolo,Jared	(2421 ACC)	Biggio,Cavan (3o)	(2301 CBA)	**Allen,Nick**	**(1413 AAB)**
	Clemens,Kody	**(2211 ABB)**	**Baty,Brett**	**(1003 BBB)**	Escobar,Eduardo (5)	(2211 AAC)	**Rojas,Miguel**	**(1333 BAB)**
	Joe,Connor (o)	(2233 BAC)	**Rivera,Emmanuel**	**(1233 ABA)**	Sosa,Lenyn	(2023 ABC)	Marcano,Tucupita	(1321 CCB)
	Schanuel,Nolan	(0433 AFF)	Miranda,Jose	(1033 CAD)	Urías,Luis	(2103 DBC)	Perdomo,Geraldo (4)	(1403 AAC)
			Senzel,Nick (o)	(1321 FCA)	Wisely,Brett	(2201 ACA)	Walls,Taylor (45)	(1403 BAC)
			Freeman,Tyler	(0431 ADD)	**Miller,Owen (53)**	**(1323 ABA)**	Wendle,Joey	(1433 DBB)
			Segura,Jean	(0321 DAC)	**Rojas,Josh (5)**	**(1321 BAB)**		
					Alu,Jake (o)	(1333 AAC)		
					Espinal,Santiago (5)	(1241 BBC)		
					Monasterio,Andruw (5)	(1403 AAC)		
					Peterson,Jace (5)	(1411 CAB)		
					Solano,Donovan (3)	(1133 DAA)		
Fringe	Pratto,Nick (o)	(3203 BAC)	Longoria,Evan	(3001 FCB)	**Villar,David**	**(4201 AAB)**	**Short,Zack (45)**	**(3201 ABB)**
	Sheets,Gavin (o)	**(2203 ABB)**	**Vargas,Ildemaro**	**(1251 BBB)**	**Gonzales,Nick**	**(3201 ABA)**	**DeJong,Paul**	**(2101 BBB)**
	Toglia,Michael	**(2201 ABA)**	Anderson,Brian (o)	(1201 FBB)	Maton,Nick (5)	(3211 DBB)	**Farmer,Kyle (45)**	**(2121 BAA)**
	Loftin,Nick	**(1333 ABB)**	Kieboom,Carter	(1103 FDA)	Ibanez,Andy (o)	(2221 ABF)	Crawford,Brandon	(2211 DAF)
	Gurriel,Yulieski	(1331 AAD)	Newman,Kevin	(1331 DBC)	Trejo,Alan (5)	(2221 ACA)	Schmitt,Casey (5)	(2121 ACD)
					Batten,Matthew	**(1301 AAA)**	Smith,Kevin	(2201 BBD)
					Castro,Harold	**(1123 ABB)**	**Amaya,Jacob**	**(1301 AAA)**
					Kemp,Tony (o)	(1431 AAC)	**Castro,Rodolfo (4)**	**(1101 ABB)**
					Lopez,Nicky (5)	(0441 AAD)	Barrero,Jose	(1401 BBF)
							Diaz,Aledmys (5)	(1233 DBB)
							Grissom,Vaughn	(1431 ACA)
							Rocchio,Brayan	(1331 AAC)
							Smith,Josh H. (5o)	(1201 ACC)
							Williams,Alika	(1211 ADD)

Universal Draft Grid

TIER	CATCHER		DH		OUTFIELD			
Elite			Ohtani,Shohei	(5455 AAF)	Judge,Aaron	(5055 DAF)	Rodríguez,Julio	(4445 AAC)
					Arozarena,Randy	**(4435 AAA)**	Soto,Juan	(4255 AAF)
					Harris II,Michael	**(4455 AAA)**	Tatis Jr.,Fernando	(4445 FAF)
					Acuña Jr.,Ronald	(4455 CAF)	Tucker,Kyle	(4455 AAD)
					Carroll,Corbin	(4545 AAD)	Ruiz,Esteury	(1525 BAC)
Gold					Alvarez,Yordan	(5155 DAD)	**Thomas,Lane**	**(3425 AAB)**
					Garcia,Adolis	**(4325 AAB)**	**Yelich,Christian**	**(3445 BAB)**
					Hernández,Teoscar	**(4225 BAB)**	Duran,Jarren	(3535 BBC)
					Castellanos,Nick	(4335 BAF)	Greene,Riley	(3435 CAF)
					Jones,Nolan	(4435 AAF)	Reynolds,Bryan	(3445 AAC)
					Lowe,Josh	(4525 AAD)	Springer,George	(2335 CAC)
					Robert Jr.,Luis	(4435 DAD)	Yoshida,Masataka	(2355 AAC)
					Suzuki,Seiya	(4345 BAD)	**Kwan,Steven**	**(1555 AAA)**
Stars	**Contreras,William**	**(3435 AAB)**	Martinez,J.D.	(5345 BAC)	**Schwarber,Kyle**	**(5125 BAB)**	**McCormick,Chas**	**(3325 BAB)**
	Realmuto,J.T.	**(3435 AAB)**	Ozuna,Marcell	(4145 DAD)	Trout,Mike	(5445 FBF)	Nimmo,Brandon	(3335 CAA)
	Rutschman,Adley	**(3155 AAA)**			**Happ,Ian**	**(4335 AAA)**	**Taveras,Leody**	**(2425 AAB)**
	Smith,Will	**(3335 AAA)**			**Santander,Anthony**	**(4135 BAB)**	Lee,Jung-hoo	(2455 AAC)
					Chisholm Jr.,Jazz	(4523 FAB)	Marte,Starling	(2445 FAD)
					Morel,Christopher	(4425 AAC)	Mullins II,Cedric	(2425 BAC)
					Ward,Taylor	(4235 CAC)	McCarthy,Jake	(1525 AAC)
					Gurriel Jr.,Lourdes	**(3255 BAA)**		
Regulars	**Álvarez,Francisco**	**(4115 ABA)**	Buxton,Byron	(5523 FBF)	Duvall,Adam	(5223 FBC)	Kepler,Max	(3235 CAC)
	Contreras,Willson	**(4145 BAA)**	Jimenez,Eloy	(3035 FAB)	Rooker,Brent	(5215 AAC)	Marsh,Brandon	(3515 AAC)
	Murphy,Sean	**(4145 AAB)**			Velázquez,Nelson	(5333 ABC)	Olivares,Edward	(3343 DBB)
	Raleigh,Cal	**(4125 AAB)**			**Siri,Jose**	**(4513 BBB)**	Walker,Jordan	(3325 AAC)
	Diaz,Yainer	(4353 ABD)			**Waters,Drew**	**(4515 BBA)**	**Canha,Mark**	**(2335 BAA)**
	Naylor,Bo	(4225 AAC)			Carpenter,Kerry	(4135 BAC)	**De La Cruz,Bryan**	**(2235 AAA)**
	Perez,Salvador (3)	(3135 DAB)			Sánchez,Jesús	(4235 BAD)	**Verdugo,Alex**	**(2255 AAA)**
	Heim,Jonah	(2135 AAC)			Soler,Jorge	(4025 DAD)	Blackmon,Charlie	(2353 CAB)
	Moreno,Gabriel	(1245 ABD)			**Hays,Austin**	**(3235 BAB)**	Friedl,T.J.	(2525 AAC)
	Ruiz,Keibert	(1145 AAC)			**Nootbaar,Lars**	**(3435 BAB)**	Rosario,Eddie	(2235 DAD)
					Outman,James	**(3305 AAB)**	**Brennan,Will**	**(1245 AAB)**
					Pham,Tommy	(3335 BAB)	Benintendi,Andrew	(1335 CAC)
					Varsho,Daulton	(3325 AAB)	Frelick,Sal	(1435 ACC)
					Carter,Evan	(3515 ACF)	Rojas,Johan	(1513 ACD)
					Kelenic,Jarred	(3215 BAC)		
Mid-Level	**Langeliers,Shea**	**(4215 AAB)**	Aranda,Jonathan	(2213 AAC)	**Brown,Seth**	**(4115 BAA)**	Pederson,Joc	(3233 BAD)
	Sanchez,Gary	**(4223 BBB)**	Lux,Gavin	(2335 FDC)	**Renfroe,Hunter**	**(4125 BAB)**	**Abreu,Wilyer**	**(2413 ABB)**
	Jansen,Danny	(4233 FCD)	McCutchen,Andre	(2223 DAC)	**Suwinski,Jack**	**(4305 AAB)**	**Conforto,Michael**	**(2225 BAA)**
	Jeffers,Ryan	(4223 BBC)	**Meneses,Joey**	**(1225 AAA)**	**Wallner,Matt**	**(4115 ABB)**	**Doyle,Brenton**	**(2505 ABA)**
	Rogers,Jake	(4413 FCC)	Ramírez,Harold	(1133 CAB)	Benson,Will	(4505 ABC)	**Meadows,Parker**	**(2513 AAA)**
	Wong,Connor	**(3513 ABA)**			Garrett,Stone	(4313 ABC)	**Rafaela,Ceddanne**	**(2533 ABA)**
	O'Hoppe,Logan	(3013 FDA)			Haniger,Mitch	(4323 FBC)	**Thomas,Alek**	**(2545 AAB)**
	Rodríguez,Endy	(2433 ACF)			Moniak,Mickey	(4403 CBC)	Baddoo,Akil	(2403 BBC)
	Stephenson,Tyler	(2235 DAD)			Stanton,Giancarlo	(4013 FAC)	Butler,Lawrence	(2513 ACF)
	Campusano,Luis	(1235 DDF)			Taylor,Tyrone	(4333 DCB)	Gordon,Nick	(2533 CDD)
					Yastrzemski,Mike	(4225 CAB)	Isbel,Kyle	(2425 BBC)
					Taylor,Michael A.	**(3413 AAA)**	Kiermaier,Kevin	(2433 DAB)
					Bryant,Kris	(3235 FAD)	Bader,Harrison	(1513 FBC)
					Crow-Armstrong,Pete	(3503 ADF)	Brantley,Michael	(1253 FDB)
					Domínguez,Jasson	(3421 ACF)	Hicks,Aaron	(1403 FBB)
					Fraley,Jake	(3333 FBA)	Margot,Manuel	(1333 DAA)
					Grisham,Trent	(3215 AAC)	Matos,Luis	(1535 ACF)
					Laureano,Ramón	(3413 DAC)	Robles,Victor	(1413 FCC)
					Melendez Jr.,MJ	(3215 AAC)	**Straw,Myles**	**(0515 AAB)**
					O'Neill,Tyler	(3323 FBC)		
Bench	**Sabol,Blake (o)**	**(4301 ABA)**	**Hiura,Keston**	**(4101 ABB)**	Larnach,Trevor	(4103 DBA)	Pereira,Everson	(2403 ADA)
	Garver,Mitch	(4023 FCF)	**Vientos,Mark**	**(3003 AAA)**	**Florial,Estevan**	**(3401 AAA)**	Ramos,Heliot	(2301 CBD)
	Amaya,Miguel	(3303 AFA)	**Vogelbach,Daniel**	**(3113 BBB)**	**Grichuk,Randal**	**(3233 BAA)**	Tauchman,Mike	(2223 ACD)
	d'Arnaud,Travis	(3133 DBC)	Kjerstad,Heston	(3233 ACF)	Davis,Henry	(3125 FCF)	**Burleson,Alec**	**(1233 AAB)**
	Wells,Austin	(3201 ACA)	Soderstrom,Tyler	(1105 ACA)	Fairchild,Stuart	(3321 ACA)	**Cabrera,Oswaldo**	**(1303 ABB)**
	Bethancourt,Christian	**(2311 ABB)**			Grossman,Robbie	(3213 AAD)	**Profar,Jurickson**	**(1331 AAB)**
	Bailey,Patrick	(2313 ADF)			Meadows,Austin	(3221 FDC)	Meckler,Wade	(1421 AFF)
	Díaz,Elias	(2113 AAC)			Slater,Austin	(3321 CCB)	Mitchell,Garrett	(1503 FFD)
	Fermin,Freddy	(2033 ACD)			**Bleday,JJ**	**(2205 BAB)**	Refsnyder,Rob	(1221 CCC)
	Gomes,Yan	(2333 BAC)			**Wiemer,Joey**	**(2303 ABA)**	Jankowski,Travis	(0511 DCF)
	Knizner,Andrew	(2211 ACC)			Canzone,Dominic	(2123 ABD)		
	Kirk,Alejandro	**(1133 BAB)**			Carlson,Dylan	(2323 DAB)		
	Vázquez,Christian	**(1123 AAB)**			Cowser,Colton	(2203 ACB)		
					Garcia,Avisail	(2303 FCC)		
					Heyward,Jason	(2123 FBD)		
					Meyers,Jake	(2211 CBC)		
					Palacios,Joshua	(2333 ACC)		
Fringe	Adams,Riley	(4011 ADF)	**Ford,Mike**	**(4111 ABB)**	Stewart,D.J.	(4011 ACB)	Adams,Jordyn	(2501 ACA)
	Maldonado,Martín	**(3103 AAA)**	Baker,Luken	(2211 AAF)	**Cave,Jake**	**(3211 BBB)**	Call,Alex	(2211 AAC)
	Thaiss,Matt	**(2201 ABB)**	Lewis,Kyle	(2201 FDD)	Adell,Jo	(3403 CBB)	Goodman,Hunter	(2101 ACF)
	Fortes,Nick	**(1203 ABB)**	Winker,Jesse	(1021 FBF)	Thompson,Trayce	(3301 CCF)	Pillar,Kevin	(2231 FDA)
	Lee,Korey	**(1103 ABA)**			**Fletcher,Dominic**	**(2211 AAA)**	**Gonzalez,Oscar**	**(1121 AAB)**
	Bart,Joey	(1201 BCB)			**Palacios,Richie**	**(2331 AAB)**	**Julks,Corey**	**(1401 AAB)**
	Delay,Jason	(1211 AFC)			**Peralta,David**	**(2243 BAA)**	Colás,Oscar	(1103 ACC)
	Grandal,Yasmani	(1201 CAF)			**Smith,Pavin**	**(2321 AAB)**		
	McGuire,Reese	(1223 BDA)						
	Trevino,Jose	(1133 DDB)						

Universal Draft Grid

TIER	STARTING PITCHERS				RELIEF PITCHERS			
Elite	**Cole,Gerrit**	**(5405 AAA)**						
Gold	**Burnes,Corbin**	**(5405 AAB)**						
	Kirby,George	**(5205 ABA)**						
Stars	Castillo,Luis	(5305 CAB)	**Wheeler,Zack**	**(5305 BAA)**	**Clase,Emmanuel**	**(5231 AAB)**		
	Musgrove,Joe	(5303 FAA)	Gallen,Zac	(4305 CAB)	Duran,Jhoan	(5531 ABF)		
	Rodriguez,Grayson	(5305 ADD)	**Gausman,Kevin**	**(4305 BAA)**	Iglesias,Raisel	(5531 DAA)		
	Strider,Spencer	(5505 AAC)	**Nola,Aaron**	**(4305 AAB)**	**Scott,Tanner**	**(5531 BAB)**		
	Valdez,Framber	(5205 CAB)			**Williams,Devin**	**(5530 AAB)**		
Regulars	Eflin,Zach	(5203 FAA)	Ryan,Joe	(4405 CAB)	Díaz,Edwin	(5530 FAD)	**Sewald,Paul**	**(4531 BAA)**
	Fried,Max	(5203 FAA)	Bassitt,Chris	(3203 CAA)	**Doval,Camilo**	**(5431 AAA)**	**Díaz,Alexis**	**(3431 BBA)**
	Glasnow,Tyler	(5503 FCA)	Bibee,Tanner	(3305 BDC)	**Hader,Josh**	**(5530 AAA)**		
	López,Pablo	(5305 CAA)	**Gilbert,Logan**	**(3205 AAA)**	Holmes,Clay	(5331 DAB)		
	Peralta,Freddy	(5503 DAA)	Kelly,Merrill	(3205 CAA)	Muñoz,Andres	(5530 FCC)		
	Skubal,Tarik	(5403 FAB)	Pérez,Eury	(3403 BDA)	Pressly,Ryan	(5430 DAA)		
	Webb,Logan	(5105 CAA)	**Senga,Kodai**	**(3305 AAB)**	Romano,Jordan	(5430 CAA)		
	Bradish,Kyle	(4205 CBB)	Urías,Julio	(3205 DAA)	**Bednar,David**	**(4431 BAA)**		
	Luzardo,Jesus	(4305 DAD)	**Yamamoto,Yoshinobu**	**(3205 AAA)**	Helsley,Ryan	(4431 FBC)		
	Miller,Bobby	(4103 ADA)			Phillips,Evan	(4331 ABD)		
Mid-Level	Bieber,Shane	(4203 FAA)	Steele,Justin	(4205 DAA)	Adam,Jason	(5421 CBB)		
	Buehler,Walker	(4203 FBA)	**Berríos,José**	**(3205 AAA)**	Cano,Yennier	(5121 ADD)		
	Darvish,Yu	(4303 DAA)	Imanaga,Shota	(3203 AAC)	Fairbanks,Peter	(5520 FCD)		
	Garrett,Braxton	**(4205 BBB)**	**Montgomery,Jordan**	**(3205 BAB)**	Stephenson,Robert	(5520 DCB)		
	Gray,Sonny	(4203 DAA)	Ober,Bailey	(3203 DCB)	Alzolay,Adbert	(4330 FCC)		
	Kikuchi,Yusei	**(4305 BAA)**	Rodriguez,Eduardo	(3203 DAA)	**Kimbrel,Craig**	**(4421 BAB)**		
	King,Michael	(4303 FBC)	Varland,Louie	(3103 ACB)	Nardi,Andrew	(4411 BDB)		
	Maeda,Kenta	(4303 FCA)	Woo,Bryan	(3303 BFF)	**Finnegan,Kyle**	**(3231 BAB)**		
	Pivetta,Nick	**(4305 AAA)**	Javier,Cristian	(2305 AAC)	Jansen,Kenley	(3430 CAB)		
	Scherzer,Max	(4303 FAA)	Pepiot,Ryan	(2203 FCB)				
	Snell,Blake	(4503 DAA)						
Bench	Lodolo,Nick	(5403 FBA)	Lugo,Seth	(3203 DBA)	Abreu,Bryan	(5420 BCB)	Robertson,David	(3321 DAA)
	Sánchez,Cristopher	(5203 BCB)	Lynn,Lance	(3303 DAB)	Alvarado,José	(5510 DCC)	Swanson,Erik	(3310 DCC)
	Baz,Shane	(4301 FDD)	Manaea,Sean	(3203 CAA)	Brash,Matt	(5521 ADC)	**Estévez,Carlos**	**(2321 BBA)**
	Brown,Hunter	(4303 ABF)	Olson,Reese	(3203 ADB)	Chapman,Aroldis	(5520 DBD)	Leclerc,José	(2321 FCA)
	Greene,Hunter	(4503 FAB)	Ragans,Cole	(3303 BCF)	Graterol,Brusdar	(5011 DCA)	Jiménez,Dany	(1321 FCB)
	Martinez,Nick	**(4203 AAB)**	Rodón,Carlos	(3303 FAC)	Hall,DL	(5411 ADB)		
	Montas,Frankie	(4303 FAD)	Sheehan,Emmet	(3403 AFF)	Hicks,Jordan	(5311 FCB)		
	Allen,Logan	(3203 ADB)	Silseth,Chase	(3303 CDA)	Martin,Christopher	(5210 DCC)		
	Bello,Brayan	(3103 CBB)	Stroman,Marcus	(3103 FAA)	**Matsui,Yuki**	**(5520 AAA)**		
	Cabrera,Edward	(3303 DCD)	Wacha,Michael	(3203 FAA)	Puk,A.J.	(5411 DBD)		
	Canning,Griffin	(3303 FCB)	Wicks,Jordan	(3101 ADA)	**Gallegos,Giovanny**	**(4420 BAA)**		
	Cease,Dylan	**(3405 AAA)**	Williams,Gavin	(3203 ADA)	**García,Yimi**	**(4311 BBA)**		
	Civale,Aaron	(3203 FAB)	Cortes,Nestor	(2203 FAB)	Ginkel,Kevin	(4311 ADC)		
	Crawford,Kutter	(3303 CCC)	Hendricks,Kyle	(2005 FAA)	Harvey,Hunter	(4321 FCB)		
	Detmers,Reid	**(3303 BAA)**	Miller,Bryce	(2103 ADF)	Merryweather,Julian	(4411 FDB)		
	Eovaldi,Nathan	(3203 FAA)	**Morton,Charlie**	**(2203 BAA)**	Santos,Gregory	(4220 DDC)		
	Germán,Domingo	(3301 FBB)	Pfaadt,Brandon	(2205 ACF)	Strahm,Matt	(4311 DCB)		
	Gore,MacKenzie	(3303 DCA)	Sears,JP	(2203 ABD)	Topa,Justin	(4111 FDF)		
	Gray,Jonathan	(3203 CAB)	Verlander,Justin	(2203 FAC)	Whitlock,Garrett	(4211 FBB)		
	Keller,Mitch	(3205 AAC)			Lange,Alex	(3420 ABD)		
Fringe	deGrom,Jacob	(5500 FCA)	Ashcraft,Graham	(2003 DBB)	Hamilton,Ian	(5311 DDC)	Burke,Brock	(3201 CBC)
	Hurt,Kyle	(5500 ADF)	Brito,Jhony	(2101 ADD)	Hentges,Sam	(5301 CCC)	Foley,Jason	(3010 ACC)
	Cobb,Alex	(4103 FAB)	Littell,Zack	(2103 DCA)	Johnson,Pierce	(5510 FCB)	Hoffman,Jeff	(3410 FCB)
	McCullers,Lance	(4201 FCA)	Lorenzen,Michael	(2103 FAB)	Kahnle,Tommy	(5510 FDD)	Holton,Tyler	(3100 ADD)
	Paddack,Chris	(4201 FDB)	McKenzie,Triston	(2201 FAB)	Mayza,Tim	(5200 CCA)	Houck,Tanner	(3203 FBA)
	Rasmussen,Drew	(4201 FAA)	Mikolas,Miles	(2005 FAB)	Romero,JoJo	(5210 FDB)	Karinchak,James	(3400 DCA)
	Ray,Robbie	(4401 FAF)	Quintana,José	(2103 FAB)	Schreiber,John	(5411 DBD)	McMillon,John	(3410 CFF)
	Springs,Jeffrey	(4400 FAB)	Ryu,Hyun-Jin	(2003 FCA)	Speier,Gabe	(5310 BDF)	Miller,Mason	(3401 FFF)
	DeSclafani,Anthony	(3101 FBA)	Sandoval,Patrick	(2203 CAB)	Stewart,Brock	(5510 FFF)	**Neris,Hector**	**(3400 ABB)**
	Dunning,Dane	(3105 CAA)	Schmidt,Clarke	(2103 DCF)	Uribe,Abner	(5510 AFF)	Ottavino,Adam	(3311 ABC)
	Flaherty,Jack	(3303 FCA)	Taillon,Jameson	(2103 DAB)	**Barlow,Scott**	**(4420 AAB)**	Payamps,Joel	(3111 CCB)
	García,Luis	(3201 FAA)	Waldichuk,Ken	(2203 ABF)	Coulombe,Daniel	(4310 FDD)	Peguero,Elvis	(3111 ADB)
	Gibson,Kyle	**(3105 BAA)**	Walker,Taijuan	(2103 DAB)	Cruz,Fernando	(4511 CDA)	Pérez,Cionel	(3111 BCC)
	Giolito,Lucas	(3305 CAA)	Yarbrough,Ryan	(2001 FBB)	Ferguson,Caleb	(4410 FDA)	Poche,Colin	(3310 FCA)
	Heaney,Andrew	(3303 FAC)	Gonzales,Marco	(1003 FAA)	Floro,Dylan	(4210 CBA)	Raley,Brooks	(3310 DCB)
	Matz,Steven	(3201 FBA)	Manning,Matt	(1003 FCF)	Holderman,Colin	(4211 DDB)	**Rogers,Tyler**	**(3011 ABA)**
	Mize,Casey	(3003 FDD)	Means,John	(1003 FCB)	Jax,Griffin	(4211 ABC)	**Smith,Will**	**(3310 BAA)**
	Paxton,James	(3301 FFF)	Miley,Wade	(1003 FBC)	Jiménez,Joe	(4510 BCC)	**Soto,Gregory**	**(3311 AAA)**
	Peterson,David	(3301 DCB)	Urquidy,José	(1003 FAB)	Kelly,Kevin	(4101 BDD)	Stephan,Trevor	(3311 ABC)
	Rogers,Trevor	(3201 FCC)	Wells,Tyler	(1203 DBB)	Leiter,Mark	(4311 ACB)	**Stratton,Chris**	**(3211 BBA)**
	Singer,Brady	(3103 CAB)			López,Reynaldo	(4311 BCC)	Suarez,Robert	(3210 FBC)
	Soroka,Michael	(3101 FDD)			McArthur,James	(4121 DDF)	Tonkin,Michael	(3200 BDA)
	Suárez,Ranger	(3203 DAA)			**McGough,Scott**	**(4310 BAA)**	Vesia,Alex	(3410 ACC)
	Wood,Alex	(3101 FAB)			Milner,Hoby	(4100 ACB)	Walker,Ryan	(3311 ADA)
	Abbott,Andrew	(2305 ADB)			**Minter,A.J.**	**(4411 BBB)**	Cosgrove,Tom	(2110 BDC)
	Cecconi,Slade	(2001 ADA)			Moreta,Dauri	(4310 ADF)	Domínguez,Seranthony	(2211 FCF)
	Clevinger,Michael	(2103 FAA)			Rogers,Taylor	(4410 DAB)	Graveman,Kendall	(2201 DBB)
	Elder,Bryce	**(2003 ABB)**			Vest,Will	(4210 DCB)	Sandlin,Nick	(2301 CCA)
	France,J.P.	(2101 ADA)			Armstrong,Shawn	(3300 DCC)		

Universal Draft Grid

TIER								
Below Fringe	May,Dustin	(4100 FDC)	Gomber,Austin	(1001 DAB)	Grove,Michael	(4301 FCD)	Bido,Osvaldo	(1101 ADA)
	Winn,Keaton	(4100 ADA)	Gray,Josiah	**(1205 AAA)**	Loáisiga,Jonathan	(4100 FCB)	Bielak,Brandon	(1101 ACB)
	Kershaw,Clayton	(3200 FAA)	Hancock,Emerson	(1000 CDC)	Middleton,Keynan	(4300 FDD)	Blanco,Ronel	(1201 ADB)
	Mahle,Tyler	(3300 FAA)	Henry,Tommy	(1001 DCC)	Soriano,José	(4411 DFF)	Curry,Xzavion	(1001 ACC)
	Márquez,Germán	(3100 FAA)	Hill,Rich	(1100 DAB)	White,Brendan	(4200 ADF)	Farmer,Buck	(1210 ACC)
	Sánchez,Sixto	(3100 FFF)	Irvin,Jake	(1001 ADB)	Bird,Jake	(3100 ACA)	Fujinami,Shintaro	(1301 AAD)
	Stone,Gavin	(3201 ADF)	Kaprielian,James	(1100 FAB)	Chafin,Andrew	(3310 CBB)	Hoeing,Bryan	(1000 ACB)
	Stripling,Ross	(3101 FAB)	Kluber,Corey	(1101 FAC)	De Los Santos,Enyel	(3301 ACC)	Joyce,Ben	(1310 CFF)
	Thompson,Zack	(3203 ADF)	Kopech,Michael	(1201 FAC)	Hernandez,Jose	(3300 CDA)	Kinley,Tyler	(1210 FDD)
	Allard,Kolby	(2100 FCA)	Kremer,Dean	(1103 DAC)	Hughes,Brandon	(3300 FDD)	Pearson,Nate	(1200 FFB)
	Assad,Javier	(2001 ACC)	Lambert,Peter	(1001 FFC)	Junis,Jakob	(3201 DBC)	Smith,Drew	(1301 FCB)
	Blackburn,Paul	(2103 FBF)	Lauer,Eric	(1201 CAD)	López,Jorge	(3110 CAC)	Toussaint,Touki	(1201 DDB)
	Bradford,Cody	(2100 ADA)	Lively,Ben	(1000 DDB)	Montero,Rafael	(3301 DBC)	Wentz,Joey	(1100 CDF)
	Bradley,Taj	(2201 ADF)	Lucchesi,Joey	(1101 FDB)	Morgan,Eli	(3201 ACB)	**Wilson,Bryse**	**(1001 BBB)**
	Carrasco,Carlos	(2100 FAC)	Lyles,Jordan	**(1003 AAB)**	**Pallante,Andre**	**(3001 ABA)**	Wilson,Steven	(1301 DCC)
	Cavalli,Cade	(2200 FDD)	Lynch,Daniel	(1001 FAC)	Richards,Trevor	(3501 CBA)	Bard,Daniel	(0310 DAF)
	Contreras,Roansy	(2101 ACD)	Manoah,Alek	(1203 AAD)	Wesneski,Hayden	(3201 ACD)	Keller,Brad	(0000 FAB)
	Faedo,Alex	(2101 CCD)	Medina,Luis	(1201 BDC)	Winckowski,Josh	(3100 ACB)		
	Greinke,Zack	(2001 FAA)	Nelson,Ryne	(1003 ACB)	Yates,Kirby	(3500 FDF)		
	Harrison,Kyle	(2301 ADB)	Ortiz,Luis	(1003 ACF)	Alexander,Tyler	(2100 FAA)		
	Houser,Adrian	(2101 FAA)	Perez,Martin	**(1001 BAB)**	Baker,Bryan	(2300 ACC)		
	Liberatore,Matthew	(2101 ACA)	Phillips,Connor	(1301 ADB)	Cabrera,Génesis	(2200 ACA)		
	Marsh,Alec	(2201 ADB)	Quantrill,Cal	(1003 FAA)	Castro,Miguel	(2201 DCA)		
	Megill,Tylor	(2103 FCC)	Scholtens,Jesse	(1000 ADB)	Clarke,Taylor	(2211 FCC)		
	Odorizzi,Jake	(2101 FBA)	Senzatela,Antonio	(1000 FBA)	Cuas,Jose	(2201 ADA)		
	Oviedo,Johan	**(1101 ABB)**	Smith-Shawver,AJ	(1200 AFF)	Falter,Bailey	(2101 BCC)		
	Priester,Quinn	(2001 ADF)	Syndergaard,Noah	(1001 FAB)	Gibaut,Ian	(2210 ADF)		
	Rea,Colin	(2101 ADA)	Teheran,Julio	(1001 FFA)	Hernández,Carlos	(2211 ACB)		
	Rom,Drew	(2201 ADB)	Waldron,Matt	(1001 ADA)	**Irvin,Cole**	**(2001 BAB)**		
	Severino,Luis	(2101 FBC)	White,Owen	(1100 ADF)	Lawrence,Justin	(2211 ACC)		
	Vásquez,Randy	(2101 ADB)	Williams,Trevor	(1101 CAC)	Machado,Andrés	(2100 ADA)		
	Winans,Allan	(2001 ADF)	Williamson,Brandon	(1201 ADB)	Murphy,Chris	(2201 ADC)		
	Adon,Joan	(1101 ACA)	Anderson,Chase	(0000 FCB)	Nelson,Kyle	(2300 DDA)		
	Anderson,Tyler	(1103 DAC)	Harris,Hogan	(0101 ADF)	Rainey,Tanner	(2310 FCF)		
	Butto,José	(1101 ACC)	Hudson,Dakota	(0001 FCF)	Smyly,Drew	(2201 DAA)		
	Chirinos,Yonny	(1001 FDD)	Muller,Kyle	(0101 ACD)	Weaver,Luke	(2201 FCA)		
	Corbin,Patrick	**(1003 AAA)**	Rutledge,Jackson	(0001 CFF)	Zerpa,Angel	(2001 FDC)		
	Cueto,Johnny	(1000 FBF)	Seabold,Connor	(0000 ACC)	Bachman,Sam	(1000 DFA)		
	Davies,Zach	(1001 FAB)	Shuster,Jared	(0000 ADF)	Barria,Jaime	(1000 BBC)		
	Feltner,Ryan	(1103 FCB)	Weathers,Ryan	(0001 ACC)	Baumann,Mike	(1100 ACA)		
	Freeland,Kyle	(1003 DAA)			Beck,Tristan	(1000 ADB)		

RotoLab
Draft Software

RotoLab is both a draft preparation program and an in-draft management tool. Just make the roster moves and player selections, and the program handles the rest... automatically! All budget calculations, inflation changes, player lists, team stats and standing totals are a single mouse click away. And... **RotoLab comes loaded with industry-leading player projections from BaseballHQ.com!**

FREE DEMO at www.rotolab.com
HUGE discount for Baseball HQ subscribers!

- Easy to use interface
- Sort, search and filter data at the click of a mouse
- Five years of historical and projected stats
- User notes for each player
- Drag-and-drop player moves
- Two-click operation to draft players
- Flexible league setup options
- Customizable valuation process
- User-definable player list
- Roster management from a single screen
- Cheat Sheet and full stat views to draft from

SIMULATION LEAGUE DRAFT

TOP 500+

NAME	POS	RAR
Freeman,Freddie	3	70.2
Judge,Aaron	9	61.4
Soto,Juan	7	61.1
Alvarez,Yordan	7	60.7
Betts,Mookie	49	60.3
Acuña Jr.,Ronald	9	60.2
Ohtani,Shohei	0	60.1
Harper,Bryce	3	54.0
Olson,Matt	3	53.4
Seager,Corey	6	50.3
Trout,Mike	8	46.4
Riley,Austin	5	43.8
Tucker,Kyle	9	42.9
Ramírez,José	5	41.5
Arraez,Luis	4	40.3
Devers,Rafael	5	40.1
Rutschman,Adley	2	39.8
Tatis Jr.,Fernando	9	38.2
Rodríguez,Julio	8	37.9
Altuve,Jose	4	36.1
Díaz,Yandy	3	36.0
Carroll,Corbin	789	35.7
Casas,Triston	3	35.0
Suzuki,Seiya	9	34.8
Alonso,Pete	3	34.5
Contreras,William	2	34.3
Marte,Ketel	4	34.2
Franco,Wander	6	33.7
Bichette,Bo	6	33.6
Bogaerts,Xander	6	33.1
Goldschmidt,Paul	3	32.9
Lewis,Royce	5	32.3
Cole,Gerrit	P	31.8
Henderson,Gunnar	56	31.6
Schwarber,Kyle	7	31.4
Albies,Ozzie	4	31.3
Jones,Nolan	79	30.6
Machado,Manny	5	30.5
Bregman,Alex	5	30.2
Turner,Trea	6	30.1
Smith,Will	2	29.9
Harris II,Michael	8	29.6
Guerrero Jr.,Vladimir	3	29.3
Nimmo,Brandon	8	29.1
Murphy,Sean	2	28.8
Contreras,Willson	2	28.6
Yoshida,Masataka	7	28.3
Burnes,Corbin	P	28.2
Reynolds,Bryan	7	28.1
Semien,Marcus	4	28.1
Witt Jr.,Bobby	6	27.8
Yelich,Christian	7	27.5
Bellinger,Cody	38	26.7
Lindor,Francisco	6	26.7
Kirby,George	P	26.4
Greene,Riley	8	25.9
Fried,Max	P	25.8
Arenado,Nolan	5	25.8
Rodriguez,Grayson	P	25.7
Happ,Ian	7	24.5
Torres,Gleyber	4	24.4
Lowe,Nathaniel	3	23.9
Ward,Taylor	7	23.8

NAME	POS	RAR
Realmuto,J.T.	2	23.6
Julien,Edouard	4	23.4
Gausman,Kevin	P	23.3
Hoskins,Rhys	3	23.2
Valdez,Framber	P	22.8
Lee,Jung-hoo	7	22.7
Ozuna,Marcell	0	22.7
Martinez,J.D.	0	22.7
Moreno,Gabriel	2	22.6
Bibee,Tanner	P	22.6
Webb,Logan	P	21.9
Musgrove,Joe	P	21.8
Diaz,Yainer	2	21.5
Wheeler,Zack	P	21.4
Bradish,Kyle	P	21.2
Naylor,Josh	3	21.2
Arozarena,Randy	7	21.1
Gurriel Jr.,Lourdes	7	20.7
Senga,Kodai	P	20.4
Gallen,Zac	P	20.2
Castillo,Luis	P	19.9
Robert Jr.,Luis	8	19.6
Turner,Justin	3	19.5
López,Pablo	P	19.4
Lowe,Josh	9	19.2
Burger,Jake	5	19.1
Drury,Brandon	34	19.0
McLain,Matt	46	19.0
Walker,Christian	3	18.7
Correa,Carlos	6	18.7
Muncy,Max	5	18.6
Naylor,Bo	2	18.5
Paredes,Isaac	35	18.4
Snell,Blake	P	18.3
Yamamoto,Yoshinobu	P	18.1
Kelly,Merrill	P	17.8
Glasnow,Tyler	P	17.8
Jeffers,Ryan	2	17.7
Flores,Wilmer	35	17.7
Adames,Willy	6	17.5
India,Jonathan	4	17.3
Pasquantino,Vinnie	3	17.2
Swanson,Dansby	6	17.2
Hoerner,Nico	46	17.0
Cruz,Oneil	6	16.9
Crawford,J.P.	6	16.8
Jung,Josh	5	16.7
Springer,George	9	16.7
Soler,Jorge	9	16.6
Strider,Spencer	P	16.2
Nootbaar,Lars	789	16.1
Gray,Sonny	P	16.1
Luzardo,Jesus	P	16.0
Raleigh,Cal	2	16.0
Álvarez,Francisco	2	16.0
Kwan,Steven	7	15.9
Hernández,Teoscar	9	15.8
Montgomery,Jordan	P	15.6
Duran,Jarren	78	15.6
Pérez,Eury	P	15.6
Marsh,Brandon	78	15.6
Bassitt,Chris	P	15.5
Bednar,David	P	15.4

NAME	POS	RAR
Castellanos,Nick	9	15.3
Belt,Brandon	3	15.2
McCormick,Chas	789	15.2
Garrett,Braxton	P	15.2
King,Michael	P	15.2
Buehler,Walker	P	15.2
Nola,Aaron	P	15.2
Nardi,Andrew	P	15.0
Candelario,Jeimer	35	15.0
Bieber,Shane	P	14.9
Donovan,Brendan	47	14.8
Sanchez,Gary	2	14.7
Bell,Josh	3	14.7
Jimenez,Eloy	0	14.7
Miller,Bobby	P	14.6
Steele,Justin	P	14.6
Carter,Evan	O	14.5
Hayes,Ke'Bryan	5	14.5
McNeil,Jeff	479	14.5
Williams,Devin	P	14.5
Peralta,Freddy	P	14.5
Heim,Jonah	2	14.3
Santander,Anthony	9	14.3
Kepler,Max	9	14.1
Blackmon,Charlie	9	14.1
Rodgers,Brendan	4	13.9
Lowe,Brandon	4	13.8
Gorman,Nolan	4	13.8
Garcia,Adolis	9	13.7
O'Hoppe,Logan	2	13.7
Gilbert,Logan	P	13.5
Polanco,Jorge	4	13.5
Eflin,Zach	P	13.4
Perez,Salvador	23	13.4
Bohm,Alec	35	13.3
Mountcastle,Ryan	3	13.3
Stephenson,Tyler	2	13.2
Woo,Bryan	P	13.2
Kirk,Alejandro	2	13.1
Steer,Spencer	357	13.1
Bryant,Kris	9	13.1
Chisholm Jr.,Jazz	8	13.0
Jansen,Danny	2	13.0
Skubal,Tarik	P	12.9
Williams,Gavin	P	12.9
Scott,Tanner	P	12.8
McMahon,Ryan	45	12.7
Duran,Jhoan	P	12.5
Schneider,Davis	4	12.5
Mayza,Tim	P	12.3
Ginkel,Kevin	P	12.2
Ruiz,Keibert	2	12.2
Chapman,Matt	5	12.0
Varland,Louie	P	11.9
Verdugo,Alex	9	11.6
Pepiot,Ryan	P	11.5
Clase,Emmanuel	P	11.5
Giménez,Andrés	4	11.5
Sale,Chris	P	11.5
De La Cruz,Elly	56	11.4
Abreu,Bryan	P	11.4
Kim,Ha-Seong	456	11.4
Díaz,Edwin	P	11.4

NAME	POS	RAR
Rengifo,Luis	456O	11.2
Ober,Bailey	P	11.2
Civale,Aaron	P	11.2
Doval,Camilo	P	11.2
Urshela,Giovanny	35	11.1
Hader,Josh	P	11.1
Caminero,Junior	5	11.1
Muñoz,Andres	P	11.0
Benintendi,Andrew	7	11.0
Edman,Tommy	468	10.9
Torkelson,Spencer	3	10.8
Stott,Bryson	4	10.8
Brash,Matt	P	10.7
Scherzer,Max	P	10.7
Fairbanks,Peter	P	10.6
Carpenter,Kerry	9	10.5
Ottavino,Adam	P	10.5
Rogers,Jake	2	10.4
Urías,Julio	P	10.4
Sánchez,Jesús	9	10.4
Baz,Shane	P	10.4
Iglesias,Raisel	P	10.3
Martinez,Nick	P	10.3
Stroman,Marcus	P	10.3
Story,Trevor	6	10.3
Berríos,José	P	10.2
Adam,Jason	P	10.2
Garver,Mitch	2	10.2
Imanaga,Shota	P	10.1
Graterol,Brusdar	P	10.1
Phillips,Evan	P	10.0
Stephenson,Robert	P	10.0
Rodriguez,Eduardo	P	10.0
Hays,Austin	7	9.9
Lux,Gavin	0	9.9
Duvall,Adam	89	9.9
Arcia,Orlando	6	9.9
Cabrera,Edward	P	9.8
Kirilloff,Alex	3O	9.7
Brantley,Michael	7	9.7
Allen,Logan	P	9.7
Suarez,Eugenio	5	9.6
Canha,Mark	79	9.6
Cano,Yennier	P	9.6
Thomas,Lane	9	9.6
Holmes,Clay	P	9.6
Estrada,Thairo	46	9.5
Sewald,Paul	P	9.5
Kikuchi,Yusei	P	9.4
Wade Jr.,LaMonte	3O	9.4
Martin,Christopher	P	9.4
Silseth,Chase	P	9.3
Pederson,Joc	7	9.2
Friedl,T.J.	78	9.2
Helsley,Ryan	P	9.2
Montas,Frankie	P	9.
Swanson,Erik	P	9.
Detmers,Reid	P	9.
Melendez Jr.,MJ	79	9.
Garcia,Luis	4	8.
Hall,DL	P	8.
Vaughn,Andrew	3	8.
Mead,Curtis	5	8.

SIMULATION LEAGUE DRAFT — TOP 500+

NAME	POS	RAR
Suwinski,Jack	89	8.8
Sánchez,Cristopher	P	8.7
Pivetta,Nick	P	8.7
Eovaldi,Nathan	P	8.7
Alvarado,José	P	8.7
Leclerc,José	P	8.6
Payamps,Joel	P	8.6
Cron,C.J.	3	8.6
Wallner,Matt	79	8.5
Davis,J.D.	5	8.5
Marte,Noelvi	5	8.4
Romano,Jordan	P	8.4
Hamilton,Ian	P	8.4
Fraley,Jake	79	8.4
Pham,Tommy	7	8.3
Gelof,Zack	4	8.3
Buxton,Byron	0	8.2
Cease,Dylan	P	8.2
Whitlock,Garrett	P	8.2
Hicks,Jordan	P	8.2
Volpe,Anthony	6	8.1
Abreu,José	3	8.1
Ryan,Joe	P	8.1
Schreiber,John	P	8.1
Cooper,Garrett	3	8.1
Peguero,Elvis	P	8.0
Yastrzemski,Mike	89	8.0
McCullers,Lance	P	8.0
Rodríguez,Endy	2	8.0
Wicks,Jordan	P	8.0
Keller,Mitch	P	8.0
Campusano,Luis	2	8.0
Darvish,Yu	P	8.0
Strahm,Matt	P	7.9
Taylor,Chris	567	7.9
Kelenic,Jarred	79	7.9
Javier,Cristian	P	7.8
Uribe,Abner	P	7.8
Johnson,Pierce	P	7.8
Harvey,Hunter	P	7.8
LeMahieu,DJ	35	7.7
Miller,Mason	P	7.7
Domínguez,Jasson	8	7.7
Santana,Carlos	3	7.7
Morton,Charlie	P	7.6
Encarnacion-Strand,Chr	3	7.6
Topa,Justin	P	7.6
Minter,A.J.	P	7.6
Olivares,Edward	7	7.5
Walker,Ryan	P	7.5
Armstrong,Shawn	P	7.5
Canning,Griffin	P	7.4
Rizzo,Anthony	3	7.4
Conforto,Michael	9	7.3
ugo,Seth	P	7.2
angeliers,Shea	2	7.2
asmussen,Drew	P	7.2
Moreta,Dauri	P	7.1
enson,Will	79	7.1
ressly,Ryan	P	7.1
Merryweather,Julian	P	7.0
Walker,Jordan	9	7.0
ello,Brayan	P	6.9

NAME	POS	RAR
deGrom,Jacob	P	6.9
Moncada,Yoán	5	6.9
Poche,Colin	P	6.9
Miley,Wade	P	6.9
Morel,Christopher	O	6.9
Ragans,Cole	P	6.9
Robertson,David	P	6.8
Ferguson,Caleb	P	6.8
Jax,Griffin	P	6.8
Haniger,Mitch	7	6.8
Olson,Reese	P	6.8
De La Cruz,Bryan	7	6.7
Alzolay,Adbert	P	6.7
Romero,JoJo	P	6.7
Graveman,Kendall	P	6.6
Kelly,Kevin	P	6.6
Maeda,Kenta	P	6.6
Lodolo,Nick	P	6.6
Díaz,Alexis	P	6.5
Cronenworth,Jake	34	6.5
Rendon,Anthony	5	6.4
Milner,Hoby	P	6.4
García,Yimi	P	6.4
Ramírez,Harold	0	6.3
Berti,Jon	56	6.3
Neris,Hector	P	6.3
Pfaadt,Brandon	P	6.2
Garrett,Stone	7	6.2
Rosario,Amed	46	6.2
Assad,Javier	P	6.1
Cosgrove,Tom	P	6.1
Chapman,Aroldis	P	6.1
López,Reynaldo	P	6.0
Santos,Gregory	P	5.9
Wisdom,Patrick	5	5.9
d'Arnaud,Travis	2	5.9
Hentges,Sam	P	5.8
Valdez,Enmanuel	4	5.8
France,Ty	3	5.8
Outman,James	8	5.8
Marte,Starling	9	5.8
Foley,Jason	P	5.7
Rogers,Tyler	P	5.7
Matos,Luis	8	5.7
Fermin,Freddy	2	5.7
Puk,A.J.	P	5.7
Renfroe,Hunter	9	5.6
Bauers,Jake	379	5.6
Gomes,Yan	2	5.6
Finnegan,Kyle	P	5.6
Springs,Jeffrey	P	5.6
Velázquez,Nelson	9	5.6
Castro,Willi	578	5.6
Westburg,Jordan	45	5.6
Coulombe,Daniel	P	5.5
Cortes,Nestor	P	5.5
Suarez,Robert	P	5.5
Cobb,Alex	P	5.4
Abreu,Wilyer	O	5.4
Verlander,Justin	P	5.4
Gallegos,Giovanny	P	5.2
Vogelbach,Daniel	0	5.2
Holderman,Colin	P	5.2

NAME	POS	RAR
Mullins II,Cedric	8	5.1
Hoffman,Jeff	P	5.1
Ibanez,Andy	40	5.1
Jansen,Kenley	P	5.1
Tovar,Ezequiel	6	5.1
Stewart,Brock	P	5.1
Houck,Tanner	P	5.1
McKenzie,Triston	P	5.1
Speier,Gabe	P	5.0
O'Hearn,Ryan	39	5.0
Grossman,Robbie	79	5.0
Joe,Connor	379	5.0
Vest,Will	P	4.9
Rooker,Brent	79	4.9
Matsui,Yuki	P	4.9
Quintana,José	P	4.9
Karinchak,James	P	4.8
Kershaw,Clayton	P	4.8
Waters,Drew	89	4.8
Garcia,Maikel	5	4.8
Kimbrel,Craig	P	4.8
McGough,Scott	P	4.7
Suárez,Ranger	P	4.7
Hurt,Kyle	P	4.7
Amaya,Miguel	2	4.7
Wong,Connor	2	4.7
Holton,Tyler	P	4.7
Sandoval,Patrick	P	4.6
Grissom,Vaughn	6	4.6
Burke,Brock	P	4.6
Raley,Brooks	P	4.5
Dunning,Dane	P	4.5
Soto,Gregory	P	4.5
García,Luis	P	4.5
Pérez,Cionel	P	4.5
Abrams,CJ	6	4.5
Matz,Steven	P	4.5
McCutchen,Andrew	0	4.5
Solano,Donovan	34	4.4
Hughes,Brandon	P	4.4
Wood,Alex	P	4.4
Ray,Robbie	P	4.4
Adams,Riley	2	4.3
Winckowski,Josh	P	4.2
Wells,Tyler	P	4.2
Mize,Casey	P	4.2
Díaz,Elias	2	4.1
O'Neill,Tyler	7	4.1
Vesia,Alex	P	4.1
Means,John	P	4.1
Taveras,Leody	8	4.1
Gray,Jonathan	P	4.0
Harrison,Kyle	P	4.0
Germán,Domingo	P	3.9
Rogers,Trevor	P	3.9
Leiter,Mark	P	3.8
Jiménez,Joe	P	3.8
Soriano,José	P	3.8
Barlow,Scott	P	3.8
Junis,Jakob	P	3.8
Kiermaier,Kevin	8	3.8
Domínguez,Seranthony	P	3.8
Neto,Zach	6	3.8

NAME	POS	RAR
Stephan,Trevor	P	3.7
Slater,Austin	78	3.6
Hicks,Aaron	789	3.6
Clevinger,Michael	P	3.6
Stratton,Chris	P	3.6
Aranda,Jonathan	0	3.5
Hendricks,Kyle	P	3.5
Miller,Bryce	P	3.5
De Los Santos,Enyel	P	3.5
Grichuk,Randal	789	3.4
Loáisiga,Jonathan	P	3.4
Gore,MacKenzie	P	3.4
May,Dustin	P	3.4
Kahnle,Tommy	P	3.4
Littell,Zack	P	3.3
Rogers,Taylor	P	3.2
Donaldson,Josh	5	3.2
Sheehan,Emmet	P	3.2
Rojas,Josh	45	3.1
Kjerstad,Heston	0	3.0
Cruz,Fernando	P	3.0
Anderson,Tim	6	3.0
Wacha,Michael	P	3.0
Sandlin,Nick	P	3.0
Brown,Hunter	P	2.9
McMillon,John	P	2.9
Siri,Jose	8	2.9
Merrifield,Whit	47	2.8
Floro,Dylan	P	2.8
Madrigal,Nick	5	2.7
Smith,Drew	P	2.7
Lange,Alex	P	2.6
Peterson,David	P	2.6
White,Brendan	P	2.6
Sears,JP	P	2.6
Crawford,Kutter	P	2.6
Baker,Bryan	P	2.6
Pearson,Nate	P	2.6
Chafin,Andrew	P	2.6
McArthur,James	P	2.5
Morgan,Eli	P	2.5
Vargas,Miguel	4	2.5
Winn,Keaton	P	2.5
Peña,Jeremy	6	2.4
Greene,Hunter	P	2.4
Thomas,Alek	8	2.4
Hampson,Garrett	689	2.3
Heyward,Jason	89	2.3
Brito,Jhony	P	2.2
Knizner,Andrew	2	2.2
Peralta,David	7	2.2
Yates,Kirby	P	2.1
Middleton,Keynan	P	2.1
Noda,Ryan	3	2.1
Montero,Elehuris	3	2.1
Pallante,Andre	P	2.1
Grandal,Yasmani	2	2.0
Rodón,Carlos	P	2.0
Ryu,Hyun-Jin	P	2.0
Montero,Rafael	P	2.0
Wong,Kolten	4	1.9
Soroka,Michael	P	1.9
Duran,Ezequiel	567	1.9

MULTI-POSITION ELIGIBILITY

*Position player eligibility for leagues that use 5 games, 10 games and 20 games as their requirements. *Qualified based on the position played the most.*

NAME	5-Gm	10-Gm	20-Gm
Alberto,Hanser	2B 3B	2B 3B	3B *
Alu,Jake	2B 3B OF	2B OF	2B OF
Anderson,Brian	3B OF	3B OF	3B OF
Andrus,Elvis	2B SS	2B SS	2B SS
Arauz,Jonathan	2B 3B SS	3B	3B *
Arias,Gabriel	1B 3B SS OF	1B 3B SS OF	1B SS
Arraez,Luis	1B 2B	1B 2B	2B
Bae,Ji-Hwan	2B OF	2B OF	2B OF
Barrero,Jose	SS OF	SS OF	SS
Basabe,Osleivis	3B SS	SS	SS
Batten,Matt	1B 2B 3B	2B 3B	2B *3B *
Bauers,Jake	1B OF	1B OF	1B OF
Bellinger,Cody	1B OF	1B OF	1B OF
Berti,Jon	2B 3B SS OF	2B 3B SS OF	3B SS
Betts,Mookie	2B SS OF	2B SS OF	2B OF
Biggio,Cavan	1B 2B 3B OF	1B 2B 3B OF	1B 2B OF
Bohm,Alec	1B 3B	1B 3B	1B 3B
Bride,Jonah	1B 3B	3B	3B
Brown,Seth	1B OF	1B OF	OF
Brujan,Vidal	2B SS OF	2B	2B *
Bryant,Kris	1B OF	OF	OF
Burger,Jake	1B 2B 3B	3B	3B
Burleson,Alec	1B OF	1B OF	OF
Caballero,Jose	2B 3B SS	2B SS	2B SS
Cabbage,Trey	1B OF	OF	OF*
Cabrera,Oswaldo	2B 3B SS OF	3B OF	OF
Candelario,Jeimer	1B 3B	1B 3B	1B 3B
Canha,Mark	1B OF	1B OF	OF
Castro,Harold	2B OF	2B OF	2B
Castro,Rodolfo	2B 3B SS	2B 3B SS	2B SS
Castro,Willi	2B 3B SS OF	2B 3B OF	3B OF
Cave,Jake	1B OF	1B OF	OF
Chavis,Michael	1B 2B 3B	2B	2B
Clement,Ernie	2B SS	SS	SS *
Cronenworth,Jake	1B 2B	1B 2B	1B 2B
Davis,J.D.	1B 3B	1B 3B	3B
De La Cruz,Elly	3B SS	3B SS	3B SS
Diaz,Aledmys	1B 2B 3B SS OF	1B 2B 3B SS OF	3B SS
Diaz,Jordan	1B 2B 3B	2B 3B	2B 3B
Diaz,Yainer	CA 1B	CA	CA
Diaz,Yandy	1B 3B	1B	1B
Dixon,Brandon	1B OF	1B OF	1B *
Donovan,Brendan	1B 2B 3B OF	1B 2B OF	2B OF
Dozier,Hunter	1B 3B OF	3B	3B *
Drury,Brandon	1B 2B	1B 2B	1B 2B
Dubon,Mauricio	2B SS OF	2B OF	2B OF
Duffy,Matt	1B 2B 3B	1B 2B 3B	2B 3B
Duran,Ezequiel	2B 3B SS OF	3B SS OF	3B SS OF
Edman,Tommy	2B SS OF	2B SS OF	2B SS OF
Encarnacion-Strand,C	1B 3B	1B	1B
Escobar,Eduardo	1B 2B 3B	2B 3B	2B 3B
Espinal,Santiago	2B 3B SS	2B 3B SS	2B 3B
Estrada,Thairo	2B SS	2B SS	2B SS
Farmer,Kyle	2B 3B SS	2B 3B SS	2B 3B SS
Fermin,Jose	2B 3B	2B	2B *
Fletcher,David	2B SS	2B SS	SS *
Flores,Wilmer	1B 2B 3B	1B 3B	1B 3B
Frazier,Adam	2B OF	2B OF	2B
Freeman,Tyler	2B 3B SS	2B 3B SS	3B
Fry,David	CA 1B OF	CA 1B	CA
Gallo,Joey	1B OF	1B OF	1B OF
Garcia,Maikel	3B SS	3B SS	3B

NAME	5-Gm	10-Gm	20-Gm
Gonzales,Nick	2B SS	2B	2B
Gonzalez,Romy	2B OF	2B OF	2B
Goodman,Hunter	1B OF	OF	OF*
Gordon,Nick	2B OF	2B OF	OF
Gorman,Nolan	2B 3B	2B 3B	2B
Grandal,Yasmani	CA 1B	CA	CA
Guillorme,Luis	2B 3B SS	2B 3B	2B
Haase,Eric	CA OF	CA OF	CA OF
Haggerty,Sam	2B OF	2B OF	OF
Hampson,Garrett	2B 3B SS OF	2B SS OF	SS OF
Harrison,Josh	2B 3B OF	2B 3B	3B *
Henderson,Gunnar	3B SS	3B SS	3B SS
Hensley,David	1B 2B	2B *	2B *
Hernandez,Enrique	1B 2B 3B SS OF	1B 2B 3B SS OF	2B SS OF
Heyward,Jason	1B OF	OF	OF
Hoerner,Nico	2B SS	2B SS	2B SS
Ibanez,Andy	2B 3B OF	2B 3B OF	2B OF
Joe,Connor	1B OF	1B OF	1B OF
Jones,Nolan	1B OF	1B OF	OF
Kemp,Anthony	2B OF	2B OF	2B OF
Kessinger,Grae	1B 2B 3B SS	3B *SS *	3B *SS *
Kim,Ha-Seong	2B 3B SS	2B 3B SS	2B 3B SS
Kiner-Falefa,Isiah	3B OF	3B OF	3B OF
Kirilloff,Alex	1B OF	1B OF	1B OF
LeMahieu,DJ	1B 2B 3B	1B 3B	1B 3B
Loftin,Nick	1B 2B	1B *	1B *
Lopez,Nicky	2B 3B SS	2B 3B SS	2B 3B
Madrigal,Nick	2B 3B	2B 3B	3B
Mancini,Trey	1B OF	1B	1B
Marcano,Tucupita	2B SS	2B SS	SS
Mastrobuoni,Miles	2B 3B OF	3B	3B
Maton,Nick	2B 3B	2B 3B	2B 3B
Mauricio,Ronny	2B 3B	2B	2B
McKinstry,Zach	2B 3B SS OF	2B 3B SS OF	2B 3B SS OF
McLain,Matt	2B SS	2B SS	2B SS
McMahon,Ryan	2B 3B	2B 3B	2B 3B
McNeil,Jeff	2B OF	2B OF	2B OF
Melendez Jr.,MJ	CA OF	CA OF	OF
Mendick,Danny	2B 3B	2B	2B *
Merrifield,Whit	2B OF	2B OF	2B OF
Miller,Owen	1B 2B 3B OF	1B 2B 3B	1B 2B 3B
Monasterio,Andruw	2B 3B SS	2B 3B	2B 3B
Montero,Elehuris	1B 3B	1B 3B	1B
Moore,Dylan	2B SS OF	2B OF	2B OF
Morel,Christopher	2B 3B OF	2B OF	OF
Motter,Taylor	2B 3B	2B 3B	2B *
Moustakas,Mike	1B 3B	1B 3B	1B 3B
Myers,Wil	1B OF	1B OF	OF
Nevin,Tyler	1B 3B OF	3B	3B *
Newman,Kevin	1B 2B 3B SS	2B 3B SS	3B
Noda,Ryan	1B OF	1B	1B
O Hearn,Ryan	1B OF	1B OF	1B OF
Odor,Rougned	2B 3B OF	2B	2B
Paredes,Isaac	1B 2B 3B	1B 2B 3B	1B 3B
Peguero,Liover	2B SS	2B SS	2B SS
Peraza,Oswald	2B 3B SS	2B 3B	3B
Perdomo,Geraldo	2B 3B SS	2B 3B SS	2B SS
Perez,Carlos	CA 1B	CA 1B	CA
Perez,Salvador	CA 1B	CA 1B	CA 1B
Peterson,Jace	2B 3B	2B 3B	2B 3B
Polanco,Jorge	2B 3B	2B 3B	2B
Pratto,Nick	1B OF	1B OF	1B OF

NAME	5-Gm	10-Gm	20-Gm
Profar,Jurickson	1B OF	OF	OF
Rafaela,Ceddanne	SS OF	OF	OF
Raley,Luke	1B OF	1B OF	1B OF
Ramirez,Harold	1B OF	OF	OF *
Remillard,Zach	2B 3B OF	2B OF	2B
Renfroe,Hunter	1B OF	OF	OF
Rengifo,Luis	2B 3B SS OF	2B 3B SS OF	2B 3B SS OF
Reyes,Pablo	2B SS	2B SS	2B SS
Rivera,Emmanuel	1B 3B	1B 3B	3B
Rocchio,Brayan	3B SS	SS	SS *
Rojas,Josh	2B 3B	2B 3B	2B 3B
Rosario,Amed	2B SS	2B SS	2B SS
Sabol,Blake	CA OF	CA OF	CA OF
Santander,Anthony	1B OF	1B OF	OF
Schmitt,Casey	2B 3B SS	2B 3B SS	3B SS
Schoop,Jonathan	2B 3B	2B 3B	2B 3B
Senzel,Nick	2B 3B OF	3B OF	3B OF
Sheets,Gavin	1B OF	1B OF	1B OF
Short,Zack	2B 3B SS	2B 3B SS	2B 3B SS
Smith,Josh	3B SS OF	3B SS OF	3B SS OF
Smith,Kevin	3B SS	3B SS	SS
Smith,Pavin	1B OF	1B OF	OF
Soderstrom,Tyler	CA 1B	CA 1B	C *
Solano,Donovan	1B 2B 3B	1B 2B 3B	1B 2B
Sosa,Edmundo	3B SS	3B SS	3B
Sosa,Lenyn	2B 3B	2B 3B	2B
Steer,Spencer	1B 2B 3B OF	1B 2B 3B OF	1B 3B OF
Stefanic,Michael	2B 3B	2B	2B *
Stephenson,Tyler	CA 1B	CA	CA
Taylor,Chris	3B SS OF	3B SS OF	3B SS OF
Taylor,Samad	2B OF	2B OF	OF*
Toglia,Michael	1B OF	1B OF	1B
Trejo,Alan	2B 3B SS	2B 3B	2B 3B
Triolo,Jared	1B 2B 3B	2B 3B	3B
Turang,Brice	2B SS	2B SS	2B SS
Turner,Justin	1B 2B 3B	1B 2B	1B
Urias,Luis	2B 3B	2B 3B	2B
Urias,Ramon	1B 2B 3B	1B 2B 3B	2B 3B
Urshela,Giovanny	1B 3B SS	1B 3B	1B 3B
Vargas,Ildemaro	2B 3B SS OF	2B 3B SS OF	3B
Vargas,Miguel	1B 2B	2B	2B
Vazquez,Christian	CA 1B	CA	CA
Velazquez,Andrew	2B SS	2B SS	SS
Vientos,Mark	1B 3B	1B 3B	3B *
Vierling,Matt	3B OF	3B OF	3B OF
Villar,David	1B 2B 3B	2B 3B	2B
Wade,LaMonte	1B OF	1B OF	1B OF
Wade,Tyler	SS OF	SS	SS *
Walls,Taylor	2B 3B SS	2B 3B SS	2B 3B SS
Walsh,Jared	1B OF	1B	1B
Westburg,Jordan	2B 3B	2B 3B	2B 3B
Wisdom,Patrick	1B 3B OF	1B 3B	3B
Wisely,Brett	2B OF	2B OF	2B

2023 PLAYING TIME MEASUREMENT CHARTS BY POSITION

Quickstart Key: AW: active weeks; PAAW: plate appearances per active week; SAW: starts per active week; PAS: plate appearances per start; EAW: extra PA per active week. Players are sorted by descending PAAW. See Encyclopedia entry on page 31 and Research articles beginning on page 70 for additional detail into the terms and concepts used here.

First Base

Name	A	B	PA	AW	PAAW	SAW	PAS	EAW	%vR	%vL	vR	vL	Pos
Freeman, Freddie,	34	L	730	27	27.0	6.0	4.53	0.0	99%	100%	4.58	4.43	
Lowe, Nathaniel	28	L	724	27	26.8	6.0	4.50	0.0	100%	98%	4.47	4.57	
Olson, Matt	29	L	720	27	26.7	6.0	4.44	0.0	98%	100%	4.43	4.52	
Goldschmidt, Paul	36	R	686	27	25.4	5.7	4.45	0.0	93%	98%	4.46	4.44	
Torkelson, Spencer	24	R	684	27	25.3	5.9	4.30	0.0	95%	97%	4.27	4.39	
Guerrero Jr., Vladin	24	R	682	27	25.3	5.7	4.42	0.1	95%	92%	4.40	4.48	
Alonso, Pete	29	R	658	26	25.2	5.8	4.30	0.0	95%	96%	4.33	4.22	
Harper, Bryce, A	31	L	546	22	24.8	5.7	4.36	0.0	94%	88%	4.43	4.19	
France, Ty	29	R	666	27	24.7	5.7	4.30	0.1	93%	100%	4.31	4.26	
Steer, Spencer	26	R	665	27	24.6	5.6	4.34	0.2	91%	98%	4.27	4.48	5o
Walker, Christian	32	R	660	27	24.4	5.7	4.25	0.3	92%	100%	4.23	4.30	
Cronenworth, Jake	29	L	521	22	23.7	5.6	4.15	0.3	98%	88%	4.16	4.11	4
Pasquantino, Vinni	26	L	259	11	23.5	5.5	4.30	0.1	96%	83%	4.27	4.40	
Bohm, Alec	27	R	611	26	23.3	5.4	4.27	0.2	86%	98%	4.25	4.31	5
Drury, Brandon, S	31	R	523	22	23.2	5.4	4.27	0.1	85%	97%	4.26	4.29	4
Turner, Justin, M	39	R	626	27	23.2	5.3	4.33	0.1	86%	90%	4.34	4.32	
Bellinger, Cody	28	L	556	24	23.2	5.3	4.30	0.2	89%	89%	4.30	4.33	o
Diaz, Yandy	32	R	600	26	23.1	5.1	4.47	0.2	82%	91%	4.44	4.55	
Candelario, Jeimer	30	B	575	25	23.0	5.6	4.12	0.1	96%	85%	4.11	4.16	5
Santana, Carlos	37	B	619	27	22.9	5.3	4.26	0.2	90%	87%	4.29	4.17	
Abreu, Jose	36	R	594	26	22.8	5.3	4.20	0.6	89%	87%	4.09	4.44	
Bell, Josh	31	B	615	27	22.8	5.5	4.14	0.1	90%	92%	4.13	4.16	
Vaughn, Andrew	25	R	615	27	22.8	5.4	4.15	0.3	86%	97%	4.12	4.24	
Rizzo, Anthony	34	L	421	19	22.2	5.2	4.25	0.0	89%	82%	4.26	4.22	
Encarnacion-Stran	24	R	241	11	21.9	5.4	3.97	0.6	85%	88%	3.89	4.20	
Smith, Dominic	28	L	586	27	21.7	5.2	4.11	0.3	99%	63%	4.11	4.08	
Noda, Ryan	27	L	495	23	21.5	4.7	4.31	1.3	91%	43%	4.33	4.18	
Perez, Salvador	33	R	578	27	21.4	5.2	4.13	0.0	85%	85%	4.09	4.24	2
Naylor, Josh	26	L	495	23	21.3	4.9	4.27	0.4	89%	70%	4.27	4.26	
Mountcastle, Ryan	26	R	470	22	21.3	4.9	4.27	0.4	76%	94%	4.24	4.30	
Paredes, Isaac	24	R	571	27	21.1	4.9	4.21	0.7	76%	100%	4.15	4.37	5
LeMahieu, DJ	35	R	562	27	20.8	4.8	4.27	0.3	76%	90%	4.26	4.30	5
Calhoun, Kole	36	L	174	8	20.8	4.9	4.21	0.3	100%	43%	4.17	4.33	
Kirilloff, Alex	26	L	319	15	20.3	4.7	4.03	1.5	87%	43%	4.05	3.89	o
Casas, Triston	23	L	502	25	20.1	4.7	4.08	1.0	88%	43%	4.12	3.82	
Schanuel, Nolan	21	L	132	6	19.7	4.2	4.56	0.7	78%	40%	4.52	4.75	
Pratto, Nick	25	L	345	17	19.4	4.6	4.09	0.4	82%	57%	4.03	4.31	o
Wade Jr., LaMonte	30	L	519	27	19.2	4.3	4.20	1.2	90%	26%	4.25	3.75	o
Urshela, Gio	32	R	228	12	19.0	4.7	3.96	0.5	75%	79%	3.90	4.13	5
Votto, Joey, D	40	L	242	13	18.3	4.5	3.95	0.4	86%	48%	3.92	4.10	
Cooper, Garrett	33	R	457	25	18.1	4.2	4.08	1.0	65%	85%	4.08	4.07	
oe, Connor	31	R	472	27	17.5	3.7	4.23	1.8	44%	95%	4.11	4.34	o
Flores, Wilmer	32	R	454	26	17.5	3.7	4.27	1.5	48%	98%	4.25	4.29	5
Cron, C.J.	34	R	278	16	17.4	4.3	4.04	0.2	70%	91%	4.02	4.10	
Belt, Brandon	35	L	404	24	16.8	4.0	4.10	0.3	80%	22%	4.08	4.43	
Solano, Donovan	36	R	450	27	16.7	3.4	4.04	2.7	45%	97%	4.25	3.73	4
Tellez, Rowdy	28	L	351	21	16.4	3.8	3.95	1.3	81%	23%	3.97	3.78	
Bosler, Jason	30	L	65	4	16.3	3.8	3.87	1.8	94%	0%	3.87		
Toglia, Michael	25	B	152	9	16.2	3.9	3.91	1.0	68%	53%	3.92	3.89	
Montero, Elehuris	25	R	307	19	16.2	4.1	3.91	0.3	53%	89%	3.95	3.85	
Raley, Luke	29	L	406	26	15.6	3.9	3.82	0.8	77%	18%	3.81	4.00	o
Miller, Owen	27	R	314	20	15.6	3.7	4.03	0.9	48%	94%	4.00	4.06	45
Gallo, Joey, N	30	L	332	22	15.1	3.7	3.62	1.6	78%	19%	3.59	4.00	o
Loftin, Nick	25	R	68	4	15.0	3.8	3.73	1.0	47%	100%	3.78	3.67	
O'Hearn, Ryan	30	L	368	25	14.7	3.6	3.83	1.1	82%	10%	3.85	3.60	o
Moustakas, Mike	35	L	386	26	14.7	3.3	4.07	1.2	69%	21%	4.05	4.20	5
Mervis, Matt	25	L	99	6	14.2	3.8	3.57	0.5	81%	10%	3.55	4.00	
Walsh, Jared	30	L	116	7	14.1	3.1	3.73	2.4	65%	17%	3.70	4.00	
Mancini, Trey	31	R	261	19	13.7	3.3	3.79	1.2	42%	86%	3.97	3.61	
Wauers, Jake	28	L	272	20	13.4	3.3	3.80	0.9	58%	24%	3.75	4.40	o

Third Base

Name	A	B	PA	AW	PAAW	SAW	PAS	EAW	%vR	%vL	vR	vL	Pos
Bregman, Alex, D	29	R	725	27	26.9	6.0	4.50	0.0	99%	100%	4.43	4.67	
Riley, Austin	26	R	715	27	26.5	5.9	4.50	0.0	96%	100%	4.48	4.55	
Caminero, Junior	20	R	36	1	26.0	5.0	5.20	0.0	100%	100%	5.33	5.00	
Suarez, Eugenio	32	R	694	27	25.7	6.0	4.30	0.0	99%	100%	4.24	4.48	
Ramirez, Jose	31	B	691	27	25.6	5.8	4.43	0.0	94%	97%	4.45	4.39	
De La Cruz, Elly	21	B	427	17	25.1	5.6	4.44	0.1	94%	89%	4.46	4.38	6
Steer, Spencer	26	R	665	27	24.6	5.6	4.34	0.2	91%	98%	4.27	4.48	3o
Jung, Josh	25	R	515	21	24.5	5.7	4.27	0.1	95%	100%	4.19	4.48	
Devers, Rafael	27	L	656	27	24.3	5.6	4.32	0.1	93%	86%	4.36	4.22	
Machado, Manny	31	R	601	25	23.6	5.4	4.36	0.0	90%	91%	4.29	4.53	
Arenado, Nolan	32	R	612	26	23.5	5.5	4.27	0.0	88%	100%	4.24	4.35	
Garcia, Maikel	23	R	515	22	23.4	5.4	4.31	0.3	85%	94%	4.30	4.32	
Bohm, Alec	27	R	611	26	23.3	5.4	4.27	0.2	86%	98%	4.25	4.31	3
Chapman, Matt	30	R	581	25	23.2	5.6	4.17	0.0	92%	93%	4.15	4.25	
McMahon, Ryan	29	L	627	27	23.2	5.4	4.26	0.0	96%	78%	4.23	4.33	4
Kim, Ha-seong	28	R	626	27	23.2	5.3	4.30	0.3	86%	96%	4.27	4.37	46
Muncy, Max	33	L	579	25	23.2	5.2	4.38	0.2	92%	74%	4.48	4.11	
Henderson, Gunna	22	L	622	27	23.0	5.3	4.30	0.4	94%	76%	4.33	4.24	6
Candelario, Jeimer	30	B	575	25	23.0	5.6	4.12	0.1	96%	85%	4.11	4.16	3
Hayes, Ke'Bryan	26	R	525	23	22.8	5.2	4.36	0.1	83%	88%	4.26	4.53	
Lewis, Royce	24	R	239	11	21.7	5.1	4.20	0.4	85%	75%	4.23	4.08	
Burger, Jake	27	R	540	25	21.4	5.2	3.99	0.5	81%	93%	3.96	4.07	
Vierling, Matt	27	R	531	25	21.2	4.8	4.25	0.7	74%	95%	4.12	4.56	o
Paredes, Isaac	24	R	571	27	21.1	4.9	4.21	0.7	76%	100%	4.15	4.37	3
LeMahieu, DJ	35	R	562	27	20.8	4.8	4.27	0.3	76%	90%	4.26	4.30	3
Moncada, Yoan	28	B	357	17	20.3	4.9	4.05	0.3	82%	77%	4.03	4.12	
Davis, J.D.	30	R	544	27	20.1	4.6	4.11	1.3	71%	89%	4.12	4.10	
Marte, Noelvi	22	R	123	6	19.8	5.0	3.93	0.2	78%	90%	4.00	3.78	
McKinstry, Zach	28	L	518	27	19.2	4.3	4.08	1.7	88%	10%	4.07	4.25	o46
Urshela, Gio	32	R	228	12	19.0	4.7	3.96	0.5	75%	79%	3.90	4.13	3
Baty, Brett	24	L	386	20	18.9	4.8	3.82	0.6	93%	50%	3.91	3.50	
Miranda, Jose	25	R	152	8	18.8	4.6	3.97	0.4	76%	89%	4.07	3.63	
Rengifo, Luis	26	B	445	24	18.5	4.3	3.96	1.4	70%	78%	3.88	4.17	46o
Triolo, Jared	25	R	209	11	18.3	4.5	4.04	0.3	72%	75%	3.97	4.17	
Segura, Jean	33	R	326	18	18.1	4.6	3.92	0.1	77%	81%	3.84	4.14	
Castro, Willi	26	B	409	23	17.7	4.0	4.12	1.4	55%	94%	4.17	4.03	o
Flores, Wilmer	32	R	454	26	17.5	3.7	4.27	1.5	48%	98%	4.25	4.29	3
Monasterio, Andru	26	R	315	18	17.4	4.3	3.91	0.7	61%	97%	3.98	3.79	4
Peraza, Oswald	23	R	191	11	17.3	4.4	3.90	0.3	61%	100%	3.94	3.77	
Rendon, Anthony,	33	R	183	10	17.1	4.0	4.28	0.0	63%	78%	4.12	4.57	
Anderson, Brian, W	30	R	361	21	17.1	4.2	4.00	0.3	66%	75%	4.03	3.93	o
Duran, Ezequiel	24	R	439	26	16.8	4.0	3.92	1.1	57%	95%	3.95	3.87	6o
Donaldson, Josh	38	R	189	11	16.5	4.1	3.96	0.3	70%	74%	3.81	4.29	
Rojas, Josh	29	L	348	21	16.3	4.0	3.75	1.1	91%	12%	3.73	4.20	4
Westburg, Jordan	24	R	228	14	16.3	3.8	3.89	1.6	48%	89%	3.79	4.00	4
Walls, Taylor	27	B	349	21	16.2	4.1	3.87	0.4	62%	88%	3.86	3.91	46
Peterson, Jace	33	L	430	27	15.9	3.8	3.78	1.5	83%	20%	3.80	3.60	4
Maton, Nick	26	L	293	18	15.9	3.8	3.64	1.9	76%	4%	3.65	3.00	4
Diaz, Jordan	23	R	293	18	15.9	4.3	3.52	0.8	59%	97%	3.68	3.30	4
Taylor, Chris	33	R	384	24	15.8	3.4	4.00	2.2	40%	91%	4.00	4.00	o6
Berti, Jon	33	R	425	27	15.7	3.7	3.89	1.5	51%	90%	3.90	3.86	6
Kieboom, Carter	26	R	94	6	15.7	3.8	3.91	0.7	50%	100%	4.14	3.56	
Schmitt, Casey	24	R	277	17	15.6	4.0	3.56	1.4	53%	97%	3.63	3.46	6
Miller, Owen	27	R	314	20	15.6	3.7	4.03	0.9	48%	94%	4.00	4.06	43
Urias, Ramon	29	R	396	25	15.5	3.7	3.90	1.0	61%	65%	3.82	4.06	4
Farmer, Kyle	33	R	369	24	15.4	3.3	3.91	2.7	42%	94%	3.96	3.84	46
Moustakas, Mike	35	L	386	26	14.7	3.3	4.07	1.2	69%	21%	4.05	4.20	3
Senzel, Nick	28	R	330	22	14.5	3.3	3.95	1.5	37%	95%	3.92	3.97	o
Madrigal, Nick	26	R	294	19	14.5	3.3	3.94	1.5	51%	63%	3.90	4.00	
Rivera, Emmanuel	27	R	283	20	14.0	3.3	3.94	1.0	44%	83%	3.97	3.90	

2023 PLAYING TIME MEASUREMENT CHARTS BY POSITION

Quickstart Key: AW: active weeks; PAAW: plate appearances per active week; SAW: starts per active week; PAS: plate appearances per start; EAW: extra PA per active week.

Players are sorted by descending PAAW. See Encyclopedia entry on page 31 and Research articles beginning on page 70 for additional detail into the terms and concepts used here.

Second Base

Name	A	B	PA	AW	PAAW	SAW	PAS	EAW	%vR	%vL	vR	vL	Pos
Semien, Marcus, A	33	R	752	27	27.9	6.0	4.64	0.0	100%	100%	4.55	4.88	
McLain, Matt	24	R	403	15	26.9	5.9	4.58	0.0	94%	96%	4.55	4.67	6
Albies, Ozzie	26	B	658	25	26.3	5.9	4.45	0.0	97%	100%	4.42	4.55	
Gelof, Zack	24	R	300	11	26.2	6.0	4.36	0.0	98%	100%	4.34	4.42	
Hoerner, Nico	26	R	688	26	26.0	5.6	4.61	0.1	93%	94%	4.56	4.72	6
Betts, Mookie	31	R	693	27	25.7	5.6	4.58	0.1	91%	98%	4.64	4.44	o
India, Jonathan	27	R	529	21	25.0	5.5	4.49	0.2	92%	95%	4.43	4.63	
Torres, Gleyber	27	R	672	27	24.9	5.7	4.35	0.2	92%	97%	4.36	4.31	
Estrada, Thairo	27	R	530	21	24.8	5.6	4.45	0.0	89%	97%	4.44	4.49	6
Mauricio, Ronny	22	B	108	4	24.3	5.8	4.22	0.0	86%	92%	4.08	4.36	
Marte, Ketel	30	B	650	27	24.1	5.3	4.47	0.2	88%	92%	4.48	4.46	
McNeil, Jeff	31	L	648	27	24.0	5.6	4.24	0.3	97%	81%	4.34	3.98	o
Stott, Bryson	26	L	640	27	23.7	5.3	4.35	0.5	97%	66%	4.37	4.30	
Cronenworth, Jake	29	L	521	22	23.7	5.6	4.15	0.3	98%	88%	4.16	4.11	3
Altuve, Jose	33	R	410	17	23.4	5.1	4.60	0.1	76%	90%	4.53	4.75	
Drury, Brandon, S	31	R	523	22	23.2	5.4	4.27	0.1	85%	97%	4.26	4.29	3
McMahon, Ryan	29	L	627	27	23.2	5.4	4.26	0.0	96%	78%	4.23	4.33	5
Kim, Ha-seong	28	R	626	27	23.2	5.3	4.30	0.3	86%	96%	4.27	4.37	56
Arraez, Luis	26	L	617	27	22.9	5.2	4.33	0.3	91%	70%	4.33	4.32	
Gimenez, Andres	25	L	616	27	22.8	5.4	4.16	0.5	96%	75%	4.19	4.09	
Edman, Tommy	28	B	528	24	22.0	5.4	4.02	0.2	85%	100%	3.86	4.41	6o
Merrifield, Whit	34	R	592	27	21.9	5.1	4.25	0.4	80%	100%	4.20	4.39	o
Garcia, Luis	23	L	482	22	21.5	5.0	4.19	0.5	94%	64%	4.22	4.10	
Rodgers, Brendan	27	R	192	9	21.3	4.9	4.27	0.4	78%	71%	4.25	4.33	
Polanco, Jorge	30	B	343	15	21.1	4.8	4.35	0.2	79%	74%	4.35	4.35	
Donovan, Brendan	26	L	371	18	20.6	4.5	4.41	0.8	86%	40%	4.44	4.20	o
Vargas, Miguel	24	R	303	15	20.2	4.7	4.09	1.1	70%	100%	4.11	4.04	
Rosario, Amed	28	R	545	27	20.2	4.4	4.35	1.2	60%	92%	4.45	4.22	6
Gorman, Nolan	23	L	464	23	19.9	4.5	4.25	0.7	89%	37%	4.27	4.08	
Lowe, Brandon	29	L	436	22	19.8	4.6	4.20	0.5	91%	28%	4.22	4.00	

Shortstop

Name	A	B	PA	AW	PAAW	SAW	PAS	EAW	%vR	%vL	vR	vL	Pos
McLain, Matt	24	R	403	15	26.9	5.9	4.58	0.0	94%	96%	4.55	4.67	4
Hoerner, Nico	26	R	688	26	26.0	5.6	4.61	0.1	93%	94%	4.56	4.72	4
Witt Jr., Bobby	23	R	694	27	25.7	5.8	4.41	0.0	95%	98%	4.42	4.41	
Turner, Trea, V	30	R	691	27	25.6	5.7	4.46	0.0	91%	100%	4.43	4.52	
Lindor, Francisco, N	30	B	687	27	25.4	5.9	4.31	0.0	96%	98%	4.42	4.10	
Bichette, Bo	25	R	602	23	25.3	5.7	4.47	0.1	94%	93%	4.42	4.68	
Swanson, Dansby	29	R	638	25	25.2	5.8	4.34	0.0	94%	96%	4.27	4.50	
De La Cruz, Elly	21	B	427	17	25.1	5.6	4.44	0.1	94%	89%	4.46	4.38	5
Estrada, Thairo	27	R	530	21	24.8	5.6	4.45	0.0	89%	97%	4.44	4.49	4
Bogaerts, Xander, J	31	R	666	27	24.7	5.7	4.32	0.0	94%	98%	4.29	4.38	
Franco, Wander	22	B	491	20	24.6	5.5	4.47	0.2	90%	95%	4.43	4.65	
Crawford, J.P.	28	L	638	26	24.5	5.5	4.42	0.0	92%	95%	4.38	4.55	
Adames, Willy, R	28	R	636	26	24.5	5.7	4.27	0.0	96%	93%	4.31	4.16	
Seager, Corey, D	29	L	536	22	24.4	5.4	4.51	0.2	89%	94%	4.53	4.45	
Pena, Jeremy	26	R	631	27	23.4	5.5	4.23	0.0	93%	90%	4.13	4.48	
Kim, Ha-seong	28	R	626	27	23.2	5.3	4.30	0.3	86%	96%	4.27	4.37	45
Henderson, Gunna	22	L	622	27	23.0	5.3	4.30	0.4	94%	76%	4.33	4.24	5
Tovar, Ezequiel	22	R	615	27	22.8	5.6	4.05	0.0	92%	96%	3.97	4.20	
Abrams, CJ	23	L	614	27	22.7	5.5	4.13	0.1	99%	75%	4.16	4.05	
Correa, Carlos	29	R	580	26	22.3	5.2	4.33	0.0	86%	86%	4.35	4.26	
Volpe, Anthony	22	R	601	27	22.3	5.6	3.96	0.3	90%	97%	3.94	4.03	
Arcia, Orlando, J	29	R	533	24	22.0	5.6	3.90	0.1	92%	96%	3.89	3.92	
Edman, Tommy	28	B	528	24	22.0	5.4	4.02	0.2	85%	100%	3.86	4.41	4o
Story, Trevor, J	31	R	168	8	21.0	5.1	4.10	0.0	75%	85%	4.10	4.09	
Winn, Masyn	21	R	137	6	21.0	5.5	3.82	0.0	89%	90%	3.88	3.67	
Anderson, Tim, D	30	R	524	25	21.0	4.7	4.36	0.4	75%	86%	4.31	4.53	
Neto, Zach	22	R	329	15	20.3	5.0	3.97	0.5	77%	81%	4.03	3.76	
Baez, Javier	31	R	546	27	20.2	4.9	4.08	0.3	76%	90%	4.00	4.31	
Rosario, Amed	28	R	545	27	20.2	4.4	4.35	1.2	60%	92%	4.45	4.22	4
Cruz, Oneil	25	L	40	2	20.0	4.5	4.44	0.0	100%	100%	4.50	4.00	

Catcher

Name	A	B	PA	AW	PAAW	SAW	PAS	EAW	%vR	%vL	vR	vL	Pos
Rutschman, Adley	25	B	687	27	25.4	5.5	4.56	0.3	93%	91%	4.58	4.53	
Contreras, William	26	R	611	27	22.6	5.1	4.41	0.3	79%	98%	4.42	4.38	
Smith, Will	28	R	554	25	21.6	4.6	4.57	0.6	78%	76%	4.59	4.54	
Perez, Salvador	33	R	578	27	21.4	5.2	4.13	0.0	85%	85%	4.09	4.24	3
Raleigh, Cal	27	B	569	27	21.1	4.7	4.25	0.9	90%	48%	4.24	4.30	
Ruiz, Keibert	25	B	562	27	20.8	4.9	4.23	0.1	88%	68%	4.23	4.23	
Realmuto, J.T.	32	R	538	27	19.9	4.8	4.10	0.2	75%	88%	4.15	4.00	
Heim, Jonah	28	B	501	25	19.9	4.9	4.02	0.2	86%	69%	4.04	3.96	
Diaz, Elias, D	33	R	526	27	19.5	4.5	4.11	0.9	71%	82%	4.06	4.21	
Stephenson, Tyler	27	R	517	27	19.1	4.5	4.08	0.7	71%	83%	4.01	4.23	
Contreras, Willson,	31	R	495	26	19.0	4.6	4.12	0.2	72%	88%	4.07	4.23	
O'Hoppe, Logan	23	R	199	10	19.0	4.7	4.02	0.1	77%	88%	3.94	4.21	
Rodriguez, Endy	23	B	204	11	18.5	4.2	4.13	1.3	73%	55%	4.10	4.19	
Bailey, Patrick	24	B	353	19	18.2	4.3	4.02	0.8	63%	91%	4.04	4.00	
Langeliers, Shea	26	R	490	27	18.1	4.6	3.89	0.4	69%	93%	3.89	3.88	
Garver, Mitch	32	R	343	19	17.5	4.2	4.06	0.6	61%	97%	4.00	4.18	
Alvarez, Francisco	22	R	423	25	16.8	4.1	3.88	0.9	58%	85%	3.93	3.80	
Sanchez, Gary	31	R	267	16	16.4	3.9	4.00	0.7	59%	79%	3.98	4.05	
Kirk, Alejandro	25	R	422	26	16.2	3.7	3.99	1.3	57%	80%	3.93	4.14	
Murphy, Sean	29	R	438	27	16.2	3.8	4.22	0.3	60%	70%	4.23	4.17	
Moreno, Gabriel	23	R	380	24	15.8	3.9	3.89	0.5	62%	73%	3.85	3.97	
Gomes, Yan	36	R	419	27	15.5	3.8	3.94	0.6	51%	88%	3.98	3.89	
Wells, Austin	24	L	74	4	15.5	3.8	4.07	0.3	58%	33%	4.07	4.00	
Grandal, Yasmani	35	B	405	26	15.3	3.7	3.94	0.9	60%	59%	3.88	4.13	
Maldonado, Marti	37	R	407	27	15.1	4.3	3.51	0.0	71%	73%	3.43	3.69	
Wong, Connor	27	R	403	27	14.9	3.9	3.65	0.7	58%	81%	3.72	3.50	
Naylor, Bo	23	L	230	15	14.9	3.7	3.84	0.8	75%	34%	3.93	3.50	
Jansen, Danny, R	28	R	301	21	14.3	3.4	4.01	0.6	55%	66%	4.04	3.95	
Diaz, Yainer	25	R	377	27	14.0	3.1	4.17	1.0	51%	53%	4.07	4.38	
Rogers, Jake	28	R	365	27	13.5	3.5	3.78	0.4	49%	82%	3.76	3.81	

Designated Hitter

Name	A	B	PA	AW	PAAW	SAW	PAS	EAW	%vR	%vL	vR	vL	Pos
Meneses, Joey	31	R	657	27	24.3	5.6	4.34	0.1	91%	96%	4.33	4.35	
Martinez, J.D.	36	R	477	20	22.8	5.3	4.28	0.1	90%	88%	4.28	4.30	
Ozuna, Marcell	33	R	592	27	21.9	5.3	4.15	0.1	86%	88%	4.16	4.14	
Jimenez, Eloy	27	R	489	23	20.5	5.0	4.11	0.1	82%	82%	4.16	3.96	
McCutchen, Andre	37	R	473	23	20.3	4.5	4.47	0.3	66%	88%	4.39	4.57	
Buxton, Byron	30	R	347	18	19.3	4.4	4.28	0.3	70%	91%	4.29	4.24	
Ramirez, Harold, A	29	R	434	27	16.1	3.6	4.11	1.1	50%	100%	4.14	4.06	
Vientos, Mark	24	R	233	14	15.7	4.1	3.77	0.4	56%	83%	3.82	3.71	
Ford, Mike	31	L	251	17	14.4	3.7	3.54	1.3	79%	4%	3.55	3.00	
Cabrera, Miguel	40	R	370	27	13.7	3.5	3.86	0.1	48%	87%	3.84	3.91	
Soderstrom, Tyler	22	L	138	9	13.7	3.6	3.53	1.1	73%	21%	3.59	3.00	
Calhoun, Willie	29	L	149	11	13.5	3.3	3.92	0.7	60%	0%	3.92		
Reyes, Franmil	28	R	65	5	13.0	3.2	3.94	0.4	55%	57%	3.83	4.25	
Aranda, Jonathan	25	L	103	7	12.7	2.9	3.90	1.6	73%	8%	3.89	4.00	
Winker, Jesse	30	L	197	15	12.6	2.9	3.89	1.2	68%	8%	3.88	4.00	
Vogelbach, Daniel	31	L	319	25	12.4	3.0	3.71	1.2	72%	0%	3.71		
Ruf, Darin	37	R	57	5	11.4	2.8	3.36	2.0	0%	93%		3.36	
Lewis, Kyle	28	R	54	4	11.3	2.3	4.11	2.0	13%	88%	4.50	4.00	
Carpenter, Matt	38	L	236	21	11.2	2.8	3.71	1.0	66%	3%	3.70	4.00	
Cruz, Nelson, R	43	R	152	14	10.9	2.4	3.88	1.7	15%	83%	3.63	3.96	
Kjerstad, Heston	24	L	32	3	10.7	2.7	3.38	1.7	50%	0%	3.38		
Baker, Luken	26	R	99	10	9.5	2.2	3.73	1.3	26%	59%	4.00	3.40	
Hensley, David	27	R	94	10	9.1	2.2	3.91	0.5	30%	61%	3.82	4.00	
Horwitz, Spencer	26	L	44	4	8.5	1.8	3.86	1.8	37%	0%	3.86		
Madris, Bligh	27	L	30	4	6.5	1.3	4.20	1.3	38%	0%	4.20		
Hummel, Cooper	29	B	26	4	6.5	1.5	3.67	1.0	25%	33%	3.75	3.50	
Canario, Alexander	23	R	17	3	5.7	1.3	3.75	0.7	7%	60%	4.00	3.67	
Miller, Brad	34	L	67	12	5.5	1.3	3.56	0.8	31%	0%	3.56		
Almonte, Abraham	34	B	16	3	5.3	0.7	4.00	2.7	13%	0%	4.00		
La Stella, Tommy	34	L	24	5	4.8	1.2	3.00	1.2	30%	0%	3.00		

2023 PLAYING TIME MEASUREMENT CHARTS BY POSITION

Quickstart Key: AW: active weeks; PAAW: plate appearances per active week; SAW: starts per active week; PAS: plate appearances per start; EAW: extra PA per active week. Players are sorted by descending PAAW. See Encyclopedia entry on page 31 and Research articles beginning on page 70 for additional detail into the terms and concepts used here.

Outfield

Name	A	B	PA	AW	PAAW	SAW	PAS	EAW	%vR	%vL	vR	vL	Pos
Acuna Jr., Ronald	26	R	735	27	27.2	5.9	4.62	0.0	98%	94%	4.59	4.74	
Schwarber, Kyle, J	30	L	720	27	26.7	5.9	4.50	0.0	97%	98%	4.50	4.51	
Kwan, Steven	26	L	718	27	26.6	5.7	4.65	0.3	97%	87%	4.68	4.58	
Tatis Jr., Fernando	25	R	635	24	26.5	5.8	4.52	0.1	96%	98%	4.45	4.70	
Rodriguez, Julio	23	R	714	27	26.4	5.7	4.61	0.1	94%	98%	4.60	4.63	
Soto, Juan	25	L	708	27	26.2	6.0	4.39	0.0	99%	100%	4.34	4.52	
Betts, Mookie	31	R	693	27	25.7	5.6	4.58	0.1	91%	98%	4.64	4.44	4
Happ, Ian	29	B	691	27	25.6	5.8	4.40	0.1	97%	92%	4.40	4.40	
Nimmo, Brandon, T	30	L	682	27	25.3	5.6	4.53	0.1	95%	85%	4.61	4.36	
Thomas, Lane	28	R	682	27	25.3	5.7	4.42	0.1	94%	95%	4.40	4.44	
Springer, George, C	34	R	681	27	25.2	5.5	4.55	0.3	91%	89%	4.53	4.63	
Hernandez, Teosca	31	R	678	27	25.1	5.9	4.26	0.0	98%	100%	4.22	4.36	
Judge, Aaron	31	R	458	18	24.9	5.7	4.38	0.1	89%	90%	4.42	4.22	
Castellanos, Nick	31	R	671	27	24.9	5.8	4.29	0.0	93%	98%	4.26	4.37	
Tucker, Kyle	26	L	667	27	24.7	5.8	4.27	0.0	96%	96%	4.17	4.49	
Steer, Spencer	26	R	665	27	24.6	5.6	4.34	0.2	91%	98%	4.27	4.48	35
Reynolds, Bryan	28	B	640	26	24.5	5.5	4.46	0.1	91%	89%	4.39	4.61	
Garcia, Adolis	30	R	632	26	24.3	5.6	4.32	0.2	93%	95%	4.30	4.38	
Santander, Anthon	29	B	656	27	24.3	5.6	4.33	0.1	96%	87%	4.38	4.23	
Arozarena, Randy	28	R	654	27	24.2	5.5	4.37	0.1	91%	94%	4.33	4.52	
Meadows, Parker	24	L	145	6	24.2	5.8	4.14	0.0	100%	67%	4.21	3.83	
McNeil, Jeff	31	L	648	27	24.0	5.6	4.24	0.3	97%	81%	4.34	3.98	4
Carroll, Corbin	23	L	646	27	23.9	5.4	4.32	0.4	96%	78%	4.37	4.18	
Suzuki, Seiya	29	R	583	24	23.7	5.5	4.30	0.1	84%	100%	4.21	4.44	
Alvarez, Yordan	26	L	496	21	23.6	5.4	4.38	0.0	87%	92%	4.33	4.50	
Yelich, Christian	32	L	632	27	23.4	5.2	4.45	0.1	94%	71%	4.52	4.24	
Young, Jacob	24	R	121	5	23.4	6.2	3.77	0.0	100%	100%	3.71	4.00	
De La Cruz, Bryan	27	R	626	27	23.2	5.4	4.22	0.2	90%	88%	4.21	4.23	
Bellinger, Cody	28	L	556	24	23.2	5.3	4.30	0.2	89%	89%	4.30	4.33	3
Benintendi, Andrew	29	L	621	27	23.0	5.3	4.35	0.1	89%	77%	4.36	4.30	
Blackmon, Charlie	37	L	413	18	22.9	4.9	4.56	0.7	86%	62%	4.57	4.52	
Jones, Nolan	25	L	424	18	22.9	5.4	4.18	0.4	91%	85%	4.19	4.14	
Nootbaar, Lars	26	L	503	21	22.8	5.1	4.40	0.4	91%	68%	4.49	4.09	
Ward, Taylor	30	R	409	18	22.7	4.9	4.49	0.5	79%	97%	4.39	4.71	
Robert, Luis	26	R	590	26	22.7	5.4	4.16	0.1	87%	95%	4.15	4.19	
Chisholm Jr., Jazz	25	L	385	17	22.6	5.5	4.11	0.2	95%	68%	4.12	4.06	
Trout, Mike	32	R	362	16	22.6	5.1	4.46	0.1	83%	85%	4.43	4.52	
Greene, Riley	23	L	416	18	22.6	5.1	4.34	0.4	92%	67%	4.41	4.00	
Davis, Henry	24	R	255	11	22.5	5.3	4.24	0.2	81%	96%	4.24	4.25	
Harris II, Michael	22	L	539	24	22.4	5.7	3.93	0.1	92%	96%	3.95	3.88	
Carter, Evan	21	L	75	3	22.3	5.3	3.63	3.0	100%	0%	3.63		
Verdugo, Alex, B	27	L	602	27	22.3	5.0	4.43	0.1	85%	74%	4.48	4.26	
Melendez, MJ	25	L	602	27	22.3	5.2	4.19	0.4	92%	68%	4.21	4.11	
Taveras, Leody	25	B	554	25	22.2	5.5	3.96	0.3	88%	98%	3.90	4.10	
Soler, Jorge	31	R	580	26	22.2	5.1	4.33	0.2	82%	90%	4.33	4.34	
Edman, Tommy	28	B	528	24	22.0	5.4	4.02	0.2	85%	100%	3.86	4.41	46
Merrifield, Whit	34	R	592	27	21.9	5.1	4.25	0.4	80%	100%	4.20	4.39	4
Gurriel Jr., Lourdes	30	R	592	27	21.9	5.1	4.21	0.3	84%	90%	4.19	4.24	
Renfroe, Hunter	31	R	548	25	21.9	5.1	4.18	0.7	82%	93%	4.15	4.26	
Friedl, T.J.	28	L	556	25	21.8	4.8	4.33	1.1	92%	50%	4.39	4.05	
Mullins II, Cedric	29	L	455	20	21.8	5.0	4.28	0.6	90%	71%	4.39	4.03	
Walker, Jordan	21	R	465	21	21.5	5.3	4.02	0.1	86%	100%	4.02	4.00	
Yoshida, Masataka	30	L	581	27	21.5	4.9	4.31	0.3	88%	60%	4.34	4.16	
Frelick, Sal	23	L	223	10	21.5	4.7	4.30	1.3	89%	41%	4.35	4.00	
Varsho, Daulton	27	L	580	27	21.5	5.2	4.01	0.5	93%	64%	4.00	4.09	
Vierling, Matt	27	R	531	25	21.2	4.8	4.25	0.7	74%	95%	4.12	4.56	5
Carpenter, Kerry	26	L	459	21	21.2	5.1	4.06	0.3	93%	58%	3.99	4.44	
Grichuk, Randal	32	R	471	22	21.0	5.0	4.08	0.5	79%	97%	4.01	4.22	
Outman, James	26	L	567	27	21.0	5.1	3.99	0.8	91%	69%	4.02	3.88	
Hays, Austin	28	R	566	27	21.0	5.0	4.14	0.4	78%	93%	3.94	4.48	

Outfield, cont.

Name	A	B	PA	AW	PAAW	SAW	PAS	EAW	%vR	%vL	vR	vL	Pos
Ruiz, Esteury	24	R	490	23	20.9	4.9	4.15	0.7	73%	95%	4.15	4.16	
Marte, Starling	35	R	341	16	20.8	5.0	4.15	0.1	80%	97%	4.29	3.90	
Kelenic, Jarred	24	L	416	20	20.8	4.9	4.12	0.6	95%	52%	4.11	4.18	
Tauchman, Mike	33	L	401	19	20.8	4.4	4.32	1.7	97%	19%	4.36	3.86	
Donovan, Brendan	26	L	371	18	20.6	4.5	4.41	0.8	86%	40%	4.44	4.20	4
Pereira, Everson	22	R	103	5	20.6	5.2	3.96	0.0	70%	100%	3.95	4.00	
Grisham, Trent	27	L	554	27	20.5	5.2	3.83	0.5	94%	71%	3.86	3.74	
Profar, Jurickson	30	B	520	25	20.4	4.4	4.50	0.4	77%	70%	4.48	4.56	
Morel, Christopher	24	R	429	21	20.4	4.8	4.17	0.4	81%	75%	4.14	4.23	
Stanton, Giancarlo	34	R	415	20	20.4	4.8	4.21	0.2	78%	90%	4.25	4.05	
Kirilloff, Alex	26	L	319	15	20.3	4.7	4.03	1.5	87%	43%	4.05	3.89	3
Kepler, Max	30	L	491	24	20.2	4.6	4.24	0.8	89%	38%	4.27	4.00	
Bryant, Kris, L	32	R	335	16	20.1	4.8	4.21	0.1	82%	76%	4.22	4.18	
Duran, Jarren	27	L	361	18	20.1	4.6	4.07	1.5	88%	35%	4.08	4.00	
Dominguez, Jasson	20	B	33	1	20.0	5.0	4.00	0.0	75%	100%	4.00	4.00	
Suwinski, Jack	25	L	534	27	19.8	4.7	4.05	0.6	95%	46%	4.03	4.12	
Rooker, Brent	29	R	526	27	19.5	4.5	4.12	0.9	67%	96%	4.14	4.09	
Pratto, Nick	25	L	345	17	19.4	4.6	4.09	0.4	82%	57%	4.03	4.31	3
Wallner, Matt	26	L	254	13	19.3	4.9	3.80	0.6	81%	71%	3.85	3.58	
Wade Jr., LaMonte	30	L	519	27	19.2	4.3	4.20	1.2	90%	26%	4.25	3.75	3
Straw, Myles	29	R	518	27	19.2	5.1	3.70	0.3	81%	90%	3.77	3.60	
McKinstry, Zach	28	L	518	27	19.2	4.3	4.08	1.7	88%	10%	4.07	4.25	456
Duvall, Adam	35	R	353	18	19.2	4.4	4.18	0.6	66%	100%	4.24	4.04	
Rosario, Eddie, M	32	L	516	27	19.1	4.9	3.80	0.6	96%	18%	3.83	3.17	
Bader, Harrison	29	R	344	18	19.1	4.7	3.92	0.8	73%	88%	3.87	4.04	
Conforto, Michael	30	L	470	24	19.1	4.7	3.97	0.5	89%	51%	4.00	3.85	
Yastrzemski, Mike	33	L	381	20	19.1	4.5	4.01	1.0	89%	47%	4.03	3.94	
McCormick, Chas	28	R	457	24	19.0	4.5	4.18	0.3	68%	89%	4.07	4.34	
Bleday, J.J.	26	L	303	16	18.9	4.6	3.90	1.1	89%	44%	3.94	3.73	
Laureano, Ramon	29	R	404	21	18.9	4.4	4.11	0.7	67%	85%	4.33	3.74	
Hernandez, Kike	32	R	508	27	18.8	4.4	3.99	1.4	61%	96%	4.07	3.88	64
Canha, Mark, D	34	R	507	27	18.8	4.5	3.96	1.0	68%	90%	4.01	3.87	
Doyle, Brenton	25	R	431	23	18.7	5.0	3.62	0.5	79%	91%	3.68	3.51	
Marsh, Brandon	26	L	472	25	18.7	4.6	3.88	0.9	93%	35%	3.89	3.81	
Lowe, Josh	25	L	501	27	18.6	4.3	4.17	0.6	86%	20%	4.14	4.71	
Rengifo, Luis	26	B	445	24	18.5	4.3	3.96	1.4	70%	78%	3.88	4.17	456
Pederson, Joc, R	31	L	425	23	18.3	4.0	4.02	2.0	94%	8%	4.06	3.00	
Waters, Drew	25	B	337	18	18.3	4.8	3.78	0.2	84%	59%	3.81	3.63	
Dubon, Mauricio	29	R	492	27	18.2	3.9	4.39	1.1	67%	59%	4.30	4.62	4
Moniak, Mickey	25	L	323	17	18.1	4.3	4.12	0.4	77%	50%	4.10	4.25	
Brown, Seth	31	L	378	21	18.0	4.4	3.79	1.4	93%	26%	3.82	3.56	
Bae, Ji-Hwan	24	L	371	20	17.9	4.5	3.85	0.7	83%	55%	3.84	3.91	4
Pham, Tommy	35	R	481	27	17.8	4.2	4.10	0.7	56%	96%	4.21	3.96	
Rafaela, Ceddanne	23	R	89	5	17.8	3.2	4.44	3.6	39%	100%	4.45	4.40	
Florial, Estevan	26	L	71	4	17.8	4.5	3.94	0.0	78%	0%	3.94		
Castro, Willi	26	B	409	23	17.7	4.0	4.12	1.4	55%	94%	4.17	4.03	5
O'Neill, Tyler	28	R	266	15	17.7	3.9	4.24	1.1	58%	83%	4.15	4.40	
Haniger, Mitch, E	33	R	229	13	17.6	4.2	4.06	0.8	60%	82%	4.17	3.83	
Fletcher, Dominic	26	L	102	5	17.6	4.2	4.10	0.4	67%	78%	4.00	4.29	
Call, Alex	29	R	439	25	17.6	4.4	3.90	0.6	63%	91%	3.90	3.90	
Colas, Oscar	25	L	263	15	17.5	4.3	3.78	1.1	83%	52%	3.85	3.50	
Joe, Connor	31	R	472	27	17.5	3.7	4.23	1.8	44%	95%	4.11	4.34	3
Thomas, Alek	23	L	402	23	17.5	4.4	3.75	0.9	88%	44%	3.81	3.44	
Anderson, Brian, W	30	R	361	21	17.1	4.2	4.00	0.3	66%	75%	4.03	3.93	5
Ibanez, Andy	30	R	383	22	17.0	4.0	3.78	1.9	54%	94%	3.82	3.71	4
Larnach, Trevor	26	L	212	12	17.0	3.8	4.04	1.5	76%	29%	4.10	3.60	
Fitzgerald, Tyler	26	R	34	2	17.0	5.0	3.40	0.0	75%	100%	3.50	3.25	
Brennan, Will	25	L	455	27	16.9	4.0	3.90	1.4	88%	26%	3.89	3.94	
Duran, Ezequiel	24	R	439	26	16.8	4.0	3.92	1.1	57%	95%	3.95	3.87	65
Butler, Lawrence	23	L	129	7	16.7	4.3	3.50	1.7	88%	17%	3.50	3.50	

BASEBALL HQ .COM®

RADIO

Fantasy Sports Writers Association

Podcast of the Year (2013)

Join host **Patrick Davitt**, BaseballHQ.com's top analysts and other industry experts for interviews, news and insights on how to win your league.

These FREE twice-weekly (Tue/Fri) podcasts are each 45-80 minutes, and available via download or subscription through iTunes or other podcatchers.

Guests who appeared on BaseballHQ Radio in 2023 include:

- Ron Shandler, Baseball Forecaster
- Ray Murphy, BaseballHQ
- Todd Zola, Mastersball
- Joe Sheehan, Joe Sheehan Newsletter
- Nick Pollack, PitcherLIst
- Eno Sarris, The Athletic
- Vlad Sedler, FTN
- Paul Sporer, FanGraphs
- Mike Gianella, Baseball Prospectus
- Jeff Zimmerman, FanGraphs

Looking for weekly, in-season prospect reports from the field?

A BASEBALLHQ PODCAST

Join Chris Blessing, Brent Hershey and the staff at BaseballHQ for a podcast feautring weekly live looks at many of the game's top prospects.

Available wherever you get your podcasts.

BASEBALLHQ.COM's

MINOR LEAGUE BASEBALL ANALYST

Presented by BASEBALLHQ.COM

Brent Hershey, Editor

Chris Blessing and Jeremy Deloney, Assoc. Editors

The first book to integrate sabermetrics and scouting. For baseball analysts and those who play in fantasy leagues with farm systems, the *Minor League Baseball Analyst* is the perfect complement to the *Baseball Forecaster* and is designed exactly for your needs, with:

Performance Trends • Scouting Reports
Major League Equivalents • Mega-Lists
Player Potential Ratings • Essays and more!

$19.95 plus $8.00 Priority Mail S&H. To order:

www.baseballhq.com/mlba2024

Get Forecaster Insights In a New Package!

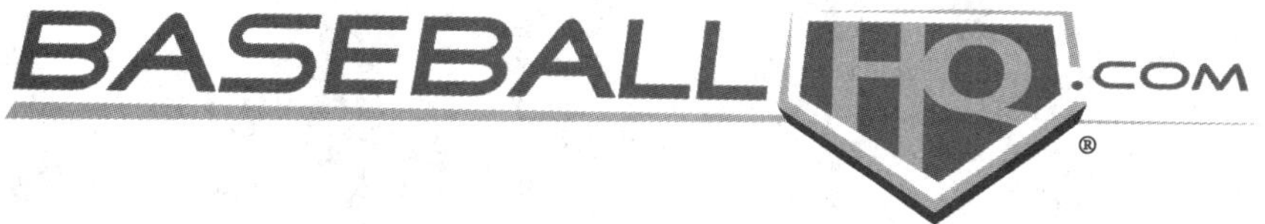

The **Baseball Forecaster** provides the core concepts in player evaluation and gaming strategy. You can maintain that edge all season long.

For over 25 years, **BaseballHQ.com** builds on the insights found in the Forecaster and covers all aspects of what's happening on the field—all with the most powerful fantasy slant on the Internet, from spring training to the season's last pitch. And in 2024, a new mobile-friendly website design will make it even easier to get ahead of the competition! Though it will have a modern look and feel, our signature features will be as sharp as ever:

- Nationally-renowned baseball analysts.
- MLB news analysis; including anticipating the **next** move.
- Dedicated columns on starting pitching, relievers, batters, and our popular Fact or Fluke? player profiles.
- Minor-league coverage beyond just scouting and lists.
- FAB targets, starting pitcher reports, strategy articles, daily game resources, call-up profiles and more!

Plus, **BaseballHQ.com** gets personal, with customizable tools and valuable resources:

- New and improved Team Stat Tracker and Power Search tools
- Custom Draft Guide for YOUR league's parameters
- Sortable and downloadable stats and projection files

Visit **www.baseballhq.com/subscribe**
to lock down your path to a 2024 championship!

Full Season subscription **$99**
(prorated at the time of order; auto-renews each October)

Draft Prep subscription **$45**
(complete access from mid-January through April 30, 2024)

Please read our Terms of service at www.baseballhq.com/terms.html

Baseball Forecaster & BaseballHQ.com: Your (updated!) season-long championship lineup.

FANTASY EXPERT

IS A FASCINATING AND WIDE-RANGING LOOK AT THE MODERN GROWTH AND DEVELOPMENT OF THE GAME THAT WENT FROM COTTAGE INDUSTRY TO NATIONAL OBSESSION.

"*Fantasy Expert* is a thorough and thoroughly interesting odyssey through the history of fantasy baseball and the visionary who did so much to popularize and legitimize it."

—PATRICK DAVITT,
BASEBALL HQ RADIO

"Two thumbs up...one for his compelling personal story and the other for his interesting and entertaining perspective on the earlier days of fantasy baseball. If I had three thumbs, I'd also point to how humorous it is."

—LARRY SCHECHTER,
AUTHOR, *WINNING FANTASY BASEBALL*

"A delightful historical lesson about the growing fantasy baseball industry. Enlightening and informative, this book introduces you to new people on every page who had a hand in growing this fabulous industry."

—GREG AMBROSIUS,
NATIONAL FANTASY BASEBALL CHAMPIONSHIP

AVAILABLE FEBRUARY 2024

TRIUMPHBOOKS.COM
@TRIUMPHBOOKS

Returning to Tampa!

March 1-3, 2024

St. Petersburg Clearwater Marriott, St. Petersburg, FL

Featuring:

Interactive sessions on topics like player analysis, injury warning signs, and 2024 breakout picks

Current ADP discussions, plus strategies for auctions and drafts

Spring training games just a few miles away

Drafts! Live, in-person, plus the LABR experts leagues

... all with a group of the friendliest, most passionate baseball fans around!

Make your Spring Training Plans NOW and include First Pitch Florida weekend!

More details: www.baseballhq.com/first-pitch-florida

2024 CHEATER'S BOOKMARK

BATTING STATISTICS

Abbrv	Term	Formula / Desc.	BENCHMARKS BAD UNDER	'23 LG AVG AL	'23 LG AVG NL	BEST OVER
Avg	Batting Average	h/ab	225	247	250	275
xBA	Expected Batting Average	*See glossary*		248	252	
OB	On Base Average	(h+bb)/(ab+bb)	285	311	318	330
Slg	Slugging Average	total bases/ab	350	412	417	450
OPS	On Base plus Slugging	OB+Slg	650	723	735	800
bb%	Walk Rate	bb/(ab+bb)	6%	9%	9%	10%
ct%	Contact Rate	(ab-k) / ab	70%	74%	75%	80%
Eye	Batting Eye	bb/k	0.30	0.36	0.39	0.50
PX	Power Index	Normalized power skills	80	100	100	120
Spd	Speed Score	Normalized speed skills	80	100	100	120
SBA	Stolen Base Attempt Rate %	(sb+cs)/(singles+bb+hbp)		9.8%	10.0%	
G	Ground Ball Per Cent	gb / balls in play		42%	43%	
L	Line Drive Per Cent	ld / balls in play		20%	20%	
F	Fly Ball Per Cent	fb / balls in play		38%	37%	
HR/F	Home runs per fly ball	HR/FB		12%	13%	
Brl%	Barrel rate	barrels/batted ball event		8.2%	8.0%	
RAR	Runs Above Replacement	*See glossary*	0.0			10.0

PITCHING STATISTICS

Abbrv	Term	Formula / Desc.	BENCHMARKS BAD OVER	'23 LG AVG AL	'23 LG AVG NL	BEST UNDER
ERA	Earned Run Average	er*9/ip	5.00	4.28	4.38	3.50
xERA	Expected ERA	*See glossary*		3.93	3.97	
WHIP	Baserunners per Inning	(h+bb)/ip	1.45	1.30	1.33	1.15
PC	Pitch Counts per Start		100	85	85	
H%	BatAvg on balls in play	(h-hr)/((ip*2.82)+h-k-hr)		29%	30%	
BB%	Walk percentage	BB/total batters faced	11%	9%	9%	7%
Ball%	Ball%	Balls/total pitches	38%	36%	36%	34%
HR/F	Homerun per Fly ball	HR/FB		12%	13%	
S%	Strand Rate	(h+bb-er)/(h+bb-hr)		71%	71%	
DIS%	PQS Disaster Rate	% GS that are PQS 0/1		32%	38%	15%
			BAD UNDER	**'23 LG AVG AL**	**'23 LG AVG NL**	**BEST OVER**
RAR	Runs Above Replacement	*See glossary*	-0.0			+10
K%	Strikeout percentage	K/total batters faced	20%	23%	22%	28%
K-BB%	K rate minus BB rate	K%-BB%	10%	15%	14%	18%
SwK	Swinging Strike Percentage	swinging strikes/pitches		11.9%	11.3%	13.0%
DOM%	PQS Dominance Rate	% GS that are PQS 4/5		21%	18%	50%
Sv%	Saves Conversion Rate	(saves / save opps)		62%	63%	80%

NOTES